UPS FOR UPS S

# Minor English Poets
# 1660-1780

A selection from the twenty-one volume *"The Works of the English Poets,"*
edited by Alexander Chalmers, first published London 1810.

## Compiled, with a new Introduction by David P. French

# Minor English Poets

## 1660-1780

A Selection from Alexander Chalmers'
*The English Poets* [1810]

Compiled, with an Introduction by
David P. French

Vol. 6

Benjamin Blom
*Publishers*

First issued London 1810 as
*The Works of the English Poets*
in 21 volumes, selected and edited by Alexander Chalmers

New edition compiled and edited with
a new Introduction by David P. French
First published in 10 volumes 1967 by Benjamin Blom, Inc., New York 10452
©Copyright 1967 by Benjamin Blom, Inc.
Library of Congress Catalog Card No. 66-29423

# CONTENTS

## Vol. VI

## Poems of Smollett.

## Poems of Wilkie.

# CONTENTS

## Poems of Cunningham.

# CONTENTS

## Poems of Lyttleton.

# CONTENTS

## Poems of Harte.

## Poems of P Whitehead.

# CONTENTS

## Poems of Lovibond.

# CONTENTS

## Poems of Fawkes.

# CONTENTS

## Poems of Armstrong.

## Poems of Langhorne.

# CONTENTS

## Poems of Jago.

# CONTENTS

## Poems of Brooke.

# CONTENTS

## Poems of Scott.

# CONTENTS

# LIFE OF TOBIAS SMOLLETT, M.D.

## BY MR. CHALMERS.

———

THE grandfather of our poet was sir James Smollett of Bonhill, a member of the Scotch parliament, and one of the commissioners for framing the treaty of union. He married Jane, daughter of sir Aulay Macauley, bart. of Ardincaple, by whom he had four sons and two daughters. The fourth son, Archibald, married, without asking his father's consent, Barbara Cunningham, daughter of Mr. Cunningham of Gilbertfield, in the neighbourhood of Glasgow. His father, however, allowed him an income of about £300 a year. He unfortunately died, after the birth of two sons and a daughter, who with their mother were left dependent on the grandfather, and we do not find that he neglected them. Tobias, the subject of this memoir, and the youngest of these children, was born in the house of Dalquhurn, near Renton, in the parish of Cardross, in 1721, and christened Tobias George: but this latter name he does not appear to have used.

The scenery amidst which he passed his early years, and cultivated the Muses, he has described, in Humphrey Clinker, with picturesque enthusiasm. He was first instructed in classical learning at the school of Dumbarton, by Mr. John Love, one of the ablest schoolmasters of that country, and to whom Mr. Chalmers has done ample justice in his life of Ruddiman.

While at this school, Smollett exhibited symptoms of what more or less predominated through life, a disposition to prove his superiority of understanding at the expense of those whose weaknesses and failings he thought he could turn into ridicule with impunity. The verses which he wrote at this early age were principally satires on such of his schoolfellows as happened to displease him. He wrote also a poem to the memory of the celebrated Wallace, whose praises he found in the story-books and ballads of every cottage. From Dumbarton he was removed to Glasgow, where, after some hesitation, he determined in favour of the study of medicine, and, according to the usual practice, was bound apprentice to Mr. John Gordon, then a surgeon and afterwards a physician of considerable eminence, whom he was unjustly accused of ridiculing under the name of Potion, in his novel of Roderick Random.

From his medical studies, which he cultivated with assiduity, he was occasionally se-
duced by a general love of polite literature, and seemed inconsciously to store his mind
with that fund of extensive, though perhaps not profound knowledge, which enabled
him afterwards to execute so many works in various branches. His satirical disposition
also followed him to Glasgow, by which he made a few admirers, and many enemies.
Dr. Moore has related, with suitable gravity, that he once threw a snowball with such
dexterity that it gave both a blow and a repartee. But such frolics were probably not frequent, and his time was in general more profitably or at least more seriously employed.
Before he had reached his eighteenth year, he began to feel the ambition of a dramatic
poet, and wrote the tragedy of the Regicide, which is now reprinted among his poems.
It was considered as an extraordinary production for a person of his years, but we do
not read it as originally composed, nor was it made public until nearly ten years after.

On the death of his grandfather, who had hitherto supported him in his studies, but
left no permanent provision for the completion of them, he removed to London, in
quest of employment in the army or navy, and strengthened his hopes by carrying his
tragedy with him. The latter, however, was in all respects an unfortunate speculation.
After being amused and cajoled by all the common and uncommon tricks of the theatrical managers, for nearly ten years, he was under the necessity of sending it to the
press in vindication of his own importunities, and the opinions of his friends. His preface may yet be read with advantage by the candidates for stage favour, although
modern managers are said to be less fastidious than their predecessors, and from the liberality of their admissions leave it somewhat doubtful whether they have not lost the
privilege of rejection. In this preface, Smollett was not sparing of his indignation, but
he reserved more substantial revenge for a more favourable opportunity.

In the mean time, in the year 1741, he procured the situation of surgeon's mate on
board a ship of the line, and sailed on the unfortunate expedition to Carthagena, which
he described in his Roderick Random, and afterwards more historically in a Compendium
of Voyages published in seven volumes, 12mo, in 1756. The issue of that expedition could
not be more humiliating to Smollett than his own situation, so averse to the disposition of
a young man of his taste and vivacity. He accordingly quitted the service, while his ship
was in the West Indies, and resided for some time in Jamaica, but in what capacity or
how supported, his biographers have not informed us. Here, however, he first became
acquainted with the lady whom he afterwards married.

In 1746, he returned to London, and having heard many exaggerated accounts of the
severities practised in suppressing the rebellion in Scotland, he gave vent to his feelings
and love for his country, in a beautiful and spirited poem, entitled the Tears of Scotland.
The subject was doubtless attractive as a poet, but as he had been bred a Whig, he was
rather inconsistent in his principles, and certainly very unfortunate in his predictions.
His friends wished him to suppress this piece as having a tendency to offend the Whigs
on whose patronage he had some reliance, and although his enthusiasm was at present
rather too warm for advice, and he had from this time declared war against the Whig-
ministers under George II. yet it does not appear that it was published with his name
for many years after.

In 1746 he first presented himself to the public as the author of Advice, a satire, in
which he endeavoured to excite indignation against certain public characters, by accusa-
tions which a man of delicacy would disdain to bring forward under any circumstances,
and which are generally brought forward under the very worst. What this production

contributed to his fame, we are not told. His friends, however, were alarmed and disgusted, and his enemies probably increased.

About this time he wrote (for Covent-Garden theatre) an opera called Alceste, which was never acted or printed, owing, it is said, to a dispute between the author and the manager. Sir John Hawkins, who, in all his writings trusts too much to his memory, informs us, that Handel set this opera to music, and, that his labour might not be lost, afterwards adapted the airs to Dryden's second Ode on St. Cecilia's Day. But Handel composed that ode in 1739, according to Dr. Burney's more accurate and scientific history of music. In 1747 our author published Reproof, a satire, as a second part to Advice, and consisting of the same materials, with the addition of some severe lines on Rich, the manager of Covent-Garden theatre, with whom he had just quarrelled.

In the same year, he married miss Ann Lascelles, the lady whom he had courted in Jamaica, and with whom he had the promise of three thousand pounds. Of this sum, however, he obtained but a small part, and that after a very expensive law-suit. As he had, upon his marriage, hired a genteel house, and lived in a more hospitable style than the possession of the whole of his wife's fortune could have supported, he was again obliged to have recourse to his pen, and produced, in 1748, The Adventures of Roderick Random, in two volumes, 12mo. This was the most successful of all his writings, and perhaps the most popular novel of the age. This it owed, partly to the notion that it was in many respects a history of his own life, and partly to its intrinsic merit, as a delineation of real life, manners and characters, given with a force of humour to which the public had not been accustomed. If, indeed, we consider its moral tendency, there are few productions more unfit for perusal; yet such were his opinions of public decency that he seriously fancied he was writing to humour the taste, and correct the morals of the age. That it contains a history of his own life was probably a surmise artfully circulated to excite curiosity, but that real characters are depicted was much more obvious. Independent of those whom he introduced out of revenge, as Lacy and Garrick for rejecting his tragedy, there are traits of many other persons more or less disguised, in the introduction of which he was incited merely by the recollection of foibles which deserved to be exposed. Every man who draws characters, whether to complete the fable of a novel, or to illustrate an essay, will be insensibly attracted by what he has seen in real life, and real life was Smollett's object in all his novels. His only monster is Count-Fathom, but he deals in none of those perfect beings who are the heroes of the more modern novels.

In 1749, his tragedy, The Regicide, as already noticed, was published, very much to his emolument, but certainly without any injury to the judgment of the managers who had rejected it. Extraordinary as it might have appeared, if published as he wrote it at the age of eighteen, it seemed no prodigy in one of more advanced years, who had adopted every improvement which his critical friends could suggest. The preface has been mentioned as containing his complaints of delay and evasion, and he had now more effectually vented his rage on lord Lyttleton and Mr. Garrick in Roderick Random. With Garrick, however, he lived to be reconciled in a manner which did credit to their respective feelings.

In 1750, he took a trip to Paris, where he renewed his acquaintance with Dr. Moore, one of his biographers, who informs us that he indulged the common English prejudices against the French nation, and never attained the language so perfectly as to be able to mix familiarly with the inhabitants. His stay here was not long, for in 1751 he published his second most popular novel, Peregrine Pickle, in four volumes, 12mo. which was received with great avidity. In the second edition, which was called for within a few months, he speaks, with more craft than truth, of certain booksellers and others who misrepresented the work and calumniated the author. He could not, however, conceal, and his biographers have told the shameless tale for him, that, " he received a handsome reward" for inserting the profligate memoirs of lady Vane. It is only wonderful that after this he could " flatter himself that he had expunged every adventure, phrase, and insinuation, that could be construed, by the most delicate readers, into a trespass upon the rules of decorum." In this work, as in Roderick Random, he indulged his unhappy propensity to personal satire and revenge by introducing living characters. He again endeavoured to degrade those of Garrick and Quin, who, it is said, had expressed a more unfavourable opinion of the Regicide than even Garrick; and was yet more unpardonable in holding up Dr. Akenside to ridicule.

Smollett had hitherto derived his chief support from his pen, but after the publication of Peregrine Pickle, he appears to have had a design of resuming his medical profession, and announced himself as having obtained the degree of doctor, but from what university has not been discovered. In this character, however, he endeavoured to begin practice at Bath, and published a tract on The External Use of Water. In this, his object was to prove that pure water, both for warm and cold bathing, may be preferred to waters impregnated with minerals, except in certain cases where the vapour bath is requisite. He enters also into a vindication of the plan of Mr. Cleland, a surgeon at Bath, for remedying the inconveniencies relating to the baths at that place. Whatever was thought of this pamphlet, he failed in his principal object : he had, indeed, obtained considerable fame, as his own complaints, and the contemporary journals plainly evince; but it was not of that kind which usually leads to medical practice.

Disappointed in this design, he determined to devote himself entirely to literary undertakings, for many of which he was undoubtedly better qualified by learning and genius than most of the authors by profession in his day. He now fixed his residence at Chelsea, on an establishment of which he has given the public a very just picture in his novel of Humphrey Clinker. If the picture be at the same time rather flattering, it must be recollected that it was Smollett's peculiar misfortune to make enemies in every step of his progress, and to be obliged to say those handsome things of himself which no other man would say for him. Dr. Moore, however, assures us that his mode of living at Chelsea was genteel and hospitable, without being extravagant, and that what he says of his liberality is not over-charged.

His first publication, in this retirement, if it may be so called, was the Adventures of Ferdinand Count Fathom, in 1753. This novel, in the popular opinion, has been reckoned greatly inferior to his former productions, but merely, as I conceive, because it is unlike them. There is such a perpetual flow of sentiment and expression in this production, as must give a very high idea of the fertility of his mind ; but in the delineation of characters he departs too much from real life, and many of his incidents are highly improbable. Mr. Cumberland, in the Memoirs of his own Life, lately published, takes credit to himself for the character of Abraham Adams, and of Sheva in his comedy of the Jew, which are, however, correct transcripts of Smollett's Jew. It would not have greatly lessened the merit of his benevolent views towards that depressed nation, had Mr. Cumberland frankly made this acknowledgement.

In 1755, Smollett published by subscription, a translation of Don Quixote, in two elegant quarto volumes. It is unnecessary to say much on a translation which has so long superseded every other. But since the appearance of lord Woodhouselee's admirable Essay on the Principles of Translation, a new edition of that by Jarvis has been published, and will serve to prove what his lordship has advanced, that Smollett's was merely an improved edition of that forgotten work. Let not this, however, detract greatly from Smollett's merit. Writing as he did for bread, dispatch was not only his primary object, as lord Woodhouselee has observed, but dispatch was probably required of him. He has excelled Jarvis while he availed himself of his labours, and such was his strong sense of ridicule, and ample fund of humour, that could he have fixed upon a proper subject, and found the requisite leisure, it is not too much to suppose that he might have been the rival of Cervantes himself.

After the publication of this translation, he visited his relations in Scotland, and on his return to England, was engaged to undertake the management of the Critical Review, which was begun in 1756, in dependence, as has been asserted, upon the patronage of the Tories and the high church party. It does not appear, however, that any extraordinary aid came from those quarters, and the mode in which it was long conducted proves, that the success of the Monthly Review was the only object; or, if that could not be rivalled, the hope that the public might support two publications of the kind.

To this task, Smollett brought many necessary qualifications: a considerable portion of general knowledge, a just taste in works of criticism, and a style flowing, easy, and popular. He had also much acquaintance with the literary history of his times, and could translate with readiness from some of the modern languages. But on the other hand, it was his misfortune here, as in every stage of his life, that the fair display of his talents, and perhaps the genuine sentiments of his heart, were perverted by the prejudices of friendship, or by the more inexcusable impulses of jealousy, revenge, and all that enters into the composition of an irritable temper. He had already suffered by provoking unnecessary animosity, and was now in a situation where it would have been impossible to escape invidious imputation, had he practised the utmost candour and moderation. How much more dangerous such a situation to one who was always too regardless of past experience, and who seems to have gladly embraced the opportunity, which secrecy afforded, of dealing his blows around without discrimination and without mercy. It is painful to read in the early volumes of this Review, the continual personal abuse he levelled at his rival, Mr. Griffiths, who very rarely took any notice of it: and the many vulgar and coarse sarcasms he directed against every author who presumed to doubt the infallibility of his opinion. It is no less painful to contemplate the self-sufficiency displayed on every occasion where he can introduce his own character and works.

Among others whom he provoked to retaliate were the noted political quack, Dr. Shebbeare, Churchill the poet, and Grainger[1]. But the contest in which he was involved with admiral Knowles terminated in a more honourable manner. That officer thought proper to prosecute the printer of the Critical Review (the late Mr. Hamilton) for a paragraph in the Review reflecting on his character, declaring at the same time that his only object was to discover the author, and if he proved to be a *gentleman*, to obtain the satisfaction of a gentleman from him. Smollett, by applying to persons acquainted with Knowles, endeavoured to avert the prosecution; but finding that im-

[1] See the Lives of Churchill and Grainger in Vol. XIV. of this collection. *C.*

possible, the moment sentence was about to be pronounced against the printer, he stept forth in open court, and avowed himself the author. After this spirited action, which yet, in Knowles' opinion, did not constitute him a *gentleman*, he was prosecuted, and sentenced to pay £100, and be imprisoned for three months.

Soon after the commencement of the Review, he published, but without his name, the Compendium of Voyages, already noticed, in seven volumes, 12mo. a work not eminently successful, and which has not since been reprinted. This was a species of compilation, however, for which he was well qualified. He knew how to retrench superfluities, and to bring forward the most pleasing parts of the narrative in an elegant style, and in drawing characters, when they fell in his way, he discovered much judgment and precision.

In 1757 he attempted the stage a second time, by a comedy, or rather farce, entitled The Reprisal, or The Tars of Old England, which Garrick, notwithstanding their former animosity, accepted, and produced upon the stage, where it had a temporary success. Davies, in his life of Garrick, gives an account of the manager's behaviour on this occasion, which reflects much honour on him, and so touched Smollett's feelings, that he embraced every opportunity of doing justice to the merits of that eminent actor, and of convincing him " that his gratitude was as warm as any other of his passions."

Notwithstanding his numerous engagements, he produced a work in 1758, which is an extraordinary instance of literary industry. This was his Complete History of England, from the earliest Times to the Treaty of Aix-la-Chapelle, in 1748, published in four quarto volumes[2]. This he is said to have composed and finished for the press in the short space of fourteen months. It was immediately after reprinted in octavo, in weekly numbers, of which an impression of ten thousand was bought up with avidity.

It would be superfluous to dwell long on the merits of a work so well known, and undoubtedly entitled to high praise as a compilation, but beyond this his warmest admirers cannot judiciously extend their encomiums. Although it may be allowed to excel the histories of Carte or Guthrie, and on account of its brevity, to be preferable to Rapin, and far more to his continuator Tindal, yet it is impossible to place it on a level with the histories of Hume, Robertson, Gibbon, or Henry. In the Critical Review it was highly praised, as might be expected, but with an affectation of candour and moderation which Smollett could not long preserve. In the Review for September 1758, we have a piece of querulous declamation, which is far more fully characteristic of the man and of the author. It is here extracted as a general specimen of the indignation which he felt against any serious attack, and it may serve to explain the relative position in which he stood with his contemporaries. The cause of the following effusion was a pamphlet published by the rev. T. Comber, in which he censures the characters Smollett had given of king William and queen Mary, &c.

Smollett's answer begins thus—

" Tell me your company, and I'll describe your manners, is a proverbial apothegm among our neighbours; and the maxim will generally hold good; but we apprehend the adage might be more justly turned to this purpose, Name your enemies, and I'll guess your character. If the Complete History of England were to be judged in this manner, we imagine the author would gladly submit to the determination of the

---

[2] Three only were published at this time, and the fourth was afterwards given gratis to the purchasers of the former. *C.*

public. Let us then see who are the professed enemies of that production: the sage, the patriot, the sedate Dr. Shebbeare: the serene Griffiths and his spouse, proprietors and directors of the Monthly Review: the profound, the candid, the modest Dr. Hill: the wise, the learned, and the temperate Thomas Comber, A. B. whose performance we are at present to consider. This is indeed a formidable group of adversaries, enough to daunt the heart of any young adventurer in the world of letters; but the author of the Complete History of England has been long familiar with such seas of trouble. The assault, however, which he has sustained from some of those heroes, was not altogether unprovoked. Shebbeare had been chastised in the Critical Review, for his insolent and seditious appeals to the public. He took it for granted, that the lash was exercised by the author of the Complete History of England: therefore he attacked that performance tooth and nail. He declared that there was neither grammar, meaning, composition, or reflection, either in the plan or the execution of the work itself. Griffiths was enraged against the same gentleman, because he was supposed to have set up the Critical Review, in opposition to the Monthly, of which he (Griffiths) was proprietor; accordingly he employed an obscure grub, who wrote in his garret, to bespatter the History of England. Hill, for these ten years, has, by turns, praised and abused Dr. Smollett, whom he did not know, without being able to vanquish that silent contempt, in which this gentleman ever held him and all his productions: piqued at this indifference and disdain, the said Hill has, in a weekly paper, thrown out some dirty insinuations against the author of the Complete History of England. We cannot rank the proprietors of R———n[3], and other histories, among the personal enemies of Dr. Smollett; because they were actuated by the dictates of self-interest, to decry his performance. This, however, they have pursued in the most sordid, illiberal, and ridiculous manner: they have caballed: they have slandered: they have vilified: they have prejudiced, misrepresented, and used undue influence among their correspondents in different parts of the kingdom: they have spared neither calumny nor expense, to prejudice the author and his work: they have had the effrontery to insinuate in a public advertisement that he was no better than an inaccurate plagiary from Rapin: and they have had the folly to declare, that Rapin's book was the most valuable performance, just immediately after they had taxed Dr. Smollett with having, by a specious plan, anticipated the judgment of the public. Finally, finding all their endeavours had proved abortive, we have reason to believe they hired the pen of the rev. Thomas Comber, of York, A. B. to stigmatize and blacken the character of the work which has been to them such a source of damage and vexation. Accordingly, this their champion has earned his wages with surprising eagerness and resolution: he has dashed through thick and thin, without fear of repulse; without dread of reputation. Indeed he writes with a degree of acrimony that seems to be personal; perhaps, if the truth was known, he would be found one of those obscure authors, who have occasionally received correction in some number of the Critical Review, and looks upon Dr. Smollett as the administrator of that correction; but this we only mention as a conjecture."—The concluding paragraph of this review of Comber's pamphlet, is not less characteristic of Smollett's temper, and style, when he wished to be thought above all petty resentments.

—Comber "very modestly says, he hopes he has kept within the bounds of good breeding, and employed none of that virulence which the Critical Reviewers have exer-

---

[3] Most of the names in this passage are printed only with the initial and final letters, except that of Rapin, which follows. This R—n may mean Robertson, whose first history was then in the press. C.

cised against the *most respectable characters*. One can hardly refrain from laughing when he reads this declaration. Mr. Comber may always be assured, that it is not in his power to excite the indignation of the Critical Reviewers: there are some objects too contemptible to excite resentment. We should be glad, however, to know what those *most respectable characters* are, that we have treated with indecency. Those *most respectable* personages are Drs. Shebbeare and Hill, Griffiths and his spouse; a group, to which the rev. Mr. Comber will make a very proper addition. We think we see this formidable band, forgetting the distinctions of party, sitting in close divan, animated with double pots, encouraged with double pay, by the right worshipful the proprietors of R——n, to renew their attacks against the Complete History of England. We shall prophecy, however, that the author of that work will never deign to take any public notice of what may be advanced against him by writers of their class. He considers them as little inconsiderable curs barking at the Moon. Nevertheless, in order to whet their spleen, we will inform the rev. Mr. Comber, that notwithstanding the uncommon arts, and great expense, with which his honest employers have puffed[4] and advertised his pamphlet, the Complete History of England continues to rise in the estimation of the public; and that above ten thousand numbers of the work are weekly purchased by the subjects of Great Britain, besides those that are sold in Ireland and the plantations."—

During his confinement in the King's Bench for the libel on admiral Knowles, he amused himself in writing the Adventures of Sir Launcelot Greaves, a sort of English Quixote. This he gave in detached parts in the British Magazine, one of those periodical works in which he was induced to engage by the consideration of a regular supply. This novel was afterwards published in two volumes, 12mo. but had not the popularity of his former works of that kind, and as a composition, whether in point of fable, character, or humour, is indeed far inferior to any of them.

The success of his History encouraged him to write a continuation of it, from 1748 to 1764. The volume for 1765, his biographer seems not to have known, was written by Guthrie during Smollett's absence on the continent. By the History and Continuation he is said to have cleared £2000. He is also supposed to have written the accounts of France, Italy, and Germany for the Universal History, when published in octavo volumes. A writer of the Gentleman's Magazine states, that he received fifteen hundred guineas for preparing a new edition of the same History, but this must be a mistake, as he was dead some years before that edition was undertaken.

When lord Bute was promoted to the office of first minister, Smollett's pen was engaged to support him against the popular clamour excited by Wilkes and his partizans. With this view our author commenced a weekly paper, called The Briton, which was answered by Wilkes in his more celebrated North Britain. Had this been a contest of argument, wit, or even mere personal and political recrimination, Smollett would have had little to fear from the talents of Wilkes; but the public mind, inflamed by every species of misrepresentation, was on the side of Wilkes, and the Briton was discontinued, when lord Bute, its supposed patron, could no longer keep his seat. Before this short contest, Smollett had lived on terms of intimacy with Wilkes, who, having no animosities that were not absolutely necessary to serve a temporary interest, probably did not think the worse of Smollett for giving him an opportunity to triumph over the author of the Complete History of England. Smollett, however, was not disposed to view the matter

---

4 Comber's pamphlet was reviewed in the Monthly in September, and Smollett could not have seen it when he wrote this. *C.*

with this complacency. He expected a reward for his services, and was disappointed, and his chagrin on this occasion he soon took an opportunity to express.

About the years 1763 and 1764 we find his name to a translation of Voltaire's works, and to a compilation entitled The Present State of all Nations, in eight volumes, 8vo. What he contributed, besides his name, to either of these undertakings cannot now be ascertained. The translation of Voltaire is in all respects beneath his talents.

In the month of June 1763, he went abroad, partly on account of his health, and partly to relieve his and Mrs. Smollett's grief for the loss of their only child, an amiable young lady who died in her fifteenth year. He pursued his journey through France and Italy about two years, and soon after his return in 1766, gave the public the result of his observations, in two volumes, 8vo. entitled, Travels through France and Italy. This work, although it attained no high degree of popularity, was read with sympathetic interest, as exhibiting a melancholy picture of the author's mind, " traduced" as he informs us, " by malice, persecuted by faction, and overwhelmed by the sense of domestic calamity." On this account, the natural and artificial objects which make travelling delightful, had no other effect on him than to excite his spleen, which he has often indulged in representations and opinions unworthy of his taste. These, however, are not unmixed with observations of another kind, acute, just, and useful. It is remarkable that in a subsequent publication (Humphrey Clinker) he makes his principal character, Matthew Bramble, describe what he saw in England in the same unvaried language of spleen and ill-humour.

Soon after his arrival from the continent, his health still decaying, he undertook a journey to Scotland, and renewed his attachment to his relations and friends. During this journey, Dr. Moore informs us, that " he was greatly tormented with rheumatic pains, and afflicted besides with an ulcer on his arm which had been neglected on its first appearance. These disorders confined him much to his chamber, but did not prevent his conversation from being highly entertaining, when the misery of which they were productive, permitted him to associate with his friends." From Scotland he went to Bath, and about the beginning of 1767 had recovered his health and spirits in a very considerable degree.

His next production, which appeared in 1769, proved that he had not forgotten the neglect with which he was treated by that ministry, in whose favour he wrote the Briton. This was entitled the Adventures of an Atom. Under fictitious names, of Japanese structure, he reviews the conduct of the eminent politicians who had conducted or opposed the measures of government from the year 1754, and retracts the opinion he had given of some of these statesmen in his history, particularly of the earl of Chatham and lord Bute. His biographer allows that many of the characters are grossly misrepresented, for which no other reason can be assigned than his own disappointment. The whole proves, what has often been seen since his time, that the measures which are right and proper when a reward is in view, are wrong and abominable when that reward is withheld.

The publication of this work, while it proclaimed that his sincerity as a political writer was not much to be depended on, afforded another instance of that imprudence which his biographer has ingeniously carried over to the account of independence. His health again requiring the genial influences of a milder climate, the expense of which he was unable to bear, his friends solicited the very persons whom he had just satyrized, to obtain for him the office of consul at Nice, Naples, or Leghorn. Dr. Moore informs us, with more acrimony than truth, " that these applications were fruitless. Dr. Smollett had never *spanielled* ministers; he could not endure the insolence of office, or stoop to cultivate the favour of any person merely on account of his power: and besides he was a man of genius."

He set out, however, for Italy early in 1770, with a debilitated body, and a mind probably irritated by his recent disappointment, but not without much of the ease which argues firmness, since during this journey he could so pleasantly divert his sorrows by writing The Expedition of Humphrey Clinker. This novel, if it may be so called, for it has no regular fable, in point of genuine humour, knowledge of life and manners, and delineation of character, is inferior only to his Roderick Random and Peregrine Pickle. It has already been noticed that Matthew Bramble, the principal character, displays the cynical temper and humane feelings of the author on his tour on the continent; and it may now be added that he has given another sketch of himself in the character of Serle in the first volume. This account of the ingratitude of Paunceford to Smollett is strictly true; and as his biographers seem unacquainted with the circumstances, the following may not be uninteresting, which was related to me by the late intimate friend of Smollett, Mr. Hamilton, the printer and proprietor of the Critical Review.

" Paunceford was a John C——l, who was fed by Smollett when he had not bread to eat, nor clothes to cover him. He was taken out to India as private secretary to a celebrated governor-general, and as essayist; and after only three years absence, returned with forty thousand pounds. From India he sent several letters to Smollett, professing that he was coming over to lay his fortune at the feet of his benefactor. But on his arrival, he treated Smollett, Hamilton, and others, who had befriended him, with the most ungrateful contempt. The person who taught him the art of essaying became reduced in circumstances, and is now (1792) or lately was collector of the toll on carts at Holborn Bars. C——l never paid him, or any person to whom he was indebted. He died in two or three years after at his house near Hounslow, universally despised. At the request of Smollett, Mr. Hamilton employed him to write in the Critical Review, which, with Smollett's charity, was all his support, previously to his departure for India."

Such kindness and such ingratitude ought not to be concealed, but it is less necessary to point out the very flattering account he has given of his hospitality and patronage of inferior authors, while he resided at Chelsea. While full credit, however, is given for these virtues, it cannot be a disrespectful wish that he had found another panegyrist than himself. There is no instance of any man of Dr. Smollett's rank in the literary world taking so many opportunities to sound his own praises, and that without any of the disguises which are employed by men who wish to acquire a factitious character. At this time, perhaps, he was desirous of recovering the reputation which envy and malice had suppressed or darkened, and might not be without hopes that as he was now approaching the close of life, his enemies would relent, and admit his evidence.

In the neighbourhood of Leghorn, he lingered through the summer of 1771, in the full possession of his faculties, and died on the 21st of October, in the 51st year of his age. Dr. Armstrong, who visited him at Leghorn, honoured his remains with a Latin inscription, elegantly noticing his genius and virtues, and severely reflecting on the " times, in which hardly any literary merit but such as was in the most false or futile taste, received any encouragement from the mock Mæcenases of Britain." In the year 1774, a column was erected to his memory on the banks of the Leven, near the house in which he was born. The inscription on this was the joint production of lord Kames, professor George Stuart, and John Ramsay, esq. and was revised by Dr. Johnson. It is elegant, affecting and modest.

Dr. Moore's opinion of his personal character is thus given :

" The person of Smollett was stout and well proportioned, his countenance engaging, his manner reserved, with a certain air of dignity that seemed to indicate that he was not unconscious of his own powers. He was of a disposition so humane and generous, that he was ever ready to serve the unfortunate, and on some occasions to assist them beyond what his circumstances could justify. Though few could penetrate with more acuteness into character, yet none was more apt to overlook misconduct when attended with misfortune.

" He lived in an hospitable manner, but he despised that hospitality which is founded on ostentation, which entertains only those whose situation in life flatters the vanity of the entertainer, or such as can make returns of the same kind, that hospitality which keeps a debtor and creditor account of dinners. Smollett invited to his plain but plentiful table the persons whose characters he esteemed, in whose conversation he delighted, and many for no other reason than because they stood in need of his countenance and protection.

" As nothing was more abhorrent to his nature than pertness or intrusion, few things could render him more indignant than a cold reception: to this however he imagined he had sometimes been exposed on his application in favour of others : for himself he never made an application to any great man in his life.

" Free from *vanity*, Smollett had a considerable share of pride, and great sensibility: his passions were easily moved, and too impetuous when roused : he could not conceal his contempt of folly, his detestation of fraud, nor refrain from proclaiming his indignation against every instance of oppression.

" Though Smollett possessed a versatility of style in writing, which he could accommodate to every character, he had no suppleness in his conduct. His learning, diligence, and natural acuteness would have rendered him eminent in the science of medicine, had he persevered in that profession ; other parts of his character were ill-suited for augmenting his practice. He could neither stoop to impose on credulity, nor humour caprice.

" He was of an intrepid, independent, imprudent disposition, equally incapable of deceit and adulation, and more disposed to cultivate the acquaintance of those he could serve, than of those who could serve him. What wonder that a man of his character was not, what is called, successful in life !"

How far this character agrees with the facts detailed in this narrative, and which are principally taken from Dr. Moore, may be now safely left to the determination of the reader.

As an author, Dr. Smollett is universally allowed the praise of original genius displayed with an ease and variety which are rarely found. Yet this character belongs chiefly to his novels. In correct delineation of life and manners, and in drawing characters of the humorous class, he has few equals. But when this praise is bestowed, every critic who values what is more important than genius itself, the interest of morals and decency, must surely stop.   It can be of no use to analyze each individual scene, incident, or character in works which, after all, must be pronounced unfit to be read.

But if the morals of the reader were in no danger, his taste can hardly escape being insulted or perverted.   Smollett's humour is of so low a cast, and his practical jokes so frequently end in what is vulgar, mean, and filthy, that it would be impossible to acquire a relish for them, without injury done to the chaster feelings, and to the just respect due to genuine wit.   No novel writer seems to take more delight in assembling images and incidents that are gross and disgusting: nor has he scrupled to introduce, with more than slight notice, those vices which are not fit even to be named.   If this be a just representation of his most favourite novels, it is in vain to oppose it by pointing out passages which do credit to his genius, and more vain to attempt to prove that virtue and taste are not directly injured by such productions.

As a historian, Smollett's reputation has certainly not been preserved.   When he published his History, something of the kind was wanted, and it was executed in a manner not unworthy of his talents.   But the writings of Hume, Robertson, and Gibbon have introduced a taste for a higher species of historical composition: and, if I am not mistaken, there has been no complete edition of Smollett's History, but that which he published.   Had he been allowed the proper time for revision and reflection, it cannot be doubted that he might have produced a work deserving of more lasting fame.   His History, even as we have it, when we advert to the short time he took for its completion, is a very extraordinary effort, and instead of blaming him for occasionally following his authorities too servilely, the wonder ought to be that he found leisure to depart from them so frequently, and to assign reasons, which are not those of a superficial thinker.   It is impossible, however, to quit this subject without adverting to the mode of publication which dispersed the work among a class of persons, the purchasers of sixpenny numbers, whom Smollett too easily took for the learned and discerning part of the public.   This fallacious encouragement afforded fuel to his irritable temper, by inciting him, not only to the arts of puffing, by which the literary character is degraded, but to those vulgar and splenetic recriminations of which a specimen has been given, and which must have lowered him yet more in the opinion of the eminent characters of his day.

Smollett was not successful in his dramatic attempts.   Those who judged from the ease and vivacity of his pictures of life and manners in his novels, no doubt thought themselves justified in encouraging him in this species of composition.   But all experience shows that the talents necessary for the prose epic, and those for the regular drama, are essentially different, and have rarely met in one man.   Fielding, a novelist greatly superior, and who after the trials of more than half a century, may be pronounced inimitable, was yet foiled in his dramatic attempts, although he returned to the charge with fresh courage and skill.

As a poet, in which character only Smollett is here introduced, although his pieces are few, they must be allowed to confer a very high rank.   It is, indeed, greatly to be lamented that he did not cultivate his poetical talents more frequently and more extensively.   The Tears of Scotland and the Ode to Independence, particularly the latter, are equal to the highest efforts in the pathetic and sublime.   In the Ode to Independence there is evidently the inspiration of real genius, free from all artificial aid, or meretricious ornament.   It may be questioned whether there are many compositions in our language which more forcibly charm by all the enchantments of taste, expression, and sentiment. Some observations on this ode, and usually printed with it, are the production of professor Richardson. It may be necessary to add that this ode was left in manuscript by Smollett, and published at Glasgow and London in 1773.

Advice and Reproof have already been noticed, and are more remarkable for their satirical aim, than for poetical beauties. His songs and other small pieces were introduced principally in his novels and in the Reprisal. To our regret we may add some degree of surprise, that one who could write so well should write so little in a department which generally confers a much higher degree of fame than he could expect from most of his other productions.

The original works of Smollett were published by the London proprietors in 1797, in eight volumes, 8vo. To this edition Dr. Moore was engaged to furnish a life. Another life about the same time was published at Edinburgh by Dr. Anderson. I have availed myself of both, as far as regards matters of fact. If I have not been able to join in their opinion of Dr. Smollett, it is some excuse that I have been indebted to them for the principal reasons which have induced me to differ.

# POEMS

OF

# DR. SMOLLETT,

---

## THE REGICIDE; OR, JAMES THE FIRST OF SCOTLAND.

### A TRAGEDY.

### PREFACE.

WHATEVER reluctance I have to trouble the public with a detail of the mortifications I have suffered, in my attempts to bring the ensuing performance on the stage, I think it a duty incumbent upon me, to declare my reasons for presenting it in this extraordinary manner; and, if the explanation shall be found either tedious or trifling, I hope the candid reader will charge my impertinence upon those who drove me to the necessity of making such an ineffectual appeal.

Besides, I flatter myself, that a fair representation of the usage I have met with will be as a beacon, to caution other inexperienced authors against the insincerity of managers, to which they might otherwise become egregious dupes; and, after a cajoling dream of good fortune, wake in all the aggravation of disappointment.

Although I claim no merit from having finished a tragedy at the age of eighteen, I cannot help thinking myself entitled to some share of indulgence for the humility, industry, and patience I have exerted during a period of ten years, in which this unfortunate production hath been exposed to the censure of critics of all degrees; and in consequence of their several opinions, altered, and (I hope) amended, times without number.

Had some of those who were pleased to call themselves my friends been at any pains to deserve the character, and told me ingenuously what I had to expect in the capacity of an author, when I first professed myself of that venerable fraternity, I should, in all probability, have spared myself the incredible labour and chagrin I have since undergone: but, as early as the year 1739, my play was taken into the protection of one of those little fellows who are sometimes called great men; and, like other orphans, neglected accordingly.

Stung with resentment, which I mistook for contempt, I resolved to punish this barbarous indifference, and actually discarded my patron; consoling myself with the barren praise of a few associates, who, in the most indefatigable manner, employed their time and influence in collecting from all quarters observations on my piece, which, in consequence of those suggestions, put on a new appearance almost every day, until my occasions called me out of the kingdom.

Soon after my return, I and my production were introduced to a late patentee, of courteous memory, who (rest his soul!) found means to amuse me a whole season, and then declared it impracticable to bring it on till next year; advising me to make my application more early in the winter; that we might have time to concert such alterations as should be thought necessary for its successful appearance on the stage.—But I did not find my account in following this wholesome advice; for, to me, he was always less and less at leisure. In short, after sundry promises, and numberless evasions, in the course of which he practised upon me the whole art of procrastination, I demanded his final answer, with such obstinacy and warmth, that he could no longer

17

resist my importunity, and refused my tragedy in plain terms.—Not that he mentioned any material objections to the piece itself, but seemed to fear my interest was not sufficient to support it in the representation; affirming, that no dramatic composition, however perfect, could succeed by its own merit only; but must entirely depend upon a faction raised in its behalf.—Incensed at this unexpected declaration, I reproached him bitterly for having trifled with me so long; and, like my brother Bayes, threatened to carry my performance to the other house.

This was actually my intention, when I was given to understand by a friend, that a nobleman of great weight had expressed an inclination to peruse it; and that, as interest was requisite, I could not do better than gratify his desire with all expedition. I committed it accordingly to the care of my counsellor, who undertook to give me a good account of it in less than a fortnight: but four months elapsed before I heard any tidings of my play; and then it was retrieved by pure accident (I believe) from the most dishonourable apartment of his lordship's house.

Enraged at the behaviour of this supercilious peer, and exceedingly mortified at the miscarriage of all my efforts, I wreaked my resentment upon the innocent cause of my disgraces, and forthwith condemned it to oblivion, where, in all probability, it would have for ever slept, like a miserable abortion, had not a young gentleman of learning and taste waked my paternal sense, and persuaded me not only to rescue it from the tomb, where it had lain two whole years, but also to new model the plan, which was imperfect and undigested before, and mould it into a regular tragedy, confined within the unities of the drama.

Thus improved, it fell into the hands of a gentleman who had wrote for the stage, and happened to please him so much, that he spoke of it very cordially to a young nobleman, since deceased, who, in the most generous manner, charged himself with the care of introducing it to the public; and, in the mean time, honoured me with his own remarks, in conformity to which, it was immediately altered, and offered by his lordship to the new manager of Drury-lane theatre. It was about the latter end of the season when this candid personage, to whom I owe many obligations for the exercises of patience he has set me, received the performance, which, some weeks after, he returned, assuring my friend that he was pre-engaged to another author, but if I could be prevailed upon to reserve it till the ensuing winter, he would bring it on.—In the interim, my noble patron left London, whither he was doomed never to return; and the conscientious manager next season, instead of fulfilling his own promise and my expectation, gratified the town with the production of a player, the fate of which every body knows.

I shall leave the reader to make his reflections on this event, and proceed to relate the other particulars of fortune, that attended my unhappy issue, which, in the succeeding spring, had the good luck to acquire the approbation of an eminent wit, who proposed a few amendments, and recommended it to a person, by whose influence, I laid my account with seeing it appear at last,

with such advantage as should make ample amends for all my disappointments.

But here too I reckoned without my host. The master of Covent Garden theatre bluntly rejected it, as a piece altogether unfit for the stage; even after he had told me, in presence of another gentleman, that he believed he should not venture to find fault with any performance which had gained the good opinion of the honourable person who approved and recommended my play.

Baffled in every attempt, I renounced all hopes of its seeing the light, when a humane lady of quality interposed, so urgently in its behalf, with my worthy friend the other manager, that he very complaisantly received it again, and had recourse to the old mystery of protraction, which he exercised with such success, that the season was almost consumed, before he could afford it a reading. My patience being by this time quite exhausted, I desired a gentleman, who interested himself in my concerns, to go and expostulate with the vaticide: and indeed, this piece of friendship he performed with so much zeal, upbraiding him with his evasive and presumptuous behaviour, that the sage politician was enraged at his reprimand; and in the mettle of his wrath, pronounced my play a wretched piece, deficient in language, sentiment, character, and plan. My friend, who was surprised at the hardiness and severity of this sentence, asking how he came to change his opinion, which had been more favourable when the tragedy was first put into his hands; he answered, that his opinion was not altered, neither had he ever uttered an expression in its favour.

This was an unlucky assertion—for, the other immediately produced a letter which I had received from the young nobleman two years before, beginning with these words——

" Sir, I have received Mr. L——'s answer; who says, he thinks your play has indubitable merit, but has prior promises to Mr. T——n, that as an honest man, cannot be evaded."——And concluding thus, " As the manager has promised me the choice of the season next year, if you'll be advised by me, rest it with me."

After having made some remarks suitable to the occasion, my friend left him to chew the cud of reflection, the result of which was, a message to my patroness, importing, (with many expressions of duty) that neither the circumstances of his company, nor the advanced season of the year, would permit him to obey her command, but if I would wait till next winter, and during the summer, make such alterations as I had agreed to, at a conference with some of his principal performers, he would assuredly put my play in rehearsal, and in the mean time give me an obligation in writing, for my further satisfaction.—I would have taken him at his word, without hesitation, but was persuaded to dispense with the proffered security, that I might not seem to doubt the influence or authority of her ladyship.—The play, however, was altered and presented to this upright director, who renounced his engagement, without the least scruple, apology, or reason assigned.

Thus have I in the most impartial manner, (perhaps too circumstantially) displayed the conduct of those playhouse managers with whom I have had any concern, relating to my tragedy: and whatever disputes have happened between the actors and me, are suppressed as frivolous animosities unworthy of the reader's attention.

Had I suffered a repulse when I first presented my performance, I should have had cause to complain of my being excluded from that avenue to the public favour, which ought to lie open to all men of genius; and how far I deserve that distinction, I now leave the world to decide; after I have, in justice to myself, declared that my hopes of success were not derived from the partial applause of my own friends only, but inspired (as some of my greatest enemies know) by the approbation of persons of the first note in the republic of taste, whose countenance, I vainly imagined, would have been an effectual introduction to the stage.

Be that as it will, I hope the unprejudiced observer will own, with indignation and disdain, that every disappointment I have endured was an accumulated injury; and the whole of my adversary's conduct, a series of the most unjustifiable equivocation and insolent absurdity: for, though he may be excusable in refusing a work of this kind, either on account of his ignorance or discernment, surely, neither the one nor the other can vindicate his dissimulation and breach of promise to the author.

Abuse of prerogative, in matters of greater importance, prevails so much at present, and is so generally overlooked, that it is almost ridiculous to lament the situation of authors, who must either, at once, forego all opportunities of acquiring reputation in dramatic poetry, or humble themselves so, as to sooth the pride, and humour the petulance of a mere Goth, who, by the most preposterous delegation of power, may become sole arbiter of this kind of writing.

Nay, granting that a bard is willing to prostitute his talents so shamefully, perhaps he may never find an occasion to practise this vile condescension to advantage: for, after he has gained admission to a patentee (who is often more difficult of access than a sovereign prince) and even made shift to remove all other objections, an insurmountable obstacle may be raised by the manager's avarice, which will dissuade him from hazarding a certain expense on an uncertain issue, when he can fill his theatre without running any risk, or disobliging his principal actors, by putting them to the trouble of studying new parts—

Besides, he will be apt to say within himself, " If I must entertain the town with variety, it is but natural that I should prefer the productions of my friends, or of those who have any friends worth obliging, to the works of obscure strangers, who have nothing to recommend them but a doubtful superiority of merit, which, in all likelihood, will never rise in judgment against me."

That such have been the reflections of patentees, I believe no man of intelligence and veracity will deny; and I will venture to affirm, that on the strength of interest or connection with the stage, some people have commenced dramatic authors, who otherwise would have employed their faculties in exercises better adapted to their capacity.

After what has been said, any thing by way of application would be an insult on the under-standing of the public, to which I owe and acknowledge the most indelible obligation for former favours as well as for the uncommon encouragement I have received in the publication of the following play.

---

## PERSONS OF THE DRAMA.

### MEN.

King of Scotland.
Angus.
Dunbar.
Ramsay.
Athol.
Stuart.
Grime.
Cattan.

### WOMEN.

Queen.
Eleonora.

GUARDS, ATTENDANTS, ETC.

---

## ACT I. SCENE I.

A Convent in Perth.

ANGUS, DUNBAR.

### DUNBAR.

But that my duty calls, I would decline
Th' unwelcome office.—Now, when Justice waves
Her flaming sword, and loudly claims her due,
Thus to arrest her arm, and offer terms
Of peace to traitors, who avow their crime,
Is to my apprehension weak, and suits
But little with the majesty of kings.——
Why sleeps the wonted valour of our prince?

### ANGUS.

Not to th' ensanguin'd field of death alone
Is Valour limited: she sits serene
In the delib'rate council; sagely scans
The source of action; weighs, prevents, provides,
And scorns to count her glories, from the feats
Of brutal force alone,—
　　　　　—What frenzy were it
To risk our fortune on th' unsure event
Of one occurrence, naked as we are
To unforeseen disaster, when the terms
We proffer may retard th' impending blow?
—Better to conquer by delay: the rage
Of Athol's fierce adherents, flush'd with hope
Of plunder and revenge, will soon abate,
And ev'ry hour bring succour to our cause.

### DUNBAR.

Well hast thou taught me, how the piercing eye
Of calm sagacity, excels the dint
Of headstrong resolution.——Yet, my soul
Pants for a fair occasion to revenge
My father's wrongs on Athol's impious head!
Yes, Angus, while the blood of March revolves
Within my veins, the traitor shall not find
His perfidy forgot—But what of this?
What are my private injuries compar'd

To those he meditates against the state!
Against a prince with ev'ry virtue grac'd
That dignifies the throne, to whom the ties
Of kindred and allegiance could not bind
His faithless heart: not ev'n the sacred bond
Of friendship unreserv'd!—For well thou know'st,
The king securely listen'd to his voice,
As to an oracle.

#### ANGUS.

'Twas there indeed
He triumph'd in his guile!—Th' unwary prince,
Sooth'd by his false professions, crown'd his guilt
With boundless confidence; and little thought
That very confidence supply'd his foe
With means to shake his throne!—While Athol led
His royal kinsman thro' the dang'rous path
Of sudden reformation, and observ'd
What murmurs issu'd from the giddy crowd.
Each popular commotion he improv'd
By secret ministers; and disavow'd
Those very measures he himself devised!
Thus cherish'd long by his flagitious arts,
Rebellion glow'd in secret, 'till at length
His scheme mature, and all our loyal thanes
At their own distant homes repos'd secure,
The flame burst out.—Now from his native hills,
With his accomplice Grime, and youthful heir,
Impet'ous Stuart, like a sounding storm
He rushes down with five revolting clans;
Displays a spurious title to the crown,
Arraigns the justice of this monarch's sway,
And by this sudden torrent, means, no doubt,
To sweep him from the throne.

#### DUNBAR.

Aspiring villain!
A fit associate has he chose: a wretch
Of soul more savage breathes not vital air,
Than Grime:—but Stuart 'till of late, maintain'd
A fairer fame.

#### ANGUS.

A cherish'd hope expires
In his dishonour too!—While Stuart's ear
Was deaf to vicious counsel, and his soul
Remained unshaken, by th' enchanting lure
Which vain ambition spread before his eye,
He bloom'd the pride of Caledonia's youth,
In virtue, valour, and external grace:—
For thou, sole rival of his fame, wast train'd
To martial deeds, in climes remote.

#### DUNBAR.

O thane!
Whatever wreaths from danger's steely crest
My sword hath won; whatever toils sustain'd
Beneath the sultry noon, and cold, damp night,
Could ne'er obtain for me one genial smile
Of her, who bless'd that happy rival's vows
With mutual love!—Why should I dread to own
The tender throbbings of my captive heart!
The melting passion which has long inspir'd
My breast for Eleonora, and implore
A parent's sanction to support my claim?

#### ANGUS.

Were she more fair and gentle than she is,
And to my partial eye nought e'er appear'd
So gently fair, I would approve thy claim
To her peculiar smiles.

#### DUNBAR.

Then will I strive,
With unremitted ardour, to subdue
Her coy reluctance; while I scorn the threats
Of frantic jealousy that flames unrein'd
In Stuart's breast!—But see! the fair one comes,
In all the pride of dazzling charms array'd.

### SCENE II.

#### ANGUS, DUNBAR, ELEONORA.

#### ELEONORA.

Something of moment, by a fresh dispatch
Imparted to the king, requires in haste
The presence of my sire.

#### ANGUS.

Forbear a while
Thy parley with the foe; and here attend
Our consultation's issue.——

[Exit Angus.

### SCENE III.

#### DUNBAR, ELEONORA.

#### DUNBAR.

I!! it suits
A soldier's tongue to plead the cause of love,
In phrase adapted to the tender theme:
But trust me, beauteous wonder! when I swear
Not the keen impulse and impatient hope
Of glory, glowing in the warrior's breast,
With more awaken'd transport, fill'd my soul
When the fierce battle rag'd, than that I feel
At thy approach!—My tongue has oft reveal'd
The dictates of my heart; but thou, averse
With cold disdain, hast ever chill'd my hopes,
And scorn'd my proffer'd vows!——

#### ELEONORA.

O youth, beware!
Let not the flow'ry scenes of joy and peace,
That faithless passion to the view presents,
Ensnare thee into woe!—Thou little know'st
What mischief lurks in each deceitful charm;
What griefs attend on love.—

#### DUNBAR.

Keen are the pangs
Of hapless love, and passion unapprov'd:
But where consenting wishes meet, and vows
Reciprocally breath'd confirm the tie,
Joy rolls on joy, an inexhausted stream!
And virtue crowns the sacred scene with peace!

#### ELEONORA.

Illusion all! the phantoms of a mind
That, o'er its present fate repining, courts
The vain resource of fancy's airy dreams.—
War is thy province.—War be thy pursuit.—

#### DUNBAR.

O! thou wouldst tell me, I am savage all—
Too much estrang'd to the soft arts of life,
To warm thy breast?——Yes, war has been my
War's rough sincerity, unskill'd in modes [school—
Of peaceful commerce—Soften'd not the less
To pious truth, humanity, and love.

#### ELEONORA.

Yes:—I were envious to refuse applause,
When ev'ry mouth is open'd in thy praise.—
I were ungrateful not to yield thee more,
Distinguish'd by thy choice; and tho' my heart
Denies thee love, thy virtues have acquir'd
Th' esteem of Eleonora.

#### DUNBAR.

O! thy words
Would fire the hoary hermit's languid soul
With ecstasies of pride!—How then shall I,
Elate with every vainer hope that warms
Th' aspiring thought of youth, thy praise sustain
With moderation?——Cruelly benign!
Thou hast adorn'd the victim; 'but, alas!
Thou likewise giv'st the blow!——
— Tho' Nature's hand
With so much art has blended ev'ry grace
In thy enchanting form, that ev'ry eye
With transport views thee, and conveys unseen
The soft infection to the vanquish'd soul,
Yet wilt thou not the gentle passion own,
That vindicates thy sway! —

#### ELEONORA.

O gilded curse!
More fair than rosy Morn, when first she smiles
O'er the dew-brighten'd verdure of the spring!
But more deceitful, tyrannous, and fell
Than syrens, tempests, and devouring flame!
May I ne'er sicken, languish, and despair
Within thy dire domain!—Listen, ye powers!
And yield your sanction to my purpos'd vow—
—If e'er my breast—— [kneeling.

#### DUNBAR.

For ever let me pine
In secret misery, divorc'd from hope!
But ah, forbear! nor forfeit thy own peace
Perhaps in one rash moment.——

### SCENE IV.

#### DUNBAR, ELEONORA, HERALD.

#### HERALD.

————From the tower
That fronts the hills, due north, a moving host
Is now descry'd: and from the southern gate
A cloud of dust is seen to roll, the gleam
Of burnish'd arms oft thro' the dusky sphere
Salutes the dazzled eye;—a loyal band
With valiant Ramsay, from the banks of Tweed,
That hastens to our aid.—The first, suppos'd
The rebel train of Athol.—By command
Of Angus, I attend thee, to demand
An audience of the foe.

#### DUNBAR.

I follow straight.
[Exit Herald.
Whate'er is amiably fair—whate'er
Inspires the gen'rous aim of chaste desire,
My soul contemplates and adores in thee!
Yet will I not with vain complainings vex
Thy gentle nature.—My unblemish'd love
Shall plead in my behalf. [Exit Dunbar.

### SCENE V.

#### ELEONORA.

Adieu, brave youth!
Why art thou doom'd to suffer fruitless pains?

And why, alas! am I the destin'd wretch
That must inflict them?—Agonizing thought!
I yielded up my fond, believing heart
To him who basely left it, for the charms
Of treacherous ambition! hapless Stuart!
How art thou chang'd! how lost! thy cruel fate,
Like a false harlot, smiles thee into ruin!

### SCENE VI.

*Enter* STUART *disguised like a priest.*

#### STUART, ELEONORA.

#### STUART.

The mighty schemes of empire soar too high
For your distinction, daughter.—Simple woman
Is weak in intellect, as well as frame,
And judges often from the partial voice
That soothes her wishes most.
[Discovering himself.

#### ELEONORA.

Ha, frantic youth!
What guilty purpose leads thy daring steps
To this forbidden place?—Art thou not come
Beneath that sacred veil, the more to brave
Th' avenging hand of Heav'n?

#### STUART.

No—that I tread
The paths of danger, where each bosom pants
With keen revenge against me, speaks aloud
The fervour of my love—My love misplac'd!
Else, would'st thou not receive the gen'rous proof
With anger and disdain.—

#### ELEONORA.

Have I not cause
To drive thee from my heart?—Hast thou not
chas'd
All faith, and truth, and loyalty from thine?
Say, hast thou not conspir'd against thy prince?
A prince! who cherish'd thee with parent's zeal,
With friendship honour'd thee, and ev'ry day
With bounteous favour crown'd thy rising wish?

#### STUART.

Curse on his arts!—his aim was to enslave
Th' aspiring soul, to stifle and repress
Th' energing dictates of my native right,
To efface the glowing images within,
Awak'd by glory, and retain by fraud
The sceptre he usurps!

#### ELEONORA.

Insidious charge!
As feeble as unjust!-for, clear as day,
In course direct——

#### STUART.

In idle argument
Let us not now consume the precious hour;
The middle stream is pass'd; and the safe shore
Invites our dauntless footsteps—Yonder Sun
That climbs the noon-tide arch, already sees
Twelve thousand vassals, marching in the train
Of warlike Athol; and before the shades
Of ev'ning deepen, Perth's devoted walls
Will shake before them—E'er the tempest roars,
I come to snatch thee from th' impending storm—

#### ELEONORA.

O impotent of thought!—O! dead to shame!
Shall I for pompous infamy forego
Th' internal peace that virtue calls her own?

#### STUART.

Or say, thy love, inconstant as the wave,
Another object claims.—False—perjur'd maid!
I mark'd thy minion, as he charm'd thine ear
With grov'ling adulation.—Yes, I saw
Thy looks, in artful languishment, disclose
Thy yielding soul, and heard thy tongue proclaim
The praises of Dunbar.—

#### ELEONORA.

Away—away!
I scorn thy mean suspicion, and renounce
Thy passion with thy crimes.—Tho' bred in camps,
Dunbar is gentle, gen'rous, and humane;
Possess'd of ev'ry manly grace, to win
The coyest virgin's heart,——

#### STUART.

Perdition whelm
The prostrate sycophant!—may Heav'n exhaust
Its thunder on my head—may Hell disgorge
Infernal plagues to blast me, if I cease
To persecute the caitiff, 'till his blood
Assuage my parch'd revenge!—Perfidious slave!
To steal between me and my darling hope!—
The traitor durst not, had I been—O vows!
Where is your obligation?—Eleonora!
O lovely curse! restore me to myself!—

#### ELEONORA.

Rage on, fierce youth, more savage than the storm
That howls on Thule's shore!—th' unthrifty maid
Too credulously fond! who gave away
Her heart so lavishly, deserves to wed
The woes that from her indiscretion flow!—
—Yet ev'n my folly should, with thee, obtain
A fairer title and a kinder fate!—

#### STUART.

Ha! weep'st thou?—witness all ye sacred pow'rs!
Her philtres have undone me!—lo, my wrath
Subsides again to love!—Enchantress! say,
Why hast thou robb'd me of my reason thus?

#### ELEONORA.

Has Eleonora robb'd thee?—O recall
Those flatt'ring arts thy own deceit employ'd
To wreck my peace?—recal thy fervent vows
Of constant faith—thy sighs and ardent looks!
Then whisper to thy soul, those vows were false—
Those sighs unfaithful, and those looks disguis'd!

#### STUART.

Thou—thou art chang'd—but Stuart still the same!
Ev'n whilst thou chid'st me, ev'ry tender wish
Awakes anew, and in my glowing breast
Unutterable fondness pants again!—
—Wilt thou not smile again, as when, reclin'd
By Tay's smooth-gliding stream, we softly breath'd
Our mutual passion to the vernal breeze?

#### ELEONORA.

Adieu—dear scenes, adieu!—ye fragrant paths
So courted once!—ye spreading boughs, that wave
Your blossoms o'er the stream!—delightful shades!
Where the bewitching music of thy tongue,
First charm'd my captive soul!—when gentle love
Inspir'd the soothing tale!—Love—sacred Love,
That lighted up his flame at Virtue's lamp!—

#### STUART.

In Time's eternal round, shall we not hail
Another season equally serene?——

—To day, in snow array'd, stern Winter rules
The ravag'd plain—Anon the teeming Earth
Unlocks her stores, and Spring adorns the year:
And shall not we—while Fate, like Winter, frowns,
Expect revolving bliss?

#### ELEONORA.

—Would'st thou return
To loyalty and me—my faithful heart
Would welcome thee again!—

#### ANGUS *within*.

Guard ev'ry gate,
That none may 'scape—

#### ELEONORA.

Ha!—whither wilt thou fly?
Discover'd and beset!

#### STUART.

Let Angus come—
His short-liv'd pow'r I scorn—
                    [*Throws away his disguise.*

### SCENE VII.

*Enter* ANGUS *with guards*, STUART, ELEONORA.

#### ANGUS.

What dark resolve,
By gloomy Athol plann'd, has hither led
Thy steps presumptuous?—Eleonora, hence,—
It ill befits thee—but, no more—away—
I'll brook no answer——    [*Exit Eleonora.*
                    —Is it not enough,
To lift Rebellion's impious brand on high,
And scorch the face of Faith; that ye thus creep
In ruffian ambush, seeking to perform
The deed ye dare not trust to open war?

#### STUART.

Thou little know'st me—or thy rankling hate
Defrauds my courage.—Wherefore should I skulk
Like the dishonour'd wretch, whose hireling steel
In secret lifted, wreaks with human gore,
When valiant Athol hastens, at the head
Of warlike thousands, to assert our cause?

#### ANGUS.

The cause of treason never was confin'd
To deeds of open war; but still adopts
The stab of crouching murder.—Thy revolt,
The stern contraction of thy sullen brow,
And this disguise, apostate! speak thee bent
On fatal errand.—

#### STUART.

That thou seest me here
Unarm'd, alone, from Angus might obtain
A fair interpretation—Stuart's love
Pleads not in mystic terms; nor are my vows
To Eleonora cancell'd or unknown——
Vows by thyself indulg'd, e'er envy yet,
Or folly had induc'd thee, to embrace
The fortunes of our foe.—Thy foul reproach
My soul retorts on thee! and mark, proud lord,
Revenge will have its turn!—

#### ANGUS.

Ha! must I bear
A beardless traitor's insults?—'tis not mine
To wage a fruitless war of words with thee, [just,
Vain glorious stripling.—While thine aims were
I seal'd thy title to my daughter's love;
But now, begrim'd with treason, as thou art,

By Heav'n! not diadems and thrones shall bribe
My approbation!—but the king himself
Shall judge thy conduct!—Guards—

## SCENE VIII.

*Enter* ELEONORA, *who kneels.*

—————— O! let me thus
Implore compassion, at a parent's knees.
Who ne'er refus'd—

### ANGUS.

—Convey him hence.—
[*Stuart is led off.*
—Arise—
Remember, Eleonora, from what source
Thine origin is drawn.—Thy mother's soul
In purity excell'd the snowy fleece
That clothes our northern hills!—her youthful
　　charms,
Her artless blush, her look severely sweet,
Her dignity of mien and smiles of love
Survive in thee—Let me behold thee too
Her honour's heiress— [*Exit Angus.*

## SCENE IX.

### ELEONORA.

—Yes—I will adhere
To this ill-omen'd honour! sacrifice
Life's promis'd joys to its austere decree;
And vindicate the glories of my race,
At the sad price of peace!—If Athol's arms
(Which Heav'n avert!) to treason add success,
My father's death will join his sov'reign's fall!
And if the cause of royalty prevail,
Each languid hope with Stuart must expire!—
　From thought to thought, perplex'd, in vain I
　　stray,
To pining anguish doom'd, and fell dismay!

## ACT II. *Scene continues.*

### ANGUS, DUNBAR.

#### DUNBAR.

BY Heav'n it glads me, that my sword shall find
An ample field to day.—The king arous'd,
Chafes like a lion in the toils betray'd!

#### ANGUS.

I mark'd his indignation, as it rose
At Athol's proud reply, from calm concern
To anxious tumult, menacing disdain,
And overboiling wrath.—But say, my friend,
How move the rebels?—Are their ranks dispos'd
By military skill?—Or come they on
In undistinguish'd crowds?—

#### DUNBAR.

In concourse rude
They swarm undisciplin'd—all arm'd alike
With sword and target.—On their first assault
(Fearless indeed and headlong!) all their hopes
Of conquest must depend.—If we, unbroke,
Sustain their onset; little skill'd in war,
To rally and renew the charge,
Confusion, havock and dismay will seize
Th' astonish'd rout.

#### ANGUS.

What numbers bring they on?

VOL. XV.

#### DUNBAR.

Ten thousand, as I guess.—

#### ANGUS.

Ours scarce amount
To half the number: yet, with those, we mean
To hazard an encounter.—Thou, mean while,
Shalt visit ev'ry passage, sound th' alarm,
And man the city-walls.—Here I attend
The king—and lo! he comes.— [*Exit Dunbar.*

## SCENE II.

### KING. ANGUS.

#### KING.

—The commonweal
Has been consulted.—Tenderness and zeal
B' came the parent.—Those have nought avail'd,—
Now, let correction speak the king incens'd!

#### ANGUS.

Not without cause, my liege shall dread rebuke
Attend your royal wrath.—What reign shall 'scape
Rebellion's curse, when your paternal sway
Has hatch'd the baneful pest?

#### KING.

Let Heaven decide
Between me and my foes.—That I would spare
The guiltless blood which must our quarrel dye,
No other proof requires, than my advance
To reconcilement—opposite perhaps
To my own dignity.—But I will rise
In vengeance mighty! and dispel the clouds
That have bedim'd my state.

#### ANGUS.

The odds are great
Between the numbers: but our cause is just:
Our soldiers regularly train'd to war,
And not a breast among us, entertains
A doubt of victory.

#### KING.

O valiant thane!
Experienc'd oft, and ever trusty found!
Thy penetrating eye, and active zeal
First brought this foul conspiracy to light;
And now thy faithful vassals first appear
In arms for my defence!—Thy recompence
My love shall study.

#### ANGUS.

Blotted be my name
From honour's records, when I stand aloof,
Regardless of the danger that surrounds
The fortunes of my prince!

#### KING.

I know thee well.—
Mean time our care must be, to obviate,
With circumspection and preventive skill,
Their numbers.—In unequal conflict joins
Th' unwieldy spear that loads the borderer,
With the broad targe and expeditious sword:
The loyal band that from the hills of Lorn
Arriv'd, shall in our front advance, and stand
With targe to targe, and blade to blade oppos'd;
The spears extended form the second line,
And our light archers hover to and fro,
To gall their flanks.—Whatever accident
In battle shall befal, thy vigilance
Will remedy.—Myself will here remain
　　　　　　O O

To guard the town, and with a small reserve,
(If need requires) thine exigence supply.

ANGUS.

With joy, the glorious task I undertake! [*Exeunt.*

## SCENE III.

DUNBAR, RAMSAY.

RAMSAY.

They halt, and occupy the narrow pass
Form'd by the river and th' impending hill;
With purpose, as I deem, to charge our host
On the small plain that skirts the town.—

DUNBAR.

'Tis well.—
Thus hemm'd, their useless numbers will involve
Themselves in tumult, to our arms secure
An easy conquest, and retard their flight.—
To Angus hie thee straight with this advice.—
My task perform'd, I wait the king's command
In this appointed place.—        [*Exit Ramsay.*

## SCENE IV.

ELEONORA, DUNBAR.

ELEONORA.

I sought thee, youth.—
Ere yet this dreadful crisis shall decide
The public fate, let us to private woe
Devote one moment!—Tell me, brave Dunbar,
Wilt thou not, from the hurry of the day,
One moment snatch to hear me, and condole
The anguish of my soul?—

DUNBAR.

O Eleonora!
Sooner shall the parch'd traveller refuse
The gelid fountain, than my raptur'd soul
The music of thy tongue!—What grief profanes
Thy spotless bosom?—happy! far above
The pride of conquerors, were I to ease
Thy sorrow's pangs!—

ELEONORA.

Thy gen'rous heart alone
Can brook the enterprize—

DUNBAR.

O! task my love;
That I more swift than gales that sweep the plain,
May fly to thy relief!

ELEONORA.

Then summon up
Those elevated thoughts that lift the soul
To virtue's highest pinnacle; the boon
My misery demands, will crave them all!—

DUNBAR.

Be it to brave the menaces of death
In shape however horrid, so my faith
And love remain inviolate, my heart
Beats with unusual ardor; and demands
The test, impatient!—

ELEONORA.

Friendless and forlorn
In fetters Stuart lies!—

DUNBAR.

Ha!

ELEONORA.

From the snares
Of gloomy fate release him.—

DUNBAR.

Cruel maid!—
Nay, let me call thee barbarous! in spite
Of adoration.—Could thy mind suggest
No forward slave, to set thy lover free,
But a despairing rival?—'Tis not giv'n
Th' impassion'd soul of man to execute
A deed so fatal to its own repose!

ELEONORA.

I sought not—witness ye celestial powers!
To aggravate thy pain.—My mind, perplex'd,
Revolv'd in silent woe, nor could unload
Her burthen to another.—Thou alone,
Hast won my fair opinion and my trust;
And to thy word indebted, honour claims
Th' engagement all her own.—

DUNBAR.

Yet, with reserve
Was that impawn'd: my loyalty and love
Were sacred ev'n from that: nor can I loose
His chains, without an injury to both!—

ELEONORA.

Cold—unaspiring is the love that dwells
With tim'rous caution; and the breast untouch'd
By glory's godlike fervour, that retains
The scruples of discretion.—Let the winds
That have dispers'd thy promise, snatch thy
vows!—

DUNBAR.

Shall I, thro' rash enthusiasm, wed
Eternal anguish?—Shall I burst asunder
The bonds of awful justice, to preserve
The serpent that has poison'd all my peace!—
No, Eleonora!—blasted be——

ELEONORA.

Take heed!
Nor by an oath precipitate, involve
Thy fate beyond resource: For know, Dunbar,
The love of Stuart, with his guilt abjur'd,
This morn, my solemn vow to Heav'n appeal'd,
Hath sever'd us for ever.

DUNBAR.

Then, I'm still!
Still as the gentle calm, when the hush'd wave
No longer foams before the rapid storm!—
Let the young traitor perish, and his name
In dark oblivion rot.

ELEONORA.

Shall I, alas!
Supinely savage, from my ears exclude
The cries of youthful woe?—of woe intail'd
By me too!—If my heart denies him love,
My pity, sure, may flow!—Has he not griefs
That wake ev'n thy compassion?—Say, Dunbar,
Unmov'd could'st thou survey th' unhappy youth
(Whom but this morn beheld in pride of hope
And pow'r magnificent!) stretch'd on the ground
Of a damp dungeon, groaning with despair
With not one friend his sorrows to divide,
And cheer his lone distress?

**DUNBAR.**

Can I resist
So fair a motive, and so sweet a tongue!
When thy soft heart with kind compassion glows,
Shall I the tender sentiment repress?—
No!—let me rather hail the social pang;
And ev'ry selfish appetite subdu'd,
Indulge a flame so gen'rous and humane!—
—Away with each emotion that suggests
A rival favour'd and a traitor freed!
My love unbounded reigns, and scorns to own.
Reflection's narrow limits!—Yes, my fair,
This hour he shall be free.—        [*Exit Dunbar.*

## SCENE V.

**ELEONORA.**

O wond'rous power
Of love beneficent!—O gen'rous youth!
What recompense (thus bankrupt as I am!)
Shall speak my grateful soul!—A poor return
Cold friendship renders to the fervid hope
Of fond desire! and my invidious fate
Allows no more.—But let me not bewail,
With avarice of grief, my private woe;
When pale with fear, and harass'd with alarm,
My royal mistress, still benign to me,
The zealous tender of my duty claims.        [*Exit.*

## SCENE VI.

*Discovers* Stuart *in chains.*

**STUART.**

Curse on my headstrong passion!—I have earn'd
The wages of my folly!—Is it thus
My faithless destiny requites my hope?

## SCENE VII.

**STUART, DUNBAR.**

**STUART.**

Ha! com'st thou to insult my chains?—'Twas well
My unpropitious demon gave me up
To your resentment, tamely.—

**DUNBAR.**

To exult
Ev'n o'er an enemy oppress'd, and heap
Affliction on th' afflicted, is the mark
And the mean triumph of a dastard soul.—
'Tis what Dunbar disdains.—Perhaps, I come
To pity, not rejoice at Stuart's fate.—

**STUART.**

To pity!—Torture! am I fall'n so low!—
Ha! recreant!—move thy pity!—Hell untie
These slavish manacles, that I may scourge
This wretched arrogant!—

**DUNBAR.**

True courage scorns
To vent her prowess in a storm of words:
And to the valiant, actions speak alone:
Then let my deeds approve me.—I am come
To give thee instant freedom.—

**STUART.**

Mean'st thou death?
I shall be free then.—An apt minister
Th' usurper has ordain'd to perpetrate
His secret murders.—

**DUNBAR.**

Why wilt thou belie
Thy own intelligence?—Thou know'st, my sword
Was ne'er accustom'd to the bravo's stab;
Nor the designs of him so falsely styl'd
Usurper, ever sully'd with a stain
Of cruelty or guile.—My purpose is,
To knock thy fetters off, conduct thee safe
Without the city-confines, and restore thee
To liberty and Athol.—

**STUART.**

Fawning coward!
Thou—thou restore me!—thou unbind my chains!
Impossible!—Thy fears that I may 'scape,
Like vultures gnaw thee!—

**DUNBAR.**

When the battle joins,
Thou shalt be answer'd.—

**STUART.**

When the battle joins!—
—Away, dissembler!—Sooner would'st thou beard
The lion in his rage, than fairly meet
My valour on the plain!

**DUNBAR.**

Ha! who art thou,
That I should dread thy threats?—By Heav'n's
high throne!
I'll meet thee in a desert, to thy teeth
Proclaim thy treachery, and with my sword
Explore thy faithless heart!—Meanwhile, my steps
Shall guide thee to the field.
        [*Stuart is unchained, and presented with a sword.*

**STUART.**

No!—Lightning blast me
If I become thy debtor, proud Dunbar!
Thy nauseous benefits shall not enslave
My free-born will.—Here, captive as I am,
Thy lavish'd obligation shall not buy
My friendship!—No! nor stifle my revenge

**DUNBAR.**

Alike unpleasant would it be to me,
To court thy love, or deprecate thy hate:—
What I have proffer'd, other motives urg'd—
The gift is Eleonora's.—

**STUART.**

Sacred powers!
Let me not understand thee!—Thou hast rous'd
My soul's full fury!—In the blood that warms
Thine heart, perfidious, I will slake mine ire!

**DUNBAR.**

In all my conduct, insolent of heart!
What hast thou mark'd so abject and so mean,
That thy foul tongue its licence thus avows?
To boundless passion subject, as thyself,
Wild tumult oft my reason overwhelms!—
Then tempt me not too far, lest blindfold wrath
Transport my soul, and headlong ruin crush
Thy pride ev'n here!—

**STUART.**

In this accursed place
Let me be shackled—rivetted with bolts,
'Till the rust gnaw my carcase to the bone,
If my heart throbs not for the combat, here!—
Ev'n here, where thou art, lord!—Ha! dost thou
  shake?
By Heav'n, thy quiv'ring lip and haggard look
Confess pale terrour and amaze!—

**DUNBAR.**

—Away!—
Away, lewd railer!—not thy sland'rous throat,
So fruitful of invectives, shall provoke me
To wreak unworthy vengeance on thee, safe
In thy captivity:—But soon as war      [out
Shall close the encountering hosts, I'll find thee
Assert my claim to Eleonora's love,
And tell thee, what thou art.

**STUART.**

I burn—I rage!
My fell revenge consumes me!—But no more—
Thou shalt not 'scape me—Goaded by my wrongs,
I'll hunt thee thro' the various scenes of death!—
Thou shalt be found!—

**DUNBAR.**

I triumph in that hope.
[*Exeunt.*

SCENE VIII. *Changes.*

KING, QUEEN, *attended.*

**KING.**

Courageous Angus shall not be o'erpower'd—
Myself will bring him aid.—

**QUEEN.**

Alas! my prince!

**KING.**

What means the gentle partner of my heart?
Dismiss thy fears.—This day will dissipate
The cause of thy dismay.—Ev'n now, I go
To pluck the wreath of victory, and lay
Fresh laurels in thy lap.

**QUEEN.**

Ah! why let in
A train of harpy sorrows to my breast!—
—Ah! why in your own precious life, expose
Your kingdom's safety, and your consort's peace!
—Let me restrain you from the field to day.—
There is no fame—no glory to be won
From a revolter's brow.—

**KING.**

The public weal
Commands to arm—dishonour taint my name,
When I reject the call!—

**QUEEN.**

Ill-omen'd call!
That like the raven's croak invades my quiet!
O! wou'd to Heaven, our minutes smoothly roll'd
In humble solitude, with meek-ey'd peace!
Remote from royalty, and all the cares
That brood around the throne!—

**KING.**

No, let us scorn
Unfeeling ease, and private bliss forego,
When public misery implores our aid.—
What dignity of transport feels the prince,
Who, from the pangs of fierce oppressive power,
A people rescues?

**QUEEN.**

What a dreadful host
Of dangers 'circle him!

**KING.**

Disease confers
The stamp of value upon health; and glory
Is the fair child of peril.—Thou thyself
My conduct wilt applaud, soon as thy mind
Its native calm regains, and reason sways
Uncheck'd by fear——Secure 'till my return
Remain within, and ev'ry thought indulge
Foreboding my success.—

**QUEEN.**

Adieu—Adieu!
Heav'n crown your valour with a wreath.
[*Exit Queen.*

**KING,** *to an attendant.*

Swift, hie thee to Dunbar, and bid him lead
The chosen citizens——

*Enter* RAMSAY.

SCENE IX.

KING *attended,* RAMSAY.

**RAMSAY.**

O fatal chance!
The traitor Grime, with a selected band,
(While Angus, press'd on every side, sustains
Th' unequal fight) a secret path pursu'd
Around the hills, and pouring all at once,
Surpris'd the eastern gate;—the citizens,
With consternation smote, before his arms
In rout disorder'd fly!—

**KING.**

Ha! then the wheel
Of fate full circle rolls to crush me down!
Nor leaves one pause for conduct!—Yet I'll bear
My fortunes like a king—haste and collect
The scattered parties—Let us not submit
'Ere yet subdu'd—to arms! [*Drawing.*

**RAMSAY.**

Alas my prince!
The convent is beset—Hark! while we speak
The gates are burst—Behold—

**KING.**

We must prevent
The pangs of ling'ring misery, and fall
With honour, as we liv'd—

SCENE X.

KING *attended,* RAMSAY. GRIME *with followers bursting in.*

**KING.**

What bold contempt

Of majesty, thus rudely dares intrude
Into my private scenes?

GRIME.

The hour is fled,.
That saw thy wanton tyranny impose
The galling yoke—Yes, I am come to wrest
The prostituted sceptre from thy hand,
And drag thee fetter'd to the royal throne
Of Walter, whom I serve.

KING.

Outrageous wretch!
Grown old in treachery! whose soul untam'd,
No mercy softens, and no laws restrain!
Tny life thrice forfeited, my pity thrice
From justice hath redeem'd; yet art thou found
Still turbulent—a rugged rebel still,
Unaw'd, and unreclaim'd!—

GRIME.

That I yet breathe
This ambient air, and tread this Earth at will,
Not to thy mercy but thy dread I owe.—
Wrong'd as I was—my old possessions reft
By thy rapacious power, my limbs enchain'd
Within a loathsome dungeon, and my name
Thy loud reproach thro' all the groaning land;
Thou durst not shed my blood!—the purple stream
Had swell'd—a tide of vengeance! and o'erwhelm'd
The proud oppressor.—

KING.

Traitor to thy prince,
And foe perverse to truth!—how full thy crimes,
Thy doom how just—my pardon how humane,
Thy conscious malice knows—But let me not
Degrade my name, and vindicate to thee
The justice of my reign.

GRIME.

Vain were th' attempt
With artifice of words to sooth my rage,
More deaf to mercy, than the famish'd wolf
That tears the bleating kid!—My starv'd revenge
Thy blood alone can satiate!—Yield thee then:
Or sink beneath mine arm.

KING.

Heav'n shall not see
A deed so abject vilify my name—
While yet I wield this sword, and the warm blood
Still streams within my veins; my courage soars
Superior to a ruffian's threats.—

GRIME.

Fall on,
And hew them piece-meal.

[King, Ramsay, and attendants drive
off Grime and his followers; but
are afterwards overpowered and dis-
armed.

GRIME.

Wilt thou yet maintain
Thy dignity of words?—Where are thy slaves,
Thy subjects, guards an I thunder of thy throne,
Reduc'd usurper?—Guard these captives.

[Exeunt King, Ramsay, &c. guarded.

SCENE XI.

Enter a Soldier to Grime.

SOLDIER.

A troop of horsemen have possessed the gate
By which we gain'd the city.—

GRIME.

Blast them, Hell!
We must retreat another way, and leave
Our aim unfin sh'd!—Our victorious swords
At least shall guard the treasure they have won.
When the fierce parent-lion bites our chain,
His whelps forlorn, an easy prey remain.

———

ACT III. SCENE I.

QUEEN, ELEONORA, CAPTAIN;

QUEEN.

WHAT from the battlements hast thou descry'd?

CAPTAIN.

Nothing distinct, my queen—Involv'd in clouds
Impervious to the view, the battle long
Continued doubtful, 'midst the mingling sounds
Of trumpets, neighing steeds, tumultuous shouts
Of fierce assailants, doleful cries of death,
And clatt'ring armour; 'till at length, the noise
In distant murmurs dy'd—O'er all the plain,
Now a dread stillness reigns!

QUEEN.

Then all is lost!
Why pauses ruin, and suspends the stroke!—
Is it to lengthen out affliction's term,
And feed productive woe?—Where shall the groans
Of innocence deserted find redress!
Shall I exclaim to Heav'n?—A ready Heav'n
Its pity and protection has withdrawn!
Earth yield me refuge then!—give me to lie
Within thy cheerless bosom!—there, put off
Th' uneasy robe of being—there, lay down
The load of my distress!

ELEONORA.

Alas! my queen,
What consolation can the wretched bring!
How shall I from my own despair collect
Assuasive balm?—Within my lonely breast
Mute sorrow and despondence long have dwelt!
And while my sire, perhaps, this instant bleeds,
The dim, exhausted fountains of my grief
Can scarce afford a tear!

QUEEN.

O luxury
Of mutual ill!—Let us enjoy the feast!
To groan re-echo groan, in concert raise
Our lamentation; and when sorrow swells
Too big for utterance, the silent streams
Shall flow in common!—When the silent streams
Forbear to flow, the voice again shall wail;
O my lost lord!—O save him—save him, powers!

ELEONORA

Is there no gentle remedy to sooth

The soul's disorder; lull the jarring thoughts,
And with fair images amuse the mind?
—Come, smiling Hope—divine illusion! come
In all thy pride of triumph o'er the pangs
Of misery and pain!

QUEEN.
                    Low—low indeed,
Have our misfortunes plung'd us; when no gleam
Of wand'ring hope, how vain soe'er or false,
Our invocation flatters!—When—O when
Will death deliver me? —Shall I not rest
Within the peaceful tomb, where may I sleep
In calm oblivion, and forget the wrecks
Of stormy life!—No sounds disturb the grave
Of murder'd husbands!—Or the dismal scream
Of infants perishing.—Ha! whither leads
Imagination!—Must ye perish then,
Ye tender blossoms?—Must the lofty oak
That gave you life, and shelter'd you from harm,
Yield to the traitor's axe?—O agony
Of fond distraction!

ELEONORA.
                    Ha!—behold where comes
The warlike son of March!—What, if he brings
The news of victory!

QUEEN.
                    My soul alarm'd
With eagerness and terrour waits her doom!

SCENE II.
QUEEN, ELEONORA, DUNBAR.
QUEEN.
Say, youth, how fares the king!

DUNBAR.
                    Fair princess, hail!
To you my duty and my speed were bent—
Your royal consort triumphs.

QUEEN.
                    Lives he then!
Lives he, deliver'd from the fatal snares
Which had enclos'd him!

DUNBAR.
                    To their hills repell'd,
The vanquish'd rebels curse his conqu'ring arm—
He bade me fly before him to the queen;
With the glad tidings cheer her drooping soul;
And bear his kindest wishes to the shrine
Himself will soon adore.

QUEEN.
                    Will he then come
And wipe the tear of sorrow from my cheek!—
Ah, no!—thy pity flatters me in vain!

DUNBAR.
Let me not dally with my queen's distress.—
What were it, but to lift incumbent woe,
That it might fall more grievous.—By the faith
Of my allegiance, hither speeds the king,
By love attended, and by conquest crown'd.

QUEEN.
O welcome messenger!—How sweetly sounds
Thy prelude!—Thus, the warbler of the morn,
To the sick wretch who moan'd the tedious night,
Brings balmy slumber, ease and hope and health!
O wondrous destiny!

ELEONORA.
                    Thus on my queen
May fortune ever smile.—May bliss to bliss
Succeed, a tranquil scene!—Say, noble youth,
Returns my sire in safety from the field?—

DUNBAR.
Safe as thy fondest filial wish can form.—
In war's variety, mine eyes have seen
Variety of valour and of skill:
But such united excellence of both—
Such art to baffle and amuse the foe;—
Such intrepidity to execute
Repeated efforts,—never, save in him,
My observation trac'd!—Our monarch's acts
My feeble praise would sully and profane.

ELEONORA.
Thy words, like genial showers to the parch'd
Refresh my languid soul!—            [earth,

QUEEN.
                    The trumpet swells!
My conqueror approaches!—Let me fly
With ecstacy of love into his arms!—
He comes!—the victor comes!

SCENE III.
KING, QUEEN, ELEONORA, DUNBAR.
KING, embracing the queen.
                    My better part!
My soul's chief residence!—My love! my queen!
Thou hast been tender overmuch, and mourn'd
Ev'n too profusely!

QUEEN.
                    Celebrate this hour
Ye songs of angels! and ye sons of Earth,
Keep festival!—My monarch is return'd!
I fold him in these arms!—I hear his voice—
His love soft-chiding!—

KING.
                    O ye powers benign!
What words can speak the rapture of my soul!
Come to my breast, where, cherish'd by my love,
Thy fair idea rooted, blossoms forth
And twines around my heart!

QUEEN.
                    Mysterious fate!
My wishes are complete!—Yet, I must ask
A thousand things impertinently fond!      [king,
How did you 'scape?—What angel's hand, my
Preserv'd you from destruction?

KING.
                    Heav'n, indeed,
Espous'd my cause, and sent to my relief
The son of March, who, with a chosen few,
Deliver'd me from Grime:—Thence to the field
We speeded, and accomplish'd what the sword
Of Angus had well nigh achiev'd before.

QUEEN to DUNBAR.
How shall acknowledgment enough reward
Thy worth unparallel'd?

KING.
                    Now, by my throne!
Not my own issue shall engross me more

Than thou, heroic youth!—Th' insulting foe,
In spite of fresh supplies, with slaughter driven
To the steep hills that bound the plain, have sent
An herald, in their turn, to sue for peace.—
An audience have I promis'd.—Ere the hour
Arrives, I will retire, and in the bath
Refresh my weary'd limbs.—

*[Exeunt King, Queen, attendants.*

## SCENE IV.

### DUNBAR, ELEONORA.

#### ELEONORA.

Renown to day
Has lavish'd all her honours on thy head.

#### DUNBAR.

What boots it, that my fortune decks me thus
With unsubstantial plumes; when my heart groans
Beneath the gay caparison, and love
With unrequited passion wounds my soul!

#### ELEONORA.

Is unpropitious love unknown to me?
To me for ever doom'd (alas!) to nurse
The slow-consuming fire.—

#### DUNBAR.

Heav'n's!—what are all
The boasted charms, that with such wond'rous
Attach thee to my rival?—Far from me   [power
Be the vain arrogance of pride, to vaunt
Excelling talents; yet I fain would learn,
On what admir'd accomplishment of Stuart,
Thy preference is fix'd.—

#### ELEONORA.

Alas! Dunbar,
My judgment, weak and erring as it is,
Too well discerns on whom I should bestow
My love and my esteem:—But trust me, youth,
Thou little know'st how hard it is to wean
The mind from darling habits long indulg'd!
I know that Stuart sinks into reproach:
Immers'd in guilt, and, more than once, subdu'd
By thy superior merit and success:
Yet ev'n this Stuart,—for I would not wrong
Thine expectation,—still retains a part
Of my compassion—nay, I fear, my love! [kings,
Would'st thou, distinguish'd by th' applause of
Disgrace thy qualities, and brook the prize
Of a divided heart?—

#### DUNBAR.

No!—witness Heav'n
I love not on such terms!—Am I then doom'd,
Unfeeling maid! for ever, to deplore
Thy unabating rigour!—The rude flint
Yields to th' incessant drop; but Eleonora,
Inflexibly severe, unchang'd remains—
Unmov'd by my complaint!

#### ELEONORA.

My father comes!
Let me, with pious ravishment, embrace
His martial knees, and bless the guardian power
That screen'd him in the battle!

## SCENE V.  •

### ANGUS, DUNBAR, ELEONORA.

#### ANGUS.

Rise, my child,
Thou hast been always dutiful, and mild
As the soft breeze that fans the summer eve!
Such innocence endearing gently stole
Into my youthful bosom, and awak'd
Love's tender languishment, when to my view
Thy mother first display'd her virgin bloom!

*[Turning to Dunbar.*

Come to my arms, Dunbar!—To shield from death
A parent, is the venerable act
Of the most pious duty.—Thus adopted,
Henceforward be my son!—The rebel chiefs
Secure in my safe conduct, wait without
The promis'd audience.—To the king repair,
And signify their presence.—     *[Exit Dunbar.*

## SCENE VI.

### ANGUS, ELEONORA.

#### ANGUS.

Eleonora,
Behold the undaunted youth, who stept between
The stroke of fate and me.—O'erpow'r'd, unhors'd,
And by the foe surrounded, I had sunk
A victim to barbarity enrag'd;
If brave Dunbar, to his own peril blind,
Had not that instant to my rescue sprung.—
Nay, when that youthful traitor—by whose arm
Releas'd, I know not, headlong rush'd against me,
My vigilant deliverer oppos'd
The fierce aggressor, whose aspiring crest
Soon prostrate fell.—

#### ELEONORA.

Ha! fell—Is Stuart slain?
O! speak, my father.—

#### ANGUS.

Wherefore this alarm!
Let me not find thy bosom entertain
A sentiment unworthy of thy name!—
The gen'rous victor gave him back his life;
And cry'd aloud, " This sacrifice I make
For Eleonora's love."—

#### ELEONORA.

O matchless youth!
His virtues conquer'd my esteem, before:
But now, my grateful sentiment inflames
Ev'n to a sister's zeal!

#### ANGUS.

With rigid power
I would not bridle thy reluctant thought:
Yet, let me, with parental care, commend
The passion of Dunbar.—

#### ELEONORA.

A fairer garb
His title could not wear:—But when I think
What rocks in secret lie—what tempests rise
On love's deceitful voyage; my timid soul
Recoils affrighted, and with horror shuns
Th' inviting calm!—

#### ANGUS.

Retire, my child, and weigh
The diff'rent claims.—Here, glory, love, and truth

Implore thy smiles :—there, vice with brutal rage
Would force thee to his wishes—But too long
I tarry in this place.—I must attend
My sov'reign in his interview with Athol.

              [*Exeunt*

SCENE VII.    *Changes to another apartment.*

ATHOL, GRIME.

ATHOL.

What we to fortune ow'd, our arms have paid :
But let us now the changeling pow'r renounce.—
Unhappy those, who hazard their designs
On her without reserve !

GRIME.

          Our plan pursu'd
A purpose more assur'd :—With conquest crown'd,
Our aim indeed, a fairer wreath had worn:
But that deny'd, on terms of darker hue
Our swords shall force success !—

ATHOL.

          Th' approaching scene
Demands our utmost arts ! not with tame sighs
To bend before his throne, and supplicate
His clemency, like slaves; nor to provoke
With pride of speech his anger half appeas'd :
But with submission mingle (as we speak)
A conscious dignity of soul, prepar'd
For all events.—

GRIME.

          Without the city-walls,
The southern troops encamp'd, already fill
The festal bowl, to celebrate the day.—

ATHOL.

By Heav'n! their flush'd intemperance will yield
Occasion undisturb'd.—For while they lie, [lurk
With wine and sleep o'erwhelm'd, the clans that
Behind th' adjacent hills, shall, in the dark,
Approach the gate when our associate Cattan
Commands the guard; then, introduc'd by him,
We take, with ease, possession of the town,
And hither move unmark'd.—

GRIME.

          Here, if we fail,
May my shrunk sinew never more unsheath
My well-try'd dagger; nor my hungry hate
Enjoy the savoury steam of hostile gore !

ATHOL.

How my fir'd soul anticipates the joy !
I see me seated in the regal chair,
Enthron'd by Grime, the partner of my power!—
But this important enterprise demands
More secret conference.—The sword of Stuart
Will much avail : but his unpractis'd youth
To doubts and scruples subject, hitherto
Declines our last resolve.—

GRIME.

          It shall be mine,
To rouse his passion to the pitch requir'd.—
But soft !—who comes ?—Ten thousand curses load
Th' ambitious stripling !

*Enter* DUNBAR.

          By the king's command,
I come to guide you to the throne.

ATHOL.

          'Tis well.—         *Exeunt.*

SCENE VIII.

*Discovers the* KING *seated.* ANGUS, *attendants.*

*Enter* ATHOL, GRIME, *introduced by* DUNBAR.

KING.

It is not well—it is not well we meet
On terms like these!—I should have found in Athol
A trusty counsellor and steady friend:
And better would it suit thy rev'rend age,
Thy station, quality, and kindred blood,
To hush ill-judging clamour, and cement
Divided factions to my throne again,
Than thus embroil the state.—

ATHOL.

          My present aim
Is to repair, not widen more, the breach
That discord made between us : this, my liege,
Not harsh reproaches, or severe rebuke
Will e'er effectuate:—No—let us rather,
On terms which equally become us both,
Our int'rests re-unite.

KING.

          Hah !—reunite !
By Heav'n, thy proud demeanor more befits
A sov'reign than a subject !—Reunite !—
How durst thou sever from thy faith, old lord!
And with an helmet load that hoary head
To wage rebellious war !

ATHOL.

          The sword of Athol
Was never drawn but to redress the wrongs
His country suffer'd.—

KING.

          Dar'st thou to my face
Impeach my conduct, baffled as thou art,
Ungrateful traitor ? Is it thus thy guilt
My clemency implores?

ATHOL.

          Not yet so low
Has fate reduc'd us, that we need to crawl
Beneath your footstool:—In our camp remain
Ten thousand vig'rous mountaineers, who long
Their honours to retrieve.—

KING, *rising hastily.*

          Swift, hie thee to them,
And lead thy fugitive adherents back !—
Away.—Now, by the mighty soul of Bruce !
Thou shalt be met.—And if thy savage clans
Abide us in the plain, we soon will tread
Rebellion into dust.—Why move ye not ?
Conduct them to their camp.—

ATHOL.

          Forgive, my prince,
If on my own integrity of heart
Too far presuming, I have gall'd the wound
Too much inflam'd already.—Not with you,
But with your measures ill-advis'd, I warr'd:
Your sacred person, family, and throne
My purpose still rever'd.—

**KING.**

O wretched plea!
To which thy blasted guilt must have recourse!
Had thy design been laudable, thy tongue
With honest freedom boldly should have spoke
Thy discontent.—Ye live not in a reign
Where truth, by arbitrary pow'r depress'd,
Dares not maintain her state.—I charge thee, say
What lawless measures has my pow'r pursu'd?

**ATHOL.**

I come, to mitigate your royal wrath
With sorrow and submission; not to sum
The motives which compell'd me to the field.—

**KING.**

I found your miserable state reduc'd
To ruin and despair:—your cities drench'd
In mutual slaughter, desolate your plains:
All order banish'd, and all arts decay'd:—
No industry, save what with hands impure
Distress'd the commonwealth:—no laws in force,
To screen the poor and check the guilty great;
While squalid Famine join'd her sister fiend,
Devouring Pestilence, to curse the scene!—
I came—I toil'd—reform'd—redress'd the whole:
And lo! my recompense!—But I relapse.—
What is your suit?—

**ATHOL.**

We sue, my liege, for peace.—

**KING.**

Say, that my lenity shall grant your prayer,
How, for the future, shall I rest assur'd
Of your allegiance?

**ATHOL.**

Stuart shall be left
The pledge of our behaviour.—

**KING.**

And your arms,
Ere noon to morrow, shall be yielded up.

**ATHOL.**

This, too, shall be perform'd.—

**KING.**

Then mark me, thane,—
Because the loins, from whence my father sprung,
On thee too life bestow'd; enjoy the gift.—
I pardon what is past.—In peace consume
The winter of thy days.—But, if ye light
Th' extinguish'd brand again, and brave my throne
With new commotions—by th' eternal power!
No future guile, submission, or regard
Shall check my indignation!—I will pour
My vengeance in full volley; and the earth
Shall dread to yield you succour or resource!
Of this, no more.—Thy kinsman shall remain
With us, an hostage of thy promis'd faith.—
So shall our mercy with our prudence join,
United brighten, and securely shine.

**ACT IV. SCENE I.**

**STUART.**

THIS solitude but more foments despair!
Recals—compares—and to th' incessant pangs
Of spite, revenge, and shame, condemns my soul!—
O! what a miserable slave am I!—
Precipitated from the tow'ring hope

Of eagle-ey'd Ambition, to th' abyss   [thought.
Of mutt'ring Horrour, curs'd from thought to
—Hah, Jealousy!—I feel th' infernal power!
Her hissing snakes arouse—her torch inflames
My madd'ning soul!—Yes,—if he thus permits
My feet to range at will; my 'vengeful hand
Will soon requite him.—   [Enter Grime.

**SCENE II.**

STUART, GRIME.

**GRIME.**

Wherefore thus alone?
Thy noble kinsman, who now parted hence,
Observes a sudden cloud o'erhang thy brow.—
Since from the dungeon to his wish restor'd,
A mute aversion to his love, secludes
Thy lonely steps—

**STUART.**

Yes,—thou thyself hast nam'd
The cause accurs'd!—ha, from the dungeon freed!—
And freed by whom!—there's poison in the thought!
—Am I not hostage of my uncle's shame?

**GRIME.**

Thou dwell'st on that too much.—Few live exempt
From disappointment and disgrace, who run
Ambition's rapid course.—Inur'd to pain,
The harden'd soul, at last, forgets to feel
The scourge of fate; and fearless rushes on
To deeds advent'rous.—

**STUART.**

Who shall frame th' attempt
That Stuart dreads t' achieve?—Not pestilence,
Not raging seas, nor livid flames can bound
My dauntless undertaking!—Tell me, Grime,
For thou wast train'd to feats of horrid proof,
Since, not the voice of Heav'n itself can lure
My honour back again—what pow'r of Hell
Shall I invoke to deepen my revenge?—

**GRIME.**

Ha! didst thou say revenge?—Hail, sable pow'r,
To me more dear than riches or renown!
What gloomy joy, to drench the dagger deep
In the proud heart of him who robb'd my fame!
My fortune thwarted; or essay'd by fraud
To poison my delights!—

**STUART.**

Ha! thou hast rous'd
The scorpion-thought that stings me!—
—Mark me, Grime,—
Our baffled cause could not alarm me thus:
If conquest for the foe declar'd to day,
Our arms again the vagrant might compel,
And chain her to our side.—But know, my love
Has been defrauded!—Eleonora's heart
That wretch invades.—That ravisher, who cropp'd
My budding fame and sunk me to reproach!
He, whom my jealousy, in all its rage,
Hath singled for destruction!—

**GRIME.**

He shall die!—

**STUART.**

Yes, he shall die!—He shall be flea'd—impal'd!
And his torn bowels thrown to beasts of prey;—
My savage hate shall on his tortures feed!
I will have vengeance!

GRIME.

Would'st thou have it full,
Include his patrons.—

STUART.

Ha!—What shall my arm
Unsheath the secret steel!

GRIME.

Yes.—Strike at once,
For liberty, ambition, and revenge.—
Let the proud tyrant yield his haughty soul;
And all his offspring swell the sanguine stream.
Let Angus perish too.—

STUART.

O wond'rous plan
Of unrestrain'd barbarity!—It suits
The horrours of my bosom!—All!—What all?
In slaughter'd heaps!—The progeny and sire!—
To sluice them in th' unguarded hour of rest!—
Infernal sacrifice!—dire—ev'n too dire
For my despair!—To me what have they done
To merit such returns?—No, my revenge
Demands the blood of one, and he shall fall.—

GRIME.

It shall suffice—Dunbar shall bleed alone.—
But let us seize him on the verge of bliss;
When the fond maid's enkindling looks confess
The flames of bashful love: when eager joy,
And modest fear, by turns exalt the blush
To a more fervid glow.—When Eleonora
Unfolds Elysium to his raptur'd view,
And smiles him to her arms.—

STUART.

Hah!—Light'ning sooth
Thy tongue, blasphemer!—Sooner may this globe
Be hurl'd to the profound abyss of Hell!—
But vain are words.—This is no place—remember,
He shall not triumph thus!—Thou hast bely'd him—
He means it not.—Nor will the syren smile—
No, Grime,—she dares not smile him to her arms!

GRIME.

Reproach, or mute disgust, is the reward
Of candid friendship, that disdains to hide
Unpalatable truth!—I tell thee, youth,
Betroth'd by Angus to Dunbar, she yields
Her plighted faith, this hour.—But see!—the maid
Moves hitherward alone!—

STUART.

Haste, leave me, Grime!
My soul is up in arms!—my vengeance boils!
Love, jealousy, implacable despair
In tempests wheel.—

GRIME.

Thou shalt not tarry here!—
Thy frantic rage may rashly overturn
Our whole design!—

STUART.

Let me not urge again
Thy swift departure!—hence—I come anon.—
[Exit Grime.

SCENE III.

STUART, ELEONORA.

STUART.

When last we parted, love had reconcil'd
Our mutual jealousies; and breath'd anew
The soul of harmony within our breasts.—
Hast thou not, since that period, entertain'd
One adverse thought to constancy and me?

ELEONORA.

Say, who invested thee with pow'r supreme
O'er Eleonora's conduct; that thou com'st
With frowning aspect, thus, to judge my fame?—
Hast thou not forfeited all claim to me?
Have I not seen thee stray from honour's path?
And shall my love be to the breast confin'd
Where treason in her darkest hue presides!—
No!—let me wipe thee, blotted as thou art,
From my abhorrent thoughts!—

STUART.

Not all this pride
Of mimic virtue—not all th' assembled host
Of female wiles, how exquisite soe'er,
Shall shelter thee, deceiver!—What new stain
Defiles my bosom, since the morning saw
Thy tenderness o'erflow; and heard thy tongue
Seduce me to thy faithless arms, again?

ELEONORA.

Is this the testimony of thy love?
This thy asserted honour! to revile
Defenceless innocence?—But this will aid
My duty—to forget thee —Dost thou ask
What recent outrage has estrang'd my heart?—
There needed none.—The measure of thy guilt
Was full enough before.—Yet thou hast heap'd
Offences to excess: in battle fought
Against thy king; and sought, with lifted arm,
My father's life—ungrateful as thou art!
Know then, the honour of my name forbids
Our fates to join! and it shall ne'er be said,
That Eleonora, lost to glory, took
A traitor to her bed!—

STUART.

Perfidious witch!
Thy charms shall not avail thee; for I come
Th' avenging minister of broken faith!
To claim the promis'd fruitage of my love—
Or—mark me—punish, with thy guilty blood,
Thy perjury and fraud!

ELEONORA.

Wilt thou attempt
To gain, by menaces, what the soft sigh
Of plaintive anguish would implore in vain?
Here strike—and let thy ruthless poniard drink
The blood of Douglas, which has often flow'd
In virtue's cause; and ev'ry soil enrich'd,
From wintry Scania to the sacred vale
Where Lebanon exalts his lofty brow.—

STUART.

Egregious sorc'ress!—give me back my peace—
Bid yesterday return, that saw my youth
Adorn'd in all its splendour, and elate
With gen'rous pride and dignity of soul!—
Ere yet thy spells had discomposed my brain,
Unstrung my arm, and laid me in the dust,
Beneath a rival's feet!

ELEONORA.

Hear all ye powers!
He claims of me, what his own conscious guilt
Hath robb'd him of.—And dost thou look for peace

In my afflicted bosom?—There, indeed,
Thine image dwells with solitude and care,
Amid the devastation thou hast made!    [*Weeps.*

### STUART.

O crocodile!—Curse on these faithless drops
Which fall, but to ensnare!—Thy specious words
Shall sooner lull the sounding surge, than check
The fury that impels me!—Yet— by Heav'n,
Thou art divinely fair! and thy distress
With magic softness ev'ry charm improves!—
Wert thou not false as Hell, not Paradise
Could more perfection boast!—O! let me turn
My fainting eyes from thy resistless face;
And from my sense exclude the soothing sound
Of thy enchanting tongue.—Yet—yet renounce
Thine infidelity—To thine embrace
Receive this wanderer—this wretch forlorn!—
Speak peace to his distracted soul; and ease
The tortures of his bosom!—

### ELEONORA.

                          Hapless youth!
My heart bleeds for thee!—careless of her own,
Bleeds o'er thy sorrows! 'mid the flinty rocks
My tender feet would tread to bring thee balm:
Or, unrepining, tempt the pathless snow!—
O! could my death recall thy banish'd quiet!
Here would I kneel, a suppliant to Heav'n,
In thy behalf; and offer to the grave
The price of thy repose!—Alas! I fear
Our days of pleasure are for ever past!

### STUART.

O thou hast joy and horrour in thy gift!
And sway'st my soul at will!—bless'd in thy love,
The memory of sorrow and disgrace,
That preys upon my youth, would soon forsake
My raptur'd thought, and Hell should plot in vain,
To sever us again!—O! let me clasp thee,
Thou charm ineffable!

### ELEONORA,

                'Forbear, fond youth,
Our unrelenting destiny hath rais'd
Eternal bars between us;

### STUART.

                    Ha!—what bars?

### ELEONORA.

A sacrifice demanded by my sire—
A vow—

### STUART.

              Perdition!—Say what vow, rash maid!

### ELEONORA.

A fatal vow! that blasts our mutual love—

### STUART.

Infernal vipers gnaw thy heart!—A vow!—
A vow that to my rival gives thee up!--
Shall he then trample on my soul at last!—
Mock my revenge, and laugh at my despair!
Ha! shall he rifle all thy sweets, at will,
And riot in the transports due to me?
Th' accursed image whirls around my brain!—
He pants with rapture!—Horrour to my soul!
He surfeits on delight!—

### ELEONORA.

                  O gentle Heav'n!
Let thy soft mercy on his soul descend

In dews of peace!—Why roll with fiery gleam
Thy starting eye-balls?—Why on thy pale cheek
Trembles fell rage!—and why sustains thy frame
This universal shock?—Is it, alas!
That I have sworn, I never will be thine?—
True, this I swore—

### STUART.

                  Hah!—never to be mine!
Th' awaken'd hurricane begins to rage!—I means
Be witness, Heav'n, and Earth, and Hell! she
To glad the bosom of my foe!—Come then
Infernal vengeance! aid me to perform
A deed that fiends themselves will weep to see!
                                          [*Draws.*
Thus, let me blast his full-bloom'd——

*Enter* DUNBAR, *who interposes.*

## SCENE IV.

### DUNBAR, STUART, ELEONORA.

### DUNBAR.

                        Ruffian, hold
Thy desp'rate hand!--What fury, 'scap'd from Hell,
Inspires thy rage to wanton in the blood
Of such excelling goodness?—

### STUART.

                      Infamy
Like mine deface the glories of thy name!
What busy demon sent thee hither, now,
My vengeance to defeat?—The hour is come—
The hour is come at last, that must decide
For ever our pretentions!

### DUNBAR.

                    Whatsoe'er
Thy hate could meditate against my life,
My nature might forgive: but this attempt
Divests my soul of mercy—

### STUART.

                    Guide my point
Ye pow'rs of darkness, to my rival's heart,
Then take me to yourselves.         [*They fight.*

### ELEONORA.

                  Restrain—restrain
Your mutual frenzy!—Horrour!—help—behold—
Behold this miserable bosom!—plunge
Your poniards here! and in its fatal source
Your enmity assuage!—

### STUART, *falling.*

                  It will not be—
Thy fortune hath eclips'd me: and the shades
Of death environ me.—Yet, what is death
When honour brings it, but th' eternal seal
Of glory, never—never to be broke!—
O thou hast slain me in a dreadful hour!
My vengeance frustrated—my prospect curs'd
With thy approaching nuptials! and my soul
Dismiss'd in all her—Eleonora!—Oh!    [*Dies.*

## SCENE V.

### DUNBAR, ELEONORA.

### DUNBAR.

Ah! wherefore dost thou wring thy tender hands
In woeful attitude?—ah! wherefore lift
Thy streaming eyes to Heav'n; while the deep
Dilates thy lab'ring breast?         [*groan*

ELEONORA.

This is too much—
This is too much to bear!—thou hast destroy'd
My last remains of peace!

DUNBAR.

And, was thy peace
Deposited in him?—In him who rais'd
His impious hand to kill thee!—'s it well
To mourn his fall, and thus accuse the blow
That rescu'd thee from death?

ELEONORA.

I blame not thee,
No, Heav'n forbid!—I blame not my protector—
Yet thy protection has undone me quite!,
And I will mourn—for ever mourn the hour—
'Th' ill-omen'd hour, that on thy sword conferr'd
Such terrible success—How pale appear
These clay-cold cheeks where grace and vigour
O dismal spectacle!—How humble now [glow'd!
Lies that ambition which was late so proud!—
Did he not call me with his latest breath!—
He would have said—but cruel fate control'd
His faultering tongue!——He would have said,
' For thee,
For thee, false maid, I perish undeplor'd!"
O! hadst thou known how obstinately true
My heart remain'd to thee, when thy own guilt,
My duty, and thy rival's worth, conspir'd
To banish thee from thence, thy parting soul
Would have acquitted—nay, perhaps, bewail'd
My persecuted truth!

DUNBAR.

O turn thine eyes
From the sad object!—Turn thy melting thoughts
From the disast'rious theme, and look on me—
On me who would with ecstacy resign
This wretched being, to be thus embalm'd
With Eleonora's tears!—Were I to fall,
Thy pity would not thus lament my fate!

ELEONORA.

Thy death such lamentation would not move,
More envy'd than bemoan'd; thy memory
Would still be cherish'd; and thy name survive
To latest ages in immortal bloom—
Ah, 'tis not so with him!—He leaves behind
No dear remembrance of unsully'd fame!
No monument of glory, to defy        [shame!
The storms of time!—Nought but reproach and
Nought, but perpetual slander, brooding o'er
His reputation lost!—O fearful scene
Of dire existence, that must never close!

SCENE VI.

ANGUS entering, ELEONORA, DUNBAR, attendants.

ANGUS.

What sound of female woe—Ha! Stuart slain!
Alas! I fear thou art the fatal cause!—
                                [To Eleonora.

ELEONORA.

Too well my father has divin'd the cause
Of their unhappy strife!—Wherefore, ye powers!
Am I to misery deliver'd up!
What kindred crime, alas! am I decreed
To expiate, that misfortunes fall so thick
On my poor head!
        ANGUS to Dunbar.
            How durst your lawless rage
Profane this sacred place with private brawl?

DUNBAR.

By Heav'n! no place, how much soe'er rever'd,
Shall screen th' assassin who, like him, would aim
The murd'rous steel at Eleonora's breast!

ANGUS.

Ha! were his aims so merciless?—Too just
The vengeance that o'ertook him!  But the event
With this unstable juncture ill accords!—
Remove the body.—Thou meanwhile retire,
Thy presence may awake, or aggravate
The rage of Athol.        [The body is removed.

DUNBAR.

Therefore I obey.—
And O thou lovely mourner! who now droop'st
Like the spread rose beneath th' inclement shower,
When next we meet, I hope to see thee bloom
With vernal freshness, and again unfold
Thy beauties to the Sun!        [Exit Dunbar.

SCENE VII.

ANGUS, ELEONORA.

ANGUS.

                Let us, my child,
Lament with steadiness those ills that flow
From our mishap  yet therefore not ascribe
To self-demerit, impotently griev'd,
The guilt of accident.—Thou hast enough
Denoted thy concern—Let me not think
Thy sorrow hath espoused a traitor's cause.

ELEONORA.

Ah! what avails to me the hard-won palm
Of fruitless virtue—Will it lull to rest
Internal anguish?—Will it yield me peace?—

ANGUS.

Thy indiscreet affliction shall not plead
Against thee, with me, now.—Remember this,
If thou art weak enough to harbour still
A guilty flame; to thy assistance call
That noble pride and dignity of scorn,
Which warms, exalts, and purifies the soul—
But I will trust thee to thyself.—Withdraw;
For Athol comes, and on his visage low'rs
A storm of wrath.        [Exit Eleonora.

SCENE VIII.

ANGUS, ATHOL.

ATHOL.

                Are these the fair effects
Of our submission!—These the promis'd fruits
Of amity restor'd!—To violate
The laws of hospitality—To guide
The midnight murderer's inhuman blow,
And sacrifice your guests!

ANGUS.

                That Athol mourns
This unforeseen severity of fate,
I marvel not.—My own paternal sense
Is wak'd by sympathy; and I condole
His interesting loss.——But thus to tax
Our blameless faith with traitorous design,
Not with our pure integrity conforms,
Nor with thy duty, thane.

**ATHOL.**

Ha! who art thou,
That I should bear thy censure and reproof?—
Not protestation, nor th' affected air
Of sympathy and candour, shall amuse
My strong conception, nor elude the cry
Of justice and revenge!

**ANGUS.**

Had justice crav'd
With rigid voice, the debt incur.'d by thee,
How hadst thou far'd?—Say, what has plac'd thy deeds
Above my censure?—Let this day's event
Proclaim how far I merit thy disdain.—
That my humanity is mis conceived
Not much alarms my wonder: conscious fraud
Still harbours with suspicion.—Let me tell thee—
The fate of Stuart was supremely just.
Th' untimely stroke his savage heart prepar'd
Against the guiltless breast of Eleonora,
Avenging Heav'n retorted on himself.

**ATHOL.**

I thought where all thy probity would end,
Disguis'd accomplice!—But remember, lord,
Should this blood-spotted bravo 'scape, secure
In thy protection, or th' unjust extent
Of regal pow'r, by all my wrongs! I'd spread
The seeds of vengeance o'er th' affrighted land,
And blood shall answer blood!

**ANGUS.**

How far thy threats
Are to be fear'd, we know.—But see, the king!—

**SCENE IX.**

KING, ANGUS, ATHOL.

**KING.**

Tell me—proud thanes, why are you found oppos'd
In loud revilings?—You, that should promote
By fair example, unity and peace!

**ATHOL.**

Have I not cause to murmur and complain?
Stuart, the latest gift and dearest pledge
Of love fraternal, sooth'd my bending age:
Him hath the unrelenting dagger torn
From my parental arms; and left, alas!
This sapless trunk, to stretch its wither'd boughs
To you for justice!—Justice then I crave.

**KING.**

To send the injur'd unredress'd away,
How great soe'er the offender, or the wrong'd
Howe'er obscure, is wicked—weak and vile:
Degrades, defies, and should dethrone a king!
Say, freely, thane, who has aggriev'd thee thus,
And were he dear as her who shares our throne,
Thou shalt have ample vengeance.

**ATHOL.**

Then I charge
The son of March with perfidy and murder.

**ANGUS.**

Were I with mean indifference to hear
Th' envenom'd tongue of calumny traduce
Defenceless worth, I should but ill deserve
Your royal confidence.—Dunbar has slain
The kinsman of this thane; yet fell he not
By murder, cowardice, or foul design.

The sword of Stuart was already drawn
To sacrifice my daughter, when Dunbar,
By Heav'n dir cted hither, interpos'd,
Redeem'd the trembling victim, and repell'd
His rival's fury on his hapless head.

**ATHOL.**

Must I refer me to the partial voice
Of an invet'rate foe?—No, I reject
The tainted evidence, and rather claim
The combat proof.—Enfeebled are my limbs
With age that creeps along my nerves unstrung,
Yet shall the justice of my cause recall
My youthful vigour, rouse my loit'ring blood,
Swell ev'ry sinew, strengthen ev'ry limb,
And crown me with success—Behold my gage,
I wait for justice.

**KING.**

Justice shalt thou have—
Nor shall an equitable claim depend
On such precarious issue.—Who shall guard
The weak from violence, if brutal force
May vindicate oppression.—Truth alone
Shall rule the fair decision, and thy wrongs,
If thou art wrong'd, in my unbiass'd sway
Shall find a just avenger.—Let Dunbar
Appear when urg'd, and answer to the charge.
[To Angus. Exeunt King, Angus.

**SCENE X.**

ATHOL, GRIME.

**ATHOL.**

Curse on the smooth dissembler!——Welcome,
My soul is wrought to the sublimest rage [Grime,
Of horrible revenge!—If aught remain'd
Of cautious scruple, to the scatt'ring winds
I give the phantom.—May this carcase rot,
A loathsome banquet to the fowls of Heav'n,
If e'er my breast admit one thought to bound
The progress of my hate!

**GRIME.**

What means my prince?

**ATHOL.**

Th' unhappy youth is slain!

**GRIME.**

Ha!—Hell be prais'd—
He was a peevish stripling, prone to change.
[Aside.
—Vain is condolence.—Let our swords be swift
To sate his hov'ring shade.—I have conferr'd
With trusty Cattan, our design explain'd,
And his full aid secur'd.—To night he rules
The middle watch.—The clans already move
In silence o'er the plain.

**ATHOL.**

Come then, ye powers
That dwell with night, and patronize revenge!
Attend our invocation, and confirm
Th' exterminating blow!—My boughs are lopp'd,
But they will sprout again: my vig'rous trunk
Shall flourish from the wound my foes have made,
And yet again, project an awful shade

**ACT V. SCENE I.**

KING, QUEEN, DUNBAR.

**QUEEN.**

O! THIS was more than the ill-sorted train

Of undetermin'd fancy!—This convey'd
No loose imperfect images: but all
Was dreadfully distinct! as if the hand
Of Fate had wrought it.—Profit by those signs—
Your guardian angel dictates.—O, my prince!
Let not your blind security disgrace
The merit of your prudence.

### KING.

No, my queen,
Let us avoid the opposite extremes
Of negligence supine, and prostrate fear.—
Already hath our vigilance perform'd
What caution justifies: and for thy dream;
As such consider it—the vain effect
Of an imagination long disturb'd.—
Life with substantial ills enough is curs'd:
Why should we then, with frantic zeal, pursue
Unreal care; and, with th' illusive form
Which our own teeming brain produc'd, affright
Our reason from her throne?

### QUEEN.

In all your course
Of youthful glory, when the guiding hand
Of warlike Henry led you to the field;
When my fond soul suffer'd the successive pangs
Of fond impatience and repressive fear;
When ev'ry reeking messenger from France,
Wreath'd a new garland for Albania's prince,
And shook my bosom with the dreadful tale
That spoke your praise; say, did my weak despair
Recal you from the race?—Did not my heart
Espouse your fame, and patiently await
The end of your career?—O! by the joys
I felt at your return, when smiling love
Secure, with rapture reign'd.—O! by these tears,
Which seldom plead; indulge my boding soul!
Arouse your conqu'ring troops; let Angus guard
The convent with a chosen band.—The soul
Of treason is abroad!

### KING.

Ye ruling powers!
Let me not wield the sceptre of this realm,
When my degen'rate breast becomes the haunt
Of haggard fear.—O! what a wretch is he,
Whose fev'rous life, devoted to the gloom
Of superstition, feels the incessant throb
Of ghastly panic!—In whose startled ear
The knell still deepens, and the raven croaks!

### QUEEN.

Vain be my terrours—my presages vain—
Yet with my fond anxiety comply,
And my repose restore!—Not for myself—
Not to prolong the season of my life,
Am I thus suppliant! Ah no! for you—
For you whose being gladdens and protects
A grateful people.—You, whose parent boughs
Defend your tender offspring from the blasts
That soon would tear them up!--For you the source
Of all our happiness and peace I fear!    [*Kneels.*

### KING.

Arise, my queen—O! thou art all compos'd
Of melting pity and of tender love!
Thou shalt be satisfy'd.—Is ev'ry guard
By Angus visited?—

### DUNBAR.

Ev'n now, my liege,
With Ramsay and his troop, he scours the plain.

### KING.

Still watchful o'er his charge—the lib'ral hand
Of bounty will have nothing to bestow,
Ere Angus cease to merit!—Say, Dunbar,
Who rules the nightly watch?

### DUNBAR.

To Cattan's care
The city guard is subject.

### KING.

I have mark'd
Much valour in him.—Hie thee to him, youth,
And bid him with a chosen few surround
The cloisters of the convent; and remain
'Till morn full streaming shall relieve his watch.
[*Exit Dunbar.*
Thus shall repose, with glad assurance, waft
Its balmy blessing to thy troubled breast.
[*Exeunt.*

## SCENE II.

### GRIME, CATTAN.

### GRIME.

Thus far, brave Cattan, fortune seems inclin'd
To recompense us for the day's disgrace.---
Our band, conceal'd within the cloisters, wait
With eagerness and joy the auspicious hour,
To perpetrate the deed.  It now remains,
To regulate our conduct, and to each
His share of this great enterprise assign.—
If Angus lives, in vain our arms devote
The usurper and his progeny to death:
His power and principles will still supply
Fresh obstacles, which all our future efforts
Can ne'er surmount.

### CATTAN.

Then let our swords prevent
All further opposition, and at once
Dismiss him to the shades.

### GRIME.

Thine be the task—
I know with what just indignation burns
Thy gen'rous hate, against the partial thane,
Who, to thine age and services, preferr'd
A raw unpractis'd stripling.

### CATTAN.

Ha!—no more.
The bare remembrance tortures me!—O Grime!
How will my soul his mortal groans enjoy!

### GRIME.

While we within perform th' intrepid blow,
To his apartment thou shalt move alone;
Nor will pretence be wanting: say, thou bring'st
Intelligence important, that demands
His instant ear:—Then shalt thou find thy foe
Unarm'd and unattended.—Need my tongue
Instruct thee further?

### CATTAN.

No, let my revenge
Suggest what follows—By the pow'rs of Hell!
I will be drunk with vengeance!

### GRIME.

To thy guard
Meanwhile repair, and watch 'till he returns

With Ramsay from the plain.—But see! they
We must avoid them, and retire unseen.  [come,
[*Exeunt.*

### SCENE III.  *An apartment.*

#### ANGUS, RAMSAY.

##### ANGUS.

By Heav'ns it much alarms me!—Wide o'er all
The dusky plain, by the fires half extinct,
Are seen the soldiers, roll'd in heaps confus'd,
The slaves of brutal appetite.—Save those
Beneath thy discipline, scarce one remains
From the contagion free.

##### RAMSAY.

When we return'd
Fatigu'd from battle, numbers brought, unask'd,
Refreshments for the wounded from the town:
Thence the temptation spread from rank to rank,
And few resisted.

##### ANGUS.

But that I consult
My king's tranquillity, and would not wake
The affrighted citizens with alarm,
An hundred trumpets should this instant raise
Their brazen throats together, and arouse
Th' extended sluggards.—Go, my valiant friend,
And with thy uninfected troops attend
To ev'ry motion of th' incertain night.
[*Exit Ramsay.*

### SCENE IV.

##### ANGUS.

Now, the loud tempest of the toilful day
Subsides into a calm.—And yet my soul
Still labours thro' the storm!—By day or night,
In florid youth, or mellow age, scarce fleets
One hour without its care!—Not sleep itself
Is ever balmy: for the shadowy dream
Oft bears substantial woe!

### SCENE V.

#### ANGUS, CATTAN.

##### CATTAN.

My noble lord,
Within the portal as I kept my watch,
Swift gliding shadows by the glimm'ring Moon
I could perceive, in forms of armed men,
Possess the space that borders on the porch—
I question'd thrice; they yielded no reply:
And now the soldiers, rang'd in close array,
Wait your command.

##### ANGUS.

Quick, lead me to the place—
Foul treason is at work!—

##### CATTAN.

It were not good
To venture forth unarm'd,—Courageous thane,
Receive this dagger,—
[*Attempts to stab Angus, who wrests the
dagger from him and kills him.*]

##### ANGUS.

Ha, perfidious slave!
What means this base attempt?—Thou shalt not
'scape.

##### CATTAN.

Curse on my feeble arm that fail'd to strike
The poniard to thy heart!—How like a dog
I tamely fall despis'd!

##### ANGUS.

Fell ruffian! say,
Who set thee on?—This treachery, I fear,
Is but the prelude to some dreadful scene!—

##### CATTAN.

Just are thy terrours.—By the infernal gulph
That opens to receive me! I would plunge
Into the abyss with joy, could the success
Of Athol feast my sense!
[*A noise of clashing swords and shrieks.*

—Hah!—now the sword
Of slaughter smoaks!—Th' exulting thane surveys
Th' imperial scene; while grimly smiling Grime
With purple honour deck'd—

##### ANGUS.

Tremendous powers!

##### CATTAN.

O'er the fall'n tyrant strides.—
[*Dies.*

##### ANGUS.

Heav'n shield us all!
Amazing horrour chills me!—Ha, Dunbar!
Then treason triumphs!—O my soul! my son!

### SCENE VI.

#### ANGUS, DUNBAR *wounded.*

##### DUNBAR.

I sought thee, noble thane, while yet my limbs
Obey their lord.—I sought thee, to unfold
My zealous soul, ere yet she takes her flight—
Stretch'd on the ground, these eyes beheld the king
Transfix'd a lifeless corse! and saw this arm
Too late to save—too feeble to avenge him!—

##### ANGUS.

Weep Caledonia, weep!—thy peace is slain—
Thy father and thy king!—O! this event,
Like a vast mountain, loads my stagg'ring soul,
And crushes all her pow'rs!—But say, my friend,
If yet thy strength permits, how this befel.

##### DUNBAR.

A band of rebels, glean'd from the defeat
By Athol, lurk'd behind the adjacent hills:
These, faithless Cattan, favour'd by the night,
Admitted to the city, join'd their power
With his corrupted guard, and hither led them
Unmark'd, where soon they enter'd unoppos'd.—
Alarm'd, I strove—but strove, alas! in vain.
To the sad scene, ere I could force my way,
Our monarch was no more! Around him lay
A heap of traitors, whom his single arm
Had slain before he fell.—Th' unhappy queen,
Who, to defend her consort's, had oppos'd
Her own defenceless frame, expiring, pour'd
Her mingling blood in copious stream with his!

##### ANGUS.

Illustrious victims!—O disast'rous fate!
Unfeeling monsters! execrable fiends!
To wanton thus in royal blood!

DUNBAR.

O thane!
How shall I speak the sequel of my tale!
How will thy fond parental heart be rent
With mortal anguish, when my tongue relates
The fate of Eleonora!

ANGUS.

                                Ha!—my fears
Anticipate thy words!—O say, Dunbar,
How fares my child!

DUNBAR.

                The shades of endless night
Now settle o'er her eyes!—heroic maid!
She to th' assaulted threshold bravely ran,
And with her snowy arms supply'd a bolt
To bar their entrance:—But the barb'rous crew
Broke in impetuous, crush'd her slender limb,
When Grime, his dagger brandishing, exclaim'd,
" Behold the sorc'ress whose accursed charms
Betray'd the youth; and whose invet'rate sire
This day revers'd our fortune in the field!—
This for revenge!"—then plung'd it in her breast!—

ANGUS.

Infernal homicide!

DUNBAR.

                There—there I own
He vanquish'd me indeed!—What though I rush'd
Thro' many a wound, and in th' assassin's heart
Imbru'd my faithful steel.—But see, where comes,
By her attendants led, the bleeding fair!

SCENE VII.

ANGUS, DUNBAR, ELEONORA *wounded and
supported.*

ELEONORA.

Here set me down—vain is your kind concern.—
Ah! who with parent tenderness will bless
My parting soul, and close my beamless eyes!
Ah! who defend me, and with pious care
To the cold grave commit my pale remains!
                                    [*Swoons.*

ANGUS.

O misery!—look up—thy father calls—
                                [*Embracing her.*

ELEONORA.

What angel borrows that paternal voice!
Ha! lives my father!—Ye propitious powers!
He folds me in his arms—Yes, he survives
The havoc of this night!—O let me now
Yield up my fervent soul with raptur'd praise!
For Angus lives t' avenge his murder'd prince,
To save his country, and protract his blaze
Of glory farther still!

ANGUS.

                        And is it thus,
The melting parent clasps his darling child!
My heart is torn with agonizing pangs
Of complicated woe!

DUNBAR.

                The public craves

Immediate aid from thee—But I wax weak,—
Our infant king, surrounded in the fort,
Demands thy present help.—

ANGUS.

                        Yes, loyal youth!
Thy glorious wounds instruct me what I owe
To my young sov'reign, and my country's peace!
But how shall I sustain the rav'nous tribe
Of various griefs, that gnaw me all at once?
My royal master falls, my country groans,
And cruel fate has ravish'd from my side
My dearest daughter and my best-lov'd friend!

DUNBAR.

Thy praise shall be thy daughter; and thy friend
Survive unchang'd in ev'ry honest breast.

ANGUS.

Must we then part for ever!—What a plan
Of peaceful happiness my hope had laid
In thee and her!—alas! thou fading flower,
How fast thy sweets consume!—come to my arms,
That I may taste them ere they fleet away!
                                [*Embracing her.*
O exquisite distress!

ELEONORA.

                        For me, my father,
For me let not the bootless tear distil.—
Soon shall I be with those, who rest secure
From all th' inclemencies of stormy life.

ANGUS.

Adieu, my children!—never shall I hear
Thy cheering voice again!—a long farewell!
                                [*Exit Angus.*

SCENE VIII.

DUNBAR, ELEONORA.

DUNBAR.

Soon shall our shorten'd race of life be run.—
Our day already hastens to its close;
And night eternal comes.—Yet, tho' I touch
The land of peace, and backward view, well
    pleas'd,
The tossing wave from which I shall be free,
No rest will greet me on the silent shore,
If Eleonora sends me hence unbless'd.

ELEONORA.

Distemper'd passion, when we parted last,
Usurp'd my troubled bosom, and Dunbar
With horrour was beheld: but reason now
With genial mildness beams upon my soul,
And represents thee justly, as thou art—
The tend'rest lover and the gentlest friend.

DUNBAR.

O transport, to my breast unknown before!
Not the soft breeze upon its fragrant wings
Wafts such refreshing gladness to the heart
Of panting pilgrims, as thy balmy words
To my exhausted spirits!—but, alas!
Thy purple stream of life forsakes apace
Its precious channels!—on thy polish'd cheek
The blowing roses fade; and o'er thine eyes
Death sheds a misty languor!

ELEONORA.

                            Let me lean

Upon thy friendly arm—Yet, O retire !
That guilty arm—Say, did it ne'er rebel
Against my peace ?—But let me not revolve
Those sorrows now.—Were Heav'n again to raise
That once-lov'd head that lies, alas ! so low !
And from the verge of death my life recall,
What joy could visit my forlorn estate,
Self-doom'd to hopeless woe !

### DUNBAR.

Must I then wander,
A pensive shade, along the dreary vale,
And groan for ever under thy reproach !

### ELEONORA.

Ah no, thou faithful youth ! shall I repay
Thy love and virtue with ungrateful hate ?
These wounds that waste so lavishly thy life,
Were they not all receiv'd in my defence ?
May no repose embrace me in the tomb,
If my soul mourns not thy untimely fall
With sister-woe !—thy passion has not reap'd
The sweet returns its purity deserv'd.

### DUNBAR.

A while forbear, pale minister of Fate,
Forbear a while; and on my ravish'd ear
Let the last music of this dying swan
Steal in soft blanishment, divinely sweet !
'Then strike th' unerring blow.—

### ELEONORA.

That thus our hopes,
Which blossom'd num'rous as the flow'ry spring,
Are nipp'd untimely, ere the sun of joy
Matured them into fruit, repine not, youth.—
Life hath its various seasons, as the year;
And after clust'ring autumn—but I faint—
Support me nearer—in rich harvest's rear
Bleak winter must have lagg'd.—Oh ! now I feel
The leaden hand of Death lie heavy on me.—
Thine image swims before my straining eye.—
—And now it disappears.—Speak—bid adieu
To the lost Eleonora.—Not a word !
—Not one farewel !—Alas ! that dismal groan
Is eloquent distress !—Celestial powers,
Protect my father, show'r upon his —— Oh !
[Dies.

### DUNBAR.

There fled the purest soul that ever dwelt
In mortal clay !—I come, my love ! I come—
Where now the rosy tincture of these lips !
The smile that grace ineffable diffus'd !
The glance that smote the soul with silent wonder !
The voice that sooth'd the anguish of disease,
And held attention captive !—Let me kiss
This pale deserted temple of my joy !
This, Chastity, this, thy unspotted shade
Will not refuse.—I feel the grisly king—
Thro' all my veins he shivers like the north—
O Eleonora ! as my flowing blood
Is mix'd with thine—so may our mingling souls
To bliss supernal wing our happy——Oh !
[Dies.

### SCENE the last.

ANGUS, RAMSAY. ATHOL, &c. prisoners.

### ANGUS.

Bright deeds of glory hath thine arm achiev'd,
VOL. XV,

Courageous Ramsay; and thy name shall live
For ever in the annals of renown.—
—But see, where silent as the noon of night
These lovers lie !—rest—rest, ill-fated pair !
Your dear remembrance shall for ever dwell
Within the breast of Angus; and his love
Oft with paternal tears bedew your tomb!

### RAMSAY.

O fatal scene of innocence destroy'd !

### ANGUS, to Athol.

O bloody author of this night's mishap !
Whose impious hands are with the sacred blood
Of majesty distain'd !—Contemplate here
The havoc of thy crimes ! and then bethink thee
What vengeance craves.—

### ATHOL.

With insolence of speech
How dares thy tongue licentious, thus insult
Thy sov'reign, Angus?—Madly hath thy zeal
Espous'd a sinking cause.—But thou may'st still
Deserve my future favour.—

### ANGUS.

O thou stain
Of fair nobility !—thou bane of faith !
Thou woman-killing coward, who hast crept
To the unguarded throne, and stabb'd thy prince !
What hath thy treason, blasted as it is,
To bribe the soul of Angus to thy views ?

### ATHOL.

Soon shalt thou rue th' indignity now thrown
On me thy lawful prince.—Yes, talking lord,
The day will soon appear, when I shall rise
In majesty and terrour, to assert
My country's freedom; and at last, avenge
My own peculiar wrongs.—When thou and all
Those grov'ling sycophants, who bow'd the knee
To the usurper's arbitrary sway,
Will fawn on me.—Ye temporizing slaves !
Unchain your king; and teach your humble
mouths
To kiss the dust beneath my royal feet.—
[To the guard.

### ANGUS.

The day will soon appear !—Day shall not thrice
Return, before thy carcase be cast forth,
Unbury'd, to the dogs and beasts of prey—
Or, high-exalted, putrify in air,
The monument of treason.—

### ATHOL.

Empty threat !
Fate hath foretold that Athol shall be crown'd.

### ANGUS.

Then Hell hath cheated thee.—Thou shalt be
An iron crown intensely hot shall gird [crown'd—
Thy hoary temples; while the shouting crowd
Acclaims thee king of traitors.

### ATHOL.

Lakes of fire !—
Ha ! said'st thou, lord !—a glowing iron crown
Shall gird my hoary temples !—Now I feel
Myself awake to misery and shame !
Ye sceptres, diadems, and rolling trains [dreams
Of flatt'ring pomp, farewell !—Curse on those
P P

Of idle superstition, that ensnare
Th' ambitious soul to wickedness and woe!
Curse on thy virtue, which hath overthrown
My elevated hopes! and may despair
Descend in pestilence on all mankind!

#### ANGUS.

Thy curse just Heav'n retorts upon thyself!
To separate dungeons lead the regicides. —
    [*Exit guard with the prisoners.*
From thirst of rule what dire disasters flow!
How flames that guilt ambition taught to glow!
Wish gains on wish, desire surmounts desire!
Hope fans the blaze, and envy feeds the fire:
From crime to crime aspires the madd'ning soul!
Nor laws, nor oaths, nor fears its rage control;
'Till Heav'n at length awakes, supremely just,
And levels all its tow'ring schemes in dust!

---

### PROLOGUE TO THE REPRISAL,

#### SPOKEN BY MR. HAVARD.

An ancient sage, when Death approach'd his bed,
Consign'd to Pluto his devoted head;
And, that no fiend might hiss, or prove uncivil,
With vows and pray'rs, he fairly brib'd the devil:
Yet neither vows nor pray'rs, nor rich oblation,
Cou'd always save the sinner—from damnation.
   Thus authors, tottering on the brink of fate,
The critic's rage with prologues deprecate;
Yet oft the trembling bard implores in vain,
The wit profess'd turns out a dunce in grain:
No plea can then avert the dreadful sentence,
He must be damn'd—in spite of all repentance.
   Here Justice seems from her straight line to vary,
No guilt attends a fact involuntary;
This maxim the whole cruel charge destroys,
No poet sure was ever dull—by choice.
So pleads our culprit in his own defence,
You cannot prove his dullness is—prepense.
   He means to please—he owns no other view;
And now presents you with—a sea ragout.
A dish—howe'er you relish his endeavours,
Replete with a variety of flavours.
A stout Hibernian, and ferocious Scot,
Together boil in our enchanted pot;
To taint these viands with the true fumet,
He shreds a musty, vain, French—martinet.
This stale ingredient might our porridge mar
Without some acid juice of English tar.
To rouse the appetite the drum shall rattle,
And the dessert shall be a bloodless battle.
What heart will fail to glow, what eye to brighten,
When Britain's wrath arous'd begins to lighten!
Her thunders roll—her fearless sons advance,
And her red ensigns wave o'er the pale flow'rs of
     France.
Such game our fathers play'd in days of yore,
When Edward's banners fann'd the Gallic shore;
When Howard's arm Eliza's vengeance hurl'd,
And Drake diffus'd her fame around the world:
Still shall that god-like flame your bosoms fire,
The gen'rous son shall emulate the sire;
Her ancient splendour England shall maintain,
O'er distant realms extend her genial reign,
And rise—th' unrival'd empress of the main.

### SONG

#### FROM THE REPRISAL.

Ye swains of the Shannon, fair Sheelah is gone,
Ye swains of the Shannon, fair Sheelah is gone,
    Ochone my dear jewel;
    Why was you so cruel
Amidst my companions to leave me alone?

Tho' Teague shut the casement in Bally-clough
    hall;       [hall;
Tho' Teague shut the casement in Bally-clough
    In the dark she was groping,
    And found it wide open;
Och! the devil himself could not stand such a fall.

In beholding your charms, I can see them no more,
In beholding your charms, I can see them no more,
    If you're dead do but own it;
    Then you'll hear me bemoan it;
For in loud lamentations your fate I'll deplore.

Devil curse this occasion with tumults and strife!
Devil curse this occasion with tumults and strife!
    O! the month of November,
    She'll have cause to remember,
As a black letter day all the days of her life.

With a rope I could catch the dear creature I've
    lost!       [lost!
With a rope I could catch the dear creature I've
    But, without a dismission,
    I'd lose my commission,
And be hang'd with disgrace for deserting my post.

---

#### SONG FROM THE SAME.

From the man whom I love, tho' my heart I dis-
I will freely describe the wretch I despise, [guise,
And if he has sense but to balance a straw,
He will sure take the hint from the picture I draw.

A wit without sense, without fancy a beau,
Like a parrot he chatters, and struts like a crow;
A peacock in pride, in grimace a baboon,
In courage a hind, in conceit a gascoon.

As a vulture rapacious, in falsehood a fox,
Inconstant as waves, and unfeeling as rocks;
As a tiger ferocious, perverse as a hog,
In mischief an ape, and in fawning a dog.

In a word, to sum up all his talents together,
His heart is of lead, and his brain is of feather:
Yet, if he has sense but to balance a straw,
He will sure take the hint from the picture I draw.

---

#### SONG FROM THE SAME.

Let the nymph still avoid, and be deaf to the swain
Who in transports of passion affects to complain;
For his rage, not his love, in that frenzy is shown;
And the blast that blows loudest is soon o'erblown.

But the shepherd whom Cupid has pierc'd to the
    heart
Will submissive adore, and rejoice in the smart;
Or in plaintive soft murmurs, his bosom-felt woe
Like the smooth gliding current of rivers will flow.

Tho' silent his tongue, he will plead with his eyes,
And his heart own your sway in a tribute of sighs;
But, when he accosts you in meadow or grove,
His tale is all tenderness, rapture, and love.

---

### SONG FROM THE SAME.

BEHOLD! my brave Britons, the fair springing
Fill a bumper and toss off your glasses: [gale,
Buss and part with your frolicksome lasses;
Then aboard and unfurl the wide flowing sail.

#### CHORUS.

While British oak beneath us rolls,
And English courage fires our souls;
To crown our toils, the Fates decree
The wealth and empire of the sea.

Our canvas and cares to the winds we display,
Life and fortune we cheerfully venture;
And we laugh, and we quaff, and we banter;
Nor think of to morrow while sure of to day.

#### CHORUS.

While British oak, &c.

The streamers of France at a distance appear!
We must mind other music than catches;
Man our quarters, and handle our matches;
Our cannon produce, and for battle prepare.

#### CHORUS.

While British oak, &c.

Engender'd in smoke and deliver'd in flame,
British vengeance rolls loud as the thunder!
Let the vault of the sky burst asunder,
So victory follows with riches and fame.

#### CHORUS.

While British oak beneath us rolls,
And English courage fires our souls;
To crown our toils, the Fates decree
The wealth and empire of the sea.

---

## EPILOGUE TO THE REPRISAL.

### SPOKEN BY MISS MACKLIN.

AYE—now I can with pleasure look around,
Safe as I am, thank Heaven, on English ground—
In a dark dungeon to be stow'd away,
Midst roaring, thund'ring, danger and dismay;
Expos'd to fire and water, sword and bullet—
Might damp the heart of any virgin pullet—
I dread to think what might have come to pass,
Had not the British lion quell'd the Gallic ass—
By Champignon a wretched victim led
To cloister'd cell, or more detested bed,
My days in pray'r and fasting I had spent.
As nun or wife, alike a penitent.
His gallantry, so confident and eager,
Had prov'd a mess of delicate soupe—maigre:
To bootless longings I had fallen a martyr:
But Heav'n be prais'd, the Frenchman caught a
    tartar.
    Yet soft—our author's fate you must decree:
Shall he come safe to port or sink at sea?
Your sentence, sweet or bitter, soft or sore,
Floats his frail bark, or runs it bump ashore.—

Ye wits above, restrain your awful thunder:
In his first cruise, 'twere pity he should founder,
        [To the gal.
Safe from your shot he fears no other foe,
Nor gulph, but that which horrid yawns below,
        [To the pit.
The bravest chiefs, ev'n Hannibal and Cato,
Have here been tam'd with—pippin and potatoe.
Our bard embarks in a more Christian cause,
He craves not mercy; but he claims applause.
His pen against the hostile French is drawn,
Who damns him is no Antigallican.
Indulg'd with fav'ring gales and smiling skies,
Hereafter he may board a richer prize.
But if this welkin angry clouds deform,
        [Looking round the house.
And hollow groans portend the approaching storm:
Should the descending show'rs of hail redouble,
        [To the gal.
And these rough billows hiss, and boil, and bubble,
        [To the pit.
He'll lanch no more on such fell seas of trouble.

---

## ADVICE AND REPROOF:

### TWO SATIRES.

First published in the year 1746 and 1747.

——— ——— Sed podice levi
Cæduntur tumidæ medico ridente Mariscæ.———
O Proceres! censore opus est an haruspice nobis?
                **JUVENAL.**
——— ——— nam quis
Peccandi finem posuit sibi? quando recepit
Ejectum semel attritâ de fronte ruborem?
                Ibid,

---

## ADVICE: A SATIRE.

### POET, FRIEND.

#### POET.

ENOUGH, enough; all this we knew before;
'Tis infamous, I grant it, to be poor:
And who so much to sense and glory lost,
Will hug the curse that not one joy can boast!
From the pale hag, O! could I once break loose;
Divorc'd, all Hell shall not re-tie the noose!
Not with more care shall H —— avoid his wife,
Not Cope fly swifter[1], lashing for his life;
Than I to leave the meagre fiend behind.

#### FRIEND.

Exert your talents; Nature, ever kind,
Enough for happiness, bestows on all;
'Tis sloth or pride that finds her gifts too small—
Why sleeps the Muse? is there no room for praise,
When such bright names in constellation blaze?
When sage Newcastle[2], abstinently great,
Neglects his food to cater for the state;

[1] A general famous for an expeditious retreat, though not quite so deliberate as that of the ten thousand Greeks from Persia; having unfortunately forgot to bring his army along with him.
[2] Alluding to the philosophical contempt which this great personage manifested for the sensual delights of the stomach.

And Grafton [3], tow'ring Atlas of the throne,
So well rewards a genius like his own :
Granville and Bath [4] illustrious, need I name
For sober dignity and spotless fame ;
Or Pitt, th' unshaken Abdiel [5], yet unsung :
Thy candour, Chomdly ! and thy truth, O Younge!

#### POET.

Th' advice is good; the question only, whether
These names and virtues ever dwelt together?
But what of that? the more the bard shall claim,
Who can create as well as cherish fame.
But one thing more,—how loud must I repeat,
To rouse th' ingag'd attention of the great,
Amus'd, perhaps, with C——'s prolific bum [6],
Or rapt amidst the transports of a drum [7];
While the grim porter watches ev'ry door,
Stern foe to tradesmen, poets, and the poor.
Th' Hesperian dragon not more fierce and fell;
Nor the gaunt, growling janitor of Hell.
Ev'n Atticus (so wills the voice of fate)
Inshrines in clouded majesty, his state ;
Nor to th' adoring crowd vouchsafes regard,
Tho' priests adore, and ev'ry priest a bard.
Shall I then follow with the venal tribe,
And on the threshold the base mongrel bribe ?
Bribe him, to feast my mute-imploring eye,
With some proud lord, who smiles a gracious lie !
A lie to captivate my heedless youth,
Degrade my talents, and debauch my truth;
While fool'd with hope, revolves my joyless day,
And friends, and fame, and fortune fleet away ;
'Till scandal, indigence, and scorn, my lot,
The dreary jail entombs me, where I rot!
Is there, ye varnish'd ruffians of the state!
Not one among the millions whom ye cheat,

[3] This noble peer, remarkable for sublimity of parts, by virtue of his office, lord chamberlain, conferred the laureat on Colly Cibber, esq. a delectable bard, whose character has already employed, together with his own, the greatest pens of the age.

[4] Two noblemen famous in their day, for nothing more than their fortitude in bearing the scorn and reproach of their country.

[5] Abdiel, according to Milton, was the only seraph that preserved his integrity in the midst of corruption—

> Among the innumerable false, unmov'd,
> Unshaken, unseduc'd, unterrify'd—

[6] This alludes to a phenomenon, not more strange than true. The person here meant, having actually laid upwards of forty eggs, as several physicians and fellows of the Royal Society can attest; one of whom, we hear, has undertaken the incubation, and will, no doubt, favour the world with an account of his success. Some virtuosi affirm, that such productions must be the effect of a certain intercourse of organs not fit to be named.

[7] This is a riotous assembly of fashionable people, of both sexes, at a private house, consisting of some hundreds; not unaptly styled a drum, from the noise and emptiness of the entertainment. There are also drum-major, rout, tempest and hurricane, differing only in degrees of multitude and uproar, as the significant name of each declares.

Who, while he totters on the brink of woe,
Dares, ere he falls, attempt th' avenging blow?
A steady blow! his languid soul to feast;
And rid his country of one curse at least!

#### FRIEND.

What! turn assassin?

#### POET.

Let th' assassin bleed:
My fearless verse shall justify the deed.
'Tis he, who lures th' unpractis'd mind astray,
Then leaves the wretch to misery a prey;
Perverts the race of virtue just begun,
And stabs the public in her ruin'd son.

#### FRIEND.

Heav'ns, how you rail! the man's consum'd by spite!
If Lockman's fate [8] attends you, when you write ;
Let prudence more propitious arts inspire:
The lower still you crawl, you'll climb the higher.
Go then, with ev'ry supple virtue stor'd,
And thrive, the favour'd valet of my lord.
Is that denied? a boon more humble crave;
And minister to him who serves a slave:
Be sure you fasten on promotion's scale;
Ev'n if you seize some footman by the tail:
Th' ascent is easy, and the prospect clear,
From the smirch'd scullion to th' embroider'd peer,
Th' ambitious drudge preferr'd, postillion rides,
Advanc'd again, the chair benighted guides;
Here doom'd, if nature strung his sinewy frame,
The slave, perhaps, of some insatiate dame;
But if exempted from th' Herculean toil,
A fairer field awaits him, rich with spoil;
There shall he shine, with mingling honours bright,
His master's pathic, pimp, and parasite;
Then strut a captain, if his wish be war,
And grasp, in hope, a truncheon and a star:
Or if the sweets of peace his soul allure,
Bask at his ease in some warm sinecure;
His fate in consul, clerk, or agent, vary,
Or cross the seas, an envoy's secretary:
Compos'd of falsehood, ignorance, and pride,
A prostrate sycophant shall rise a L——d [9]:
And won from kennels to th' impure embrace,
Accomplish'd Warren triumph o'er disgrace [10].

#### POET.

Eternal infamy his name surround,
Who planted first that vice on British ground!
A vice that 'spite of sense and nature reigns,
And poisons genial love, and manhood stains!
Pollio ! the pride of science and its shame,
The Muse weeps o'er thee, while she brands thy
Abhorrent views that prostituted groom, [name!
Th' indecent grotto and polluted doom!
There only may the spurious passion glow,
Where not one laurel decks the caitiff's brow,
Obscene with crimes avow'd, of every dye,
Corruption, lust, oppression, perjury:

[8] To be little read, and less approved.

[9] This child of dirt, (to use a great author's expression) without any other quality than grovelling adulation, has arrived at the power of insulting his betters every day.

[10] Another son of fortune, who owes his present affluence to the most infamous qualifications; commonly called Brush Warren, from having been a shoe-black: it is said he was kept by both sexes at one time.

Let Chardin with a chaplet round his head [11],
The taste of Maro and Anacreon plead;
" Sir, Flaccus knew to live as well as write,
And kept, like me, two boys array'd in white."
Worthy to feel that appetence of fame
Which rivals Horace only in his shame!
Let Isis wail in murmurs, as she runs [12],
Her tempting fathers and her yielding sons;
While Dullness screens [13] the failings of the church,
Nor leaves one sliding rabbi in the lurch:
Far other raptures let the breast contain,
Where heav'n-born taste and emulation reign.

#### FRIEND.

Shall not a thousand virtues, then, atone
In thy strict censure for the breach of one ?
If Bubo keeps a catamite or whore,
His bounty feeds the beggar at his door:
And though no mortal credits Curio's word,
A score of lacquies fatten at his board:
To Christian meekness sacrifice thy spleen,
And strive thy neighbour's weaknesses to screen.

#### POET.

Scorn'd be the bard, and wither'd all his fame,
Who wounds a brother weeping o'er his shame!
But if an impious wretch with frantic pride
Throws honour, truth, and decency aside,
If, nor by reason aw'd, nor check'd by fears,
He counts his glories from the stains he bears;
Th' indignant Muse to virtue's aid shall rise,
And fix the brand of infamy on vice.
What if, arous'd at his imperious call,
An hundred footsteps echo through his hall;
And, on high columns rear'd, his lofty dome
Proclaims th' united art of Greece and Rome:
What tho' whole hecatombs his crew regale,
And each dependant slumbers o'er his ale;
While the remains through mouths unnumber'd [past,
Indulge the beggar and the dogs at last:
Say, friend, is it benevolence of soul,
Or pompous vanity, that prompts the whole?
These sons of sloth, who by profusion thrive,
His pride inveigled from the public hive :
And numbers pine in solitary woe,
Who furnish'd out this phantasy of show.
When silent misery assail'd his eyes,
Did e'er his throbbing bosom sympathize?
Or his extensive charity pervade
To those who languish in the barren shade,
Where oft, by want and modesty suppress'd,
The bootless talent warms the lonely breast?
No! petrify'd by dullness and disdain,
Beyond the feeling of another's pain,.

[11] This genial knight wore at his own banquet a garland of flowers, in imitation of the ancients; and kept two rosy boys robed in white, for the entertainment of his guests.

[12] In allusion to the unnatural orgies said to be solemnized on the banks of this river; particularly at one place, where a much greater sanctity of morals and taste might be expected.

[13] This is a decent and parental office, in which Dullness is employed; namely, to conceal the failings of her children: and exactly conformable to that instance of filial piety, which we meet with in the son of Noah, who went backward, to cover the nakedness of his father, when he lay exposed from the scoffs and insults of a malicious world.

The tear of pity ne'er bedew'd his eye,
Nor his lewd bosom felt the social sigh!

#### FRIEND.

Alike to thee his virtue or his vice,
If his hand lib'ral, owns thy merit's price.

#### POET.

Sooner, in hopeless anguish would I mourn,
Than owe my fortune to the man I scorn!—
What new resource?

#### FRIEND.

A thousand yet remain
That bloom with honours, or that teem with gain:
These arts,—are they beneath—beyond thy care?
Devote thy studies to th' auspicious fair:
Of truth divested, let thy tongue supply
The hinted slander, and the whisper'd lie;
All merit mock, all qualities depress,
Save those that grace th' excelling patroness;
Trophies to her, on others' follies raise,
And heard with joy, by defamation praise:
To this collect each faculty of face,
And ev'ry feat perform of sly grimace;
Let the grave sneer sarcastic speak thee shrewd,
The smutty joke ridiculously lewd;
And the loud laugh, thro' all its changes rung,
Applaud th' abortive sallies of her tongue:
Enroll'd a member in the sacred list,
Soon shalt thou sharp in company, at whist;
Her midnight rites and revels regulate [14],
Priest of her love, and demon of her hate.

#### POET.

But say, what recompense for all this waste
Of honour, truth, attention, time, and taste?
To shine confess'd, her zany and her tool,
And fall by what I rose, low ridicule?
Again shall Handel raise his laurel'd brow,
Again shall harmony with rapture glow!
The spells dissolve, the combination breaks,
And Punch no longer Frasi's rival squeaks.
Lo, Russel [15] falls a sacrifice to whim,
And starts amaz'd in Newgate from his dream:

[14] These are mysteries performed, like those of the Dea Bona, by females only; consequently it cannot be expected that we should here explain them: we have, notwithstanding, found means to learn some anecdotes concerning them, which we shall reserve for another opportunity.

[15] A famous mimic and singer. The person here meant, by the qualifications above described, had insinuated himself into the confidence of certain ladies of quality, who engaged him to set up a puppet-show, in opposition to the oratorios of Handel, against whom they were unreasonably prejudiced. But the town not seconding the capricious undertaking, they deserted their manager, whom they had promised to support, and let him sink under the expense they had entailed upon him: he was accordingly thrown into prison, where his disappointment got the better of his reason, and he remained in all the ecstasy of despair; till at last, his generous patronesses, after much solicitation, were prevailed upon to collect five pounds, on the payment of which he was admitted into Bedlam, where he continued bereft of his understanding, and died in the utmost misery.

With trembling hands implores their promis'd aid;
And sees their favour like a vision fade!
Is this, ye faithless Syrens!—this the joy
To which, your smiles th' unwary wretch decoy?
Naked and shackled, on the pavement prone,
His mangled flesh devouring from the bone;
Rage in his heart, distraction in his eye!
Behold, inhuman hags! your minion lie!
Behold his gay career to ruin run,
By you seduc'd, abandon'd and undone!
Rather in garret pent[16], secure from harm,
My Muse with murders shall the town alarm;
Or plunge in politics with patriot zeal,
And snarl like Gutherie for the public weal,
Than crawl an insect, in a beldame's power,
And dread the crush of caprice ev'ry hour!

### FRIEND.

'Tis well;—enjoy that petulance of style,
And, like the envious adder, lick the file[17]:
What tho' success will not attend on all!
Who bravely dares, must sometimes risk a fall.
Behold the bounteous board of Fortune spread;
Each weakness, vice and folly yields thee bread;
Wouldst thou with prudent condescension strive
On the long-settled terms of life to thrive.

### POET.

What! join the crew that pilfer one another,
Betray my friend, and persecute my brother:
Turn usurer o'er cent per cent to brood,
Or quack, to feed like fleas, on human blood?

### FRIEND.

Or if thy soul can brook the gilded curse,
Some changeling heiress steal——

### POET.

Why not a purse?
Two things I dread, my conscience and the law.

### FRIEND.

How? dread a mumbling bear without a claw?
Nor this, nor that is standard right or wrong,
'Till minted by the mercenary tongue;
And what is conscience, but a fiend of strife,
That chills the joys, and damps the schemes of life?
The wayward child of vanity and fear,
The peevish dam of poverty and care;
Unnumber'd woes engender in the breast
That entertains the rude, ungrateful guest.

### POET.

Hail, sacred pow'r! my glory and my guide!
Fair source of mental peace, what e'er betide;
Safe in thy shelter, let disaster roll
Eternal hurricanes around my soul;
My soul serene, amidst the storms shall reign,
And smile to see their fury burst in vain!

### FRIEND.

Too coy to flatter, and too proud to serve[18],
Thine be the joyless dignity to starve.

16 These are the dreams and fictions of Grub-
street, with which the good people of this metropolis are daily alarmed and entertained.
17 This alludes to the fable of the viper and file,
applicable to all the unsuccessful efforts of malice
and envy.
18 This, surely, occasioned Churchill's

Too proud to flatter, too sincere to lie.

### POET.

No;—thanks to discord, war shall be my friend;
And moral rage, heroic courage lend
To pierce the gleaming squadron of the foe,
And win renown by some distinguish'd blow.

### FRIEND.

Renown! ay, do——unkennel the whole pack
Of military cowards on thy back.        [stood 19,
What difference, say, 'twixt him who bravely
And him who sought the bosom of the wood[20]?
Envenom'd calumny the first shall brand,
The last enjoy a ribbon and command.

### POET.

If such be life, its wretches I deplore,
And long to quit th' unhospitable shore.

--------

## REPROOF: A SATIRE.

### POET, FRIEND.

### POET.

HOWE'ER I turn, or wheresoe'er I tread,
This giddy world still rattles round my head!
I pant for silence ev'n in this retreat—
Good Heav'n! what demon thunders at the gate?

### FRIEND.

In vain you strive, in this sequester'd nook,
To shroud you from an injur'd friend's rebuke.

### POET.

An injur'd friend!—who challenges the name?
If you, what title justifies the claim?
Did e'er your heart o'er my affliction grieve,
Your int'rest prop me, or your purse relieve?
Or could my wants my soul so far subdue,
That in distress she crawl'd for aid to you?
But let us grant th' indulgence e'er so strong;
Display without reserve th' imagin'd wrong:
Among your kindred have I kindled strife,
Deflow'r'd your daughter, or debauch'd your wife;
Traduc'd your credit, bubbled you at game;
Or soil'd with infamous reproach your name?

### FRIEND.

No; but your cynic vanity (you'll own)
Expos'd my private counsel to the town.

### POET.

Such fair advice 'twere pity sure to lose;
I grant I printed it for public use.

### FRIEND.

Yes, season'd with your own remarks between,
Inflam'd with so much virulence of spleen,
That the mild town (to give the devil his due)
Ascrib'd the whole performance to a Jew.

19 and 20 This last line relates to the behaviour
of a general on a certain occasion, who discovered
an extreme passion for the cool shade during the
heat of the day: the Hanoverian general, in the
battle of Dettingen.

**POET.**

Jews, Turks, or Pagans, hallowed be the mouth
That teems with moral zeal and dauntless truth!
Prove that my partial strain adopts one lie,
No penitent more mortify'd than I;
Not ev'n the wretch in shackles, doom'd to groan
Beneath th' inhuman scoffs of Williamson[1].

**FRIEND.**

Hold—let us see this boasted self-denial—
The vanquish'd knight[2] has triumph'd in his trial.

**POET.**

What then?

**FRIEND.**

Your own sarcastic verse unsay,
That brands him as a trembling runaway.

**POET.**

With all my soul!—th' imputed charge rehearse;
I'll own my errour and expunge the verse.
Come, come,—howe'er the day was lost or won,
The world allows the race was fairly run.
But lest the truth too naked should appear,
A robe of sable shall the goddess wear:
When sheep were subject to the lion's reign,
Ere man acquir'd dominion o'er the plain,
Voracious wolves, fierce rushing from the rocks,
Devour'd without control th' unguarded flocks:
The suff'rers crowding round the royal cave,
Their monarch's pity and protection crave:
Not that they wanted valour, force or arms,
To shield their lambs from danger and alarms;
A thousand rams, the champions of the fold,
In strength of horn, and patriot virtue bold,
Engag'd in firm association, stood,
Their lives devoted to the public good:
A warlike chieftain was their sole request,
To marshal, guide, instruct, and rule the rest:
Their pray'r was heard, and by consent of all,
A courtier ape appointed general.—
He went, he led, arrang'd the battle stood,
The savage foe came pouring like a flood;
Then pug aghast, fled swifter than the wind,
Nor deign'd, in threescore miles, to look behind;
While ev'ry band for orders bleat in vain,
And fall in slaughter'd heaps upon the plain:
The scar'd baboon (to cut the matter short)
With all his speed could not out-run report;
And to appease the clamours of the nation,
'Twas fit his case should stand examination.
The board was nam'd—each worthy took his place;
All senior members of the horned race[3].—
The wether, goat, ram, elk, and ox were there,
And a grave, hoary stag possess'd the chair.—

[1] Governor of the Tower.
[2] Sir John Cope.
[3] It is not to be wondered at, that this board
consisted of horned cattle only, since, before the
use of arms, every creature was obliged in war to
fight with such weapons as nature afforded it,
consequently those supplied with horns bid fairest
for signalizing themselves in the field, and carrying off the first posts in the army.—But I observe,
that among the members of this court, there is no
mention made of such of the horned family as
were chiefly celebrated for valour; namely, the
bull, unicorn, rhinoceros, &c. which gives reason
to suspect, that these last were either out of fa-

Th' inquiry past, each in his turn began
The culprit's conduct variously to scan.
At length, the sage uprear'd his awful crest,
And pausing, thus his fellow chiefs address'd.—
"If age, that from this head its honours stole,
Hath not impair'd the functions of my soul,
But sacred wisdom with experience bought,
While this weak frame decays, matures my thought;
Th' important issue of this grand debate
May furnish precedent for your own fate;
Should ever fortune call you to repel
The shaggy foe, so desperate and fell—
'Tis plain, you say, his excellence sir Ape
From the dire field accomplish'd an escape;
Alas! our fellow-subjects ne'er had bled,
If every ram that fell, like him had fled;
Certes, those sheep were rather mad than brave,
Which scorn'd th' example their wise leader gave.
Let us, then, ev'ry vulgar hint disdain,
And from our brother's laurel wash the stain."
Th' admiring court applauds the president,
And pug was clear'd by general consent.

**FRIEND.**

There needs no magic to divine your scope,
Mark'd as you are a flagrant misanthrope:
Sworn foe to good and bad, to great and small,
Thy rankling pen produces nought but gall:
Let virtue struggle, or let glory shine,
Thy verse affords not one approving line.—

**POET.**

Hail sacred themes! the Muse's chief delight!
O bring the darling objects to my sight!
My breast with elevated thought shall glow,
My fancy brighten, and my numbers flow!
Th' Aonian grove with rapture would I tread,
To crop unfading wreaths for William's head;
But that my strain, unheard amidst the throng,
Must yield to Lockman's ode and Hanbury's song[4].
Nor would th' enamour'd Muse neglect to pay
To Stanhope's worth[5] the tributary lay;
The soul unstain'd, the sense sublime to paint,
A people's patron, pride and ornament!
Did not his virtues eterniz'd remain
The boasted theme of Pope's immortal strain.
Not ev'n the pleasing task is left, to raise
A grateful monument to Barnard's praise;
Else should the venerable patriot stand
Th' unshaken pillar of a sinking land.
The gladd'ning prospect let me still pursue:
And bring fair virtue's triumphs to the view!
Alike to me, by fortune blest or not,
From soaring Cobham to the melting Scot[6].

vour with the ministry, laid aside on account of
their great age, or that the ape had interest
enough at court to exclude them from the number
of his judges.

[4] Two productions resembling one another very
much in that cloying mediocrity, which Horace
compares to—Crassum ungentum, et sardo cum
melle papaver.

[5] The earl of Chesterfield.

[6] Daniel Mackercher, esq. a man of such primitive simplicity, that he may be said to have
exceeded the Scripture injunction, by not only
parting with his cloak and coat, but with his shirt
also, to relieve a brother in distress: Mr. Annes-
ley, who claimed the Anglesea title and estate.

But fo! a swarm of harpies intervene,
To ravage, mangle, and pollute the scene!
Gorg'd with our plunder, yet still gaunt for spoil,
Rapacious Gideon fastens on our isle;
Insatiate Lascelles, and the fiend Vaneck[7],
Rise on our ruins, and enjoy the wreck;
While griping Jasper[8] glories in his prize,
Wrung from the widow's tears and orphan's cries.

FRIEND.

Relaps'd again! strange tendency to rail!
I fear'd this meekness would not long prevail.

POET.

You deem it rancour then?—Look round and see
What vices flourish still, unprun'd by me:
Corruption, roll'd in a triumphant car,
Displays his burnish'd front and glitt'ring star;
Nor heeds the public scorn, or transient curse,
Unknown alike to honour and remorse.
Behold the leering belle[9], caress'd by all,
Adorn each private feast and public ball;
Where peers attentive listen and adore,
And not one matron shuns the titled whore.
At Peter's obsequies[10] I sung no dirge;
Nor has my satire yet supply'd a scourge
For the vile tribes of usurers and bites,
Who sneak at Jonathan's and swear at White's.
Each low pursuit, and slighter folly b.ed
Within the selfish heart and hollow head,
Thrives uncontrol'd, and blossoms o'er the land,
Nor feels the rigour of my chast'ning hand:
While Codrus shivers o'er his bags of gold,
By famine wither'd, and benumb'd by cold;
I mark his haggard eyes with frenzy roll,
And feast upon the terrours of his soul;
The wrecks of war, the perils of the deep,
That curse with hideous dreams the caitiff's sleep;
Insolvent debtors, thieves, and civil strife,
Which daily persecute his wretched life;
With all the horrours of prophetic dread,
That rack his bosom while the Mail is read.
Safe from the rod, untainted by the school,
A judge by birth, by destiny a fool,
While the young lordling struts in native pride,
His party-coloured tutor by his side[11],
Pleas'd, let me own the pious mother's care,
Who to the brawny sire commits her heir.

[7] A triumvirate of contractors, who, scorning the narrow views of private usury, found means to lay a whole state under contribution, and pillage a kingdom of immense sums, under the protection of law.

[8] A Christian of bowels, who lends money to his friends in want at the moderate interest of 50 per cent. A man famous for buying poor seamens' tickets.

[9] A wit of the first water, celebrated for her talent of repartee and double entendre.

[10] Peter Waters, esq. whose character is too well known to need description.

[11] Whether it be for the reason assigned in the subsequent lines, or the frugality of the parents, who are unwilling to throw away money in making their children wiser than themselves, I know not: but certain it is, that many people of fashion commit the education of their heirs to some trusty footman, with a particular command to keep master out of the stable.

Fraught with the spirit of a Gothic monk,
Let Rich, with dulness and devotion drunk,
Enjoy the peal so barbarous and loud,
While his brain spues new monsters to the crowd[12];
I see with joy, the vaticide deplore
An hell-denouncing priest and sov'reign whore.
Let ev'ry polish'd dame, and genial lord
Employ the social chair[13], and venal board[14];
Debauch'd from sense, let doubtful meanings run,
The vague conundrum and the prurient pun;
While the vain fop, with apish grin, regards
The gig'ling minx half chok'd behind her cards:
These, and a thousand idle pranks, I deem
The motley spawn of ignorance and whim.
Let pride conceive and folly propagate,
The fashion still adopts the spurious brat:
Nothing so strange that fashion cannot tame;
By this dishonour ceases to be shame:
This weans from blushes lewd Tyrawly's face,
Gives Hawley[15] praise and Ingoldsby disgrace,
From Mead to Thompson shifts the palm at once,
A meddling, prating, blund'ring, busy dunce!
And may (should taste a little more decline)
Transform the nation to an herd of swine.

FRIEND.

The fatal period hastens on apace!
Nor will thy verse th' obscene event disgrace;
Thy flow'rs of poetry, that smell so strong,
The keenest appetites have loath'd the song;
Condemn'd by Clark, Banks, Barrowby, and Chitty[16]
And all the crop-ear'd critics of the city:
While sagely neutral sits thy silent friend,
Alike averse to censure or commend.

POET.

Peace to the gentle soul, that could deny
His invocated voice to fill the cry!
And let me still the sentiment disdain
Of him, who never speaks but to arraign;
The sneering son of calumny and scorn,
Whom neither arts, nor sense, nor soul adorns.

[12] Monsters of absurdity.

He look'd, and saw a sable sorc'rer rise,
Swift to whose hand a winged volume flies:
All sudden, gorgons hiss, and dragons glare,
And ten-horn'd fiends and giants rush to war.
Hell rises, Heaven descends, and dance on Earth,
Gods, imps and monsters, music, rage and mirth,
A fire, a jig, a battle, and a ball,
'Till one wide conflagration swallows all.
                                        Dunciad.

[13] This is no other than an empty chair, carried about with great formality, to perform visits, by the help of which a decent correspondence is often maintained among people of fashion, many years together, without one personal interview; to the great honour of hospitality and good neighbourhood.

[14] Equally applicable to the dining and card-table, where every guest must pay an extravagant price for what he has.

[15] A general so renowned for conduct and discipline, that, during an action in which he had a considerable command, he is said to have been seen rallying three fugitive dragoons, five miles from the field of battle.

[16] A fraternity of wits, whose virtue, modesty, and taste, are much of the same dimension.

Or his, who to maintain a critic's rank,
Tho' conscious of his own internal blank,
His want of taste unwilling to betray,
'Twixt sense and nonsense hesitates all day;
With brow contracted hears each passage read,
And often hums and shakes his empty head;
Until some oracle ador'd, pronounce
The passive bard a poet or a dunce;
Then, in loud clamour echoes back the word,
'Tis bold! insipid—soaring or absurd.
These, and th' unnumber'd shoals of smaller fry
That nibble round, I pity and defy.

## THE TEARS OF SCOTLAND.

### Written in the Year 1746.

MOURN, hapless Caledonia, mourn
Thy banish'd peace, thy laurels torn!
Thy sons, for valour long renown'd,
Lie slaughter'd on their native ground;
Thy hospitable roofs no more,
Invite the stranger to the door;
In smoky ruins sunk they lie,
The monuments of cruelty.

The wretched owner sees afar
His all become the prey of war;
Bethinks him of his babes and wife,
Then smites his breast, and curses life.
Thy swains are famish'd on the rocks,
Where once they fed their wanton flocks:
Thy ravish'd virgins shriek in vain;
Thy infants perish on the plain.

What boots it then, in every clime,
Thro' the wide-spreading waste of time,
Thy martial glory, crown'd with praise,
Still shone with undiminish'd blaze?
Thy tow'ring spirit now is broke,
Thy neck is bended to the yoke.
What foreign arms could never quell,
By civil rage and rancour fell.

The rural pipe and merry lay
No more shall cheer the happy day:
No social scenes of gay delight
Beguile the dreary winter night:
No strains but those of sorrow flow,
And nought be heard but sounds of woe,
While the pale phantoms of the slain
Glide nightly o'er the silent plain.

O baneful cause, oh, fatal morn,
Accurs'd to ages yet unborn!
The sons against their fathers stood,
The parent shed his children's blood.
Yet, when the rage of battle ceas'd,
The victor's soul was not appeas'd:
The naked and forlorn must feel
Devouring flames, and murd'ring steel!

The pious mother doom'd to death,
Forsaken wanders o'er the heath,
The bleak wind whistles round her head,
Her helpless orphans cry for bread;
Bereft of shelter, food, and friend,
She views the shades of night descend,
And, stretch'd beneath th' inclement skies,
Weeps o'er her tender babes and dies.

While the warm blood bedews my veins,
And unimpair'd remembrance reigns,
Resentment of my country's fate
Within my filial breast shall beat;
And, spite of her insulting foe,
My sympathizing verse shall flow:
" Mourn, hapless Caledonia, mourn
Thy banish'd peace, thy laurels torn."

## VERSES

### ON A YOUNG LADY PLAYING ON A HARPSICHORD AND SINGING.

WHEN Sappho struck the quiv'ring wire,
The throbbing breast was all on fire:
And when she rais'd the vocal lay,
The captive soul was charm'd away!

But had the nymph, possest with these,
Thy softer, chaster, pow'r to please;
Thy beauteous air of sprightly youth,
Thy native smiles of artless truth;

The worm of grief had never prey'd
On the forsaken love-sick maid:
Nor had she mourn'd a hapless flame,
Nor dash'd on rocks her tender frame.

## LOVE ELEGY.

### IN IMITATION OF TIBULLUS.

WHERE now are all my flatt'ring dreams of joy?
  Monimia, give my soul her wonted rest;
Since first thy beauty fix'd my roving eye,
  Heart-gnawing cares corrode my pensive breast.

Let happy lovers fly where pleasures call,
  With festive songs beguile the fleeting hour;
Lead beauty thro' the mazes of the ball,
  Or press her wanton in love's roseate bower.

For me, no more I'll range th' empurpled mead,
  Where shepherds pipe, and virgins dance around,
Nor wander thro' the woodbine's fragrant shade,
  To hear the music of the grove resound.

I'll seek some lonely church, or dreary hall,
  Where fancy paints the glimm'ring taper blue,
Where damps hang mould'ring on the ivy'd wall,
  And sheeted ghosts drink up the midnight dew:

There leagued with hopeless anguish and despair,
  Awhile in silence o'er my fate repine:
Then, with a long farewel to love and care,
  To kindred dust my weary limbs consign.

Wilt thou, Monimia, shed a gracious tear
  On the cold grave where all my sorrows rest?
Strew vernal flow'rs, applaud my love sincere,
  And bid the turf lie easy on my breast?

## SONG.

WHILE with fond rapture and amaze,
On thy transcendent charms I gaze,

My cautious soul essays in vain
Her peace and freedom to maintain:
Yet let that blooming form divine,
Where grace and harmony combine,
Those eyes, like genial orbs, that move,
Dispensing gladness, joy, and love,
In all their pomp assail my view,
Intent my bosom to subdue;
My breast, by wary maxims steel'd,
Not all those charms shall force to yield.

But, when invok'd to beauty's aid,
I see th' enlighten'd soul display'd;
That soul so sensibly sedate
Amid the storms of froward fate!
Thy genius active, strong and clear,
Thy wit sublime, tho' not severe,
The social ardour void of art,
That glows within thy candid heart;
My spirits, sense and strength decay,
My resolution dies away,
And ev'ry faculty opprest,
Almighty love invades my breast!

### SONG.

To fix her—'twere a task as vain
To count the April drops of rain,
To sow in Afric's barren soil,
Or tempests hold within a toil.

I know it, friend, she's light as air,
False as the fowler's artful snare;
Inconstant as the passing wind,
As winter's dreary frost unkind.

She's such a miser too in love,
It's joys she'll neither share nor prove;
Tho' hundreds of gallants await
From her victorious eyes their fate.

Blushing at such inglorious reign,
I sometimes strive to break her chain;
My reason summon to my aid,
Resolv'd no more to be betray'd.

Ah! friend! 'tis but a short-liv'd trance,
Dispell'd by one enchanting glance;
She need but look, and, I confess,
Those looks completely curse or bless.

So soft, so elegant, so fair,
Sure something more than human's there;
I must submit, for strife is vain,
'Twas destiny that forg'd the chain.

### ODES.

#### BURLESQUE ODE[1].

WHERE wast thou, wittol Ward, when hapless
fate
From these weak arms mine aged grannam tore:
These pious arms essay'd too late,
To drive the dismal phantom from the door.

[1] Dr. Smollett, imagining himself ill treated by
lord Lyttleton, wrote the above burlesque on
that nobleman's monody on the death of his lady.

Could not thy healing drop, illustrious quack,
Could not thy salutary pill prolong her days;
For whom, so oft, to Marybone, alack!
Thy sorrels dragg'd thee thro' the worst of ways!

Oil-dropping Twick'nham did not then detain
Thy steps, tho' tended by the Cambrian maids;
Nor the sweet environs of Drury-lane;
Nor dusty Pimlico's embow'ring shades;
Nor Whitehall, by the river's bank,
Beset with rowers dank;
Nor where th' Exchange pours forth its tawny sons;
Nor where to mix with offal, soil, and blood,
Steep Snow-hill rolls the sable flood;
Nor where the Mint's contaminated kennel runs:

Ill doth it now beseem,
That thou shouldst doze and dream,
When Death in mortal armour came,
And struck with ruthless dart the gentle dame.
Her lib'ral hand and sympathising breast
The brute creation kindly bless'd:
Where'er she trod grimalkin purr'd around,
The squeaking pigs her bounty own'd;
Nor to the waddling duck or gabbling goose
Did she glad sustenance refuse;
The strutting cock she daily fed,
And turky with his snout so red;
Of chickens careful as the pious hen,
Nor did she overlook the tomtit or the wren;
While redbreast hopp'd before her in the hall,
As if she common mother were of all.

For my distracted mind,
What comfort can I find?
O best of grannams! thou art dead and gone,
And I am left behind to weep and moan,
To sing thy dirge in sad funereal lay,
Ah! woe is me! alack! and well-a-day!

#### TO MIRTH.

PARENT of joy! heart-easing Mirth!
Whether of Venus or Aurora born;
Yet goddess sure of heavenly birth,
Visit benign a son of Grief forlorn:
    Thy glittering colours gay,
    Around him, Mirth, display;
    And o'er his raptur'd sense
    Diffuse thy living influence:
So shall each hill in purer green array'd,
And flower adorn'd in new-born beauty glow;
    The grove shall smooth the horrours of the
        shade,
And streams in murmurs shall forget to flow.
Shine, goddess, shine with unremitted ray,
And gild (a second sun) with brighter beam our day.

    Labour with thee forgets his pain,
    And aged Poverty can smile with thee;
    If thou be nigh, Grief's hate is vain,
    And weak th' uplifted arm of Tyranny.
        The Morning opes on high
        His universal eye;
        And on the world doth pour
        His glories in a golden shower,
    Lo! Darkness trembling 'fore the hostile ray
        Shrinks to the cavern deep and wood forlorn:
    The brood obscene, that own her gloomy sway,
Troop in her rear, and fly th' approach of Morn.

Pale shivering ghosts, that dread th' all-cheering
          light,           [night.
Quick, as the lightnings flash, glide to sepulchral

But whence the gladdening beam
That pours his purple stream
  O'er the long prospect wide?
'Tis Mirth. I see her sit
In majesty of light,
  With Laughter at her side.
Bright-ey'd Fancy hovering near
Wide waves her glancing wing in air;
And young Wit flings his pointed dart,
That guiltless strikes the willing heart.
  Fear not now Affliction's power,
  Fear not now wild Passion's rage,
  Nor fear ye aught in evil hour,
  Save the tardy hand of Age.
Now Mirth hath heard the suppliant poet's prayer;
No cloud that rides the blast, shall vex the
  troubled air.

---

### TO SLEEP.

SOFT Sleep, profoundly pleasing power,
Sweet patron of the peaceful hour,
O listen from thy calm abode,
And hither wave thy magic rod;
Extend thy silent, soothing sway,
And charm the canker Care away.
Whether thou lov'st to glide along,
Attended by an airy throng
Of gentle dreams and smiles of joy,
Such as adorn the wanton boy;
Or to the monarch's fancy bring
Delights that better suit a king;
The glittering host, the groaning plain,
The clang of arms, and victor's train;
Or should a milder vision please,
Present the happy scenes of peace;
Plump Autumn, blushing all around,
Rich Industry with toil embrown'd,
Content, with brow serenely gay,
And genial Art's refulgent ray.

---

### TO LEVEN-WATER.

ON Leven's banks, while free to rove,
And tune the rural pipe to love;
I envied not the happiest swain
That ever trod the Arcadian plain.
  Pure stream! in whose transparent wave
My youthful limbs I wont to lave;
No torrents stain thy limpid source;
No rocks impede thy dimpling course,
That sweetly warbles o'er its bed,
With white, round, polish'd pebbles spread;
While, lightly pois'd, the scaly brood
In myriads cleave thy crystal flood;
The springing trout in speckled pride;
The salmon, monarch of the tide;
The ruthless pike, intent on war;
The silver eel, and mottled par[1].
Devolving from thy parent lake,
A charming maze thy waters make,

[1] The par is a small fish, not unlike the smelt,
which it rivals in delicacy and flavour.

By bowers of birch, and groves of pine,
And edges flower'd with eglantine.
Still on thy banks so gaily green,
May num'rous herds and flocks be seen,
And lasses chanting o'er the pail,
And shepherds piping in the dale,
And ancient Faith that knows no guile, [1]
And Industry imbrown'd with toil,
And hearts resolv'd, and hands prepar'd,
The blessings they enjoy to guard.

---

### TO BLUE-EY'D ANN.

WHEN the rough North forgets to howl,
And Ocean's billows cease to roll;
When Lybian sands are bound in frost,
And cold to Nova Zembla's lost!
When heav'nly bodies cease to move,
My blue-ey'd Ann I'll cease to love.

No more shall flowers the meads adorn;
Nor sweetness deck the rosy thorn;
Nor swelling buds proclaim the spring;
Nor parching heats the dog-star bring;
Nor laughing lilies paint the grove,
When blue-ey'd Ann I cease to love.

No more shall joy in hope be found;
Nor pleasures dance their frolic round;
Nor love's light god inhabit Earth;
Nor beauty give the passion birth;
Nor heat to summer sunshine cleave,
When blue-ey'd Nanny I deceive.

When rolling seasons cease to change,
Inconstancy forgets to range;
When lavish May no more shall bloom;
Nor gardens yield a rich perfume;
When Nature from her sphere shall start,
I'll tear my Nanny from my heart.

---

### TO INDEPENDENCE.

#### STROPHE.

THY spirit, Independence, let me share!
Lord of the lion-heart and eagle-eye,
Thy steps I follow with my bosom bare,
Nor heed the storm that howls along the sky.
Deep in the frozen regions of the north,
A goddess violated brought thee forth,
Immortal Liberty, whose look sublime
Hath bleach'd the tyrant's cheek in every varying
    clime.
What time the iron-hearted Gaul
With frantic Superstition for his guide,
Arm'd with the dagger and the pall,
The sons of Woden to the field defy'd:
The ruthless hag, by Weser's flood,
In Heaven's name urg'd th' infernal blow;
And red the stream began to flow:
The vanquish'd were baptiz'd with blood[1].

[1] Charlemagne obliged four thousand Saxon
prisoners to embrace the Christian religion, and
immediately after they were baptized ordered their
throats to be cut.—Their prince Vitikind fled for
shelter to Gotric king of Denmark.

#### ANTISTROPHE.

The Saxon prince in horrour fled
From altars stain'd with human gore;
And Liberty his routed legions led
In safety to the bleak Norwegian shore.
There in a cave asleep she lay,
Lull'd by the hoarse-resounding main;
When a bold savage past that way,
Impell'd by Destiny, his name Disdain.
Of ample front the portly chief appear'd:
The hunted bear supply'd a shaggy vest;
The drifted snow hung on his yellow beard;
And his broad shoulders brav'd the furious
     blast.
He stopt: he gaz'd; his bosom glow'd,
And deeply felt the impression of her charms: ｉ
He seiz'd th' advantage Fate allow'd;
And straight compress'd her in his vig'rous arms.

#### STROPHE.

The curlieu scream'd, the Tritons blew
Their shells to celebrate the ravish'd rite;
Old Time exulted as he flew;
And Independence saw the light.
The light he saw in Albion's happy plains,
Where under cover of a flowering thorn,
While Philomel renew'd her warbled strains,
The auspicious fruit of stol'n embrace was born—
The mountain Dryads seiz'd with joy,
The smiling infant to their charge consign'd;
The Doric Muse caress'd the favourite boy;
The hermit Wisdom stor'd his opening mind.
As rolling years matur'd his age,
He flourish'd bold and sinewy as his sire;
While the mild passions in his breast asswage
The fiercer flames of his maternal sire.

#### ANTISTROPHE.

Accomplished thus, he wing'd his way,
And zealous roved from pole to pole,
The rolls of right eternal to display,
And warm with patriot thoughts the aspiring
     soul.
On desert isles[2] it was he that rais'd
Those spires that gild the Adriatic wave,
Where Tyranny beheld amaz'd
Fair Freedom's temple, where he mark'd her
     grave,
He steel'd the blunt Batavian's arms
To burst the Iberian's double chain[3];
And cities rear'd, and planted farms,
Won from the skirts of Neptune's wide domain.
He, with the generous rustics, sate
On Uri's rocks in close divan[4];
And wing'd that arrow sure as fate,
Which ascertain'd the sacred rights of man.

    2 Although Venice was built a considerable
time before the era here assigned for the birth of
Independence, the republic had not yet attained
to any great degree of power and splendour.
    3 The Low Countries were not only oppressed
by grievous taxations, but likewise threatened
with the establishment of the Inquisition, when
the Seven Provinces revolted, and shook off the
yoke of Spain.
    4 Alluding to the known story of William Tell
and his associates, the fathers and founders of the
confederacy of the Swiss Cantons.

#### STROPHE.

Arabia's scorching sands he cross'd ,
Where blasted nature pants supine,
Conductor of her tribes adust,
To Freedom's adamantine shrine;
And many a Tartar hord forlorn, aghast[6]!
He snatch'd from under fell Oppression's wing;
And taught amidst the dreary waste
The all-cheering hymns of Liberty to sing.
He virtue finds, like precious ore,
Diffus'd thro' every baser mould,
Even now he stands on Calvi's rocky shore,
And turns the dross of Corsica to gold[7].
He, guardian genius, taught my youth
Pomp's tinsel livery to despise:
My lips by him chastis'd to truth,
Ne'er pay'd that homage which the heart denies.

#### ANTISTROPHE.

Those sculptur'd halls my feet shall never tread,
Where varnish'd Vice and Vanity combin'd,
To dazzle and seduce, their banners spread;
And forge vile shackles for the free-born mind.
Where Insolence his wrinkl'd front uprears,
And all the flowers of spurious fancy blow;
And Title his ill-woven chaplet wears,
Full often wreath'd around the miscreant's brow:
Where ever-dimpling Falshood, pert and vain,
Presents her cup of stale profession's froth;
And pale Disease, with all his bloated train,
Torments the sons of Gluttony and Sloth.

#### STROPHE.

In Fortune's car behold that minion ride,
With either India's glittering spoils opprest:
So moves the sumpter-mule, in harness'd pride,
That bears the treasure which he cannot taste.
For him let venal bards disgrace the bay,
And hireling minstrels wake the tinkling string;
Her sensual snares let faithless Pleasure lay;
And all her jingling bells fantastic Folly ring;
Disquiet, Doubt, and Dread shall intervene;
And Nature, still to all her feelings just,
In vengeance hang a damp on every scene,
Shook from the baleful pinions of Disgust.

#### ANTISTROPHE.

Nature I'll court in her sequester'd haunts
By mountain, meadow, streamlet, grove, or cell,
Where the poised lark his evening ditty chaunts,
And Health, and Peace, and Contemplation dwell.
There Study shall with Solitude recline;
And Friendship pledge me to his fellow-swains;
And Toil and Temperance sedately twine
The slender chord that fluttering life sustains:
And fearless Poverty shall guard the door;
And Taste unspoil'd the frugal table spread;
And Industry supply the humble store;
And Sleep unbribed his dews refreshing shed:

    5 The Arabs, rather than resign their indepen-
dency, have often abandoned their habitations,
and encountered all the horrours of the desert.
    6 From the tyranny of Jenghis-Khan, Timur-
Bec, and other eastern conquerors, whole tribes
of Tartars were used to fly into the remoter wastes
of Cathay, where no army could follow them.
    7 The noble stand made by Paschal Paoli and
his associates against the usurpations of the French
king, must endear them to all the sons of liberty
and independence.

White-mantled Innocence, ethereal sprite,
Shall chase far off the goblins of the night;
And Independence o'er the day preside,
Propitious power! my patron and my pride.

## OBSERVATIONS

### ON DR. SMOLLETT'S ODE TO INDEPENDENCE.

LYRIC poetry imitates violent and ardent passions. It is therefore bold, various, and impetuous. It abounds with animated sentiments, glowing images, and forms of speech often unusual, but commonly nervous and expressive. The composition and arrangement of parts may often appear disordered, and the transitions sudden and obscure; but they are always natural, and are governed by the movements and variations of the imitated passion. The foregoing ode will illustrate these observations.

The introduction is poetical and abrupt.

" Thy spirit, Independence, let me share!
Lord of the lion-heart and eagle-eye,
Thy steps I follow with my bosom bare,
Nor heed the storm that howls along the sky."

The picture exhibited in these lines is striking, because the circumstances are happily chosen, briefly, and distinctly delineated. It is. sublime, because the images are few, and in themselves great and magnificent. The " lion-heart and eagle-eye" suggest an idea of the high spirit and commanding aspect of Independence: and the poet following with " bosom bare" denotes, in a picturesque manner, the eagerness and enthusiasm of the votary. The last circumstance is peculiarly happy.

" Nor heed the storm that howls along the sky."

It marks the scene: it is unexpected, and excites surprise: it is great and awful, and excites astonishment. Combined with the preceding circumstance, it conveys a beautiful allegorical meaning; and signifies that a mind truly independent is superior to adversity, and unmoved by external accidents. We may observe too, in regard to the diction, that the notions of sound and motion communicated by the words " howl" and " along," contribute, in a peculiar manner, to the sublimity of the description.

" Lord of the lion-heart and eagle-eye,
Thy steps I follow with my bosom bare,
Nor heed the storm that howls along the sky."

These lines are written in the true spirit of lyric poetry. Without preparing the mind by a cool artificial introduction, rising gradually to the impetuosity of passion, they assail the imagination by an abrupt and sudden impulse; they vibrate through the soul, and fire us instantaneously with all the ardour and enthusiasm of the poet. Many of the odes of Horace are composed in the same spirit, and produce similar effects. Without any previous argument or introduction, in the fulness of passion and imagination, he breaks out in bold, powerful, and impetuous figures.

Quo me, Bacche, rapis, tui
Plenum? Quæ nemora aut quos agor in specus
Velox mente nova?———
Qualem ministrum fulminis alitem———

The poet, full of enthusiasm and admiration, continues his prosopopeia; and, in a strain of poetry exceedingly wild and romantic, gives us the genealogy of Independence.

" A goddess violated brought thee forth,
Immortal Liberty, whose look sublime
Hath bleach'd the tyrant's cheek in every varying
          clime."

According to the acceptation of our author, liberty means the security of our lives and possessions, and freedom from external force: independence is of higher import, and denotes that internal sense and consciousness of freedom which beget magnanimity, fortitude, and that becoming pride which leads us to respect ourselves, and do nothing unworthy of our condition. Liberty therefore is, with perfect propriety, said to be the mother of Independence, and Disdain his father—Disdain arising from indignation against an oppressor, and triumph on having frustrated or escaped his malice. This stern personage is strongly characterized in the following direct description.

" Of ample front the portly chief appear'd:
The hunted bear supply'd a shaggy vest;
The drifted snow hung on his yellow beard;
And his broad shoulders braved the furious blast."

Men may enjoy liberty without independence: they may be secure in their persons and possessions, without feeling any uncommon elevation of mind, or any sense of their freedom. But if their liberty is attacked, they are alarmed, they feel the value of their condition, they are moved with indignation against their oppressors, they exert themselves, and if they are successful, or escape the danger that threatened them, they triumph, they reflect on the happiness and dignity conferred by freedom, they applaud themselves for their exertions, become magnanimous and independent. There is therefore no less propriety in deducing the origin of Independence from Disdain and Liberty, than in fixing the era of his birth. The Saxons, according to our author, free, simple, and inoffensive, were attacked, escaped the violence of their adversary, reflected on the felicity of their condition, and learned independence.

The education of Independence, and the scene of his nativity, are suited to his illustrious lineage, and to the high achievements for which he was destined.

" The light he saw in Albion's happy plains,
Where under cover of a flowering thorn,
While Philomel renew'd her warbled strains,
The auspicious fruit of stol'n embrace was born—
The mountain Dryads seiz'd with joy,
The smiling infant to their charge consign'd;
The Doric Muse caress'd the favourite boy;
The hermit Wisdom stor'd his opening mind."

The imagery in these lines is soft and agreeable, the language smooth, and the versification numerous.

Independence thus descended, and thus divinely instructed and endowed, distinguishes himself accordingly by heroic and beneficent actions.

" Accomplish'd thus, he winged his way,
And zealous rov'd from pole to pole,
The rolls of right eternal to display,
And warm with patriot thoughts the aspiring soul."

The ode may be divided into three parts. The poet sets out with a brief address to Independence, imploring his protection. He sees, in idea, the high object of his adoration, and transported by an ardent and irresistible impulse, he rehearses his birth, education, and qualities. He proceeds, in the second place, to celebrate his office and most renowned achievements; and returns, at the end of the third strophe, to acknowledge with gratitude the protection he had requested, and the power of Independence in preserving him untainted by the debasing influences of grandeur, and the admiration of vain magnificence. Animated with this reflection, and conscious of the dignity annexed to an independent state of mind, he inveighs against those "minions of Fortune" who would impose upon mankind by the ostentation of wealth, and the parade of pageantry.

" In Fortune's car behold that minion ride,
With either India's glittering spoils opprest:
So moves the sumpter-mule, in harness'd pride,
That bears the treasure which he cannot taste.
For him let venal bards disgrace the bay ;
And hireling minstrels wake the tinkling string:
Her sensual snares let faithless Pleasure lay ;
And all her jingling bells fantastic Folly ring ;
Disquiet, Doubt, and Dread, shall intervene ;
And Nature, still to all her feelings just,
In vengeance hang a damp on every scene,
Shook from the baleful pinions of Disgust."

These lines, embellish'd by fancy, and recommended to the heart by harmony, are the invective of truth and honest indignation.

In the last antistrophe the poet descends from his enthusiasm; he is less impetuous; the illustrious passions that animated and impelled him are exhausted; but they leave his mind full of their genuine and benign influences, not agitated and disordered, as if their tendency had been vicious, but glowing with self-approbation, soft, gentle and composed,

THE

# POEMS

OF

## *WILLIAM WILKIE, D. D.*

# LIFE OF WILLIAM WILKIE,

## *BY MR. CHALMERS.*

WILLIAM WILKIE was born in the parish of Dalmeny, in the county of West Lothian, on the 5th of October, 1721. His father, although a small farmer, and poor and unfortunate, endeavoured to give him a liberal education, which he appears to have improved by diligence. In the ninth volume of Sir John Sinclair's Statistical Account of Scotland, are some verses said to have been written by him in his tenth year. Dr. Gleig, who has inserted a very candid life of Wilkie in the Supplement to the Encyclopedia Britannica, doubts the probability of this report, as the verses contain more knowledge of electricity than had then been acquired either by boys or men. A very few of these verses will, however, convince the reader, that Wilkie is not to be ranked among *les enfans celebres.*

> What penetrating mind can rightly form
> A faint idea of a raging storm?
> Who can express of elements the war,
> And noisy thunder roaring from afar?
> This subject is superior to my skill:
> Yet I'll begin, to show I want not will, &c.

At the age of thirteen, he was sent to the university of Edinburgh, where he was soon distinguished for originality of thought, and rapid progress in learning. Among his associates here, we have the names of Robertson, Home (the dramatic poet), Hume, Ferguson, and Adam Smith. With these he continued in habits of friendship and correspondence for many years; but I know not whether it will be accounted a proof of his judgment, that he considered Adam Smith as excelling Hume and Robertson in the powers of invention.

Before he completed his education, his father died, leaving him no other inheritance than his small farm, and the care of three sisters. Necessity thus turned his attention to the study of agriculture, which he cultivated with so much success, although upon a confined scale, that he acquired a solid reputation as a practical farmer, and was enabled to provide for himself and his sisters. He still, however, prosecuted his studies, and at the accustomed period was admitted a preacher in the church of Scotland.

For some years this made no alteration in his mode of life. Being admitted a preacher not implying, as in England, the cure of souls, he had only to exercise his ministerial office occasionally for the clergymen in his neighbourhood, and could employ the principal part of his time on his farm and his studies. He appears to have been early ambitious of the character of a poet, and having read Homer, as Don Quixote read romances, he determined to sally forth as his rival, or continuator; and this enthusiasm produced the Epigoniad, published in 1753. On this poem he is said to have employed fourteen years, which ill agrees with what his biographers tell us of his propensity to poetry, and the original vigour of his mind, for it appeared with all the imperfections of a rough sketch. It is more probable that he wrote by snatches as he found time and inclination, and had perhaps long finished the work before he ventured to publish it. Its reception by the English public was not very flattering, but in his own country the Epigoniad succeeded so well, that a second edition was called for in 1759, to which he added a dream in the manner of Spenser.

A few years before this, he was ordained minister of Ratho, in consequence of a presentation from the late earl of Lauderdale, who knew his worth, and admired his genius. By an assiduous attention to the public and private duties of his sacred function, we are told, he became popular and useful. Yet it is difficult to conceive how a clergyman could preserve the reverence due to his character or office, " who generally preached with his hat on his head, and often forgot to pronounce the blessing after public service: and who has been seen to dispense the sacrament without consecrating the elements." Such indecent negligence cannot surely be excused on the plea of absence of mind, allowable enough in the common intercourse of life, but which in the present case implies a careless abstraction of mind from that which ought to have occupied it entirely.

In 1759, he was chosen professor of natural philosophy in the university of St. Andrews, a proof that he had acquired a character for higher attainments than are discoverable in the Epigoniad. When he removed to St. Andrews, his whole fortune did not exceed two hundred pounds, with which he purchased a few acres of land in the neighbourhood of the city, and cultivated them with his usual judgment, still continuing to maintain his sisters, whom he brought from Ratho to reside with him. As a teacher, he is said to have displayed great knowledge of science, with an easy and familiar mode of demonstration which fixed the regard as well as the attention of his scholars[1]. In 1766, the university conferred upon him the degree of Doctor in Divinity.

In 1768, he published his Fables, which had less success than even his Epigoniad, although they are rather happy imitations of the manner of Gay, and the

[1] Travels in Scotland, by the Rev. James Hall, vol. i. p. 131, et seq.—C.

thoughts, if not always original, are yet sprightly and just. After a lingering illness, he died Oct. 10, 1772.

The character of Dr. Wilkie appears to have been distinguished for those singularities which are sometimes found in men of genius, either from early indulgence or affectation. His biographers have multiplied instances of his disgusting manners, which it would have been more prudent to bury in oblivion, as the reader of such tales is too apt to imagine that what was only occasional must have been uniform.

He is said to have died worth £3000, accumulated by penurious living; but those who knew him more intimately have vindicated his character in this respect. Much of his life was spent in poverty, and a strong sense of the value of independence induced him to become saving, as soon as he could spare any thing from his immediate wants and the necessity of his sisters, for whom he appears to have provided with all the affectionate concern of a parent. By avoiding the expenses of hospitality, in a hospitable country, he incurred the suspicion of avarice ; but he was known to be liberal to the poor, and ought not to be blamed if he preferred the silent dictates of his heart to the ostentatious fashion of society.

His learning, according to every account, was extensive, and much of it acquired at a very early age. His conversation was enriched by original sentiments, delivered in a bold, and sometimes coarse manner : and there were few good judges who did not leave his company impressed with a high opinion of his talents. He must have been indeed an extraordinary man, who could preserve the respect of his contemporaries and of his scholars, notwithstanding such indelicate and disgusting habits, as we read of in the life of no other man. Some men have been slovenly from negligence, but Wilkie, where he had a choice, is said to have given a decided preference to what was dirty.

When the Epigoniad made its appearance, it was attacked by the Monthly and Critical Reviewers with apparent severity ; but the extracts and specimens by which they confirmed their opinions, satisfied the public that they had examined the poem with impartiality, and decided with justice. It would, therefore, have probably sunk into oblivion, had not the sale in Scotland exhausted the first edition, and encouraged the author to publish a second, in which he made a few alterations, chiefly in the versification. Yet as the principal objections remained in full force, this would have contributed little to extend our author's fame; and the new edition was but slowly called for, when an extraordinary appeal from the general opinion was preferred by the celebrated Mr. Hume, who wrote a very long encomium on the Epigoniad, addressed to the editor of the Critical Review, and published in the seventh volume of that journal. As I have nothing to oppose to the neglect with which Wilkie's poems have been treated, I hope I shall be pardoned for inserting Mr. Hume's very elaborate criticism, whatever effect it may produce. The analysis he gives of the fable may at least assist the readers of the Epigoniad. As to the very high praise he bestows, those who knew Mr. Hume's taste, friendship, or sincerity, will be best enabled to determine whether he is serious.

" TO THE AUTHORS OF THE CRITICAL REVIEW.

" Gentlemen,                                          " April, 1759.

" The great advantages which result from literary journals have recommended the use of them all over Europe ; but as nothing is free from abuse, it must be confessed that some inconveniences have also attended these undertakings. The works of the learned multiply in such a surprising manner, that a journalist, in order to give an account to the public of all new performances, is obliged to peruse a small library every month, and as it is impossible for him to bestow equal attention on every piece which he criticises, he may readily be surprised into mistakes, and give to a book such a character as, on a more careful perusal, he would willingly retract. Even performances of the greatest merit are not secure against this injury ; and, perhaps, are sometimes the most exposed to it. An author of genius scorns the vulgar arts of catching applause : he pays no court to the great : gives no adulation to those celebrated for learning : takes no care to provide himself of partisans, or *proneurs,* as the French call them : and by that means his work steals unobserved into the world : and it is some time before the public, and even men of penetration, are sensible of its merit. We take up the book with prepossession, peruse it carelessly, are feebly affected by its beauties, and lay it down with neglect, perhaps with disapprobation.

" The public has done so much justice to the gentlemen engaged in the Critical Review, as to acknowledge that no literary journal was ever carried on in this country with equal spirit and impartiality : yet, I must confess that an article published in your Review of 1757, gave me great surprise, and not a little uneasiness. It regarded a book called the Epigoniad, a poem of the epic kind, which was at that time published with great applause at Edinburgh, and of which a few copies had been sent up to London. The author of that article had surely been lying under strong prepossessions, when he spoke so negligently of a work which abounds in such sublime beauties, and could endeavour to discredit a poem, consisting of near six thousand lines, on account of a few mistakes in expression and prosody, proceeding entirely from the author's being a Scotchman, who had never been out of his own country. As there is a new edition published of this poem, wherein all or most of these trivial mistakes are corrected, I flatter myself that you will gladly lay hold of this opportunity of retracting your oversight, and doing justice to a performance, which may, perhaps, be regarded as one of the ornaments of our language. I appeal from your sentence, as an old woman did from a sentence pronounced by Philip of Macedon :—I appeal from Philip, ill-counselled and in a hurry, to Philip, well-advised, and judging with deliberation. The authority which you possess with the public makes your censure fall with weight : and I question not but you will be the more ready, on that account, to redress any injury into which either negligence, prejudice, or mistake, may have betrayed you. As I profess myself to be an admirer of this performance, it will afford me pleasure to give you a short analysis of it, and to collect a few specimens of those great beauties in which it abounds.

" The author, who appears throughout his whole work to be a great admirer and imitator of Homer, drew the subject of this poem from the fourth Iliad, where

Sthēnelus gives Agamemnon a short account of the sacking of Thebes. After the fall of those heroes, celebrated by Statius, their sons, and among the rest Diomede, undertook the siege of that city, and were so fortunate as to succeed in their enterprize, and to revenge on the Thebans and the tyrant Creon the death of their fathers. These young heroes were known to the Greeks under the title of the Epigoni, or the descendants; and for this reason the author has given to his poem the title of Epigoniad, a name, it must be confessed somewhat unfortunately chosen, for as this particular was known only to a very few of the learned, the public were not able to conjecture what could be the subject of the poem, and were apt to neglect what it was impossible for them to understand.

"There remained a tradition among the Greeks, that Homer had taken the siege of Thebes for the subject of a poem, which is lost; and our author seems to have pleased himself with the thought of reviving the work, as well as of treading in the footsteps of his favourite author. The actors are mostly the same with those of the Iliad : Diomede is the hero : Ulysses, Agamemnon, Menelaus, Nestor, Idomeneus, Merion, even Thersites, all appear in different passages of the poem, and act parts suitable to the lively characters drawn of them by that great master. The whole turn of this new poem would almost lead us to imagine that the Scottish bard had found the lost manuscript of that father of poetry, and had made a faithful translation of it into English. Longinus imagines that the Odyssey was executed by Homer in his old age; we shall allow the Iliad to be the work of his middle age ; and we shall suppose that the Epigoniad was the essay of his youth, where his noble and sublime genius breaks forth by frequent intervals, and gives strong symptoms of that constant flame which distinguished its meridian.

"The poem consists of nine books. We shall open the subject of it in the author's own words :

> Ye pow'rs of song ! with whose immortal fire
> Your bard enraptur'd sung Pelides' ire,
> To Greece so fatal, when in evil hour,
> He brav'd in stern debate, the sov'reign pow'r,
> By like example teach me now to show
> From love, no less, what dire disasters flow.
> For when the youth of Greece, by Theseus led,
> Return'd to conquer where their fathers bled,
> And punish guilty Thebes, by Heav'n ordain'd
> For perfidy to fall, and oaths profan'd ;
> Venus, still partial to the Theban arms,
> Tydeus' son seduc'd by female charms ;
> Who, from his plighted faith by passion sway'd,
> The chiefs, the army, and himself betray'd.
>   This theme did once your fav'rite bard employ,
> Whose verse immortaliz'd the fall of Troy :
> But time's oblivious gulf, whose circle draws
> All mortal things by fate's eternal laws,
> In whose wide vortex worlds themselves are tost,
> And rounding swift successively are lost,
>   his song hath snatch'd. I now resume the strain,
> Not from proud hope and emulation vain,

By this attempt to merit equal praise
With worth heroic, born in happier days.
Sooner the weed, that with the Spring appears,
And in the Summer's heat its blossom bears,
But, shriv'ling at the touch of Winter hoar,
Sinks to its native earth, and is no more;
Might match the lofty oak, which long hath stood,
From age to age, the monarch of the wood.
But love excites me, and desire to trace
His glorious steps, tho' with unequal pace.
Before me still I see his awful shade,
With garlands crown'd of leaves which never fade;
He points the path to fame, and bids me scale
Parnassus' slipp'ry height, where thousands fail:
I follow trembling; for the cliffs are high,
And hov'ring round them watchful harpies fly,
To snatch the poet's wreath with envious claws,
And hiss contempt for merited applause.

"The poet supposes that Cassandra, the daughter of the king of Pelignium in Italy, was pursued by the love of Echetus, a barbarous tyrant in the neighbourhood; and as her father rejected his addresses, he drew on himself the resentment of the tyrant, who made war upon him, and forced him to retire into Etolia, where Diomede gave him protection. This hero falls himself in love with Cassandra, and is so fortunate as to make equal impression on her heart; but before the completion of his marriage, he is called to the siege of Thebes, and leaves, as he supposes, Cassandra in Etolia with her father. But Cassandra, anxious for her lover's safety, and unwilling to part from the object of her affections, had secretly put on a man's habit, had attended him in the camp, and had fought by his side in all his battles. Meanwhile the siege of Thebes is drawn out to some length, and Venus, who favours that city, in opposition to Juno and Pallas, who seek its destruction, deliberates concerning the proper method of raising the siege. The fittest expedient seems to be the exciting in Diomede a jealousy of Cassandra, and persuading him that her affections were secretly engaged to Echetus, and that the tyrant had invaded Etolia in pursuit of his mistress. For this purpose Venus sends down Jealousy, whom the author personifies under the name of Zelotype. Her person and flight are painted in the most splendid colours that poetry affords:

First to her feet the winged shoes she binds,
Which tread the air and mount the rapid winds:
Aloft they bear her thro' th' ethereal plain,
Above the solid Earth and liquid main:
Her arrows next she takes of pointed steel,
For sight too small, but terrible to feel:
Rous'd by their smart, the savage lion roars,
And mad to combat rush the tusky boars.
Of wounds secure; for where their venom lights,
What feels their power all other torment slights.
A figur'd zone, mysteriously design'd,
Around her waist her yellow robe confin'd:
There dark Suspicion lurk'd, of sable hue;
There hasty Rage his deadly dagger drew;

Pale Envy inly pin'd: and by her side
Stood Phrenzy, raging with his chains unty'd ;
Affronted Pride with thirst of vengeance burn'd,
And Love's excess to deepest hatred turn'd.
All these the artist's curious hand express'd,
The work divine his matchless skill confess'd.
The virgin last, around her shoulders flung
The bow ; and by her side the quiver hung;
Then, springing up, her airy course she bends,
For Thebes; and lightly o'er the tents descends.
The son of Tydeus, 'midst his bands, she found
In arms complete, reposing on the ground :
And, as he slept, the hero thus address'd,
Her form to fancy's waking eye express'd.

" Diomede, moved by the instigations of jealousy, and eager to defend his mistress and his country, calls an assembly of the princes, and proposes to raise the
siege of Thebes, on account of the difficulty of the enterprize, and dangers which
surround the army. Theseus, the general, breaks out into a passion at this proposal : but is pacified by Nestor. Idomeneus rises, and reproaches Diomede for
his dishonourable counsel, and among other topics, upbraids him with his degene-
racy from his father's bravery.

Should now, from hence arriv'd, some warrior's ghost
Greet valiant Tydeus on the Stygian coast,
And tell, when danger or distress is near,
That Diomede persuades the rest to fear :
He'd shun the synod of the mighty dead,
And hide his anguish in the deepest shade :
Nature in all an equal course maintains :
The lion's whelp succeeds to awe the plains :
Pards gender pards : from tigers tigers spring,
Nor doves are hatch'd beneath a vulture's wing :
Each parent's image in his offspring lives :
But nought of Tydeus in his son survives.

"The debate is closed by Ulysses, who informs the princes that the Thebans are
preparing to march out in order to attack them ; and that it is vain for them to
deliberate any longer concerning the conclusion of the war.

" We have next a description of a battle between the Thebans, under Creon, and
the confederate Greeks, under Theseus. The battle is full of the spirit of Homer.
We shall not trouble our reader with particulars, which would appear insipid in
prose especially if compared to the lively poetry of our author. We shall only
transcribe one passage, as a specimen of his happy choice of circumstances :

Next Arcas, Cleon, valiant Chromius dy'd;
With Dares, to the Spartan chiefs ally'd.
And Phœmius, whom the gods in early youth
Had form'd for virtue and the love of truth ;
His gen'rous soul to noble deeds they turn'd,
And love to mankind in his bosom burn'd :
Cold thro' his throat the hissing weapon glides,
And on his neck the waving locks divides.

His fate the Graces mourn'd.   The gods above,
Who sit around the starry throne of Jove,
On high Olympus bending from the skies,
His fate beheld with sorrow-streaming eyes.
Pallas alone, unalter'd and serene,
With secret triumph saw the mournful scene:
Not hard of heart : for none of all the pow'rs,
In earth or ocean, or th' Olympian tow'rs,
Holds equal sympathy with human grief,
Or with a freer hand bestows relief:
But conscious that a mind by virtue steel'd
To no impression of distress will yield;
That still unconquer'd, in its awful hour
O'er death it triumphs with immortal pow'r.

" The battle ends with advantage to the confederate Greeks : but the approach of night prevents their total victory.

" Creon, king of Thebes, sends next an embassy to the confederate Greeks, desiring a truce of seven days, in order to bury the dead. Diomede, impatient to return home, and stimulated by jealousy, violently opposes this overture, but is over-ruled by the other princes, and the truce is concluded. The author, in imitation of Homer, and the other ancient poets, takes here an opportunity of describing games celebrated for honouring the dead. The games he has chosen are different from those which are to be found among the ancients, and the incidents are new and curious.

" Diomede took no share in these games : his impatient spirit could not brook the delay which arose from the truce : he pretends that he consented not to it, and is not included in it: he therefore proposes to his troops to attack the Thebans while they are employed in performing the funeral rites of the dead: but is opposed in this design by Deïphobus his tutor, who represents to him in the severest terms the rashness and iniquity of his proposal. After some altercation, Diomede, impatient of contradiction in his favourite object, and stung by the free reproaches of his tutor, breaks out into a violent passion, and throws his spear at Deïphobus, which pierced him to the heart.

" This incident, which is apt to surprize us, seems to have been copied by our author, from that circumstance in the life of Alexander, where this heroic conqueror, moved by a sudden passion, stabs Clytus his ancient friend, by whom his life had been formerly saved in battle. The repentance of Diomede is equal to that of Alexander. No sooner had he struck the fatal blow than his eyes are opened : he is sensible of his guilt and shame ; he refuses all consolation ; abstains even from food : and shuts himself up alone in his tent. His followers, amazed at the violence of his passion, keep at a distance from him : all but Cassandra, who enters his tent with a potion, which she had prepared for him. While she stands before him alone, her timidity and passion betray her sex ; and Diomede immediately perceives her to be Cassandra, who had followed him to the camp, under a warlike disguise. As his repentance for the murder of Deïphobus was now the ruling passion in his breast, he is not moved by tenderness for Cassandra : on the contrary, he considers her as the cause, however innocent, of the murder of his friend, and of his own guilt; and he treats her with such coldness that she retires in confusion. She even leaves the camp, and resolves to return to her father in Etolia; but is taken on the road by a party of Thebans, who carry her to Creon. That tyrant determines to make the most political use of this incident: he sends privately a message to Diomede, threatening to put Cassandra to death, if that hero would not agree to a separate truce with Thebes. This proposal is at first rejected by Dio- mede, who threatens immediate destruction to Creon and all his race. Nothing can be more artfully managed by the poet than this incident. We shall hear him in his own words :

> Sternly the hero ended, and resign'd,
> To fierce disorder, all his mighty mind,
> Already in his thoughts, with vengeful hands,
> He dealt destruction 'midst the Theban bands,
> In fancy saw the tott'ring turrets fall,
> And led his warriors o'er the level'd wall.
> Rous'd with the thought, from his high seat he sprung;
> And grasp'd the sword, which on a column hung ;
> The shining blade he balanc'd thrice in air ;
> His lances next he view'd, and armour fair.
> When, hanging 'midst the costly panoply,
> A scarf embroider'd met the hero's eye,
> Which fair Cassandra's skilful hands had wrought,
> A present for her lord, in secret brought
> That day, when first he led his martial train
> In arms, to combat on the Theban plain.
> As some strong charm, which magic sounds compose,
> Suspends a downward torrent as it flows ;
> Checks in the precipice its headlong course,
> And calls it trembling upwards to its source :
> Such seem'd the robe, which, to the hero's eyes,
> Made the fair artist in her charms to rise.
> His rage, suspended in its full career,
> To love resigns to grief and tender fear.
> Glad would he now his former words revoke,
> And change the purpose which in wrath he spoke ;
> From hostile hands his captive fair to gain,
> From fate to save her, or the servile chain :
> But pride, and shame, the fond design supprest ;
> Silent he stood, and lock'd it in his breast.
> Yet had the wary Theban well divin'd,
> By symptoms sure, each motion of his mind :
> With joy he saw the heat of rage suppress'd ;
> And thus again his artful words address'd.

" The truce is concluded for twenty days; but the perfidious Creon, hoping that Diomede would be overawed by the danger of his mistress, resolves to surprise the Greeks ; and accordingly makes a sudden attack upon them, breaks into their camp, and carries every thing before him. Diomede at first stands neuter ; but when Ulysses suggests to him, that after the defeat of the confederate Greeks, he has no security ; and that so treacherous a prince as Creon will not spare, much less restore Cassandra, he takes to arms, assaults the Thebans, and obliges them to seek shelter within their walls.   Creon, in revenge, puts Cassandra to death, and shews her head over the walls.   This sight so inflames Diomede, that he attacks Thebes with double fury, takes the town by scalade, and gratifies his vengeance by the death of Creon.

" This is a short abstract of the story on which this new poem is founded.  The reader may perhaps conjecture (what I am not very anxious to conceal) that the execution of the Epigoniad is better than the design, the poetry superior to the fable, and the colouring of the particular parts more excellent than the general plan of the whole.   Of all the great epic poems which have been the admiration of mankind, the Jerusalem of Tasso alone would make a tolerable novel, if reduced to prose, and related without that splendour of versification and imagery by which it is supported: yet in the opinion of many great judges, the Jerusalem is the least perfect of all these productions : chiefly, because it has least nature and simplicity in the sentiments, and is most liable to the objection of affectation and conceit.   The story of a poem, whatever may be imagined, is the least essential part of it : the force of the versification, the vivacity of the images, the justness of the descriptions, the natural play of the passions, are the chief circumstances which distinguish the great poet from the prosaic novelist, and give him so high a rank among the heroes in literature ; and I will venture to affirm, that all these advantages, especially the three former, are to be found in an eminent degree in the Epigoniad. The author, inspired with the true genius of Greece, and smit with the most profound veneration for Homer, disdains all frivolous ornaments ; and relying entirely on his sublime imagination, and his nervous and harmonious expression, has ventured to present to his reader the naked beauties of nature, and challenges for his partizans all the admirers of genuine antiquity.

"There is one circumstance in which the poet has carried his boldness of copying antiquity beyond the practice of many, even judicious moderns.   He has drawn his personages, not only with all the simplicity of the Grecian heroes, but also with some degree of their roughness, and even of their ferocity.   This is a circumstance which a mere modern is apt to find fault with in Homer, and which perhaps he will not easily excuse in his imitator.   It is certain, that the ideas of manners are so much changed since the age of Homer, that though the Iliad was always among the ancients conceived to be a panegyric on the Greeks, yet the reader is now almost always on the side of the Trojans, and is much more interested for the humane and soft manners of Priam, Hector, Andromache, Sarpedon, Æneas, Glaucus, nay, even of Paris and Helen, than for the severe and cruel bravery of Achilles, Agamemnon, and the other Grecian heroes.   Sensible of this inconvenience, Fenelon, in his elegant romance, has softened extremely the harsh manners of the heroic ages, and has contented himself with retaining that amiable simplicity by which those ages were distinguished.   If the reader be displeased, that the British poet has not followed the example of the French writer, he must, at least, allow that he has drawn a more exact and faithful copy of antiquity, and has made fewer sacrifices of truth to ornament.

" There is another circumstance of our author's choice which will be liable to dispute.   It may be thought that by introducing the heroes of Homer, he has lost all the charms of novelty, and leads us into fictions which are somewhat stale and thread-bare. Boileau, the greatest critic of the French nation, was of a very different opinion :

> La fable offre a l'esprit mille agréments divers
> . Là tous les noms heureux semblent nez pour les vers :
> Ulysse, Agamemnon, Oreste, Idomenée,
> Helene, Menelas, Paris, Hector, Enee.

" It is certain that there is in that poetic ground a kind of enchantment which allures every person of a tender and lively imagination ; nor is this impression diminished, but rather much increased, by our early introduction to the knowledge of it in our perusal of the Greek and Latin classics.

" The same great French critic makes the apology of our poet in his use of the ancient mythology :

> Ainsi dans cet amas de nobles fictions,
> Le poet s' egeye en mille inventions,
> Orne, eleve, embellit, aggrandit toutes choses,
> Et trouve sous sa main des fleurs toujours ecloses.

" It would seem, indeed, that if the machinery of the heathen gods be not admitted, epic poetry, at least all the marvellous part of it, must be entirely abandoned. The Christian religion, for many reasons, is unfit for the fabulous ornaments of poetry : the introduction of allegory, after the manner of Voltaire, is liable to many objections : and though a mere historical epic poem, like Leonidas, may have its beauties, it will always be inferior to the force and pathetic of tragedy, and must resign to that species of poetry the precedency which the former composition has always challenged among the productions of human genius. But with regard to these particulars, the author has himself made a sufficient apology in the judicious and spirited preface which accompanies his poem.

" But though our poet has in general followed so successfully the footsteps of Homer, he has, in particular passages, chosen other ancient poets for his model. His seventh book contains an episode, very artfully inserted, concerning the death of Hercules : where he has plainly had Sophocles in his view, and has ventured to engage in a rivalship with that great master of the tragic scene. If the sublimity of our poet's imagination, and the energy of his style, appear any where conspicuous, it is in this episode, which we shall not scruple to compare with any poetry in the English language. Nothing can be more pathetic than the complaint of Hercules, when the poison of the centaur's robe begins first to prey upon him :

> Sov'reign of heav'n and earth ! whose boundless sway
> The fates of men and mortal things obey,
> If e'er delighted from the courts above,
> In human form you sought Alcmene's love ;
> If fame's unchanging voice to all the earth,
> With truth, proclaims you author of my birth ;
> Whence, from a course of spotless glory run,
> Successful toils and wreaths of triumph won,
> Am I thus wretched ? better that before
> Some monster fierce had drank my streaming gore ;

Or crush'd by Cacus, foe to gods and men,
My batter'd brains had strew'd his rocky den:
Than, from my glorious toils and triumphs past,
To fall subdu'd by female arts, at last.
O cool my boiling blood, ye winds, that blow
From mountains loaded with eternal snow,
And crack the icy cliffs: in vain! in vain!
Your rigour cannot quench my raging pain!
For round this heart the furies wave their brands,
And wring my entrails with their burning hands.
Now bending from the skies, O wife of Jove!
Enjoy the vengeance of thy injur'd love:
For fate, by me, the Thund'rer's guilt atones;
And, punish'd in her son, Alcmene groans:
The object of your hate shall soon expire;
Fix'd on my shoulders preys a net of fire;
Whom nor the toils nor dangers could subdue,
By false Eurystheus dictated from you;
Nor tyrants lawless, nor the monstrous brood
Which haunts the desert or infests the flood,
Nor Greece, nor all the barb'rous climes that lie
Where Phœbus ever points his golden eye,
A woman hath o'erthrown!—ye gods! I yield
To female arts, unconquer'd in the field.
My arms—alas! are these the same that bow'd
Anteus, and his giant force subdu'd?
That dragg'd Nemea's monster from his den?
And slew the dragon in his native fen?
Alas! alas! their mighty muscles fail,
While pains infernal ev'ry nerve assail:
Alas, alas! I feel in streams of woe
These eyes dissolve, before untaught to flow.
Awake my virtue, oft in dangers try'd,
Patient in toils, in deaths unterrify'd,
Rouse to my aid; nor let my labours past,
With fame atchiev'd, be blotted by the last:
Firm and unmov'd, the present shock endure;
Once triumph, and for ever rest secure.

"Our poet, though his genius be in many respects very original, has not disdained to imitate even modern poets. He has added to his heroic poem a dream, in
the manner of Spenser, where the poet supposes himself to be introduced to Homer,
who censures his poem in some particulars, and excuses it in others. This poem
is indeed a species of apology for the Epigoniad, wrote in a very lively and elegant
manner: it may be compared to a well-polished gem, of the purest water, and cut
into the most beautiful form. Those who would judge of our author's talents for
poetry, without perusing his larger work, may satisfy their curiosity, by running
over this short poem. They will see the same force of imagination and harmony
of numbers, which distinguish his longer performance: and may thence, with small
application, receive a favourable impression of our author's genius.

"D. H."

That Wilkie may not be deprived of any favourable opinion, nor the admission of his works into this collection stand in need of any further apology, I shall subjoin the opinion of a very elegant and candid critic of the present day.—" The Epigoniad of Wilkie is the bold attempt of an energetic mind to try its powers in the most arduous path of poetry, the epic ; without that correctness of judgment, and previous discipline in the practice of harmonious numbers, which can alone ensure success in an age of polish and refinement. It has accordingly been measured by that standard of criticism, which the most unqualified judges can easily apply,—a comparison with the most perfect productions of its kind : and its palpable defects have involved in an indiscriminate condemnation its less obvious, but real merits [2]."

[2] Lord Woodhouslee's Life of Lord Kaimes, vol. i. p. 178. 4to. 1807.—C.

# AUTHOR'S PREFACE

## *EPIGONIAD.*

---

As there is no class of writers more freely censured than poets, and that by judges of all sorts, competent and incompetent; I shall attempt to answer some objections that may be made to the following performance, by persons not sufficiently acquainted with epic poetry, and the rules upon which it ought to be formed.

The beauties of the piece, if it has any, shall be left to be discovered by the reader for himself. This is his undoubted privilege; and I have no intention to break in upon it: neither would it be of any advantage to do so; for poetical beauties, if they are real, will make themselves observed, and have their full effect without a comment.

Some will object to the choice of the subject, That it is taken from the history of an age and nation, the particular manners of which are not now well known, and therefore incapable of being justly represented by any modern author. This objection will appear to be of little consequence, when we consider that the fact upon which it proceeds is so far from being strictly true, that there are none who have any tolerable share of classical learning, that are not better acquainted with the manners and customs of the heroic ages, than with those of their own country, at the distance of a few centuries. Neither is this knowledge of ancient manners confined to the learned; the vulgar themselves, from the books of Moses, and other accounts of the first periods of the Jewish state, are sufficiently instructed in the customs of the earliest times, to be able to relish any work where these are justly represented. With what favour, for instance, has Mr. Pope's translation of the Iliad been received by persons of all conditions? and how much is it commonly preferred to the Fairy Queen, a poem formed upon manners of a much more modern cast. But supposing the fact upon which the objection proceeds to be true, and that the customs and manners peculiar to the times from which the subject of the poem is taken are not now well understood, I do not apprehend that, even with this concession, the objection amounts to any thing considerable; for manners are to be distinguished into two kinds, universal and particular. Universal manners, are those which arise from the original frame and constitution of the human nature, and which consequently are the same in all nations and periods of the world. Particular manners, on the other hand, consist of such customs and modes of behaviour as proceed from the influence of partial causes, and that shift and vary as those causes do upon which they depend. To make myself understood by an example: it is agreeable to common or universal manners, to be angry and resent an injury; but particular manners, in ordinary cases, determine the methods of revenge. For great offences, an Italian poisons his enemy; a Spaniard stabs him over the shoulder; and a Frenchman seeks satisfaction in a duel. From this example, it will be easy to see that particular manners ought to appear but very little, either in epic poetry, tragedy, or any other of the higher kinds of poetical composition; for they are vulgar and depend upon custom: but great passions and high characters reject ordinary forms; and therefore must, upon every occasion, break through all the common modes both of speech and behaviour. Though ancient manners, therefore, were not so precisely known as they are, I should imagine, that a story taken from the accounts which we have of the heroic ages, might very well serve for the subject of an epic poem, and have all the advantages necessary in respect of that species of composition.

It may likewise be alleged, that I have done wrong in choosing for my subject a piece of history which has no connection with present affairs ; and that, if I had done otherwise, my work would have been more interesting and useful.

This objection, seemingly a very material one, admits, notwithstanding, of an easy answer, viz. that subjects for epic poetry ought always to be taken from periods too early to fall within the reach of true history. And, if this rule is shown to be essential, which I shall attempt to do in what follows, it will be found to be impossible that any subject proper for that kind of writing should have a connection with present affairs. The proper business of epic poetry is to extend our ideas of human perfection, or, as the critics express it, to excite admiration. In order to do this in any tolerable degree, characters must be magnified, and accommodated rather to our notions of heroic greatness, than to the real state of human nature. There appears a certain littleness in all men, when truly known, which checks admiration, and confines it to very narrow limits ; heroes, themselves, though possessed of the greatest qualities, are, in most circumstances of their condition, so much upon a level with the ordinary run of mankind, that such as have an opportunity of being intimately acquainted with them, do not admire them at the same rate that others do, who view them only at a distance. The common conditions of humanity lessen every man ; and there are many little circumstances inseparably connected with our state of being, which we cannot easily reconcile with our idea of Epaminondas, Plato, Scipio, or Cæsar. From all this it p'ainly appears, that admiration claims for its object something superior to mere humanity ; and therefore such poems as have it for their end to excite admiration, ought to celebrate those persons only that never have been treated of by regular historians. For history gives to all things their just and natural dimensions ; and, if it should interfere with poetical fiction, would effectually confute those beautiful legends which are invented to raise our ideas of character and action, above the standard at which experience has fixed them.

Let it be observed, as a further confirmation of the maxim which I am establishing, that there is in our minds a principle which leads us to admire past times, especially those which are most remote from our own. This prejudice is strong in us ; and, without being directed or assisted by art, forms in the mere vulgar of all countries, the most extravagant notions of the stature, strength, and other heroic qualities of their remote ancestors. This prejudice, so favourable to poetical fiction, true history effectually destroys ; and therefore poets, that they may have the advantage of it, ought to celebrate those persons and events only that are of so great antiquity, as not to be remembered with any degree of certainty and exactness.

But, instead of a thousand arguments to this purpose, let us only consider the machinery which must be employed in an epic poem : how Heaven and Hell must both be put in motion, and brought into the action, how events altogether out of the common road of human affairs, and no ways countenanced either by reason or by experience, must be offered to men's imagination, so as to be admitted for true. Let us consider all this, and it will appear, that there is nothing which poets ought more carefully to avoid, than interfering with such regular and well vouched accounts of things as would effectually confute their fable, and make the meanest reader reject it with contempt. This is a point of prudence which no poet has yet neglected with impunity. Lucan, according to his usual rashness, has taken for the subject of an epic poem, one of the best known events which he could have pitched upon in the whole series of human affairs ; and in order to distinguish himself from a mere historian, is often under a necessity of starting from his subject, and employing the whole force of a very lively and fruitful invention, in unnecessary descriptions and trifling digressions. This, besides other inconveniences of greater importance, gives such an appearance of labour and straining to his whole performance, as takes much from the merit of it, with all who have any notion of ease, majesty, and simplicity in writing. He, and all other poets who have fallen into the same errour, find always this disadvantage attending it, that the true and fictitious parts of their work refuse to unite, and standing as it were at a distance, upon terms of mutual aversion, reproach each other with their peculiar defects. Fiction accuses truth of narrowness and want of dignity ; and this again represents the other as vain and extravagant. Spenser, who, in his Fairy Queen, not only treats of matters within the sphere of regular history, but describes even the transactions of his own time, in order to avoid the inconveniences which he knew to be almost inseparable from such an attempt, covers his story with a veil of allegory, that few of his readers are able to penetrate. This stratagem leaves him at full liberty in the exercise of his invention ; but he pays, in my opinion, too dear for that privilege, by sacrificing to it all the weight and authority which a mixture of received tradition and real geography would have given to his fable. Milton takes the subjects of both his great poems from true history, yet does not succeed the worse upon that account. But it is to be remembered, that his chief actors are not men, but divine and angelical beings; and that it is the human nature only which suffers by a just representation, and loses in point of dignity, when truly known. Besides, the historical circumstances upon which he builds are so few, and of so extraordinary a nature, that they are easily accommodated to poetical fiction; and therefore, instead of limiting him, and setting bounds to his invention, they serve only to countenance and give a degree of credibility to whatever he pleases to feign. Shakespeare may likewise be quoted as an exception to the general rule, who takes the subjects of many of his pieces from periods of the English history not very remote, and, notwithstanding, succeeds remarkably in exciting the heroic passion. That Shakespeare makes us admire his heroes is undeniable; and no man of common sense will ever pretend to assert, that real characters of great men, touched up and heightened by a poetical fancy, will not very naturally excite admiration. But there are different degrees of this passion, as well as of all others: and it is evident, that the degree of it which Shakespeare intends to raise, is not equal to that which Homer aims at, and the other writers of the epic tribe. We admire no character in Shakespeare's works more than that of Henry V. but the idea which Homer gives us of Achilles is still more noble and august. The tragedian mixes so much of the ordinary man in the character of his hero, that we become too familiar with him to admire him in a high degree: for in those very pieces in which he is represented as performing his most remarkable exploits, he is often found at his leisure hours amusing himself with a knot of humourists, pickpockets, and buffoons. I do not pretend to censure Shakespeare for this conduct; because it is not the business of a tragedian to make us admire, but to interest our other affections: and, to make his heroes very much objects of admiration, would possibly be one of the greatest errours that an author of that kind could fall into: for the principle of compassion, to which tragedy is peculiarly addressed, is incompatible with high admiration; and a man, in order either to be loved or pitied, must appear with evident symptoms of the weaknesses common to the rest of the human kind. It is our own image in distress which afflicts us; and we never pity one under calamities, who is not weak enough to be moved by them. Homer, upon this account, never attempts to excite pity, but from such private and domestic distresses as show his heroes in the light of ordinary men. Sophocles likewise, from a just apprehension that the heroic passion interferes with the proper spirit of tragedy, lessens on purpose the great characters which he introduces, and strips them of more than half their dignity. Though therefore Shakespeare makes us admire his heroes as much as a tragedian ought to do, and even more, in some instances, than the rules of art would justify; yet, as the degree of admiration which he excites is less by far than that which epic poetry aims at, it may well be raised from subjects that are strictly historical, though the higher degrees of that passion cannot. Were my judgment of sufficient authority in matters of criticism, I would have it understood as a rule, that the subjects of epic poetry should be taken from tradition only; that tragedy should keep within the limits of true history; and that comedy, without meddling at all with historical facts, should expose vice and folly in recent instances, and from living examples. That part of the rule which regards epic poetry, is sufficiently justified from what has been already said; and, concerning tragedy, I have likewise observed, that it ought not to exalt its greatest characters above the standard of real life. From this it will follow, that it may be strictly historical without losing any real advantage, and attain its full perfection without the assistance of fable. I believe it will be easily allowed, that where truth and fiction are equally subservient to the purposes of poetry, the first ought always to be preferred; for true history carries a weight and authority with it, which seldom attend stories that are merely fictitious, and has many other advantages for interesting our affections above the legends of remote antiquity. But as tragedy should never go so far back as the fabulous ages, neither should it, in my opinion, approach too near to the present times; for though it does not aim at raising and gratifying the passion of admiration, yet it has a degree of dignity to maintain, which it would endanger by treating of events too recent, and characters too particularly remembered. Comedy, on the other hand, and indeed every species of satire whatsoever, ought to attack living characters only, and the vices and follies of present times. That imperfection which appears in every thing when viewed near, a circumstance so unfavourable to the genius of epic poetry and tragedy, falls in precisely with that of comedy, a kind of writing which has no dignity to support, points always at what is ridiculous, and marks its objects with characters of littleness and contempt. We naturally admire past times, and reverence the dead; and consequently are not so much disposed to laugh at fools, who have already finished their parts, and retired, as at fools who are yet upon the stage. The ancient comedy of the Greeks, which proceeded upon this maxim, was certainly, upon that account, the most perfect species of satire that ever was invented. Homer, as he exceeds all other poets in merit, has likewise the advantage of them in point of good fortune; the condition of the age in which he wrote gave him an opportunity of celebrating, in his poems, events, which though they were in his days of no great antiquity, and consequently the more interesting, yet had fallen, through the want of authentic records, into so happy a degree of obscurity, that he was at full liberty to feign concerning them what he pleased, without any danger of confutation. This is an advantage which succeeding poets could not boast of; and therefore have found themselves under a necessity, either of taking their subjects from remote antiquity, as I have done, or, (which, in my opinion, is worse) of attempting to mix fable with true history, which never can be done with success.

The mythology in the following poem will probably give offence to some readers, who will think it indecent for a Christian to write in such a manner as to suppose the truth of a Heathen religion. They will be of opinion, that it would have been better, either to have introduced no religious system at all, or to have chosen such a subject as would have admitted of the true system. I shall endeavour to answer this objection, by establishing two maxims directly opposite to what is proposed in the preceding alternative, and show not only that divine beings are necessary characters in an epic poem, but likewise that it is highly improper to introduce the true God into a work of that nature. If these two points are fully made out, the force of the objection will be taken away. As to the first of them, let us again consider the end which epic poetry proposes to itself: it aims at exciting admiration, by setting before us images of whatever is great and noble in the human character: it is necessary for this purpose that a poet should give his heroes, not only all those intrinsic qualities which make men admired, but that he should magnify them likewise by a skilful management of outward circumstances. We do not form our notions either of persons or things from their real qualities only; circumstances of a foreign nature, and merely accessory, have as great an influence as these in determining our approbation and dislike. This observation shows the importance of mythology to epic poetry; for nothing can render a person of greater consequence in the eye of the world, than an opinion that the gods regard him with a peculiar degree of attention, and are much interested in all that relates to him. If people are once considered as the favourites of Heaven, or instruments chosen for the accomplishment of its important purposes; poets may tell of them what great things they please, without seeming to exaggerate, or say any thing that exceeds the bounds of probability. Homer was certainly of this opinion, when he ascribed, to his heroes, valour and other great qualities in so immoderate a degree; for, had the gods never interposed in any of the events which he celebrates; had his chief actors been no ways connected with them, either in point of favour or consanguinity, and represented, at the same time, as performing the high exploits which he ascribes to them, instead of being applauded as the first of poets, he would have been censured as the most false and most credulous of historians. This argument in favour of poetical mythology, with another which might be taken from the advantage it is of in point of ornament, and a third from its use in allegory, has determined almost all the writers who have followed the epic or heroic style, to allow it a place in their compositions: such of them as have taken their subject from Greek or Roman story, have adopted the mythology of Homer; and the rest, in celebrating more modern heroes, have, instead of that, made use of the true religion, corrupted by an unnatural mixture of northern superstition and Grecian fable. From a practice therefore so universal, we may justly infer, that poets have looked upon mythology as a thing of great use in their compositions, and almost essential to the art.

It may be alleged, after all that has been said, that, to bring gods into epic poetry, is inconvenient on many accounts; that it prevents a proper display of character in the human actors, turning them all into so many machines, to be moved and guided by the immediate impulses of deity; that it breaks in upon the order of natural causes, and renders all art, either in the plan or conduct of a work, superfluous and unnecessary. If what this objection supposes were true, and that the mixing of gods with men in the action of an epic poem, necessarily turned the whole into miracle; if it were an unavoidable consequence of this method, that the human actors should be governed in all they do by divine impulse determining them, without regard to their natural characters, and the probable motives which ought to influence them: in short, if mythology could have no place in a poem, but at the expense of manners, order, connection, and every other thing that can render a work either beautiful or instructive, it would be an argument against it of such weight, as nothing alleged in its favour would be able to counterbalance. But the objection is by no means well founded ; for, though there may be an indiscreet application of mythology, productive of all those ill effects which have been mentioned ; yet it is obvious, both from reason and experience, that mythology may be managed in such a manner as to be attended with none of them. And this will appear from a very obvious example : the greatest part of mankind, in every age, have believed that gods and superior beings govern and direct the course of human affairs. Many individuals, and even whole nations, have thought that all the actions and events of our lives are predetermined by an over-ruling power, and that we suffer the control of an irresistible necessity in all we do : yet this opinion never changes the moral feelings of such as entertain it, and their judgment of characters and actions ; they love and hate, approve and disapprove, admire and despise, in the same manner as others do who believe that men are absolutely free, and that their final determinations proceed only from themselves. But when it is understood, that people act without consciousness, or that the organs of their bodies are not under the dominion of their own wills, but actuated by some other being without their consent ; in short, when mere physical necessity is substituted in place of moral, all idea of character, all sense of approbation and disapprobation immediately ceases. From this fact, the truth of which nobody will dispute, it is easy to judge in what cases the interposition of gods in the action of a poem will prevent a proper display of the human characters, and when not. Volition, as appears by the example now given, is that upon which all our moral ideas are founded : so long then as volition is exerted, there is a character, and, when that ceases, the character is lost. If therefore the deities in a poem are employed in animating and deterring the heroes, only by suggesting such motives as are proper to influence their wills ; such interposition by no means interferes with the display of character, but rather favours it ; for the quality of every mind may be known from the motives by which it is determined ; and Minerva's prevailing with Pandarus to be guilty of a piece of treachery, by suggesting that Paris would reward him for it, discovered the venality of his temper as much as if he had done the same action from a like motive occurring to himself.

Poets often make the gods infuse an uncommon degree of vigour into their heroes, for answering some great occasion, and add to the grace and dignity of their figure. Sometimes they make a second-rate hero the first in a particular action, and, with their assistance, he distinguishes himself above such as are at other times more remarkable for valour and success ; all this is so agreeable to what happens naturally, and from mere mechanical causes, that we forget the gods, and interpret what happens as if they had not interposed at all. For every body knows, that when people are roused to any remarkable exertion of force, they become stronger than they are at other times; and that, when in this manner the spirits rise to an uncommon height, the whole body acquires new graces. Valour is not a fixed and permanent quality, nor is it found in any one always in the same degree. Plutarch observes, that of all the virtues it exerts itself most irregularly, and rises by fits like a divine inspiration. The sense which every man has of these things, makes him look upon the interposition of gods in such cases as a mythological way of expressing what is merely natural, and allow such as perform the great actions in a poem to possess the whole merit of them. It never lessens our opinion of Hector's valour, for instance, that Apollo often assists him ; nor do we think Ulysses less prudent, because he is guided by the influence of Minerva. We have as clear impressions of those, and the other Homeric characters, as we have of any characters whatsoever, and discern their limits and distinguishing marks as clearly, as if they had acted altogether of themselves. That superior beings should be employed in governing the events of things, and interposing by thunder, earthquakes, inundations, pestilences, and the like, can never be thought unnatural in poetry, by any one who believes that Providence actually manages the affairs of the world by such means. It belongs to men to design and act, but to Heaven alone to determine events. Though a poet, therefore, should represent an army weaker and worse conducted, prevailing, in consequence of that kind of interposition which has been mentioned, over another, evidently better and stronger; there would be nothing unnatural in such an account, or contrary to what is often experienced in real affairs.

After all that has been said, it must be owned, that if gods are brought in upon slight occasions, and for trifling purposes ; if they are put upon working miracles in order to cover blunders either in the plan or execution of a poem, and employed in cutting such knots as the author himself has not the skill or patience to untie ; it must be owned, I say, that this is a very wrong application of mythology, and attended with all the disadvantages which the objection mentions. It is a stratagem, which, if often practised, would teach the reader at last to disregard all appearances, and, when the most important periods of affairs were approaching, to remain quite secure and uninterested, trusting that a god would always be at hand in time of need to manage every thing as the poet would have it, and put all to rights by the shortest and most effectual methods. I have considered this objection at greater length, because at first view it appears very plausible; and shall proceed to what remains, after I have taken notice of another, which has likewise some appearance of force. It will be thought inconvenient, as it is the design of epic poetry to raise and dignify human characters, that gods should appear with men in the same scenes of action. It will be alleged, that in this case the divine persons will necessarily overshadow the human, lessen them by a comparison, and consequently produce an effect directly opposite to what is intended. This objection, however plausible, does not seem to be supported by experience; at least I never found in any instance, that the splendour of the divine characters in a poem eclipsed the human. Besides, this is what cannot easily happen; for, let us suppose two parties of boys engaged in some trial, either of force or skill, and that a few men take part in the debate, dividing themselves between the opposite sides, and assisting them against each other, would the exploits of the full-grown men, however remarkable, lessen those of the boys? by no means; for things that are confessedly unequal, never come into competition, and therefore cannot be either lessened or magnified by appearing together. Are we less disposed to admire the valour of Achilles, because it is understood he was not a match for Jupiter? or the sagacity of Ulysses, because his penetration was not equal to that of Minerva? But there is one circumstance which renders it absolutely impossible for the gods in epic poetry to eclipse the men in point of heroism; and it is this, that the gods are immortal, and consequently cannot exert that in which heroism chiefly consists, viz. the contempt of death. Homer, in order to give his deities as much of that quality as possible, has made them vulnerable and susceptible of pain; a freedom which has shocked some of the critics, who did not attend to the reason of his doing so. But Homer was too good a judge of propriety, not to be sensible that no person could appear with advantage in military actions, who ventur'd nothing in point of personal safety; and that stature, force, magnificent armour, and even the highest achievements, will never constitute the heroic character, where patience and a contempt of danger have no opportunity of appearing. It is this circumstance which gives the mortals in epic poetry a manifest advantage over the immortals; and Mars, when ushered into the field with all the pomp and magnificence of Homeric description, is an object less to be admired than Diomed, Ajax, and many others who combat bravely, though conscious of mortality. Homer, who has managed his great characters with the truest judgment and strictest attention to circumstances, takes care to have Achilles early informed that he was to perish at Troy, else he might seem too conscious of safety, from his matchless valour and the armour which he wore, to be great in that which is most to be admired, the contempt of death, when the danger of it is imminent. It must be acknowledged, that in Milton's Paradise Lost, the persons in machinery over-shadow the human characters, and that the heroes of the poem are all of them immortals: but then it is to be remembered, that Paradise Lost is a work altogether irregular; that the subject of it is not epic, but tragic; and that Adam and Eve are not designed to be objects of admiration, but of pity: it is tragic in its plot, and epic in its dress and machinery: as a tragedy, it does not fall under the present question; and as an epic poem, it evades it likewise, by a circumstance very uncommon, viz. that in the part of it which is properly epic, there are no human persons at all.

I have in this manner endeavoured to prove that mythology is necessary to an epic poem, and that the chief objections to the use of it are of little consequence. I proceed to establish the other proposition which I mentioned, and show, that the true God ought not to be brought into a work of that nature. And if this proposition can be made out, it will easily appear from it and the preceding one taken together, that poets are under a necessity of having recourse to a false theology, and that they are not to be blamed for doing what the nature of epic poetry on the one hand, and respect to the true religion on the other, render necessary and unavoidable. For proving the point in question, I need only observe, that no person can appear with advantage in poetry, who is not represented according to the form and condition of a man. This art addresses itself chiefly to the imagination, a faculty which apprehends nothing in the way of character that is not human, and according to the analogy of that nature of which we ourselves are conscious. But it would be equally impious and absurd to represent the deity in this manner, and to contrive for him a particular character, and method of acting, agreeable to the prejudices of weak and ignorant mortals. In the early ages of the church, he thought fit to accommodate himself, by such a piece of condescension, to the notions and apprehensions of his creatures: but it would be indecent in any man to use the same freedom, and do that for God, which he only has a right to do for himself. The author of Paradise Lost has offended nototiously in this respect; and, though no encomiums are too great for him as a poet, he is justly chargeable with impiety, for presuming to represent the Divine Nature, and the mysteries of religion, according to the narrowness of human prejudice: his dialogues between the Father and the Son; his employing a Being of infinite wisdom in discussing the subtleties of school divinity; the sensual views which he gives of the happiness of Heaven, admitting into it, as a part, not only real eating and drinking, but another kind of animal pleasure too by no means more refined: these, and such like circumstances, though perfectly poetical, and agreeable to the genius of an art which adapts every thing to the human mode, are, at the same time, so inconsistent with truth, and the exalted ideas which we ought to entertain of divine things, that they must be highly offensive to all such as have just impressions of religion, and would not choose to see a system of doctrine revealed from Heaven, reduced to a state of conformity with heathen superstition. True theology ought not to be used in an epic poem, for another reason, of no less weight than that which has been mentioned, viz. That the human characters which it represents should never be formed upon a perfect moral plan, but have their piety (for instance) tinctured with superstition, and their general behaviour influenced by affection, passion, and prejudice. This will be thought a violent paradox, by such as do not know that imperfect characters interest us more than perfect ones, and that we are doubly instructed when we see, in one and the same example, both what we ought to follow and what we ought to avoid. Accordingly Horace, in his Epistle to Lollius, where he bestows the highest encomiums upon the Iliad, as a work which delineated vice and virtue better than the writings of the most celebrated philosophers, says of it, notwithstanding, that it is taken up in describing the animosities of foolish kings and infatuated nations. To go to the bottom of this matter, it will be proper to observe, that men are capable of two sorts of character, which may be distinguished by the names of natural and artificial. The natural character implies all those feelings, passions, desires, and opinions, which men have from nature and common experience, independent of speculation and moral refinement. A person of this character looks upon outward prosperity as a real good, and considers the calamities of life as real evils; loves his friends, hates his enemies, admires his superiors, is assuming with respect to his inferiors, and stands upon terms of rivalship with his equals; in short, is governed by all those passions and opinions that possess the hearts and determine the actions of ordinary men. The force and magnitude of this character is in proportion to the strength of these natural dispositions; and its virtue consists in having the generous and beneficent ones predominant. As to that sort of character, again, which I distinguished by the name of artificial; it consists in a habit of mind formed by discipline, according to the cool and dispassionate dictates of reason. This character is highly moral, but, in my opinion, far less poetical than the other, by being less fit for interesting our affections, which are formed by the wise Author of our nature for embracing such beings as are of the same temper and complexion with ourselves, and are marked with the common infirmities of human nature. Persons of the high philosophic character, are too firm and unmoved, amidst the calamities they meet with, to excite much sympathy, and are too much superior to the sallies of passion and partial affection, the popular marks of generosity and greatness of mind, ever to be much admired by the bulk of mankind. If the most accomplished poet in the world should take a rigid philosopher for the chief character either of an epic poem or a tragedy, it is easy to conjecture what would be the success of such an attempt; the work would assume the character of its hero, and be cold, dispassionate, and uninteresting. There is, however, a species of panegyric proper for such sort of perfection, and it may be represented to advantage, either in history or prose dialogue, but it will never strike the bulk of mankind. Plato, in his apology of Socrates, deceives us; as Mr. Addison likewise does in his tragedy of Cato: for both of them attempt to persuade us, that we are affected with the contemplation of unshaken fortitude, while we are only sympathizing with suffering innocence. The tenderness of humanity appearing through the hardness of the philosophic character, is that which affects us in both instances, and not that unconquered greatness of mind, which occasions rather wonder and astonishment than genuine affection.

From what has been said, it is easy to infer, that the great characters, both in epic poetry and tragedy, ought not to be formed upon a perfect moral plan; and therefore heroes themselves must often be represented as acting from such motives, and governed by such affections, as impartial reason cannot approve of: but it would be highly indecent to make a being, whom religion teaches us to consider as perfect, enter into the views of such persons, and exert himself in order to promote their extravagant enterprizes. This would be to bring down the infinite wisdom of God to the level of human folly, and to make him altogether such an one as ourselves.

A false theology, therefore, ought rather to be employed in poetical compositions than the true; for, as the superior beings which are introduced must of necessity be represented as assuming the passions and opinions of those whom they favour, it is surely much safer to employ a set of imaginary beings for this purpose, than God himself, and the blessed angels, who ought always to be objects of our reverence.

The same reasoning which leads to this conclusion, will likewise make us sensible, that among false religions, those ought to be preferred which are least connected with the true; for the superstitions which priests and poets have built upon the Christian faith, dishonour it, and therefore should, if possible, be buried in oblivion. The ancient Greek theology seems upon all accounts the fittest. It has no connection with the true system, and therefore may be treated with the greatest freedom, without indecency or ground of offence. It consists of a number of beautiful fables, suited to the taste of the most lively and ingenious people that ever existed, and so much calculated to ravish and transport a warm imagination, that many poets in modern times, who proceeded upon a different theology, have notwithstanding been so bewitched with its charms, as to admit it into their works, though it clashed violently with the system which they had adopted. Milton is remarkable in this respect; and the more so, as his poem is altogether of a religious nature, and the subject of it taken from holy writ.

Some may possibly imagine, that the following work would have had greater merit, if it had offered to the world a set of characters entirely new, and a story no ways connected with any thing that is already known. I am not of this opinion, but persuaded, on the contrary, that, to invent a story quite new, with a catalogue of names never before heard of, would be an attempt of such a nature, as could not be made with tolerable success; for every man must be sensible, that the wonders which epic poetry relates, will shock even the ignorant vulgar, and appear altogether ridiculous, if they are not founded upon something which has already gained a degree of credit. Our first ideas are taken from experience; and, though we may be brought to receive notions, not only very different from those which experience suggests, but even directly contrary to them, yet this is not to be done suddenly and at one attempt: such, therefore, as would have their fictions favorably received, must lay it down as a rule, to accommodate what they feign to established prejudices, and build upon stories which are already in some measure believed. With this precaution, they may go great lengths without appearing absurd, but will soon shock the meanest understandings, if they neglect it. Had there been no fabulous accounts concerning the Trojan expedition current in Greece and Asia, at the time when Homer wrote, the stories which he tells, though the most beautiful that ever were invented, would have appeared to his cotemporaries altogether ridiculous, and never been admired, till antiquity had procured them credit, or a tradition been formed afterwards to vouch for them to the world; for, in matters of an extraordinary kind, not only reason, but even imagination, requires more than a single testimony to ground its assent upon; and therefore, though I should have invented a set of characters entirely new, and framed a story for the subject of my poem no ways connected with any thing that has yet been heard of, and been so happy in this attempt as to produce what might equal, in point of perfection, any of the most beautiful fables of antiquity; it would have wanted, notwithstanding, what is absolutely necessary in order to success, viz. that credit which new invented fictions derive from their connection with such as are already become familiar to men's imaginations.

Tradition is the best ground upon which fable can be built, not only because it gives the appearance of reality to things that are merely fictitious, but likewise because it supplies a poet with the most proper materials for his invention to work upon. There are some fabulous stories that please more universally than others; and of this kind are the wonders which tradition reports; for they are accommodated to the affections and passions of the bulk of mankind, in the same manner as national proverbs are to their understandings. The strict accommodation in both instances proceeds from the same cause, viz. that nothing of either sort is the work of one man, or of one age, but of many. Traditions are not perfected by their first inventors, nor proverbs established upon a single authority. Proverbs derive their credit from the general consent of mankind; and tradition is gradually corrected and improved in the hands of such as transmit it to each other through a succession of ages. In its first periods, it is a narrow thing, but extends itself afterwards, and, with the advantage of time and experiments often repeated, adapts itself so precisely to the affections, passions, and prejudices, natural to the human species, that it becomes at last perfectly agreeable to the sentiments of every heart. No one man, therefore, can pretend to invent fables that will please so universally as those which are formed by the progress of popular tradition. The faculties of any individual must be too narrow for that purpose, and have too much of a peculiar cast to be capable of producing what will be so strictly adapted to the common feelings and sentiments of all. It is this sort of perfection which pleases us in archaiology, or the traditional accounts which we have of the origins of nations; for we are often more agreeably entertained with stories of that kind, though we know them to be absolutely false, than with the justest representations of real events. But as tradition, while it continues in the hands of the people, must be but rude and disagreeable in respect of its form, and have many things low and absurd in it, necessary to be palliated or suppressed, it does not arrive at that perfection of which it is capable, till it comes under the management of the poets, and from them receives its last improvement. By means of this progress, tales that, in the mouths of their first inventors, were the most absurd that can be imagined, the effects of mere superstition, ignorance, and national prejudice, rise up at last to astonish the world, and draw the admiration of all ages, in the form of an Iliad or Odyssey. It is not the business of a poet, then, to make fable, but to form, correct, and improve tradition: and it is to his following this method, that Homer undoubtedly owes his success; for it is obvious to any one who considers his works with attention, that he only collected the various traditions that were current in his days, and reduced them to a system. That infinite variety of independent stories which occur in his works, is a proof of this: these are told with so minute, and often so unnecessary a detail of circumstances, that it is easy to see that he followed accounts already current, and did not invent what he has recorded. I could as easily believe that Prometheus made a man of clay, and put life into him, or assent to any other of the most absurd fictions of antiquity; I could even as soon be persuaded that all that Homer has written is strict matter of fact, as believe that any one mortal man was capable of inventing that infinite variety of historical circumstances which occur in the works of that celebrated poet: for invention is by no means an easy thing; and to contrive a tale that will please universally is certainly one of the most difficult undertakings that can be imagined. Poets, therefore, have found themselves under a necessity of trusting to something more powerful than their own invention in this important article, *viz.* the joint endeavours of many, regulated and directed by the censure of ages.

What has been said, is not only sufficient to justify me in forming my poem upon historical circumstances already known, and introducing characters which the reader is before acquainted with; but shows the necessity likewise of taking many of the historical circumstances from the antient poets. For tradition, the proper foundation of epic poetry, is now to be found only in their writings; and therefore must be used like a common stock, and not considered as the property of individuals.

For the immoderate length of the two episodes, *viz.* those in the fourth and seventh books, all that I can say, is, that they are both brought in for very important purposes, and therefore may be permitted to take up more room than is ordinarily allowed to things of that sort. Besides, the first of them is intended as an experiment in that kind of fiction which distinguishes Homer' sOdyssey, and the other as an attempt to heroic tragedy, after the manner of Sophocles.

The language is simple and artless. This I take to be an advantage, rather than a defect; for it gives an air of antiquity to the work, and makes the style more suitable to the subject.

My learned readers will be surprised to find Agamemnon and Menelaus at the siege of Thebes, when, according to Homer, they were not there: and, at the same time, no notice taken of Sthenelus, the friend and companion of Diomed, whom the same author mentions as present in that expedition.

With respect to the first circumstance; I did not choose, for the sake of a fact of so little consequence, and that too depending only upon poetical authority, to deprive myself of two illustrious names very proper for adorning my catalogue of heroes. And as to the second; it will be easily allowed, that I could not have made Sthenelus appear, without assigning him that place in Diomed's friendship, and consequently in the action of the poem, which Ulysses now possesses; and which is the only part in the whole suited to his peculiar character. I must have put a second-rate hero in the place of a first-rate one; and a name little known in the place of one which every body is acquainted with. Besides, I must have transferred to Sthenelus, the valour, firmness, and address of Ulysses; because the part he was to act would have required these, and must, at the same time, have sunk Ulysses into the character of Sthenelus, for want of a proper opportunity of displaying him in his own. These are inconveniences too great to be incurred for the sake of a scrupulous agreement with Homer in point of fact; and are therefore, in my opinion, better avoided.

I have explained myself upon the foregoing particulars, for the sake of the learned part of my readers only: and shall now drop a hint for such of them as do not fall under that denomination.

The following poem is called the Epigoniad, because the heroes, whose actions it celebrates, have got the name of The Epigoni (or descendants), being the sons of those who attempted the conquest of Thebes in a former expedition.

Thus far I have endeavoured to apologise for the following performance. It may be censured, no doubt, upon many accounts besides those that have been mentioned: but I am persuaded, that what has been said will determine every candid reader, not to be peremptory in condemning what at first view he may dislike; for the specimen of criticism which has been given, will convince him that the real faults of epic poetry are not easily ascertained, and distinguished from those inconveniences that must be allowed to take place, in order to prevent greater faults, and produce, upon the whole, a higher degree of perfection.

# POEMS

OF

## WILLIAM WILKIE.

THE

### EPIGONIAD.

#### BOOK I.

Ye pow'rs of song! with whose immortal fire
Your bard enraptur'd sung Pelides' ire,
To Greece so fatal, when in evil hour,
He brav'd, in stern debate, the sov'reign pow'r,
By like example teach me now to show
From love, no less, what dire disasters flow.
For when the youth of Greece, by Theseus led,
Return'd to conquer where their fathers bled,
And punish guilty Thebes, by Heav'n ordain'd
For perfidy to fall, and oaths profan'd ;
Venus, still partial to the Theban arms,
Tydeus' son seduc'd by female charms ;
Who, from his plighted faith by passion sway'd,
The chiefs, the army, and himself betray'd.
This theme did once your fav'rite bard employ,
Whose verse immortaliz'd the fall of Troy :
But time's oblivious gulf, whose circle draws
All mortal things by fate's eternal laws,
In whose wide vortex worlds themselves are tost,
And rounding swift successively are lost,
This song hath snatch'd. I now resume the strain,
Not from proud hope and emulation vain,
By this attempt to merit equal praise
With worth heroic, born in happier days.
Sooner the weed, that with the Spring appears,
And in the Summer's heat its blossom bears,
But, shriv'ling at the touch of Winter hoar,
Sinks to its native earth, and is no more;
Might match the lofty oak, which long hath stood,
From age to age, the monarch of the wood.
But love excites me, and desire to trace
His glorious steps, tho' with unequal pace.
Before me still I see his awful shade,
With garlands crown'd of leaves which never fade;
He points the path to fame, and bids me scale
Parnassus' slipp'ry height, where thousands fail :
I follow trembling ; for the cliffs are high,
And hov'ring round them watchful harpies fly,
To snatch the poet's wreath with envious claws,
And hiss contempt for merited applause.

But if great Campbell, whose auspicious smile
Bids genius yet revive to bless our isle,
Who, from the toils of state, and public cares,
Oft with the Muses to the shade repairs,
My numbers shall approve, I rise to fame :
For what he praises, envy dares not blame.
    Where high Olympus' hundred heads arise,
Divide the clouds, and mingle with the skies,
The gods assembled met : and view'd from far,
Thebes and the various combats of the war.
From all apart the Paphian goddess sat,
And pity'd in her heart her fav'rite state,
Decreed to perish, by the Argive bands,
Pallas's art, Tydides' mighty hands :
Pensive she sat, and every art explor'd
To charm the victor, and restrain his sword ;
But veil'd her purpose from the piercing ray
Of Pallas, ever jealous of her sway :
Unseen the goddess, from th' Olympian height
To shady Cyprus bent her rapid flight,
Down the steep air, as, from the setting skies,
At ev'n's approach, a streaming meteor flies.
Where lofty shores the tempest's rage restrain,
And sleeps, in peace dissolv'd, the hoary main ;
In love's fam'd isle a deep recess is found,
Which woods embrace, and precipices bound,
To Venus sacred ; there her temple stands,
Where azure billows wash the golden sands,
A hollow cave ; and lifts its rocky head,
With native myrtle crown'd, a lofty shade ;
Whither resort the Naiads of the flood,
Assembl'd with the nymphs from ev'ry wood,
Her heifers there they tend, and fleecy store,
Along the windings of the desert shore.
Thither the goddess, from the Olympian height
Descending swift, precipitates her flight ;
Conspicuous, on the yellow sand, she stood,
Above the margin of the azure flood.
From ev'ry grove and stream the nymphs attend,
And to their queen in cheerful homage bend.
Some hast'ning to the sacred grot repair,
And deck its rocky walls with garlands fair ;
Others produce the gifts which Autumn brings,
And sparkling nectar quench'd with mountain
            springs.

79

And now the queen, impatient to explain
Her secret griefs, address'd her list'ning train:
　" Ye rural goddesses, immortal fair !
Who all my triumphs, all my sorrows share ;
I come, afflicted, from th' ethereal tow'rs,
Where Thebes is doom'd to fall by partial pow'rs.
Nor can entreaty save my fav'rite state,
Avert or change the rigour of her fate ;
Though, breathing incense, there my altar stands,
With daily gifts supply'd from virgin's hands.
Juno now rules the senate of the skies,
And with her dictates ev'ry pow'r complies ;
Her jealous hate the guiltless town condemns
To wasteful havoc, and the rage of flames ;
Since, thither tempted by a stranger's charms,
The mighty thunderer forsook her arms.
Jove's warlike daughter too promotes her aim,
Who for Tydides seeks immortal fame ;
For him employs a mother's watchful cares,
And the first honours of the war prepares:
To frustrate both, a monument would raise
Of lasting triumph and immortal praise ;
To draw the son of Tydeus from the field,
To whose victorious hands the town must yield ;
For, by the all-decreeing will of fate,
He only can o'erthrow the Theban state.
A way which promises success I'll name:
The valiant youth adores a lovely dame,
Alcander's daughter, whom the graces join'd
With gifts adorn above the human kind :
She with her sire forsook th' Hesperian strand,
By hostile arms expell'd their native land :
For Echetus who rules, with tyrant force,
Where Aufidus directs his downward course,
And high Garganus, on th' Apulian plain,
Is mark'd by sailors, from the distant main ;
Oft from her sire had claim'd the lovely maid,
Who, still averse, to grant his suit delay'd :
For, barb'rous in extreme, the tyrant feeds
With mangl'd limbs of men his hungry steeds :
Impatient of his love, by hostile arms
And force declar'd, he claim'd her matchless charms,
Pelignium raz'd, the hero's royal seat,
Who sought in foreign climes a safe retreat :
His flight, Ætolia's friendly shore receives,
Her gen'rous lord protects him and relieves;
Three cities to possess, the chief obtains,
With hills for pasture fit, and fruitful plains.
Cassandra for his bride Tydides claim'd ;
For hymeneal rites the hour was nam'd ;
When, call'd to arms against the Theban tow'rs,
The chief reluctant led his martial pow'rs.
Hence jealousy and fear his breast divide,
Fear for the safety of an absent bride ;
Lest, by his passion rous'd, the tyrant rise,
And unoppos'd usurp the lovely prize.
He knows not, that, in martial arms conceal'd,
With him she braves the terrours of the field ;
True to his side, noon's sultry toil endures,
And the cold damps that chill the midnight hours.
If dreams, or signs, could jealousy impart,
And whets the cares that sting the hero's heart,
Impatient of his pain, he'd soon prepare,
With all its native bonds, to quit the war."
　　The goddess thus : a Paphian nymph reply'd,
And drew the list'ning crow'd on ev'ry side:
Zelotypé, whom fell Alecto bore,
With Cupid mixing on th' infernal shore.

　" Goddess ! these shafts shall compass what
　　　　　you aim,
My mother dipt their points in Stygian flame ;
Where'er my father's darts their way have found,
Mine follow deep, and poison all the wound.
By these, we soon, with triumph, shall behold
Pallas deceiv'd, and Juno's self control'd."
　They all approve ; and, to the rural fane,
Around their sov'reign, moves the joyful train ;
The goddess plac'd, in order each succeeds,
With song and dance the genial feast proceeds ;
While to the sprightly harp, the voice explains
The loves of all the gods in wanton strains:
But when arriv'd the silent hour, which brings
The shades of ev'ning on its dewy wings,
Zelotypé, impatient to pursue
Her journey, hast'ning to her cave, withdrew.
First to her feet the winged shoes she binds,
Which tread the air, and mount the rapid winds;
Aloft they bear her through th' ethereal plain,
Above the solid earth and liquid main :
Her arrows next she takes of pointed steel,
For sight too small, but terrible to feel :
Rous'd by their smart, the savage lion roars,
And mad to combat rush the tusky boars,
Of wounds secure ; for where their venom lights,
What feels their power all other torment slights.
A figur'd zone, mysteriously design'd,
Around her waist her yellow robe confin'd :
There dark Suspicion lurk'd, of sable hue ;
There hasty Rage his deadly dagger drew ;
Pale Envy inly pin'd ; and by her side
Stood Phrenzy, raging with his chains unty'd ;
Affronted Pride with thirst of vengeance burn'd,
And Love's excess to deepest hatred turn'd.
All these the artist's curious hand express'd,
The work divine his matchless skill confess'd.
The virgin last, around her shoulders flung
The bow ; and by her side the quiver hung :
Then, springing up, her airy course she bends
For Thebes; and lightly o'er the tents descends.
The son of Tydeus, 'midst his bands, she found
In arms complete, reposing on the ground ;
And, as he slept, the hero thus address'd,
Her form to fancy's waking eye express'd.
　" Thrice happy youth ! whose glory 'tis to
The Paphian goddess's peculiar care;　　[share
But happy only, as you now improve
The warning sent as earnest of her love.
Her messenger I am : if in your heart
The fair Hesperian virgin claims a part :
If, with regret, you'd see her matchless charms
Destin'd to bless a happier rival'. arms ;
Your coasts defenceless, and unguarded tow'rs
Consum'd and ravag'd by the Latian pow'rs ;
Withdraw your warriors from the Argive host,
And save whate'er you value, ere 'tis lost.
For Echetus, who rules with tyrant force,
Where Aufidus directs his downward course ;
And high Garganus on th' Apulian strand
Marks to the mariner the distant land,
Prepares, by swift invasion, to remove
Your virgin bride, and disappoint your love.
Before, excited by her matchless charms,
He claim'd her from her sire by hostile arms ;
Pelignium raz'd, the hero's royal seat,
When in your land he sought a safe retreat.
Cassandra follow'd with reluctant mind,
To love the tyrant secretly inclin'd ;

Though fierce and barb'rous in extreme, he feeds
With mangl'd limbs of men, his hungry steeds.
And now at anchor on the Latian tide,
With all their train on board, his galleys ride:
Prepar'd when favour'd by the western breeze,
With course direct to cross the narrow seas.
This to your ear the Paphian goddess sends;
The rest upon your timely care depends."
    She said; and turning, fix'd upon the bow
A venom'd shaft, the cause of future woe:
Then, with reverted aim, the subtile dart,
Dismiss'd, and fix'd it in the hero's heart.
Amaz'd he wak'd; and, on his arm reclin'd,
With sighs, thus spoke the anguish of his mind.
    "What dire disasters all my ways beset!
How close around me pitch'd the fatal net!
Here if I stay, nor quit the Argive host,
Etolia's ravag'd, and Cassandra's lost:
For sure the pow'rs immortal ne'er in vain
To mortals thus the secret fates explain.
If I retire, the princes must upbraid
My plighted faith infring'd, the host betray'd;
And, to succeeding times, the voice of fame,
With cowardice and sloth, will blot my name.
Between these sad alternatives I find
No distant hopes to sooth my anxious mind;
Unless I could persuade the Argive pow'rs
To quit at once these long contested tow'rs:
Nor want I reasons specious in debate
To move the boldest warriors to retreat.
Divided thus, the shame would lighter fall;
Reproach is scarce reproach which touches all."
    Thus pond'ring in his mind the hero lay,
Till darkness fled before the morning ray:
Then rose; and, grasping in his mighty hand
The regal staff, the sign of high command,
Pensive and sad forsook his lofty tent,
And sought the son of Dares as he went:
Talthybius he sought, nor sought in vain;
He found the hero 'midst his native train;
And charg'd him to convene, from tent to tent,
The kings to Eteon's lofty monument.
    Obedient to the charge, he took his way,
Where Theseus 'midst the bold Athenians lay,
The king of men; in whose superior hand,
Consenting princes plac'd the chief command.
Adrastus next he call'd, whose hoary hairs
By age were whiten'd and a length of cares;
Who first to Thebes the Argive warriors led:
In vain for Polynices' right they bled,
By fate decreed to fall; he now inspires
The sons to conquer, and avenge their sires.
Ulysses heard, who led his martial train,
In twenty ships, across the sounding main:
The youth, in Ithaca, Zacynthus, bred,
And Cephalenia crown'd with lofty shade.
The Spartan monarch, with his brother, heard
The herald's call; and at the call appear'd:
Yet young in arms, but destin'd to command
All Greece, assembled on the Trojan strand.
The Cretan chief appear'd; and he whose sway
Messenia and the Pylian realms obey.
Oileus next he call'd, whose martial pow'rs
From Bessa move and Scarphe's lofty tow'rs.
Elpenor too, who from the Chalcian strand
And fair Eretria led his martial band,
Appear'd; and all who merited renown
In ten years war before the Trojan town.
Achilles only, yet unfit to wield
The Pelian jav'lin, and the pond'rous shield,

In Phthia staid; to Chiron's care resign'd,
Whose wise instructions form'd his mighty mind.
The chiefs were plac'd. Superior to the rest
The monarch sat, and thus the peers addrest.
    "Princes! let Tydeus' valiant son declare
What cause convenes the senate of the war.
If of himself, or from advice he knows
Some secret mischief plotted by our foes,
Which prudence may prevent, or force resist,
We come prepar'd to counsel and assist:"
The monarch thus. Tydides thus reply'd,
And drew attention deep on ev'ry side.
    "Princes! I have not now the host conven'd,
For secrets by intelligence obtain'd;
But openly my judgment to express
Of mischiefs seen, which prudence must redress:
By war's devouring rage, our martial pow'rs
Grow thin and waste before these hostile tow'rs;
While Thebes, secure, our vain attempts with-
By daily aid sustain'd from distant lands. [stands,
Shall we proceed to urge this dire debate,
And press, with hostile arms, the Theban state?
Or, by experience taught the worst to fear,
Consult the public safety, and for bear?
Had our great sires, by happier counsels sway'd,
As prudence taught, necessity obey'd;
Renounc'd in time this fatal strife, which brings
Alike to nations mischief, and to kings;
Those heroes had not, with their martial train,
Distinguish'd by their fall a foreign plain.
The gods themselves, in vengeance for our crimes,
With such disasters lash the guilty times;
In judgment just, they sow'd the seeds of strife,
To sweep transgressors from the seats of life.
Let him, who obstinately will, proceed,
And wait the vengeance hov'ring o'er his head;
Since Thebes grows stronger; and the Argive pow'rs
Decrease, as famine or the sword devours,
To morrow I withdraw my martial train;
Nor stay to perish, like my sire, in vain."
    Thus as the hero spoke, the kings divide,
And mingled murmurs round th' assembly glide,
Heard like the sound which warn the careful
                                         swain
Of sudden winds or thick-descending rain;
When mountain echoes catch the sullen roar
Of billows bursting on the sandy shore,
And hurl it round in airy circles tost,
Till in the distant clouds the voice is lost.
The king of men to sudden rage resign'd,
At once, the empire of his mighty mind,
With sharp reproaches hast'ning to reply;
But, more sedate, the Pylian monarch nigh,
In act to rise, the angry chief confin'd;
And, whisp'ring, thus address'd with head de-
                                        clin'd:
    "It ill becomes the prince, whose sov'reign hand
Sways the dread sceptre of supreme command,
To be the first in discord; and obey
As headlong passion blindly leads the way.
For when the kings in rash debate engage,
'Tis yours to check and moderate their rage;
Since, of the various ills that can distress
Confed'rate councils, and prevent success,
Discord is chief; where'er the fury sways,
The parts she severs, and the whole betrays."
    The hero thus. The king of men remain'd
By sound advice persuaded, and restrain'd.
Crete's valiant monarch rose; and to the rest,
Thus spoke the dictates of his gen'rous breast.

'Confed'rate kings, when any leader here
The war dissuades, and warns you to forbear,
I might approve; for, safe beyond the sea,
Creon and Thebes can never injure me.
And when the barb'rous tyrant, unwithstood,
His hot revenge shall quench in Grecian blood;
When Thrace and Macedon, by his command,
Shall ravage Argos and the Pylian strand;
Secure and guarded by the ocean's stream,
Crete's hundred towns shall know it but by fame.
Yet would not I, though many such were found,
For open war, advise a peace unsound.
Let Macedon to Thebes her succours send,
And Thrace, with all her barb'rous tribes, descend;
By foreign aids the more our foes increase,
The greater glory waits us from success.
You all remember, on the Isthmean strand,
Where neighb'ring seas besiege the straiten'd
    land,
When Greece enleagu'd a full assembly held,
By public justice to the war compell'd;
That blood of slaughter'd victims drench'd the
    ground,
While oaths divine the willing nations bound,
Ne'er to return, till our victorious pow'rs
Had level'd with the dust the Theban tow'rs.
Jove heard, and bid applauding thunders roll,
Loud on the right; they shook the starry pole:
For Jove himself is witness of our vows,
And him, who violates, his wrath pursues.
Our joyful shouts the earth, the ocean heard;
We claim'd the omen, and the God rever'd:
In confidence of full success we came,
To conquer Thebes, and win immortal fame.
But if the gods and fate our fears distrust,
To public justice and ourselves unjust;
Dishonour'd to our native seats we go,
And yield a lasting triumph to the foe.    [ghost
Should now, from hence arriv'd, some warrior's
Greet valiant Tydeus on the Stygian coast,
And tell, when danger or distress is near,
That Diomed persuades the rest to fear;
He'd shun the synod of the mighty dead,
And hide his anguish in the deepest shade:
Nature in all an equal course maintains;
The lion's whelp succeeds to awe the plains;
Pards gender pards; from tigers tigers spring;
No doves are hatch'd beneath a vulture's wing:
Each parent's image in his offspring lives;
But nought of Tydeus in his son survives."
  He said; and by his sharp reproaches stung,
And wav'ring in suspence the hero hung,
In words now prone to vent his kindl'd ire,
Or fix'd in sullen silence to retire.
As when a current, from the ocean wide,
Rolls, through the Cyclades, its angry tide;
Now here, now there, in circling eddies tost,
The certain tenour of its course is lost,
Each wary pilot for his safety fears
In mute suspense, and trembles as he steers:
Such seem'd the tumult of the hero's breast,
And such amazement long restrain'd the rest.
Laertes' son at last the silence broke,
And, rising, thus with prudent purpose spoke:
  "Princes! I counsel war; but will not blame
The chief dissenting, whose illustrious name
We all must honour: yet, with patience, hear
What now I offer to the public ear:

I freely own th' unnumber'd ills that wait
On strife prolong'd, and war's disastrous state.
With war lean famine and diseases dwell,
And Discord fierce, escap'd the bounds of Hell,
Where'er on Earth her course the fury bends,
A crowd of mischiefs still her steps attends;
Fear flies before her swifter than the wind,
And desolation marks her path behind.
Yet her, attended thus, the Gods ordain
Stern arbitress of right to mortal men;
To awe injustice with her lifted spear,
And teach the tyrants of the Earth to fear.
If Thebes is perjur'd, and exerts her might
For usurpation in contempt of right;
(If oaths despis'd, and all the ties which bind
The great society of human kind;)
For Eteocles in the war she stood,
And drench'd her thirsty fields with Grecian
    blood;        [vain
The gods themselves have err'd, and plac'd in
The scepter'd kings injustice to restrain;
Else she deserves the last extremes to feel
Of wasteful fire and keen devouring steel.
Though prudence urg'd and equity approv'd,
Joining to second what Tydides mov'd,
We could not hope the war for peace to change,
Thebes thinks not now of safety, but revenge.
Last night, disguis'd, I mingled with the foe,
Their secret hopes and purposes to know;
And found that Creon, with his martial train,
This day intends to brave us on the plain.
Greece too, I heard, by barb'rous sovereigns
    claim'd,
Some Athens, Argos, some Mycæne nam'd;
Sparta and Pylos, with the various towns
Which grace, in prospect fair, th' Arcadian
    downs:
Others Etolia challeng'd for their lot;
Nor was even Ithaca itself forgot.
From such vain hopes to boasting they proceed;
Each promises to win some hero's head.
Leophron too, distinguished from the rest,
Superior pride and insolence express'd;
In form a god he 'midst th' assembly stood,
By all ador'd, the idol of the crowd;
And promis'd, if he chanc'd in fight to meet
Th' Etolian chief, to stretch him at his feet;
Unless some god oppos'd, or dastard fear
By sudden flight, should snatch him from his
    spear.
Can we then hope by peace to end our toils,
When foes secure already share our spoils;
Peace to expect from flight itself were vain;
And flight, I know, your gen'rous souls disdain."
  He said. The chiefs with indignation burn'd;
And Diomed submitting thus return'd:
  " Princes! I need not for myself profess,
What all have witness'd, all must sure confess;
That in the front of battle still engag'd,
I never shunn'd to mingle where it rag'd.
Nor now does fear persuade me to retire,
False Creon safe, and guilty Thebes entire;
But war and famine thin our martial pow'rs,
Whilst adverse fates protect the Theban tow'rs.
And as the careful shepherd turns his flock
Back from the dangers of the slipp'ry rock,
And from the haunts where foxes mark **the**
    ground,
Or rapid rivers flow with banks unsound;

So kings should warn the people to forbear
Attempts, when symptoms mark destruction near.
But since the leaders, with consenting voice,
For war already fix the public choice;
I freely yield, nor ever will divide,
Where all deliberate, and all decide."
   The hero thus, and ceas'd. And thus the rest,
From his high seat, the king of men address'd:
" Since war is now decreed, 'tis next our care
That all should speedily for fight prepare;
Creon, this day, intends with all his train
To try our valour on the equal plain;
And will, with diligence, improve an hour,
Which finds us inattentive and secure.
First let each leader with his bands in haste
Snatch, as the time allows, a short repast;
Then arm for fight, and to the field proceed,
The phalanx following as the chariots lead.
Who arms the first, and first to combat goes,
Though weaker, seems superior to his foes;
But such as lag are more than half o'erthrown,
Less in the eyes of others and their own."
   The monarch thus. The princes all assent.
Straight from the council through the host they
      went,
To arm their bands with diligence and care;
They all obey, and all for fight prepare.

---

THE

## EPIGONIAD.

### BOOK II.

Assembl'd on the plain, the Theban pow'rs
In order'd ranks appear before the tow'rs;
Creon their leader, whose superior sway,
The martial sons of sacred Thebes obey.
The chiefs obedient to his high command,
Rul'd the whole war, and marshall'd every band.
His valiant son the first, his country's boast,
Her noblest hope, the bulwark of her host,
Leophron, to the field the warriors led,
Whom Thebes herself within her ramparts bred:
Peneleus, who from Medeon led his pow'rs,
Œchalia low, and Arne's lofty tow'rs:
Leitus from Thespia, where the verdant shades
Of Helicon invite the tuneful maids:
Porthenor rich, whose wide possessions lay
Where fam'd Æsopus winds his wat'ry way;
Beneath Cytheron's height, the lofty mound
Which parts Bœotian plains from hostile ground:
Phericles, who the valiant warriors led
In Mycallessus, Harma, Aulis, bred:
Andremon, leader of his native band,
From lofty Schœnus on th' Ismenian strand:
And Anthedon, where swift Euripus pent
Divides Eubœa from the continent:
These rul'd the Theban pow'rs beneath the care
Of Creon, chief and sov'reign of the war.
   The aids from Macedon the next were plac'd;
Their shining casques with waving plumage
      grac'd;
A wolf's grey hide, around their shoulders flung,
With martial grace above their armour hung:
From high Dodona's sacred shades they came;
Cassander led them to the fields of fame.

The Thracians next, a formidable band;
Nations and tribes distinct, in order stand :
Byzantines fierce, whose crooked keels divide
The Pontic gulf, and stem the downward tide:
In Grecian arms the hardy warriors move,
With pond'rous shields and glitt'ring spears
      above.
The Thynians next were marshall'd on the field;
Each with a falchion arm'd and lunar shield,
Whose bending horns a verge of silver bound;
And figures fierce their brazen helmets crown'd:
With these the Daci came, a martial race;
Fierce as their clime, they rear the pond'rous
      mace;
In giant strength secure, they scorn the spear,
And crush, with weighty blows, the ranks of war :
From Ister's icy streams, a barb'rous crowd,
In shaggy furs, a herd promiscuous stood;
Swift as their savage game; for wide they roam
In tribes and nations, ignorant of home;
Excelling all who boast superior skill
To send the winged arrow swift to kill :
These Rhœsus rul'd, of various tribes compos'd,
By various leaders on the field dispos'd.
   To fight the Argives mov'd in close array;
Bright shone their arms and flash'd redoubl'd
      day;
Resolv'd, and still as silent night, they go;
Nor with insulting shouts provoke the foe.
Thick from their steps, in dusky volumes, rise
The parched fields, and darken all the skies.
Beneath the shade, the ardent warriors close;
Their shields and helmets ring with sounding
      blows.
   First Menelaus struck a Theban lord;
His armed breast the weighty lance explor'd;
Burst the close mail; the shining breast-plate
      tore;
And from life's fountain drew a stream of gore.
Supine he fell amidst his native bands,
And wrench'd the fixed dart with dying hands.
To spoil the slain the son of Atreus flies;
The Thebans interpose with hostile cries;
And Creon's valiant son his buckler spread,
An orb of triple brass, to guard the dead :
As Jove's imperial bird her wings extends,
And from the shepherd's rage her young defends;
So stern Leophron bore his ample shield;
Like Mars he stood, the terrour of the field.
With dread unusual check'd, the Spartan band
Recoil'd; Atrides only dar'd to stand.
He thus began: " Presumptuous youth ! forbear
To tempt the fury of my flying spear.
That warrior there was by my javelin slain,
His spoils to guard you interpose in vain."
Atrides thus; and Creon's son replies:
" Thy lance I dread not, and thy threats despise.
This hand hath many a chief of high renown,
And braver warriors oft in fight o'erthrown:
Like theirs, thy fall shall dignify my spear,
And future boasters thence be taught to fear."
Thus as he spoke his weighty lance he threw
At Atrens' son ; which rising as it flew
Upon the hero's crest with furious sway,
Glanc'd as it pass'd and shav'd the plumes away.
Hissing amidst the Spartan ranks it came,
And struck a youth of undistinguish'd name:
Cold, through his breast, the steel and polish'd
      wood
A passage forc'd, and drew a stream of blood.

His lance Atrides next prepares to throw;
Poises it long, and meditates the blow:
Then, from his hand dismissed with happier aim,
Thund'ring against the Theban shield it came;
Where wreath'd around a mimic serpent twin'd,
With plates of polish'd silver lightly join'd:
Thence turn'd with course oblique it drove along,
And spent its fury on the vulgar throng.    .
Leophron straight his flaming falchion drew,
And at his foe, with eager fury, flew:
As stooping from above, an eagle springs
To snatch his prey, and shoots upon his wings.
The Spartan warrior dreads impending fate;
And, turning, meditates a quick retreat.
As when a shepherd swain, in desert shades,
The blood-nurs'd offspring of the wolf invades;
If, from the opening of some thicket near,
With rage inflam'd, the angry dam appear,
With darts at first, and threat'ning shouts he
    tries,
To awe the guardian, and assert the prize:
But, when she springs, the close encounter dreads,
And, trembling, from the angry foe recedes.
So Menelaus fled.  His native train,
In wild disorder, scatters o'er the plain.

His valiant brother heard upon the right,
Where in his lofty car he rul'd the fight;
And to his squire Nichomachus: " With speed,
Turn to the left, and urge the flying steed:
For, if these sounds deceive not, Sparta fails;
And, with a tide of conquest, Thebes prevails."
Quick as the word, the silver reins he drew,
And through the fight the bounding chariot flew.
Like some quick vessel, when a prosp'rous gale
Favours her course, and stretches ev'ry sail;
Above the parting waves she lightly flies,
And smooth behind a tract of ocean lies:
So, 'midst the combat, rush'd the lofty car;
Pierc'd the thick tumult, and disjoin'd the war.
But Clytodemon's son a jav'lin threw;
With force impell'd, it lighten'd as it flew,
And struck the right-hand courser to the ground,
Ethon, for swiftness in the race renown'd.
Behind his ear the deadly weapon stood,
Loos'd his high neck, and drew a stream of blood.
Groaning he sunk; and spread his flowing mane,
A shining circle, on the dusty plain.
Intangled deep the royal chariot stood,
With hostile spears beset, an iron wood.

From his high seat the Spartan hero sprung
Amid the foe; his clanging armour rung.
Before the king, the armed bands retire;
As shepherd swains avoid a lion's ire,
When fierce from famine on their darts he turns,
And rage indignant in his eye-balls burns.
Amid the fight, distinguish'd like the star
Of ev'ning, shone his silver arms afar;
Which, o'er the hills it setting light displays;
And marks the ruddy west with silver rays.
Pale and amaz'd his brother chief he found,
An armed circle of his friends around.
"Alas, my brother! have I liv'd to see
Thy life redeem'd with deathless infamy!"
(The hero cry'd) " far better that a ghost
You now had wander'd on the Stygian coast,
And by a glorious fall preserv'd your name
Safe and unblasted by the breath of fame;
Which soon shall tell the world, amaz'd to hear,
That Menelaus taught the host to fear."

By conscious guilt subdu'd the youth ap-
    pear'd;
Without reply, the just reproach he heard:
Confounded, to the ground he turn'd his eyes;
Indignant thus the great Atrides cries:
" Mycæneans! Spartans! taught to seek renown
From dangers greatly brav'd and battles won;
Ah warriors! will ye fly, when close behind
Dishonour follows swifter than the wind!
Return to glory: whether Jove ordains,
With wreaths of conquest, to reward your pains,
Or dooms your fall; he merits equal prize,
With him who conquers, he who bravely dies."
The hero thus; and, like swift light'ning driv'n
Through scatter'd clouds along the vault of Heav'n
By Jove's dread arm, his martial voice inspir'd
The fainting host, and ev'ry bosom fir'd.
Again upon the conquering foe they turn'd:
The war again, in all its fury, burn'd.
As when the deep, which, ebbing from the land,
Along the coast displays a waste of sand,
Returns; and, blown by angry tempests, roars
A stormy deluge 'gainst the rocky shores:
So, rushing to the fight, the warriors came;
Ardent to conquer, and retrieve their fame.
Before his host the son of Creon stood,
With labour'd dust obscure, and hostile blood;
He thus exclaim'd: " And shall this dastard
    train
(Warriors of Thebes!) dispute the field again?
Their better chief, I know him, leads the band;
But fate shall soon subdue him by my hand."
He said; and, at the king, his jav'lin threw;
Which, aim'd amiss, with erring fury flew.
Across the armed ranks it swiftly drove,
The warriors stooping as it rush'd above.
The Spartan hero aim'd his weighty spear;
And thus to Jove address'd an ardent prayer.
" Hear me, great sire of gods! whose boundless
    sway
The fates of men and mortal things obey;
Whose sov'reign hand, with unresisted might,
Depresses or exalts the scales of fight:
Now grant success to my avenging hand,
And stretch this dire destroyer on the sand.
Jove, grant me now to reach his hated life,
And save my warriors in this doubtful strife."
The hero thus; and sent his weighty spear;
With speed it flew, and pierc'd the yielding air;
Swift, as a falcon to her quarry springs,
When down the winds she stretches on her wings.
Leophron, stooping, shun'd the deadly stroke,
Which on the shield of Hegisander broke.
Vain now his lute; in vain his melting strains,
Soft as Apollo's on the Lycian plains:
His soul excluded, seeks the dark abodes
By Styx embrac'd, the terrour of the gods;
Where surly Charon, with his lifted oar,
Drives the light ghosts, and rules the dreary
    shore.
With grief Leophron saw the warrior slain.
He snatch'd a pond'rous mace from off the
    plain,
Cut in the Thracian woods, with snags around
Of pointed steel with iron circles bound.
Heav'd with gigantic force the club to throw,
He swung it thrice, and hurl'd it at his foe.
Thund'ring upon his armed head it fell;
The brazen helmet rung with stunning knell.

As when a rock by forceful engines thrown,
Where hostile arms invest a frontier town,
Threat'ning destruction, rolls along the skies ;
And war itself stands wond'ring as it flies :
Falls on some turret's top, the structure bends
Beneath the tempest, and at once descends
With hideous crash; thus, stooping to the ground,
Atrides sunk; his silver arms resound.
But Pallas, mixing in the dire debate,
A life to rescue yet not due to fate,
Had o'er his head her cloudy buckler held ;
And half the fury of the blow repell'd.
The son of Creon rush'd to seize his prize,
The hero's spoils ; and thus exulting cries :
" Warriors of Thebes ! your labours soon shall
      cease,
And final victory restore your peace ;
For great Atrides, by my valour slain,
A lifeless corse, lies stretch'd upon the plain.
Only be men ! and make the Argive bands
Dread in succeeding times your mighty hands ;
That foes no more, when mad ambition calls,
With dire alarms may shake your peaceful walls."
Exulting thus, the hero rush'd along;
And kindled with his shouts, the vulgar throng.
Resolv'd and firm the Spartan warriors stand
Around their king, a formidable band.
Their spears, protended thick, the foe restrain'd ;
Their bucklers join'd, the weighty war sustain'd.
But as a mountain wolf, from famine bold,
On prey intent, surveys the midnight fold ;
Where, in the shelter of some arching rock,
At ev'n the careful shepherd pens his flock ;
On spoil and ravage bent, he stalks around,
And meditates to spring the lofty mound :
Impatient thus the Theban chief survey'd
The close-compacted ranks on ev'ry side;
To find where least the serred orb could bear
The strong impression of a pointed war.
Him Menelaus saw, with anguish stung ;
And, from amidst his armed warriors, sprung
With wrath inflam'd ; as starting from a brake,
Against some trav'ller, darts some crested snake.
His rage in vain the Theban ranks withstand ;
The bravest warriors sink beneath his hand.
Clytander, Iphitus, Palemon, fam'd
For chariots rul'd and fiery coursers tam'd ;
And Iphialtes, like the god of light,
Whose pointed arrows thinn'd the lines of fight :
These the first transports of his fury feel.
Against Leophron now he lifts his steel,
And speeds to vengeance ; but, in full career,
He stood arrested by a vulgar spear.
Fix'd in his thigh the barbed weapon hung,
Relax'd the muscles, and the nerves unstrung.
The Spartan warriors to his succour flew;
Against the darts their ample shields they
      threw,            [war,
Which storm'd around ; and, from the rage of
Convey'd the wounded hero to his car.
    With fierce impatience Creon's son beheld
The Spartan warriors still dispute the field.
Before their leader fall'n the heroes stood ;
Their spears erected, like the sacred wood
Which round some altar rises on the plain,
The mystic rites to hide from eyes profane.
Thither his native bands the hero turn'd ;
Drawn to a wedge, again the combat burn'd.

Through all the air a storm of jav'lins sung ;
With sounding blows each hollow buckler rung.
First Enopæus felt a deadly wound,
Who in Amycle till'd the fruitful ground ;
To great Andremon's spear he yields his breath,
And starts and quivers in the grasp of death.
Next Hegesippus press'd th' ensanguin'd plain ;
Leophron's jav'lin mix'd him with the slain.
On Malea's cliffs he fed his fleecy store,
Along the windings of the craggy shore.
He vow'd to Phœbus, for a safe return,
An hundred victims on his hearth to burn.
In vain ! the god, in justice, had decreed,
His gifts contemn'd, the offerer to bleed :
For violence augmented still his store ;
And, unreliev'd, the stranger left his door.
Prone on the bloody ground the warrior fell,
His soul indignant sought the shades of Hell.
Next Arcas, Cleon, valiant, Chromius dy'd ;
With Dares, to the Spartan chiefs ally'd.
And Phœmius, whom the gods in early youth
Had form'd for virtue and the love of truth ;
His gen'rous soul to noble deeds they turn'd,
And love to mankind in his bosom burn'd :
Cold thro' his throat the hissing weapon glides,
And on his neck the waving locks divides.
His fate the Graces mourn'd.   The gods above,
Who sit around the starry throne of Jove,
On high Olympus bending from the skies,
His fate beheld with sorrow-streaming eyes.
Pallas alone, unalter'd and serene,
With secret triumph saw the mournful scene :
Not hard of heart : for none of all the pow'rs,
In earth ôr ocean, or th' Olympian tow'rs,
Holds equal sympathy with human grief,
Or with a freer hand bestows relief :
But conscious that a mind by virtue steel'd
To no impression of distress will yield ;
That, still unconquer'd, in its awful hour
O'er death it triumphs with immortal pow'r.
    Now Thebes prevailing, Sparta's host retreats ;
As falls some rampart where the ocean beats :
Unable to resist its stormy way,            [way ;
Mounds heap'd on mounds, and bars of rock give
With inundation wide the deluge reigns, [plains.
Drowns the deep valleys, and o'erspreads the
Thus o'er the field, by great Leophron led,
Their foes repuls'd, the Theban squadrons spread.
The hero, stooping where Atrides lay,
Rent from his head the golden casque away;
His mail unlock'd ; and loos'd the golden chains,
The zone which by his side the sword sustains.
The monarch now amid the vulgar dead,
For wheels to crush and armed hoofs to tread,
Defenceless lay.   But stern Leophron's hate
Retriev'd him, thus expos'd, from certain fate.
In semblance dead, he purpos'd to convey
The body naked to some public way ;
Where dogs obscene, and all the rav'nous race,
With wounds unsightly, might his limbs disgrace.
Straight he commands ; and to a neighb'ring
      grove,
His warriors charg'd, the Spartan chief remove,
On their broad shields they bore him from the
      plain,
To sense a corse, and number'd with the slain.
His fixed eyes in hov'ring shades were drown'd ;
His mighty limbs in death-like fetters bound.

The shouts tumultuous and the din of war,
His ear receiv'd like murmurs heard afar ;
Or as some peasanc hears, securely laid
Beneath a vaulted cliff or woodland shade,
When o'er his head unnumber'd insects sing
In airy rounds, the children of the Spring.
Adrastus' valiant son, with grief, beheld
The Spartans to inglorious flight compell'd ;
Their valiant chief resign'd to hostile hands,
He thus aloud address'd the scatt'ring bands :
" What shame, ye warriors ! if ye thus expose
Your leader to the injuries of foes !
Though all should quit him, honour bids you bring
His reliques back, or perish with your king.
Leophron sure injuriously ordains,
With insults, to deface his dear remains ;
Spurn'd by the feet of men, expos'd and bare,
For dogs obscene and rav'nous birds to share."
Exclaiming thus, through all the field he flew ;
And call'd the host the conflict to renew.
They stop, they charge ; again the combat burns :
They bleed, they conquer, and retreat by turns.
Hegialus excites the dire debate ;
And, by example, leads the work of fate :
For now he sees Atrides borne afar,
By hostile hands, beyond the lines of war.
With indignation fierce his bosom glows ;
He rushes fearless 'midst a host of foes ;
And now had merited a deathless name,
And with a deed immortal crown'd his fame,
Atrides sav'd ; but fate's supreme command
That honour destin'd for a mightier hand.
Leophron vex'd, that twice constrain'd to yield,
The Spartan warriors re-assum'd the field,
His pow'rs address'd : " For ever lost our fame,
Dishonour foul will blot the Theban name ;
If dastard foes, twice routed and pursu'd,
Shall brave the victors still with rage renew'd.
Your glory gain'd with vigour now maintain ;
Nor let us conquer thus and bleed in vain."
He said, and 'gainst the Argive hero turn'd ;
With martial wrath his ardent bosom burn'd ;
Who, fearless and undaunted, dar'd to wait ;
Nor by ignoble flight declin'd his fate.
For, at the Theban chief, his lance he threw,
Which, aim'd amiss, with erring fury flew :
Beyond the hostile ranks the weapon drove ;
The warriors stooping as it rush'd above.
Not so the Theban spear ; with happier aim,
Full to the centre of the shield it came ;
And rising swiftly from the polish'd round,
His throat transfix'd, and bent him to the ground.
To spoil the slain the ardent victor flew ;
The Spartan bands the bloody shock renew ;
Fierce to the charge with tenfold rage return,
And all at once with thirst of vengeance burn.
O'er all the field the raging tumult grows ;
And ev'ry helmet rings with sounding blows :
But most around the Argive hero dead ;
There toil the mightiest, there the bravest bleed.
As when outrageous winds the ocean sweep,
And from the bottom stir the hoary deep ;
O'er all the wat'ry plain the tempest raves,
Mixing in conflict loud the angry waves :
But where some pointed cliff the surface hides,
Whose top unseen provokes the angry tides,
With ten fold fury there the billows fly,
And mount in smoke and thunder to the sky.

Adrastus, by unactive age restrain'd,
Behind the army on a mount remain'd ;
Under an oak the hoary warrior sat,
And look'd and listen'd to the dire debate.
Now, tam'd by age, his coursers stood unbound ;
His useless arms lay scatter'd on the ground ;
Two aged heralds there the chief obey'd ;
The squire attending by his master stay'd. [ear?
And thus the king : " What sounds invade mine
My friends ! what sad disaster must we hear ?
Some hero's fall ; for with the shouts, I know
Loud lamentation mixt, and sounds of woe.
So were we told, when mighty Tydeus fell,
And Polynices trod the path to Hell ;
So rag'd the combat o'er the heroes slain,
And such the din and tumult of the plain."
He said ; and list'ning (what he greatly fear'd)
Hegialus's name at last he heard
Mix'd with the noise ; and, sick'ning at the
                        sound,
By grief subdu'd, fell prostrate on the ground.
But rage astonish'd and despair, he rose
Eager to rush amid the thickest foes.
His spear he grasp'd, impatient for the fight ;
And pond'rous shield, unequal to the weight.
Him frantic thus his wise attendants held ;
And to retire with prudent care compell'd.
Impatient of his state, by quick returns,
With grief he melts, with indignation burns.
And thus at last : " Stern ruler of the sky !
Whose sport is man, and human misery ;
What deed of mine has stirr'd thy boundless rage,
And call'd for vengeance on my helpless age ?
Have I, by sacrilege, your treasures drain'd ?
Your altars slighted, or your rites profan'd ?
Did I forget my holy vows to pay ?
Or bid you witness, and my faith betray ?
Has lawless rapine e'er increas'd my store,
Or unreliev'd the stranger left my door ?
If not ; in justice, can your stern decree
With wrath pursue my guiltless race and me ?
Here valiant Tydeus, Polynices fell ;
In one sad hour they trod the path to Hell :
For them my daughters mourn, their sorrows
                        flow
Still fresh, and all their days are spent in woe.
Hegialus remain'd my hopes to raise ;
The only comfort of my joyless days :
In whom I saw my vigorous youth return,
And all our native virtues brighter burn.
He's now no more ; and to the nether skies,
Banish'd by fate, a bloodless spectre flies.
For what, ye gods ! has unrelenting fate
Curs'd my misfortunes with so long a date,
That thus I live to see our antient race
At once extinguish'd, and for ever cease ?
Gods ! grant me now the only boon I crave,
For all my sorrows past, a peaceful grave :
Now let me perish, that my fleeting ghost
May reach my son in Pluto's shady coast ;
Where, join'd for ever, kindred souls enjoy
An union fix'd, which nothing can destroy."
He said, and sinking prostrate on the ground,
His furrow'd cheeks with floods of sorrow drown'd ;
And, furious in the rage of grief, o'erspread
With dust the reverend honors of his head.

THE
EPIGONIAD.
BOOK III.

THE Spartan bands, with thirst of vengeance
[spir'd. fir'd,
The fight maintain'd; nor from their toils re-
Before the hero fall'n the warriors stand,
Firm as the chains of rock which guard the strand;
Whose rooted strength the angry ocean braves,
And bounds the fury of his bursting waves.
So Sparta stood; their serred bucklers bar
The Theban phalanx, and exclude the war.
While from the field, upon their shoulders laid,
His warriors sad the Argive prince convey'd;
Leophron saw, with indignation fir'd,
And, with his shouts, the ling'ring war inspir'd,
Again the rigour of the shock returns;
The slaughter rages, and the combat burns;
Till, push'd and yielding to superior sway,
In slow retreat the Spartan ranks gave way.
As, in some channel pent, entangled wood
Reluctant stirs before the angry flood;
Which, on its loaded current, slowly heaves
The spoils of forests mix'd with harvest sheaves.
    Pallas observ'd, and from the Olympian height
Precipitated swift her downward flight.
Like Cleon's valiant son, the goddess came;
The same her stature, and her arms the same.
Descending from his chariot to the ground,
The son of Tydeus, 'midst his bands, she found;
His steeds unrul'd: for stretch'd before the
    wheel,
Lay the bold driver pierc'd with Theban steel.
On the high car her mighty hand she laid;
And thus address'd the valiant Diomed: [fight,
"The Spartan warriors, prince! renounce the
O'ermatch'd by numbers and superior might:
While adverse fate their valiant chief restrains,
Who dead or wounded with the foe remains;
Hegialus lies lifeless on the earth,
Brother to her from whom you claim your birth:
The great Atrides, as he press'd to save,
Leophron's jav'lin mark'd him for the grave.
To vengeance haste; and, ere it is too late,
With speedy succour stop impending fate:
For stern Leophron, like the rage of flame,
With ruin threatens all the Spartan name."
    The goddess thus: Tydides thus replies:
" How partial are the counsels of the skies!
For vulgar mer't oft the gods with care
Honour and peace and happiness prepare;
While worth, distinguish'd, by their partial hate,
Submits to all the injuries of fate.
Adrastus thus, with justice, may complain
His daughters widow'd, sons in battle slain.
In the devoted line myself I stand;
And here must perish by some hostile hand:
Yet not, for this, I shun the works of war,
Nor sculk inglorious when I ought to dare.
And now I'll meet yon terrour of the plain;
To crown his conquests, or avenge the slain.
But wish some valiant youth, to rule my car
And push the horses through the shock of war,
Were present; for, extended in his gore,
The brave Speusippus knows his charge no more."
    Thus as the hero spoke, Cassandra heard,
And present, to assume the charge, appear'd.

By love inspir'd, she sought the fields of war;
Her hero's safety was her only care.
A polish'd casque her lovely temples bound,
With flow'rs of gold and various plumage crown'd;
Confus'dly gay, the peacock's changeful train,
With gaudy colours mix'd of ev'ry grain;
The virgin white, the yellow's golden hue,
The regal purple, and the shining blue,
With female skill compos'd. The shield she bore
With flow'rs of gold was mark'd and spangled
    o'er:
Light and of slend'rest make, she held a lance:
Like some mock warrior armed for the dance,
When spring's return and music's cheerful strain
The youth invite to frolic on the plain.
    " Illustrious chief," the armed virgin said,
" To rule your steeds on me the task be laid;
Skill'd to direct their course with steady rein,
To wake their fiery mettle, or restrain;
To stop, to turn, the various arts I know;
To push them on direct, or shun the foe.
With ready hand your voice I shall obey;
And urge their fury where you point the way."
The virgin thus: and thus Tydides said:
" Your zeal I honour, but reject your aid.
Fierce are my steeds; their fury to restrain
The strongest hand requires and stiffest rein:
For oft, their mettle rous'd, they rush along;
Nor feel the biting curb, or sounding thong.
Oft have I seen you brave the toils of fight,
With dauntless courage but unequal might.
Small is your force; and, from your arm un-
    strung,
The harmless lance is impotently flung.
Yet not for this you shun the martial strife,
Patient of wounds and prodigal of life.
Where'er I combat, faithful to my side,
No danger awes you, and no toils divide.
Yet grudge not that your service I decline;
Homocleon's better hand shall guide the rein:
His manly voice my horses will obey,
And move submissive to his firmer sway."
Th' Etolian warrior thus; and, with a bound,
Rose to his lofty chariot from the ground.
The goddess to the driver's seat proceeds;
Assumes the reins, and winds the willing steeds.
On their smooth sides the sounding lash she plies;
And through the fight the smoking chariot flies.
Th' Athenians soon they pass'd; and Phocians
    strong,
Who from fair Crissa led their martial throng.
Th' Arcadians next from Alpheus' silver flood,
And hardy Eleans, grim with dust and blood,
In order rang'd. As when some pilot spies
The rocky cliffs in long succession rise,
When near the land his galley scours the shores,
By prosp'rous winds impell'd and speeding oars:
So, hastening to the fight, the hero flew.
And now the Spartan host appears in view:
By wounds subdu'd, their bravest warriors lay;
Others, by shameful flight, their fear obey;
The rest, in slow retreat, forsake the field,
O'ermatch'd by numbers, and constrain'd to yield.
Th' Etolian hero saw, and rais'd his voice,
Loud as the silver trumpet's martial noise;
And rush'd to fight: through all the field it flew;
The host at once the happy signal knew;
And joy'd, as they who, from the found'ring ship
Escap'd, had struggled long amid the deep:

Faint from despair, when hope and vigour fail,
If, hast'ning to their aid, appears a sail;
With force renew'd their weary limbs they strain,
And climb the slipp'ry ridges of the main.
So joy'd the Spartans to repulse the foe;
With hope restor'd, their gen'rous bosoms glow:
While Thebes, suspended 'midst her conquest,
 stands;
And feels a sudden check through all her bands.
   Leophron only, far before the rest,
Tydides waited with a dauntless breast.
Firm and unaw'd the hardy warrior stood;
Like some fierce boar amid his native wood,
When armed swains his gloomy haunts invade,
And trace his footsteps through the lonely shade;
Resolv'd he hears approach the hostile sound,
Grinds his white teeth, and threat'ning glares
 around:
So stood Leophron trusting in his might,
And shook his armour, eager for the fight.
Tydides saw; and, springing from his car,
Thus brav'd the hero, as he rush'd to war:
" O son unhappy, of a sire accurst!
The p'ague of all, and fated to the worst!
The injuries of Greece demand thy breath;
See, in my hand, the instrument of death.
Hegialus's ghost shall less deplore
His fate untimely on the Stygian shore,
When banish'd from the light, your shade shall
To mingle with the dark infernal gloom." [come
Tydides thus: and Creon's son replies:
" Your fear in vain, by boasting, you disguise;
Such vulgar art a novice yet confounds,
To scenes of battle new and martial sounds;
Though lost on me, who dwell amid alarms,
And never met a greater yet in arms."
   Thus as the warrior spoke, his lance with care
He aim'd, and sent it hissing through the air.
On Diomed's broad shield the weapon fell;
Loud rung the echoing brass with stunning knell:
But the strong orb, by Vulcan's labour bound,
Repell'd, and sent it blunted to the ground.
Tydides next his pond'rous jav'lin threw:
With force impell'd, it brighten'd as it flew;
And pierc'd the border of the Theban shield,
Where, wreath'd around, a serpent guards the
 field;
Through the close mail an easy passage found,
And mark'd his thigh, in passing, with a wound.
Now in close fight the angry chiefs engage;
Like two fell griffins rous'd to equal rage;
Pois'd on their rolling trains they fiercely rise,
With blood-bespotted crests and burning eyes;
With poison fraught they aim their deadly stings,
Clasp their sharp fangs, and mix their rattling
 'wings.
In combat thus, the ardent warriors clos'd,
With shield to shield, and foot to foot oppos'd.
First at his foe Leophron aim'd a stroke;
But, on his polish'd casque, the falchion broke:
From the smooth steel the shiver'd weapon
 sprung;
Aloft in air its hissing splinters sung.
Not so, Tydides, did thy weapon fail;
With force impell'd it pierc'd the silver mail,
Whose sliding plates the warrior's neck surround:
A tide of gore came rushing from the wound.
Stagg'ring to earth he sunk with head declin'd;
And life in long convulsive throbs resign'd.

Nor stopp'd Tydides to despoil the slain;
The warrior goddess led him cross the plain,
Towards the grove where great Atrides lay;
Th' immortal spear she stretch'd, and mark'd the
 way.
   Thither amid surrounding foes they haste;
Who shun'd them, still retreating, as they pass'd:
And ent'ring found the Spartan hero laid
On the green sward, beneath the bow'ring shade.
The guard secure, lay stretch'd upon the ground;
Their shields resign'd, their lances pitch'd
One only near a winding riv'let stood, [around:
Which turn'd its wandring current through the
 wood;
His helmet fill'd with both his hands he rear'd,
In act to drink; when in the grove appear'd
Th' Etolian prince. His armour's fiery blaze
The dark recess illumin'd with its rays.
Amaz'd the Theban stood; and, from his hand,
The helmet slipp'd, and roll'd upon the sand.
Not more afraid the wond'ring swain descries,
'Midst night's thick gloom, a flaming meteor
 rise;
Sent by the furies, as he deems, to sow
Death and diseases on the Earth below. [cry'd.
" Tydides comes!" with fault'ring voice he
And straight to flight his willing limbs apply'd.
With sudden dread surpris'd the guards retire;
As shepherd swains avoid a lion's ire,
Who roams the heights and plains, from famine
 bold,
The stall to ravage or assault the fold.
   Now, lifeless as he lay, the martial maid
Atrides, with a pitying eye, survey'd;
And, with her spear revers'd, the hero shook:
The touch divine his iron slumber broke:
As when his drowsy mate the shepherd swain
Stirs with his crook, and calls him to the plain;
When in the east he sees the morning rise,
And redd'ning o'er his head the colour'd skies.
When from the ground his head the hero rais'd,
In full divinity the goddess blaz'd;
Her left, reveal'd, the dreadful ægis rears,
Whose ample field the snaky Gorgon bears;
Th' immortal lance stood flaming in the right,
Which scatters and confounds the ranks of fight.
Speechless the chiefs remain'd; amazement
 strong,
In mute suspence and silence, held them long.
And thus the goddess: " Atreus' son! arise,
Confess the partial favour of the skies.
For thee I leave the thund'rer's lofty seat,
To wake thee slumb'ring on the verge of fate:
To you let Diomed his arms resign;
Unequal were your force to govern mine;
His stronger arm shall bear this pond'rous shield;
His better hand the weighty jav'lin wield.
Arise! be sudden, for your foes draw near;
Assur'd to conquer when the gods appear."
   The goddess thus; and, mixing with the wind,
Left in a heap her shining arms behind
Upon the field; with loud harmonious peal,
Th' immortal buckler rung, and golden mail,
And thus Atrides, rising from the ground:
" In this approv'd is hoar tradition found;
That oft, descending from th' ethereal tow'rs,
To mix with mortals, come the heav'nly pow'rs:
But ne'er till now I saw a god appear,
Or more than human voice did ever hear.

Do you, my friend, assume these arms divine ;
The mortal and inferior shall be mine.''
Atrides thus ; and Diomed reply'd :
" To Heav'n obedience must not be deny'd ;
Else you yourself th' immortal arms should
wield,
And I with these attend you on the field.
But of the pow'rs above, whose sov'reign sway
The fates of men and mortal things obey,
Pallas, with surest vengeance, still pursues
Such as obedience to her will refuse." [bound,
  He said ; and straight his shining arms un-
The casque,the mail,the buckler's weighty round;
With secret joy th' immortal helmet took :
High on its crest the waving plumage shook.
This whosoever wears, his sharpen'd eyes
All dangers mock of ambush and surprise ;
Their ray unquench'd, the midnight shade di-
vides ;
No cunning covers, and no darkness hides.
The breast-plate next he takes, whose matchless
art
Firm courage fixes in the bounding heart ;
The rage of war unmov'd the wearer braves,
And rides serene amid the stormy waves :
The glitt'ring mail a starry baldric bound,
His arm sustain'd the buckler's weighty round ;
Impenetrably strong, its orb can bear
And turn, like softest lead, the pointed spear ;
Nor yields to aught, in Earth or Heav'n above,
But the dread thunder of almighty Jove.
Th' immortal spear the hero last did wield,
Which fixes conquest, and decides a field ;
Nor strength nor numbers can its rage withstand,
Sent by a mortal or immortal hand.
  Thus arm'd to meet the foe Tydides mov'd,
And glory'd conscious of his might improv'd ;
Like the proud steed rejoicing in his force,
When the shrill trumpet wakes him to the
course ;
Fierce and impatient of restraint, he strains
With stiffen'd neck against the galling reins.
Taller he seem'd ; as when the morning spread,
With golden lustre, crowns some mountain's
head
In early spring ; when, from the meads below,
A wreath of vapours binds his rocky brow ;
In cloudy volumes settling as they rise,
They lift the lofty prospect to the skies :
So in immortal arms the chief appear'd,
His stature broad display'd, and higher rear'd.
  Now from the field approaching to the grove,
Embattl'd thick, the Theban warriors move ;
Slowly they move, as swains with doubtful steps
Approach the thicket where a lion sleeps.
Tydides saw ; and, rushing from the shade,
The Spartan call'd, and to the combat led.
Unaw'd the hero met the hostile band ;
Nor could united force his rage withstand.
They wheel'd aloof ; as when a dragon springs
From his dark den, and rears his pointed wings
Against approaching swains, when summer burns,
And the fresh lakes to parched deserts turns ;
They fly dispers'd, nor tempt his fatal ire,
His wrath-swoln neck and eyes of living fire :
So fled the Thebans, nor escap'd by flight.
Amid their squadrons, like a faulcon light,
The hero sprung ; who, stooping from the skies,
The feather'd race disperses as he flies,

Still from his hand th' immortal weapon flew ;
And ev'ry flight an armed warrior slew.
Andremon first, beneath his mighty hand,
Of life bereft, lay stretch'd upon the sand.
Pherecydes gigantic press'd the plain ;
And valiant Tereus sunk amid the slain.
Warriors to these of vulgar names succeed ;
And all his path is mark'd with heaps of dead.
As when some woodman, by incessant strokes,
Bestrews a mountain with its falling oaks ;
Fells the thick planes, the hawthorn's flow'ry
shade,
The poplar fair by passing currents fed,
The laurel with unfading verdure crown'd ;
Heaps roll'd on heaps, the forest sinks around :
So spreads the slaughter as the chief proceeds ;
At ev'ry stroke an armed warrior bleeds,
Atrides combats by the hero's side,
To share his glory and the toil divide :
Unmov'd amidst the hostile ranks they go ;
Before them far retreats the routed foe.
  And now the Spartan host appear'd in sight,
By toil subdu'd and ling'ring in the fight.
Their valiant leader saw, and rais'd his voice,
Loud as the silver trumpet's martial noise,
With hopes of victory his bands to cheer ;
It swiftly flew : the distant Spartans hear
With glad surprise.   Polyctes thus addrest,
And rous'd the languid valour of the rest.
" Myceneans ! Spartans ! taught to seek renown
From dangers greatly brav'd, and battles won ;
With sorrow and regret I see you yield,
And Thebes victorious drive you from the field.
Atrides calls us ; to his aid repair :
No foe subdues you but your own despair.
He yet survives, beset with hostile bands,
And, from your valour, present aid demands."
He said.  The rigour of the shock returns ;
The slaughter rages, and the combat burns.
As when a reaping train their sickles wield,
Where yellow harvest loads some fruitful field ;
The master's heart, with secret joy, o'erflows ;
He prompts the work, and counts the length'ning
rows ;
So 'midst the war, the pow'r of battles stood,
Pleas'd with the carnage and the streams of
blood.
  Elpenor first lay lifeless on the plain,
By stern Plexippus with a jav'lin slain,
A grief to Thebes.  Euryalus the bold,
Rich in his flocks and rich in sums of gold,
Beneath the arm of Aristæus fell ;
Loud rung his silver arms with echoing knell :
And like some flow'r, whose painted foliage fair
With fragrant breath perfumes the vernal air,
If the rude scythe its tender root invades,
It falls dishonour'd and its lustre fades.
Thus fell Euryalus ; whose matchless grace,
In youth's full bloom, surpass'd the human race ;
For Cynthius only could with him compare,
In comely features, shape, and flowing hair.
  Now o'er the fields the rage of war is spread ;
And heaps on heaps ascend the hills of dead.
Ranks meeting ranks oppose with equal rage :
As when the north and stormy south engage,
Beneath their strife the troubled ocean roars ;
And rushing waves o'erwhelm the rocky shores ;
So rag'd the fight ; when bursting from a crowd
Of thick opposing foes, the princes stood

Between the hosts.   And thus th' Etolian lord:
" Spartans ! behold your valiant chief restor'd ;
Ye owe his safety to Minerva's care ;
Let hecatombs your gratitude declare,
Soon as from Thebes you reach your native
                                      ground,
Where flocks and herds for sacrifice abound ;
Now fight and conquer ;  let this signal day
Your tedious toils, with victory, repay ;
And, for Hegialus, let thousands dead
With ample vengeance gratify his shade."
As thus the hero spoke, the warriors heard,
And hope rekindling through the host appear'd ;
With joyful shouts they rent the trembling air,
And bless'd the gods, and own'd Minerva's care.
    Now, tow'ring in the midst, Atrides stood,
And call'd his warriors to the fight aloud :
As mariners with joy the Sun descry,
Ascending, in his course, the eastern sky ;
Who all night long, by angry tempests tost,
Shunn'd with incessant toil some faithless coast ;
So to his wishing friends Atrides came ;
Their danger such before, their joy the same.
Again the rigour of the shock returns ;
The slaughter rages and the combat burns;
With thirst of vengeance ev'ry bosom glows.
Tydides leads, and rushes on his foes ;
Around his head a ray of light'ning shone
From the smooth helmet and the glitt'ring cone;
Like that by ight which streams with fiery
                                      glare,
When some red meteor glides along the air,
Sent by the angry gods with tainted breath,
To sow the seeds of pestilence and death :
From look to look infectious terrour spreads ;
And ev'ry wretch th'impending vengeance dreads.
    Before the chief the Theban bands retire,
As shepherd swains avoid the lion's ire.
Clytander only by the fates impell'd,
Oppos'd him single and disdain'd to yield ;
Lycaon's son ;  deceiv'd by glory's charms,
Superior might he brav'd and matchless arms.
Nor was his brother present by his side,
To share the danger and the toil divide ;
Himself a youth, and yet by time unsteel'd,
Single he met Tydides in the field.
Against th' immortal shield his lance he flung,
Whose hollow orb with deaf'ning clangour rung :
The tow'rs of Thebes re-echo'd to the sound ;
The spear repuls'd fell blunted on the ground.
Tydides next th' immortal jav'lin threw ;
With force impell'd, it brighten'd as it flew ;
And pierc'd the Theban helmet near the cone ;
Behind his ear the starting weapon shone.
Supine the warrior fell, his spirit fled,
And mix'd with heroes in th' Elysian shade.
To spoil the slain the ardent victor flew :
First from the wound the fixed lance he drew,
The helmet loos'd, the costly mail unbound,
And shining shield with sculptur'd figures
                                      crown'd.
These spoils the hero, in his grateful mind,
A present for the gen'rous youth design'd ;
Who still in perilous battle sought his side,
And proffer'd late his warlike steeds to guide.
Fatal the gift, the cause of future woe !
But good and ill th' immortals only know.
The armour to a vulgar hand consign'd,
Again the hero, swifter than the wind,

To combat rush'd.
              But, from his throne above
Declin'd, the all-surveying eye of Jove
His progress mark'd. The herald pow'r, who brings
His sov'reign mandates on immortal wings,
He thus address'd : " To yonder sphere descend ;
Bid Phœbus straight his ev'ning charge attend :
For, with reverted eye, he views the war,
And checks the progress of his downward car.
Let him not linger in th' ethereal way,
But lash his steeds, and straight conclude the day;
For, if the gods descend not to her aid,
Or ev'ning interpose with friendly shade,
Thebes now must perish : and the doom of fate,
Anticipated, have an earlier date
Than fate ordains ; for, like devouring flame,
Tydides threatens all the Theban name ;
Immortal arms his native force improve,
Conferr'd by Pallas, partial in her love.
These to retrieve must be your next essay ;
Win them by art, and hither straight convey :
For man with man an equal war shall wage,
Nor with immortal weapons arm his rage."
    He said.  And Maia's son, with speed, ad-
                                      drest
His flight to Phœbus hov'ring in the west.
Upon a cloud his winged feet he stay'd ;
And thus the mandates of his sire convey'd.
" Ruler of light !  let now thy car descend,
And silent night her peaceful shade extend,
Else Thebes must perish ;  and the doom of fate,
Anticipated, have an earlier date
Than fate decrees : for, like devouring flame,
Tydides threatens all the Theban name ;
Immortal arms his native force improve,
Conferr'd by Pallas, partial in her love."
    The son of Maia thus.  The god obey'd ;
The sounding lash upon his steeds he lay'd.
Swift to the goal with winged feet they flew ;
The night ascending as the day withdrew.
To Thebes the herald next pursu'd his way ;
Shot like a meteor with the setting ray.
Behind Tydides in the fight he stay'd ;
And on his head the potent sceptre lay'd;
Whose magic pow'r on waking sense prevails ;
Or, in profoundest sleep, the eye unseals ;
The struggling ghost unbinds from mortal clay,
And drives it down the dark Tartarean way.
Subdu'd the hero stood by pow'rful charms,
Till Hermes stript him of th' immortal arms ;
And, mounting to the starry roofs above,
Dispos'd them in the armoury of Jove.
And, recollected, thus Tydides spoke :  [woke :
" Whate'er they give, th' immortals may re-
I own their favour ;  that, of mortal line
The first,  I wore a panoply divine.
But if the day were lengthen'd to my will,
With light to point my jav'lin where to kill,
Thebes now should perish ;  but the morning ray
Shall finish what the ev'ning shades delay."
    And now the night began her silent reign ;
Ascending, from the deep, th' ethereal plain ;
O'er both the hosts she stretch'd her ample shade,
Their conflict to suspend :  the hosts obey'd.
The field no more a noisy scene appears,
With steeds and chariots throng'd, and glitt'ring
                                      spears ;
But still and silent : like the hoary deep,
When, in their caves, the angry tempests sleep,

Peaceful and smooth it spreads from shore to
    shore,        [fore:
Where storms had rag'd and billows swell'd be-
Such seem'd the field; the martial clangors
    cease;
And war tumultuous lulls itself to peace.

---

THE

## EPIGONIAD.

### BOOK IV.

And now the princes of the Theban state
In council sat, assembled in the gate,
Where rows of marble pillars bound the space,
To judgment sacred in the days of peace.
And Creon thus, with public cares oppress'd
And private griefs, the senators address'd.
  "Princes of Thebes, and valiant aids from far,
Our firm associates in the works of war,
Heroes, attend! I shall not now propose
To supplicate, for peace, our haughty foes;
No peace can grow, no friendship e'er be found,
When mutual hate has torn so wide a wound.
Yet for a truce of seven days space I plead,
And fun'ral obsequies to grace the dead.
Nor were it just, that they, who greatly fall
From rage of foes to guard their native wall,
Should want the honours which their merits
    claim,
Sepulchral rites deny'd and fun'ral flame."
  Thus as he spoke, parental grief supprest
His voice, and swell'd within his lab'ring breast.
Silent amidst th' assembled peers he stands,
And wipes his falling tears with trembling hands;
For great Leophron, once his country's boast,
The glory and the bulwark of her host,
Pierc'd by a foe and lifeless on the plain,
Lay drench'd in gore and mix'd with vulgar slain:
Silent he stood; the Theban lords around
His grief partake, in streams of sorrow drown'd;
Till sage Palantes rose, and to the rest,
The monarch seconding, his words addrest.
  "Princes! renown'd for wisdom and for might,
Rever'd in council and approv'd in fight;
What Creon moves the laws themselves require,
With obsequies to grace and fun'ral fire
Each warrior, who in battle bravely falls
From rage of foes to guard his native walls.
If all approve, and none will sure withstand
What Creon counsels and the laws command,
Charg'd with the truce, Apollo's priest shall go
To offer and conclude it with the foe.
His silver hairs a mild respect may claim,
And great Apollo's ever honor'd name."
  The rest assent. The venerable man,
Slow from his seat arising, thus began :
" Princes of Thebes! and thou, whose sov'reign
    hand
Sways the dread sceptre of supreme command ;
Though well I might this perilous task refuse,
And plead my feeble age a just excuse;
Yet nothing shall restrain me, for I go,
Pleas'd with the pious charge, to meet the foe.
Willing I go; our bleeding warriors claim
Sepulchral honours and the fun'ral flame.
If all approve, let Clytophon attend;
With just success our labours thus shall end:

For sure no Theban boasts an equal skill,
With pleasing words, to bend the fixed will."
  Sooth'd with the friendly praise, the hero said,
" No self-regard shall hold me or dissuade;
The pious charge my inmost thoughts approve."
He said; and slow thro' yielding crowds they
    move;
While Thebes on ev'ry side assembled stands,
And supplicates the gods with lifted hands:
" O grant that wrathful enemies may spare
These rev'rend heads; nor wrong the silver hair !"
  And now they pass'd the lofty gates, and came
Where slow Ismenus winds his gentle stream ;
Amphion's grove they pass'd, whose umbrage
His rural tomb defends on ev'ry side.  [wide
The scene of fight they reach'd, and spacious
    fields    [shields.
With mangled slaughter heap'd, and spears and
Under their feet the hollow bucklers sound ;
And splinter'd falchions glitter on the ground.
And now the stations of the camp appear,
Far as a shaft can wound the flying deer.
Thither, amid the wrecks of war, they go
With silent steps; and scape the watchful foe.
Now full in view before the guards they stand;
The priest displays his ensigns in his hand,
The laurel wreath, the gold bespangled rod
With stars adorn'd, the symbols of the god.
He thus began : " Ye Argive warriors, hear !
A peaceful message to your tents we bear :
A truce is ask'd, till the revolving Sun,
Seven times from east to west his journey run,
Again ascends; and from the ocean's streams,
Crowns the green mountains with his golden
That mutually secure, with pious care, [beams;
Both hosts funereal honours may prepare
For ev'ry hero, whom the rage of fight
Has swept to darkness and the shores of night."
  Thus, as he spoke, the list'ning warriors heard
With approbation, and the priest rever'd.
The chief of Salamis, their leader, went
Himself to guide them to the royal tent ;
Which shone conspicuous; through the shades
    of night
Its spacious portal pour'd a stream of light.
Thither conducted by the chief, they found
The king of men with all his peers around,
On thrones with purple spread each royal guest
In order sat, and shar'd the genial feast.
Silent they enter'd. From his chair of state,
Full in the midst opposed to the gate,
The monarch saw; and rising thus exprest
The gen'rous dictates of his royal breast.
  " My guests, approach! no enemy is near ;
This roof protects you, straight forget your fear.
Ev'n though from yon devoted walls you come,
For vengeance mark'd by fate's eternal doom;
Here in my tent, with safety, you shall rest,
And with the princes, share the genial feast.
You freely then your message may propose,
When round the board the cheering vintage
    flows,
Which sooths impatience, and the open'd ear,
With favour and attention, bends to hear."
  The hero thus. Apollo's priest replies :
" Humane thy manners, and thy words are wise;
With thee the noblest gifts the gods have plac'd,
And pow'r supreme with equal wisdom grac'd
                            L

Though oft, by parts, for others they ordain,
The arts of sway, the privilege to reign ;
In thee their partial favour has combin'd
The highest fortune with the greatest mind."
  As thus the sage reply'd, the princely band
By turns presented each his friendly hand,
The sign of peace. For each a sp'endid throne,
Where fring'd with gold the purple cov'ring
    shone,
The ready waiters, by command, prepar'd ;
There sat the envoys and the banquet shar'd.
On ev'ry side the sparkling vintage flows,
The momentary cure of human woes.
The rage of thirst and hunger thus suppress'd,
To Nestor turning Clytophon address'd.
  " Illustrious chief! an honour now I'll claim,
Which not to publish, sure, would merit blame.
Your father's guest, I was ; by fortune led,
When from Trinacria's desert shores I fled
With ills beset : but, in his friendly land,
His gen'rous heart I prov'd and lib'ral hand.
A grateful mind excites me to reveal
His sov'reign bounty, and attempt a tale
Of dear remembrance. But the fond design,
Prudence dissenting, warns me to decline ;
For when to public cares your thoughts you bend,
A private story mingled must offend."
  The artful Theban thus. The chief reply'd,
Whose sov'reign mandates all the host obey'd.
"My honour'd guest! proceed; nor aught conceal
Which gratitude enjoins you to reveal :
For gen'rous deeds, imprudently supprest,
Lie unapplauded in the grateful breast :
And now the feast, short interval of care,
To vocal symph'ony unbends the ear ;
Or sweet discourse, which to the soul conveys
Sublimer joys than music's tuneful lays."
The monarch thus. The prudent sage sup-
    press'd
His inward joy, and thus the peers address'd :
Each chief he strove to gain, but Nestor most,
Whose wisdom sway'd the councils of the host.
  " Confed'rate kings ! and thou whose sov'reign
    hand
Sways the dread sceptre of supreme command,
Attend and hearken ! since you seek to know,
The sad beginnings of a life of woe.
In Rhodes my father once dominion claim'd,
Orsilochus, for deeds of valour fam'd.
The Sporades his sov'reign sceptre own'd,
And Carpathus with waving forests crown'd.
His youngest hope I was, and scarce had seen
The tenth returning summer clothe the green,
When pirates snatch'd me from my native land :
While with my infant equals on the strand
I play'd, of harm secure, and from the deep
With pleasure saw approach the fatal ship ;
Pleas'd with the whiteness of the sails we stood,
And the red streamers shining on the flood ;
And fearless saw the hostile galley land,
Where from the hills a current seeks the strand.
They climb'd the rocky beach, and far around,
Intent on spoil and rapine, view'd the ground ;
If any herd were near, or fleecy store,
Or lonely mansion on the winding shore.
My young companions straight their fear obey.
I, bold and unsuspecting, dar'd to stay.   [toil
Me straight they seiz'd ; and doom'd to servile
A wretched captive in a foreign soil.

Struggling in vain, they bore me down the bay,
Where, anchor'd near the beach, their vessel lay ;
And plac'd me on the deck. With bitter cries,
To speeding gales I saw the canvass rise ;
The boundless ocean far before me spread ;
And from my reach the shores at distance fled.
All day I wept ; but when the setting light
Retir'd, and yielded to the shades of night,
Sleep stole upon my grief with soft surprise,
Which care ne'er banish'd long from infant eyes.
  " Nine days we sail'd ; the tenth returning ray
Show'd us Trinacria rising in our way,
Far in the west ; where, with his ev'ning beams,
The Sun descending gilds the ocean's streams.
Thither the sailors ply, and blindly run
On hidden dangers which they ought to shun ;
For whom the gods distinguish by their hate,
They first confound and then resign to fate.
All day we sail'd ; and with the ev'ning hour,
Which calls the shepherd to his rural bow'r,
Approach'd the shore. The forests on the land
We mark'd, and rivers op'ning from the strand.
Then gladness touch'd my heart ; the first I knew
Since fate had mix'd me with that lawless crew :
With joy I saw the rising shores appear ;
And hop'd to find some kind deliv'rer near ;
Some gen'rous lord, to whom I might relate,
Low bending at his knees, my wretched fate.
Vain was the hope ; the Cyclopes ne'er know
Compassion, nor to melt at human woe.
  " Near on the left, and where the parted tides
A promontory's rocky height divides,
A bay they found ; and on the fatal strand
Descending, fix'd their vessel to the land.
The valleys straight and mountains they explore,
And the long windings of the desert shore ;
And find, of sheep and goats, a mingled flock,
Under the shelter of a cavern'd rock.
The largest and the best the pirate band
Seiz'd, and prepar'd a banquet on the strand.
With joy they feasted ; while the goblet, crown'd
With Mithymnean vintage, flow'd around.
Of harm secure they sat ; and void of fear
To mirth resign'd ; nor knew destruction near.
  "Amid them there I meditating sat ;
Some god inspir'd me, or the pow'r of fate,
To 'scape their hated hands : and soon I found
The wish'd occasion ; when along the ground,
Each where he sat, the ruffians lay supine,
With sleep oppress'd and sense-subduing wine ;
Softly I rose, and to a lofty grove,
Which shaded all the mountain tops above
Ascending, in a rocky cavern lay,
Till darkness fled before the morning ray.
Then from above I saw the pirate band,
In parties, roaming o'er the desert strand ;
The mountain goats they drove and fleecy store,
From all the pastures, crowded to the shore.
Me too by name they call'd ; and oft, in vain,
Explor'd each grove and thicket on the plain ;
While from above I saw, with careless eye,
Them searching round and list'ning for reply.
Some to the ship the bleating spoil convey'd ;
While others to prepare a banquet stay'd,
And call'd their mates : to share with full repast
With mirth they came, nor knew it was their
    last.
  " Then from the rocky summit where I lay,
A flock appear'd descending to the bay ;

Which through a narrow valley rush'd along,
Oxen and sheep, an undistinguish'd throng.
With these the sloping hills were cover'd o'er,
And the long windings of the sandy shore.
Behind a Cyclops came ; and by degrees,
Rose to my view, and tower'd above the trees.
His giant stature, like a lofty rock,
Appear'd : and in his hand a knotted oak
Of tallest growth ; around his shoulder flung
His bag enormous, by a cable hung.
Panting I lay ; as when a lurking deer,
From some close thicket, sees the hunter near.
By dread subdu'd, confounded, and amaz'd,
My fixed eye-balls darken'd as I gaz'd.
Soon from above my wretched mates he knew,
As on the level shore, in open view,
They sat secure, with flow'ry garlands crown'd ;
The signs of spoil and ravage scatter'd round.
With indignation, for his wasted flock,
Inflam'd, he thus, like distant thunder, spoke.
" Whoe'er these are, who from their native soil
To foreign climates thus, in quest of spoil,
Licentious roam ; they soon shall feel my hand,
And rue that e'er they touch'd Trinacria's
            strand."
As mutt'ring thus, along the craggy road
He came, the mountain trembled as he trode.
The wretches saw with horrour and affright ;
Each limb enfeebled lost the pow'r of flight.
Their cries in vain the monster mov'd to spare ;
His club he rear'd and swung it thrice in air,
Then hurl'd it cross the bay : it swiftly drove
O'er the smooth deep, and raz'd the beach
            above.
Threat'ning it rush'd along ; but, bending low,
Each, where he sat, escap'd the weighty blow.
Beyond them far it pitch'd upon the land, [sand.
Tore the green sward, and heav'd a mount of
Now starting from the ground they strove to fly,
Press'd by despair and strong necessity ;
The woody summits of the cliffs to gain,
With falt'ring haste they fled across the plain.
But the impending mountains barr'd their flight,
High and projecting from their airy height ;
Back from the slipp'ry arch, in heaps, they fall;
And with imploring cries for mercy call,
In vain. The monster with gigantic strides,
At twenty steps, the spacious bay divides ;
Around his knees the whit'ning billows roar,
And his rude voice like thunder shakes the shore.
" There thirty youths he slew; against the
            stones
And ragged cliffs, he dash'd their crackling bones.
Twenty his feet and heavy hands pursue,
As to the ocean in despair they flew ;
Striving the summit of the beach to gain,
With headlong course to rush into the main :
For there they hop'd a milder fate to have,
And less abhorr'd, beneath the whelming wave.
These too he reach'd; and with his weighty
            hand, [sand,
Their flight oppress'd, and mix'd them with the
Two yet surviv'd ; who supplicating strove,
With humble suit,'his barb'rous soul to move.
With trembling knees the sandy beach they
            press'd ;
And, as they came, the monster thus address'd.
" 'O thou ! with whom no mortal can compare
For strength resistless, pity now and spare.

O let the blood, already shed, atone
For our provoking guilt, and trespass done !
O spare and pity ! sure the gods above,
Who sit around the starry throne of Jove,
Are won by pray'r ; and he whose matchless
            might
The solid Earth sustains and starry height,
Oft spares the guilty ; for his soul approves
Compassion, and the works of mercy loves.
Let sov'reign pity touch thy mighty breast ;
And him revere, the greatest and the best ;
Who pardons oft, but measures grief and pain
To such as hear the wretched plead in vain.'
" As thus to touch his iron heart they try'd,
The Cyclops smiling, scornful thus reply'd :
' The praise of mercy well your words proclaim ;
And vengeance mark,though merited, with blame;
Well have you spoken ; therefore, from my hand,
More favour hope than any of your band ;
They, on the desert shore expos'd and bare,
The wolves shall feast and ev'ry bird of air ;
But ye, preferr'd above the rest, shall have
This body for your monument and grave.'
" He said, and seizing lifts them both on high,
With hands and feet extended in the sky :
Then dash'd them thrice against the rocky shore ;
Gnaw'd their warm flesh, and drank their stream-
            ing gore.
Oft have I seen the havoc of the plain,
The rage of tempests and the stormy main ;
But fate, in such a form, ne'er met my eyes,
And, while I speak, afresh its horrours rise
To chill my veins : nor can the vary'd state
Of sprightly youth, and middle age sedate,
Or life's last stage with all its griefs opprest,
Banish the dire impression from my breast.
For still I see the monster, as he stood,
His hairy visage dy'd in human blood :
As the grim lion leaves the wasted plains,
Red from the ravage of the flocks and swains.
" With vengeance pleas'd he view'd the shores
            around ;
And, riding near the beach, our vessel found :
Her by the mast he seiz'd : and to the land,
With all her anchors, dragg'd along the strand.
Exploring, next the solid deck he tore,
And found, conceal'd below, his fleecy store.
With scornful smiles he saw the theft bewray'd ;
And sidelong on the beach the galley laid ;
And call'd his flock : to open light they strain,
Through the wide beach, and crowd upon the
            plain :
Still, as they pass'd, his weighty hands he laid
On their soft backs, and, stroking gently, said :
" Go now, my flock ! enjoy the verdant hills,
The rivers cool, the sweet refreshing rills,
The meads and shady forests, safe from harm ;
Your foes lie crush'd beneath your master's
            arm."
The giant thus ; and next the hold explor'd :
Four jars he found with Lesbian vintage stor'd.
These first he drain'd ; then to his lips apply'd
His flute, which like a quiver by his side,
Of size enormous, hung. Its hollow sound
The woods repeated and the caves around.
Its music such, as when a stormy gale
Roars through a hollow cliff with hideous peal,
Resounding deep, along the level shore ;
He play'd, and drove his pasturing flock before.

" Horrour and grief at once my heart assail'd ;
Presages sad o'er ev'ry hope prevail'd.
My distant country rush'd upon my mind ;
My friends, my weeping parents, left behind.
Now lost to hope, and furious from despair,
With both my hands I rent my rooted hair ;
And, in an agony of sorrow, prest,
With strokes repeated oft, my heaving breast.
All day I mourn'd ; but when the setting ray
Retir'd, and ev'ning shades expell'd the day ;
Encourag'd by the night, I sought the plain ;
And, wand'ring anxious 'midst the mangled slain,
Oft call'd to know if any of the band
Did yet survive, escap'd the monster's hand :
But none reply'd.  Along the desert shore
All night I wander'd, 'midst the sullen roar
Of bursting billows ; till the morning ray
Appear'd to light my solitary way.
'Twas then I reach'd a mountain's height o'er-spread
W'th thickets close, and dark impending shade,
Hung o'or a valley, where a river leads
His wand'ring current through a grove of reeds.
" Thither I went ; and, op'ning to the deep,
A cavern found beneath the rocky steep:
The haunt of mountain goats, when wint'ry rains
Have chas'd them from the hills and naked plains.
Gladly I enter'd ; for, deceiv'd by fear,
I always thought the barb'rous Cyclops near ;
His form descry'd in ev'ry tree behind,
And heard his voice approaching in the wind.
Of honey there a sweet repast I found,
In clusters hanging from the cliffs around.
My hunger soon appeas'd, the gentle pow'r
Of sleep subdu'd me till the ev'ning hour.
'Twas then I wak'd ; and to the deep below,
Through thickets, creep'd with careful steps and slow ;
And gaz'd around if any hut were there,
Or solitary wretch my grief to share :
But none appear'd.  I climb'd a mountain's head,
Where, wide before me, lay the ocean spread ;
A'd there no object met my wishing eyes,
But billows bounded by the setting skies.
Yet still I gaz'd, till night's prevailing sway
Extinguish'd, in the west, the ev'ning ray.
Hopeless and sad, descending from my stand,
I wander'd on the solitary strand,          [roar
Through the thick gloom ; and heard the sullen
Of billows bursting on the desert shore.
" Thus ten long years I liv'd conceal'd by day,
Under a rock on wither'd leaves I lay ;
At dawn and twilight on the mountains stood,
Exploring with my eyes the pathless flood ;
Impatient till some friendly sail should come,
To waft me to my sire and native home :
But none appear'd.  The pilots shun the shores
Where Ætna flames, and dire Charybdis roars ;
And where the curs'd Cyclopean brothers reign,
The lonely tyrants of the desert plain.
Press'd by despair, at last I dar'd to brave,
E'en in a skiff, the terrours of the wave ;
Contemning all the perils in my way,
For worse it seem'd than death itself to stay.
" Of oziers soft the bending hull I wove ;
And ply'd the skins of mountain goats above.

A slender fir, ten cubit lengths, I found
Fall'n from a mould'ring bank, and stript it round.
This for the mast, with bulrush ropes I ty'd ;
A pole to steer the rudder's use supply'd :
Four goat-skins join'd I fitted for the sail,
And spread it with a pole to catch the gale.
Each chink with gum, against the brine I clos'd ;
And the whole work beneath a shade dispos'd,
Where, from the hills descending to the main,
A winding current cuts the sandy plain.
Nuts and dry'd figs in baskets next I shar'd ;
And liquid stores in bags of skin prepar'd :
And waited anxious till the southern gale,
From the dire coast, should bear my flying sail.
Nine days I stay'd ; and still the northern breeze,
From great Hesperia, swept the whit'ning seas :
But on the tenth it chang'd ; and when the hour
Of twilight call'd the giant to his bow'r,
Down from my grotto to the shore I came,
And call'd the god who rules the ocean's stream ;
Oblations vow'd, if, by his mighty hand
Conducted safe, I found my native land.
And, turning where conceal'd my vessel lay,
The rope I loos'd, and push'd her to the bay ;
The sail unfurl'd, and, steering from the strand,
Behind me left with joy the hated land.
" All night, by breezes sped, the prow divides
The deep, and o'er the billows lightly glides.
But when the dawn, prevailing o'er the night,
Had ting'd the glowing east with purple light,
The air was hush'd : deserted by the gale,
Loose to the mast descends the empty sail.
And full against my course a current came,
Which hurl'd me backwards, floating on its stream,
Towards the land.    I saw the shores draw near ;
And the long billows on the beach appear.
The cruel Cyclops spy'd me, as he drove
His past'ring flock along the hills above ;
And winding through the groves his secret way,
Conceal'd behind a promontory lay ;
Prepar'd to snatch me, when his arm could reach
My skiff, which drove ungovern'd to the beach.
I mark'd his purpose ; furious from despair,
With both my hands I rent my rooted hair ;
And on the poop with desp'rate purpose stood,
Prepar'd to plunge into the whelming flood.
But Neptune sav'd me in that perilous hour ;
The headlong current felt his present pow'r :
Back from the shore it turn'd at his command,
And bore me joyful from the fatal strand.
The Cyclops vex'd, as when some fowler spies,
Safe from his cover'd snares, the quarry rise,
His seat forsook, and, leaning o'er the steep,
Strove with soft words to lure me from the deep.
'Stranger, approach ! nor fly this friendly strand ;
Share the free blessings of a happy land :
Here, from each cliff, a stream of honey flows ;
And ev'ry hill with purple vintage glows.
Approach ; your fear forget ; my bounty share ;
My kindness prove and hospitable care.'
As to allure me thus the monster try'd,
His fraud I knew ; and rashly thus reply'd :
' Talk not of friendship ; well I know the doom
Of such as to your dire dominions come :
These eyes beheld when, with a ruthless hand,
My wretched mates you murder'd on the strand.
Two su'd for mercy ; but their limbs you tore
With brutal rage, and drank their streaming gore.

If Heav'n's dread sov'reign to my vengeful hand
His wasting flames would yield, and forked brand,
Scorch'd on the cliffs, your giant limbs should
    feed
The mountain wolves, and all the rav'nous breed.'
  " I said ; and from the south a rising breeze
Brush'd the thick woods, and swept the curling
    seas.
Above the waves my vessel lightly flew ;
The ocean widen'd, and the shores withdrew.
Inrag'd the Cyclops, rushing down the steep,
Eager to snatch me, plung'd into the deep:
My flight he follow'd with gigantic strides,
And stem'd with both his knees the rushing tides.
Soon had I perish'd, but escap'd again,
Protected by the god who rules the main.
He sent a spectre from his wat'ry caves ;
Like mist it rose and hover'd o'er the waves.
A skiff like mine, by art divine, it grew ;
And to the left across the ocean flew.
With course divided, where the pilot spies
Amid the deep two desert islands rise,
In shape, like altars, so by sailors nam'd,
A mark for pilots, else for nothing fam'd ;
The angry giant doubting stood, nor knew
Which to forsake, the shadow or the true :
For both seem'd equal. By the fates misled,
He chac'd the airy image as it fled ;
Nor reach'd it : for it led him through the main,
As the bright rainbow mocks some simple swain:
Who still intent to catch it where it stands,
And grasp the shining meteor with his hands,
Along the dewy meadows holds his way ;
But still before him flies the colour'd ray.
The Cyclops so, along the wat'ry plain,
The shadowy phantom chas'd and chas'd in vain:
The billows bursted on his hairy sides,
And far behind him rush'd the parted tides.
Dissolv'd at last, its airy structure broke,
And vanish'd hov'ring like a cloud of smoke.
His errour then, and my escape, he knew ;
For, favour'd by the breeze, my vessel flew
Far to the deep : yet plunging in the waves,
Torn from its bed a pond'rous rock he heaves,
Craggy and black, with dangling sea-weed hung;
Push'd from his hand the weighty mass he flung,
To crush my flight: along th' ethereal plain
It roll'd, and thund'ring downwards shook the
    main.
Behind it fell ; and farther from the shore,
Hurl'd on the mounting waves, my vessel bore
Towards the deep. The giant saw, with pain,
His fraud detected, force essay'd in vain.
He curs'd the partial pow'rs, and lash'd on high,
With both his hands, the ocean to the sky.
  " Now safe beyond his reach, a prosp'rous gale
Blew fresh behind, and stretch'd my flying sail :
The shores retir'd ; but, from the distant main,
I saw him tow'ring on the wat'ry plain,
Like a tall ship ; and moving to the shore,
Sullen and sad, to tend his fleecy store.
Seven days I sail'd ; the eighth returning light
The Pylian shores presented to my sight,
Far in the east ; and where the Sun displays,
Along the glitt'ring waves, his early rays.
Thither I steer'd, and, where a point divides
Extended in the deep, the parted tides,
A fane I mark'd ; whose tow'ring summit, rear'd
High in the air, with gilded spires appear'd.

To Neptune sacred on the beach it stands,
Conspicuous from the sea and distant lands.
Assembled on the shore the people stood
On every side extended, like a wood :
And in the midst I saw a pillar rise,
Of sacred smoke, ascending to the skies.
'Twas there I reach'd the hospitable strand,
And, joyful, fix'd my vessel to the land.
  "There, with his peers, your royal sire I found;
And fell before him prostrate on the ground,
Imploring aid ; my lineage I reveal'd,
Nor aught of all my tedious toils conceal'd.
Attentive as I spoke the hero heard,
Nor credulous nor diffident appear'd ;
For prudence taught him, neither to receive
With easy faith, or rashly disbelieve.
  " O son of Neleus ! though you justly claim,
For eloquence and skill, superior fame ;
Yet to an equal glory ne'er aspire :
Vain were the hope to emulate your sire.
Eight days we feasted ; still the flowing bowl
Return'd, and sweet discourse, to glad the soul,
With pleasure heard ; as comes the sound of rain,
In summer's drought, to cheer the careful swain.
And when the ninth returning morn arose,
Sixty bold mariners the hero chose,
Skill'd, through the deep, the flying keel to guide,
And sweep, with equal oars, the hoary tide :
They trimm'd a vessel, by their lord's com-
    mand,
To waft me to my sire and native land.
With gifts enrich'd of robes and precious ore,
He sent me joyful from the Pylian shore.
Such Neleus was ! and such his signal praise
For hospitable deeds in former days ;
The friend, the patron, destin'd to redress
The wrongs of fate, and comfort my distress.
  " But what is man ! a reptile of the Earth ;
To toils successive fated from his birth ;
Few are our joys ; in long succession flow
Our griefs ; we number all our days in woe.
Misfortune enter'd with my infant years ;
My feeble age a load of sorrow bears.
Driv'n from my country by domestic foes,
Thebes but receiv'd me to partake her woes.
The sword I've seen and wide devouring fire,
Against her twice in fatal league conspire.
The public griefs, which ev'ry heart must share,
By nature taught to feel another's care,
Augment my own : our matrons weeping stand ;
Our rev'rend elders mourn a ruin'd land ;
Their furrow'd cheeks with streams of sorrow
    flow ;
And wailing orphans swell the gen'ral woe ;
They mourn their dearest hopes, in battle slain,
Whose limbs unbury'd load their native plain ;
And now by us entreat that war may cease,
And, for seven days successive, yield to peace :
That mutually secure, with pious care,
Both hosts funereal honours may prepare
For ev'ry warrior, whom the rage of fight
Has swept to darkness and the coasts of night.
To ratify the truce, if ye approve,
We come alike commission'd, as to move."
    Thus Clytophon ; and he, whose sov'reign
    sway
The warriors of the Pylian race obey,
Nestor, his partial favour thus express'd,
And to the Theban chief himself address'd,

"The truth you speak, nor do your words appear
Prepar'd with art, or dictated by fear;
For what you tell, my memory recalls,
When young I saw you at my native walls,
Yourself a youth; though now a length of years,
Imprinted deep, in all your form appears;
Yet still, with sure remembrance, can I trace
Your voice the same and lineaments of face.
An infant then upon your knees I hung,
And catch'd the pleasing wonders from your
    tongue:
  our woes I pity'd, as I pity still;
And, were the chiefs determin'd by my will,
The truce should stand: for piety conspires
With justice, to demand what Thebes requires."
  The hero thus; the king of men replies:
"Princes, in fight approv'd, in council wise!
What Thebes propounds 'tis yours alone to chuse
Whether ye will accept it or refuse:
For though your votes consenting in my hand
Have plac'd the sceptre of supreme command;
Yet still my pow'r, obedient to your choice,
Shall with its sanction join the public voice."
  The monarch thus; and thus the chief re-
    ply'd,
Whom fair Etolia's martial sons obey'd:
"Princes, attend! and thou,whose sov'reign hand
Sways the dread sceptre of supreme command!
What Thebes requires I do not now oppose,
Because, insensible to human woes,
The widow's tears I scorn, the mother's sighs,
The groans of fathers, or the orphan's cries,
Whose dearest hopes, in rage of battle slain,
With wounds defac'd, lie scatter'd on the plain:
Compassion for the host, which fruitless toil
So long has wasted in a foreign soil,
What Thebes propounds, impels me to dissuade,
And, for the living, disregard the dead.
How long has war and famine thin'd our pow'rs,
Inactive camp'd around the Theban tow'rs?
And pestilence, whose dire infection flies,
Blown by the furies through the tainted skies?
Many now wander on the Stygian shore,
Whom sires and consorts shall behold no more;
And many still, who yet enjoy the day,
Must follow down the dark Tartarean way,
If, blinded by the fates, our counsels bar
The course of conquest and protract the war.
Since equity and public right demands
That Thebes should fall by our avenging hands,
Now let us combat, till the gods above,
Who sit around the starry throne of Jove,
The judges of the nations, crown our toil,
So long endur'd, with victory and spoil;
Or, destine us to fall in glorious fight,
Elate and dauntless in the cause of right.
Shall we delay till dire infection spreads
Her raven wings o'er our devoted heads?
Till gen'rous wrath, by slow disease supprest,
Expires inactive in the warrior's breast,
And life, the price of glory, paid in vain,
We die forgotten on a foreign plain."
  Tydides thus; and he, whose sov'reign sway
The warriors of the Pylian race obey,
Nestor, reply'd, for eloquence approv'd,
By Pallas and the tuneful sisters lov'd:
"Confed'rate kings! and thou, whose sov'reign
    hand
Sways the dread sceptre of supreme command,

With patience hear the reasons which I plead
For fun'ral rites, the honours of the dead.
Well have you heard the various ills that wait
On strife prolong'd, and war's disastrous state:
And they, who choose to dwell amid alarms,
The rage of slaughter and the din of arms,
Know little of the joys, when combats cease,
That crown with milder bliss the hours of peace.
Though gladly would I see, in vengeance just,
The Theban tow'rs confounded with the dust;
That, from the war releas'd, we might again
Each share the pleasures of his native reign:
Yet let us not presumptuously withstand
What piety alike and right command,
The honours of the dead; nor tempt the gods,
To curse our labours, from their bright abodes.
Far in the Heav'ns, above this mortal scene,
In boundless light, the thund'rer sits serene;
He views the works of men; the good he knows,
And on their just attempts success bestows;
But blasts impiety, and mocks its aim,
With disappointment sure, and lasting shame.
  "Attend, ye princes! and I shall unfold
What sage Harmonius taught my sire of old.
The Locri summon'd all their martial pow'rs,
And fought around the Orchomenian tow'rs.
From oxen seiz'd, began the dire debate;
And wide and wasteful was the work of fate.
The Orchomenians oft a truce propos'd
For fun'ral rites; the Locrian chiefs oppos'd.
Nine days expir'd, the bleeding warriors lay;
Their wounds hot streaming to the solar ray.
From Styx's sable shore their ghosts implor'd,
With suppliant cries, Hell's dread avenging
    lord.
He heard, and from the gloomy deep below
Of Erebus profound, the house of woe,
A fury sent, the fiercest of the crew,
Whose iron scourges human crimes pursue:
Discord her name; among th' infernal gods
She dwells, excluded from the blest abodes;
Though oft on Earth she rears her baleful head,
To kindle strife, and make the nations bleed.
The fury came; and, hov'ring o'er the plain,
Devoted with her eyes the Locrian train.
In form a raven, to a tow'r she flew,
Which rose upon a precipice in view,
And on the airy summit took her seat,
With potent charms, to kindle dire debate.
The howling dogs her presence first declare;
The war-horse trembling snorts aloft in air;
On man at last the dire infection fell,
The awful vengeance of the pow'rs of Hell,
Confusion straight through all the camp is found;
The wand'ring centinel deserts his ground,
Fatally gay and crown'd with ev'ry weed,
Which weeping matrons scatter o'er the dead;
Of dire portent: but when the silent reign
Of night possess'd the mountains and the plain,
Above the camp her torch the fury rear'd,
Red, in the air, its baleful flame appear'd,
Kindling debate: outrageous strife arose,
Loud as the ocean when a tempest blows,
O'er all the plain, and stun'd the ear of night
With shouts tumultuous and the din of fight.
Down from her airy stand the goddess came,
Shot like a meteor, with a stream of flame,
To kindle fiercer strife, with stronger charms,
To swell the tumult and the rage of arms.

The combat burn'd: the Orchomenians heard
With horrour, nor beyond their walls appear'd,
By awe divine restrain'd: but when the light
Return'd successive on the steps of night,
From ev'ry tow'r they saw the spacious plain
With havoc heap'd, and mountains of the slain.
The secret cause the augurs first declar'd;
The justice of the gods they own'd and fear'd.
No fun'ral rite the Orchomenian state
On them bestow'd, the vulgar or the great;
In one deep pit, whose mouth extended wide
Four hundred cubit length from side to side,
They whelm'd them all; their bucklers and their
                                        spears,
The steeds, the chariots, and the charioteers,
One ruin mix'd; for so the will of Jove
The priests declar'd; and heap'd a mount above:
Such was the fate, by Heav'n and Hell decreed,
To punish bold contemners of the dead.
And let us not their fatal wrath provoke,
Nor merit by our guilt an equal stroke;
But seal the truce, and piously bestow
What to the reliques of the dead we owe."
    He said; the peers their joint assent declare,
The dead to honour, and the gods revere.
The king of men commands a herald straight
The priests to call, and hasten ev'ry rite.
While thus the sov'reign mandate they obey'd,
Th' Etolian leader rose, and frowning said:
    "O blind to truth! and fated to sustain
A length of woes, and tedious toils in vain!
By sounds deceiv'd, as to her fatal den
Some vocal sorc'ress lures the steps of men;
O eloquence! thou fatal charm! how few,
Guided by thee, their real good pursue!
By thee, our minds, with magic fetters bound,
In all decisions, true and false confound.
Not the unnumber'd wrecks, which lie along
The Syrens' coast the trophies of their song,
Nor there where Circe from the neighb'ring deep,
With strong enchantments, draws the passing
                                        ship,
Can match thy spoils: O let me ne'er obey,
And follow blindly, as you point the way!
Confed'rate kings! since nothing can oppose
The truce you purpose with our treach'rous foes,
With mischief pregnant; I alone am free,
Nor these my eyes the fatal rite shall see;
Lest it be said, when mischief shall succeed,
Tydides saw it, and approv'd the deed."
    Speaking he grasp'd his spear and pond'rous
                                shield;            [field,
And mov'd like Mars, when, 'midst th' imbattled
Sublime he stalks to kindle fierce alarms,
To swell the tumult and the rage of arms.
Such seem'd the chief: the princes with sur-
                                prize
Turn on the king of men, at once their eyes.
    He thus began: " Since now the public choice
The truce approves, with one consenting voice;
Tydides only, with superior pride,
Tho' youngest, still the readiest to decide,
Our gen'ral sense condemns; his haughty soul
Must not the counsels of the host control,
Brave though he is: the altars ready stand;
In order waits the consecrated band;
Straight let us seal the truce with blood and wine,
And, to attest it, call the pow'rs divine."
    The monarch thus; Tydides to his tent,
Thro' the still host, in sullen sorrow went.

Fix'd in his mind the fatal vision stay'd,
Snatch'd by invading force his lovely maid;
The fraud of Cytherea; still his heart
Incessant anguish felt, and lasting smart:
And, as a lion, when his side retains
A barbed shaft, the cause of bitter pains,
Growls in some lonely shade; his friends declin'd,
He breath'd in groans the anguish of his mind.
    Now round the flaming hearth th' assembly
                                stands,
And Theseus thus invokes with lifted hands:
"Hear me, ye pow'rs, that rule the realms of light!
And ye dread sov'reigns of the shades of night!
If, till the eighth succeeding Sun displays,
Above the eastern hills, his early rays,
Any bold warrior of the Argive bands,
Against a Theban lifts his hostile hands
By us approv'd; let ev'ry curse succeed
On me, and all, for perjury decreed.
And as by blood our mutual oath we seal,
The blood of victims drawn by deathful steel;
So let their blood be shed, who, scorning right,
Profanely shall presume its ties to slight."
Apollo's priest, for Thebes, resum'd the vow,
The gods above invoking, and below,
Their vengeance to inflict, if force, or art,
The truce should violate on either part.
    The rites concluded thus, the king commands
Two younger warriors of his native bands
A chariot to prepare; the driver's place
Sophronimus assum'd; with tardy pace,
Ascend the sage ambassadors; before
A lighted torch Asteropæus bore,
And led the way; the tents, the field of war,
They pass'd, and at the gate dismiss'd the car.

---

THE
### EPIGONIAD.
#### BOOK V.

Soon as the Sun display'd his orient ray,
And crown'd the mountain tops with early day;
Through ev'ry gate the Theban warriors flow,
Unarm'd and fearless of th' invading foe:
As when, in early spring, the shepherd sees
Rush from some hollow rock a stream of bees,
Long in the cliffs, from winter's rage, conceal'd,
New to the light, and strangers to the field;
In compass wide their mazy flight they steer,
Which wings of balmy zephyrs lightly bear
Along the meads, where some soft river flows,
Or forests, where the flow'ry hawthorn blows;
To taste the early spring their course they bend,
And lightly with the genial breeze descend:
So o'er the heights and plains the Thebans
                                spread;            [dead,
Some, 'midst the heaps of slaughter, sought their
Others with axes to the woods repair'd,
Fell'd the thick forests, and the mountains bar'd.
    With like intent the Argive warriors mov'd,
By Theseus led, whom virgin Pallas lov'd.
Ten thousand oxen drew the harness'd wains,
In droves collected from the neighb'ring plains;
Slow up the mountains move the heavy wheels,
The steep ascent each groaning axle feels:
In ev'ry grove the temper'd axes sound;
The thick trees crackle, and the caves resound.
Now to the plain the moving woods descend,
Under their weight a thousand axles bend:

And round the camp, and round the Theban
    walls,
Heaps roll'd on heaps, the mingled forest falls.
Of this the Spartan chief, his native bands,
With speed to rear a lofty pile, commands;
Which for Hegialus, with grateful mind,
Adrastus' valiant son, the chief design'd ;
Who to his aid, when ev'ry warrior fled,
Repair'd, and for his rescue greatly bled :
His native bands the hero thus addrest,
While sighs incessant labor'd from his breast,
  " The chief of Argos, warriors ! first demands
Funereal honours from our grateful hands ;
For him this lofty structure is decreed,
And ev'ry rite in order shall succeed :
His dear remains in my pavilion rest;
Nor can Adrastus at the rites assist ;
Who to despairs and phrenzy has resign'd,
By age and grief subdu'd, his generous mind.:
The other princes of the army wait
The obsequies to grace, with mournful state."
  He said ; and to his tent the warriors led,
Where stood already deck'd the fun'ral bed :
With Syrian oil bedew'd, the corse they found
Fresh from the bath, and breathing fragrance
For Menelaus, with divided care,   [round :
Each rite domestic hast'ned to prepare.
Twelve princes to the pile the corse sustain'd ;
The head on Agamemnon's hand reclin'd :
With mournful pomp the slow procession mov'd ;
For all the hero honour'd and approv'd.
  First on the top the fun'ral bed they place ;
And next, the sad solemnity to grace,
And gratify the manes of the slain,   [plain.
The blood of steeds and bullocks drench'd the
The four fair steeds which drew the rapid car,
That bore the hero through the ranks of war,
Their lofty necks the pointed falchion tore,
With force impell'd, and drew a stream of gore :
Three groaning fell ; but, fiercer from the stroke,
The silver reins the fourth with fury broke,
And fled around the field : his snowy chest,
Was dash'd with streaming blood, and lofty crest.
In circles still he wheel'd ! at ev'ry round,
Still nearer to the pile himself he found ;
Till drain'd of life, by blood alone supply'd,
Just where he felt the blow, he sunk, and dy'd.
  By awe divine subdu'd, the warriors stand ;
And silent wonder fixes ev'ry band :
Till thus Atrides : " Sure th' immortal gods,
The glorious synod of the blest abodes,
Approve our rites ; the good their favour share,
In death and life the objects of their care."
  Atrides thus : and, further to augment
The mournful pomp, the martial goddess went
Through all the camp, in Merion's form ex-
    press'd;
And thus aloud the public ear address'd :
" Warriors and friends ! on yonder lofty pyre,
Hegialus expects the fun'ral fire :
For such high merit, public tears should flow ;
And Greece assembled pour a flood of woe.
Now let us all his obsequies attend ;
And, with the mournful rites, our sorrows blend."
Proclaiming thus aloud the goddess went ;
The army heard ; and each forsakes his tent ;
Her voice had touch'd their hearts ; they mov'd
    along,
Nations and tribes, an undistinguish'd throng.

Around the pile the wid'ning circle grows ;
As, spreading, in some vale, a deluge flows,
By mountain torrents fed, which stretches wide,
And floats the level lands on ev'ry side.
Distinguish'd in the midst the princes stand,
With sceptres grac'd, the ensigns of command.
Atrides, with superior grief oppress'd,
Thus to the sire of gods his pray'r address'd,
  " Dread sov'reign, hear ! whose unresisted
    sway
The fates of men and mortal things obey :
From thee the virtue of the hero springs ;
Thine is the glory and the pow'r of kings.
If e'er by thee, and virgin Pallas, led,
To noble deeds this gen'rous youth was bred :
If love to men, or piety, possest,
With highest purpose, his undaunted breast ;
Command the winds in bolder gusts to rise,
And bear the flames, I kindle, to the skies."
  The hero thus ; and with the fun'ral brand
The structure touch'd ; ascending from his hand,
Spreads the quick blaze : the ruler of the sky
Commands ; at once the willing tempests fly :
Rushing in streams invisible, they came,
Drove the light smoke, and rais'd the sheeted
    flame.
The favour of the gods the nations own,
And, with their joint applause, the hero crown.
From morn till noon the roaring flames aspire,
And fat of victims added feeds the fire ;
Then fall their lofty spires, and, sinking low,
O'er the pale ashes tremulously glow.
With wine, the smoke, and burning embers lay'd;
The bones they glean'd, and to a tomb convey'd
Under an oak, which, near the public way,
Invites the swains to shun the noontide ray.
  Now twenty warriors of Atrides' train,
Loaded with treasure, brought a harness'd wain ;
Vases and tripods in bright order plac'd,
And splendid arms with fair devices grac'd :
These for the games the Spartan chief decreed,
The fun'ral games in honour of the dead.
Amid the princes first a polish'd yew,
Unbent upon the ground the hero threw,
Of work divine ; which Cynthius claim'd before,
And Chiron next upon the mountains bore ;
His sire the third receiv'd it : now it lies,
For him who farthest shoots, the destin'd prize.
  " Heroes, approach !" Atrides thus aloud,
" Stand forth, distinguish'd from the circling
    crowd,
Ye who, by skill or manly force, may claim
Your rivals to surpass and merit fame.
This bow, worth twenty oxen, is decreed
For him who farthest sends the winged reed :
This bowl, worth eight, shall be reserv'd to
    grace
The man whose merit holds the second place."
He spoke. His words the bold Ajaces fir'd ;
Crete's valiant monarch to the prize aspir'd ;
Teucer for shooting fam'd ; and Merion strong,
Whose force enormous drag'd a bull along :
Prompt to contend, and rais'd with hope, they
    stood,
Laertes' son the last forsook the crowd.
Tydides too had join'd them, and obtain'd
Whatever could by skill or force be gain'd ;
But in his tent, indulging sad despair,
He sat, subdu'd by heart-consuming care.

Straight in a casque the equal lots were thrown;
Each hero with his name had mark'd his own:
These, mix'd with care, the chief of Sparta drew;
Idmenëus's the first he knew:
Teucer, with hope inspir'd, the second claim'd:
The third Oileus, much for shooting fam'd;
Next claim'd the wearer of the seven-fold shield,
Though young in arms, distinguish'd in the field;
Ulysses! thine came next; and, last of all,
Bold Merion with a smile receiv'd his ball.

Press'd with incumbent force, the Cretan lord
Strain'd the stiff bow, and bent it to the cord;
Then, from the full-stor'd quiver, chose with art,
Wing'd for th' aerial flight, a pointed dart.
Theseus commands the warriors to divide,
Who crowded thick and press'd on ev'ry side;
Straight they retire; as, at the word of Jove,
From day's bright face the scatt'ring clouds remove;
And through the host appear'd a spacious way,
Where woods and fields in distant prospect lay.
With force immense, the Cretan monarch drew,
Stretch'd the tough cord, and strain'd the circling yew;
From his firm gripe the starting arrow sprung,
The stiff bow crack'd, the twanging cordage sung.
Up the light air the hissing weapon flies,
Pierces the winds, and streams along the skies:
Far to the distant plain it swiftly drove;
The host stood wond'ring as it rush'd above:
Descending there upon a mount it stood;
A depth of soil receiv'd the trembling wood.
Applause from all, tumultuous shouts declare,
By echoes wafted through the trembling air.
Such joy the hero feels, as praise inspires,
And to the circle of the kings retires.

The valiant Teucer next receiv'd the bow,
And to Apollo thus address'd a vow:
" Hear me, dread king! whose unresisted sway
Controls the Sun, and rules the course of day;
Great patron of the bow! this shaft impel;
And hecatombs my gratitude shall tell;
Soon as to Salamis our martial pow'rs
Return, victorious, from the Theban tow'rs."
He said, and bid the winged arrow fly;
It pierc'd the winds, and swept a length of sky;
In compass, like the colour'd arch, which shines
Exalted, as the setting Sun declines;
From north to south it marks th' ethereal space,
And woods and mountains fill its wide embrace:
Beyond the Cretan shaft, it reach'd the plain;
As far before, as now a shepherd swain,
Hurl'd from a sling, the sounding flint can throw,
From his young charge, to drive the deadly crow.

Oilean Ajax next the weapon claim'd,
For skill above the rest, and practice fam'd;
But Phœbus, chief and patron of the art,
Retarded in its flight the winged dart:
For, nor by pray'rs, nor holy vows, he strove,
Of grateful sacrifice, the god to move.
Downwards he turn'd it, where a cedar fair
Had shot its spiring top aloft in air;
Caught in a bough the quiv'ring weapon stood,
Nor forc'd a passage through the closing wood.

Ajax the next appear'd upon the plain,
With strength untaught, and emulous in vain;
With sinewy arms the solid yew he bends;
Near and more near approach the doubling ends:

The arrow sprung; but erring took its way,
Far to the left, where oozy marshes lay,
And groves of reeds; where slow Ismenus strays,
And winds, through thickets green, his wat'ry maze.
Abash'd the youth, with painful steps, retires;
And now Ulysses to the prize aspires.

In silence thus the prudent warrior pray'd,
And, in his heart, address'd the martial maid:
"Great queen of arts! on thee my hopes depend;
With favour, to thy suppliant's suit, attend!
By thee my infant arms were taught to throw
The dart with certain aim, and bend the bow:
Oft on my little hands, immortal maid!
To guide the shaft, thy mighty hands were laid:
Now, goddess, aid me, while I strive for fame;
Wing the swift weapon, and assert my claim."
He pray'd: the goddess, at his suit, descends;
And present from th' Olympian courts attends.
With force divine his manly limbs she strung.
The bow he strain'd: the starting arrow sung;
As when the sire of gods, with wrathful hand,
Drives the swift lightning and the forked brand,
To waste the labours of the careful swains,
Consume the mountain flocks, or scorch the plains;
With sudden glare appears the fiery ray;
No thought can trace it through th' ethereal way:
So swift thy winged shaft, Ulysses! flew,
Nor could the following eye its speed pursue.
The flight of Teucer's arrow far surpast,
Upon a rural hearth it pitch'd at last,
To Ceres built; where swains, in early spring,
With joy were wont their annual gifts to bring;
When first to view, above the furrow'd plain,
With pleasing verdure, rose the springing grain,
Through all the host applauding shouts resound;
The hills repeat them, and the woods around.

The bended bow bold Merion next assumes,
A shaft selects, and smooths its purple plumes:
He plac'd it on the string, and bending low,
With all his force collected, strain'd the bow.
Up the light air the starting arrow sprung;
The tough bow crack'd; the twanging cordage sung.
Beyond the reach of sight the weapon drove,
And tow'r'd amid th' ethereal space above:
But as it rose, a heron cross'd before,
From inland marshes steering to the shore;
Under the wing it reach'd her with a wound;
Screaming she wheel'd, then tumbled to the ground.

And thus the youth: "Illustrious chiefs! I claim
If not the prize, at least superior fame:
Ungovern'd strength alone the arrow sends;
To hit the mark, the shooter's art commends.
In mirthful mood the hero thus address'd;
And all their favour and applause express'd.

" Ulysses! take the bow," Atrides cries,
" The silver bowl, brave Teucer! be thy prize.
In ev'ry art, my friends! you all excel;
And each deserves a prize for shooting well:
For though the first rewards the victors claim,
Glory ye merit all, and lasting fame."
He said; and pond'ring in his grateful mind,
Distinguish'd honours for the dead design'd.

"Warriors of Greece, and valiant aids from far,
Our firm associates in the works of war!
Here from a rock the Theban stream descends,
And to a lake its silver current sends;

Whose surface smooth, unruffled by the breeze,
The hills inverted show and downward trees:
Ye daring youths! whose manly limbs divide
The mounting surge, and brave the rushing tide;
All ye, whom hopes of victory inspire,
Stand forth distinguish'd ; let the crowd retire.
This costly armour shall the youth obtain,
Who comes victorious from the wat'ry plain ;
That island compass'd, where the poplar grows,
And in the lake its wav'ring image shows,
Who measuring back the liquid space, before
His rivals, shall regain the flow'ry shore.
This golden bowl is fix'd the second prize,
Esteem'd alike for fashion and for size."

The hero thus: with thirst of glory fir'd,
Crete's valiant monarch to the prize aspir'd;
With Sparta's younger chief; Ulysses came;
And brave Clearchus emulous of fame,
A wealthy warrior from the Samian shore.
In cattle rich, and heaps of precious ore:
Distinguish'd in the midst the heroes stood,
Eager to plunge into the shining flood,
His brother's ardour purpos'd to restrain,
Atrides strove, and counsel'd thus, in vain :
" Desist, my brother ! shun th' unequal strife;
For late you stood upon the verge of life:
No mortal man his vigour can retain,
When flowing wounds have empty'd ev'ry vein.
If now you perish in the wat'ry way,
Grief upon grief shall cloud this mournful day :
Desist, respect my counsel, and be wise ;
Some other Spartan in your place will rise."
To change his brother's purpose thus he try'd ;
But nothing mov'd, the gen'rous youth reply'd :
" Brother ! in vain you urge me to forbear,
From love and fond affection prompt to fear;
For firm, as e'er before, my limbs remain,
To dash the fluid waves, or scour the plain."
He said, and went before. The heroes move
To the dark covert of a neighb'ring grove ;
Which to the bank its shady walks extends,
Where mixing with the lake a riv'let ends.
Prompt to contend, their purple robes they loose,
Their figur'd vests and gold embroider'd shoes ;
And through the grove descending to the strand,
Along the flow'ry bank in order stand.
As when, in some fair temple's sacred shrine,
A statue stands, express'd by skill divine,
Apollo's or the herald-pow'rs, who brings
Jove's mighty mandates on his airy wings ;
The form majestic awes the bending crowd :
In port and stature such, the heroes stood.
Starting at once, with equal strokes, they
    sweep
The smooth expanse, and shoot into the deep;
The Cretan chief, exerting all his force,
His rivals far surpass'd, and led the course;
Behind Atrides, emulous of fame ;
Clearchus next ; and last Ulysses came.
And now they measur'd back the wat'ry space,
And saw from far the limits of the race.
Ulysses then, with thirst of glory fir'd,
The Samian left, and to the prize aspir'd ;
Who, emulous, and dreading to be last,
With equal speed, the Spartan hero pass'd.
Alarm'd, the Cretan monarch strove, with pain,
His doubtful hopes of conquest to maintain ;
Exerting ev'ry nerve, his limbs he ply'd,
And wishing, from afar, the shore descry'd:

For near and nearer still Ulysses prest ;
The waves he felt rebounding from his breast.
With equal zeal for victory they strove ;
When, gliding sudden from the roofs of Jove,
Pallas approach'd ; behind a cloud conceal'd,
Ulysses only saw her form reveal'd.
Majestic by the hero's side she stood ;
Her shining sandals press'd the trembling flood.
She whisper'd soft, as when the western breeze
Stirs the thick reeds, or shakes the rustling trees:
" Still shall thy soul, with endless thirst of fame,
Aspire to victory, in ev'ry game.
The honours, which from bones and sinews rise;
Are lightly valu'd by the good and wise :
To envy still they rouse the human kind ;
And oft, than courted, better far decliu'd.
To brave Idomenëus yield the race,
Contented to obtain the second place."
The goddess thus : while, stretching to the land,
With joy the Cretan chief approach'd the strand;
Ulysses next arriv'd ; and, spent with toil,
The weary Samian grasp'd the welcome soil.

But far behind the Spartan warrior lay,
Fatigu'd, and fainting, in the wat'ry way.
Thrice struggling, from the lake, his head he
    rear'd ;
And thrice, imploring aid, his voice was heard.
The Cretan monarch hastes the youth to save,
And Ithacus again divides the wave ;
With force renew'd their manly limbs they ply ;
And from their breasts the whit'ning billows fly.
Full in the midst a rocky isle divides
The liquid space, and parts the silver tides ;
Once cultivated, now with thickets green
O'erspread, two hillocks and a vale between.
Here dwelt an aged swain ; his cottage stood
Under the cliffs, encompass'd by a wood.
From poverty secure, he heard afar,
In peace profound, the tumults of the war.
Mending a net before his rural gate,
From other toils repos'd, the peasant sat ;
When first the voice of Menelaus came,
By ev'ning breezes wafted from the s ream.
Hast'ning, his skiff he loos'd, and spread the sail;
Some present god supply'd a prosp'rous gale:
For, as the Spartan chief, with toil subdu'd,
Hopeless of life, was sinking in the flood,
The swain approach'd, and in his barge receiv'd
Him safe from danger imminent retriev'd.

Upon a willow's trunk Thersites sat,
Contempt in laughter fated to create,
Where, bending from a hollow bank, it hung,
And rooted to the mould'ring surface clung ;
He saw Atrides safe ! and thus aloud,
With leer malign, address'd the list'ning crowd.
" Here on the flow'ry turf a hearth shall stand ;
A hecatomb the fav'ring gods demand,
Who sav'd Atrides in this dire debate,
And snatch'd the hero from the jaws of fate :
Without his aid we all might quit the field ;
Ulysses, Ajax, and Tydides, yield :
His mighty arm alone the host defends,
But dire disaster still the chief attends :
Last Suu beheld him vanquish'd on the plain ;
Then warriors sav'd him, now a shepherd swain.
Defend him still from persecuting fate !
Protect the hero who protects the state ;
In martial conflicts watch with prudent fear,
And, when he swims, let help be always near !"

He said; and, scorn and laughter to excite,
His features foul he writh'd, with envious spite,
Smiling contempt; and pleas'd his ranc'rous
    heart
With aiming thus oblique a venom'd dart.
But joy'd not long; for soon the faithless wood,
Strain'd from the root, resign'd him to the flood.
Plunging and sputt'ring as his arms he spread,
A load of soil came thund'ring on his head,
Slipt from the bank: along the winding shore,
With laughter loud he heard the echoes roar,
When from the lake his crooked form he rear'd:
With horrour pale, with bloating clay besmear'd:
Then clamb'ring by the trunk, in sad dismay,
Which half immers'd with all its branches lay,
Confounded, to the tents he sculk'd along,
Amid the shouts and insults of the throng.

Now cloth'd in public view the heroes stand,
With sceptres grac'd, the ensigns of command.
The Cretan monarch, as his prize, assumes
The polish'd helmet, crown'd with waving plumes,
The silver mail, the buckler's weighty round,
Th' embroider'd belt, with golden buckles bound.
The second prize Laertes' son receiv'd,
With less applause from multitudes deceiv'd;
The first he could have purchas'd; but declin'd
And yielded, to the martial maid resign'd.

Thus they. The Thebans, near the eastern
Around their pyres in silent sorrow wait: [gate:
Hopeless and sad they mourn'd their heroes slain,
The best and bravest on their native plain.
The king himself, in deeper sorrow, mourn'd;
With rage and mingled grief his bosom burn'd.
Like the grim lion, when his offspring slain
He sees, and round him drawn the hunter's train;
Couch'd in the shade with fell intent he lies,
And glares upon the foes with burning eyes:
Such Creon seem'd: hot indignation drain'd
Grief's wat'ry sources, and their flow restrain'd.
Upon a turret o'er the gate he stood,
And saw the Argives, like a shady wood,
Extended wide; and dreading fraud design'd,
Still to the plain his watchful eyes confin'd,
Suspicious from his hatred, and the pow'r
Of restless passions, which his heart devour:
And, when at ev'n's approach the host retir'd,
And from the labours of the day respir'd;
Within the walls he drew his martial pow'rs,
And kept with strictest watch the gates and tow'rs.

Soon as the night possess'd th' ethereal plain,
And o'er the nations stretch'd her silent reign,
The guards were plac'd, and to the gentle sway
Of sleep subdu'd, the weary warriors lay.
Tydides only wak'd, by anxious care
Distracted, still he mourn'd his absent fair,
Deeming her lost; his slighted counsel mov'd
Lasting resentment, and the truce approv'd:
Contending passions shook his mighty frame;
As warring winds impel the ocean's stream,
When south and east with mingled rage contend,
And in a tempest on the deep descend:
Now, stretch'd upon the couch, supine he lay;
Then, rising anxious, wish'd the morning ray.
Impatient thus, at last, his turbid mind,
By various counsels variously inclin'd,
The chief address'd: " Or shall I now recall
Th' Etolian warriors from the Theban wall;
Obey the warning by a goddess giv'n,
Nor slight her counsel dictated from Heav'n?

Or shall I try, by one deciding blow,
The war at once to end, and crush the foe?
This pleases most; nor shall the voice of fame
The daring deed, in after ages, blame.
No truce I swore, but shun'd it, and remov'd,
Alone dissenting while the rest approv'd.
Soon as the morn, with early light reveal'd,
Has call'd the Theban warriors to the field;
Against the town I'll lead my martial pow'rs,
And fire with flaming brands her hated tow'rs:
The bane of Greece, whence dire debate arose
To bid the peaceful nations first be foes;
Where Tydeus fell, and many heroes more,
Banish'd untimely to the Stygian shore.
The public voice of Greece for vengeance calls;
And shall applaud the stroke by which she falls."
He purpos'd: but the gods, who honour right,
Deny'd to treason what is due to might.

When from the east appear'd the morning fair,
The Theban warriors to the woods repair,
Fearless, unarm'd; with many a harness'd wain,
The woody heights were crowded and the plain.
Tydides saw; and, issuing from his tent,
In arms compleat, to call his warriors, went.
Their leader's martial voice the soldiers heard
Each in his tent, and at the call appear'd
In shining arms. Dëiphobus began,
For virtue fam'd, a venerable man.
Him Tydeus lov'd; and in his faithful hand
Had plac'd the sceptre of supreme command,
To rule the state; when, from his native tow'rs,
To Thebes the hero led his martial pow'rs;
His son, an infant, to his care resign'd,
With sage advice to form his tender mind.
The hero thus: " Illustrious chief! declare
What you intend, and whither point the war.
The truce commenc'd, you cannot, and be just,
The Thebans now assault, who freely trust
To public faith engag'd: unarm'd they go
Far through the woods and plains, nor fear a
    foe."

His leader's purpose thus the warrior try'd;
And, inly vex'd, Tydides thus reply'd:
" Father! thy words from ignorance proceed;
The truce I swore not, nor approv'd the deed.
The rest are bound, and therefore must remain
Ling'ring inactive on this hostile plain:
The works of war abandon'd, let them shed
Their unavailing sorrows o'er the dead:
Or aim the dart, or hurl the disk in air;
Some paltry presents shall the victors share.
Warriors we came, in nobler strife to dare;
To fight and conquer in the lists of war;
To conquer Thebes: and Jove himself ordains,
With wreaths of triumph, to reward our pains.
Wide to receive us stand the Theban gates;
A spacious entry, open'd by the fates,
To take destruction in; their turrets stand
Defenceless, and expect the flaming brand.
Now let us snatch th' occasion while we may,
Years waste in vain and perish by delay,
That, Thebes o'erthrown, our tedious toils may
    cease,
And we behold our native walls in peace."

Tydides thus: the ancient warrior burns
With indignation just, and thus returns:
" O son! unworthy of th' illustrious line
From which you spring: your sire's reproach
    and mine!

Did I e'er teach you, justice to disclaim ;
And steal, by treachery, dishonest fame ?
The truce subsists with all the rest ; are we
Alone excepted, unengag'd and free ?
Why, warriors ! do not then these hostile tow'rs,
Against us, send at once their martial pow'rs ?
And are we safe, but that the treaty stands,
And from unequal force protects our bands ?
In this our foes confide ; the dead they burn,
And mix with tears their ashes in the urn.
Their tow'rs defenceless, and their gates unbarr'd,
Shall we with wrongs their confidence reward ?
No ; though each warrior of this num'rous
　　　　band
Should yield to execute what you command;
Yet would not I, obedient to thy will,
Blot my long labours with a deed so ill.
Whatever hard or dang'rous you propose,
Though old and weak, I shun not, nor oppose:
But what the gods command us to forbear,
The prudent will avoid, the bravest fear."
He said ; and to the ground his buckler flung;
On the hard soil the brazen orbit rung:
The rest, approving, dropt upon the field
His pond'rous jav'lin, each, and shining shield.
The warlike son of Tydeus straight resign'd,
To dire disorder, all his mighty mind,
And sudden wrath ; as when the troubled air,
From kindled lightning, shines with fiery glare:
With fury so inflam'd, the hero burn'd,
And frowning to Dëiphobus return'd :　　[aim,
" I know thee, wretch ! and mark thy constant
To teach the host their leader thus to blame.
Long have I borne your pride ; your rev'rend
　　　　age,　　　　　　　　　[rage:
A guardian's name, suppress'd my kindling
But to protect your insolence, no more
Shall these avail, and skreen it as before."
　　He said ; and more his fury to provoke,
Replying thus, the aged warrior spoke :
" Vain youth ! unmov'd thy angry threats I
　　hear ;
When tyrants threaten, slaves alone should fear :
To me is ev'ry servile part unknown,
To glory in a smile, or fear a frown,
Your mighty sire I knew by council rul'd ;
His fiercest transports sober reason cool'd.
But wild, and lawless, like the stormy wind,
The sport of passion, impotent, and blind,
The desp'rate paths of folly you pursue,
And scorn instruction with a lofty brow :
Yet know, proud prince ! my purpose I retain,
And see thy threat'ning eye-balls roll in vain :
Never, obsequious to thy mad command,
Against the foe I'll lift a hostile hand ;
Till, righteously fulfill'd, the truce expire
Which Heav'n has witness'd and the sacred fire."
　　He said ; and, by his sharp reproaches stung,
With sudden hand, his lance the hero flung:
Too sure the aim ; his faithful friend it found,
And open'd in his side a deadly wound :
Stagg'ring he fell ; and, on the verge of death,
In words like these resign'd his parting breath :
" O Diomed, my son ! for thee I fear :
Sure Heav'n is angry, and its vengeance near:
For whom the gods distinguish by their hate,
Themselves are made the ministers of fate;
Far from their side, the destin'd victims drive
Their friends intent to succour and retrieve,

Ere yet their vengeance falls, the pow'rs invoke,
While uninflicted hangs the fatal stroke :
And rule the transports of your wrath, lest fear
Make sound advice a stranger to your ear."
Speaking he dy'd ; his gen'rous spirit fled
To mix with heroes in th' Elysian shade.
　　Amaz'd, at first, th' Etolian warriors stood ;
No voice, no action, through the wand'ring
　　crow'd ;
Silent they stood, like rows of forest trees,
When Jove's dread thunder quells the summer
But soon on ev'ry side a tumult rose,　[breeze:
Loud as the ocean when a tempest blows ;
Disorder wild the mingling ranks confounds,
The voice of sorrow mix'd with angry sounds.
On ev'ry side against the chief appears
A brazen bulwark rais'd of shields, and spears,
Fast closing round.　But from his thigh he drew
His shining blade, and on the phalanx flew ;
With gesture fierce the threat'ning steel he
　　wav'd ;
But check'd its fury, and the people sav'd :
As the good shepherd spares his tender flock,
And lightens, when he strikes, the falling crook.
The crowd dividing shunn'd the hero's ire ;
As from a lion's rage the swains retire,
When dreadful o'er the mangled prey he stands,
By brandish'd darts unaw'd and flaming brands.
　　And now the flame of sudden rage supprest,
Remorse and sorrow stung the hero's breast.
Distracted through the scatt'ring crowd he went,
And sought the dark recesses of his tent ;
He enter'd : but the menial servants, bred
To wait his coming, straight with horrour fled.
Against the ground he dash'd his bloody dart ;
And utter'd thus the swellings of his heart :
" Why fly my warriors ? why the menial train,
Who joy'd before to meet me from the plain,
Why shun they now their lord's approach ; nor
　　bring,
To wash my bloody hands, the cleansing spring ?
Too well, alas ! my fatal rage they know,
To them more dreadful now than to the foe ;
No enemy, alas ! this spear has stain'd ;
With hostile gore in glorious battle drain'd :
My guardian's blood it shows, whose hoary hairs
Still watch'd my welfare with a father's cares.
Thou pow'r supreme ! whose unresisted sway
The fates of men and mortal things obey !
If wise and good, why did thy hand impart
So fierce an impulse to this bounding heart ?
By fury rul'd and impotent of mind,
No awe restrains me, and no tie can bind :
Hence, by the madness of my rage o'erthrown,
My father's friend lies murder'd, and my own."
He said ; and, yielding to his fierce despair,
With both his hands he rent his rooted hair ;
And where his locks in shining ringlets grew,
A load of ashes from the hearth he threw,
Rolling in dust : but now around the slain
His warriors stood assembled on the plain ;
For total insurrection ripe they stood ;
Their angry murmurs rose to tumult loud.
　　Ulysses soon the dire disorder heard ;
And present to explore the cause appear'd :
The hero came, and, 'midst the warriors found,
Dëiphobus extended on the ground.
A flood of sorrow started to his eyes,
But soon he check'd each symptom of surprise,

With prudent care; while pressing round the chief
Each strove to speak the universal grief:
Their mingled spears in wild disorder shook;
Like the sharp reeds along some winding brook,
When through the leafless woods the north wind
Parent of ice and thick descending snows:
Now fell revenge had bath'd in streams of blood,
And pow'r in vain her desp'rate course withstood:
But Ithacus, well skill'd in ev'ry art
To fix, or change each purpose of the heart,
Their stern decrees by soft persuasion broke;
And answ'ring, thus with prudent purpose spoke:
" Warriors ! your gen'rous rage approve I
    must;
Dire was the deed; the purpos'd vengeance just;
But, when the kings in full assembly sit,
To them the crime, and punishment commit:
For rash procedure wrongs the fairest cause;
And private justice still insults the laws.
Now to your tents your shields and lances bear;
Theseus expects us, and the hour is near:
The altars flame; the priests in order stand,
With sacrifice, to hallow ev'ry band:
But to the covert of a tent convey,
Sav'd from the scorching winds and solar ray,
These dear remains; till Theseus has decreed
Distinguish'd obsequies to grace the dead."
The hero thus; and, from his shoulders, threw
The regal cloak of gold, and shining blue;
Which o'er the slain, with prudent care, he
    spread,
His ghastly features, from the crowd, to shade.
Thrice to his eyes a flood of sorrow came;
Thrice on the brink he check'd the gushing
    stream,
In act to flow; his rising sighs supprest;
Patient of grief, he lock'd it in his breast.

THE

## EPIGONIAD.

### BOOK VI.

To sad despair th' Etolian chief resign'd,
And dire remorse, which stung his tortur'd mind,
From early dawn, in dust extended lay,
By all abandon'd till the setting ray.
'Twas then Cassandra came; and, at the door,
Thrice call'd her lord: he started from the floor:
In sullen majesty his chair of state,
Full in the midst opposed to the gate,
The hero press'd: the anxious maid drew near,
By love excited, and restrained by fear:
Trembling before the chief she stood; and held
A bowl of wine with temp'ring mixtures quell'd;
The fragrant juice which fam'd Thesprotia yields,
The vintage of her cliffs, and sunny fields.
And thus: " Dread lord ! reject not with disdain
A present offer'd by a humble swain.
This bowl receive, of gentle force to charm
Distress, and of its rigour grief disarm.
How vain to grieve for ever for the past?
No hour recalls the actions of the last:
Nor groans, nor sighs, nor streams of sorrow shed,
From their long slumber can awake the dead.

When death's stern pow'r his iron sceptre lays
On the cold lips, the vital spirit strays
To worlds unknown: and can the dead perceive
The tears of friends or lovers when they grieve?"
  To sooth his passion, thus the virgin try'd;
With wonder, thus th' Etolian chief reply'd :
" Say who you are, who thus approach my seat,
Unaw'd by good Dëiphobus's fate ?
When all avoid my presence, nor appear,
By indignation banish'd, or by fear.      [bind
What is thy name ? what deed of mine could
To friendship such unchang'd thy constant mind;
Still to survive the horrour of a crime,
Whose colour blots the registers of time ?"
  The hero thus.   Cassandra thus replies :
" Iphicles is my name; my country lies
Where Antirrihum's rocky shores divide,
Extended in the deep, th' Ionian tide.
There dwells my sire possest of ample store,
In flocks and herds and gold's refulgent ore.
Oeneus his name; his vessels on the main,
From rich Hesperia waft him yearly gain,
And that fam'd land, whose promontories run
Far to the west, beneath the setting Sun;
Where ev'ry cliff with veins of silver gleams,
And sands of gold lie glitt'ring in the streams.
In Hymen's sacred ties two sons he bred,
Me, and my valiant brother Lycomed.
The youngest I, was charg'd his flocks to keep;
My brother rul'd his galleys on the deep.
Once as he left Iberia's wealthy shore,
With Bœtic fleeces fraught and precious ore;
Phœnician pirates waited on the strand,
Where high Pachynus stretches from the land;
In that fam'd isle where Ætna lifts his spires,
With smoke obscure, and blows his sulph'rous
    fires.
Behind the cliffs conceal'd, the treach'rous band
Waited the Greeks descending on the strand :
My brother there with twenty youths they slew;
Their sudden arrows from an ambush flew.
Dire was the deed; and still my sorrows stream,
Whene'er that argument of woe I name,
And grief prevails; but, in your presence, most;
You still recall the brother whom I lost:
For such he was in lineaments of face,
In martial stature, and majestic grace;
Though less in all; in form inferior far;
And still, though valiant, less in works of war.
Hence, deeply rooted in my constant heart,
You challenge, as your own, a brother's part:
And I alone, of all the host, remain
To share your grief and suffer in your pain."
  Thus by an artful tale, the virgin strove
To shun discov'ry, and conceal her love.
Yet still her looks, her gestures, all express'd
The maid; her love in blushes stood confess'd,
Tydides saw; and quickly, to his thought,
Each circumstance the fair Cassandra brought.
Silent he sat; and fix'd in deep surprise,
Her flushing features mark'd and downcast eyes.
He thus reply'd : " The native truth reveal;
And, what I ask you, hope not to conceal.
Or shall I credit what you now have said;
Oeneus your sire, your brother Lycomed ?
Or art thou she, whose beauty first did move,
Within my peaceful breast, the rage of love ?"
  With look and voice severe, the hero spoke.
Aw'd and abash'd, the conscious virgin shook;

She dropt the silver goblet on the ground ;
The fragrant liquor drench'd the pavement
　　round,
And thus Tydides with a frown address'd :
" Thy art is useless, and the truth confess'd ;
Nor can that fair disguise of martial arms
And male attire, conceal thy fatal charms.
Those eyes I see, whose soft enchantment stole
My peace, and stirr'd a tempest in my soul :
By their mild sight, in innocence array'd,
To guilty madness was my heart betray'd.
Dëiphobus is dead ; his mournful ghost,
Lamenting, wanders on the Stygian coast ;
And blames my wrath. Oh ! that the Sun, which
　　gave
Light to thy birth, had set upon thy grave ;
And he had liv'd ! now lifeless on the plain
A corse he lies, and number'd with the slain."
　　The hero ended thus ; with melting eye,
The virgin turn'd, unable to reply.
In sorrow graceful, as the queen of love
Who mourn'd Adonis in the Syrian grove,
Confounded and abash'd, she left the tent,
And thro' the host in silent anguish went,
Far to the left ; where, in a lonely wood,
To Ceres built, a rural temple stood ;
By swains frequented once, but now the place
Unsightly shrubs o'erspread and weeds disgrace.
Thither Cassandra went ; and at the shrine,
With suppliant voice address'd the power divine :
" Hear me, dread genius of this sacred grove !
Let my complaints thy sov'reign pity move.
To seek the friendly shelter of thy dome,
With heart unstain'd, and guiltless hands, I come :
Love is my crime ; and, in thy rural seat,
From infamy I seek a safe retreat.
By blame unmerited, and cold neglect,
Banish'd I come ; receive me and protect !"
She pray'd, and ent'ring, 'gainst a pillar, staid
Her lance ; and on the floor her armour laid.
Then falling prostrate pour'd a flood of tears,
With present ills oppress'd and future fears.
　　'Twas then the herald of the queen of love,
Zelotypé, descended in the grove,
By Venus sent ; but still her counsels fail'd ;
And Pallas with superior sway prevail'd :
The phantom enter'd, and assum'd a form,
Pale as the Moon appearing thro' a storm ;
In Amyclea's shape disguis'd she came ;
The same her aspect, and her voice the same.
Cassandra saw ; a sudden horrour froze
Her veins ; erect her parted locks arose,
Stirr'd from the root : impatient thus the maid,
With trembling lips, in falt'ring accents, said :
" My lov'd, my honour'd parent ! have my groans,
From death's deep slumber, rous'd thy sacred
　　bones :
I hop'd that nothing could your peace molest ;
Nor mortal cares disturb eternal rest ;
That safe for ever on th' Elysian shore,
You heard of human misery no more."
　　Cassandra thus ; and thus the Paphian maid :
" Your gen'rous love, my child, is ill repaid ;
Your griefs I feel, and bear a parent's part ;
Tho' blood no more returns to warm my heart ;
And that, which first your mortal being bred,
To dust lies mould'ring in its earthy bed.
To Calydon, my child, with speed return ;
Your father grieves ; your gay companions mourn ;

He deems you lost, and desp'rate of his state,
By grief subdu'd invokes his ling'ring fate :
Incessant tears bedew his wrinkled face,
And ashes foul his hoary locks disgrace.
Return, return ! nor let misjudging pride,
With further errours, strive the past to hide.
Return, once more to bless his aged eyes,
Or, by your guilty stay a parent dies."
　　She ended thus. Her arms Cassandra spread
To fold, in close embrace, the parting shade ;
In vain ; for, starting from her grasp, it flew,
And, gliding thro' the shady walks, withdrew.
The virgin now awaits the rising morn,
With purpose fix'd impatient to return :
And when, thro' broken clouds, a glimm'ring ray
Of early dawn foretold approaching day ;
The spear she grasp'd, and on her temples plac'd
The golden casque, with various plumage grac'd ;
Tydides' gift ; when in the ranks of fight
The brave Clytander sunk beneath his might.
The gods she call'd ; and, bending to the ground,
Their aid invok'd with reverence profound.
Then left the dome ; and where Ismenus strays,
Winding thro' thickest woods his wat'ry maze,
Her way pursu'd : a hostile band drew near ;
Their tread she heard, and saw their armour
　　clear ;
Chief of the Theban youth ; the herds they drove,
And flocks collected from the hills above.
For thus the Paphian goddess had betray'd,
To hands of cruel foes, the guiltless maid.
　　By sudden terrour check'd, at first she stood :
Then turn'd, and sought the covert of the wood ;
Nor so escap'd : her glitt'ring armour shone,
The starry helmet and the lofty cone,
Full to the glowing east ; its golden rays
Her winding flight betray'd thro' all its maze.
The Thebans saw ; and, rushing 'midst the shade
With shouts of triumph, seiz'd the trembling
　　maid.
Amaz'd and pale, before the hostile band,
She stood ; and dropt the jav'lin from her hand.
" O spare my life !" she cry'd, " nor wealth, nor
　　fame
To purchase in the works of war, I came.
No hate to you I bear, or Creon's sway,
Whose sov'reign will the sons of Thebes obey :
Me hapless friendship hither led, to share,
With Diomed, the dangers of the war.
I now return and quit the martial strife,
My sire to succour on the verge of life ;
Who crush'd beneath a load of sorrow bends,
And to the grave, with painful steps, descends.
But if the plea of pity you reject,
The stronger ties of equity respect :
A truce we swore ; Jove witnesses the deed ;
On him who breaks it, vengeance will succeed."
　　Thus as the virgin spoke, Phericles ey'd
The arms she wore ; and sternly thus reply'd :
" Ill-fated wretch ! that panoply to wear ;
The same my brother once in fight did bear ;
Whom fierce Tydides, with superior might,
O'erthrew and vanquish'd in the ranks of fight.
If with his foe my brother's spoils you shar'd,
A mark of love, or merited reward ;
Prepare to yield them and resign thy breath ;
To vengeance due : Clytander claims thy death."
　　Frowning he spoke, and drew his shining blade ;
Beneath the lifted steel, th' unhappy maid
Confounded stoop'd : Menœtius caught the stroke
On his broad shield ; and interposing spoke :

" Brave youth! respect my counsel, and suspend
The sudden vengeance which you now intend.
The chiefs of Thebes, the rulers of the state,
In full assembly, at the Cadmean gate,
A monument for great Leophron rear;
His name, achievements, and descent to bear.
Thither let this devoted youth be led,
An off'ring grateful to the hero's shade:
Nor shall Clytander less the deed approve;
Or friendly zeal applaud, and feel our love;
When fame shall tell, in Pluto's gloomy reign,
How stern Tydides mourns this warriour slain."
Thus ignorantly they; nor knew the peace
Of happy patriots, when their labors cease;
That fell revenge and life-consuming hate
Find no admittance, to molest their state.

And now they led the captive cross the plain;
Scarce could her trembling knees their load sustain;
Thrice had her falt'ring tongue her sex reveal'd,
But conscious shame oppos'd it and conceal'd.
Their monarch at the Cadmean gate they found,
In mournful state, with all his peers around.
Oblations to Leophron's mighty shade,
In honey, milk, and fragrant wines they paid.
And thus Lycaon's son address'd the king:
" A grateful off'ring to your rites we bring.
This youth, the friend of Diomed, we found
Clad in the armour which Clytander own'd;
My brother's spoils, by Diomed possest,
When his keen jav'lin pierc'd the hero's breast.
Soon had my rage the hostile deed repaid,
With vengeance grateful to his kindred shade;
But public griefs the first atonements claim,
And heroes of a more distinguish'd name.
Leophron, once his country's pride and boast;
Andremon too, the bulwark of the host,
His blood demands; for when their souls shall
    know
The sweet revenge, in Pluto's shades below,
Pleas'd with our zeal, will each illustrious ghost,
With lighter footsteps, press th' Elysian coast."

He spoke; the princes all at once incline;
The rest, with shouts, applaud the dire design.
An altar soon of flow'ry turf they raise:
On ev'ry side the sacred torches blaze:
The bowls, in shining order, plac'd around;
The fatal knife was whetted for the wound.
Decreed to perish, stood the helpless fair;
Like some soft fawn, when, in the hunter's snare
Involv'd, she sees him from his seat arise, [cries:
His brandish'd truncheon dreads, and hears his
Silent she stands, to barb'rous force resign'd,
In anguish soft, dissolv'd her tender mind.
The priests in order ev'ry rite prepar'd;
Her neck and bosom, for the blow, they bar'd;
The helmet loos'd, the buckled mail unbound,
Whose shining circles fenc'd her neck around.
Down sunk the fair disguise; and full to sight
The virgin stood, with charms divinely bright.
The comely ringlets of her flowing hair,
Such as the wood-nymphs wear, and Naiades fair
Hung loose; her middle by a zone embrac'd,
Which fix'd the floating garment round her waist.
Venus herself divine effulgence shed
O'er all her stature, and her lovely head;
Such as in spring the colour'd blossoms show,
When on their op'ning leaves the zephyrs blow:
Amazement seiz'd the chiefs; and all around

With murmurs mix'd the wond'ring crowds resound.
Most vote to spare: the angry monarch cries:
" Ye ministers, proceed; the captive dies.
Shall any here, by weak compassion mov'd,
A captive spare by stern Tydides lov'd ? [hand
The scourge of Thebes, whose wide-destroying
Has thinn'd our armies in their native land,
And slain my son: by all the gods I swear,
Whose names, to cite in vain, the nations fear,
That none, he loves, shall ever 'scape my rage:
The vulgar plea I scorn, of sex, or age,
Ev'n she, who now appears with ev'ry grace
Adorn'd, each charm of stature and of face:
Ev'n though from Venus she could claim the prize,
Her life to vengeance forfeited, she dies."
Sternly the monarch ended. All were still,
With mute submission to the sov'reign will:
Lycaon's valiant son except; alone
His gen'rous ardour thus oppos'd the throne:
" Dread sov'reign! listen with a patient ear,
And what I now shall offer, deign to hear.
When first by force we seiz'd this captive maid,
The truce was vi'lated, our faith betray'd;
And justice, which, in war and peace, prevails
Alike, and weighs their deeds with equal scales,
Her freedom claims, with presents to atone
For what our rage perfidiously has done:
Let us not, now, to further wrongs proceed;
But fear the curse for perjury decreed."
Phericles thus: and, with a stern regard,
His indignation thus the king declar'd:
" Vain giddy youth! forbear with factious breath,
To rouse my justice to pronounce thy death:
In opposition, first of all you move,
While others hear in silence, and approve.
Your bold presumption check, and learn to dread
My vengeance thunder'd on your wretched head."
Frowning he ended thus: his threats defy'd,
With gen'rous heat Phericles thus reply'd:
" Princes! attend, and trust my words sincere;
The king I honour, and his will revere,
When truth gives sanction to his just commands,
No common right in opposition stands:
Yet gen'rous minds a principle retain,
Which promises and threats attempt in vain,
Which claims dominion, by the gods imprest,
The love of justice in the human breast:
By this inspir'd, against superior might,
I rise undaunted in the cause of right.
And now, by all th' avenging gods, I swear,
Whose names, to cite in vain, the nations fear;
That no bold warrior of the Theban bands,
This maid shall violate with hostile hands; [wield,
While these my arms have force the lance to
And lift in her defence this pond'rous shield,
Not ev'n the king himself, whose sov'reign sway
The martial sons of sacred Thebes obey."
He said; and, by his bold example fir'd,
Twelve warriors rose, with equal zeal inspir'd.
With shining steel the altar they surround,
The fire now flaming, and the victim crown'd.
On ev'ry side in wild disorder move
The thick compacted crouds: as when a grove,
Rock'd by a sudden whirlwind, bends and strains
From right to left, along the woodland plains:
Fell discord soon had rag'd, in civil blood,
With wide destruction not to be withstood;
For from his seat the angry monarch sprung,

And lifted, for the blow, the sceptre hung:
But 'midst the tumult Clytophon appear'd,
Approv'd for wisdom, and with rev'rence heard.
Straight, by the robe, the furious chief he seiz'd,
And thus, with sage advice, his wrath appeas'd:
" Hear, mighty prince! respect the words of age,
And calm the wasteful tempest of thy rage;
The public welfare to revenge prefer,
For nations suffer when their sov'reigns err.
It ill becomes us now, when hostile pow'rs
With strictest siege invest our stait'ned tow'rs!
It ill becomes us thus, with civil arms,
To wound the state, and aggravate our harms.
Hear, all ye princes! what to me appears
A prudent counsel, worthy of your ears:
Let us inquire, if in our hands we hold
A life esteem'd by Diomed the bold:
If, in his breast, those tender passions reign,
Which charms like these must kindle and main-
Our mandates freely to his tent we send, [tain;
For to our will his haughty soul must bend:
Nor dares he, while the Theban walls enclose
A pledge so dear, invade us or oppose;
But must submit, whenever we require,
Or with his pow'rs to aid us, or retire."
He said; the monarch painfully supprest
His burning rage, and lock'd it in his breast.
He thus reply'd: " Thy prudent words inspire
Pacific councils, and subdue mine ire:
But if in peace I rul'd the Theban state,
Nor hostile armies thunder'd at my gate;
They had not dar'd, with insolence and spite,
My purpose to oppose and scorn my might."
He said, and to his seat again retir'd;
While sudden transport ev'ry breast inspir'd;
As swains rejoice, when, from the troubled skies,
By breezes swept, a gather'd tempest flies;
With wish'd return the Sun exerts his beams
To cheer the woods and gild the shining streams.
   Mean while the son of Tydeus, through the
              plain,
With wishing eyes, Cassandra sought in vain;
At ev'ry leader of the bands inquir'd;
Then, sad and hopeless, to his tent retir'd.
'Twas then his grief the bounds of silence broke,
And thus in secret to himself he spoke:
"Me sure, of all men's sons, the gods have curst
With their chief plagues, the greatest and the
              worst;
Doom'd to disasters, from my earliest hour;
Not wise to shun nor patient to endure.
From me the source, unnumber'd ills proceed
To all my friends; Dëiphobus is dead!
His soul excluded seeks the nether skies,
And wrong'd Cassandra from my presence flies.
Me surely, at my birth, the gods design'd
Their rod of wrath, to scourge the human kind;
For slaughter form'd, with brutal fury brave,
Prompt to destroy, but impotent to save.
How could my madness blame thee, gen'rous
              maid!
And, with my crime, thy innocence upbraid?
Dëiphobus is fall'n! but not by thee;
Thy only fault, alas! was love to me;
For this, in plated steel thy limbs were dress'd,
A weighty shield thy tender arm oppress'd;
For this, thou didst to hostile fields repair,
And court such objects as distract the fair;

Patient above thy sex! an ill reward,
Blame and unjust reproach, was all you shar'd.
By my unkindness banish'd, now you roam,
And seek, through paths unknown, your distant
              home:
To mountain wolves expos'd, a helpless prey,
And men unjust more terrible than they.
Save her, ye gods! and let me stand the aim
Of Jove's all-dreaded bolt, and scorching flame."
   Thus plain'd the hero till the setting ray
Withdrew, and ev'ning shades expell'd the day;
Then in his tent, before his lofty seat,
Appear'd a herald from the Theban state;
The hero's knees, with trembling hands, he
              press'd,
And with his message thus the chief address'd:
" Hear, mighty prince! the tidings which I bring,
From Thebes assembled, and the Theban king:
An armed warrior of your native train,
At early dawn, was seiz'd upon the plain.
What others did, forgive, if I relate;
Creon commands me and the Theban state.
A fairer youth, in martial arms, ne'er came
To court bright honour in the fields of fame.
A casque of polish'd steel his temples press'd,
The golden cone with various plumage dress'd;
A silver mail embrac'd his body round,
And greaves of brass his slender ancles bound:
To Thebes well known the panoply he wore,
The same, which once, renown'd Clytander
              bore.
Our warriors dragg'd him to the Cadmean gate,
Where Creon, with the rulers of the state,
Assembled sat; the trembling captive stood,
With arms surrounded, and th' insulting crowd:
' O spare my life!' he cry'd, ' nor wealth, nor
To purchase in the works of war, I came. [fame
No hate to you I bear, or Creon's sway,
Whose sov'reign will the sons of Thebes obey.
Me luckless friendship hither led, to share,
With Diomed, the dangers of the war.
I now return, and quit the martial strife,
My sire to succour on the verge of life;
Whose feeble age the present aid demands,
And kind assistance of my filial hands.'
His words inclin'd the wisest and the best,
And some their gen'rous sympathy exprest:
But others, nothing mov'd, his guiltless head
With threats demanded, to avenge the dead:
And thus the king: ' My countrymen, attend!
In this, let all your loud contention end:
If Diomed, to save this valu'd life,
The field abandons and the martial strife;
The captive safe, with presents, I'll restore,
Of brass, and steel, and gold's refulgent ore:
But if these terms the haughty chief shall slight,
And for the Argives still exert his might;
Before our hero's tombs, this youth shall bleed,
To please the living, and avenge the dead.'
His sentence all approv'd; and to your ear,
As public herald, I the message bear;
And must your answer crave, without delay;
Creon and Thebes already blame my stay."
   Thus as he spoke, contending passions strove,
With force oppos'd, the hero's soul to move;
As shifting winds impel the ocean's tide,
And sway the reeling waves from side to side:
Rage dictated revenge; but tender fear,
From love and pity, warn'd him to forbear:

Till, like a lion, fiercer from his pain,
These words broke forth in wrath and high dis-
    dain :
" Go, tell your tyrant, that he tempts a soul
Which presents cannot win, nor threats control :
Not form'd, like his, to mock at ev'ry tie ;
With perjury to sport, and Heav'n defy.
A common league the Argive warriors swore,
And seal'd the sacred tie with wine and gore ;
My faith was plighted then, and ne'er shall fail,
Nor Creon's arts, to change me, aught avail.
But tell him loud, that all the host may hear,
And Thebes through all her warriors learn to
    fear,
If any, from himself, or by command,
The captive violates with hostile hand ;
That all shall quickly rue the guilty deed,
When, to requite it, multitudes shall bleed."
Sternly the hero ended, and resign'd,
To fierce disorder, all his mighty mind.
Already in his thoughts, with vengeful hands,
He dealt destruction 'midst the Theban bands,
In fancy saw the tott'ring turrets fall,
And led his warriors o'er the level'd wall.
Rous'd with the thought, from his high seat he
    sprung ;
And grasp'd the sword, which on a column hung ;
The shining blade he balanc'd thrice in air ;
His lances next he view'd, and armour fair.
When, hanging 'midst the costly panoply,
A scarf embroider'd met the hero's eye,
Which fair Cassandra's skilful hands had wrought,
A present for her lord, in secret brought,
That day, when first he led his martial train
In arms, to combat on the Theban plain. [pose,
As some strong charm, which magic sounds com-
Suspends a downward torrent as it flows ;
Checks in the precipice its headlong course,
And calls it trembling upwards to its source :
Such seem'd the robe, which, to the hero's eyes,
Made the fair artist in her charms to rise.
His rage, suspended in its full career,
To love resigns, to grief and tender fear.
Glad would he now his former words revoke,
And change the purpose which in wrath he spoke ;
From hostile hands his captive fair to gain,
From fate to save her, or the servile chain :
But pride, and shame, the fond design supprest ;
Silent he stood, and lock'd it in his breast.
Yet had the wary Theban well divin'd,
By symptoms sure, each motion of his mind :
With joy he saw the heat of rage suppress'd ;
And thus again his artful words address'd. [ear,
" Illustrious prince ! with patience bend thine
And what I now shall offer, deign to hear.
Of all the griefs, distressful mortals prove,
The woes of friendship most my pity move.
You much I pity, and the youth regret,
Whom you too rigidly resign to fate ;
Expos'd alone, no hope of comfort near,
The scorn and cruelty of foes to bear.
O that my timely counsel might avail,
For love, and sympathy, to turn the scale !
That Thebes releas'd from thy devouring sword,
The captive honor'd, and with gifts restor'd,
We yet might hope for peace, and you again
Enjoy the blessings of your native reign."
Insinuating thus, the herald try'd
His aim to compass ; and the chief reply'd :

" In vain you strive to sway my constant mind ;
I'll not depart while Theseus stays behind :
Me nothing e'er, to change my faith, shall move,
By men attested, and the gods above :
But since your lawless tyrant has detain'd
A valu'd hostage, treacherously gain'd ;
And dire injustice only will restore
When force compels, or proffer'd gifts implore :
A truce I grant, till the revolving Sun,
Twice ten full circuits of his journey run,
From the red ocean, points the morning ray,
And on the steps of darkness pours the day :
Till then, from fight and council I abstain,
Nor lead my pow'rs to combat on the plain :
For this, your monarch to my tent shall send
The captive, and from injuries defend.
This proffer is my last ; in vain will prove
All your attempts my fixed mind to move :
If Thebes accepts it, let a sign declare,
A flaming torch, display'd aloft in air,
From that high tow'r, whose airy top is known
By trav'lers from afar, and marks the town ;
The fane of Jove : but if they shall reject
The terms I send, nor equity respect,
They soon shall feel the fury of mine ire,
In wasteful havoc, and the rage of fire."
The hero thus ; and round his shoulders flung
A shaggy cloak, with vulgar trappings hung ;
And on his head a leathern helmet plac'd,
A boar's rough front with grisly terrours grac'd ;
A spear he next assum'd, and pond'rous shield,
And led the Theban, issuing to the field.
Amid surrounding guards they pass'd unseen,
For night had stretch'd her friendly shade be-
    tween ;     [knew ;
Till nearer, through the gloom, the gate they
The herald enter'd, and the chief withdrew ;
But turning oft to Thebes his eager eyes,
The signal, on the tow'r, at last he spies ;
A flaming torch, upon the top, expos'd,
Its ray at once his troubled mind compos'd :
Such joy he felt, as when a watch-tow'r's light,
Seen through the gloom of some tempestuous
Glads the wet mariner, a star to guide   [night,
His lab'ring vessel, through the stormy tide.

---

## THE
## EPIGONIAD.
### BOOK II.

Now silent night the middle space possest,
Of Heav'n, or journey'd downwards to the west ;
But Creon, still with thirst of vengeance fir'd,
Repose declin'd, nor from his toils respir'd ;
But held his peers in council to debate
Plans for revenge, suggested by his hate.
Before the king Dienices appear'd ;
To speak his tidings sad, the hero fear'd ;
Return'd from Oeta ; thither sent to call
Alcides to protect his native wall.
  And Creon thus : " Dienices ! explain
Your sorrow ; are our hopes of aid in vain ?
Does Hercules neglect his native soil ;
While strangers reap the harvest of his toil ?
We from your silence cannot hope success ;
But further ills your falling tears confess :

Cleon my son is dead; his fate you mourn;
I must not hope to see his safe return.
Sure, if he liv'd, he had not come the last;
But found his father with a filial haste.
His fate, at once, declare, you need not fear,
With any tale of grief, to wound mine ear,
Proof to misfortune: for the man, who knows
The whole variety of human woes,
Can stand unmov'd though loads of sorrow press;
Practis'd to bear, familiar with distress."
   The monarch question'd thus: and thus the
       youth:
" Too well thy boding fear has found the truth.
Cleon is dead; the hero's ashes lie
Where Pelion's lofty head ascends the sky.
For as, on Oeta's top, he vainly strove
To win the arrows of the son of Jove;
Compelling Philoctetes to resign,
The friend of Hercules, his arms divine;
The insult to repel, an arrow flew,
And from his heart the vital current drew:
Prostrate he sunk; and welling from the wound,
A flood of gore impurpled all the ground."
  Thus spoke Dienices. The king supprest
His big distress, and lock'd it in his breast:
Sighing he thus reply'd: " The cause declare,
Which holds the great Alcides from the war;
And why another now, the bow commands
And arrows, sacred from his mighty hands.
Nor fear my valiant son's untimely fate,
With all its weight of sorrow, to relate:
All I can bear. Against my naked head,
I see the vengeance of the gods decreed;
With hostile arms beset my tott'ring reign;
The people wasted, and my children slain.
Attempts prove fruitless; ev'ry hope deceives;
Success in prospect, disappointment gives:
With swift approach, I see destruction come;
But with a mind unmov'd, I'll meet my doom;
Nor stain this war-worn visage with a tear,
Since all that Heav'n has purpos'd, I can bear."
The monarch thus his rising grief suppress'd;
And thus the peers Dienices address'd:
  " Princes of Thebes! and thou, whose sov'-
    reign hand
Sways the dread sceptre of supreme command!
To what I offer, lend an equal ear; [hear.
The truth I'll speak, and judge me when you
If Cleon, by my fault, no more returns,
For whom, her second hope, his country mourns;
No doom I deprecate, no torture fly,
Which justice can denounce, or rage supply:
But if my innocence appears, I claim
Your censure to escape, and public blame.
  "From Marathon by night our course we steer'd,
And pass'd Gerastus when the day appear'd;
Andros we saw, with promontories steep,
Ascend; and Delos level with the deep.
A circuit wide; for where Euripus roars
Between Euboea and the Theban shores,
The Argives had dispos'd their naval train;
And prudence taught to shun the hostile plain.
Four days we sail'd; the fifth our voyage ends,
Where Oeta, sloping to the sea, descends.
The vales I search'd, and woody heights above,
Guided by fame, to find the son of Jove;
With Cleon only: for we charg'd the band
To stay, and guard our vessel on the strand.
In vain we search'd; but when the lamp of day
Approach'd the ocean with its setting ray,

A cave appear'd, which from a mountain steep,
Through a low valley, look'd into the deep.
Thither we turn'd our weary steps, and found
The cavern hung with savage spoils around;
The wolf's grey fur, the wild boar's shaggy hide,
The lion's mane, the panther's speckled pride:
These signs we mark'd; and knew the rocky seat,
Some solitary hunter's wild retreat.
Farther invited by a glimm'ring ray,
Which through the darkness shed uncertain day,
In the recesses of the cave we found
The club of Hercules; and wrapt around,
Which, seen before, we knew, the lion's spoils,
The mantle which he wore in all his toils.
Amaz'd we stood; in silence each his mind
To fear and hope alternately resign'd:
With joy we hop'd to find the hero near;
The club and mantle found, dispos'd to fear.
His force invincible in fight we knew,
Which nought of mortal kind could e'er subdue,
But fear'd Apollo's might, or his who heaves
The solid earth, and rules the stormy waves.
  "Pond'ring we stood; when on the roof above,
The tread of feet descending thro' the grove
Which crown'd the hollow cliff, amaz'd we heard;
And straight before the cave a youth appear'd.
A bleeding buck across his shoulders flung,
Ty'd with a rope of twisted rushes, hung.
He dropt his burden in the gate, and plac'd,
Against the pillar'd cliff, his bow unbrac'd.
'Twas then our footsteps in the cave he heard,
And thro' the gloom our shining arms appear'd.
His bow he bent; and backwards from the rock
Retir'd, and, of our purpose quest'ning, spoke;
' Say who you are, who seek this wild abode,
Thro' desert paths, by mortals rarely trod?
If just, and with a fair intent you come,
Friendship expect, and safety in my dome:
But if for violence, your danger learn,
And trust my admonition when I warn:
Certain as fate, where'er this arrow flies,
The hapless wretch, who meets its fury, dies:
No buckler to resist its point avails, [fails;
The hammer'd cuirass yields, the breast-plate
And where it once has drawn the purple gore,
No charm can cure, no med'cine health restore.'
  " With threats he question'd thus; and Cleon
    said:
' We come to call Alcides to our aid;
By us the senators of Thebes entreat
The hero, to protect his native state:
For hostile arms invest the Theban tow'rs:
Famine within, without the sword, devours.
If you have learn'd where Hercules remains,
In mountain caves, or hamlets on the plains,
Our way direct; for, led by gen'ral fame,
To find him in these desert wilds we came.'
  " He spoke; and Philoctetes thus again:
' May Jove, for Thebes, some other aid ordain;
For Hercules no more exerts his might,
Against oppressive force, for injur'd right:
Retir'd, among the gods, he sits serene,
And views, beneath him far, this mortal scene:
But enter now this grotto, and partake
What I can offer, for the hero's sake:
With you from sacred Thebes he claim'd his
    birth,
For god-like virtue fam'd thro' all the Earth;
Thebes therefore and her people still shall be,
Like fair Trachines and her sons to me.

Enter; for now the double twilight fails;
And o'er the silent Earth the night prevails:
From the moist valleys noxious fogs arise,
To wrap the rocky heights, and shade the skies.'
  " The cave we enter'd, and his bounty shar'd;
A rural banquet by himself prepar'd.
But soon the rage of thirst and hunger stay'd,
My mind still doubtful, to the youth I said:
' Must hapless Thebes, despairing and undone,
Want the assistance of her bravest son?
The hero's fate explain, nor grudge mine ear
The sad assurance of our loss to hear.'
I question'd thus. The youth, with horror pale,
Attempted to recite an awful tale;
Above the fabled woes which bards rehearse,
When sad Melpomene inspires the verse.
  " ' The wife of Jove' (Pœonides reply'd)
' All arts in vain to crush the hero try'd;
For brighter from her hate his virtue burn'd;
And disappointed still, the goddess mourn'd.
His ruin to effect at last she strove
By jealousy, the rage of injur'd love.
The bane to Deianira's breast convey'd,
Who, as a rival, fear'd th' Oechalian maid.
The goddess knew, that, jealous of her lord,
A robe she kept with latent poisons stor'd;
The centaur's gift, bequeath'd her, to reclaim
The hero's love, and light his dying flame;
If e'er devoted to a stranger's charms,
He stray'd inconstant, from her widow'd arms;
But giv'n with treacherous intent to prove
The death of nature, not the life of love.
Mad from her jealousy, the charm she try'd;
His love to change, the deadly robe apply'd:
And guiltless of the present which he bore,
Lychas convey'd it to Cenœnum's shore:
Where to the pow'rs immortal, for their aid,
A grateful hecatomb the hero paid:
When favor'd from above, his arm o'erthrew
The proud Eurytus, and his warriors slew.
The venom'd robe the hero took, nor fear'd
A gift by conjugal respects endear'd:
And straight resign'd the lion's shaggy spoils,
The mantle which he wore in all his toils.
No sign of harm the fatal present show'd;
Till rous'd by heat its secret venom glow'd:
Straight on the flesh it seiz'd, like stiffest glue,
And scorching deep, to ev'ry member grew.
Then tearing with his hands th' infernal snare,
His skin he rent, and laid the muscles bare;
While streams of blood, descending from the wound,
Mix'd with the gore of victims on the ground.
The guiltless Lychas, in his furious mood,
He seiz'd, as trembling by his side he stood:
Him, by the slender ancle snatch'd, he swung;
And 'gainst a rocky promontory flung:
Which, from the dire event, his name retains;
Thro' his white locks impurpled rush'd the brains.
Aw'd by the deed, his desp'rate rage to shun,
Our bold companions from his presence run:
I too, conceal'd behind a rock, remain'd;
My love and sympathy by fear restrain'd:
For furious 'midst the sacred fires he grew;
The victims scatter'd, and the hearths o'erthrew.
Then sinking prostrate, where a tide of gore
From oxen slain had blacken'd all the shore,

His form divine he roll'd in dust and blood;
His groans the hills re-echo'd and the flood.
Then rising furious, to the ocean's streams
He rush'd, in hope to quench his raging flames;
But burning still the unextinguish'd pain,
The shore he left, and stretch'd into the main.
A galley anchor'd near the beach we found;
Her curled canvass to the breeze unbound;
And trac'd his desp'rate course, till far before
We saw him land on Oeta's desert shore.
Towards the skies his furious hands he rear'd,
And thus, across the deep, his voice we heard:
  " ' Sov'reign of Heav'n and Earth! whose boundless sway
The fates of men and mortal things obey,
If e'er delighted from the courts above,
In human form you sought Alcmene's love;
If fame's unchanging voice to all the Earth,
With truth, proclaims you author of my birth;
Whence, from a course of spotless glory run,
Successful toils and wreaths of triumph won,
Am I thus wretched? better that before
Some monster fierce had drank my streaming gore;
Or crush'd by Cacus, foe to gods and men,
My batter'd brains had strew'd his rocky den;
Than, from my glorious toils and triumphs past,
To fall subdu'd by female arts, at last.
O cool my boiling blood, ye winds, that blow
From mountains loaded with eternal snow,
And crack the icy cliffs: in vain! in vain!
Your rigour cannot quench my raging pain!
For round this heart the furies wave their brands,
And wring my entrails with their burning hands.
Now bending from the skies, O wife of Jove!
Enjoy the vengeance of thy injur'd love:
For fate, by me, the thund'rer's guilt atones;
And, punish'd in her son, Alcmene groans:
The object of your hate shall soon expire;
Fix'd on my shoulders preys a net of fire;
Whom nor the toils nor dangers could subdue,
By false Eurystheus dictated from you;
Nor tyrants lawless, nor the monstrous brood
Which haunts the desert or infests the flood,
Nor Greece, nor all the barb'rous climes that lie
Where Phœbus ever points his golden eye;
A woman hath o'erthrown!—ye gods! I yield
To female arts, unconquer'd in the field.
My arms—alas! are these the same that bow'd
Anteus, and his giant force subdu'd?
That dragg'd Nemea's monster from his den?
And slew the dragon in his native fen?
Alas! alas! their mighty muscles fail,
While pains infernal ev'ry nerve assail:
Alas, alas! I feel in streams of woe
These eyes dissolve, before untaught to flow.
Awake my virtue, oft in dangers try'd,
Patient in toils, in deaths unterrify'd,
Rouse to my aid; nor let my labours past,
With fame achiev'd, be blotted by the last:
Firm and unmov'd, the present shock endure;
Once triumph, and for ever rest secure.'
  " ' The hero thus; and grasp'd a pointed rock
With both his arms, which straight in pieces broke,
Crush'd in his agony: then on his breast
Descending prostrate, further plaint supprest.
And now the clouds, in dusky volumes spread,
Had darken'd all the mountains with their shade:

The winds withhold their breath; the billows
The sky's dark image on the deep imprest. [rest;
A bay for shelter, op'ning in the strand,
We saw, and steer'd our vessel to the land.
Then mounting on the rocky beach above,
Thro' the thick gloom, descry'd the son of Jove.
His head, declin'd between his hands, he lean'd;
His elbows on his bended knees sustain'd.
Above him still a hov'ring vapour flew,
Which, from his boiling veins, the garment drew.
Thro' the thick woof we saw the fumes aspire;
Like smoke of victims from the sacred fire,
Compassion's keenest touch my bosom thrill'd;
My eyes, a flood of melting sorrow fill'd:
Doubtful I stood; and pond'ring in my mind,
By fear, and pity, variously inclin'd,
Whether to shun the hero, or essay,
With friendly words, his torment to allay:
When bursting from above with hideous glare,
A flood of lightning kindled all the air.
From Oeta's top it rush'd in sudden streams;
The ocean redden'd at its fiery beams.
Then, bellowing deep, the thunder's awful sound
Shook the firm mountains and the shores around.
Far to the east it roll'd, a length of sky;
We heard Euboea's rattling cliffs reply.
As at his master's voice a swain appears,
When wak'd from sleep his early call he hears,
The hero rose; and to the mountain turn'd,
Whose cloud-involved top with lightning burn'd,
And thus his sire address'd; 'With patient
Thy call I hear, obedient and resign'd; [mind
Faithful and true the oracle! which spoke,
In high Dodona, from the sacred oak;
That twenty years of painful labours past,
On Oeta's top I should repose at last:
Before, involved, the meaning lay conceal'd;
But now I find it in my fate reveal'd.
Thy sov'reign will I blame not, which denies,
With length of days, to crown my victories:
Though still with danger and distress engag'd,
For injur'd right eternal war I wag'd;
A life of pain, in barb'rous climates, led,
The Heav'ns my canopy, a rock my bed:
More joy I've felt than delicacy knows,
Or all the pride of regal pomp bestows.
Dread sire! thy will I honour and revere,
And own thy love with gratitude sincere,
Which watch'd me in my toils, that none could
To raise a trophy from my glory lost:     [boast
And though at last, by female arts, o'ercome,
And unsuspected fraud, I find my doom;
There to have fail'd, my honour ne'er can shake,
Where vice is only strong and virtue weak.'
    " 'He said; and turning to the cloudy height,
The seat of thunder, wrapt in sable night,
Firm and undaunted trod the steep ascent;
An earthquake rock'd the mountain as he went.
Back from the shaking shores retir'd the flood;
In horror lost, my bold companions stood,
To speech or motion: but the present pow'r
Of love inspir'd me, in that awful hour;
With trembling steps, I trac'd the son of Jove;
And saw him darkly on the steep above, [noise
Through the thick gloom. The thunder's awful
Ceas'd; and I call'd him thus with feeble voice:
'O son of mighty Jove! thy friend await,
Who comes to comfort thee, or share thy fate.
In ev'ry danger and distress before,
His part your faithful Philoctetes bore.

O let me still attend you, and receive
The comfort which a present friend can give,
Who come obsequious for your last commands,
And tenders to your need his willing hands.'
    " 'My voice he heard; and from the mountain's
Saw me ascending on the steep below.     [brow
To favour my approach his steps he stay'd;
And pleas'd, amidst his anguish, smiling said:
'Approach, my Philoctetes! Oft I've known
Your friendly zeal in former labours shown:
The present, more than all, your love proclaims,
Which braves the thund'rer's bolts and volley'd
                                flames;
With daring step, the rocking earthquake treads,
While the firm mountains shake their trembling
                                heads.
As my last gift, these arrows, with the bow,
Accept; the greatest which I can bestow;
My glory all my wealth; of pow'r to raise
Your name to honour and immortal praise;
If for wrong'd innocence your shafts shall fly,
As Jove by signs directs them from the sky.'
    " 'Straight from his mighty shoulders, as he
                                spoke,
He loos'd and lodg'd them in a cavern'd rock;
To lie untouch'd, till future care had drain'd
Their poison from the venom'd robe retain'd.
And thus again: 'The only aid I need,
For all my favours past, the only meed,
Is, that, with vengeful hand, you fix a dart
In cruel Deianira's faithless heart:
Her treach'rous messenger already dead,
Let her, the author of his crime, succeed.
This awful scene forsake without delay;
In vain to mingle with my fate you stay:
No kind assistance can my state retrieve,
Nor any friend attend me, and survive.'
    " 'The hero thus his tender care exprest,
And spread his arms to clasp me to his breast;
But soon withdrew them, lest his tainted veins
Infection had convey'd and mortal pains:
Silent I stood in streams of sorrow drown'd,
Till from my heart these words a passage found:
'O bid me not forsake thee, nor impose
What wretched Philoctetes must refuse.
By him I swear, whose presence now proclaim
The thunder's awful voice and forked flame,
Beneath whose steps the trembling desert quakes,
And Earth affrighted to her centre shakes;
I never will forsake thee, but remain
While struggling life these ruin'd limbs retain:
No form of fate shall drive me from thy side,
Nor, death with all its terrours e'er divide;
Though the same stroke our mortal lives should
                                end,
One flash consume us, and our ashes blend.'
    " 'I spoke; and to the cloudy steep we turn'd;
Along its brow the kindled forest burn'd.
The savage brood, descending to the plains,
The scatter'd flocks and dread distracted swains,
Rush'd from the shaking cliffs: we saw them
                                come,
In wild disorder mingled, through the gloom.
And now appear'd the desert's lofty head,
A narrow rock with forest thinly spread.
His mighty hands display'd aloft in air,
To Jove the hero thus address'd a pray'r
'Hear me, dread pow'r! whose nod controls
                                the skies,
At whose command the winged lightning flies:

Almighty sire! if yet you deign to own
Alcmena's wretched offspring as your son ;
Some comfort in my agony impart,
And bid thy forked thunder rend this heart :
Round my devoted head it idly plays ;
And aids the fire, which wastes me, with its rays :
By heat inflam'd, this robe exerts its pow'r,
My scorched limbs to shrivel and devour ;
Upon my shoulders, like a dragon, clings,
And fixes in my flesh a thousand stings.
Great sire ! in pity to my suit a tend,
And with a sudden stroke my being end.'

"'As thus the hero pray'd, the lightning ceas'd,
And thicker darkness all the hill embrac'd.
He saw his suit deny'd : in fierce despair,
The rooted pines he tore, and cedars fair ;
And from the crannies of the rifted rocks,
Twisted with force immense the stubborn oaks.
Of these upon the cliff a heap he laid,
And thus address'd me, as I stood dismay'd :
' Behold, my friend ! the ruler of the skies,
In agony invok'd, my suit denies :
But sure the oracle inspir'd from Heaven,
Which in Dodona's sacred grove was given,
The truth declar'd : that now my toils shall
And all my painful labours end in peace : [cease,
Peace, death can only bring : the raging smart,
Wrapt with my vitals, mocks each healing art.
Not all the plants that clothe the verdant field,
Not all the health a thousand mountains yield,
Which on their tops the sage physician finds,
Or digging from the veins of flint unbinds,
This fire can quench.   And therefore, to obey
My last commands, prepare without delay.
When on this pile you see my limbs compos'd,
Shrink not, but hear what must not be oppos'd ;
Approach, and, with an unrelenting hand,
Fix, in the boughs beneath, a flaming brand.
I must not longer trust this madding pain,
Lest some rash deed should all my glory stain.
Lychas I slew upon the Cœnian shore,
Who knew not, sure, the fatal gift he bore :
His guilt had taught him else to fly, nor wait,
Till from my rage he found a sudden fate.
I will not Deianira's action blame ;
Let Heav'n decide, which only knows her aim :
Whether from hate, with treacherous intent,
This fatal garment to her lord she sent ;
Or, by the cunning of a foe betray'd,
His vengeance, thus imprudently convey'd.
If this, or that, I urge not my command,
Nor claim her fate from thy avenging hand :
To lodge my lifeless bones, is all I crave,
Safe and uninjur'd in the peaceful grave.'

" ' This with a hollow voice and alter'd look,
In agony extreme, the hero spoke.
I pour'd a flood of sorrow, and withdrew,
Amid the kindled groves, to pluck a bough ;
With which the structure at the base I fir'd :
On ev'ry side the pointed flames aspir'd.
But ere involving smoke the pile enclos'd,
I saw the hero on the top repos'd ;
Serene as one who, near the fountain laid,
At noon enjoys the cool refreshing shade.
The venom'd garment hiss'd ; its touch the fires
Avoiding, slop'd oblique their pointed spires :
On ev'ry side the parted flame withdrew,
And level'd, round the burning structure flew.
At last victorious to the top they rose ;
Firm and unmov'd the hero saw them close.

His soul unfetter'd, sought the blest abodes,
By virtue rais'd to mingle with the gods.
His bones in earth, with pious hands, I laid ;
The place to publish nothing shall persuade ;
Lest tyrants now unaw'd, and men unjust,
With insults, should profane his sacred dust.
E'er since, I haunt this solitary den,
Retir'd from all the busy paths of men ;
For these wild mountains only suit my state,
And sooth, with kindred gloom, my deep regret.'

" He ended thus : amazement long suppress'd
My voice ; but Cleon answ'ring thus address'd :
' Brave youth ! you offer, to our wond'ring ears,
Events more awful than tradition bears.
Fix'd in my mind the hero's fate remains,
I see his agonies, and feel his pains.
Yet suffer, that for hapless Thebes I mourn,
Whose fairest hopes the envious fates o'erturn.
If great Alcides liv'd, her tow'rs should stand
Safe and protected by his mighty hand :
On you, brave youth ! our second hopes depend ;
To you the arms of Hercules descend.
He did not, sure, those glorious gifts bestow,
The shafts invincible, the mighty bow ;
From which the innocent protection claim,
To dye the hills with blood of savage game.
Such toils as these your glory ne'er can raise,
Nor crown your merit with immortal praise ;
And with the great Alcides place your name,
To stand distinguish'd in the rolls of fame.'

" The hero thus.   The son of Pœan said :
' Myself, my arms, I offer for your aid ;
If fav'ring from the skies, the signs of Jove
Confirm what thus I purpose and approve.
For when Alcides, with his last commands,
His bow and shafts committed to my hands ;
In all attempts he charg'd me to proceed
As Jove by signs and auguries should lead.
But these the rising Sun will best disclose ;
The season now invites to soft repose.'

" He said ; and, from the hearth a flaming bough,
To light us through the shady cavern, drew.
Far in the deep recess, a rocky bed
We found, with skins of mountain monsters spread.
There we compos'd our weary limbs, and lay,
Till darkness fled before the morning ray.
Then rose, and climb'd a promontory steep,
Whose rocky brow, impending o'er the deep,
Shoots high into the air, and lifts the eye,
In boundless stretch, to take a length of sky.
With hands extended to th' ethereal height,
The pow'r we call'd, who rules the realms of light ;
That symbols sure his purpose might explain,
Whether the youth should aid us, or refrain :
We pray'd ; and on the left along the vales,
With pinions broad display'd, an eagle sails.
As near the ground his level flight he drew,
He stoop'd, and brush'd the thickets as he flew ;
When starting from the centre of a brake,
With horrid hiss appear'd a crested snake :
Her young to guard, her venom'd fangs she rear'd ;
Above the shrubs her wavy length appear'd ;
Against his swift approaches, as he flew,
On ev'ry side her forked tongue she threw,
And armed jaws ; but wheeling from the snare
The swift assailant still escap'd in air ;
But, stooping from his pitch, at last he tore
Her purple crest, and drew a stream of gore.
She writh'd ; and, in the fierceness of her pain,
Shook the long thickets with her twisted train ;

Relax'd at last, its spires forgot to roll,
And, in a hiss, she breath'd her fiery soul :
In haste to gorge his prey, the bird of Jove
Down to the bottom of the thicket drove ;
The young defenceless from the covert drew ;
Devour'd them straight, and to the mountains
This omen seen, another worse we hear :    [flew.
The subterraneous thunder greets our ear :
The worst of all the signs which augurs know ;
A dire prognostic of impending woe.

" Amaz'd we stood, till Philoctetes broke
Our long dejected silence thus, and spoke :
' Warriors of Thebes ! the auguries dissuade
My purpose, and withhold me from your aid ;
Though pity moves me, and ambition draws,
To share your labours and assert your cause ;
In fight the arms of Hercules to show,
And from his native ramparts drive the foe.
But vain it is against the gods to strive ;
Whose counsels ruin nations or retrieve ;
Without their favour, valour nought avails,
And human prudence self-subverted fails ;
For irresistibly their pow'r presides
In all events, and good and ill divides.
Let Thebes assembled at the altars wait,
And long processions crowd each sacred gate :
With sacrifice appeas'd, and humble pray'r,
Their omens frustrated, the gods may spare.
To day, my guests, repose ; to morrow sail,
If Heav'n propitious sends a prosp'rous gale :
For, shifting to the south, the western breeze
Forbids you now to trust the faithless seas.'

" The hero thus ; in silence sad, we mourn'd ;
And to the solitary cave return'd,
Despairing of success ; our grief he shar'd,
And for relief a cheering bowl prepar'd ;
The vintage which the grape spontaneous yields,
By art untutor'd, on the woodland fields,
He sought with care, and mingled in the bowl
A plant, of pow'r to calm the troubled soul ;
Its name nepenthe ; swains, on desert ground,
Do often glean it, else but rarely found ;
This in the bowl he mix'd ; and soon we found,
In soft oblivion, all our sorrows drown'd :
We felt no more the agonies of care,
And hope, succeeding, dawn'd upon despair.
From morn we feasted, till the setting ray
Retir'd, and ev'ning shades expell'd the day ;
Then in the dark recesses of the cave,
To slumbers soft, our willing limbs we gave :
But ere the morning, from the east, appear'd,
And sooner than the early lark is heard,
Cleon awak'd, my careless slumber broke,
And bending to my ear, in whispers spoke :
' Dienices ! while slumbering thus secure,
We think not what our citizens endure. [pears
The worst the signs have threaten'd, nought ap-
With happier aspect to dispel our fears ;
Alcides lives not, and his friend in vain
To arms we call, while auguries restrain :
Returning thus, we bring the Theban state
But hopes deceiv'd, and omens of her fate :
Better success our labours shall attend,
Nor all our aims in disappointment end ;
If you approve my purpose, nor dissuade
What now I counsel for your country's aid.
Soon as the Sun displays his early beam,
The arms of great Alcides let us claim ;
Then for Bœotia's shores direct our sails ;
And force must second if persuasion fails :

Against reproach necessity shall plead ;
Censure confute, and justify the deed.'
" The hero thus, and ceas'd : with pity mov'd,
And zeal for Thebes, I rashly thus approv'd.
' You counsel well ; but prudence would advise
To work by cunning rather, and surprise,
Than force declar'd ; his venom'd shafts you know,
Which fly resistless from th' Herculean bow ;
A safe occasion now the silent hour
Of midnight yields ; when, by the gentle pow'r
Of careless slumber bound, the hero lies,
Our necessary fraud will 'scape his eyes ;
Without the aid of force shall reach its aim,
With danger less incurr'd, and less of blame.'

" I counsel'd thus ; and Cleon straight ap-
In silence from the dark recess we mov'd ; [prov'd.
Towards the hearth, with wary steps, we came,
The ashes stirr'd, and rous'd the slumb'ring flame.
On ev'ry side in vain we turn'd our eyes,
Nor, as our hopes had promis'd, found the prize :
Till to the couch, where Philoctetes lay,
The quiver led us by its silver ray ;
For in a panther's fur together ty'd,
His bow and shafts, the pillow's place supply'd :
Thither I went with careful steps and slow ;
And by degrees obtain'd th' Herculean bow :
The quiver next to disengage essay'd ;
It stuck entangled, but at last obey'd.
The prize obtain'd, we hasten to the strand,
And rouse the mariners, and straight command
The canvass to unfurl : a gentle gale
Favour'd our course, and fill'd the swelling sail :
The shores retir'd ; and when the morning ray
Ascended, from the deep, th' ethereal way ;
Upon the right Centeum's beach appear'd,
And Pelion on the left his summit rear'd.
All day we sail'd ; but when the setting light
Approach'd the ocean, from th' Olympian height,
The breeze was hush'd ; and, stretch'd across
                              the main,
Like mountains rising on the wat'ry plain,
The clouds collected on the billows stood,
And, with incumbent shade, obscur'd the flood.
Thither a current bore us ; soon we found
A night of vapour closing fast around.
Loose hung the empty sail : we ply'd our oars,
And strove to reach Eubœa's friendly shores ;
But strove in vain ; for erring from the course,
In mazes wide, the rower spent his force.
Seven days and nights we try'd some port to gain,
Where Greek or barb'rous shores exclude the
                              main ;
But knew not, whether backwards, or before,
Or on the right, or left, to seek the shore :
Till, rising on the eighth, a gentle breeze
Drove the light fog, and brush'd the curling seas.
Our canvass to its gentle pow'r we spread ;
And fix'd our oars, and follow'd as it led.
Before us soon, impending from above,
Through parting clouds, we saw a lofty grove.
Alarm'd, the sail we slacken, and explore
The deeps and shallows of the unknown shore.
Near on the right a winding creek appear'd,
Thither directed by the pole, we steer'd ;
And landed on the beach, by fate misled,
Nor knew again the port from which we fled.
The gods themselves deceiv'd us : to our eyes
New caverns open, airy cliffs arise ;
That Philoctetes might again possess
His arms, and Heav'n our injury redress.

" The unknown region purpos'd to explore,
Cleon, with me alone, forsakes the shore ;
Back to the cave we left, by angry fate
Implicitly conducted, at the gate
The injur'd youth we found ; a thick disguise
His native form conceal'd, and mock'd our eyes ;
For the black locks in waving ringlets spread,
A wreath of hoary white involv'd his head,
Beneath a load of years, he seem'd to bend,
His breast to sink, his shoulders to ascend.
He saw us straight, and, rising from his seat,
Began with sharp reproaches to repeat
Our crime ; but could not thus suspicion give ;
So strong is errour when the gods deceive !
We question'd of the country as we came,
By whom inhabited, and what its name ;
How far from Thebes: that thither we were bound;
And thus the wary youth our errour found.
Smooth'd to deceive, his accent straight he
    turn'd,
While in his breast the thirst of vengeance burn'd;
And thinking now his bow and shafts regain'd,
Reply'd with hospitable kindness feign'd :
' On Ida's sacred height, my guests ! you stand;
Here Priam rules, in peace, a happy land.
Twelve cities own him, on the Phrygian plain,
Their lord, and twelve fair islands on the main.
From hence to Thebes in seven days space you'll
If Jove propitious sends a prosp'rous gale.  [sail,
But now accept a homely meal, and deign
To share, what Heav'n affords a humble swain.'
" He said ; and brought a bowl with vintage
    fill'd,
From berries wild, and mountain grapes distill'd,
Of largest size ; and plac'd it on a rock,
Under the covert of a spreading oak ;
Around it autumn's mellow stores he laid,
Which the Sun ripens, in the woodland shade.
Our thirst and hunger thus at once allay'd,
To Cleon turning, Philoctetes said :
' The bow you wear of such unusual size,
With wonder still I view and curious eyes ; [art,
For length, for thickness, and the workman's
Surpassing all I've seen in ev'ry part.'
" Dissembling, thus inquir'd the wary youth,
And thus your valiant son declar'd the truth :
' Father ! the weapon, which you thus commend,
The force of great Alcides once did bend ; [du'd,
These shafts the same which monsters fierce sub-
And lawless men with vengeance just pursu'd.'
" The hero thus ; and Pœan's son again :
' What now I ask, refuse not to explain :
Whether the hero still exerts his might,
For innocence oppress'd: and injur'd right ?
Or yields to fate ; and with the mighty dead,
From toil reposes in the Elysian shade !
Sure, if he liv'd, he would not thus forego
His shafts invincible and mighty bow,
By which he oft immortal honour gain'd
For wrongs redress'd and lawless force re-
    strain'd.'
" The rage suppress'd, which in his bosom
    burn'd,
He question'd thus ; and Cleon thus return'd :
' What we have heard of Hercules, I'll show ;
What by report we learn'd, and what we know.
From Thebes to Oeta's wilderness we went,
With supplications, to the hero, sent
From all our princes ; that he would exert
His matchless valour on his country's part,

Against whose state united foes conspire,
And waste her wide domain with sword and fire.
There on the cliffs, which bound the neighb'ring
We found the mansion of a lonely swain ; [main,
Much like to this, but that its rocky mouth,
The cooling north respects, as this the south ;
And, in a corner of the cave conceal'd,
The club which great Alcides us'd to wield.
Wrapt in his shaggy robe, the lion's spoils,
The mantle which he wore in all his toils.
At ev'n a hunter in the cave appear'd ;
From whom the fate of Hercules we heard.
He told us that he saw the chief expire,
That he himself did light his fun'ral fire ;
And boasted, that the hero had resign'd,
To him, this bow and quiver, as his friend :
Oft seen before, these deadly shafts we know,
And tipp'd with stars of gold th' Herculean bow :
But of the hero's fate, the tale he told,
Whether 'tis true, I cannot now unfold.'
" He spoke. The youth with indignation burn'd,
Yet calm in outward semblance, thus return'd :
' I must admire the man who could resign
To you, these arms so precious and divine,
Which, to the love of such a friend, he ow'd ;
Great was the gift if willingly bestow'd :
By force they could not easily be gain'd,
And fraud, I know, your gen'rous souls disdain'd.'
" Severely smiling, thus the hero spoke ;
With conscious shame we heard, nor silence
    broke :
And thus again : ' The only boon I claim,
Which, to your host deny'd, would merit blame;
Is, that my hands that weapon may embrace,
And on the flaxen cord an arrow place ;
An honour which I covet ; though we mourn'd,
By great Alcides, once our state o'erturn'd :
When proud Laomedon the hero brav'd,
Nor paid the ransom for his daughter sav'd.'
" Dissembling thus did Philoctetes strive
His instruments of vengeance to retrieve ;
And, by the Fates deceiv'd, in evil hour,
The bow and shafts we yielded to his pow'r,
In mirthful mood, provoking him to try
Whether the weapon would his force obey ;
For weak he seem'd, like those whose nerves have
    lost,      [boast,
Through age, the vigour which in youth they
The belt around his shoulders first he flung,
And, glitt'ring by his side the quiver hung :
Compress'd with all his force the stubborn yew
He bent, and from the case an arrow drew :
And yielding to his rage in furious mood,
With aim direct against us full he stood,  [guise,
For vengeance arm'd ; and now the thick dis-
Which veil'd his form before, and mock'd our
Vanish'd in air ; our errour then appear'd; [eyes,
I saw the vengeance of the gods, and fear'd.
Before him on the ground my knees I bow'd,
And, with extended hands, for mercy su'd.
But Cleon, fierce and scorning to entreat,
His weapon drew, and rush'd upon his fate :
For as he came, the fatal arrow flew,
And from his heart the vital current drew :
Supine he fell : and, welling from the wound,
A tide of gore impurpled all the ground.
The son of Pœan stooping drew the dart,
Yet warm with slaughter, from the hero's heart ;
And turn'd it full on me : with humble pray'r,
And lifted hands, I mov'd him still to spare.

At last he yielded, from his purpose sway'd,
And answer'ring thus in milder accents, said:
' No favour, sure, you merit ; and the cause,
Of right infring'd and hospitable laws,
Would justify revenge ; but as you claim,
With Hercules, your native soil the same ;
I now shall pardon for the hero's sake,
Nor, though the gods approve it, vengeance take :
But straight avoid my presence, and unbind,
With speed, your flying canvass to the wind.
For if again to meet these eyes you come,
No pray'rs shall change, or mitigate your doom.'
" With frowning aspect thus the hero said.
His threats I fear'd, and willingly obey'd.
Straight in his purple robe the dead I bound,
Then to my shoulders rais'd him from the ground:
And from the hills descending to the bay,
Where anchor'd near the beach our galley lay,
The rest conven'd, with sorrow to relate
This anger of the gods and Cleon's fate:
The hero's fate his bold companions mourn'd,
And ev'ry breast with keen resentment burn'd.
They in their heady transports straight decreed,
His fall with vengeance to requite or bleed.
I fear'd the angry gods ; and gave command,
With sail and oar, to fly the fatal strand ;
Enrag'd and sad, the mariners obey'd,
Unfurl'd the canvass, and the anchor weigh'd.
Our course, behind, the western breezes sped,
And from the coast with heavy hearts we fled.
All day they favour'd, but with ev'ning ceas'd ;
And straight a tempest, from the stormy east,
In opposition loud, began to blow,
And rear in ridges high the deep below.
Against its boist'rous sway in vain we strove ;
Obliquely to the Thracian coast we drove :
Where Pelion lifts his head aloft in air,
With pointed cliffs and precipices bare ;
Thither our course we steer'd, and on the strand
Descending, fix'd our cable to the land.
There twenty days we stay'd, and wish'd, in vain,
A favourable breeze, to cross the main ;
For with unceasing rage the tempest rav'd,
And o'er the rocky beach the ocean heav'd.
At last with care the hero's limbs we burn'd,
And, water'd with our tears, his bones inurn'd.
There, where a promontory's height divides,
Extended in the deep, the parted tides,
His tomb is seen, which, from its airy stand,
Marks to the mariner the distant land.   [will
" This, princes ! is the truth ; and though the
Of Heav'n, the sov'reign cause of good and ill,
Has dash'd our hopes, and, for the good in view,
With griefs afflicts us and disasters new ;
Yet, innocent of all, I justly claim
To stand exempt from punishment, or blame.
That zeal for Thebes 'gainst hospitable laws
Prevail'd, and ardour in my country's cause,
I freely have confess'd ; but sure, if wrong
Was e'er permitted to inducement strong,
This claims to be excus'd : our country's need,
With all who hear it, will for favour plead."
He ended thus. Unable to subdue
His grief, the monarch from the throne withdrew:
In silent wonder fix'd, the rest remain'd ;
Till Clytophon the gen'ral sense explain'd:
" Your just defence, we mean not to refuse ;
Your prudence censure, or your zeal accuse :
To Heav'n we owe the valiant Cleon's fate,
With each disaster which afflicts the state.

Soon as the Sun forsakes the eastern main,
At ev'ry altar let a bull be slain ;
And Thebes assembled move the pow'rs to spare,
With vows of sacrifice and humble pray'r :
But now the night invites to soft repose,
The momentary cure of human woes ;
The stars descend ; and soon the morning ray
Shall rouse us to the labours of the day."
The hero thus. In silence all approv'd,
And rising, various, from th' assembly mov'd.

## THE
## EPIGONIAD.

### BOOK VIII.

BEHIND the palace, where a stream descends,
Its lonely walks a shady grove extends ;
Once sacred, now for common use ordain'd,
By war's wide licence and the ax profan'd :
Thither the monarch, from th' assembly, went
Alone, his fury and despair to vent,
And thus to Heav'n : " Dread pow'r ! whose
    sov'reign sway
The fates of men and mortal things obey !
From me expect not such applause to hear,
As fawning vot'ries to thine altars bear ;
But truth severe. Although the forked brand,
Which for destruction arms thy mighty hand,
Were level'd at my head ; a mind I hold,
By present ills, or future, uncontrol'd.
Beneath thy sway, the race of mortals groan ;
Felicity sincere is felt by none :
Delusive hope th' unpractis'd mind assails,
And, by ten thousand treach'rous arts, prevails :
Through all the Earth the fair deceiver strays,
And wretched man to misery betrays.
Our crimes you punish, never teach to shun,
When, blind from folly, on our fate we run :
Hence sighs and groans thy tyrant reign confess,
With ev'ry rueful symptom of distress.
Here war unchain'd exerts his wasteful pow'r ;
Here famine pines ; diseases there devour,
And lead a train of all the ills that know
To shorten life, or lengthen it in woe.
All men are curst ; but I, above the rest,
With tenfold vengeance, for my crimes, opprest :
With hostile pow'rs beset my tott'ring reign,
The people wasted, and my children slain ;
In swift approach, I see destruction come,
But, with a mind unmov'd, I'll meet my doom ;
For know, stern pow'r ! whose vengeance has
    decreed
That Creon, after all his sons, should bleed ;
As from the summit of some desert rock,
The sport of tempests, falls the leafless oak,
Of all its honours stript, thou ne'er shalt find,
Weakly submiss, or stupidly resign'd
This dauntless heart ; but purpos'd to debate
Thy stern decrees, and burst the chains of fate."
    He said ; and turning where the herals dstand
All night by turns, and wait their lord's command ;
Menestheus there and Hegesander found,
And Phæmius sage, for valour once renown'd ;
He charg'd them thus : " Beyond the eastern
    tow'rs,
Summon to meet in arms our martial pow'rs.
In silence let them move ; let signs command,
And mute obedience reign through ev'ry band ;
For when the east with early twilight glows,
We rush, from cover'd ambush, on our foes

Secure and unprepar'd : the truce we swore,
Our plighted faith, the seal of wine, and gore,
No ties I hold; all piety disclaim :
Adverse to me the gods, and I to them."
The angry monarch thus his will declar'd ;
His rage the heralds fear'd, and straight repair'd
To rouse the warriors. Now the morning light
Begins to mingle with the shades of night :
In every street a glitt'ring stream appears,
Of polish'd helmets mix'd with shining spears :
Towards the eastern gate they drive along,
Nations and tribes, an undistinguish'd throng :
Creon himself superior, in his car,
Receiv'd them coming, and dispos'd the war.

And now the Argives from their tents proceed,
With rites sepulchral to intomb the dead.
The king of men, amid the fun'ral fires,
The chiefs assembles, and the work inspires.
And thus the Pylian sage, in counsel wise :
" Princes ! I view, with wonder and surprise,
Yon field abandon'd, where the foe pursu'd
Their fun'ral rites before, with toil renew'd :
Not half their dead interr'd, they now abstain,
And silence reigns through all the smoky plain :
Thence jealousy and fear possess my mind
Of faith infring'd, and treachery design'd :
Behind those woody heights, behind those tow'rs,
I dread, in ambush laid, the Theban pow'rs ;
With purpose to assault us, when they know
That we, confiding, least expect a foe :
Let half the warriors arm, and stand prepar'd,
From sudden violence, the host to guard ;
While, in the mournful rites, the rest proceed,
Due to the honour'd reliques of the dead."

Thus as he spoke ; approaching from afar,
The hostile pow'rs, embattled for the war,
Appear'd; and streaming from their polish'd shields
A blaze of splendour brighten'd all the fields.
And thus the king of men, with lifted eyes,
And both his hands extended to the skies :
" Ye pow'rs supreme ! whose unresisted sway
The fate of men and mortal things obey !
Let all the plagues, which perjury attend,
At once, and sudden, on our foes descend :
Let not the sacred seal of wine and gore,
The hands we plighted, and the oaths we swore,
Be now in vain; but, from your bright abodes,
Confound the bold despisers of the gods."

He pray'd ; and nearer came the hostile train,
With swift approach advancing on the plain;
Embattled thick ; as when, at fall of night,
A shepherd, from some promontory's height,
Approaching from the deep, a fog descries,
Which hov'ring lightly o'er the billows flies ;
By breezes borne, the solid soon it gains,
Climbs the steep hills, and darkens all the plains :
Silent and swift the Theban pow'rs drew near ;
The chariots led, a phalanx clos'd the rear.
Confusion straight through all the host arose,
Stirr'd like the ocean when a tempest blows.
Some arm for fight; the rest to terrour yield,
Inactive stand, or trembling quit the field.
On ev'ry side, assaults the deafen'd ear
The discord loud of tumult, rage, and fear.
Superior in his car, with ardent eyes,
The king of men through all the army flies ;
The rash restrains, the cold with courage fires,
And all with hope and confidence inspires ;
As when the deep, in liquid mountains hurl'd,
Assaults the rocky limits of the world ;

When tempests with unlicens'd fury rave,
And sweep from shore to shore the flying wave :
If he to whom each pow'r of ocean bends,
To quell such uproar, from the deep ascends,
Serene, amidst the wat'ry war, he rides,
And fixes, with his voice, the moving tides :
Such seem'd the monarch. From th' Olympian
The martial maid precipitates her flight; [height,
To aid her fav'rite host the goddess came,
Mentor she seem'd, her radiant arms the same;
Who with Ulysses brought a chosen band
Of warriors from the Cephalenian strand ;
Already arm'd the valiant youth she found,
And arming for the fight his warriors round.
And thus began : " Brave prince ! our foes appear
For battle order'd, and the fight is near.
Dauntless they come superior and elate,
While fear unmans us, and resigns to fate.
Would some immortal from th' Olympian height
Descend, and for a moment stop the fight ;
From sad dejection rous'd, and cold despair,
We yet might arm us, and for war prepare;
But if on human aid we must depend,
Nor hope to see the fav'ring gods descend,
Great were the hero's praise, who now could boast
From ruin imminent to save the host !
The danger near some prompt expedient claims,
And prudence triumphs oft in worst extremes."

Thus, in a form assum'd, the martial maid ;
The generous warrior, thus replying, said :
" In youth, I cannot hope to win the praise,
With which experience crowns a length of days :
Weak are the hopes that on my counsels stand,
To combats new, nor practis'd in command :
But as the gods, to save a sinking state,
Or snatch an army from the jaws of fate,
When prudence stands confounded, oft suggest
A prompt expedient to some vulgar breast ;
To your discerning ear I shall expose
What now my mind excites me to disclose.
Sav'd from th' unfinish'd honours of the slain,
The mingled spoils of forests load the plain;
In heaps contiguous, round the camp they lie,
A fence too weak to stop the enemy :
But if we mix them with the seeds of fire,
Which unextinguish'd glow in ev'ry pyre,
Against the foe a sudden wall shall rise,
Of flame and smoke ascending to the skies :
The steed dismay'd shall backward hurl the car;
Mix with the phalanx, and confound the war."

He said. The goddess, in her conscious breast,
A mother's triumph for a son possess'd,
Who emulates his sire in glorious deeds,
And, with his virtue, to his fame succeeds :
Graceful the goddess turn'd, and with a voice,
Bold and superior to the vulgar noise,
O'er all the field commands the woods to fire ;
Straight to obey a thousand hands conspire.
On ev'ry side the spreading flame extends,
And, roll'd in cloudy wreaths, the smoke ascends.

Creon beheld ; enrag'd to be withstood :
Like some fierce lion when he meets a flood
Or trench defensive, which his rage restrains
For flocks unguarded, left by careless swains ;
O'er all the field he sends his eyes afar,
To mark fit entrance for a pointed war :
Near on the right a narrow space he found,
Where fun'ral ashes smok'd upon the ground :
Thither the warriors of the Theban host,
Whose martial skill he priz'd and valour most,

The monarch sent, Chalcidamus the strong,
Who from fair Thespia led his martial throng,
Where Helicon erects his verdant head,
And crowns the champaign with a lofty shade :
Oechalia's chief was added to the band,
For valour fam'd and skilful in command ;
Erithæus, with him, his brother, came,
Of worth unequal, and unequal fame.
Rhesus, with these, the Thracian leader, went,
To merit fame, by high achievements, bent ;
Of stature tall, he scorns the pointed spear,
And crushes with his mace the ranks of war :
With him twelve leaders of his native train,
In combats, taught the bounding steed to rein,
By none surpass'd who boast superior skill
To send the winged arrow swift to kill,
Mov'd to the fight. The rest of vulgar name,
Though brave in combat, were unknown to fame.
  Their bold invasion dauntless to oppose,
Full in the midst, the bulk of Ajax rose ;
Unarm'd he stood ; but, in his mighty hand,
Brandish'd, with gesture fierce, a burning brand,
Snatch'd from the ashes of a fun'ral fire ;
An olive's trunk, five cubit lengths entire.
Arm'd for the fight, the Cretan monarch stood ;
And Merion, thirsting still for hostile blood ;
The prince of Ithaca, with him who led
The youth, in Sycion, and Pellene, bred.
But ere they clos'd, the Thracian leader prest,
With eager courage, far before the rest ;
Him Ajax met, inflam'd with equal rage :
Between the wond'ring hosts the chiefs engage ;
Their weighty weapons round their heads they
          throw,
And swift, and heavy falls each thund'ring blow ;
As when in Ætna's caves the giant brood,
The one-ey'd servants of the Lemnian god,
In order round the burning anvil stand,
And forge, with weighty strokes, the forked brand:
The shaking hills their fervid toil confess,
And echoes rattling through each dark recess:
So rag'd the fight ; their mighty limbs they strain;
And oft their pond'rous maces fall in vain :
For neither chief was destin'd yet to bleed ;
But fate at last the victory decreed.
The Salaminian hero aim'd a stroke,
Which thund'ring on the Thracian helmet broke;
Stunn'd by the boist'rous shock, the warrior reel'd
With giddy poise, then sunk upon the field.
Their leader to defend, his native train
With speed advance, and guard him on the plain.
Against his foe, their threat'ning lances rise,
And aim'd at once, a storm of arrows flies ;
Around the chief on ev'ry side they sing ;
One in his shoulder fix'd its barbed sting.
Amaz'd he stood, nor could the fight renew ;
But slow and sullen from the foe withdrew.
Straight to the charge Idomeneus proceeds,
With hardy Merion, try'd in martial deeds,
Laertes' valiant son, and he who led
The youth in Sycion, and Pellene, bred ;
With force united, these the foe sustain,
And wasteful havoc loads the purple plain :
In doubtful poise the scales of combat sway'd,
And various fates alternately obey'd.
  But now the flames, which barr'd th' invading
Sunk to the wasted wood, in ashes glow ;    [foe,
Thebes rushes to the fight ; their polish'd shields
Gleam through the smoke, and brighten all the
      fields ;

Thick fly the embers, where the coursers tread,
And cloudy volumes all the welkin shade.
The king of men, to meet the tempest, fires
His wav'ring bands, and valour thus inspires.
  " Gods ! shall one fatal hour deface the praise
Of all our sleepless nights, and bloody days ?
Shall no just meed for all our toils remain ?
Our labours, blood, and victories in vain ?
Shall Creon triumph, and his impious brow
Claim the fair wreath, to truth and valour due?
No, warriors ! by the heav'nly pow'rs, is weigh'd
Justice with wrong, in equal balance laid :
From Jove's high roof depend th' eternal scales,
Wrong mounts defeated still, and right prevails.
Fear then no odds ; on Heav'n itself depend,
Which falsehood will confound, and truth defend."
  He said ; and sudden in the shock they close,
Their shields and helmets ring with mutual blows:
Disorder dire the mingling ranks confounds,
And shouts of triumph mix with dying sounds ;
As fire, with wasteful conflagration, spreads,
And kindles, in its course, the woodland shades,
When, shooting sudden from the clouds above,
On some thick forest fall the flames of Jove ;
The lofty oaks, the pines and cedars burn,
Their verdant honours all to ashes turn ;
Loud roars the tempest ; and the trembling swains
See the wide havoc of the wasted plains :
Such seem'd the conflict ; such the dire alarms,
From shouts of battle mix'd with din of arms.
Phericles, first, Lycaon's valiant son,
The sage whose counsels propp'd the Theban
          throne,
Rose in the fight, superior to the rest,
And brave Democleon's fall his might confest,
The chief and leader of a valiant band,
From fair Eione and th' Asinian strand.
Next Asius, Iphitus, and Crates fell ;
Terynthian Podius trode the path to Hell :
And Schedius, from Mazeta's fruitful plain,
Met there his fate, and perish'd with the slain.
Aw'd by their fall, the Argive bands give way ;
As yields some rampart to the ocean's sway,
Whe n rous'd to rage, it scorns opposing mounds,
And sweeps victorious through forbidden grounds.
  But Pallas, anxious for her fav'rite host,
Their best already wounded, many lost,
Ulysses sought : she found him, in the rear,
Wounded and faint, and leaning on his spear.
And thus in Mentor's form ; " Brave prince ! I
          dread
Our hopes defeated, and our fall decreed :
For conqu'ring on the right the foe prevails,
And all defence against their fury fails ;
While here, in doubtful poise, the battle sways,
And various fates alternately obeys ;
If great Tydides, who beholds from far
Our danger imminent, yet shuns the war,
Held by resentment, or some cause unknown,
Regardless of our safety and his own,
Would rise to aid us ; yet we might respire,
And Creon, frustrated, again retire.
Great were his praise, who could the chief per-
In peril so extreme, the host to aid.    [suade,
The fittest you, who boast the happy skill,
With pleasing words, to move the fixed will :
Though Nestor justly merits equal fame,
A friend the soonest will a friend reclaim."
  And thus Ulysses to the martial maid :
  " I cannot hope the hero to persuade :

The source unknown from which his rage pro-
    ceeds,
Reason in vain from loose conjecture pleads;
The fatal truce, with faithless Creon made,
Provokes him not, nor holds him from our aid;
He easily resign'd whate'er he mov'd,
Till now, approving as the rest approv'd,
Some dire disaster, some disgrace unseen,
Confounds his steady temper, else serene:
But with my utmost search, I'll strive to find
The secret griefs which wound his gen'rous mind;
If drain'd of blood, and spent with toils of war,
My weary limbs can bear their load so far."
    He spoke; his words the martial maid admir'd;
With energy divine his breast inspir'd;
Lightly the hero mov'd, and took his way
Where broad encamp'd th' Etolian warriors lay:
Already arm'd he found the daring band,
Fierce and impatient of their lord's command;
Some, murm'ring, round the king's pavilion
    stood,
While others, more remote, complain'd aloud:
With pleasing words he sooth'd them as he went,
And sought their valiant leader in his tent:
Him pond'ring deep in his distracted mind,
He found, and sitting sad, with head declin'd.
He thus address'd him: "Will the news, I bring,
Afflict, or gratify, th' Etolian king?
' That wav'ring on the brink of foul defeat,
Without the hopes of success or retreat,
Our valiant bands th' unequal fight maintain;
Their best already wounded, many slain.'
If treach'rous Thebes has brib'd you with her
    store,
And bought the venal faith which once you swore;
Has promis'd precious ore, or lovely dames,
And pays to lust the price which treason claims:
Name but the proffers of the perjur'd king,
And more, and better, from your friends I'll bring;
Vast sums of precious ore, and greater far
Than Thebes, in peace, had treasur'd for the war;
Or, though, to gratify thy boundless mind,
Her private wealth and public were combin'd.
If beauty's pow'r your am'rous heart inflames,
Unrival'd are Achaia's lovely dames;
Her fairest dames Adrastus shall bestow,
And purchase thus the aid you freely owe.
Gods! that our armies e'er should need to fear
Destruction, and the son of Tydeus near!"
    Ulysses thus; and Tydeus' son again:
" Your false reproaches aggravate my pain
Too great already: in my heart I feel
Its venom'd sting, more sharp than pointed steel.
No bribe persuades, or promise from the foe,
My oath to vi'late, and the war forego:
In vain for this were all the precious store,
Which trading Zidon wafts from shore to shore;
With all that rich Iberia yet contains,
Safe and unrifled in her golden veins.
The source from which my miseries arise,
The cause, which to the host my zeal denies,
With truth I shall relate; and hope to claim
Your friendly sympathy, for groundless blame.
In yonder walls a captive maid remains,
To me more dear than all the world contains;
Fairer she is than nymph was ever fair;
Pallas in stature and majestic air;
As Venus soft, with Cynthia's sprightly grace,
When on Taïgetus she leads the chase,

Or Erymanthus; while in fix'd amaze,
At awful distance held, the satyrs gaze.
With oaths divine our plighted faith we bound;
Hymen had soon our mutual wishes crown'd;
When, call'd to arms, against the Theban tow'rs,
From Calydon I led my martial pow'rs.
Her female form in martial arms conceal'd,
With me she brav'd the terrours of the field:
Unknown and unrewarded, from my side
No toil could drive her, and no shock divide.
But now proud Thebes injuriously detains
The lovely virgin, lock'd in hostile chains;
Doom'd and reserv'd to perish, for my sake,
If of your counsel s, I, or works, partake;
Till twenty mornings in the east shall rise,
And twenty ev'nings gild the western skies.
See then the cause which holds me, and confines
My arm, to aid you, though my heart inclines;
Love mix'd with pity, whose restraints I feel
Than adamant more strong, and links of steel."
    The hero thus. Laertes' son reply'd:
" Oft have I heard what now is verify'd;
That still when passion reigns without control,
Its sway confounds and darkens all the soul.
If Thebes, by perjury, the gods provok'd,
The vengeance slighted, by themselves invok'd,
Assaulted us, secure, with hostile arms,
And mix'd our pious rites with dire alarms:
With better faith, by faithless Creon sway'd,
Will they at last restore the captive maid?
When from their battlements and lofty spires,
They see their champaign shine with hostile
    fires;
And, pitch'd around them, hosts of armed foes,
With strict embrace, their straiten'd wallsenclose;
The gods they scorn as impotent, and vain:
What will they do, when you alone remain?
Our princes fall'n, the vulgar warriors fled,
Shall to your tent the captive fair be led?
Or rather must you see her matchless charms
Reserv'd to bless some happier rival's arms:
While rage and jealousy divide your breast,
No present friend to pity or assist?
Now rather rise; and, ere it is too late,
Rescue our armies from impending fate.
The captive maid uninjur'd you'll regain;
Force oft obtains what justice asks in vain.
With success thus your wishes shall be crown'd,
Which trust in Thebes would frustrate and con-
    found."
    Ulysses thus: his weighty words inclin'd,
Long tortur'd with suspense, the hero's mind;
As settling winds the moving deep control,
And teach the wav'ring billows how to roll.
Straight from his seat th' Etolian warrior rose;
His mighty limbs the martial greaves enclose;
His breast and thighs in polish'd steel he dress'd;
A plumed helmet next his temples press'd:
From the broad baldric, round his shoulders
    flung,
His shining sword and starry falchion hung:
The spear he last assum'd, and pond'rous shield,
With martial grace, and issu'd to the field:
To mingle in the fight, with eager haste
He rush'd, nor call'd his warriors as he past.
Ulysses these conven'd; his prudent care
Their ranks dispos'd, and led them to the war.
Afar distinguish'd by his armour bright,
With shouts Tydides rous'd the ling'ring fight;

Through all the host his martial voice resounds,
And ev'ry heart with kindling ardour bounds;
As when the Sun ascends, with gladsome ray,
To light the weary trav'ler on his way;
Or cheer the mariner by tempests tost
Amidst the dangers of some per'lous coast:
So to his wishing friends Tydides came;
Their danger such before, their joy the same.

Phericles saw; and, springing from the throng,
Call'd the bold Thebans, as he rush'd along:
" Ye gen'rous youths! whom fair Bœotia breeds,
The nurse of valour and heroic deeds;
Let not, though oft renew'd, these tedious toils
Your martial ardour quench, and damp your
        souls.
Tydides comes; and leads, in armour bright,
His native bands, impatient for the fight;
Myself the first the hero's arm shall try,
And teach you how to conquer, or to die.
We strive not now, as when, in days of peace,
Some prince's hymeneal rites to grace,
In listed fields bedew'd with fragrant oil,
In combat feign'd, the mimic warriors toil;
Alike the victors, and the vanquish'd fare,
And genial feasts, to both, conclude the war:
We now must conquer; or it stands decreed
That Thebes shall perish, and her people bleed.
No hopes of peace remain; nor can we find
New gods to witness, or new oaths to bind,
The first infring'd: and therefore must prepare
To stand or perish by the lot of war:
Then let us all undaunted brave our fate:
To stop is doubtful, desp'rate to retreat."

The hero thus; and to the battle led;
Like Mars, he seem'd, in radiant armour clad,
Tow'ring sublime; behind his ample shield,
He mov'd to meet Tydides on the field:
As when at noon, descending to the rills,
Two herds encounter, from the neighb'ring hills;
Before the rest, the rival bulls prepare,
With awful prelude, for th' approaching war;
With desp'rate horns they plough the smoking
        ground;
Their hideous roar the hollow caves resound;
Heav'd o'er their backs the streaming sand as-
        cends;
Their stern encounter both the herds suspends:
So met the chiefs; and such amazement quell'd
The rest, and in suspense the combat held.
Tydides first his weighty weapon threw,
Wide of the mark with erring force it flew.
Phericles! thine succeeds with happier aim,
Full to the center of the shield it came:
But slightly join'd, unequal to the stroke,
Short from the steel, the staff in splinters broke.
With grief Tydides saw his aim deceiv'd;
From off the field a pond'rous rock he heav'd;
With figures rude of antique sculpture grac'd,
It mark'd the reliques of a man deceas'd.
Push'd at his foe the weighty mass he flung;
Thund'ring it fell; the Theban helmet rung:
Deep with the brain the dinted steel it mix'd,
And lifeless, on the ground, the warrior fix'd.
Aw'd by his fall, the Theban bands retire;
As flocks defenceless shun a lion's ire;
At once they yield, unable to withstand
The wide destruction of Tydides' hand.
Disorder soon, the form of war confounds,
And shouts of triumph mix with dying sounds.

Creon perceiv'd, where ruling on the right
In equal poise he held the scales of fight,
Blaspheming Heav'n, he impiously resign'd,
To stern despair, his unsubmitting mind:
Yet, vers'd in all the various turns of fate,
The brisk assault to rule, or safe retreat,
He drew his firm battalions from the foe,
In martial order, regularly slow.
The Argive leaders, thund'ring in the rear,
Still forwards on the yielding squadrons bear:
The strife with unabated fury burns,
They stop, they combat, and retreat by turns;
As the grim lion sourly leaves the plains,
By dogs compell'd, and bands of armed swains;
Indignant to his woody haunts he goes,
And with retorted glare restrains his foes.

Mean while Tydides, near the Cadmean gate,
Urg'd with incessant toil the work of fate;
Towards the walls, an undistinguish'd throng,
The victors and the vanquish'd, rush'd along.
Access to both the guarded wall denies;
From ev'ry tow'r, a storm of jav'lins flies;
Thick as the hail descends, when Boreas flings
The rattling tempest from his airy wings:
So thick the jav'lins fell, and pointed spears;
Behind them close, another host appears,
In order'd columns rang'd, by Creon led:
Ulysses saw; and thus to Diomed:
" Bold as you are, avoid these guarded tow'rs,
From loose pursuit recal your scatter'd pow'rs:
See Creon comes; his thick embattled train,
In phalanx join'd, approaches from the plain.
Here if we stay th' unequal fight to prove,
The tow'rs and ramparts threaten from above
With darts and stones; while to th' invading foe,
In order loose, our scatter'd ranks we show;
Nor by your matchless valour hope, in vain,
Such odds to conquer, and the fight maintain;
Against an army single force must lose;
Immod'rate courage still like folly shows.
See where into the field yon turret calls,
Drawn to a point the long-extended walls:
There force your way, and speedily regain
The space, and safety of the open plain."

Ulysses thus; and, by his prudence sway'd,
The martial son of Tydeus straight obey'd.
Thrice to the height the hero rais'd his voice,
Loud as the silver trumpet's martial noise,
The signal of retreat; his warriors heard,
And round their chief in order'd ranks appear'd,
Drawn from the mingled tumult of the plain;
As, sever'd on the floor, the golden grain
Swells to a heap; while, whirling through the
        skies,
The dusty chaff in thick disorder flies;
Tydides leads; between the guarded tow'rs
And hostile ranks, he draws his martial pow'rs
Towards the plain; as mariners, with oar
And sail, avoid some promontory's shore;
When, caught between the ocean and the land,
A sudden tempest bears them on the strand;
The stem opposing to its boist'rous sway,
They shun the cape and stretch into the bay:
So scap'd Tydides. Cover'd by their tow'rs,
In safety stood retir'd the Theban pow'rs,
For from above an iron tempest rain'd,
And the incursions of the foe restrain'd.

THE

*EPIGONIAD.*

BOOK IX.

And now the king of men his army calls
Back from the danger of th' impending walls ;
They quit the combat, and in order long
The field possess, a phalanx deep and strong.
Rank following rank, the Theban squadrons
    move
Still to the rampart, and the tow'rs above :
Creon himself, unwilling, quits the field,
Enrag'd, defeated, and constrain'd to yield :
'Gainst all his foes, his indignation burns,
But first on Diomed its fury turns.
He call'd a vulgar warrior from the crowd,
A villain dark, and try'd in works of blood,
Erembus nam'd, of huge gigantic size,      [eyes ;
With cloudy features mark'd, and down-cast
Cold and inactive still in combat found,
Nor wont to kindle at the trumpet's sound ;
But bold in villany when pow'r commands ;
A weapon fitted for a tyrant's hands.      [sword,
And thus the wrathful monarch : " Take this
A sign, to all my servants, from their lord ;
And hither bring the fair Etolian's head ;
I, who command you, will reward the deed :
But let not pity, or remorse, prevail ;
Your own shall answer, if in aught you fail."

    He said ; the murth'rer, practis'd to obey,
The royal sword receiv'd, and took his way
Straight to the palace, where the captive fair,
Of hope bereft, and yielding to despair,
Lamenting sat.   Their mutual griefs to blend,
The queen and all the royal maids attend.
And thus the queen : " Fair stranger ! shall your
All hopes reject of comfort and relief ?      [grief
Your woes I've measur'd, all your sorrows known ;
And find them light when balanc'd with my own.
In one sad day my valiant sire I mourn'd ;
My brother slain ; my native walls o'erturn'd ;
Myself a captive, destin'd to fulfil,
In servile drudgery, a master's will ;
Yet to a fall so low, the gods decreed
This envy'd height of greatness to succeed.
The pow'rs above, for purposes unknown,
Oft raise the fall'n, and bring the lofty down ;
Elude the vigilance of all our care :
Our surest hopes deceive, and mock despair.
Let no desponding thoughts your mind possess,
To banish hope, the med'cine of distress :
For nine short days your freedom will restore,
And break the bondage which you thus deplore.
But I, alas ! unhappy still, must mourn
Joys once possess'd, which never can return ;
Four valiant sons, who perish'd on the plain
In this dire strife, a fifth on Oeta slain :
These shall return to bless my eyes no more ;
The grave's dark mansion knows not to restore,
For time, which bids so oft the solar ray
Repeat, with light renew'd, th' ethereal way,
And from the soil, by heat and vernal winds,
To second life the latent plant unbinds,
Again to flourish, nurs'd by wholesome dews,
Never to mortal man his life renews.
These griefs are sure ; but others still I fear ;
A royal husband lost, and bondage near ;

Myself, my daughters, dragg'd by hostile hands ;
Our dignity exchang'd for servile bands :
All this the gods may purpose, and fulfil ;
And we with patience must endure their will."
    As thus Laodice her sorrow try'd
With sympathy to sooth ; the maid reply'd :
" Great queen ! on whom the sov'reign pow'rs
A gen'rous heart to feel another's woe ;     [bestow
Let still untouch'd through life your honours last,
With happier days to come for sorrows past !
Yet strive not thus a hopeless wretch to cheer,
Whom sure conjecture leads the worst to fear.
Shall Diomed a public cause forego,
His faithful friends betray, and trust a foe ?
By treachery behold the host o'erthrown,
Renounce the public interest and his own ?
Shall kings and armies, in the balance laid,
Avail not to out-weigh a single maid ?
One, whom his fury falsely did reprove
For crimes unknown, whose only crime was love ?
No, sure ere this he triumphs in the field ;
Your armies to his matchless valour yield :
And soon submitting to the fatal blow,
This head must gratify a vanquish'd foe.
If symbols e'er the secret fates explain,
If visions do not always warn in vain,
If dreams do ever true prognostics prove,
And dreams, the sages say, descend from Jove,
My fate approaches : late at dead of night ;
My veins yet freeze with horrour and affright !
I thought that, all forsaken and alone,
Pensive I wander'd far through ways unknown ;
A gloomy twilight, neither night nor day,
Frown'd on my steps, and sadden'd all the way :
Long dreary vales I saw on ev'ry side,
And caverns sinking deep, with entrance wide ;
On ragged cliffs the blasted forests hung ;
Her baleful note the boding screech-owl sung.
At last, with many a weary step, I found
This melancholy country's outmost bound,
An ocean vast : upon a cliff I stood,
And saw, beneath me far, the sable flood ;
No islands rose the dull expanse to grace,
And nought was seen, through all the boundless
    space,                          [frown'd,
But low-brow'd clouds, which on the billows
And, in a night of shade, the prospect drown'd.
The winds, which seem'd around the cliffs to
    blow,
With doleful cadence, utter'd sounds of woe,
Wafting, from ev'ry cave and dreary den,
The wail of infants mix'd with groans of men :
Amaz'd, on ev'ry side my eyes I turn,
And see depending from the craggy bourn
Wretches unnumber'd ; some the mould'ring
    soil,                              [toil ;
Some grasp'd the slipp'ry rock, with fruitless
Some hung suspended by the roots, which pass
Through crannies of the cliffs, or wither'd grass.
Still from the steep they plung'd into the main ;
As from the eves descends the trickling rain.
Amaz'd I turn'd, and strove in vain to fly ;
Thickets oppos'd, and precipices high
To stop my flight : and, from the airy steep,
A tempest snatch'd, and hurl'd me to the deep.
The sudden violence my slumber broke ;
The waves I seem'd to touch, and straight awoke.
With sleep the vision fled ; but, in my mind,
Imprinted deep, its image left behind.

For had the frightful scene which fancy drew,
And what I seem'd to suffer, all been true ;
Had fate appear'd, in blackest colours dress'd,
No deeper had its horrours been impress'd.
When thus the gods by certain symbols warn,
And sure, from dreams, their purposes we learn,
No blame I merit, that to fear resign'd,
Fate's dead approach sits heavy on my mind."
  Cassandra thus ; Laodice again :
" Futurity, in dreams, we seek in vain ;
For oft, from thoughts disturb'd, such phan-
       toms rise,
As fogs from marshes climb, to blot the skies:
With a dark veil, the cheerful face of day
They sadden, and eclipse the solar ray ;
But soon, in dews and soft descending rains,
Fall to refresh the mountains and the plains.
For Diomed's offence you ne'er can bleed ;
Favour, your sex and innocence will plead,
Ev'n with the worst : nor will a gen'rous foe
His rage, in cruelty and baseness, show.
Now to the tow'rs I haste, to view from far
The danger or success of this day's war.
Let Clymene with me the walls ascend ;
The rest at home domestic cares attend."
  She ended thus ; and from her seat arose ;
The royal maid attends her, as she goes
Towards the western gate ; where full to view
Expos'd, the armies and the camp she knew.
And now appear'd within the lofty gate,
By Creon sent, the messenger of fate.
His shining blade, for execution bar'd,
And aspect dark, his purpose straight declar'd.
Alarm'd at once the royal virgins rise,
And scatt'ring, fill the dome with female cries :
But, bolder from despair, Cassandra staid,
And to th' assassin thus, undaunted, said :
" Approach ! divide this neck with deathful
       steel,
A tyrant's vassal no remorse should feel.
O Diomed ! let this example prove,
In man, that stubborn honour conquers love :
With weight superior, great ambition draws
The scale for glory, and a public cause.
I blame thee not for this ; nor will impeach
A great example, which I could not reach :
For had whole armies, in the balance laid,
And kings and mighty states with thee been
       weigh'd,
And I the judge appointed to decree,
They all had perished to ransom thee."
Cassandra thus ; and for the blow prepar'd,
With both her hands, her shining neck she bar'd,
And round her head a purple garment roll'd,
With leaves of silver mark'd, and flow'rs of gold.
Rais'd for the stroke, the glitt'ring falchion
       hung,
And swift descending, bore the head along.
A tide of gore, diffus'd in purple streams,
Dashes the wall, and o'er the pavement swims,
Prone to the ground the headless trunk reclines,
And life, in long convulsive throbs, resigns.
  Now on the open plain before the walls,
The king of men the chiefs to council calls.
And Diomed, with secret griefs oppress'd,
Impatient, thus the public ear address'd :
" Confed'rate kings ! and thou, whose sov'reign
       hand
Sways the dread sceptre of supreme command !

What holds us, and restrains our martial pow'rs;
While haughty Thebes insults us, from her
       tow'rs?
In vain we conquer thus, and bleed in vain,
If victory but yields the empty plain.
Behind his walls, perfidious Creon lies,
And safely meditates a new surprise :
When on the urn our pious tears we pour ;
Or mirth disarms us, and the genial hour ;
No, let us rather, now when fortune calls,
With bold assault, attempt to mount the walls ;
Myself the first a chosen band shall lead,
Where yon low rampart sinks into the mead :
There will I gain the battlements, and lay,
For others to succeed, an open way,
If bars of steel have force their works to tear,
Or, from their hinges heav'd the gates can
       bear."
  Tydides thus.   His counsel to oppose,
The leader of the Cretan warriors rose :
" Confed'rate kings : and thou, whose sov'reign
       hand
Sways the dread sceptre of supreme command !
Let not Tydides now, with martial rage,
In measures hot and rash, the host engage.
To sober reason, still let passion yield,
Nor here, admit the ardour of the field :
If Thebes could thus with one assault be won,
Her armies vanquish'd, and her wall o'erthiown;
Could this one signal day reward our toil,
So long endur'd, with victory and spoil :
No soldier in the ranks, no leader here,
Would shun the fight, or counsel to forbear.
But if for victory, a foul defeat,
With all the shame and danger of retreat,
Should be the issue, which the wise must dread,
To stop is better, sure, than to proceed.
On yonder walls and lofty turrets, stand,
Not, sav'd from shameful flight, a heartless band,
Who, desp'rate of their state, would soon forego
Their last defences, and admit a foe ;
But who, from fight recall'd, without dismay,
A safe retreat maintain'd, in firm array.
Secure they combat from protecting walls ;
Thrown from above each weapon heavier falls;
Against such odds, can we the fight maintain,
And with a foe found equal on the plain ?
Though we desist, no leader will oppose
That thus the fruits of victory we lose ;
When, pent within their battlements and tow'rs,
In narrow space, we hold the Theban pow'rs :
For oftener, than by arms, are hosts o'erthrown
By dearth and sickness, in a straiten'd town.
He who can only wield the sword and spear,
Knows less than half the instruments of war.
Heart-gnawing hunger, enemy to life,
Wide-wasting pestilence, and civil strife,
By want inflam'd, to all our weapons claim
Superior force, and strike with surer aim :
With these, whoever arm'd to combat goes,
Instructed how to turn them on his foes,
Shall see them soon laid prostrate on the ground,
His aims accomplish'd, and his wishes crown'd.
Our warriors, therefore, let us straight recall,
Nor, by assault, attempt to force the wall ;
But with a rampart, to the gates oppos'd,
Besiege, in narrow space, our foes enclos'd."
  The hero thus ; and, eager to reply,
Tydides rose : when on a turret high

Creon appear'd; Cassandra's head, display'd
Upon a lance's point, he held, and said:
" Ye Argive warriors ! view this sign; and know,
That Creon never fails to quit a foe.
This bloody trophy mark; and if it brings
Grief and despair to any of the kings,
Let him revenge it on the man who broke
His faith, and dar'd my fury to provoke."
He ended thus. Tydides, as he heard,
With rage distracted, and despair, appear'd.
Long on the tow'r he fix'd his burning eyes;
The rest were mute with wonder and surprise;
But, to the counsel turning, thus at last :
" If any favour claim my merits past;
If, by a present benefit, ye'd bind
To future services a grateful mind;
Let what I urge in council, now prevail,
With hostile arms yon rampart to assail:
Else, with my native bands, alone I'll try
The combat, fix'd to conquer or to die."
The hero thus. Ulysses thus exprest
The prudent dictates of his generous breast :
" Princes ! shall dire contention still preside
In all our councils, and the kings divide ?
Sure, of the various ills that can distress
United armies and prevent success,
Discord is chief: where'er the fury strays,
The parts she severs and the whole betrays.
Now let Tydides lead his native pow'rs
To combat, and assault the Theban tow'rs;
The rest, on various parts, their forces show,
By mock approaches to distract the foe.
If he prevails, to victory he leads ;
And safe behind him all the host succeeds:
If Jove forbids and all-decreeing fate,
The field is open, and a safe retreat."
Ulysses thus. The princes all assent ; [went,
Straight from the council through the host they
Review'd its order, and in front dispos'd
The slingers; and the rear with bowmen clos'd;
Arming the rest with all that could avail,
The tow'rs and battlements to sap or scale.
Tydides first his martial squadrons leads ;
Ulysses, with his native band, succeeds.
Upon them, as they came, the Thebans pour
A storm of jav'lins, shot from ev'ry tow'r ;
As from the naked heights the feather'd kind,
By bitter show'rs compell'd, and wintry wind,
In clouds assembled, from some mountain's head,
To shelter crowd, and dive into the shade;
Such and so thick the winged weapons flew,
And many warriors wounded, many slew.
Now on their ranks, by forceful engines thrown,
Springs, from the twisted rope, the pond'rous
    stone,
With wide destruction through the host to roll,
To mix its order and confound the whole.
Intrepid still th' Etolian chief proceeds ;
And still Ulysses follows as he leads.
They reach'd the wall. Tydides, with a bound,
Twice strove in vain to mount it from the ground.
Twice fled the foe ; as, to the boist'rous sway
Of some proud billow, mariners give way ;
Which, rous'd by tempests, 'gainst a vessel
    bends
Its force, and mounting o'er the deck ascends:
Again he rose : the third attempt prevail'd ;
But, crumbling in his grasp, the rampart fail'd :
For thunder there its fury had imprest,
And loos'd a shatter'd fragment from the rest.

Supine upon the earth the hero falls,
Mix'd with the smoke and ruin of the walls.
By disappointment chaf'd, and fierce from pain,
Unable now the rampart to regain,
He turn'd, and saw his native bands afar,
By fear restrain'd, and ling'ring in the war.
From Creon straight and Thebes, his anger
    turns,
And 'gainst his friends, with equal fury, burns;
As when, from snows dissolv'd or sudden rains,
A torrent swells and roars along the plains ;
If, rising to oppose its angry tide,
In full career, it meets a mountain's side;
In foaming eddies, backwards to its source,
It wheels, and rages with inverted course:
So turn'd at once, the fury, in his breast,
Against Ulysses, thus itself exprest :
" Author accurs'd, and source of all my woes?
Friend more pernicious than the worst of foes !
By thy suggestions from my purpose sway'd,
I slew Cassandra, and myself betray'd ;
Hence, lodg'd within this tortur'd breast, remains
A fury, to inflict eternal pains.
I need not follow, with vindictive spear,
A traitor absent, while a worse is near:
Creon but acted what you well foreknew,
When me unwilling to the fight you drew.
To you the first my vengeance shall proceed,
And then on Creon and myself succeed:
Such sacrifice Cassandra's ghost demands,
And such I'll offer with determin'd hands."
Thus as he spoke, Ulysses pond'ring stood,
Whether by art to sooth his furious mood,
Or, with a sudden hand, his lance to throw,
Preventing, ere it fell, the threaten'd blow.
But, gliding from above, the martial maid
Between them stood, in majesty display'd;
Her radiant eyes with indignation burn'd,
On Diomed their piercing light she turn'd ;
And frowning thus : " Thy frantic rage restrain ;
Else by dread Styx I swear, nor swear in vain,
That proof shall teach you whether mortal might
This arm invincible can match in fight.
Is 't not enough that he whose hoary hairs
Still watch'd your welfare with a father's cares,
Who dar'd, with zeal and courage, to withstand
Your fatal phrenzy, perish'd by your hand ?
That, slighting ev'ry tie which princes know,
You leagu'd in secret with a public foe ?
And, from your faith by fond affection sway'd,
The kings, the army, and yourself betray'd ?
Yet, still unaw'd, from such atrocious deeds,
To more and worse your desp'rate rage proceeds,
And dooms to perish, by a mad decree,
The chief who sav'd alike the host and thee.
Had Thebes prevail'd, and one decisive hour
The victory had fix'd beyond thy pow'r;
These limbs, ere now, had captive fetters worn,
To infamy condemn'd, and hostile scorn;
While fair Cassandra, with her virgin charms,
A prize decreed, had blest some rival's arms.
Did not the worth of mighty Tydeus plead,
Approv'd when living, and rever'd when dead,
For favour to his guilty son, and stand
A rampart to oppose my vengeful hand ;
You soon had found how mad it is to wage
War with the gods, and tempt immortal rage.
This Thebes shall know, ere to the ocean's
    streams
The Sun again withdraws his setting beams ;

For now the gods consent, in vengeance just,
For all her crimes, to mix her with the dust."
The goddess thus ; and turning to the field,
Her deity in Mentor's form conceal'd :
With courage new each warrior's heart inspires,
And wakes again, in all, their martial fires.
  Conscious of wrong, and speechless from
            surprise,
Tydides stood, nor dar'd to lift his eyes,
Of fate regardless ; though from ev'ry tow'r,
Stones, darts, and arrows fell, a mingled show'r :
For awe divine subdu'd him, and the shame
Which virtue suffers from the touch of blame.
But to Ulysses turning, thus at last :
  " Prince ! can thy gen'rous love forget the past;
And all remembrance banish from thy mind,
Of what my fury and despair design'd ?
If you forgive me, straight our pow'rs recall
Who shun the fight, while I attempt the wall.
Some present god inspires me ; for I feel
My heart exulting knock the plated steel :
In brisker rounds the vital spirit flies,
And ev'ry limb with double force supplies."
  Tydides thus.  Ulysses thus again:
" Shall Heav'n forgive offences, man retain;
Though born to err, by jarring passions tost ?
The best, in good, no steadiness can boast :
No malice therefore in my heart shall live ;
To sin is human ; human to forgive.
But do not now your single force oppose
To lofty ramparts and an host of foes;
Let me at least, attending at your side,
Partake the danger, and the toil divide :
For see our pow'rs advancing to the storm !
Pallas excites them in a mortal form.
Let us, to mount the rampart, straight proceed ;
They of themselves will follow as we lead."
  Ulysses thus ; and, springing from the ground,
Both chiefs at once ascend the lofty mound.
Before him each his shining buckler bears
'Gainst flying darts, and thick portended spears.
Now, on the bulwark's level top, they stand,
And charge on ev'ry side the hostile band :
There many warriors in close fight they slew,
And many headlong from the rampart threw.
Pallas her fav'rite champions still inspires, [fires.
Their nerves confirms, and wakes their martial
With course divided, on the foe they fall,
And bare between them leave a length of wall ;
As fire, when kindled on some mountain's head,
Where runs, in long extent, the woodland shade,
Consumes the middle forest, and extends
Its parted progress to the distant ends :
So fought the leaders, while their scatter'd pow'rs,
In phalanx join'd, approach'd the Theban tow'rs;
With hands, and heads against the rampart lean'd,
The first, upon their shields, the rest sustain'd :
Rank above rank the living structure grows,
As settling bees the pendent heap compose,
Which to some cavern's roof united clings,
Woven thick with complicated feet and wings :
Thus mutually sustain'd, the warriors bend ;
While o'er their heads the order'd ranks ascend.
  And now the martial goddess with delight,
Plac'd on a turret's top, survey'd the fight.
Thrice to the height she rais'd her awful voice ;
The tow'rs and bulwarks trembled at the noise:
Both warring hosts alike the signal hear;
To this, the cause of hope, to that, of fear.

And Theseus thus address'd his martial train :
" Here shall we wage a distant war in vain,
When now Tydides, from the conquer'd tow'rs
Descending, on the town his warriors pours ?
Your glory if ye would assert, nor yield
At once the praise of many a well-fought field;
Ascend these lofty battlements, and claim
With those who conquer now an equal fame."
The monarch thus ; and to the combat leads;
With emulation fir'd, the host proceeds;
Under a show'r of falling darts they go,
Climb the steep ramparts, and assault the foe ;
As winds outrageous, from the ocean wide,
Against some mole impel the stormy tide,
Whose rocky arms, opposed to the deep,
From tempests, safe the anchoring vessel keep;
Wave heap'd on wave, the stormy deluge tow'rs,
And o'er it, with resistless fury, pours :
Such seem'd the fight, the Theban host o'er
            thrown,
The wall deserts, and mingles with the town.
  Creon in vain the desp'rate rout withstands
With sharp reproaches and vindictive hands ;
His rage they shun not, nor his threat'nings
            hear,
From stunning clamours deaf, and blind from fear.
And thus the monarch with uplifted eyes,
And both his hands extended to the skies.
" Ye pow'rs supreme, whose unresisted sway
The fates of men and mortal things obey !
Against your counsels, vain it is to strive,
Which only ruin nations or retrieve.
Here in your sight, with patience I resign
That envy'd royalty which once was mine ;
Renounce the cares, that wait upon a crown,
And make my last attention all my own.
Seven virgin daughters in my house remain,
Who must not live to swell a victor's train ;
Nor shall my wretched queen, in triumph borne,
Be lifted to the eye of public scorn :
One common fate our miseries shall end,
And, with the dust of Thebes, our ashes blend."
  His fix'd decree the monarch thus exprest ;
One half the fates confirm'd, deny'd the rest :
For now surrounded by the hostile crowd
His captive queen, an humble suppliant, stood.
Tydides found her as she left the walls ;
Before the hero to the ground she falls ;
With trembling hands, his mighty knees she
            press'd,
And, supplicating, thus with tears address'd :
" Illustrious chief ! for sure your gallant mien
No less proclaims you, spare a wretched queen ;
One whom the gods with endless hate pursue,
To griefs already sumless adding new ;
O spare a helpless wretch, who humbly bends,
And for protection on thy might depends !"
As supplicating thus her suit she press'd,
Ulysses heard, and thus the chief address'd :
" See how th' immortals, by a just decree,
Cassandra's fall avenge, and honour thee !
See, at thy feet, the wife of Creon laid,
A victim offer'd for the injur'd maid.
Let her the first your just resentment feel;
By Heav'n presented to your vengeful steel."
  Ulysses thus.  With sighs the hero said :
" Enough is offer'd to Cassandra's shade ;
With wide destruction, wasting sword and fire,
To plague the authors of her fall, conspire,

Yet all in vain. No sacrifice recalls
The parted ghost from Pluto's gloomy walls.
Too long, alas! has lawless fury rul'd,
To reason deaf, by no reflection cool'd:
While I unhappy, by its dictates sway'd,
My guardian murder'd, and the host betray'd.
No victim, therefore, to my rage I'll pay;
Nor ever follow as it points the way."
   The son of Tydeus thus; and to his tent,
From insults safe, the royal matron sent.
Himself again the course of conquest led
Till Thebes was overthrown, and Creon bled.

---

## A DREAM.

### IN THE MANNER OF SPENSER.

ONE ev'ning, as by pleasant Forth I stray'd,
   In pensive mood, and meditated still
On poets' learned toil, with scorn repaid
   By envy's bitter spite, and want of skill;
   A cave I found, which open'd in a hill.
The floor was sand, with various shells yblended,
   Through which, in slow meanders, crept a rill;
he roof, by Nature's cunning slight suspended:
Thither my steps I turn'd, and there my journey
   ended.

Upon the ground my listless limbs I laid,
   Lull'd by the murmur of the passing stream:
Then sleep, soft stealing, did my eyes invade;
   And waking thought soon ended in a dream.
   Transported to a region I did seem,
Which with Thessalian Tempe might compare;
   Of verdant shade compos'd, and wat'ry gleam:
Not ev'n Valdarno, thought so passing fair,
Might match this pleasant land in all perfec-
   tions rare.

One, like a hoary palmer, near a brook,
   Under an arbour, seated did appear;
A shepherd swain, attending, held a book,
   And seem'd to read therein that he mote hear.
   From curiosity I stepped near;
But ere I reach'd the place where they did sit,
   The whisp'ring breezes wafted to my ear
The sound of rhymes which I myself had writ:
Rhymes much, alas, too mean, for such a judge
   unfit.

For him he seem'd who sung Achilles' rage,
   In lofty numbers that shall never die,
And wise Ulysses' tedious pilgrimage,
   So long the sport of sharp adversity:
   The praises of his merit, Fame on high,
With her shrill trump, for ever loud doth sound;
   With him no bard, for excellence, can vie,
Of all that late or ancient e'er were found;
So much he doth surpass ev'n bards the most re-
   nown'd.

The shepherd swain invited me to come
   Up to the arbour where they seated were;
For Homer call'd me: much I fear'd the doom
   Which such a judge seem'd ready to declare.
As I approach'd, with meikle dread and care,
He thus address'd me: "Sir, the cause explain
   Why all your story here is told so bare?
Few circumstances mix'd of various grain;
Such, surely, much enrich and raise a poet's
   strain."

"Certes," quoth I, "the critics are the cause
   Of this and many other mischiefs more;
Who tie the Muses to such rigid laws,
   That all their songs are frivolous and poor.
   They cannot now, as oft they did before,
Ere pow'rful prejudice had clipt their wings,
   Nature's domain with boundless flight explore,
And traffic freely in her precious things:
Each bard now fears the rod, and trembles while
   he sings.

"Though Shakespear, still disdaining narrow rules,
   His bosom fill'd with Nature's sacred fire,
Broke all the cobweb limits fix'd by fools,
   And left the world to blame him and admire;
   Yet his reward few mortals would desire;
For, of his learned toil, the only meed
   That ever I could find he did acquire,
Is that our dull, degenerate, age of lead,
Says that he wrote by chance, and that he scarce
   could read."

"I ween," quoth he, "that poets are to blame
   When they submit to critics' tyranny:
For learned wights there is no greater shame,
   Than blindly with their dictates to comply.
   Who ever taught the eagle how to fly,
Whose wit did e'er his airy tract define;
   When with free wing he claims his native sky,
Say, will he steer his course by rule and line?
Certes, he'd scorn the bound that would his flight
   confine.

"Not that the Muses' art is void of rules:
   Many there are, I wot, and stricter far,
Than those which pedants dictate from the
   schools,
   Who wage with wit and taste eternal war:
For foggy ignorance their sight doth mar;
   Nor can their low conception ever reach
To what dame Nature, crown'd with many a
   star,
Explains to such as know her learned speech;
But few can comprehend the lessons she doth
   teach.

"As many as the stars that gild the sky,
   As many as the flow'rs that paint the ground,
In number like the insect tribes that fly,
   The various forms of beauty still are found;
   That with strict limits no man may them
   bound,
And say that this, and this alone, is right:
   Experience soon such rashness would confound,
And make its folly obvious as the light;
For such presumption sure becomes not mortal
   wight.

"Therefore each bard should freely entertain
   The hints which pleasing fancy gives at will;
Nor curb her sallies with too strict a rein,
   Nature subjecting to her hand-maid Skill:
   And you yourself in this have done but ill;
With many more, who have not comprehended
   That genius, crampt, will rarely mount the
   hill,
Whose forked summit with the clouds is blended:
Therefore, when next you write, let this defect be
   mended.

"But, like a friend, who candidly reproves
   For faults and errours which he doth espy,
Each vice he freely marks; yet always loves
   To mingle favour with severity.

Certes," quoth he, " I cannot well deny,
That you in many things may hope to please :
You force a barbarous northern tongue to ply,
And bend it to your purposes with ease ;
Though rough as Albion's rocks, and hoarser
     than her seas.

" Nor are your tales, I wot, so loosely yok'd,
As those which Colin Clout [1] did tell before ;
Nor with description crowded so, and chok'd,
Which, thinly spread, will always please the
     more.
Colin, I wot, was rich in Nature's store ;
More rich than you, had more than he could use :
But mad Orlando [2] taught him bad his lore :
Whose flights, at random, oft misled his Muse :
To follow such a guide, few prudent men would
     chuse.

" Me you have follow'd : Nature was my guide ;
   To this the merit of your verse is owing :
And know for certain, let it check your pride,
That all you boast of is of my bestowing.
The flow'rs I see through all your garden
     blowing,
Are mine ; most part, at least : I might demand,
Might claim them, as a crop of my own
     sowing,
And leave but few, thin scatter'd o'er the land :
A claim so just, I wot, you could not well with-
     stand."

" Certes," quoth I, " that justice were full hard,
Which me alone would sentence to restore ;
When many a learned sage, and many a bard,
Are equally your debtors, or much more.
Let Tityrus [3] himself produce his store,
Take what is thine, but little will remain :
Little, I wot, and that indebted sore
To Ascra's bard [4], and Arethusa's swain [5] ;
And others too beside, who lent him many a strain.

" Nor could the modern bards afford to pay,
Whose songs exalt the champions of the Cross :
Take from each hoard thy sterling gold away,
And little will remain but worthless dross.
Not bards alone could ill support the loss ;
But sages too, whose theft suspicion shunn'd :
E'en that sly Greek[6], who steals and hides so
     close,
Were half a bankrupt, if he should refund.
While these are all forborn, shall I alone be
     dunn'd."

He smil'd ; and from his wreath, which well
     could spare      [were clad,
Such boon, the wreath with which his locks
Pluck'd a few leaves to hide my temples bare ;
The present I receiv'd with heart full glad.
" Henceforth," quoth I, " I never shall be sad ;
For now I shall obtain my share of fame :
Nor will licentious wit, or envy bad,
With bitter taunts, my verses dare to blame :
This garland shall protect them, and exalt my
     name."

[1] Spenser.
[2] Ariosto, so called from his hero.
[3] Virgil.     [4] Hesiod.     [5] Theocritus.
[6] Plato, reckoned, by Longinus, one of the
greatest imitators of Homer.

But dreams are short ; for as I thought to lay
My limbs at ease upon the flow'ry ground,
And drink, with greedy ear, what he might say,
As murm'ring waters sweet, or music's sound ;
My sleep departed ; and I, waking, found
Myself again by Fortha's pleasant stream.
Homewards I stepp'd, in meditation drown'd,
Reflecting on the meaning of my dream :
Which let each wight interpret as him best doth
     seem.

# FABLES.

TO THE

## EARL OF LAUDERDALE.

MY LORD,

IT is undoubtedly an uneasy situation to lie
under great obligations without being able to
make suitable returns: all that can be done in
this case is, to acknowledge the debt, which
(though it does not entitle to an acquittance)
is looked upon as a kind of compensation, being
all that gratitude has in its power.

This is in a peculiar manner my situation with
respect to your lordship. What you have done
for me with the most uncommon favour and
condescension, is what I never shall be able to
repay ; and therefore have used the freedom to
recommend the following performance to your
protection, that I might have an opportunity of
acknowledging my obligations in the most public
manner.

It is evident that the world will hardly allow
my gratitude upon this occasion to be disinter-
ested. Your distinguished rank, the additional
honours derived from the lustre of your ancestors, your own uncommon abilities, equally
adapted to the service of your country in peace
and in war, are circumstances sufficient to make
any author ambitious of your lordship's patronage. But I must do myself the justice to insist,
it is upon the account of distinctions less splendid, though far more interesting (those, I mean,
by which you are distinguished as the friend of
human nature, the guide and patron of unexpe-
rienced youth, and the father of the poor), that
I am zealous of subscribing myself,

     my lord,

         your lordship's

            most humble, and

               most devoted servant,

                 WILLIAM WILKIE.

## THE YOUNG LADY AND THE LOOKING-GLASS.

YE deep philosophers who can
Explain that various creature, man,
Say, is there any point so nice,
As that of offering an advice ?

To bid your friend his errours mend,
Is almost certain to offend :
Though you in softest terms advise,
Confess him good ; admit him wise ;
In vain you sweeten the discourse,
He thinks you call him fool, or worse ;
You paint his character, and try
If he will own it, and apply.
Without a name reprove and warn :
Here none are hurt, and all may learn.
This too must fail, the picture shown,
No man will take it for his own.
In moral lectures treat the case,
Say this is honest, that is base ;
In conversation none will bear it;
And for the pulpit, few come near it.
And is there then no other way
A moral lesson to convey ?
Must all that shall attempt to teach,
Admonish, satyrize, or preach ?
Yes, there is one, an ancient art,
By sages found to reach the heart,
Ere science with distinctions nice
Had fixt what virtue is, and vice,
Inventing all the various names
On which the moralist declaims :
They wou'd by simple tales advise,
Which took the hearer by surprise ;
Alarm'd his conscience, unprepar'd,
Ere pride had put it on its guard ;
And made him from himself receive
The lessons which they meant to give.
That this device will oft prevail,
And gain its end, when others fail,
If any shall pretend to doubt,
The tale which follows makes it out.
    There was a little stubborn dame
Whom no authority could tame,
Restive by long indulgence grown,
No will she minded but her own :
At trifles oft she'd scold and fret,
Then in a corner take a seat,
And sourly moping all the day,
Disdain alike to work or play.
Papa all softer arts had try'd,
And sharper remedies apply'd ;
But both were vain, for every course
He took still made her worse and worse.
'Tis strange to think how female wit,
So oft shou'd make a lucky hit,
When man with all his high pretence
To deeper judgment, sounder sense,
Will err, and measures false pursue—
'Tis very strange I own, but true.—
Mama observ'd the rising lass,
By stealth retiring to the glass,
To practise little airs unseen,
In the true genius of thirteen :
On this a deep design she laid
To tame the humour of the maid ;
Contriving like a prudent mother
To make one folly cure another.
Upon the wall against the seat
Which Jessy us'd for her retreat,
Whene'er by accident offended,
A looking-glass was straight suspended,
That it might show her how deform'd
She look'd, and frightful when she storm'd ;
And warn her, as she priz'd her beauty,
To bend her humour to her duty.

All this the looking glass achiev'd,
Its threats were minded and believ'd.
    The maid, who spurn'd at all advice,
Grew tame and gentle in a trice.
So when all other means had fail'd,
The silent monitor prevail'd.
    Thus, fable to the human-kind
Presents an image of the mind ;
It is a mirror where we spy
At large our own deformity,
And learn of course those faults to mend,
Which but to mention would offend.

_____

## THE KITE AND THE ROOKS.

You say 'tis vain in verse or prose
To tell what ev'ry body knows,
And stretch invention to express
Plain truths which all men will confess:
Go on the argument to mend,
Prove that to know is to attend,
And that we ever keep in sight
What reason tells us once is right :
Till this is done you must excuse
The zeal and freedom of my Muse,
In hinting to the human-kind
What few deny but fewer mind :
There is a folly which we blame,
'Tis strange that it should want a name,
For sure no other finds a place
So often in the human race ;
I mean the tendency to spy
Our neighbour's faults with sharpen'd eye,
And make his lightest failings known,
Without attending to our own.
The prude, in daily use to vex
With groundless censure half the sex,
Of rigid virtue, honour nice,
And much a foe to every vice,
Tells lies without remorse and shame,
Yet never thinks herself to blame.
A scriv'ner, though afraid to kill,
Yet scruples not to forge a will ;
Abhors the soldier's bloody feats,
While he as freely damns all cheats.
The reason's plain, 'tis not his way
To lie, to cozen and betray.
But tell me if to take by force,
Is not as bad at least, or worse.
The pimp who owns it as his trade
To poach for letchers, and be paid,
Thinks himself honest in his station,
But rails at rogues that sell the nation:
Nor would he stoop in any case,
And stain his honour for a place.
To mark this errour of mankind
The tale which follows is design'd.
    A flight of rooks one harvest morn
Had stopt upon a field of corn,
Just when a kite, as authors say,
Was passing on the wing that way:
His honest heart was fill'd with pain,
To see the farmer lose his grain,
So lighting gently on a shock
He thus the foragers bespoke.
" Believe me, sirs, you're much to blame,
'Tis strange that neither fear nor shame

Can keep you from your usual way
Of stealth, and pilf'ring ev'ry day.
No sooner has th' industrious swain
His field turn'd up and sow'd the grain,
But ye come flocking on the wing,
Prepar'd to snatch it ere it spring:
And after all his toil and care
Leave every furrow spoil'd and bare:
If aught escapes your greedy bills,
Which nurs'd by summer grows and fills,
'Tis still your prey: and though ye know
No rook did ever till or sow,
Ye boldly reap, without regard
To justice, industry's reward,
And use it freely as your own,
Though men and cattle shou'd get none.
I never did in any case
Descend to practises so base;
Though stung with hunger's sharpest pain,
I still have scorn'd to touch a grain,
Even when I had it in my pow'r,
To do 't with safety every hour:
For, trust me, nought that can be gain'd
Is worth a character unstain'd."
    Thus with a face austerely grave
Harangu'd the hypocrite and knave;
And answering from amidst the flock
A rook with indignation spoke.
    " What has been said is strictly true,
Yet comes not decently from you;
For sure it indicates a mind
From selfish passions more than blind,
To miss your greater crimes, and quote
Our lighter failings thus by rote.
I must confess we wrong the swain,
Too oft by pilf'ring of his grain:
But is our guilt like yours, I pray,
Who rob and murder every day?
No harmless bird can mount the skies
But you attack him as he flies;
And when at eve he lights to rest,
You stoop and snatch him from his nest.
The husbandman who seems to share
So large a portion of your care,
Say, is he ever off his guard,
While you are hov'ring o'er the yard?
He knows too well your usual tricks,
Your ancient spite to tender chicks,
And that you, like a felon, watch
For something to surprise and snatch.'"
    At this rebuke so just, the kite
Surpris'd, abash'd, and silenc'd quite,
And prov'd a villain to his face,
Straight soar'd aloft and left the place.

------

## THE MUSE AND THE SHEPHERD.

Let every bard who seeks applause
Be true to virtue and her cause,
Nor ever try to raise his fame
By praising that which merits blame;
The vain attempt he needs must rue,
For disappointment will ensue.
Virtue with her superior charms
Exalts the poet's soul and warms,
His taste refines, his genius fires,
Like Phœbus and the Nine inspires;

While vice, though seemingly approv'd,
Is coldly flatter'd, never lov'd.
    Palemon once a story told,
Which by conjecture must be old:
I have a kind of half conviction
That at the best 'tis but a fiction;
But taken right and understood,
The moral certainly is good.
    A shepherd swain was wont to sing
The infant beauties of the spring,
The bloom of summer, winter hoar,
The autumn rich in various store;
And prais'd in numbers strong and clear
The Ruler of the changeful year.
To human themes he'd next descend,
The shepherd's harmless life commend,
And prove him happier than the great
With all their pageantry and state:
Who oft for pleasure and for wealth,
Exchange their innocence and health;
The Muses listen'd to his lays
And crown'd him as he sung with bays.
Euterpe, goddess of the lyre,
A harp bestow'd with golden wire:
And oft wou'd teach him how to sing,
Or touch with art the trembling strings.
His fame o'er all the mountains flew,
And to his cot the shepherds drew;
They heard his music with delight,
Whole summer days from morn to night:
Nor did they ever think him long,
Such was the magic of his song:
Some rural present each prepar'd,
His skill to honour and reward;
A flute, a sheep-hook, or a lamb
Or kidling follow'd by its dam:
For bards it seems in earlier days,
Got something more than empty praise.
All this continu'd for a while,
But soon our songster chang'd his style,
Infected with the common itch,
His gains to double and grow rich:
Or fondly seeking new applause,
Or this or t'other was the cause;
One thing is certain, that his rhymes
Grew more obsequious to the times,
Less stiff and formal, alter'd quite
To what a courtier calls polite,
Whoe'er grew rich, by right or wrong,
Became the hero of a song:
No nymph or shepherdess could wed,
But he must sing the nuptial bed,
And still was ready to recite
The secret transports of the night,
In strains too luscious for the ear
Of sober chastity to bear.
Astonish'd at a change so great,
No more the shepherds sought his seat,
But in their place, a horned crowd
Of satyrs flock'd from every wood,
Drawn by the magic of his lay,
To dance, to frolic, sport and play.
The goddess of the lyre disdain'd
To see her sacred gift profan'd,
And gliding swiftly to the place,
With indignation in her face,
The trembling shepherd thus address'd,
In awful majesty confess'd.
    " Thou wretched fool, that harp resign,
For know it is no longer thine;

It was not given you to inspire
A herd like this with loose desire,
Nor to assist that venal praise,
Which vice may purchase, if it pays:
Such offices my lyre disgrace;
Here take this bag-pipe in its place.
'Tis fitter far, believe it true,
Both for these miscreants and you."
The swain dismay'd, without a word,
Submitted, and the harp restor'd.

---

## THE GRASSHOPPER AND THE GLOWWORM.

When ignorance possess'd the schools,
And reign'd by Aristotle's rules,
Ere Verulam, like dawning light,
Rose to dispel the Gothic night:
A man was taught to shut his eyes,
And grow abstracted to be wise.
Nature's broad volume fairly spread,
Where all true science might be read
The wisdom of th' Eternal Mind,
Declar'd and publish'd to mankind,
Was quite neglected, for the whims
Of mortals and their airy dreams:
By narrow principles and few,
By hasty maxims, oft untrue,
By words and phrases ill-defin'd,
Evasive truth they hop'd to bind;
Which still escap'd them, and the elves
At last caught nothing but themselves.
Nor is this folly modern quite,
'Tis ancient too: the Stagirite
Improv'd at first, and taught his school
By rules of art to play the fool.
Ev'n Plato, from example bad,
Would oft turn sophist and run mad;
Make Socrates himself discourse
Like Clarke and Leibnitz, oft-times worse;
'Bout quirks and subtilties contending,
Beyond all human comprehending.
From some strange bias men pursue
False knowledge still in place of true,
Build airy systems of their own,
This moment rais'd, the next pull'd down;
While few attempt to catch those rays
Of truth which nature still displays
Throughout the universal plan,
From moss and mushrooms up to man.
This sure were better, but we hate
To borrow when we can create;
And therefore stupidly prefer,
Our own conceits, by which we err,
To all the wisdom to be gain'd
From nature and her laws explain'd.

One ev'ning when the Sun was set,
A grasshopper and glowworm met
Upon a hillock in a dale,
As Mab the fairy tells the tale.
Vain and conceited of his spark,
Which brighten'd as the night grew dark,
The shining reptile swell'd with pride
To see his rays on every side,
Mark'd by a circle on the ground
Of livid light some inches round.
Quoth he, " If glowworms never shone,
To light the Earth when day is gone,

In spite of all the stars that burn,
Primeval darkness wou'd return:
They're less and dimmer, one may see,
Besides much farther off than we;
And therefore thro' a long descent
Their light is scatter'd quite and spent:
While ours, compacter and at hand,
Keeps night and darkness at a stand,
Diffus'd around in many a ray,
Whose brightness emulates the day."
This pass'd and more without dispute,
The patient grasshopper was mute:
But soon the east began to glow
With light appearing from below,
And level from the ocean's streams
The Moon emerging shot her beams.
To gild the mountains and the woods,
And shake and glitter on the floods.
The glowworm, when he found his light
Grow pale and faint and vanish quite
Before the Moon's prevailing ray,
Began his envy to display.
"That globe," quoth he, "which seems so fair,
Which brightens all the Earth and air,
And sends its beams so far abroad,
Is nought, believe me, but a clod;
A thing which, if the Sun were gone,
Has no more light in't than a stone,
Subsisting merely by supplies
From Phœbus in the nether skies:
My light indeed, I must confess,
On some occasions will be less;
But spite itself will hardly say
I'm debtor for a single ray;
'Tis all my own, and on the score
Of merit, mounts to ten times more
Than any planet can demand
For light dispens'd at second hand."
To hear the paltry insect boast,
The grasshopper all patience lost.
Quoth he, " My friend, it may be so,
The Moon with borrow'd light may glow;
That your faint glimm'ring is your own,
I think, is question'd yet by none:
But sure the office to collect
The solar brightness and reflect,
To catch those rays that wou'd be spent
Quite useless in the firmament,
And turn them downwards on the shade
Which absence of the Sun has made,
Amounts to more in point of merit
Than all your tribe did e'er inherit:
Oft by that planet's friendly ray
The midnight trav'ler finds his way;
Safe by the favour of her beams,
'Midst precipices, lakes and streams;
While you mislead him, and your light,
Seen like a cottage-lamp by night,
With hopes to find a safe retreat,
Allures and tempts him to his fate:
As this is so, I needs must call
The merit of your light but small:
You need not boast on 't though your own;
'Tis light indeed, but worse than none;
Unlike to what the Moon supplies,
Which you call borrow'd, and despise."

## THE APE, THE PARROT, AND THE JACKDAW.

I HOLD it rash at any time
To deal with fools dispos'd to rhyme ;
Dissuasive arguments provoke
Their utmost rage as soon as spoke :
Encourage them, and for a day
Or two you're safe by giving way ;
But when they find themselves betray'd,
On you at last the blame is laid.
They hate and scorn you as a traitor,
The common lot of those who flatter :
But can a scribbler, sir, be shunn'd ?
What will you do when teas'd and dunn'd ?
When watch'd, and caught, and closely press'd,
When complimented and caress'd,
When Bavius greets you with a bow,
" Sir, please to read a line or two ;"
If you approve and say they're clever,
" You make me happy, sir, for ever."
What can be done ? the case is plain,
No methods of escape remain :
You're fairly noos'd, and must consent
To bear, what nothing can prevent,
A coxcomb's anger ; and your fate
Will be to suffer soon or late.
　An ape that was the sole delight
Of an old woman day and night,
Indulg'd at table and in bed,
Attended like a child and fed :
Who knew each trick, and twenty more
Than ever monkey play'd before,
At last grew frantic and wou'd try,
In spite of nature's laws, to fly.
Oft from the window wou'd he view
The passing swallows as they flew,
Observe them fluttering round the walls,
Or gliding o'er the smooth canals :
He too must fly, and cope with these ;
For this and nothing else wou'd please :
Oft thinking from the window's height,
Three stories down to take his flight :
He still was something loth to venture,
As tending strongly to the centre :
And knowing that the least mistake
Might cost a limb, perhaps his neck.
The case you'll own was something nice ;
He thought it best to ask advice ;
And to the parrot straight applying,
Allow'd to be a judge of flying,
He thus began : " You'll think me rude,
Forgive me if I do intrude,
For you alone my doubts can clear
In something that concerns me near :
Do you imagine, if I try,
That I shall e'er attain to fly ?
The project's whimsical, no doubt,
But ere you censure hear me out :
That liberty's our greatest blessing
You'll grant me without farther pressing ;
To live confin'd, 'tis plain and clear,
Is something very hard to bear :
This you must know, who for an age
Have been kept pris'ner in a cage,
Deny'd the privilege to soar
With boundless freedom as before.
I have, 'tis true, much greater scope
Than you my friend, can ever hope ;

I traverse all the house and play
My tricks and gambols ev'ry day :
Oft with my mistress in a chair
I ride abroad to take the air ;
Make visits with her, walk at large,
A maid or footman's constant charge.
Yet this is noth ng, for I find
Myself still hamper'd and confin'd ;
A grov'ling thing : I fain would rise
Above the Earth and mount the skies :
The meanest birds, and insects too,
This feat with greatest ease can do.
To that gay creature turn about
That's beating on the pane without ;
Ten days ago, perhaps but five,
A worm, it scarcely seem'd alive :
By threads suspended, tough and small,
'Midst dusty cobwebs on a wall ;
Now dress'd in all the diff'rent dyes
That vary in the ev'ning skies,
He soars at large, and on the wing
Enjoys with freedom all the spring ;
Skims the fresh lakes, and rising sees
Beneath him far the loftiest trees ;
And when he rests, he makes his bow'r
The cup of some delicious flow'r.
Shall creatures so obscurely bred,
On mere corruption nurs'd and fed,
A glorious privilege obtain,
Which I can never hope to gain ?
Shall I, like man's imperial race
In manners, customs, shape and face,
Expert in all ingenious tricks,
To tumble, dance, and leap o'er sticks ;
Who know to sooth and coax my betters,
And match a beau, at least in letters ;
Shall I despair, and never try
(What meanest insects can) to fly ?
Say, mayn't I without dread or care
At once commit me to the air,
And not fall down and break my bones
Upon those hard and flinty stones ?
Say, if to stir my limbs before
Will make me glide along or soar ?
All things they say are learn'd by trying ;
No doubt it is the same with flying.
I wait your judgment with respect,
And shall proceed as you direct."
　Poor Poll, with gen'rous pity mov'd,
The Ape's fond rashness thus reprov'd :
For, though instructed by mankind,
Her tongue to candour still inclin'd.
　" My friend, the privilege to rise
Above the Earth and mount the skies,
Is glorious sure, and 'tis my fate
To feel the want on't with regret ;
A pris'ner to a cage confin'd,
Though wing'd and of the flying kind.
With you the case is not the same,
You're quite terrestrial by your frame,
And shou'd be perfectly content
With your peculiar element :
You have no wings, I pray reflect,
To lift you and your course direct ;
Those arms of yours will never do,
Not twenty in the place of two ;
They ne'er can lift you from the ground,
For broad and long, they're thick and round ;
And therefore if you choose the way,
To leap the window, as you say,

'Tis certain that you'll be the jest
Of every insect, bird and beast,
When you lie batter'd by your fall
Just at the bottom of the wall.
Be prudent then, improve the pow'rs
Which nature gives in place of ours.
You'll find them readily conduce
At once to pleasure and to use.
But airy whims and crotchets lead
To certain loss, and ne'er succeed:
As folks, though inly vex'd and teas'd,
Will oft seem satisfy'd and pleas'd."
  The ape approv'd of every word,
At this time utter'd by the bird:
But nothing in opinion chang'd,
Thought only how to be reveng'd.
It happen'd when the day was fair,
That Poll was set to take the air,
Just where the monkey oft sat poring
About experiments in soaring:
Dissembling his contempt and rage,
He stept up softly to the cage,
And with a sly malicious grin,
Accosted thus the bird within.
  "You say, I am not form'd for flight;
In this you certainly are right;
'Tis very plain upon reflection,
But to yourself there's no objection,
Since flying is the very trade
For which the winged race is made;
And therefore for our mutual sport,
I'll make you fly, you can't be hurt."
With that he slyly slipt the string
Which held the cage up by the ring.
In vain the parrot begg'd and pray'd,
No word was minded that she said;
Down went the cage, and on the ground
Bruis'd and half-dead poor Poll was found.
Pug who for some time had attended
To that alone which now was ended,
Again had leisure to pursue
The project he had first in view.
  Quoth he, "A person if he's wise
Will only with his friends advise,
They know his temper and his parts,
And have his interest near their hearts.
In matters which he should forbear,
They'll hold him back with prudent care,
But never from an envious spirit
Forbid him to display his merit;
Or judging wrong, from spleen and hate
His talents slight or underrate:
I acted sure with small reflection
In asking counsel and direction
From a sly minion whom I know
To be my rival and my foe:
One who will constantly endeavour
To hurt me in our lady's favour,
And watch and plot to keep me down,
From obvious interests of her own:
But on the top of that old tow'r
An honest daw has made his bow'r;
A faithful friend whom one may trust,
My debtor too for many a crust,
Which in the window oft I lay
For him to come and take away:
From gratitude no doubt he'll give
Such counsel as I may receive;
Well back'd with reasons strong and plain
To push me forward or restrain."

One morning when the daw appear'd,
The project was propos'd and heard:
And though the bird was much surpris'd
To find friend Pug so ill advis'd,
He rather chose that he shou'd try
At his own proper risk to fly,
Than hazard, in a case so nice,
To shock him by too free advice.
  Quoth he, "I'm certain that you'll find
The project answer to your mind;
Without suspicion, dread or care,
At once commit you to the air;
You'll soar aloft, or, if you please,
Proceed straight forwards at your ease:
The whole depends on resolution,
Which you possess from constitution;
And if you follow as I lead,
'Tis past a doubt you must succeed."
  So saying, from the turret's height
The Jack-daw shot with downward flight,
And on the edge of a canal,
Some fifty paces from the wall,
'Lighted obsequious to attend
The monkey when he should descend:
But he, altho' he had believ'd
The flatterer and was deceiv'd,
Felt some misgivings at his heart
In vent'ring on so new an art:
But yet at last, 'tween hope and fear,
Himself he trusted to the air;
But far'd like him whom poets mention
With Dedalus's old invention:
Directly downwards on his head
He fell, and lay an hour for dead.
The various creatures in the place,
Had diff'rent thoughts upon the case,
From some his fate compassion drew,
But those I must confess were few;
The rest esteem'd him rightly serv'd,
And in the manner he deserv'd,
For playing tricks beyond his sphere,
Nor thought the punishment severe.
They gather'd round him as he lay,
And jeer'd him when he limp'd away.
  Pug, disappointed thus and hurt,
And grown besides the public sport,
Found all his different passions change
At once to fury and revenge:
The daw 'twas useless to pursue;
His helpless brood, as next in view,
With unrelenting paws he seiz'd,
One's neck he wrung, another squeez'd,
Till of the number four or five,
No single bird was left alive.
  Thus counsellors, in all regards
Though different, meet with like rewards,
The story shews the certain fate
Of every mortal soon or late,
Whose evil genius for his crimes
Connects with fop that rhymes.

## THE BOY AND THE RAINBOW.

DECLARE, ye sages, if ye find
'Mongst animals of ev'ry kind,
Of each condition, sort, and size,
From whales and elephants to flies,
A creature that mistakes his plan,
And errs so constantly as man?

Each kind pursues his proper good,
And seeks for pleasure, rest, and food,
As nature points, and never errs
In what it chooses and prefers;
Man only blunders, though possest
Of talents far above the rest.
   Descend to instances and try;
An ox will scarce attempt to fly,
Or leave his pasture in the wood,
With fishes to explore the flood.
Man only acts, of every creature,
In opposition to his nature.
The happiness of human kind,
Consists in rectitude of mind,
A will subdu'd to reason's sway,
And passions practis'd to obey;
An open and a gen'rous heart,
Refin'd from selfishness and art;
Patience which mocks at fortune's pow'r,
And wisdom never sad nor sour:
In these consist our proper bliss;
Else Plato reasons much amiss:
But foolish mortals still pursue
False happiness in place of true;
Ambition serves us for a guide,
Or lust, or avarice, or pride;
While reason no assent can gain,
And revelation warns in vain.
Hence through our lives, in every stage,
From infancy itself to age,
A happiness we toil to find,
Which still avoids us like the wind;
Ev'n when we think the prize our own,
At once 'tis vanish'd, lost, and gone.
You'll ask me why I thus rehearse
All Epictetus in my verse,
And if I fondly hope to please
With dry reflections such as these,
So trite, so hackney'd, and so stale?
I'll take the hint and tell a tale.
   One ev'ning as a simple swain
His flock attended on the plain,
The shining bow he chanc'd to spy,
Which warns us when a show'r is nigh;
With brightest rays it seem'd to glow,
Its distance eighty yards or so.
This bumpkin had it seems been told
The story of the cup of gold,
Which Fame reports is to be found
Just where the rainbow meets the ground;
He therefore felt a sudden itch
To seize the goblet and be rich;
Hoping, (yet hopes are oft but vain):
No more to toil through wind and rain,
But sit indulging by the fire,
'Midst ease and plenty, like a 'squire:
He mark'd the very spot of land
On which the rainbow seem'd to stand,
And stepping forwards at his leisure
Expected to have found the treasure.
But as he mov'd, the colour'd ray
Still chang'd its place and slipt away,
As seeming his approach to shun;
From walking he began to run,
But all in vain, it still withdrew
As nimbly as he cou'd pursue;
At last through many a bog and lake,
Rough craggy road and thorny brake,
It led the easy fool, till night
Approach'd, then vanish'd in his sight,

And left him to compute his gains,
With nought but labour for his pains.

------

## CELIA AND HER MIRROR.

As there are various sorts of minds,
So friendships are of diff'rent kinds:
Some, constant when the object's near,
Soon vanish if it disappear.
Another sort, with equal flame,
In absence will be still the same:
Some folks a trifle will provoke,
Their weak attachment soon is broke;
Some great offences only move
To change in friendship or in love.
Affection, when it has its source
In things that shift and change of course,
As these diminish and decay,
Must likewise fade and melt away.
But when 'tis of a nobler kind,
Inspir'd by rectitude of mind,
Whatever accident arrives,
It lives, and death itself survives;
Those different kinds reduc'd to two,
False friendship may be call'd, and true.
   In Celia's drawing-room of late
Some female friends were met to chat;
Where after much discourse had past,
A portrait grew the theme at last:
'Twas Celia's you must understand,
And by a celebrated hand.
Says one, "That picture sure must strike,
In all respects it is so like;
Your very features, shape and air
Express'd, believe me, to a hair:
The price I'm sure cou'd not be small,"—
"Just fifty guineas frame and all."—
"That mirror there is wond'rous fine."—
"I own the bauble cost me nine;
I'm fairly cheated you may swear,
For never was a thing so dear."—
"Dear!"—quoth the looking-glass—and spoke,
"Madam, it wou'd a saint provoke:
Must that same gaudy thing be own'd
A pennyworth at fifty pound;
While I at nine am reckon'd dear,
'Tis what I never thought to hear.
Let both our merits now be try'd,
This fair assembly shall decide;
And I will prove it to your face,
That you are partial in the case.
I give a likeness far more true
Than any artist ever drew:
And what is vastly more, express
Your whole variety of dress:
From morn to noon, from noon to night,
I watch each change and paint it right;
Besides I'm mistress of the art,
Which conquers and secures a heart.
I teach you how to use those arms,
That vary and assist your charms,
And in the triumphs of the fair,
Claim half the merit for my share:
So when the truth is fairly told,
I'm worth at least my weight in gold;
But that vain thing of which you speak
Becomes quite useless in a week,
For, though it had no other vice,
'Tis out of fashion in a trice:

The cap is chang'd, the cloke, the gown;
It must no longer stay in town;
But goes in course to hide a wall
With others in your country-hall.''
   The mirror thus :—the nymph reply'd,
" Your merit cannot be deny'd:
The portrait too, I must confess,
In some respects has vastly less.
But you yourself will freely grant
That it has virtues which you want.
'Tis certain that you can express
My shape, my features, and my dress,
Not just as well, but better too
Than Kneller once or Ramsay now.
But that same image in your heart
Which thus excels the painter's art,
The shortest absence can deface,
And put a monkey's in its place:
That other which the canvas bears,
Unchang'd and constant, lasts for years,
Wou'd keep its lustre and its bloom
Though it were here and I at Rome.
When age and sickness shall invade
Those youthful charms and make them fade,
You'll soon perceive it, and reveal
What partial friendship shou'd conceal:
You'll tell me, in your usual way,
Of furrow'd cheeks and locks grown gray;
Your gen'rous rival, not so cold,
Will ne'er suggest that I am old;
Nor mark when time and slow disease
Have stol'n the graces wont to please;
But keep my image to be seen
In the full blossom of sixteen :
Bestowing freely all the praise
I merited in better days.
You will (when I am turn'd to dust,
For beauties die, as all things must,
And you remember but by seeing)
Forget that e'er I had a being :
But in that picture I shall live,
My charms shall death itself survive,
And figur'd by the pencil there
Tell that your mistress once was fair.
Weigh each advantage and defect,
The portrait merits most respect :
Your qualities would recommend
A servant rather than a friend;
But service sure, in every case,
To friendship yields the higher place."

---

## THE FISHERMEN.

### IMITATED FROM THEOCRITUS.

By all the sages 'tis confest
That hope when moderate is best:
But when indulg'd beyond due measure,
It yields a vain deceitful pleasure,
Which cheats the simple, and betrays
To mischief in a thousand ways :
Just hope assists in all our toils,
The wheels of industry it oils;
In great attempts the bosom fires,
And zeal and constancy inspires.
False hope, like a deceitful dream,
Rests on some visionary scheme,
And keeps us idle to our loss,
Enchanted with our hands across.

   A tale an ancient bard has told
Of two poor fishermen of old,
Their names were (lest I should forget
And put the reader in a pet,
Lest critics too shou'd make a pother)
The one Asphelio, Gripus t'other.
The men were very poor, their trade
Cou'd scarce afford them daily bread:
Though ply'd with industry and care
Through the whole season, foul and fair.
Upon a rock their cottage stood,
On all sides bounded by the flood :
It was a miserable seat,
Like cold and hunger's worst retreat:
And yet it serv'd them both for life,
As neither cou'd maintain a wife ;
Two walls were rock, and two were sand,
Ramm'd up with stakes and made to stand.
A roof hung threat'ning o'er their heads
Of boards half-rotten, thatch'd with reeds.
And as no thief e'er touch'd their store,
A hurdle serv'd them for a door.
Their beds were leaves ; against the wall
A sail hung drying, yard and all.
On one side lay an old patch'd wherry
Like Charon's on the Stygian ferry :
On t' other, baskets and a net,
With sea-weed foul and always wet.
These sorry instruments of trade
Were all the furniture they had:
For they had neither spit nor pot,
Unless my author has forgot.
   Once, some few hours ere break of day,
As in their hut our fishers lay,
The one awak'd and wak'd his neighbour,
That both might ply their daily labour;
For cold and hunger are confest
No friends to indolence or rest.
   " Friend," quoth the drowsy swain, and swore,
" What you have done has hurt me more
Than all your service can repay
For years to come by night and day;
You've broke—the thought on't makes me mad—
The finest dream that e'er I had."    [prove
   Quoth Gripus : " Friend your speech wou'd
You mad indeed, or else in love;
For dreams shou'd weigh but light with those
Who feel the want of food and clothes:
I guess, though simple and untaught,
You dream'd about a lucky draught,
Or money found by chance: they say,
That hungry foxes dream of prey."
   " You're wond'rous shrewd, upon my troth,"
Asphelio cry'd, " and right in both :
My dream had gold in't, as you said,
And fishing too, our constant trade;
And since your guess has hit so near,
In short the whole on't you shall hear.
   " Upon the shore I seem'd to stand,
My rod and tackle in my hand ;
The baited hook full oft I threw,
But still in vain, I nothing drew :
A fish at last appear'd to bite,
The cork div'd quickly out of sight,
And soon the dipping rod I found
With something weighty bent half round :
Quoth I, ' Good luck has come at last,
I've surely made a happy cast:
This fish, when in the market sold,
In place of brass will sell for gold:'

To bring it safe within my reach
I drew it safely to the beach,
But long ere it had come so near,
The water gleam'd with something clear;
Each passing billow caught the blaze,
And glitt'ring shone with golden rays.
Of hope and expectation full
Impatient, yet afraid to pull,
To shore I slowly brought my prize,
A golden fish of largest size:
'Twas metal all from head to tail,
Quite stiff and glitt'ring ev'ry scale.
Thought I, ' My fortune now is made ;
'Tis time to quit the fishing trade,
And choose some other, where the gains
Are sure, and come for half the pains.
Like creatures of amphibious nature
One hour on land and three in water;
We live 'midst danger, toil and care,
Yet never have a groat to spare :
While others, not expos'd to harm,
Grow rich, though always dry and warm ;
This treasure will suffice, and more,
To place me handsomely on shore,
In some snug manor; now a swain,
My steers shall turn the furrow'd plain,
While on a mountain's grassy side
My flocks are past'ring far and wide :
Beside all this, I'll have a seat
Convenient, elegant and neat,
A house not over-great nor small,
Three rooms, a kitchen, and a hall.
The offices contriv'd with care
And fitted to complete a square:
A garden well laid out ; a-wife,
To double all the joys of life ;
With children pratt'ling at my knees,
Such trifles as are sure to please.'
Those gay designs, and twenty more,
I in my dream was running o'er,
While you, as if you ow'd me spite,
Broke in and put them all to flight,
Blew the whole vision into air,
And left me waking in despair.
Of late we have been poorly fed,
Last night went supperless to bed,
Yet, if I had it in my pow'r
My dream to lengthen for an hour,
The pleasure mounts to such a sum,
I'd fast for fifty yet to come.
Therefore to bid me rise is vain ,
I'll wink and try to dream again."

"If this," quoth Gripus, " is the way
You choose, I've nothing more to say ;
'Tis plain that dreams of wealth will serve
A person who resolves to starve;
But sure, to hug a fancy'd case,
That never did nor can take place,
And for the pleasures it can give
Neglect the trade by which we live,
Is madness in its greatest height,
Or I mistake the matter quite :
Leave such vain fancies to the great,
For folly suits a large estate:
The rich may safely deal in dreams,
Romantic hopes and airy schemes.
But you and I, upon my word,
Such pastime cannot well afford ;
And therefore if you would be wise,
Take my advice, for once, and rise."

## CUPID AND THE SHEPHERD.

Who sets his heart on things below,
But little happiness shall know ;
For every object he pursues
Will vex, deceive him, and abuse:
While he whose hopes and wishes rise
To endless bliss above the skies,
A true felicity shall gain,
With freedom from both care and pain.
He seeks what yields him peace and rest,
Both when in prospect and possest.

A swain, whose flock had gone astray,
Was wand'ring far out of the way
Through deserts wild, and chanc'd to see
A stripling leaning on a tree.
In all things like the human-kind,
But that upon his back behind
Two wings were from his shoulders spread
Of gold and azure ting'd with red ;
Their colour like the ev'ning sky:
A golden quiver grac'd his thigh :
His bow unbended in his hand
He held, and wrote with on the sand;
As one whom anxious cares pursue,
In musing oft is wont to do.
He started still with sudden fear,
As if some danger had been near,
And turn'd on every side to view
A flight of birds that round him flew,
Whose presence seem'd to make him sad,
For all were ominous and bad ;
The hawk was there, the type of spite,
The jealous owl that shuns the light,
The raven, whose prophetic bill
Denounces woe and mischief still ;
The vulture hungry to devour,
Though gorg'd and glutted ev'ry hour ;
With these confus'd an ugly crew
Of harpies, bats, and dragons flew,
With talons arm'd, and teeth, and stings,
The air was darken'd with their wings.
The swain, though frighten'd, yet drew near,
Compassion rose in place of fear ;
He to the winged youth began,—
" Say, are you mortal and of man,
Or something of celestial birth,
From Heaven descended to the Earth ?"
" I am not of terestrial kind,"
Quoth Cupid, " nor to Earth confin'd :
Heav'n is my true and proper sphere,
My rest and happiness are there:
Through all the boundless realms of light
The phœnix waits upon my flight,
With other birds whose names are known
In that delightful place alone.
But when to Earth my course I bend,
At once they leave me and ascend ;
And for companions, in their stead,
Those winged monsters there succeed,
Who hov'ring round me night and day,
Expect and claim me as their prey."
" Sir," quoth the shepherd, " if you'll try,
Your arrows soon will make them fly ;
Or if they brave them and resist,
My sling is ready to assist."
" Incapable of wounds and pain,"
Reply'd the winged youth again,

" These foes our weapons will defy;
Immortal made, they never die;
But live to haunt me every where,
While I remain within their sphere."
  " Sir," quoth the swain, " might I advise,
You straight show'd get above the skies:
It seems indeed your only way,
For nothing here is worth your stay:
Beside, when foes like these molest,
You'll find but little peace or rest."

---

## THE SWAN AND OTHER BIRDS.

Each candidate for public fame
Engages in a desp'rate game:
His labour he will find but lost,
Or less than half repaid at most:
To prove this point I shall not choose
The arguments which Stoics use ;
That human life is but a dream,
And few things in it what they seem:
That praise is vain and little worth,
An empty bauble, and so forth.
I'll offer one, but of a kind
Not half so subtil and refin'd ;
Which, when the rest are out of sight,
May sometimes chance to have its weight.
The man who sets his merits high
To glitter in the public eye,
Shou'd have defects but very small,
Or strictly speaking, none at all:
For that success which spreads his fame,
Provokes each envious tongue to blame,
And makes his faults and failings known
Where'er his better parts are shown.
  Upon a time, as poets sing,
The birds all waited on their king,
His hymeneal rites to grace;
A flow'ry meadow was the place ;
They all were frolicsome and gay
Amidst the pleasures of the day,
And ere the festival was clos'd,
A match at singing was propos'd ;
The queen herself a wreath prepar'd,
To be the conqueror's reward ;
With store of pinks and daisies in it,
And many a songster try'd to win it,
But all the judges soon confest
The swan superior to the rest,
He got the garland from the bride,
With honour and applause beside :
A tattling goose, with envy stung,
Although herself she ne'er had sung,
Took this occasion to reveal
What swans seem studious to conceal,
And, skill'd in satire's artful ways,
Invective introduc'd with praise.
  " The swan," quoth she, " upon my word,
Deserves applause from ev'ry bird :
By proof his charming voice you know,
His feathers soft and white as snow ;
And if you saw him when he swims
Majestic on the silver streams,
He'd seem complete in all respects :
But nothing is without defects;
For that is true, which few wou'd think,
His legs and feet are black as ink—"

  " As black as ink !— if this be true,
To me 'tis wonderful and new,"
The sov'reign of the birds reply'd ;
" But soon the truth on't shall be try'd.
Sir, show your limbs, and for my sake,
Confute at once this foul mistake,
For I'll maintain, and I am right,
That, like your feathers, they are white."
  " Sir," quoth the swan, " it wou'd be vain
For me a falsehood to maintain ;
My legs are black, and proof will show
Beyond dispute that they are so :
But if I had not got a prize
Which glitters much in some folks eyes,
Not half the birds had ever known
What truth now forces me to own."

---

## THE LOVER AND HIS FRIEND.

### TO THE POETS.

'Tis not the point in works of art
With care to furnish every part,
That each, to high perfection rais'd,
May draw attention and be prais'd,
An object by itself respected,
Though all the others were neglected:
Not masters only this can do,
But many a vulgar artist too :
We know distinguish'd merit most
When in the whole the parts are lost,
When nothing rises up to shine,
Or draw us from the chief design.
When one united full effect
Is felt before we can reflect,
And mark the causes that conspire
To charm, and force us to admire.
This is indeed a master's part,
The very summit of his art,
And therefore when ye shall rehearse
To friends for trial of your verse,
Mark their behaviour and their way,
As much, at least, as what they say ;
If they seem pleas'd, and yet are mute,
The poem's good beyond dispute ;
But when they babble all the while,
Now praise the sense, and now the style,
'Tis plain that something must be wrong,
This too weak or that too strong.
The art is wanting which conveys
Impressions in mysterious ways,
And makes us from a whole receive
What no divided parts can give :
Fine writing, therefore, seems of course
Less fit to please at first than worse.
A language fitted to the sense
Will hardly pass for eloquence.
One feels its force, before he sees
The charm which gives it pow'r to please,
And ere instructed to admire,
Will read and read and never tire.
But when the style is of a kind
Which soars and leaves the sense behind,
'Tis something by itself, and draws
From vulgar judges dull applause.
They'll yawn, and tell you as you read,
" Those lines are mighty fine indeed;"

But never will your works peruse
At any time, if they can choose.
'Tis not the thing which men call wit,
Nor characters, though truly hit,
Nor flowing numbers soft or strong,
That bears the raptur'd soul along ;
'Tis something of a diff'rent kind,
'Tis all those skilfully combin'd,
To make what critics call a whole,
Which ravishes and charms the soul.
  Alexis, by fair Celia's scorn
To grief abandon'd and forlorn,
Had sought in solitude to cover
His anguish, like a hopeless lover :
With his fond passion to debate,
Gay Strephon sought his rural seat,
And found him with the shepherd's plac'd
Far in a solitary waste.—
  " My friend," quoth he, " you're much to
This foolish softness quit for shame ;   [blame ;
Nor fondly doat upon a woman,
Whose charms are nothing more than common.
That Celia's handsome I agree,
But Clara's handsomer than she :
Euanthe's wit, which all commend,
Does Celia's certainly transcend :
Nor can you find the least pretence
With Phebe's to compare her sense ;
With better taste Belinda dresses,
With truer step the floor she presses ;
And for behaviour soft and kind,
Melissa leaves her far behind :
What witchcraft then can fix the chain
Which makes you suffer her disdain,
And not attempt the manly part
To set at liberty your heart ?
Make but one struggle, and you'll see
That in a moment you'll be free."
  This Strephon urg'd, and ten times more,
From topics often touch'd before :
In vain his eloquence he try'd ;
Alexis, sighing, thus reply'd :—
  " If Clara's handsome and a toast,
'Tis all the merit she can boast :
Some fame Euanthe's wit has gain'd,
Because by prudence not restrain'd,
Phebe I own is wondrous wise,
She never acts but in disguise :
Belinda's merit all confess
Who know the mystery of dress :
But poor Melissa on the score
Of mere good-nature pleases more :
In those the reigning charm appears
Alone, to draw our eyes and ears,
No other rises by its side
And shines, attention to divide ;
Thus seen alone it strikes the eye,
As something exquisite and high:
But in my Celia you will find
Perfection of another kind.;
Each charm so artfully exprest
As still to mingle with the rest :
Averse and shunning to be known,
An object by itself alone,
But thus combin'd they make a spell
Whose force no human tongue can tell ;
A pow'rful magic which my breast
Will ne'er be able to resist :
For as she slights me or complies,
Her constant lover lives or dies."

## THE RAKE AND THE HERMIT.

A youth, a pupil of the town,
Philosopher and atheist grown,
Benighted once upon the road,
Found out a Hermit's lone abode,
Whose hospitality in need
Reliev'd the trav'ler and his steed,
For both sufficiently were tir'd,
Well drench'd in ditches and bemir'd.
Hunger the first attention claims ;
Upon the coals a rasher flames,
Dry crusts, and liquor something stale,
Were added to make up a meal ;
At which our trav'ler as he sat,
By intervals began to chat.—
  " 'Tis odd," quoth he, " to think what strains
Of folly govern some folks' brains :
What makes you choose this wild abode ?
You'll say, 'tis to converse with God :
Alas, I fear, 'tis all a whim ;
You never saw or spoke with him.
They talk of Providence's pow'r,
And say it rules us every hour ;
To me all nature seems confusion,
And such weak fancies mere delusion.
Say, if it rul'd and govern'd right,
Cou'd there be such a thing as night ;
Which, when the Sun has left the skies,
Puts all things in a deep disguise ?
If then a trav'ler chance to stray
The least step from the public way,
He's soon in endless mazes lost,
As I have found it to my cost.
Besides, the gloom which nature wears,
Assists imaginary fears
Of ghosts and goblins from the waves
Of sulph'rous lakes, and yawning graves,
All sprung from superstitious seed,
Like other maxims of the creed.
For my part, I reject the tales
Which faith suggests when reason fails ;
And reason nothing understands,
Unwarranted by eyes and hands.
These subtle essences, like wind,
Which some have dreamt of and call mind,
It ne'er admits ; nor joins the lie
Which says men rot, but never die.
It holds all future things in doubt,
And therefore wisely leaves them out :
Suggesting what is worth our care,
To take things present as they are,
Our wisest course : the rest is folly,
The fruit of spleen and melancholy."—
  " Sir," quoth the hermit, " I agree
That reason still our guide shou'd be :
And will admit her as the test,
Of what is true and what is best :
But reason sure wou'd blush for shame
At what you mention in her name ;
Her dictates are sublime and holy :
Impiety's the child of folly :
Reason with measur'd steps and slow
To things above from things below
Ascends, and guides us through her sphere
With caution, vigilance, and care.
Faith in the utmost frontier stands,
And reason puts us in her hands,
But not till her commission giv'n
Is found authentic, and from Heav'n.

'Tis strange that man, a reas'ning creature,
Shou'd miss a God in viewing nature :
Whose high perfections are display'd
In ev'ry thing his hands have made :
Ev'n when we think their traces lost,
When found again, we see them most ;
The night, itself which you would blame
As something wrong in nature's frame,
Is but a curtain to invest
Her weary children, when at rest :
Like that which mothers draw to keep
The light off from a child asleep.
Beside, the fears which darkness breeds,
At least augments, in vulgar heads,
Are far from useless, when the mind
Is narrow and to Earth confin'd ;
They make the wordling think with pain
On frauds and oaths and ill got gain ;
Force from the ruffian's hand the knife
Just rais'd against his neighbour's life ;
And in defence of virtue's cause
Assist each sanction of the laws.
But souls serene, where wisdom dwells
And superstitious dread expels,
The silent majesty of night
Excites to take a nobler flight ;
With saints and angels to explore
The wonders of creating pow'r ;
And lifts on contemplation's wings
Above the sphere of mortal things :
Walk forth and tread those dewy plains
Where night in awful silence reigns ;
The sky's serene, the air is still,
The woods stand list'ning on each hill,
To catch the sounds that sink and swell
Wide-floating from the ev'ning bell,
While foxes howl and beetles hum,
Sounds which make silence still more dumb :
And try if folly rash and rude
Dares on the sacred hour intrude.
Then turn your eyes to Heav'n's broad frame,
Attempt to quote those lights by name,
Which shine so thick and spread so far ;
Conceive a sun in every star,
Round which unnumber'd planets roll,
While comets shoot athwart the whole.
From system still to system ranging,
Their various benefits exchanging,
And shaking from their flaming hair
The things most needed every where.
Explore this glorious scene, and say
That night discovers less than day ;
That 'tis quite useless, and a sign
That chance disposes, not design :
Whoe'er maintains it, I'll pronounce
Him either mad, or else a dunce.
For reason, though 'tis far from strong,
Will soon find out that nothing's wrong,
From signs and evidences clear
Of wise contrivance every where."
    The hermit ended, and the youth
Became a convert to the truth ;
At least, he yielded, and confest
That all was order'd for the best.

## PHEBUS AND THE SHEPHERD.

I cannot think but more or less
True merit always gains success ;

That envy, prejudice, and spite,
Will never sink a genius quite.
Experience shows beyond a doubt
That worth, though clouded, will shine out
The second name for epic song,
First classic of the English tongue,
Great Milton, when he first appear'd,
Was ill receiv'd and coldly heard :
In vain did faction damn those lays
Which all posterity shall praise :
Is Dryden or his works forgot,
For all that Buckingham has wrote ?
The peer's sharp satire, charg'd with sense,
Gives pleasure at no one's expense :
The bard and critic, both inspir'd
By Phebus, shall be still admir'd :
'Tis true that censure, right or wrong,
May hurt at first the noblest song,
And for a while defeat the claim
Which any writer has to fame :
A mere book-merchant with his tools
Can sway with ease the herd of fools,
Who on a moderate computation
Are ten to one in every nation.—
" Your style is stiff—your periods halt—
In every line appears a fault—
The plot and incidents ill sorted—
No single character supported—
Your similes will scarce apply ;
The whole misshapen, dark and dry.—"
All this will pass, and gain its end
On the best poem e'er was penn'd :
But when the first assaults are o'er,
When fops and witlings prate no more,
And when your works are quite forgot
By all who praise or blame by rote :
Without self-interest, spleen, or hate,
The men of sense decide your fate :
Their judgment stands, and what they say
Gains greater credit ev'ry day ;
Till groundless prejudices past,
True merit has its due at last.
The hackney scribblers of the town,
Who were the first to write you down,
Their malice chang'd to admiration,
Promote your growing reputation,
And to excess of praise proceed ;
But this scarce happens till you're dead,
When fame for genius, wit, and skill,
Can do you neither good nor ill ;
Yet, if you would not be forgot,
They'll help to keep your name afloat.
    An aged swain that us'd to feed
His flock upon a mountain's head,
Drew crouds of shepherds from each hill,
To hear and profit by his skill ;
For ev'ry simple of the rock,
That can offend or cure a flock,
He us'd to mark, and knew its pow'r
In stem and foliage, root and flow'r.
Beside all this, he cou'd foretel
Both rain and sunshine passing well ;
By deep sagacity he'd find,
The future shiftings of the wind ;
And guess more shrewdly ev'ry year
If mutton wou'd be cheap or dear.
To tell his skill in every art,
Of which he understood a part,
His sage advice was wrapt in tales,
Which oft persuade when reason fails.

To do him justice every where
Wou'd take more time than I can spare,
And therefore now shall only touch
Upon a fact which authors vouch;
That Phebus oft wou'd condescend
To treat this shepherd like a friend:
Oft when the solar chariot past,
Provided he was not in haste,
He'd leave his steeds to take fresh breath,
And crop the herbage of the heath;
While with the swain a turn or two
He'd take, as landlords use to do,
When, sick of finer folks in town,
They find amusement in a clown.
One morning when the god alighted,
His winged steeds look'd wild and frighted;
The whip it seems had not been idle,
One's traces broke, another's bridle:
All four were switch'd in very part,
Like common jades that draw a cart,
Whose sides and haunches all along
Show the just measure of the thong.
　"Why, what's the matter," quoth the swain,
"My lord, it gives your servant pain;
Sure some offence is in the case,
I read it plainly in your face."
　"Offence," quoth Phebus, vex'd and heated;
"'Tis one indeed and oft repeated:
Since first I drove through Heav'n's highway,
That's before yesterday you'll say,
The envious clouds in league with night
Conspire to intercept my light;
Rank vapours breath'd from putrid lakes,
The streams of common-sew'rs and jakes,
Which under-ground shou'd be confin'd,
Nor suffer'd to pollute the wind;
Escap'd in air by various ways,
Extinguish or divert my rays.
Oft in the morning, when my steeds
Above the ocean lift their heads,
And when I hope to see my beams
Far glittering on the woods and streams:
A ridge of lazy clouds that sleep
Upon the surface of the deep,
Receive at once and wrap me round
In fogs extinguish'd half and drown'd.
But mark my purpose, and by Styx
I'm not soon alter'd when I fix;
If things are suffer'd at this pass,
I'll fairly turn my nags to grass:
No more this idle round I'll dance,
But let all nature take its chance."
　"If," quoth the shepherd, "it were fit
To argue with the god of wit,
I cou'd a circumstance suggest
That wou'd alleviate things at least.
That clouds oppose your rising light
Full oft and lengthen out the night,
Is plain; but soon they disappear,
And leave the sky serene and clear;
We ne'er expect a finer day,
Than when the morning has been gray;
Besides, those vapours which confine
Yon issuing from your eastern shrine,
By heat sublim'd and thinly spread,
Streak all the ev'ning sky with red:
And when your radiant orb in vain
Wou'd glow beneath the western main,
And not a ray cou'd reach our eyes,
Unless reflected from the skies,

Those watry mirrors send your light
In streams amidst the shades of night:
Thus length'ning out your reign much more
Than they had shorten'd it before.
As this is so, I must maintain
You've little reason to complain:
For when the matter's understood,
The ill seems balanc'd by the good;
The only diff'rence in the case
Is that the mischief first takes place,
The compensation when you're gone
Is rather somewhat late, I own:
But since 'tis so, you'll own 'tis fit
To make the best on't, and submit."

－－－－－－－

### THE BREEZE AND THE TEMPEST.

That nation boasts a happy fate
Whose prince is good as well as great,
Calm peace at home with plenty reigns,
The law its proper course obtains;
Abroad the public is respected,
And all its int'rests are protected:
But when his genius, weak or strong,
Is by ambition pointed wrong,
When private greatness has possess'd
In place of public good his breast,
'Tis certain, and I'll prove it true,
That ev'ry mischief must ensue.
On some pretence a war is made,
　he citizen must change his trade;
His steers the husbandman unyokes,
The shepherd too must quit his flocks,
His harmless life and honest gain,
To rob, to murder, and be slain:
The fields, once fruitful, yield no more
Their yearly produce as before:
Each useful plant neglected dies,
While idle weeds licentious rise
Unnumber'd, to usurp the land
Where yellow harvests us'd to stand.
Lean famine soon in course succeeds;
Diseases follow as she leads.
No infant bands at close of day
In ev'ry village sport and play.
The streets are throng'd with orphans dying
For want of bread, and widows crying:
Fierce rapine walks abroad unchain'd,
By civil order not restrain'd:
Without regard to right and wrong,
The weak are injur'd by the strong;
The hungry mouth but rarely tastes
The fatt'ning food which riots wastes,
All ties of conscience lose their force,
Ev'n sacred oaths grow words of course.
By what strange cause are kings inclin'd
To heap such mischiefs on mankind?
What pow'rful arguments control
The native dictates of the soul?
The love of glory and a name
Loud-sounded by the trump of Fame:
Nor shall they miss their end, unless
Their guilty projects want success.
Let one possess'd of sov'reign sway
Invade and murder and betray,
Let war and rapine fierce be hurl'd
Through half the nations of the world;

And prove successful in a course
Of bad designs, and actions worse,
At once a demi-god he grows,
And, incens'd both in verse and prose,
Becomes the idol of mankind ;
Though to what's good he's weak and blind ;
Approv'd, applauded, and respected,
While better rulers are neglected.

Where Shotts's airy tops divide
Fair Lothian from the vale of Clyde,
A tempest from the east and north
Fraught with the vapours of the Forth,
In passing to the Irish seas,
Once chanc'd to meet the western breeze.
The tempest hail'd him with a roar,
" Make haste and clear the way before;
No paltry zephyr must pretend
To stand before me, or contend :
Begone, or in a whirlwind tost
Your weak existence will be lost."

The tempest thus :—The breeze reply'd,
" If both our merits shou'd be try'd,
Impartial justice wou'd decree
That you shou'd yield the way to me."

At this the tempest rav'd and storm'd,
Grew black and ten times more deform'd.
" What qualities," quoth he, " of thine,
Vain flatt'ring wind, can equal mine ?
Breath'd from some river, lake, or bog,
Your rise at first is in a fog;
And creeping slowly o'er the meads
Scarce stir the willows or the reeds;
While those that feel you hardly know
The certain part from which you blow.
From Earth's deep womb, the child of fire,
Fierce, active, vigorous, like my sire,
I rush to light ; the mountains quake
With dread, and all their forests shake:
The globe itself convuls'd and torn,
Feels pangs unusual when I'm born :
Now free in air, with sov'reign sway
I rule, and all the clouds obey:
From east to west my pow'r extends,
Where day begins and where it ends :
And from Bootes downwards far,
Athwart the track of ev'ry star.
Through me the polar deep disdains
To sleep in winter's frosty chains ;
But rous'd to rage, indignant heaves
Huge rocks of ice upon its waves ;
While dread tornados lift on high
The broad Atlantic to the sky.
I rule the elemental roar,
And strew with shipwrecks ev'ry shore:
Nor less at land my pow'r is known
From Zembla to the burning zone.
I bring Tartarian frosts to kill
The bloom of summer ; when I will
Wide desolation doth appear
To mingle and confound the year:
From cloudy Atlas wrapt in night,
On Barca's sultry plains I light,
And make at once the desert rise
In dusty whirlwinds to the skies ;
In vain the trav'ler turns his steed,
And shuns me with his utmost speed;
I overtake him as he flies,
O'erblown he struggles, pants, and dies.
Where some proud city lifts in air
Its spires, I make a desert bare;

And when I choose, for pastime's sake,
Can with a mountain shift a lake ;
The Nile himself, at my command.
Oft hides his head beneath the sand,
And midst dry deserts blown and tost,
For many a sultry league is lost.
All this I do with perfect ease,
And can repeat whene'er I please :
What merit makes you then pretend
With me to argue and contend,
When all you boast of force or skill
Is scarce enough to turn a mill,
Or help the swain to clear his corn,
The servile tasks for which you're born ?"
" Sir," quoth the breeze, " if force alone
Must pass for merit, I have none ;
At least I'll readily confess
That yours is greater, mine is less.
But merit rightly understood
Consists alone in doing good ;
And therefore you yourself must see
That preference is due to me :
I cannot boast to rule the skies
Like you, and make the ocean rise,
Nor e'er with shipwrecks strew the shore,
For wives and orphans to deplore.
Mine is the happier task, to please
The mariner, and smooth the seas,
And waft him safe from foreign harms
To bless his consort's longing arms.
With you I boast not to confound
The seasons in their annual round,
And marr that harmony in nature
That comforts ev'ry living creature.
But oft from warmer climes I bring
Soft airs to introduce the spring ;
With genial heat unlock the soil,
And urge the ploughman to his toil:
I bid the op'ning blooms unfold
Their streaks of purple, blue and gold,
And waft their fragrance to impart
That new delight to ev'ry heart,
Which makes the shepherd all day long
To carrol sweet his vernal song:
The summer's sultry heat to cool,
From ev'ry river, lake and pool,
I skim fresh airs. The tawny swain,
Who turns at noon the furrow'd plain,
Refresh'd and trusting in my aid,
His task pursues and scorns the shade :
And ev'n on Afric's sultry coast,
Where such immense exploits you boast,
I blow to cool the panting flocks
'Midst deserts brown and sun-burnt rocks,
And health and vigour oft supply
To such as languish, faint and die :
Those humbler offices you nam'd,
To own I'll never be asham'd,
With twenty others that conduce
To public good or private use,
The meanest of them far outweighs
The whole amount of all your praise ;
If to give happiness and joy,
Excels the talent to destroy."
The tempest, that till now had lent
Attention to the argument,
Again began (his patience lost)
To rage, to threaten, huff and boast :
Since reason fail'd, resolv'd in course
The question to decide by force,

And his weak opposite to brave.—
The breeze retreated to a cave
To shelter, till the raging blast
Had spent its fury and was past.

---

### THE CROW AND THE OTHER BIRDS.

CONTAINING AN USEFUL HINT TO THE CRITICS.

In ancient times, tradition says,
When birds like men would strive for praise;
The bullfinch, nightingale, and thrush,
With all that chant from tree or bush,
Wou'd often meet in song to vie;
The kinds that sing not, sitting by.
A knavish crow, it seems, had got
The nack to criticise by rote;
He understood each learned phrase,
As well as critics now-a-days:
Some say, he learn'd them from an owl,
By list'ning where he taught a school.
'Tis strange to tell, this subtil creature,
Though nothing musical by nature,
Had learn'd so well to play his part,
With nonsense couch'd in terms of art,
As to be own'd by all at last
Director of the public taste.
Then puff'd with insolence and pride,
And sure of numbers on his side,
Each song he freely criticis'd;
What he approv'd not, was despis'd:
But one false step in evil hour
For ever stript him of his pow'r.
Once when the birds assembled sat,
All list'ning to his formal chat;
By instinct nice he chanc'd to find
A cloud approaching in the wind,
And ravens hardly can refrain
From croaking when they think of rain;
His wonted song he sung: the blunder
Amaz'd and scar'd them worse than thunder;
For no one thought so harsh a note
Cou'd ever sound from any throat;
They all at first with mute surprise
Each on his neighbour turn'd his eyes:
But scorn succeeding soon took place,
And might be read in ev'ry face.
All this the raven saw with pain,
And strove his credit to regain.
Quoth he, "The solo which ye heard
In public shou'd not have appear'd;
The trifle of an idle hour,
To please my mistress once when sour:
My voice, that's somewhat rough and strong,
Might chance the melody to wrong,
But, try'd by rules, you'll find the grounds,
Most perfect and harmonious sounds."—
He reason'd thus; but to his trouble,
At every word the laugh grew double.
At last o'ercome with shame and spite,
He flew away quite out of sight.

---

### THE HARE AND THE PARTAN.[1]

The chief design of this fable is to give a true specimen of the Scotch dialect, where it may be supposed to be most perfect, namely, in

[Partan] A Crab,

Mid-Lothian, the seat of the capital. The style is precisely that of the vulgar Scotch; and that the matter might be suitable to it, I chose for the subject a little story adapted to the ideas of peasants. It is a tale commonly told in Scotland among the country people; and may be looked upon as of the kind of those aniles fabellæ, in which Horace observes his country neighbours were accustomed to convey their rustic philosophy.

A canny man[2] will scarce provoke
Ae[3] creature livin, for a joke;
For be they weak or be they strang[4],
A jibe[5] leaves after it a stang[6]
To mak them think on't; and a laird[7]
May find a begger sae prepar'd,
Wi pawks[8] and wiles, whar pith[9] is wantin,
As soon will mak him rue his tauntin.
Ye hae my moral, if am able
All fit it nicely wi a fable.
A hare, ae morning, chanc'd to see
A partan creepin on a lee[10],
A fishwife[11] wha was early oot
Had drapt[12] the creature thereaboot.
Mawkin[13] bumbas'd[14] and frighted sair[15]
To see a thing but hide and hair[16],
Which if it stur'd not might be taen[17]
For naething ither than a stane[18].
A squunt-wise[19], wambling[20] sair beset
Wi gerse and rashes[21] like a net,

---

* *A canny man*] A canny man signifies nearly the same thing as a prudent man: but when the Scotch say that a person is *not* canny, they mean not that they are imprudent, but mischievous and dangerous. If the term *not canny* is applied to persons without being explained, it charges them with sorcery and witchcraft.

[3] *Ae*] One.

[4] *Strang*] Strong. The Scotch almost always turn *o* in the syllable *ong*, into *a*. In place of *long*, they say *lang*; in place of *tongs*, *tangs*; as here *strang*, for *strong*.

[5] *A jibe*] A satirical jest.

[6] *Stang*] Sting.

[7] *Laird*] A gentleman of an estate in land.

[8] *Pawks*] Stratagems.

[9] *Pith*] Strength.

[10] *Lee*] A piece of ground let run into grass for pasture.

[11] *Fishwife*] A woman thats sells fish. It is to be observed that the Scotch always use the word woman.

[12] *Drapt*] Dropt.

[13] *Mawkin*] A cant name for a hare, like that of Reynard for a fox, or Grimalkin for a cat, &c.

[14] *Bumbas'd*] Astonish'd.

[15] *Sair*] Sore. I shall observe, once for all that the Scotch avoid the vowels *o* and *u*; and have in innumerable instances supplied their places with *a* and *e*, or diphthongs in which these letters are predominant.

[16] *But hide and hair*] Without hide and hair.

[17] *Taen*] Taken.

[18] *Naething ither than a stane*] Nothing other than a stone.

[19] *A squunt-wise*] Obliquely or asquat.

[20] *Wambling*] A feeble motion like that of a worm or serpent.

[21] *Gerse and rashes*] Grass and rushes. The

First thought to rin [22] for't ; (for bi kind
A hare's nae fechter [23], ye maun mind [24])
But seeing, that wi [25] aw its strength
It scarce cou'd creep a tether length [26],
The hare grew baulder [27] and cam near,
Turn'd playsome, and forgat her fear.
Quoth Mawkin, " Was there ere in nature
Sae feckless [28] and sae poor a creature ?
It scarcely kens [29], or am mistaen,
The way to gang [30] or stand its lane [31].
See how it steitters [32]; all be bund [33]
To rin a mile of up-hill grund
Before it gets a rig-braid frae [34]"
The place its in, though doon the brae [35]."
    Mawkin wi this began to frisk,
And thinkin [36] there was little risk,
Clapt baith her feet on Partan's back,
And turn'd him awald [37] in a crack.
To see the creature sprawl, her sport
Grew twice as good, yet prov'd but short.
For patting wi her fit [38], in play,
Just whar the Partan's nippers lay,
He gript it fast, which made her squeel,
And think she bourded [39] wi the deil.
She strave to rin, and made a fistle :
The tither catch'd a tough bur thristle [40] :

vowel e which comes in place of a is by a meta-
thesis put between the consonants g and r to
soften the sound.

[22] *Rin*] Run.
[23] *Fechter*] Fighter.
[24] *Ye maun mind*] You must remember.
[25] *Wi aw*] With all.
[26] *A tether length*] The length of a rope used
to confine cattle when they pasture to a particular spot.
[27] *Baulder*] Bolder.
[28] *Feckless*] Feeble. *Feckful* and *feckless*
signify strong and weak, I suppose from the verb
*to effect*.
[29] *Kens, or am mistaen*] Knows, or I am in a
mistake.
[30] *Gang*] Go.
[31] *Its lane*] Alone, or without assistance.
[32] *Steitters*] Walks in a weak stumbling way.
[33] *All be bund*] I will be bound.
[34] *A rig-braid frae*] The breadth of a ridge
from. In Scotland about four fathoms.
[35] *Brae*] An ascent or descent. It is worth
observing, that the Scotch when they mention a
rising ground with respect to the whole of it,
they call it a *knau* if small, and a *hill* if great ;
but if they respect only one side of either, they
call it a *brae* : which is probably a corruption of
the English word *brow*, according to the analogy
I mentioned before.
[36] *Thinkin*] Thinking. When polysyllables
terminate in *ing*, the Scotch almost always neglect the g, which softens the sound.
[37] *Awald*] Topsy-turvy.
[38] *Fit*] Foot.
[39] *Bourded*] To *bourd* with any person is to
attack him in the way of jest.
[40] *Thristle*] Thistle. The Scotch, though
they commonly affect soft sounds, and throw out
consonants and take in vowels in order to obtain
them, yet in some cases, of which this is an example, they do the very reverse: and bring in

Which held them baith, till o'er a dyke
A herd came stending [41] wi his tyke [42],
And fill'd poor Mawkin, sairly rueen,
Whan forc'd to drink of her ain brewin [43].

## A DIALOGUE.

### THE AUTHOR AND A FRIEND.

" Here take your papers."—"Have you look'd
    them o'er ?"
" Yes, half a dozen times, I think, or more."
" And will they pass ?"—"They'll serve but for a
    day ;
Few books can now do more : you know the way;
A trifle's puff'd till one edition's sold,
In half a week at most a book grows old.
The penny turn'd 's the only point in view,
So ev'ry thing will pass if 'tis but new."—
    " By what you say I easily can guess
You rank me with the drudges for the press ;
Who from their garrets show'r Pindarics down,
Or plaintive elegies to lull the town."—
    " You take me wrong : I only meant to say,
That ev'ry book that 's new will have its day ;
The best no more : for books are seldom read ;
The world 's grown dull, and publishing, a trade.
Were this not so, cou'd Ossian's deathless strains,
Of high heroic times the sole remains,
Strains which display perfections to our view,
Which polish'd Greece and Italy ne'er knew,
With modern epics share one common lot,
This day applauded and the next forgot ?"
    " Enough of this ; to put the question plain,
Will men of sense and taste approve my strain ?
Will my old-fashion'd sense and comic ease
With better judges have a chance to please ?"
    "The question's plain, but hard to be resolv'd ;
One little less important can be solv'd :
The men of sense and taste, believe it true,
Will ne'er to living authors give their due.
They 're candidates for fame in diff'rent ways ;
One writes romances and another plays,
A third prescribes you rules for writing well,
Yet bursts with envy if you shou'd excel.
Through all fame's walks, the college and the
    court,
The field of combat and the field of sport ;
The stage, the pulpit, senate-house and bar,
Merit with merit lives at constant war."
    " All who can judge affect not public fame ;
Of those that do the paths are not the same :
A grave historian hardly needs to fear
The rival glory of a sonnetteer :
The deep philosopher, who turns mankind
Quite inside outwards, and dissects the mind,
Wou'd look but whimsical and strangely out,
To grudge some quack his treatise on the gout."—

superfluous consonants to roughen the sound,
when such sounds are more agreeable to the
roughness of the thing represented.
[41] *Stending*] Leaping.
[42] *Tyke*] Dog.
[43] *Brewin*] Brewing. " To drink of one's
own brewing," is a proverbial expression for suffering the effects of one's own misconduct. The
English say, " As they bake, so let them brew."

O

"Hold, hold, my friend, all this I know, and
    more;
An ancient bard [1] has told us long before;
And by examples easily decided,
That folks of the same trades are most divided.
But folks of diff'rent trades that hunt for fame
Are constant rivals, and their ends the same:
It needs no proof, you'll readily confess,
That merit envies merit more or less:
The passion rules alike in those who share
Of public reputation, or despair.
Varrus has knowledge, humour, taste, and sense,
Cou'd purchase laurels at a small expense;
But wise and learn'd, and eloquent in vain,
He sleeps at ease in pleasure's silken chain:
Will Varrus help you to the Muse's crown,
Which, but for indolence, might be his own?
Timon with art and industry aspires
To fame; the world applauds him, and admires:
Timon has sense, and will not blame a line
He knows is good, from envy or design:
Some gen'ral praise he'll carelessly express,
Which just amounts to none, and sometimes less:
But if his penetrating sense should spy
Such beauties as escape a vulgar eye,
So finely couch'd, their value to enhance,
That all are pleas'd, yet think they're pleas'd by
    chance;
Rather than blab such secrets to the throng,
He'd lose a finger, or bite off his tongue.
Narcissus is a beau, but not an ass,
He likes your works, but most his looking-glass;
Will he to serve you quit his favourite care,
Turn a book-pedant and offend the fair?
Clelia to taste and judgment may pretend;
She will not blame your verse, nor dares com-
    mend:
A modest virgin always shuns dispute;
Soft Strephon likes you not, and she is mute.
Stern Aristarchus, who expects renown
From ancient merit rais'd, and new knock'd
    down,
For faults in every syllable will pry,
Whate'er he finds is good he'll pass it by."
    "Hold, hold, enough! All act from private
    ends;
Authors and wits were ever slipp'ry friends:"
    "But say, will vulgar readers like my lays?
When such approve a work, they always praise."
    "To speak my sentiments, your tales I fear
Are but ill suited to a vulgar car.
Will city readers, us'd to better sport,
The politics and scandals of a court, [pore,
Well vouch'd from Grub-street, on your pages
For what they ne'er can know, or knew before?
Many have thought, and I among the rest,
That fables are but useless things at best:
Plain words without a metaphor may serve
To tell us that the poor must work or starve.
We need no stories of a cock and bull
To prove that graceless scribblers must be dull.
That hope deceives; that never to excel,
'Gainst spite and envy is the only spell—
All this, without an emblem, I suppose
Might pass for sterling truth in verse or prose."—
    "Sir, take a seat, my answer will be long;
Yet weigh the reasons and you'll find them strong.

[1] Hesiod.

At first [2] when savage men in quest of food,
Like lions, wolves and tigers, rang'd the wood,
They had but just what simple nature craves,
Their garments skins of beasts, their houses
    caves.
When prey abounded, from its bleeding dam
Pity would spare a kidling or a lamb,
Which, with their children nurs'd and fed at
    home,
Soon grew domestic and forgot to roam:
From such beginnings flocks and herds were seen
To spread and thicken on the woodland green:
With property, injustice soon began,   [man.
And they that prey'd on beasts now prey'd on
Communities were fram'd, and laws to bind
In social intercourse the human kind.
These things were new, they had not got their
    names,
And right and wrong were yet uncommon themes
The rustic senator, untaught to draw
Conclusions in morality or law,
Of every term of art and science bare,
Wanted plain words his sentence to declare;
Much more at length to manage a dispute,
To clear, inforce, illustrate and confute;
Fable was then found out, 'tis worth your heed
And answer'd all the purposes of pleading. [ing,
It won the head with unsuspected art,
And touch'd the secret springs that move the
    heart:
With this premis'd, I add, that men delight
To have their first condition still in sight.
Long since the sires of Brunswick's line forsook
The hunter's bow, and dropt the shepherd's
    crook:
Yet, 'midst the charms of royalty, their race
Still loves the forest, and frequents the chase.
The high-born maid, whose gay apartments shine
With the rich produce of each Indian mine,
Sighs for the open fields, the past'ral hook,
To sleep delightful near a warbling brook;
And loves to read the ancient tales that tell
How queens themselves fetch'd water from the
    well.
If this is true, and all affect the ways
Of patriarchal life in former days,
Fable must please the stupid, the refin'd,
Wisdom's first dress to court the op'ning mind."
    "You reason well, cou'd nature hold her course,
Where vice exerts her tyranny by force:
Are natural pleasures suited to a taste,
Where nature's laws are alter'd and defac'd?
The healthful swain who treads the dewy mead,
Enjoys the music warbled o'er his head;
Feels gladness at his heart while he inhales
The fragrance wafted in the balmy gales.
Not so Silenus from his night's debauch,
Fatigu'd and sick, he looks upon his watch
With rheumy eyes and forehead aching sore,
And staggers home to bed to belch and snore;
For such a wretch in vain the morning glows,
For him in vain the vernal zephyr blows:

[2] The author speaks of those only who upon
the dispersion of mankind fell into perfect barba-
rism, and emerged from it again in the way
which he describes, and not of those who had
laws and arts from the beginning by divine tradition.

Gross pleasures are his taste, his life a chain
Of feverish joys, of lassitude and pain.
Trust not to nature in such times as these,
When all is off the hinge, can nature please ?
Discard all useless scruples, be not nice ;
Like some folks laugh at virtue, flatter vice,
Boldly attack the mitre or the crown ;
Religion shakes already, push it down :
Do every thing to please ?—You shake your head :
Why then 'tis certain that you'll ne'er succeed :
Dismiss your Muse, and take your full repose ;
What none will read 'tis useless to compose."—
   " A good advice ! to follow it is hard.—
Quote one example, name me but a bard
Who ever hop'd Parnassus' heights to climb,
That dropt his Muse, till she deserted him.
A cold is caught, this med'cine can expel,
The dose is thrice repeated, and you're well.
In man's whole frame there is no crack or flaw
But yields to Bath, to Bristol, or to Spa :
No drug poetic frenzy can restrain,
Ev'n hellebore itself is try'd in vain :
'Tis quite incurable by human skill ;
And though it does but little good or ill,
Yet still it meets the edge of reformation,
Like the chief vice and nuisance of the nation.
The formal quack, who kills his man each day,
Passes uncensur'd, and receives his pay.
Old Aulus, nodding 'midst the lawyers strife,
Wakes to decide on property and life.
Yet not a soul will blame him, and insist
That he should judge to purpose, or desist.
At this address how would the courtiers laugh !
' My lord, you're always blundering: quit your
      staff:
You've lost some reputation, and 'tis best
To shift before you grow a public jest.'
This none will think of, though 'tis more a crime
To mangle state-affairs, than murder rhyme.
The quack, you'll say, has reason for his killing,
He cannot eat unless he earns his shilling.
The worn-out lawyer clambers to the bench
That he may live at ease, and keep his wench ;
The courtier toils for something higher far,
And hopes for wealth, new titles and a star ;

While moon-struck poets in a wild-goose chase
Pursue contempt, and begg'ry, and disgrace."
   " Be't so ; I claim by precedent and rule
A free-born Briton's right, to play the fool :
My resolution's fix'd, my course I'll hold
In spite of all your arguments when told :
Whether I'm well and up, or keep my bed,
Am warm and full, or neither cloth'd nor fed,
Whether my fortune's kind, or in a pet,
Am banish'd by the laws, or fled for debt ;
Whether in Newgate, Bedlam, or the Mint,
I'll write as long as publishers will print."
   " Unhappy lad, who will not spend your time
To better purpose than in useless rhyme:
Of but one remedy your case admits,
The king is gracious, and a friend to wits ;
Pray write for him, nor think your labour lost,
Your verse may gain a pension or a post."
   " May Heav'n forbid that this auspicious reign
Shou'd furnish matter for a poet's strain :
The praise of conduct steady, wise, and good,
In prose is best express'd and understood.
Nor are those sov'reigns blessings to their age
Whose deeds are sung, whose actions grace the
      stage.
A peaceful river, whose soft current feeds
The constant verdure of a thousand meads,
Whose shaded banks afford a safe retreat
From winter's blasts and summer's sultry heat,
From whose pure wave the thirsty peasant drains
Those tides of health that flow within his veins,
Passes unnotic'd ; while the torrent strong
Which bears the shepherds and their flocks along,
Arm'd with the vengeance of the angry skies,
Is view'd with admiration and surprise ;
Employs the painter's hand, the poet's quill,
And rises to renown by doing ill.
Verse form'd for falshood makes ambition shine,
Dubs it immortal, and almost divine;
But qualities which fiction ne'er can raise
It always lessens when it strives to praise."
   " Then take your way, 'tis folly to contend
With those who know their faults, but will not
      mend."

THE

# POEMS

OF

# *JOHN CUNNINGHAM.*

Fælix ille, quem, semotum longe e strepitu et popularibus
  undis, interdum molli rus accipii umbra !

RAPIN.

Silvestrem tenui musam meditabor avena.

# LIFE OF CUNNINGHAM.

## BY MR. CHALMERS.

THE only account we have of Mr. Cunningham appeared originally in the London Magazine for 1773, from which it has been repeatedly copied without acknowledgment.

He was born in 1729, in Dublin, where his father and mother, both descendants of Scotch parents, then resided. His father was a wine-cooper, and becoming enriched by a prize in the lottery, commenced wine-merchant, and failed. The little education our author received was from a Mr. Clarke, who was master of the grammar-school of the city of Drogheda; and when his father's affairs became embarrassed, he was recalled to Dublin, where he produced many of his lesser poems at a very early age. At seventeen he wrote a farce, entitled, Love in a Mist, which was acted for several nights at Dublin in the year 1747. Garrick is said to have been indebted to this farce for the fable or plot of his Lying Valet.

The success of his little drama procured him the freedom of the theatre, to which he became immoderately attached, and, mistaking inclination for ability, commenced actor without one essential qualification either natural or acquired, if we except a knack at personating the mock French character, in which he is said to have been tolerable. His passion for the stage, however, predominated so strongly, that without any intimation of his intentions, he left his family and embarked for England, where he obtained a precarious and unprofitable employment in various companies of strolling comedians. Frequent want made him at length sensible of his imprudence, but pride prevented his return to his friends; and the death of his father, in circumstances of distress, probably reconciled him to a way of life which he could not now exchange for a better. About the year 1761 we find him a performer at Edinburgh, under the direction of Mr. Love, and here he published his Elegy on a Pile of Ruins, which, although obviously an imitation of Gray's Elegy, contains many passages conceived in the true spirit of poetry, and obtained considerable reputation. He soon afterwards borrowed five stanzas from this Elegy, and placed them in his Elegiac Ode on the Death of his late Majesty, an instance of taking freedom with a recent poem for which it is not easy to account. During his theatrical engagement at Edinburgh, although insignificant as an actor, he was of some value to the manager, by furnishing prologues and other occasional addresses, which were much applauded.

About this time he received an invitation from certain booksellers in London, who proposed to engage him in such works of literature as might procure him a more easy and honourable employment than he had hitherto followed. He repaired accordingly to the metropolis, but was disappointed in the promised undertaking by the bankruptcy of the principal person concerned in it, and, after a short stay, was glad to return to his friends in the north.

This was the only effort he ever made to emerge from the abject situation in which youthful imprudence had originally placed him. But with this state, says his biographer, he appeared by no means dissatisfied. Competence and obscurity were all he desired. He had no views of ambition; and indolence had possessed him so entirely, that he never made a second attempt. In a letter to a friend, he describes himself in these terms: " You may remember my last expedition to London. I think I may be convinced by it that I am not calculated for the business you mention. Though I scribble (but a little neither) to amuse myself, the moment I consider it as my duty it would cease to be an amusement, and I should of consequence be weary on't. I am not enterprizing: and tolerably happy in my present situation."

In 1762 he published The Contemplatist, but with less success than his Elegy. This is indeed the worst of all his productions, and was censured with much force of ridicule by a writer in the Monthly Review. It abounds with glittering and absurd conceits, and had it been published now, might have been mistaken for a satire on the maukish namby-pamby stuff which the author of The Baviad and Mæviad has chastised with equal justice and humour. It may here be mentioned that in 1765 he published Fortune, an Apologue, in which there are some poetical beauties, particularly the description of avarice, but not much consistency of plan; and in the following year collected his poems into a volume, which was honoured by a numerous list of subscribers.

For some time, he was a performer in Mr. Digges's company at Edinburgh, and on that gentleman's quitting Scotland, returned to Newcastle upon Tyne, a spot which had been his residence for many years, and which he considered as his home. Here and in the neighbouring towns he earned a scanty subsistence. Although his mode of life was not of the reputable kind, his blameless and obliging conduct procured him many friends, and in their society he passed his days without any effort to improve his situation. Yet in the verses he wrote about three weeks before he died, it appears that he was not quite so contented as his biographer has represented.

A few months before his death, being incapable of any theatrical exertion, he was removed to the house of his friend, Mr. Slack of Newcastle, who with great kindness received him under his roof, and paid every attention to him which his state required. After lingering some time under a nervous disorder, during which he burnt all his papers, he died on the 18th of September, 1773, and was buried in St. John's church yard, Newcastle. On a tomb-stone erected to his memory is the following inscription :

Here lie the remains of
JOHN CUNNINGHAM.
Of his excellence
As a pastoral poet,
His works will remain a monument
For ages
After this temporary tribute of esteem
Is in dust forgotten.
He died in Newcastle, Sept. 18, 1773,
Aged 44.

Although Cunningham cannot be admitted to a very high rank among poets, he may be allowed to possess a considerable share of genius. His poems have a peculiar sweetness and elegance; his sentiments are generally natural, and his language simple, and appropriate to his subject, except in some of his longer pieces, where he accumulates epithets that appear to be laboured, and are sometimes uncouth compounds, either obsolete or unauthorized. As he contemplated Nature with a fond and minute attention, and had familiarized his mind to rural scenes and images, his pastorals will probably continue to be his most favoured efforts. He has informed us that Shenstone, with whose correspondence he was honoured, encouraged him to cultivate this species of poetry. His Landscape is a cluster of beauties which every reader must feel, but such as only a very accurate observer of nature could have grouped with equal effect. His fables are ingenious, and his lyric pieces were at one time in very high estimation, and certainly cannot suffer by a comparison with their successors on the stage and public gardens. His love-verses and his tributes of affection bespeak considerable ardour, with sometimes an attempt at conceits to which he seems to have been led by imitation. If he does not often move the passions, he always pleases the fancy, and his works have lost little of the popularity with which they were originally favoured.

A

# CARD FROM THE AUTHOR,

TO

## *DAVID GARRICK, ESQ.*

————————

REMOTENESS of situation, and some other circumstances, have hitherto deprived the author of that happiness he might receive from seeing Mr. Garrick.

'Tis the universal regard his character commands, occasions this address.

It may be thought by many, (at a visit so abrupt as this is) that something highly complimentary should be said on the part of the intruder; but according to the ideas the author has conceived of Mr. Garrick's delicacy and good sense, a single period in the garb of flattery would certainly offend him.

He therefore takes his leave;—and after having stept (perhaps a little too forward) to offer his tribute of esteem, respectfully retires.

NEWCASTLE,
*Aug.* 1771.

# POEMS

OF

## *JOHN CUNNINGHAM.*

### *DAY:*

#### A PASTORAL.

......... Carpe diem.     Hor.

##### MORNING.

In the barn the tenant cock,
  Close to Partlet perch'd on high,
Briskly crows, (the shepherd's clock!)
  Jocund that the morning's nigh.

Swiftly from the mountain's brow,
  Shadows, nurs'd by night, retire:
And the peeping sun-beam, now,
  Paints with gold the village spire.

Philomel forsakes the thorn,
  Plaintive where she prates at night;
And the lark, to meet the morn,
  Soars beyond the shepherd's sight.

From the low-roof'd cottage ridge,
  See the chatt'ring swallow spring;
Darting through the one-arch'd bridge,
  Quick she dips her dappled wing.

Now the pine-tree's waving top
  Gently greets the morning gale:
Kidlings, now, begin to crop
  Daisies, in the dewy dale.

From the balmy sweets, uncloy'd,
  (Restless till her task be done)
Now the busy bee's employ'd
  Sipping dew before the Sun.

Trickling through the crevic'd rock,
  Where the limpid stream distills,
Sweet refreshment waits the flock
  When 'tis sun-drove from the hills.

Colin, for the promis'd corn
  (Ere the harvest hopes are ripe)
Anxious, hears the huntsman's horn,
  Boldly sounding, drown his pipe.

Sweet,—O sweet, the warbling throng,
  On the white emblossom'd spray !
Nature's universal song
  Echoes to the rising day.

---

##### NOON.

Fervid on the glitt'ring flood,
  Now the noon-tide radiance glows:
Dropping o'er its infant bud,
  Not a dew-drop's left the rose.

By the brook the shepherd dines;
  From the fierce meridian heat
Shelter'd, by the branching pines,
  Pendent o'er his grassy seat.

Now the flock forsakes the glade,
  Where, uncheck'd, the sun-beams fall;
Sure to find a pleasing shade
  By the ivy'd abbey wall.

Echo in her airy round,
  O'er the river, rock, and hill,
Cannot catch a single sound,
  Save the clack of yonder mill.

Cattle court the zephyrs bland,
  Where the streamlet wanders cool;
Or with languid silence stand
  Midway in the marshy pool.

But from mountain, dell, or stream,
  Not a flutt'ring zephyr springs:
Fearful lest the noon-tide beam
  Scorch its soft, its silken wings.

Not a leaf has leave to stir,
  Nature 's lull'd—serene—and still !
Quiet e'en the shepherd's cur,
  Sleeping on the hearth-clad hill.

Languid is the landscape round,
  Till the fresh descending shower,
Grateful to the thirsty ground,
  Raises ev'ry fainting flower.

Now the hill—the hedge—is green,
  Now the warblers' throats in tune!
Blithsome is the verdant scene,
  Brighten'd by the beams of noon!

-----

### EVENING.

O'er the heath the heifer strays
  Free;—(the furrow'd task is done)
Now the village windows blaze,
  Burnish'd by the setting Sun.

Now he hides behind the hill,
  Sinking from a golden sky:
Can the pencil's mimic skill
  Copy the refulgent dye?

Trudging as the ploughmen go,
  (To the smoking hamlet bound)
Giant-like their shadows grow,
  Lengthen'd o'er the level ground.

Where the rising forest spreads,
  Shelter for the lordly dome!
To their high-built airy beds,
  See the rooks returning home!

As the lark, with vary'd tune,
  Carols to the evening loud;
Mark the mild resplendent Moon,
  Breaking through a parted cloud!

Now the hermit Howlet peeps
  From the barn, or twisted brake:
And the blue mist slowly creeps,
  Curling on the silver lake.

As the trout in speckled pride,
  Playful from its bosom springs;
To the banks, a ruffled tide
  Verges in successive rings.

Tripping through the silken grass,
  O'er the path divided dale,
Mark the rose-complexion'd lass,
  With her well-pois'd milking pail.

Linnets, with unnumber'd notes,
  And the cuckoo bird with two,
Tuning sweet their mellow throats,
  Bid the setting Sun adieu.

-----

### THE CONTEMPLATIST:

#### A NIGHT PIECE.

Nox erat ................
Cum tacet omnis ager, pecudes, pictæque volucres.

The queen of Contemplation, Night,
  Begins her balmy reign;
Advancing in their varied light
  Her silver-vested train.

'Tis strange, the many marshall'd stars,
  That ride yon sacred round,
Should keep, among their rapid cars,
  A silence so profound!

A kind, a philosophic calm,
  The cool creation wears!
And what day drank of dewy balm,
  The gentle night repairs.

Behind their leafy curtains hid,
  The feather'd race how still!
How quiet now the gamesome kid,
  That gambol'd round the hill!

The sweets, that, bending o'er their banks,
  From sultry day declin'd,
Revive in little velvet ranks,
  And scent the western wind.

The Moon, preceded by the breeze
  That bade the clouds retire,
Appears amongst the tufted trees,
  A phœnix nest on fire.

But soft—the golden glow subsides!
  Her chariot mounts on high!
And now, in silver'd pomp, she rides
  Pale regent of the sky!

Where Time, upon the wither'd tree
  Hath carv'd the moral chair,
I sit, from busy passions free,
  And breathe the placid air.

The wither'd tree was once in prime;
  Its branches brav'd the sky!
Thus, at the touch of ruthless Time,
  Shall youth and vigour die.

I'm lifted to the blue expanse!
  It glows serenely gay!
Come, Science, by my side, advance,
  We'll search the milky way.

Let us descend—the daring flight
  Fatigues my feeble mind;
And Science, in the maze of light,
  Is impotent and blind.

What are those wild, those wand'ring fires,
  That o'er the moorland ran?
Vapours.——How like the vague desires
  That cheat the heart of man!

But there's a friendly guide!——a flame,
  That, lambent o'er its bed,
Enlivens, with a gladsome beam,
  The hermit's osier shed.

Among the russet shades of night,
  It glances from afar!
And darts along the dusk; so bright,
  It seems a silver star!

In coverts, (where the few frequent)
  If Virtue deigns to dwell,
'Tis thus, the little lamp, Content,
  Gives lustre to her cell.

How smooth that rapid river slides
  Progressive to the deep!
The poppies, pendent o'er its sides,
  Have charm'd the waves to sleep.

Pleasure's intoxicated sons!
  Ye indolent! ye gay!
Reflect——for as the river runs,
  Life wings its trackless way.

That branching grove of dusky green
  Conceals the azure sky;
Save where a starry space between
  Relieves the darken'd eye.

Old Errour, thus, with shades impure,
  Throws sacred Truth behind:
Yet sometimes, through the deep obscure,
  She bursts upon the mind.

Sleep and her sister Silence reign,
  They lock the shepherd's fold;
But hark—I hear a lamb complain,
  'Tis lost upon the wold!

To savage herds, that hunt for prey,
  An unresisting prize!
For having trod a devious way,
  The little rambler dies.

As luckless is the virgin's lot,
  Whom pleasure once misguides:
When hurried from the halcyon cot,
  Where Innocence presides——

The passions, a relentless train!
  To tear the victim run:
She seeks the paths of peace in vain,
  Is conquer'd——and undone.

How bright the little insects blaze,
  Where willows shade the way:
As proud as if their painted rays
  Could emulate the day!

'Tis thus, the pigmy sons of Pow'r
  Advance their vain parade!
Thus, glitter in the darken'd hour,
  And like the glow-worms fade!

The soft serenity of night,
  Ungentle clouds deform!
The silver host that shone so bright,
  Is hid behind a storm!

The angry elements engage!
  An oak (an ivied bower!)
Repels the rough wind's noisy rage,
  And shields me from the shower.

The rancour, thus, of rushing fate,
  I 've learnt to render vain:
For whilst Integrity 's her seat,
  The soul will sit serene.

A raven, from some greedy vault,
  Amidst that cloister'd gloom,
Bids me, and 'tis a solemn thought!
  Reflect upon the tomb.
    VOL. XIV.

The tomb!——the consecrated dome!
  The temple rais'd to Peace!
The port, that to its friendly home
  Compels the human race!

Yon village, to the moral mind,
  A solemn aspect wears;
Where sleep hath lull'd the labour'd hind,
  And kill'd his daily cares:

'Tis but the church-yard of the night;
  An emblematic bed!
That offers to the mental sight,
  The temporary dead.

From hence, I 'll penetrate, in thought,
  The grave's unmeasur'd deep;
And tutor'd, hence, be timely taught,
  To meet my final sleep.

'Tis peace——(the little chaos past!)
  The gracious Moon restor'd!
A breeze succeeds the frightful blast,
  That through the forest roar'd!

The nightingale, a welcome guest!
  Renews her gentle strains;
And Hope, (just wand'ring from my breast)
  Her wonted seat regains.

Yes——when yon lucid orb is dark,
  And darting from on high;
My soul, a more celestial spark,
  Shall keep her native sky.

Fann'd by the light—the lenient breeze,
  My limbs refreshment find;
And moral rhapsodies, like these,
  Give vigour to the mind.

————————

THE

*THRUSH AND PIE:*

A TALE.

Conceal'd within an hawthorn bush,
We 're told, that an experienc'd Thrush
Instructed, in the prime of spring,
Many a neighbouring bird to sing.
She caroll'd, and her various song
Gave lessons to the list'ning throng:
But (the entangling boughs between)
'Twas her delight to teach unseen.
  At length, the little wond'ring race
Would see their fav'rite face to face;
They thought it hard to be deny'd,
And begg'd that she 'd no longer hide.
O'er-modest, worth's peculiar fault,
Another shade the tut'ress sought;
And loth to be too much admir'd,
In secret from the bush retir'd.
  An impudent, presuming Pie,
Malicious, ignorant, and sly,
Stole to the matron's vacant seat,
And in her arrogance elate,
Rush'd forward—with—" My friends, you see
The mistress of the choir in me:
    F f

Here, be your due devotion paid,
I am the songstress of the shade."
    A Linnet, that sat list'ning nigh,
Made the impostor thus reply :
" I fancy, friend, that vulgar throats
Were never form'd for warbling notes:
But if these lessons came from you,
Repeat them in the public view;
That your assertions may be clear,
Let us behold as well as hear."
    The length'ning song, the soft'ning strain,
Our chatt'ring Pie attempts in vain,
For to the fool's eternal shame,
All she could compass was a *scream.*
    The birds, enrag'd, around her fly,
Nor shelter nor defence is nigh.
    The caitiff wretch, distress'd—forlorn!
On every side is peck'd and torn,
Till for her vile, atrocious lies,
Under their angry beaks she dies.
    Such be his fate, whose scoundrel claim
Obtrudes upon a neighbour's fame.
    Friend E——n [1], the tale apply,
You are—yourself—the chatt'ring Pie:
Repent, and with a conscious blush,
Go make atonement to the Thrush [2].

---

## PALEMON:

### A PASTORAL.

PALEMON, seated by his fav'rite maid,
The sylvan scenes, with ecstasy, survey'd;
Nothing could make the fond Alexis gay,
For Daphne had been absent half the day:
Dar'd by Palemon for a pastoral prize,
Reluctant, in his turn, Alexis tries.

#### PALEMON.

This breeze by the river how charming and soft!
    How smooth the grass carpet! how green!
Sweet, sweet sings the lark! as he carols aloft,
    His music enlivens the scene!
A thousand fresh flow'rets unusually gay
    The fields and the forests adorn;
I pluck'd me some roses, the children of May,
    And could not find one with a thorn.

#### ALEXIS.

The skies are quite clouded, too bold is the breeze,
    Dull vapours descend on the plain;
The verdure 's all blasted that cover'd yon trees,
    The birds cannot compass a strain:
In search for a chaplet my temples to bind,
    All day as I silently rove,
I can't find a flow'ret (not one to my mind)
    In meadow, in garden, or grove.

#### PALEMON.

I ne'er saw the hedge in such excellent bloom,
    The lambkins so wantonly gay;
My cows seem to breathe a more pleasing perfume,
    And brighter than common the day:

[1] A Y—shire bookseller, who pirated an edition of the Pleasing Instructor.
[2] The compiler, and reputed authoress of the original essays in that book.

If any dull shepherd should foolishly ask,
    So rich why the landscapes appear?
To give a right answer, how easy my task!
    Because my sweet Phillida's here.

#### ALEXIS.

The stream that so muddy moves slowly along,
    Once roll'd in a beautiful tide;
It seem'd o'er the pebbles to murmur a song,
    But Daphne sat then by my side.
See, see the lov'd majd, o'er the meadows she hies,
    Quite alter'd already the scene!
How limpid the stream is! how gay the blue skies!
    The hills and the hedges how green!

---

## THE

## HAWTHORN BOWER.

PALEMON, in the hawthorn bower,
    With fond impatience lay;
He counted every anxious hour
    That stretch'd the tedious day.
The rosy dawn, Pastora nam'd,
    And vow'd that she 'd be kind;
But, ah! the setting Sun proclaim'd
    That women's vows are—wind.

The fickle sex, the boy defy'd;
    And swore, in terms profane,
That Beauty in her brightest pride
    Might sue to him in vain.
When Delia from the neighb'ring glade
    Appear'd in all her charms,
Each angry vow Palemon made
    Was lost in Delia's arms.

The lovers had not long reclin'd
    Before Pastora came:
" Inconstancy," she cry'd, " I find
    In every heart 's the same;
For young Alexis sigh'd and prest,
    With such bewitching power,
I quite forgot the wishing guest
    That waited in the bower. ·

---

## THE

## ANT AND CATERPILLAR,

### A FABLE.

As an Ant, of his talents superiorly vain,
Was trotting, with consequence, over the plain,
A Worm, in his progress remarkably slow,
Cry'd——" Bless your good worship wherever you
    go;
I hope your great mightiness won't take it ill,
I pay my respects with an hearty good-will."
With a look of contempt and impertinent pride,
" Begone, you vile reptile," his *antship* replied;
" Go—go and lament your contemptible state,
But first——look at me——see my limbs how
    complete;

I guide all my motions with freedom and ease,
Run backward and forward, and turn when I please;
Of Nature (grown weary) you shocking essay !
I spurn you thus from me——crawl out of my
    way."
    The reptile insulted, and vext to the soul,
Crept onwards, and hid himself close in his hole ;
But Nature, determin'd to end his distress,
Soon sent him abroad in a butterfly's dress.
    Ere long the proud Ant, as repassing the road,
(Fatigu'd from the harvest, and tugging his load)
The beau on a violet bank he beheld,
Whose vesture, in glory, a monarch's excell'd ;
His plumage expanded—'twas rare to behold
So lovely a mixture of purple and gold.
    The Ant, quite amaz'd at a figure so gay,
Bow'd low with respect, and was trudging away.
" Stop, friend," says the Butterfly——" don't be
    surpris'd,
I once was the reptile you spurn'd and despis'd ;
But now I can mount, in the sun-beams I play,
While you must, for ever, drudge on in your way."

MORAL.

A wretch, though to day he's o'erloaded with sorrow,
May soar above those that oppress'd him——to
    morrow.

## PHILLIS:

### A PASTORAL BALLAD.

I said,—on the banks by the stream,
    I 've pip'd for the shepherds too long :
Oh grant me, ye Muses, a theme,
    Where glory may brighten my song !
But Pan [1] bade me stick to my strain,
    Nor lessons too lofty rehearse ;
Ambition befits not a swain,
    And Phillis loves pastoral verse.

The rose, though a beautiful red,
    Looks faded to Phillis's bloom ;
And the breeze from the bean-flower bed
    To her breath 's but a feeble perfume:
The dew-drop so limpid and gay,
    That loose on the violet lies,
Though brighten'd by Phœbus's ray,
    Wants lustre, compar'd to her eyes.

A lily I pluck'd in full pride,
    Its freshness with her's to compare ;
And foolishly thought (till I try'd)
    The flow'ret was equally fair.
How, Corydon, could you mistake ?
    Your fault be with sorrow confest,
You said the white swans on the lake
    For softness might rival her breast.

While thus I went on in her praise,
    My Phyllis pass'd sportive along :
Ye poets, I covet no bays,
    She smil'd——a reward for my song !

[1] The author intends the character of Pan for
the late Mr. Shenstone, who favoured him with a
letter or two, advising him to proceed in the pastoral manner.

I find the god Pan 's in the right,
    No fame 's like the fair-ones' applause!
And Cupid must crown with delight
    The shepherd that sings in his cause.

## POMONA:

### A PASTORAL.

#### ON THE CIDER BILL BEING PASSED.

From orchards of ample extent,
    Pomona 's compell'd to depart ;
And thus, as in anguish she went,
    The goddess unburthen'd her heart:

" To flourish where Liberty reigns,
    Was all my fond wishes requir'd ;
And here I agreed with the swains
    To live till their freedom expir'd.

" Of late you have number'd my trees,
    And threaten'd to limit my store :
Alas—from such maxims as these,
    I fear that your freedom 's no more.

" My flight will be fatal to May :
    For how can her gardens be fine :
The blossoms are doom'd to decay,
    (The blossoms, I mean, that were mine.)

" Rich Autumn remembers me well :
    My fruitage was fair to behold ;
My pears—how I ripen'd their swell !
    My pippins !—were pippins of gold !

" Let Ceres drudge on with her ploughs !
    She droops as she furrows the soil ;
A nectar I shake from my boughs,
    A nectar that softens my toil.

" When Bacchus began to repine,
    With patience I bore his abuse ;
He said that I plunder'd the vine,
    He said that I pilfer'd his juice.

" I know the proud drunkard denies
    That trees of my culture should grow :
But let not the traitor advise ;
    He comes from the climes of your foe.

" Alas ! in your silence I read
    The sentence I 'm doom'd to deplore :
'Tis plain the great Pan has decreed,
    My orchard shall flourish no more."

The goddess flew off in despair ;
    As all her sweet honours declin'd :
And Plenty and Pleasure declare,
    They 'll loiter no longer behind.

## MAY-EVE:

### OR, KATE OF ABERDEEN.

The silver-Moon's enamour'd beam
    Steals softly through the night,
To wanton with the winding stream,
    And kiss reflected light.

To beds of state go, balmy Sleep,
('Tis where you've seldom been)
May's vigil while the shepherds keep
    With Kate of Aberdeen.

Upon the green the virgins wait,
    In rosy chaplets gay,
Till Morn unbar her golden gate,
    And give the promis'd May.
Methinks I hear the maids declare,
The promis'd May, when seen,
Not half so fragrant, half so fair,
    As Kate of Aberdeen.

Strike up the tabor's boldest notes,
    We 'll rouse the nodding grove ;
The nested birds shall raise their throats,
    And hail the maid I love:
And see—the matin lark mistakes,
    He quits the tufted green:
Fond bird ! 'tis not the morning breaks,
    'Tis Kate of Aberdeen.

Now lightsome o'er the level mead,
    Where midnight Fairies rove,
Like them, the jocund dance we 'll lead,
    Or tune the reed to love :
For see the rosy May draws nigh;
    She claims a virgin queen;
And hark, the happy shepherds cry,
    'Tis Kate of Aberdeen.

### KITTY FELL.

The courtly bard, in verse sublime,
    May praise the toasted belle ;
A country maid (in careless rhyme)
    I sing—my Kitty Fell !

When larks forsake the flow'ry plain,
    And Love's sweet numbers swell,
My pipe shall join the morning strain,
    In praise of Kitty Fell.

Where woodbines twist their fragrant shade,
    And noontide beams repel,
I 'll rest me on the tufted mead,
    And sing of Kitty Fell.

When moon-beams dance among the boughs
    That lodge sweet Philomel,
I 'll pour with her my tuneful vows,
    And pant for Kitty Fell.

The pale-faced pedant burns his books ;
    The sage forsakes his cell :
The soldier smooths his martial looks,
    And sighs for Kitty Fell.

Were mine, ye great, your envy'd lot,
    In gilded courts to dwell;
I 'd leave them for a lonely cot
    With Love and Kitty Fell.

### THYRSIS.

The pendent forest seem'd to nod,
    In drowsy fetters bound ;
And fairy elves in circles trod
    The daisy-painted ground :
When Thyrsis sought the conscious grove,
    Of slighted vows to tell,
And thus (to soothe neglected love)
    Invok'd sad Philomel :

" The stars their silver radiance shed,
    And silence charms the plain ;
But where 's my Philomela fled,
    To sing her love-lorn strain ?
Hither, ah, gentle bird, in haste
    Direct thy hov'ring wing :
The vernal green 's a dreary waste,
    Till you vouchsafe to sing.

" So thrilling sweet thy numbers flow,
    (Thy warbling song distrest !)
The tear that tells the lover's woe
    Falls cold upon my breast.
To hear sad Philomel complain,
    Will soften my despair ;
Then quickly swell the melting strain,
    And soothe a lover's care."

" Give up all hopes, unhappy swain,"
    A list'ning sage reply'd,
" For what can constancy obtain,
    From unrelenting pride ?"
The shepherd droop'd—the tyrant Death
    Had seiz'd his trembling frame ;
He bow'd, and with departing breath
    Pronounc'd Zaphira's name.

### CLARINDA.

Clarinda's lips I fondly press'd,
    While rapture fill'd each vein ;
And as I touch'd her downy breast,
    Its tenant slept serene.

So soft a calm, in such a part,
    Betrays a peaceful mind ;
Whilst my uneasy, flutt'ring heart,
    Would scarcely be confin'd.

A stubborn oak the shepherd sees,
    Unmov'd, when storms descend;
But, ah ! to ev'ry sporting breeze,
    The myrtle bough must bend.

### FANNY OF THE DALE.

Let the declining damask rose
    With envious grief look pale;
The summer bloom more freely glows
    In Fanny of the Dale.

Is there a sweet that decks the field,
    Or scents the morning gale;
Can such a vernal fragrance yield,
    As Fanny of the Dale ?

The painted belles, at court rever'd,
　Look lifeless, cold, and stale :
How faint their beauties, when compar'd
　With Fanny of the Dale !

The willows bind Pastora's brows,
　Her fond advances fail :
For Damon pays his warmest vows
　To Fanny of the Dale.

Might honest truth, at last, succeed,
　And artless love prevail ;
Thrice happy cou'd he tune his reed,
　With Fanny of the Dale !

## A SONG.

### SENT TO CHLOE WITH A ROSE.

#### TUNE—THE LASS OF PATIE'S MILL.

YES, every flower that blows,
　I pass unheeded by,
Till this enchanting rose
　Had fix'd my wand'ring eye.
It scented every breeze,
　That wanton'd o'er the stream,
Or trembled through the trees,
　To meet the morning beam.

To deck that beauteous maid,
　Its fragrance can't excel,
From some celestial shade
　The damask charmer fell:
And as her balmy sweets,
　On Chloe's breast she pours,
The Queen of Beauty greets
　The gentle Queen of Flowers.

## STANZAS

### ON THE FORWARDNESS OF SPRING.

　　......... tibi, flores, plenis
　　Ecce ferunt nymphæ calathis.　　　Virg.

O'ER Nature's fresh bosom, by verdure unbound,
　Bleak Winter blooms lovely as Spring :
Rich flow'rets (how fragrant!) rise wantonly round,
　And Summer's wing'd choristers sing !

To greet the young monarch of Britain's blest isle,
　The groves with gay blossoms are grac'd !
The primrose peeps forth with an innocent smile,
　And cowslips crowd forward in haste.

Dispatch, gentle Flora, the nymphs of your train
　Through woodlands, to gather each sweet:
Go——rob, of young roses, the dew-spangled plain,
　And strew the gay spoils at his feet.

Two chaplets of laurel, in verdure the same,
　For George, oh ye virgins, entwine !　　　[came,
From Conquest's own temples these ever-greens
　And those from the brows of the Nine !

What honours, ye Britons ! (one emblem implies)
　What glory to George shall belong !
What Miltons, (the other) what Addisons rise,
　To make him immortal in song !

To a wreath of fresh oak, England's emblem of
　　　　　　　　　　　　　　　　power !
　Whose honours with time shall increase !
Add a fair olive sprig, just unfolding its flow'r,
　Rich token of concord and peace !

Next give him young myrtles, by Beauty's bright
　Collected—the pride of the grove !　　　[queen
How fragrant their odour ! their foliage how green !
　Sweet promise of conjugal love !

Let Gaul's captive lilies, cropt close to the ground,
　As trophies of conquest be ty'd :
The virgins all cry, " There 's not one to be found !
　Out-bloom'd by his roses—they dy'd."

Ye foes of Old England, such fate shall ye share,
　With George, as our glories advance—　[despair,
Through envy you'll sicken,—you'll droop—you'll
　And die—like the lilies of France.

### ON

## THE APPROACH OF MAY.

THE virgin, when soften'd by May,
　Attends to the villager's vows ;
The birds sweetly bill on the spray,
　And poplars embrace with their boughs :
On Ida bright Venus may reign,
　Ador'd for her beauty above !
We shepherds that dwell on the plain,
　Hail May as the mother of Love.

From the west as it wantonly blows,
　Fond Zephyr caresses the vine ;
The bee steals a kiss from the rose,
　And willows and woodbines entwine :
The pinks by the rivulet side,
　That border the vernal alcove,
Bend downward to kiss the soft tide :
　For May is the mother of Love.

May tinges the butterfly's wing,
　He flutters in bridal array !
And if the wing'd foresters sing,
　Their music is taught them by May.
The stock-dove, recluse with her mate,
　Conceals her fond bliss in the grove,
And murmuring seems to repeat
　That May is the mother of Love.

The goddess will visit you soon,
　Ye virgins be sportive and gay:
Get your pipes, oh ye shepherds ! in tune,
　For music must welcome the May.
Would Damon have Phillis prove kind,
　And all his keen anguish remove,
Let him tell her soft tales, and he 'll find
　That May is the mother of Love.

## THE VIOLET.

SHELTER'D from the blight, ambition,
　Fatal to the pride of rank,
See me in my low condition,
　Laughing on the tufted bank.

On my robes (for emulation)
　No variety 's imprest :
Suited to an humble station,
　Mine 's an unembroider'd vest.

Modest though the maids declare me,
　May in her fantastic train,
When Pastora deigns to wear me,
　Ha'n't a flow'ret half so vain.

## THE NARCISSUS.

As pendent o'er the limpid stream
　I bow'd my snowy pride,
And languish'd in a fruitless flame,
　For what the Fates deny'd ;
The fair Pastora chanc'd to pass,
　With such an angel air,
I saw her in the wat'ry glass,
　And lov'd the rival fair.

Ye Fates, no longer let me pine,
　A self-admiring sweet,
Permit me, by your grace divine,
　To kiss the fair-one's feet :
That if by chance the gentle maid
　My fragrance should admire,
I may,—upon her bosom laid,
　In sister sweets expire.

## THE MILLER.

### A BALLAD.

IN a plain pleasant cottage, conveniently neat,
With a mill and some meadows—a freehold estate,
A well-meaning miller by labour supplies
Those blessings, that grandeur to great ones denies :
No passions to plague him, no cares to torment,
His constant companions are Health and Content ;
Their lordships in lace may remark, if they will,
He 's honest, though daub'd with the dust of his
　　mill.

Ere the lark's early carols salute the new day,
He springs from his cottage as jocund as May ;
He cheerfully whistles, regardless of care,
Or sings the last ballad he bought at the fair :
While courtiers are toil'd in the cobwebs of state,
Or bribing elections, in hopes to be great,
No fraud or ambition his bosom e'er fill,
Contented he works, if there 's grist for his mill.

On Sunday, bedeck'd in his homespun array,
At church he 's the loudest to chant or to pray ;
He sits to a dinner of plain English food,
Though simple the pudding, his appetite 's good.

At night, when the priest and exciseman are gone,
He quaffs at the alehouse with Roger and John,
Then reels to his pillow, and dreams of no ill ;
No monarch more blest than the man of the mill.

## A LANDSCAPE.

Rura mihi et irrigui placeant in vallibus amnes.
　　　　　　　　　　　　　　　Virg.

Now that Summer's ripen'd bloom
　Frolics where the Winter frown'd,
Stretch'd upon these banks of broom,
　We command the landscape round.

Nature in the prospect yields
　Humble dales, and mountains bold,
Meadows, woodlands, heaths,—and fields
　Yellow'd o'er with waving gold.

Goats upon that frowning steep,
　Fearless, with their kidlings browse !
Here a flock of snowy sheep !
　There an herd of motley cows !

On the uplands, every glade
　Brightens in the blaze of day ;
O'er the vales, the sober shade
　Softens to an evening grey.

Where the rill, by slow degrees,
　Swells into a crystal pool,
Shaggy rocks and shelving trees
　Shoot to keep the waters cool.

Shiver'd by a thunder-stroke,
　From the mountain's misty ridge,
O'er the brook a ruin'd oak,
　Near the farm-house, forms a bridge.

On her breast the sunny beam
　Glitters in meridian pride ;
Yonder as the virgin stream
　Hastens to the restless tide :——

Where the ships by wanton gales
　Wafted, o'er the green waves run,
Sweet to see their swelling sails
　Whiten'd by the laughing Sun !

High upon the daisied hill,
　Rising from the slope of trees,
How the wings of yonder mill
　Labour in the busy breeze !——

Cheerful as a summer's morn,
　(Bouncing from her loaded pad)
Where the maid presents her corn,
　Smirking, to the miller's lad.

O'er the green a festal throng
　Gambols, in fantastic trim !
As the full cart moves along,
　Hearken——'tis their harvest hymn !

Linnets on the crowded sprays
　Chorus,—and the wood-larks rise,
Soaring with a song of praise,
　Till the sweet notes reach the skies.

Torrents in extended sheets
  Down the cliffs, dividing, break:
'Twixt the hills the water meets,
  Setting in a silver lake !

From his languid flocks, the swain,
  By the sunbeams sore opprest,
Plunging on the wat'ry plain,
  Ploughs it with his glowing breast.

Where the mantling willows nod,
  From the green bank's slopy side,
Patient, with his well-thrown rod,
  Many an angler breaks the tide !

On the isles, with osiers drest,
  Many a fair-plum'd halcyon breeds !
Many a wild bird hides her nest,
  Cover'd in yon crackling reeds.

Fork-tail'd prattlers, as they pass
  To their nestlings in the rock,
Darting on the liquid glass,
  Seem to kiss the mimick'd flock.

Where the stone cross lifts its head,
  Many a saint and pilgrim hoar,
Up the hill was wont to tread,
  Barefoot, in the days of yore.

Guardian of a sacred well,
  Arch'd beneath yon reverend shades,
Whilome, in that shatter'd cell,
  Many an hermit told his beads.

Sultry mists surround the heath
  Where the gothic dome appears,
O'er the trembling groves beneath,
  Tott'ring with a load of years.

Turn to the contrasted scene,
  Where, beyond these hoary piles,
Gay, upon the rising green,
  Many an attic building smiles!

Painted gardens—grots—and groves,
  Intermingling shade and light;
Lengthen'd vistas, green alcoves,
  Join to give the eye delight.

Hamlets—villages, and spires,
  Scatter'd on the landscape lie,
Till the distant view retires,
  Closing in an azure sky.

## MELODY.

Lightsome as convey'd by sparrows,
  Love and Beauty cross'd the plains,
Flights of little pointed arrows
  Love dispatch'd among the swains:
But so much our shepherds dread him,
  (Spoiler of their peace profound)
Swift as scudding fawns they fled him,
  Frighted, though they felt no wound.

Now the wanton god grown slier,
  And for each fond mischief ripe,
Comes disguis'd in Pan's attire,
  Tuning sweet an oaten pipe:
Echo, by the winding river,
  Doubles his delusive strains:
While the boy conceals his quiver,
  From the slow-returning swains.

As Palemon, unsuspecting,
  Prais'd the sly musician's art,
Love, his light disguise rejecting,
  Lodg'd an arrow in his heart:
Cupid will enforce your duty,
  Shepherds, and would have you taught,
Those who timid fly from Beauty,
  May by Melody be caught.

## DELIA.

### A PASTORAL.

The gentle swan with graceful pride
  Her glossy plumage laves,
And sailing down the silver tide,
  Divides the whisp'ring waves:
The silver tide, that wand'ring flows,
  Sweet to the bird must be !
But not so sweet—blithe Cupid knows,
  As Delia is to me.

A parent bird, in plaintive mood,
  On yonder fruit-tree sung,
And still the pendent nest she view'd,
  That held her callow young:
Dear to the mother's flutt'ring heart
  The genial brood must be ;
But not so dear (the thousandth part!)
  As Delia is to me.

The roses that my brow surround
  Were natives of the dale ;
Scarce pluck'd, and in a garland bound,
  Before their sweets grew pale !
My vital bloom would thus be froze,
  If luckless torn from thee ;
For what the root is to the rose,
  My Delia is to me.

Two doves I found, like new-fall'n snow,
  So white the beauteous pair !
The birds to Delia I 'll bestow,
  They 're like her bosom fair !
When, in their chaste connubial love,
  My secret wish she 'll see ;
Such mutual bliss as turtles prove,
  May Delia share with me.

## THE SYCAMORE SHADE.

### A BALLAD.

T'other day as I sat in the sycamore shade,
  Young Damon came whistling along,
I trembled—I blush'd—a poor innocent maid !
  And my heart caper'd up to my tongue :

"Silly heart," I cry'd, "fie! What a flutter is here!
Young Damon designs you no ill;
The shepherd 's so civil, you 've nothing to fear,
Then prythee, fond urchin, lie still."

Sly Damon drew near, and knelt down at my feet,
One kiss he demanded—No more!
But urg'd the soft pressure with ardour so sweet,
I could not begrudge him a score;
My lambkins I 've kiss'd, and no change ever found,
Many times as we play'd on the hill;
But Damon's dear lips made my heart gallop round,
Nor would the found urchin lie still.

When the Sun blazes fierce, to the sycamore shade
For shelter, I 'm sure to repair;
And, virgins, in faith I 'm no longer afraid,
Although the dear shepherd be there:
At ev'ry fond kiss that with freedom he takes,
My heart may rebound if it will;
There 's something so sweet in the bustle it makes,
I 'll die ere I bid it lie still.

---

## DAMON AND PHILLIS.

### A PASTORAL DIALOGUE.

Donec gratus eram, &c.            Hor.

#### DAMON.

When Phillis was faithful, and fond as she 's fair,
I twisted young roses in wreaths for my hair;
But ah! the sad willow 's a shade for my brows,
For Phillis no longer remembers her vows!
To the groves with young Colin the shepherdess flies,
While Damon disturbs the still plains with his sighs.

#### PHILLIS.

Bethink you, false Damon, before you upbraid,
When Phœbe's fair lambkin had yesterday stray'd,
Through the woodlands you wander'd, poor Phillis
                                forgot!
And drove the gay rambler quite home to her cot;
A swain so deceitful no damsel can prize;
'Tis Phœbe, not Phillis, lays claim to your sighs.

#### DAMON.

Like summer 's full season young Phœbe is kind,
Her manners are graceful, untainted her mind!
The sweets of contentment her cottage adorn,
She 's fair as the rose-bud, and fresh as the morn!
She smiles like Pomona—These smiles I 'd resign,
If Phillis were faithful, and deign'd to be mine.

#### PHILLIS.

On the tabor young Colin so prettily plays,
He sings me sweet sonnets, and writes in my praise!
He chose me his true-love last Valentine-day,
When birds sat like bridegrooms all pair'd on the
                        spray;              [mind,
Yet I 'd drive the gay shepherd far, far from my
If Damon, the rover, were constant and kind.

#### DAMON.

Fine folks, my sweet Phillis, may revel and range,
But fleeting 's the pleasure that 's founded on
                        change!
In the villager's cottage such constancy springs,
That peasants with pity may look down on kings.

To the church then let 's hasten, our transports to
                        bind,
And Damon will always prove faithful and kind.

#### PHILLIS.

To the church then let 's hasten, our transports to
                        bind,
And Phillis will always prove faithful and kind.

---

## THE WARNING.

Young Colin once courted Myrtilla the prude,
If he sigh'd or look'd tender, she cry'd he was
                        rude;
Though he begg'd with devotion, some ease for his
                        pain,
The shepherd got nothing but frowns and disdain.
Fatigu'd with her folly, his suit he gave o'er,
And vow'd that no female should fetter him more.

He strove with all caution to 'scape from the net,
But Chloe soon caught him,—a finish'd coquet!
She glanc'd to his glances, she sigh'd to his sighs,
And flatter'd his hope—in the language of eyes.
Alas for poor Colin! when put to the test,
Himself and his passion prov'd both but her jest.

By the critical third he was fix'd in the snare;
By Fanny—gay, young, unaffected, and fair;
When she found he had merit, and love took his
                        part,
She dally'd no longer—but yielded her heart.
With joy they submitted to Hymen's decree,
And now are as happy—as happy can be.

As the rose-bud of beauty soon sickens and fades,
The prude and coquet are two slighted old maids;
Now their sweets are all wasted,—too late they
                        repent,
For transports untasted, for moments misspent!
Ye virgins, take warning, improve by my plan,
And fix the fond youth when you prudently can.

---

## HOLIDAY GOWN.

In holiday gown, and my new fangled hat,
Last Monday I tript to the fair;
I held up my head, and I 'll tell you for what,
Brisk Roger I guess'd wou'd be there:
He woos me to marry whenever we meet,
There 's honey sure dwells on his tongue!
He hugs me so close, and he kisses so sweet,
I 'd wed—if I were not too young.

Fond Sue, I 'll assure you, laid hold on the boy,
(The vixen wou'd fain be his bride)
Some token she claim'd, either ribbon or toy,
And swore that she 'd not be deny'd:
A top-knot he bought her, and garters of green,
Pert Susan was cruelly stung;
I hate her so much, that, to kill her with spleen,
I 'd wed—if I were not too young.

He whisper'd such soft pretty things in mine ear!
  He flatter'd, he promis'd, and swore!
Such trinkets he gave me, such laces and geer,
  That, trust me,—my pockets ran o'er:
Some ballads he bought me, the best he cou'd find,
  And sweetly their burthen he sung;
Good faith! he's so handsome, so witty, and kind,
  I'd wed—if I were not too young.

The Sun was just setting, 'twas time to retire,
  (Our cottage was distant a mile)
I rose to be gone—Roger bow'd like a 'squire,
  And handed me over the stile:
His arms he threw round me—love laugh'd in his eye,
  He led me the meadows among,
There prest me so close, I agreed, with a sigh,
  To wed—for I was not too young.

## DAPHNE:

### A SONG.

No longer, Daphne, I admire
  The graces in thine eyes;
Continu'd coyness kills desire,
  And famish'd passion dies.
Three tedious years I've sigh'd in vain,
Nor could my vows prevail;
With all the rigours of disdain,
  You scorn'd my amorous tale.

When Celia cry'd, "How senseless she,
  That has such vows refus'd;
Had Damon giv'n his heart to me,
  It had been kinder us'd.
The man's a fool that pines and dies
  Because a woman's coy;
The gentle bliss that one denies,
  A thousand will enjoy."

Such charming words, so void of art,
  Surprising rapture gave;
And though the maid subdu'd my heart,
  It ceas'd to be a slave:
A wretch condemn'd, shall Daphne prove;
  While blest without restraint,
In the sweet calendar of love
  My Celia stands—a saint.

## CORYDON:

### A PASTORAL.

#### TO THE MEMORY OF WILLIAM SHENSTONE, ESQ.

Come, shepherds, we'll follow the hearse,
  We'll see our lov'd Corydon laid:
Though sorrow may blemish the verse,
  Yet let a sad tribute be paid.

They call'd him the pride of the plain;
  In sooth he was gentle and kind!
He mark'd on his elegant strain
  The graces that glow'd in his mind.

On purpose he planted yon trees,
  That birds in the covert might dwell;
He cultur'd his thyme for the bees,
  But never wou'd rifle their cell.

Ye lambkins that play'd at his feet,
  Go bleat—and your master bemoan;
His music was artless and sweet,
  His manners as mild as your own.

No verdure shall cover the vale,
  No bloom on the blossoms appear;
The sweets of the forest shall fail,
  And winter discolour the year.

No birds in our hedges shall sing,
  (Our hedges so vocal before)
Since he that should welcome the spring,
  Salutes the gay season no more.

His Phillis was fond of his praise,
  And poets came round in a throng;
They listen'd——they envy'd his lays,
  But which of them equal'd his song?

Ye shepherds, henceforward be mute,
  For lost is the pastoral strain;
So give me my Corydon's flute,
  And thus——let me break it in twain.

## DAMON AND PHŒBE.

When the sweet rosy morning first peep'd from
    the skies,
A loud singing lark bade the villagers rise;
The cowslips were lively—the primroses gay,
And shed their best perfumes to welcome the
    May:
The swains and their sweethearts all rang'd on the
    green,
Did homage to Phœbe—and hail'd her their queen.

Young Damon step'd forward: he sung in her
    praise,
And Phœbe bestow'd him a garland of bays:
" May this wreath," said the fair-one, "dear lord
    of my vows,
A crown for true merit, bloom long on thy brows:"
The swains and their sweethearts that danc'd on
    the green,
Approv'd the fond present of Phœbe their queen.

'Mongst lords and fine ladies, we shepherds are
    told,
The dearest affections are barter'd for gold;
That discord in wedlock is often their lot,
While Cupid and Hymen shake hands in a cot:
At the church with fair Phœbe since Damon has
    been,
He's rich as a monarch—she's blest as a queen.

## A PASTORAL HYMN TO JANUS.

### ON THE BIRTH OF THE QUEEN.

Te primum pia thura rogent—te vota salutent,
......... te colat omnis honos.     Mart. ad Janum.

To Janus, gentle shepherds! raise a shrine:
    His honours be divine!
And as to mighty Pan with homage bow:
    To him, the virgin troop shall tribute bring;
Let him be hail'd like the green-liveried Spring,
Spite of the wintry storms that stain his brow.

The pride, the glowing pageantry of May,
    Glides wantonly away:
But January, in his rough-spun vest,
    Boasts the full blessings that can never fade,
    He that gave birth to the illustrious maid,
Whose beauties make the British monarch blest!

Could the soft Spring with all her sunny showers,
    The frolic nurse of flowers!
Or flaunting Summer, flush'd in ripen'd pride,
    Could they produce a finish'd sweet so rare:
    Or from his golden stores, a gift so fair,
Say, has the fertile Autumn e'er supply'd?

Henceforward let the hoary month be gay
    As the white-hawthorn'd May!
The laughing goddess of the Spring disown'd,
    HER rosy wreath shall on HIS brows appear,
    Old Janus, as he leads, shall fill the year,
And the less fruitful Autumn be dethron'd.

Above the other months supremely blest,
    Glad Janus stands confest!
He can behold with retrospective face
    The mighty blessings of the year gone by:
    Where, to connect a monarch's nuptial tie,
Assembled ev'ry glory, ev'ry grace!

When he looks forward on the flatt'ring year,
    The golden hours appear,
As in the sacred reign of Saturn, fair:
    Britain shall prove from this propitious date,
    Her honours perfect, victories complete,
And boast the brightest hopes, a BRITISH HEIR.

The above little poem was written on supposition that her majesty's birth-day was *really* in the
month of January.

---

## AN INSCRIPTION

### ON THE HOUSE AT MAVIS-BANK, NEAR EDINBURGH, SITUATED IN A GROVE.

Parva domus! nemerosa quies!
    Sis tu, quoque nostris
Hospitium, laribus, subsidiumque diu!
Flora tuas ornet postes, Pomonaque mensas!
Conferat ut varias fertilis hortus opes!
Et volucres pictæ cingentes voce canora,
Retia sola canent quæ sibi tendit amor!

Floriferi colles, dulces mihi sæpe recessus
Dent, atque hospitibus gaudia plena meis!
Concedatque Deus nunquam, vel sero senescas,
Seroque terrenas experiare vices!
Integra reddantur quæ plurima sæcula rodaut
Detur, et ut senio pulchrior eniteas.

---

### THE INSCRIPTION IMITATED.

PEACE has explor'd this sylvan scene,
    She courts your calm retreat,
Ye groves of variegated green,
    That grace my genial seat!
Here, in the lap of lenient ease,
    (Remote from mad'ning noise)
Let me delude a length of days,
    In dear domestic joys!

Long may the parent queen of flow'rs
    Her fragrance here display!
Long may she paint my mantling bow'rs,
    And make my portals gay!
Nor you—my yellow gardens, fail
    To swell Pomona's hoard!
So shall the plenteous, rich regale—
    Replenish, long, my board!

Pour through the groves your carols clear,
    Ye birds, nor bondage dread:
If any toils entangle here,
    'Tis those which Love hath spread.
Where the green hill so gradual slants,
    Or flowery glade extends,
Long may these fair, these fav'rite haunts
    Prove social to my friends!

May you preserve perpetual bloom,
    My happy halcyon seat!
Or if fell Time denounce thy doom,
    Far distant be its date!
And when he makes, with iron rage,
    Thy youthful pride his prey,
Long may the honours of thy age
    Be reverenc'd in decay!

---

## ANOTHER INSCRIPTION

### ON THE SAME HOUSE.

HANC in gremio resonantis sylvæ
    Aquis, hortis, aviumque garritu,
Cæterisque ruris honoribus,
    Undique renidentem villam,
Non magnificam——non superbam;
    At qualen vides,
Commodam, mundam, genialem
    Naturæ parem, socians artem.
    Sibi, suisque
    Ad vitam placide,
    Et tranquille agendum
Designavit, instruxitque.
        D. I. C.

## IMITATED.

In the deep bosom of my grove
    A sweet recess survey!
Where birds, with elegies of love,
    Make vocal every spray.
A sylvan spot, with woods—with waters crown'd,
With all the rural honours blooming round!

This little, but commodious seat
    (Where Nature weds with Art)
A'nt to the EYE superbly great,
    Its beauties charm the HEART.
Here, may the happy founder and his race
Pass their full days in harmony and peace!

## CONTENT.

### A PASTORAL.

O'er moorlands and mountains, rude, barren, and
    As wilder'd and weary'd I roam,      [bare,
A gentle young shepherdess sees my despair,
    And leads me—o'er lawns—to her home:
Yellow sheaves from rich Ceres her cottage had
        crown'd,
    Green rushes were strew'd on her floor,
Her casement, sweet woodbines crept wantonly
    And deck'd the sod seats at her door.   [round,

We sate ourselves down to a cooling repast,
    Fresh fruits! and she cull'd me the best;
While thrown from my guard by some glances she
    Love slily stole into my breast!      [cast,
I told my soft wishes; she sweetly reply'd,
    (Ye virgins, her voice was divine!)
" I've rich ones rejected, and great ones deny'd,
    But take me, fond shepherd—I'm thine."

Her air was so modest, her aspect so meek!
    So simple, yet sweet, were her charms!
I kiss'd the ripe roses that glow'd on her cheek,
    And lock'd the dear maid in my arms.
Now jocund together we tend a few sheep,
    And if, by yon prattler, the stream,
Reclin'd on her bosom, I sink into sleep,
    Her image still softens my dream.

Together we range o'er the slow rising hills,
    Delighted with pastoral views,
Or rest on the rock whence the streamlet distils,
    And point out new themes for my Muse.
To pomp or proud titles she ne'er did aspire,
    The damsel 's of humble descent;
The cottager, PEACE, is well known for her sire,
    And shepherds have nam'd her CONTENT.

## CORYDON AND PHILLIS.

### A PASTORAL.

Her sheep had in clusters crept close by the grove,
    To hide from the rigours of day;
And Phillis herself, in a woodbine alcove,
    Among the fresh violets lay:
A youngling, it seems, had been stole from its dam,
    ('Twixt Cupid and Hymen a plot)
That Corydon might, as he search'd for his lamb,
    Arrive at this critical spot.

As through the gay hedge for his lambkin he peeps,
    He saw the sweet maid with surprise;
" Ye gods, if so killing," he cry'd, " when she
        sleeps,
    I'm lost when she opens her eyes!
To tarry much longer would hazard my heart,
    I'll onwards, my lambkin to trace:"
In vain honest Corydon strove to depart,
    For love had him nail'd to the place.

" Hush, hush'd be these birds, what a bawling they
        keep!"
    He cry'd, " you're too loud on the spray,
Don't you see, foolish lark, that the charmer 's
        asleep?
    You'll wake her as sure as 'tis day:
How dare that fond butterfly touch the sweet maid!
    Her cheek he mistakes for the rose;
I'd pat him to death, if I was not afraid
    My boldness would break her repose."

Young Phillis look'd up with a languishing smile,
    " Kind shepherd," she said, " you mistake;
I laid myself down just to rest me a while,
    But trust me, have still been awake:"
The shepherd took courage, advanc'd with a bow,
    He plac'd himself close by her side,
And manag'd the matter, I cannot tell how,
    But yesterday made her his bride.

## AN

### ELEGY ON A PILE OF RUINS.

Aspice murorum moles, præruptaque saxa!
                    Janus Vitalis.
Omnia, tempus edax depascitur, omnia carpit.
                    Seneca.

In the full prospect yonder hill commands,
    O'er barren heaths, and cultivated plains;
The vestige of an ancient abbey stands,
    Close by a ruin'd castle's rude remains.

Half buried, there, lie many a broken bust,
    And obelisk, and urn, o'erthrown by Time;
And many a cherub, there, descends in dust
    From the rent roof, and portico sublime.

The rivulets, oft frighted at the sound
    Of fragments, tumbling from the tow'rs on high,
Plunge to their source in secret caves profound,
    Leaving their banks and pebbly bottoms dry.

Where rev'rend shrines in gothic grandeur stood,
    The nettle, or the noxious night-shade spreads;
And ashlings, wafted from the neighb'ring wood,
    Through the worn turrets wave their trembling
        heads.

There Contemplation, to the crowd unknown,
    Her attitude compos'd, and aspect sweet!
Sits musing on a monumental stone,
    And points to the MEMENTO at her feet.

Soon as sage ev'ning check'd day's sunny pride,
    I left the mantling shade in moral mood;
And seated by the maid's sequester'd side,
    Sigh'd, as the mould'ring monuments I view'd.

Inexorably calm, with silent pace
Here Time has pass'd—What ruin marks his way!
This pile, now crumbling o'er its hallow'd base,
Turn'd not his step, nor could his course delay.

Religion rais'd her supplicating eyes
In vain; and Melody her song sublime:
In vain, Philosophy, with maxims wise,
Would touch the cold unfeeling heart of Time.

Yet the hoar tyrant, though not mov'd to spare,
Relented when he struck its finish'd pride;
And partly the rude ravage to repair,
The tott'ring tow'rs with twisted ivy ty'd.

How solemn is the cell o'ergrown with moss,
That terminates the view, yon cloister'd way!
In the crush'd wall, a time-corroded cross,
Religion like, stands mould'ring in decay!

Where the mild Sun, through saint-encypher'd glass,
Illum'd with mellow light yon dusky isle,
Many rapt hours might Meditation pass,
Slow moving 'twixt the pillars of the pile!

And Piety, with mystic-meaning beads,
Bowing to saints on every side inurn'd,
Trod oft the solitary path that leads
Where now the sacred altar lies o'erturn'd!

Through the grey grove, between those with'ring
trees,
'Mongst a rude group of monuments, appears
A marble-imag'd matron on her knees,
Half wasted, like a Niobe in tears:

Low levell'd in the dust her darling 's laid!
Death pitied not the pride of youthful bloom;
Nor could maternal piety dissuade,
Or soften the fell tyrant of the tomb.

The relics of a mitred saint may rest,
Where, mould'ring in the niche, his statue stands;
Now nameless as the crowd that kiss'd his vest,
And crav'd the benediction of his hands.

Near the brown arch, redoubling yonder gloom,
The bones of an illustrious chieftain lie;
As trac'd among the fragments of his tomb,
The trophies of a broken Fame imply.

Ah! what avails, that o'er the vassal plain,
His rights and rich demesnes extended wide!
That Honour and her knights compos'd his train,
And Chivalry stood marshal'd by his side!

Though to the clouds his castle seem'd to climb,
And frown'd defiance on the desp'rate foe;
Though deem'd invincible, the conqueror, Time,
Levell'd the fabric, as the founder, low.

Where the light lyre gave many a soft'ning sound,
Ravens and rooks, the birds of discord, dwell;
And where Society sat sweetly crown'd,
Eternal Solitude has fix'd her cell.

The lizard, and the lazy lurking bat,
Inhabit now, perhaps, the painted room,
Where the sage matron and her maidens sat,
Sweet-singing at the silver-working loom.

The traveller 's bewilder'd on a waste;
And the rude winds incessant seem to roar,
Where, in his groves with arching arbours grac'd,
Young lovers often sigh'd in days of yore.

His aqueducts, that led the limpid tide
To pure canals, a crystal cool supply!
In the deep dust their barren beauties hide: [dry!
Time's thirst, unquenchable, has drain'd them

Though his rich hours in revelry were spent,
With Comus, and the laughter-loving crew;
And the sweet brow of Beauty, still unbent,
Brighten'd his fleecy moments as they flew:

Fleet are the fleecy moments! fly they must;
Not to be stay'd by masque or midnight roar!
Nor shall a pulse among that mould'ring dust
Beat wanton at the smiles of Beauty more!

Can the deep statesman, skill'd in great design,
Protract, but for a day, precarious breath?
Or the tun'd follower of the sacred Nine
Soothe, with his melody, insatiate Death!

No—though the palace bar her golden gate,
Or monarchs plant ten thousand guards around;
Unerring, and unseen, the shaft of Fate
Strikes the devoted victim to the ground!

What then avails Ambition's wide-stretch'd wing,
The schoolman's page, or pride of Beauty's bloom?
The crape-clad hermit, and the rich-rob'd king,
Levell'd, lie mix'd promiscuous in the tomb.

The Macedonian monarch, wise and good,
Bade, when the morning's rosy reign began,
Courtiers should call, as round his couch they stood,
"Philip! remember thou 'rt no more than man.

"Though glory spread thy name from pole to pole:
Though thou art merciful, and brave, and just;
Philip, reflect, thou 'rt posting to the goal,
Where mortals mix in undistinguish'd dust!"

So Saladin, for arts and arms renown'd,
(Egypt and Syria's wide domains subdu'd)
Returning with imperial triumphs crown'd,
Sigh'd, when the perishable pomp he view'd:

And as he rode, high in his regal car
In all the purple pride of conquest drest;
Conspicuous, o'er the trophies gain'd in war,
Plac'd, pendent on a spear, his burial vest:

While thus the herald cry'd—" This son of Pow'r,
This Saladin, to whom the nations bow'd,
May, in the space of one revolving hour,
Boast of no other spoil but yonder shroud!"

Search where Ambition rag'd, with rigour steel'd,
Where Slaughter, like the rapid lightning, ran;
And say, while Memory weeps the blood-stain'd
field,                                        [man?
Where lies the chief, and where the common

Vain then are pyramids, and motto'd stones,
And monumental trophies rais'd on high!
For Time confounds them with the crumbling bones,
That mix'd in hasty graves unnotic'd lie.

Rests not beneath the turf the peasant's head,
  Soft as the lord's beneath the labour'd tomb?
Or sleeps one colder, in his close clay bed,
  Than t'other in the wide vault's dreary womb?

Hither, let Luxury lead her loose-rob'd train;
Here flutter Pride, on purple-painted wings:
And from the moral prospect learn—how vain
The wish, that sighs for sublunary things!

---

### A SONG.

He that Love hath never try'd,
Nor had Cupid for his guide,
Cannot hit the passage right
To the palace of delight.

What are honours, regal wealth,
Florid youth, and rosy health?
Without Love his tribute brings,
Impotent, unmeaning things!

Gentle shepherds, persevere,
Still be tender, still sincere;
Love and Time, united, do
Wonders, if the heart be true.

---

### SAPPHO'S HYMN TO VENUS

#### IMITATED.

Hail! (with eternal beauty blest!
  O'er Heav'n and Earth ador'd!)
Hail, Venus! 'tis thy slave's request,
  Her peace may be restor'd:
Break the fond bonds, remove the rankling smart,
And bid thy tyrant son from Sappho's soul depart.

Once you descended, queen of love,
  At Sappho's bold desire,
From the high roofs of sacred Jove,
  Thy ever glorious sire!
I saw thy dusky pinion'd sparrows bear
Thy chariot, rolling light, through the rejoicing air.

No transient visit you design'd,
  Your wanton birds depart;
And with a look, divinely kind,
  That sooth'd my flutt'ring heart:
" Sappho," say you, " what sorrow breaks thy rest?
How can I give relief to thy conflicting breast?

" Is there a youth severely coy,
  My fav'rite would subdue?
Or has she lost some wand'ring boy,
  To plighted vows untrue?
Spread thy soft nets, the rambler shall return,
And with new lighted flames, more fond, more
    fiercely burn.

" Thy proffer'd gifts though he deride,
  And scorn thy glowing charms,
Soon shall his every art be try'd
  To win thee to his arms:
Though he be now as cold as virgin snow,
The victim, in his turn, shall like rous'd Ætna glow."

Thee, goddess, I again invoke,
  These mad desires remove!
Again I 've felt the furious stroke
  Of irresistless love:
Bid gentle peace to Sappho's breast return,
Or make the youth she loves with mutual ardour
    burn.

---

### IMITATIONS FROM ANACREON.

#### ODE LVIII.

As I wove, with wanton care,
Fillets for a virgin's hair,
Culling for my fond design
What the fields had fresh and fine:
Cupid,—and I mark'd him well,
Hid him in a cowslip bell;
While he plum'd a pointed dart,
Fated to inflame the heart.
  Glowing with malicious joy,
Sudden I secur'd the boy;
And, regardless of his cries,
Bore the little frighted prize
Where the mighty goblet stood,
Teeming with a rosy flood.
  " Urchin," in my rage I cry'd,
" What avails thy saucy pride?
From thy busy vengeance free,
Triumph now belongs to me!
Thus—I drown thee in my cup;
Thus—in wine I drink thee up."
  Fatal was the nectar'd draught
That to murder Love I quaff'd,
O'er my bosom's fond domains
Now the cruel tyrant reigns:
On my heart's most tender strings,
Striking with his wanton wings,
I'm for ever doom'd to prove
All the insolence of love.

---

#### ODE IX.

##### THE DOVE.

" Tell me," said I, " my beauteous Dove
(If an ambassadress from Love)
Tell me, on what soft errand sent,
Thy gentle flight is this way bent?
  " Ambrosial sweets thy pinions shed
As in the quivering breeze they spread!"
  " A message," says the bird, " I bear
From fond Anacreon to the fair;
A virgin of celestial grace!
The Venus of the human race!
  " Me, for an hymn, or amorous ode,
The Paphian Venus once bestow'd
To the sweet bard; for whom I'd fly
Unwearied to the furthest sky.
  " Through the soft air he bade me glide,
(See, to my wing his billet 's ty'd)
And told me, 'twas his kind decree,
When I return'd, to set me free.
  " 'Twould prove me but a simple bird
To take Anacreon at his word:
Why should I hide me in the wood,
Or search for my precarious food,

When I 've my master's leave to stand
Cooing upon his friendly hand;
When I can be profusely fed
With crumbs of his ambrosial bread,
And, welcom'd to his nectar bowl,
Sip the rich drops that fire the soul;
Till, in fantastic rounds I spread
My fluttering pinions o'er his head?
　" Or if he strike the trembling wire,
I perch upon my fav'rite lyre;
Till, lull'd into luxuriant rest,
Sleep steals upon my raptur'd breast.
　" Go, stranger—to your business—go,
I've told you all you wish'd to know:
Go, stranger,—and I think you 'll say,
This prattling Dove 's an arrant Jay."

### THE DANCE.

HARK! the speaking strings invite,
Music calls us to delight:
See the maids in measures move,
Winding like the maze of love.
As they mingle, madly gay,
Sporting Hebe leads the way.
　On each glowing cheek is spread
Rosy Cupid's native red;
And from ev'ry sparkling eye
Pointed darts at random fly.
Love, and active Youth, advance
Foremost in the sprightly dance.
　As the magic numbers rise,
Through my veins the poison flies;
Raptures, not to be exprest,
Revel in my throbbing breast.
Jocund as we beat the ground,
Love and Harmony go round.
　Every maid (to crown his bliss)
Gives her youth a rosy kiss;
Such a kiss as might inspire
Thrilling raptures—soft desire
Such Adonis might receive,
Such the queen of beauty gave,
When the conquer'd goddess strove
(In the conscious myrtle grove)
To inflame the boy with love.
　Let not pride our sports restrain,
Banish hence the prude, Disdain!
Think—ye virgins, if you 're coy,
Think—ye rob yourselves of joy;
Every moment you refuse,
So much ecstasy you lose:
Think—how fast these moments fly:
If you should too long deny,
Love and Beauty both will die.

### ODE XIV.

WHY did I with Love engage!
Why provoke his mighty rage!
　True it is, the wand'ring child
Met me with an aspect mild,
And besought me, like a friend,
At his gentle shrine to bend.
True, from my mistaken pride,
Due devotion was deny'd,
Till (because I would not yield)
Cupid dar'd me to the field.

　Now I'm in my armour clasp'd,
Now the mighty lance is grasp'd,
But an *Achileian* spear
Would be ineffectual here,
While the poison'd arrows fly
Hot, as lightning from the sky.
　Wounded, through the woods I run,
Follow'd still by Beauty's son,
Arrows in malignant showers
Still the angry urchin pours;
Till, exhausting all his store,
(When the quiver yields no more)
See the god—a living dart,
Shoots *himself* into my heart.
　Freedom I must, now, resign,
Victory, oh Love, is thine!
What can outward actions win
When the battle burns within!

FILL me that capacious cup,
Fill it, to the margin up;
From my veins the thirsty day
Quaffs the vital strength away.

Let a wreath my temples shield,
Fresh from the enamell'd field;
These declining roses bow,
Blasted by my sultry brow.

Flow'rets, by their friendly aid,
From the sunbeams form a shade:
Let me from my heart require,
(Glowing with intense desire)
Is there, in the deepest grove,
Shel'er from the BEAMS of Love?

### ODE XXXIII.

#### TO THE SWALLOW.

SOON as summer glads the sky,
Hither, gentle bird, you fly;
And with golden sunshine blest,
Build your pretty plaster'd nest.
　When the seasons cease to smile,
(Wing'd for Memphis or the Nile)
Charming bird, you disappear
Till the kind succeeding year.
　Like the Swallow, Love, depart!
Respite for a while my heart.
No, he 'll never leave his nest,
Tyrant tenant of my breast!
There a thousand WISHES try
On their callow wings to fly;
There you may a thousand tell,
Pertly peeping through the shell:
In a state unfinish'd, rise
Thousands of a smaller size.
Till their noisy chirpings cease,
Never shall my heart have peace.
　Feather'd ones the younglings feed,
Till mature they 're fit to breed;
Then, to swell the crowded store,
They produce their thousands more:
Nor can mighty numbers count
In my breast their vast amount.

## THE PICTURE:

### A TALE.

A PORTRAIT, at my lord's command,
Completed by a curious hand:
For dabblers in the nice *vertù*
His lordship set the piece to view,
Bidding their connoisseurships tell,
Whether the work was finish'd well.
"Why"—says the loudest, " on my word,
'Tis not a *likeness*, good my lord ;
Nor, to be plain, for speak I must,
Can I pronounce one feature just."
Another effort straight was made,
Another portraiture essay'd ;
The judges were again besought,
Each to deliver what he thought.
" Worse than the first"—the critics bawl ;
" O what a mouth ! how *monstrous* small !
Look at the cheeks—how lank and thin !
See, what a most prepost'rous chin !"
After remonstrance made in vain,
" I'll," says the painter, " once again,
(If my good lord vouchsafes to sit)
Try for a more successful hit:
If you 'll to morrow deign to call,
We 'll have a piece to please you all."
To morrow comes—a picture 's plac'd
Before those spurious sons of Taste——
In their opinions all agree,
This is the vilest of the three.
" Know—to confute your envious pride,
(His lordship from the canvass cry'd)
" Know—that it is my real face,
Where you could no resemblance trace :
I've try'd you by a lucky trick,
And prov'd your GENIUS to the quick.
Void of all judgment—justice—sense,
Out—ye pretending varlets—hence."
The connoisseurs depart in haste,
Despis'd—detected—and disgrac'd.

## THE WITCH:

### A TALE.

A WITCH, that from her ebon chair
Could hurl destruction through the air,
Or, at her all-commanding will,
Make the tumultuous ocean still :
Once, by an incantation fell,
(As the recording Druids tell)
Pluck'd the round Moon, whose radiant light
Silver'd the sober noon of night,
From the domain she held above,
Down to a dark, infernal grove.
" Give me," the goddess cry'd, "a cause,
Why you disturb my sacred laws ?
Look at my train,—yon wand'ring host !
See how the trembling stars are lost !
Through the celestial regions wide,
Why do they range without a guide !
*Chaos*, from our confusion, may
Hope for his old detested sway."
" I 'm," says the Witch, " severely crost,
Know that my fav'rite squirrel 's lost :

Search——for I' ll have creation torn,
If he 's not found before the morn."
Soon as the impious charge was giv'n—
From the tremendous stores of Heaven,
Jove with a bolt——revengeful !——red !
Struck the detested monster dead.
If there are slaves to pity blind,
With power enough to plague mankind,
That for their own nefarious ends
Tread upon Freedom and her friends,
Let 'em beware the Witch's fate !
When their presumption 's at the height,
Jove will his angry powers assume,
And the curs'd miscreants meet their doom.

## REPUTATION:

### AN ALLEGORY.

To travel far as the wide world extends,
Seeking for objects that deserv'd their care,
Virtue set forth, with two selected friends,
Talent refin'd, and Reputation fair.

As they went on, in their intended round,
Talent first spoke, " My gentle comrades, say,
Where each of you may probably be found,
Should accident divide us on the way.

" If torn (she added) from my lov'd allies,
A friendly patronage I hope to find,
Where the fine arts from cultivation rise,
And the sweet Muse hath harmoniz'd mankind."

Says Virtue, " Did Sincerity appear,
Or meek-ey'd Charity among the great ;
Could I find courtiers from corruption clear,
'Tis among these I 'd seek for my retreat.

" Could I find patriots, for the public weal
Assiduous, and without their selfish views ;
Could I find priests of undissembled zeal,
'Tis among those my residence I 'd choose.

" In glitt'ring domes let Luxury reside ;
I must be found in some sequester'd cell,
Far from the paths of Avarice or Pride,
Where homebred Happiness delights to dwell."

" Ye may be trac'd, my gentle friends, 'tis true,
But who," says Reputation, " can explore
My slipp'ry steps ?——Keep, keep *me* in your view,
If *I'm* once lost, you 'll never find me more. "

## THE ROSE AND BUTTERFLY:

### A FABLE.

AT day's early dawn a gay Butterfly spied
A budding young Rose, and he wish'd her his bride:
She blush'd when she heard him his passion declare,
And tenderly told him—he need not despair.
Their faith was soon plighted, as lovers will do,
He swore to be constant, she vow'd to be true.
It had not been prudent to deal with delay,
The bloom of a rose passes quickly away,
And the pride of a butterfly dies in a day.

When wedded, away the wing'd gentleman hies,
From flow'ret to flow'ret he wantonly flies;
Nor did he revisit his bride, till the Sun
Had less than one-fourth of his journey to run.
The Rose thus reproach'd him—" Already so cold !
How feign'd, O you false one, the passion you told !
'Tis an age since you left me:" she meant a few
    hours;
But such we 'll suppose the fond language of flowers:
" I saw when you gave the base violet a kiss :
How—how could you stoop to a meanness like this ?
Shall a low, little wretch, whom we Roses despise,
Find favour, O Love ! in my Butterfly's eyes ?
On a tulip, quite tawdry, I saw your fond rape,
Nor yet could the pitiful primrose escape :
Dull daffodils too were with ardour address'd,
And poppies, ill-scented, you kindly caress'd.'"
The coxcomb was piqu'd, and reply'd with a sneer,
" That you 're first to complain, I commend you,
    my dear !
But know, from your conduct my maxims I drew,
And if I 'm inconstant, I copy from you.
I saw the boy Zephirus rifle your charms,
I saw how you simper'd and smil'd in his arms ;
The honey-bee kiss'd you, you cannot disown,
You favour'd besides—O dishonour !—a drone ;
Yet worse—'tis a crime that you must not deny,
Your sweets were made common, false Rose, to a fly."

MORAL.

This law, long ago, did Love's providence make,
That ev'ry coquet should be curs'd with a rake.

THE SHEEP AND THE BRAMBLE-BUSH:

A FABLE.

A THICK-TWISTED brake, in the time of a storm,
    Seem'd kindly to cover a sheep:
So snug, for a while, he lay shelter'd and warm,
    It quietly sooth'd him asleep.

The clouds are now scatter'd—the winds are at
    The sheep to his pasture inclin'd :        [peace;
But, ah ! the fell thicket lays hold of his fleece,
    His coat is left forfeit behind.

My friend, who the thicket of law never try'd,
    Consider before you get in;
Though judgment and sentence are pass'd on your
    By Jove, you 'll be fleec'd to the skin.    [side,

THE FOX AND THE CAT.

A FABLE.

THE Fox and the Cat, as they travell'd one day,
With moral discourses cut shorter the way :
" 'Tis great," says the Fox, " to make justice our
    guide !"
" How godlike is mercy !" Grimalkin reply'd.
    Whilst thus they proceeded,—a wolf from the
Impatient of hunger, and thirsting for blood, [wood,
Rush'd forth—as he saw the dull shepherd asleep,
And seiz'd for his supper an innocent sheep.
" In vain, wretched victim, for mercy you bleat,
When mutton 's at hand," says the wolf. " I must
    eat."

Grimalkin 's astonish'd,—the Fox stood aghast,
To see the fell beast at his bloody repast.
" What a wretch," says the Cat,—" 'tis the vilest
    of brutes :
Does he feed upon flesh, when there 's herbage
    —and roots ?"
Cries the Fox—" While our oaks give us acorns so
    good,
What a tyrant is this, to spill innocent blood !"
    Well, onward they march'd, and they moraliz'd
    still,
Till they came where some poultry pick'd chaff by
    a mill;
Sly Renard survey'd them with gluttonous eyes,
And made (spite of morals) a pullet his prize.
A mouse too, that chanc'd from her covert to
The greedy Grimalkin secur'd as her prey.  [stray,
    A spider that sat in her web on the wall,
Perceiv'd the poor victims, and pity'd their fall ;
She cry'd—" Of such murders how guiltless am I!"
So ran to regale on a new taken fly.

MORAL.

The faults of our neighbours with freedom we blame,
But tax not ourselves, though we practise the same.

HYMEN.

WHEN Chloe, with a blush, comply'd
To be the fond Nicander's bride,
His wild imagination ran
On raptures never known by man.
How high the tides of fancy swell,
Expression must despair to tell.
    A painter call'd,——Nicander cries,
Descending from the radiant skies,
" Draw me a bright, a beauteous boy,
The herald of connubial joy !
Draw him with all peculiar care,
Make him beyond Adonis fair ;
Give to his cheeks a roseate hue,
Let him have eyes of heav'nly blue,
Lips soft'ning in nectarious dew ;
A lustre o'er his charms display,
More glorious than the beams of day.
Expect, sir, if you can succeed,
A premium for a prince indeed." ·
    His talents straight the painter try'd,
And ere the nuptial knot was ty'd,
A picture in the noblest taste
Before the fond Nicander plac'd.
    The lover thus arraign'd his skill,
" Your execution 's monstrous ill !
A different form my fancy made ;
You 're quite a bungler at the trade.
Where is the robe's luxuriant flow ?
Where is the cheek's celestial glow ?
Where are the looks so fond and free ?
'Tis not an Hymen, sir, for me."
    The painter bow'd—with this reply,
" My colours an't, your honour, dry;
When time has mellow'd ev'ry tint,
'Twill please you—or the deuce is in 't :
I 'll watch the happy change, and then
Attend you with my piece again."
    In a few months the painter came
With a performance—(still the same :)

" Take it away,"—the husband cry'd,
" I have repeated cause to chide:
Sir, you should all excesses shun;
This is a picture overdone!
There 's too much ardour in that eye,
The tincture on the cheeks too high!
The robes have a lascivious play,
The attitude 's too loosely gay.
Friend, on the whole, this piece, for me,
Is too luxuriant—far too free."
The painter thus—" The faults you find
Are form'd in your capricious mind;
To passion a devoted slave,
The first directions, sir, you gave;
Possession has repell'd the flame,
Nor left a sentiment the same.
" My picture is design'd to prove
The changes of precarious love.
" On the next stair-case rais'd on high,
Regard it with a curious eye;
As to the first steps you proceed,
'Tis an accomplish'd piece indeed!
But as you mount some paces higher,
Is there a grace that don't expire?"
So various is the human mind,
Such are the frailties of mankind,
What at a distance charm'd our eyes,
After attainment—droops—and dies.

---

## FORTUNE:

### AN APOLOGUE.

#### FABULA NARRATUR.

Jove and his senators, in sage debate
For man's felicity, were settling laws,
When a rude roar, that shook the sacred gate,
Turn'd their attention to inquire the cause.

A long-ear'd wretch, the loudest of his race,
In the rough garniture of grief array'd,
Came brawling to the high imperial place,
" Let me have justice, Jupiter!"—he bray'd.

" I am an ass, of innocence allow'd
The type, yet Fortune persecutes me still;
While foxes, wolves, and all the murd'ring crowd,
Beneath her patronage can rob and kill.

" The pamper'd horse (he never toil'd so hard!)
Favour and friendship from his owner finds;
For endless diligence,—(a rough reward!)
I 'm cudgel'd by a race of paltry hinds.

" On wretched provender compell'd to feed!
The rugged pavement ev'ry night my bed!
For me, dame Fortune never yet decreed
The gracious comforts of a well-thatch'd shed.

" Rough and unseemly 's my irreverent hide!
Where can I visit, thus uncouthly drest?
That outside elegance the dame deny'd,
For which her fav'rites are too oft caress'd.

" To suff'ring virtue, sacred Jove, be kind!
From Fortune's tyranny pronounce me free!
She 's a deceiver if she says she 's blind,
She sees, propitiously sees all—but me."

The plaintiff could articulate no more:
His bosom heav'd a most tremendous groan!
The race of long-ear'd wretches join'd the roar,
Till Jove seem'd to tott'ring on his high-built throne.

The monarch, with an all-commanding sound,
(Deepen'd like thunder through the rounds of
space)
Gave order—" That dame Fortune should be found,
To answer, as she might, the plaintiff's case."

Soldiers and citizens, a seemly train!
And lawyers and physicians, sought her cell:
With many a schoolman—but their search was vain:
Few can the residence of Fortune tell.

Where the wretch Avarice was wont to hide
His gold, his emeralds, and rubies rare;
'Twas rumour'd that dame Fortune did reside,
And Jove's ambassadors were posted there.

Meagre and wan, in tatter'd garments drest,
A feeble porter at the gate they found:
Doubled with wretchedness—with age distrest,
And on his wrinkled forehead Famine frown'd.

" Mortals avaunt," (the trembling spectre cries)
" Ere you invade those sacred haunts, beware!
To guard lord Avarice from rude surprise,
I am the centinel—my name is Care.

" Doubts, Disappointments, Anarchy of Mind,
These are the soldiers that surround his hall:
And ev'ry fury that can lash mankind,
Rage, Rancour, and Revenge attend his call.

" Fortune's gone forth, you seek a wand'ring dame,
A settled residence the harlot scorns:
Curse on such visitants, she never came,
But with a cruel hand she scatter'd thorns!

" To the green vale, yon shelt'ring hills surround,
Go forward, you 'll arrive at Wisdom's cell:
Would you be taught where Fortune may be found,
None can direct your anxious search so well."

Forward they went, o'er many a dreary spot:
(Rough was the road, as if untrod before)
Till from the casement of a low-roof'd cot
Wisdom perceiv'd them, and unbarr'd her door.

Wisdom (she knew of Fortune but the name)
Gave to their questions a serene reply:
" Hither," she said, " if e'er that goddess came,
I saw her not—she pass'd unnotic'd by.

" Abroad with Contemplation oft I roam,
And leave to Poverty my humble cell:
She 's my domestic, never stirs from home,
If Fortune has been here, 'tis she can tell.

" The matron eyes us from yon mantling shade,
And see her sober footsteps this way bent!
Mark by her side a little rose-lipp'd maid,
'Tis my young daughter, and her name's Content."

As Poverty advanc'd with lenient grace, [here:
" Fortune," she cry'd, " hath never yet been
But Hope, a gentle neighbour of this place,
Tells me, her highness may, in time, appear.

" Felicity, no doubt, adorns their lot,
  On whom her golden bounty beams divine !
Yet though she never reach our rustic cot,
  Patience will visit us—we sha'n't repine."

After a vast (but unavailing) round,
  The messengers, returning in despair,
On an high hill a fairy mansion found,
  And hop'd the goddess, Fortune, might be there.

The dome, so glitt'ring, it amaz'd the sight,
  ('Twas adamant, with gems encrusted o'er)
Had not a casement to admit the light,
  Nor could Jove's deputies descry the door.

But eager to conclude a tedious chase,
  And anxious to return from whence they came,
Thrice they invok'd the Genius of the place,
  Thrice utter'd, awfully, Jove's sacred name.

As Echo from the hill amounc'd high Jove,
  Illusion and her fairy dome withdrew:
(Like the light mists by early sunbeams drove)
  And Fortune stood reveal'd to public view.

Oft for that nappiness high courts deny'd,
  To this receptacle dame Fortune ran :
When harass'd, it was here she us'd to hide,
  From the wild suits of discontented man.

Prostrate, the delegates their charge declare,
  (Happy the courtier that salutes her feet !)
Fortune receiv'd them with a flatt'ring air,
  And join'd them till they reach'd Jove's judgment
    seat.

Men of all ranks at that illustrious place   [keen :
  Were gather'd; though from diff'rent motives
Many—to see dame Fortune's radiant face,
  Many—by radiant Fortune to be seen.

Jove smil'd, as on a fav'rite he esteems,
  He gave her, near his own, a golden seat :
Fair Fortune 's an adventurer, it seems,
  The deities themselves are glad to greet,

" Daughter," says Jupiter, " you 're sore accus'd !
  Clamour incessantly reviles your name !
If by the rancour of that wretch abus'd,
  Be confident, and vindicate your fame.

" Though pester'd daily with complaints from man,
  Through this conviction I record them not—
Let my kind providence do all it can,
  None of that species ever lik'd his lot.

" But the poor quadruped that now appeals !
  Can wanton cruelty the weak pursue !
Large is the catalogue of woes he feels,
  And all his wretchedness he lays to you."

" Ask him, high Jupiter," reply'd the dame,
  " In what he has excell'd his long-ear'd class
Is Fortune (a divinity) to blame
  That she descends not to regard——an ass ?' "

Fame enter'd in her rolls the sage reply ;
  The dame, defendant, was discharg'd with grace !
" Go"—(to the plaintiff) said the sire, " and try
  By merit to surmount your low-born race,

" Learn from the lion to be just and brave,
  Take from the elephant instruction wise ;
With gracious breeding like the horse behave,
  Nor the sagacity of hounds despise.

" These useful qualities with care imbibe,
  For which some quadrupeds are justly priz'd :
Attain those talents that adorn each tribe,
  And you 'll no longer be a wretch despis'd."

---

## A MAN TO MY MIND.

### (WROTE AT THE REQUEST OF A LADY.)

Since wedlock 's in vogue, and stale virgins despis'd,
To all batchelors greeting, these lines are premis'd ;
I 'm a maid that would marry, but where shall I find
(I wish not for fortune) a man to my mind ?

Not the fair-weather fop, fond of fashion and lace ;
Not the 'squire that can wake to no joys but the
    chase ;
Not the free-thinking rake, whom no morals can bind :
Neither this—that—nor t' other 's the man to my
    mind.

Not the ruby-fac'd sot, that topes world without end,
Not the drone, who can't relish his bottle and friend ;
Not the fool, that 's too fond ; nor the churl that 's
    unkind :
Neither this—that—nor t' other 's the man to my
    mind.

Not the wretch with full bags, without breeding or
    merit ;
Not the flash, that 's all fury without any spirit ;
Not the fine master Fribble, the scorn of mankind ;
Neither this—that—nor t' other 's the man to my
    mind.

But the youth in whom merit and sense may conspire,
Whom the brave must esteem, and the fair should
    admire ;
In whose heart love and truth are with honour
    combin'd :
This—this—and no other 's the man to my mind.

---

## WITH A PRESENT.

Let not the hand of Amity be nice !
  Nor the poor tribute from the heart disclaim ;
A trifle shall become a pledge of price,
  If Friendship stamps it with her sacred name.

The little rose that laughs upon its stem,
  One of the sweets with which the gardens teem,
In value soars above an eastern gem,
  If tender'd as the token of esteem.

Had I vast hoards of massy wealth to send,
  Such as your merits might demand—their due !
Then should the golden tribute of your friend
  Rival the treasures of the rich Peru.

## FANCY:

### A SONG IN A PANTOMIME ENTERTAINMENT.

FANCY leads the fetter'd senses
  Captives to her fond control;
Merit may have rich pretences,
  But 'tis Fancy fires the soul.

Far beyond the bounds of meaning
  Fancy flies, a fairy queen!
Fancy, wit and worth disdaining,
  Gives the prize to Harlequin.

If the virgin 's false, forgive her,
  Fancy was your only foe:
Cupid claims the dart and quiver,
  But 'tis Fancy twangs the bow.

---

## LOVE AND CHASTITY:

### A CANTATA.

#### RECITATIVE.

FROM the high mount[1], whence sacred groves depend,
Diana and her virgin troop descend;
And while the buskin'd maids with active care
The business of the daily chase prepare,
A favourite nymph steps forward from the throng,
And thus, exulting, swells the jovial song.

#### AIR.

Jolly Health springs aloft at the loud sounding horn,
  Unlock'd from soft Slumber's embrace;
And Joy sings an hymn to salute the sweet Morn,
  That smiles on the nymphs of the chase:
The rage of fell Cupid no bosom profanes,
  No rancour disturbs our delight,
All the day with fresh vigour we sweep o'er the plains,
  And sleep with contentment all night.

#### RECIT.

Their clamour rouse the slighted god of Love:
He flies, indignant, to the sacred grove:
Immortal myrtles wreath his golden hair,
His rosy wings perfume the wanton air;
Two quivers fill'd with darts his fell designs declare.
A crimson blush o'erspread Diana's face,
A frown succeeds—she stops the springing chase,
And thus forbids the boy the consecrated place.

#### AIR.

Fond disturber of the heart,
From these sacred shades depart:
Here 's a blooming troop disdains
Love, and his fantastic chains.
Sisters of the silver bow,
Pure and chaste as virgin snow,
Melt not at thy feeble fires,
Wanton god of wild desires!

#### RECIT.

Rage and revenge divide Love's little breast,
Whilst thus the angry goddess he addrest:

[1] Mount Latmos.

#### AIR.

Virgin snow does oft remain
Long unmelted on the plain,
Till the glorious god of day
Smiles, and wastes its pride away.
What is Sol's meridian fire
To the darts of strong desire!
Love can light a raging flame
Hotter than his noon-tide beam.

#### RECIT.

Now, through the forest's brown-embower'd ways,
With careless steps the young Endymion strays:
His form erect!—loose flows his lovely hair,
His glowing cheeks like youthful Hebe's fair!
His graceful limbs with ease and vigour move,
His eyes—his ev'ry feature form'd for love:
Around the list'ning woods attentive hung,
Whilst thus, invoking sleep, the shepherd sung:

#### AIR.

Where the pebbled streamlet glides,
  Near the wood-nymph's rustic grot,
If the god of sleep resides,
  Or in Pan's sequester'd cot:
Hither if he 'll lightly tread,
  Follow'd by a gentle dream,
We 'll enjoy this grassy bed,
  On the bank beside the stream.

#### RECIT.

As on the painted turf the shepherd lies,
Sleep's downy curtain shades his lovely eyes;
And now a sporting breeze his bosom shows,
As marble smooth, and white as Alpine snows:
The goddess gaz'd, in magic softness bound;
Her silver bow falls useless to the ground!
Love laugh'd, and, sure of conquest, wing'd a dart
Unerring, to her undefended heart.
She feels in ev'ry vein the fatal fire,
And thus persuades her virgins to retire:

#### AIR.

Ye tender maids be timely wise!
  Love's wanton fury shun!
In flight alone your safety lies,
  The daring are undone!

Do blue-ey'd doves, serenely mild,
  With vultures fell engage!
Do lambs provoke the lion wild,
  Or tempt the tiger's rage!

No, no, like fawns, ye virgins fly,
  To secret cells remove;
Nor dare the doubtful combat try
  'Twixt Chastity and Love.

---

## AMPHITRION.

#### RECITATIVE.

AMPHITRION and his bride, a godlike pair!
He brave as Mars, and she as Venus fair;
On thrones of gold in purple triumph plac'd,
With matchless splendour held the nuptial feast:
Whilst the high roof with loud applauses rung,
Enraptur'd, thus, the happy hero sung:

#### AIR,

Was mighty Jove descending,
　In all his wrath divine,
Enrag'd at my pretending
　To call this charmer mine:
His shafts of bolted thunder
　With boldness I 'd deride;
Not Heav'n itself can sunder
　The hearts that love has ty'd.

#### RECIT.

The thunderer heard,—he look'd with vengeance
　down,
Till Beauty's glance disarm'd his awful frown.
The magic impulse of Alcmene's eyes
Compell'd the conquer'd god to quit his skies;
He feign'd the husband's form, possess'd her charms,
And punish'd HIS presumption in HER arms,

#### AIR.

He deserves sublimest pleasure,
　Who reveals it not, when won:
Beauty 's like the miser's treasure;
　Boast it—and the fool 's undone!

Learn by this, unguarded lover,
　When your secret sighs prevail,
Not to let your tongue discover
　Raptures that you should conceal,

---

### ANACREON.

##### ODE XIX.　IMITATED,

OLD Earth, when in a tippling vein,
Drinks torrents of ambrosial rain,
Which the tall trees, by heat opprest,
Drink from her kind maternal breast:

Lest angry Ocean should be dry,
The river-gods their stores supply:
The monarch of the glowing day
Drinks large potations from the sea:

And the pale empress of the night
Drinks from his orb propitious light:
All—all things drink—abstemious sage!
Why should not we our thirst assuage?

---

### NEWCASTLE BEER.

WHEN Fame brought the news of Great Britain's
　success,
And told at Olympus each Gallic defeat;
Glad Mars sent by Mercury orders express,
　To summon the deities all to a treat:
　　Blithe Comus was plac'd
　　To guide the gay feast,
And freely declar'd there was choice of good cheer;
　　Yet vow'd, to his thinking,
　　For exquisite drinking,
Their nectar was nothing to Newcastle beer.

The great god of war, to encourage the fun,
　And humour the taste of his whimsical guest,
Sent a message that moment to Moor's [1] for a tun
　Of stingo, the stoutest, the brightest, and best:

> [1] Moor's, at the sign of the Sun, Newcastle,

No gods—they all swore,
Regal'd so before,
With liquor so lively, so potent, and clear:
　　And each deified fellow
　　Got jovially mellow,
In honour, brave boys, of our Newcastle beer.

Apollo perceiving his talents refine,
　Repents he drank Helicon water so long:
He bow'd, being ask'd by the musical Nine,
　And gave the gay board an extempore song:
　　But ere he began,
　　He toss'd off his can:
There 's nought like good liquor the fancy to
　clear:
　　Then sang with great merit,
　　The flavour and spirit,
His godship had found in our Newcastle beer.

'Twas stingo like this made Alcides so bold,
　It brac'd up his nerves, and enliven'd his pow'rs;
And his mystical club, that did wonders of old,
　Was nothing, my lads, but such liquor as ours,
　　The horrible crew
　　That Hercules slew,
Were Poverty—Calumny—Trouble—and Fear:
　　Such a club would you borrow,
　　To drive away sorrow,
Apply for a jorum of Newcastle beer.

Ye youngsters, so diffident, languid, and pale,
　Whom love, like the cholic, so rudely infests;
Take a cordial of this, 'twill probatum prevail,
　And drive the cur Cupid away from your breasts:
　　Dull whining despise,
　　Grow rosy and wise,
Nor longer the jest of good fellows appear;
　　Bid adieu to your folly,
　　Get drunk and be jolly,
And smoke o'er a tankard of Newcastle beer.

Ye fanciful folk, for whom physic prescribes,
　Whom bolus and potion have harass'd to death!
Ye wretches, whom Law and her ill-looking tribes
　Have hunted about till you 're quite out of
　　breath!
　　Here 's shelter and ease,
　　No craving for fees,
No danger,—no doctor,—no bailiff is near!
　　Your spirits this raises,
　　It cures your diseases,
There's freedom and health in our Newcastle beer,

---

### THE TOAST:

##### A CATCH.

GIVE THE TOAST—my good fellow, be jovial and gay,
And let the brisk moments pass jocund away!
HERE 's THE KING—take your bumpers, my brave
　British souls,
Who guards your fair freedom should crown your
　full bowls,
LET HIM LIVE—long and happy, see Lewis brought
　down,
And taste all the comforts, no cares of a crown

## A THREE-PART CATCH.

'Tis in view—(the rich blessing kind Nature be-
 stow'd,
To conquer our sorrows, or lighten the load)
A full flask !—the rich nectar this bottle contains
In a flood of fresh rapture shall roll through our
 veins.
Let it bleed—and carousing this liquor divine,
Sing an hymn to the god that first cultur'd the vine.

ON

## SIR W—— B——T'S BIRTH-DAY.

Does true Felicity on Grandeur wait ?
 Delights she in the pageantry of show ?
Say, can the glitt'ring gewgaws of the great
 An hour of inborn happiness bestow ?

He that is just, benevolent, humane,
 In conscious rectitude supremely blest,
O'er the glad hearts of multitudes shall reign,
 Though the gay star ne'er blaz'd upon his
  breast.

Ye happy children of the hoary North,
 Hail the glad day that saw your patron born ;
Whose private virtues, and whose public worth,
 Might the rich seats of royalty adorn.

## STANZAS

SPOKEN AT A PLAY AT THE THEATRE IN SUNDERLAND,
FOR THE BENEFIT OF THE CORSICANS.

Who can behold with an unpitying eye
 The glorious few (with patriotic fire)
Distrest—invaded—and resolv'd to die,
 Or keep their independent rights entire ?
Shackled themselves, the servile Gauls would
 bind,
In their ignoble fetters, half mankind.

The gentle homage that, to night, you 've paid
 To Freedom, and her ever sacred laws,
The humble off'ring at her altar made,
 Prove that your hearts beat nobly in her cause.
All-gracious Freedom, O vouchsafe to smile,
Through future ages, on this favourite isle !

Far may the boughs of Liberty expand,
 For ever cultur'd by the brave and free !
For ever blasted be that impious hand,
 That lops one branch from this illustrious tree !
Britons !—'tis your's to make her verdure thrive,
And keep the roots of Liberty alive.

O may her rich, her ripening fruits of gold,
 Britannia, bloom perpetually for thee !
May you ne'er want a dragon, as we 're told
 Defended, once, the fam'd Hesperian tree !
A dragon fix'd, for your imperial sake,
With anxious eyes, eternally awake.

## THE RESPITE.

A PASTORAL.

Ah, what is 't to me that the grasshopper sings !
 Or what, that the meadows are fair !
That (like little flow'rets, if mounted on wings)
 The butterflies flaunt it in air !
Ye birds, I 'll no longer attend to a lay ;
 Your haunts in the forest resign !
Shall you, with your true loves, be happy all day,
 Whilst I am divided from mine ?

Where woodbines and willows inclin'd to unite,
 We twisted a blooming alcove ;
And oft has my Damon, with smiles of delight,
 Declar'd it the mantle of Love.
The roses that crept to our mutual recess,
 And rested among the sweet boughs,
Are faded—they droop—and they cannot do less,
 For Damon is false to his vows.

This oak has for ages the tempest defy'd,
 We call it—the king of the grove ;
He swore, a light breeze should its centre divide,
 When he was not true to his love :
Come, come, gentle Zephyr, in justice descend,
 His falsehood you 're bound to display ;
This oak and its honours you 'll easily rend,
 For Damon has left me——a day.

The shepherd rush'd forth from behind the thick
 Prepar'd to make Phillida blest,      [tree,
And, clasping the maid, from an heart full of glee,
 The cause of his absence confest :
High raptures, 'twas told him by masters in love,
 Too often repeated, would cloy ;      [prove,
And respites——he found were the means to im-
 And lengthen the moments of joy.

AN

## IRREGULAR ODE ON MUSIC.

Cease, gentle sounds, nor kill me quite,
With such excess of sweet delight !
Each trembling note invades my heart,
And thrills through every vital part ;
 A soft—a pleasing pain
Pursues my heated blood through ev'ry vein ;
What—what does the enchantment mean ?
Ah ! give the charming magic o'er,
My beating heart can bear no more.

 Now wild with fierce desire,
 My breast is all on fire !
 In soften'd raptures, now, I die !
Can empty sound such joys impart !
Can music thus transport the heart,
 With melting ecstasy !
O art divine ! exalted blessing !
Each celestial charm expressing !
 Kindest gift the gods bestow !
 Sweetest good that mortals know !

When seated in the verdant shade
(Like tuneful Thyrsis) Orpheus play'd ;
 The distant trees forsake the wood,
 The list'ning beasts neglect their food,

To hear the heav'nly sound;
　The Dryads leave the mountains,
　The Naiads quit the fountains,
And in a sprightly chorus dance around.

To raise the stately walls of ancient Troy,
Sweet Phœbus did his tuneful harp employ;
　See what soft harmony can do!
　The moving rocks the sound pursue,
　Till in a large collected mass they grew:
Had Thyrsis liv'd in these remoter days,
His were the chaplet of immortal bays!
　　Apollo's harp unknown!
　The shepherd had remain'd of song
　　The deity alone.

------

FROM

## A TRUANT TO HIS FRIENDS.

'Tis not in cells, or a sequester'd cot,
　The mind and morals properly expand;
Let youth step forward to a busier spot,
　Led by Discretion's cool, conducting hand.

To learn some lessons from the schools of man,
　(Forgive me!) I forsook my darling home;
Not from a light, an undigested plan,
　Nor from a youthful appetite to roam.

In your affections—(let resentment fly!)
　Restore me to my long-accustom'd place;
Receive me with a kind, forgiving eye,
　And press me in the parent's fond embrace.

------

TO

## THE AUTHOR OF POEMS.

WRITTEN BY NOBODY [1].

Advance to fame—advance reveal'd!
　Let conscious worth be bold:
Why have you lain so long conceal'd,
　And hid Peruvian gold?

Dan Phœbus did with joy discern
　Your genius brought to light:
And many a Somebody should learn,
　From Nobody to write.

------

## A BIRTH-DAY ODE:

PERFORMED AT THE CASTLE OF DUBLIN.

RECITATIVE.

Hark—how the soul of music reigns,
　As when the first great birth of Nature sprung,
When Chaos burst his massy chains,
　'Twas thus the cherubs sung:

------

[1] J. Robertson, an actor belonging to the York
company.

AIR.

Hail—hail, from this auspicious morn
Shall British glories rise!
Now are the mighty treasures born,
That shall Britannia's fame adorn,
　And lift her to the skies.

RECIT.

Let George's mighty banners spread,
　His lofty clarions roar;
Till warlike Echo fills with dread
　The hostile Gallic shore.

AIR.

Mark—how his name with terrour fills!
The magic sound Rebellion kills,
And brightens all the northern hills,
　Where pallid treasons dwell;
The monster shall no more arise,
Upon the ground she panting lies!
Beneath his, William's, foot she dies,
　And now, she sinks to Hell.

RECIT.

Haste—let Ierne's harp be newly strung,
And after mighty George be William sung.

AIR.

Talk no more of Grecian glory,
　William stands the first in story:
He, with British ardour glows!
　See—the pride of Gallia fading!
　See—the youthful warrior leading
Britons, vengeful, to their foes!

RECIT.

Fair is the olive-branch Hibernia boasts,
Nor shall the din of war disturb her coasts;
While Stanhope smiles, her sons are blest,
In native loyalty confest!

AIR.

See—O see, thrice happy isle!
　See what gracious George bestow'd;
Twice [2] have you seen a Stanhope smile,
　These are gifts become a god!

How the grateful island glows!
　Stanhope's name shall be rever'd;
Whilst by subjects, and by foes,
　Sacred George is lov'd and fear'd.

CHORUS.

Like Persians to the rising Sun,
　Respectful homage pay;
At George's birth our joys begun:
　Salute the glorious day!

------

## THE BROKEN CHINA.

Soon as the Sun began to peep,
　And gild the morning skies,
Young Chloe from disorder'd sleep
　Unveil'd her radiant eyes.

------

[2] Earl of Chesterfield, and earl of Harrington,
both successively lords lieutenant of Ireland.

# TO MR. ———....ON THE LATE ABSENCE OF MAY. 175

A guardian Sylph, the wanton sprite
That waited on her still,
Had teas'd her all the tedious night
With visionary ill.

" Some shock of Fate is surely nigh,"
Exclaim'd the tim'rous maid:
" What do these horrid dreams imply?
  My Cupid can't be dead!"

She call'd her Cupid by his name,
In dread of some mishap;
Wagging his tail, her Cupid came,
And jump'd into her lap.

And now the best of brittle ware
Her sumptuous table grac'd:
The gentle emblems of the fair,
In beauteous order plac'd!

The kettle boil'd, and all prepar'd
To give the morning treat,
When Dick, the country beau, appear'd,
And, bowing, took his seat.

Well—chatting on, of that and this,
The maid revers'd her cup;
And, tempted by the forfeit kiss,
The bumpkin turn'd it up.

With transport he demands the prize;
Right fairly it was won!
With many a frown the fair denies:
Fond baits to draw him on!

A man must prove himself polite,
In such a case as this;
So Richard strives with all his might
To force the forfeit kiss.

But as he strove—O dire to tell!
(And yet with grief I must)
The table turn'd—the china fell,
A heap of painted dust!

" O fatal purport of my dream!"
The fair afflicted cry'd,
" Occasion'd (I confess my shame)
By childishness and pride!

" For in a kiss, or two, or three,
No mischief could be found:
Then had I been more frank and free,
My china had been sound."

## TO MR. ———.

Yes, Colin, 'tis granted, you flutter in lace,
  You whisper and dance with the fair;
But merit advances, 'tis your's to give place;
  Stand off, and at distance revere:
Nor tease the sweet maid with your jargon of
      chat,
  By her side as you saunter along;
Your taste—your complexion—your this—and your
      that,
  Nor lisp out the end of your song.

For folly and fashion you barter good sense,
  (If sense ever fell to your share)
'Tis enough you could pert *petit maitre* commence,
  Laugh—loiter—and lie with an air.
No end you can answer, affections you 've none,
  Made only for prattle and play;
Like a butterfly, bask'd for a while in the Sun,
  You 'll die undistinguish'd away.

## ON
### THE LATE ABSENCE OF MAY.
(WRITTEN IN THE YEAR 1771.)

The rooks in the neighbouring grove
  For shelter cry all the long day;
Their huts in the branches above
  Are cover'd no longer by May:
The birds that so cheerfully sung,
  Are silent, or plaintive each tone!
And, as they chirp, low, to their young,
  They want of their goddess bemoan.

No daisies, on carpets of green,
  O'er Nature's cold bosom are spread!
Not a sweet-briar sprig can be seen,
  To finish this wreath for my head:
Some flow'rets, indeed, may be found,
  But these neither blooming nor gay;
The fairest still sleep in the ground,
  And wait for the coming of May.

December, perhaps, has purloin'd
  Her rich, though fantastical geer;
With Envy the Months may have join'd,
  And jostled her out of the year:
Some shepherds, 'tis true, may repine,
  To see their lov'd gardens undress'd;
But I—whilst my Phillida's mine,
  Shall always have May in my breast.

## AN EULOGIUM ON MASONRY.
SPOKE BY MR. DIGGS, AT EDINBURGH.

Say, can the garter, or the star of state,
That on the vain, or on the vicious wait,
Such emblems, with such emphasis impart,
As an insignium near the Mason's heart?
  Hail sacred Masonry, of source divine,
Unerring mistress of the faultless line,
Whose plumb of Truth, with never-failing sway,
Makes the join'd parts of Symmetry obey!
  Hail to the Craft, at whose serene command
The gentle Arts in glad obedience stand:
Whose magic stroke bids fell Confusion cease,
And to the finish'd Orders yield its place;
Who calls Creation from the womb of Earth,
And gives imperial cities glorious birth.
  To works of art her merit 's not confin'd,
She regulates the morals, squares the mind;
Corrects with care the tempest-working soul,
And points the tide of passions where to roll;
On Virtue's tablets marks each sacred rule,
And forms her lodge an universal school;
Where Nature's mystic laws unfolded stand,
And Sense and Science, join'd, go hand in hand.

O! may her social rules instructive spread,
Till Truth erect her long-neglected head;
Till, through deceitful Night she dart her ray,
And beam, full glorious, in the blaze of day!
Till man by virtuous maxims learn to move;
Till all the peopled world her laws approve,
And the whole human race be bound in brother's
love.

---

## PROLOGUES AND EPILOGUES.

---

### A PROLOGUE,

SPOKE AT THE OPENING OF THE THEATRE AT YORK, AFTER
IT WAS ELEGANTLY ENLARGED.

ONCE on a time his earthly rounds patrolling,
(Your heathen gods were always fond of strolling)
Jove rambled near the cot of kind Philemon,
When night, attended by a tempest, came on;
And as the rain fell pattering, helter skelter,
The deity implor'd the hind for shelter.
　　Philemon plac'd his godship close beside him,
While goody Baucis made the fire that dry'd·him;
With more benevolence than one that 's richer,
He spread the board, he fill'd the friendly pitcher;
And, fond to give his guest a meal of pleasure,
Sung a rough song, in his rude country measure.
　　Jove was so pleas'd with these good-natur'd sallies,
Philemon's cot he conjur'd to a palace.
　　Taste, like great Jupiter, came here to try us,
(Oft from the boxes we perceiv'd her spy us)
Whether she lik'd us and our warm endeavours,
Whether she found that we deserv'd her favours,
I know not : but 'tis certain she commanded
Our humble theatre should be expanded.
　　The orders she pronounc'd were scarcely ended,
But, like Philemon's house, the stage extended:
And thus the friendly goddess bids me greet ye;
'Tis in that circle [pointing to the boxes] she designs
　　to meet ye:
Pedants would fix her residence with heathens,
But she prefers old York to Rome or Athens.

---

### A PROLOGUE,

SPOKE AT THE OPENING AN ELEGANT LITTLE THEATRE
AT WHITBY.

FROM Shakspeare—Jonson—Congreve—Rowe—
　　and others—
The laurel'd list, the true Parnassian brothers!
Hither we 're sent, by their supreme direction,
To court your favour, and to claim protection.
　　Our hopes are flatter'd with the fair's compliance;
Beauty and Wit were always in alliance!
Their mutual sway reforms the rude creation,
And Taste 's determin'd by their approbation.
　　The tragic Muse presents a stately mirror,
Where Vice surveys her ugly form with terrour:
And as the fiend departs—abash'd—discarded—
Imperial Virtue 's with the palm rewarded.
The comic glass, from modern groups collected,
Shows fops and fools of every class—dissected:
It marks the fair coquet's unfaithful dealings,
And proves that haughty prudes may have their
　　failings.

For faults that flow from habit more than nature,
We 'll blend, with honest mirth, some wholesome
　　satire.
　　Now for our bark—the vessel 's tight and able!
New built!—new rigg'd!—[Pointing to the scenes]
　　with canvass—mast—and cable!
Let her not sink,—or be unkindly stranded,
Before the moral freight be fairly landed!
For though with heart and hand we heave together,
'Tis your kind plaudit must command the weather:
Nor halcyon seas,—nor gentle gales attend us,
Till this fair circle with their smiles befriend us.

---

### A PROLOGUE,

ON OPENING THE THEATRE AT WHITBY THE ENSUING
SEASON.

O'ER the wild waves, unwilling more to roam,
And by his kind affections call'd for home;
When the bold youth that ev'ry climate tries
'Twixt the blue bosoms—'twixt the seas and skies—
When he beholds his native Albion near,
And the glad gale gives wings to his career,
What glowing ecstasies, by Fancy drest,
What filial sentiments expand his breast!
In the full happiness he forms on shore,
Doubts—dangers—and fatigues are felt no more.
　　Such are the joys that in our bosoms burn!
Such the glad hopes that glow at our return!
With such warm ardours you behold us meet,
To lay, once more, our labours at your feet.
　　(Not without hopes your patronage will last)
We bend with gratitude for favours past.
That our light bark defy'd the rage of winter,
Rode ev'ry gale—nor started ev'n a splinter;
We bow to Beauty—('twas those smiles secur'd her)
And thank our patrons who so kindly moor'd her.
Still—still—extend your gentle cares to save her,
That she may anchor long in Whitby's—favour.

---

### A PROLOGUE,

SPOKE IN THE CHARACTER OF A SAILOR, ON OPENING
THE NEW THEATRE AT NORTH SHIELDS.

　　　　　　　　　　　　　　[Without.
HOLLO! my masters, where d'ye mean to stow us?
We 're come to see what pastime ye can show us;
Sal, step aloft—you shan't be long without me,
I 'll walk their quarter deck and look about me.
　　　　　　　　　　　　　　[Enters.
　　Tom and Dick Topsail are above—I hear 'em,
Tell 'em to keep a birth, and, Sal—sit near 'em.
Sal 's a smart lass—I 'd hold a butt of stingo
In three weeks' time she'd learn the playhouse lingo:
She loves your plays, she understands their meaning,
She calls 'em—MORAL RULES made entertaining:
Your Shakspeare books, she knows 'em to a tittle;
And I, myself (at sea) have read—a little.
　　At London, sirs, when Sal and I were courting,
I tow'd her ev'ry night a playhouse sporting:
Mass! I could like 'em and their whole 'paratus,
But for their fiddlers and their damn'd sonatas;
Give me the merry sons of guts and rosin,
That play——God save the King, and Nancy Daw-
　　son.　　　　　　　　　　　　[Looking about.

Well——though the frigate's not so much be-
    doyzen'd,
'Tis snug enough !—'Tis clever for the size on 't:
And they can treat with all that's worth regarding
On board the Drury Lane or Common Garden.
                    [ *Bell rings.*
  Avast !—A signal for the lanch, I fancy :
What say you, Sam, and Dick, and Doll, and Nancy[1],
Since they have trimm'd the pleasure-barge so
    tightly,
Sha'n't you, and I, and Sal, come see them nightly ?
The jolly crew will do their best endeavours,
They 'll grudge no labour to deserve your favours.
A luckier fate they swear can ne'er behap 'em
Than to behold you pleas'd, and hear you—clap 'em.

---

### AN EPILOGUE,

SPOKE AT NORWICH, IN THE CHARACTER OF MRS. DEBORAH
WOODCOCK, IN LOVE IN A VILLAGE.

AFTER the dangers of a long probation,
When, Sybil like, she 's skill'd in penetration ;
When she has conquer'd each unruly passion,
And rides above the rocks that others dash on ;
When deeply mellow'd with reserve and rigour,
When decent gravity adorns her figure,
Why an old maid, I wish the wise would tell us,
Should be the standing jest of flirts and fellows !
  In maxims sage ! in eloquence how clever !
Without a subject she can talk—for ever !
Rich in old saws, can bring a sentence pat in,
And quote, upon occasion, lawyer's latin.
  Set up that toast, that culprit, *nobus corum,*
'Tis done—and she 's demolish'd in *turrorum.*
  If an old maid 's a dragoness on duty,
To guard the golden fruit of rip'ning beauty ;
'Tis right, for fear the giddy sex should wander,
To keep them in restraint by decent slander.
When slips are made, 'tis easy sure to find 'em ;
We can detect before the fair design'd them.
  As for the men, whose satire oft hath stung us,
Many there are that may be rank'd among us.
LAW, with long suits and busy mischiefs laden,
In rancour far exceeds the ancient maiden.
'Tis undeny'd, and the assertion 's common,
That modern PHYSIC is a mere old woman.
The puny fop that simpers o'er his tea dish,
And cries,—" Indeed—Miss Deb'rah 's—quite old
Of doubtful sex, of undetermin'd nature, [maidish!"
In all respects is but a virgin *cretur.*
  Jesting apart, and moral truths adjusting !
There 's nothing in the state itself disgusting ;
Old maids, as well as matrons bound in marriage,
Are valu'd from propriety of carriage :
If gentle sense, if sweet discretion guide 'em,
It matters not though coxcombs may deride 'em ;
And virtue 's virtue, be she maid or wedded,
A certain truth ! say——Deb'rah Woodcock said it.

---

### A PROLOGUE TO THE MUSE OF OSSIAN ;

A LITTLE PIECE, ADAPTED TO THE STAGE BY D. E. BAKER,
FROM THE CELEBRATED POEM OF OSSIAN, THE SON OF
FINGAL.

To form a little work of nervous merit,
To give the sleepy stage a nobler spirit ;

    [1] To the gallery.

To touch a sacred Muse, and not defile her,
This was the plan propos'd by our compiler.
  Though Caution told him—the presumption 's
    glaring !
Dauntless, he cry'd, " It is but nobly daring !
Can we peruse a pathos more than Attic,
Nor wish the golden measure stamp'd dramatic !
Here are no lines—in measur'd pace that trip it,
No modern scenes—so lifeless ! so insipid !
Wrought by a Muse—(no sacred fire debarr'd her)
'Tis nervous ! noble ! 'tis true northern ardour !
  " Methinks I hear the Grecian bards exclaiming,
(The Grecian bards no longer worth the naming)
In song, the northern tribes so far surpass us,
One of their Highland hills they 'll call Parnassus ;
And from the sacred mount decrees should follow,
That Ossian was himself—the true Apollo."
  Spite of this flash—this high poetic fury,
He trembles for the verdict of his jury :
As from his text he ne'er presum'd to wander,
But gives the native Ossian to your candour,
To an impartial judgment we submit him,
Condemn—or rather (if you can) acquit him.

---

### AN

### EPILOGUE TO THE MUSE OF OSSIAN.

IN fond romance let Fancy reign creative !
Valour among the northern hills is native ;
The northern hills, 'tis prov'd by Ossian's story,
Gave early birth to 'Caledonian glory ;
Nor could the stormy clime, with all its rigour,
Repel, in love or war, the hero's vigour.
  When honour call'd, the youth disdain'd to ponder,
And as he fought, the fav'rite maid grew fonder.
The brave, by beauty were rejected never,
For girls are gracious when the lads are clever.
If the bold youth was in the field vindictive,
The bard, at home, had ev'ry power descriptive ;
He swell'd the sacred song, enhanc'd the story,
And rais'd the warrior to the skies of glory.
  That northern lads are still unconquer'd fellows,
The foes of Britain to their cost can tell us ;
The sway of northern beauty, if disputed,
Look round, ye infidels, and stand confuted :
And for your bards, the letter'd world have known
    'em,
They 're such—the sacred Ossian can't disown 'em.
  To prove a partial judgment does not wrong you,
And that your usual candour reigns among you,
Look with indulgence on this crude endeavour,
And stamp it with the sanction of your favour.

---

### AN EPILOGUE,

SPOKE IN THE CHARACTER OF LADY TOWNLEY, IN THE
PROVOKED HUSBAND.

AT lady—let me recollect—whose night is 't ?
No matter—at a circle the politest ;
Taste summons all the satire she is able,
And canvasses my conduct to the table.
  " A wife reclaim'd, and by an husband's rigour !
A wife with all her appetites in vigour !
Lard ! she must make a lamentable figure !
  " Where was her pride ? Of ev'ry spark divested !
To mend, because a prudish husband press'd it !

What! to prefer his dull domestic quiet,
To the dear scenes of hurricane and riot!
Parties disclaim'd, the happy rout rejected!
Because at ten she's by her spouse expected!
Oh, hideous! how immensely out of nature!
Don't you, my dears, despise the servile creature?"
  Prudence, although the company be good,
Is often heard, and sometimes understood.
Suppose, to justify my reformation,
She'd give the circle this concise oration.
  " Ye giddy group of fashionable wives,
That in continued riot waste your lives;
Did ye but see the demons that descend,
The cares convulsive that on cards attend;
The midnight spectres that surround your chairs,
(Rage reddens here—there Avarice despairs)
You'd rush for shelter where contentment lies,
To the domestic blessings you despise.
  " Or if you 've no regard to moral duty,
('Tis trite but true)—quadrille will murder beauty."
  Taste is abash'd, (the culprit) I 'm acquitted,
They praise the character they lately pity'd;
They promise to reform—relinquish play,
So break the tables up at—break of day.

---

AN EPILOGUE,

SPOKE AT EDINBURGH, IN THE CHARACTER OF LADY
FANCIFUL.

FANCY, we 're told, of parentage Italic,
And Folly, whose original is Gallic,
Set up to sale their vast misshapen daughter,
And Britain, by a large subscription, bought her.
  The fertile soil grew fond of this exotic,
And nurs'd her, till her pow'r became despotic;
Till ev'ry would-be beauty in the nation
Did homage at the shrine of Affectation.
But Common-Sense will certainly dethrone her,
And (like the fair-ones of this place) disown her.
If she attempts the dimpled smile, delightful!
The dimpled smile of Affectation 's frightful:
Mark but her bagatelles—her whine—her whim-
  per—
Her loll—her lisp—her saunter, stare—her simper;
All outrés, all—no native charm about her,
And Ridicule would soon expire without her.
  Look for a grace, and Affectation hides it;
If Beauty aims an arrow, she misguides it:
So awkwardly she mends unmeaning faces,
To Insipidity she gives——grimaces.
  Without her dear coquetish arts to aid 'em,
Fine ladies would be just as—Nature made 'em,
Such sensible—sincere—domestic creatures,
The jest of modern belles, and petit maitres.
  Safe with good sense, this circle 's not in danger,
But as the foreign phantom 's—here a stranger,
I gave her portrait, that the fair may know her,
And if they meet, be ready to forego her;
For trust me, ladies, she 'd deform your faces,
And with a single glance destroy the graces.

---

AN EULOGIUM ON CHARITY.

SPOKE AT ALNWICK, IN NORTHUMBERLAND, AT A CHARI-
TABLE BENEFIT PLAY, 1765.

To bid the rancour of Ill-fortune cease,
To tell Anxiety—I give thee peace,

To quell Adversity—or turn her darts,
To stamp fraternity on gen'rous hearts:
For these high motives—these illustrious ends,
Celestial Charity to night descends.
  Soft are the graces that adorn the maid,
Softer than dew-drops to the sun-burnt glade!
She 's gracious as an unpolluted stream,
And tender as a fond young lover's dream!
Pity and Peace precede her as she flies,
And Mercy beams benignant in her eyes!
From her high residence, from realms above,
She comes, sweet harbinger of heavenly love!
  Her sister's [1] charms are more than doubly
  bright,
From the kind cause that call'd her here to night.
An artless grace the conscious heart bestows,
And on the generous cheek a tincture glows,
More lovely than the bloom that paints the vernal
  rose.
  The lofty pyramid shall cease to live!
Fleeting the praise such monuments can give!
But Charity, by tyrant Time rever'd,
Sweet Charity, amidst his ruins spar'd,
Secures her votaries unblasted fame,
And in celestial annals saves their name.

---

AN EPILOGUE,

DESIGNED TO BE SPOKE AT ALNWICK, ON RESIGNING THE
PLAYHOUSE TO A PARTY DETACHED FROM THE EDIN-
BURGH THEATRE.

To Alnwick's lofty seat, a sylvan scene!
To rising hills from distance doubly green,
" Go,"—says the god of wit, " my standard bear,
These are the mansions of the great and fair [2],
'Tis my Olympus now, go spread my banners
  there."
  Led by fond Hope, the pointed path we trace,
And thank'd our patron for the flowery place;
Here—we behold a gently waving wood!
There—we can gaze upon a wand'ring flood!
The landscape smiles!—the fields gay fragrance
  wear!
Soft scenes are all around—refreshful air!
Slender repast indeed, and but cameleon fare!
  A troop, at certain times compell'd to shift,
And from their northern mountains turn'd adrift;
By tyrant managers a while consign'd,
To fatten on what forage they can find;
With lawless force our liberty invades,
And fain would thrust us from these fav'rite shades;
But we (since Prejudice erects her scale,
And puffs and petty artifice prevail)
To stronger holds with cool discretion run,
And leave the conquerors to be—undone.
  With gratitude, still we 'll acknowledge the fa-
  vours
So kindly indulg'd to our simple endeavours;
To the great and the fair we rest thankfully debtors,
And wish we could say, we gave place to our betters.

---

[1] The countess of Northumberland, who honoured
the charity with her presence.

[2] The earl and countess of Northumberland, lord
and lady Warkworth, &c.

## A PROLOGUE TO LOVE AND FAME.

### SPOKE AT SCARBOROUGH.

[*Entering.*

WHERE is this author?—Bid the wretch appear,
Let him come in, and wait for judgment—*here.*
This awful jury, all impatient, wait;
Let him come in, I say, and meet his fate!
Strange, very strange, if such a piece succeeds!
(Punish the culprit for his vile misdeeds)
Know ye to night, that his presumptuous works
Have turn'd good Christians into—Heathen Turks?
And if the genius an't corrected soon,
In his next trip, he 'll mount us to the Moon.
   Methinks I hear him say—" For mercy's sake
Hold your rash tongue—my love and fame 's at
      stake;
When you behold me—diffident—distrest !
'Tis cruelty to make my woes a jest :
Well—if you will—but why should I distrust?
My judges are as merciful as just ; .
I know them well, have oft their friendship try'd,
And their protection is my boast—my pride."
   Hoping to please, he form'd this bustling plan;
Hoping to please !. 'tis all the moderns can:
Faith ! let him 'scape, let Love and Fame survive,
With your kind sanction keep his scenes alive ;
Try to approve (applaud we will exempt)
Nor crush the bardling in this hard attempt.
Could he write up to an illustrious theme,
There 's mark'd upon the register of Fame
A subject—but beyond the warmest lays !
Wonder must paint, when 'tis a G—nby's praise.

----

## A PROLOGUE TO RULE A WIFE.

### SPOKEN AT EDINBURGH.

'TIS an odd portrait that the poet drew !
A strange irregular he sets in view !
'Mongst us—thank Heaven—the character 's un-
      known,
(Bards have creative faculties we own)
And this appears a picture from his brain,
Till we reflect the lady liv'd in Spain.
   Should we the portrait with the sex compare,
'Twould add new honours to the northern fair ;
Their merit, by the foil, conspicuous made,
And they seem'd brighter from contrasting shade.
   Rude were the rules our fathers form'd of old,
Nor should such antiquated maxims hold ;
Shall subject man assert superior sway,
And dare to bid the angel sex obey ?
Or if permitted to partake the throne,
Despotic, call the reins of power his own ?
Forbid it, all that 's gracious—that 's polite !
(The fair to liberty have equal right)
Nor urge the tenet, though from Fletcher's school,
That every husband has a right to rule.
   A matrimonial medium may be hit,
Where neither governs, but where both submit. ,
   The nuptial torch with decent brightness burns,
Where male and female condescend by turns ;
Change then the phrase, the horrid text amend,
And let the word obey,——be condescend.

## A PROLOGUE,

### ON REVIVING THE MERCHANT OF VENICE, AT THE TIME THE BILL HAD PASSED FOR NATURALIZING THE JEWS.

'TWIXT the sons of the stage, without pensions or
      places,
And the vagabond Jews, are some similar cases;
Since time out of mind, or they 're wrong'd much
      by slander,
Both lawless, alike, have been sentenc'd to wander;
Then faith 'tis full time we appeal to the nation,
To be join'd in this bill for na-tu-ra-li-za-ti-on ;
Lard, that word 's so uncouth !—'tis so irksome to
      speak it !                    [take it.
But 'tis Hebrew, I believe, and that 's taste, as I
   Well—now to the point—I 'm sent here with com-
      mission,
To present this fair circle our humble petition :
But, conscious what hopes we should have of suc-
      ceeding,
Without (as they phrase it) sufficiently bleeding;
And convinc'd we 've no funds, nor old gold we can
      rake up,
Like our good fathers—Abraham, Isaac, and Jacob;
We must frankly confess we have nought to pre-
      sent ye,
But Shakspeare's old sterling—pray let it content ye.
   This Shylock, the Jew, whom we mean to re-
      store ye,
Was naturaliz'd oft by your fathers before ye ;
Then take him to night to your kindest compassion,
For to countenance Jews is the pink of the fashion.

----

## A PROLOGUE,

### FOR SOME COUNTRY LADS, PERFORMING THE DEVIL OF A, WIFE, IN THE CHRISTMAS HOLIDAYS.

IN days of yore, when round the jovial board,
With harmless mirth, and social plenty stor'd,
Our parent Britons quaff'd their nut-brown ale,
And carols sung, or told the Christmas tale;
In struts St. George, old England's champion knight,
With hasty steps, impatient to recite
" How he had kill'd the dragon, once in fight."
   From ev'ry side—from Troy—from ancient
Princes pour in to swell the motley piece; [Greece,
And while their deeds of prowess they rehearse,
The flowing bowl rewards their hobbling verse.
   Intent to raise this evening's cordial mirth,
Like theirs, our simple stage-play comes to birth.
Our want of art we candidly confess,
But give you Nature in her homespun dress ;
No heroes here—no martial men of might !
A cobler is the champion of to night;
His strap, more fam'd than George's lance of old,
For it can tame that dragoness, a scold :
Indulgent, then, support the cobler's cause,
And though he may n't deserve it, smile applause.

----

## A PROLOGUE,

### ON OPENING THE NEW THEATRE IN NEWCASTLE, 1766.

IF to correct the follies of mankind,
To mend the morals—to enlarge the mind,
To strip the self-deceiving passions bare,
With honest mirth to kill an evening's care ;

If these kind motives can command applause,
For these the motley stage her curtain draws.
  Does not the poet, that exists by praise,
Like to be told that he has reach'd the bays ?
Is not the wretch (still trembling for his store)
Pleas'd when he grasps a glitt'ring thousand more?
Cheers not the mariner propitious seas?
Likes not the lawyer to be handling fees?
Lives not the lover but in hopes of bliss ?
To ev'ry question we'll reply with—yes.
  Suppose them gratified—their full delight
Falls short of ours on this auspicious night;
When rich in happiness—in hopes elate,
Taste has receiv'd us to our fav'rite seat.
O that the soul of action were but ours,
And the vast energy of vocal powers !
That we might make a grateful off'ring, fit
For these kind judges that in candour sit.
  Before such judges, we confess with dread,
These new dominions we presume to tread ;
Yet if you smile, we 'll boldly do our best,
And leave your favours to supply the rest.

---

AN INTRODUCTION,

SPOKE AT THE THEATRE IN SUNDERLAND, TO A PLAY PER-
FORMED THERE FOR THE BENEFIT OF THE WIDOWS AND
ORPHANS OF THAT PLACE.

ON widows—orphans—left, alas ! forlorn,
(From the rack'd heart its every comfort torn)
Humanity, to night, confers relief,
And softens, though she can't remove their grief :
Blasted her hopes, her expectations, kill'd,
The sons of Sympathy (with sorrow chill'd)
Behold the wretched matron—madly weep,
And hear her cry—" My joys are in the deep !"
To the tremendous Power that rules mankind,
Lord of the seas—the calm and boist'rous wind,
We bow, obedient, and with awe resign'd.
His ways, inscrutable, we can't explore,
No—we may wonder, but we must adore.
Happy, for ever, be the generous breast,
That feels compassion for the poor distrest ;
Happy the hand that stops the sufferer's tear !
Such hands there are, and such, we find, are here.

---

AN ELEGIAC ODE

ON THE

DEATH OF HIS LATE MAJESTY.

Pallida mos æquo pulsat pede pauperum tabernas,
Regumque turres.                         Horace.

ENGLAND ! thy Genius, vested like Despair,
  With loud distress alarms the chalky shore :
" Britons !" he cries, and rends his hoary hair,
  "Britons ! your much-lov'd monarch is no more !"

The sea-gods from their pearl-embroider'd beds,
  Who to great George the green dominion gave,
No longer lift their coral-crowned heads,
  But dive distress'd beneath the trembling wave.

Hark, how the winds, erst bounteous to his will,
  That bore his thund'ring fleets to Gallia's shore,
Pause,—for a while, pathetically still,
  Then let their sorrows burst in pealy roar.

The nymphs that in the sacred groves preside,
  Where Britain's conqu'ring oaks eternal spring,
In their embrown'd retreats their sorrows hide,
  And silent mourn the venerable king.

Tenants of liberty, on Britain's plain,
  With flocks enrich'd, a vast unnumber'd store !
'Tis gone, the mighty George's golden reign ;
  Your Pan, your great protector is no more !

The British swains, e'er whiles a blithsome throng,
  No more in Laughter's band, to revel seen !
No more the shepherd tunes his cheerful song,
  Or dances sportful on the dew-dress'd green.

Beauty, no more the toy of fashion wears,
  (So late by love's designful labour drest ;)
But from her brow the lustr'd diamond tears,
  And with the sable cypress veils her breast.

Religion, lodg'd high on her pious pile,
  Laments the fading state of CROWNS below ;
While Melancholy fills the vaulted isle
  With the slow music of heart-wounding woe.

See the detestful owl, ill-omen'd, rise !
  Dragg'd, by Despair, from her sequestr'd cell;
And, by the discord of shrill shrieking cries,
  Doubling the horrours of the deep-ton'd bell.

The choral Muses droop ! their harps unstrung,
  The lutes and laurel wreaths neglected fall !
Commerce—bestill'd her many-nation'd tongue,
  Whilom so busy in her bustling hall[1] !

Behold the Virtues rang'd, a sorrowing band !
  They mourn with grief dejected eyes,
See Art and sister Science, weeping stand !
  For, ah ! their patron, their defender dies ;

On Conquest's cheek see how the roses fail !
  Grief makes, alas ! the fairest blossoms bow !
And Honour's fire ethereal burns but pale,
  That erst beam'd glorious on our George's brow.

The dreary paths of unrelenting Fate,
  Must monarchs, mix'd with common mortals, try !
Is there no refuge for the good and great ?
  And must the gracious and the godlike die ?

Must gilded courts be chang'd for Horrour's cave !
  And scepter'd kings, who keep the world in awe,
Conquer'd by time, and the unpitying grave,
  Scarce sav'd their laurels from its rig'rous law !

Search where fell Carnage rag'd with rigour steel'd,
  Where Slaughter, like the rapid lightning, ran;
And say, when you 've bewept the blood-stain'd field,
  Which is the monarch? which the common man ?

The Macedonian monarch[2], wise and good,
  Bade (when the morning's rosy reign began)
Courtiers should call, as round his couch they stood,
  " Philip, remember thou 'rt no more than man."

[1] The hall of commerce, the Royal Exchange.

[2] Philip, king of Macedon, the father of Alexander the Great, appointed the pages of his chamber,
to remind him every morning, that, notwithstand-

" Though glory spread thy name from pole to pole,
  Though thou art merciful, and brave, and just,
Philip, reflect thou 'rt posting to the goal,
  Where mortals mix in undistinguish'd dust."

What then avails Ambition's wide-stretch'd wing!
  The schoolman's page, or pride of beauty's
     bloom!
The crape-clad hermit, and the rich-rob'd king,
  Mingle promiscuous in the levelling tomb.

So Saladin [3], for arts and arms renown'd,
  The Syrians and Egyptians both subdu'd;
Returning, with imperial triumphs crown'd,
  Sigh'd, when the perishable pomp he view'd.

And as he rode, high on his regal car,
  In all the purple pride of Conquest drest,
Conspicuous o'er the trophies gain'd in war,
  Plac'd on a pendant spear his burial vest.

While thus the herald cry'd, " This son of Pow'r,
  This Saladin, to whom the nations bow'd,
May, in the space of a revolving hour,
  Boast of no other spoil but yonder shroud."

Can the deep statesman, skill'd in great design,
  Save, for the smallest space, precarious breath?
Or the tun'd follower of the sacred Nine,
  Soothe, with his melody, the tyrant Death?

No! though the palace bar her golden gate,
  Or monarchs plant ten thousand guards around,
Unerring, and unseen, the shaft of Fate
  Strikes the devoted victim to the ground.

If in the tent retir'd, or battle's rage,
  Britannia's sighs shall reach great Fred'ric's [4] ear;
He 'll drop the sword, or shut the sophic page,
  And pensive pay the tributary tear.

Then shall the monarch weigh the moral thought,
  (As he laments the parent, friend, ally,)
The solemn truth, by sage Reflection taught,
  That, spite of glory, Fred'ric's self must die.

Crowns, like the glow-worm's scarce distinguish'd
    light,
  For a short moment glance their twinkling fires,
But there 's a deathless wreath, divinely bright,
  Whose more than diamond lustre, ne'er expires.

Such is the starry meed that Virtue ty'd
  With her own hands on George's gracious brow;
Eternal shall its golden beams abide,
  Though the bright Sun should from its orbit bow.

Nor is the sacred gift to kings confin'd,
  The wretch, to fortune, friends, and fame unknown,
Shall, if sweet piety adorn his mind,
  Mount to the highest step of Glory's throne.

ing his glory and power, he was no more than a
mere mortal man.
  [3] Saladin, a famous eastern emperor, in his
triumphant return from the most remarkable conquests, had a shroud carried before him, while
proclamation was made, That the victor, after all
his glory, could lay real claim to nothing but that
wretched linen to wrap his body in for the tomb.
  [4] Frederic, king of Prussia.

The parent's face Apelles [5] prudent hides,
  While Death devours the darling of his age:
Nature the pencil'd stroke of art derides,
  When grief distracts with agonizing rage.

Then let the Muse her sablest curtain spread,
  By Sorrow taught her nerveless pow'r to know:
When nations cry, their king, their parent's dead,
  The rest is dumb, unutterable woe.

Mercy, co-partner of great George's throne,
  Through the embrighted air ascendant flies,
Duteous, the peace-bestowing maid is flown
  To smooth his halcyon progress to the skies.

But see a sacred radiance beams around!
  That with returning hope a people cheers!
Behold you youth, with grace imperial crown'd,
  How awful! yet how lovely in his tears!

Mark how his bosom heaves the filial sigh!
  He droops distress'd like a fair frost-chill'd flower,
Till Glory, from her radiant sphere on high,
  Hails him to hold the reins of regal Power.

The sainted sire to realms of bliss remov'd,
  Like the fam'd phenix from his pyre shall
    spring
Another George, as gracious, as belov'd,
  As good, and glorious, as the parent king.

---

## HORACE. ODE X. BOOK IV.

### IMITATED.

CHLOE, my most tender care,
Always coy, and always fair,
Should unwish'd-for languor spread
O'er that beauteous white and red;
Should these locks, that sweetly play
Down these shoulders, fall away,
And that lovely bloom, that glows
Fairer than the fairest rose,
Should it fade, and leave thy face
Spoil'd of every killing grace:
Should your glass the charge betray,
Thus, my fair, you 'd weeping say,
" Cruel gods! does beauty fade?
Now warm desires my breast invade;
And why, while blooming youth did glow,
Was this heart as cold as snow?"

---

## SENT TO MISS BELL H———,

### WITH A PAIR OF BUCKLES.

HAPPY trifles, can ye bear
Sighs of fondness to the fair;
If your pointed tongues can tell,
How I love my charming Bell?
Fondly take a lover's part,
Plead the anguish of my heart.

  [5] Apelles finding it impossible to express with his
pencil the distress of Agamemnon, while his daughter Iphigenia was offered as a sacrifice, painted him
with a veil spread over his face.

Go—ye trifles—gladly fly,
(Gracious in my fair-one's eye)
Fly—your envy'd bliss to meet;
Fly, and kiss the charmer's feet.
Happy there, with waggish play,
Though you revel day by day,
Like the donor, ev'ry night,
(Robb'd of his supreme delight)
To subdue your wanton pride,
Useless, you 'll be thrown aside.

## TO CHLOE,

### ON A CHARGE OF INCONSTANCY.

How can Chloe think it strange,
Time should make a lover change?
  Time brings all things to an end,
Courage can't the blow defend.
See, the proud aspiring oak
Falls beneath the fatal stroke:
If on Beauty's cheek he preys,
Straight the rosy bloom decays:
Joy puts out his lambent fires,
And at Time's approach—expires.
  How can Chloe think it strange,
Time should make a lover change?

## INCANTATION.

PERFORMED AT THE THEATRE IN SUNDERLAND, IN A NEW
PANTOMIME.

RECITATIVE.—HECATE.

From the dark, tremendous cell,
Where the fiends of magic dwell,
Now the Sun hath left the skies,
Daughters of Enchantment, rise.

AIR.
[The Witches appear.
Welcome from the shades beneath!
Welcome to the blasted heath!
Where the spectre and the sprite
Glide along the glooms of night.
Beldams!—with attention keen,
Wait the wish of Harlequin:
Many a wonder must be done
For my first, my fav'rite son.

CHORUS OF WITCHES.

Many a wonder shall be done,
Hecate, for your fav'rite son.

## FORTUNE TO HARLEQUIN.

IN A PANTOMIME.

From my favour, sense rejected,
Fools by Fortune are protected:
Fortune, Harlequin, hath found you,
Happiness will hence surround you.

Should a thousand ills enclose you,
Quick contrivance this [1] bestows you!
Valour makes the fair adore you;
This [2] shall drive your foes before you.

Gold 's the mighty source of pleasure!
Take this purse of magic treasure;
Go—for while my gifts befriend you,
Joy and jollity attend you.

## ACROSTIC.

" P-ray tell me," says Venus, one day to the
      Graces,                    [places]
(O-n a visit they came, and had just ta'en their
" L-et me know why of late I can ne'er see your
      faces:                     [ye:
L-adies, nothing, I hope, happen'd here to affright
Y-ou've had compliment cards ev'ry day to invite
      ye."

S-ays Cupid, who guess'd their rebellious proceed-
      ing,                 [a-breeding:
" U-nderhand, dear mamma, there 's some mischief
T-here 's a fair-one at Lincoln, so finish'd a beauty,
T-hat your loves and your graces all swerve from
      their duty."              [thus put on,
" O-n my life," says dame Venus, " I 'll not be
N-ow I think on 't, last night, some one call'd me
      Miss Sutton."

## ON THE DEATH OF MRS. SLEIGH,

OF STOCKTON.

Much lov'd, much honour'd, much lamented
      Sleigh!
The kindred Virtues had expir'd with thee,
Were it ordain'd the daughters of the sky,
Like the frail offspring of the Earth, could die:
Trembling they stand at thy too early doom,
And mingling tears to consecrate thy tomb.

## ACROSTIC.

W-here no ripen'd summer glows,
I-n the lap of northern snows;
D-eserts gloomy, cold, and drear,
(O-nly let the nymph be there)
W-reaths of budding sweets would wear.

M-ay would every fragrance bring,
A-ll the vernal bloom of spring:
D-ryads, deck'd with myrtles green,
D-ancing, would attend their queen:
E-very flower that Nature spreads,
R-ising where the charmer treads!

## ON THE DEATH OF LORD GRANBY.

For private loss the lenient tear may flow,
  And give a short, (perhaps) a quick relief;
While the full heart, o'ercharg'd with public woe,
  Must labour through a long, protracted grief.

A hat.            A sword.

This sudden stroke ('twas like the lightning's blast)
  The sons of Albion can't enough deplore;
Think, Britons, think on all his triumphs past,
  And weep——your warrior is——alas! no more.

Blight, we are told, respects the conq'ror's tree,
  And through the laurel grove with caution flies:
Vague—and how vain must that assertion be,
  Cover'd with laurels when a Granby dies!

## ON THE DEATH OF MR. ———

### OF SUNDERLAND.

Go, breath of Sorrow,—go attending sighs,
  Acquaint the natives of the northern shore,
The man they lov'd, the man they honour'd, dies,
  And Charity's first steward—is no more.

Where shall the poor a friendly patron find?
  Who shall relieve them from their loads of pain?
Say, has he left a feeling heart behind,
  So gracious—good—so tenderly humane?

Yes—there survives his darling offspring—young,
  Yet in the paths of Virtue, steady—sure!
'Twas the last lesson from his parent's tongue,
  " Think, (O remember) think upon my poor."

## A PETITION

TO THE WORSHIPFUL FREE MASONS, DELIVERED FROM THE
STAGE, BY A LADY, AT A COMEDY COUNTENANCED BY
THAT FRATERNITY.

BROTHERS!—'tis bold to interrupt your meeting,
But from the female world I wait you—greeting:
                                   [*Curtsies.*
  The ladies can advance a thousand reasons,
That make them hope to be received as Masons:
To keep a secret,—not one hint expressing,
To rein the tongue—O husbands, there's a blessing!
As virtue seems the Mason's sole foundation,
Why should the fair be barr'd from—installation?
If you suppose us weak, indeed you wrong us;
Historians, Sapphos too, you'll find among us;
Think—brothers—think, and graciously admit us;
Doubt it not, sirs, we 'll gloriously acquit us:
How to be wiser, and more cautious, teach us,
Indeed 'tis time that your instructions reach us:
The faults of late, and every foul miscarriage,
Committed in the sphere of modern marriage,
Were caus'd, (if I 've a grain of penetration)
From each great lady's not being made a Mason.
Accept us, then, to brotherhood receive us,
And Virtue, we're convinc'd, will never leave us.

## AN ODE

FOR THE BIRTH DAY OF THE KING OF PRUSSIA.

Arma, virumque cano.          Virg.

### RECIT.

MORE glorious than the comet's blaze,
That through the starry region strays:

From Zembla to the torrid zone,
The mighty name of Prussia's known.

### AIR.

Be banish'd from the books of Fame,
  Ye deeds in distant ages done;
Lost and inglorious is the name
  Of Hannibal, or Philip's son:
Could Greece, or conquering Carthage sing
A hero great as Prussia's king!

Where restless Envy can't explore,
  Or flatter'd Hope presume to fly;
Fate bade victorious Fred'ric soar,
  For laurels that can never die.
Could Greece, &c.

His rapid bolts tremendous break,
  Through nations arm'd in dread array,
Swift as the furious blasts that shake
  The bosom of the frighted sea.
Could Greece, &c.

In vain, to shake the throne of Jove,
  With impious rage, the giants try'd;
'Gainst Fred'ric's force the nations strove
  In vain—their haughty legions dy'd.
Could Greece, &c.

While Prudence guides his chariot wheels,
  Through Virtue's sacred paths they roll;
Immortal Truth his bosom steels,
  And guards him glorious to the goal.
Could Greece, &c.

The vengeful lance Britannia wields,
  In consort with her brave ally,
Saves her fair roses in the fields,
  Where Gaul's detested lilies die.
Wreaths of eternal friendship spring,
'Twixt mighty George and Prussia's king.

The jocund bowl let Britons raise,
  And crown the jovial board with mirth;
Fill—to great Frederic's length of days,
  And hail the hero's glorious birth—
Could Greece, or conquering Carthage sing
A chieftain fam'd like Prussia's king?

## AN ODE,

COMPOSED FOR THE BIRTH-DAY OF THE LATE GENERAL
LORD BLAKENEY.

THE Muses' harps, by Concord strung!
  Loud let them strike the festal lay,
Wak'd by Britannia's grateful tongue,
  To hail her hero's natal day.
Arise, paternal glory rise,
And lift your Blakeney to the skies!

Behold his warlike banners wave!
  Like Britain's oak the hero stands:
The shield—the shelter of the brave!
  The guardian o'er the British bands;
Arise, paternal, &c.

He wrests the wreath from Richlieu's [1] brows,
Which Fraud or Faction planted there;
France to the gallant hero bows,
And Europe's chiefs his name revere.
Arise, paternal, &c.

With partial conquest on their side!
The sons of Gaul—a pageant crew!
Rank, but inglorious in their pride,
To Blakeney, and his vanquish'd few.
Arise, paternal, &c.

Hibernia [2], with maternal care,
His labour'd statue lifts on high:
Be partial, Time!—the trophy spare,
That Blakeney's name may never die!
Arise, paternal glory, rise!
And lift your Blakeney to the skies!

## ON A VERY YOUNG LADY.

See how the buds and blossoms shoot:
How sweet will be the summer fruit!
Let us behold the infant rose;
How fragrant when its beauty blows!
The morning smiles, serenely gay;
How bright will be the promis'd day!
Contemplate next the charming maid,
In early innocence array'd!
If, in the morning of her years,
A lustre so intense appears,
When time shall point her noon-tide rays,
When her meridian charms shall blaze,
None but the eagle-ey'd must gaze.

## A SONNET:

### ADDRESSED TO MISS S———.

When Flora decks the mantling bowers,
In elegant array,
And scatters all her opening flowers,
A compliment to May!
With glowing joy my bosom beats;
I gaze delighted round,
And wish to see the various sweets
In one rich nosegay bound.
'Tis granted—and their bloom display'd,
To bless my wond'ring view;
I see them all—my beauteous maid,
I see them all in—you.

## ANACREON. ODE V.

### IMITATED.

### THE ROSE.

Shed roses in the sprightly juice,
Prepar'd for every social use!
So shall the earthly nectar prove
A draught for all-imperial Jove.
Ourselves, with rosy chaplets bound,
Shall sing, and set the goblet round.

[1] Richlieu, commander of the expedition against Port Mahon.
[2] A statue was erected in Dublin to the memory of general Blakeney, who was a native of Ireland.

Thee, ever gentle Rose, we greet,
We worship thee, delicious sweet!
For though by mighty gods caress'd,
You deign to make us mortals blest.
The Cupids, and the Graces fair,
With myrtle sprigs adorn their hair;
And nimbly strike celestial ground,
Eternal roses blooming round.
Bring us more sweets, ere these expire,
And reach me that harmonious lyre;
Gay Bacchus, Jove's convivial son,
Shall lead us to his fav'rite ton:
Among the sporting youths and maids,
Beneath the vine's auspicious shades,
For ever young—for ever gay,
We'll dance the jovial hours away.

## MOSCHUS. IDYLLIUM VII.

### (AS TRANSLATED BY DR. BROOME.)

### TO THE EVENING STAR.

Hail, golden star, of ray serene!
Thou fav'rite of the Cyprian queen!
O Hesper! glory of the night,
Diffusing through the gloom, delight!
Whose beams, all other stars outshine,
As much as silver Cynthia, thine:
O guide me, speeding o'er the plain,
To him I love, my shepherd swain;
He keeps the mirthful feast, and soon
Dark shades will cloud the splendid Moon.
Of lambs I never robb'd the fold,
Nor the lone traveller of gold:
Love is my crime: O! lend thy ray
To guide a lover on her way.
May the bright star of Venus prove
The gentle harbinger of Love!

\*\*\* To this Idyllium (translated by Dr. Broome) the author owns himself indebted for a hint, from which the following Pastoral proceeds.

## A PASTORAL.

Where the fond Zephyr through the woodbine
plays,
And wakes sweet fragrance in the mantling bow'r,
Near to that grove my lovely bridegroom stays
Impatient—for 'tis past—the promis'd hour!

Lend me thy light, O ever-sparkling star!
Bright Hesper! in thy glowing pomp array'd,
Look down, look down, from thy all-glorious car,
And beam protection on a wand'ring maid.

'Tis to escape the penetrating spy,
And pass, unnotic'd, from malignant sight,
This dreary waste, full resolute I try,
And trust my footsteps to the shades of night.

The Moon has slipp'd behind an envious cloud,
Her smiles, so gracious, I no longer view;
Let her remain behind that envious shroud,
My hopes, bright Hesperus, depend on you.

No rancour ever reach'd my harmless breast;
I hurt no birds, nor rob the bustling bee:
Hear, then, what Love and Innocence request,
And shed your kindest influence on me.

Thee—Venus loves—first twinkler of the sky,
Thou art her star—in golden radiance gay!
On my distresses cast a pitying eye,
Assist me—for, alas! I 've lost my way.

I see the darling of my soul—my love!
Expression can't the mighty rapture tell :
He leads me to the bosom of the grove:
Thanks, gentle star—kind Hesperus, farewell!

## TO CHLOE,

### IN AN ILL HUMOUR.

Consider, sweet maid, and endeavour
To conquer that pride in thy breast;
It is not an haughty behaviour
Will set off thy charms to the best.

The ocean, when calm, may delight you,
But should a bold tempest arise,
The billows enrag'd would affright you :
Loud objects of awful surprise!

'Tis thus, when good humour diffuses
Its beams o'er the face of a fair;
With rapture his heart a man loses,
While frowns turn love to despair.

## EPIGRAMS, &c.

### AN EPIGRAM.

A member of the modern great
Pass'd Sawney with his budget,
The peer was in a car of state,
The tinker forc'd to trudge it.

But Sawney shall receive the praise
His lordship would parade for;
One 's debtor for his dapple greys,
And t'other's shoes are paid for.

### ANOTHER.

To Wasteall, whose eyes were just closing in death,
Doll counted the chalks on the door;
" In peace," cry'd the wretch, " let me give up my [breath,
And Fate will soon rub out my score."
" Come, bailiffs," cries Doll, " (how I 'll hamper
Let the law be no longer delay'd, [this cheat!)
I never once heard of that fellow call'd Fate,
And by G—d he sha'n't die till I 'm paid."

### ON MR. CHURCHILL'S DEATH.

Says Tom to Richard, " Churchill 's dead;"
Says Richard, " Tom, you lie,
Old Rancour the report hath spread,
But Genius cannot die."

### A POSTSCRIPT.

Would honest Tom G——d¹ get rid of a scold,
The torture, the plague of his life!
Pray tell him to take down his lion of gold,
And hang up his brazen-fac'd wife.

¹ Landlord of the Golden Lion, an inn in Yorkshire.
VOL XIV.

### EPIGRAPH FOR DEAN SWIFT'S MONUMENT.

EXECUTED BY MR. P. CUNNINGHAM, STATUARY IN DUBLIN.

Say, to the Drapier's vast unbounded fame,
What added honours can the sculptor give?
None—'tis a sanction from the Drapier's name
Must bid the sculptor and his marble live.

### EPIGRAM.

Could Kate for Dick compose the Gordian string,
The Tyburn knot how near the nuptial ring!
A loving wife, obedient to her vows,
Is bound in duty to exalt her spouse.

### APOLLO TO MR. C—— F,——

ON HIS BEING SATIRIZED BY AN IGNORANT PERSON.

Whether he 's worth your spleen or not,
You 've ask'd me to determine:
I wish my friend a nobler lot
Than that of trampling vermin.

A blockhead can't be worth our care,
Unless that we 'd befriend him:
As you 've some common sense to spare,
I 'll pay what you may lend him.

### ON SEEING J. C——FT, ESQ. ABUSED IN A NEWS-
PAPER.

When a wretch to public notice
Would a man of worth defame;
Wit, as threadbare as his coat is,
Only shows his want of shame.

Busy, pert, unmeaning parrot!
Vilest of the venal crews!
Go—and in your Grub-street garret,
Hang yourself and paltry Muse.

Pity too the meddling sinner
Should for hunger hang or drown :
F——x, (he must not want a dinner)
Send the scribbler half a crown.

## VERSES,

WRITTEN ABOUT THREE WEEKS BEFORE HIS DEATH.

Dear lad, as you run o'er my rhyme,
And see my long name at the end,
You 'll cry—" And has Cunningham time
To give so much verse to his friend?"

'Tis true, the reproof (though severe)
Is just from the letters I owe;
But blameless I still may appear,
For nonsense is all I bestow.
H h

However, for better for worse,
  As Damons their Chloes receive,
Ev'n take the dull lines I rehearse—
  They 're all a poor friend has to give.

The Drama and I have shook hands,
  We 've parted, no more to engage;
Submissive I met her commands—
  For nothing can cure me of age.

My sunshine of youth is no more!
  My mornings of pleasure are fled!
'Tis painful my fate to endure—
  A pension supplies me with bread!

Dependant at length on the man
  Whose fortunes I struggled to raise!
I conquer my pride as I can—
  His charity merits my praise!

His bounty proceeds from his heart;
  'Tis principle prompts the supply—
His kindness exceeds my desert,
  And often suppresses a sigh.

But like the old horse in the song,
  I 'm turn'd on the common to graze—
To Fortune these changes belong,
  And contented I yield to her ways!

She ne'er was my friend; through the day
  Her smiles were the smiles of deceit—
At noon she 'd her favours display,
  And at night let me pine at her feet.

No longer her presence I court,
  No longer I shrink at her frowns!
Her whimsies supply me with sport—
  And her smiles I resign to the clowns!

Thus lost to each worldly desire,
  And scorning all riches—all fame,
I quietly hope to retire
  When Time shall the summons proclaim.

I 've nothing to weep for behind!
  To part with my friends is the worst!
Their numbers, I grant, are confin'd;
  But you are, still, one of the first.

THE

# POEMS

OF

## *LORD LYTTELTON.*

# LIFE OF LYTTELTON.

## BY DR. JOHNSON.

GEORGE LYTTELTON, the son of sir Thomas Lyttelton, of Hagley in Worcestershire, was born in 1709. He was educated at Eton, where he was so much distinguished, that his exercises were recommended as models to his schoolfellows.

From Eton he went to Christ-church, where he retained the same reputation of superiority, and displayed his abilities to the public in a poem on Blenheim.

He was a very early writer, both in verse and prose. His Progress of Love, and his Persian Letters, were both written when he was very young ; and indeed the character of a young man is very visible in both. The verses cant of shepherds and flocks, and crooks dressed with flowers ; and the letters have something of that indistinct and headstrong ardour for liberty which a man of genius always catches when he enters the world, and always suffers to cool as he passes forward.

He staid not long in Oxford ; for in 1728 he began his travels, and saw France and Italy. When he returned, he obtained a seat in parliament, and soon distinguished himself among the most eager opponents of sir Robert Walpole, though his father, who was commissioner of the admiralty, always voted with the court.

For many years the name of George Lyttelton was seen in every account of every debate in the house of commons. He opposed the standing army ; he opposed the excise ; he supported the motion for petitioning the king to remove Walpole. His zeal was considered by the courtiers not only as violent, but as acrimonious and malignant ; and, when Walpole was at last hunted from his places, every effort was made by his friends, and many friends he had, to exclude Lyttelton from the secret committee.

The prince of Wales, being (1737) driven from St. James's, kept a separate court, and opened his arms to the opponents of the ministry. Mr. Lyttelton became his secretary, and was supposed to have great influence in the direction of his conduct. He persuaded his master, whose business it was now to be popular, that he would advance his character by patronage. Mallet was made under-secretary, with 200*l.* ; and Thomson had a pension of 100*l.* a year. For Thomson, Lyttelton always retained his kindness, and was able at last to place him at ease.

M

Moore courted his favour by an apologetical poem, called The Trial of Selim; for which he was paid with kind words, which, as is common, raised great hopes, that were at last disappointed.

Lyttelton now stood in the first rank of opposition; and Pope, who was incited, it is not easy to say how, to increase the clamour against the ministry, commended him among the other patriots. This drew upon him the reproaches of Fox, who, in the house, imputed to him as a crime his intimacy with a lampooner so unjust and licentious. Lyttelton supported his friend; and replied, that he thought it an honour to be received into the familiarity of so great a poet.

While he was thus conspicuous, he married (1741) Miss Lucy Fortescue, of Devonshire, by whom he had a son, the late lord Lyttelton, and two daughters, and with whom he appears to have lived in the highest degree of connubial felicity: but human pleasures are short; she died in childbed about five years afterwards; and he solaced himself by writing a long poem to her memory.

He did not, however, condemn himself to perpetual solitude and sorrow; for, after a while, he was content to seek happiness again by a second marriage with the daughter of sir Robert Rich; but the experiment was unsuccessful.

At length, after a long struggle, Walpole gave way, and honour and profit were distributed among his conquerors. Lyttelton was made (1744) one of the lords of the treasury; and from that time was engaged in supporting the schemes of the ministry.

Politics did not, however, so much engage him as to withhold his thoughts from things of more importance. He had, in the pride of juvenile confidence, with the help of corrupt conversation, entertained doubts of the truth of Christianity; but he thought the time now come when it was no longer fit to doubt or believe by chance, and applied himself seriously to the great question. His studies, being honest, ended in conviction. He found that religion was true; and what he had learned he endeavoured to teach (1747) by Observations on the Conversion of St. Paul; a treatise to which infidelity has never been able to fabricate a specious answer. This book his father had the happiness of seeing, and expressed his pleasure in a letter which deserves to be inserted.

" I have read your religious treatise with infinite pleasure and satisfaction. The style is fine and clear, the arguments close, cogent, and irresistible. May the King of kings, whose glorious cause you have so well defended, reward your pious labours, and grant that I may be found worthy, through the merits of Jesus Christ, to be an eye-witness of that happiness which I don't doubt he will bountifully bestow upon you. In the mean time, I shall never cease glorifying God, for having endowed you with such useful talents, and giving me so good a son.

" Your affectionate father,

" THOMAS LYTTELTON."

A few years afterward, (1751) by the death of his father, he inherited a baronet's title with a large estate, which, though perhaps he did not augment, he was careful to adorn by a house of great elegance and expense, and by much attention to the decoration of his park.

As he continued his activity in parliament, he was gradually advancing his claim to profit and preferment; and accordingly was made in time (1754) cofferer and privy counsellor: this place he exchanged next year for the great office of chancellor of the exchequer; an office, however, that required some qualifications which he soon perceived himself to want.

The year after, his curiosity led him into Wales; of which he has given an account, perhaps rather with too much affectation of delight, to Archibald Bower, a man of whom he has conceived an opinion more favourable than he seems to have deserved, and whom, having once espoused his interest and fame, he was never persuaded to disown. Bower, whatever was his moral character, did not want abilities; attacked as he was by an universal outcry, and that outcry, as it seems, the echo of truth, he kept his ground; at last, when his defences began to fail him, he sallied out upon his adversaries, and his adversaries retreated.

About this time Lyttelton published his Dialogues of the Dead, which were very eagerly read, though the production rather, as it seems, of leisure than of study: rather effusions than compositions. The names of his persons too often enable the reader to anticipate their conversation; and, when they have met, they too often part without any conclusion. He has copied Fenelon more than Fontenelle.

When they were first published, they were kindly commended by the critical reviewers; and poor Lyttelton, with humble gratitude, returned, in a note which I have read, acknowledgments which can never be proper, since they must be paid either for flattery or for justice.

When, in the latter part of the last reign, the inauspicious commencement of the war made the dissolution of the ministry unavoidable, sir George Lyttelton, losing with the rest his employments was recompensed with a peerage; and rested from political turbulence in the house of lords.

His last literary production was his History of Henry the Second, elaborated by the searches and deliberations of twenty years, and published with such anxiety as only vanity can dictate.

The story of this publication is remarkable. The whole work was printed twice over, a great part of it three times, and many sheets four or five times. The booksellers paid for the first impression; but the charges and repeated operations of the press were at the expense of the author, whose ambitious accuracy is known to have cost him at least a thousand pounds. He began to print in 1755. Three volumes appeared in 1764, a second edition of them in 1767, a third edition in 1768, and the conclusion in 1771.

Andrew Reid, a man not without considerable abilities, and not unacquainted with letters or with life, undertook to persuade Lyttelton, as he had persuaded himself, that he was master of the secret of punctuation; and, as fear begets credulity, he was employed, I know not at what price, to point the pages of Henry the Second. The book was at last pointed and printed, and sent into the world. Lyttelton took money for his copy, of which, when he had paid the pointer, he probably gave the rest away; for he was very liberal to the indigent.

When time brought the history to a third edition, Reid was either dead or discarded; and the superintendence of typography and punctuation was committed to a man originally a comb-maker, but then known by the style of Doctor. Something uncommon was probably expected, and something uncommon was at last done; for to the doctor's edition is appended, what the world has hardly seen before, a list of errours in nineteen pages.

But to politics and literature there must be an end. Lord Lyttelton had never the appearance of a strong or of a healthy man; he had a slender uncompacted frame, and a meagre face; he lasted, however, sixty years, and was then seized with his last illness. Of his death a very affecting and instructive account has been given by his physician [1], which will spare me the task of his moral character.

" On Sunday evening the symptoms of his lordship's disorder, which for a week past had alarmed us, put on a fatal appearance, and his lordship believed himself to be a dying man. From this time he suffered by restlessness rather than pain; though his nerves were apparently much fluttered, his mental faculties never seemed stronger, when he was thoroughly awake.

" His lordship's bilious and hepatic complaints seemed alone not equal to the expected mournful event; his long want of sleep, whether the consequence of the irritation in the bowels, or, which is more probable, of causes of a different kind, accounts for his loss of strength, and for his death, very sufficiently.

" Though his lordship wished his approaching dissolution not to be lingering, he waited for it with resignation, He said, ' It is a folly, a keeping me in misery, now to attempt to prolong life;' yet he was easily persuaded, for the satisfaction of others, to do or take any thing thought proper for him. On Saturday he had been remarkably better, and we were not without some hopes of his recovery.

" On Sunday, about eleven in the forenoon, his lordship sent for me, and said he felt a great hurry, and wished to have a little conversation with me, in order to divert it. He then proceeded to open the fountain of that heart, from whence goodness had so long flowed, as from a copious spring. ' Doctor,' said he, ' you shall be my confessor: when I first set out in the world, I had friends who endeavoured to shake my belief in the Christian religion. I saw difficulties which staggered me ; but I kept my mind open to conviction. The evidences and doctrines of Christianity, studied with attention, made me a most firm and persuaded believer of the Christian religion. I have made it the rule of my life, and it is the ground of my future hopes. I have erred and sinned : but have repented, and never indulged any vicious habit. In politics, and public life, I have made public good the rule of my conduct. I never gave counsels which I did not at the time think the best. I have seen that I was sometimes in the wrong; but I did not err designedly. I have endeavoured, in private life, to do all the good in my power, and never for a moment could indulge malicious or unjust designs upon any person whatsoever.'

" At another time he said, ' I must leave my soul in the same state it was in before this illness; I find this a very inconvenient time for solicitude about any thing.'

" On the evening, when the symptoms of death came on, he said, ' I shall die; but it will not be your fault.' When lord and lady Valentia came to see his lordship, he gave them his solemn benediction, and said, ' Be good, be virtuous, my lord; you must come to this.' Thus he continued giving his dying benediction to all around him. On Monday morning a lucid interval gave some small hopes, but these vanished in the evening; and he continued dying, but with very little uneasiness, till Tuesday morning, August 22, when, between seven and eight o'clock, he expired, almost without a groan."

His lordship was buried at Hagley; and the following inscription is cut on the side of his lady's monument.

[1] Dr. Johnstone of Kidderminster. C.

This unadorned stone was placed here
by the particular desire and express
directions of the Right Honourable
GEORGE Lord LYTTELTON,
who died August 22, 1773, aged 64.

Lord Lyttelton's poems are the works of a man of literature and judgment, devoting part of his time to versification. They have nothing to be despised, and little to be admired. Of his Progress of Love, it is sufficient blame to say that it is pastoral. His blank verse in Blenheim has neither much force nor much elegance. His little performances, whether songs or epigrams, are sometimes sprightly, and sometimes insipid. His epistolary pieces have a smooth equability, which cannot much tire, because they are short, but which seldom elevates or surprises. But from this censure ought to be excepted his Advice to Belinda, which, though for the most part written when he was very young, contains much truth and much prudence, very elegantly and vigorously expressed, and shows a mind attentive to life, and a power of poetry which cultivation might have raised to excellence.

# POEMS

OF

# *LORD LYTTELTON.*

## THE PROGRESS OF LOVE,

### IN FOUR ECLOGUES.

1. Uncertainty. To Mr. Pope.
2. Hope. To the hon. George Doddington.
3. Jealousy. To Edward Walpole, esq.
4. Possession. To the right hon. the lord viscount Cobham.

## UNCERTAINTY.

### ECLOGUE I.

#### TO MR. POPE.

POPE, to whose reed beneath the beachen shade,
The nymphs of Thames a pleas'd attention paid;
While yet thy Muse, content with humbler praise,
Warbled in Windsor's grove her sylvan lays;
Though now, sublimely borne on Homer's wing
Of glorious wars and godlike chiefs she sing :
Wilt thou with me revisit once again
The crystal fountain, and the flowery plain?
Wilt thou, indulgent, hear my verse relate
The various changes of a lover's state ;
And, while each turn of passion I pursue,
Ask thy own heart if what I tell be true?
To the green margin of a lonely wood,
Whose pendent shades o'erlook'd a silver flood,
Young Damon came, unknowing where he stray'd,
Full of the image of his beauteous maid :
His flock, far off, unfed, untended, lay,
To every savage a defenceless prey ;
No sense of interest could their master move,
And every care seem'd trifling now but love.
A while in pensive silence he remain'd,
But, though his voice was mute, his looks complain'd;
At length the thoughts within his bosom pent
Forc'd his unwilling tongue to give them vent.

"Ye nymphs," he cried, "ye Dryads, who so long
Have favour'd Damon, and inspir'd his song;
For whom, retir'd, I shun the gay resorts
Of sportful cities, and of pompous courts ;
In vain I bid the restless world adieu,
To seek tranquillity and peace with you.
Though wild Ambition and destructive Rage
No factions here can form, no wars can wage :
Though Envy frowns not on your humble shades,
Nor Calumny your innocence invades :
Yet cruel Love, that troubler of the breast,
Too often violates your boasted rest;
With inbred storms disturbs your calm retreat,
And taints with bitterness each rural sweet.
"Ah, luckless day! when first with fond surprise
On Delia's face I fix'd my eager eyes!
Then in wild tumults all my soul was tost,
Then reason, liberty, at once were lost :
And every wish, and thought, and care, was gone,
But what my heart employ'd on her alone.
Then too she smil'd : can smiles our peace destroy,
Those lovely children of Content and Joy !
How can soft pleasure and tormenting woe
From the same spring at the same moment flow :
Unhappy boy ! these vain inquiries cease,
Thought could not guard, nor will restore, thy peace :
Indulge the frenzy that thou must endure,
And sooth the pain thou know'st not how to cure.
Come, flattering Memory ! and tell my heart
How kind she was, and with what pleasing art
She strove its fondest wishes to obtain,
Confirm her power, and faster bind my chain.
If on the green we danc'd, a mirthful band ;
To me alone she gave her willing hand :
Her partial taste, if e'er I touch'd the lyre,
Still in my song found something to admire.
By none but her my crook with flowers was crown'd,
By none but her my brows with ivy bound :
The world, that Damon was her choice, believ'd,
The world, alas ! like Damon, was deceiv'd.
When last I saw her, and declar'd my fire
In words as soft as passion could inspire,
Coldly she heard, and full of scorn withdrew,
Without one pitying glance, one sweet adieu.

The frighted hind, who sees his ripen'd corn
Up from the roots by sudden tempests torn,
Whose fairest hopes destroy'd and blasted lie,
Feels not so keen a pang of grief as I.
Ah, how have I deserv'd, inhuman maid,
To have my faithful service thus repaid?
Were all the marks of kindness I receiv'd,
But dreams of joy, that charm'd me and deceiv'd?
Or did you only nurse my growing love,
That with more pain I might your hatred prove?
Sure guilty treachery no place could find
In such a gentle, such a generous mind:
A maid brought up the woods and wilds among
Could ne'er have learnt the art of courts so young:
No; let me rather think her anger feign'd,
Still let me hope my Delia may be gain'd;
'Twas only modesty that seem'd disdain,
And her heart suffer'd when she gave me pain."

Pleas'd with this flattering thought, the lovesick
Felt the faint dawning of a doubtful joy;   [boy
Back to his flock more cheerful he return'd,
When now the setting Sun more fiercely burn'd,
Blue vapours rose along the mazy rills,
And light's last blushes ting'd the distant hills.

-----

## HOPE.

### ECLOGUE II.

TO MR. DODDINGTON, AFTERWARDS LORD MELCOMBE
REGIS.

HEAR, Doddington, the notes that shepherds sing,
Like those that warbling hail the genial Spring.
Nor Pan, nor Phœbus, tunes our artless reeds:
From Love alone their melody proceeds.
From Love, Theocritus, on Enna's plains,
Learnt the wild sweetness of his Doric strains,
Young Maro, touch'd by his inspiring dart,
Could charm each ear, and soften every heart:
Me too his power has reach'd, and bids with thine
My rustic pipe in pleasing concert join [1].

Damon no longer sought the silent shade,
No more in unfrequented paths he stray'd,
But call'd the swains to hear his jocund song,
And told his joy to all the rural throng.
"Blest be the hour," he said, "that happy hour,
When first I own'd my Delia's gentle power;
Then gloomy discontent and pining care
Forsook my breast, and left soft wishes there;
Soft wishes there they left, and gay desires,
Delightful languors, and transporting fires,
Where yonder limes combine to form a shade,
These eyes first gaz'd upon the charming maid;
There she appear'd, on that auspicious day,
When swains their sportive rites to Bacchus pay:
She led the dance—Heavens! with what grace she
mov'd!                                [mov'd!
Who could have seen her then, and not have lov'd?
I strove not to resist so sweet a flame,
But gloried in a happy captive's name;
Nor would I now, could Love permit, be free,
But leave to brutes their savage liberty.

[1] Mr. Doddington had written some very pretty
love verses, which have never been published.
Lyttelton.

" And art thou then, fond youth, secure of joy?
Can no reverse thy flattering bliss destroy?
Has treacherous Love no torment yet in store?
Or hast thou never prov'd his fatal power?
Whence flow'd those tears that late bedew'd thy
cheek?
Why sigh'd thy heart as if it strove to break?
Why were the desert rocks invok'd to hear
The plaintive accent of thy sad despair?
From Delia's rigour all those pains arose,
Delia, who now compassionates my woes,
Who bids me hope; and in that charming word
Has peace and transport to my soul restor'd.

" Begin my pipe, begin the gladsome lay;
A kiss from Delia shall thy music pay;
A kiss obtain'd 'twixt struggling and consent,
Given with forc'd anger, and disguis'd content.
No laureat wreaths I ask, to bind my brows,
Such as the Muse on lofty bards bestows:
Let other swains to praise or fame aspire;
I from her lips my recompense require.

" Why stays my Delia in her secret bower?
Light gales have chas'd the late impending shower;
Th' emerging Sun more bright his beams extends;
Oppos'd, its beauteous arch the rainbow bends!
Glad youths and maidens turn the new-made hay:
The birds renew their songs on every spray!
Come forth, my love, thy shepherd's joys to crown:
All nature smiles.—Will only Delia frown?
Hark how the bees with murmurs fill the plain,
While every flower of every sweet they drain:
See, how beneath yon hillock's shady steep,
The shelter'd herds on flowery couches sleep:
Nor bees, nor herds, are half so blest as I,
If with my fond desires my love comply;
From Delia's lips a sweeter honey flows,
And on her bosom dwells more soft repose.

" Ah! how, my dear, shall I deserve thy charms?
What gift can bribe thee to my longing arms?
A bird for thee in silken bands I hold,
Whose yellow plumage shines like polish'd gold;
From distant isles the lovely stranger came,
And bears the fortunate Canaries name;
In all our woods none boasts so sweet a note,
Not ev'n the nightingale's melodious throat.
Accept of this; and could I add beside
What wealth the rich Peruvian mountains hide:
If all the gems in eastern rocks were mine,
On thee alone their glittering pride should shine.
But, if thy mind no gifts have power to move,
Phœbus himself shall leave th' Aonian grove:
The tuneful Nine, who never sue in vain,
Shall come sweet suppliants for their favourite
swain.
For him each blue-ey'd Naiad of the flood,
For him each green-hair'd sister of the wood,
Whom oft beneath fair Cynthia's gentle ray
His music calls to dance the night away.
And you, fair nymphs, companions of my love,
With whom she joys the cowslip meads to rove,
I beg you, recommend my faithful flame,
And let her often hear her shepherd's name:
Shade all my faults from her inquiring sight,
And show my merits in the fairest light;
My pipe your kind assistance shall repay,
And every friend shall claim a different lay.

" But see! in yonder glade the heavenly fair
Enjoys the fragrance of the breezy air—
Ah, thither let me fly with eager feet;
Adieu, my pipe; I go my love to meet.

O, may I find her as we parted last,
And may each future hour be like the past!
So shall the whitest lamb these pastures feed,
Propitious Venus, on thy altars bleed."

---

## JEALOUSY.
### ECLOGUE III.
#### TO MR. EDWARD WALPOLE.

THE gods, O Walpole, give no bliss sincere;
Wealth is disturb'd by care, and power by fear:
Of all the passions that employ the mind,
In gentle love the sweetest joys we find:
Yet ev'n those joys dire Jealousy molests,
And blackens each fair image in our breasts.
O may the warmth of thy too tender heart
Ne'er feel the sharpness of his venom'd dart!
For thy own quiet, think thy mistress just,
And wisely take thy happiness on trust.
   Begin, my Muse, and Damon's woes rehearse,
In wildest numbers and disorder'd verse.
   On a romantic mountain's airy head
(While browzing goats at ease around him fed)
Anxious he lay, with jealous cares opprest;
Distrust and anger labouring in his breast—
The vale beneath a pleasing prospect yields
Of verdant meads and cultivated fields;
Through these a river rolls its winding flood,
Adorn'd with various tufts of rising wood;
Here, half conceal'd in trees, a cottage stands,
A castle there the opening plain commands;
Beyond, a town with glittering spires is crown'd,
And distant hills the wide horizon bound:
So charming was the scene, a while the swain
Beheld delighted, and forgot his pain:
But soon the stings infix'd within his heart
With cruel force renew'd their raging smart:
His flowery wreath, which long with pride he wore,
The gift of Delia, from his brows he tore,
Then cried, " May all thy charms, ungrateful maid,
Like these neglected roses, droop and fade!
May angry Heaven deform each guilty grace,
That triumphs now in that deluding face!
Those alter'd looks may every shepherd fly,
And ev'n thy Daphnis hate thee worse than I!
   " Say, thou inconstant, what has Damon done,
To lose the heart his tedious pains had won?
Tell me what charms you in my rival find,
Against whose power no ties have strength to bind?
Has he, like me, with long obedience strove
To conquer your disdain, and merit love?
Has he with transport every smile ador'd,
And died with grief at each ungentle word?
Ah, no! the conquest was obtain'd with ease;
He pleas'd you, by not studying to please:
His careless indolence your pride alarm'd;
And, had he lov'd you more, he less had charm'd.
   " O pain to think! another shall possess
Those balmy lips which I was wont to press:
Another on her panting breast shall lie,
And catch sweet madness from her swimming eye!—
I saw their friendly flocks together feed,
I saw them hand in hand walk o'er the mead:
Would my clos'd eye had sunk in endless night,
Ere I was doom'd to bear that hateful sight!
Where'er they pass'd, be blasted every flower,
And hungry wolves their helpless flocks devour!—

Ah, wretched swain, could no examples move
Thy heedless heart to shun the rage of love?
Hast thou not heard how poor Menalcas [2] died
A victim to Parthenia's fatal pride?
Dear was the youth to all the tuneful plain,
Lov'd by the nymphs, by Phœbus lov'd in vain:
Around his tomb their tears the Muses paid;
And all things mourn'd, but the relentless maid.
Would I could die like him, and be at peace?
These torments in the quiet grave would cease;
There my vex'd thoughts a calm repose would find,
And rest, as if my Delia still were kind.
No, let me live, her falsehood to upbraid:
Some god perhaps my just revenge will aid.—
Alas! what aid, fond swain, wouldst thou receive?
Could thy heart bear to see its Delia grieve?
Protect her, Heaven! and let her never know
The slightest part of hapless Damon's woe:
I ask no vengeance from the powers above;
All I implore is never more to love.—
Let me this fondness from my bosom tear,
Let me forget that e'er I thought her fair.
Come, cool Indifference, and heal my breast;
Wearied, at length, I seek thy downy rest:
No turbulence of passion shall destroy
My future ease with flattering hopes of joy.
Hear, mighty Pan, and, all ye sylvans, hear
What by your guardian deities I swear;
No more my eyes shall view her fatal charms,
No more I'll court the traitoress to my arms;
Not all her arts my steady soul shall move,
And she shall find that reason conquers love!"—
Scarce had he spoke, when through the lawn below
Alone he saw the beauteous Delia go;
At once transported, he forgot his vow,
(Such perjuries the laughing gods allow!)
Down the steep hills with ardent haste he flew;
He found her kind, and soon believ'd her true.

---

## POSSESSION.
### ECLOGUE IV.
#### TO LORD COBHAM.

COBHAM, to thee this rural lay I bring,
Whose guiding judgment gives me skill to sing:
Though far unequal to those polish'd strains,
With which thy Congreve charm'd the listening
   plains:
Yet shall its music please thy partial ear,
And sooth thy breast with thoughts that once were
   dear;
Recall those years which time has thrown behind,
When smiling Love with Honour shar'd thy mind:
When all thy glorious days of prosperous fight
Delighted less than one successful night.
The sweet remembrance shall thy youth restore,
Fancy again shall run past pleasures o'er;
And, while in Stowe's enchanting walks you stray,
This theme may help to cheat the summer's day.
   Beneath the covert of a myrtle wood,
To Venus rais'd, a rustic altar stood.
To Venus and to Hymen, there combin'd,
In friendly league to favour human-kind.
With wanton Cupids, in that happy shade,
The gentle Virtues and mild Wisdom play'd.

[2] See Mr. Gay's Dione.

Nor there in sprightly Pleasure's genial train,
Lurk'd sick Disgust, or late-repenting Pain,
Nor Force, nor Interest, join'd unwilling hands,
But Love consenting tied the blissful bands.
Thither, with glad devotion, Damon came,
To thank the powers who bless'd his faithful flame:
Two milk-white doves he on their altar laid,
And thus to both his grateful homage paid:
" Hail, bounteous god ! before whose hallow'd shrine
My Delia vow'd to be for ever mine,
While, glowing in her cheeks, with tender love,
Sweet virgin modesty reluctant strove !
And hail to thee, fair queen of young desires !
Long shall my heart preserve thy pleasing fires,
Since Delia now can all its warmth return,
As fondly languish, and as fiercely burn.
" O the dear bloom of last propitious night !
O shade more charming than the fairest light !
Then in my arms I clasp'd the melting maid,
Then all my pains one moment overpaid ;
Then first the sweet excess of bliss I prov'd,
Which none can taste but who like me have lov'd.
Thou too, bright goddess, once, in Ida's grove,
Didst not disdain to meet a shepherd's love ;
With him, while frisking lambs around you play'd,
Conceal'd you sported in the secret shade :
Scarce could Anchises' raptures equal mine,
And Delia's beauties only yield to thine.
" What are ye now, my once most valued joys ?
Insipid trifles all, and childish toys—
Friendship itself ne'er knew a charm like this,
Nor Colin's talk could please like Delia's kiss,
" Ye Muses, skill'd in every winning art,
Teach me more deeply to engage her heart ;
Ye nymphs, to her your freshest roses bring,
And crown her with the pride of all the Spring :
On all her days let health and peace attend ;
May she ne'er want, nor ever lose, a friend !
May some new pleasure every hour employ :
But let her Damon be her highest joy !
" With thee, my love, for ever will I stay,
All night caress thee, and admire all day ;
In the same field our mingled flocks we 'll feed,
To the same spring our thirsty heifers lead,
Together will we share the harvest toils,
Together press the vine's autumnal spoils.
Delightful state, where Peace and Love combine,
To bid our tranquil days unclouded shine !
Here limpid fountains roll through flowery meads;
Here rising forests lift their verdant heads ;
Here let me wear my careless life away,
And in thy arms insensibly decay.
" When late old age our heads shall silver o'er,
And our slow pulses dance with joy no more ;
When Time no longer will thy beauties spare,
And only Damon's eye shall think thee fair ;
Then may the gentle hand of welcome Death,
At one soft stroke, deprive us both of breath !
May we beneath one common stone be laid,
And the same cypress both our ashes shade !
Perhaps some friendly Muse, in tender verse,
Shall deign our faithful passion to rehearse
And future ages, with just envy mov'd,
Be told how Damon and his Delia lov'd."

## SOLILOQUY

### OF A BEAUTY IN THE COUNTRY.

#### WRITTEN AT ETON SCHOOL.

'Twas night ; and Flavia, to her room retir'd,
With evening chat and sober reading tir'd ;
There, melancholy, pensive, and alone,
She meditates on the forsaken town :
On her rais'd arm reclin'd her drooping head,
She sigh'd, and thus in plaintive accents said :
" Ah ! what avails it to be young and fair ;
To move with negligence, to dress with care ?
What worth have all the charms our pride can
boast,
If all in envious solitude are lost ?
Where none admire, 'tis useless to excel ;
Where none are beaux, 'tis vain to be a belle ;
Beauty, like wit, to judges should be shown ;
Both most are valued, where they best are known.
With every grace of Nature or of Art,
We cannot break one stubborn country heart :
The brutes, insensible, our power defy :
To love, exceeds a 'squire's capacity.
The town, the court, is Beauty's proper sphere ;
That is our Heaven, and we are angels there :
In that gay circle thousand Cupids rove,
The court of Britain is the court of Love.
How has my conscious heart with triumph glow'd,
How have my sparkling eyes their transport show'd,
At each distinguish'd birth-night ball, to see
The homage, due to empire, paid to me !
When every eye was fix'd on me alone,
And dreaded mine more than the monarch's
frown ;
When rival statesmen for my favour strove,
Less jealous in their power than in their love.
Chang'd is the scene ; and all my glories die,
Like flowers transplanted to a colder sky :
Lost is the dear delight of giving pain,
The tyrant joy of hearing slaves complain.
In stupid indolence my life is spent,
Supinely calm, and dully innocent :
Unblest I wear my useless time away ;
Sleep (wretched maid !) all night, and dream all
day ;
Go at set hours to dinner and to prayer
(For dullness ever must be regular.)
Now with mamma at tedious whist I play ;
Now without scandal drink insipid tea ;
Or in the garden breathe the country air,
Secure from meeting any tempter there ;
From books to work, from work to books, I rove,
And am, alas ! at leisure to improve !—
Is this the life a beauty ought to lead ?
Were eyes so radiant only made to read ?
These fingers, at whose touch ev'n age would
glow,
Are these of use for nothing but to sew ?
Sure erring Nature never could design
To form a housewife in a mould like mine !
O Venus, queen and guardian of the fair,
Attend propitious to thy votary's prayer :
Let me revisit the dear town again :
Let me be seen !—could I that wish obtain,
All other wishes my own power would gain."

## BLENHEIM.

WRITTEN AT THE UNIVERSITY OF OXFORD, IN THE
YEAR 1727.

PARENT of arts, whose skilful hand first taught
The towering pile to rise, and form'd the plan
With fair proportion; architect divine.
Minerva, thee to my adventurous lyre
Assistant I invoke, that means to sing
Blenheim, proud monument of British fame,
Thy glorious work! for thou the lofty towers
Didst to his virtue raise, whom oft thy shield
In peril guarded, and thy wisdom steer'd
Through all the storms of war.—Thee too I call,
Thalia, sylvan Muse, who lov'st to rove
Along the shady paths and verdant bowers
Of Woodstock's happy grove: there tuning sweet
Thy rural pipe, while all the Dryad train
Attentive listen; let thy warbling song
Paint with melodious praise the pleasing scene,
And equal these to Pindus' honour'd shades.
     When Europe freed, confess'd the saving power
Of Marlborough's hand; Britain, who sent him forth
Chief of confederate hosts, to fight the cause
Of Liberty and Justice, grateful rais'd
This palace, sacred to her leader's fame:
A trophy of success; with spoils adorn'd
Of conquer'd towns, and glorying in the name
Of that auspicious field, where Churchill's sword
Vanquish'd the might of Gallia, and chastis'd
Rebel Bavar.—Majestic in its strength,
Stands the proud dome, and speaks its great design.
     Hail, happy chief, whose valour could deserve
Reward so glorious! grateful nation, hail,
Who paid'st his service with so rich a meed!
Which most shall I admire, which worthiest praise,
The hero or the people? Honour doubts,
And weighs their virtues in an equal scale.
Not that Germania pays th' uncancell'd debt
Of gratitude to us—Blush, Cæsar, blush,
When thou behold'st these towers; ingrate, to thee
A monument of shame! Canst thou forget
Whence they are nam'd, and what an English arm
Did for thy throne that day? But we disdain
Or to upbraid or imitate thy guilt.
Still thy obdurate heart against the sense
Of obligation infinite; and know,
Britain, like Heaven, protects a thankless world
For her own glory, nor expects reward.
     Pleas'd with the noble theme, her task the Muse
Pursues untir'd, and through the palace roves
With ever-new delight. The tapestry rich
With gold, and gay with all the beauteous paint
Of various colour'd silks, dispos'd with skill,
Attracts her curious eye, Here Ister rolls
His purple wave; and there the Granick flood
With passing squadrons foams: here hardy Gaul
Flies from the sword of Britain; there to Greece
Effeminate Persia yields.—In arms oppos'd,
Marlborough and Alexander vie for fame
With glorious competition; equal both
In valour and in fortune: but their praise
Be different, for with different views they fought:
This to *subdue*, and that to *free* mankind.
     Now, through the stately portals issuing forth,
The Muse to softer glories turns, and seeks
The woodland shade, delighted. Not the vale
Of Tempe fam'd in song, or Ida's grove,

Such beauty boasts. Amid the mazy gloom
Of this romantic wilderness once stood
The bower of Rosamonda, hapless fair,
Sacred to grief and love; the crystal fount
In which she us'd to bathe her beauteous limbs
Still warbling flows, pleas'd to reflect the face
Of Spencer, lovely maid, when tir'd she sits
Beside its flowery brink, and views those charms
Which only Rosamond could once excel.
But see where, flowing with a nobler stream,
A limpid lake of purest waters rolls
Beneath the wide-stretch'd arch, stupendous work,
Through which the Danube might collected pour
His spacious urn! Silent a while and smooth
The current glides, till with an headlong force
Broke and disorder'd, down the steep it falls
In loud cascades; the silver-sparkling foam
Glitters relucent in the dancing ray.
     In these retreats repos'd the mighty soul
Of Churchill, from the toils of war and state,
Splendidly private, and the tranquil joy
Of contemplation felt, while Blenheim's dome
Triumphal ever in his mind renew'd
The memory of his fame, and sooth'd his thoughts
With pleasing record of his glorious deeds.
So, by the rage of Faction home recall'd,
Lucullus, while he wag'd successful war
Against the pride of Asia, and the power
Of Mithridates, whose aspiring mind
No losses could subdue, enrich'd with spoils
Of conquer'd nations, back return'd to Rome,
And in magnificent retirement past
The evening of his life.—But not alone,
In the calm shades of honourable ease,      [ven
Great Marlborough peaceful dwelt: indulgent Hea-
Gave a companion to his softer hours,
With whom conversing, he forgot all change
Of fortune, or of state, and in her mind
Found greatness equal to his own, and lov'd
Himself in her.—Thus each by each admir'd,
In mutual honour, mutual fondness join'd,
Like two fair stars, with intermingled light,
In friendly union they together shone,
Aiding each other's brightness, till the cloud
Of night eternal quench'd the beams of one.
Thee, Churchill, first the ruthless hand of Death
Tore from thy consort's side, and call'd thee hence
To the sublimer seats of joy and love;
Where Fate again shall join her soul to thine,
Who now, regardful of thy fame, erects
The column to thy praise, and soothes her woe
With pious honours to thy sacred name
Immortal. Lo! where, towering in the height
Of yon aërial pillar, proudly stands
Thy image, like a guardian god, sublime,
And awes the subject plain: beneath his feet,
The German eagles spread their wings; his hand
Grasps Victory, its slave. Such was thy brow
Majestic, such thy martial port, when Gaul
Fled from thy frown, and in the Danube sought
A refuge from thy sword.—There, where the field
Was deepest stain'd with gore, on Hochstet's plain,
The theatre of thy glory, once was rais'd
A meaner trophy, by the imperial hand;
Extorted gratitude! which now the rage
Of malice impotent, beseeming ill
A regal breast, has levell'd to the ground:
Mean insult! This, with better auspices,
Shall stand on British earth to tell the world
How Marlborough fought, for whom, and how repaid

His services. Nor shall the constant love
Of her who rais'd this monument be lost
In dark oblivion : that shall be the theme
Of future bards in ages yet unborn,
Inspir'd with Chaucer's fire, who in these groves
First tun'd the British harp, and little deem'd
His humble dwelling should the neighbour be
Of Blenheim, house superb; to which the throng
Of travellers approaching shall not pass
His roof unnoted, but respectful hail
With reverence due. Such honour does the Muse
Obtain her favourites.—But the noble pile
(My theme) demands my voice.—O shade ador'd,
Marlborough ! who now above the starry sphere
Dwell'st in the palaces of Heaven, enthron'd
Among the demi-gods, deign to defend
This thy abode, while present here below,
And sacred still to thy immortal fame,
With tutelary care. Preserve it safe
From Time's destroying hand, and cruel stroke
Of factious Envy's more relentless rage.
Here may, long ages hence, the British youth,
When Honour calls them to the field of war,
Behold the trophies which thy valour rais'd;
The proud reward of thy successful toils
For Europe's freedom, and Britannia's fame ;
That fir'd with generous envy, they may dare
To emulate thy deeds.—So shall thy name,
Dear to thy country, still inspire her sons
With martial virtue; and to high attempts
Excite their arms, till other battles won,
And nations sav'd, new monuments require,
And other Blenheims shall adorn the land.

---

## TO THE REVEREND DR. AYSCOUGH,

AT OXFORD.

WRITTEN FROM PARIS IN THE YEAR 1728.

Say, dearest friend, how roll thy hours away?
What pleasing study cheats the tedious day ?
Dost thou the sacred volumes oft explore
Of wise Antiquity's immortal lore,
Where virtue, by the charms of wit refin'd,
At once exalts and polishes the mind ?
How different from our modern guilty art,
Which pleases only to corrupt the heart ;
Whose curst refinements odious vice adorn,
And teach to honour what we ought to scorn !
Dost thou in sage historians joy to see
How Roman greatness rose with liberty :
How the same hands that tyrants durst control
Their empire stretched from Atlas to the pole ;
Till wealth and conquest into slaves refin'd
The proud luxurious masters of mankind ?
Dost thou in letter'd Greece each charm admire,
Each grace, each virtue, Freedom could inspire ;
Yet in her troubled state see all the woes,
And all the crimes, that giddy Faction knows ;
Till, rent by parties, by corruption sold,
Or weakly careless, or too rashly bold,
She sunk beneath a mitigated doom,
The slave and tutoress of protecting Rome ?
Does calm Philosophy her aid impart,
To guide the passions, and to mend the heart ?
Taught by her precepts, hast thou learnt the end
To which alone the wise their studies bend ;
For which alone by Nature were design'd
The powers of thought—to benefit mankind ?

Not, like a cloyster'd drone, to read and dose,
In undeserving, undeserv'd, repose ;
But reason's influence to diffuse; to clear
Th' enlighten'd world of every gloomy fear;
Dispel the mists of errour, and unbind
Those pedant chains that clog the freeborn mind.
Happy who thus his leisure can employ !
He knows the purest hours of tranquil joy ;
Nor vext with pangs that busier bosoms tear,
Nor lost to social virtue's pleasing care ;
Safe in the port, yet labouring to sustain
Those who still float on the tempestuous main.
  So Locke the days of studious quiet spent ;
So Boyle in wisdom found divine content ;
So Cambray, worthy of a happier doom,
The virtuous slave of Louis and of Rome.
  Good Wor'ster [1] thus supports his drooping age,
Far from court-flattery, far from party-rage;
He, who in youth a tyrant's frown defy'd,
Firm and intrepid on his country's side,   [guide !
Her boldest champion then, and now her mildest
O generous warmth ! O sanctity divine !
To emulate his worth, my friend, be thine:
Learn from his life the duties of the gown ;
Learn, not to flatter, nor insult the crown ;
Nor, basely servile, court the guilty great,
Nor raise the church a rival to the state:
To errour mild, to vice alone severe,
Seek not to spread the *law of love* by fear.
The priest who plagues the world can never mend:
No foe to man was e'er to God a friend.
Let reason and let virtue faith maintain;
All force but theirs is impious, weak, and vain,
  Me other cares in other climes engage,
Cares that become my birth, and suit my age ;
In various knowledge to improve my youth,
And conquer prejudice, worst foe to truth ;
By foreign arts domestic faults to mend,
Enlarge my notions, and my views extend ;
The useful science of the world to know,
Which books can never teach, or pedants show.
  A nation here I pity and admire,
Whom noblest sentiments of glory fire,
Yet taught, by custom's force and bigot fear,
To serve with pride, and boast the yoke they bear:
Whose nobles, born to cringe and to command,
(In courts a mean, in camps a generous band)
From each low tool of power, content receive
Those laws, their dreaded arms to Europe give.
Whose people (vain in want, in bondage blest ;
Though plunder'd, gay ; industrious, though opprest)
With happy follies rise above their fate,
The jest and envy of each wiser state.
  Yet here the Muses deign'd a while to sport
In the short sunshine of a favouring court :
Here Boileau, strong in sense and sharp in wit,
Who, from the ancients, like the ancients writ,
Permission gain'd inferior vice to blame,
By flattering incense to his master's fame.
Here Moliere, first of comic wits, excelled
Whate'er Athenian theatres beheld ;
By keen, yet decent, satire skill'd to please,
With morals mirth uniting, strength with ease.
Now, charm'd, I hear the bold Corneille inspire
Heroic thoughts, with Shakspeare's force and fire !
Now sweet Racine, with milder influence, move
The soften'd heart to pity and to love.

[1] Bishop Hough.

With mingled pain and pleasure, I survey
The pompous works of arbitrary sway;
Proud palaces, that drain'd the subjects' store,
Rais'd on the ruins of th' opprest and poor;
Where ev'n mute walls are taught to flatter state,
And painted triumphs style Ambition GREAT [2].
With more delight those pleasing shades I view,
Where Condé from an envious court withdrew [3];
Where, sick of glory, faction, power, and pride,
(Sure judge how empty all, who all had tried!)
Beneath his palms the weary chief repos'd,
And life's great scene in quiet virtue clos'd.

With shame that other fam'd retreat I see,
Adorn'd by art, disgrac'd by luxury [4]:
Where Orleans wasted every vacant hour,
In the wild riot of unbounded power;
Where feverish debauch and impious love
Stain'd the mad table and the guilty grove.

With these amusements is thy friend detain'd,
Pleas'd and instructed in a foreign land;
Yet oft a tender wish recalls my mind
From present joys to dearer left behind.
O native isle, fair Freedom's happiest seat!
At thought of thee, my bounding pulses beat;
At thought of thee, my heart impatient burns,
And all my country on my soul returns.
When shall I see thy fields, whose plenteous grain
No power can ravish from th' industrious swain?
When kiss, with pious love, the sacred earth
That gave a Burleigh or a Russel birth?
When, in the shade of laws, that long have stood,
Propt by their care, or strengthen'd by their blood,
Of fearless independence wisely vain,
The proudest slave of Bourbon's race disdain?

Yet, oh! what doubt, what sad presaging voice,
Whispers within, and bids me not rejoice;
Bids me contemplate every state around,
From sultry Spain to Norway's icy bound;
Bids their lost rights, their ruin'd glory see;
And tells me, " These, like England, once were free!"

---

## TO MR. POYNTZ,

AMBASSADOR AT THE CONGRESS OF SOISSONS, IN 1728.

WRITTEN AT PARIS.

O thou, whose friendship is my joy and pride,
Whose virtues warm me, and whose precepts guide;
Thou to whom greatness, rightly understood,
Is but a larger power of being good;
Say, Poyntz, amidst the toil of anxious state,
Does not thy secret soul desire retreat?
Dost thou not wish (the task of glory done)
Thy busy life at length might be thy own;
That, to thy lov'd philosophy resign'd,
No care might ruffle thy unbended mind?
Just is the wish. For sure the happiest meed,
To favour'd man by smiling Heaven decreed,
Is, to reflect at ease on glorious pains,
And calmly to enjoy what virtue gains.

Not him I praise, who, from the world retir'd,
By no enlivening generous passion fir'd,

[2] The victories of Louis the Fourteenth, painted in the galleries of Versailles.

[3] Chantilly.

[4] St. Cloud.

On flowery couches slumbers life away,
And gently bids his active powers decay;
Who fears bright Glory's awful face to see,
And shuns renown as much as infamy.
But blest is he, who, exercis'd in cares,
To private leisure public virtue bears:
Who tranquil ends the race he nobly run,
And decks repose with trophies Labour won.
Him Honour follows to the secret shade,
And crowns propitious his declining head;
In his retreats their harps the Muses string,
For him in lays unbought spontaneous sing;
Friendship and Truth on all his moments wait,
Pleas'd with retirement better than with state;
And round the bower, where humbly great he lies,
Fair olives bloom, or verdant laurels rise.

So when thy country shall no more demand
The needful aid of thy sustaining hand;
When Peace restor'd shall, on her downy wing,
Secure repose and careless leisure bring;
Then, to the shades of learned ease retir'd,
The world forgetting, by the world admir'd,
Among thy books and friends, thou shalt possess
Contemplative and quiet happiness:
Pleas'd to review a life in honour spent,
And painful merit paid with sweet content.
Yet, though thy hours unclogg'd with sorrow roll,
Though wisdom calm, and science feed thy soul,
One dearer bliss remains to be possest,
That only can improve and crown the rest.—

Permit thy friend this secret to reveal,
Which thy own heart perhaps would better tell;
The point to which our sweetest passions move
Is, to be truly lov'd, and fondly love.
This is the charm that smooths the troubled breast,
Friend of our health, and author of our rest:
Bids every gloomy vexing passion fly,
And tunes each jarring string to harmony.
Ev'n while I write, the name of Love inspires
More pleasing thoughts, and more enlivening fires;
Beneath his power my raptur'd fancy glows,
And every tender verse more sweetly flows.
Dull is the privilege of living free;
Our hearts were never form'd for liberty:
Some beauteous image, well imprinted there,
Can best defend them from consuming care.
In vain to groves and gardens we retire,
And Nature in her rural works admire;
Though grateful these, yet these but faintly charm;
They may delight us, but can nerve warm.
May some fair eyes, my friend, thy bosom fire
With pleasing pangs of ever-gay desire;
And teach thee that soft science, which alone
Still to thy searching mind rests slightly known!
Thy soul, though great, is tender and refin'd,
To friendship sensible, to love inclin'd,
And therefore long thou canst not arm thy breast
Against the entrance of so sweet a guest.
Hear what th' inspiring Muses bid me tell,
For Heaven shall ratify what they reveal:
" A chosen bride shall in thy arms be plac'd,
With all th' attractive charms of beauty grac'd,
Whose wit and virtue shall thy own express,
Distinguish'd only by their softer dress;
Thy greatness she, or thy retreat, shall share;
Sweeten tranquillity, or soften care;
Her smiles the taste of every joy shall raise,
And add new pleasure to renown and praise;
Till charm'd you own the truth my verse would prove,
That happiness is near allied to love."

*VERSES*

TO BE WRITTEN UNDER A PICTURE OF MR. POYNTZ.

Such is thy form, O Poyntz, but who shall find
A hand, or colours, to express thy mind ?
A mind unmov'd by every vulgar fear,
In a false world that dares to be sincere;
Wise without art; without ambition great;
Though firm, yet pliant; active, though sedate;
With all the richest stores of learning fraught,
Yet better still by native prudence taught;
That, fond the griefs of the distress to heal,
Can pity frailties it could never feel;
That, when Misfortune sued, ne'er sought to know
What sect, what party, whether friend or foe;
That, fix'd on equal virtue's temperate laws,
Despises calumny, and shuns applause :
That, to its own perfe .ions singly blind,
Would for another time. is praise design'd.

---

*AN EPISTLE TO MR. POPE.*

FROM ROME, 1730.

Immortal bard ! for whom each Muse has wove
The fairest garlands of th' Aonian grove;
Preserv'd our drooping genius to restore,
When Addison and Congreve are no more;
After so many stars extinct in night,
The darken'd age's last remaining light !
To thee from Latian realms this verse is writ,
Inspir'd by memory of ancient wit;
For now no more these climes their influence boast,
Fall'n is their glory, and their virtue lost;
From tyrants, and from priests, the Muses fly,
Daughters of Reason and of Liberty !
Nor Baiæ now nor Umbria plain they love,
Nor on the banks of Nar or Mincio rove;
To Thames's flowery borders they retire,
And kindle in thy breast the Roman fire.
So in the shades, where, cheer'd with summer rays,
Melodious linnets warbled sprightly lays,
Soon as the faded, falling leaves complain
Of gloomy Winter's unauspicious reign,
No tuneful voice is heard of joy or love,
But mournful silence saddens all the grove.
 Unhappy Italy ! whose alter'd state
Has felt the worst severity of Fate :
Not that barbarian hands her fasces broke,
And bow'd her haughty neck beneath their yoke;
Nor that her palaces to earth are thrown,
Her cities desert, and her fields unsown ;
But that her ancient spirit is decay'd,
That sacred Wisdom from her bounds is fled ;
That there the source of science flows no more,
Whence its rich streams supplied the world before.
 Illustrious names ! that once in Latium shin'd,
Born to instruct and to command mankind ;
Chiefs, by whose virtue mighty Rome was rais'd,
And poets, who those chiefs sublimely prais'd;
Oft I the traces you have left explore,
Your ashes visit, and your urns adore;
Oft kiss, with lips devout, some mouldering stone,
With ivy's venerable shade o'ergrown ;
Those horrid ruins better pleas'd to see
Than all the pomp of modern luxury.

As late on Virgil's tomb fresh flowers I strow'd,
While with th' inspiring Muse my bosom glow'd,
Crown'd with eternal bays, my ravish'd eyes
Beheld the poet's awful form arise:
" Stranger," he said, " whose pious hand has paid
These grateful rites to my attentive shade,
When thou shalt breathe thy happy native air,
To Pope this message from his master bear:
" Great bard, whose numbers I myself inspire,
To whom I gave my own harmonious lyre,
If, high exalted on the throne of wit,
Near me and Homer thou aspire to sit,
No more let meaner satire dim the rays
That flow majestic from thy nobler bays ;
In all the flowery paths of Pindus stray,
But shun that thorny, that unpleasing way ;
Nor, when each soft engaging Muse is thine,
Address the least attractive of the Nine.
" Of thee more worthy were thy task, to raise
A lasting column to thy country's praise ;
To sing the land, which yet alone can boast
That liberty corrupted Rome has lost;
Where Science in the arms of Peace is laid,
And plants her palm beneath the olive's shade.
Such was the theme for which my lyre I strung,
Such was the people whose exploits I sung ;
Brave, yet refin'd, for arms and arts renown'd,
With different bays by Mars and Phœbus crown'd;
Dauntless opposers of tyrannic sway,
But pleas'd a mild Augustus to obey.
" If these commands submissive thou receive,
Immortal and unblam'd thy name shall live,
Envy to black Cocytus shall retire ;
And howl with furies in tormenting fire ;
Approving Time shall consecrate thy lays,
And join the patriot's to the poet's praise."

---

*TO LORD' HERVEY.*

IN THE YEAR 1730.    FROM WORCESTERSHIRE.

Strenua nos exercet inertia : navibus atque
Quadrigis petimus bene vivere: quod petis, hic est;
Est ulubris, animus si te non deficit æquus.   Hor.

Favourite of Venus and the tuneful Nine,
Pollio, by Nature form'd in courts to shine,
Wilt thou once more a kind attention lend,
To thy long absent and forgotten friend ;
Who, after seas and mountains wander'd o'er,
Return'd at length to his own native shore,
From all that's gay retir'd, and all that's great,
Beneath the shades of his paternal seat,
Has found that happiness he sought in vain
On the fam'd banks of Tiber and of Seine ?
'Tis not to view the well-proportion'd pile,
The charms of Titian's and of Raphael's style ;
At soft Italian sounds to melt away ;
Or in the fragrant groves of myrtle stray ;
That lulls the tumults of the soul to rest,
Or makes the fond possessor truly blest.
In our own breasts the source of pleasure lies,
Still open, and still flowing to the wise;
Not forc'd by toilsome art and wild desire
Beyond the bounds of Nature to aspire,
But, in its proper channels gliding fair;
A common benefit, which all may share.
Yet half mankind this easy good disdain,
Nor relish happiness unbought by pain;   [is vain.
False is their taste of bliss, and thence their search

So idle, yet so restless, are our minds,
We climb the Alps, and brave the raging winds;
Through various toils to seek content we roam,
Which with but *thinking right* were ours at home.
For not the ceaseless change of shifted place
Can from the heart a settled grief erase,
Nor can the purer balm of foreign air
Heal the distemper'd mind of aching care.
The wretch, by wild impatience driven to rove,
Vext with the pangs of ill-requited love,
From Pole to Pole the fatal arrow bears,
Whose rooted point his bleeeding bosom tears;
With equal pain each different clime he tries,
And is himself that torment which he flies.

For how should ills, which from our passions flow,
Be chang'd by Afric's heat, or Russia's snow?
Or how can aught but powerful reason cure
What from unthinking folly we endure?
Happy is he, and he alone, who knows
His heart's uneasy discord to compose;
In generous love of others' good, to find
The sweetest pleasures of the social mind;
To bound his wishes in their proper sphere;
To nourish pleasing hope, and conquer anxious fear:
This was the wisdom ancient sages taught,
This was the sovereign good they justly sought;
This to no place or climate is confin'd,
But the free native produce of the mind.

Nor think, my lord, that courts to you deny
The useful practice of philosophy:
Horace, the wisest of the tuneful choir,
Not always chose from greatness to retire;
But, in the palace of Augustus, knew
The same unerring maxims to pursue,
Which, in the Sabine or the Velian shade,
His study and his happiness he made.

May you, my friend, by his example taught,
View all the giddy scene with sober thought;
Undazzled every glittering folly see,
And in the midst of slavish forms be free;
In its own centre keep your steady mind,
Let Prudence guide you, but let Honour bind.
In show, in manners, act the courtier's part,
But be a country gentleman at heart.

---

## ADVICE TO A LADY.

### M.DCC.XXXI.

THE counsels of a friend, Belinda, hear,
Too roughly kind to please a lady's ear,
Unlike the flatteries of a lover's pen,
Such truths as women seldom learn from men.
Nor think I praise you ill, when thus I show
What female vanity might fear to know.
Some merit's mine, to dare to be sincere;
But greater your's, sincerity to bear.

Hard is the fortune that your sex attends;
Women, like princes, find few real friends:
All who approach them their own ends pursue;
Lovers and ministers are seldom true.
Hence oft from Reason heedless Beauty strays,
And the most trusted guide the most betrays,
Hence, by fond dreams of fancied power amus'd,
When most ye tyrannise, you 're most abus'd.

What is your sex's earliest, latest care,
Your heart's supreme ambition?—To be fair.
For this, the toilet every thought employs,
Hence all the toils of dress, and all the joys:

For this, hands, lips, and eyes, are put to school,
And each instructed feature has its rule:
And yet how few have learnt, when this is given,
Not to disgrace the partial boon of Heaven!
How few with all their pride of form can move!
How few are lovely, that are made for love!
Do you, my fair, endeavour to possess
An elegance of mind as well as dress;
Be that your ornament, and know to please
By graceful Nature's unaffected ease.

Nor make to dangerous wit a vain pretence,
But wisely rest content with modest sense;
For wit, like wine, intoxicates the brain,
Too strong for feeble woman to sustain:
Of those who claim it more than half have none;
And half of those who have it are undone.

Be still superior to your sex's arts,
Nor think dishonesty a proof of parts:
For you, the plainest is the wisest rule:
A *cunning woman* is a *knavish fool*.

Be good yourself, nor think another's shame
Can raise your merit, or adorn your fame.
Prudes rail at whores, as statesmen in disgrace
At ministers, because they wish their place.
Virtue is amiable, mild, serene;
Without, all beauty; and all peace within:
The honour of a prude is rage and storm,
'Tis ugliness in its most frightful form.
Fiercely it stands, defying gods and men,
As fiery monsters guard a giant's den.

Seek to be good, but aim not to be great:
A woman's noblest station is retreat:
Her fairest virtues fly from public sight,
Domestic worth, that shuns too strong a light.

To rougher man Ambition's task resign:
'Tis ours in senates or in courts to shine;
To labour for a sunk corrupted state,
Or dare the rage of Envy, and be great.
One only care your gentle breasts should move,
Th' important business of your life is love;
To this great point direct your constant aim,
This makes your happiness, and this your fame.

Be never cool reserve with passion join'd;
With caution choose; but then be fondly kind.
The selfish heart, that but by halves is given,
Shall find no place in Love's delightful Heaven;
Here sweet extremes alone can truly bless:
The virtue of a lover is excess.
A maid unask'd may own a well-plac'd flame;
Not loving *first*, but loving *wrong*, is shame.

Contemn the little pride of giving pain,
Nor think that conquest justifies disdain.
Short is the period of insulting power:
Offended Cupid finds his vengeful hour;
Soon will resume the empire which he gave,
And soon the tyrant shall become the slave.

Blest is the maid, and worthy to be blest,
Whose soul, entire by him she loves possest,
Feels every vanity in fondness lost,
And asks no power but that of pleasing most:
Hers is the bliss, in just return, to prove
The honest warmth of undissembled love;
For her, inconstant man might cease to range,
And gratitude forbid desire to change.

But, lest harsh Care the lover's peace destroy,
And roughly blight the tender buds of joy,
Let Reason teach what Passion fain would hide,
That Hymen's bands by Prudence should be tied,
Venus in vain the wedded pair would crown,
If angry Fortune on their union frown:

Soon will the flattering dream of bliss be o'er,
And cloy'd imagination cheat no more.
Then, waking to the sense of lasting pain,
With mutual tears the nuptial couch they stain;
And that fond love, which should afford relief,
Does but increase the anguish of their grief:
While both could easier their own sorrows bear,
Than the sad knowledge of each other's care.
　　Yet may you rather feel that virtuous pain,
Than sell your violated charms for gain;
Than wed the wretch whom you despise or hate,
For the vain glare of useless wealth or state.
The most abandoned prostitutes are they,
Who not to love, but avarice, fall a prey:
Nor aught avails the specious name of *wife ;*
A maid so wedded is *a whore for life.*　　　[ven
　　Ey'n in the happiest choice, where favouring Hea-
Has equal love and easy fortune given,
Think not, the husband gain'd, that all is done:
The prize of happiness must still be won:
And oft, the careless find it to their cost,
The *lover* in the *husband* may be lost;
The Graces might *alone* his heart *allure ;*
*They* and the Virtues *meeting* must *secure.*
　　Let ev'n your *prudence* wear the pleasing dress
Of care for *him,* and anxious *tenderness.*
From kind concern about his weal or woe,
Let each domestic duty seem to flow.
The *household sceptre* if he bids you bear,
Make it your pride his *servant* to appear:
Endearing thus the common acts of life,
The *mistress* still shall charm him in the *wife ;*
And wrinkled age shall unobserv'd come on,
Before his eye perceives one beauty gone:
Ev'n o'er your cold, your ever-sacred urn,
His constant flame, shall unextinguish'd burn.
　　Thus I, Belinda, would your charms improve,
And form your heart to all the arts of love.
The task were harder, to secure my own
Against the power of those already known:
For well you twist the secret chains that bind
With gentle force the captivated mind,
Skill'd every soft attraction to employ,
Each flattering hope, and each alluring joy.
I own your genius; and from you receive
The rules of pleasing, which to you I give.

## SONG.

### WRITTEN IN THE YEAR 1732.

When Delia on the plain appears,
Aw'd by a thousand tender fears,
I would approach, but dare not move:
Tell me, my heart, if this be love?

Whene'er she speaks, my ravish'd ear
No other voice but her's can hear,
No other wit but her's approve:
Tell me, my heart, if this be love?

If she some other youth commend,
Though I was once his fondest friend,
His instant enemy I prove:
Tell me, my heart, if this be love?

When she is absent, I do more
Delight in all that pleas'd before,

The clearest spring, or shadiest grove:
Tell me, my heart, if this be love?

When, fond of power, of beauty vain,
Her nets she spread for every swain,
I strove to hate, but vainly strove:
Tell me, my heart, if this be love?

## SONG.

### WRITTEN IN THE YEAR 1733.

The heavy hours are almost past
　　That part my love and me:
My longing eyes may hope at last
　　Their only wish to see.

But how, my Delia, will you meet
　　The man you 've lost so long?
Will love in all your pulses beat,
　　And tremble on your tongue?

Will you in every look declare
　　Your heart is still the same;
And heal each idly-anxious care
　　Our fears in absence frame?

Thus, Delia, thus I paint the scène,
　　When shortly we shall meet;
And try what yet remains between
　　Of loitering time to cheat.

But, if the dream that soothes my mind
　　Shall false and groundless prove;
If I am doom'd at length to find
　　You have forgot to love:

All I of Venus ask, is this;
　　No more to let us join:
But grant me here the flattering bliss,
　　To die, and think you mine.

## DAMON AND DELIA.

### IN IMITATION OF HORACE AND LYDIA.

### WRITTEN IN THE YEAR 1732.

#### DAMON.

Tell me, my Delia, tell me why
My kindest, fondest looks you fly?
What means this cloud upon your brow?
Have I offended? Tell me how! —
Some change has happen'd in your heart,
Some rival there has stol'n a part;
Reason these fears may disapprove:
But yet I fear, because I love.

#### DELIA.

First tell me, Damon, why to day
At Belvidera's feet you lay?
Why with such warmth her charms you prais'd,
And every trifling beauty rais'd,
As if you meant to let me see
Your flattery is not all for me?
Alas! too well your sex I knew,
Nor was so weak to think you true.

### DAMON.

Unkind ! my falsehood to upbraid,
When your own orders I obey'd ;
You bid me try, by this deceit,
The notice of the world to cheat,
And hide, beneath another name,
The secret of our mutual flame.

### DELIA.

Damon, your prudence I confess,
But let me wish it had been less ;
Too well the lover's part you play'd,
With too much art your court you made ;
Had it been only art, your eyes
Would not have join'd in the disguise.

### DAMON.

Ah ! cease thus idly to molest
With groundless fears thy virgin breast.
While thus at fancied wrongs you grieve,
To me a real pain you give.

### DELIA.

Though well I might your truth distrust,
My foolish heart believes you just :
Reason this faith may disapprove ;
But I believe, because I love.

## ODE.

IN IMITATION OF PASTOR FIDO.

(O primavera gioventu del anno.)

WRITTEN ABROAD IN 1729.

Parent of blooming flowers and gay desires,
Youth of the tender year, delightful Spring,
At whose approach, inspir'd with equal fires,
The amorous nightingale and poet sing !

Again dost thou return, but not with thee
Return the smiling hours I once possest ;
Blessings thou bring'st to others, but to me
The sad remembrance that I once was blest.

Thy faded charms, which Winter snatch'd away,
Renew'd in all their former lustre shine ;
But, ah ! no more shall hapless I be gay,
Or know the vernal joys that have been mine.

Though linnets sing, though flowers adorn the green,
Though on their wings soft Zephyrs fragrance bear:
Harsh is the music, joyless is the scene,
The odour faint : for Delia is not there.

Cheerless and cold I feel the genial Sun,
From thee while absent I in exile rove ;
Thy lovely presence, fairest light, alone
Can warm my heart to gladness and to love.

## PARTS OF AN ELEGY OF TIBULLUS.

TRANSLATED, 1729-30.

(Divitias alius fulvo sibi congerat auro.)

Let others heap of wealth a shining store,
And, much possessing, labour still for more ;
Let them, disquieted with dire alarms,
Aspire to win a dangerous fame in arms :

VOL. XIV.

Me tranquil poverty shall lull to rest,
Humbly secure, and indolently blest ;
Warm'd by the blaze of my own cheerful hearth,
I' ll waste the wintry hours in social mirth ;
In summer pleas'd attend to harvest toils,
In autumn press the vineyard's purple spoils,
And oft to Delia in my bosom bear
Some 'kid, or lamb, that wants its mother's care :
With her I 'll celebrate each gladsome day,
When swains their sportive rites to Bacchus pay :
With her new milk on Pales' altar pour,
And deck with ripen'd fruits Pomona's bower.
At night, how soothing would it be to hear,
Safe in her arms, the tempest howling near ;
Or, while the wintry clouds their deluge pour,
Slumber, assisted by the beating shower!
Ah! how much happier, than the fool who braves,
In search of wealth, the black tempestuous waves!
While I, contented with my little store,
In tedious voyage seek no distant shore ;
But, idly lolling on some shady seat,
Near cooling fountains shun the dog-star's heat :
For what reward so rich could Fortune give,
That I by absence should my Delia grieve?
Let great Messalla shine in martial toils,
And grace his palace with triumphal spoils ;
Me Beauty holds, in strong though gentle chains,
Far from tumultuous war and dusty plains.
With thee, my love, to pass my tranquil days,
How would I slight Ambition's painful praise !
How would I joy with thee, my love, to yoke
The ox, and feed my solitary flock !
On thy soft breast might I but lean my head,
How downy should I think the woodland bed !
The wretch, who sleeps not by his fair-one's
side,
Detests the gilded couch's useless pride,
Nor knows his weary weeping eyes to close,
Though murmuring rills invite him to repose.
Hard were his heart, who thee, my fair, could leave
For all the honours prosperous war can give ;
Though through the vanquish'd East he spread his
fame,
And Parthian tyrants tremble at his name ;
Though, bright in arms, while hosts around him bleed,
With martial pride he prest his foaming steed.
No pomps like these my humble vows require ;
With thee I 'll live, and in thy arms expire.
Thee may my closing eyes in death behold !
Thee may my faultering hand yet strive to hold !
Then, Delia, then, thy heart will melt in woe,
Then o'er my breathless clay thy tears will flow ;
Thy tears will flow, for gentle is thy mind,
Nor dost thou think it weakness to be kind.
But, ah ! fair mourner, I conjure thee, spare
Thy heaving breasts and loose dishevell'd hair :
Wound not thy form ; lest on th' Elysian coast
Thy anguish should disturb my peaceful ghost.
But now nor death nor parting should employ
Our sprightly thoughts, or damp our bridal joy :
We 'll live, my Delia ; and from life remove
All care, all business, but delightful love.
Old age in vain those pleasures would retrieve
Which youth alone can taste, alone can give :
Then let us snatch the moment to be blest,
This hour is Love's—be Fortune's all the rest.

N

### SONG.

WRITTEN IN THE YEAR 1732.

SAY, Myra, why is gentle love
  A stranger to that mind,
Which pity and esteem can move,
  Which can be just and kind?

Is it, because you fear to share
  The ills that love molest;
The jealous doubt, the tender care,
  That rack the amorous breast?

Alas! by some degree of woe
  We every bliss must gain:
The heart can ne'er a transport know,
  That never feels a pain.

### VERSES,

WRITTEN AT MR. POPE'S HOUSE AT TWICKENHAM, WHICH
HE HAD LENT TO MRS. GREVILLE.

IN AUGUST 1735.

GO, Thames, and tell the busy town,
  Not all its wealth or pride
Could tempt me from the charms that crown
  Thy rural flowery side:

Thy flowery side, where Pope has plac'd
  The Muses' green retreat,
With every smile of Nature grac'd,
  With every art complete.

But now, sweet bard, thy heavenly song
  Enchants us here no more;
Their darling glory lost too long
  Thy once-lov'd shades deplore.

Yet still, for beauteous Greville's sake,
  The Muses here remain;
Greville, whose eyes have power to make
  A Pope of every swain.

### EPIGRAM.

NONE without hope e'er lov'd the brightest fair:
But Love can hope, where Reason would despair.

### TO MR. WEST, AT WICKHAM[1].

WRITTEN IN THE YEAR 1740.

FAIR Nature's sweet simplicity,
  With elegance refin'd,
Well in thy seat, my friend, I see,
  But better in thy mind.

[1] See the Inscriptions in Mr. West's Poems.

To both, from courts and all their state,
  Eager I fly, to prove
Joys far above a courtier's fate,
  Tranquillity and love.

### TO MISS LUCY FORTESCUE.

ONCE, by the Muse alone inspir'd
  I sung my amorous strains:
No serious love my bosom fir'd;
  Yet every tender maid, deceiv'd,
The idly-mournful tale believ'd,
  And wept my fancied pains.

But Venus now, to punish me
  For having feign'd so well,
Has made my heart so fond of thee,
That not the whole Aonian choir
Can accents soft enough inspire,
  Its real flame to tell.

### TO THE SAME;

WITH HAMMOND'S ELEGIES.

ALL that of love can be express'd,
  In these soft numbers see;
But, Lucy, would you know the rest,
  It must be read in me.

### TO THE SAME.

To him who in an hour must die,
Not swifter seems that hour to fly,
Than slow the minutes seem to me,
Which keep me from the sight of thee.

Not more that trembling wretch would give,
Another day or year to live,
Than I to shorten what remains
Of that long hour which thee detains.

Oh! come to my impatient arms,
Oh! come, with all thy heavenly charms,
At once to justify and pay
The pain I feel from this delay.

### TO THE SAME.

To ease my troubled mind of anxious care,
  Last night the secret casket I explor'd,
Where all the letters of my absent fair
  His richest treasure careful love had stor'd.

In every word a magic spell I found
  Of power to charm each busy thought to rest;
Though every word increas'd the tender wound
  Of fond desire still throbbing in my breast.

So to his hoarded gold the miser steals,
  And loses every sorrow at the sight;
Yet wishes still for more, nor ever feels
  Entire contentment, or secure delight.

Ah! should I lose thee, my too lovely maid,
  Couldst thou forget thy heart was ever mine,
Fear not thy letters should the change upbraid;
  My hand each dear memorial shall resign:

Not one kind word shall in my power remain,
  A painful witness of reproach to thee;
And lest my heart should still their sense retain,
  My heart shall break, to leave thee wholly free.

---

### A PRAYER TO VENUS.

#### IN HER TEMPLE AT STOW.

#### TO THE SAME.

Fair Venus, whose delightful shrine surveys
  Its front reflected in the silver lake,
These humble offerings, which thy servant pays,
  Fresh flowers, and myrtle wreaths, propitious take.

If less my love exceeds all other love,
  Than Lucy's charms all other charms excel,
Far from my breast each soothing hope remove,
  And there let sad Despair for ever dwell.

But if my soul is fill'd with her alone;
  No other wish nor other object knows:
Oh! make her, goddess, make her all my own,
  And give my trembling heart secure repose!

No watchful spies I ask, to guard her charms,
  No walls of brass, no steel-defended door:
Place her but once within my circling arms,
  *Love's surest fort*, and I will doubt no more.

---

#### TO THE SAME.

#### ON HER PLEADING WANT OF TIME.

On Thames's bank, a gentle youth
For Lucy sigh'd, with matchless truth,
  Ev'n when he sigh'd in rhyme;
The lovely maid his flame return'd,
And would with equal warmth have burn'd,
  But that she had not time.

Oft he repair'd with eager feet
In secret shades his fair to meet,
  Beneath th' accustom'd lime:
She would have fondly met him there,
And heal'd with love each tender care,
  But that she had not time.

" It was not thus, inconstant maid!
You acted once," the shepherd said,
  " When love was in its prime:"
She griev'd to hear him thus complain;
And would have writ, to ease his pain,
  But that she had not time.

" How can you act so cold a part?
No crime of mine has chang'd your heart,
  If love be not a crime.—
We soon must part for months, for years"—
She would have answer'd with her tears,
  But that she had not time.

---

#### TO THE SAME.

Your shape, your lips, your eyes, are still the same,
Still the bright object of my constant flame;
But where is now the tender glance, that stole,
With gentle sweetness, my enchanted soul?
Kind fears, impatient wishes, soft desires,
Each melting charm that love alone inspires?
These, these are lost: and I behold no more
The maid my heart delighted to adore.
Yet, still unchang'd, still doating to excess,
I ought, but dare not try, to love you less;
Weakly I grieve, unpitied I complain;
But not unpunish'd shall your change remain;
For you, cold maid, whom no complaints can move,
Were far more blest, when you like me could love.

---

#### TO THE SAME.

When I think on your truth, I doubt you no more,
I blame all the fears I gave way to before:
I say to my heart, " Be at rest, and believe
That whom once she has chosen she never will
    leave."

But, ah! when I think on each ravishing grace
That plays in the smiles of that heavenly face;
My heart beats again; I again apprehend
Some fortunate rival in every friend.

These painful suspicions you cannot remove,
Since you neither can lessen your charms nor my
    love;
But doubts caus'd by passion you never can blame;
For they are not ill founded, or you feel the same.

---

#### TO THE SAME.

#### WITH A NEW WATCH.

With me while present may thy lovely eyes
  Be never turn'd upon this golden toy:
Think every pleasing hour too swiftly flies;
  And measure time, by joy succeeding joy!

But when the cares that interrupt our bliss
  To me not always will thy sight allow;
Then oft with kind impatience look on this,
  Then every minute count—as I do now.

---

#### AN IRREGULAR ODE.

#### WRITTEN AT WICKHAM IN 1746.

#### TO THE SAME.

Ye sylvan scenes with artless beauty gay,
  Ye gentle shades of Wickham, say,
What is the charm that each successive year,
  Which sees me with my Lucy here,
    Can thus to my transported heart
A sense of joy unfelt before, impart?

Is it glad Summer's balmy breath, that blows
From the fair jasmine and the blushing rose?
Her balmy breath, and all her blooming store
Of rural bliss, was here before:
Oft have I met her on the verdant side
Of Norwood-hill, and in the yellow meads,
  Where Pan the dancing Graces leads,
  Array'd in all her flowery pride.
No sweeter fragrance now the gardens yield,
No brighter colours paint th' enamel'd field.

Is it to Love these new delights I owe?
  Four times has the revolving Sun
His annual circle through the zodiac run;
  Since all that Love's indulgent power
  On favour'd mortals can bestow,
Was given to me in this auspicious bower.

Here first my Lucy, sweet in virgin charms,
  Was yielded to my longing arms;
  And round our nuptial bed,
Hovering with purple wings, th' Idalian boy
Shook from his radiant torch the blissful fires
  Of innocent desires,
While Venus scatter'd myrtles o'er her head.
Whence then this strange increase of joy?
He, only he, can tell, who, match'd like me,
(If such another happy man there be)
  Has by his own experience tried
How much *the wife* is dearer than *the bride*.

TO THE

## MEMORY OF THE SAME LADY.

A MONODY.   A. D. 1747.

Ipse cavà solans ægrum testudine amorem,
Te dulcis conjux, te solo in littore secum,
Te veniente die, te decedente canebat.

At length escap'd from every human eye,
  From every duty, every care,
That in my mournful thoughts might claim a share,
Or force my tears their flowing stream to dry;
Beneath the gloom of this embowering shade,
This lone retreat, for tender sorrow made,
I now may give my burden'd heart relief,
  And pour forth all my stores of grief;
Of grief surpassing every other woe,
Far as the purest bliss, the happiest love
Can on th' ennobled mind bestow,
Exceeds the vulgar joys that move
Our gross desires, inelegant and low.

Ye tufted groves, ye gently-falling rills,
  Ye high o'ershadowing hills,
Ye lawns gay-smiling with eternal green,
  Oft have you my Lucy seen!
But never shall you now behold her more:
  Nor will she now with fond delight
And taste refin'd your rural charms explore.
Clos'd are those beauteous eyes in endless night,
Those beauteous eyes where beaming us'd to shine
Reason's pure light and Virtue's spark divine.

Oft would the Dryads of these woods rejoice.
  To hear her heavenly voice;

For her despising, when she deign'd to sing,
  The sweetest songsters of the spring:
The woodlark and the linnet pleas'd no more;
  The nightingale was mute,
  And every shepherd's flute
  Was cast in silent scorn away,
While all attended to her sweeter lay.
Ye larks and linnets, now resume your song,
  And thou, melodious Philomel,
  Again thy plaintive story tell;
For Death has stopt that tuneful tongue,
Whose music could alone your warbling notes excel.

  In vain I look around
  O'er all the well-known ground,
My Lucy's wonted footsteps to descry;
  Where oft we us'd to walk,
  Where oft in tender talk
We saw the summer Sun go down the sky;
  Nor by yon fountain's side,
  Nor where its waters glide
Along the valley, can she now be found:
In all the wide-stretch'd prospect's ample bound
  No more my mournful eye
  Can aught of her espy,
But the sad sacred earth where her dear relics lie.

O shades of Hagley, where is now your boast?
Your bright inhabitant is lost.
You she preferr'd to all the gay resorts
Where female vanity might wish to shine,
The pomp of cities, and the pride of courts.
Her modest beauties shunn'd the public eye:
  To your sequester'd dales
  And flower embroider'd vales
From an admiring world she chose to fly:
With Nature there retir'd, and Nature's God,
  The silent paths of wisdom trod,
And banish'd every passion from her breast,
  But those, the gentlest and the best,
Whose holy flames with energy divine
The virtuous heart enliven and improve,
The conjugal and the maternal love.

Sweet babes, who, like the little playful fawns,
Were wont to trip along these verdant lawns
  By your delighted mother's side,
Who now your infant steps shall guide?
Ah! where is now the hand whose tender care
To every virtue would have form'd your youth,
And strew'd with flowers the thorny ways of
    truth?
  O loss beyond repair!
  O wretched father! left alone,
To weep their dire misfortune, and thy own!
How shall thy weaken'd mind, oppress'd with woe,
  And drooping o'er thy Lucy's grave,
Perform the duties that you doubly owe!
  Now she, alas! is gone,
From folly and from vice their helpless age to save?

Where were ye, Muses, when relentless Fate
From these fond arms your fair disciple tore;
  From these fond arms, that vainly strove
  With hapless ineffectual love
To guard her bosom from the mortal blow?
  Could not your favouring power, Aonian
    maids,
Could not, alas! your power prolong her date,
For whom so oft in these inspiring shades,

Or under Camden's moss-clad mountains hoar,
  You open'd all your sacred store,
  Whate'er your ancient sages taught,
  Your ancient bards sublimely thought,
And bade her raptur'd breast with all your spirit
    glow?

  Nor then did Pindus or Castalia's plain,
  Or Aganippe's fount your steps detain,
  Nor in the Thespian vallies did you play;
    Nor then on Mincio's bank [1]
    Beset with osiers dank,
  Nor where Clitumnus [2] rolls his gentle stream,
  Nor where through hanging woods,
  Steep Anio [3] pours his floods,
  Nor yet where Meles [4] or Ilissus [5] stray.
    Ill does it now beseem,
    That, of your guardian care bereft,
To dire disease and death your darling should be left.

  Now what avails it that in early bloom,
    When light fantastic toys
    Are all her sex's joys,    [Rome ;
  With you she search'd the wit of Greece and
  And all that in her latter days
    To emulate her ancient praise
  Italia's happy genius could produce;
    Or what the Gallic fire
    Bright sparkling could inspire,
  By all the Graces temper'd and refin'd;
    Or what in Britain's isle,
  Most favour'd with your smile,
  The powers of Reason and of Fancy join'd
  To full perfection have conspir'd to raise?
    Ah! what is now the use
  Of all these treasures that enrich'd her mind,
To black Oblivion's gloom for ever now consign'd.

  At least, ye Nine, her spotless name
    'Tis yours from death to save,
  And in the temple of immortal Fame
  With golden characters her worth engrave.
    Come then, ye virgin sisters, come,
  And strew with choicest flowers her hallow'd tomb:
  But foremost thou, in sable vestment clad,
    With accents sweet and sad,
  Thou, plaintive Muse, whom o'er his Laura's urn
    Unhappy Petrarch call'd to mourn;
  O come, and to this fairer Laura pay
A more impassion'd tear, a more pathetic lay.

  Tell how each beauty of her mind and face
  Was brighten'd by some sweet peculiar grace!
    How eloquent in every look    (spoke!
  Through her expressive eyes her soul distinctly
  Tell how her manners, by the world refin'd,
  Left all the taint of modish Vice behind,

[1] The Mintio runs by Mantua, the birth place of Virgil.

[2] The Clitumnus is a river of Umbria, the residence of Propertius.

[3] The Anio runs through Tibur or Tivoli, where Horace had a villa.

[4] The Meles is a river of Ionia, from whence Homer, supposed to be born on its banks, is called Melisigenes.

The Ilissus is a river at Athens.

And made each charm of polish'd courts agree
  With candid Truth's simplicity,
  And uncorrupted Innocence!
  Tell how to more than manly sense
    She join'd the softening influence
    Of more than female tenderness:
  How, in the thoughtless days of wealth and
    joy,
  Which oft the care of others' good destroy,
    Her kindly-melting heart,
    To every want and every woe,
    To guilt itself when in distress,
    The balm of pity would impart,
  And all relief that bounty could bestow!
  Ev'n for the kid or lamb that pour'd its life
    Beneath the bloody knife,
    Her gentle tears would fall,
Tears from sweet Virtue's source, benevolent to
    all.

    Not only good and kind,
  But strong and elevated was her mind:
    A spirit that with noble pride
    Could look superior down
    On Fortune's smile or frown;
  That could without regret or pain
    To Virtue's lowest duty sacrifice
  Or Interest or Ambition's highest prize;
  That, injur'd or offended, never tried
    Its dignity by vengeance to maintain,
    But by magnanimous disdain.
  A wit that, temperately bright,
    With inoffensive light
    All pleasing shone; nor ever past
  The decent bounds that Wisdom's sober hand,
  And sweet Benevolence's mild command,
  And bashful Modesty, before it cast.
  A prudence undeceiving, undeceiv'd,
  That nor too little nor too much believ'd,
  That scorn'd unjust Suspicion's coward fear,
  And without weakness knew to be sincere.
  Such Lucy was, when, in her fairest days,
  Amidst th' acclaim of universal praise,
    In life's and glory's freshest bloom,
Death came remorseless on, and sunk her to the
    tomb.

  So, where the silent streams of Liris glide,
  In the soft bosom of Campania's vale,
  When now the wintry tempests all are fled,
  And genial Summer breathes her gentle gale,
  The verdant orange lifts its beauteous head:
  From every branch the balmy flowerets rise,
  On every bough the golden fruits are seen;
  With odours sweet it fills the smiling skies,
  The wood-nymphs tend, and th' Idalian queen.
  But, in the midst of all its blooming pride,
    A sudden blast from Apenninus blows,
    Cold with perpetual snows:
The tender blighted plant shrinks up its leaves, and
    dies.

  Arise, O Petrarch, from th' Elysian bowers,
    With never-fading myrtles twin'd,
    And fragrant with ambrosial flowers,
  Where to thy Laura thou again art join'd;
  Arise, and hither bring the silver lyre,
    Tun'd by thy skilful hand,
    To the soft notes of elegant desire,
    With which o'er many a land

Was spread the fame of thy disastrous love;
To me resign the vocal shell,
And teach my sorrows to relate
Their melancholy tale so well,
As may ev'n things inanimate,
Rough mountain oaks and desert rocks, to pity move.

What were, alas! thy woes compar'd to mine?
To thee thy mistress in the blissful band
Of Hymen never gave her hand;
The joys of wedded love were never thine:
In thy domestic care
She never bore a share,
Nor with endearing art
Would heal thy wounded heart
Of every secret grief that fester'd there:
Nor did her fond affection on the bed
Of sickness watch thee, and thy languid head
Whole nights on her unwearied arm sustain,
And charm away the sense of pain:
Nor did she crown your mutual flame
With pledges dear, and with a father's tender name.

O best of wives! O dearer far to me
Than when thy virgin charms
Were yielded to my arms,
How can my soul endure the loss of thee?
How in the world, to me a desert grown,
Abandon'd and alone,
Without my sweet companion can I live?
Without thy lovely smile,
The dear reward of every virtuous toil,
What pleasures now can pall'd Ambition give?
Ev'n the delightful sense of well-earn'd praise,
Unshar'd by thee, no more my lifeless thoughts
could raise.

For my distracted mind
What succour can I find?
On whom for consolation shall I call?
Support me, every friend;
Your kind assistance lend,
To bear the weight of this oppressive woe.
Alas! each friend of mine,
My dear departed love, so much was thine,
That none has any comfort to bestow.
My books, the best relief
In every other grief,
Are now with your idea sadden'd all:
Each favourite author we together read
My tortur'd memory wounds, and speaks of Lucy
dead.

We were the happiest pair of human kind:
The rolling year its varying course perform'd,
And back return'd again;
Another and another smiling came,
And saw our happiness unchang'd remain:
Still in her golden chain
Harmonious Concord did our wishes bind:
Our studies, pleasures, taste, the same.
O fatal, fatal stroke,
That all this pleasing fabric Love had rais'd
Of rare felicity,
On which ev'n wanton Vice with envy gaz'd,
And every scheme of bliss our hearts had form'd,
With soothing hope, for many a future day,
In one sad moment broke!—
Yet, O my soul, thy rising murmurs stay;

Nor dare the all-wise Disposer to arraign,
Or against his supreme decree
With impious grief complain.
That all thy full blown joys at once should fade;
Was his most righteous will—and be that will obey'd.

Would thy fond love his grace to her control,
And in these low abodes of sin and pain
Her pure exalted soul
Unjustly for thy partial good detain?
No—rather strive thy groveling mind to raise
Up to that unclouded blaze,
That heavenly radiance of eternal light,
In which enthron'd she now with pity sees
How frail, how insecure, how slight,
Is every mortal bliss;
Ev'n love itself, if rising by degrees
Beyond the bounds of this imperfect state,
Whose fleeting joys so soon must end,
It does not to its sovereign good ascend.
Rise then, my soul, with hope elate,
And seek those regions of serene delight,
Whose peaceful path and ever-open gate
No feet but those of harden'd Guilt shall miss,
There Death himself thy Lucy shall restore,
There yield up all his power ne'er to divide you more.

---

### ON THE SAME LADY,

To the
Memory of Lucy Lyttelton,
Daughter of Hugh Fortescue of Filleigh
In the county of Devon, esq.
Father to the present earl of Clinton,
By Lucy his wife,
The daughter of Matthew lord Aylmer,
Who departed this life the 19th of Jan. 1746-7,
Aged twenty-nine,
Having employed the short time assigned to
her here
In the uniform practice of religion and virtue.

Made to engage all hearts, and charm all eyes;
Though meek, magnanimous; though witty, wise;
Polite, as all her life in courts had been;
Yet good, as she the world had never seen;
The noble fire of an exalted mind,
With gentle female tenderness combin'd.
Her speech was the melodious voice of Love,
Her song the warbling of the vernal grove;
Her eloquence was sweeter than her song,
Soft as her heart, and as her reason strong;
Her form each beauty of her mind express'd,
Her mind was Virtue by the Graces dress'd.

---

### HORACE. BOOK IV, ODE IV.

WRITTEN AT OXFORD 1725 [1].

Qualem ministrum fulminis alitem, &c,

As the wing'd minister of thundering Jove,
To whom he gave his dreadful bolts to bear,
Faithful assistant [2] of his master's love,
King of the wandering nations of the air,

[1] First printed with Mr. West's translation of
Pindar. See the preface to that gentleman's
poems.

[2] In the rape of Ganymede, who was carried up

When balmy breezes fann'd the vernal sky,
  On doubtful pinions left his parent nest,
In slight essays his growing force to try,
  While inborn courage fir'd his generous breast;

Then, darting with impetuous fury down,
  The flocks he slaughter'd, an unpractis'd foe;
Now his ripe valour to perfection grown
  The scaly snake and crested dragon know:

Or, as a lion's youthful progeny,
  Wean'd from his savage dam and milky food,
The gazing kid beholds with fearful eye,
  Doom'd first to stain his tender fangs in blood:

Such Drusus, young in arms, his foes beheld,
  The Alpine Rhæti, long unmatch'd in fight:
So were their hearts with abject terrour quell'd;
  So sunk their haughty spirit at the sight.

Tam'd by a boy, the fierce barbarians find
  How guardian Prudence guides the youthful flame,
And how great Cæsar's fond paternal mind
  Each generous Nero forms to early fame;

A valiant son springs from a valiant sire:
  Their race by mettle sprightly coursers prove;
Nor can the warlike eagle's active fire
  Degenerate to form the timorous dove.

But education can the genius raise,
  And wise instructions native virtue aid;
Nobility without them is disgrace,
  And honour is by vice to shame betray'd.

Let red Metaurus, stain'd with Punic blood,
  Let mighty Asdrubal subdued, confess
How much of empire and of fame is ow'd
  By thee, O Rome, to the Neronian race.

Of this be witness that auspicious day,
  Which, after a long, black, tempestuous night,
First smil'd on Latium with a milder ray,  [light.
  And cheer'd our drooping hearts with dawning

Since the dire African with wasteful ire
  Rode o'er the ravag'd towns of Italy;
As through the pine-trees flies the raging fire,
  Or Eurus o'er the vext Sicilian sea.

From this bright era, from this prosperous field,
  The Roman glory dates her rising power;
From hence 'twas given her conq'ering sword to wield,
  Raise her fall'n gods, and ruin'd shrines restore.

Thus Hannibal at length despairing spoke:
  " Like stags to ravenous wolves an easy prey,
Our feeble arms a valiant foe provoke,
  Whom to elude and 'scape were victory:

" A dauntless nation, that from Trojan fires,
  Hostile Ausonia, to thy destin'd shore
Her gods, her infant sons, and aged sires,
  Through angry seas and adverse tempests bore:

" As on high Algidas the sturdy oak,
  Whose spreading boughs the axe's sharpness feel,
Improves by loss, and, thriving with the stroke,
  Draws health and vigour from the wounding steel.

to Jupiter by an eagle, according to the Poetical History.

" Not Hydra sprouting from her mangled head
  So tir'd the baffled force of Hercules;
Nor Thebes, nor Colchis, such a monster bred,
  Pregnant of hills, and fam'd for prodigies.

" Plunge her in ocean, like the morning Sun,
  Brighter she rises from the depths below:
To earth with unavailing ruin thrown,
  Recruits her strength, and foils the wondering foe.

" No more of victory the joyful fame
  Shall from my camp to haughty Carthage fly;
Lost, lost, are all the glories of her name!
  With Asdrubal her hopes and fortune die!

" What shall the Claudian valour not perform
  Which Power Divine guards with propitious care,
Which Wisdom steers through all the dangerous storm,  [war?"
  Through all the rocks and shoals of doubtful

## VIRTUE AND FAME.

TO THE COUNTESS OF EGREMONT.

Virtue and Fame, the other day,
Happen'd to cross each other's way;
Said Virtue, " Hark ye! madam Fame,
Your ladyship is much to blame;
Jove bids you always wait on me,
And yet your face I seldom see:
The Paphian queen employs your trumpet,
And bids it praise some handsome strumpet;
Or, thundering through the ranks of war,
Ambition ties you to her car."
Saith Fame, " Dear madam, I protest,
I never find myself so blest
As when I humbly wait behind you!
But 'tis so mighty hard to find you!
In such obscure retreats you lurk!
To seek you is an endless work."
  " Well,", answer'd Virtue, " I allow
Your plea. But hear, and mark me now.
I know (without offence to others)
I know the best of wives and mothers;
Who never pass'd an useless day
In scandal, gossiping, or play:
Whose modest wit, chastis'd by sense,
Is lively cheerful innocence;
Whose heart nor envy knows, nor spite,
Whose duty is her sole delight;
Nor rul'd by whim, nor slave to fashion,
Her parents' joy, her husband's passion."
  Fame smil'd and answer'd, " On my life,
This is some country parson's wife,
Who never saw the court nor town,
Whose face is homely as her gown;
Who banquets upon eggs and bacon—"
  " No, madam, no—you're much mistaken—
I beg you'll let me set you right—
'Tis one with every beauty bright;
Adorn'd with every polish'd art
That rank or fortune can impart:
'Tis the most celebrated toast
That Britain's spacious isle can boast;
'Tis princely Petworth's noble dame;
'Tis Egremont—Go, tell it, Fame."

### ADDITION, EXTEMPORE,

#### BY EARL HARDWICKE.

FAME heard with pleasure—straight replied,
" First on my roll stands Wyndham's bride;
My trumpet oft I 've rais'd, to sound
Her modest praise the world around !
But notes were wanting—Canst thou find
A Muse to sing her face, her mind ?
Believe me, I can name but one,
A friend of yours—'tis Lyttelton."[1]

#### LETTER TO EARL HARDWICKE:

##### OCCASIONED BY THE FOREGOING VERSES.

##### MY LORD,

A THOUSAND thanks to your lordship for your addition to my verses. If you can write such *extempore*, it is well for other poets, that you chose to be lord chancellor, rather than laureat. They explain to me a vision I had the night before.

Methought I saw before my feet,
With countenance serene and sweet,
The Muse, who, in my youthful days,
Had oft inspir'd my careless lays.
She smil'd, and said, " Once more I see
My fugitive returns to me ;
Long had I lost you from my bower,
You scorn'd to own my gentle power ;
With me no more your genius sported,
The grave historic Muse you courted ;
Or, rais'd from Earth, with straining eyes ;
Pursued Urania through the skies;
But now, to my forsaken track,
Fair Egremont has brought you back :
Nor blush, by her and Virtue led,
That soft, that pleasing path, to tread ;
For there, beneath to morrow's ray,
Ev'n Wisdom's self shall deign to play.
Lo ! to my flowery groves and springs
Her favourite son the goddess brings,
The council's and the senate's guide,
Law's oracle, the nation's pride :
He comes, he joys with thee to join,
In singing Wyndham's charms divine :
To thine he adds his nobler lays ;
Ev'n thee, my friend, he deigns to praise,
Enjoy that praise, nor envy Pitt
His fame with burgess or with cit ;
For sure one line from such a bard,
Virtue would think her best reward."

### HYMEN TO ELIZA.

MADAM, before your feet I lay
This ode upon your wedding-day,
The first indeed I ever made,
For writing odes is not my trade :
My head is full of household cares,
And necessary dull affairs;
Besides that sometimes jealous frumps
Will put me into doleful dumps.
And then no clown beneath the sky
Was e'er more ungallant than I ;

For you alone I now think fit
To turn a poet and a wit—
For you whose charms, I know not how,
Have power to smooth my wrinkled brow,
And make me, though by nature stupid,
As brisk, and as alert, as Cupid.
These obligations to repay,
Whene'er your happy nuptial day
Shall with the circling years return,
For you my torch shall brighter burn
Than when you first my power ador'd,
Nor will I call myself your lord,
But am, (as witness this my hand)
Your humble servant at command.

HYMEN.

Dear child, let Hymen not beguile
You, who are such a judge of style,
To think that he these verses made,
Without an abler penman's aid ;
Observe them well, you 'll plainly see,
That every line was writ by me.

CUPID.

### ON

### READING MISS CARTER'S POEMS

#### IN MANUSCRIPT.

SUCH were the notes that struck the wondering ear
Of silent Night, when, on the verdant banks
Of Siloë's hallow'd brook, celestial harps,
According to seraphic voices, sung
*Glory to God on high, and on the earth*
*Peace and good-will to men !*—Resume the lyre,
Chauntress divine, and every Briton call
Its melody to hear—so shall thy strains,
More powerful than the song of Orpheus, tame
The savage heart of brutal Vice, and bend
At pure Religion's shrine the stubborn knees
Of bold Impiety.—Greece shall no more
Of Lesbian Sappho boast, whose wanton Muse,
Like a false Syren, while she charm'd, seduc'd
To guilt and ruin. For the sacred head
Of Britain's poetess, the Virtues twine
A nobler wreath, by them from Eden's grove
Unfading gather'd, and direct the hand
Of —— to fix it on her brows.

### MOUNT EDGECUMBE.

THE gods, on thrones celestial seated,
By Jove, with bowls of nectar heated,
All on Mount Edgecumbe turn'd their eyes ;
" That place is mine," great Neptune cries ;
" Behold ! how proud o'er all the main
Those stately turrets seem to reign !
No views so grand on Earth you see !
The master too belongs to me :
I grant him my domain to share,
I bid his hand my trident bear."
" The sea is your's, but mind the land,"
Pallas replies ; " by me were plann'd
Those towers, that hospital, those docks,
That fort, which crowns those island rocks:
The lady too is of my choir,
I taught her hand to touch the lyre ;

With every charm her mind I grac'd,
I gave her prudence, knowledge, taste."
" Hold, madam," interrupted Venus,
" The lady must be shar'd between us:
And surely mine is yonder grove,
So fine, so dark, so fit for love.;
Trees, such as in th' Idalian glade,
Or Cyprian lawn, my palace shade."
   Then Oreads, Dryads, Naiads, came ;
Each nymph alleg'd her lawful claim.
   But Jove, to finish the debate,
Thus spoke, and what he speaks is fate:
" Nor god nor goddess, great or small,
That dwelling his or her's may call;
I made Mount Edgecumbe for you all."

---

## INVITATION.

##### TO THE DOWAGER DUTCHESS D'AIGUILLON.

WHEN Peace shall, on her downy wing,
To France and England Friendship bring,
Come, Aiguillon, and here receive
That homage we delight to give
To foreign talents, foreign charms,
To worth which Envy's self disarms
Of jealous hatred : come and love
That nation which you now approve.
So shall by France amends be made
(If such a debt can e'er be paid)
For having with seducing art
From Britain stol'n her Hervey's heart.

---

### TO
## COLONEL DRUMGOLD.

DRUMGOLD, whose ancestors from Albion's shore
Their conquering standards to Hibernia bore,
Though now thy valour, to thy country lost,
Shines in the foremost ranks of Gallia's host,
Think not that France shall borrow all thy fame—
From British sires deriv'd thy genius came:
Its force, its energy, to these it ow'd,
But the fair polish Gallia's clime bestow'd:
The Graces there each ruder thought refin'd,
And liveliest wit with soundest sense combin'd.
They taught in sportive Fancy's gay attire
To dress the gravest of th' Aonian choir,
And gave to sober Wisdom's wrinkled cheek
The smile that dwells in Hebe's dimple sleek.
Pay to each realm the debt that each may ask:
Be thine, and thine alone, the pleasing task,
In purest elegance of Gallic phrase
To clothe the spirit of the British lays.
Thus every flower which every Muse's hand
Has rais'd profuse in Britain's favourite land,
By thee transplanted to the banks of Seine,
Its sweetest native odours shall retain.
And when thy noble friend, with olive crown'd,
In Concord's golden chain has firmly bound
The rival nations, thou for both shalt raise
The grateful song to his immortal praise.
Albion shall think she hears her Prior sing ;
And France, that Boileau strikes the tuneful string,

Then shalt thou tell what various talents join'd,
Adorn, embellish, and exalt his mind ;
Learning and wit, with sweet politeness grac'd ;
Wisdom by guile or cunning undebas'd ;
By pride unsullied, genuine dignity ;
A nobler and sublime simplicity.
Such in thy verse shall Nivernois be shown:
France shall with joy the fair resemblance own;
And Albion sighing bid her sons aspire
To imitate the merit they admire.

---

## EPITAPH ON CAPTAIN GRENVILLE[1] ;

#### KILLED IN LORD ANSON'S ENGAGEMENT IN 1747.

YE weeping Muses, Graces, Virtues, tell
If, since your all-accomplish'd Sydney fell,
You, or afflicted Britain, e'er deplor'd
A loss like that these plaintive lays record !
Such spotless honour ; such ingenuous truth;
Such ripen'd wisdom in the bloom of youth !
So mild, so gentle, so compos'd a mind,
To such heroic warmth and courage join'd ;
He too, like Sydney, nurs'd in Learning's arms,
For nobler War forsook her softer charms:
Like him, possess'd of every pleasing art,
The secret wish of every female's heart:
Like him, cut off in youthful glory's pride,
He, unrepining, *for his country dy'd*.

---

## ON GOOD-HUMOUR.

#### WRITTEN AT ETON-SCHOOL, 1729.

TELL me, ye sons of Phœbus, what is this
Which all admire, but few, too few, possess ?
A virtue 'tis to ancient maids unknown,
And prudes, who spy all faults except their own.
Lov'd and defended by the brave and wise,
Though knaves abuse it, and like fools despise.
Say, Wyndham, if 'tis possible to tell,
What is the thing in which you most excel ?
Hard is the question, for in all you please ;
Yet sure good-nature is your noblest praise ;
Secur'd by this, your parts no envy move,
For none can envy him whom all must love.
This magic power can make ev'n folly please,
This to Pitt's genius adds a brighter grace,
And sweetens every charm in Cælia's face.

[1] These verses having been originally written
when the author was in opposition, concluded thus,
(much better, perhaps, than at present):

But nobler far, and greater is the praise
So bright to shine in these degenerate days:
An age of heroes kindled Sidney's fire ;
His inborn worth alone could Grenville's deeds in-
spire.

But some years after, when his lordship was
with ministry, he erased these four lines. See
Gent. Mag. vol. xlix. p. 601.    N.

SOME ADDITIONAL STANZAS

TO

### ASTOLFO'S VOYAGE TO THE MOON,

IN ARIOSTO.

WHEN now Astolfo, stor'd within a vase,
　Orlando's wits had safely brought away;
He turn'd his eyes towards another place,
　Where, closely cork'd, unnumber'd bottles lay.

Of finest crystal were those bottles made,
　Yet what was there enclos'd he could not see:
Wherefore in humble wise the saint he pray'd,
　To tell what treasure there conceal'd might be.

" A wondrous thing it is," the saint replied,
　" Yet undefin'd by any mortal wight;
An airy essence, not to be descried,
　Subtle and thin, that MAIDENHEAD is hight.

" From Earth each day in troops they hither
　　come,
And fill each hole and corner of the Moon;
For they are never easy while at home,
　Nor ever owner thought them gone too soon.

" When here arriv'd, they are in bottles pent,
　For fear they should evaporate again;
And hard it is a prison to invent,
　So volatile a spirit to retain.

" Those that to young and wanton girls belong
　Leap, bounce, and fly, as if they 'd burst the
　　glass:
But those that have below been kept too long
　Are spiritless, and quite decay'd, alas !"

So spake the saint, and wonder seiz'd the knight,
　As of each vessel he th' inscription read ;
For various secrets there were brought to light;
　Of which report on Earth had nothing said.

Virginities, that close confin'd he thought
　In t' other world, he found above the sky;
His sister's and his cousin's there were brought,
　Which made him swear, though good St. John
　　was by.

But much his wrath increas'd, when he espied
　That which was Chloe's once, his mistress dear:
" Ah, false and treacherous fugitive !" he cried,
　" Little I deem'd that I should meet thee here.

" Did not thy owner, when we parted last,
　Promise to keep safe for me alone ?
Scarce of our absence three short months are past,
　And thou already from thy post art flown.

" Be not enrag'd," replied th' apostle kind—
　" Since that this maidenhead is thine by right,
Take it away; and, when thou hast a mind,
　Carry it *thither* whence it took its flight."

" Thanks, holy father !" quoth the joyous knight,
　" The Moon shall be no loser by your grace :
Let me but have the use on 't for a night,
　And I 'll restore it to its present place."

### TO A YOUNG LADY.

WITH THE TRAGEDY OF VENICE PRESERVED.

IN tender Otway's moving scenes we find
What power the gods have to your sex assign'd :
Venice was lost, if on the brink of fate
A woman had not propt her sinking state :
In the dark danger of that dreadful hour,
Vain was her senate's wisdom, vain its power;
But, sav'd by Belvidera's charming tears,
Still o'er the subject main her towers she rears,
And stands a great example to mankind,
With what a boundless sway you rule the mind,
Skilful the worst or noblest ends to serve,
And strong alike to ruin or preserve.
　In wretched Jaffier, we with pity view
A mind, to honour false, to virtue true,
In the wild storm of struggling passions tost,
Yet saving innocence, though fame was lost;
Greatly forgetting what he ow'd his friend—
His country, which had wrong'd him, to defend.
But she, who urg'd him to that pious deed,
Who knew so well the patriot's cause to plead,
Whose conquering love her country's safety won,
Was, by that fatal love, herself undone.
[1] " Hence may we learn, what passion fain would
　hide,
That Hymen's bands by prudence should be tied,
Venus in vain the wedded pair would crown,
If angry Fortune on their union frown :
Soon will the flattering dreams of joys be o'er,
And cloy'd imagination cheat no more ;
Then, waking to the sense of lasting pain,
With mutual tears the bridal couch they stain :
And that fond love, which should afford relief,
Does but augment the anguish of their grief :
While both could easier their own sorrows bear,
Than the sad knowledge of each other's care."
　May all the joys in Love and Fortune's power
Kindly combine to grace your nuptial hour !
On each glad day may plenty shower delight,
And warmest rapture bless each welcome night !
May Heaven, that gave you Belvidera's charms,
Destine some happier Jaffier to your arms,
Whose bliss misfortune never may allay,
Whose fondness never may through care decay ;
Whose wealth may place you in the fairest light,
And force each modest beauty into sight !
So shall no anxious want your peace destroy,
No tempest crush the tender buds of joy ;
But all your hours in one gay circle move,
Nor Reason ever disagree with Love !

───────

### ELEGY.

TELL me, my heart, fond slave of hopeless love,
And doom'd its woes, without its joys to prove,
Canst thou endure thus calmly to erase
The dear, dear image of thy Delia's face?

[1] The twelve following lines, with some small
variations, already have been printed in Advice to
a Lady, p. 175; but, as lord Lyttelton chose to
introduce them here, it was thought more eligible
to repeat these few lines, than to suppress the rest
of the poem.

Canst thou exclude that habitant divine,
To place some meaner idol in her shrine ?
O task, for feeble reason too severe !
O lesson, nought could teach me but despair !
Must I forbid my eyes that heavenly sight,
They 've view'd so oft with languishing delight ?
Must my ears shun that voice, whose charming sound
Seem'd to relieve, while it increas'd, my wound ?
    O Waller ! Petrarch ! you who tun'd the lyre
To the soft notes of elegant desire ;
Though Sidney to a rival gave her charms,
Though Laura dying left her lover's arms,
Yet were your pains less exquisite than mine,
'Tis easier far to lose, than to resign !

---

## INSCRIPTION

### FOR A BUST OF LADY SUFFOLK ;

#### DESIGNED TO BE SET UP IN A WOOD AT STOWE.

#### 1732.

Her wit and beauty for a court were made :
But truth and goodness fit her for a shade.

---

## SULPICIA TO CERINTHUS,

### IN HER SICKNESS.

#### FROM TIBULLUS.

#### (SENT TO A FRIEND, IN A LADY'S NAME.)

Say, my Cerinthus, does thy tender breast
Feel the same feverish heats that mine molest ?
Alas ! I only wish for health again,
Because I think my lover shares my pain :
For what would health avail to wretched me,
If you could, unconcern'd, my illness see ?

---

#### SULPICIA TO CERINTHUS.

I 'm weary of this tedious dull deceit ;
Myself I torture, while the world I cheat :
Though Prudence bids me strive to guard my fame,
Love sees the low hypocrisy with shame ;
Love bids me all confess, and call thee mine,
Worthy my heart, as I am worthy thine :
Weakness for thee I will no longer hide ;
Weakness for thee is woman's noblest pride.

---

## CATO'S SPEECH TO LABIENUS,

### IN THE NINTH BOOK OF LUCAN.

#### (Quid quæri, Labiene, jubes, &c.)

What, Labienus, would thy fond desire,
Of horned Jove's prophetic shrine inquire ?
Whether to seek in arms a glorious doom,
Or basely live, and be a king in Rome ?
If life be nothing more than death's delay ;
If impious force can honest minds dismay,
Or probity may Fortune's frown disdain ;
If well to mean is all that virtue can ;
And right, dependant on itself alone,
Gains no addition from success ?—'Tis known :

Fix'd in my heart these constant truths I bear,
And Ammon cannot write them deeper there.
    Our souls, allied to God, within them feel
The secret dictates of the almighty will :
This is his voice, be this our oracle.
When first his breath the seeds of life instill'd,
All that we ought to know was then reveal'd.
Nor can we think the omnipresent mind
Has truth to Libya's desert sands confin'd,
There, known to few, obscur'd, and lost, to lie—
Is there a temple of the Deity,
Except earth, sea, and air, yon azure pole ;
And chief, his holiest shrine, the virtuous soul ?
Where'er the eye can pierce, the feet can move,
This wide, this boundless universe is Jove.
Let abject minds, that doubt because they fear,
With pious awe to juggling priests repair ;
I credit not what lying prophets tell—
Death is the only certain oracle.
Cowards and brave must die one destin'd hour—
This Jove has told ; he needs not tell us more.

---

## TO MR. GLOVER ;

### ON HIS POEM OF LEONIDAS.

#### WRITTEN IN THE YEAR 1734.

Go on, my friend, the noble task pursue,
And think thy genius is thy country's due ;
To vulgar wits inferior themes belong,
But liberty and virtue claim thy song.
Yet cease to hope, though grac'd with every charm,
The patriot verse will cold Britannia warm ;
Vainly thou striv'st our languid hearts to raise,
By great examples drawn from better days :
No longer we to Sparta's fame aspire,
What Sparta scorn'd, instructed to admire ;
Nurs'd in the love of wealth, and form'd to bend
Our narrow thoughts to that inglorious end :
No generous purpose can enlarge the mind,
No social care, no labour for mankind,
Where mean self-interest every action guides,
In camps commands, in cabinets presides ;
Where Luxury consumes the guilty store,
And bids the villain be a slave for more.
    Hence, wretched nation, all thy woes arise,
Avow'd corruption, licens'd perjuries,
Eternal taxes, treaties for a day,
Servants that rule, and senates that obey.
    O people, far unlike the Grecian race,
That deems a virtuous poverty disgrace,
That suffers public wrongs and public shame,
In council insolent, in action tame !
Say, what is now th' ambition of the great ?
Is it to raise their country's sinking state ;
Her load of debt to ease by frugal care,
Her trade to guard, her harass'd poor to spare ?
Is it, like honest Somers, to inspire
The love of laws, and freedom's sacred fire ?
Is it, like wise Godolphin, to sustain
The balanc'd world, and boundless power restrain ?
Or is the mighty aim of all their toil,
Only to aid the wreck, and share the spoil ?
On each relation, friend, dependant, pour,
With partial wantonness, the golden shower,
And, fenc'd by strong corruption, to despise
An injur'd nation's unavailing cries !

Rouze, Britons, rouze! if sense of shame be weak,
Let the loud voice of threatening danger speak.
Lo!, France, as Persia once, o'er every land
Prepares to stretch her all-oppressing hand.
Shall England sit regardless and sedate,
A calm spectatress of the general fate;
Or call forth all her virtue, and oppose,
Like valiant Greece, her own and Europe's foes?
O let us seize the moment in our power,
Our follies now have reach'd the fatal hour;
No later term the angry gods ordain;
This crisis lost, we shall be wise in vain.
  And thou, great poet, in whose nervous lines
The native majesty of freedom shines,
Accept this friendly praise; and let me prove
My heart not wholly void of public love;
Though not like thee I strike the sounding string
To notes which Sparta might have deign'd to sing,
But, idly sporting in the secret shade,
With tender trifles soothe some artless maid.

---

### TO WILLIAM PITT, ESQUIRE,

ON HIS LOSING HIS COMMISSION,

IN THE YEAR 1736.

Long had thy virtues mark'd thee out for fame,
Far, far superior to a cornet's name;
This generous Walpole saw, and griev'd to find
So mean a post disgrace that noble mind.
The servile standard from thy freeborn hand
He took, and bade thee lead the patriot band.

---

### PROLOGUE TO THOMSON'S CORIOLANUS.

SPOKEN BY MR. QUIN.

I come not here your candour to implore.
For scenes, whose author is, alas! no more;
He wants no advocate his cause to plead;
You will yourselves be patrons of the dead.
No party his benevolence confin'd,
No sect—alike it flow'd to all mankind.
He lov'd his friends (forgive this gushing tear:
Alas! I feel I am no actor here)
He lov'd his friends with such a warmth of heart,
So clear of interest, so devoid of art,
Such generous friendship, such unshaken zeal,
No words can speak it: but our tears may tell.—
O candid truth, O faith without a stain,
O manners gently firm, and nobly plain,
O sympathizing love of others' bliss,
Where will you find another breast like his?
Such was the man—the poet well you know:
Oft has he touch'd your hearts with tender woe:
Oft in this crowded house, with just applause,
You heard him teach fair Virtue's purest laws;
For his chaste Muse employ'd her heaven-taught lyre
None but the noblest passions to inspire,
Not one immoral, one corrupted thought,
One line, which dying he could wish to blot.
 Oh! may to-night your favourable doom
Another laurel add, to grace his tomb:
Whilst he, superior now to praise or blame,
Hears not the feeble voice of human fame.

Yet, if to those whom most on Earth he lov'd,
From whom his pious care is now remov'd,
With whom his liberal hand, and bounteous heart,
Shar'd all his little fortune could impart;
If to those friends your kind regard shall give
What they no longer can from his receive;
That, that, ev'n now, above yon starry pole,
May touch with pleasure his immortal soul.

---

### EPILOGUE TO LILLO'S ELMERICK.

You, who, supreme o'er every work of wit,
In judgment here, unaw'd, unbiass'd, sit,
The *palatines* and guardians of the pit;
If to your minds this merely modern play
No useful sense, no generous warmth convey;
If *fustian* here, through each unnatural scene,
In *strain'd* conceits *sound high*, and *nothing mean* ;
If *lofty dullness* for your vengeance call:
Like *Elmerick* judge, and let *the guilty fall*.
But if simplicity, with force and fire,
Unlabour'd thoughts and artless words inspire:
If, like the action which these scenes relate,
The whole appear irregularly great;
If master-strokes the nobler passions move;
Then, like the *king, acquit* us, and *approve*.

---

### INSCRIPTIONS AT HAGLEY.

---

I.

ON A VIEW FROM AN ALCOVE.

........................... VIRIDANTIA TEMPE!
TEMPE, QVAE SYLVAE CINGVNT SVPERIMPENDENTES.

---

II.

ON A ROCKY FANCY SEAT.

........................... EGO LAVDO RVRIS AMOENI,
RIVOS, ET MVSCO CIRVMLITA SAXA NEMVSQVE.

---

III.

TO THE MEMORY OF
WILLIAM SHENSTONE, ESQUIRE;
IN WHOSE VERSES
WERE ALL THE NATURAL GRACES,
AND IN WHOSE MANNERS
WAS ALL THE AMIABLE SIMPLICITY,
OF PASTORAL POETRY,
WITH THE SWEET TENDERNESS
OF THE ELEGIAC.

---

IV.

ON THE PEDESTAL OF AN URN [1].

ALEXANDRO POPE;
POETARVM ANGLICANORVM
ELEGANTISSIMO DVLCISSIMOQVE;

[1] A Doric portico in another part of the park is honoured with the name of Pope's Building, and inscribed, QVIETI ET MVSIS.

VIRORVM CASTIGATORI ACERRIMO,
SAPIENTIAE DOCTORI SVAVISSIMO,
SACRA ESTO.
ANN. DOM. M.DCC.XLIV.

---

## V.

### ON A BENCH.

LIBET IACERE MODO SVB ANTIQVA ILICE,
MODO IN TENACE GRAMINE ;
LABVNTER ALTIS INTERIM RIVIS AQVAE ;
QVAERVNTVR IN SYLVIS AVES :
PONTESQVE LYMPHIS OBSTREPVNT MANANTIBVS
SOMNOS QVOD INVITET LEVES.

## VI.

### ON THOMSON'S SEAT [2].

INGENIO IMMORTALI
IACOBI THOMSON,
POETAE SVBLIMIS,
VIRI BONI ;
AEDICVLAM HANC, QVEM VIVVS DILEXIT,
POST MORTEM EIVS CONSTRVCTAM,
DICAT DEDICATQVE
GEORGIVS LYTTELTON.

[2] A very handsome and well-finished building, in an octagonal line.

# THE

# POEMS

OF

# *WALTER HARTE.*

# LIFE OF WALTER HARTE,

## BY MR. CHALMERS.

THE following desultory information, perhaps improperly called a life, is derived principally from the notes on Mr. Nicholls's collection of poems, augmented by various notices in the Gentleman's Magazine, the author's works, and the writings of his contemporaries. His learning and personal worth, neither of which have ever been called in question, would have procured him a more particular narrative, if it had been possible to recover the requisite materials.

His father the rev. Walter Harte was fellow of Pembroke College, Oxford, prebendary of Wales, canon of Bristol, and vicar of St. Mary Magdalen, Taunton, Somersetshire. Refusing to take the oaths after that revolution which placed a new family on the throne, he relinquished all his preferments, in 1691, and retired to Kentbury in Buckinghamshire, where he died February 10, 1736, aged eighty-five. His son informs us, that when judge Jefferies came to Taunton assizes in the year 1685, to execute his commission upon the unfortunate persons concerned in Monmouth's rebellion, Mr. Harte, then minister of St. Mary Magdalen's, waited on him in private, and remonstrated much against his severities. The judge listened to him calmly, and with some attention, and, though he had never seen him before, advanced him in a few months to a prebendal stall in the cathedral church of Bristol. " I thought," says Dr. Warton, who has introduced this story in his notes on Pope, " the reader might not dislike to hear this anecdote of Jefferies, the only one action of his life that I believe does him any credit."

Old Mr. Harte was so much respected for his piety and learning, that the prelates Kidder, Hooper, and Wynne, who successively filled the see of Bath and Wells, contrived that he should receive the profits of his prebend of Wells as long as he lived : and Mr. Simon Harco urt, afterwa the celebrated lord chancellor, offered him a bishopric in queen Anne's time, which he declined with grateful acknowledgements.   According  to  his  son's account,  he was  a most laborious student, employing ten or twelve hours  a day, without any interruption, but that of casual sickness, for fifty years successively.   His  principal  business was in re-ferring every difficult part  of scripture to those particular passages  in the fathers, and eminent modern divines, who had explained them expressly or  occasionally.

The time of our poet's birth has not been settled.   A writer  in the Gentleman's Magazine fixes it about  the  year 1707, but an  earlier date will correspond better with circumstances.   If he was born in  1707, his lines to lady Hertford must have been written at eleven, which is highly improbable;  yet there is some difficulty in adjusting the date of this poem.   In Lintot's  edition, it is subscribed September 30, 1725, but Francis, the late  marquis of  Hertford, was born in 1719, a year after his father's marriage, and when Mr. Harte, according to the  above account, could have been only eleven years  of age.   We have  his  own authority that all the poems published in  this volume  were  written when  he  was  under nineteen, consequently the date of 1725 must be an errour, especially if Collins's account of the Hertfort family be correct.   But here, too, there is something that requires ex-planation, for the title of Beauchamp was not conferred on the family for many years after the publication of these poems.

He received his education at Marlborough school, under the rev. Mr. Hildrop, to whom  he dedicates the few  divine  poems in the volume published in 1727.   At what time  he went to Oxford does  not appear, but he  took  his  master's degree June 30, 1720, according to the last edition  of  the graduates of that  university, a clear proof that he must have been  born  long before 1707.   With Pope he acquired  an  early intimacy, and shared rather more  of  his friendship than that poet was wont to bestow on his brethren.   Pope encouraged his  poetical enthu-siasm, and  inserted many  lines in his  poems, and  Harte repaid the instructions of so distinguished a preceptor, by compliments introduced not without elegance and propriety in his Essays on Painting and on  Satire, and elsewhere.

In 1727, he published the volume of poems, already mentioned, dedicated to the gallant and eccentric earl of Peterborough who was, as  the author acknowledges, the first " who took notice of  him."  This volume was ushered in  by a very nu-merous list of subscribers, among whom is the name of  Alexander Pope, for four copies.  An edition of these poems may be sometimes picked up,  dated 1739, and printed for John Cecil, instead of Barnard Lintot the original publisher.   As the same  list of subscribers is  repeated, it is probable that these were the remaining copies bought at Lintot's sale, (who died in 1737) and were at this time published with a  new title  page.

In 1730 he published his Essay on Satire, 8vo. and in 1735, the Essay on Reason, folio, to which Pope contributed  very considerably, although no part of his share can be exactly ascertained, except the first two lines.   He afterwards published two sermons, the one  entitled the Union and Harmony of Reason, Morality, and revealed Religion, preached at St. Mary's Oxford, February 27, 1736—7, which excited  so much admiration, or curiosity, as  to  pass  through five editions.   The other was a fast sermon, preached at the  same place, January 9, 1739—40. He was afterwards vice-principal of St. Mary Hall, and held in so much reputa-tion as a tutor, that lord Lyttelton, who was one of his earliest friends, recommended him to the earl of Chesterfield, as a private and travelling preceptor to his natural son. With this young man, to whom his lordship addressed those letters which have so much injured his reputation, Mr. Harte travelled from the year 1746 to 1750. Lord Chesterfield is said to have procured for him a canonry of Windsor, in 1751, " with much difficulty" arising from his college connections, St. Mary Hall, of which Dr. King was principal, being at that time noted for jacobitism.

In 1759, he published his history of Gustavus Adolphus, 2 vols. 4to. a work on which he had bestowed much labour, and in which he has accumulated very valuable materials. An edition was soon published in German by George Henry Martini, with a preface, notes,and corrections, from the pen of the translator John Gotlieb Bohme, Saxon historiographer, and professor of history in the university of Leipzic. The success, however, at home, was far inferior to his hopes, yet sufficient to encourage him to publish an octavo edition in 1763, corrected and improved. At this time he resided at Bath, dejected and dispirited between real and imaginary distempers. In November 1766, a paralytic stroke deprived him of the use of his right leg, affected his speech, and in some degree his head. He employed, however, his intervals of health, in preparing the Amaranth for the press, which was published in 1767. In the following year, he had entirely lost the use of his left side, and he languished in this melancholy condition till March 1774, when he breathed his last, having just outlived the publication of the celebrated letters addressed to his pupil Mr. Stanhope, but which it is hoped he did not see. At the time of his death he was vicar of St. Austel and St. Blazy in Cornwall.

Frequent mention of his character and writings occurs in Chesterfield's letters.

" Next week Harte will send you his Gustavus Adolphus (March 30, 1759,) in two quartos : it will contain many new particulars of the life of that real hero, as he had abundant and authentic materials which have never yet appeared. It will, upon the whole, be a very curious and valuable history : though, between you and me, I could have wished that he had been more correct and elegant in his style. You will find it dedicated to one of your acquaintance, who was forced to prune the luxuriant praises bestowed upon him, and yet has left enough of all conscience to satisfy a reasonable man. Harte has been very much out of order, these last three or four months, but is not the less intent upon sowing his lucerne, of which he had six crops last year, to his infinite joy, and, as he says, profit."

April 16, 1759. " I am very sorry to tell you, that Harte's Gustavus Adolphus does not take at all,and consequently sells very little : it is certainly informing, and full of good matter : but it is as certain too, that the style is execrable : where the d——l he picked it up, I cannot conceive, for it is a bad style, of a new and singular kind : it is full of Latinisms, Gallicisms, Germanisms, and all *isms* but Anglicisms : in some places pompous, in others vulgar and low."

November 27, 1762. " Harte is going to publish a new edition of his Gustavus, in octavo : which, he tells me he has altered, and which, I could tell him, he should translate into English, or it will not sell better than the former."

December 18, 1763. " Harte has a great poetical work to publish, before it be long : he has shown me some parts of it ; he had entitled it Emblems : but I persuaded him to alter that name for two reasons : the first was, because they were not emblems, but fables: the second was, that, if they had been emblems, Quarles had degraded and vilified that name to such a degree, that it is impossible to make use of it after him: so they are to be called fables, though moral tales would, in my mind, be the properest name; if you ask me what I think of those I have seen, I must say that *sunt plura bona : quædam mediocria, et quædam.*"—

September 3, 1764. " I have received a book for you, and one for myself, from Harte. It is upon agriculture, and will surprise you, as I confess it did me. This work is not only English, but good and elegant English : he has even scattered graces upon his subject: and in prose, has come very near Virgil's Georgics in verse, I have written to him, to congratulate his happy transformation."

November 28, 1765. " Poor Harte is very ill, and condemned to the Hotwell at Bristol. He is a better poet than a philosopher: for all this illness and melancholy proceeds originally from the ill success of his Gustavus Adolphus. He is grown extremely devout, which I am very glad of, because that is always a comfort to the afflicted."

July 2, 1767. " Poor Harte is in a most miserable condition : he has lost one side of himself, and in a great measure his speech : notwithstanding which, he is going to publish his *Divine Poems*, as he calls them. I am sorry for it, as he had not time to correct them, before this stroke, nor abilities to do it since."—

In these opinions there is some truth and some flippancy. His lordship, however, must have entertained a very high opinion of Mr. Harte's learning and integrity, when he confided to him the early and most interesting years of that son on whom all his hopes were fixed; yet Dr. Maty expresses his wonder, that he should not have chosen a tutor who understood a little better the external decorations which his lordship prized so highly. " Harte," says Dr. Maty, " had none of the amiable connecting qualifications, which the earl wished in his son."

" It was impossible he should succeed in finishing the polish of his education in the manner lord Chesterfield wished: and it is a matter of astonishment that the earl should not have perceived how much the tutor's example must have defeated his precepts. The three principal articles he recommended to his son, were his appearance, his elocution and his style. Mr. Harte, long accustomed to a college life, was too awkward both in his person and address to be able to familiarize the graces with his young pupil. An unhappy impediment in his speech, joined to his total want of ear, rendered him equally unfit to perceive as to correct any defects of pronounciation, a careful attention to which was so strongly recommended in all lord Chesterfield's letters, as absolutely necessary for an orator."

All this, however, lord Chesterfield knew, and yet appointed Mr. Harte, appears to have been perfectly satisfied with his conduct, and treated him with great kindness, and condescending familiarity as long as he lived. Dr. Maty seems to have forgot that Harte left his pupil before his lordship had fully developed that abominable plan of hypocrisy and profligacy which, notwithstanding his biographers' softenings, has irrecoverably disgraced his memory ; and as it is acknowledged that Mr. Stanhope did not practise the system which his father so elegantly and artfully recommended, let us hope that he was preserved by the better foundation Mr. Harte had laid.

His life of Gustavus Adolphus was a very unfortunate publication. He had learning, industry, and the spirit of research : and he had acquired a considerable degree of political and military knowledge. He had besides access to the most valuable materials, and his work may be considered as in many respects original. But either through affectation, or by means of some desultory course of reading in every language but his own, he was led to adopt a style peculiarly harsh and pedantic, and often unintelligible by the irregular construction of his sentences, by new words of his own coinage, or by old words used in a new sense. The wonder is, that in all this he fancied himself " writing in a style less laboured and ornamental than is usually exhibited by the fluent writers of the present age." George Hawkins, his bookseller, we are told, sometimes objected to his uncouth words or phrases, while the work was in the press, but Harte refused to change them, and used to add with a complaisant sneer, " George, that's what we call writing!" It is, such writing, however, as we do not find in his sermons printed in 1737, and 1740, far less in his Essays on Husbandry, which ought to have been mentioned as printed in 1764, and which, with very few exceptions, are distinguished for perspicuity of style, and for more elegance than that subject is generally supposed to admit.

The life of Gustavus probably employed many of his years, at least the plan must have occupied his mind for a very considerable time before he began to collect his materials. The undertaking was suggested to him by lord Peterborough, with whom he could have had no communication, except previously to the year 1734, when his lordship's growing infirmities deprived him of the pleasures of society, and in the following year of life. When travelling with Mr. Stanhope, our author procured access to various sources of information, and dwelt so long on his subject with a fond regard, that when he found how coolly his work was received by the world, and how harshly by the critics, he became uneasy, fretful, and according to lord Chesterfield, seriously ill with disappointment. Dr. Johnson was of opinion, that the defects of his history proceeded not from imbecility, but from foppery : and it is certain that the critics, while they pointed out the defects in his style, paid due encomiums on the merit of the history in other respects.

According to Boswell, Dr. Johnson said, " he was excessively vain. He put copies of his book in manuscript into the hands of lord Chesterfield and lord Granville, that they might revise it. Now how absurd was it to suppose that two such noblemen would revise so big a manuscript. Poor man! he left London the day of the publication of his book, that he might be out of the way of the great praise he was to receive : and he was ashamed to return, when he found how ill his book had succeeded. It was unlucky in coming out the same day with Robertson's History of Scotland."—

Not the same day, for Robertson's History was published a month sooner, but Hume's House of Tudor came out the same week ; and after perusing these, poor Harte's style could not certainly be endured. It was not, however, so very absurd to submit his manuscript to lord Chesterfield or lord Granville, if they permitted him, and the former certainly did peruse it, although he might think it too generally contaminated for a few friendly hints or corrections.

With Pope, Harte appears to have been on very intimate terms, and we find his encomiastic lines among the testimonies of authors prefixed to the Dunciad.

He had even attained so much character both as a poet and a philosopher, that the Essay on Man was at first attributed to him. It may not be impertinent to introduce, here an anecdote, related by Dr. Warton, who was very intimate with Harte. Pope told Mr. Harte, that in order to disguise his being the author of the Second Epistle of the Essay on Man, he made, in the first edition, the following bad rhyme :

A cheat! a whore! that starts not at the *name*,
In all the inns of court, or *Drury-Lane*.

" And Harte remembered to have often heard it urged, in inquiries about the author, whilst he was unknown, that it was impossible it could be Pope's, on account of this very passage."— Warton, it may be added, always spoke with respect of Harte's abilities.

From every evidence, he appears to have been a man of extensive learning, and acquainted not only with the best authors of his time, but with the classics, the fathers of the church, and other eminent writers of antiquity, which Dr. Maty, rather inconsiderately, calls " Gothic erudition." It is true that he often discovers that kind of reading which is seldom read, but the illustrations he has appended to the poems in the Amaranth from the fathers, &c. are generally apt and judicious. Towards the close of life, he cheered his painful and solitary hours by devotional reading.

He died unmarried, and at one time seems to have considered the married state as unfavourable to the exertions of genius. In his Essay on Painting, he very ungallantly recommends that the artist should be

" Untouch'd by cares, uncumber'd with a wife."

Notwithstanding the unfortunate reception of his history, he projected another undertaking of the same kind. This we learn from the concluding passage of his Gustavus : in which he says his intention was to carry the history of Germany down to the peace of Munster, but that he was deterred by the magnitude of the undertaking. He adds, however, in a note, that he had completed the history of the thirty years war, from the breaking out of the troubles in Bohemia in 1618 to the death of Gustavus in 1632. These papers, with whatever else he left, are supposed to have fallen into the hands of his servant Edward Dore, who afterwards kept an inn in Bath. Dore and his family are no more, and the manuscripts are probably irrecoverably lost. We have his own authority also, that he intended to have written a criticism on the poetry of Dryden, which he seems to have appreciated with just taste. The Advertisement to Religious Melancholy, from which this information is taken, is inserted almost entire, by Dr. Warton in his edition of Pope, as the result of a conference between Pope and Harte.

Harte's poems in general are entitled to considerable praise, although it may probably be thought that he was a better critic than a poet, and exhibited more taste than genius. His attachment to Pope led him to an imitation of that writer's manner, particularly in the Essay on Reason and that on Satire, which are now added to his other works. His Essay on Reason has been somewhere called a fine philosophical poem. It might with more propriety be called a fine Christian poem, as it has more of religion than philosophy, and might have been aptly entitled An Essay on Revelation. The Essay on Satire has some elegant passages, but is desultory, and appears to have been written as a compliment to the Dunciad of Pope, whose opinions he followed as far as they respected the merits of the dunces whom Pope libelled.

For his Essay on Painting, he pleads that it was written at intervals, upon such remarks as casually occurred in his reading, and is therefore deficient in connection. He adds that he had finished the whole before he saw Du Fresnoy, which may readily be believed. He discovers, however, a very correct notion of an art which was not at that time much studied in this country, and has laid down many precepts which, if insufficient to form a good painter, will at least prevent his falling into gross improprieties. So much knowledge of the art, and acquaintance with the works of the most eminent painters, argues a taste surprising at his early age. He had some turn for drawing, and made several sketches when abroad, which were afterwards engraved as head pieces for the poems in the Amaranth. In this Essay, he delights in images, which although in general pleasing and just, are perhaps too frequently, and as it were periodically introduced. With all his admiration of Pope, he was not less attached to Dryden as a model, and if he has less harmony than Pope, has at the same time less monotony.

His translations are faithful and not inelegant. His acquaintance with the classics was very intimate, and he has decorated his Essays on Husbandry with a profusion of apt illustrations.

The Soliloquy occasioned by the chirping of a Grasshopper is tender and playful, but his other small pieces are not entitled to particular notice.

The Amaranth was written, as he informs us " for his private consolation under a lingering and dangerous state of health." There is something so amiable, and we may add so heroic in this, that it is impossible not to make every allowance for defects ; but this collection of poems does not upon the whole stand so much in need of indulgence as may be expected. Some of them were sketched when he was abroad, and now were revised and prepared, but others may perhaps be the effusions of a man in sickness and pain. Yet there are more animated passages of genuine poetry scattered over this volume than we find in his former works.

The whole of the Amaranth is of the serious cast, such as became the situation of the author. We have, indeed, heard of authors who have sported with unusual glee in their moments of debility and decay, and seemed resolved to meet death with an air of good humour and levity. Such a state of mind, where it does really occur, and is not affectation, is rather to be wondered at, than envied. It is not the feeling of a rational, and an immortal creature.

In these poems he adopts various measures, according to his subject. The transition from the ode to the heroic, in the Ascetic, he justifies by the example of Cowley, and from the nature of the precepts, which are most suitable to the solemnity of heroic verse. The Ode to Contentment has many splendid passages and the recurrence of " All, all from Thee, &c." is particularly graceful. The exclamation of " Bless me," is, however, a puerility unworthy of the general strain of this poem.

In the Vision of Death, he professes to imitate Dryden by the introduction of more triplets and alexandrines than " he might otherwise have done." But if by this he avoids the perpetual restraint of the couplet, there is too much of visible artifice in the method he takes to relieve himself. This, however, is one of the most ingenious fables of which immortality is the subject; the figure and habitation of Death, are poetically conceived and expressed, and the address of Death is energetic and striking.

The Courtier and Prince is one of the most instructive and interesting fables in our language.   Its length will perhaps be objected, but not by those who attend to the many scattered beauties of sentiment and imagination, and whatever opinion may be entertained on the merit of this and his other poems, it ought not to be forgot that in all he prefers no higher claims than

" The sounds of verse, and voice of Truth."

# POEMS

## OF

## *WALTER HARTE.*

---

TO THE RIGHT HONOURABLE

### CHARLES EARL OF PETERBOROW AND MONMOUTH.

My lord,

I FANCY the public will be much surprised, when I say your lordship was the first person who was pleased to take notice of me. How little I deserve so much partiality, I leave the world to judge. Yet thus much I can affirm; I only wish that these poems may live to posterity, to be a memorial of the gratitude rather than the genius

Of your lordship's
most humble, most obliged,
and most dutiful servant,
W. HARTE.

---

### ADVERTISEMENT.

IT will be necessary to inform the reader, that the author was under nineteen when all these poems were written.

I ought here to say a word or two of my Essay on Painting. This performance is by no means correct in all its parts; I had neither health, leisure, nor abilities equal to my design. 'Twas written at intervals, upon such remarks as casually occurred in my reading. Of course no exact connexion must be expected: though I might allege, that Horace uses as little in his Art of Poetry. I had finished the whole, before ever I saw Du Fresnoy; as will appear by comparison.

## *AN ESSAY ON PAINTING.*

TO THE RIGHT HONOURABLE THOMAS EARL OF PEMBROKE.

Μιμητικὴ [Ποιήσεως] τέχνη καὶ δύναμίς ἐςιν ἀν-
τίςροφος τῆ ζωῖραφίᾳ ζωῖραφίαν μὲν λέγυσιν ἵναι
ΦΘΕΓΓΟΜΈΝΗΝ τὴν Ποίησιν, Ποίησιν δὲ
ΣΙΓΩΣΑΝ τὴν ζωγραφίαν.
Plutarch. de audiend. Poet.

————————————Poema
Est pictura loquens, mutum pictura poema.

WHATEVER yet in poetry held true,
If duly weigh'd holds just in painting too :
Alike to profit, and delight they tend ;
The means may vary, but the same their end.
Alike from Heav'n, congenial first they came,
The same their labours, and their praise the same :
Alike by turns they touch the conscious heart,
And each on each reflects the lights of art.
You nobler youths who listen to my lays,
And scorn by vulgar arts to merit praise :
Look cautious round, your genius nicely know,
And mark how far its utmost stretch will go ;
Pride, envy, hatred, labour to conceal,
And sullen prejudice, and party-zeal ;
Approve, examine, and then last believe——
For friends mislead, and critics still deceive.
Who takes his censure, or his praise on trust,
Is kind, 'tis true, but never can be just.
But where's the man with gen'rous zeal inspir'd,
Dear in each age, in ev'ry art admir'd ?

Blest with a genius strong, [1] but unconfin'd,
A spritely wit, with sober judgment join'd,
A love of learning, and a patient mind;
A vig'rous fancy, such as youth requires,
And health, and ease, and undisturb'd desires.
Who spares no pains his own defects to know,
Who not forgives, but ev'n admires a foe;
By manners sway'd, which stealing on the heart,
Charm more through ease, and happiness, than
    art.
Such Titian was, by nature form'd to please,
Blest in his fortunes, born to live at ease:
Who felt the poet's, or the painter's fire,
Now dipp'd the pencil, and now tun'd the lyre:
Of gentlest manners in a court refin'd,
A friend to all, belov'd of all mankind;
The Muse's glory, as a monarch's care, [2]
Dear to the gay, the witty, and the fair!
    But ah! how long will nature ask to give
A soul like his, and bid a wonder live?
Rarely a Titian, or a Pope appears,
The forming glory of a thousand years!
    A proper taste we all derive from Heav'n,
Wou'd all but bless, and manage what is giv'n.
Some secret impulse moves in ev'ry heart,
And nature's pleas'd with gentle strokes of art;
Most souls, 'tis true, this blessing faintly charms;
A distant flame, that rather shines, than warms:
Like rays, through wintry streams reflected,
    falls
Its dubious light, in glimm'ring intervals.
    Like Maro first with trembling hand design
Some humble work, and study line by line:
A Roman urn, a grove encircled bow'r,
The blushing cherry, or the bending flow'r.
Painful, and slow to noble arts we rise,
And long long labours wait the glorious prize;
Yet by degrees your steadier hand shall give
A bolder grace, and bid each object live.
So in the depths of some sequester'd vale,
The weary peasant's heart begins to fail:
Slowly he mounts the huge high cliff with pain,
And prays in thought he might return again:
'Till opening all at once beneath his eyes,
The verdant trees, and glittering turrets rise:
He springs, he triumphs, and like light'ning flies.
Ev'n Raphael's self from rude essays began,
And shadow'd with a coal his shapeless man.
Time was, when Pope for rhymes would knit his
    brow,
And write as tasteless lines—as I do now.
    'Tis hard a sprightly fancy to command,
And give a respite to the lab'ring hand;
Hard as our eager passions to restrain,
When priests, and self-denial plead in vain:
When pleasures tempt, and inclinations draw,
When vice is nature, and our will the law.
As vain we strive each trivial fault to hide,
That shows but little judgment, and more pride.
Like some nice prude, offensive to the sight,
Exactness gives at best a cold delight; [3]

Each painful stroke disgusts the lively mind;
For art is lost, when overmuch refin'd.
So nice reformers their own faith betray,
And school-divines distinguish sense away.
To err is mortal, do whate'er we can,
Some faulty trifles will confess the man.
Dim spots suffuse the lamp that gilds the sky,
If nicely trac'd through Galileo's eye.
Wisest are they, who each mad whim repress,
And shun gross errours, by committing less.
    Still let due decencies preserve your fame,
Nor must the pencil speak the master's shame.
Each nobler soul in ev'ry age was giv'n
To bless mankind, for arts descend from Heav'n.
Gods! shall we then their pious use profane,
'T' oblige the young, the noble, or the vain!
Whoever meditates some great design,
Where strength and nature dawn at ev'ry line,
Where art and fancy full perfection give,
And each bold figure glows, and seems to live:
Where lights and shades in sweet disunion play,
Rise by degrees, or by degrees decay;
Far let him shun the busy noise of life,
Untouch'd by cares, uncumber'd with a wife.
Bear him, ye Muses! to sequester'd woods,
To bow'ry grottoes, and to silver floods [4]! [reign,
Where Peace, and Friendship hold their gentle
And Love unarm'd sits smiling on the plain.
Where Nature's beauties variously unite,
And in a landscape open on the sight.
Where Contemplation lifts her silent eye,
And lost in vision travels o'er the sky.
Soft as his ease the whisp'ring Zephyrs blow,
Calm as his thoughts the gentle waters flow:
Hush'd are his cares, extinct are Cupid's fires,
And restless hopes, and impotent desires.
    But Nature [5] first must be your darling care;
Unerring Nature, without labour fair.
Art from this source derives her true designs,
And sober judgment cautiously refines.
No look, no posture must mishap'd appear:
Bold be the work, but boldly regular.
When mercy pleads, let softness melt the eyes;
When anger storms, the swelling muscles rise.
A soft emotion breathes in simple love,
The heart just seems to beat, the eye to move.
Gently, ah! gently, Languor seems to die,
Now drops a tear, and now steals out a sigh.
Let awful Jove his lifted thunders wield;
Place azure Neptune in the watry field.
Round smiling Venus draw the faithless boy,
Surmise, vain hopes, and short-enduring joy.
But should you dress a nymph in monstrous ruff,
Or saintly nun profane with modish snuff:
Each fool will cry, O horridly amiss!
The painters mad, mend that, and alter this.
    From Heav'n descending, beauteous Nature
        came,
One clear perfection, one eternal flame,

---

[1] Sit vir talis, qualis verè sapiens appellari
possit, nec moribus modo perfectus, sed etiam
scientià, & omni facultate dicendi, qualis for-
tasse adhuc nemo fuerit.  Quintilian.

[2] Titian was created count Palatine by Charles
V. and most intimately acquainted with Ariosto,
Aretine, &c.

[3] Odiosa cura est—Optima enim sunt minimè

accersita, & simplicibus ab ipsâ veritate pro-
fectis similia. Quintil. Lib. 8. Cap. 3. in Proem.

[4] Aptissima sunt in hoc nemora, sylvæque;
quòd illa coeli libertas, locorumque; amænitas
sublimem animum, & beatiorem spiritum parent.
Quintilian.

[5] Videantur omnia ex Naturâ rerum hominumque fluere—Hoc opus, hic labor est; sine
quo, cætera nuda, jejunga, infirma, ingrata,
Quintil. Lib. 6. cap. 2.

Whose lovely lights on ev'ry object fall
By due degrees, yet still distinguish all.
Yet as the best of mortals are sometimes,
Not quite exempt from folly or from crimes;
There are, who think that nature is not free
From some few symptoms of deformity.
Hence springs a doubt, if painters may be
To err, who copy nature in a fault, [thought
Led by some servile rule, whose pow'r prevails
On imitation, when th' example fails.
Poets, and painters here employ your skill;
Be this the doctrine of your good and ill,
Enough to pose the critics of a nation,
Nice as the rules of Puritan-salvation.
Yet if the seeds of art we nicely trace 6;
There dawns a heav'nly, all-inspiring grace,
No tongue expresses it, no rule contains;
(The glorious cause unseen) th' effect remains:
Fram'd in the brain, it flows with easy art,
Steals on the sense, and wins the yielding heart,
A pleasing vigour mixt with boldness charms,
And happiness completes what passion warms.
Nor is it thought a trifle, to express
The various shapes, and foldings of the dress 7,
With graceful ease the pencil to command,
And copy nature with a hasty hand.
Through the clear robe the swelling muscles rise,
Or heaving breasts, that decently surprise;
As some coy virgin with dejected mien [seen,
Conceals her charms, yet hopes they may be
Be ev'ry person's proper habit known 8,
Peculiar to his age, or sex alone.
In flowing robes the monarch sweeps along,
Large are the foldings, natural, and strong:
Wide ample lights in spreading glories play,
And here contrasted, deeper shades decay.
The virgin-pow'rs who haunt the silver floods,
And hoary hills, and consecrated woods,
Soft strokes, and graceful negligence demand,
The nice resultance of an easy hand;
Loose to the winds their airy garments fly
Like filmy dews, too tender for the eye.
But e'er these charms are to perfection wrought,
Adapted manuals must be nicely sought.
Gay vivid colours must the draught inspire,
Now melt with sweetness and now burn with fire.
A northern sky must aid the steady sight,
Else the shades alter with the transient light.
Methinks the loaded table stands display'd,
Each nicer vase " in mystic order laid."
Here ocean's mistress heaps around her shells
Beauteous, and recent from the sea-green cells;
The taper pencils here are rang'd apart,
There chalk, lead, vials, and loose schemes of
    art.
So when bold Churchill with a gen'ral's care
Eyes his brave Britons crowding to the war;

6 Tradi omnia, quæ ars efficit, non possunt.
                    Quintil. Lib. 8. cap. 10.
Vide etiam quæ sequuntur de Pictore.
7 Non refert quid facias, sed quo loco. Nam
ornatus omnis non tam suâ, quam rei cui ad-
hibetur, conditione constat.
                    Quintil. Lib. 11. cap. 1.

8 Reddere personæ scit convenientia cuique;
Respicere exemplar vitæ morumque, jubebo
Doctum imitatorem.
                    Horat. de Art. Poet.

Watchful, and silent move the duteous bands,
One look excites them, and one breath com-
    mands,
Hail happy Painting! to confirm thy sway,
Ocean, and air their various tributes pay.
The purple insect 9 spreads her wings to thee,
Wafts o'er the breeze, or glitters on the tree.
Earth's winding veins unnumber'd treasures hold,
And the warm champian ripens into gold.
A clearer blue the lazuli bestows,
Here umber deepens, there vermillion glows.
For thee, her tender greens, and flourets rise,
Whose colours change in ever-mingling dyes;
Ev'n those fair groves (for Eden first design'd)
Weep in soft fragrance through their balmy rind:
Transparent tears! that glitter as they run,
Warm'd with the blushes of the rising Sun.
    Here cease my song—a gentler theme in-
        spires
Each tender thought, and wakes the lover's fires.
Once more your aid celestial Muses bring;
Sacred the lays! nor to the deaf we sing.
    In ancient Greece 10 there liv'd, unknown to
A nymph, and Mimicina was her name. [fame,
Smit by a neighb'ring youth betimes she fell
Victim to love, and bade the world farewell.
Thoughtful and dull she pin'd her bloom away
In lonely groves, nor saw the cheerful day.
This might be borne—but lo! her lovely swain
Must part, ah, never to return again!
One mutual kiss must mutual passion sever,
One look divide 'em, and divide for ever!
See, now she lies abandon'd to despair,
And to rude winds unbinds her flowing hair:
Beauteous neglect! when melting to her woes,
A Sylvan maid from her dark grotto rose:
(Long had she view'd the solitary fair,
Her bleeding bosom heav'd with equal care)
A heav'nly picture in her hand she bore,
She smil'd, she gave it, and was seen no more
Pleas'd Mimicina, speechless with surprise,
Ey'd the fair form, and lightning of the eyes:
She knew—and sighing gave a tender kiss;
Her noble passion was content with this:
No more his absence, or her woes deplor'd,
And as the living, she the dead ador'd.
    Thus Painting rose, to nourish soft desires,
And gentle hopes, and friendship's purer fires:
Thus still the lover must his nymph adore,
And sigh to charms, that ought to charm no
        more.
Thus when these eyes, with kind illusions blest,
Survey each grace Parthenia once possest:
Her winning sweetness, and attractive ease,
And gentle smiles that never fail'd to please;
Heav'ns! how my fancy kindles at the view,
And my fond heart relents, and bleeds anew!
Fair faithless virgin! with constraint unkind,
Misled by duty, and through custom blind:
Perhaps ev'n now, from pride and int'rest free,
Thou shar'st each pang of all I felt for thee;
Ah, no—my pray'rs, my tears, my vows resign,
Alas, 'tis now a crime to call me thine,
To act the tender, or the friendly part;
No—hate, forget me, tear me from my heart.

9 The cochineel.
10 This story, with several others, is mentioned by most ancient writers. I have chosen it as
the most poetical.

Yet still thy smiles in breathing paint inspire,
Still thy kind glances set my soul on fire.
Thither each hour I lift my thoughtful eye.
Now drop a tear, now softly breathe a sigh;
Sacred 'till death my gentlest vows shall be,
And the last gasp of life be breath'd for thee !
    You too, O Sculpture, shall exalt my lays,
Pictura's sister-candidate for praise !
Soft Raphael's air divine, Antonio [11] shows;
And all Le Brun in mimic Picart [11] glows.
Hither ye nations, now direct your eyes,
Rise crown'd with lustre, gentle Albion rise !
Now thy soft Hollar, now thy Smith appears,
A faultless pattern to succeeding years;
There sacred domes [12] in length'ning vistas
        charm,
And British beauties here for ever warm.
    Most painters, of less judgment than caprice,
Are like old maidens infamously nice :
It matters nought if rules be false or true,
All shou'd be modish, whimsical and new;
Fond of each change, the present still they praise,
So women love—and actors purchase plays.
As if self-love, or popular offence,
Receiv'd a sanction to mislead our sense ;
Or party-notions, vapours, faith, and zeal
Were all, at proper times, infallible.
True wit, and true religion are but one,
Tho' some pervert 'em, and ev'n most have none.
Who thinks what others never thought before,
Acts but just that his sons will act no more.
Yet on a time, when vig'rous thoughts demand,
Indulge a warmth, and prompt the daring hand :
On purpose deviate from the laws of art,
And boldly dare to captivate the heart;
Breasts warm'd to rapture shall applaud your fire,
May disapprove you, but shall still admire.
The Grecian artist at one dash supply'd
What patient touches, and slow art deny'd.
So when pale Florio in the gloomy grove
Sits sadly musing on the plagues of love,
When hopes and fears distract his tim'rous mind,
And fancy only makes the nymph unkind:
Desp'rate at last he rushes from the shade,
By force and warm address to win the maid:
His brisk attack the melting nymph receives
With equal warmth, he presses, she forgives ;
One moment crowns whole tedious years of pain,
And endless griefs, and health consum'd in vain.
    Of ev'ry beauty that conspires to charm
Man's nicer judgment, and his genius warm,
To just invention be the glory giv'n,
A particle of light deriv'd from Heav'n.
Unnumber'd rules t' improve the gift are shown
By ev'ry critic, to procure it, none.
    Some colours often to the rest impart
New graces, more thro' happiness, than art.
This, nicely study'd, will your fame advance,
The greatest beauties seldom come by chance.
    Some gaze at ornament alone, and then
So value paint, as women value men.
It matters nought to talk of truth, or grace,
Religion, genius, customs, time, and place.
So judge the vain, and young; nor envy we :
They cannot think indeed—but they may see.

[11] Two engravers, famous for their prints copied from Raphael and Le Brun.
[12] Alluding to Hollar's Etchings in the Mo-
nasticon.

Excessive beauty, like a flash of light,
Seems more to weaken, than to please the sight.
In one gay thought luxuriant Ovid writ,
And Voiture tires us, but with too much wit.
    Some all their value for grotesque express,
Beauty they prize, but beauty in excess :
Where each gay figure seems to glare apart,
Without due grace, proportion, shades, or art.
(The sad remains of Goths in ancient times,
And rev'rend dulness, and religious rhymes)
So youthful poets ring their music round
On one eternal harmony of sound.
"The lines are gay," and whosoe'er pretends
To search for more, mistakes the writer's ends.
    Colours, like words, with equal care are sought,
These please the sight, and those express the
        thought,
But most of all, the landscape seems to please
With calm repose, and rural images.
See, in due lights th' obedient objects stand,
As happy ease exalts the master's hand.
See, absent rocks hang trembling in the sky,
See, distant mountains vanish from the eye ;
A darker verdure stains the dusky woods ;
Floats the green shadow in the silver floods ;
Fair visionary worlds surprise the view,
And fancy forms the golden age a-new.
    True just designs will merit honour still ;
Who begins well, can scarcely finish ill.
Unerring truth must guide your hand aright,
Art without this is violence to sight.—
    The first due postures of each figure trace
In swelling out-lines with an easy grace.
But the prime person mostly will demand
Th' unweary'd touches of thy patient hand :
There thought, and boldness, strength, and art
        conspire,
The critic's judgment, and the painter's fire :
It lives, it moves, it swells to meet the eye :
Behind, the mingling groupes in softer shadows
        die.
    Never with self-design your merits raise,
Nor let your tongue be echo to your praise.
To wiser heads commit such points as these,
A modest blush will tell how much they please.
    In days of yore, a prating lad, they say,
Met glorious Reubens journeying on the way:
Sneering, and arch he shakes his empty head,
(For half-learn'd boys will talk a Solon dead)
"Your servant, good sir Paul, why, what, the devil,
The world to you is more than fairly civil;
No life, no gusto in your pieces shine,
Without decorum, as without design"—
    Sedate to this the Heav'n-born artist smil'd,
" Nor thine, nor mine to speak our praise, my
        child !
Each shall expose his best to curious eyes,
And let th' impartial world adjust the prize."
    Let the soft colours sweeten and unite
To one just form, as all were shade, or light.
    Nothing so frequent charms th' admiring eyes
As well tim'd fancy, and a sweet surprise.
So when the Grecian [13] labour'd to disclose
His nicest art, a mimic lark arose:
The fellow-birds in circles round it play'd,
Knew their own kind, and warbled to a shade.

[13] See Pliny's Natural History, lib. 35. cap.
10.

So Vandervaart in later times excell'd,
And nature liv'd in what our eyes beheld.
He too can oft (in optics deeply read)
A noon-day darkness o'er his chamber spread : [14]
The transient objects sudden as they pass
O'er the small convex of the visual glass,
Transferr'd from thence by magic's pow'rful call,
Shine in quick glories on the gloomy wall ;
Groves, mountains, rivers, men surprise the
    sight,     [wavy light.
Trembles the dancing world, and swims the
Each varying figure in due place dispose [15],
These boldly heighten, touch but faintly those.
Contiguous objects place with judgment nigh,
Each due proportion swelling on the eye.
Remoter views insensibly decay,
And lights, and shadows sweetly drop away.
In bluish white the farthest mounts arise,
Steal from the eye, and melt into the skies.
Hence sacred domes in length'ning ailes extend,
Round columns swell, and rising arches bend :
Obliquer views in side-long vistas glance,
And bending groves in fancy seem to dance.
  Two equal lights descending from the sky,
O'erpow'r each other, and confuse the eye.
The greatest pleasures tire the most, and such
Still end in vices if enjoy'd too much.
Tho' painters often to the shades retire,
Yet too long ease but serves to quench the fire.
Wing'd with new praise, methinks they boldly
O'er airy Alps, and seem to touch the sky.  [fly
Still true to fame, here well-wrought busts de-
High turrets nod, and arches sink away.   [cay,
Ev'n the bare walls, whose breathing figures
    glow'd
With each warm stroke that living art bestow'd,
Or slow decay, or hostile time invades,
And all in silence the fair fresco fades.
Each image yet in fancy'd thoughts we view,
And strong idea forms the scene a-new :
Delusive, she, Paulo's free stroke supplies, [eyes.
Revives the face, and points th' enlight'ning
  'Tis thought each science, but in part, can
A length of toils for human life at most :   [boast
(So vast is art !) if this remark prove true,
'Tis dang'rous sure to think at once of two,
And hard to judge if greater praise there be
To please in painting, or in poetry ;
Yet Painting lives less injur'd, or confin'd,
True to th' idea of the master's mind :
In ev'ry nation are her beauties known,
In ev'ry age the language is her own :
Nor time, nor change diminish from her fame ;
Her charms are universal, and the same.
O, could such blessings wait the poet's lays,
New beauties still, and still eternal praise !
Ev'n though the Muses ev'ry strain inspire,
Exalt his voice, and animate his lyre :
Ev'n tho' their art each image shou'd combine
In one clear light, one harmony divine ;

[14] This practice is of no late invention. Baptista Porta, who flourished about the year 1500, gives an ingenious account of it in his Natural Magic, lib. 17. How useful this may be to young painters, is not my province to determine.
[15] Singula quæque, locum teneant sortita decenter.
Hoc amat obscurum, vult hoc sub luce videri.
                        orat.

Yet ah, how soon the casual bliss decays,
How great the pains, how transient is the praise !
Language, frail flow'r, is in a moment lost,
(That only product human wit can boast)
Now gay in youth, its early honours rise,
Now hated, curst, it fades away, and dies.
  Yet verse first rose to soften human kind,
To mend their manners, and exalt their mind.
See, savage beasts stand list'ning to the lay,
And men more furious, and more wild than they;
Ev'n shapeless trees a second birth receive,
Rocks move to form, and statues seem to live.
Immortal Homer felt the sacred rage,
And pious Orpheus taught a barb'rous age ;
Succeeding painters thence deriv'd their light,
And durst no more than those vouchsaf'd to write.
At last t' adorn the gentler arts, appears
Illustrious Zeuxis from a length of years.
Parrhasius' hand with soft'ning strokes exprest
The nervous motions, and the folded vest :
Pregnant of life his rounded figures rise,
With strong relievo swelling on the eyes.
Evenor bold, with fair Apelles came,
And happy Nicias crown'd with deathless fame.
  At length from Greece, of impious arms afraid,
Painting withdrew, and sought th' Italian shade;
What time each science met its due regard,
And patrons took a pleasure to reward.
But ah, how soon must glorious times decay,
One transient joy, just known, and snatch'd
    away !
By the same foes. which Painting shunn'd before,
Ev'n here she bleeds, and arts expire once more.
Ease, lust, and pleasures shake a feeble state,
Gothic invasions, and domestic hate ;   [sume,
Time's slow decays, what these ev'n spare, con-
And Rome lies bury'd in the depths of Rome !
  Long slumber'd Painting in a stupid trance
Of heavy zeal, and monkish ignorance :
(When faith itself for mere dispute was giv'n,
Subtile was wise, and wranglers went to Heav'n.)
'Till glorious Cimabue [16] restor'd her crown,
And dipp'd the pencil, studious of renown.
Masaccio taught the finish'd piece to live,
And added ev'ry grace of perspective.
Exact correctness Titian's hand bestow'd,
And Vinci's stroke with living labour glow'd.
Next Julio rose, who ev'ry language knew,
Liv'd o'er each age, and look'd all nature
    through.
  In happy Paulo strength and art conspire,
The Graces please us, and the Muses fire.
Each nobler secret others boast alone,
By curious toil Caracci made his own :
Raphael's nice judgment, Angelo's design,
Correggio's warmth, and Guido's pleasing line.
Thrice glorious times, when ev'ry science charms,
When rapture lifts us, and religion warms !
Vocal to Heav'n the swelling organs blow,
A shriller consort aids the notes below ;
Above, around the pictur'd saints appear,
And list'ning seraphs smile and bend to hear.
  Thence Painting, by some happy genius led,
O'er the cold North in slow approaches spread.
Ev'n Britain's isle, that blush'd with hostile gore,
Receiv'd her laws, unknown to yield before;

[16] Giovanni Cimabue, born at Florence in the year 1240. He was the person who revived painting after its unfortunate extirpation.

Relenting now, her savage heroes stand,
And melt at ev'ry stroke from Reubens' hand.
Still in his right the graceful Jervas sways,
Sacred to beauty, and the fair one's praise,
Whose breathing paint another life supplies,
And calls new wonders forth from Mordaunt's
       eyes.
And Thornhill, gen'rous as his art, design'd
At once to profit, and to please mankind.
Thy dome, O Paul's, which heav'nly views adorn,
Shall guide the hands of painters yet unborn;
Each melting stroke shall foreign eyes engage,
And shine unrival'd through a future age.
Hail happy artists! in eternal lays
The kindred-muses shall record your praise;
Whose heav'nly aid inspir'd you first to rise,
And fix'd your fame immortal in the skies;
There sure to last, 'till Nature's self expires,
Increasing still, and crown'd with clearer fires :
High-rais'd above the blasts of public breath,
The voice of hatred, and the rage of death.
Ah, thus, for ever may my numbers shine,
Bold as your thoughts, but easy as your line!
Then might the Muse to distant ages live,
Contract new beauty, and new praise receive:
Fresh strength, and light ev'n time itself bestow,
Soften each line, and bid the thought to glow ;
(Fame's second life) whose lasting glory fears
Nor change, nor envy, nor devouring years.
    Then should these strains to Pembroke's hands
       be borne—
Whom native graces, gentle arts adorn,
Honour unshaken, piety resign'd,
A love of learning, and a gen'rous mind.
    Yet if by chance, enamour'd of his praise,
Some nobler bard shall rise in future days,
(When from his Wilton walls the strokes decay,
And all art's fair creation dies away :
Or solid statues, faithless to their trust,
In silence sink, to mix with vulgar dust;)
Ages to come shall Pembroke's fame adore,
Dear to the Muse, 'till Homer be no more.

## ACONTIUS TO CYDIPPE.

### FROM OVID.

#### ARGUMENT.

In a religious assembly at the temple of Diana in
Delos, Acontius was much enamoured with
Cydippe, a lady of remarkable wit and beauty. Besides this, her fortune and family
were much above his own : which made him
solicitous how to discover his passion in a
successful manner. At last he procured a very
beautiful apple, upon which he wrote a dys-
tic to this purpose, " I swear by chaste Diana
I will for ever be thy wife." So soon as he
had written it, he threw the apple directly at
the feet of Cydippe, who imagining nothing of
the deceit, took it up, and having read the inscription, found herself obliged by a solemn
oath to marry Acontius. For in those times
all oaths which were made in the temple of
Diana were esteemed inviolable. Some time
afterwards, her father, who knew nothing of
what had happened, espoused her to another
lover. The marriage was just upon the point

of celebration, when Cydippe was seized with
a violent fever. Acontius writes to her, he
reminds her of a former solemn obligation, and
artfully insinuates that her distemper is inflicted as a just punishment from Diana.

ONCE more, Cydippe, all thy fears remove,
'Tis now too late to dread a cheat in love.
Those rosy lips, in accents half divine,
Breath'd the soft promise in the Delian shrine ;
Dear awful oath! enough Cydippe swore,
No human ties can bind a virgin more.
So may kind Heav'n attend a lover's pray'r,
Soften thy pains, and comfort my despair.
See, the warm blush your modest cheeks inflame;
Yet is there cause for anger or for shame !
Recal to mind those tender lines of love,
Deny you cannot—tho' your heart disprove.
Still must I waste in impotent desires,
And only hope revive the fainting fires ?
Yet did'st thou promise to be ever mine—
A conscious horrour seem'd to shake the shrine,
The pow'r consenting bow'd ; a beam of light
Flash'd from the skies, and made the temple
       bright.
Ah! then Cydippe, dry thy precious tears:
The more my fraud, the more my love appears.
Love ever-watchful, ev'n by nature charms;
Inflames the modest, and the wise disarms;
Fair yet dissembling, pleasing but to cheat
With tender blandishment, and soft deceit,
Kind speaking motions, melancholy sighs,
Tears that delight, and eloquence of eyes.
Love first the treach'rous dear design inspir'd,
My hopes exalted, and my genius fir'd :
Ah! sure I cannot—must not guilty prove ;
Deceit itself is laudable in love!
Once more inspir'd such tender lines I send,
See, my hand trembles lest my thoughts offend.
Heroes in war inflam'd by beauty's charms,
Tear the sad virgin from her parents arms;
I too, like these, feel the fierce flames of love,
Yet check my rage, and modestly reprove.
Ah, teach me, Heav'n, some language to persuade,
Some other vows to bind the faithless maid ;
O Love all-eloquent, you only know
To touch the soul with elegies of woe !
If treach'ry fail, by force I urge my right,
Sheath'd in rough armour, formidably bright:
So Paris snatch'd his Spartan bride away,
A half denying, half consenting prey;
I too resolve——whate'er the dangers be,
For death is nothing when compar'd to thee.
Were you less fair, I then might guiltless prove,
And moderate the fury of my love ;
But ah ! those charms for ever must inspire :
Each look, each motion sets my soul on fire.
Heav'n's with what pleasing ecstasies of pain
Trembling I gaze, and watch thy glance in vain.
How can I praise those golden curls that deck
Each glowing cheek, or wave around thy neck:
Thy swelling arms, and forehead rising fair,
Thy modest sweetness, and attractive air ;
Adjoin to these a negligence of grace,
A winning accent, and enchanting face.
Dear matchless charms ! I cease to name the rest,
Nor wonder thou that love inflames my breast.
    Since all alike to Hymen's altars bend,
Ah, bless at once the lover, and the friend.

Let envy rage, and int'rest disapprove,
Envy and int'rest must submit to love.
By pray'rs and vows Hesione was won
To share the joys of hostile Telamon.
Soft gen'rous pity touch'd the captive dame
Who arm'd Achilles with a lover's flame.
To bless the wretched, shows a soul divine—
Be ever angry—but be ever mine.
Yet can no pray'rs thy firm resentment move?
Wretch that I was so ill to fix my love!
See, at thy feet despairing, wild I roll,
Grief swells my heart, and anguish racks my soul:
There fix my doom; relentless to my sighs,
And lifted hands, and supplicating eyes.
Then wilt thou say (for pity sure must move
A virgin's breast) " How patient is his love!
Ev'n my heart trembles, as his tears I see;
The youth who serves so well, is worthy me."
Still must I then in sad destruction moan?
My cause unheeded, and my grief unknown.
Ah, no—Acontius cannot write in vain:
Sure ev'ry wretch has licence to complain!
But if you triumph in a lover's woe,
Remember still Diana is your foe:
Diana listen'd to the vows you made,
And trembled at the change her eyes survey'd.
Ah, think, repent, while yet the time is giv'n,
Fierce is the vengeance of neglected Heav'n!
By Dian's hand the Phrygian matron fell,
Sent with her race, an early shade to Hell.
Chang'd to a stag, Acteon pour'd away,
In the same morn the chaser and the prey.
Althea rag'd with more than female hate,
And hurl'd into the flames the brand of fate.
Like these offensive, punish'd too like these,
Heav'n blasts thy joys, and heightens the disease.
Nor think Cydippe, (as my fears foresee)
A thought unworthy of thyself, or me!
Think not I frame this seeming truth, to prove
Thy stern disdain, a pious fraud in love;
Rather than so, I yet abjure thy charms,
And yield thee, scornful, to another's arms!
Alas, for this pale sickness haunts thy bed,
And shooting aches seem to tear thy head;
A sudden vengeance waits thy guilty loves;
Absent is Hymen, Dian'disapproves.
Think then, repent—recal the parting breath
O'er thy lips hov'ring in the hour of death,
See, on thy cheeks the fading purple dies,
And shades of darkness settle on thy eyes.
But whence, ye pow'rs, or wherefore rose that
    pray'r?
Still must I mourn in absence, or despair;
Forc'd, if she dies, the promise to resign——
Ev'n if she lives, I must not call her mine!
  Like some pale ghost around thy house I rove,
Now burn in rage, and now relent with love:
A thousand needless messages I make,
A thousand mournful speeches give, and take.
O that my skill the sov'reign virtues knew
Of ev'ry herb that drinks the early dew,
Then might I hear thy moans, thy sickness see,
Nor were it sure a crime to gaze on thee.
Perhaps ev'n now, (as fear foresees too well)
The wretch I curse, detest, avoid like Hell,
Beside thee breathes a love-dejected sigh,
And marks the silent glances of thy eye.

    ¹ Briseïs.

Some faint excuse he raises, to detain
Thy swelling arm, and press the beating vein:
Now o'er thy neck his glowing fingers rove,
Too great a pleasure for so mean a love!
Villain beware! the sacred nymph resign,——
Avoid, detest her, dread whate'er is mine;
Elsewhere a lover's preference I give,
But cease to rival here, or cease to live.
The vows you claim by right of human laws,
At best but serve to vindicate my cause.
To thee alone by duty is she kind;
Can parents alienate a daughter's mind?
First weigh the crime, the vengeance next explore,
The father promis'd, but the daughter swore:
That merely vain on human faith relies;
But this obtests the sanction of the skies.
  Here cease my woes—ah, whither am I born,
A woman's triumph, and a rival's scorn?
Vain are my vows, unheeded is my pray'r,
The scatt'ring winds have lost 'em all in air;
Yet think Cydippe, e'er thy lover dies!
Banish that wretch for ever from thy eyes;
Scorn, envy, censures are confer'd on me,
And pain,—and death is all he brings to thee.
Gods! may some vengeance crimes like these atone,
And snatch his life, to mediate for thy own!
Nor think to please avenging Cynthia's eyes
With streams of blood in holy sacrifice:
Heav'n claims the real, not the formal part,
A troubled spirit, and repenting heart.
For ease, and health, the patient oft requires
The piercing steel, and burns alive in fires;
Not so with you—ah, but confirm the vow!
One look, one promise can restore thee now;
Again thy smiles eternal joys bestow,
And thy eyes sparkle, and thy blushes glow.
  Suppose from me for ever you remove,
Once must you fall a sacrifice to love;
And then, ah, then will angry Cynthia close
Thy wakeful eyes, or ease a matron's throes?
Yet wilt thou ever find a cause for shame?
No sure——a mother cannot, must not blame.
Tell her the vow, the place, the sacred day
I gaz'd on thee, and gaz'd I heart away:
Then will she surely say (if e'er she knew
But half that tender love I feel for you)
" Ah, think Cydippe, and his consort be;
The youth who pleas'd Diana, pleases me!"
Yet if she asks (as women oft inquire)
Tell her my life, my nation, and my sire:
Not void of youthful vanities I came,
Nor yet inglorious in the world of fame;
From ancient race I drew my gen'rous blood,
Where Cea's isle o'erlooks the watry flood:
Add, that I study ev'ry art to please,
Blest in my genius, born to live at ease.
Wit, merit, learning cannot fail to move,
And all those dearer blessings lost in love!
Ah! had you never sworn, 'twere hard to chuse
A love like mine ——and will you now refuse?
  In midnight dreams when wakeful fancy keeps
Its dearest thoughts, and ev'n in slumber weeps,
Diana's self these mournful strains inspir'd,
And Cupid when I wak'd, my genius fir'd.
Methinks, ev'n now, his piercing arrows move
My tender breast, and spread the pains of love.
Like me beware, unhappy is thy art!
Direct at thee Diana aims her dart
To drink the blood that feeds thy faithless heart

The loves thou never can'st enjoy, resign;
Nor rashly lose another life with thine.
Then will we, eager as our joys, remove
To Dian's shrine, the patroness of love !
High o'er her head in triumph shall be plac'd
The golden fruit, with this inscription grac'd ;
" Ye hapless lovers, hence, for ever know
Acontius gain'd the nymph who caus'd his woe !"
Here cease my hand—I tremble, lest each line
Should wound a soul so griev'd, so touch'd as thine.
No more my thoughts th' ungrateful toil pursue ;
Pleasure farewell, and thou, my dear, adieu !

## PART OF PINDAR'S FIRST PYTHIAN ODE PARAPHRASED.

Χρυσέα φόρμιγξ 'Απολλω ——

### ARGUMENT.

This ode is address'd to Hieron king of Sicily, as
is also the first of the Olympics. Pindar takes
occasion to begin with an encomium on music,
finely describing its effects upon the passions.
We must suppose this art to be one of his hero's
more distinguishable excellencies ; as it appears from several passages in the ode above.
From thence he expatiates in the praise of
poetry ; and inveighs very severely upon those
who either contemn, or have no taste for that
divine science. Their misfortunes and punish-
ments are instanc'd by those of Typhœus :
whom the poets imagine to be imprisoned by
Jupiter under mount Ætna. The digressions in this ode are the most inartificial and
surprising of any in the whole author. We
are once more in the hero's native country ;
every thing opens agreeably to the eye, and
the poem proceeds after Pindar's usual manner.

### STROPHE I.

Gentle lyre, begin the strain ;
Wake the string to voice again.
Music rules the world above ;
Music is the food of love.
Soft'ned by the pow'r of sound,
Human passions melt away :
Melancholy feels no wound,
Envy sleeps, and fears decay.
Entranc'd in pleasure Jove's dread eagle lies,
Nor grasps the bolt, nor darts his fiery eyes.

### ANTISTROPHE I.

See, Mars awak'd by loud alarms
Rolls o'er the field his sanguine eyes,
His heart tumultuous beats to arms,
And terrours glare, and furies rise !
Hark the pleasing lutes complain,
In a softly-breathing strain ;
Love and slumber seal his eye
By the gentle charms opprest :
From his rage he steals a sigh,
Sinking on Dione's breast.

### EPODE I.

Verse, gentle Verse from Heav'n descending came,
Curst by the wicked, hateful to the vain :
Tyrants and slaves profane his sacred name,
Deaf to the tender lay, or vocal strain....

In fires of Hell Typhœus glows,
Imprison'd by the wrath of Jove ;
No ease his restless fury knows,
Nor sounds of joy, nor pleasing love.
Where, glitt'ring faintly on the eye,
Sicilian Ætna props the sky
With mountains of eternal snow ;
He darts his fiery eyes in vain,
And heaves, and roars, and bites his chain
In impotence of woe.

### STROPHE II.

Angry flames like scarlet glowing.
Fiery torrents ever flowing,
Smoke along the with'ring plain
Ere they rush into the main.
When the sable veil of night
Stretches o'er the shaded sky,
Fires of sulphur gleam with light,
Burning rocks disparted fly.
Sudden, by turns the flashing flames arise,
Pour down the winds, or tremble up the skies.

### ANTISTROPHE II.

In fair Sicilia's rich domain,
Where flow'rs and fruits eternal blow,
Where Plenty spreads her peaceful reign,
And seas surround, and fountains flow,
Bright Religion lifts her eye,
Wand'ring through the kindred-sky.
Hail thou, everlasting Jove,
Parent of th' Aonian quire ;
Touch my raptur'd soul with love,
Warm me with celestial fire !

### EPODE II.

The pious mariner when first he sweeps
The foaming billows, and exalts his sails,
Propitiates ev'ry pow'r that rules the deeps,
Led by new hopes, and borne by gentle gales.
So ere the Muse, disus'd to sing,
Emblazons her fair hero's praise :
(What time she wakes the trembling string,
Attemper'd to the vocal lays)
Prostrate in humble guise she bends,
While some celestial pow'r descends
To guide her airy flights along :
God of the silver bow, give ear ;
(Whom Tenedos, and Chrysa fear)
Observant of the song !

### STROPHE III.

Gentle wishes, chaste desires,
Holy Hymen's purer fires :
Lives of innocence and pleasure,
Moral virtue's mystic treasure ;
Wisdom, eloquence, and love,
All are blessings from above.
Hence regret, distaste, dispraise,
Guilty nights, uneasy days :
Repining jealousies, calm friendly wrongs,
And fiercer envy, and the strife of tongues.

### ANTISTROPHE III.

When Virtue bleeds beneath the laws,
Or ardent nations rise in arms,
Thy mercies judge the doubtful cause,
Thy courage ev'ry breast alarms.
Kindling with heroic fire
Once again I sweep the lyre.

Fair as summer's evening skies,
En-ls thy life serene, and glorious ;
Happy hero, great and wise,
O'er thy foes, and self victorious.

---

## THE EPISODE OF ORPHEUS AND
## EURYDICE,

#### TRANSLATED FROM THE FOURTH GEORGIC OF
#### VIRGIL.

At chorus æqualis Dryadum—

Her sudden death the mountain-Dryads mourn'd
And Rhodope's high brow the dirge return'd:
Bleak Orythya trembled at their woe,
And silver Hebrus murmur'd in his flow.
While to his mournful harp, unseen, alone,
Despairing Orpheus warbled out his moan.
With rosy dawn his plaintive lays begun,
His plaintive voice sung down the setting Sun.
    Now in the frantic bitterness of woe
Silent he treads the dreary realms below,
His loss in tender numbers to deplore,
And touch'd the souls who ne'er were touch'd
                                        before.
Mov'd with the pleasing harmony of song,
The shadowy spectres round the poet throng :
Num'rous as birds that o'er the forest play,
(When evening Phœbus rolls the light away :
Or when high Jove in wintry seasons pours
A sudden deluge from descending show'rs.)
The mother's ghost, the father's rev'rend shade,
The blooming hero, and th' unmarry'd maid:
The new-born heir who soon lamented dies,
And feeds the flames before his parent's eyes ;
All whom Cocytus' sable water bounds,
And Styx with thrice three wand'ring streams
                                        surrounds.
    See, the dread regions tremble and admire !
Ev'n Pain unmov'd stands heark'ning to the lyre.
Intent, Ixion stares, nor seems to feel
The rapid motions of the whirling wheel.
Th' unfolding snakes around the furies play,
As the pale sisters listen to the lay.
    Nor was the poet's moving suit deny'd,
Again to realms above he bears his bride,
When (stern decree !) he turns his longing eyes...
'Tis done, she's lost, for ever ever flies—
Too small the fault, too lasting was the pain,
Could love but judge, or Hell relent again !
Amaz'd he stands, and by the glimpse of day
Just sees th' unbody'd shadow flit away.
When thus she cry'd—" Ah, too unthoughtful
Thus for one look to violate thy vows !     [spouse,
Fate bears me back, again to Hell I fly,
Eternal darkness swims before my eye !
Again the melancholy plains I see,          [thee !"
Ravish'd from life, from pleasure, and from
She said, and sinking into endless night,
Like exhalations vanish'd from the sight.
In vain he sprung to seize her, wept, or pray'd,
Swift glides away the visionary shade.
    How wilt thou now, unhappy Orpheus, tell
Thy second loss, and melt the pow'rs of Hell ?
Cold are those lips that blest thy soul before,
And her fair eyes must roll on thine no more.
Sev'n tedious moons despairing, wild he stood,
And told his woes to Strymon's freezing flood.

Beneath his feet eternal snows were spread,
And airy rocks hang nodding o'er his head,
The savage beasts in circles round him play,
And rapid streams stand list'ning to the lay.
    So when the shepherd swain with curious eyes
Marks the fair nest, and makes the young his
Sad Philomel, in poplar shades alone,    [prize:
In vain renews her lamentable moan.
From night to morn she chants her tender love,
And mournful music dies along the grove.
    No thoughts of pleasure now his soul employ,
Averse to Venus and the nuptial joy :
Wild as the winds o'er Thracia's plains he roves,
O'er the bleak mountains, and the leafless groves.
When stung with rage the Bacchanalian train
Rush'd to the bard, and stretch'd him on the
                                        plain ;
(Nor sounds, nor pray'rs their giddy fury move,
And he must cease to live, or learn to love)
See, from his shoulders in a moment flies
His bleeding head, and now, ah now he dies !
Yet as he dy'd, Eurydice he mourn'd,
Eurydice, the trembling banks return'd;
Eurydice, with hollow voice he cry'd,
Eurydice, ran murm'ring down the tide.

---

## TO THE RIGHT HONOURABLE LADY
## HERTFORD,

#### UPON THE BIRTH OF LORD BEAUCHAMP.

Once more inspir'd, I touch the trembling
                                        string ;
What Muse for Hertford will refuse to sing ?
Thine are the fav'rite strains, and may they be
Sacred to praise; to beauty, and to thee !
    Sudden, methinks, in vision I survey
The glorious triumphs of th' expected day :
Fair lovely sights in opening scenes appear,
And airy music trembles on my ear ;
Surrounding eyes devour the beauteous boy,
And ev'ry bosom beats with sounds of joy.
    Rise from thy slumbers, gentle infant, rise !
Lift thy fair head, unfold thy radiant eyes,
Whose lovely light must other courts adorn,
And wound the hearts of beauties yet unborn,
Subdue the sex, that triumphs in its pride,
And humble those, who charm the world beside.
    Descend, ye gentle Nine ! descend, and spread
Laurels and bays around his infant-head.
Bid noble passions in his bosom roll,
And beams of fancy dawn upon his soul ;
In soften'd music bid his accents flow,
Piercing, and gentle as descending snow :
Bid him be all that can his birth commend ;
The daring patriot, and unshaken friend ;
Admir'd, yet humble, modest, though severe,
Abroad obliging, and at home sincere ;
Good, just, and affable in each degree:
Such is the father, such the son shall be !
    These humble strains, indulgent Hertford,
                                        spare ;
Forgive the Muse, O fairest of the fair !
First in thy shades (where silver Kennet glides,
Fair Marlbro's turrets trembling in his tides:
Where Peace and Plenty hold their gentle reign,
And lavish Nature decks the fruitful plain :
Where the fam'd mountain lifts its walks on high,
As varying prospects open on the eye)

To love's soft theme I tun'd the warbling lyre,
And borrow'd from thy eyes poetic fire.
    September the
      30th, 1725.

## THE ARMY OF ADRASTUS,

### AND HIS ALLIES, MARCHING FROM ARGOS TO THE SIEGE OF THEBES.

#### FROM THE 4TH THEBIAD OF STATIUS.

*Jamque snos circum————*

Around the pomp in mourning weeds array'd,
Weeps the pale father, and the trembling maid:
The screaming infants at the portals stand,
And clasp, and stop the slow-proceeding band.
Each parting face a settled horrour wears,
Each low-held shield receives a flood of tears.
Some with a kiss (sad sign of future harms)
Round the clos'd beaver glue their clasping arms,
Hang on the spear, detain 'em as they go.
With lifted eyes, and eloquence of woe.
Those warlike chiefs, whom dread Bellona steel'd,
And arm'd with souls unknowing once to yield,
Now touch'd with sorrows, hide their tearful
    eyes,
And all the hero melts away and dies.
  So the pale sailor lanching from the shore,
Leaves the dear prospects that must charm no
    more :
Here shrieks of anguish pierce his pitying ears—
There strangely wild, a floating world appears—
Swift the fair vessel wings her watry flight,
And in a mist deceives the aking sight :
The native train in sad distraction weep,
Now beat their breasts, now tremble o'er the deep,
Curse ev'ry gale that wafts the fleet from land,
Breathe the last sigh, and wave the circling hand.
  You now, fair ancient Truth! conduct along
Th' advent'rous bard, and animate his song:
Each godlike man in proper lights display,
And open all the war in dread array.
You too, bright mistress of th' Aonian quire,
Divine Calliope! resume the lyre :
The lives and deaths of mighty chiefs recite,
The waste of nations, and the rage of fight.

## A SIMILIE,

#### UPON A SET OF TEA-DRINKERS.

So fairy elves their morning-table spread
O'er a white mushroom's hospitable head :
In acorn cups the merry goblins quaff,
The pearly dews, they sing, they love, they laugh;
Melodious music trembles through the sky,
And airy sounds along the green-wood die.

## THE SAME.

#### DIVERSIFYED IN AUNCIENT METRE.

So, yf deepe clerkes in tymes of yore saine trew,
Or poets eyne, perdie, mought sothly yew,

The dapper elfins theyr queint festes bedight
Wyth mickle plesaunce on a mushroom lite :
In acorne cuppes they quaffen daint liquere,
And rowle belgardes, and defflie daunce yfere;
Ful everidele they makin muskie sote,
And sowns aeriall adowne the grene woode flote.

## A SOLILOQUY,

#### OCCASIONED BY THE CHIRPING OF A GRASSHOPPER.

Happy insect! ever blest
With a more than mortal rest,
Rosy dews the leaves among,
Humble joys, and gentle song !
Wretched poet! ever curst,
With a life of lives the worst,
Sad despondence, restless fears,
Endless jealousies and tears.
  In the burning summer, thou
Warblest on the verdant bough,
Meditating chearful play,
Mindless of the piercing ray;
Scorch'd in Cupid's fervours, I
Ever weep and ever die.
  Proud to gratify thy will,
Ready Nature waits thee still :
Balmy wines to thee she pours,
Weeping through the dewy flow'rs :
Rich as those by Hebe giv'n
To the thirsty sons of Heav'n.
  Yet alas, we both agree,
Miserable thou like me !
Each alike in youth rehearses
Gentle strains, and tender verses;
Ever wand'ring far from home;
Mindless of the days to come,
(Such as aged Winter brings
Trembling on his icy wings)
Both alike at last we die;
Thou art *starv'd*, and so am I !

## THE STORY OF ARETHUSA.

#### TRANSLATED FROM THE 5TH BOOK OF OVID'S METAMORPHOSES.

#### Connection to the former.

The poet describes Ceres wandering over the world in great affliction, to search after her daughter Proserpina, who was then lost. At last Arethusa (a river of Sicily) informs the goddess that her daughter was stolen away by Pluto, and carried down into Hell. Now it was ordained by fate, that Proserine should return again, if she tasted not of any fruit in the other world. But temptations were strong, and the woman could not resist eating six or seven kernels of a pomegranate. However, to mitigate the sentence, Jupiter decreed that she should reside but half the year with Pluto, and pass the rest with her mother. Upon these terms Ceres is very well pacified, and in complaisance desires Arethusa to relate her life, and for what reasons she was changed into a river.

Hush'd in suspence the gath'ring waters stood,
When thus began the parent of the flood ;
What time emerging from the wave, she prest
Her verdant tresses dropping on her breast.
  " Of all the nymphs Achaia boasts," (she said)
" Was Arethusa once the fairest maid.
None lov'd so well, to spread in early dawn
The trembling meshes o'er the dewy lawn :
Tho' dress and beauty scarce deserv'd my care,
Yet ev'ry tongue confess'd me to be fair.
The charms which others strive for, I resign,
And think it ev'n a crime to find them mine !
  " It chanc'd one morn, returning from the
Weary I wander'd by a silver flood :      [wood,
The gentle waters scarce were seen to glide,
And a calm silence still'd the sleeping tide ;
High o'er the banks a grove of watry trees
Spread its dark shade that trembled to the breeze.
(My vest suspended on the boughs) I lave
My chilly feet, then plunge beneath the wave ;
A ruddy light my blushing limbs dispread,
And the clear stream half glows with rosy-red.
When from beneath in awful murmurs broke
A hollow voice, and thus portentous spoke :
  " ' My lovely nymph, my Arethusa stay,
Alpheüs calls ;" it said, or seem'd to say—
"Naked and swift I flew, (my clothes behind)
Fear strung my nerves, and shame enrag'd my
      mind :
So wing'd with hunger the fierce eagle flies,
To drive the trembling turtles through the skies :
So wing'd with fear the trembling turtles spring,
When the fierce eagle shoots upon the wing.
  " Swift-bounding from the god, I now survey
Where breezy Psophis and Cyllene lay.
Elis' fair structures open'd on my eyes ;
And waving Erymanthus cools the skies.
At length unequal for the rapid chase
Tremble my limbs, the god maintains the race :
O'er hills and vales with furious haste I flew :
O'er hills and vales the god behind me drew.
Now hov'ring o'er, his length'ning shadow bends,
(His length'ning shadow the low Sun extends)
And sudden now, his sounding steps drew near ;
At least I seem'd his sounding steps to hear.
Now sinking, in short sobs I gasp'd for breath,
Just in the jaws of violence and death.
' Ah, Cynthia help !' ('twas thus in thought I pray'd)
' Ah, help a ravish'd, miserable maid !'
The virgin-pow'r consenting to my pray'r,
Diffus'd around a veil of clouded air :
Lost in the gloom he wanders o'er the plain,
And Arethusa calls, but calls in vain ;
In misty steams th' impervious vapours rise,
Perplex his guesses, and deceive his eyes.
  " What fears I felt as thus enclos'd I stood,
What chilling horrours trembled thro' my blood?
So pants the fawn in silence and despair,
When the grim wolf runs howling thro' the lair :
So sits the lev'ret, when the hound pursues
His trembling prey, and winds the tainted dews.
"Sudden my cheek with flashing colour burns,
Pale swoons, and sickly fears succeed by turns :
Cold creeps my blood, its pulses beat no more :
Big drops of sweat ascend from ev'ry pore ;
Adown my locks the pearly dews distill,
And each full eye pours forth a gushing rill ;
Now all at once my melting limbs decay,
In one clear stream dissolving fast away."

  " The god soon saw me floating o'er the plain,
And straight resum'd his warry form again—
Instant, Diana smote the trembling ground ;
Down rush my waters with a murm'ring sound ;
Thence darkling thro' th' infernal regions stray,
And in the Delian plains review the day."

---

## ANGERIANUS DE CÆLIA,

### (EPIG. 40.)

Quum dormiret Amor, rapuit clam pulchra
      pharetram
Cælia, surreptâ flevit Amor pharetrâ.
" Noli (Cypris ait) sic flere Cupido ; pharetram
Pulchra tibi rapuit Cælia, restituet,
Non opus est illi calamis, non ignibus : urit
Voce, manu, gressu, pectore, fronte, oculis."

---

## CUPID MISTAKEN.

#### FROM THE SPORTS OF CUPID, WRITTEN BY AN-GERIANUS.

##### IMITATED AND ENLARGED.

As fast beside a murm'ring stream,
In blissful visions Cupid lay,
    Chloë, as she softly came,
    Snatch'd his golden shafts away.

From place to place in sad surprize
The little angry godhead flew :
    Trembling in his ruddy eyes
    Hung the pearly drops of dew.

So on the rose (in blooming May,
When purple Phœbus rises bright)
    Liquid gems of silver lay,
    Pierc'd with glitt'ring streams of light.

Fair Venus with a tender languish
Smiling, thus her son addrest,
    As he murmur'd out his anguish
    Trembling on her snowy breast :

" Peace, gentle infant, I implore,
Nor lavish precious tears in vain ;
    Chloë, when the jest is o'er,
    Brings the useless shafts again.

" Can Chloë need the shafts of love,
Young, blooming, witty, plump, and fair ?
    Charms and raptures round her move,
    Murm'ring sighs, and deep despair.

" Millions for her unheeded die,
Millions her their blessings owe ;
    Ev'ry motion of her eye
    Murders more than Cupid's bow."

---

## TO A YOUNG LADY,

#### WITH MR. FENTON'S MISCELLANY.

These various strains, where ev'ry talent charms,
Where humour pleases, or where passion warms :
(Strains ! where the tender and sublime conspire,
A Sappho's sweetness, and a Homer's fire
Attend their doom, and wait with glad surprise
Th' impartial justice of Cleora's eyes.

'Tis hard to say, what mysteries of fate,
What turns of fortune on good writers wait.
The party-slave will wound 'em as he can,
And damns the merit, if he hates the man.
Nay, ev'n the bards with wit and laurels crown'd,
Bless'd in each strain, in ev'ry art renown'd,
Misled by pride, and taught to sin by pow'r,
Still search around for those they may devour;
Like savage monarchs on a guilty throne,
Who crush all might that can invade their own.
Others who hate, yet want the soul to dare,
So ruin bards—as beaus deceive the fair:
On the pleas'd ear their soft deceits employ;
Smiling they wound, and praise but to destroy.
These are th' unhappy crimes of modern days,
And can the best of poets hope for praise?
   How small a part of human blessings share
The wise, the good, the noble, or the fair!
Short is the date unhappy wit can boast,
A blaze of glory in a moment lost,
Fortune, still envious of the great man's praise,
Curses the coxcomb with a length of days.
So (Hector dead) amid the female quire,
Unmanly Paris tun'd the silver lyre.
   Attend ye Britons! in so just a cause
'Tis sure a scandal, to withhold applause;
Nor let posterity reviling say,
Thus unregarded Fenton pass'd away!
Yet if the Muse may faith or merit claim,
(A Muse too just to bribe with venal fame)
Soon shalt thou shine " in majesty avow'd;
As thy own goddess breaking thro' a cloud." [1]
Fame, like a nation-debt, tho' long delay'd,
With mighty int'rest must at last be paid.
   Like Vinci's strokes, thy verses we behold;
Correctly graceful, and with labour bold.
At Sappho's woes we breathe a tender sigh,
And the soft sorrow steals from ev'ry eye.
Here Spenser's thoughts in solemn numbers roll,
Here lofty Milton seems to lift the soul.
There sprightly Chaucer charms our hours away
With stories quaint, and gentle roundelay.
   Muse! at that name each thought of pride
     recall,
Ah, think how soon the wise and glorious fall!
What though the sisters ev'ry grace impart,
To smooth thy verse, and captivate the heart:
What though your charms, my fair Cleora! shine
Bright as your eyes, and as your sex divine!
Yet shall the verses, and the charms decay,
The boast of youth, the blessing of a day!
Not Chaucer's beauties could survive the rage
Of wasting envy, and devouring age:
One mingled heap of ruin now we see:
Thus Chaucer is, and Fenton thus shall be!

## TO MR. POPE.

To move the springs of nature as we please,
To think with spirit, but to write with ease:
With living words to warm the conscious heart,
Or please the soul with nicer charms of art,
For this the Grecian soar'd in epic strains,
And softer Maro left the Mantuan plains:
Melodious Spenser felt the lover's fire,
And awful Milton strung his Heav'nly lyre.

[1] Epistle to Southerne.

'Tis yours, like these, with curious toil to trace
The pow'rs of language, harmony, and grace,
How nature's self with living lustre shines;
How judgment strengthens, and how art refines;
How to grow bold with conscious sense of fame,
And force a pleasure which we dare not blame:
To charm us more thro' negligence than pains,
And give ev'n life and action to the strains:
Led by some law, whose pow'rful impulse guides
Each happy stroke, and in the soul presides:
Some fairer image of perfection, giv'n
T' inspire mankind, itself deriv'd from Heav'n.
   O ever worthy, ever crown'd with praise;
Blest in thy life, and blest in all thy lays!
Add that the sisters ev'ry thought refine:
Or ev'n thy life be faultless as thy line;
Yet envy still with fiercer rage pursues,
Obscures the virtue, and defames the Muse.
A soul like thine, in pains, in grief resign'd,
Views with vain scorn the malice of mankind:
Not critics, but their planets prove unjust:
And are they blam'd who sin because they must?
   Yet sure not so must all peruse thy lays;
I cannot rival—and yet dare to praise.
A thousand charms at once my thoughts engage,
Sappho's soft sweetness, Pindar's warmer rage,
Statius' free vigour, Virgil's studious care,
And Homer's force, and Ovid's easier air.
So seems some picture, where exact design,
And curious pains, and strength and sweetness
     join:                          [tows,
Where the free thought its pleasing grace bes-
And each warm stroke with living colour glows;
Soft without weakness, without labour fair;
Wrought up at once with happiness and care!
   How blest the man that from the world removes
To joys that Mordaunt, or his Pope approves;
Whose taste exact each author can explore,
And live the present and past ages o'er:
Who free from pride, from penitence, or strife,
Move calmly forward to the verge of life:
Such be my days, and such my fortunes be,
To live by reason, and to write by thee!
   Nor deem this verse,tho' humble, thy disgrace;
All are not born the glory of their race:
Yet all are born t' adore the great man's name,
And trace his footsteps in the paths to fame.
The Muse, who now this early homage pays,
First learn'd from thee to animate her lays:
A Muse as yet unhonour'd, but unstain'd,
Who prais'd no vices, no preferment gain'd;
Unbiass'd or to censure or commend,
Who knows no envy, and who grieves no friend;
Perhaps too fond to make those virtues known,
And fix her fame immortal on thy own.

## THE SIXTH THEBAID OF STATIUS.

TRANSLATED INTO ENGLISH; WITH NOTES.

Curritur ad vocem jucundam, & carmen amicæ
Thebaïdos, lætam fecit cum Statius urbem,
Promisitque diem: tantâ dulcedine captos
Afficit ille animos——            Juv. Sat. 7.

ARGUMENT TO THE WHOLE THEBAID.

OEDIPUS the son of Laius, king of Thebes, was

in his infancy expos'd to wild beasts upon the mountains; but by some miraculous preservation he escaped this danger, and afterwards, by mistake, slew his own father, as they contended for the way. He then married Jocasta, queen of Thebes, whom he knew not to be his mother, and had by her two sons, Etheocles and Polynices; who, after their father had put out his eyes, and banished himself from Thebes, agreed between themselves to govern year by year interchangeably. But this agreement was ill observed. Etheocles, when his date of government was expired, refused to resign it to Polynices: who, in his rage, fled to Adrastus, king of Argos, to implore assistance against his brother. Adrastus received the young prince with all imaginable tenderness, and gave him in marriage to his fair daughter Deipyle, as the oracles had appointed. He then, with the assistance of his allies, undertakes to settle Polynices on the throne, and to depose Etheocles. Upon this, Thebes is besieged, and after several encounters, the difference is at last decided by the duel and death of the two brothers. This is the main action of the poem. '

Besides this, by way of an under-action, the poet has interwoven another distinct story. The goddess Venus is resolved to revenge herself upon the Lemnians, because they neglected all sacrifices to her. She first disgusts the men with their wives, and then in return spirits up the women into a resolution of murdering their husbands. This horrible design was executed by each of them, except Hypsipyle, who saved her father Thoas. Some time afterwards this also was discovered. Hypsipyle, to avoid the fury of the women fled to the sea-shore; where she was taken by the pirates, and presented by them to king Lycurgus, who made her nurse to his son Archemorus. The dominions of this prince lay directly in the way from Argos to Thebes. As Adrastus and his allies were marching thither, the troops were ready to perish for want of water. They chanced in a wood to meet Hypsipyle, who pitying their misfortunes, lays down in haste her young child, and shows them a spring that could never be drained. She receives the thanks of Adrastus, and having at his request recited her own adventures, returns back, and finds the young infant Archemorus just kill'd by a serpent. Her confusion and fears are described in an excellent speech upon that occasion. The Grecians kill the serpent, and in honour of the dead prince perform all the rites of burial; which is the subject of this present book.

First of all it begins with an historical account of the Nemæan games, then follows the funeral, with a more particular description of hewing the forests, and offering their hair to the deceased. The anguish of Adrastus, the lamentations of Eurydice, and the silence of Hypsipyle, are extremely well adapted to nature. A monument is erected to the memory of Archemorus, which is ornamented with the whole story in sculpture. After this succeed the funeral games; the chariot-race, the

foot-race, the discus, the fight with the cæstus, the wrestling, and shooting of arrows; which last ends with a prodigy, foreboding that none of the confederate princes should return from the war, except Adrastus.

———

Soon mournful fame through ev'ry town proclaims
The rites of sepulture, and Grecian games :
What mighty chiefs should glory give or gain,
Prepar'd to combat on the listed plain.
These honours first the great Alcides paid
To please old Pelop's venerable shade :
What time near Pisa he inhum'd the dead,
And bound with olive-wreaths his dusty head.
These, with new hopes glad Phocis next bestow'd,
When Python sunk beneath her bowyer god.
These still religion to Palæmon pays
(Religion blinded with a length of days)
When hanging o'er the deep in anguish raves
His royal mother [1] to the sounding waves;
O'er either Isthmus floats the mingled moan,
And distant Thebè answers groan for groan.
The pious games begin, with loud alarms,
Here the young warriours first prelude in arms:
Each blooming youth Aonia sends to fame,
And each dear object to the Tyrian dame;
Who once embru'd in blood, shall heap around
High hills of slain, and deluge all the ground.
The youthful sailors thus with early care
Their arms experience, and for sea prepare :
On some smooth lake their lighter oars essay,
And learn the dangers of the watry way;
But once grown bold, they lanch before the wind
Eager and swift, nor turn their eyes behind.
Aurora now, fair daughter of the day,
Warm'd the clear orient with a blushing ray;
Swift from mankind the pow'r of slumbers flew;
And the pale Moon her glimm'ring beams withdrew.
O'er the long woods the matin dirges run,
And shrieks of sorrow wake the rising Sun.
Th' unhappy father, father now no more,
His bosom beat, his aged hairs he tore:
Beside him lay each ornament of state,
To make him wretched, as they made him great.
With more than female grief the mother cries,
And wringing both her hands, obtests the skies;
Bending she weeps upon th' extended slain,
Bathes ev'ry wound, returns, and weeps again.
But when the kings in sad and solemn woe,
Enter'd the dome, majestically slow :
(As if just then the trembling babe was found,
And life's last blood came issuing thro' the wound)
Breast took from breast the melancholy strain,
And pausing nature wept, and sob'd again.
Confus'd each Grecian hangs his guilty head,
And weeps a flood of tears to wail the dead.
Mean while Adrastus bears the friendly part,
And with kind words consoles the father's heart.
He marks th' eternal orders of the sky,
And proves that man was born to grieve and die;
Now tells him Heav'n will future children send
To heir his kingdom, and his years defend.

[1] Leucothöe.

In vain the charmer pleads, unbounded flow
The parent's tears, in violence of woe.
He hears no more than storms that thund'ring
Regard the sailors vows, or piercing cries, [rise,
And the wild horrour of their stony eyes.

Apart, a crowd of friends the bier bestrow
With cypress-boughs: then place the straw be-
       low.              [spread,
The second rank with short-liv'd flow'rs they
Which soon must fade, and wither like the dead.
Arabian odours from the third diffuse
A grateful smoke, and weep in fragrant dews.
Above from heaps of gold bright colours stream,
And deeper purple shoots a sanguine gleam.
Inwoven on the pall, young Linus lay
In lonely woods, to mangling dogs a prey.
Heart-wounded at the sight, in anguish stands
Eurydice, and spreads her trembling hands;
Then turns her eyes, half dying with a groan,
For kindred miseries so like her own.
Arms, scepters, jewels, on the dead they throw,
And sacrifice all grandeur to their woe.
As if the hero, deck'd with warlike spoil,
Was borne in triumph to the fun'ral pyle.
Yet as due rites, with kind affection paid,
Can add some honours to the infant-shade;
Hence rose magnificence, and solemn tears,
With presents suited to maturer years.

Long time with early hopes Lycurgus fed
A breed of coursers sacred to the dead.
A glitt'ring helm was safely plac'd apart,
And purple trappings of Sidonian art:
And consecrated spears, (a deadly store)
Radiant and keen, as yet unstain'd with gore.
The pious mother thus, deceiv'd too late
Like her fond spouse, reserv'd a crown of state,
And royal robes, o'erwrought with rising flow'rs;
The silent growth of solitary hours.
These and the rest at once, the furious sire
Dooms in distraction to the greedy fire.

Meanwhile, assembled by the seer's commands,
To raise the pyre, crowd thick the Grecian
        bands,
From Nemee these, and Tempe's lofty crown,
Tumble whole heaps of crashing forests down:
Their airy brows the naked hills display,
And earth once more beholds the face of day.
Deep groan the groves: on ruffling pinions rise
Birds after birds; the angry savage flies.
Sacred through time, from age to age it stood,
A wide-spread, gloomy, venerable wood;
Older than man, and ev'ry sylvan maid,
Who haunts the grot, or skims along the glade.
Stretch'd o'er the ground the tow'ring oaks were
        seen,
The foodful beech, and cypress ever green:
The nuptial elm, and mountain-holm entire,
The pitchy tree that feeds the fun'ral fire:
The resin soft, and solitary yew,
For ever dropping with unwholesome dew;
The poplar trembling o'er the silver flood,
The warrior ash that reeks in hostile blood,
Th' advent'rous fir that sails the vast profound,
And pine, fresh bleeding from th' odorous
        wound—
All at one time the nodding forests bend,
And with a crash together all descend,
Loud as when blust'ring Boreas issues forth,
To bring the sweeping whirlwind from the north:

Sudden and swift as kindling flames arise,
Float o'er the fields, and blaze unto the skies.
The sinking-grove resounds with frequent groans,
Sylvanus starts, and hoary Pales moans.
Trembling and slow the guardian-nymphs retire,
Or clasp the tree, and perish in the fire.

So when some chief (the city storm'd) com-
        mands
Revenge and plunder to his furious bands:
Ere yet he speaks the domes in ruin lay;
They strike, they level, seize and bear away,
Sacred to Heav'n and Hell, the mourners rear
Two massy altars, pointing in the air.
The pious rites begin, in mournful strains
The music of the Phrygian fife complains;
Whose pow'rful sounds th' unwilling ghosts obey,
And, pale and shiv'ring, mount the realms of day.
First Pelops taught these melancholy strains,
When Niobe's fond offspring prest the plains:
Six blooming youths, and six fair virgins fell,
Sent by fierce Cynthia to the shades of Hell.
Incence and oil upon the pile they throw,
And mighty monarchs mighty gifts bestow.
High-rais'd in air the mournful bier is born,
Dejected chiefs Lycurgus' train adorn;
The female sex around the mother crowd,
And weep and sob, and vent their griefs aloud:
Behind, Hypsipyle's soft sorrows flow
Silent, and fast, in eloquence of woe.
Each heaving bosom draws a deeper sigh,
And the big passion bursts from ev'ry eye.
Thus while the crystal tears unbounded, ran,
In piercing shrieks Eurydice began.

   "Ah! dearest child! amid these mournful
        dames
I never thought to give thee to the flames!
How could I dream of sorrows and of death
In the first moments of thy infant breath?
How could I dread these bloody wars to see;
Or deem that Thebes should ever murder thee?
What sudden vengeance wing'd with wrath di-
Pursues me still, and curses all my line? [vine
Yet Cadmus' sons in ease and plenty live,
Blest with each joy th' indulging pow'rs can give;
No mourning dames in sable weeds appear,
To bathe the last cold ashes with a tear.

   "Wretch that I was, too fondly to believe
A faithless slave, a wand'ring fugitive!
Pious she told the melancholy tale
With fair invention, pow'rful to prevail;
Is this that guardian of the Lemnian state,
Who snatch'd her father from the jaws of fate?
   "Ah no! herself the bloody furies join'd,
And vow'd like those, destruction to mankind!
Is this her care; to leave in woods alone
Her prince, nay more, an infant not her own?
Suppose through pity or neglect she stray'd,
(While my dear child lay trembling in the shade)
Unknowing of the monsters wild and vast,
Who haunt the gloomy groves, or dreary waste;
Each murm'ring fount that quivers to the breeze,
Each dying gale that pants upon the trees,
Sudden by turns distract an infant's ears,
And death attends th' imaginary fears.

   "Hail thou dear infant! wretched, early ghost,
Murder'd by her who ought to love thee most.
Whose hands sustain'd thee, and whose music
        charm'd,       [warm'd:
Whose eye o'ersaw thee, and whose bosom

Who dry'd thy cheeks with streams of crystal
    drown'd,     [sound.
And taught thy voice to frame the fault'ring
Ungrateful wretch, may grief thy years consume,
And pains eternal bend thee to the tomb !
Tear her, ye warriors, tear her from my eyes,
Deaf to her vows, her penitence, or cries:
Deep in her bosom drive th' avenging dart,
To drink the blood that feeds her faithless heart.
In the same moment I'll resign my breath,
Satiate with fury, and content in death !"
  She spake, and starting saw the Lemnian maid,
As in the silence of her soul she pray'd:
Sudden her rage rekindles at the view,
And trickling down her cheeks descend the drops
    of dew.
" Bear, oh ye chiefs, this female curse away,
Who adds a horrour to the fun'ral day,
Who with a smile profanes the matron's moan,
And triumphs in misfortunes not her own."
She said, and sinking drew a fainter sigh.
Rage stop'd her voice, and grief o'erwhelmed
    her eye ;
Thence slowly moving thro' the crowd she went
By silent steps, in sullen discontent.
  So when the holy priest with curious eyes,
Dooms some fair heifer to the sacrifice,
Or the gaunt lion bears her thro' the wood,
As down her side distils the life-warm blood:
The mother-beast, dejected and alone,
Pours to the winds her lamentable moan,
With mournful looks she paces from the plain,
And often goes, and often turns again.
  The father now unbares his rev'rend head ;
His silver locks he scatters o'er the dead :
Then with a sigh, the venerable man
Thus to the parent of the gods began.
" If Jove's almighty wisdom can deceive,
Curst is the man who fondly will believe !
These sacred hairs, long from the razor free,
I bore, a pious gift reserv'd for thee:
What time Opheltes' youthful cheeks resign
Their tender down, an off'ring at thy shrine.
In vain—the sullen priest refus'd my pray'r,
And scatt'ring winds disperst it all in air.
Tear them my fingers, tear them from my head,
The last sad office to the worthy dead!"
  Mean while the kindling brand awakes the
Th' unwilling parents silently retire ;  [fire,
High-lifted shields, that intercept the light
In one dark circle, hide the mournful sight.
The flying em'ralds crackle in the blaze,
And fiery rubies stream with sanguine rays.
In shining rills the trembling silver flows,
And clearer gold with flaming lustre glows.
In balmy clouds Arabia's odours rise,
To waft their grateful fragrance to the skies.
Rich urns of milk, tott'ring, their streams in-
    cline,
Mingling with blood, and ting'd with sable wine.
Sev'n mournful cohorts (as their chieftains
    lead)
With arms reverst pace slowly round the dead ;
Now moving to the left, enclose the pyre,
And scatter heaps of dust to sink the fire,
Thrice join their spears, thrice clash their sound-
    ing shields ;
Four times the females shriek, and clamour fills
    the fields.

  Remote from these, another fire they feed
With firstling victims of the woolly breed.
Intent in thought the pious augur stands,
Approves the rites, inspires the fainting bands :
Calmly dissembling in his anxious mind
Each sad presage of miseries behind.
Returning from the right with loud alarms,
Again the warriors beat their clatt'ring arms:
Shields, lances, helms, the sinking flames o'er-
    spread,
A friend's last pledges to the warlike dead.
Full on the winds the swelling music floats,
And Nemee's shades pour back the length'ning
    notes,
So when the trumpeter with lab'ring breath
Shakes the wide fields, and sounds the charge of
    death :
The blood fermenting feels a gentle heat,
Quick roll the eyes, and fast the pulses beat :
E'er yet their rage the martial god controls,
Nor swells their nerves, nor rushes on their souls.
  Now careful Night in sober weeds array'd,
O'er the clear skies extends her dusky shade.
They bend the copious goblet o'er the pyre,
And quench with wine the yet remaining fire.
Nine times his course bright Lucifer had roll'd,
And ev'ning Vesper deck'd his rays with gold :
Now o'er the urn the sacred earth they spread:
And raise a monument to grace the dead.
Here in relief the Lemnian virgin stands,
Who points the grateful spring to Grecia's bands:
There young Opheltes breathes his dying moan,
And seems to shiver, and turn pale in stone ;
In waving spires the serpent floats along,
And rolls his eyes in death, and darts his forky
    tongue.
  By this, the pleas'd spectators in a row,
Throng the green Circus, and enjoy the show.
Deep in the bosom of a vale it stood,
Sacred to sports, and overhung with wood :
A darker green its grassy surface crowns,
And smoothly swims the car along the downs.
Long ere the dawn of morn the mingling throng
Spreads o'er the plain, and man bears man along :
(Not half such numbers crowd the sacred space.
Where yearly honours dead Palæmon grace ;)
Confus'd delight ! the fair, the gay, the sage,
And boastful youth, and deep-discerning age.
Twice fifty steers along the plains they drew,
As many mother-cows of sable hue ;
As many heifers raise their youthful horns,
Whose front as yet, no blaze of white adorns.
  High o'er the people, wrought with lively
    grace,
Shine the fair glories of their ancient race :
Each speaking figure seems to touch the soul,
And life and motion animate the whole.
Here lab'ring Hercules with anguish prest
The roaring lion to his manly breast.
Inspir'd with art th' historic figures rise,
And ev'n in sculpture live, and meet the eyes.
Here rev'rend Inachus extends his side
O'er the green margin of his silver tide :
Transform'd, behind him fearful Iö stood,
And cropt the grass beside her father's flood ;
She mixes with the herd her mournful cries,
And often turns, and watches Argus' eyes.
Her, from the Pharian coast indulging Jove
Transferr'd immortal, to the realms above.

Still in her fanes the sable Memphian bows,
And eastern Magi pay their early vows.
Here Tantalus amid the pow'rs divine
Lifts the deep goblet crown'd with sparkling wine:
Nor stands (as poets sing) in streams below,
Still curst with life, yet fated still to woe,
The wretch for ever pines, the streams for ever
        flow.
There Pelops lashes on with loos'ned reins
Neptune's fleet coursers o'er the smoking plains;
Behind his rival o'er the rapid steed
Hangs imminent—and drives with equal speed.
Acrysius here in thoughtful posture stands:
There brave Choræbus lifts his bleeding hands.
Here am'rous Jove descending as of old,
Impregnates Danäe with a show'r of gold.
Her blushes Amymóne strives to hide,
Comprest by Neptune in the silver tide.
Alcmena there young Hercules admires,
As her head blazes with three lambent fires.
Here Belus' sons at Hymen's altars stand,
And join with hearts averse the friendly hand:
A faithless smile of ill-dissembled grace
Seem'd most to flatter in Egysthus' face:
As the calm villain with severe delight
Acts in his mind the murders of the night.
Now ev'ry bosom beats with hopes, or fear,
The clamours thicken, and the crowd draws near.
Inspire the muse, to sing each hero's deeds,
O pow'r of verse! and name, and gen'rous steeds.
Before, afar, Arion beats the plain; [mane :
Loose to the breeze high-danc'd his floating
Immortal steed! whom first th' earth-shaker's
        hand
Tam'd to the lash, and drove along the strand:
Though restless as the wintry surges roll,
And furious still, and unsubdu'd of soul.
Mix'd with his watry steeds the god he bore
To Lybian Syrtes, or th' Ionian shore:
Swift flew the rapid car, and left behind
The noise of tempests, and the wings of wind.
To glory next great Hercules he drew,
O'er hills, and vales, and craggy rocks he flew :
Then to Adrastus' government was giv'n
Th' immortal courser, and the gift of Heav'n.
The royal hand by due degrees reclaim'd,
And length of years his stubborn spirit tam'd :
Him now with many a wish, and many a pray'r,
Adrastus lends to Polynices' care ;
Shows him to urge his fiery soul along
With tim'rous hand, and gentleness of tongue :
The reins to guide, the circling lash to wield,
And drive victorious o'er the dusty field.
So sad Apollo with a boding sigh
Told his fond child the danger of the sky :
Careful the parent, such advice to give;
Could fate be chang'd, or headstrong youth
        believe !
Th' Œbalian priest moves second o'er the
        plain, •
Who boasts his coursers of immortal strain :
Sprung from fair Cyllarus in days of yore :
(The guilty product of a stol'n amour)
When Castor griev'd in bitterness of soul, [pole.
Where seas scarce flow beneath the Scythian
White were the steeds that drew him o'er the
        field,
White was his helm, his ribbands, and his shield.
Next, bold Admetus, whirling from above
The sounding scourge, his female coursers drove :

Nor strokes nor blandishment their rage con-
        trols,              [souls,
They bound and swell with more than female
Sprung from the cloud-born Centaurs, such their
        force,
Their lustful heat, and fury in the course.
Then fair Hypsipile's bold offspring came,
Two lovely twins, alike intent on fame, [same.
Their steeds, their chariots, and their arms the
(This Thoas call'd, the name his grandsire bore ,
And Euneos that, to sail from shore to shore)
Each wish'd the glorious victory his own,
If not—his brother to be blest alone.
Last Chromis and Hippodamus succeed,
Each checks the reins, and each inspires his
        steed :
Alike with martial eminence they shone,
Œnomäus' this, and that Alcides' son ;
One drove the coursers erst at Pisa bred,
And one the savage steeds of Diomed.
Whence first they start, a stony fragment
Of old, a limit to contiguous lands.   [stands,
An aged oak of leaves and branches bare,
Presents a goal to guide the circling car.
Their distance such, as the wing'd arrow flies
Thrice from the bow sent hissing through the
        skies.
Mean while, high-thron'd amid th' Aonian
Divine Apollo strikes the silver lyre ;    [quire
He sung the wars on Phlegra's fatal plain,
And Python, o'er Castalia's fountain slain.
He sung what order rules the worlds on high,
Who bids the thunder roar, and lightning fly :
Who feeds the stars, or gave the winds to blow :
What springs eternal swell the seas below ;.
Who spread the clouds, who rolls the lamp of
        light
O'er Heav'n's blue arch, or wraps the world in
        night.
Here ceas'd th' harmonious god, his lyre he
With decent care beneath a laureat shade ; [laid
Then in rich robes his beauteous limbs he drest :
A starry zone hung blazing o'er his breast.
Sudden a shout confus'dly strikes his ears—
He bends his awful eyes, the crowd appears.
Each chief he knows, and honours each, but most
The [2] priest, and ruler of Thessalia's host, [3]
" What pow'r," (he cries) " has fir'd with thirst of
These two adorers of Apollo's name ?     [fame
Equally dear and good, alike renown'd
For piety, alike with favours crown'd.
When once a swain the lowing herds I drove,
(Such was the doom of fate, and wrath of Jove)
Still did Admetus' pious altars blaze,
And ev'ry temple rung with hymns of praise;
While at my shrine Amphiaräus stands,
And lifts his eyes, and spreads his trembling
        hands ;
O dearest, best of men ; alas no more—
Black fate impends, and all thy joys are o'er.
Soon must the Theban earth in sunder rend
Her opening jaws, and thou to Hell descend !
Admetus' life to distant times shall last,
And ev'ry year add glories to the past :
Unknowing of repentance, cares, and strife,
These hands shall guide him to the verge of life.
Each bird of omen told the fatal day—"
He said, and weeping turn'd his eyes away :

* Amphiaräus.     [3] Admetus.

Then sudden from Olympus' airy height,
To Nemee's shade precipitates his flight;
Swift, as a sudden flash of light'ning flies,
Bending he shoots adown the shining skies:
Ev'n while on Earth the god pursues his way,
Behind, aloft, the streams of glory play,
Dance on the winds, or in a blaze decay.

Now in his helm impartial Prothöus throws
The flying lots, and as the lots dispose,
Around him rang'd in beauteous order came
Each ardent youth, a candidate for fame.
Here wild mistrust, and jealousies appear,
And pale surprise, and self-suspecting fear:
Restless impatience, cold in ev'ry part,
And a sad dread that seems to sink the heart.
There shouts of triumph rend the vaulted sky,
And fame and conquest brighten ev'ry eye.
Th' impatient coursers pant in ev'ry vein,
And pawing seem to beat the distant plain:
The burning foam descends, the bridles ring,
And from the barrier-bounds in thought they
  spring;
The vales, the floods appear already crost,
And e'er they start, a thousand steps are lost.
T' exalt their pride, a crowd of servants deck
Their curling manes, and stroke the shining
  neck.
Instant, (the signal giv'n) the rival throng
Starts sudden with a bound—and shoots along.
Swift as a vessel o'er the waters flies,
Swift as an arrow hisses through the skies:
Swift as a flame devours the crackling wood,
Swift as the headlong torrents of a flood.
Now in one cloud they vanish from the eye,
Nor see nor know their rivals as they fly:
They turn the goal: again with rapid pace
The wheels roll round, and blot their former
  trace;
Now on their knees they steer a bending course,
Now hang impatient o'er the flying horse.
From groaning earth the mingling clamours rise,
Confusion fills their ears, and darkness blinds
  their eyes.
Instinct with prescience, or o'eraw'd by fear,
Arion feels an unknown charioteer
Pois'd on the reins; to sudden thought restor'd,
He dreads the fury of his absent lord:
Enrag'd now runs at random, and disdains
To bear a stranger: wonder fills the plains.
All think the steed too eager for the prize;
The steed breathes vengeance, from the driver
  flies,
And seeks his master round with wishful eyes.
  The next, though mighty far the next, suc-
    ceeds
Amphiaräus with his snow-white steeds:
Close by his side Admetus whirls along,
Euneos and Thoas join the flying throng:
Next Chromas and Hippodamus appear,
Who wage a dreadful conflict in the rear:
Skill'd of themselves, in vain they urge the chase,
(Their steeds too heavy for so swift a race)
Hippodamus flew first, and full behind
Impatient Chromis blows the sultry wind.
Admetus now directs the side-long horse
To turn the goal, and intercept the course:
His equal art the priest of Phœbus tries,
The goal he brushes, as his chariot flies;
While mad Arion wanders o'er the plain,
Nor minds the race, nor hears the curbing rein.

Unable to control, the trembling chief
Sits sadly silent, and indulges grief:
Pleas'd with his liberty the sea-born horse
Springs with a bound, and thunders o'er the
  course:
Loud shouts the multitude; in wild debate
Of fears and terrours Polynices sate,
Flings up the reins, and waits th' event of fate.
So spent with toils, and gasping after breath,
Pants the pale sailor in the arms of death;
In sad despair gives ev'ry labour o'er,
And marks the skies and faithless winds no more.
  Now horse with horse, to chariot chariot clos'd,
Wheels clash'd with wheels, and chief to chief
  oppos'd.          [ways—
War, war it seem'd! and death ten thousand
So dreadful, is the sacred lust of praise!
Each chief by turns his panting coursers fires,
With praise now pleases, now with rage inspires.
By fair address Admetus sooths along
Iris the swift, and Pholöe the strong.
Amphiaräus hastens with a blow
Fierce Aschetos to rush before the foe,
And Cycnus whiter than the new-fal'n snow.
With vows and pray'rs Hippodamus excites
Slow moving Calydon, renown'd in fights:
Strimon encourag'd by bold Chromis flies,
And swift Æchion starts at Euneos' cries:
And fair Podarcè fleck'd with purple stains,
By Thoas summon'd, beats the sounding plains.
In silence Polynices drives alone,
Sighs to himself, and trembles to be known.
  Three times the smoking car with rapid pace
Had turn'd the goal, the fourth concludes the
  race.
Fast and more fast the panting coursers blow,
And streams of sweat from ev'ry member flow.
  Now Fortune first the crown of conquest
    brings
(Suspending in mid air her trembling wings).
In act to hurl Admetus to the plain,
Revengful Thoas gives up all the rein;
Hippodamus survey'd the fraud from far:
Full in its course he met the driving car,
Loud clash'd the wheels; Hippodamus withdrew
To turn the chariot, ardent Chromas flew
Instant before, in angry fight oppos'd,
Chief strove with chief, to chariot chariot clos'd.
In vain th' impatient coursers urge along,
Lock'd in th' embrace, indissolubly strong.
  So when the summer winds in silence sleep,
And drowsy Neptune stills the watry deep:
O'er the clear verdant wave extended lies
Th' unmoving vessel, till the gales arise.
  Again the warriors strive, the fields resound:
Hippodamus, all sudden with a bound
Shock'd—from his chariot tumbled to the ground.
The Thracian coursers (but their chief withstood)
Spring to devour his limbs, and drink his blood:
Instant the gen'rous victor turn'd away,
And gain'd more glory though he lost the day.
  Mean while the god who gilds th' ethereal
    space
Descends, himself a partner of the race:
(Just where the steeds their stretching shade
And the long labours of the Circus end)  [extend,
A Gorgon's head aloft in air he bore,
Horrid with snakes, and stain'd with human gore:
One ghastly look were able to dismay
The steeds of Mars, or those that lead the day;

Ev'n Hell's grim guardian might surcease to roar;
And furies fear, unknown to fear before.
    Sudden Arion ey'd the sight from far,
And loudly snorting stopp'd the driving car:
Cold darts of ice shot thrilling through his blood,
His fearful flesh all trembled as they stood:
Abruptly shock'd, and mindless of the rein,
Th' Aonian hero tumbled to the plain ;
Again recover'd, fleeter than the wind
Arion flies, and leaves his chief behind.
Beside the prostrate chief, the rival throng
Obliquely bending, swiftly rush'd along.
Slow from the dust he rose, and sadly went
Through the long crowd in sullen discontent.
O happy hour ! had fate but deign'd to close
Thy eyes in death ; the period of our woes !
Thee Thebes should honour, and her tyrant shed
Some tears in public to bewail the dead.
Larissa's groves should fall, to raise thy pyre
And Nemee's woods augment the fun'ral fire.
All Greece a nobler monument should raise
Than this, now sacred to Opheltes' praise.
    Furious the prophet drove with rapid pace
Sure of the prize, yet second in the race:
Before, afar the sea-born courser drew
His empty chariot rat'ling as he flew.
Yet still the prophet thunders o'er the plain,
Eager of praise, amaz'd, enrag'd,—in vain ;
The pow'r of wisdom more than mortal strong,
Swells ev'ry nerve to lash the steeds along :
Instinct with rage divine his steeds renew
The rapid labour bath'd in streams of dew.
The glowing axle kindles as they fly,
And drifts of rising dust involve the sky.
Earth opening seems to groan, (a fatal sign !)
Still they rush on, advancing in a line :
Now with redoubled swiftness Cycnus flies,
But partial Neptune the whole palm denies :
Arion won the race, the prophet bore the prize.
    A massy bowl (the pledge design'd to grace
The gen'rous chief victorious in the race)
Two youths present him : antique was the mould,
Blazing with gems, and rough with rising gold :
In this, Alcides each revolving night
Was wont to drown the labours of the fight :
Grav'd on the sides was seen the dreadful fray
When brutal Centaurs snatch'd the bride away.
With living terrours stare the chiefs around,
These aim the dart, and those receive the wound:
Each in distorted postures heaves for breath,
And seems to threaten in the pangs of death.
    A costly vesture was reserv'd to grace
Admetus, next in merit as in place ;
Embroider'd figures o'er the texture shine,
And Tyrian purple heightens the design.
Here pale and trembling with the wintry air,
Leander stands, an image of despair.
Now bending from the beach, he seems to glide
With eyes uplifted through the rolling tide ;
Aloft, alone the melancholy dame
Eyes the rough waters, and extends the flame.
Half-weeping Polynices takes his prize,
A beauteous handmaid with celestial eyes.
    August rewards are destin'd next to grace
The spritely youth contending in the race.
A blameless sport ! and sacred sure the praise
To grace a festival in peaceful days :
Nor yet unuseful in th' embattel'd plain
When death is certain, and resistance vain.

First cheerful Idas in the lists appears,
Idas, a lovely boy in blooming years
(Idas who late his honour'd temples bound
With palms that flourish'd on th' Olympian
        ground).
Loud shouts each chief that from high Elis leads
His native train, and Pisa's watry meads:
Then Phædimus proclaim'd-in Isthmian games,
And Alcon first of Sicyonian names ;
Next aged Dymas rose, whose youthful speed
Surpass'd the swiftness of the flying steed :
And last in infamous disorder came
A clam'rous multitude unknown to fame.
    But ev'ry voice cheers Atalanta's son,
And ev'ry eye devours him ere they run.
Lives there a warrior in the world of fame,
Who never heard of Atalanta's name ?
Like Cynthia's self she seem'd, a sylvan grace :
Matchless alike in beauty or the race.
The mother's glories all their thoughts employ,
And raise expectance from the lovely boy.
He too in speed out-strips the wings of wind,
As thro' the lawns he drives the panting hind :
Or when he catches sudden with a bound
The flying jav'lin e'er it touch the ground.
    The modest youth unbinds with decent care
His damask vesture dancing to the air :
Then by degrees unveils to public view
His snowy limbs like marble, vein'd with blue.
His rosy cheeks that glow'd with warmth before,
His tresses wav'd in ringlets please no more ;
A thousand charms appear ! in stupid gaze
The crowd devours him, silent with amaze.
Conscious he stands, his head declining down,
And blushes oft ; and chides them with a frown :
Decent confusion ! mindful of the toil
He bathes his shining limbs in streams of oil ;
Alike the chiefs—Intent, th' encircling host
Admires 'em all, Parthenopæus most.
    So when the night in solemn silence reigns,
And one clear blue o'erspreads th' etherial plains:
The glitt'ring stars with living splendours glow,
And dance and tremble on the seas below ;
High o'er them all exalted Hesper rolls,
Itself a sun, and gilds the distant poles.
    The next in beauty, as in speed, appears
Fair Idas, in the strength of youthful years :
A party-coloured down but just began
To shade his chin, the promise of a man.
    A signal sounds. The ready racers start,
Double their speed, and summon all their art.
Low at each step their straining knees they bend,
Then springing with a bound, again ascend,
Swifter than thought ; nor seem to run, but fly,
Stretch'd on the winds, half-vanish'd from the
        eye.
Now side by side, or breast to breast they close,
While each alike by turns outstrips his foes.
Scarce half so swiftly o'er the Nemean plains
Just now, the courser pour'd with loos'ned reins,
Each, like an arrow from the Parthian yew
Sent with full force, along the Circus flew.
    So when a tim'rous herd of list'ning deer
The roaring lion hears, or seems to hear,
(What time the lordly savage haunts the wood,
And longs to bathe his thirsty jaws in blood)
Close and more close they join, a trembling
        train,
And wildly stare, and scour along the plain,

Yet furious still, Parthenopæus flies ;
Him step by step impatient Idás plies,
And pants aloud, with vengeance in his eyes;
Now hanging o'er, his hov'ring shade is seen,
That lengthens still, and floats along the green :
And sudden now, by unperceiv'd degrees
Full on his neck he blows the sultry breeze.
Next Phædimus and aged Dymes past
Along the circus, Alcon came the last.

As the fair offspring of the sylvan Grace
With matchless swiftness speeds along the race,
His golden tresses wav'd in curls, behind
Flow loosely down, and dance upon the wind :
(These from a child with pious hopes he bore,
Sacred to her who treads the Delian shore[4];
What time from Thebe's distant plains he came
Renown'd for conquests of immortal fame :
Too fondly pious ! in a Theban urn
Soon must thou sleep, ah, never to return!)
These vengeful Idas saw with ardent eyes :
Resolv'd by force or fraud t'obtain the prize;
Sudden he stretch'd his impious arm, and drew
Supine on earth the stripling, as he flew :
Then starting reach'd the goal, and claim'd the
        prize.
Arms ! arms ! aloud th' Arcadian nation cries:
Vengeance at once they vow, or else prepare
To leave the Circus and renounce the war.
Tumultuous murmurs echo thro' the crowd,
Those praise the fraud, and these detest aloud.

Slow-rising from the plains the youth appears,
His eyes half angry, and half drown'd with tears,
He bends his head, the tears in silence flow ;
A mournful image, beautiful in woe!
Now beats his bosom, frantic with despair ;
And rends the ringlets of his golden hair.

A busy murmur deafens ev'ry ear,
Nor yet the crowd the royal judgment hear.
At last Adrastus rose with awful grace,
And thus bespoke the rivals in the race.
" Cease, gen'rous youths ! once more your
        fortunes try,
In sep'rate paths, each starting from the eye."

So spake the king : and sudden from the view,
In sep'rate paths the ready racers flew.
But first th' Arcadian youth with lifted eyes
Thus sent his soul in whispers to the skies.
" Queen of the silver bow, and wood-land
        glades ;                [shades ;
The Heav'ns fair light, and empress of the
Sacred to thee alone, with decent care
I nurs'd these curls of loug-descending hair :
At thy desires I fell ; yet hear my pray'r !
If e'er my mother pleas'd thee in the chase,
If e'er I pleas'd thee—banish my disgrace ;
Nor let these omens prophesy my fall
( As sure they must) beneath the Theban wall !"
So pray'd the youth. The goddess heard his
        pray'r,
Rapid he shot along, half pois'd in air :
Fast and more fast the flying fields withdrew ;
Scarce rose the dust beneath him as he flew.
Shouting, he reach'd the goal : with transport
        fir'd,
Soon sought Adrastus, and his right requir'd.
Panting and pale he seiz'd the palm. At hand
To close the game the ready prizes stand.

[4] Diana.

Th' Arcadian youth a brass-hoof'd courser gain'd:
A buckler fraudful Idas next obtain'd:
But Lycian quivers for the rest remain'd.

Adrastus next demands what chiefs prepare
To whirl the massy discus through the air.
A herald, bending with the burthen, threw
Th' enormous circles down in public view.
Starts ev'ry Grecian speechless with surprise ;
Much wond'ring at the weight and shapeless
        size.
First two Achaians round the labour came,
With ardent Phlegyas, candidates for fame :
An Acarnanian next accepts the toil,
And three brave chieftains from Ephyre's soil,
With numbers more—but eager of renown,
Sudden Hippomedon flings thund'ring down
A disk of double weight ; amaz'd they stand;
The vast orb rings, and shakes the trembling
        land.                [nown'd,
" Warriors" (he cries) " in fighting fields re-
Whose arms must strike Thebe's bulwarks to
        the ground :
On tasks like these your mighty prowess try :"—
Boastful he spoke, and whirl'd it up the sky.
Amaz'd each chief the wond'rous cast admires,
And conscious of th' event betimes retires.
Pisæan Phlegyas only keeps the field,
With great Menestheus, yet untaught to yield :
Brave warriors each, too noble to disgrace
By one mean act the glories of their race.
The rest inglorious leave the listed ground,
And tremble to survey th' enormous round.
First Phlegyas rose the mighty toil to try :
Dumb was each voice, attentive ev'ry eye ;
He rolls the quoit in dust with prudent care,
And poises oft, and marks its course in air.
Ev'n from a child, (where old Alphëus leads
His mazy stream through Pisa's lowly meads)
Not only when with mighty chiefs he strove
At sacred games to please Olympian Jove :
Thus with full force the massy weight he threw
Far o'er the stream, half shaded, as it flew.
At first he marks the skies and distant plain,
Then summons all his strength from ev'ry vein.
Couch'd on his knees the pond'rous orb he swung
High o'er his head, along the air it sung.
Now wasting by degrees, with hollow sound
Fell heavily, and sunk beneath the ground.
Fond of his art and strength in days of yore,
Well-pleas'd he stands, and waits th' event once
        more.
Loud shout the Greeks, and dwell on Phlegyas'
        praise.
Hippomedon with scorn the chief surveys.
Some nobler arm the pond'rous orb must throw
With care, directly in a line below.
But fortune soon his mighty hopes withstood,
Fortune still envious to the brave or good !
Alas, can man confront the pow'rs on high ?
While distant fields are measur'd in his eye,
Just when his arm he stretch'd at full extent,
Couch'd on one knee, his side obliquely bent ;
Struck by some force unseen, th' enormous round
Dropt from his hand, and idly prints the ground.
Much griev'd the pitying host, yet griev'd not all;
Some inly smil'd to see the discus fall.
    Next, sage Menestheus stands prepared to
        fling
The disk, and rolls it in the dusty ring :

Z

Intent of mind he marks its airy way,
And much implores the progeny of May.
Well-aim'd it flew half o'er the cirque; at last
Heavy it fell.  An arrow mark'd the cast.
    Slow rose Hippomedon, and e'er he rose
Much weigh'd the fate and fortune of his foes.
He pois'd, and rear'd the mighty orb on high;
Swung round his arm, and whirl'd it thro' the
        sky,
Forth-springing with the cast.  Aloft it sung
Far o'er the mark where er'st Menestheus flung:
And o'er those hills with grassy verdure crown'd,
Whose airy summits shade the circus round—
There sunk, and sinking shook the trembling
        ground.
    So Polyphemus, more than mortal strong,
Hurl'd a huge rock to crush th' Ulyssean throng:
Blind as he was, the vengeful weight he threw,
The vessel trembled, and the waters flew.
    Soon good Adrastus rises, to repay
With sumptuous gifts the labours of the fray.
Safe for Hippomedon apart was roll'd
A tiger's skin, the paws o'erwrought with gold.
His Gnossian bows and darts Menestheus took;
Then thus to Phlegyas with a mournful look
He said.  " This sword, unhappy chief, re-
        ceive;
(A boon so just Hippomedon might give:)
This sword which once immortal honours gain'd,
Which sav'd Pelasgus,and his pow'r maintain'd."
    A warlike toil Adrastus next demands,
In iron gloves to sheath their hardy hands:
First Capaneus prepar'd for combat stands;
A mighty giant, large, and tow'ring high,
Dreadful in fight, and hideous to the eye.
Around his wrists the hard bull-hides he binds,
And vaunts his strength, and deals his blows in
        winds:                    [there be,
" Stand forth some chief," he cries, " (if such
Who dares oppose an enemy like me!)
Yet might some Theban sink beneath my blow;
Glorious and sweet is vengeance on a foe."
    So spake the chief.  Half-trembling with amaze,
In speechless horrour all the circle gaze.
At last Alcidimas, with gen'rous ire
Sprung forth, unask'd.  The Doric bands admire.
All but his friends.  They knew the daily care
Which Pollux us'd, to train him to the war.
(He taught him first to bind the gauntlets round
His nervous wrists, and aim the crashing wound:
Oppos'd in fight, he heav'd him high, or prest
The youth loud-panting on his naked breast.)
    Him Capaneus survey'd with scornful eyes,
Insults his years, and claims a nobler prize.
Provok'd, he turns to fight.  Each warrior stands
At full extent, and lifts his iron hands.  [round,
Well-temper'd casques their hardy brows sur-
To break at least the fury of the wound.
This tow'r like Tytius on the Stygian shore,
When the fierce vultures cease to drink his gore:
So high in air his spreading shoulders rise,
So swell his muscles, and so flame his eyes;
That at his side in blooming youth appears,
Yet promis'd wonders from maturer years:
The favours of the crowd alike succeed
On either side: none wish'd the chiefs to bleed.
    Low'ring at first they met, nor silence broke,
Each lifts his arm, and only aims the stroke.
Some moments thus they gaz'd in wild surprise,
A hasty fury sparkled in their eyes;

Now conscious fear succeeds.  The chiefs essay
Their arms, and slowly first provoke the fray.
This on nice art and diffidence relies,
That on mere courage and stupendous size;
Void of all fear, and without conduct brave,
He wastes that strength himself has pow'r to
        save:
Still blindly drives where fury leads the way,
And storms, and falls the victor and the prey.
With stedfast glances this surveys his foe,
And either shuns, or wards th' impending blow:
Now lowly bends (his elbow o'er him spread)
The stroke impetuous sings above his head.
Now nearer draws, the more he seems to fly;
So much his motion varies from his eye!
Now with full force he aims a pond'rous blow,
And tow'ring high o'ershades his mighty foe.
Thus in some storm the broken billows rise
Round the vast rock, and thunder to the skies.
    Once more with wary footsteps wheeling
        round,
Full on his front he deals a mortal wound:
Crashing it falls—unfelt the trickling blood
Spreads o'er his helmet in a crimson flood.
A sudden whisper murmurs round; alone
To Capaneus the cause remains unknown.
At last he lifts his hand on high, the gore
Forth-welling fast distains his cæstus o'er.
Grief swells his heart, and vengeance and dis-
        dain—
So foams the lion, monarch of the plain,
And loudly roaring with indignant pride,
Gnaws the barb'd jav'lin griding in his side:
Now springs with rage; supine along the ground
Pants the bold youth whose hand infix'd the
        wound.
    Fast and more fast his lifted arms he throws
Around his head, and doubles blows on blows.
Part waste in air, part on the cæstus fall
With mighty force; his foe returns 'em all.
Still seems to fear him with dissembling eyes,
Yet still persists, and combats, while he flies.
Panting they reel; the youth retreats more slow,
The weary giant scarcely aims a blow,
They sink at once—so sailors on the main
Who long have toil'd through adverse waves in
        vain,                        [more,
All drop their hands.  The signal sounds once
Again they start, and stretch the lab'ring oar.
    Thus rose the chiefs, with recollected might
Rush'd Capaneus like thunder to the fight.
Low bends Alcidimas with watchful eyes:
Short of his aim the giant o'er him flies;
Up starts the youth, and as he stagger'd round,
Clasp'd firm his neck, and bow'd him to the
        ground.
As rising from th' inglorious plain contends
Fierce Capaneus, a second blow descends
Full on his head: beneath the stroke he bent;
The youth turn'd pale, and trembled at th'
        event.
    Loud shout the Greeks: the shore and forest
        rings.
Then thus in haste exclaims the king of kings
(As from the ground the furious Argive rose,
And vow'd, and aim'd intolerable blows):
" Seize him, ye chiefs,his bloody hands restrain,
Give all the palm, but lead him from the plain.
Haste, see, he raves! ah, tear him from my eyes,
He lives, he rises, the Laconian dies!"

He said. Hippomedon, and Tydeus rose :
Scarce both their hands restrain his mighty
    blows.          [give :
Then thus they spoke. "The prize is thine, for-
'Tis double fame to bid the vanquish'd live ;
A friend, and our ally"—he storms the more,
Rejects the prize, and thus devoutly swore :
" By all this blood, at present my disgrace,
These hands shall crush that more than female
    face ;         [plain"—
These hands shall dash him headlong to the
To Pollux then he weeps, but weeps in vain.
He said. By force they turn'd his steps away.
Stubborn he still persists, nor yields the day.
Far off in secret, the Laconian host
Smile at his fury, and their hero boast.
    Mean while with conscious virtue Tydeus
    burns,
Renown and praise inflame his heart by turns :
Swift in the race he still the guerdon bore,
Now toss'd the discus, now the gauntlets wore ;
But most for Pales' active arts renown'd,
To hurl his foe supine along the ground.
By Hermes tutor'd, on th' Œtolian plain,
He made whole nations bite the dust in vain.
    Full terrible he look'd. For arms he wore
The savage trophies of a mountain-boar,
Once Calydonia's dread ! the bristly hide [pride.
Broad o'er his shoulders hung, with barb'rous
Unbound, he flings it down, then waits his
    foes.
Besides him, tow'ring, huge Agylleus rose,
A monstrous giant, dreadful to mankind ;
Yet weak he seem'd, his limbs were loosely
    join'd.
Low Tydeus was. What Nature there deny'd,
Strong nerves, and mighty courage well supply'd;
For Nature never since the world began
Lodg'd such a spirit in so small a man !
Soon as their shining limbs are bath'd in oil,
Down rush the heroes to the wrestling toil.
Deform'd with dust (their arms at distance
    spread)
Each on his shoulder half reclines his head.
    Now bending 'till he almost touch'd the plain,
Tydeus the giant heav'd, but heav'd in vain.
The mountain-cypress thus, that firmly stood
From age to age, the empress of the wood,
By some strong whirlwind's sudden blast declin'd,
Bends arching down, and nods before the wind :
The deep roots tremble till the gust blows o'er,
And then she rises, stately as before.
    So vast Agylleus scarcely mov'd below,
Hangs imminent upon th' Œtolian foe.
Breast, shoulders, thighs, with mighty strokes
    resound,
And all appears an undistinguish'd wound.
On tiptoe rais'd, their heads obliquely bent,
Each hangs on each, stretch'd out at full ex-
    tent.
Not half so bloody, or with half such rage,
Two furious monarchs of the herd engage.
Apart the milk-white heifer views the fight,
And waits to crown the victor with delight.
Their chests they gore, the mighty shock re-
    sounds ;        [wounds.
Love swells their hate, and heals the gaping
    So shaggy bears in strict embraces roll,
And from each corse squeeze forth th' unwilling
    soul.

    Thus Tydeus storm'd ; nor heats nor toils as-
    swage
His furious strength, or mitigate his rage.
Agylleus pants aloud, nor scarce contends;
Black'ned with dust a stream of sweat descends.
Tydeus press'd on, and seem'd to aim a blow
Full at his neck : the force was meant below,
Where well-knit nerves the knees firm strength
    supply ;
Short of their reach, his hands the blow deny.
He sinks ; o'er him, like some vast mountain fell
Agylleus, and half squeez'd his soul to Hell.
    So when th' Iberian swain in search of ore
Descends, and views the light of Heav'n no more:
If some strong earthquake rocks the mould'ring
    ground,
(High o'er him hung) down rush the ruins round,
Deep under earth his batter'd carcase lies,.
Nor breathes its spirit to congenial skies.
    Full of disdain Œtolian Tydeus rose ;
No peace, no bounds his fierce resen'ment
    knows :        [wind,
Swift from th' inglorious hold he springs like
And circles round, then firmly fix'd behind.
His hand embrac'd his side, his knees surround
The giant's knees, and bend 'em to the ground.
Nought boots resistance now. Agylleus makes
One more essay. That moment Tydeus takes,
And rears him high. The mingling shouts arise,
And loud applause runs rattling thro' the skies.
    So Hercules, who long had toil'd in vain,
Heav'd huge Anthëus from the Lybian plain ;
Erect in air th' expiring savage hung,
Nor touch'd the kindred earth, from whence he
    sprung.
    Long Tydeus held him thus. At length he found
The point of time, and hurl'd him to the
    ground
Side-long—Himself upon the giant lies,
And grasps his neck, and firmly locks his thighs.
Prone o'er th' inglorious dust, Agylleus quakes
Half-dead : his shame alone resistance makes :
Then rose at last, and stagg'ring thro' the
    throng,
Slowly he trail'd his feeble legs along.
    When Tydeus thus. (His nobler hand sustain'd
The palm, his left the warlike gifts he gain'd :)
" What though my blood o'erflow'd yon guilty
    ground,        [round ;
When singly arm'd, whole numbers press'd me
(So prov'd all contracts with the Theban name,
Their honour such) yet Tydeus lives the same."
He spoke, and speaking sent the prize away ;
Aside, a breast-plate for the vanquish'd lay.
    Others in arms their manly limbs enclose;
To combat Epidaurian Agreus rose :
Him with his shining blade the Theban waits,
An exile still by unrelenting fates.
    Then thus Adrastus. "Gen'rous youths give o'er;
Preserve all rage: and thirst for hostile gore.
Ye gods ! what slaughter and what combats call !
Then waste your fury, Thebes demands it all.
But you, O prince ! a kinsman, and our friend,
Whose cause such numbers with their lives defend;
For whom, our native towns, and countries lay
Unpeopled half, to other foes a prey ;
Trust not th' event of fight ; nor bleed, to please
Th' inhuman hopes of base Etheocles.
Avert it Heav'n !" The ready chiefs obey'd:
Their brave attempt a glitt'ring helm repaid.

Howe'er in sign of conquest and renown,
He bids the warriors Polynices crown
With wreaths, and hail him victor—no portent,
(So will'd the Sisters) prophesy'd th' event.
Him too the chiefs with kind persuasions pray
To rise, and close the honours of the day :
(And lest one victory be lost) to throw
The missile lance, or bend the Lycian bow.
Well-pleas'd Adrastus to the plain descends
In pomp, his steps a youthful crowd attends.
Behind, a squire the royal quiver bore,
Deep fill'd with shafts, a formidable store.
'Tis plain (Shall man deny ?) each human
        cause
Proceeds, unseen, from Heav'n's eternal laws.
All fate appear'd : the chiefs perversely blind
Neglect the sign, nor see th' event behind.
We deem from chance unerring omens flow ;
While fate draws near, and aims a surer blow.
By this the monarch strain'd the bending yew:
Full on its mark the feather'd weapon flew,
Nor enter'd there.  Th' impassive ash resounds :
Again with double force the shaft rebounds,
In the same line wing'd back its airy way,
Then prone on earth before Adrastus lay.
Each reasons, as his wayward thoughts decree;
These think the shaft rebounded from the tree ;
And those, that winds with unresisted force
Drove clouds on clouds, to intercept its course.
Mean while th' event and dreadful omen lies
Deep wrapt in night, nor seen by human eyes.
One chief in safety must return alone,
Through woes, and blood, and dangers yet un-
known.

---

NOTES

UPON THE

## SIXTH THEBAID OF STATIUS.

### NOTE 1.

Mr. Dryden, in his excellent preface to the
Æneid, takes occasion to quarrel with Statius, and
calls the present book an ill-timed, and injudicious episode.  I wonder so severe a remark
could pass from that gentleman, who was an admirer of our author even to superstition.  I own
I can scarce forgive myself, to contradict so great
a poet, and so good a critic ; talium enim virorum
ut admiratio maxima, ita censura difficilis.  However the present case may admit of very allevi-
ating circumstances.  It may be replied in general, that the design of this book was to give a
respite to the main action, introducing a mournful, but pleasing variation from terrour to pity.
It is also highly probable, that Statius had an eye
to the funeral obsequies of Polydore, and Anchises, mentioned in the 3d and 5th books of Virgil.
We may also look upon them as a prelude, opening the mind by degrees to receive the miseries
and horrour of a future war.  This is intimated
in some measure by the derivation of the word
Archemorus.
  Besides the reasons above mentioned, we have
a fine opportunity of remarking upon chief of
the heroes who must make a figure hereafter ;
this is represented to the eye in a lively sketch
that distributes to each person his proper lights,
with great advantage.

### 2.

It must certainly be an infinite pleasure to
peruse the most ancient piece of history now extant, excepting that in holy scripture.  This
remark must be understood of the action of the
Thebaid only, which Statius, without question,
faithfully recited from the most authentic chro-
nicles in his own age.  The action of the Iliad
and Odyssey happened several years after.  This
is evident from Homer's own words.  Agamemnon, in the 4th Iliad, recites with great transport
the expedition of Tydeus : and Ulysses mentions
the story of Jocasta (or Epicaste, as he calls her)
in a very particular manner.  It is in his descent
to Hell, Odyssey the eleventh :

Μητέρα δ' Οιδιπόδαο ἴδον, καλὴν Επικάϛην,
"Η μέγα ἔργον ἔρεξεν ἀϊδρείησι νόοιο,
Γημαμένη ῷ ὗεῖ. ὁ δ' ὃν πατέρ' ἐξαναρίξας
Γῆμεν.
'Αλλ' ὁ μὲν ἐν Θήβη πολυηράτῳ ἄλγεα πάχων
Καδμείων ἤνασσε, θεῶν ὀλοὰς διὰ βουλάς,
'Η δ' ἔβη εἰς ἀϊδαο πυλάρταο κρατεροῖο
῀Ωι ἀχέϊ χομένη, τῷ δ' ἄλγεα κάλλιπ' ὀπίσσω
Πολλὰ μάλ', ὅσσα τὲ μητρὸς ἐρίννυες 'ετελεῦσι.

### 3.

The antiquity of the Thebaid may be considered also in another view.  As the poet was
obliged to conform the manners of his heroes to
the time of action, we in justice ought not to
be so much shock'd with those insults over the
dead which run through all the battles.  This
softens a little the barbarity of Tydeus, who
expired gnawing the head of his enemy ; and the
impiety of Capaneus, who was thunderstruck
while he blasphemed Jupiter.  Whoever reads
the books of Joshua and Judges will find about
those times the same savage spirit of insolence
and fierté.

### 4.

The Nemæan games.    v. 4.

I beg to be excused from giving a long account
of the Nemæan games.  What the world calls
learning, differs very little from pedantry ; and
I am sensible many an honest man may deserve
that imputation when he means no manner of
harm : so much harder 'tis to conceal knowledge,
than first get it.  The best and most ancient
information now extant is to be collected from
Pindar's odes in general.  However I must just
take notice of a funeral oration spoken in honour
of Archemorus, as it is mentioned by Clemens
Alexandrinus, in his admonit. ad Gentes.

### 5.

The youthful sailors thus with early care
Their arms experience—    v. 23.

'Tis worth while here to take notice of Statius's similies in general.  They are sometimes
proper, but not often : a common fault with most
young authors, who can reject nothing ; though
a more judicious writer at the same time would
either suppress the thought, or at most content
himself with a metaphor.  I am apt to think
similies must seldom be used, except they convey to the mind some very pleasing, or strong
piece of painting.  For all similies are descrip-

tions (or pictures) whose only beauty proceeds from an excellence in the imagery. In these cases, painting must always be consulted.

Another oversight in Statius is want of parity in the circumstances: but this is owing to the irregularity of his genius, which was above insisting upon particulars, and gave only some bold strokes of likeness.

If a translator can leave out such similies (or other passages) in Statius as are not proper, without violating the context: or if he can supply any of their defects in a very short compass, I think he ought. Though these liberties are not to be taken with more correct writers.

**6.**

Swift from mankind the Pow'r of slumbers flew. v. 31.

This place is not translated exactly to the letter, nor indeed would our language bear it. The original is extremely poetical, and correspondent to the best paintings in those times:

——cornu fugiebat somnus inani.

For Somnus (or sleep) was represented as a deity pouring dews out of a horn, over the temples of the sleeping person. Statius alludes to this in another passage, upon the same occasion;

——cornu perfuderat omni.

This remark I owe to Lactantius, who has given us the only tolerable comment upon Statius. Care has been taken to read him entirely over, though to little purpose. His notes are learned, short, and clear, but seldom poetical. Most of them are like the old Scholia upon Homer, explaining one word by another. He is full of apostrophes and exclamations, yet gives no reasons. Such as, exquisitè dictum! pictum egregiè! &c.

**7.**

Mean while Adrastus bears the friendly part, And with kind words consoles, &c. v. 51.

Chaucer, who was perhaps the greatest poet among the moderns, has translated these verses almost word for word in his Knight's Tale. I shall make this remark once for all: as nothing particularises the fine passages in Homer more than that Virgil vouchsafed to imitate them: so scarce any thing can exalt the reputation of Statius higher, than the verbal imitations of our great countryman. I prefer this to a volume of criticisms; no man would imitate what he could exceed.

**8.**

Inwoven on the pall, young Linus lay In lonely woods—— v. 70.

Linus was the son of Apollo, and the nymph Psamathe. No picture could be introduced with more propriety; his death was almost exactly the same with that of Archemorus. The story is related at large by Adrastus in the first Thebaid; and admirably translated by Mr. Pope:

How mean a fate, unhappy child! is thine ? Ah how unworthy those of race divine ? On flow'ry herbs in some green covert laid, His bed the ground, his canopy the shade,

He mixes with the bleating lambs his cries; While the rude swain his rural music tries, To call soft slumbers on his infant eyes. Yet ev'n in those obscure abodes to live, Was more, alas! than cruel fate would give! For on the grassy verdure as he lay And breath'd the freshness of the rising day; Devouring dogs the helpless infant tore, Fed on his trembling limbs, and lapt the gore.

**9.**

The pious mother thus, deceiv'd too late Like her fond spouse—— v. 90.

I scarce ever met with a more incoherent passage than this, in any author. The sense is fine, and easily apprehended by the context: the words are obscure to a fault, and the transition too sudden and violent:

Namque illi & pharetras, brevioraque tela dicarat Festinus voti pater, insontesque sagittas. Jam tunc & notâ stabulis de gente probatos In nomen pascebat equos, cinctusque sonantes, Armaque majores expectatura lacertos— Spes avidæ! quas non in nomen credula vestes Urgebat studio? &c.

Spes avidæ, must certainly be spoken of the mother, or else credula has nothing to agree with. In short, it must never be defended, but by one of these two excuses, either that Statius left his poem unfinished, or that the verse immediately preceding, is now lost. It might mean perhaps no more than this, " thus too was the unhappy mother deceived! with what care—&c." This consideration clears the sense, and solves all objections at once. However 'tis a mere conjecture, and may be truer to the author's reputation, than his first meaning.

All grave readers will reject this as a whimsical young man's notion; nor do I lay any stress upon it. To show I can be serious on occasion, I shall just refer them to Virgil's third Georgic, where will be found a transition from horses to cows, as obscure almost as this in Statius.

Gronovius (without any authority) thinks we should read spes avidi, instead of avidæ, still preserving the context, and referring credula to spes. I cannot approve of this emendation for many reasons; we at once lose half the beauty. Besides, the repetition of in nomen would be tautology, if it did not refer to another person: nor can urgere vestes be so properly applied to the father.

Whoever reads this positive Dutchman's preface to Ammianus Marcellinus, will never think him to be a man of sense, or candour.

**10.**

Stretch'd o'er the ground the tow'ring oaks were seen, &c. v. 108.

This description is inimitably beautiful, and I might spend a whole page in admirations. 'Twere easy also, by drawing parallel places, (a common, but unfair practice) to prefer Statius to all the ancients, and moderns. Most of the poets have exercised their genius upon this occasion; particularly Ovid in the 10th book of his Metamorphosis:

————Non Chaonis absuit arbos,
Non nemus Heliadum, non frondibus esculus
    altis :
Non tiliæ molles, non fagus, & innuba laurus,
Et coryli fragiles, & fraxinus utilis hastis,
Enodisque abies curvataque glandibus ilex,
Et platanus genialis, acerque coloribus impar,
Amnicolæque simul salices, & aquatica lotos.

As also Claudian, in the Rape of Proserpina,
Lib. the 2d. Chaucer seems to have a particular eye to this passage throughout all his poems.
See his Knight's Tale, the Assembly of Fowls, and
Complaint of the Black Knight. I am also much
pleased to find this passage finely imitated by two
other of our ancient English poets. I shall first
cite Fairfax, who understood the harmony of
numbers better than any person then living, except Spenser. All the world knows his excellent
version (or paraphrase rather) of Tasso's Gieru-
salem liberata. The other, whom I mean, is
M. Drayton, whose Fairy-tale is a master-piece
in those grotesque writings :

Down fall the sacred palms, and ashes wild—
The fun'ral cypress, holly ever green ;
  The weeping fir, thick beech, and sailing
    pine ;
The married elm fell with his fruitful vine ;
The shooter-yew, the broad-leav'd sycamore,
The barren platine, and the wallnut sound ;
The myrrh that her foul sin doth still deplore;
The alder, owner of all watrish ground ;
Sweet juniper, whose shadow hurteth sore ;
Proud cedar; oak, the king of forests crown'd.
              Fairfax.

The tufted cedar, and the branching pine. . . .
  Under whose covert, (thus divinely made)
Phœbus' green laurel flourish'd in the shade :
Fair Venus' myrtle, Mars his warlike fir,
Minerva's olive, and the weeping myrrh ;
The patient palm that strives in spite of hate,
The poplar to Alcides consecrate, &c.
              Drayton.

I ask pardon for the tediousness of this note,
and the reader in justice ought to acknowledge I
writ it to gratify my pleasure, rather than my
vanity ; and surely no person who has the least
taste can be displeased with so much variety. I
insist only to produce one description more out
of Statius. The verses are extremely natural,
and carry something with them as awful and
venerable as the subject :

Sylva capax ævi, validâque incurva senectâ,
Æternum intonsæ frondis, stat pervia nullis
Solibus.
Subter opaca quies, vacuusque silentia servat
Horror, & exclusæ pallet mala lucis imago,
Nec caret umbra Deo.
              Thebaid 4.

### 11.

Sacred to Heav'n and Hell the mourners rear
Two massy altars———— v. 131.

It may be asked why the Grecians raised two
altars. Lactantius answers that one only was
for Archemorus, and the other for the serpent
that killed him.
If the reader supposes this to be too much honour

for the latter, it must be remembered, that those
creatures were almost always esteemed by the
ancients, as sacred to some deity. But Statius
mentions this in particular. See the death of
Archemorus, in the 5th Thebaid :

————Nemoris sacer horror Achæi
Erigitur Serpens.

And a little afterwards,

——Inachio sanctum dixêre Tonanti
Agricolæ——

So Virgil, speaking of the two serpents that
strangled Laocoon, Eneid the 2d :

Their task perform'd the serpents quit their
    prey,
And to the tow'r of Pallas make their way :
Couch'd at her feet they lie protected there
By her large buckler, and protended spear.
              Dryden.

### 12.

————In mournful strains
The music of the Phrygian fife complains. v.
137.

The Phrygian measure in music was made use
of, to call the spirits of the deceased from Hades.
Pelops was the first person who invented, and set
it to the lyre, and from him it came to the Grecians.
              Lactantius.

### 13.

Behind Hypsypile's soft sorrows flow
Silent, and fast—— v. 147.

Nothing can be more finely imaged than this
character of Hypsypile ; it seems a perfect picture of beauty in distress. Her very silence is
eloquent : she knows her innocence, but must
not speak one word to defend it. She moves
along by herself the very last of them all, while
every eye seems to threaten and accuse her.
And even after all this, there is still a dejected
sweetness, a tenderness, a confusion that cannot
be expressed. I know not how to make the
reader any ways sensible of my own images,
except I refer him to the character of Briseïs in
Homer's first Iliad, and the picture of Sisigambis
in Darius's tent.
This puts me in mind of some fine strokes in
Spenser, though upon a different occasion. What
I mean, is the silence and confusion of Britomart,
when the Red-cross knight discovers her to be a
lady, and inquires after her adventures :

Thereat she sighing softly, had no pow'r
To speak awhile, ne ready answer make,
But with heart-thrilling throbs, and bitter
As if she had a fever-fit, did quake,   [stow'r,
And ev'ry dainty limb with horror shake ;
And ever and anon the rosie red
Flash'd through her face, as it had been a flake
Of lightning, through bright Heaven fulmined.
        Fairy Queen, Lib. 3. Cant. 2.

See also the same canto, stanza the 15th.

### 14.

Speech of Eurydice. v. 153.

Statius has equally shown his conduct in this

speech of Eurydice. She is injured, and indeed deserves a liberty to resent it. She condoles, she repents, she heightens her misfortunes, and then seems to wonder why Providence should inflict them. This she aggravates by considering the prosperity of her neighbours, which certainly gives the deepest remorse in all afflictions. Nothing can be finer than these two last particulars. They arise immediately from human nature, and give a lively picture of self-respect, and indulgency to our own frailties. What follows is more abrupt and violent; she draws the author of her misery in the most disagreeable colours, makes her treacherous, negligent, and even insensible of gratitude or pity.

### 15.

Whose hands sustain'd thee, and whose music charm'd,
Whose eye o'ersaw thee—v. 185.

I am far from being disgusted with these little particularities that attend the most serious and noble passions. Nothing has a better effect in poetry, or painting. An incident may be small, and at the same time not trifling. This puts me in mind of an observation in Longinus: it is made upon Sappho's love-ode, translated afterwards by Catullus. " The poetess" (says he) " has assembled with admirable skill all the little accidents to that passion. Her heart beats fast, her tongue trembles, her sight seems to swim, and her colour vanishes all in one moment."
This confusion suits admirably well with the wandering irresolutions of the soul upon such occasions.

Longinus, Chap. 8.

### 16.

So when the holy priest with curious eyes
Dooms some fair heifer, v. 209.

I must not forget that Statius has copied this simile from Lucretius. 'Tis hard to say which is the more excellent. Lucretius his lines are these, after he has described the young heifer slain in sacrifice:

At mater virideis saltus orbata peragrans,
Omnia convisens oculis loca, si queat usquam
Conspicere amissum fœtum, completque querelis
Frondiferum nemus adsistens, & crebra revisit
Ad stabulum, desiderio perfixa juvenci,
Non teneræ ulla saluces, atque herbæ rore vigentes
Fluminave ulla queunt summis labentia ripis
Oblectare animum, subitamque avertere curam:
Nec vitulorum aliæ species per pabula læta
Derivare queunt alio, curâve levare.   Lib. 2.

### 17.

The father now unbares his rev'rend head;
His silver locks he scatters o'er the dead. v. 217.

The practice of cutting off the hair, and strewing it over the deceased, was so common with the ancients, that all testimonies are needless. It prevails among the Sclavonians to this day, who, (as lord Busbeque observes in his Epistles) neque modo capillos, sed etiam supercilia sibi (in luctu) demunt.

### 18.

If Jove's almighty wisdom can deceive,
Curs'd is the man who fondly will believe!
v. 221.

This apostrophe contains a fine picture of human nature in distress. Heaven itself cannot escape our censure: its unerring justice is called into question, and we fancy more to be inflicted on us, than we ought to suffer.
Much of this kind is the speech of Asius in Homer's 12th Iliad. Eustathius makes a very moral remark upon it, which I shall transcribe, as I find it admirably translated to my hands.
" The speech of Asius is very extravagant: he exclaims against Jupiter for a breach of promise, not because he had broken his word, but because he had not fulfilled his own vain imaginations. This conduct, though very blameable in Asius, is very natural to persons under disappointments, who are ever ready to blame Heaven, and turn their misfortunes into a crime." Thus far Eustathius.
Æneas (whose chief character is piety) could not help accusing men and gods when he lost Creusa. Though in justice to Virgil it ought to be observed, that he softens, or rather disapproves of the impiety at the same time; for so the word amens must be understood.

Quem non incusavi, amens, hominumque deorumque?

As this note is capable of very serious reflections, it may not perhaps be amiss to look a little into the holy scriptures. The impatience of Job's wife, as also the diffidence and irresolution of David in the 73d Psalm, are extraordinary instances of this sort. But Jeremiah carries it yet farther: he proceeds to an expostulation with his Maker. " Let me talk with thee, O Lord, of thy judgments. Thou hast planted (the wicked) yea, they have taken root: they grow, yea, they bring forth fruit. But thou, O Lord, knowest me, thou hast seen me, and tried my heart towards thee. I have forsaken my house, &c." Chap. 12. v. 1, 2, 3, & 8.
Lactantius solves the extravagance of this speech of Lycurgus very oddly, by a reflection on his priesthood. His words are these, " priests may be as angry as they will," for so must he be understood according to the purport of the original. I much question whether his name-sake would have allowed this concession to the c'ergy: and if the translator may have leave to give his opinion, he thinks them to have less need of it, than any other part of the nation.

### 19.

Nine times his course bright Lucifer had roll'd
And ev'ning Vesper deck'd his rays with gold.
v. 271.

This particularity is so far from being ornamental, that it preserves a valuable piece of antiquity; namely the closing of the funeral games after nine days end: which ceremony the old Romans called Novemdialia.

Bernartius.

**20.**

High o'er the people wrought with lively grace,
Shine the fair glories of their ancient race.
v. 297.

I don't remember any thing more noble, or judicious than this historical picture. The description of a shield was already worn out : 'twas impossible to add any thing of moment after Homer and Virgil. Nor is it introduced merely for ornament ; it contains, no less than the story of their ancestors, magnanimûm series antiqua parentum. Its effects are visible : to inspire them with courage in the funeral games. Besides, it happily avoids most of the objections that have been made against the shields of Achilles and Æneas. Its size answers all multiplicity of figures ; and even every figure bears a plain reference to the subject of action. The rules of painting are exactly preserved : we have not only a contrast of passions in different persons, but variety of place in each distinct compartiment.

'Tis reasonable to think our author designed this as a compliment to a common ceremony then among the Romans : who used at all solemn funerals to carry before the corps of the deceased the pictures of their ancestors. Thus Horace, Epode the 8th ;

——Funus atque imagines
Ducunt triumphales tuum.

See also Cicero's oration for Milo, and the 35th book of Pliny. Perhaps Statius owed the first hint of his historical picture to the custom we now mention.

**21.**

——Brave Choræbus lifts his bleeding hands—
v. 324.

Lactantius gives two meanings to this hemystic ; the *venerable* or *undaunted* figure of Choræbus. I have chosen the latter, because it agrees best with his character in the first Thebaid. The story is too long to be transcribed.

**22.**

Here Belus' sons at Hymen's altars stand,
And join with hearts averse the friendly hand.
v. 351.

The contract of Danaus and Egypt is too well known to be repeated. However for the sake of the curious I shall not pass by the epistle of Hypermnestra to Linus, and some remarkable passages in Pindar's ninth Pythian Ode. Statius seems pleased with this story, and has chosen it in another place to ornament the shield of Hippomedon. There is something very masterly in the expression, and the tout-ensemble makes a fine piece of night-painting :

——humeros, & pectora latè
Flammeus orbis habet——vivit in auro
Nox Danai, sontes furiarum lampade nigrâ
Quinquaginta ardent thalami, pater ipse cruentis
In foribus, laudatque nefas, atque inspicit enses.
Theb. 4.

**23.**

Swift flew the rapid car, and left behind
The noise of tempests, and the wings of wind.
v. 349.

These verses are somewhat too bold in the original :

——stupuère relicta
Nubila, certantes Eurique Notique sequuntur.

Whoever translates Statius must have liberty to soften some of these hyperboles. Yet Lactantius was of another opinion, who admires this place in the true spirit of criticism. Divinè dictum ! dedit illis victoriæ votum, sed ademit effectum. His remark is not worth translating.

**24.**

So sad Apollo with a boding sigh.
Told his fond child—— v. 363.

We may perceive something very remarkable in this simile, not without a fine commiseration for unhappy Polynices. Instead of accusing the rashness, or folly of Phaeton, all is attributed to fatal destiny. As much as to say, Polynices lost not the race through his own imprudence, but by the interposition of a deity.

**25.**

Admetus' life, &c. v. 431.

This alludes chiefly to the story of Alceste, Admetus his wife, who was so honourable (it seems) as to lay down her life to atone for her husband's. Juvenal makes an agreeable use of this female gallantry :

——spectant subeuntem fata mariti
Alcesten.
Lactantius.

Euripides has written a tragedy upon this occasion. I am afraid few modern ladies would give such an example, but indeed husbands are much alter'd since the days of Admetus. I may add, that Statius takes notice of the death of Alceste in his Sylva, entituled the Tears of Etruscus, Lib. 3. I the rather cite this poem because it contains some fine strokes of humanity, and filial affection. Of the same nature is his Epicedion in Patrem. I wonder that these two admirable copies have never yet beeen translated.

**26.**

" Th' impatient coursers pant in ev'ry vein,
And pawing seem to beat the distant plain.
The vales, the floods appear already crost,
And e'er they start, a thousand steps are lost."
v. 454.

The Latin of these verses is wonderfully fine, as Mr. Dryden acknowledges in his preface to Du Fresnoy. He cites them as a true image of our author :

Stare adeò miserum est, pereunt vestigia mille
Ante fugam, absentemque ferit gravis ungula campum.

" Which would cost me" (says he) " an hour to translate, there is so much beauty in the original."

Since that, Mr. Pope has imitated these verses almost verbatim in his Windsor Forest: and I thought fit to transfer them hither, rather than expose my own weakness. I never was heartily mortified before; I just know how to admire him and to despise myself! the reader may be assured, I durst not presume to do this without that gentleman's consent; who not only gave me leave to use his translation, but also to alter any circumstances that might not correspond with the original. I remember a paper in the Guardian that consists chiefly of parallel descriptions upon this occasion; and thither I refer the curious.

Balde the Jesuit has some bold strokes in an ode whose title I forgot, though 'tis written partly in imitation of the war-horse in Job. I mention this, purely to do justice to that poet's memory, who (notwithstanding some extravagances) came nearer to the spirit and abruptness of Pindar, than any of his cotemporaries.

## 27.

Earth opening seem'd to groan (a fatal sign!)
v. 600.

Because Amphiaraus was afterwards to be swallowed under ground. See the latter end of the seventh Thebaid :

Illum ingens haurit specus, & transire parantes
Merget equos : non arma manu, non fræna
remisit
Sicut erat, rectos defert in Tartara currus :
Respexitque cadens cœlum, campumque coire
Ingemuit——

I take this to be one of the most noble descriptions I ever met with in any language.

## 28.

Loud shouts each chief that from high Elis
leads
His native train, &c. v. 639.

I have open'd this passage a little, but with due respect to geography. See the fourth Theb. Resupina Elis, demissa Pisa.

## 29.

Lives there a warrior in the world of fame,
Who never heard of Atalanta's name ? v. 649.

The commentators are all mighty merry upon these verses. It seems Statius has confounded the history of Atalanta (there being two of that name) and takes the wife of Hippomenes for that of Pelops; the famous racer in days of yore. This (say they) is a remarkable oversight, and very few of them can heartily forgive it. The matter is hardly worth debate: poets were never thought infallible. Whoever reads the critical discourse upon the Iliad, will find many errours even in Homer; though not so many as La Motte fancied. Aristotle, Cicero, and Dionysius of Halicarnassus were seldom right in their quotations. Macrobius tells us, that Virgil ran into many palpable mistakes, purely to disengage himself from too much exactness, and to imitate Homer. Mons. la Mothe le Vayer has written an entire treatise upon this subject: and I think it worth reading, merely as a mortification for human vanity.

In deference to the above-mentioned criticism, I thought fit to leave out, vestigia cunctis inde-prensa procis; for there lies all the confusion.

## 30.

Foot-race. v. 766.

I must own, I think this foot-race an inimitable piece of poetry. The design itself is equally as just; the circumstances perhaps are more beautiful than those upon the same subject in the Greek or Roman poet. Had Statius given the prize to Idas, (than which nothing was more easy) I cannot but think the moral would have been highly defective. Yet Euryalus in Virgil wins the race by downright fraudulence. In the descriptive parts our author borrows nothing considerable from either of the above cited poets. I wish he had taken one circumstance from Homer, which pleases me much. It is the passage where Ulysses follows Ajax :

——αὐτὰρ ὄπισθεν
Ἴχνια τύπτε πόδεσσι πάρος κόνιν ἀμφιχυθῆναι.

——His foe he plies,
And treads each footstep, e'er the dust can rise.

## 31.

Thus in some storm the broken billows rise
Round the vast rock—— v. 909.

'Tis with great judgment the poet introduces this simile, which admirably paints the size and unmoveableness of Capaneus. I have endeavoured to give it this turn, adding the epithet vast, to strengthen the idea. A translator can seldom do his author this justice, and I see no reasons against it, if the deviation exceeds not one word. However, it is manifest the original alludes only to the noise, and sudden overflowing of the waters. 'Tis impossible to give a more lively image of Alcidamas. Statius has comprized himself also into a shorter pass than usual, that the mind might not be too much suspended in the midst of so important an action. Besides, there is a particular beauty in the versification: it seems to run by starts, short and violent :

Assilit, ut præceps cumulo salir unda, minaces
In scopulos, & fracta redit——

## 32.

The fight of the cæstus. v. 966.

I have taken notice in the foot-race, that Statius has varied from Virgil, with admirable judgment. The same may be advanced here in respect to Homer, who in his fight of the cæstus, rewards insolence and pride, instead of punishing them. There is an exact parity of character between Capaneus and Epëus: but not the same success. The boaster in this place meets with the most manifest disadvantage: a great improvement of the moral.

Upon the whole: it may be required I should attempt something like a comparison between the descriptions of this game in Homer, Virgil, and Statius. To speak my own sentiments, I cannot but prefer the latter, not only for its greater variety of incidents, but for the character of arrogance, which is wrought up to much more perfection: it was this they all laboured at. Capaneus is so far blinded with his own admiration, that he still fancies himself the conqueror: though the odds appeared visibly against him: so apt is pride to magnify. This is superadded to the characters in Homer and Virgil: and I think it a most natural improvement.

### 33.

The mountain-cypress thus, that firmly stood
From age to age——　　　v. 994.

Originally;

Ille autem Alpini veluti regina cupressus
Verticis——

I have read in one of our modern critics, or in some book of travels, that no cypresses grow upon the Alps. The author upon this takes occasion to fall foul upon an eminent Roman poet, and wonders at his ignorance. It is no matter where I met with this remark, it not being of much consequence: yet I thought fit to leave out Alpinus; and added a more indefinite epithet.

Since my writing this note, I chanc'd to read Bernartius's comment upon Statius. He is much chagrined at this oversight. As a specimen of his humanity and taste for criticism, I shall transcribe his own words at length: " Attigit ut videtur Papinius hic guttam è flumine Lethes. Nam in Alpibus nusquam cupressi : nisi forte speciem pro genere posuit, quod non inepte affirmare possumus.

### 34.

Not half so bloody: or with half such rage
Two mighty monarchs of the herd engage.
　　　　　　　　　　　v. 1006.

Statius seems to have copied this simile from the combat of Hercules and Achelöus in the ninth book of Ovid's Metamorphoses. I shall pleasure the reader with them both. And first Ovid;

Non aliter vidi fortes concurrere tauros,
Cum pretium pugnæ, toto nitidissima saltu
Expetitur conjux: spectant armenta, paventque
Nescia quem tanti maneat victoria regni.

Non sic ductores gemini gregis, horrida tauri
Bella movent: medio conjux stat candida prato
Victorem expectans; rumpunt obnixa surentes.
Pectora——

The latter in my opinion is far more natural than the former. There is a beautiful contrast, or variation of numbers, very tender and flowing, in

——medio conjux——&c.

Which is somewhat faintly preserved in the translation.

Spenser has a simile something of this nature in the combat between the Red-cross knight and Sansfoy, Lib. 1. Canto 2.

### 35.

Nor breath'd its spirit to congenial skies.
　　　　　　　　　　　v. 1029.

Or to congenial stars more literally, according to the philosophy of Pythagoras. The wicked, says Lactantius, were punished by their stars (ab ipsis astris, stellisque are his words); the good enjoyed their light for ever. For a farther explication of this ancient doctrine, I refer the reader to Servius and Ruæus's notes upon the 227th line of Virgil's 4th Georgic, Syderis in numerum, &c. See also Plato in Timæo.

### 36.

So Hercules, who long had toil'd in vain,
Heav'd huge Anthëus. v. 1040.

I cannot but admire this noble simile; besides the parity of circumstances, the savage character of Anthëus suits admirably well with the brutal fury of Agylleus: nor is it a small compliment to little Tydeus, to compare him with Hercules for strength. I fancy Spenser drew the story of Maleger at large from this picture. I am the more inclined to think so, because in the combat of prince Arthur, and Pyrrhocles, he translates almost literally from Statius those verses that describe Agylleus after his fall: though it must be owned, he has interwoven a simile that much improves them :

Nought booted it the Paynim then to strive,
But as a bittour in an eagle's claw,
That may not hope by flight to 'scape alive,
Still hopes for death, with dread and trembling
So he now subject to the victor's law,　[awe :
Did not once move, nor upwards cast his eye.

### 37.

Here end the funeral games, which are put off (as in Virgil) by a prodigy, foreboding that none of the seven captains should return, except Adrastus: as that in Virgil foretold the burning of the ships by the Trojan matrons.

To conclude, whosoever will read the original impartially, will find Statius to be a much better poet than the world imagines. What the translation is, I know not: nor can the notes be extraordinary, when no body has written any thing tolerable before me. The reader may believe, or disbelieve them as he pleases; I deliver conjectures, not doctrines. If my present version has the fortune to please, I may perhaps proceed farther: if not, I cannot but think myself happy in reviving at least so fine a piece of poetry. I have but just given the sketch of a picture, it remains for others to deepen the strokes, and finish the whole. Whoever can take such pains, will oblige me, as much as the world.

# DIVINE POEMS.

## DEDICATION.

To the reverend Mr. Hildrop, master of Marleborough-School, (under whom I had the

-honour of receiving my education) these Divine Poems are humbly dedicated by his
most obliged,
and obedient servant,
W. HARTE.

---

## PSALM THE CIV'th,

### PARAPHRASED.

Awake my soul! in hallow'd raptures praise
Th' Almighty God, who in th' empyreal height
Majestic shines, too glorious to behold.
Methinks the broad expansion of the sky
O'erspreads thy throne: in air thy chambers
hang
Eternal, and unmov'd. Clouds roll'd on clouds
Thy chariot form; in thund'rings wrapt and fires
Thou walk'st, incumbent on the wings of wind.
Active as flames, all intellect, God forms
Angels of essence pure, whose finer parts
Invisible, and half dissolv'd in light, [hand
Should fleet through worlds of air. Th' Almighty
Fixt earth's eternal basis, and prescrib'd
Its utmost limits to the raging main.
Forth from their deeps a world of waters rose
And delug'd earth. He spoke, the waves obey'd
In peace, subsiding to their ancient springs.
Part murmur headlong down the mountain's
sides:
Part through the vales in slow mæanders play,
As pleas'd, yet loth to leave the flow'ry scene.
Thither by instinct savage beasts repair
To slake their thirst. Along the margin trees
Wave in the watry gleam, amid whose boughs
The winged songsters chant their Maker's pow'r.
God with prolific dews, and genial rain
Impregnates earth, then crowns the smiling fields
With lively green: the vegetative juice
Flows briskly through the trees; the purple grape
Swells with nectareous wines t' inspire the soul.
With verdant fruits the clust'ring olive bends
Whose spritely liquor smooths the shining face.
On Lebanon the sacred cedar waves,
And spiry fir-tree, where the stork conceals
Her clam'rous young. The rocks bare, unadorn'd,
Have uses too: there goats in quest of food
Hang pendulous in air, there rabbits form
Their mazy cells—in constant course the Moon
Nocturnal sheds her kindly influence down,
Marks out the circling year, and rules the
tides.
In constant regularity the Sun
Purples the rosy east, or leaves the skies.
Then awful night o'er all the globe extends
Her sable shades: the woods and deserts ring
With hideous yell, what time the lions roar
And tear their prey; but when the glimm'ring
morn
Dawns o'er the hills, their depredations cease
And sacred silence reigns. The painful man
Commences with the Sun his early toil,
With him retires to rest. O Pow'r supreme!
How wonderful thy works! the bounteous earth
Pours from its fruitful surface plants and herbs
Adapt for ev'ry use: its bowels hold
Rich veins of silver, and the golden ore.
Unnumber'd wonders in the deeps appear,

Incredible to thought. There tow'rs of oak
Float o'er the surges; there enormous whales
In awkward gambols play, th' inferior fry
Sportive through groves of shining coral glide.
These with observance due, when hunger calls
Expect their meat from God, who sometimes
A just sufficiency, or more profuse [gives
Show'rs down his bounty with a copious hand.
When God withholds his all-sustaining care,
To dust, their former principle, they fall.
Then thy prolific spirit forms anew
Each undecaying species. Mighty God! [is,
How great, how good thy pow'r; that was, and
And e'er shall be immutably the same!
Earth at thy look with reverential fear
Ev'n to the centre shakes: the mountains blaze
Beneath thy touch. Hail awful pow'r of Heav'n,
Eternal three and one! The slaves of vice
Thy vengeance, like a sudden whirlwind's rage,
Sweeps from mankind. My Muse, thrice glo-
rious task!
While my blest eyes behold the cheerful Sun,
While life shall animate this mortal frame,
In Heav'nly flights shall spread a bolder wing,
And sing to Him, who gave her first to sing!

---

## PSALM THE CVIIth,

### PARAPHRASED.

Mortals, rejoice! with raptures introduce
Your grateful songs, and tell what mercies God
Deigns to bestow on man: but chiefly you
The progeny of David, whom the Lord
Selected from each region of the globe
Beneath the arctic or antarctic pole:
Or where the purple Sun with orient beams
Strikes parallel on Earth, or prone descends
T' illumine worlds beyond th' Hesperian main.
With weary feet, and mournful eyes they
pass'd
Erroneous through the dreary waste of plains,
Immeas'rable: the broad expanse of Heav'n
Their canopy, the ground, of damp malign,
Their bed nocturnal. Thus in wild despair
Anxious they sought some hospitable town.
In shame and bitterness of soul once more
They recognized the Lord, and trembling cry'd
" Have mercy on us!" he, the source of mercy,
Kindly revisited his fav'rite race,
Consol'd their woes, and led the weary train
Through barren wilds to the long-promis'd land,
Then plac'd 'em there in peaceful habitations.

### CHORUS.

" O that the sons of men in grateful songs,
Wou'd praise th' unbounded goodness of the
Lord,
Declare his miracles, and laud his pow'r!"

He cheers the sad, and bids the famish'd soul
Luxuriant feast till nature craves no more.
He often saves th' imprison'd wretch that lies
Tortur'd in iron chains, no more to see
The cheerful light, or breathe the purer air.
(The due reward imperious mortals find, [pise
When swell'd with earthly grandeur, they des-
The Pow'r supreme) thus Jesse's sacred seed,
Elated with the num'rous gifts of Heav'n,

Slighted the giver: then the wrathful Lord
With-held his hand. They, impotent to save
Their forfeit lives, in piercing accents cry'd,
" Help Lord, we die !" he soon with aspect mild
Commiserates their anguish, and reliev'd
Those limbs, which sedentary numbness e'rst
Had crampt, when they in doleful shades of
    death,
Sate inconsolable—" O then that men    [Lord,
Wou'd praise th' unbounded goodness of the
Declare his miracles, and laud his pow'r !"
    Man, thoughtless of his end, in anguish reaps
The fruits of folly, and voluptuous life.
Sated with luxury his stomach loaths
Most palatable meats: with heavy pain
His eyes roll slowly ; if he drops to rest,
He starts delirious, and still seems to see
Horrible fiends, that tear him from mankind.
His flushing cheeks now glow like flames of fire :
Now chill'd, he trembles with extremes of cold
That shoot, like darts of ice, through every vein.
Ev'n then, when art was conquer'd, pray'rs
    and vows
Lenient of anger soon appeas'd the Lord,
Whose saving providence restor'd his health,
And snatch'd th' expiring from the jaws of death.
    But mostly they who voyage o'er the deeps
Observe the works of God. Sudden, from high
Down pours a rushing storm, more dreadful
    made
By darkness: save what light the flashing waves
Disclose. The vessel rides sublime in air
High on the surging billows, or again
Precipitous through yawning chasms descends.
Heart-thrilling plaints, and hands up-rear'd to
    Heav'n,
Speak well their anguish, and desire to live.
Shock'd by each bursting wave that whirls 'em
    round,
They stagger in amaze, like reeling men
Intoxicated with the fumes of wine,
Yet when they cry to God, his saving pow'r
Hushes the winds, and bids the main subside.
Instead of storms the whisp'ring zephyrs fan
The silent deep, and wave their pendent sails.
Then ev'ry heart exults : joyous repose
Dismisses each terrific thought, when once
(At Heav'n's command) the weary vessel makes
Her long-expected haven.—" O that men
Would praise th' unbounded goodness of the
    Lord,
Declare his miracles, and laud his pow'r !"
    To him once more address your songs of praise
In ev'ry temple sacred to his name,
Or where the rev'rend senators conven'd
In council sit. He turns the limpid streams,
And flow'ry meadows to a dreary waste.
Where corn has grown, and fragrant roses fill'd
The skies with odoriferous sweets, he bids
The baleful aconite up-lift its head
(The curse of impious nations): and again
In lonely deserts at his high behests
Soft-purling rills in sportive mazes glide
Mæander'd through the valleys: there he bids
The hungry souls increase and multiply.    [down
His bounteous hand the while pours goodness
Ineffable, and guards their num'rous herds.
Though thousands fall, his mercy still renews
The never-ending race.—When tyrants, proud

Of arrogated greatness, without law
Unpeople realms, and breathe but to destroy ;
Then God his high prerogative asserts,
Resumes his pow'r, and blasts their guilty heads :
Then raises from the dust the humble soul
Who meekly bore indignities and woe.

## TO MY SOUL.

### FROM CHAUCER.

FAR from mankind, my weary soul, retire,
Still follow truth, contentment still desire.
Who climbs on high, at best his weakness shows,
Who rolls in riches, all to fortune owes.
Read well thy self, and mark thy early ways,
Vain is the Muse, and envy waits on praise.

Wav'ring as winds the breath of fortune blows,
No pow'r can turn it, and no pray'rs compose.
Deep in some hermit's solitary cell
Repose and ease and contemplation dwell.
Let conscience guide thee in the days of need ;
Judge well thy own, and then thy neighbour's
    deed.

What Heav'n bestows with thankful eyes receive ;
First ask thy heart, and then through faith be-
Slowly we wander o'er a toilsome way,    [lieve.
Shadows of life, and pilgrims of a day.
" Who wrestles in this world, receives a fall ;
Look up on high, and thank thy God for all !"

## AN ESSAY ON SATIRE:

### PARTICULARLY ON THE DUNCIAD.

#### PRINTED 1730.

## CONTENTS.

    I. The origin and use of satire. The excellency of epic satire above others, as adding example to precept, and animating by fable and sensible images. Epic satire compared with epic poem, and wherein they differ : of their extent, action, unities, episodes, and the nature of their morals. Of parody : of the style, figures and wit, proper to this sort of poem, and the superior talents requisite to excel in it.
    II. The characters of the several authors of satire. 1. The ancients; Homer, Simonides, Archilochus, Aristophanes, Menippus, Ennius, Lucilius, Varro, Horace, Persius, Petronius, Juvenal, Lucian, the emperor Julian. 2. The moderns: Tassone, Coccaius, Rabelais, Regnier, Boileau, Dryden, Garth, Pope.
    III. From the practice of all the best writers and men in every age and nation, the moral justice of satire in general, and of this sort in particular, is vindicated. The necessity of it shown in this age more especially, and why bad writers are at present the most proper objects of satire. The true causes of bad writers. Characters of several sorts of them now abounding. Envious critics, furious pedants, secret libellers, obscene poetesses, advocates for corruption,

scoffers at religion, writers for deism, desitical and Arian clergymen.

Application of the whole discourse to the Dunciad, concluding with an address to the author of it.

———

T' EXALT the soul, or make the heart sincere,
To arm our lives with honesty severe,
To shake the wretch beyond the reach of law,
Deter the young, and touch the bold with awe,
To raise the fallen, to hear the sufferer's cries,
And sanctify the virtues of the wise,
Old Satire rose from probity of mind,
The noblest ethics, to reform mankind.
As Cynthia's orb excels the gems of night,
So epic satire shines, distinctly bright.
Here genius lives, and strength in ev'ry part,
And lights and shades, and fancy fix'd by art.
A second beauty in its nature lies,
It gives not things, but beings to our eyes,
Life, substance, spirit animate the whole :
Fiction and fable are the sense and soul.
The common dulness of mankind array'd
In pomp, here lives and breathes, a wond'rous
        maid :
The poet decks her with each unknown grace,
Clears her dull brain, and brightens her dark
        face.
See! father Chaos o'er his first-born nods,
And mother Night, in majesty of gods.
See Querno's throne, by hands pontific rise,
And a fools' pandæmonium strike our eyes.
Ev'n what on Curl the public bounteous pours
Is sublimated here to golden show'rs.
  A Dunciad or a Lutrin is compleat,
And one in action ; ludicrously great.
Each wheel rolls round in due degrees of force ;
Ev'n episodes are needful, and of course :
Of course when things are virtually begun
E'er the first ends, the father and the son !
Or else so needful, and exactly grac'd,
That nothing is ill-suited, or ill-plac'd.
  True epic's a vast world, and this a small,
One has its proper beauties, and one all.
Like Cynthia, one in thirty days appears ;
Like Saturn, one rolls round in thirty years.
There opens a wide tract, a length of floods,
A height of mountains, and a waste of woods:
Here but one spot : nor leaf nor green depart
From rules ; e'en Nature seems the child of Art.
As unities in epic works appear,
So may they shine in full distinction here,
Ev'n the warm Iliad moves with slower pow'rs ;
That forty days demands, this forty hours.
  Each other satire humbler arts has known,
Content with meaner beauties, though its own :
Enough for that, if rugged in its course
The verse but rolls with vehemence and force ;
Or nicely pointed in th' Horatian way,
Wounds keen, like Sirens mischievously gay.
Here all has wit, yet must that wit be strong
Beyond the turns of epigram or song.
The thought must rise, exactly from the vice,
Sudden, yet finish'd ; clean, and yet concise.
One harmony must first with last unite :
As all true paintings have their place and light.
Transitions must be quick, and yet design'd,
Not made to fill, but just retain the mind :

And similies, like meteors of the night,
Just give one flash of momentary light.
As thinking makes the soul, low things exprest
In high-rais'd terms, define a Dunciad best.
Books and the man, demand as much, or more,
Than he who wander'd on the Latian shore :
For here (eternal grief to Duns's soul,
And B——'s thin ghost) the part contains the
        whole :
Since in mock-epic none succeeds, but he
Who tastes the whole of epic poesy.
  The moral must be clear and understood :
But finer still, if negatively good :
Blaspheming Capaneus obliquely shows
T' adore those gods Æneas fears and knows.
A fool's the hero : but the poets end
Is to be candid, modest, and a friend.
  Let classic learning sanctify each part,
Not only show your reading, but your art.
The charms of parody, like those of wit,
If well contrasted, never fail to hit ;
One half in light, and one in darkness drest,
(For contraries oppos'd still shine the best.)
When a cold pause half breaks the writer's heart,
By this, it warms, and brightens into art.
When rhet'ric glitters with too pompous pride,
By this, like Circe, 'tis undeify'd.
So Berecynthia, while her offspring vie
In homage to the mother of the sky,        [flow'rs,
(Deck'd in rich robes of trees, and plants, and
And crown'd illustrious with a hundred tow'rs)
O'er all Parnassus casts her eyes at once,
And sees an hundred sons—and each a dunce.
  The language next : from hence new pleasure
        springs :
For styles are dignified as well as things.
Tho' sense subsists, distinct from phrase or sound,
Yet gravity conveys a surer wound.
The chymic secret which your pains would find,
Breaks out, unsought for, in Cervantes' mind :
And Quixote's wildness, like that king's of old,
Turns all he touches into pomp and gold.
Yet in this pomp discretion must be had :
Though grave, not stiff ; though whimsical, not
        mad :
In works like these if fustain might appear,
Mock-epics, Blackmore, would not cost thee
        dear.
  We grant, that Butler ravishes the heart,
As Shakespeare soar'd beyond the reach of art :
(For Nature form'd those poets without rules
To fill the world with imitating fools.)
What burlesque could, was by that genius done;
Yet faults it has, impossible to shun :
Th' unchanging strain for want of grandeur cloys,
And gives too oft the horse-laugh mirth of boys :
The short-legg'd verse, and double-gingling sound,
So quick surprise us, that our heads run round :
Yet in this work peculiar life presides,
And wit, for all the world to glean besides.
  Here pause, my Muse, too daring and too
        young,
Nor rashly aim at precepts yet unsung.
Can man the master of the Dunciad teach ?
And these new bays what other hopes to reach ?
'Twere better judg'd, to study and explain
Each ancient grace he copies not in vain :
To trace thee, Satire, to thy utmost spring,
Thy form, thy changes, and thy authors sing.

All nations with this liberty dipense,
And bid us shock the man that shocks good sense.
   Great Homer first the mimic sketch design'd:
What grasp'd not Homer's comprehensive mind?
By him who virtue prais'd, was folly curst,
And who Achilles sung, drew Dunce the first [1].
   Next him Simonides, with lighter air
In beasts, and apes, and vermin, paints the fair:
The good Scriblerus in like forms displays
The reptile rhymsters of these later days.
   More fierce, Archilochus, thy vengeful flame:
Fools read, and died: for blockheads then had
       shame.
   The comic satirist [2] attack'd his age,
And found low arts, and pride, among the sage:
See learned Athens stand attentive by,
And stoics learn their foibles from the eye.
   Latium's fifth Homer [3] held the Greeks in
      view:
Solid, though rough, yet incorrect as new.
Lucilius, warm'd with more than mortal flame,
Rose next, and held a torch to ev'ry shame.
See stern Menippus, cynical, unclean;
And Grecian centos, mannerly obscene.
Add the last efforts of Pacuvius' rage,
And the chaste decency of Varro's page.
   See Horace next, in each reflection nice,
Learn'd, but not vain: the foe of fools, not vice.
Each page instructs, each sentiment prevails,
All shines alike, he rallies, but ne'er rails:
With courtly ease conceals a master's art,
And least expected steals upon the heart.
Yet Cassius [4] felt the fury of his rage,
(Cassius, the Welsted of a former age);
And sad Alpinus ignorantly read,
Who murder'd Memnon, tho' for ages dead.
   Then Persius came: whose line tho' roughly
      wrought,
His sense o'erpaid the stricture of his thought.
Here in clear light the stoic-doctrine shines,
Truth all subdues, or patience all resigns.
A mind supreme: impartial, yet severe:
Pure in each act, in each recess sincere!
Yet rich ill poets urg'd the stoic's frown,
And bade him strike at dulness and a crown [5].
   The vice and luxury Petronius drew
In Nero meet: th' imperial point of view:
The Roman Wilmot, that could vice chastise,
Pleas'd the mad king he serv'd to satirise.
   The next in satire [6] felt a nobler rage,
What honest heart could bear Domitian's age?
See his strong sense, and numbers masculine!
His soul is kindled, and he kindles mine:
Scornful of vice, and fearless of offence,
He flows a torrent of impetuous sense.
   So savage tyrants who blasphem'd their god,
Turn suppliants now, and gaze at Julian's rod [7].
   Lucian, severe, but in a gay disguise,
Attacks old faith, or sports in learned lyes [8];
Sets heroes and philosophers at odds;
And scourges mortals, and dethrones the gods.
   Then all was right—But Satire rose once more
Where Medici and Leo arts restore.

[1] Margites.        [2] Aristophanes.
[3] Ennius.          [4] Epod. 6.
[5] See his first satire of Nero's verses, &c.
[6] Juvenal.
[7] The Cæsars of the emperor Julian.
[8] Lucian's True History.

Tassonè shone fantastic, but sublime:
And he, who form'd the Macaronic-rhyme.
   Then westward too by slow degrees confest,
Where boundless Rabelais made the world his
      jest:
Marot had nature, Regnier force and flame,
But swallow'd all in Boileau's matchless fame!
Extensive soul! who rang'd all learning o'er,
Present and past—and yet found room for more.
Full of new sense, exact in ev'ry page,
Unbounded, and yet sober in thy rage.
Strange fate! Thy solid sterling of two lines,
Drawn to our tinsel, thro' whole pages shines [9].
   In Albion then, with equal lustre bright,
Great Dryden rose, and steer'd by Nature's light.
Two glimm'ring orbs he just observ'd from far,
The ocean wide, and dubious either star.
Donne teem'd with wit, but all was maim'd and
      bruis'd,
The periods endless, and the sense confus'd:
Oldham rush'd on, impetuous and sublime,
But lame in language, harmony and rhyme:
These (with new graces) vig'rous Nature join'd
In one, and center'd them in Dryden's mind.
How full thy verse! Thy meaning how severe!
How dark thy theme! Yet made exactly clear.
Not mortal is thy accent, nor thy rage,
Yet mercy softens, or contracts each page.
Dread bard! instruct us to revere thy rules,
And hate like thee, all rebels, and all fools.
   His spirit ceas'd not (in strict truth) to be:
For dying Dryden breath'd, O Garth, on thee,
Bade thee to keep alive his genuine rage,
Half sunk in want, oppression and old age:
Then, when thy pious hands [10] repos'd his head,
When vain young lords and ev'n the flamen fled.
For well thou knewst his merit and his art,
His upright mind, clear head, and friendly heart.
Ev'n Pope himself (who sees no virtue bleed
But bears th' affliction) envies thee the deed,
   O Pope! instructor of my studious days,
Who fix'd my steps in virtue's early ways;
On whom our labours, and our hopes depend,
Thou more than patron, and ev'n more than
Above all flattery, all thirst of gain,    [friend!
And mortal but in sickness, and in pain!
Thou taught'st old Satire nobler fruits to bear,
And check'd her licence with a moral care,
Thou gav'st the thought new beauties not its own,
And touch'd the verse with graces yet unknown;
Each lawless branch thy level eye survey'd,
And still corrected Nature as she stray'd:
Warm'd Boileau's sense with Britain's genuine
      fire,
And added softness to Tassonè's lyre.
   Yet mark the hideous nonsense of the age,
And thou thyself the subject of its rage.
So in old times, round godlike Scæva ran
Rome's dastard sons, a million, and a man.
   Th' exalted merits of the wise and good
Are seen, far off, and rarely understood.
The world's a father to a dunce unknown,
And much he thrives, for, Dulness! he's thy own.
No hackney brethren e'er condemn'd him twice:
He fears no enemies, but dust and mice.

[9] Roscommon, reversed.
[10] Dr. Garth took care of Mr. Dryden's funeral, which some noblemen, who undertook it, had neglected.

If Pope but writes, the devil, Legion raves,
And meagre critics mutter in their caves:
(Such critics of necessity consume
All wit, as hangmen ravish'd maids at Rome.)
Names he a scribbler? all the world's in arms;
Augusta, Granta, Rhedecyna swarms:
The guilty reader fancies what he fears,
And every Midas trembles for his ears.

See all such malice, obloquy and spite,
Expire e'er morn, the mushroom of a night.
Transient as vapours glimm'ring thro' the glades,
Half-form'd and idle, as the dreams of maids.
Vain as the sick man's vow, or young man's sigh,
Third-nights of bards, or Henley's [11] sophistry.
These ever hate the poet's sacred line:
These hate whate'er is glorious or divine.
From one eternal fountain beauty springs,
The energy of wit and truth of things.
That source is God : from him they downwards
    tend,
Flow round—yet in their native centre end.
Hence rules, and truth, and order, dunces strike;
Of arts, and virtues, enemies alike.

Some urge, that poets of supreme renown
Judge ill to scourge the refuse of the town;
Howe'er their casuists hope to turn the scale,
These men must smart, or scandal will prevail.
By these the weaker sex still suffer most;
And such are prais'd who rose at honour's cost:
The learn'd they wound, the virtuous, and the
    fair;
No fault they cancel, no reproach they spare:
The random shaft, impetuous in the dark,
Sings on unseen, and quivers in the mark.
'Tis justice, and not anger, makes us write,
Such sons of darkness must be dragg'd to light:
Long-suff'ring nature must not always hold:
In virtue's cause 'tis gen'rous to be bold.
To scourge the bad, th' unwary to reclaim,
And make light flash upon the face of shame.

Others have urg'd (but weigh it, and you'll
    find
'Tis light as feathers blown before the wind)
That poverty, the curse of Providence,
Atones for a dull writer's want of sense:
Alas! his dulness 'twas which made him poor :
Not vice versa: we infer no more.
Of vice and folly poverty's the curse,
Heav'n may be rigid, but the man was worse,
By good made bad, by favours more disgrac'd,
So dire th' effects of ignorance misplac'd !
Of idle youth, unwatch'd by parents' eyes !
Of zeal for pence, and dedication lies !
Of conscience modell'd by a great man's looks,
And arguings in religion—from no books !

No light the darkness of that mind invades,
Where Chaos rules, enshrin'd in genuine shades:
Where in the dungeon of the soul enclos'd,
True Dulness nods, reclining and repos'd.
Sense, grace, or harmony, ne'er enter there,
Nor human faith, nor piety sincere:
A midnight of the spirits, soul and head,
(Suspended all) as thought itself lay dead.
Yet oft a mimic gleam of transient light
Breaks thro' this gloom, and then they think
    they write;

[11] In the original H——; probably orator
Henley. C.

From streets to streets th' unnumber'd pam-
    phlets fly;
Then tremble Warner, Brown and Billinsly [12].
O thou most gentle deity appear,
Thou who still hear'st, and yet art prone to hear:
Whose eye ne'er closes, and whose brains ne'er
    rest,
(Thy own dear Dulness bawling at thy breast)
Attend, O Patience, on thy arm reclin'd,
And see wit's endless enemies behind !
And ye, our Muses, with a hundred tongues;
And thou, O Henley ! blest with brazen lungs:
Fanatic Withers! fam'd for rhymes and sighs,
And Jacob Behmen! most obscurely wise:
From darkness palpable, on dusky wings
Ascend! and shroud him who your offspring
    sings.

The first with Egypt's darkness in his head,
Thinks wit the devil, and curses books unread.
For twice ten winters he has blunder'd on,
Thro' heavy comments, yet ne'er lost nor won:
Much may be done in twenty winters more,
And let him then learn English at threescore.
No sacred Maro glitters on his shelf,
He wants the mighty Stagyrite himself.
See vast Coimbrias' [13] comments pil'd on high;
In heaps Soncinas [14], Sotus, Sanchez lie;
For idle hours, Sa's [15] idle casuistry.
Yet worse is he, who in one language read,
Has one eternal jingling in his head,
At night, or morn, in bed, and on the stairs—
Talks flights to grooms, and makes lewd songs
    at pray'rs;
His pride, a pun, a guinea his reward,
His critic Gildon, Jemmy Moore his bard.

What artful hand the wretch's form can hit,
Begot by Satan on a Manley's wit:
In parties furious at the great man's nod,
And hating none for nothing, but his God:
Foe to the learn'd, the virtuous, and the sage,
A pimp in youth, an atheist in old age;
Now plung'd in bawdry and substantial lies,
Now dabbling in ungodly theories:
But so, as swallows skim the pleasing flood,
Grows giddy, but ne'er drinks to do him good :
Alike resolv'd to flatter, or to cheat,
Nay worship onions, if they cry, "come eat :"
A foe to faith, in revelation blind,
And impious much, as dunces are by kind.

Next see the master-piece of flatt'ry rise,
Th' anointed son of dulness and of lies;
Whose softest whisper fills a patron's ear,
Who smiles unpleas'd, and mourns without a
Persuasive, tho' a woful blockhead he:    [tear;
Truth dies before his shadow's sophistry;
For well he knows the vices of the town,
The schemes of state, and int'rest of the gown:
Immoral afternoons, indecent nights,
Inflaming wines, and second appetites.

But most the theatres with dulness groan;
Embrios half form'd, a progeny unknown:

[12] Three booksellers.
[13] The society of Coimbria in Spain, which
published commentaries on Aristotle.
[14] Soncinas, a schoolman.
[15] Eman. de Sa. See Paschal's Mystery of
Jesuitism.

Fine things for nothing, transports out of season,
Effects uncaus'd, and murders without reason.
Here worlds run round, and years are taught to
Each scene an elegy, each act a play.    [stay,
Can the same pow'r such various passions move?
Rejoice or weep, 'tis ev'ry thing for love.
The self-same cause produces Heav'n and Hell :
Things contrary, as buckets in a well :
One up, one down, one empty and one full :
Half high, half low, half witty, and half dull.
So on the borders of an ancient wood,
Or where some poplar trembles o'er the flood,
Arachne travels on her filmy thread,
Now high, now low, or on her feet or head.
    Yet these love verse, as croaking comforts
        frogs,
And mire and ordure are the heav'n of hogs.
As well might nothing bind immensity,
Or passive matter immaterials see,
As these should write by reason, rhyme and rule,
Or he turn wit, whom Nature doom'd a fool.
If Dryden err'd, 'twas human frailty once,
But blundering is the essence of a dunce.
    Some write for glory, but the phantom fades:
Some write as party, or as spleen invades :
A third because his father was well read,
And, murd'rer like, calls blushes from the dead.
Yet all for morals and for arts contend—
They want them both, who never prais'd a friend.
More ill, than dull : for pure stupidity
Was ne'er a crime in honest Banks, or me.
    See next a crowd in damasks, silks, and crapes,
Equivocal in dress, half belles, half-trapes :
A length of night-gown rich Phantasia trails,
Olinda wears one shift, and pares no nails :
Some in Curll's cabinet each act display,
When Nature in a transport dies away :
Some more refin'd transcribe their Opera-loves
On iv'ry tablets, or in clean white gloves :
Some of Platonic, some of carnal taste,
Hoop'd or unhoop'd, ungarter'd or unlac'd.
Thus thick in air the wing'd creation play,
When vernal Phœbus rolls the light away,
A motley race, half insects, and half fowls,
Loose-tail'd and dirty, may-flies, bats and owls.
    Gods ! that this native nonsense was our worst !
With crimes more deep, O Albion, art thou
        curst.
No judgment open prophanation fears,
For who dreads God, that can preserve his fears?
O save me, Providence, from vice refin'd,
That worst of ills, a speculative mind !
Not that I blame divine philosophy
(Yet much we risk, for pride and learning lye):
Heav'n's paths are found by nature more than
        art,
The schoolman's head misleads the layman's
        heart.
    What unrepented deeds has Albion done?
Yet spare us, Heav'n ! return, and spare thy
Religion vanishes to types and shade,    [own.
By wits, by fools, by her own sons betray'd.
Sure 'twas enough, to give the dev'l his due,
Must such men mingle with the priesthood too?
So stood Onias at th' Almighty's throne,
Profanely cinctur'd in a harlot's zone.
    Some Rome, and some the Reformation blame;
'Tis hard to say from whence such licence came :
From fierce enthusiasts, or Socinians sad?
Collins the soft, or Bourignon the mad?

From wayward nature, or lewd poets' rhymes?
From praying, canting, or king-killing times?
From all the dregs which Gallia could pour forth,
(These sons of schism) landed in the north?—
From whence it came, they and the d—l best
        know,
Yet thus much, Pope, each atheist is thy foe.
    O Decency, forgive these friendly rhymes,
For raking in the dung-hill of their crimes.
To name each monster would make printing
        dear,
Or tire Ned Ward, who writes six books a year.
Such vicious nonsense, impudence, and spite,
Would make a hermit, or a father write.
Though Julian rul'd the world, and held no more
Than deist Gildon taught, or Toland swore,
Good Gregory [16] prov'd him execrably bad,
And scourg'd his soul, with drunken reason mad.
Much longer Pope restrain'd his awful hand,
Wept o'er poor Nineveh, and her dull band,
'Till fools like weeds rose up, and chok'd the
        land.
Long, long he slumber'd e'er th' avenging hour :
For dubious mercy half o'er-rul'd his pow'r :
Till the wing'd bolt, red-hissing from above,
Pierc'd millions thro'—for such the wrath of
        Jove.
Hell, Chaos, Darkness, tremble at the sound,
And prostrate fools bestrow the vast profound;
No Charon wafts them from the farther shore,
Silent they sleep, alas ! to rise no more.
    O Pope, and sacred Criticism, forgive [live !
A youth, who dares approach your shrine, and
Far as he wander'd in an unknown night,
No guide to lead him, but his own dim light.
For him more fit in vulgar paths to tread,
To show th' unlearned what they never read,
Youth to improve, or rising genius tend,
To science much, to virtue more, a friend.

## AN ESSAY ON REASON.

Cœlestis rationis opus deducere mundo aggrediar.
                        MANIL. Lib. 1.

FROM Time's vast length, eternal and unknown,
Essence of God, coeval Reason shone :
Mark'd each recess of providence and fate,
Weighing the present, past, and future state :
'Ere Earth to start from nothing was decreed,
'Ere man had fall'n, or God vouchsaf'd to bleed;
Part of herself in Eden's pair she saw,
Where virtue was but practice, nature's law;
Where truth was almost felt as well as seen,
(Perception half) and scarce a mist between :
Where homage strove in praise and pray'r
        t'adore,
By one to honour, and by one implore : [bowl,
While temp'rance cropt the herb, and mixt the
And health warm'd sense, and sense sublim'd the
        soul.
    Fear was not then, nor malady, nor age,
Nor public hatred, nor domestic rage :
No fancied want, no lust of taste decreed
The honest ox to groan, the lamb to bleed :

[16] Gregory Nazianzen who wrote two satires,
or invectives against Julian.

No earth-born pride had snatch'd th' Almighty's
    rod,
O'erturn'd the balance, or blasphem'd the God :
No vice (for vice is only truth deny'd)  ·
Nurs'd ignorance, or nature's voice bely'd.
    Hail, blissful pair ! whose sense if farther
        wrought,
Had weaken'd,stretch'd,and agoniz'd the thought,
Created both to know and to possess
What we, unhappy, can but barely guess :
Truth to survey in clearest lights arrang'd,
Ere frauds were form'd to rules, or words were
Ere every act a double aspect bore,    [chang'd,
Or doubts intending well, perplext us more :
    You saw the source of actions and the end ;
Why things are opposite, and why they blend ;
How from eternal causes good and ill
Subsist: how mingle, yet are diff'rent still :
How modes unnumber'd soften and unite ;
How strength of falsehood glares, and strength of
        light :
    Half of the God came open to your view ;
You hail'd his presence, and his voice you knew;
That God, whose light is truth, whose vast extent
Of pleasure, good—self-form'd and self-content !
Unhurt by years, unlimited by place,
At once o'erflowing time and thought and space.
    By knowing him, you knew him to be best,
(For the first attribute infers the rest),
Knew from his mind why boundless virtues rose,
Why his unerring will that virtue chose,
Not something sep'rate (as the deist dreams)
To circumscribe his pow'r, contract his schemes :
For reason though it binds th' immortal will,
Is but a portion of the Godhead still :
This learn, ye wits, by sacred myst'ry aw'd,
And know that God is only guide to God.
    This the first knew, their heart, their knowledge
        clear;
Their reason perfect, as their frame could bear:
Till lust of change and more than mortal pride
Infring'd the law, the penalty defy'd :
Curst by themselves in Eden's blest abodes,
Possessing all, yet raging to be gods :
Thence sin unnerv'd the sense, obscur'd the soul,
And still increas'd, like rivers as they roll :
For nature once deprav'd, like motion crost,
Ne'er of herself can gain the pow'rs she lost.
    But here the moderns eagerly dispute,—
" Why in a state of knowledge absolute,
(Where unmix'd truth came naked to the view,
And the first glance could pierce all nature thro',)
God should an edict positive decree
And guard so strict th' inviolable tree ?
This were for trifles sagely to contend,
To barter truth for show, for means the end."
    Agreed : but first our mighty sect should
        prove
God has no title to our faith or love :
To awe submissive, reverential fear,
To hope, to homage, to the grateful tear :
That truth omniscient may sometimes deceive,
That all-wise bounty knows not what to give :
First let the critics of the Godhead make
Such theorems clear, and then this answer take :
    That Adam, though all moral truth he saw,
· Yet scarce a motive had t' infringe that law :
How could he honour other gods than one ?
How change a spirit into sculptur'd stone ?

How, the first morning life inform'd his frame,
Durst he profane his Maker's sacred name ?
How without parents could intemp'rate rage
Spurn the hoar head, or mock the tears of age ?
Why should he covet ? when supremely blest—
Or why defraud ? when all things he possest—
The bridal bed for whom should he deceive ?
Or whom assassin, but his much-lov'd Eve ?—
Hence 'twas that man by positives was try'd :
And hence beheld the Godhead justifi'd.
    Add, that the reasoning faculty of man
Serv'd not as now, when Adam first began :
Much though he saw, yet little had he try'd,
Nor known experience, nature's surest guide :
See then a previous cause and reason giv'n
Why a reveal'd instinct should come from Heav'n,
Which op'd at once the natures and the pow'rs
Of earth, air, sea, beasts, reptiles, fruits, and
        flow'rs.
    Effects, as yet uncaus'd, thence Adam knew,
The rage of poisons, and the balms of dew :
Smil'd when the gen'rous courser paw'd the
        plains,
Yet shun'd the tygress and her beauteous stains :
Nurs'd the soft dove that slumber'd on his breast,
Nor touch'd the dipsas' poison-flaming crest.
    How had he trembled in that bless'd abode,
Had not his sovereignty been taught by God ?
Or how, unlicens'd, durst he wanton tread
Ev'n the green insect in its herbal bed ?
For life, like property, is no man's slave,
And only he can reassume that gave.
(This by the way :) the hist'ry of the fall,
And how the first-form'd loins contain'd us all,
Dread points ! which none explain, and few con-
        ceive,
We wave for ever, doctors, by your leave.
Ethnics and Christians a corruption grant,
The manner how, still wicked wits may want,
So, if they doubt what sound, or vision be,
Thence let them prove we cannot hear, or see.
'Spite of their mock'ry also, plain is this,
That no man had a plea to Adam's bliss.
Grant that the parent wastes a vast estate—
Is he for that, just object of our hate,
Provided all remains that use requires,
Or need can crave, for ends and for desires,
To point out evil, virtue's heights to reach,
This life to soften, or the next to teach ?
    Shall man, because he wants a seraph's flame,
Not taste the joys proportion'd to his frame ?
Knowledge enough for use, for pride is giv'n ;
Strong, but not sensitive as truth in Heav'n :
Clear yet adapted to the mental sight:
For too much truth o'erpow'rs, as too much light,
    Reason, like virtue, in a medium lies : [wise,
A hair's-breadth more might make us mad, not
Out-know ev'n knowledge, and out-polish art,
Till Newton drops down giddy—a Descartes !
For reason, like a king who thirsts for pow'r,
Leaves realms unpeopled,while it conquers more:
Admit our eye-sight as the lynx's clear :
T' attain the distant, we o'ershoot the near :
(For art too nice, like tubes revers'd, extends
Things beyond things, till ev'n the object ends.)
Hence nature, like Alcides, saw 'twas fit
To fix th' extremest stretch of human wit ;
Wit, like an insect clamb'ring up a ball,
Mounts to one point,and then of course must fall,

No wiser, if its pains proceed, than end,
And all its journey only to descend.
The question is not therefore, how much light
God's wisdom gives us, but t'exert it right:
Enough remains for ev'ry social end,
For practice, theory, self, neighbour, friend:
Then call not knowledge narrow, Heav'n unkind;
One curse there is, 'tis wantonness of mind.—
To human plummets can abysses sound:
greed: yet rocks they reach and shelving
   ground:
Thus reason, where 'tis dang'rous,steers us right,
And then dissolves amidst th' abyss of light.
'Tis reason finds th' horizon's glimm'ring line
Where realms of truth,and realms of errour join:
Views its own hemisphere with thankful eyes,
Thinks nature good in that which she denies:
While-pride amidst the vast abrupt must soar—
Alas! to fathom God is to be more!
Then dare be wise, into thyself descend,
Sage to some purpose, studious to some end:
Search thy own heart, the well where knowledge
   lies:         [skies:
Thence (not from higher earth) we catch the
Leave myst'ry to the seraph's purer thought
Which takes in truth, as forms by streams are
   caught:
Leaves lust to brutes whose unhurt sense is such,
That tenfold transport thrills at ev'ry touch:
Holding the middle sphere where reason lies,
Than these more temp'rate, as than those less
   wise.
Each pow'r of animals in each degree,
Ev'n second instinct, knowledge is to thee:
Th' effect as certain, tho' the birth more slow,
For like the rose it must expand and blow:
Time must call forth the manhood of the mind,
By study strengthen'd, and by taste refin'd:
Its action open, as its purpose true,
Slow to resolve, but constant to pursue:
Weeded from passion, prejudice and pride,
Mod'rate to ail, yet steady to one side.
Such once was Knight: in word, in action clear,
Ev'n in the last recess of thought sincere:
Great without titles, virtuous without show,
Learn'd without pride, and just without a foe:
Alike humane, to pity, or impart:
The coolest head, and yet the warmest heart.
O early lost! With ev'ry grace adorn'd!
By me (so Heav'n ordain'd it) always mourn'd;
In life's full joy, and virtues' fairest bloom
Untimely check'd, and hurry'd to the tomb:
Torn ev'n from her whom all the world approv'd,
More blest than man, and more than man be-
   lov'd.
  How few, like thee, truth's arduous paths can
   tread,           [head?
Trace her slow streams, and taste them at their
See how scarft sages, and pale schoolmen roam
From art to art? their mind a void at home.
For oft our understanding opes our eyes,
Forgets itself, tho' all things it descries.
Minds like fine pictures are by distance prov'd,
And objects proper, only as remov'd.
  Yet reason has a fund of charms t' engage
Art, study, meditation, youth and age:
Beauty,which must the slave, the monarch strike;
Homage, which paid not, injures both alike:
Virtue at once to please, and to befriend,
(Great Nature's clue, observant of its end);

Such were the paths, the rubric ancients trod,
The friends of virtue and the friends of God.
  Science like this, important and divine,
The good man offers, Reason, at thy shrine:
Sees thee,God, Nature (well explain'd) the same:
Not chang'd when thought on, varying but in
   name:
Sees whence each aptitude,each diff'rence springs,
How thought ev'n acts, and meaning lives in
   things:
Or else examines at less studious hours
The thinking faculty, its source, its pow'rs:
How stretch'd like Kneller's canvas first it lies,
'Ere the soft tints awake, or outlines rise:
How till the finishing of thrice sev'n years,
The master figure Reason scarce appears:
Sighs to survey a realm by right its own,
While passion, fierce co-heir, usurps the throne:
A second Nero, turbulent in sway,
His pleasure, noise, his life one stormy day:
Headstrong in love, and headstrong too in hate,
Resolv'd t' enslave the mob, or sink the state:
Sad farce of pow'r, sad anarchy of things,
Where brutes are subjects, and where tyrants
   kings!
  Yet in this infant state, by stealth, by chance,
Th' increasing mind still feels a slow advance,
Thro' the dark void ev'n gleams of truth can
And love of liberty upheave at root:   [shoot,
No more the tender seeds unquicken'd lie,
But stretch their form and wait for wings to fly.
Sensation rst, the ground-work of the whole,
Deals ray by ray each image to the soul:
Perception true to every nerve, receives
The various impulse, now exults, now grieves:
Thought works and ends, and dares afresh be-
   gin:          [in;
So whirlpools pour out streams, and suck them
That thought romantic Memory detains
In unknown cells, and in aerial chains:
Imagination thence her flow'rs translates;
And Fancy, emulous of God, creates:
Experience slowly moving next appears,
Wise but by habit, judging but from years:
Till Knowledge comes, a wise and gen'rous heir,
And opes the reservoir, averse to spare:
And Reason rises, the Newtonian sun,
Moves all, guides all, and all sustains in one.
  Bright emanation of the Godhead, hail!
Fountain of living lustre, ne'er to fail:
As none deceiving, so of none deceiv'd:
Beheld, and in the act of sight believ'd;
In truth, in strength, in majesty array'd,
No change to turn thee, and no cloud to shade.
Such in herself is Reason—deist, say,
What hast thou here t' object, t' explain away?
Thinkst thou thy reason this unerring rule?
Then live a madman—and yet die a fool!
God gave us reason as the stars were giv'n,
Not to discard the Sun, but mark out Heav'n;
At once a rule of faith, if well employ'd,
A source of pleasure, if aright enjoy'd,
A point, round which th' eternal errour lies
Of fools too credulous, and wits too wise:
A faithful guide to comfort and to save,
Till the mind floats, like Peter on the wave:
Then bright-ey'd Hope descends, of heav'nly
And Faith our immortality on Earth.   [birth,
A Saviour speaks! lo! darkness low'rs no more,
And the hush'd billows sleep against the shore.

If this be hardship, let the dying heir
Spurn back his father's aid, and curse his care:
If this be cruel, partial and unwise,
Then perish infidel, and God despise.
Nor flows it hence, that revelation's force
Chains reason down, or thwarts it in its course:
Since obligation, first of moral ties,
Binds thus, and yet no tyranny implies:
We grant that men th' eternal motive see,
Yet motive, where there's choice, still leaves
    them free:
True liberty was ne'er by licence gain'd,
Nor are liege-subjects slaves because restrain'd;
Restriction shows the check, but none creates:
So prescience finds, but not necessitates.
Yet still the wits with partial voice exclaim,
" What art thou truth? What knowledge, but a
    ' name?
In short, are mortals free, or they are bound?
Tell us, is reason something, or a sound?"
    Friends, 'tis agreed: behold the gen'rous part,
My soul at once unfolded, and my heart;
Too brave to be by superstition aw'd,
And yet too modest to confront the God:
Chain'd to no int'rest, bigot to no cause,
Slave of no hope, preferment, or applause:
For those who cleave to truth for virtue's sake,
Enjoy all party-good, yet nothing stake.
    Thou then, O source of uncreated light,
Hallow my lips, and guard me while I write.
    First in that Pow'r (to whose eternal thought
No outward image e'er one image brought,
The part, the whole, the seer and the seen,
No distance, inference, or act between),
Reason presides, diffusing thence abroad
Thro' truth, thro' things—the test, the point of
    God.
    As perfect reason from the Godhead springs,
(And still unchang'd if perfect): so from things,
Truths, actions—in their kind and their degree,
Starts real meaning, difference, harmony.
These all imply a reason, reason still
A duty; good, if sought; if sought not, ill:
Hence in the chain of causes, virtue, vice,
And hence religion, take their gen'ral rise.
    God first creates; the ref'rence, nature, force
Of things created must result of course:
As well might sense its evidence disclaim,
Or chance sketch out Earth's, Heav'n's stupen-
    dous frame;
As well might motion to be rest consent,
As well might matter fill without extent,
As things (instead of being what they ought)
Sink into hazard, whim, caprice, or nought.
    Hence in each art, the great, the glorious
For science only copies moral charms, [warms,
Mysterious excellence! the dome, the draught,
The lay, the concert swell upon the thought.
    The mind to nobler beauty thence proceeds,
The union, colouring, and force of deeds;
Swells in the hero's cause with vast esteem,
Pants for the patriot, and would more than seem;
Labours with Brutus in the stern decree, [free!"
Yet whispers 'midst his tears, " O Rome be
Envies at Utica the stoic sword,
Or bleeds at Carthage, martyr to its word.
    These truths congenial, nor devis'd though
    found,
Live in each age, and shoot from ev'ry ground:

Bloom or on Albion's, or on India's coast,
Midst Abyssinia's flames, or Zembla's frost.
    Yet still the wits and moralists exclaim,
" That virtue's casual oft, and oft a name:
At Esperanza's cape (or Jesuits lie)
Their baptism's urine, and their god a fly:
Old Cato, sagely vers'd in stoic laws,
Still hackney'd out his wife to serve the cause:
And incest, for th' advantage of a nation
Was sacred made by Spartan toleration:
Midst Tart'ry's deserts, and Cathaya's sands,
In their horse-soup their natives wash their
    hands:
One drop of wine but in their chamber spilt,
Is certain death, inexpiable guilt[1]!
For a huge whore, see heroes, kings, at strife,
But never virgin there was made a wife[2]."
    Of all assertions, these indeed are chief
T' excite compassion, tho' not shake belief:
Since from an agent's want of taste and skill
It flows not that the rule must needs be ill;
For truth exists abstracted from the mind,
And Nature's laws are laws, tho' man be blind,
    Reason, at most, but imitates the Sun,
To each is various, and to all is one:
Perfect, consider'd in itself, 'tis true,
And yet imperfect as exerted too:
The mental pow'r eternal, equal, fixt,
The human act unequal, casual, mixt;
And if such dormant reason bears no fruit,
Dead in the branch, tho' real at the root,
Defect and actual ignorance are one,
For useless talents are the same as none:
All men may catch the heights of truths,'tis true,
But the great question is, if all men do.
    " Oh but:" says one, " if reason comes from
    Heav'n,
" Nature, or God, must deal the blessing ev'n.'
Agreed: and in a prior sense they do;
But still t' improve the gift devolves on you:
Reason in this respect, I boldly say— [lay)—
(And so do thousands, schoolmen, churchmen,
No more is natural, and inly born
Than love, or lust, or pride, or hate, or scorn:
'Tis man's t' exert, exalt, subject, impart:
Here lies the honesty and here the art.
    'Tis his, t' improve good sense, but none create,
Ty'd down to spend no more than his estate:
To strike no notion out, no truth deduce,
But just as nature sow'd the seeds for use.
    This instance urg'd and drawn from mental
    pow'rs,
Earth each day testifies in trees and flowers:
Culture with skill, and science join'd with toil,
Teach Persia's peach to bloom in Albion's soil;
As truly nature's produce here, as there,
In its own sunshine and its spicy air.—
For truth, like earth made barren by the fall,
Just as men labour, tribute pays to all:
Plain, if kind Heav'n two blessings shall impart,
A reasonable head, and upright heart:
For plainness rises in a giv'n degree
As men are honest, and as men can see:
Quarles may be harder to th' unletter'd clown
Than Hed'lin, or Bossu to wits in town.
What's ethic to the true pains-taking man,
Who never thinks, and cheats but all he can?"

[1] Voyages de Carpin.
[2] Histoire des Gheriffs.

What's Shaftsbury's hairs-breadth morals at the
　　'change?
Or Tindal's fitness at Philemon's Grange?
Or solid reasoning to the headstrong youth,
His tutor, pain, experiment his truth?
　　In short one sentence may the whole discuss—
As we with truth, truth coincides with us :
This boults the matter fairly to the bran,
And nothing more wits, bards, deans, doctors
　　can.
　　Nature, like God, ne'er felt the least decay :
But human nature has, and oft she may :
Full in the child th' unsinew'd sire appears,
More weak by growth, more infantine by years ;
And ductile vice each new impression takes,
Passive as air, with ev'ry motion shakes.
　　Like some true Roman dome mankind appears,
The pile impair'd, but not o'erwhelm'd by years:
Ev'n the remains, strength, beauty, use, impart,
And faint, or rough, are equal proofs of art :
Yet nothing but the first creating hand
Shall fill the shadowy lines, or new command,
Bid the stretch'd roof to swell, the arch to bend,
The wings to widen, and the front extend.
Yet as true madmen most their friends suspect,
So wits for this, shal! ev'n their God reject.
　　Not that my verse right reason would control,
True freedom limit, or contract the soul :
Th' exchange were one to bigotry from pride,
A hair's-breadth serves to join them, or divide :
Yet proper decencies must still be had,
Not meanly pious we, nor vainly mad:
Reason, like Israel, Horeb's place descries,
But if she gazes wantonly, she dies :
If well-attemper'd, her etherial light
Will fix our slippery steps, and gild our night :
Or else at most we run a rash career,
Or fare like pilots, who by meteors steer.
For like a mark she's faithful to the view,
But just as distance, force, and aim are true :
Then guide and judge, and guardian of our ways,
Test of our deeds, and umpire of our praise,
Source of our joy, and bound'ry of our grief,
Anchor of hope, and pilot of belief,
True to the clear, unbiass'd, humble soul,
Which trembling seeks her, as the steel its pole.
　　Yet ah! how few ev'n ancient times beheld,
(When Greece and Rome in arms and arts ex-
　　cell'd)
Who thro' life's maze the steps of Nature trod,
Reason their guide, and truth their unknown god.
The Stagyrite, who bold to Heav'n would soar,
Trembled at last to die and be no more :
Gods, angels, glories op'd on Plato's view,
Yet judgment quench'd the flames which rapture
　　blew :
Midst myriads, who but Socrates appears
The birth, pride, effort, of three thousand years !
Nothing the rest, or worse than nothing meant:
God was but chance, and vi: tue but content :
At best the hero's was an impious name:
Free patriots while they bled were slaves to fame:
Even Hell was fable, and their blest abodes,
Of brutes a synod, or a mob of gods.
　　What bramin yet, what sage of Rome or
　　　　Greece,
Ere form'd one moral system of a piece?
Or half an altar rais'd, or duty paid,
Unmix'd with rituals, homage, myst'ry, shade?

He therefore best infers who steers by fact,
And weighs not reason's pow'r, but folly's act:
　　Which of these godlike ancients even drew,
The whole of ethics justly round and true?
Had mission or to prophecy or preach,
Sanction t' excite, authority to teach?
Nay ev'n their rule of morals and of life
Was often wrong, oft various, oft at strife.
'Gainst state or priest they little durst impart,
Their lips scarce breath'd the truths that scorch'd
　　their heart.
Hence Samos' sage the current faith advis'd,
Hence Plato trimm'd his creeds, and temporiz'd,
And Greece for one man's [3] head, in holy rage,
(A strange example in that mod'rate age!)
More art employ'd, more premiums issu'd forth,
Than all our modern deists' heads are worth.
　　Nay half the source of most the ancients knew,
From Noah they, as he from Eden drew :
Whence truth in secret pipes to Memphis pass ;
Thence strain'd thro' Jewry, water'd Asia last.
So Nilus wanders mystic in its flow,
And columns tost from Tempe feed the Po.
　　Now too, wit's Titans, spite of all their boast,
But combat God with his own arms at most:
The truths they boast of, and the rules they
　　know,
Seen not, or own'd not, first from Scripture flow.
So painters, us'd to copy, seem t' invent,
Of aid unconscious, and in theft content.
Faith strikes the light, but pride assumes the
　　fame,
Sure, like th' oblig'd, t'efface her patron's name ;
For as when vig'rous breezes drive a fleet,
Earth seems to stretch, and lab'ring floats to
　　meet,
(Solid herself and fix): so here 'tis thus :
Nor we to God, but God accedes to us.
　　For, ah! ev'n here, where life a journey runs,
Blest with new day-light and with nearer suns,
Virtue's dim lights by God's own hand supplied,
With sanction strengthen'd, honour'd with a
　　guide,
How few (except instructed first and led)
Can thread the maze, or touch the fountain's
Observe a mean twixt bigotry and pride, [head !
Hit the strait way, or err not in the wide !
If reason then scarce finishes the best,
Th' unbias'd few, how fares it with the rest?
Where errour holds at least a dubious sway,
A war of thoughts, and twilight of a day :
Where prepossession warps the ductile mind,
Where blindfold education leads the blind :
Where interest biasses, ill customs guide,
And strong desires pour on us like a tide :
Where insolence is never at a loss,
But saunters on to Heav'n, a saint in gross :
Where wit must mince a gnat (its throat so
　　small):
Where ignorance, an ostrich, gorges all:
Where zeal her unknown vow of fury keeps,
And superstition like an idiot weeps :
Where persecution lifts its iron rod,
Bad for good ends, the butcher of the God :
Where pride still list'ning to herself appears,
New forms Earth's orbit, and new rolls the
　　spheres,

　　　　　[3] Diagoras.

Holds ev'n th' Almighty in her airy chain,
Gives back his laws, well meant, but meant in
Its bravery at best a blundering hit,         [vain;
Its freedom treason, obloquy its wit :
Its vast request just purely to declaim,
And the dear little licence—to blaspheme :—
Say, can cool virtue here dissuade from ill?
Or exil'd reason—pander to the will ?
At most a voice or miracle may save,
And only terrours snatch us from the grave.
  Suppose (though we disown it oft to be)
Man from these errours and these passions free :
Well taught by art, by nature well inclin'd,
Steady of judgment, tractable of mind,
The first step is, the giving folly o'er ;
The last, to practice truth, is ten times more,
  Ah me ! what lengths of valley yet remain,
What hills to climb, ere reason's height he gain?
What strength to toil, what labour to pursue,
Still out of reach, and often out of view.
  Then, gracious God, how well dost thou provide
For erring reason an unerring guide !
To silence explanation (myst'ry's foe),
To lead the tim'rous, and exalt the low :
Ev'n to the best (as all are oft perplext)
Instructive, as true comments on a text.
    Then let each hour's new whim the witlings
                                        swell,
Heav'n let them tutor, and extinguish Hell :
Refuse to trust Omniscience on its troth,
Yet take a lawyer's word, or harlot's oath :
Then bigots, when 'gainst bigots they complain ;
And only singular, because they're vain.
Grant none but they the narrow path can hit—
When will two wits allow each other wit ?
    Far other views the solid mind employ,
A bounded prospect, but a surer joy :—
True knowledge when she conquers or abstains,
Like the true hero, equal glory gains.
This, this is science, sacred in its end,
True to the views of Heav'n,one's self, and friend,
The earliest study, as the latest care,
The surest refuge, and the only pray'r.
    O thou, the God, who high in Heav'n pre-
                    sides,              [guides,
Whose eye o'ersees me, and whose wisdom
Deal me that portion of content and rest, [best :
That unknown health, and peace, which suit me
Save me from all the guilt and all the pain,
That lust of pleasure brings, and lust of gain :
In trial fix me, and in peril shade,
'Gainst foes protect me, 'gainst my passions aid :
In wealth my guardian, and in want my guide,
'Twixt a mean flattery, and drunken pride :
With life's more dear sensations warm my heart,
Transport to feel, benevolence t' impart,
Each homefelt joy, each public duty send,
Make me, and give me, all things in the friend.
    But most protect and guard me in a mind
Not rashly bold, nor abjectly resigned.

And oh, when interest every virtue hides,
When errour blinds, and prejudice misguides,
Alike thy grace, alike thy truth impart,
Beam on my soul, and triumph o'er my heart.
    Thus let me live unheard of, or forgot,
My wealth content, praise, silence, truth my lot:
Thy word, O God ! my science and delight,
Task of my day and transport of my night :
There taught that he who suffers is but tried,
And he who wonders still may find a guide ;
Sanction with truth, reward with virtue join'd,
Life without end,and laws that reach the mind !
Happy the man that such a guide can take,
Whose character is, never to forsake.

---

## TO THE PRINCE OF ORANGE,

ON HIS PASSING THROUGH OXFORD IN HIS RETURN
FROM BATH [1].

At length, in pity to a nation's prayer,
Thou liv'st, O Nassau, Providence's care !
Life's sun, which lately with a dubious ray
Gave the last gleams of a short glorious day,
Again with more than noon tide lustre burns ;
The dial brightens, and the line returns.
    Some guardian power, who o'er thy fate pre-
                                        sides,
Whose eyes unerring Albion's welfare guides,
Taught yonder streams with new-felt force to flow,
And bade th' exalted minerals doubly glow.
Thus cold and motionless Bethesda stood,
Till heavenly influence brooded o'er the flood.
Lo ! while our isle with one loud pæan rings,
Equal, though silent, homage Isis brings ;
Isis, whose erring on the modest side
Th' unkind and ignorant mistake for pride.
Here's the task of reason, not of art,
Words of the mind, and actions of the heart !
    And sure that unbought praise which learning
                                        brings
Outweighs the vast acclaim that deafens kings ;
For souls, supremely sensible and great,
See through the farce of noise,and pomp of state;
Mark when the fools huzza, or wise rejoice,
And judge exactly between sound and voice.
    Hail, and proceed ! be arts like ours thy care,
Nor slight those laurels thou wert born to wear :
Adorn and emulate thy glorious line,
Take thy forefather's worth, and give them thine.
Blest with each gift that human hearts can move,
In science blest, but doubly blest in love.
    Power, beauty, virtue, dignify thy choice,
Each public suffrage, and each private voice.

[1] From the Epithalamia Oxoniensia, &c.
1734. *K.*

# THE AMARANTH,

### OR, RELIGIOUS POEMS;

#### CONSISTING OF FABLES, VISIONS, EMBLEMS, &c.

———Deus ora movet : Sequar ora moventem
Rite Deum !———

THE AMARANTHINE CROWN DESCRIBED BY MILTON.

A crown inwove with amaraut and gold ;
Immortal Amarant ! a flow'r which once
In Paradise fast by the tree of life
Began to bloom ; but soon for man's offence
To Heav'n remov'd, where first it grew ; there
      grows,
And flow'rs aloft, shading the fount of life.
                              Par. Lost, l. III, v. 352.

## PREFACE.

I shall not trouble the public with excuses for venturing to send these Religious Poems into the world ; having long since observed, that all apologies made by authors, far from gaining the end proposed, serve only to supply an ill-natured critic with weapons to attack them. This being the case, it shall suffice me to say, that I drew up the present writings for my own private consolation under a lingering and dangerous state of health, which it has pleased God to make my portion: nor had I any better opportunity or power of discharging the duties of my profession to mankind. The goodness of my cause may perhaps supply the defects of my poetry ; since, in this sense, "the very gleanings of the grapes of Ephraim will be better than the vintage of Abiezer." I promise my readers no extraordinary art in composition or style ; but flatter myself they will find some nature, some flame, and some truth.

Parables, fables, emblematic visions, &c. are the most ancient method of conveying truth to mankind. Upwards of forty of the finest and most poetical parts of the Old and New Testament are of this cast, and force their way upon the mind and heart irresistibly, though they are written in prose.

From a just sense of this humble simplicity, I have here translated the plainest and least figurative parable that our Blessed Saviour has delivered to us, relating only to a few un-ornamented circumstances in agriculture.

To express such humble allusions with clearness, propriety, and dignity, was, it must be confessed, one of the hardest pieces of poetry I ever yet undertook ; nevertheless, I flattered myself that I was in some degree master of one part of the subject (namely, the culture of land) upon which the parable is founded.

Yet the great and real difficulty still recurred ;

Difficile est propriè communia dicere.———

How far I have succeeded in this, or any other particular, is more than I shall take upon me to conjecture. Nor shall it be dissembled, but that I had a great inclination to give a paraphrase (or metaphrase rather) of the xxviiith chapter of Deuteronomy ; which, I believe, hath never yet been turned into English verse. It is doubtless one of the noblest pieces of poetry in Holy Scripture ; being at the same time sublime, and yet plain ; seemingly familiar, and yet richly diversified.

In this chapter, the change of ideas and events from a state of obedience to a state of disobedience, exhibits a power of language, imagery, and just thinking, which no un-inspired writings ever have laid claim to with justice, or ever shall. But, when I came to take a closer view of the precipice and its dangers, " my heart trembled," as Job says, " and was moved out of its place ;" I threw down the pencil in despair, and left the undertaking to some abler hand ; namely, to some future Milton, Dryden, or Pope.

Upon the whole, I may perhaps venture to persuade myself, that the intention of the present work is commendable, and that the work when perused, may prove useful (more or less) to my fellow-christians.

Conscious of my own inabilities, and being desirous that the reader may receive some advantage by casting his eyes over these poems, I have added in a few notes, the most remarkable passages I had an eye to in the Holy Scriptures ; and in the writings of the primitive fathers ; they being the only compass and charts which I have made use of in my navigation.

A mixture of pleasing and instructive poetry cannot fail to engage the attention of all rational and serious readers : "For, as it is hurtful to drink wine, or water, alone ; and as wine mingled with water is pleasant, and delighteth the taste ; even so speech, finely framed, delighteth the ears of them that read the story."
                              2 Maccab. Ch. ult. v. ult.

## CHRIST'S PARABLE OF THE SOWER.

I will incline mine ear to a parable : I will open my dark saying upon the harp. Psalm xlix, v. 4.

All these things spake Jesus unto the multitude in parables. Without a parable spake he not unto them. Matth. c. xiii. v. 34.

A wise man will hear, and increase learning, and a man of understanding shall attain unto wise counsels: to understand a proverb (a parable) and the interpretation; the words of the wise, and their dark sayings. Prov. c. i. v. 5, 6.

## INTRODUCTION.

Long e'er th' Ascréan bard [1] had learnt to
    sing,
Or Homer's fingers touch'd the speaking string;
Long e'er the supplemental arts had found
Th' embroid'ry of auxiliary sound;
/The Heav'n-born Muse the paths of nature chose:
Emblems and fables her whole mind disclose,
Victorious o'er the soul with energy of prose!

    True poetry, like Ophir's gold, endures
All trials, yet its purity secures;
Invert, disjoint it, change its very name,
The essence of the thoughts remains the same.
Something there is, which endless charms affords,
And stamps the majesty of truth on words.

    The son of Gideon [2], 'midst Cherizim's snow,
Unskill'd in numbers taught the stream to flow,
With conscious pride disdain'd the aids of art,
And pour'd a full conviction on the heart:
His Cedar, Fig-tree, and the Bry'r convey
The highest notions in the humblest way [3].

    In Nathan's fable strong and mild conspire,
The suppliant's meekness and the poet's fire:
Till waken'd nature bade the tears to flow,
And David's muse assum'd the voice of woe [4].

    The wise, all-knowing Saviour of mankind
Mix'd ease with strength, and truth with em-
    blem join'd:
Omniscience, vested with full pow'r to choose,
O'erlooks the strong, nor does the weak refuse [5]:
Leaves pageantry of means to feebler man,
And builds the noblest, on the plainest plan:
Divine simplicity the work befriends,
And humble causes reach sublimest ends.

    True flame of verse, O sanctifying fire [6]!
Warm not my genius, but my heart inspire!
On my cleans'd lips permit the coals to dwell
Which from thy altar on Isaiah fell [7]!
Cancel the world's applause; and give thy grace
To me, the meanest of the tuneful race.
Teach me the words of Jesus to impart
With energy of pow'r, but free from art.
Thy emanations light and heat dispense;
To sucklings speech, to children eloquence!—
Like Habakkuk [8], I copy, no indite;
Tim'rous like him, I tremble whilst I write!
But Jeremiah with new boldness sung,
When inspiration rush'd upon his tongue [9].
The pow'rs of sacred poesy were giv'n
By Him that bears the signature of Heav'n [10].

[1] Hesiod.      [2] Jotham.
[3] See the whole parable, Judg. c. ix. v. 7—21.
[4] On this occasion David composed the 50th
psalm.
[5] It is the uniform doctrine of Scripture,
"That flight shall perish from the swift, and
the strong shall not strengthen his force, neither
shall the mighty deliver himself." Amos, c. ii.
v. 14.
[6] Rom. c. xv. v. 16. 2 Thess. c. ii. v. 13. 1 Pet.
c. i. v. 2.
[7] Isaiah c. vii. v. 6.
[8] Hab. c. ii. v. 2.
[9] Jer. c. i. v. 6, &c. 8, 9.
[10] John, c. vi. ver. 27.

## PARABLE.

When vernal show'rs and sunshine had un-
The frozen bosom of the torpid ground,   [bound
When breezes from the western world repair
To wake the flow'rs and vivify the air,
Th' industrious peasant left his early bed,
And o'er the fields his seeds for harvest spread,
With equal hand, and at a distance due,
(Impartially to ev'ry furrow true)
The life-supporting grain he justly threw [1].
As was the culture, such was the return;
Of weeds a forest, or a grove of corn [2].
But, where he dealt the gift on grateful soils,
Harvests of industry o'er-paid his toils.

    Some seeds by chance on brashy [3] grounds he
    threw,
And some the winds to flinty head-lands blew;
Sudden they mounted, pre-mature of birth,
But pin'd and sicken'd, unsupply'd with earth:
Whilst burning suns their vital juice exhal'd,
And, as the roots decay'd, the foliage fail'd.

    Some seeds he ventur'd on ungrateful lands,
Tough churlish clays, and loose unthrifty sands;
The step-dame soil refus'd a nurse's care:
The plants were sickly, juiceless, pale, and bare.
On trodden paths a casual portion fell:
Condemn'd in scanty penury to dwell,
And half-deny'd the matrix of a cell;
While other seeds, less fortunate than they,
Slept, starv'd and naked, on the hard high-way,
From frost defenceless, and to birds a prey.
Here daws with riotous excesses feed,
And choughs, the cormorants of grain, succeed;
Next wily pigeons take their silent stand,
And sparrows last, the gleaners of the land.

    Another portion mock'd the seedsman's toil,
Dispens'd upon a rich, but weedy soil:
Fat unctuous juices gorg'd the rank-fed root;
And plethories of sap produc'd no fruit.
Hence, where the life-supplying grain was spread,
The rav'nous dock uprears its miscreant head;
Insatiate thistles, tyrants of the plains;
And lurid-hemloc, ting'd with pois'nous stains.
What these might spare, th' incroaching thorns
    demand;
Exhaust earth's virtue, and perplex the land [4].

    At last, of precious grain a chosen share
Was sown on pre-dilected land with care;
(A cultur'd spot, accustom'd to receive
All previous aids that industry can give;)

[1] "Bless God, who hath given thee two de-
narii, namely, the law and the gospel, in recompence for thy submission and labour."
    Chrysost. Hom. in Luc. c. 10.
[2] "They that fear the Lord are a sure seed, and
they that love him an honourable plant: they
that regard not the law, are a dishonourable
seed: they that transgress the commandments,
are a deceitful seed." Ecclus. c. x. v. 19.
[3] Brashy lands, in an husbandry-sense, signify lands that are dry, shallow, gravelly, and
pebbly. Such sort of grounds the old Romans
called glareous:

—— Jejuna quidem clivosi glarea ruris.
              Virg. Georg. II

[4] See Hosea, c. x. v. 4 and 8.

The well-turn'd soil with auburn brightness shone,
Mellow'd with nitrous air and genial sun:
An harmony of mould, by nature mixt!
Not light as air, nor as a cement fix'd:
Just firm enough t' embrace the thriving root,
Yet give free expanse to the fibrous shoot ;
Dilating, when disturb'd by lab'ring hands,
And smelling sweet, when show'rs refresh the
        lands.                                    [tain,
Scarce could the reapers' arms the sheaves con-
And the full garners swell'd with golden grain ;
Unlike the harvests of degen'rate days,
One omer sown, one hundred-fold repays :
Rich product, to a bountifel excess !—
Nor ought we more to ask, nor more possess.
The harvest overcomes the reapers' toil ;
So feeble is the hind, so strong the soil $^5$.
    Man's Saviour thus his parable exprest ;
He that hath ears to hear, may feel the rest.

### INTERPRETATION.

THE gift of knowing is to all men giv'n $^6$ ; .
All know, but few perform, the will of Heav'n ;
They hear the sound, but miss the sense convey'd,
And lose the substance, whilst they view the
        shade.
When specious doctrines hover round a mind
Which is not vitally with Heav'n conjoin'd,
The visionary objects float and pass
Transient as figures gliding o'er a glass :
Each but a momentary visit makes,
And each supplies the place the last forsakes.—
Satan for ever fond to be employ'd,
(And changing minds ev'n ask to be destroy'd $^7$,)
Marks well th' infirm of faith ; and soon supplies
Phantoms of truth, and substances of lyes :
Killing the dying, he a conquest gains ;
And, from a little, steals the poor remains.
Reason, man's guardian, by neglect, or sleep,
Loses that castle, he was meant to keep.
    The seeds upon a flinty surface cast,
Denote the worldly-wise, who think in haste :
Who change, for changing's sake, from right
        to wrong,
Constant to nothing, and in nothing long ;
To day they hear the word of God with joy,
To morrow they the word of God destroy ;
Indiff'rent, to assert or to deny :
With zeal they flatter, and with zeal decry.
Such is the fool of wit ! who strives with pains
To lose that paradise the peasant gains.—

$^5$ Imbecillior colonus quàm ager. Columella.

$^6$ " To sin against knowledge is a greater offence than an ignorant trespass ; in proportion
as a fault, which is capable of no excuse, is
more heinous than a fault which admits of a tolerable defence."        J. Mart. Resp. ad Orthod.

" Ignorance will not excuse sin, when it is a sin
in itself."                            Anon. Vet.

$^7$ " He that is idle tempts Satan to set him to
work."                            Chrysost. Hom.
Pious Jeremy Taylor once said to a lady,
" Madam, if you do not employ your children,
the devil will." The son of Sirach gives also the
following advice : " Send thy son to labour, that
he be not idle ; for idleness teacheth much evi!."
                            C. xxxiii, v. 27.

Whenever adverse fortune choaks the way,
When danger threats, or clouds o'ercast the day,
This plant of casualty, unfix'd at root,
Shakes with the blast, and casts his unripe fruit ;
But, when the storms of poverty arise,
And persecution ev'ry virtue tries,
Mindless of God, and trusting to himself a,
He strands Heav'n's freightage on a dang'rous
Averse to learn, and more averse to bear, [shelf.
He sinks, the abject victim of despair !
    The men of pow'r and pomp resemble seeds
Sown on rich earth, but choak'd with thorns and
                                            weeds.
Religion strikes them, but they shun the thought ;
Behold the profit, and yet profit nought.
Heav'n's high rewards they silently contemn,
And think the present world suffices them.
Mean-while ambition leads the soul astray,
Far from its natal walk, th' ethereal way ;
Int'rest assassins friendship ev'ry hour,
Truth warps to custom, conscience bends to pow'r,
Till all the cultivating hand receives
Is empty blossom, and death-blasted leaves.
Idiots in judgment, baffled o'er and o'er ;
Still the same bait, still circumvented more ;
Self-victims of the cunning they adore !
Wise without wisdom, busy to no end ;
Man still their foe, and Heav'n itself no friend !
    The chosen seed, on cultur'd ground, are they
Who humbly tread the evangelic way.
The road to Heav'n is uniform and plain :
All other paths are serpentine and vain.
The true disciple takes the word reveal'd,
Nor rushes on the sanctu'ry conceal'd,
Whilst empty reas'ners emptiest arts employ ;
Nothing they build, and all things they destroy !
The provident of Heav'n unlocks his store,
To clothe the naked, and to feed the poor :
To each man gen'rous, and to each man just,
Conscious of a depositary trust.
Patient of censure, yet condemning none :
Placid to all, accountable to One.
Ev'n in prosperity he fears no loss,
Expects a change, and starts not at the cross.
All injuries by patience he surmounts ;
All suff'rings God's own med'cines he accounts $^9$ :

$^8$ " We are all careful about small matters,
and negligent in the greatest ; of which this is
the reason, we know not where true felicity is."
                                    St. Hieron.
$^9$ The preacher writes beautifully upon this
subject. Ecclus. C. ii. " My son, if thou come
to serve the Lord, prepare thy soul for trial,
set thy heart aright, and constantly endure, and
make not haste in time of trouble ;" i. e. be not
impatient to get over thy trouble. " Cleave unto
him, and depart not away, that thou mayest be
increased at thy last end. Whatsoever is brought
upon thee take cheerfully, and be patient when
thou art changed to a low estate. For gold is
tried in the fire, and acceptable men in the furnace of adversity.—Look at the generations of
old, and see, did ever any trust in the Lord and
was confounded ? or did any abide in his fear
and was forsaken ? or whom did he ever despise,
that called upon him ? for the Lord is full of
compassion and mercy ; he forgiveth sins, and
saveth in time of affliction.—Wo be to the sinner
that goeth two ways ;" i. e. that hath recourse

Studious of good, and penitent for ill,
Still short of grace, yet persevering still ;
As just and true as erring nature can
(For imperfection sets its stamp on man).
Heav'n marks the saint, her mansions to adorn,
And, having purg'd the chaff, accepts the corn.

---

## THE ASCETIC;

### OR, THOMAS A KEMPIS :

#### A VISION.

In omnibus requiem quæsivi, et nusquam
Inveni, nisi in angulis, et libellis.
    Symbol. Kempisian.

At nunc, discussa rerum caligine, verum
Aspicis; illo alii rursus jactantur in alto.
At tua securos portus, blandamque quietem
Intravit, non quassa ratis.
    Stat. Sylv. L. II.

---

### ADVERTISEMENT

#### TO THE READER.

At the end of the 12th stanza in this poem, I had several inducements for venturing to change the ode into heroic measure. The first was, that I might diversify the doctrinal part from the descriptive. The second was, that our excellent and most learned poet, Cowley, had given me his authority for making this change, in his poem de Plantis. But the third and truer reason was, that I found it next to impracticable, to deliver short, unadorned, didactical sentences consistently with the copiousness, irregularity, and enthusiasm peculiar to ode-writing.—Let the reader only make the experiment, and I flatter myself he will join with me in opinion.—Nor have I departed any further than in a metaphor or two from that original simplicity which characterises my author, however difficult and self-denying such an undertaking might be in a poetical composition. What gave me warning was, that Castalio and Stanhope had both spoiled Thomas a Kempis by attempting to adorn him with flowery language, false elegance, and glaring imagery. ' And, by the way, to this cause may be attributed the miscarriages of many poets, (otherwise confessedly eminent) in their paraphrases of the Psalms of David, the Book of Job,

to man as well as God. " Wo unto him that is faint-hearted; for he believeth not, therefore shall he not be defended. Wo unto you that have lost patience: what will ye do when the Lord shall visit you?—they that fear the Lord will say, we will fall into the hands of the Lord, and not into the hands of men : for as his majesty is, so is his mercy."
In like manner St. Chrysostom informs us, " That, in proportion as God adds to our tribulation, he adds likewise to our retribution."

¹ This river takes its rise from one of the highest ice-mountains in Switzerland.
² The species of larch-tree here meant is called sempervirens: the other larches are deciduis foliis.

&c. The grandeur of scriptural sublimity, or simplicity, admits of few or no embellishments. George Sandys, in the reign of Charles I. seems only to have known this secret.

---

And in the morning, rising up a great while before day, he went and departed into a solitary place, and there prayed.
    Mark, c. i. v. 35.

Deep in a vale, where cloud-born Rhyne ¹
Through meads his Alpine waters roll'd,
Where pansies mixt with daisies shine,
And asphodels instarr'd with gold;
Two forests, skirting round the feet
Of everlasting mountains, meet,
Half parted by an op'ning glade;
Around Hercynian oaks are seen.—
Larches ², and cypress ever green,
Unite their hospitable shade.
    Impearl'd with dew, the rosy Morn
Stood tip-toe ³ on the mountain's brow ;
Gleams following gleams the Heav'ns adorn,
And gild the theatre below.:
Nature from needful slumber wakes,
And from her misty eye-balls shakes
The balmy dews of soft repose :
The pi-u-lark with grateful lays
Ascends the skies, and chants the praise
Which man to his Creator owes ⁴.

When lo ! a venerable sire appears,
With sprightly footsteps hast'ning o'er the plain;
His tresses bore the marks of fourscore years,
Yet free from sickness he, and void of pain :
His eyes with half their youthful clearness shone⁵;
Still on his cheeks health's tincture gently glow'd,
His aged voice retain'd a manly tone,
His peaceful blood in equal tenour flow'd.
At length, beneath a beechen shade reclin'd,
He thus pour'd forth to Heav'n the transports of
        his mind.

³ Tip toe. Shakespeare.
⁴ " Before we engage in worldly business, or any common amusements of life, let us be careful to consecrate the first-fruits of the day, and the very beginning of our holy thoughts unto the service of God." St. Basil.
⁵ Thomas à Kempis had no manifest infirmities of old-age, and retained his eye-sight perfect to the last.
All that I have ever been able to learn in Germany upon good authority, concerning him, is as follows : He was born at Kempis, or Kempen, a small walled town in the dutchy of Cleves, and diocese of Cologn. His family-name was Hamerlein, which signifies in the German language a little hammer. We find also that his parents were named John and Gertrude Hamerlein. He lived chiefly in the monastery of Mount St. Agnes; where his effigy, together with a prospect of the monastery, was engraven on a plate of copper that lies over his body. The said monastery is now called Bergh-Clooster, or, as we might say in English, Hill-Cloyster. Many strangers in their travels visit it. Kempis was certainly one of the best and greatest men since the primitive ages. His book of the Imitation of Christ has seen near forty editions in the ori-

" Come unto me (Messiah cries)
All that are laden and oppress'd :
To Thee I come (my heart replies)
O Patron of eternal rest !
Who walks with me (rejoins the voice)
In purest day-light shall rejoice,
Incapable to err, or fall.
With thee I walk, my gracious God ;
Long I've thy painful foot-steps trod,
Redeemer, Saviour, Friend of all [6]!

" Heav'n in my youth bestow'd each good
Of choicer sort : in fertile lands
A decent patrimony stood,
Sufficient for my just demands.
My form was pleasing ; health refin'd
My blood ; a deep-discerning mind
Crown'd all the rest,—The fav'rite child
Of un-affected eloquence,
Plain nature, un-scholastic sense :—
And once or twice the Muses smil'd !

" Blest with each boon that simpler minds desire,
Till Heav'n grows weary of their nauseous pray'rs,
I made the nobler option to retire [7],
And gave the world to worldlings and their heirs ;
The warriors laurels, and the statesman's fame,
The vain man's hopes for titles and employ,
The pomp of station, and the rich man's name,
I left for fools to seek, and knaves t'enjoy[8] ;
An early whisper did its truths impart,
And all the God conceal'd irradiated my heart.

" Happy the man who turns to Heav'n,
When on the landscape's verge of green
Old-age appears, to whom 'tis giv'n
To creep in sight, but fly, unseen !

ginal Latin, and above sixty translations have been made from it into modern languages.
Our author died August the 8th, 1471, aged 92 years.
In the engraving on copper above-mentioned, and lying over his grave, is represented a person respectfully presenting to him a label on which is written a verse to this effect :

Oh ! where is Peace ? for Thou its paths hast trod. ——

To which Kempis returns another strip of paper, inscribed as follows :

In poverty, retirement, and with God.

He was a canon regular of Augustins, and subprior of mount St. Agnes' monastery. He composed his treatise On the Imitation of Christ in the sixty-first year of his age, as appears from a note of his own writing in the library of his convent.
[6] Imitation of Christ, Lib. I. c. i.
[7] " Solitude is the best school wherein to learn the way to Heaven."               St. Jerom.

" Worldly honours are a trying snare to men of an exalted station ; of course their chief care must be, to put themselves out of the reach of envy by humility."               Nepotian.

" The pleasures of this world are only the momentary comforts of the miserable, and not the rewards of the happy."               St. August.

[8] Cætera solicitæ speciosa incommoda vitæ
    Permisi stultis quærere, habere malis.
                        Couleius de Plant.

Stealer of marches, subtile foe,
Simon of stratagem and woe !
Thy fatal blows, ah ! who can ward ?
Around thee lurks a motley train
Of wants, and fears, and chronic pain,
The hungry Croats of thy guard.

" (Thus on the flow'r-enamell'd lawn,
Unconscious of the least surprize,
In thoughtless gambols sports the fawn,
Whilst veil'd in grass the tygress lies.
The silent trait'ress crouches low,
Her very lungs surcease to blow :
At length she darts on hunger's wings ;
Sure of her distance and success,
Where Newton could but only guess,
She never misses, when she springs [9].)

" More truly wise the man, whose early youth [10]
Is offer'd a free off'ring to the Lord,
A self-addicted votary to truth,
Servant thro' choice, disciple by accord !
Heav'n always did th' unblemish'd turtle choose,
Where health conjoin'd with spirit most abounds :
Heav'n seeks the young, nor does the old refuse,
But youth acquits the debt, which age compounds !
Awkward in time, and sour'd with self-disgrace,
The spend-thrift pays his all, and takes the bankrupt's place."

Thus spoke the venerable sage
Who ne'er imbib'd Mæonian lore,
Who drew no aids from Maro's page,
And yet to nobler flights could soar.
Taught by the Solymæan maid ;
With native elegance array'd,
He gave his easy thoughts to flow ;
The charms which anxious art deny'd
Truth and simplicity supply'd,
Melodious in religious woe.

Poet in sentiment ! He feels
The flame ; nor seeks from verse his aid !
The veil which artful charms conceals,
To real beauty proves a shade.
When nature's out-lines dubious are,
Verse decks them with a slight cymarr [11] ;
True charms by art in vain are drest.
Not icy prose could damp his fire :
Intense the flame and mounting high'r,
Brightly victorious when opprest !

By this time morn in all its glory shone ;
The Sun's chaste kiss absorb'd the virgin-dew ;
Th' impatient peasant wish'd his labour done,
The cattle to th' umbrageous streams withdrew ;
Beneath a cool impenetrable shade,
Quiet, he mus'd.  So Jonas safely sate [play'd]
(When the swift gourd her palmy leaves dis-
To see the tow'rs of Ninus bow to fate [12].

[9] This parenthesis was inserted by way of imitating the famous parenthesis in Horace's Ode, which begins

    Qualem ministrum fulminis alitem, &c.

[10] " Even from the flower till the grape was ripe, hath my heart delighted in Wisdom."
                        Ecclus. c. li. v. 15.
[11] A thin covering of the gause, or sarsnetkind.           Dryd. Cymon & Iphigen.
[12] Jonah, c. iv. v. 6.

# THOMAS A KEMPIS: A VISION. 273

Th' Ascetic then drew forth a parchment-scroll,
And thus pour'd out to Heav'n th' effusions of
his soul.

---

### THE MEDITATION OF THOMAS A KEMPIS.

(1.) 'T is vanity to wish for length of days;
The art of living well is wise men's praise.
If death, not length of life, engag'd our view,
Life would be happier, and death happier too [1]
Nature foreshows our death : 'tis God's decree;
The king, the insect dies; and so must we.
What's natural, and common to us all,
What's necessary ;—none should evil call.
Check thy fond love of life, and human pride;
Shall man repine at death, when Christ has dy'd?
(2.) He that can calmly view the mask of
Will never tremble at the face beneath ; [death,
Probationer of Heav'n, he starts no more
To see the last sands ebb, than those before [2].
(3.) In vain we argue, boast, elude, descant;—
No man is honest that's afraid of want.
No blood of confessors that bosom warms [3],
Which starts at hunger, as the worst of harms [4]
(4.) The man with christian preservance fir'd [5],
Check'd but not stop'd ; retarded but not tir'd;
Straiten'd by foes, yet sure of a retreat,
In Heav'n's protection rests securely great [6];
Hears ev'ry sharp alarm without dismay;
Midst dangers dauntless, and midst terrours gay;
Indignant of obstruction glows his flame,
And, struggling, mounts to Heav'n, from whence
    it came :
Oppress'd it thrives; its own destroyers tires,
And with unceasing fortitude aspires [7].

[1] This and the following passages marked with
a note of reference are extracted almost verbatim
from Kempis's Book of the Imitation of Christ.
Lib. I, c. 1, 2. See also Lib. 1, c. 19. 23.
[2] " Death, when compared to life, seems to
be a remedy and not a punishment."
                                    St. Macar.

On the same point another primitive Christian hath observed, " That the Supreme Being
made life short; since, as the troubles of it
cannot be removed from us, we may the sooner
be removed from them." St. Bernard.
[3] " Dost thou fear poverty ? Christ calls the
poor man blessed.—
— Art thou afraid of labour ? Pains are productive of a crown, [fears no famine :
— Art thou hungry ? A true confidence in God
— for the Supreme Governor of the world beholds
thy warfare; and prepares for thee a crown of
glory and everlasting rest."—
                                    Hieron. in Epist.
[4] L. II. Thom. à Kempis.
[5] Perseverance is an image of eternity."
                                    St. Bernard.
[6] " The greatest safety man can have is to
fear nothing but God." Senec.
" Human fear depresses, the fear of God exhi-
larates." Cassian.
[7] Imitat. of Christ, L. III., c. 5. Ibid. c. 19,
N°. 1.

When man desponds, (of human hope bereft)
Patience and Christian heroism are left [8],
Let patience be thy first and last concern;
The hardest task a Christian has to learn [9]!
Life's pendulum in th' other world shall make
Advances, on the side it now goes back.
By force, a virtue of celestial kind
Was never storm'd ; by art 'tis undermin'd [10].
(5.) All seek for knowledge. Knowledge is no
    more
Than this; to know ourselves, and God adore.
Wouldst thou with profit seek, and learn with
    gain?—
Unknown thyself, in solitude remain [11].
Virtue retires, but in retirement blooms,
Full of good works, and dying in perfumes [12].
In thy own heart the living waters rise [13];
Good conscience is the wisdom of the wise ! [14]
Man's only confidence, unmixt with pride,
Is the firm trust that God is on his side [15]
Like Aaron's rod, the faithful and the just,
Torn from their tree, shall blossom in the dust.
(6.) God, says the chief of penitents [16], is One,
Who gives Himself, his Spirit, and his Son.
" Is hunger irksome ?—Thou by Him art fed
With quails miraculous, and Heav'nly bread.
Is thirst oppressive ?—Lift thy eyes, and see
Cat'racts of water fall from rocks for thee.
Art thou in darkness ?—Uncreated light
Is all thy own, and guides thy erring sight.
Is nakedness thy lot ?—Yet ne'er repine ;—
The vestments of Eternity are thine.
Art thou a widow ?—God's thy consort true.
Art thou an orphan?—He's thy father too."

[8] Ibid. c. 35, N°. 2. Ibid. c. 18, N°. 2.
[9] See also Caussin's Holy Court, Part I, L. 3.
Sect. 32, fol. 1650.
[10] "True christian piety was never made a
real captive; it may be killed, but not conquer-
ed." St. Jerom.
[11] " Imitation of Christ, L. I, c. 20. L. II,
c. 10.
[12] " The retired Christian, in seeking after an
happy life, actually enjoys one ; and possesses
that already which he only fancies he is pursuing." St. Eucher.
[13] " Drink waters out of thine own cisterns.
Prov. c. v, V. 15. See also Rev. c. xxii, v. 1.
" And he showed me a pure river of water of life,
clear as crystal." See John, c. vii, v. 38.
[14] Imitat. of Jesus Christ, L. I, c. 6.
[15] Imitat. of Jesus Christ, Lib. II, c. 10.
" The only means of obtaining true security
is to commit all our interests to God, who constantly knows and is ever willing to bestow good
things on them that ask him as they ought."
                                    Cassian.
" Security is no where but in the love and
service of God. It is neither in Heaven, nor
Paradise, much less in the present world. In
Heaven the angels fell from the divine presence :
in Paradise Adam lost his abode of pleasure: in
the world Judas fell from the school of our Saviour." St. Bernard.
[16] St. August. The ten lines marked with
inverted commas are a literal translation from
him.

(7.) The men of Science aim themselves to
　　show [17],
And know just what imports them not to know [18].
(Once having miss'd the truth, they farther stray:
As men ride fastest who have lost their way ;)
Whilst the poor peasant that with daily care
Improves his lands and offers Heav'n his pray'r,
With conscious boldness may produce his face
Where proud philosophers shall want a place[19].
Philosophy in anxious doubts expires :
Religion trims her lamp, as life retires [20].
True faith, like gold into the furnace cast,
Maintains its sterling pureness to the last.
Conscience will ev'ry pious act attest [21] :
A silent panegyrist, but the best !
　　(8.) All chastisements for private use are giv'n;
The revelations Personal of Heav'n [22] :
But man in misery mistakes his road,
Sighs for lost joys, and never turns to God [23].
Heav'n more than meets her child with sorrows
　　try'd ;
Her dove brings olive, e'er the waves subside[24].
Man gives but once, and grudges when we sue;
Heav'n makes old gifts the precedents for new.
　　(9.) Afflictions have their use of ev'ry kind ;
At once they humble, and exalt the mind :
The ferment of the soul by just degrees
Refines the true clear spirit from the lees [25].
Boast as we will, and argue as we can,
None ever knew the virtues of a man,
Except affliction sifts the flour from bran[26].

[17] " It is good to know much and live well :
but, if we cannot attain both, it is better to desire piety than learning : for knowledge makes no
man truly happy, nor doth happiness consist in
intellectual acquisitions. The only valuable
thing is a religious life."
　　　　　　　　Sti. Greg. Magn. Moral.
And again : "That only is the best knowledge
which makes us better."
　[18] Imitat. of Christ. 　　[19] Ibid.
　[20] Imitat. of Jesus Christ, L. II, c. 10.
　[21] " As in water face answereth to face, so the
heart of man to man." Prov. xxvii, v. 19.
" Thou canst avoid, sooner or later, whatever
molesteth thee, except thy own conscience."
　　　　　　　　Augustin. in Psalm xxx.
　[22] Imitat. of Jesus Christ, L. I, c. 13.
" God causeth (afflictions) to come, either
for correction, or for his land, or for mercy."
Job, c. xxxvii, v. 13.
　" It is the work and providence of God's secret counsel, that the days of the elect should
be troubled in their pilgrimage. This present
life is the way to our eternal abode : God therefore in his secret wisdom afflicts our travel with
continual trouble, lest the delights of our journey might take away the desire of our journey's
end." 　　　　　　　　St. Greg. Mag.
　" No servant of Christ is without affliction. If
you expect to be free from persecution, you have
not yet so much as begun to be a Christian."
　　　　　　　　St. August.
　[23] Imitat. of Christ, L. I, c. 11.
　[24] Imitat. of Christ, ibid. See also Gen. c.
viii, v. 11.
　[25] Imitat. of Christ, L. I, c. 13.
　[26] Ibid. Lib. I, c. 16. Lib. III, c. 12. See
also Amos, c. ix. v. 3, and Luke c. xxii, v. 31.

Say, is it much indignities to bear,
　When God for thee thy nature deign'd to wear ?
If slander vilifies the good man's name,
It hurts not; but prevents a future shame,
The censure and reproaches of mankind
Are the true christian mentors of the mind.
No other way humility is gain'd ;
No other way vain glory is restrain'd.
Nor worse, nor better we, if praise or blame
Lift or depress—the man is still the same [27].
The happy, if they're wise, must all things fear;
Nor need th' unhappy, if they're good, des-
　　pair.
　　(10.) Hard is the task 'gainst nature's strength
　　to strive :
Perfection is the lot of none alive ;
Or grant frail man could tread th' unerring road,
How could we suffer for the sake of God[28] ?
Affliction's ordeal, sharp, but brightly shines ;
Sep'rates the gold[29], and ev'ry vice calcines.
In adverse fortune, when the storm runs high,
And sickness graves death's image on the eye,
Nor wealth, nor rank, nor pow'r, assuage the
　　grief—
Ask God to send thee patience or relief[30].
The infant Moses 'scap'd his wat'ry grave[31].
Heav'n half o'erwhelms the man it means to
　　save !
　　(11.) Th' ambitious and the covetous desire[32]
More than their worth deserves, or wants re-
　　quire :
Not merely for the profit things may yield,
But, ah ! their neighbour's pittance maims their
　　field :
Thus, gain'd by force, or fraudulent design,
The grapes of Naboth yield them blood for
　　wine [33]
　　(12) Nothing but truth can claim a lasting
　　date [34];
Time is truth's surest judge, and judges late :

　[27] Imitat. of Christ, L. III, c. 5.
　[28] Ibid.
　[29] " For gold is tried in the fire, and acceptable men in the furnace of adversity."
　　　　　　　　Ecclus. c. ii, v. 5.
　[30] Imitat. of Christ, L. III, c. 5.
　[31] Exod. c. II, v. 5.
　[32] " He that gathereth by defrauding his own
soul, gathereth for others, that shall spend his
goods riotously. A covetous man's eye is not satisfied with his portion, and the iniquity of the
wicked drieth up his soul."
　　　　　　　　Ecclus. c. xiv.
　[33] " Ahab's excuse to Naboth, when he said
give me thy vineyard that I may make it a garden of herbs, represents in a lively manner the
pretences that avaricious and ambitious men
use, when they want to make new acquisitions.
They lye to their consciences ; asking a seeming
trifle, and meaning to obtain something very valuable." 　　　　　　　　St. Ambrose.
　" Woe unto them that covet fields, and take
them away by violence." Micah, c. ii, v. 2.
　" They enlarge their desire as Hell, and are as
death, and cannot be satisfied : woe unto them
that encrease that which is not theirs."
　　　　　　　　Hab. c. ii, v. 5, 6.
　[34] Imitat. of Jesus Christ, L. I, c. 3.

And, for thy guide, be he alone believ'd,
Who never can deceive, nor is deceiv'd [35] !
Thus safe thro' waves the sons of Isr'el trod ;
Their better magnet was the lamp of God : [led
And thus Heav'n's star Earth's humble shepherds
To their Messiah in his humbler bed.
(13.) Flatt'ry and fame at death the vain for-
sake,
And other knaves and fools their honours take[36].
(14.) Tease not thy mind ; nor run a restless
round
In search of science better lost than found.
Still teach thy soul a sober course to try,
And shun the track of singularity !
(15.) Presumptuous flights and sceptical debates
Foretel (Cassandra-like) the fall of states.
So Greece and Rome soon moulder'd to decay,
When Epicurus' system gain'd the day.
But those who make prophaneness stand for wit,
Desp'rate apply the pigeons to their feet :
Bankrupts of sense, and impudently bad ;
Their judgment ruin'd, and their fancy mad !
Like Daniel's [37] goat [38] in th' insolence of youth,
Stars they displace, and overturn the truth.
(16.) He, who adopts religions, wrong or right,
Is not a convert, but an hypocrite :
Him, seeming what he is not, man esteems;
God hates him, for he is not what he seems.
The bull-rush thus a specious outside wears,
Smooth as the shining rind the poplar bears :
But strip the cov'ring of its polish'd skin,
And all is insubstantial sponge within.
When not a whisper breaths upon the trees,
Unmov'd it stands, but bends with ev'ry breeze.
It boasts th' ablution of a silver flood,
But feeds on mire, and roots itself in mud.
(17.) Self-love is foolish, criminal, and vain[39],
Therefore, O man, such partial views restrain :
And often take this counsel for a rule,
To please one's self is but to please one fool[40].
(18.) The alms we give, we keep : the alms
we save
We lose : possessing only what we gave [41].

[35] ——Neque decipitur,neque decipit unquam.
Manil.
[36] " There is no work that shows more art and
industry than the texture of a spider's web. The
delicate threads are so nicely disposed, and so
curiously interwoven one with another, that you
would think it produced by the labour of a celestial being ; yet nothing in the event is more
fragil and insubstantial. A breath of wind tears
it to pieces, and carries it away. Just so are
worldly acquisitions made by men in exalted
stations, and reputedly wise and cunning."
Origen.
[37] Dan. c. viii, v. 10, 11.
[38] The prophet here means, by the goat, the
king of Greece, the region of vain philosophy.
[39] " He that loveth himself most, hath of all
then the happiness of finding the fewest rivals."
Anon. Vet.
[40] " He that pleaseth himself, pleaseth a
fool."
[41] " There is that scattereth and yet increas-
eth ; and there is that withholding more than is
meet, but it tendeth to poverty."
Prov. c. xi, v. 24.
" The riches which thou treasurest up, are

But if vain glory prompts the tongue to boast,
In vain we strive to give, the gift is lost.
Wealth, unbestow'd, is the fool's alchymy ;—
Misers have wealth, but taste it not ;—and die.
In ev'ry purse that th' avaricious bears,
There's still a rent, which wily Satan tears[42]:
A man may mend it, at returning light,
But the arch-fiend undarns the work at night.
Useless, O miser ! are thy labours found ;
And all thy vintage leaks on thirsty ground [43].
Chimeric nonsense ! Riches unemploy'd
In doing good, are riches unenjoy'd ;
The slave who sets his soul on worthless pelf,
Is a mere Dioclesian to himself;
A wretched martyr in a wretched cause ;
Alive, unhonour'd ; dead, without applause !
Boast not of homage to Earth's monarchs giv'n ;
A Paula's [44] name is better known in Heav'n.
(19.) Riches no more are ours, than are the
waves [laves.
Of yonder Rhyne, which our Mount-Agnas [45]
Th' impatient waters no continuance make ;
Adopt new owners, and their old forsake.
[46] As those who call for wines, beyond their
share,
Refund the draughts which nature cannot bear ;
(Whilst bile and gall corroding in their breast
Demand a passage, and admit no rest :)
Just so rapacious misers swell their store ;
To di'monds di'monds add, and ore to ore ;
They gulp down wealth,—and, with heart pier-
cing pain,
And clay-cold qualms, discharge the load again.
Death bursts the casket, and the farce is o'er.
(Curst is that wealth, which never eas'd the
poor !) [floor;
Whilst fools and spendthrifts sweep it from the
The gold of Ophyr [47] dazzles their weak eyes,
Turquoises [48] next their weaker minds surprise,
Rich, deeply azur'd, like Italian skies.

lost ; those which thou charitably bestowest, are
truly thine." St. August.
[42] Haggai, c. i, v. 6.
[43] ——————Ibi omnis
Effusus labor.—————— Virg.
[44] Paula was a Roman lady descended from
the Gracchi and Scipios. Her husband was of
the Julian race. After his decease, she gave
most of her possessions to the poor, and retired
from Rome to a solitude at Bethlehem. That
incomparable virgin Eustochium was her daughter. Both their histories are drawn at large by
St. Jerom, and addressed to Eustochium. Paula
has written some excellent verses on religious
subjects.
She built a temple at Emmäus in honour of
our Blessed Saviour. Her tomb is at Bethlehem.
The inscription for her and her daughter was
written by St. Jerom. Sandy's Trav. fol. 135.
139, &c.
[45] The name of the monastery where Kempis
resided.
[46] Part of this paragraph, is copied from Job,
c. xx, v. 14, 15, 18. Compare also Job, c.
xxvii, v. 19, 20, 21.
[47] Gold of Ophir. See 1 Kings c. ix, v. 28. 1
Chron. xxix, v. 4. 2 Chron. viii, v. 18. Psalm
xlv, v. 9. Isaiah xiii. v. 12.
[48] Turquoises, " The true oriental turquoise

Then are the fi'ry rubies [49] to be seen,
And em'ralds [50] tinctur'd with the rainbow's
　　　green,
Translucent beryl [51], flame-ey'd chrysolite[52],
And sardŏnix [53], refresher of the sight;
With these th' empurpled amethist combines[54],
And opaz[55], vein'd with riv'lets, mildly shines.
　　All first turns into riot, then to care :—
Whirl'd down th' impetuous torrent, call'd an heir.
　　(19.) Religion's harbour, like th' Etrurian
　　　bay [56],
Secure from storms is land-lock'd ev'ry way.
Safe, 'midst the wreck of worlds, the vessel rides,
Nor minds the absent rage of winds and tides:
Whilst from his prow the pilot looking down,
Surveys at once God's image and his own[57];
Heav'n's favour smooths th' expanse, and calm-
　　ness sleeps
On the clear mirror of the silent deep[58].
　　(20) No man at once two Edens can enjoy[59]:
Nor Earth and Heav'n the self-same mind employ.
Two diff'rent ways th' unsocial objects draw:
Flesh strives with spirit, nature combats law :
Reason and revelation live at strife,
Though meant for mutual aid, like man and
　　wife[59].
　　Religion and the world can ne'er agree :
One eye is sacrific'd, that one may see,
Canals, for pleasure made, with pleasure stray ;
But drain at length the middle stream away.
　　(21.) Life's joy and pomp at distance should
　　　appear,
Possession brings the vulgar dawbing near.
Who can rejoice to tread a devious road,
Led by false views, and serpentine from God [61] ?

comes out of the old rock in the mountains of
Piriskua, about eighty miles from the town of
Moscheda." Hist. of Gust. Adolph. vol. II, p.
342.
　[49] Rubies. " Nazarites, more ruddy than rubies." Lam. c. iv, v. 7.
　[50] Emeralds. " A rainbow in sight like an
emerald." Rev. c. iv, v. 3.
　[51] Beryl. Dan. c. x, v. 6. Rev. xxi, v. 20.
　[52] Chrysolite. Ezek. c. xxviii.
　[53] Sardŏnyx. Rev. c. xxi, v. 20.
　[54] Amethist. Exod. c. xxviii, v. 19. Ibid. c.
xxxix, v. 12.
　[55] Ezek. c. xxviii, v. 13, and Rev. xxi. v. 20.
　[56] The port of Lerichè, in Tuscany.
　[57] " One way to know God is perfectly to
know one's self." 　　　　　　Hugo de anima.
' " Why dost thou wonder, O man, at the
height of the stars, or depth of the sea ? examine
rather thine own soul, and wonder there."
　　　　　　　　　　　　　　　　Isidor.
　[58] Imitat. of Christ, L. II, c. 1—3.
　[59] " It is not only difficult but impossible to
enjoy Heaven here and hereafter ; or, in other
words, to live in pleasure and dissapation, and at
the same time attain spiritual happiness. No
man hath passed from one paradise to another :
no man hath been the mirror of felicity in both
worlds, nor shone with equal glory in Earth and
in Heaven." 　　　　　　　　　Hieron.
　[60] Imitat. of Christ, L, I, c. 24.
　[61] Ibid. L. I, c. 21.

Would'st thou be vitally with Christ conjoin'd ?
Copy his deeds, and imitate his mind [62];
No man can worldly happiness ensure ;
Heav'n's consolation all men may procure[63].
　(22.) When passions reign with arbitrary sway,
Resistance, not compliance, wins the day[64].
Here av'rice, there ambitious schemes prevail ;
Who can quench flames when double winds assail?
Boast as we will, our christian glories lie
In humble suff'ring, not proud apathy[65],
Submission an eternal crown procures ;
Heav'n's hero conquers most, who most en-
　　dures.—
　Like the four cherubs in Ezekiel's dream[66],
(What time the prophet slept by Chebar's stream)
The Christian, mov'd by energy divine,
Walks forward still, in one unvarying line[67]:
Nor wealth, nor pow'r, attract his wondering
　　sight ;
He swerves not to the left hand, nor the right.
Humbly he eats, and finds the proffer'd scroll
Sweet to the taste, inspiring to the soul [68].
So when Saul's weary'd son his fasting broke
With honey dropping from Philistian oak,
Returning strength and sprightliness arise,
Glow on his cheeks, and sparkle in his eyes [69].
　When fortune smiles within doors and without,
Man's heart, well-pleas'd, may think itself de-
　　vout :
But, when ill days, and nights of pain, succeed,
Let him bear well, and he's devout indeed[70].
　(23.) Those who revenge a deed that injures
　　them,
Copy the very sin, which they condemn[71].
Impiously wand'ring from the christian road,
They snatch God's own prerogative from God !
Michael in bitterness of strife consign'd
The final verdict to th' unerring mind[72].—
From turbulence of anger wisely keep ;
The hind who soweth winds, shall whirlwinds
　　reap[73].
　(24.) The worldling, tempter of himself, pursues
Idols of his own making; ideot's views ;

　[62] Imitat. of Christ, L. I, c. 24.
　[63] Ibid.
　[64] Ibid. L. I, c. 6.
　[65] Ibid. L. II, c. 3.
　[66] See Ezek. c. 1.
　[67] Ezek. c. i, v. 12.
　[68] Ibid. c. iii, v. 1, 2, 3.
　[69] 1 Sam. c. xiv, v. 29.
　[70] Imitat. of Christ, L. II, c. 3.
　[71] " To return one injury for another is to revenge like man : whereas to revenge like God is
to love our enemies. It is a great happiness not
to be able to hurt one's neighbour, nor to have
the power and parts to do mischief. The inge-
nuity of (what we call) men of the world, consists
in knowing how to injure others, and revenge
ourselves when injured. Whercas, on the contrary, not to return evil for evil is the true honour and vital principle of the gospel."
　　　　　　　　　　　　　　　　　　Leon.
　[72] Jude, v. 9. Zech. c. iii, v. 2.
　[73] Hosea, c. viii, v. 7. Hind is the head-ser-
vant in husbandry matters. Chaucer, Dryden,
and in the west of England at present.

Unhappy wretch! wrapt up in thin disguise!
Where all that is not impious, is unwise!
See, how he broods from night to morning's dawn
On eggs of basilisks, and scorpion-spawn[74]:
And, after all the care he can impart,
His foster'd miscreants sting him to the heart
Swift through each vein the mystic poisons roll,
Fatal alike to body and to soul[75]!

(25.) Perfect would be our nature and our joy
If man could ev'ry year one vice destroy [76] [77].
Withdraw thee from the sins that most assail,
And labour where thy virtues least prevail[78].

(26.) False joys elate, and griefs as false con-
troul
The little pismire with an human soul[79]:
Oh, were he like th' unreas'ning ant, who strives
For solid good, and but by instinct lives.

(27.) To wail and not amend a life mispent
Means to confess, but means not to repent:
Tongue-penitents, like him who too much owes,
Run more in debt, and live but to impose.

(28.) Deem not th' unhappy, vicious; nor de-
vote
To sarcasm and contempt the thread-bare coat.
Oft have we seen rich fields of genuine corn
Edg'd round with brambles, and begirt with thorn.
The pow'rs of Zeuxis' pencil are the same,
Enclos'd in gilded, or in sable frame.

(29.) The down that smoothes the great man's
anxious bed,
Was gather'd from a quiet poor man's shed:
Content and peace are found in mean estate,
And Jacob's dreams on Jacob's pillow wait[80].
So Tekoa's swain, by no vain glories led,
Nurtur'd his herds with leaves, and humbly fed[81].

(30.) Good turns of friends we scribble on the
But injuries engrav'd on marble stand[82]. [sand,

(31.) With pray'rs thy ev'ning close, thy
morn begin;
But Heav'n's true sabbath is to rest from sin.

(32.) An hermit once cry'd out in private
pray'r,
" Oh, if I knew that I should persevere !"
An angel's voice reply'd, in placid tone,
" What woulds't thou do, if the great truth were
known?
Do now [83], what thou intendest then to do,
And everlasting safety shall ensue[84]."—

[74] Isaiah, c. lix, v. 4.
[75] Matth. c. x, v. 28.
[76] Imitat. of Christ, L. I, c. 11. L. II, c. 23.
[77] " Instead of standing still, going backward,
or deviating, always add, always proceed: not
to advance, in some sense is to retire. It is better to creep in the right way than fly in the
wrong way." St. August. in Serm.
[78] Imitat. of Christ, L. I, c. 25.
[79] Man.
[80] " And Jacob took the stones of that place
and put them for his pillows."
Gen. c. xxxviii, v. 2.
[81] Amos c. vii, v. 14.
[82] Kempisii dictum commune. " Beneficia
pulveri; si quid mali patimur, marmori inscul-
pimus."
[83] " A Christian hath no to morrow; that is to
say, a Christian should put off no duty till to
morrow." Tertull.
[84] Imitat. of Christ, L. I, c. 25.

To choose, implies delay; whilst time devours
The sickly blossoms of preceding hours.
Repentance, well perform'd, confirms the more;
As bones, well set, grow stronger than before.

(33.) When Heav'n excites thee to a better
way,
Catch the soft summons, and the call obey:
Thus Mary left her solitude and tears,
When Martha whisper'd, lo! thy Christ ap-
pears [85].

(34.) The virtues of the world, which most men
move,
Are lay'rs from pride, or graftings on self-love[86]:
Whatever for itself is not esteem'd,
Proves a false choice, and is not as it seem'd[87].

(35.) The track to Heav'n is intricate and
Narrow to tread, and difficult to keep: [steep;
On either hand sharp precipices lie, /
And our steps faulter with the swerving eye;
That passage clear'd, a level road remains,
Through quiet valleys and refreshing plainsss.

(36.) Most would buy Heav'n without a price
or loss[89].
They like the paradise, but shun the cross[89].
Many participate of Christ's repast;
Few choose his abstinence, or learn to fast[90].
Few relish Christianity; and most [coast [91],
(In private) wish their Lord would leave their
Thousands may counterfeit th' apparent part;
And thousands may be Gergesenes at heart[92].
All in Christ's kingdom would the thrones part
take;
Few have the faith to suffer for his sake[93]
His tasteful bread by many mouths is sought;
Few choose to drink his passion's bitter draught[94].

[85] Imitat. of Christ, L. II, c. 28. See John
c. ii, v. 28.
[86] " There is a sort of seeming good, which, if
a rational mind loves, it sinneth; inasmuch as
it is an object beneath the consideration of such
a mind." St. August. de Ver. Relig.
" Whatever is not loved on account of its own
intrinsic worth, is not properly loved."
Idem in Soliloq. L. I, c. 13.
[87] " In this life there is no virtue but in loving
that which is truly amiable. To choose this, is
prudence; to be averted from it by no terrifying
circumstances, is fortitude. To be influenced
by no sort of temptation, is temperance; and to
be affected by no ambitious views, is considering
the thing with impartial justice as we ought to
do." Idem de Ver. Felicitat. L. II.
[88] Imitat. of Christ, L. II, c. 11, No. 1.
[89] Ibid. [90] Ibid.
[91] Matth. c. viii, v. 34. [92] Ibid.
"It is common for man to ask every blessing
that God can bestow, but he rarely desires to
possess God himself."
Aug. in Psalm lxxvi.
[93] Imitat. of Christ, L. II, c. 2. No. 1.
[94] Ibid. See also c. 12.

## CONTENTMENT, INDUSTRY, AND ACQUIESCENSE UNDER THE DIVINE WILL:

### AN ODE,

WRITTEN IN THE ALPINE PARTS OF CARNIOLA, 1749.

The wilderness and solitary place shall be glad
for them, (the children of the Lord:) and the
desert shall rejoice and blossom like the rose.
It shall blossom abundantly, and rejoice even
with joy and singing : the glory of Lebanon
shall be given unto it, the excellency of Carmel
and Sharon : they shall see the glory of the
Lord, and the excellency of our God.
　　　　　　Isaiah, c. xxxv, v. 1, 2.

**W**HY dwells my unoffended eye
On yon blank desert's trackless waste ;
All dreary earth, or cheerless sky,
Like ocean wild, and bleak, and vast ?
There Lysidor's enamour'd reed
Ne'er taught the plains Eudosia's praise :
There herds were rarely known to feed,
Or birds to sing, or flocks to graze.
Yet does my soul complacence find ;
All, all from Thee,
Supremely gracious Deity,
Corrector of the mind ! !

The high-arch'd church is lost in sky,
The base [2] with thorns and bry'rs is bound :
The yawning fragments nod from high,
With close-encircling ivy crown'd :
Heart-thrilling echo multiplies
Voice after voice, creation new !
Beasts, birds obscene, unite their cries :
Graves ope, and spectres freeze the view.
Yet nought dismays ; and thence we find
'Tis all from Thee,
Supremely gracious Deity,
Composer of the mind !

Earth's womb, half dead to Ceres' skill,
Can scarce the cake of off'ring give ;
Five acres' corn can hardly fill
The peasant's wain, and bid him live ;
The starving beldame gleans in vain,
In vain the hungry chough succeeds :
They curse the unprolific plain,
The scurf-grown moss, and tawdry weeds.
Yet still sufficiency we find ;
All, all from Thee,
Supremely gracious Deity,
Corrector of the mind !

December's Boreas issues forth,
In sullen gloom and horrour drest,
Charg'd with the nitre of the north,
Abhorr'd by man, by bird, and beast.
All nature's lovely tint embrown'd
Sickens beneath the putrid blast :
Destruction withers up the ground,
Like parchment into embers cast[3].

[1] " To be satisfied is the highest pitch of art
man can arrive to." 　　　　St. Gregor. Hom.
[2] Base for basis. See Zechar. c. v, v. 2.
[3] ————inamabile frigus aduret. 　　Virg.
Much to the same purpose is a passage in the

Yet health, and strength, and ease we find :
All, all from Thee,
Supremely gracious Deity,
Composer of the mind !

Tremble, and yonder Alp behold[4],
Where half-dead nature gasps below,
Victim of everlasting cold,
Entomb'd alive in endless snow.
The northern side is horrour all ;
Against the southern, Phœbus plays ;
In vain th' innoxious glimm'rings fall,
The frost outlives, outshines the rays.
Yet consolation still I find ;
And all from Thee,
Supremely gracious Deity,
Corrector of the mind !

Bless me ! how doubly sharp it blows,
From Zemblan and Tartarian coasts !
In sullen silence fall the snows,
The only lustre nature boasts ;
The nitrous pow'r with tenfold force
Half petrifies Earth's barren womb,
High-arch'd cascades suspend their force,
Men freeze alive, and in the tomb.
Yet warmth and happiness we find ;
All, all from Thee,
Supremely gracious Deity,
Composer of the mind !

Then, in exchange, a month or more
The Sun with fierce solsticial gleams,
Darting o'er vales his raging pow'r,
Like ray-collecting mirrors, beams.
Torrents and cataracts are dry,
Men seek the scanty shades in vain ;
The solar darts like lightning fly,
Transpierce the skull, and scorch the brain.
Yet still no restless heats we find ;
And all from Thee,
Supremely gracious Deity,
Corrector of the mind !

For Nature rarely form'd a soil
Where diligence subsistence wants :
Exert but care, nor spare the toil,
And all beyond, th' Almighty grants

Son of Sirach :—" When the cold north wind bloweth, and the water congealed into ice, he pour-
eth the hoar frost upon the earth. It abideth
upon every gathering together of water, and
clotheth the water with a breast-plate. It de-
voureth the mountain, and burneth the wilderness, and consumeth the grass as fire." c. xliii,
v. 19, 21.
[4] A glaciére, or ice-mountain.
Cuncta gelu, canáque æternùm grandine tecta,
Atque ævi glaciem cohibent : riget ardua montis
Æthenii facies, surgentique obvia Phæbo
Duratas nescit flammis mollire pruinas.
　　　　　　　　　　Sil. Ital.
[5] " The Sun parcheth the country, and who
can abide the burning heat thereof ? A man blowing a furnace is in works of heat, but the Sun
burneth the mountains three times more ; breathing out fiery vapours, and sending forth bright
beams, it dimmeth the eyes."
　　　　　　Ecclus. ch. xliii, v. 3, 4.

Each earth at length to culture yields,
Each earth its own manure 6 contains:
Thus the Corycian nurst his fields7,
Heav'n gave th' increase, and he the pains.
Th' industrious peace and plenty find :
All due to Thee,
Supremely gracious Deity,
Composer of the mind !

Scipio sought virtue in his prime,
And, having early gain'd the prize,
Stole from th' ungrateful world in time,
Contented to be low and wise !
He serv'd the state with zeal and force,
And then with dignity retir'd ;
Dismounting from th' unruly horse,
To rule himself, as sense requir'd ;
Without a sigh, he pow'r resign'd.—
All, all from Thee,
Supremely gracious Deity,
Corrector of the mind !

When Dioclesian sought repose,
Cloy'd and fatigu'd with nauseous pow'r,
He left his empire to his foes,
For fools t' admire, and rogues devour:
Rich in his poverty, he bought
Retirement's innocence and health,
With his own hands the monarch wrought,
And chang'd a throne for Ceres' wealth.
Toil sooth'd his cares, his blood refin'd.—
And all from Thee,
Supremely gracious Deity,
Composer of the mind !

He 8, who had rul'd the world, exchang'd
His sceptre for the peasant's spade,
Postponing (as thro' groves he rang'd)
Court-splendour to the rural shade.
Child of his hand, th' engrafted thorn
More than the victor-laurel pleas'd :
Heart's-ease9, and meadow-sweet 10, adorn
The brow, from civic garlands eas'd.
Fortune, however poor, was kind.—
All, all from Thee,
Supremely gracious Deity,
Corrector of the mind !

Thus Charles, with justice styled the Great 11,
For valour, piety and laws ;
Resign'd two empires to retreat,
And from a throne to shades withdraws ;
In vain (to soothe a monarch's pride)
His yoke the willing Persian bore:
In vain the Saracen comply'd,
And fierce Northumbrians stain'd with gore.

6 Du Hamel; Elem. d'Agricult. Patullo; Meliorat. des Terres.
7 Virg. Georg. IV, v. 127, &c.
8 Dioclesian.
9 Heart's-ease, viola tricolor ; called also by our old poets Love in idleness ; pansy (from the French pensée, or the Italian pensieri) ; three faces under a hood ; herb Trinity ; look up and kiss me ; kiss me at the gate, &c.
10 Spiræa, named also in ancient English poetry, mead-sweet, queen of the meads, bridewort, &c.
11 Charlemagne.

One Gallic farm his cares confin'd ;
And all from Thee,
Supremely gracious Deity,
Composer of the mind !

Observant of th' Almighty-will,
Prescient in faith, and pleas'd with toil,
Abram Chaldea left, to till
The moss-grown Haran's flinty soil 12:
Hydras of thorns absorb'd his gain,
The common-wealth of weeds rebell'd,
But labour tam'd th' ungrateful plain,
And famine was by art repell'd ;
Patience made churlish nature kind.—
All, all from Thee,
Supremely gracious Deity,
Corrector of the mind !

———Formidine nulla ;
Quippe in corde Deus—.
Stat. Theb. IV. v. 489.

## THE VISION OF DEATH.

Imperfecta tibi elapsa est, ingrataque vita :
Et nec-opinanti Mors ad caput adstitit, ante
Quam satur, at plenus possis discedere rerum.
LUCRET.

Mille modis leti miseros Mors una fatigat.
Stat. Theb. IX. v. 280.

## ADVERTISEMENT.

As this poem is an imperfect attempt to imitate Dryden's manner, I have of course admitted more triplets and Alexandrine verses than I might otherwise have done. Upon the whole, many good judges have thought, (and such was the private opinion of my much honoured friend Elijah Fenton in particular) that Dryden has too many Alexandrines and triplets, and Pope too few. The one by aiming at variety (for his ear was excellent) was betrayed into a careless diffusion ; and the other, by affecting an over-scrupulous regularity, fell into sameness and restraint.
We speak this with all due deference to the two capital poets of the last and present century : and say of them, as the successor of Virgil said of Amphiaraüs and Admetus ;
AMBO BONI, CHARIQUE AMBO.—
Theb. VI,

## INTRODUCTION.

Dryden, forgive the Muse that apes thy voice
Weak to perform, but fortunate in choice,
Who but thyself the mind and ear can please
With strength and softness, energy and ease ;
Various of numbers, new in ev'ry strain;
Diffus'd, yet terse, poetical, tho' plain :
Diversify'd 'midst unison of chime;
Freer than air, yet manacled with rhyme ?

12 Gen. ch. xii, v. 31. Nehem. ch. ix, v. 7.
Judith, ch, v. 7. Acts, ch. vii, v. 2—11.
B b

Thou mak'st each quarry which thou seek'st thy
The reigning eagle of Parnassian skies; [prize,
Now soaring 'midst the tracts of light and air,
And now the monarch of the woods and lair[1].—
Two kingdoms thy united realm compose,
The land of poetry, and land of prose,
Each orphan-muse thy absence inly mourns;
Makes short excursions, and as quick returns:
No more they triumph in their fancy'd bays,
But crown'd with wood-bine dedicate their lays.
    Thy thoughts and music change with ev'ry
       line;
No sameness of a prattling stream is thine.
Which, with one unison of murmur, flows,
Opiate of in-attention and repose;
(So Huron-leeches, when their patient lies
In fev'rish restlessness with un-clos'd eyes,
Apply with gentle strokes their osier-rod,
And tap by tap invite the sleepy god[2].)
No—'Tis thy pow'r, (thine only,) tho' in rhyme,
To vary ev'ry pause, and ev'ry chime;
Infinite descant[3]! sweetly wild and true,
Still shifting, still improving, and still new!—
In quest of classic plants, and where they grow,
We trace thee, like a lev'ret in the snow.
Of all the pow'rs the human mind can boast,
The pow'rs of poetry are latest lost:
The falling of thy tresses at threescore,
Gave room to make thy laurels show the more[4].
This prince of poets, who before us went,
Had a vast income, and profusely spent:
Some have his lands, but none his treasur'd store,
Lands un-manur'd by us, and mortgag'd o'er and
    o'er!
" About his wreaths the vulgar muses strive,
And with a touch their wither'd bays revive[5]!"
They kiss his tomb, and are enthusiasts made;
So Statius slept, inspir'd by Virgil's shade[6].
To Spencer much, to Milton much is due;
But in great Dryden we preserve the two.
What Muse but his can Nature's beauties hit,
Or catch that airy fugitive, call'd wit?
    From limbs of this great Hercules are fram'd
Whole groups of pigmies, who are verse-men
    nam'd:
Each has a little soul he calls his own,
And each enunciates with a human tone;

[1] Layer, lair, and lay.—The surface of arable
or grass-lands. Chaucer; Folkingham, 1610;
Dryden. Laire also signifies the place where
beasts sleep in the fields, and where they leave
the mark of their bodies on young corn, grass,
&c.

[2] Voyages du Baron La Hontan.

[3] Milton.

[4] The verses of Robert Waring, (a friend of
Dr. Donne's) on a poet in the beginning of the
last century, may be applied to Dryden:

Younger with years, with studies fresher
    grown,
Still in the bud, still blooming, yet full blown.

[5] Dryden's Prologue to Troilus and Cressida.

[6] ——————— tenues ignavo pollice chordas
    Pulso, Maroneique sedens in margine templi
    Sumo animum, & magni tumulis accanto
    magistri.
                Sylv. Lib. IV.

Alike in shape; unlike in strength and size;—
One lives for ages, one just breathes and dies.
    O thou, too great to rival or to praise;
Forgive, lamented shade, these duteous lays.
Lee had thy fire, and Congreve had thy wit;
And copyists, here and there, some likeness hit;
But none possess'd thy graces, and thy ease;
In thee alone 'twas natural to please!
    More still I think, and more I wish to say;
But bus'ness calls the Muse another way.

————

In those fair vales by Nature form'd to please,
Where Guadalquiver serpentines with ease,
(The richest tract the Andalusians know,
Fertile in herbage, grateful to the plow,)
A lovely villa stood; (suppose it mine;)
Rich without cost, and without labour fine;
Indulgent Nature all her beauties brought,
And Art withdrew, unask'd for, and unsought.
For lo, th' Iberians by tradition found
That the whole district once was classic ground;
Here Columella first improv'd the plains,
And show'd Ascrean arts to simple swains:
Taught by the Georgic-Muse the lyre he strung,
And sung, what dying Virgil left unsung[1].
    Fatigu'd with courts, and votary to truth,
Hither I fled, philosopher, and youth:
And, leaving Olivarez to sustain
Th' encumbring fasces of ambitious Spain,
(As one rash Phaeton usurp'd a day,
Misled the seasons, and mistook his way,)
I chose to wander in the silent wood,
Or breathe my aspirations to the flood,
Studying the humble science to be good.
From the brute beasts humanity I learn'd,
And in the pansy's life God's providence discern'd,
    'Twas now the joyous season of the year:
The Sun had reach'd the Twins in bright career;
Nature, awaken'd from six months' repose,
Sprung from her verdant couch;—and active rose
Like health refresh'd with wine; she smil'd, ar-
      ray'd         [glade,
With all the charms of sun-shine, stream and
New drest and blooming as a bridal maid.
    Yet all these charms could never lull to rest
A peevish irksomeness which teas'd my breas
The vernal torrent, murm'ring from afar,
Whisper'd no peace to calm this nervous war;
And Philomel, the siren of the plain,
Sung soporific unisons in vain.
I sought my bed, in hopes relief to find:
But restlessness was mistress of my mind.
My wayward limbs were turn'd, and turn'd in
      vain,—
Yet free from grief was I, and void of pain.
In me, as yet, ambition had no part; [heart.
Pride had not sowr'd, nor wealth debas'd my
I knew not public cares, nor private strife;—
And love, the blessing, or the curse of life,
Had only hover'd round me like a dream,
Play'd on the surface, not disturb'd the stream.
    Yet still I felt, what young men often feel;
(Impossible to tell, or to conceal,)

[1] ——————— Et quæ
Virgilius nobis post se memoranda reliquit.
             Colum. de Hortis, L. X.

When nothing makes them sick but too much
   wealth,
Or wild o'er-boiling of ungovern'd health;
Whose grievance is satiety of ease,
Freedom their pain, and plenty their disease.
By night, by day, from pole to pole they run :
Or from the setting seek the rising Sun ;
No poor deserting soldier makes such haste,
No doves pursu'd by falcons fly so fast ;
And when Automedon at length attains
The place he sought for with such cost and pains,
Swift to embrace, and eager to pursue,
He finds he has no earthly thing to do ;
Then yawns for sleep, the opium of the mind,
The last dull refuge indolence can find [2].
   Most men, like David, wayward in extremes,
Languish for Ramah's cisterns, and her streams :
The bev'rage sought for comes ; capricious, they
Loathe their own choice, and wish the boon
   away [3].
   Such was my state. "O gentle Sleep," I
" Why is thy gift to me alone deny'd ?" [cry'd,
Mildest of beings, friend to ev'ry clime,
Where lies my errour, what has been my crime ?
Beasts, birds, and cattle feel thy balmy rod ;
The drowsy mountains wave, and seem to nod
The torrents cease to chide, the seas to roar,
And the hush'd waves recline upon the shore."
Perhaps the wretch, whose god is wealth and
   care,
Rejects the precious object of my pray'r :
Th' ambitious statesman strives not to partake
Thy blessings, but desires to dream awake :
" The lover rudely thrusts thee from his arms,
And like Ixion clasps imagin'd charms.
Thence come to me.—Let others ask for more ;
I ask the slightest influence of thy pow'r :
Swiftest in flight of all terrestrial things,
Oh only touch my eye-lids with thy wings [4] !"

[2] Currit agens mannos ad villam hic præcipi-
   tanter,
   Auxilium tectis quasi ferre ardentibus instans.
   Oscitat extemplò tetigit cum limina villæ,
   Aut abit in somnum gravis, atque oblivia
   quærit.
            Lucret. L. III. v. 1076.

[3] See Sandy's Trav. p. 137, and 1 Chron. ch.
xi, v. 17, &c.
[4] All the verses in this paragraph marked with
inverted commas are imitated from a famous
passage in Statius, never yet translated into our
language. The original perhaps is as fine a
morsel of poetry as antiquity can boast of :

Crimine quo merui juvenis placidissime divum
Quóve errore miser, donis ut solus egerem
Somne tuis ? Tacet omne pecus, volucresque,
   feræque ;
Et simulant fessos curvata cacumina somnos.
Nec trucibus fluviis idem sonus. Occidit horror
Æquoris, & terris maria acclinata quiescunt.
At nunc heus aliquis longa sub nocte puellæ
Brachia nexa tenens, ultro te Somne repellit.
Inde veni. Nec te totas infundere pennas
Luminibus compello meis, (hoc turba precatur
Lætior ;) extremo me tange cacumine virgæ,
Sufficit ; aut leviter suspenso poplite transi.
              Syl. L. V.

So spoke I restless; and, then springing light
From my tir'd bed, walk'd forth in meer despite.
What impulse mov'd my steps I dare not say ;
Perhaps some guardian-angel mark'd th' way :
By this time Phospher had his lamp withdrawn,
And rising Phœbus glow'd on ev'ry lawn.
The air was gentle, (for the month was May,)
And ev'ry scene look'd innocent and gay.
In pious matins birds with birds conspire,—
Some lead the notes, and some assist the choir.
   The goat-herd, gravely pacing with his flocks,
Leads them to heaths and bry'rs, and crags and
   rocks.
Th' impatient mower with an aspect blythe
Surveys the sain-foyn-fields [5], and whets his
Ynoisa, Sanchia, Beatrix, prepare   |scythe.
To turn th' alfalsa-swarths [6] with anxious care,
(No more for Moorish sarabrands they call,
Their castanets hang idle on the wall :)
Alfalsa, whose luxuriant herbage feeds
The lab'ring ox, mild sheep, and fiery steeds :
Which ev'ry summer, ev'ry thirtieth morn,
Is six times re-produc'd, and six times shorn.
The Cembran pine-trees [7] form an awful shade,
And their rich balm perfumes the neighb'ring
   glade ?
(Whilst humbler olives, intermix'd between,
Had chang'd their fruit to filamotte from green,)
The Punic granate [8] op'd its rose-like flow'rs ;
The orange breath'd its aromatic pow'rs.
   Wand'ring still on, at length my eyes survey'd
A painted seat, beneath a larch-tree's shade.
I sate, and try'd to doze, but slumber fled ;
I then essay'd a book, and thus I read [9] :
   "Suppose, O man, great Nature's voice should
To thee, or me, or any of us all ;   [call
' What dost thou mean, ungrateful wretch ! thou
Thou mortal thing, thus idly to complain ? [vain,
If all the bounteous blessings I could give,
Thou hadst enjoy'd ; If thou hadst known to live
(And pleasure not leak'd thro' thee like a sieve) ;
Why dost thou not give thanks as at a plenteous
   feast,   [take thy rest ?
Cramm'd to the throat with life, and rise and
But, if my blessings thou hast thrown away,
If indigested joys pass'd thro' and would not
   stay,
Why dost thou wish for more to squander still ?
If life be grown a load, a real ill,
And I would all thy cares and labours end,
Lay down thy burthen, fool ! and know thy
   friend.

[5] The best species of this grass, hitherto
known, is in Andalusia.
[6] Alfalsa (from the old Arabian word alfalsa-
fat) lucerne-grass. At present the Spaniards
call it also ervaye.
[7] A sort of ever-green laryx : Pinus Cembra.
This beautiful tree grows wild on the Spanish
Appennines, and is raised by culture in less
mountainous places. What name the natives
give it I have forgotten ; but the French in the
Briançois call it meicze, and the Italians in the
bishopric of Trente, in Fiume, &c. give it the
name of cirmoli, not lariché.
[8] The pom-granate.
[9] The Spanish author introduces the following
passages from Lucretius.

To please thee, I have empty'd all my store,
I can invent and can supply no more:
But run the round again, the round I ran before.
Suppose thou art not broken yet with years,
Yet still the self-same scene of things appears,
And would be ever, cou'dst thou ever live;
For life is still but life, there's nothing new to
    give.'
What can we plead against so just a bill?
We stand convicted, and our cause goes ill.
But if a wretch, a man oppress'd by fate,
Should beg of Nature to prolong his date,
She speaks aloud to him, with more disdain;
'Be still,thou martyr-fool, thou covetous of pain.'
But if an old decrepid sot lament;    [tent?
' What thou!' she cries, 'who hast out-liv'd con-
Dost thou complain, who hast enjoy'd my store?
But this is still th' effect of wishing more!
Unsatisfy'd with all that Nature brings,
Loathing the present, liking absent things.
From hence it comes, thy vain desires at strife
Within themselves, have tantaliz'd thy life;
And ghastly death appear'd before thy sight
E'er thou hast gorg'd thy soul and senses with
    delight.
Now leave those joys, unsuiting to thy age,
To a fresh comer, and resign the stage.
Mean-time, when thoughts of death disturb thy
    head,
Consider, Ancus, great and good, is dead:
Ancus, thy better far, was born to die;
And thou, dost thou bewail mortality [10] ?' "
    Charm'd with these lines of reason and good
    sense,
(No matter who the author was, nor whence,)
I stopp'd, and into contemplation fell;
Amaz'd an impious wit should think so well;
Who often (to his own and reader's cost,
To show the atheist, half the poet lost.
(Knowing too much, makes many a muse unfit;
'Tis not the bloom, but plethory of wit.—)
At length a drowsiness arrested thought,
And sleep (as is her custom) came unsought.
    Now listen to the purport of my tale.
Methought I wander'd in a fairy vale:
Replete with people of each sex and age;
Good, bad, great, small, the foolish and the sage:
Whilst on the ground promiscuously were laid
Stars, mitres, rags, the sceptre, and the spade.
    At length a haughty dame approach'd my view,
Whom by no single attribute I knew;
For all that painters feign, and bards devise,
Is meer mock-imag'ry, and artful lyes.
Boldly she look'd, like one of high degree;
Yet never seem'd to cast a glance on me;
At which I inly joy'd; for, truth to say,
I felt an unknown awe, and some dismay.
She pass'd me: her side-face was smooth and
    fair;
(Much as fine women, turn'd of forty, are:)
When, turning short, and un-perceiv'd by me,
She grasp'd my throat, and spoke with stern au-
    thority:
" Him, whom I seek, art thou! Thy race is run:
My journey's ended, and thy bus'ness done.
Surrender up to me thy captive-breath,
My pow'r is nature's pow'r, my name is Death!"

    [10] Lucret. L. III. translated by Dryden.

Have you e'er seen th' affrighted peasant grasp
(Searching for flow'rs or fruits) th' envenom'd
    asp?
Or have you ever felt th' impetuous shock,
When the swift vessel splits upon a rock?
Or mark'd a face with horrour over-spread,
When the third apoplex invades the head?
Then form some image of my ghastly fright;
Fear stopp'd my voice, and terrour dimm'd my
    sight:
My heart flew from its place [11] in consternation,
And nature felt a short annihilation:    [eyes
Then—with a plunge—I sobb'd;—and with faint
Look'd upwards, to the Ruler of the skies [12].
    At length—recov'ring—in a broken tone—
" Princess'—I cry'd,—" Thy pris'ner is un-
Despair and misery succeed to fear:— [done.—
O had I known thy presence was so near!"
    Abrupt th' inexorable pow'r reply'd,
('Then turn'd her face, and show'd the hideous
    side:)
" Fool! 'tis too late to wish, too late to pray:
Thou hadst the means, but not the will to pay;
Each day of human life is warning-day.
The present point of time is all thou hast,
The future doubtful and the former past!
Yet as I read contrition in thy eyes,
And thy breast heaves with terrour and surprise,
(I, who as yet was never known to show
False pity to premeditated woe)
Will graciously explain great Nature's laws,
And hear thy sophisms in so plain a cause.
There is a reason, (which to time I leave)
Why I give thee alone this short reprieve [13].
Banish thy fears, urge all thy wit can find,
Suppose me what I am, suppose thyself mankind!"
    She spoke, and led me by a private way,
Where a small winding path half-printed lay:
Then, turning short, an avenue we 'spy'd,
Long, smoothly pav'd, magnificently wide.
Dark cypresses the skirting sides adorn'd,
And gloomy yew-trees, which for ever mourn'd:
Whilst on the margin of the beaten road,
Its pallid bloom sick-smelling hen-bane show'd;
Next emblematic rose-mary appear'd,
And lurid hemloc its stain'd stalks up-rear'd,
(God's signature to man in evil hour!—)
Nor were the night-shades wanting, nor the pow'r
Of thorn'd stramonium, nor the sickly flow'r
Of cloying mandrakes; the deceitful root
Of the monk's fraudful cowl [14], and Plinian
    fruit [15].
Hypericon [16] was there, the herb of war,
Pierc'd thro' with wounds,and seam'd with many
    a scar:

    [11] Job, ch. xxxvii, v. 1.
    [12] From Statius.
Stabat anhela metu, solum Natura Tonantem
Respiciens.———    Achill. I. v. 487.
    [13] The reason is, that what here happens is a
vision, and not a reality.
    [14] Napellus; monk's-hood, friar's cowl; the
most dangerous sort of aconite.
    [15] Amomum Plinii.
    [16] St. John's Wort. See Gondibert, L. I,
Canto 6. This plant is called by us the herb of
war, not merely because its juice is of a bloody
colour, but because it is one of the principal

And pale nymphæa [17] with her clay-cold breath;
And poppies, which suborn the sleep of death.
  This avenue (mysterious to relate)
Surpris'd me much, and warn'd me of my fate.
Its length at first approach enormous seem'd;
Full half a thousand stadia [18] as I deem'd:
But then the road was smooth and fair to see;
(With such insensible declivity)
That what men thought a tedious course to run,
Was finish'd oft the hour it first begun.
  Sudden, arriving at a palace-gate,
I saw a spectre in the portal wait:
An ill-shap'd monster, hideous to be seen;
She seem'd, methought, the mother of the queen. [19].
  Opening their valves, self-mov'd on either
The adamantine doors expanded wide:   [side,
When Death commands they close, when Death commands divide.
Then quick we enter'd a magnific hall,
Where groups of trophies over-spread the wall.
In sable scrawls I Nero's name perus'd,
And Herod's, with a sanguine stain suffus'd;
While Numa's name adorn'd a radiant place,
And that of Titus deck'd a milk white space.
  " Now," cry'd the Pow'r of Death, " survey me well:
Thy shame, remorse, and disappointment tell;
Why dost thou tremble still, and whence thy dread?
Why shake thy lips, and why thy colour fled?
Speak, vassal, recognize thy sov'reign queen:
Hast thou ne'er seen me? Know'st thou not me, seen?"
  " Liege-mistress, whom the greatest kings adore,
I own my homage, and confess thy pow'r.
Alone, that sov'reignty on Earth is thine,
Which justly proves its claim to right divine:
Thine is the old hereditary sway,
Which mortals ought, and mortals must obey.
But empress, thou hast not the form I deem'd:
Velasquez [20] painted lies, and Camoëns [20] dream'd:   [grant!)
I thought to meet, (as late as Heav'n might
A skeleton, ferocious, tall, and gaunt;
Whose loose teeth in their naked sockets shook,
And grinn'd terrific, a Sardonian look [21].
I thought, besides, thy right-hand aim'd a dart,
Resistless, to transpierce the human heart,

vulnerary herbs used in making the famous arquebusade-water.—And again, as its leaves are full of little punctures and holes, it is named by Latin writers porosa, and perfoliata: the French call it mille-pertuis, and the Italians, perforata.
[17] Water-lily.
[18] About threescore and ten miles: emblematical of the Psalmist's duration of human life.
[19] Sin.
[20] Two Spaniards, the one a famous painter, and the other a celebrated poet.
[21] According to the antients the herba Sardoä, or apium risûs, (by some supposed to be the water crow-foot) brought on, after being eaten, such horrid convulsions, that the party died grinning, through the extremity of agony.

And that thy likeness of a head sustain'd
A regal crown [22]: but all was false, or feign'd.
  " I see thee now, delusive as thou art,
Without one symbol to alarm the heart:
Not ev'n upon thy flowing vest is shown
An emblematic dart, or charnel-bone;
I rather see it, glorious to behold,
With rubies edg'd, and purfled o'er with gold:
Gay annual flow'rs adorn each vacant space,
Of short-liv'd beauty, and uncertain grace.—
Artificer of fraud and deep disguise!
Prompt to perform, ingenious to surprise:
In ev'ry light (as far as man can see
By thy consent) supreme hypocrisy!
Punish thy hopeless captive if he lies.—
Instead of a scalp'd skull, and empty eyes,
Bones without flesh, and (as we all suppose)
Vacuity of lips, and cheeks, and nose,
(So dextrous is thy sorcery and care!)
I see a woman tolerably fair.
  " Instead of sable robes and mournful geer
Camelion-like, a thousand garbs you wear,
Nor bear the black and solemn thrice a year;
Drest in gay robes, whose shifting colours show
The varying glories of the show'ry bow, [green,
Glowing with waves of gold; sea-tinctur'd
Rich azure, and the bloomy gridéline [23].
  " Thus in appearances you cheat us all,
Plan our disgraces, and contrive our fall;
Something you show, that ev'ry fool may hit,
With mirth you treat, and bait that mirth with wit:
False hopes, the loves and graces of your train,
(Pimps to the great, th' ambitious, and the vain,)
Summon your guests, and in attendance wait;
While you, like eastern queens, conceal'd in state,
O'erlook the whole; th' audacious jest refine,
Smile on the feast [24], and sparkle in the wine.
Arachné thus in ambush'd covert lies;
Wits, atheists, jobbers, statesmen, are the flies.
Doom'd to be lost, they dream of no deceit,
And, fond of ruin, over-look the cheat;
Pride stands for joy, and riches for delight:—
Weak men love weakness, in their own despite;
And, finding in their native funds no ease,
Assume the garb of fools and hope to please.—
Wretches when sick of life for rats-bane call:
'Twere worth our while to give them fool-bane   [all:
Since by degrees each mis-conceiving elf
Is ruin'd, not by nature, but himself.
  " Too late I see thy fraudful face entire:
One-half half-mimics health; half-means desire;
And, tho' true youth and nature have no part,
Yet paint enlivens it, and wiles, and art;
Colours laid on with a true harlot-grace;
They only show themselves, and hide the face.
The other half is hideous to behold,
Ugly as grandame-apes, and full as old.

[22] Milton's Paradise Lost, L. II, v. 672.
[23] Dryden's Flower and Leaf. " Bright crimson and pure white, sweetly mixed in waves and melting one into the other, make the colour which our ancient poets called gridéline."
[24] In speculis Mors atra sedet, dominique silentis
    Adnumerat populos.——
          Stat. Theb. L. IV, v. 527.

There time has spent the fury of his course,
And plough'd and harrow'd with repeated force :
One blinking eye with scalding rheum suffus'd,
A leg contracted, and an arm disus'd ;   •
An half-liv'd emblem, fit for man to see ;
An hemiplegia of deformity !
   " But princess, to thy cunning be it known,
This emblematic side is rarely shown ;
Man would start back if wedded to the crone.
Side-long it is your custom to advance,
Show the fair half, and hide the foul, askance ;
And, like a vet'ran tempter, cast an eye
Of glancing blandishment in passing by.
By stealing side-ways with a silent pace
Man rarely sees the moral of your face :
And (what's the dang'rous frenzy of the whim)
Concludes, you've no immediate call for him,
Adjoin to this, your necromantic pow'r,
Contracting half an age to half an hour.
Just so the cyphers from the unit fled,
When Malicorn the demon's contract read [25].
The unit in the fore-most column stood,
And the two cyphers were obscur'd with blood [26].
   ' Two other mistress-arts you make your own ;
To Circe and Urganda arts unknown :
When men look on you, and your steps survey,
You seem to glide a-slant another way :
But the first moment they withdraw their eye,
Swift you take wing, and like a vulture fly,
Which snuffs the distant quarry in the wind,
And marks the carcass she is sure to find.——
The next deception is more wond'rous still ;
O grand artificer of fraud and ill !
When the sick man up-lifts the sash t' inhale
Th' enlivening breezes of the western gale,
To snatch one glimpse of ease from flow'ry
     fields,
And (fancying) taste the joy which nature yields ;
Far as the landscape's verge admits his view,
He sees a phantom, and concludes it you.
A gleam of courage then relieves his breast,
' Be calm my soul,' he cries, ' and take thy
     rest [27] : '
When at that moment, dreadful to relate,
(For all but he that ought observe his fate,)
The wife, the son, the friend perceive thee stand
Behind his curtains with uplifted hand,
Thee, real Tnce ! to drive the deadly dart,
And at one sudden stroke transpierce the
     heart ! "

[25] D. of Guise, a Tragedy. Dryden.
[26] Malicorn was an astrologer advanced in years, but being ambitious of making a great figure in this world, made over his soul to Satan, upon condition that he enjoyed earthly grandeur for 100 years more. The contract was written, signed and sealed in due form, when lo, at the expiration of one year the evil spirit entered Malicorn's chamber, preceded by thunder and lightning, and demanded him as his forfeit. The astrologer was exceedingly terrified, and, after making many remonstrances, insisted on seeing the original contract ; but the cyphers in number 100 were written with evanescent ink, and the figure 1 only remained legible. The moral of this fiction is incomparable. See Act V, Sc. 5.
[27] Luke, ch. xii, v. 13.

   " Culprit, thou hast thy piteous story told,
As trite as Priam's tale, and twice as old,"
Reply'd the queen : "painters and bards, 'tis true,
Have neither sung me right, nor justly drew :
I am not the gaunt spectre they devise
With chap-fall'n mouth, and with extinguish'd
     eyes.——
Whether enlighten'd with an heav'nly ray,
Or whether thou hast better guess'd than they,
I say not ; yet thus much I must confess,
Thy knowledge is superior, or thy guess.
I own the feign'd retreat, th' oblique advance,
The flight I take unseen, th' illusive glance,
The blandishments of artificial grace,
The sound, the palsy'd limbs, and double face,
All I contend for, (there the question lies,)
Is this ; Let men but look thro' wisdom's eyes,
And death ne'er takes them by a false surprize.
   " Did not thy Maker, when he gave thee birth,
Create thee out of perishable earth ?
Where hot, and cold, the rough, and lenient fight,
The hard, and soft, the heavy, and the light :
Whilst ev'ry atom fretted to decay
The heterogeneous lump of jarring clay ?——
Was not just death entail'd on thee and all,
(Such the decree of Heav'n) in Adam's fall ?
The parent-plant receiv'd a taint at root,
Hence the weak branches, hence the sickly
     fruit.
   " Thus with spring's genial balm and sun-shine
The annual flouret lifts its tender head,    [fed
In summer blooming, and at winter dead ;
Nay, if by chance a lasting plant be found,
Whose roots pierce deep th' inhospitable ground ;
Whose verdant leaves, (life's common autumn
Bid fair t' out-live the bitter wintry blast, [past)
And green old-age predicts a vernal shoot ;——
I lend my hand to pluck both branch and root.——
Man is no more perennial than a flow'r ;
Some may live years, some months and some an
     hour.
   "When first thou gav'st the promise of a man,
When th' embryon-speck of entity began,
Was not death ambiguous at a strife,
'Twixt death ambiguous and a twilight life,
Struggling with dubious shade and dubious light,
Like the Moon's orb ; whilst nations in affright
Hope for new day, but fear eternal night ?
   " When motionless the half-form'd fœtus lay,
And doubtful life just gleam'd a glimm'ring ray,
When nature bade the vital tide to roll,
I cloth'd with crust of flesh that gem the soul ;
My mortal dart th' immortal stream defil'd,
And the sire's frailties flow'd into the child.
The very milk his pious mother gave,
Turn'd poison, and but nurs'd him for the grave [28].
In ev'ry atom that his frame compos'd
I weak to strong, unsound to sound oppos'd.
Cruel, and proud of a deputed reign,
I ting'd the limpid stream with gloomy pain ;
Nor yet contented, in the current threw
Discolour'd sickness of each dismal hue.

[28] " Consider, O man, what thou wert before thy birth, what thou art from thy birth to thy death, and what thou shalt be after death. Thou wast made of an impure substance, and clothed and nourished in thy mother's blood."
               St. August.

Thus from the source which first life's waters
    gave,
Till their last final home, the ocean-grave,
Infection blends itself in ev'ry wave :
Marasmus, atrophy, the gout, and stone;
Fruits of our parents' folly and our own !
    " To live in health and ease you idly feign ;
Man's sprightliest days are intermitting pain.
Changing for worse, and never warn'd by ill,
Still the same bait, the same deception still !
Youth has new times for change, and may com-
Age ventures all upon a losing hand.    [mand ;
The liberty you boast of is a cheat ;
Licentiousness lurks under the deceit :
Plenty of means you have, and pow'r to chuse ;
Yet still you take the bad, the good refuse.
The freedom of the tempests you enjoy,
Born to o'erturn, and breathing to destroy.
These injure not themselves, the reas'ning elf
Injures alike both others and himself.
Sour'd in his liveliest hours, infirm when strong,
Unsure at safest, and but short when long.
    " Hast thou with anxious care and strictest
      thought
Made that nice estimate of time you ought ?
Time, like the precious di'mond, should be
      weigh'd ;
Carats, not pounds, must in the scale be laid.
Know'st thou the value of a year, a day,
An hour, a moment, idly thrown away ?
Then had thy life been blessedly employ'd,
And all thy minutes sensibly enjoy'd !
What are they now, and whither are they flown?
Th' immortal pain subsists, the mortal pleasure's
    gone !
Can'st thou recall them ?—Impotent and vain !
Or have they promis'd to return again ?
Call (if thou can'st) the winged arrow back,
Which lately cut thro' air its viewless track;
Or bid the cataract ascend its source,   [course ;
Which pour'd from Alpine heights its furious
Ah no—Time's vanish'd ! and you only find
A cold, unsatisfying scent behind !
    " Foe to delays, economist of time,
Thrice-happy Titus, virtuous in thy prime !
In whom the noon-day—or the setting Sun
Ne'er saw a work of goodness left undone.—
Old age compounds, or (more provoking yet)
Sends a small gift, when Heav'n expects the debt.
Bring not the leavings of thy faint desires
To him who gives the best, and best requires ;
Man mocks his Maker, and derides his law :
Satan has the full ears, and God the straw.
    "Behold the wretch, who long has health enjoy'd,
With gold unsated and with pow'r uncloy'd ;
Salmoneus like, to fancy'd greatness rais'd,
With slaves surrounded, and by flatt'rers prais'd:
See him against his nature vainly strive,
The busiest, pertest, proudest thing alive !
(As if beyond the patriarchal date
Exceptive mercy had prolong'd his fate.)
When lo ! behind the variegated cloud,
Euwrapt in mists, and muffled in a shrowd,
The dissolution of old age comes on,
Gouts, palsies, asthmas, jaundice, and the stone:
An hungry, merciless, insatiate band,
Eager as Croats for Death's last command !
Which still repeat their mercenary strain,
' Lead us, to add the living to the slain.'

    " Then mark the worldling, and explore him
      well :
His grief, his shame, and self-conviction tell :
' Weak were my joys,' (he cries,) ' and short
    their stay :
Pride mark'd the race, and folly pick'd the way.
Can I revoke my mis-directed pow'r ?   [hour ?
Where's my lost hope, and where the vanish'd
Curst be that greatness which blind fortune lent;
Curst be that wealth which sprung not from con-
    tent !
Still, still my conscious memory prevails ;
And understanding paints where mem'ry fails !'
    " Allow me next with confidence to say,
(As safely with the strictest truth I may ;)
" Why dost thou, ideot, senselessly complain,
(Fond of more life, and covetous of pain,)
That I, a tyrant, seize thee by surprize ?"—
Flames, as she spoke, shot flashing from her
"Dotard ! I gave thee warning ev'ry hour; [eyes.
Announc'd my presence, and proclaim'd my
    pow'r.
One only bus'ness in the world was thine,
Born but to die ! t' exact the pay'ment mine.
If, atheist-like, you blame the just decree,
Attack thy Maker, but exculpate me !
Mortality's coeval with thy breath ;
Life is a chain of links which lead to death.
Sleep—wake—run—creep—alike to death you
    move ;     [love.
Death's in thy meat, thy wine, thy sleep, thy
Know'st thou not me, my warnings, and alarms?
Thou, who so oft hast slumber'd in my arms !
For ever seeing, can'st thou nought descry ?
Dead ev'ry night, and yet untaught to die !
    " How dar'st thou give thy impious murmurs
    vent,
Thyself a breathing, speaking monument ?
No death is sudden to a wretch like thee,
The emblem of his own mortality !
Above, beneath, within thee, and without,
All things fore-show the stroke, and clear the
The very apoplex, thy swiftest foe,   [doubt,
Forewarns his coming ; and approaches slow ;
Sudden confusions interrupt thy brain ;
Swift thro' thy temples shoots the previous pain;
Suspicion follows, and mis-giving fear.—
Death always speaks, if man would strive to
    hear.
    " Acquit me then of fraudulent surprise :
Leave sophistry to wits ; be truly wise ;
For, as the cedar falls, it ever lies [29] !
Start not at what we call our latest breath ;
The morning of man's real life is death [30]."
So spake the pow'r, Who never felt control.
Fear smote my heart, and conscience stung my
    soul ;
Remorse, vexation, shame, and anger strive.—
I wak'd :—and (to my joy) I wak'd alive.
Never was human transport more sincere ;—
And the best men may find instruction here.

[29] Eccles. ch. xi, v. 3.
[30] —————— Steriles transmisimus annos ;
    Hæc ævi mihi prima dies : hæc limina vitæ
      Stat. Sylv. L. IV.

## MORAL.

**W**HO puts off Death, to the last moments
　driv'n,
Is near the grave, but very far from Heav'n [31].
He who repents, and gains the wish'd reprieve,
Was fit to die, and is more fit to live.
Chuse a good convoy in an hostile course;
Right foresight never makes a danger worse.

---

## THE COURTIER AND PRINCE.

### ·A FABLE.

Put not your trust in princes, nor in the son of
man, in whom there is no help.
　　　　　　　Psalm cxlvi, v. 3.
Now behold, thou trusteth upon the staff of a
bruised reed—on which if a man lean, it will
go through his hand and pierce it: so is Pha-
raoh, king of Egypt, unto all that trust in him.
　　　　　2 Kings, ch. xviii, v. 21.

---

**W**ITH diffidence, O Muse, awake the string!
Proba [1], herself a Muse, commands to sing:
Divest thyself of thy pretended bays, 　[lays:
And crown'd with short-liv'd flow'rs present thy
From female archives stol'n, a tale disclose,
Verse tortur'd into rhymes from honest prose.
Short fables may with double grace be told;
So smallest glasses sweetest essence hold.
　Antonia somewhere [2] does a tale report,
Of no small use to rising men at court:
(Who seek promotion in the worldly road,
And make their titles and their wealth their
　god;)
Antonia! who the Hermit's Story fram'd [3]:
A tale to prose-men known [4], by verse-men
　fam'd [5].
A courtier, of the lucky, thriving sort,
Rose like a meteor, and eclips'd the court;
By chance or cunning ev'ry storm outbraves:
Topmost he rode, midst shoals of fools and
　knaves,
Triumphant, like an eygre [6], o'er the waves:

[31] A saying of pious Jeremy Taylor.
[1] A Roman young lady'of quality and a Christian convert. She afterwards married Adelphus,
who was a proconsul in the reign of Honorius
and Theodosius junior. She composed an History of the Old and New Testament in verse.
Her epitaph on her husband is much admired.
Both pieces were printed at Francfort in 1541.
　Her name at length was Proba Valeria Fal-
conia.
[2] Traité sur la Piété solide. Epît. xx, par
Madame Antoinette de Bourignon.
[3] Epît. de Bourignon. Partie seconde, Epit.
xvii.
[4] Dr. Patrick's Parable of the Pilgrim.
[5] Parnelle's Hermit.
[6] The tenth wave, when rivers are swollen by
floods, or agitated by storms, is called in some
parts of England an eygre.
　　See Dryden's Threnod. August.

Casually lucky, fortunately great,
Ten times his planet overcame his fate.
Riches flow'd in; and accidents were kind;
Health join'd her opium to delude the mind [7];
Whilst pride was gratify'd in ev'ry view,
And pow'r had scarce an object to pursue;
Cramm'd to the throat with happiness and ease,
Till nature's self could do no more to please.—
Vain-glorious mortal, to profusion blest!
And almost by prosperity distrest!
Whilst poets, the worst panders of the age,
Hymn'd his no-virtues in each flatt'ring page:
True parasitic plants [8], which only grow
Upon their patron trees, like miscelto:
So pella-mountain on the flax appears,
And thyme, th' epithimy [9], (her bastard) rears
Just so th' agaric from the larix springs,
And fav'rites fatten on perspiring kings.—
More might be said; but this we leave untold,
That better things their proper place may hold.
　Our mirror of good luck, whom chance had
　　claim'd
As her own offspring, was Amariel nam'd.
At his first horoscope the goddess smil'd,
And wrapp'd in her own mantle her own child;
Then, as a wit upon th' occasion said,
(Not less a wit, we hope, for being dead,)
" Gave him her blessing, put him in a way,
Set up the farce, and laugh'd at her own play."
　Fortune, the mistress of the young and bold,
Espous'd him early, but caress'd him old;
Duteous and faithful as an Indian wife,
She made appearance to be true for life:
And kept her love alive, and like to last,
Beyond the date her Pompey was disgrac'd.
But nothing certain (as the wise man [10] found)
Is to be deem'd on sublunary ground.

[7] " Prosperous health and uninterrupted ease
are often the occasion of some fatal misfortune.
Thus a long peace makes men unguarded, and
sometimes unmindful, in matters of war: it being observed, that the most signal overthrow is
usually given us, when an unexpected enemy
surpriseth us in the deep sleep of peace and security." 　　　　　St. Gregor. the Great.
[8] Parasitical plants, according to the language
of botanists, will not grow in the common matrix of the earth, but their seeds, being dispersed by winds, take root in the excrementitious
parts of a decayed tree, or arise as an excres-
cence from the exsudations of some tree or
plant. Thus the dodder (cuscuta), formerly
called pella-mountain, grows usually on flax; and
therefore the Italian peasant calls it podagra di
linio.
[9] The Arabians and Italians (imitating the
Greek word ἐπιθυμιὸν) call this adscititious plant
efitimo and epithimo; but very few of our English botanists make mention of it. As far as I
have hitherto seen, only one of our herbalists
has touched upon it, namely, Peter Treveris,
who flourished about the reign of Henry VII.
He calls it epithimy. For my own part, not
caring to invent new words in poetry, I have
thought proper to retain the word which he
(Treveris) has used, as it is well-sounding, and
not inelegant.
[10] Son of Sirach.

Join'd to good fortune, 'twas our courtier's lot
To serve a prince who ne'er his friends forgot :
Humane, discreet, compassionate, and brave ;
Not milder when he lov'd, than when forgave.
Gen'rous of promise, punctual in the deed ;
Grac'd with more candour than most monarchs
    need.
A milkiness of blood his heart possess'd ;
With grief he punish'd, and with transport
    bless'd[11].
    As noblest metals are most ductile found,
Great souls with mild compassion most abound.
The golden dye with soft complacence takes
Each speaking lineament th' engraver makes,
And wears a faithful image for mankind,
True to the features, truer to the mind :
Whilst stubborn iron (like a barren soil
To lab'ring hinds) eludes the artist's toil ;
To ev'ry stroke ungrateful and unjust,
Corrodes itself, or hardens into rust.
    Good-nature, in the language from above[12],
Is universal charity and love :
Patient of wrongs, and enemy to strife ;
Basis of virtue, and the staff of life !
Whilst av'rice, private censure, public rage,
Are th' old man's hobby-horse, and crutch of age.
Party conducts us to the meanest ends ;
Party made Herod and a Pilate friends [13].
    Scorn'd be the bard, and banish'd ev'n from
      schools,
Who first immortaliz'd man-killing fools ;
Blockheads in council, bloody in command :
Warriors—not of the head, but of the hand ;
True brethren of the iron-pated Suede[14] :
They fight like Ajax, and like Ajax read.
    Of all the great and harmless things below,
Only an elephant is truly so.
(Thus writes a wit[15], well known a cent'ry past ;   •
Forgotten now ; yet still his fame shall last.)
Kings have their follies; statesmen have their
    arts ;           [hearts ;
Wealth spoils the great; beauty ensnares our
And wits are doubly dup'd by having parts.
Some have ten times the parts they ought to use;
" A great wit's greatest work is to refuse [16] !"
Never, O bards, the warning voice despise ;—
To add is dang'rous, to retrench is wise.
Poets instead of saying what they could,
Must only say the very thing they should.
This mighty ΕΥΡΗΚΑ reserv'd for few,
Virgil and Boileau, Pope and Dryden knew.
    (Thus by the way.) Now, Muse, resume thy
      course ;
There is no wand'rer like the poet's horse :
Who quits the solid road, and well-beat lanes,
(Sick of his track, and punish'd for his pains,)
To mimic galloping on green-swarth plains

So, in the daily work she labours at,
The swallow toils, and rises with a gnat.—
    It chanc'd as through his groves our monarch
      stray'd,
T' enjoy the coolness of a summer shade,
Wrapt up in virtuous schemes of means and ends,
To reconcile his foes, or bless his friends,
He spy'd a figure, which by shape he knew,
In a lone grotto half conceal'd from view :
Thither the prudent wand'rer had retir'd,
As modesty and well bred sense requir'd :
Studious of manners, fearful to intrude
On precious hours of royal solitude.
    " Amariel," cry'd the prince, " I know thee
Invelop'd in the umbrage of a cell :     [well,
I like thy modesty, with manners fraught ;—
But, as my spirits ask a pause from thought,
Walk with thy master, and with him inhale
The cooling freshness of the western gale.
    " Amariel," added he, and gently smil'd,
" This grove's my kingdom, and each tree my
      child :
(Forgive the vanity, which thus compares
My self to Cyrus, and his rural cares [17];)
My ready pencil sketch'd the first design,
These eyes adjusted ev'ry space and line ;
These hands have fixt th' inoculated shoots,
Train'd the loose branches, and reform'd the
      roots.
Happy the monarch of the town and field,
Where vice to laws, and weeds to culture yield !
    " My human realms a tenfold care demand;
Reluctant is the staple [18] of the land :
Sour are the juices, churlish is the soil,
Of rule impatient, and averse to toil.
In vain I cherish, and in vain replace ;     [face.
Th' ungrateful branch flies back, and wounds my
Courtiers are like th' hyéna, never tame :
No bounties fix them, and no arts reclaim :
Frontless they run the muck [19] through thick and
      thin ;
Not poorer, if they lose ;—and they may win.
Patriots of their own int'rest, right or wrong :
Foes to the feeble, flatt'rers to the strong.
Stiff complaisance thro' their best homage
      spreads,           [heads.
So turn-soles [20] court the Sun with 'wry-neck'd
True as a dial, when their patrons shine ;
But blank, if the said patrons pow'r resign.
Like good sir Martin [20], when he lost his man,
They grieve—and get another as they can.
Yet, (though small real comfort is enjoy'd
Where man the ruler is, and men employ'd,)
Of all my friends and servants, you alone
Have pleas'd me best, and most reliev'd the
      throne.

[11] " Bountifulness is a most beautiful garden,
and mercifulness endureth for ever."
                         Ecclus.
[12] Eὐδοxία.  Matth. ch. ii. v. 14.
[13] Luke ch. xxii. v. 12.
[14] Demir-bash, or iron-headed: a name given
by the Turks to Charles the XIIth of Sweden.
[15] Dr. Donne's Letters in Prose, 12°, Lond.
1591.
[16] Sir John Birkenhead's epistle to Cartwright,
1668.

[17] Xenophont. Oeconomic. c. iv, &c.
[18] The staple of the soil, in an husbandry-
sense, is the upper earth, which lies within the
reach of the plough and influence of the atmosphere.
    Thus we call wool, with relation to England,
a staple commodity.
[19] Dryden's Hind and Panther.
[20] The heliotrope, or Sun-flower, called, by
the Italians, orologio dei cortegiani.
[21] Sir Martin Marr-all, in a comedy of Dryden's writing.

Whatever then my bounty can provide ;
Whatever by my friendship be supply'd ;
As far as faith can bind, or speech can say,
Ask, and I meet thy wishes half the way."
   The servant bow'd, and gratitude express'd ;
Such gratitude as dwells in courtier's breast :
Pleas'd to the height of transport he retir'd ;
His fears were calm'd, and his ambition fir'd.
Unhappy man, in both his objects wrong ;
The weak he trusted, and forgot the strong !
   Six years were past, when lo, by slow degrees,
A fever did his limbs and spirits seize :
Advancing gently, no alarm it makes, [brakes:)
(Like murd'ring Indians gliding through the
But, having mark'd her sure approaches well,
She storms, and nothing can her force repell.
Instant, a liquid fire inflames the blood,
Whilst spasms impede the self-refining flood :
Petechial spots th' approach of Death proclaim,
Redd'ning like comets with vindictive flame ;
Whilst wand'ring talk, and mopings wild, presage
Moon-struck illusion, and conclude in rage.
Inevitable Death alarms the heart :
Nature stands by, and bids her aim the dart.
   The sick man, stupify'd with fear and woe,
Had hardly words to speak, or tears to flow ;
At length in broken sounds was heard to cry,
" Grant me to see my master, e'er I die."
The master came. " Ah, prince," Amariel said,
" Now keep thy promise, and extend thy aid ;
Unfurl my tangled thread of human breath,
And call me back one year, before my death."
   The prince (for he was wise, and good withall,)
Stood like a statue mortis'd to the wall :
At length recov'ring from amazement, broke
An awful silence, and thus gravely spoke :
" Amariel, sure thy pangs disturb thy brain :
The boon you ask is blasphemous and vain :
Am I a god, to alter Death's decree ?
That's the prerogative of Heav'n, not me."
   " Then," cry'd Amariel, with an hasty tone,
" Gain me a week, three days, or gain me one."
   " Impossible !" agen the prince reply'd ;
" Sure thy disease to madness is ally'd :
Ask me for riches—freely I resign
A third, or half, and bid thee make them thine.
Whate'er the world can human greatness call,
Pow'r, rank, grants, titles, I'll bestow them all.
Then die in peace, or with contentment live,
Nor ask a gift no mortal pow'r can give."
   With eyes that flash'd with eagerness and fire
The sick man then propos'd a new desire :
" As Death's dread tyranny has no control,
Can you ensure the safety of my soul ?
Anxious and doubtful for my future state,
I read the danger, but I read too late."
The prince stood mute ; compassion and amaze
Tore his divided heart ten thousand ways :
And, having rightly weigh'd the sick man's
                              pray'r,
Thus he reply'd in sorrow and despair :
   " Salvation of the soul by grace is giv'n ;—
Unalienable is the grace of Heav'n.
I tremble at the rash request you make,
Which is not mine to grant, or yours to take."
   Amariel then, with disappointment spent,
Turn'd from his prince in mournful discontent,
And, lifting up to Heav'n his hands and eyes,
Thus in a flood of tears obtests the skies :

" Wretch that I am, unworthy of my breath ;
Deceiv'd when living, and deceiv'd in death !
Why did I waste my strength, my cares, my
To serve a master—master but in name ? [fame,
An ethnic idol, for delusion made ;
Eyes without sight, protection without aid ?
Unable to bestow the good we want,
And ready, what avails us not, to grant !
Deceitful, impotent, unuseful pow'r ;
Which can give di'monds, but not give an hour !
At Rimmon's shrine no longer will I bow,
But thus to th' all-pow'rful king address my vow :
   " O thou, the only great, and good, and wise,
Ruler of Earth, and monarch of the skies ;
Thou, whom th' intents of virtuous actions
                        please ;            [ease [22] :
Whose laws are freedom, and whose service
Whose mercy waits th' offender to the grave,
Willing to hear ; omnipotent to save !
Who ne'er forgot one meritorious deed,
Nor left a servant in the hour of need ;
To mercy and to equity inclin'd ;
Who mind'st the heart, and tenour of the mind [23].
Forgive my errour, and my life restore ;
Thee will I serve alone, and thee adore !
Farewell Earth's deities and idols all ;
Moloch and Mammon, Chiun [24], Dagon, Baal :
Whose chemarims [25] tread their fantastic rounds
O'er Aven's [26] plains, and dance to Tyrian
                        sounds.
" Hence, false Astarte [27], who the world suborns,
Life's lambent meteor glist'ring round her horns.
Let Thammuz moan his self-inflicted pain,
And Sidon's stream run purple to the main.
" No star of Remphan [28] shall attract my sight,
Shorn of its beams, and gleaming sickly light :
Malignant orb ! which tempts bewilder'd swains
To gulphs, to quicksands, and waste trackless
By thee the false Achitophel was led ;     [plains !
And Haman [29] dy'd aloft, and made a cloud
                        his bed.
   " From worldly hopes and false dependance
                        freed,
I'll seek no safety from a splinter'd reed ;
Which causes those to fall, who wish to stand ;
Or, if it aids the steps, gangrenes the hand [30].
   " How vain is all the chymic wealth of pow'r ;
Sought for an age, and squander'd in an hour !
Full late we learn, in sickness, pains, and woe,
What in high health 'twas possible to know.
   " Two ages may have two Elishas seen ;
Groups of Gehazis [31] choke the space between :

[22] Idcirco servi sumus, ut liberi esse possimus.
                              Cicero.
[23] Bishop Jer. Taylor.
[24] Chiun, probably from KΥΩN : Qu. if not
Anubis. See also Amos, ch. v. v. 26. 1 Kings,
ch. xi. v. 32.
[25] For the chemarims of Baal, see Hosea, ch.
x. v. 5, in Marg. 2 Kings, ch. xxiii. v. 5.
[26] Aven. Hosea, ch. x. v. 8. Plains of Aven.
Amos, ch. i. v. 5.
[27] Perhaps the same as Astaroth, or Venus the
goddess of the Sidonians.
[28] Acts, ch. viii. v. 43.
[29] Esther, ch. vii. v. 9.
[30] Isaiah, ch. xxxvi. v. 6.
[31] 2 Kings, ch. v, v. 20.

# THE ENCHANTED REGION. 289

Who live unthinking, and obdurate die,
Nor heed their own or children's leprosy [32].
Sin-born and blind ! Who change, protest, and
    swear,
With the same ease they draw the vital air.
Proud of the wit, and heedless of the sin,
They strip, and sell the Christian to the skin [33].
Charms irresistible the dupes behold
In vineyards, farms, and all-compelling gold.
Others (still weaker) set their truth to sale
For a mere sound, and cut off Heav'n's entail:
Whilst he, who never fails his imps, supplies
Prompt treachery, and fresh-created lies.—
Time-servers are at ev'ry man's command
For loaves and fish on Dalmanutha's strand [34]."
  He spoke: and, with a flood of tears oppress'd,
Gave anguish vent, and felt a moment's rest.
Heav'n with compassion heard the sick man
    grieve;
And Hezekiah gain'd the wish'd reprieve [35],
Once more his blood with equal pulses flow'd,
And health's contentment on his visage glow'd.
Places and honours be with joy resign'd;
(Peace-off'rings to procure a tranquil mind [36]!)
Gave all his riches to the sick and poor,
And made one patriarch-farm his only store.
To groves and brooks our new Elijah ran,
Far from the monster world, and traitor man.
Thus he surviv'd the tempest of the day,
And ev'ning-sunshine shot a glorious ray.
Diseases, sickness, disappointments, sorrow,
All lend us comfort, whilst they seem to borrow.
  Here I might paint him in a life retir'd,
Ennobled by the virtues he acquir'd;
But the true transports of the wise and good
Are best by implication understood;
Except the Muse with Dryden's strength could
    soar:——
Me, humble Prudence whispers[37] to give o'er.
A safe retreat ; plann'd and perform'd with care,
Stands for a vict'ry in poetic war.
So when the warbling lark has mounted high
With upright flight, and gain'd upon the sky,
Grown giddy, she contracts her flick'ring wings:
Thrids her descending course in spiral rings,
Less'ning her voice ; but to the ground she sings;
Resolving, on a more auspicious day,
Higher to mount, and chant a better lay [38].
  How few can still their reader's minds en-
    gage ?—
One Pope is the slow child-birth of one age.
Others write verses, but they write unblest;
Some few good lines stand sponsors for the rest:
They miss wit's depth, and on the surface skim ;
(He who seeks pearls, must dive, as well as
    swim.)

[32] Ibid. v. ult.
[33] " They pull off the robe with the garment."
Mic. ch. ii, v. 8.
[34] Mark ch. viii, v. 10.
[35] 2 Kings, ch. xx.
[36] Tranquil mind.  Shakespeare.
[37] Me, mea Calliope, cura leviore vagantem,
Jam revocat, parvoque jubet decurrere gyro.
        Columell. de Hortis, L. 10.
[38] ——————— nostra fatiscit,
Laxaturque chelys: vires instigat, alitque ;
Tempestiva quies ; major post otia virtus.
                Sylv. L. 4.

Bad bards, worse critics!—Thus we multiply
Poems and rules, but write no poetry.
Ev'n Pope, like Charlemagne, with all his fire
Made Paladins—but not an host entire[39].
Far as its pow'rs could go, thy genius went:
Good sense still kept thee in thy own extent[40].
Rare wisdom! both t' enjoy and know thy
    store ;—
Most wits, like misers, always covet more.
Leave me, lov'd bard, instructor of my youth,
Leave me the sounds of verse, and voice of truth ;
So when Elias dropp'd his mantle, ran
Elisha, and a prophet's life began [41].
  Add, that the Muses, nurst in various climes,
Yield diff'rent produce, and at diff'rent times.
Italian plants, in nature's hot-bed plac'd,
Bear fruits in spring, and riot into waste.
French flow'rs less early, (and yet early,) blow;
Their pertness is a green-house from the snow.
Cold northern wits demand a longer date ;
Our genius, like our climate, ripens late.
The fancy's solstice is at forty o'er,
The tropic of our judgment sees three-score.
Thus summer codlings yield a poignant draught,
Which frisks the palate, but ne'er warms the
    thought:    cast,)
Rough cackagees, (four months behind them
Take all bad weathers, and through autumn last;
Mellow'd from wild austerity, at length
They taste like nectar, and adopt its strength.

---

## THE ENCHANTED REGION:

### OR, MISTAKEN PLEASURES.

The mistress of witchcrafts.
                Nahum, ch. iii, v. 4.
Draw near hither, ye sons of the sorceress.
                Isaiah, ch. lvii, v. 3.
According to their pasture, so were they filled:
  they were filled, and their heart was exalted ;
Therefore they have forgotten me.
             Hosea, ch. xiii, v. 6.

[39] An answer made by Boccace, when it was
objected to him, that some of his novels had not
the spirit of the rest.
  [40] Amongst Mr. Pope's great intellectual abilities, good sense was his most distinguishing
character : for he knew precisely, and as it were
by a sort of intuition, what he had power to do,
and what he could not do.
  He often used to say, that for ten years together he firmly resisted the importunity of friends
and flatterers, when they solicited him to undertake a translation of Virgil after Dryden. Nor
did he ever mistake the extent of his talents, but
in the following trivial instance ; and that was,
when he writ his Ode to Music on St. Cecilia's day;
induced perhaps by a secret ambition of rivalling
the inimitable Dryden. In which case, if he
hath not exceeded the original, (for there is always some advantage in writing first) he hath at
least surpassed (and perhaps ever will surpass)
those that come after him, and attempt to make
the same experiment.
  [41] 2 Kings, ch. ii.

E<small>MPTY</small>, illusory life,
Pregnant with fraud, in mischiefs rife [1];
Form'd to ensnare us, and deceive us : 
Nahum's enchantress ! which beguiles
With all her harlotry of wiles !—
First she loves, and then she leaves us !

Erring happiness beguiles
The wretch that strays o'er Circe's isles ;
All things smile, and all annoy him ;
The rose has thorns, the doves can bite ;
Riot is a fatigue till night,
Sleep an opium to destroy him.

Louring in the groves of death
Yew-trees breathe funereal breath,
Brambles and thorns perplex the shade ;
Asphaltic waters creep and rest ;
Birds, in gaudy plumage drest,
Scream unmeaning through the glade [2].

Earth fallacious herbage [3] yields,
And deep in grass its influence shields ;
Acrid juices, scent annoying ;—
Corrosive crow-feet choke the plains,
And hemloc strip'd with lurid stains,
And luscious mandrakes, life-destroying.

Gaudy bella-donna [4] blowing,
Or with glossy berries glowing,
Lures th' unwise to tempt their doom :
Love's apple [5] masks the fruit of death ;
Sick hen-bane murders with her breath,
Actæa [6] with an harlot's bloom.

One plant [7] alone is wrapt in shade ;
Few eyes its privacy invade ;
Plant of joy, of life, and health !
More than the fabled lotos fam'd
Which (tasted once) mankind reclaim'd
From parents, country, pow'r, and wealth [8].

On yonder Alp I see it rise,
Aspiring to congenial skies,

[1] " Art thou arrived to maturity of life ? Look back and thou shalt see the frailty of thy youth, the folly of thy childhood, and the senseless dissipation of thy infancy !—Look forward and thou shalt behold the insincerity of the world and cares of life, the diseases of thy body and the troubles of thy mind." Annon. Vet.
" In this world death is every-where, grief every-where, and desolation every-where. The world flieth us, and yet we follow it : it falleth, and we adhere to it, and fall with it, and attempt to enjoy it falling."
St. Gregor. Hom.

[2] It is remarked, that birds adorned with rich plumage, as peacocks, parrots, &c. have, generally speaking, unmusical voices.
[3] ——— fallax herba veneni. Virg.
[4] The bella-donna lily, or deadly-shade. (Atropa Linnæi.)
[5] Amomum Plinii.
[6] Actæa ; herb Christopher.
[7] The passion-flower.
[8] See Homer's Odyssey, l. IX, v. 94, &c.

But cover'd half with ivy-walls ;—
There, where Eusebio [9] rais'd a shrine,
Snatch'd from the gulf by Pow'r Divine,
Where Reiga's tumbling torrent falls [10].

Compar'd with thee, how dimly shows
Poor Anacreon's life-less rose ?
What is Homer's plant [11] to thee?—
In vain the Mantuan poet try'd
To paint Amellus' starry [12] pride,
Emblem of wit's futility !

Men saw, alas, and knew not thee,
Mystic evangelic tree !
Thou hadst no charms for paynim-eyes ;
Till, guided by the lamp of Heav'n,
To chaste Urania pow'r was giv'n
To see, t'admire, and moralize.

All beauteous flow'r, whose centre glows
With studs of gold ; thence streaming flows.
Ray-like effulgence. Next is seen
A rich expanse of varying hue,
Enfring'd with an empurpled-blue,
And streak'd with young Pomona's green [13].

High o'er the pointal, deck'd with gold,
(Emblem mysterious to behold,)

[9] The baron De Bottoni.
[10] This alludes to a well-known fact in the dutchy of Carniola, where the present ode was written.
About the year 1675, a nobleman was riding at night upon a road which goes near the edge of the precipice here mentioned. Mistaking his way (and that for a few steps only) his horse stopped short, and refused to go on ; upon which the rider, who in all probability was heated with liquor, (otherwise he ought to have known the precipice better, it being not far from his own castle) lost both his temper and prudence, and spurred the horse with great anger ; upon which the poor beast took a desperate leap, intending, as was imagined, to have reached another angle of the precipice on the same side which the road lay. The horse fell directly into the torrent, two or three hundred feet beneath, and was hurried away with such rapidity that the body was never found. The nobleman was discovered next day in an opening of the rock, about half way down, where a few bushes grew ; and, as the saddle was found not far from him, it was supposed that the horse, by the violence of his effort he made, burst the saddle-girths. The rider lived many years after this wonderful escape, and, out of gratitude to God, erected a beautiful chapel on the edge of the precipice, dedicated (if I mistake not) to St. Anthony of Padua.
I made a drawing of the chapel, precipice, torrent, and nobleman's castle ; of which a copy was taken afterwards by the celebrated draftsman Visentini, at Venice, in 1750.
[11] Moly. Homer's Odyssey, l. XI, v. 305.
[12] Aster Atticus, or (purple Italian) star-wort.
Georg. IV, v. 271.
[13] Alluding to that particular species of green called by the French pomme-verte, or apple-green.

A radiant cross its form expands;—
Its opening arms appear t' embrace
The whole collective human race,
Refuge of all men in all lands!

Grant me, kind Heav'n, in prosp'rous hour
To pluck this consecrated flow'r,
And wear it thankful on my breast;
Then shall my steps securely stray,
No pleasures shall pervert my way [14],
No joys seduce, no cares molest.

Like Tobit (when the hand, approv'd
By Heav'n, th' obstructing films remov'd [15])
I now see objects as I ought:
Ambition's [16] hideous; pleasure vain;
Av'rice [16] is but a blockhead's gain,
Possessing all, bestowing nought.

Passions and frauds surround us all,
Their empire is reciprocal:
Shun their blandishments and wiles;
Riches but serve to steel the heart;
Want has its meanness and its art;
Health betrays, and strength beguiles,

In highest stations snares misguide;
Midst solitude they nurture pride,
Breeding vanity in knowledge;
A poison in delicious meat,
Midst wines a fraud, midst mirth a cheat,
In courts, in cabinet, and college.

The toils are fixt, the sportsmen keen:
Abroad unsafe, betray'd within,
Whither, O mortal! art thou flying?
Thy resolutions oft are snares,
Thy doubts, petitions, gifts, and pray'rs;—
Alas, there may be snares in dying!

[14] " My heart is a vain and wandering heart, whenever it is led by its own determinations. It is busy to no purpose, and occupied to no end, whenever it is not guided by divine influence: it seeketh rest and findeth none: it agreeth not with itself: it alters resolutions, changeth judgment, frames new thoughts, and suppresses old ones; pulls down every thing, and re-buildeth nothing; in short, it never continueth in the same state."
St. Bernard. Meditat.

" Seest thou the luminary of the greater world in the highest pitch of meridian glory; where it continueth not, but descends in the same proportion as it ascended? Look next and consider if the light of this lower world is more permanent? Continuance is the child of Eternity, and not of Time." Ex. Vet. Ascet.

[15] Tobit, ch. iii, v. 17.
[16] " All vices wax old by age: covetousness (and ambition) alone grow young."
Ex. Vet. Ascet.

" Why are earth and ashes proud? There is not a more wicked thing than a covetous man: for such an one setteth his own soul to sale; because, while he liveth, he casteth away his bowels;" i. e. is a stranger to compassion.
Ecclus. ch. x, v. 9.

Deceiving none, by none ensnar'd,
O Paraclete [17], be thou my guard,
Patron of ev'ry just endeavour!
The cross of Christ is man's reward [18]:
No heights obstruct, no depths retard;
Christian joys are joys for ever!

## EULOGIUS; OR, THE CHARITABLE MASON.

### AN HISTORICAL FABLE.

TAKEN FROM THE GREEK OF PAULUS SYLLOGUS, LIB. III.

—— Nos, vilis turba, caducis
Deservire bonis, semperque *optare* parati,
Spargimur in casus.     Stat. Sylvæ, L. II.

God gives us what he knows our wants require,
And better things than those which we desire.
Dryd. Palam. & Arc.

Give me neither poverty nor riches; feed me with food convenient for me: Lest I be full and deny thee, and say, Who is the Lord? Or lest I be poor and steal, and take the name of my God in vain. Agur's Prayer.
Prov. ch. xxx, v. 8, 9.

### INTRODUCTION.

Permit me, Stanhope [1], as I form'd thy youth
To classic taste and philosophic truth,
Once more, thy kind attention to engage,
And, dying, leave thee comfort for old-age;
This hist'ry may eternal truths suggest:—
I've seen thee learned, and would leave thee
One grain of piety avails us more     [blest!
Than Prussia's laurels, or Potosi's store.

How blindly to our misery we run;     [done!
Dup'd by false hopes, and by our pray'rs un-
We want, we wish, we change, we change agen;
Yet know not how to ask, nor what, nor when.
Just so, misled by liquor, drunkards stray,
They know they have a road, but miss their way;
Th' existence of their home admits no doubt;
Th' uncertainty—is where to find it out [2].

[17] ΠΑΡΑΚΛΗΤΟΣ: The Comforter; the Holy Spirit.     John, ch. xiv, v. 16—26.

Dryden first introduced the word Paraclete into the English language, in his translation of the Hymn Veni Creator Spiritus: as also in his Britannia Rediviva:

Last solemn Sabbath saw the church attend;
The Paraclete in fiery pomp descend.
But, when his wond'rous octave roll'd again—

[18] Rom. ch. viii, v. 39.
[1] Philip Stanhope, esq. late member of parliament for St. German's in Cornwall, and at present envoy extraordinary to the court of Dresden and the circle of Lower Saxony, &c. The natural son of lord Chesterfield, to whom his celebrated letters were addressed.
[2] Væ tempori illi quando non deum cognovimus!
August. Soliloq. c. 31.

Zimri ask'd wealth, and wealth o'erturn'd his
    parts.——              [hearts.
Parents for children pray, which break their
Contractors, agio-men, for villas sigh;
To day they purchase, and to morrow die.
Six cubic feet of earth are all their lot [3];
Mourn'd with hypocrisy, with ease forgot.
Their Christian-heirs the pagan-rites employ,
And give the fun'ral ilicet with joy.
Lelio [4] would be th' Angelic [5] of a school;
Kneels down a wit, and rises up a fool.
Weak hands affect to hold the statesman's scale;
As well the shrimp might emulate a whale.—
Clamb'ring, with stars averse, to fortune's
    height
Ambitious Omri rose, and dropp'd down-right—
His paunch too heavy, and his head too light.
Like fall'n Salmoneus, he perceiv'd, at length,
The mean hypocrisy of boasted strength :
To deal like Dennis his vain thunder round,
And imitate inimitable sound.—
Both ways deceitful is the wine of pow'r,
When new, 'tis heady, and, when old, 'tis sour.
Ianthe' pray'd for beauty; luckless maid!—
An idiot mind th' angelic form betray'd.
Nature profusely deck'd the out-side pile,
But starv'd the poor inhabitant the while.
D'Avenant implor'd the Muses for a tongue:
The Muses lent him theirs. He sweetly sung;
And—(but for Milton [6]) had more sweetly [7]
    swung.            [all [8],
" Learn hence," he cry'd, " my merry brethren
Tyburn's agáric stanches wit, and gall."
    Others mount Pegasus, but lose their seat:
And break their necks, before they end the heat.
Libanius try'd the streams of eloquence, [sense.
But plummet deep he sunk, unbuoy'd with
Soncinas [9] ask'd the " knack of plotting treason
Against the crown and dignity of reason [10]."

[3] Hic tibi mortis erunt metæ: domus alta
    sub Ida,
    Lyrnessi domus alta:—Solo Laurente se-
     pulcrum.         Virg. Æneid XII.
" A small space of ground after death contains both rich and poor. Nature produceth us
all alike, and makes no distinction at death.
Open the grave, view the dead bodies; move
the ashes, you will find no difference between
the patrician and the peasant, except thus far;
that by the magnificence of the tomb of the
former you may perceive he had much more to
resign and lose than the latter."
                      St. Ambrose.
[4] Late lord B***.    [5] Doctor Angelicus.
[6] Milton interceded, and saved D'Avenant,
when he was a state-prisoner at Cowes castle in
the isle of Wight, anno 1650: D'Avenant, in return, preserved Milton at the Restoration.
[7] Alluding to a passage in Dryden: " A man
may be capable, as Jack Ketch's wife said of his
servant, of a plain piece of work, bare hanging;
but, to make a malefactor die sweetly, was only
belonging to her husband."
               Dedication to Juvenal.
[8] From an old poem.
[9] A Spanish casuist.
[10] Logic: so defined by our venerable poet
Francis Quarles, 1638.

By his own art th' artificer-was try'd,
And lawyers beat him on the quibbling side.
    Now hasten, poet, to begin thy song:
" A tale," says Prior, " ne'er should be too
    long."
Ill-judging is the bard, who slacks his pace
And seeks for flow'rs, when he should run the
    race;
Or, wand'ring to enchanted castles, sleeps
On beds of down : or Cupid's vigils keeps;
Whilst the main action is by pleasures crost,
And the first purport of th' adventure lost.
Great wits may scorn the dry poetic law ;
Nor from the critic, but from Nature, draw:
Each seeming trip, and each digressive start,
Displays their ease the more, and deep-plann'd
    art:
(All study'd blandishments t' allure the heart.)
Like Santueil's [11] stream, gliding thro' flow'ry
    plains,
Th' effects are seen; the source unknown re-
    mains.

In ancient times, scarce talk'd of, and less
    known,
When pious Justin [1] fill'd the eastern throne,
In a small dorp [2] till then for nothing fam'd,
And by the neighb'ring swains Thebais nam'd,
Eulogius liv'd : an humble mason he ;
In nothing rich, but virtuous poverty.
From noise and riot he devoutly kept,
Sigh'd with the sick, and with the mourner wept;
Half his earn'd pittance to poor neighbours went:
They had his alms, and he had his content.
Still from his little he could something spare
To feed the hungry, and to clothe the bare.
He gave whilst aught he had, and knew no
    bounds;            [pounds.
The poor man's drachma stood for rich men's
He learnt with patience, and with meekness
    taught;
His life was but the comment of his thought.
Hence, ye vain-glorious Shaftesburys, allow
That men had more religion then than now.
Whether they nearer liv'd to the blest times
When man's Redeemer bled for human crimes;
Whether the hermits of the desert fraught
With living practice, by example taught;
Or whether, with transmissive virtues fir'd,
(Which Chrysostoms all-eloquent inspir'd,)
They caught the sacred flame—I spare to say.
Religion's sun still shot an ev'ning ray.
On the south aspect of a sloping hill,
Whose skirts meand'ring Peneus washes still,
Our pious lab'rer pass'd his youthful days
In peace and charity, in pray'r and praise.

[11] Alluding to his famous inscription:
Quæ dat aquas saxo letet hospita Nympha sub
    imo;
Sic tu, cum dederis dona, latere velis.
                 Santol. Poem.
[1] About the year DXXVI.
[2] Dorp, a village, or more properly an hamlet.                    Dryden.
It is a German word, and adopted by our best
writers in the beginning and middle of the last
century.

No theatres of oaks around him rise,
Whose roots Earth's centre touch, whose heads
　　the skies:
No stately larch-tree there expands a shade
O'er half a rood [3] of Larisséan glade :
No lofty poplars catch the murm'ring breeze,
Which loit'ring whispers on the cloud-capp'd
Such imag'ry of greatness ill became 　[trees;
A nameless dwelling, and an unknown name!
Instead of forest-monarchs, and their train,
The unambitious rose bedeck'd the plain :
Trifoliate cytisus restrain'd its boughs
For humble sheep to crop, and goats to browze.
On skirting heights thick stood the clust'ring
　　vine,
And here and there the sweet-leav'd eglantine;
One lilac only, with a statelier grace,
Presum'd to claim the oak's and cedar's place,
And, looking round him with a monarch's care,
Spread his exalted boughs to wave in air.
　　This spot, for dwelling fit, Eulogius chose,
And in a month a decent home-stall rose,
Something, between a cottage and a cell.—
Yet Virtue here could sleep, and Peace could
　　dwell.
From living stone, (but not of Parian rocks)
He chipp'd his pavement, and he squar'd his
　　blocks:
And then, without the aid of neighbours' art,
Perform'd the carpenter's and glazier's part.
The site was neither granted him, nor giv'n;
'Twas Nature's; and the ground-rent due to
　　Heav'n.
Wife he had none : nor had he love to spare;
An aged mother wanted all his care.
They thank'd their Maker for a pittance sent,
Supp'd on a turnip, slept upon content.
Four rooms, above, below, this mansion grac'd,
With white-wash deckt, and river-sand o'er-cast:
The first, (forgive my verse if too diffuse,)
Perform'd the kitchen's and the parlour's use:
The second, better bolted and immur'd,
From wolves his out-door family secur'd :
(For he had twice three kids, besides their dams;
A cow, a spaniel, and two fav'rite lambs :)
A third, with herbs perfum'd, and rushes spread,
Held, for his mother's use, a feather'd bed :
Two moss-matrasses in the fourth were shown;
One for himself, for friends and pilgrims one.
　　A ground-plot square five hives of bees con-
　　tains;
Emblems of industry and virtuous gains [4]!
Pilaster'd jas'mines 'twixt the windows grew,
With lavender beneath, and sage and rue.
Pulse of all kinds diffus'd their od'rous pow'rs,
Where Nature pencils butterflies [5] on flow'rs :
Nor were the cole-worts wanting, nor the root
Which after-ages call Hybernian fruit:
There, at a wish, much chamomile was had ;
(The conscience of man's stomach good or bad ;)
Spoon-wort [6] was there, scorbutics to supply ;
And centaury to clear the jaundic'd eye;

[3] See note 12.
[4] Nullus, cum per cœlum licuit, otio periit
dies. 　　　　Plin. Hist. Natural, l. 1.
[5] All leguminous plants are, as the learned
say, papilionaceous, or bear butterflied flowers.
[6] Cochlearia. Spoon-wort is the old English
word for scurvy-grass.

And that [7], which on the Baptist's vigil sends
To nymphs and swains the vision of their friends,
Else physical and kitchen-plants alone
His skill acknowledge, and his culture own.
Each herb he knew, that works or good or ill,
More learn'd than Mesva [8], half as learn'd as
　　Hill;
For great the man, and useful without doubt,
Who seasons pottage—or expells the gout;
Whose science keeps life in, and keeps death
　　out!
No flesh from market-towns our peasant sought;
He rear'd his frugal meat, but never bought :
A kid sometimes for festivals he slew :
The choicer part was his sick neighbour's due:
Two bacon-flitches made his Sunday's cheer ;
Some the poor had, and some out-liv'd the year:
For roots and herbage, (rais'd at hours to spare)
With humble milk, compos'd his usual fare.
(The poor man then was rich, and liv'd with glee;
Each barley-head un-taxt, and day-light free :)
All had a part in all the rest could spare,
The common water [9], and the common air [10].
　　Mean while God's blessings made Eulogius
　　thrive,
The happiest, most contented man alive,
His conscience cheer'd him with a life well spent,
His prudence a superfluous something lent,
Which made the poor who took, and poor who
　　gave, content.
Alternate were his labours and his rest,
For ever blessing, and for ever blest,
Such kindness left men nothing to require,
Prevented wishing, and out-ran desire.
He sought, not to prolong poor lives, but save:
And that which others lend, he always gave.
Us'ry, a canker in fair virtue's rose,
Corrodes, and blasts the blossom e'er it blows:
So fierce, O Lucre, and so keen thy edge :
Thou tak'st the poor man's mill-stones for a
　　pledge [11]!
Eusebius, hermit of a neighb'ring cell, [well:
His brother Christian mark'd, and knew him
With zeal un-envying, and with transport fir'd,
Beheld him, prais'd him, lov'd him, and admir'd.
Convinc'd, that noiseless piety might dwell
In secular retreats, and flourish well;
And that Heav'n's king (so great a master He)
Had servants ev'ry where, of each degree.
" All-gracious Pow'r," he cries, " for forty years
I've liv'd an anchorete in pray'rs and tears :

[7] In imitation of Virgil :
　　"　———— Conon, & quis fuit alter
　　Descripsit radio? &c."

[8] An Arabian physician, well skilled in botany.
[9] Quid prohibietis aquas? Usus communis
　　aquarum est. 　　　　　Ovid. Met.
[10] ———— Et cunctis undamque auramque
　　patentem. 　　　　　Virg. Æn. vii.

But Ovid is still more explicite, Met. I.

　　——————Campum
Communemque prius, ceu lumina solis, &
　　auræ.
[11] " No man shall take the nether or upper
mill-stone to pledge; for he taketh a man's life
to pledge." 　　　　　Deut. ch. xxiv, v. 6.

Yon' spring, which bubbles from the mountain's
Has all the luxury of thirst supply'd :     [side,
The roots of thistles have my hunger fed, ·
Two roods [12] of cultur'd barley give me bread.
A rock my pillow, and green moss my bed.
The midnight clock attests my fervent pray'rs,
The rising Sun my orisons declares,
The live-long day my aspiration knows,
And with the setting Sun my vespers close !
Thy truth, my hope : thy Providence, my guard:
Thy grace, my strength : thy Heav'n, my last
    reward!
But, self-devoted from the prime of youth
To life sequester'd, and ascetic truth,
With fasting mortify'd, worn out with tears,
And bent beneath the load of sev'nty years,
I nothing from my industry can gain
To ease the poor man's wants, or sick man's
My garden takes up half my daily care, [pain:
And my field asks the minutes I can spare ;
While blest Eulogius from his pittance gives
The better half, and in true practice lives.
Heav'n is but cheaply serv'd with words and
I want that glorious virtue—to bestow! [show,
True Christianity depends on fact :
Religion is not theory, but act.
Men, seraphs, all, Eulogius' praise proclaim,
Who lends both sight and feet to blind and lame:
Who sooths th' asperity of hunger's sighs,
And dissipates the tear from mournful eyes ;
Pilgrims or wand'ring angels entertains ;
Like pious Abraham on Mamre's plains.
Ev'n to brute beasts his righteous care extends[13],
He feels their suff'rings, and their wants be-
        friends ;
From one small source so many bounties spring,
We lose the peasant, and suppose a king ;
A king of Heav'n's own stamp, not vulgar make ;
Blessed in giving, and averse to take !
Not such my pow'r ! Half-useless doom'd to
Pray'rs and advice are all I have to give : [live,
But all, whate'er my means or strength deny,
The virtues of Eulogius can supply.
Each, in the compass of his pow'r, he serves ;
Nor ever from his gen'rous purpose swerves:
Ev'n enemies to his protection run,
Sure of his light, as of the rising Sun.
What pity is it that so great a soul,
An heart so bountiful, should feel control ?
Warm in itself, by icy fortune dampt,
And in the effort of exertion crampt ;
Beneficent to all men, just, and true :
As Nature bounteous, and impartial too.
Thus sometimes have I seen an angel's mind
In a weak body wretchedly confin'd ;
A mind, O Constantine, which from thy throne
Can take no honours, and yet add her own !
  " Then hear me, gracious Heav'n, and grant
     my pray'r;
Make yonder man the fav'rite of thy care:
Nourish the plant with thy celestial dew,
Like manna let it fall, and still be new :
Expand the blossoms of his gen'rous mind,
Till the rich odour reaches half mankind.

   [12] Two roods, i. e. half an acre.
   [13] " The righteous man regardeth the life of
his beast."          Prov. ch. xii, v. 10.

Give him Bizantium's wealth, which useless
    shines,
Sicilian plenty, and the Indian mines;
Instead of Peneus, let Pactolus lave
His garden's precincts with a golden wave;
Then may his soul its free-born range enjoy,
Give deed to will, and ev'ry pow'r employ :
In him the sick a second Luke shall find ;
Orphans and widows, to his care consign'd,
Shall bless the father, and the husband kind :
Just steward of the bounty he receiv'd,
And dying poorer than the poor reliev'd !"
  So pray'd he, whilst an angel's voice from
    high
Bade him surcease to importune the sky :
Fate stopp'd his ears in an ill-omen'd day,
And the winds bore the warning sounds away;
Wild indistinction did their place supply ;
Half heard, half lost, th' imperfect accents die.
Little foresaw he that th' Almighty Pow'r,
Who feeds the faithful at his chosen hour,
Consults not taste, but wholesomeness of food,
Nor means to please their sense, but do them
Great was the miracle, and fitter too,    [good.
When draughts from Cherith's brook Elijah
    drew [14] :
And wing'd purveyors his sharp hunger fed
With frugal scraps of flesh, and maslin-bread [15].
On quails the humble prophet's pride might
    swell,
And high fed lux'ry prompt him to rebell.
  Nor dreamt our anchorete, that, if his friend
Should reach, O virtuous Poverty ! thy end,
That conscience and religion soon might fly
To some forsaken clime and distant sky.
Ign'rant of happiness, and blind to ruin,
How oft are our petitions our undoing !
Jephtha, with grateful sense of vict'ry fir'd,
Made a rash vow, and thought the vow inspir'd :
In piety the first, his daughter ran,     •
To hail with duteous voice the conq'ring man :
Well meaning, but unconscious of her doom,
She sought a blessing, and she found a tomb [16] !

   [14] 1 Kings, ch. xvii, v. 4, &c.
   [15] Maslin bread, i. e. miscellane, or miscellaneous bread, an ancient English word, given to
a plain sort of household bread. When people
in a middling station used it, they generally
mixed two gallons of oats and rye with six gallons of wheat. The poorer people mixed in
equal quantities wheat, barley, oats, rye, buckwheat, pulse, &c. But such is the luxury of the
present age (even amongst the poor) that not only
the thing but the very name is forgotten ; and a
preference given to a whiter, but more unwholesome sort of bread, if alum enters into the composition ; which, indeed, cannot be concealed.
  One of the first cares of a prime-minister (who
ought also to be considered as proveditor-general
of a kingdom) is to see the people supplied with
bread, of an wholesome nature, at as reasonable
a price as possible.
  Hence the great Gustavus used to say, "That
it required more talents to feed a large army
in the field, upon easy terms, in times of war,
than to conduct the fighting part."
   [16] Judges, ch. xi, v. 31.

The Pow'r Supreme, (my author so declares)
Heard with concern the erring hermit's pray'rs;
Heard disapproving; but at length inclin'd
To give a living lesson to mankind ;
That men thence-forward should submissive live;
And leave omniscience the free pow'r to give.—
For wealth or poverty, on man bestow'd,
Alike are blessings from the hand of God!
How often is the soul ensnar'd by health?
How poor.in virtue is the man of wealth.

The hermit's pray'r permitted, not approv'd ;
Soon in an higher sphere Eulogius mov'd :
Each sluice of affluent fortune open'd soon,
And wealth flow'd in at morning, night, and noon.

One day, in turning some uncultur'd ground,
(In hopes a fiee-stone quarry might be found)
His mattock met resistance, and behold
A casket burst, with di'monds fill'd and gold.
He cramm'd his pockets with the precious store,
And ev'ry night review'd it o'er and o'er;
Till a gay conscious pride, unknown as yet,
Touch'd a vain heart, and taught it to forget:
And, what still more his stagg'ring virtue try'd,
His mother, tut'ress of that virtue, dy'd.

A neighb'ring matron, not unknown to fame,
(Historians give her Teraminta's name,)
The parent of the needy and distress'd,
With large demesnes and well-sav'd treasure blest ;                            [store
(For like th' Egyptian prince [17] she hoarded
To feed at periodic dearths the poor ;)
This matron, whiten'd with good works and age,
Approach'd the sabbath of her pilgrimage ;
Her spirit to himself th' Almighty drew ;—
Breath'd on th' alembic, and exhal'd the dew.
In souls prepar'd, the passage is a breath
From time t'eternity, from life to death [18].
But first, to make the poor her future care,
She left the good Eulogius for her heir.

Who but Eulogius now exults for joy ?
New thoughts, new hopes, new views his mind employ.
Pride push'd forth buds at ev'ry branching shoot,
And virtue shrunk almost beneath the root.
High-rais'd on fortune's hill, new Alps he spies,
O'ershoots the valley which beneath him lies,
Forgets the depths between, and travels with his eyes.

The tempter saw the danger in a trice,
(For the man slidder'd upon fortune's ice:)
And, having found a corpse half-dead, half-warm,
Reviv'd it, and assum'd a courtier's form :
Swift to Thebais urg'd his airy flight ;
And measur'd half the globe in half a night.

With flowing manners exquisitely feign'd,
And accent soft, he soon admission gain'd :
Survey'd each out-work well, and mark'd apart
Each winding avenue that reach'd the heart;

Displaying, like th' illusive fiend of old,
Thrones deckt with gems, and realms of living gold [19].
Bad spirits oft intrude upon the good ;
Adonis' grot near Christ's presepio stood [20].
Th' artificer of fraud, (tho' here he fail'd,)
Straight chang'd approaches, and the ear assail'd;
This only chink accessible he finds ;
For flatt'ry's oil pervades ev'n virtuous minds.
Virtue, like towns well-fortify'd by art,
Has (spite of fore-sight) one deficient part.
With lenient artifice, and fluent tongue,
(For on his lips the dews of Hybla hung,)
Libanius like [21], he play'd the sophist's part,
And by soft marches stole upon the heart:
Maintain'd that station, gave new birth to sense,
Aud call'd forth manners, courage, eloquence :
Then touch'd with spritely dashes here and there,
(Correctly strong, yet seeming void of care,)
The master-topic, which may most men move,
The charms of beauty and the joys of love !
Eulogius faulter'd at the first alarms,
And soon the 'waken'd passions buzz'd to arms;
Nature the clam'rous bell of discord rung,
And vices from dark caverns swift up-sprung.
So, when Hell's monarch did his summons make,
The slumb'ring demons started from the lake.

Eulogius saw with pride, or seem'd to see,
(Not yet in act, but in the pow'r to be,)
Great merit lurking dormant in his mind :
He had been negligent—but Nature kind:
Till by degrees the vain, deluded elf,
Grew out of humour with his former self.
He thought his cottage small, and built in haste;
It had convenience but it wanted taste.
His mien was awkward ; graces he had none ;
Provincial were his notions and his tone;
His manners emblems of his own rough stone.
Then, slavish copyist of his copying friend,
He ap'd him without skill, and without end :
Larissa's gutturals convuls'd his throat;
He smooth'd his voice to the Bizántine note.
With courtly suppleness unfurl'd his face ;
Or screw'd it to the bonne mine of grimace;
With dignity he sneez'd, and cough'd with grace.
The pious mason once, had time no more
To mark the wants and mis'ry of the poor!
Suspicious thoughts his pensive mind employ,
A sullen gratitude, and clouded joy.
In days of poverty his heart was light;
He sung his hymns at morning, noon, and night.
Want sharpens poesy, and grief adorns ;
The spink [22] chants sweetest in a hedge of thorns [23].

[17] Gen. ch. xli, v. 35, &c.
[18] " The time in which we now live is borrowed from the space of our existence : what is past
is dead and vanished; what remaineth is daily
made less and less; insomuch that the whole
time of our life is nothing but a passage to death."
St. August. de Civitat. Dei, X.

[19] Matth. ch. v, v. 8.
[20] See Sandys's Travels into the Holy Land, folio, p. 138.
Presepio is an Italian word, taken from the
Latin, and signifies a stable or manger. It is now
become a term of art, and denotes any picture,
drawing, or print, where Christ is represented as
born in a stable or lying in the manger.
[21] A famous Greek rhetorician in the fourth
century, whose orations are still extant.
[22] Spink, the old poetical name for finches of
every sort. See Country Farm, by Surflet and
Markham, folio, printed in 1616.
[23] Sic Orig.

Tir'd of an house too little for his pride,
Tir'd of himself, and country friends beside,
He sometimes thought to build a mansion, fit
For state, and people it with men of wit ;
Knowing (by fame) small poets, small musi-
    cians,
Small painters, and still smaller politicians ;
Nor was the fee of ten-score minæ wanting,
To purchase taste in building and in planting.
A critic too he was, and rul'd the stage ;
The fashionable judgment [24] of his age :
When Crito once a panegyric show'd,
He beat him with the staff [25] of his own ode.
" Ah, what !" (he cry'd,) " are Pindar's flights
    to me ?
I love soft home-made sing-song, duty free.
Write me the style that lords and ladies speak ;
Or give me pastorals in Doric Greek :
I read not for instruction, but for ease ;
The opium of the pen is sure to please ;
Where limpid streams are clear, and sun-shine
    bright ;     [unite :
Where woos and coos, and loves and doves
Where simply married epithets are seen,
With gentle Hyphen keeping peace between.
Whipt cream ; unfortify'd with wine or sense !
Froth'd by the slatten-muse, Indifference ;
And deck'd (as after-ages more shall see)
With poor hedge-flow'rs, y-clept Simplicity !
Pert, and yet dull ; tawdry and mean withall ;
Fools for the future will it Nature call."
    He learnt his whims, and high-flown notions
    too,
Such as fine men adopt, and fine men rue ;
(Meer singularity the point in view.)
Julian with him was statesman, bard, and wit ;
Julian, who ten times miss'd, and one time hit ;
Who reason'd blindly, and more blindly writ.
Julian, who lov'd each sober mind to shock ;—
Who laugh'd at God, and offer'd to a cock.
He learn'd no small regard for Arius too :
And hinted what—nor he, nor Arius knew.
But most (as did his pregnant parts become)
He lov'd th' old pageantry of Pagan Rome.
Pompous idolatry with him was fashion ;
Nay, he once dream'd of transubstantiation.—
    Now, Muse, return, and tread thy course again ;
I only tell the story of a swain.
    Pirasmus (for that name the demon bore
Who nurs'd our spark in fashionable lore)
Lik'd well this way-ward vanity of mind,
But thought a country-stage a niche confin'd ;
Too cold for lux'ry, nor to folly kind :
Bizantium's hot-bed better serv'd his use,
The soil less stubborn, and more rank the juice.
    " My lord," he cries, (with looks and tone
    compos'd,
Whilst he the mischief of his soul disclos'd)
" Forgive me, if that title I afford
To one, whom nature meant to be a lord ;
How ill mean neighbourhood your genius suits ?
To live like Adam 'midst an herd of brutes !

[24] Critics in the reign of Charles II. called
themselves judgments. Hence Dryden says,

    —— A brother-judgment spare,
    He is, like you, a very wolf, or bear.

[25] Staff, i. e. Stanza. See Shakespeare, Cowley, and Dryden's Rival Ladies, Act I, sc. 2.

Leave the meer country to meer country-swains
And dwell where life in all life's glory reigns.
    "At six hours' distance from Bizantium's walls,
(Where Bosphorus into the Euxine falls)
In a gay district, call'd th' Elysian Vale [26],
A furnish'd villa stands, propos'd for sale :
Thither, for summer shade, the great resort ;
Each nymph a goddess, and each house a court :
Be master of the happier Lares there,
And taste life's grandeur in a rural air."
    He spoke.   Eulogius readily agreed,
And sign'd with eager joy the purchase-deed.
Div'd in the Theban vales an home-spun swain,
And rose a tawdry fop in Asia's plain.
Dame Nature gave him comeliness and health,
And Fortune (for a pass-port) gave him wealth.
The beaux extoll'd him, the coquets approv'd ;
For a rich coxcomb is by instinct lov'd.
Swift Atalanta (as the story's told [27])
Felt her feet bird-lim'd to the earth with gold :
The youth [28] had wealth, with no unpleasing
    face ;
That, and the golden apples, won the race :
Had he been swifter than the swiftest wind,
And a poor wit,—he still had sigh'd behind.—
    Here Satin vanish'd :—he had fresh com-
    mands—
And knew, his pupil was in able hands.
    And now the treasure found, and matron's
    store,
Sought other objects than the tatter'd poor,
Part to humiliated Apicius went,
A part to gaming confessors was lent,
And part, O virtuous Thais, paid thy rent !
Poor folks have leisure hours to fast and pray,
Our rich man's bus'ness lay another way :
No farther intercourse with Heav'n had he,
But left good works to men of low degree :
Warm as himself pronounc'd each ragged man,
And bade distress to prosper as it can :
Till, grown obdurate by meer dint of time,
He deem'd all poor men rogues, and want a
    crime [29].
    By chance he ancient amities forgot,
Or else expung'd them with one wilful blot :
Nor knew he God nor man, nor faith nor friends,
But for by-purposes and worldly ends.
No single circumstance his mind dismay'd,
But his low extract, and once humble trade ;
These thoughts he strove to bury in expense,
Rich meat, rich wines, and vain magnificence :
Weak as the Roman chief, who strove to hide
His father's cot, (and once his father's pride,)

[26] Sic Orig.
[27] Ovid. Met. l. x, v. 666.
[28] Hippomenes.
[29] " Why dost thou doat on the image of a
king stamped on coin, and despisest the image
of God that shines in human nature ?"
                         St. August.
    Minutius Felix addresses himself very pathe-
tically to great and opulent men devoid of charity and alms-giving :
    " A man," says he, " asks bread of you :—
Whilst your horses champ upon bridles whose
bits are gilt with gold, the people die with hunger :—whereas one of your diamonds might save
the lives of an hundred families."

By casing a low shed of rural mould
With marble walls, and roof adorn'd with gold[30].
Who but Eulogius now is prais'd and known,
The very ignis fatuus of the town?
Our ready scholar in a single year
Could lie, forget, swear, flatter, and forswear [31].
Rough to the tim'rous, timid with the brave,
'Midst wits a witling, and with knaves a knave.

Fame, not contented with her broad high way,
Delights,for change, thro' private paths to stray;
And, wand'ring to the hermit's distant cell,
Vouchsaf'd Eulogius' history to tell.

At night a dream confirm'd the hermit more;
He started, scream'd, and sweat from ev'ry pore.
He dream'd that on his throne th' Almighty sate
In th' awful valley of Jehoshaphat [32],
Where, underneath a spreading cedar's shade,
He 'spy'd his friend on beds of roses laid;
Round him a crowd of threat'ning furies stands,
With instruments of vengeance in their hands.

The judge supreme soon cast a stedfast eye,
(Stern, yet attemper'd with benignity,)
On the rash hermit; who with impious pray'r,
Had been the sponsor of another's care.
" Wretch, thou art lost in part, and in the
whole!
Is this the mortgage for thy brother's soul?"

An apoplex of dread Eusebius shook:
Despairing Judas glar'd in all his look,
Trembling he fell before th' Almighty-throne;
Importunate as Abraham [33] t'attone
For others' crimes: " O Pow'r Supreme," said
he,                                   [see:
" Grant me, once more, th' ungrateful wretch to
Suspend thy doom till then : on Christian ground
No graceless monster, like my friend, is found."

He spoke, and wak'd aghast : he tore his hair,
And rent his sack-cloth garments in despair;
Walk'd to Constantinople, and inquir'd
Of all he met; at length the house desir'd
By chance he found, but no admission gain'd;
A Thracian slave the porter's place maintain'd,
(Sworn foe to thread-bare suppliants,) and with
pride
His master's presence, nay, his name, deny'd.

There walk'd Eusebius at the dawn of light,
There walk'd at noon, and there he walk'd at
night,
In vain.—At length, by Providence's care,
He found the door unclos'd, nor servants near.
He enter'd, and thro' sev'ral rooms of state
Pass'd gently; in the last Eulogius sate.
" Old man, good morrow," the gay courtier
cry'd;
" God give you grace, my son," the sire reply'd;

30 Sic Orig.
31 " Those who are accustomed to swear often may sometimes by chance happen to forswear: as he that indulges his tongue in talking
frequently speaks that which he blushes for in
silence."                          St. Chrysost.
   Again, St. Jerom adds, " Let thy tongue be a
stranger to lying and swearing; on the contrary,
let the love of truth be so strongly in thee, that
thou countest whatever thou sayest to be sealed
with an oath."
32 Joel, ch. iii, v. 12.
33 Gen. ch. xviii, v. 23—33.

And then, in terms as moving and as strong,
As clear, as ever fell from angel's tongue,
Besought, reprov'd, exhorted, and condemn'd:—
Eulogius knew him, and tho' known, contemn'd.
The hermit then assum'd a bolder tone;
His rage was kindled, and his patience gone.
" Without respect to titles or to place,
I call thee" (adds he) " miscreant to thy face.
My pray'rs drew down Heav'n's bounty on thy
And in an evil hour my wishes sped.   [head,
Ingratitude's black curse thy steps attend,
Monster to God, and faithless to thy friend !"

With all the rage of an insulted man
The courtier call'd his slaves, who swiftly ran;
" Androtion, Geta, seize this aged fool,
See him well-scourg'd, and send him back to
school.
Teach the old chronicle, in future times
To bear no mem'ry but of poor rogues' crimes. '

The hermit took the chastisement, and went
Back to Thebaïs full of discontent;
Saw his once impious rashness more and more,
And, victim to convinc'd contrition, bore
With Christian thankfulness the marks he wore.
And then on bended knees with tears and sighs
He thus invok'd the Ruler of the skies:
" My late request, All-gracious Pow'r, forgive!
And—that yon miscreant may repent, and live,
Give him that poverty which suits him best,
And leave disgrace and grief to work the rest."

So pray'd the hermit, and with reason pray'd.
Some plants the sun-shine ask, and some the
shade.                                [bloom
At night the nure-trees spread, but check their
At morn, and lose their verdure and perfume.
The virtues of most men will only blow,
Like coy auriculas, in Alpine snow [33];
Transplant them to the equinoctial line,
Their vigour sickens, and their tints decline.—
Heav'n to its predilected children grants
The middle space 'twixt opulence and wants.
   Meanwhile Eulogius, un-abash'd and gay,
Pursu'd his courtly track without dismay :
Remorse was hood-wink'd, conscience charm'd
away.
Reason the felon of herself was made,
And Nature's substance hid by Nature's shade!
   Our fine man, now completed, quickly found
Congenial friends in Asiatic ground.
Th' advent'rous pilot in a single year
Learn'd his state-cock-boat dextrously to steer;
Versatile, and sharp-piercing like a screw,
Made good th' old passage, and still forc'd a new:
For, just as int'rest whiffled on his mind,
He Anatolians left, or Thracians join'd;
Caught ev'ry breeze, and sail'd with ev'ry tide;
But still was mindful of the lee-ward side:
Still mark'd the pinnacle of fortune's height,
And bark'd—to be made turn-spit of the state.
   By other arts he learns the knack to thrive;
The most obsequious parasite alive:
Camelion of the court, and country too :
Pays Cesar's tax, but gives the mob their due;
And makes it, in his conscience, the same thing
To crown a tribune, or behead a king :

33 This flower was discovered under the snow,
at the feet of some ice-mountains amongst the
Alps.

All things to all men ;—and (himself to please)
Assimulates [34] each colour which he sees.
If patriots pay him, willow-wreaths he bears,
And coats of filamotte [35] complexion wears ;
If statesmen pay him better, a fresh hue
Brightens his garb ; more brilliant as more new;
Court-turquoise, and indelible of blue.
Thus weather-cocks by ev'ry wind are blown,
And int'rest oils a motion, not their own. [call,
How strangely crowds misplace things, and mis-
Madness in one is liberty in all !
    On less important days, he pass'd his time
In virtuoso-ship, and crambo-rhyme:
In gaming, jobbing, fiddling, painting, drinking,
And ev'ry art of using time, but thinking.
He gives the dinners of each up-start man,
As costly, and luxurious, as he can ;
Then weds an heiress of suburbian mould,
Ugly as apes ; but well endow'd with gold;
There Fortune gave him his full dose of strife,
A scolding woman, and a jealous wife !
    T' increase this load, some sycophant-report
Destroy'd his int'rest and good grace at court.
At this one stroke the man look'd dead in law:
His flatt'rers scamper, and his friends withdraw [36].
Some men (as Holy Writ fortelleth right)
Have one ways entrance, but have sev'n ways
    flight [37].
    "I never lik'd the wretch," says one: another
Opines [38] in the same language with his brother:
A third, with mystic shrug and winking eye,
Suspects him for a dervise and a spy.
" Pray, sir, the crime?".—The monarch frown'd
    —no more,
The fellow's guilty, and his bus'ness o'er [39].
    And now (to shorten my disast'rous tale)
Storms of affronts pour'd in as thick as hail.
Each scheme for safety mischievously sped,
And the drawn sword hung o'er him by a thread.

[34] Protinus assimulat tetigit quoscunque co-
lores.                    Ovid. Met. XV. v. 411.
[35] Filamotte (Dryden) is that " clouded mixture of crimson, yellow, and umber-colours,
which are seen in the beginning of winter on a
falling leaf." Filamotte, quasi feüeille morte.
Thus Isabella-colour denotes a certain grave colour worn by the infanta Isabella Clara Eugenia,
arch-dutchess of Austria, &c. 1625. For gride-
line, see the Vision of Death, page 373, note 23.
[36] " A friend cannot be known in prosperity,
and an enemy cannot be hidden in adversity."
                    Ecclus. ch. xii.
[37] Deut. ch. xxviii, v. 7.
[38] Opines, i. e. gives his opinion. Mr. Pope,
from the French.
[39] ——— Nunquam, si quid mihi credis, amavi
    Huncce hominem.  Sed quo cecidit sub cri-
    . mine! Quisquam
    Delator ? Quibus indiciis, quo teste proba-
    vit ?                            [venit
    Nil horum.  Verbosa, et grandis epistola
    A Capreis.  Bene habet, nil plus inter-
    rogo.—
                    Juven. Sat. X, v. 68.
    To such sort of worldly connexions may be ap-
plied the golden saying of St. Chrysostom,
" meum and tuum are almost incompatible
words."                    Orat. in Philagon.

Child he had none.  His wife with sorrow dy'd,
Few women can survive the loss of pride.
    Meanwhile the demon, who was absent far,
(Engag'd in no less work than civil war)
Perceiv'd th' approaching wreck ; and, in a trice
Appearing, gave both comfort and advice.
    " Great geniuses," he cry'd, " must ne'er
    despair;
The wise and brave usurp on Fortune's care!
The un-exhausted funds of human wit
Oft miss one object, and another hit;
The man of courts who trusts to one poor hole,
Is a low foolish fool [40], and has no soul :
Disgraces my respected patronage:   [age [41];
And, gaining Heav'n, becomes the jest of th'
Court-loyalty is a precarious thing:   [king ;
When the king's trump, time-servers serve the
But, when he's out of luck, they shift their sail,
And popularity's the fav'rite gale:
Vain popularity ! which fancy shrouds,
Like Juno's shade, in party-colour'd clouds.
Each man will go a mile to see you crown'd
With civic wreaths, till Earth and skies resound;
And each man will go two to see you drown'd.
    " Whoever hopes in dang'rous times to rise,
Must learn to shoot swift Fortune as she flies:
Capricious phantom ! never at a stay ;
Just seen, and lost; when nearest, far away !
But, to be brief; (and mark my judgment well)
Your fortunes totter'd, when old Justin fell ;
His successor [42], as you and all men know,
Is kind, when friend ; and un-appeas'd, when
    foe ;
Some sly court-vermin, wriggling in his ear,
Has whisper'd, what predicts your ruin near :
Then cast thy die of fortune all at once ;
Learn to be any thing but dupe or dunce.
Fortune assists the brave.  Plunge boldly in;
T' attempt, and fail, is a poor sneaking sin.
Hypatius (with pretensions not the worst)
Affects the throne: be thou to join the first:
'Tis not a crime too worldly wise to be ;—
Or (if it is) discharge the crime on me."
    Thus weak Eulogius, by false greatness aw'd,
Listen'd—unto th' artificer of fraud: [throne:
The doctrine came not from th' all-righteous
When Satan tells a lie, 'tis all his own [43].
    He spoke, and vanish'd.  Swift Eulogius fled,
And to the emulous of empire sped.

[40] " A fool in his folly.".
                    Prov. of Solom. ch. xvii, v. 12.
[41] The son of Sirach, in opposition to these
false and dangerous notions, justly remarks :
" Observe the opportunity, and beware of evil :
be not ashamed when it concerneth thy soul,"
                    Ecclus. ch. iv, v. 20.
    Isaiah's advice is very noble: " Fear not the
reproach of men, neither be ye afraid of their
revilings: for the moth shall eat them up as a
garment, and the worm shall eat them like
wool; but my salvation shall be for ever."
                    Ch. li, v. 7, 8.
" I, even I, am he that comforteth you.
Why shouldst thou be afraid of a man that shall
die, and forgetteth the Lord thy Maker, who
stretched forth the Heavens?" Ibid. v. 12, 13.
[42] Justinian.
[43] John, ch. viii, v. 44.

Here, were it not too long, I might declare
The motives and successes of the war,
The prowess of the knights, their martial deeds,
Their swords, their shields, their surcoats [44] and
Till Belisarius at a single blow    [their steeds:
Suppress'd the faction and repell'd the foe.
By a quick death the traitors he reliev'd ;
Condemn'd, if taken; famish'd, if repriev'd.

Now see Eulogius (who had all betray'd
Whate'er he knew) in loathsome dungeon laid :
A pris'ner, first of war, and then of state:
Rebel and traitor ask a double fate !
But good Justinian, whose exalted mind
(In spite of what Pirasmus urg'd) inclin'd
To mercy, soon the forfeit-life forgave,
And freed it from the shackles of a slave.
Then spoke with mild, but in majestic strain,
" Repent and haste thee to Larissa's plain,
Or wander thro' the world, another Cain.
Thy lands and goods shall be the poor man's lot,
Or feed the orphans you've so long forgot."

Forsaken, helpless, recognised by none,
Proscrib'd Eulogius left th' unprosp'rous town :
For succour at a thousand doors he knock'd ;
Each heart was harden'd, and each door was
                        lock'd ;
A pilgrim's staff he bore, of humble thorn ;
Pervious to winds his coat, and sadly torn:
Shoes he had none : a beggar gave a pair,
Who saw feet poorer than his own, and bare.
He drank the stream, on dew-berries he fed,
And wildings harsh supply'd the place of bread ;
Thus homeward urg'd his solitary way ;
(Four years had he been absent to a day.)
Fame thro' Thebais his arrival spread,
Half his old friends reproach'd him, and half
Of help and common countenance bereft, [fled:
No creature own'd him, but a dog he left.
Compunction touch'd his soul, and, wiser made
By bitter suff'rings, he resum'd his trade :    `
Thank'd Heav'n for want of pow'r and want of
                  pelf,
That he had lost the world, and found himself.
Conscience and charity reviv'd their part,
And true humility enrich'd the heart,
While grace celestial with enliv'ning ray
Beam'd forth, to gild the ev'ning of his day.
His neighbours mark'd the change, and each
              man strove
By slow degrees t' applaud him, and to love.
So Peter, when his tim'rous guilt was o'er,
Emerg'd, and stood twice firmer than before [45].

Eusebius, who had long in silence mourn'd,
Rejoic'd to hear the prodigal return'd ;
And with the eagerness of feeble age
Made haste t' express his joy, and griefs assuage.
" My son," he cry'd, " once more contem-
       plate me :
Behold th' unhappy wretch that ruin'd thee;
My ill-judg'd pray'rs (in luckless moments sped)
Brought down the curse of riches on thy head.
No language can express one single part
Of what I felt, and what still racks my heart.

[44] Surcoat, an upper garment of defence.
                         Dryden.

[45] See Luke, ch. xxii, v. 55—62.
" Peter stood more firmly, after he had lamented his fall, than before he fell."
                      St. Ambrose.

Vainly I thought, that, to increase thy store,
Was to increase Heav'n's manna for the poor.
Man's virtue cannot go beyond its length;
God's gifts are still proportioned to our strength.
The scripture-widow [46] gives her well-sav'd mite
With affluent joy, nor fears to suffer by't :
Whilst Dives' heaps (the barter of his soul)
Lie bury'd in some base inglorious hole,
Or on the wings of pomp and lux'ry fly,
Accurst by Heav'n, and dead to charity [47]!
The charitable few are chiefly they
Whom Fortune places in the middle way [48];
Just rich enough, with economic care,
To save a pittance, and a pittance spare :
Just poor enough to feel the poor man's moan,
Or share those suff'rings which may prove their
            own !—
Great riches, with insinuating art,
Debase the man, and petrify the heart.
Let the false friend, like Satan, be withstood,
Who wishes us more wealth—to do more good !
To this great trial some are equal found ;
Most in th' unnavigable stream are drown'd [49]."
   He spoke : and, with a flood of tears opprest,
Left his Eulogius to divine the rest.
" Father," he cry'd, (and with complacence
         smil'd)             [child,
" Heav'n's trials have at length reclaim'd its
Omniscience only can our wants fore-know,
And All-beneficence will best bestow.
Some few God's bounty on the poor employ :
There are—whom to promote, is to destroy !
Rough, thorny, barren, is pale virtue's road ;
And poisons are true cures when giv'n by God,
Spontaneous I resign, with full accord,
The empty nothings wealth and pow'r afford ;
My mind's my all, by Heav'n's free grace re-
         stor'd.
O Pow'r Supreme! unsearchable thy views!
Omniscient, or to give, or to refuse !
Grant me, as I begun, to end my days
In acts of humble charity and praise ;
In thy own paths my journey let me run,
And, as in Heav'n, on Earth thy will be done !"

[46] Luke, ch. xxi, v. 2.   2 Cor. ch. viii, v. 12.
[47] " God is not honoured with our expending
that money which is bedewed with the tears of
the oppressed.           St. Chrysost.
[48] The truly charitable man, (who happens to
be neither rich nor poor) is well painted by an
ancient classic.  I quote the verses, because I
never saw them quoted :

                —————— Cujus
Nou frontem vertêre minæ ; sed candida semper
Gaudia, & in vultu curarum ignara voluptas.
Non tibi sepositas infelix strangulat arca
Divitias ; avidéve animum dispendia torquent
Fœnoris expositi census ; sed docta fruendi
Temperies, &c.

[49] Hugo, in his excellent treatise De Anima,
makès the following remark upon greatness and
ambition:
   " The human heart is a small thing, and yet
desireth great matters.  It is barely sufficient
for a kite's dinner, and yet the whole world suf-
ficeth it not,"

Thus he maintain'd Almighty Wisdom's cause.
The Sun shone forth—The hermit pleas'd with-
draws—
And Nature wore an aspect of applause.

---

## MACARIUS; OR, THE CONFESSOR.

*Da vocem magno, Pater, ingeniumque dolori.*
Stat. Epiced. Patris.

### AN EPISTLE TO THE REV. DR. ROBERT HORT,
### CANON OF WINDSOR.

ALL sober poets with thy bard [1] agree,
Who sung, " That truth was truest poetry."—
Alike to me, and the deceas'd, a friend ;
O Hort, to these my pious strains attend.
Thou knew'st the man; and thy good sense is
uch,
I dare not say too little or too much.—
Under his eye the self same views combin'd
Our studies, and one horoscope conjoin'd.
He check'd th' impatient wand'rings of our youth,
And grafted on our fancy facts and truth.
Together we amus'd our youthful prime,
Days seem'd but hours, and time improv'd on
time:
Mindless of cares, (and how they pass'd or came)
Our sports, our labours, and our rest the same [2].
See'st thou yon yews, by pensive nature
made
For tears, and grief, and melancholy shade ;
Wide o'er the church they spread an awful light,
Than day more serious, half-compos'd as night,
(There, where the winding Kennet gently laves
Britannia's Lombardy [3] with silver waves;)
There sleeps Macarius, foe to pomp and pride;
Who liv'd contented, and contented dy'd.
Say, shall the lamp were Tullia was entomb'd,
Burn twice sev'n ages, and be un-consum'd ?
And not one verse be sacred to a name
Endear'd by virtuous deeds and silent fame ?
True fame demands not panegyric aid;
The fun'ral torch burns brightest in the shade;
Too fast it blazes, fann'd by public air ;—
Thus blossoms fall, before their tree can bear.
True fame, like porc'lain earth, for years must
lay
Bury'd, and mix'd with elemental clay [4].
His younger days were not in trifling spent,
For pious Hall [5] a kind inspection lent :

[1] Cowley. See his Davideis.
[2] These eight lines are imitated from a famous
passage in Persius, Sat. V, too well known to be
reprinted. It begins— '

Geminos horoscope— &c.

[3] Berkshire.
[4] It is reported that the Chinese beat and mix
thoroughly together the composition that makes
porcelain, and then bury it in a deep bed of clay
for an hundred years. See Dr. Donne's Letters.
See also the Discovery of Hidden Treasure, 4to.
London, 1656, p 89 ; (a very scarce and curious
work, by the famous Gabriel Plattes.)
[5] Mr. John Hall, master of Pembroke College,

He show'd him what to seek and what to shun:—
Harcourt [6] with him the thorny journey run,
Companion of his studies ; and a friend
Sincere in youth, and stedfast to the end.
Courts and the world he knew, but not admir'd;
He travell'd thro' them wisely, and retir'd :
Giving to solitude and heav'nly care
Those moments which the worldling cannot spare.
Thus, half a century, his course he run
Of pray'r and praises, daily, like the sun:
Happy! who truth invariably pursues,
And well-earn'd fame by better fame renews [7] !
His books, like friends were chosen, few and
Constantly us'd and truly understood. [good;
The Sacred Scriptures were his chief delight [8];
Task of the day, and vision of the night :
Truth's second sources he with care survey'd,
And walk'd with Hermas in the rural shade [9].
Cyprian with awful gravity he sought ;
And true simplicity Ignatius brought ;
Lively Minucius did his hours beguile ;
Lactantius charm'd with elegance of style ;
But mostly Chrysostom engag'd his mind :
Great without labour, without art refin'd !
Now see his gentle elocution flows,
Soft as the flakes of heav'n-descending snows ;
Now see him, like th' impetuous torrent, roll ;
Pure in his diction, purer in his soul :
By few men equall'd, and surpass'd by none;
A Tully and Demosthenes in one [10] !

Oxford, in 1667, and rector of St. Aldate's in the
same university. Created D D. in 1669; elected Margaret professor in 1676 ; and consecrated
bishop of Bristol the 12th of June, 1691. All
which preferments he enjoyed together.
[6] Mr. Simon Harcourt, afterwards lord chancellor Harcourt, offered him a bishopric from
queen Anne many years after the Revolution; but
the favour was declined with grateful acknowledgments.
[7] " Surely vain are all men by nature, who are
ignorant of God ; and could not, out of the good
things that are seen, know him. That is, neither, by considering the works did they acknowledge the work-master."
Wisd. of Sol. ch. xiii, v. 1.
[8] He employed ten or twelve hours a day in
study, without any interruption, but that of casual sickness for fifty years successively. His
principal business was in referring every difficult
part of Scripture to those particular passages in
the fathers, and eminent modern divines, who
had explained them expressly or occasionally.
[9] Alluding to a work entituled the Shepherd of
Hermas. Hermas was cotemporary with some
of the apostles.
[10] In order to judge a little of these two assertions, be pleased only to read St. Chrysostom's
Homily on the Ten Talents, or his Commentary
on St. Matthew ; and his Orations to the People
of Antioch. ΠΕΡΙ ΑΝΔΡΙΑΝΤΩΝ.
See also Ferrarius De Concione Veterum, and
the Eloquence Crétienne of M. Gisbert : the last
of which works was a favourite book with the late
lord Somers, and wrought a great effect on his
future way of thinking.
This anecdote was imparted to me by the
late Mr. Elijah Fenton, as matter of fact on his
own knowledge.

Something at cheerful intervals was due
To Roman classics, and Athenian too.
Plato with raptures did his soul inspire;
Plotinus fann'd the Academic ' fire
Then came the Stagyrite;—whose excellence
Beams forth in clearness, brevity, and sense!
  Next, for amusement' sake, he turn'd his
    eyes
To them, whom we despoil, and then despise:
Fore-most of these, unrivall'd Shakespeare stands;
With Hooker, Raleigh, Chillingworth, and
    Sands 12;—
(For in those days " were giants in our lands !'')
Thus, like the bee, he suck'd from ev'ry flow'r,
And hour surpass'd the predecessor hour.
Latimer's father 13 was his type of yore,
Little he had, but something for the poor;
And oft on better days the board was spread
With wholesome meat and hospitable bread.
Poor in himself, men poorer he reliev'd,
And gave the charities he had receiv'd.
  The midnight-lamp, in crystal case enclos'd,
Beams bright; nor is to winds nor rain's ex-
    pos'd:
A watch-tow'r to the wand'rers of mankind;
Forlorn, belated, and with passions blind 14,

11 Academic is used in the Horatian sense of
the word :

Atque inter sylvas Academi quærere verum.

12 Edwyn Sandys, archbishop of York, was
one of the first eminent reformers, not only of our
holy religion, (which almost every person knows)
but of our language (which circumstance few
persons are apprized of). His sermons the time
when he preached them being duly considered)
may be looked upon as a master-piece of eloquence and fine writing. They were chiefly
preached between the years 1550 and 1576.
His son George (and here let me be understood to refer chiefly to his Paraphrase on Job)
knew the true harmony of the English heroic
couplet long before Denham and Waller took up
the pen; and preserved that harmony more uniformly. Variety perhaps was wanting; which
Dryden afterwards supplied, but not till he came
to the forty-fifth year of his age; namely, till
the time he published Aurengzebe.

13 Bishop Hugh Latimer (whom I quote only
by memory, not having the original at hand)
says, in one of his sermons preached at St. Paul's
Cross, about the year ——, " that tho' his father possessed no more than 40 acres of free land,
or thereabouts, yet he had always something to
give to the poor, and now and then entertained his friends;—that he portioned out' three
daughters, at 5l. a piece, and bred up a son at
the university; (otherwise adds he,) I should not
have had the honour of appearing in this pulpit
before the king's majesty."
Note, The original edition says 4 acres, which
must be an errour of the press, instead of 40
acres. Old Latimer lived in good repute about
the year 1470, in which year his son Hugh was
born.

14 Palantesque homines passim, ac rationis
    egentes,
Despectare procul.          Ovid. Met.

Who tread the foolish round their fathers trod
And,'midst life's errours,hit on death's by-road 15.
  'Midst racking pains 16 his mind was calm and
    ev'n;
Patience and cheerfulness to him were giv'n;
Patience! the choicest gift on this side Heav'n !
His strength of parts surviv'd the sev'ntieth year,
And then, like northern fruits, left off to bear;
Nought but a vestal fire such heat contains;
Age seldom boasts so prodigal remains 17.
Some few beyond life's usual date are cast:
Prime clusters of the grape 18 till winter last.
To these a sacred preference is giv'n:
Each shaft is polish'd, and th' employer Heav'n 19.
  Jeffr**s (if that were possible) restrain'd '
His fury, when you mournfully complain'd 21
And Kirk's barbarians, hard as harden'd steel,
Forgot their Lybia, and vouchsaf'd to feel.
  When crowns were doubtful, and when num-
    bers steer'd
As honour prompted, or self-int'rest veer'd,
(Times! when the wisest of mankind might err,
And, lost in shadows, wrong or right, prefer;)
The tempter, in a vapour's form 21, arose,
And o'er his eyes a dubious twilight throws,
To lead him, puzzling, o'er fallacious ground,
Suborn his passions, and his sense confound:
Pomp to foretaste, and mitres pre-descry;
(For mists at once enlarge and multiply;)
Our hero paus'd—and, weighing either side,
Took poverty, and conscience for his guide:
For he, who thinks he suffers for his God,
Deserves a pardon, tho' he feels the rod.
Yet blam'd he none; (himself in honour clear;)
That were a crime had cost his virtue dear !
Thus all he lov'd; and party he had none,
Except with charity, and Heav'n alone.
In his own friends some frailties he allow'd;
These were too singular, and those too proud.
Rare spirit ! in the midst of party-flame,
To think well-meaning men are half the same !

Sed nil dulcius est, bene quàm munita tenere
Edita doctrinâ sapientûm templa, serena,
Despicere unde queas alios, passimque videre
Errare, atque viam palantes quærere vitæ.
                          Lucret. L. II, v. 6.

15 Wisd. of Sol. ch. i, v. 12.
16 In the last year of his life Macarius was
grievously afflicted with nephritic pains.
17 ———— Cui vix certaverit ulla
    Aut tantùm fluere, aut totidem durare per
    annos,                     Virg. Georg. 2.
18 2 Esdras, ch. xii, v. 42.
19 Isaiah xlix, v. 2. " A polished shaft in the
quiver of God."
20 When judge Jeffr**s came to Taunton assizes, in the year 1685, to execute his commission upon the unfortunate people concerned in
Monmouth's rebellion, the person here spoken
of being minister of St. Mary Magdalen's church
at Taunton, waited on him in private, and remonstrated much against his severities. The
judge listened to him calmly, and with some attention; and, though he had never seen him before, advanced him in a few months to a prebendal stall in the cathedral church of Bristol.
21 See Sandys's Paraphrase on Job, where Satan arises in form of an exhalation.

B—— sometimes would to thy cottage tend;  
An'artful enemy, but seeming friend :  
Conscious of having plann'd thy worldly fate [22],  
He could not love thee, and he durst not hate.  
But then seraphic Ken was all thy own ;  
And he [23], who long declin'd Ken's vacant throne,  
Begging with earnest zeal to be deny'd ;—  
By worldlings laught at, and by fools decry'd :  
Dodwell was thine, the humble and resign'd ;  
Nelson, with Christian elegance of mind ;  
And he [24], whose tranquil mildness from afar  
Spoke him a distant, but a brilliant star.  
These all forsook their homes—Nor sigh'd nor  
     wept ;—  
Mammon they freely gave, but God they kept.  
Ah, look on honours with Macarius' eyes,  
Snares to the good, and dangers to the wise !  
    In silence for himself, for friends in tears,  
He wander'd o'er the desert forty [25] years.  
The cloud and pillar (or by night or day)  
Reviv'd his heart, and ascertain'd the way [26].  
His sandals fail'd not ; and his robes untorn  
Escap'd the bramble and entangling thorn [27].  
Heav'n purify'd for him th' embitter'd well [28],  
And manna from aërial regions fell [29].  
At length near peaceful Pisgah [30] he retir'd,  
And found that rest his pilgrimage requir'd :  
Where, as from toils he silently withdrew,  
Half Palestina [31] open'd on his view:  
" Go, pious hermit," groves and mountains cry'd :  
" Enter, thou faithful servant," Heav'n reply'd.  
    Mild as a babe reclines himself to rest,  
And smiling sleeps upon the mother's breast,  
Tranquil, and with a patriarch's hopes, he gave  
His soul to Heav'n, his body to the grave;  
And with such gentleness resign'd his breath,  
That 'twas a soft extinction, and not death.

[22] Bishop Ken used to say, that king William and queen Mary would gladly have permitted the non-juring bishops and clergy (who had just before signalized themselves in a steady opposition to popery) to have enjoyed their preferments till death, upon their parole of honour given, that they would never disturb the government ; which favour would have been thankfully accepted of, and complied with, by the aforesaid bishops, &c. ; but somebody here alluded to (at least as Macarius thought) traversed their majesties' gracious intentions. In proof of this, bishop Ken performed the funeral service over Mr. Kettlewell in the year 1695, and prayed for king William and queen Mary.

[23] Dr. George Hooper. N. B. It must here also be remembered, that Dr. Beveridge, refused to succeed bishop Ken in 1691, and then the offer was made to R. Kidder, D. D.

[24] Mr. John Kettlewell, vicar of Coleshill in Warwickshire.

[25] See Exodus, passim. Psalm xcv, v. 10. Hebr. ch. iii, v. 17.

[26] Exod. ch. xiii, v. 21.

[27] Deut. ch. viii, v. 4.

[28] Waters of Marah. Exod. ch. xv, v. 23—25.

[29] Ibid. ch. xvi, v. 15 and 35.

[30] Deut. xxxiv, v. 1.

[31] Palestina is the Scripture word for Palestine. Isaiah twice, ch. xiv, v. 29, 31. Exod. ch. xv, v. 14.

Happy ! who thus, by unperceiv'd decay,  
Absent themselves from life, and steal away [32]  
    Accept this verse, to make thy mem'ry live,  
Lamented shade !—'Tis all thy son can give.  
Better to own the debt we cannot pay,  
Than with false gold thy fun'ral rites defray.  
Vainly my Muse is anxious to procure  
Gifts unavailing, empty sepulture [33] ;  
As vainly she expands her flutt'ring wings:  
She is no swan, nor, as she dies, she sings.  
He, that would brighten ancient di'monds, must  
Clear and re-polish them with di'mond dust:  
That task is not for me : the Muses lore  
Is lost;—For Pope and Dryden are no more !  
    O Pope ! too great to copy, or to praise ;  
(Whom envy sinks not, nor encomiums raise;)  
Forgive this grateful tribute of my lays.  
Milton alone could Eden lost re-gain ;  
And only thou portray Messiah's reign.  
O early lost ! with ev'ry grace adorn'd !  
By me (so Heav'ns ordain it) always mourn'd.  
By thee the good Macarius was approv'd:  
Whom Fenton honour'd, and Philotheüs lov'd [34].  
   My first, my latest bread, I owe to thee :  
Thou, and thy friends, preserv'd my Muse and  
      me.  
By proxy, from a gen'rous kindred spread,  
Thy Craggs's bounty fell upon my head [35]:  
Thy Mordaunt's [36] kindness did my youth en-  
      gage,  
And thy own Chesterfield protects my age.

---

## BOETIUS:

### OR, THE UPRIGHT STATESMAN,

A SUPPOSED EPISTLE FROM BOETIUS TO HIS WIFE RUSTICIANA.

———————— Pectore magno  
Spemque metumque domat, vitio sublimior omni,  
Exemptus fatis ; indignantemque repellit  
Fortunam ; dubio quem non in turbine rerum  
Deprêndit suprema dies, sed abire paratum,  
Ac plenum vitâ.       Stat. Sylv. L. I.

---

### ARGUMENT.

BOETIUS flourished in the former part of the sixth century. He was descended from the

[32] Macarius (who was born the 28th of October, 1650) was dispossessed of his preferments in 1691, and remained deprived till the time of his death, which happened in February 1735; and (which is remarkable enough) the bishops Kidder, Hooper, and Wynne all contrived that Macarius should receive the little profits from his prebend of Wells as long as he lived. A circumstance to their honour, as well as his.

[33] Hunc saltem accumulem donis, & fungar  
      inani  
Munere.              Virg.

[34] Philotheüs, bishop Ken.

[35] The late Mrs. Nugent—and Edward Eliot of Port Eliot, esq. &c. &c.

[36] Charles, late earl of Peterborow, general in Spain, &c.

Manlian family, and was one of the first persons of Rome in fortunes and dignity. He received his education at Athens; after which he was thrice consul, and always renowned for his eloquence in the senate. He was upon all occasions inflexibly honest and veracious.

His book entituled the Consolation of Philosophy, may be looked upon as a master-piece of fine writing. The poetry of it is equal to most compositions in the Augustan age; and that even in the classical purity of style: but something which manifests the declension of the Roman language may be discovered in the prose part.

In his prose writings he made Aristotle his model; and, like him, is always clear, though concise: leaving an infinite fund for the mind of the reader to work upon. Many works pass under his name: some are genuine; and some are looked upon as supposititious.

This book of Philosophical Consolation (from which a large part of the present epistle is extracted) has been universally admired in all ages, insomuch that there are many more fine manuscripts extant of it, than of Virgil, Horace, and Cicero, all taken together. The work we here speak of has been the particular delight and study of princes and good politicians. Chaucer translated it into our language, and afterwards it was translated by queen Elizabeth, &c.

Boetius had two wives: the first was Helpés a Sicilian [1], whose conjugal affection is celebrated by him in an epitaph still extant. His second wife (to whom the following letter is supposed to be addressed) was Rusticiana, the daughter of Symmachus, a Roman senator and consul; one of the most virtuous, learned, and amiable persons of that age. As to Rusticiana, historians give her all perfections of mind and body. By her Boetius had several children: and two of his sons when young had the honour to be publicly carried to the senate-house in a consular chair, by way of extraordinary compliment to their father.

When Theodoric the Goth himself master of the kingdom of Italy, he wisely made choice of Boetius to be the director of his councils, and governed for many years to the universal satisfaction of his subjects. From

[1] Edward Philips, who writ one of the best accounts we have of the poets, ancient and modern, says, "some authors assert that Helpés was daughter of a Sicilian king, and that she writ hymns in honour of the apostles after she embraced christianity."

Philips's authority carries weight with it: for Milton was the instructor of his youthful studies, and afterwards revised the work we here allude to; Philips's mother being Milton's sister.

Philips's book was published in 12mo, 1665, and entituled Theatrum Poetarum. One Winstanley, a barber, transcribed the lives of the English poets from our author's work almost verbatim, and published them in 1687. A most notorious plagiarism; it being but 22 years after the Theatrum Poetarum was published.

a principle of self-interest he had long concealed his inclination for Arianism; but a series of prosperous government made him ambitious, self-confident, and jealous of Boetius's glory. In addition to this, the Gothic chieftains that belonged to him were uneasy to see all power in the hands of a Roman; and one of them in particular, named Trigilla, having gained a new and great ascendancy over the king, contrived our statesman's ruin, by suborning false witnesses, and devising treasonable letters between him and Justin, emperor of the east.

Boetius was first banished to Pavia, and after four years confinement privately executed in prison. His father-in-law, Symmachus, incurred the same fate. Theodoric soon afterwards died with remorse, under all the agonies of a disturbed mind.

It has been looked upon by many good christians as no small misfortune, that Boetius in his Consolation has not derived his arguments from divine wisdom as well as prophane philosophy. One may perceive here and there several hints taken from Scripture, but nothing as I remember, in totidem verbis: yet his general belief of Christianity has never been suspected, nor even his orthodoxy; for he writ an express treatise on the consubstantiality of the Trinity, which is still preserved, and looked upon to be genuine.

These circumstances induced me to conclude this epistle in a manner not unworthy of our philosopher, and highly agreeable to his imitator.

It has often been thought, that a second part added to Boetius's Consolation, written in the same manner of a vision, and consisting of verse and prose interchangeably, where Divine Wisdom is introduced as the speaker and comforter, would afford us one of the finest and most instructive works that could be composed. The sieur de Ceriziers, almoner to Louis the XIIIth, made an attempt of this kind about the year 1636, and executed it with some degree of success.

Boetius was commented upon by no less a person than Thomas Aquinas, who was one of the clearest and purest writers of his time. This shows the esteem in which the scholastic ages held him.

In our country king Alfred was the first who translated the Consolation of Philosophy, and this translation is still extant. Chaucer, as we have already hinted, gave us another version; and a third, I think, was published by the monks of Tavistock, at the second press that was established in England. A fourth translation was made (as some say) by queen Elizabeth; and one or too more preceded the version published by lord Preston.

I have nothing farther to add, but that my worthy friend, to whom this elegy is addressed, will be pleased to bear in memory these beautiful verses of antiquity; which may be applied (not improperly) both to him and me.

—————— Nos facta aliena canendo,
Vergimur in senium; propriis tu pulcher ab annis

Ipse canenda geres, patriæque exempla parabis;
Poscit avus: præstatque domi novisse trium-
 phos—
Jamque vale, & penitùs noti tibi vatis amorem
Corde exire veta,—

---

## EPISTLE

### FROM BOETIUS TO HIS WIFE RUSTICIANA.

And it came to pass from the time that he (Po-
tiphar) had made him over-seer in his house,
and over all that he had, that the Lord blessed
the Egyptian's house for Joseph's sake; and
the blessing of the Lord was upon all he had
in the house and in the field.

     Gen. ch. xxxix, v. 5.

---

## INTRODUCTION.

The man, that's truly read in virtue's laws,
Improves from censure, and distrusts applause.
Firm in his hope, he yields not to despair [2];
The cube reverst is still erect and square [3].
 Eliot, to whom kind Nature did impart
The coolest head, and yet the warmest heart:
Blest in thy nuptials, blest in thy retreat,
Privately good, and amiably great;
Accept with candour these spontaneous lays,
And grant me pardon, for I ask not praise.—
In proof the Muse true oracles recites,
Hear what Boetius to his consort writes.
Mark well the man, and Heav'n thy labour
 bless;—
In all be like him, but unhappiness!
Thus he aspir'd on meditation's wings,
And to the best of consorts thus he sings:

---

Rusticiana, loveliest of thy kind,
Most in my eyes, and ever in my mind;
Exil'd from all the joys the world can give,
And—(for my greater grief!) allow'd to live:
(By him [1], I train'd to glory, basely left;)
Of all things, but my innocence, bereft:
Patrician, consul, statesman but in name;
Of honour plunder'd, and proscrib'd in fame:
(Betray'd by men my patronage had fed,
And curst by lips to which I gave their bread;)
To thee I breathe my elegies of woe;
For thee, and chiefly thee, my sorrows flow:
Joint-partner of my life, my heart's relief;
Alike partaker of my joys or grief!
All-bounteous God, how gracious was the care
To mix thy antidote with my despair!
Rusticiana lives to smooth my death,
And waft with sighs to Heav'n my parting breath,
Hence hope and fortitude inspire my breast:
Be her's the earthly part, and thine the rest!
Still I am happy, human and divine;
Th' assistant angel she, th' assistance thine.

---

[2] "The fortitude of a just man consists in
contemning the flatteries of prosperity, and
overcoming the fears of poverty."
    Sti. Gregor. Moral. L. VIII.
[3] Compositus, semperque suus.
     Stat. Sylvæ. L. II.
[1] The emperor Theodoric.

---

O wife, more gentle than the western breeze,
Which (loath to part) dwells whisp'ring on the
 trees:
Chaste as th' lamb th' indulgent pastor leads
To living streams thro' Sharon's flow'ry meads;
Mild as the voice of comfort to despair;
Fair as the spring, and yet more true than fair [a];
Delightful as the all-enlivening Sun;
Brighter than rills, that glitter as they run,
And mark thee spotless;—air thy purity
Denotes, thy clearness fire, and earth thy con-
 stancy [3].
Weep not to read these melancholy strains;
Change courts for cells, and coronets for chains.—
No greatness can be lost, where God remains!
 Say, what avails me, that I boast the fame
And deathless honours of the Manlian name;
Th' unsoil'd succession of renown'd descent,
Equal to time's historical extent [4]?
One of my ancestors receiv'd his doom
There, where he sav'd the liberties of Rome!
Did not another plunge into the wave
The Gaulish champion, and his country save?
Did not a third, (and harder was his fate)
Make his own child a victim for the state?
And did not I my wealth and life consume,
To bless at once Theodoric and Rome?—
But all is cancell'd and forgotten since;
Past merits were reproaches to my prince!
 As my own glory serv'd to ruin me,
Thy birth from Symmachus avails not thee:
Thy meekness, prudence, beauty, innocence,
Thy knowledge, and thy virtues, gave offence.
When excellence is eminent, like thine,
Our eyes are dazzled with too bright a shrine;
Death must the medium give, that makes it
 mildly shine.
 What visionary hope the wretch beguiles,
Who founds his confidence on princes' smiles?
True to their int'rest, mindless of their trust,
Convenient is the regal term for just.
The plant, my cultivating hands had made
A spreading tree, oppress'd me with its shade;
Ambition push'd forth many a vig'rous shoot,
And rancid jealousy manur'd the root:
Ingratitude a willing heart misled,
And sycophants the growing mischief fed,

---

[2] Quis te felicissimum conjugis pudore, non
 prædicavit?
    Philosophæ Verba ad Boetium,
     De Consolat. L. II, Pros. 3.
Vivit uxor ingenio modesta, pudicitiæ pudore præcellens, et, ut omnes ejus dotes brevi-
ter includam, patri (Symmacho) similis. Vivit
inquam, tibique tantùm, vitæ hujus exosa,
spiritum servat. Quoque uno felicitatem minui
tuam vel ipsa concesserim, tui desiderio lachry-
mis ac dolore tabescit.
 Ejusd. Verba. ibid. Pros. 4, edit. Juntarum
        1521.
[3] This passage was written in imitation of
Ovid's famous description of Galatea, Met. l.
XIII. and improved by an hint taken from Dr,
Donne's Poems, page 96, 12mo.
[4] Quod si quid in nobilitate bonum, id solum esse arbitror, ut imposita nobilitas necessi-
tudo videatur, nè à majorum virtute degene-
rent.        L. III, Pros. 6.

Till th' Arian sophist [5] crept thro' all restraint;
The tempter ply'd him, and there split the
saint.
Th' assassin-hand which Odoácer slew,
Once more, distain'd with blood, appêar'd to
Not foe by foe in hostile fields opprest,    [view:
But friend with friend, th' inviter and the guest[6].
And O, how weak my skill, how vain my toils,
To sow religion's seeds in courtly soils!
The few surviving plants that fix'd their root,
O'ercharg'd with specious herbage, bore no fruit,
Gorg'd to satiety with unctuous juice
From a fat earth, and form'd for bulk, not use;
Till all the cultivating hand receives
Is steril plenty of luxuriant leaves [7].—
Or, where we sow'd the grain of life, succeeds
A copious harvest of pernicious weeds.    [stands,
Where corn once stood, th' insatiate thistle
And deletereous hemloc chokes the lands.
If errours purely human are forgiv'n,
I dare present my last appeal to Heav'n,
Religion and clear honesty, combin'd,
Made up the short full system of my mind.
Nicely I mark'd the quicksands of the state,
The crown's encroachments, and the people's
hate;
Fore-warn'd my prince of arbitrary sway,
And taught his subjects willingly t' obey:
Thus ev'ry thing conspir'd to one great end,
The nation was my child, the king my friend.
Both still I serv'd with uniform intent,
The good of both with equal fervour meant;
And, wheresoe'er th' infraction first arose,
Still judg'd th' aggressors man's and nature's
foes.
Monarchs, sometimes, discard thro' fear, or
hate,    [state;
Those, whose good sense and virtues poize the
So mariners, when storms the ocean sweep,
Commit their guardian-ballast to the deep.
Methinks, in these my solitudes, I hear
Tricilla whisp'ring in the tyrant's ear [8],
" Assert the glories which are all thy own;
And lop the branch that over-shades the throne;"
When he and malice know, I taught no more
Than ev'ry righteous statesman taught before.
I show'd my prince [9]—" The first of regal arts
Was to reign monarch of the people's hearts:

[5] Theodoric in his heart was strongly inclined
to Arianism.
[6] Odoácer and Theodoric had divided by agreement the kingdom of Italy between them. The
latter invited the former to a banquet, and killed
him with his own hand.
[7] ——————— nesoia falcis
    Sylva comam tollit, fructumque expirat in
    umbras.    Stat. Sylvæ.
[8] L. I, Pros. 4.
[9] The precepts of government, comprised in
the following lines, and recommended by Boetius, are extracted almost verbatim from Cassiodorus's Letters. Cassiodorus was secretary to
Theodoric and Athalaric, kings of the Goths.
He was a statesman of great genius, and an author of wonderful invention.
'An ancient writer of the church has justly
marked out the difference betwixt a king and a
tyrant: " they have both" (says he) " absolute

(Swift to encourage, eager to redress,
The steward of a nation's happiness;)
Taught him, each gift he gave, by truth to scan;
T' adapt the man to place, not place to man;
To guard the public wealth with anxious care,
Studious of peace, but still prepar'd for war :
Taught him, that princes of celestial kind,
Like Numa, cultivate the field and mind [10]:
Warn'd him 'gainst pow'r, which suffers no con-
trol;
But mostly that, which persecutes the soul :
Then by examples, or from reason, show'd,
That none are true to man who're false to God ";
And that our lives, except by freedom blest,
Are a dull passive slavery at best."
Hence righteous kings of softer clay are made;
Not for their subjects mis'ry, but their aid [12].
True liberty, by pious monarchs giv'n,
Is emblematic manna rain'd from Heav'n :
Without it, ev'ry appetite is pall'd,
The body fetter'd, and the mind enthrall'd [13].
Thus when by chance some rustic hand invades
The nightingale's recess in poplar-shades,
And bears the pris'ner with offensive care
To Nero's house of gold, and Nero's fare;
Th' aërial chorister, no longer free,
Wails and detests man's civil cruelty:'
Still dumb th' imprison'd sylvan bard remains;
(Your human bards make music with their
chains;)
And when from his exalted cage he sees    [trees,
The hills, the dales, the lawns, the streams, the
He looks on courtly food with loathing eyes,
And sighs for liberty, and worms, and flies [14].

power and abundance of people under their command; but exert their authority and power in a
very different manner : for the former seeks only
the good of those whom he governs, and hazards
all, even his life, that they may live in peace and
safety." He then gives the contrast of their
characters in more full detail.
Synesius Bishop of Cyrené to the Emperor
Arcadius.
[10] Ovid. Met. XV, v. 482.
[11] A saying of Constantius Chlorus, the father
of Constantine the Great.
[12] The character of a just and pious prince is
finely marked by Isaiah, ch. xvi, v. 5. " In
mercy shall the throne be established, and he
shall sit upon it in truth, in the tabernacle of
David; judging and seeking judgment, and hasting righteousness."
[13] Much to this purpose is a passage in the Son
of Sirach :—" As long as thou livest, and hast
breath in thee, give not thyself over to any. In
all thy works keep to thyself the pre-eminence,
and leave not a stain in thine honour."
Ecclus. ch. xxxiii.

[14] Quæ canit altis garrula ramis
    Ales, caveæ clauditur antro.
    Huic licet illita pocula melle
    Largasque dapes dulci studio
    Ludens hominum cura ministret;
    Si tamen alto saliens tecto
    Nemorum gratas viderit umbras,
    Sparsas pedibus proterit escas;
    Sylvas tantum mœsta requirit.
        Boet. de Consolat. L. III. Metr. 2.

Such truths my crimes! But Charity's soft
　　　veil
Shall shade the hateful remnant of the tale.
The daughter of a Symmachus [16] disdains
Vindictive plaints and acrimonious strains;
Make the solemnity of grief appear
Magnificently dumb, without a tear!
Brave as our sex, and as thy own resign'd;
Unconquer'd, like thy beauty, be thy mind!—
Wretch that I was, how dar'd I to complain?
Heav'n's chastisements are never dealt in vain!
In something, or my pride or frailty err'd,
And my just doom was certain, tho' deferr'd.
The mists of twilight-sunshine, and esteem,
Made me not greater grow, but greater seem.
When I the paths of human grandeur trod,
Might not my alien heart diverge from God?
Might I not raise my kins-folk and my friends
From private reasons, and for private ends;
Exclusive of the better few, who stay
Far from the solar walk, and court's high-way [17]?
Might I not swell too much on earthly pow'r,
Man's ideot-play-thing, gewgaw of an hour?
Or might not false compliance, flatt'ry, art,
Unhinge my truth, unchristianize my heart?
　　Why nam'd I in these lines my wealth, my
　　　race [18],
The consul's station, or the statesman's place;
The confidence I gain'd, the trusts I bore?—
See, my heart sickens to review them more!
Boast as we will, dissemble as we can,
A pious peasant is the greater man.
How hard the contest, and how sharp the strife
To part the great from pageantry of life!
To wean the bearded infant from his toys,
Vain hopes, vain honours, and still vainer joys!
See the proud demi-god in triumph sit,
With nauseous incense chok'd, and hireling wit;
Hymn'd by a chorus of self-serving tools,
The Nisroch [19] of his knaves, and calf [20] of
　　　fools!—
I'll dwell no longer on this angry theme [21];—
But sketch the moral picture of a dream [22].
　　One night, with grief o'er charg'd, with cares
　　　opprest,
Like a sick child, I moan'd myself to rest:

[16] Pretiosissimum generis humani decus Sym-
　　machus socer;
　　Vir totus ex sapientia, virtutibusque factus.
　　　　Boet. de Consolat. L. II, Pros. 4.

Socer Symmachus, sanctus, atque actu ipso
　　reverendus.　　Ibid. L. I, Pros. 4.
[17] " In chusing men who are to discharge the
highest offices, the safest conduct is to take the
man who goes out of his way in order to decline
it, and not the man who intrudes boldly for it."
　　　　　　　　　St. Bernard.
[18] See the early part of the epistle.
[19] 2 Kings, ch. xix, v. 37.
[20] Exod. ch. xxxii, v. 4, 1 Kings, ch. xii, v.
28.
[21] De sceleribus ac fraudibus delatorum recte
tu quidem strictim attingendum putasti, quod ea
melius uberiusque recognoscentis omnia vulgi ce-
lebrentur.　Philosophia loquitur, L. 1, Pros. 5.
[22] What follows is extracted from the Philosophical Consolation of Boetius.

When lo, a figure of celestial mien
(Known indistinctly once, and faintly seen)
Approach'd me; fair and graceful as a queen.
Now, (strange to tell!) she seem'd of human
　　size,
And now, her form august half reach'd the skies [23].
　Sweet-smiling, with an accent soft she said,
" Is this Boetius? Or Boetius' shade?
What sudden stroke of unexpected woe
Congeals thy tears, and wants the pow'r to flow?
Incapable of comfort or relief,
See a dumb image petrify'd with grief!
Th' impetuous storm arose not by degrees,
But bursts like hurricanes on Adria's seas [24]."
　She spoke, and to my throbbing heart apply'd
Her tender hand; " My son, my son," she
　　cry'd,　　　　　　　　　　　[ease;
"Med'cines, and not complaints, thy pangs must
False greatness, and false pride, are thy disease,"
Then with her other hand she touch'd my eyes [25],
Soft, as when Zephyr's breath o'er roses flies:
Instant my sense return'd, restor'd and whole,
To re-possess its empire of the soul.
So, when o'er Phœbus low-hung clouds prevail,
Sleep on each hill, and sadden ev'ry dale;
Sudden, up-springing from the north, invades
A purging wind, which first disturbs the shades;
Thins the black phalanx; till with fury driv'n
Swift disappears the flying wreck of Heav'n:
To its own native blue the sky refines,
And the Sun's orb with double radiance shines [26].
　The dame celestial mark'd with glad surprise
Recover'd reason lab'ring in my eyes,
And, kindly smiling, said, or seem'd to say;
" At length, my son, the intellectual ray
Just gleams the hopeful promise of a day.
Patients like thee must cautiously be fed
With milk diluted, and innoxious bread:
Permit me then in gentlest strains to give
Rules to die happy, and contented live;
And, when thy stomach can strong food digest,
My prudence shall administer the rest [27].
I never leave my children on the road,
But lead each pilgrim to his blest abode [28].
" Suffice it first this wholesome truth t' im-
　　part;
Coy Fortune's absence stings thee to the heart:
A willing mistress to the young and bold,
But scornful of the tim'rous and the old:
Mere lust of change compell'd her to cashier
Her best lov'd Pompey in his fiftieth year.

[23] L. I, Pros. 1, De Consolat. Philosoph.
[24] De Consolat. Philosoph, L. I, Pros. 2.
[25] L. I, Pros. 9.

[26] Tunc me discussa liquerunt nocte tenebræ,
　　Luminibusque prior rediit vigor.
　　Ut cum præcipiti glomerantur sidera Coro
　　　Nimbosisque polus stetit imbribus:
　　Sol latet, ac nondum cœlo venientibus astris
　　　Desuper in terram nox funditur.
　　Hanc, si Threïcio Boreas emissus ab antro
　　　Verberet, & clausum reserat diem;
　　Emicat & subito vibratus lumine Phœbus,
　　　Mirantes oculos radiis ferit.
　　　　　　　　　　　L. I, Metr. 3.
[27] L. I, Pros. 2.
[28] L. I, Pros. 3.

The frowns of a capricious jilt you mourn,
Who's thine or mine, and ev'ry man's by turn :
Were Fortune constant, she's no more the same,
But, chang'd in species, takes another name.
Say, when that prodigy[29] of falsehood smil'd,
And all the sorceress thy heart beguil'd ;
When ev'ry joy that full possession gave
Rose to the highest relish man can crave ;
Wast thou then happy to thy soul's desire ?—
Something to seek, and something to require,
Still, still perplex'd thee, unforeseen before.—
Thy draughts were mighty, but thy dropsy more[30].
'Tis granted, Fortune's vanish'd—and what then ?
Thou'rt still as truly rich as all good men :
Thy mind's thy own ; (if that be calm and
　　ev'n !)—
Thy faith in Providence, thy funds in Heav'n.
The Indian only took her jingling bells,
Her rags of silk, and trumpery of shells :
Virtue's a plunder of a cumb'rous make,
She cannot, and she does not chuse to take[31].—
Accept the inconstant, if she deigns to stay ;
And, if she leaves thee, speed her on the way ;
For where's the diff'rence, mighty reas'ner, say,
When man by death of all things is bereft,
If he leaves Fortune, or by Fortune's left[32]?
Fortune to Galba's door the diadem brought ;
The door was clos'd, and other sons she sought :
Fortune's a woman, over fond or blind ;
A step-dame now, and now a mother kind.
　" Eschew the lust of pow'r, and pride of
　　life ;—
One jarring mass of counter-working strife !
Vain hopes, which only idiot minds employ ;
And fancy builds for fancy to destroy !
All must be wretched who expect too much ;
Life's chymic gold proves recreant to the touch.
　" The man who fears, nor hopes for earthly
　　things,
Disarms the tyrant, and looks down on kings :
Whilst the depending, craving, flatt'ring slave,
Makes his own chain that drags him to the
　　grave [33]."
The goddess now, with mild and sober grace
Inclining, look'd me stedfast in the face.
　" Thy exile next sits heavy on thy mind ;
Thy pomp, thy wealth, thy villas, left behind,
Ah, quit these nothings to the hungry tribe ;
States cannot banish thee ; they may proscribe.
The good man's country is in ev'ry clime,
His God in ev'ry place, at ev'ry time ;
In civiliz'd, or in barbarian lands,
Wherever Virtue breathes, an altar stands[34]!

[29] Intelligo multiformis illius prodigii fucos.
　　　　　　　　　　　　L. II, Pros. 1.
[30] Largis cum potius muneribus fluens
Sitis ardescit habendi.　　L. II, Metr. 2.
[31] L. II, Pros. 1.
[32] Quid igitur referre putes, tunè illam mo-
ricendo deseras, an te illa fugiendo?
　　　　　　　　　　　　Lib. II, Pros. 3.
[33] Quisquis composito serenus ævo
　　Nec speres aliquid, nec extimescas,
　　Exarmaveris impotentis iram.
　　At quisquis trepidus pavet, vel optat,
　　Nectit, qua valeat trahi, catenam.
　　　　　　　　　　Boet. L. I.
[34] L. I, Pros. 5, Boetius.——

　" A farther weakness in thy heart I read ;
Thy prison shocks thee with unusual dread :
Dark solitude thy wav'ring mind appalls,
Damp floors, and low hung roofs, and naked
　　walls.
Yet here the mind of Socrates could soar ;
And, being less than man, he rose to more.
Wish not to see new hosts of clients wait
In rows submissive through vast rooms of state ;
Nor, on the litter of coarse rushes spread,
Lament the absence of thy downy bed :
Nor grieve thou, that thy plunder'd books afford
No consolation to their exil'd lord :
Read thy own heart[35] ; its motions nicely scan ;
There's a sufficient library for man[36].
And yet a nobler volume still remains ;
The book of Providence all truths contains :
For ever useful, and for ever clear,
To all men open, and to all men near :
By tyrants unsuppress'd, untouch'd by fire ;
Old as mankind, and with mankind t' expire[37].
　" Next, what aggrieves thee most, is loss of
　　fame,
And the chaste pride of a once spotless name :
But mark, my son, the truths I shall impart,
And grave them on the tablets of thy heart:
The first keen stroke th' unfortunate shall find,
Is losing the opinion of mankind[38] :
Slander and accusation take their rise
From thy declining fortunes, not thy vice.
How rarely is a poor man highly deem'd ;
Or a rich upstart villain dis-esteem'd ?—
From chilly shades the gnats of fortune run
To buz in heat and twinkle in the sun ;
Till Heav'n (at Heav'n's appointed season kind,)
Sweeps off th' Egyptian plague with such a wind,
That not one blood sucker is left behind.
　" Boast not, nor grieve at good or evil fame[39] :
Be true to God, and thou art still the same.
Man cannot give thee virtues thou hast not,
Nor steal the virtues thou hast truly got.
　" And what's the applause of learning or of
　　wit ?
Critics unwrite whate'er the author writ :

　——— Ubicunque Virtus ;
　　Heic, puto, templum est.
　　　　　　　　Jac. Balde Odæ.
Heav'n, to men well dispos'd, is ev'ry where.
　　　　　　　　Dr. Donne.
[35] " There are two lessons which God instills
every day into the faithful : the one is, to see
their own faults : the other is, to comprehend the
divine goodness."　　Thom. à Kemp.
[36] "The best looking-glass wherein to see thy
God is perfectly to see thyself."
　　　　　　　　　　Hugo de Anima.
[37] L. I, Pros. 4. Boetius.
[38] At vero hic etiam nostris malis cumulus
accedit, quod existimatio plurimorum non rerum
merita, sed fortunæ spectat eventum ; eaque
tantum judicat esse provisa, quæ felicitas com-
mendaverit. Quo fit, ut existimatio bona, prima
omnium deserat infelices.
　　　　　　　　　　Boetius, Ibid.
[39] Si vis beatus esse, cogita hoc primum,
contemnere et contemni ; nondum es felix, si te
turba non deriserit.
　　　　　　　　　Antisthenis Dictum.

To a new fate this second life must yield,
And death will twice be master of the field[40].

"Nor grieve, nor murmur, nor indulge despair,
To see the villain cloth'd, and good man bare ;
To see impiety with pomp enthron'd ;—
(Virtue unsought for, honesty unown'd :)
Heav'n's dispensations no man can explore ;
In this, to fathom God, is to be more !
Meer man but guesses the divine decree ;
The most the Stagyrite himself could see,
Was the faint glimm'ring of contingency.
Yet deem not rich men happy, nor the poor
Unprosp'rous ; wait th' event, and judge no more.
True safety to Heav'n's children must belong :
With God the rich are weak, the poor are strong.
Th' irrevocable sanction stands prepar'd ;
Vice has its curse, and virtue its reward [41].
Conscience, man's centinel, forbids to stray,
Nor shows us the great gulf for Heav'n's high-
　　way.
" To serve the great, and aggrandise our pride,
We barter honour, and our faith beside :
Mindless of future bliss, and heav'nly fame,
We strip and sell the Christian to the name.
Ambition, like the sea by tempests tost,
Still makes new conquests for old conquests lost :
Court-favours lie above the common road
By modesty and humble virtue trod ;
Like trees on precipices, they display
Fair fruit, which none can reach but birds of
　　prey.
" All men from want, as from contagion, fly ;
They weary Earth, and importune the sky ;
Gain riches, and yet 'scape not poverty :
The once mean soul preserves its earthly part,
The beggar's flatt'ry, and the beggar's heart.
" In spite of titles, glory, kindred, pelf,
Lov'st thou an object better than thyself ?
You answer, No.—If that, my son, be true,
Then give to God the thanks to God are due.
No man is crown'd the fav'rite of the skies,
Till Heav'n his faith by sharp affliction tries :
Nor chains, disgrace, nor tyrants can control
Th' ability to save th' immortal soul.
How oft did Seneca deplore his fate,
Debarr'd that recollection which you hate !
How often did Papinian waste his breath
T' implore like your's, a pausing time for
　　death [42] ?—
" Place in thy sight Heav'n's confessors re-
And suffer with humility of mind : 　[sign'd,
As thy prosperities pass'd swift away,
Just so thy grief shall make a transient stay [43].

40　Cum sera vobis rapiet hoc etium dies,
　　Jam vos secunda mors manet.
　　　　　　Boetius, L. II, Metr. 7.
41 Si ea quæ paulo ante conclusa sunt, in-
convulsa sequantur, ipso de cùjus nunc regno
loquimur, auctore cognosces, semper quidem
potentes bonos esse, malos veio abjectos semper
& imbecilles ; nec sine pœna unquam esse vitia,
nec sine præmio virtutes ; bonis felicia, malis
semper infortunata contingere.
　　　　　Boetius, L. IV, Prosa 1,
　　　　　　　　De Consolat. Philosoph.
　　　　Qui semina virtù, fama raccoglie.
42 Boet. L. III, Pros. 5.
43 Quod si idcirco te fortunantum esse non

Thy life's last hour (nor is it far from thee)
Is the last hour of human misery.
Extremes of grief or joy are rarely giv'n,
And last as rarely, by the will of Heav'n."
　　So spake Philosophy, and upwards flew,
Inspiring confidence as she withdrew.
　　Here let my just resentments cease to flow,
Here let me close my elegies of woe.
　　Rusticiana, fairest of the fair,
My present object, and my future care ;
Be mindful of my children, and thy vows :—
And ('gainst thy judgment) O defend thy spouse.
My children are my other self to thee :—
Heav'n you distrust if you lament for me.
Weep not my fate : is man to be deplor'd,
From a dark prison to free air restor'd ?
Admir'd by friends, and envy'd by my foes,
I die, when glory to the highest rose.
I've mounted to the summit of a ball ;
If I go further, I descend, or fall.
Hail death, thou lenient cordial of relief ;
Preventive of my shame and of my grief !
Kind Nature crops me in full virtue's bloom[44],
Not left to shrink and wither for the tomb.
Shed not a tear, but vindicate thy pow'r,
Enrich'd like Egypt's soil without a show'r.
Fortune, which gave too much, did soon repine,
There was no solstice in a course like mine.
With calmness I my bleeding death behold ;
Suns set in crimson-streams to rise in gold.
Farewell, and may Heav'n's bounty heap on
　　thee,
(As more deserving) what it takes from me [45] !—
That peace, which made thy social virtues shine,
The peace of conscience, and the peace divine,
Be ever, O thou best of women, thine !
Forgive, Almighty Pow'r, this worldly part ;
These last convulsions of an husband's heart :
Give us thy self ; and teach our minds to see
The Saviour and the Paraclete in thee !

―――――――

## RELIGIOUS MELANCHOLY,

### AN EMBLEMATICAL ELEGY.

Shall not every one mourn that dwelleth therein?
　　　　　　　　Amos, ch. viii, v. 8.
I did mourn as a dove ; mine eyes failed with
　　looking upwards.
　　　　　　　Isaiah, ch. xxxviii, v. 14.
Fear not thou, my servant, saith the Lord ; for
　　I am with thee. I will not make a full end
　　of thee ; but correct thee in measure.
　　　　　　　　Jer. ch. xlvi, v. ult.

existimas, quoniam quæ tunc læta videbantur,
abiêrunt : non est quod te miserum putes, quoniam, quæ nunc creduntur mœsta, prætereunt."
　　　　　　　　Idem, L. II, Pros. 3.
44 ―――――― Raperis, non indigus ævi,
　　Non nimius. 　　　　　　　Stat.
45 Pars animæ victura meæ, cui linquere
　　possem,
　　O Utinam ! quo dura mihi rapit Atropos
　　annos ! 　　　　　　Stat. Sylvæ.

## ADVERTISEMENT.

If is to be hoped the reader will pardon me, if I take the liberty of prefixing to this elegy a slight advertisement, instead of inserting what might seem too long for a note in the body of the poem.

Having ventured (and I am sure it is licentia sumpta pudenter [1],) to introduce three or four new expressions in a volume of near five thousand lines, and one, namely, dew-tinged ray, in the present elegy, I thought myself obliged to make some apology on that subject; since all innovations in poets like me, (who can only pretend to a certain degree of mediocrity) are more or less of an affected cast, and rarely to be excused; inasmuch as we have the vanity to teach others what we do not thoroughly understand ourselves.

And here permit me to call that language of ours classical English, which is to be found in a few chosen writers inclusively from the times of Spencer till the death of Mr. Pope; for false refinements, after a language has arisen to a certain degree of perfection, give reasons to suspect that a language is upon the decline. The same circumstances have happened formerly, and the event has been almost invariably the same. Compare Statius and Claudian with Virgil and Horace: and yet the former was, if one may so speak, immediate heir at law to the latter.

I have known some of my cotemporary poets (and those not very voluminous writers) who have coined their one or two hundred words a man; whereas Dryden and Pope devised only about threescore words between them; many of which were compound epithets: but most of the words which they introduced into our language proved in the event to be vigorous and perennial plants, being chosen and raised from excellent offsets [2]. —Indeed the former author revived also a great number of ancient words and expressions; and this he did (beginning at Chaucer) with so much delicacy of choice, and in a manner so comprehensive, that he left the latter author (who was in that point equally judicious and sagacious) very little to do, or next to nothing.

Some few of Dryden's revived words I have presumed to continue; of which take the following instances; as gridéline, filmont, and carmine, (with reference to colours, and mixtures of colours;) cymar, eygre, trine, ΕΥΡΗΚΑ, paraclete, panoply, rood, dorp, eglantine, orisons, aspirations, &c. I mention this, lest any one should be angry with me, or pleased with me in

[1] Horat.
[2] I must here make one exception. Dryden showed some weakness, in anglicising common French words, and those not over elegant, when at the same time we had synonymous words of our own growth. Thus, for example, he introduced levee, couchee, boutéfeu, simagres, fracheur, fougue, &c. Nor was he more lucky in the Italian falsarè:

——————————— his shield
Was falsify'd, and round with jav'lins fill'd.
Dryden's Virg.

particular places, where I discover neither boldness nor invention.—I owe also to Fenton the participle meandered; and to Sir W. D'Avenant the latinism of funeral ilicet.

As to compound epithets, those ambitiosa ornamenta [3] of modern poetry, Dryden has devised a few of them, with equal diffidence and caution; but those few are exquisitely beautiful. Mr. Pope seized on them as family diamonds, and added thereto an equal number, dug from his own mines, and heightened by his own polishing.

Compound epithets first came into their great vogue about the year 1598. Shakespeare and Ben Jonson both ridiculed the ostentatious and immoderate use of them, in their prologues to Troilus and Cressida and to Every Man in his Humour. By the above-named prologues it also appears, that bombast grew fashionable about the same era. Now in both instances an affected taste is the same as a false taste. The author of Hieronimo (who as I may venture to assure the reader, was one John Smith [4]) first led up the dance. Then came the bold and self-sufficient translator of Du Bartas [5], who broke down all the flood-gates of the true stream of eloquence (which formerly preserved the river clear, within due bounds, and full to its banks) and, like the rat in the Low-Country dikes, mischievously or wantonly deluged the whole land.

Of innovated phrases and words; of words revived; of compound epithets, &c. I may one day or other say more, in a distinct criticism on Dryden's poetry. It shall therefore only suffice to observe here, that our two great poetical masters never thought that the interposition of an hyphen, without just grounds and reasons, made a compound epithet. On the contrary, it was their opinion, (and to this opinion their practice was conformable) that such union should only be made between two nouns, as patriot-king, ideot-laugh, &c.—or between an adjective and noun, or noun and adjective, vice versa, or an adjective and participle; as laughter-loving, cloud-compelling, rosy-fingered, &c.—As also by an adverb used as part of an adjective, as you may see in the words well-concocted, well-digested, &c.—But never by a full real adverb and adjective, as inly-pining, sadly-musing, and, to make free with myself, (though I only did it by way of irony) my expression of simply-marry'd epithets, of which sort of novelties modern poetry chiefly consists. Nor should such compound epithets be looked upon as the poet's making; for they owe their existence to the compositor of the press, and the intervention of an hyphen.

Much of the same analogy by which Dryden and Pope guided themselves in the present case, may be seen in the purer Greek and Roman languages: but all the hyphens in the world, (supposing hyphens had been then known) would not have truly joined together the dulce ridentem, or dulce loquentem, of Horace.

In a word, some few precautions of the pre-

[3] Horat.
[4] John Smith writ also the Hector of Germany.
[5] Joshua Sylvester.

sent kind are not unnecessary: English poetry begins to grow capricious, fantastical, and affectedly luxuriant; and therefore (as Augustus said of Haterius) sufflaminari paululùm debet.

---

## RELIGIOUS MELANCHOLY,

### AN EMBLEMATICAL ELEGY,

Pains and diseases ; stripes and labour too[1]!
"What more could Edom and proud Ashur do?"
Scourge after scourge, and blows succeeding blows?
Lord, has thy hand no mercy, and our woes
No intermission? Gracious Being, please
To calm our fears, and give the body ease !
The poor man, and the slave of ev'ry kind, [find:
'Midst pains and toils may gleams of comfort
But who can bear the sickness of the mind ?
The pow'r of Melancholy mounts the throne,
And makes the realms of wisdom half her own [2]:
Not David's lyre, with David's voice conjoin'd,
Can drive th' oppressive phantom from the mind [3] ?
No more the Sun delights, nor lawns, nor trees ;
The vernal blossoms, or the summer's breeze.
No longer Echo makes the dales rejoice
With sportive sounds, and pictures of a voice [4]:
Th' aërial choir, which sung so soft and clear,
Now grates harsh music to the froward ear:
The gently murm'ring rills offend from far,
And emulate the clangour of a war:
Books have no wit, the liveliest wits have none ;
And hope, the last of ev'ry friend, is gone !
Nor rest nor joy to Virtue's self are giv'n,
Till the disease is rectify'd by Heav'n.
And yet this Iliad of intestine woes
(So frail is man) from seeming nothings rose :
A drop of acrid juice, a blast of air,
Th' obstruction of a tube as fine as hair ;
Or spasm within a labyrinth of threads,
More subtile far than those the spider spreads [5].
What sullen planet rul'd our hapless birth,
Averse from joys, and enemy of mirth ?
Wat'ry Arcturus in a luckless place
South'd [6], and portended tears to all our race:
With him the weeping Pleiades conjoin,
And Mazzaroth made up the mournful trine [7]:

---

[1] The hint of this emblem is taken from our venerable and religious poet F. Quarles, L. III, Embl. 4. Mr. Dryden used to say, that Quarles exceeded him in the facility of rhyming.
  Quarles's book, and the emblematical prints therein contained, are chiefly taken from the Pia Desideria of Hugo Hermannus. The engravings were originally designed by that celebrated artist C. Van Sichem.
[2] Dan. ch. iv, v. 34.
[3] 1 Sam. ch. xvi, v. 23.
[4] Agreeably to this, is a lovely piece of imagery in the holy Scriptures.
  "The Earth mourneth and languisheth ; Lebanon is ashamed, and hewn down ; Sharon is like a wilderness; Bashan and Carmel shake off their fruits."          Isaiah, ch. xxxiii, v. 9.
[5] Isaiah, ch. lix, v. 5.
[6] South'd, a received term in astrology.
[7] Job, ch. xxxviii v. 31, 32. According to

Orion added noise to dumb despair,
And rent with hurricanes the driving air ;
And last Absinthion [8] his dire influence shed
Full on the heart, and fuller on the head.
  Oft have we sought (and fruitless oft) to gain
A short parenthesis 'twixt pain and pain ;
But, sick'ning at the cheerfulness of light,
The soul has languish'd for th' approach of night:
Again, immerst in shades, we seem to say,
O day-spring [9] ! gleam thy promise of a day [10].
On this side death th' unhappy sure are curst;
Who sigh for change, and think the present worst :
Who weep unpity'd, groan without relief ;
" There is no end nor measure of their grief !"
The happy have waste twelve-months to bestow ;
But those can spare all time, who live in woe !
Whose liveliest hours are misery and thrall ;
Whose food is wormwood, and whose drink is gall [11].
Banish their grief, or ease their irksome load ;
Ephraim, at length, was favour'd by his God [12].
  Ah, what is man, that demi-god on Earth ?
Proud of his knowledge, glorying in his birth ;
Profane corrector of th' Almighty's laws,
Full of th' effect, forgetful of the cause !
Why boast of reason, and yet reason ill ?
Why talk of choice, yet follow erring will ?
Why vaunt our liberty, and prove the slave
Of all ambition wants, or follies crave ?
This is the lot of him, surnam'd the wise,
Who lives mistaken, and mistaken dies !
  The sick less happy, and yet happier live ;
For pains and maladies are God's reprieve :
This respite, 'twixt the grave and cradle giv'n,
Is th' interpos'd parenthesis of Heav'n !

---

Scripture-astronomy these three were all watery signs, and emblematical of grief. The fourth constellation, named Orion, threatened mankind with hurricanes and tempests. Sandys understood the passage in the same manner as I do. See his excellent Paraphrase on Job, folio, page 49, London 1637. Mention is again made of the Seven Stars, (Pleiades) and of Orion, Amos, ch. v, v. 8—and Job, ch. ix, v. 9.
[8] The star of bitterness, called Wormwood, Rev. ch. viii, v. 11.
[9] Job, ch. xxxviii, v. 12. Luke, ch. I, v. 78. Ἀνατολὴ ἐξ ὕψυς. This poetical word, day-spring, expressing the dawn of morning, has been never adopted by our poets, as far as we can recollect.
[10] Deut. ch. xxviii, v. 66, 67.
  " And thy life shall hang in doubt before thee, and thou shalt fear day and night, and shalt have no assurance of thy life. In the morning thou shalt say, Would God it were even! and at even thou shalt say, Would God it were morning! For the fear of thine heart wherewith thou shalt fear, and for the sight of thine eyes wherewith thou shalt see." See also Job, ch. iii. v. 8.
[11] Jerem. ch. xxiii, v. 15.
[12] Ibid. ch. xxxi, v. 20. "Ephraim is my dear son ;—for, since I spake against him, I do earnestly remember him still: therefore my bowels are troubled for him : I will surely have mercy upon him, saith the Lord."

Too often we complain—but flesh is weak;
Silence would waste us, and the heart would
break.
Behold yon' rose, the poor despondent cries,
(Pain on his brow, and anguish in his eyes)
What healthy verdure paints its juicy shoots,
What equal circulation feeds the roots!
At morning dawn it feels the dew-ting'd ray,
But opens all its bosom to the day.
No art assists it, and no toil it takes[13],
Slumbers at ev'ning, and with morning wakes[14].
Why was I born? Or wherefore born a man?
Immense my wish; yet tether'd to a span!
The slave, that groans beneath the toilsome
oar,
" Obtains the sabbath of a welcome shore:"
His captive stripes are heal'd; his native soil
Sweetens the memory of foreign toil.
" Alas, my sorrows are not half so blest;"
My labours know no end, my pains no rest!
Tell me, vain-glorious Newtons, if you can,
What heterogeneous mixtures form the man?
Pleasure and anguish, ignorance and skill;
Nature and spirit, slav'ry and free will;
Weakness and strength; old age and youthful
Errour and truth; eternity and time!—[prime;
What contradictions have for ever ran
Betwixt the nether brute and upper man[15]?
Ah! what are men, who God's creation scorn?
The worm their brother[16];—brother elder born!
Plants live like them, in fairer robes array'd,
Alike they flourish, and alike they fade.
The lab'ring steer sleeps less disturb'd at night,
And eats and drinks with keener appetite,—
Restrain'd by nature just t' enjoy his fill;
Useful, and yet incapable of ill.
Say, man, what vain pre-eminence is thine?
Each sense impair'd by gluttony and wine[17]:
Thou art the beast, except thy sparing mind
Aspires to pleasures of immortal kind:
Else, boasted knowledge, hapless is thy curse,
T' approve the better, and embrace the worse!
So Annas owns the miracle, and then
(Wilfully blinded) persecutes agen[18].
To minds afflicted ever has been giv'n
A claim upon the patronage of Heav'n:
(Whilst the world's idiots ev'ry thought employ
With hopes to live and die without annoy.)
In the first agonies of heart-struck grief,
Heav'n to our parents typify'd relief[19].

[13] Matth. ch. vi, v. 28.
[14] Concerning the sleep of plants, see an ingenious Latin treatise lately published in Sweden.
[15] Poetical definition of a centaur.
[16] Job, ch. xvii, v 14.—There is a remarkable
passage in the Psalms upon this occasion, where
the worm takes place of the monarch: "O praise
the Lord, ye mountains and all hills; fruitful
trees and all cedars; beasts and all cattle; worms
and feathered fowls; kings of the Earth and all
people; princes and judges of the world."
Psalm cxlviii, v. 10, Septuagint Version.
[17] ". If we pamper the flesh too much, we
nourish an enemy; if we defraud it of lawful sustenance, we destroy a good citizen."
St. Gregor. Homil.
[18] Acts, ch. iv, v. 6, 18.
[19] Gen. ch. iii, v. 15.

Th' Almighty lent an ear to Hannah's pray'r[20],
And bless'd her with each blessing, in an heir:
Whilst Hezekiah[21], earnest in his cause,
Gain'd a suspension of great Nature's laws,
And permanence to time;—for lo! the Sun
Retrac'd the journey he had lately run.—
But most th' unhappy wretch, aggriev'd in
Rais'd pity in the Saviour of mankind[22]. [mind,
He ask'd for peace; Heav'n gave him its own
Demons were dumb, and Legion dispossest. [rest,
Wither'd with palsy'd blasts, the limbs resume,
Thy strength, O manhood; and, O youth, thy
Syro-Phenicia's maiden re-enjoy'd [bloom[23]!
That equal mind, which Satan once destroy'd[24].
And, when the heav'nly Ephphatha[25] was spoke,
The deaf-born heard, the dumb-born silence
broke.
Th' ethereal fluid mov'd, the speech return'd;
No spasms were dreaded, no despondence
mourn'd.
Then rouse, my soul, and bid the world adieu,
Its maxims, wisdom, joys and glory too;
The mighty EΥΡΗΚΑ[26] appears in view.
Just so, the gen'rous falcon[27], long immur'd
In doleful cell, by osier-bars secur'd,
Laments her fate; till, flitting swiftly by,
Th' aerial prize attracts her eager eye:
Instant she summons all her strength and fire;
Her aspect kindles fierce with keen desire;
She prunes her tatter'd plumes in conscious
pride, [side:
And bounds from perch to perch, and side to
Impatient of her jail, and long detain'd,
She breaks the bounds her liberty restrain'd:
Then, having gain'd the point by Heav'n de-
sign'd,
Soars 'midst the clouds, and proves her high-
born kind.
When Adam did his Paradise forego,
He earn'd his hard-bought bread with sweating
brow.—
Give us the labour, but suppress the woe
Merit we boast not: but Christ's sacred side
Has pour'd for all its sacramental tide.
No sin, no guile, no blemishes had he;
A self-made slave to set the captive free!
Yet pain and anguish still too far presume;
Just are Heav'n's ways, and righteous is its
doom.
All chastisement, before we reach the grave,
Are bitter med'cines, kindly meant to save.
Thus let the rhet'ric of our suff'rings move;
The voice of grief is oft the voice of love[28]!

[20] 1 Kings, ch. i.
[21] 2 Kings, ch. xx.
[22] Mark, ch. v, v. 3—9. And also " the spirit
of the Lord is upon me (saith Christ:) he sent me
to heal the broken-hearted," &c. Luke, ch. iv.
v. 18. Compare likewise Isaiah, ch. lxi, v. 1.
[23] Matth. ch. iv, v. 24, &c. Acts viii, v. 7.
[24] Mark vii, v. 26.
[25] Ibid. v. 34.
[26] See Dryden's Relig. Laici; and Prior's Ode
entitled, What is Man? EΥΡΗΚΑ signifies
finding out the great point desired.
[27] The hint of this similie is taken from
Quarles.
[28] " There is sometimes a certain pleasure in

The bed of sickness (after cares and strife)
Is weak man's cradle for a second life :
Death's but a moment ; and, before we die,
We touch the threshold of eternity !
So, stretch'd beneath the juniper's chill shade,
Th' afflicted prophet [29] in despondence pray'd :
" Oh, take the burthen of my life away,
Dead are my sires ; nor better I than they:"
At length a seraph cry'd, " Arise and eat ;
Behold thy bev'rage; and behold thy meat:
Heav'n's one repast shall future strength supply
For forty days, till Horeb meets thy eye[30]."
The good man neither fears, desponds, nor
    faints,
Arm'd with the heav'nly panoply [31] of saints.

---

## MEDITATIONS ON CHRIST'S DEATH AND PASSION.

### AN EMBLEM.

He was wounded for our transgressions, he was
bruised for our iniquities: the chastisement
of our peace was upon him.
        Isaiah, ch. liii, v. 5.

Σός εἰμι, ΧΡΙΣΤΕ· σῶσον, ὡς Αὐτὸς θέλεις.
        Greg. Naz. Carm. Iamb.

Respice dum transis, quia sis mihi causa doloris·

Haste not so fast, on worldly cares employ'd,
Thy bleeding Saviour [1] asks a short delay :
What trifling bliss is still to be enjoy'd,
What change of folly wings thee on thy way ?
Look back a moment, pause a while [2], and stay.
For thee thy God assum'd the human frame ;
For thee the guiltless pains and anguish try'd;
Thy passion (sin excepted) his became :
Like thee he suffer'd, hunger, wept, and dy'd.

Nor wealth nor plenty did he ever taste,
The moss his pillow oft, his couch the ground ;
The poor man's bread completed his repast;
Home he had none, and quiet never found,
For fell reproach pursu'd, and aim'd the wound [3]:

weeping : it is a sort of consolation to an afflicted
person to be thoroughly sensible of his affliction."
        St. Ambrose.

[29] Elijah.
[30] 2 Kings, ch. xix., v. 4—8.
[31] Eph. ch. vi, v. 14—17.——Panoply (from
the Greek), a complete suit of armour.   Mr.
Pope, Dryden.
[1] " Christ is the way, the truth, and the life.
The way wherein thou oughtest to walk ; the
truth which thou desirest to obtain : and the life
of happiness which thou longest to enjoy."
        St. August.
[2] " If you labour for a time, you will afterwards enjoy an eternity of rest. Your sufferings
are of a short duration, your joy will last for
ever : and if your resolution wavers, and is going to desert you, turn your eyes towards Mount
Calvary, and consider what Christ suffered for
you, innocent as he was. This consideration
will enable you to say in the event, that your
sufferings lasted for a moment."      Idem.
[3] " Through envy proceeded the fall of the
world, and death of Christ."      St. August.

The wise men mock'd him, and the learned
    scorn'd ;
Th' ambitious worldling other patrons try'd ;
The pow'r that judg'd him, ev'ry foe suborn'd ;
He wept un-pity'd, and un-honour'd dy'd.

For ever mournful, but for ever dear,
O love stupendous ! glorious degradation !
No death of sickness, with a common tear ;—
No soft extinction claims our sorrows here ;
But anguish, shame, and agonizing passion !
The riches of the world, and worldly praise,
No monument of gratitude can prove ;
Obedience only the great debt repays,
An imitative heart, and undivided love !

To see the image of th' All-glorious Pow'r
Suspend his immortality, and dwell
In mortal bondage, tortur'd ev'ry hour ;
A self-made pris'ner in a dolesome cell,
Victim for sin, and conqueror of Hell [4] !
Lustration for offences not his own !
Th' unspotted for th' impure resign'd his breath;
No other off'ring could thy crimes atone:
Then blame thy Saviour's love, but not his death.

From this one prospect draw thy sole relief,
Here learn submission, passive duties learn ;
Here drink the calm oblivion of thy grief:
Eschew each danger, ev'ry good discern,
And the true wages of thy virtue earn.
Reflect, O man, on such stupendous love,
Such sympathy divine, and tender care [5];
Beseech the Paraclete [6] thine heart to move,
And offer up to Heav'n this silent pray'r.

[7] " Great God, thy judgments are with justice
    crown'd,
To human crimes and errours gracious still ;
Yet, though thy mercies more and more abound,
Right reason spares not fresh-existing ill,

" For he (Pilate) knew that the chief priests
had delivered him for envy."
        Mark, ch. xv, v. 10.
An antient Heathen also hath personified envy,
and painted her in a mischievous attitude ;

———— Gnara malorum,
Invidia infelix ! animi vitalia vidit,
Lædendique vias.
[4] Nolo vivere sine vulnere, cum te videam
vulneratum.         Bonavent.
" To know God, without knowing our misery,
creates pride: to know misery, without knowing Christ, causes despondence."
        St. Augustin.
[5] " They make a free-will offering to God,
who in the midst of their sufferings preserve
their gratitude and acknowledgements."
        Cassian.
[6] " God's Holy Spirit worketh in the following manner in his rational children. It instructs,
moves, and admonishes: as for example ; it instructs the reason, moves the will, and admonishes the memory."      St. Gregor. in Moral.
[7] Translated from the famous French Ode of
M. de Barreaux.

Grand Dieu ! Tes jugements sont remplis d'
    équité, &c.

Nor can thy goodness counter-work thy will.
Ah no! The gloom of sin so dreadful shows,
That horrour, guilt, and death the conscience fill:
Eternal laws our happiness oppose;
Thy nature and our lives are everlasting foes!

" Severe thy truth, yet glorious is thy scheme;
Complete the vengeance of thy just desire;
See from our eyes the gushing torrents stream,
Yet strike us, blast us with celestial fire;
Our doom, and thy decrees, alike conspire.
Yet dying we will love thee and adore.
Where shall the flaming flashes of thy ire

Transpierce our bodies? Ev'ry nerve and pore
With Christ's immaculate blood is cover'd and
o'er."

" When we praise God we may speak much, and
yet come short: Wherefore in sum, he is all.
When you glorify him, exalt him as much
as you can: for even yet he will far exceed.
And when you exalt him, put forth all your
strength, and be not weary, for you can never
go far enough." Ecclus. ch. xliii, v, 27—
30.

THE

# POEMS

OF

## *PAUL WHITEHEAD.*

# LIFE OF PAUL WHITEHEAD,

## EY MR. CHALMERS.

PAUL WHITEHEAD, the youngest son of Edmund Whitehead, a taylor, was born at his father's house in Castle-Yard, Holborn, on the sixth day of February 1709-10, St. Paul's day, O. S. to which circumstance he is said to owe his name. As he was intended for trade, he received no other education than what a school at Hitchen in Hertfordshire afforded, and at the usual age was placed as an apprentice to a mercer or woollen-draper in London. Here he had for his associate the late Mr. Lowth of Paternoster-row, long the intimate friend, and afterwards the executor of the celebrated tragedian, James Quin. Whitehead and Lowth were both of a lively disposition and fond of amusement.; Lowth had attached himself to the theatre, and by this means Whitehead became acquainted with some of the theatrical personages of that day, and among others with Fleetwood the manager. Lowth, however, continued in business, while Whitehead was encouraged to enter himself of the Temple and study the law.

Fleetwood was always in distress, and always contriving new modes of relief; Whitehead was pliable, good natured and friendly, and being applied to by the artful manager to enter into a joint security for the payment of three thousand pounds, which he was told would not affect him, as another name besides Fleetwood's was wanted merely as a matter of form, readily fell into the snare. It is perhaps wonderful that Whitehead, who knew something of business and something of law, should have been deceived by a pretence so flimsy ; but on the other hand it is not improbable that Fleetwood, who had the baseness to lie, had also the cunning to enjoin secresy, and Whitehead might be flattered by being thus admitted into his confidence. The consequence, however, was, that Fleetwood was unable to pay, and Whitehead, considering himself as entrapt into a promise, did not look upon it as binding in honour, and therefore submitted to a long confinement in the

Fleet-prison. If this transaction happened, as one of his biographers informs us, about the year 1742, Whitehead was not unable to have satisfied Fleetwood's creditors. He had in the year 1735 married Anna Dyer, the only daughter of sir Swinnerton Dyer, bart. of Spains-hall, Essex, with whom he received the sum of ten thousand pounds. By what means he was released at last without payment, we are not told.

Long before this period', Whitehead, who from his infancy had discovered a turn for poetry, and had when at school corresponded in rhime with his father, distinguished himself both as a poet and a politician. In the latter character, he appears to have united the principles of jacobitism and republicanism in no very consistent proportions. As a jacobite, he took every opportunity of venting his spleen against the reigning family : and as a republican, he was no less outrageous in his ravings about liberty, which, in his dictionary, meant an utter abhorrence of kings, courts and ministers. His first production of this kind was the State Dunces, in 1733, inscribed to Mr. Pope, and written in a close imitation of that poet's satires. The keenness of his abuse, the harmony of his verse, and above all the personalities which he dealt about him with a most liberal hand, conferred popularity on this poem, and procured him the character of an enemy who was to be dreaded, and a friend who ought to be secured. He was accordingly favoured by the party then in opposition to sir Robert Walpole, and at no great distance of time, became patronized by Bubb Doddington and the other adherents of the prince of Wales's court. The State Dunces was answered in a few days by a Friendly Epistle to its author, in verse not much inferior. Whitehead sold his poem to Dodsley, for ten guineas, a circumstance which Dr. Johnson, who thought meanly of our poet, recollected afterwards when Dodsley offered to purchase his *London*, and conditioned for the same sum. " I might perhaps have accepted of less : but that Paul Whitehead had a little before got ten guineas for a poem : and I would not take less than Paul Whitehead²."

In 1739, Whitehead published his more celebrated poem, entitled Manners, a satire not only upon the administration, but upon all the venerable forms of the constitution, under the assumption of an universal depravity of manners. Pope had at this time taken liberties which, in the opinion of some politicians, ought to be repressed. In his second dialogue of Seventeen Hundred and Thirty-eight, he gave offence to one of the Foxes, among others; which Fox, in a reply to Lyttelton, took an opportunity of repaying, by reproaching Lyttelton with the friendship of a lampooner, who scattered his ink without fear or decency, and against whom he hoped the resentment of the legislature would quickly be discharged³. Pope, however, was formidable, and had many powerful friends. With all his preju-

---

¹ " The first whimsical circumstance, which drew the eyes of the world upon him, was his introduction of the Mock Procession of Masonry, in which Mr. 'Squire Carey gave him much assistance: and so powerful was the laugh and satire against that secret society, that the anniversary parade was laid aside from that period.'' Captain Thomson's Life of Whitehead, p. vii. But Whitehead was long known to the world before this mock procession, which did not take place till the year 1744, 'Squire Carey was a surgeon in Pall Mall, and an associate of Ralph and other minor humourists of the day. *C.*

² Boswell's Life of Johnson, vol. i. p. 102. edit. 1807.
³ Johnson's Life of Pope.

dices, he was the first poet of the age and an honour to his country. But Paul Whitehead was less entitled to respect: he was formidable rather by his calumny than his talents, and might be prosecuted with effect.

Accordingly, in the house of peers, lord Delawar, after expatiating on the gross falsehoods and injurious imputations contained in the poem, against many noblemen and prelates of high character, moved that the author and publisher should attend at the bar of the house. On the day appointed, Dodsley appeared as the publisher, Whitehead having absconded. Dodsley pleaded that he did not look into the contents of the poem, " but that imagining there might be something in it, as he saw it was a satire by its title-page, that might be laid hold of in law, he insisted that the author should affix his name to it, and that then he printed it." In consequence of this confession, he was taken into the custody of the usher of the black rod, but released after a short confinement and payment of the usual fees[4].

No farther steps were taken against the author of Manners: the whole process, indeed, was supposed to be intended rather to intimidate Pope, than to punish Whitehead, and it answered that purpose: Pope became cautious, " willing to wound and yet afraid to strike," and Whitehead for some years remained quiet.

The noise, however, which this prosecution occasioned, and its failure as to the main object, induced Whitehead's enemies to try whether he might not be assailed in another way, and rendered the subject of odium, if not of punishment. In this pursuit, the authors of some of the ministerial journals published a letter from a Cambridge student, who had been expelled for atheism, in which it was intimated that Whitehead belonged to a club of young men who assembled to encourage one another in shaking off what they termed the prejudices of education. But Whitehead did not suffer this to disturb the retirement so necessary in his present circumstances, and as the accusation had no connection with his politics or his poetry, he was content to sacrifice his character with respect to religion, which he did not value, in support of the cause he had espoused. That he was an infidel seems generally acknowledged by all his biographers, and when he joined the club at Mednam Abbey, it must be confessed that his practices did not disgrace his profession.

In 1744, he published The Gymnasiad, a just satire on the savage amusements of the boxers, which were then more publicly, if not more generally encouraged, than in our own days. Broughton, who died within these few years at Lambeth, was at that time the invincible champion, and Whitehead accordingly dedicated the poem to him in a strain of easy humour. Soon after he published Honour[5],

---

[4] In order to procure this lenity, Dodsley drew up a petition to the house, which the earl of Essex, one of the noble personages libelled in the poem, had the generosity to present. Victor, in one of his Letters, informs us that he had the boldness to suggest this measure to the earl. C.

[5] " I must tell you that the celebrated Mr. Paul Whitehead has been at Deal, with a family where I often visit: and it was my fate to be once in his company much against my will : for having naturally as strong an antipathy to a wit, as some people have to a cat, I at first fairly run away to avoid it. However, at last I was dragged in, and condemned by my perverse fortune to hear part of a *satyre* just ready for the press. Considered as poetry and wit, it had some extremely fine

another satire at the expense of the leading men in power, whom he calum₋ niates with all that relentless and undistinguishing bitterness in which Churchill afterwards excelled.

We next find him an active partizan in the contested election for Westminster, between lord Trentham, and sir George Vandeput, in 1749. He not only can₋ vassed for sir George (for whom also his patron Doddington voted) but wrote the greater part of his advertisements, handbills and paragraphs. He wrote also the case of the hon. Alexander Murray, who was sent to Newgate for heading a riot on that occasion.

In 1755, he published An Epistle to Dr. Thomson. This physician was one of the persons who shared in the convivial hours of Mr. Doddington, afterwards lord Melcombe, although it is not easy to discover what use he could make of a physician out of practice, a man of most slovenly habits, and who had neither taste nor talents. It was at his lordship's house, where Whitehead became acquainted with this man, and looked up to him as an oracle both in politics and physic, and here too he associated very cordially with Ralph, whom he had abused with so much contempt in the State Dunces. From his Diary lately published, and from some of his unpublished letters, in my posses₋ sion, it appears that Doddington had no great respect for Thomson, and merely used Whitehead, Ralph and others, as convenient tools in his various political intrigues. Whitehead's epistle is an extravagant encomium on Thomson, of whose medical talents he could be no judge, and which, if his Treatise on the Small-pox be a specimen, were likely to be more formidable to his patients than to his brethren.

Except a small pamphlet on the disputes, in 1768, between the four managers of Covent-Garden Theatre, the Epistle to Dr. Thomson was the last of our author's detached publications. The lesser pieces to be found in his works were occasional trifles written for the theatres or public gardens. He was now in easy, if not affluent circumstances. By the interest of lord le Despenser, he got the place of deputy-treasurer of the chamber, worth 800l. and held it to his death. On this acquisition, he purchased a cottage on Twickenham Common, and from a de₋ sign of his friend Isaac Ware, the architect, at a small expense improved it into an elegant villa. Here, according to sir John Hawkins, he was visited by very few of the inhabitants of that classical spot, but his house was open to all his London acquaintance, Hogarth, Lambert and Hayman, painters, Isaac Ware, Beard and Howard, &c. In such company principally he passed the remainder of his days, suffering the memory of his poetry and politics to decay gradually. His death happened at his lodgings in Henrietta Street, Covent-Garden, Dec. 30, 1774. For some time previous to this event he lingered under a severe illness, during which he employed himself in burning all his manuscripts ; among these

strokes: but the vile practice of exalting some characters, and abusing others, without any co₋ lour of truth or justice, has something so shocking in it, that the finest genius in the world, can₋ not, I think, take from the horrour of, and I had much ado to sit with any kind of patience to hear it out. Surely there is nothing more provoking than to see fine talents so wretchedly misapplied," Part of a letter from Mrs. Carter, (in her Memoirs lately published by the rev. Mr. Pennington) and dated April 1745.

were originals of many occasional pieces of poetry written for the amusement of his friends, some of which had probably been published without his name, and cannot now be distinguished. His works, as given in this collection, were published in an elegant quarto volume (in 1777) by captain Edward Thomson, who prefixed Memoirs of his Life, in which we have found very little that had not been published in the Annual Register of 1775. The character Thomson gives of him is an overstrained panegyric, inconsistent in itself, and more so when compared with some facts which he had not the sense to conceal, nor the virtue to censure.

Whitehead's character has never been in much esteem, yet it was not uniformly bad. Those who adopt the severe sentence passed by Churchill, in these lines,

> May I (can worse disgrace on manhood fall?)
> Be born a WHITEHEAD and baptised a Paul[6].

will want nothing else to excite abhorrence ; but Churchill has taken too many liberties with truth to be believed without corroborating evidence. Besides, we are to consider what part of Whitehead's conduct excited this indignation. Paul's great and unpardonable crime, in Churchill's eyes, was his accepting a place under government, and laying aside a pen, which, in conjunction with Churchill's, might have created wonders in the political world. Churchill could not dislike him because he was an infidel and a man of pleasure. In point of morals there was surely not much difference in the misfortune of being born a Whitehead or a Churchill.

How very erroneous Whitehead's life had been, is too evident from his having shared in those scenes of blasphemy and debauchery which were performed at Medmenham or Mednam Abbey, a house on the Thames near Marlow in Buckinghamshire. His noble patron, (then sir Francis Dashwood,) sir Thomas Stapleton, John Wilkes, Whitehead and others combined, at this place, in a scheme of impious and sensual indulgence unparalleled in the annals of infamy : and perhaps there cannot be a more striking proof of want of shame as well as of virtue, than the circumstance which occasioned the discovery of this refined brothel[7]. Wilkes was the first person to disclose the shocking secret, and that merely out of a pique against one of the members who had promoted the prosecution against him for writing the Essay on Woman. In the same note to one of Churchill's poems in which he published the transactions of this profligate cabal, he was not ashamed to insert his own name as a partner in the guilt.

[6] Captain Thomson, whose notions of right and wrong are more confused than those of any man who ever pretended to delineate a character, says that in these lines Churchill meant "to be neither illiberal nor ill natured." " One would conclude, that he had a very particular enmity to Paul Whitehead, but, *to do him justice,* he had enmity to no man: very few breasts ever possessed more philanthropy, charity and honour !" *C.*

[7] After such an account of the indecencies practised at this place as could become the character only of the shameless narrator, captain Thomson sums up the whole in these words, which are an additional specimen of his ability in delineating moral character.—" Now all that can be drawn from the publication of these ceremonies is, that a set of worthy, jolly fellows, happy disciples of Venus and Bacchus, got occasionally together, to celebrate women in wine: and to give more zest to the festive meeting, they plucked every luxurious idea from the ancients, and enriched their own modern pleasures with the addition of classic luxury."—It may be necessary to inform the reader, that among their modern pleasures, they assumed the names of the apostles, nothing in whose history was sacred from their impious ribaldry. *C.*

That Whitehead repented of the share he took in this club, we are not told. His character suffered, however, in common with that of the other members: and he appears to have been willing to " buy golden opinions of all men" by acts of popularity, and gain some respect from his social, if he could gain none from his personal virtues. Sir John Hawkins represents him, as by nature a friendly and kind-hearted man, well acquainted with vulgar manners and the town, but little skilled in knowledge of the world, and little able to resist the arts of designing men. He had married a woman of a good family and fortune, whom, though homely in her person, and little better than an ideot[8], he treated not only with humanity, but with tenderness, hiding, as well as he was able, those defects in her understanding, which are oftener the subjects of ridicule than compassion. At Twickenham, adds sir John, he manifested the good-ness of his nature in the exercise of kind offices, in healing breaches and com-posing differences between his poor neighbours[9].

But whatever care Whitehead took to retrieve his character, and throw ob-livion over the most blameable part of his life, he unintentionally revived the whole by a clause in his will, in which, out of *gratitude*, he bequeathed his HEART to lord le Despencer, and desired it might be deposited, if his lordship pleased, in some corner of his mausoleum. These terms were accordingly fulfilled, and the valuable relic deposited with the ceremony of a military proces-sion, vocal performers habited, as a choir, in surplices, and every other testimony of veneration. The whole was followed by the performance of an oratorio in West Wycombe church. The following incantation which was sung at the placing of the urn in the mausoleum, may be a sufficient specimen of this solemn mockery :

> From Earth to Heaven WHITEHEAD's soul is fled :
> Refulgent glories beam around his head !
> His Muse, concording with resounding strings,
> Gives angels words to praise the King of kings.

His poems were appended to the last edition of Dr. Johnson's collection, and I have not therefore ventured to displace them. Yet it may be doubtful whether any partiality can assign him a very high rank even among versifiers. He was a professed imitator of Pope in his satires, and may be entitled to all the praise which successful imitation deserves. His lines are in general harmonious and correct, and sometimes vigorous, but he owes his popularity chiefly to the personal calumnies so liberally thrown out against men of rank, in the defamation of whom a very active and extensive party was strongly inter-ested. Like Churchill's, therefore, his works were forgotten when the con-tending parties were removed or reconciled. But he had not the energetic and original genius of Churchill, nor can we find many passages in which the spirit of genuine poetry is discoverable. Of his character as a poet, he was himself

---

[8] His biographer, above mentioned, calls her " a most amiable lady." She died, however, young.

[9] Hawkins' Life of Dr. Johnson.

very careless, considering it perhaps as only the temporary instrument of his advancement to ease and independence. No persuasions could induce him to collect his works, and they would probably never have been collected, had not the frequent mention of his name in conjunction with those of his political patrons, and the active services of his pen, created a something like permanent reputation, and a desire to collect the various documents by which the history of factions may be illustrated.

# POEMS

#### OF

## PAUL WHITEHEAD.

---

THE

### STATE DUNCES:

A SATIRE. INSCRIBED TO MR. POPE, 1733.

I from my soul sincerely hate
Both kings and ministers of state.

SWIFT.

WHILE cringing crowds at faithless levees
  wait,
Fond to be fools of fame, or slaves of state;
And others, studious to increase their store,
Plough the rough ocean for Peruvian ore:
How blest thy fate, whom calmer hours attend,
Peace thy companion, fame thy faithful friend!
While in thy Twick'nham bow'rs, devoid of
  care
You feast the fancy, and enchant the ear;
Thames gently rolls her silver tide along,
And the charm'd Naiads listen to thy song.
Here, peaceful pass the gentle hours away,
While tuneful science measures out the day!
Here happy bard, as various fancies lead,
You paint the blooming maid, or flow'ry mead!
Sound the rough clangour of tumultuous war,[1]
Or sing the ravish'd tendrils of the fair[2]!
Now melting move the tender tear to flow,
And wake our sighs with Eloisa's woe[3].
But chief, to dullness ever foe decreed,
The apes of science with thy satire bleed[4];
Peers, poets, panders, mingle in the throng,
Smart with thy touch, and tremble at thy
  songs.
  Yet vain, O Pope! is all thy sharpest rage,
Still starv'ling Dunces persecute the age;
Faithful to folly, or enrag'd with spite,
Still tasteless Timons build, and Tibbalds write;

[1] Homer.  [2] Rape of the Lock.
[3] Eloisa to Abelard.  [4] Dunciad.
[5] Epistles.

Still Welstead[6] tunes his beer-inspired lays,
And Ralph, in metre, holds forth Stanhope's
Ah! hapless victim to the poet's flame, [praise,
While his eulogiums crucify thy fame.
  Shall embrio wits thy studious hours engage,
Live in thy labours, and prophane thy page;
While virtue, ever-lov'd, demands thy lays,
And claims the tuneful tribute of thy praise?
Can Pope be silent, and not grateful lend
One strain to sing the patriot, and the friend,
Who, nobly anxious in his country's cause,
Maintains her honours, and defends her laws?
Could I, my bard, but equal numbers raise,
Then would I sing—for, oh! I burst to praise—
Sing how a Pult'ney[7] charms the list'ning throng,
While senates hang enraptur'd on his tongue;
With Tully's fire how each oration glows,
In Tully's music how each period flows;
Instruct each babe to lisp the patriot's name,
Who in each bosom breathes a Roman flame.
So, when the genius of the Roman age
Stemm'd the strong torrent of tyrannic rage,
In freedom's cause each glowing breast he
  warm'd,
And, like a Pult'ney, then a Brutus charm'd.
  How blest, while we a British Brutus see,
And all the Roman stands confest in thee!
Equal thy worth, but equal were thy doom,
To save Britannia, as he rescu'd Rome:
He from a Tarquin snatch'd the destin'd prey;
Britannia still laments a Walpole's sway.
  Arise, my tuneful bard, nor thus in vain
Let thy Britannia, whom thou lov'st, complain:

[6] Still Welstead, .... And Ralph.] Two authors, remarkable for nothing so much as the
figure they make in the Dunciad, unjustly, on
the part of Welstead, who certainly was not a
despicable writer. Whitehead was afterwards
very intimate with Ralph, whom he frequently
met at Bubb Doddington's.—C.
  [7] Afterwards earl of Bath.

If thou in moanful lays relate her woe,
Each heart shall bleed, each eye with pity flow:
If to revenge you swell the sounding strain,
Revenge and fury fire each British swain :
Obsequious to thy verse each breast shall move,
Or burn with rage, or soften into love.
O let Britannia be her poet's care !
And lash the spoiler, while you save the fair.
Lo ! where he stands, amidst the servile crew,
Nor blushes stain his cheek with crimson hue ;
While dire corruption all around he spreads,
And ev'ry ductile conscience captive leads :
Brib'd by his boons, behold the venal band
Worship the idol they could once command ;
So Britain's now, as Judah's sons before,
First raise a golden calf, and then adore.
    Let dull Parnassian sons of rhyme no more
Provoke thy satire, and employ thy pow'r ;
New objects rise to share an equal fate,
The big, rich, mighty, Dunces of the State.
Shall Ralph, Cooke, Welstead, then engross thy
      rage,
While courts afford a Hervey, York, or Gage ?
Dullness no more roosts only near the sky,
But senates, drawing-rooms, with garrets vie ;
Plump peers, and breadless bards, alike are dull;
St. James's and Rag-fair club fool for fool.
    Amidst the mighty dull, behold how great
An Appius swells, the Tibbald of the state !
Long have he strove to spread his lawless sway
O'er Britain's sons, and force them to obey ;
But, blasted all his blooming hopes, he flies
To vent his woe, and mourn his lost excise.
    Pensive he sat, and sigh'd, while round him
      lay
Loads of dull lumber, all inspir'd by pay :
Here, puny pamphlets, spun from prelates'
    brains ;            [strains :
There, the smooth jingle of Cooke's lighter
Here, Walsingham's [8] soft lulling opiate spread ;
There, gloomy Osborn's [8] quintessence of lead :
With these the statesman strove to ease his
      care,
To sooth his sorrows, and divert despair :
But long his grief sleep's gentle aid denies :
At length a slumb'rous Briton clos'd his eyes.
    Yet vain the healing balm of downy rest,
To chase his woe, or ease his lab'ring breast :
Now frightful forms rise hideous to his view;
More, Strafford, Laud, and all the headless crew;
Daggers and halters boding terrour breeds,
And here a Dudley swings, there Villiers bleeds.
    Now goddess Dulness, watchful o'er his fate,
And ever anxious for her child of state ;
From couch of down slow rais'd her drowsy head,
Forsook her slumbers, and to Appius sped.
    " Awake, my son, awake," the goddess cries,
" Nor longer mourn thy darling lost excise :"
(Here the sad sound unseal'd the statesman's
    eyes)
" Why slumbers thus my son, opprest with care ?
While Dullness rules, say, shall her sons despair?
O'er all I spread my universal sway ;
Kings, prelates, peers, and rulers, all obey :
Lo ! in the church my mighty pow'r I shew,
In pulpit preach, and slumber in the pew :

[8] Names assumed by writers of two ministerial papers.

The bench and bar alike my influence owns ;
Here prate my magpies, and there doze my
    drones.
In the grave dons, how formal is my mien,
Who rule the gallipots of Warwick-lane :
At court behold me strut in purple pride,
At Hockley roar, and in Crane-court preside.
But chief in thee my mighty pow'r is seen ;
'Tis I inspire thy mind, and fill thy mien ;
On thee, my child, my duller blessings shed,
And pour my opium o'er thy fav'rite head ;
Rais'd thee a ruler of Britannia's fate,
And led thee blund'ring to the helm of state."
    Here bow'd the statesman low, and thus ad-
    drest :
" O goddess, sole inspirer of my breast !
To gall the British neck with Gallic chain,
Long have I strove, but long have strove in vain ;
While Caleb[9], rebel to thy sacred pow'r,
Unveils those eyes which thou hast curtain'd o'er;
Makes Britain's sons my dark designs foresee,
Blast all my schemes, and struggle to be free.
O, had my projects met a milder fate,
How had I reign'd a basha of the state !
How o'er Britannia spread imperial sway !
How taught each free-born Briton to obey !
No smiling freedom then had cheer'd her swains,
But Asia's deserts vy'd with Albion's plains :
Turks, Vandals, Britain ! then compar'd with
    thee,           [were free ;
Had hugg'd their chains, and joy'd that they
While wond'ring nations all around had seen
Me rise a great Mogul, or Mazarin :
Then had I taught Britannia to adore,
Then led her captive to my lawless pow'r.
Methinks, I view her now no more appear
First in the train, and fairest 'midst the fair :
Joyless I see the lovely mourner lie,
Nor glow her cheek, nor sparkle now her eye;
Faded each grace, no smiling feature warm ;
Torn all her tresses, blighted ev'ry charm :
Nor teeming plenty now each valley crowns ;
Slaves are her sons, and tradeless all her towns.
For this, behold yon peaceful army fed ;
For this, on senates see my bounty shed ;
For this, what wonders, goddess, have I wrought !
How bully'd, begg'd, how treated, and how
    fought !
What wand'ring maze of error blunder'd through,
And how repair'd old blunders still by new !
Hence the long train of never ending jars,
Of warful peaces, and of peaceful wars,
Each mystic treaty of the mighty store,
Which to explain, demands ten treaties more :
Hence scarecrow navies, floating raree-shows ;
And hence Iberia's pride, and Britain's woes.
These wond'rous works, O goddess ! have I done,
Works ever worthy Dulness' fav'rite son.
    " Lo ! on thy sons alone my favours show'r ;
None share my bounty that disdain thy pow'r :
Yon feathers, ribbons, titles light as air,
Behold, thy choicest children only share :
Each views the pageant with admiring eyes,
And fondly grasps the visionary prize ;
Now proudly spreads his leading-string of state,
And thinks—to be a wretch, is to be great.

[9] Caleb D'Anvers, the name assumed by the writers of the Craftsman.

" But turn, O goddess ! turn thine eyes, and
    view
The darling leaders of thy gloomy crew.
  " Full open-mouth'd Newcastle there behold,
Aping a Tully, swell into a scold,
Grievous to mortal ear.—As at the place
Where loud tongu'd virgins vend the scaly race,
Harsh peals of vocal thunder fill the skies,
And stunning sounds in hideous discord rise ;
So, when he tries the wond'rous power of noise,
Each hapless ear's a victim to his voice.
    [10] How blest, O Cheselden ! whose art can
      mend
    Those ears Newcastle was ordain'd to rend.
  " See Harrington secure in silence sit ;
No empty words betray his want of wit:
If sense in hiding folly is express'd,
O Harrington ! thy wisdom stands confess'd.
  " To Dullness' sacred cause for ever true,
Thy darling Caledonian, goddess, view ;
The pride and glory of thy Scotia's plains,
And faithful leader of her venal swains :
Loaded he moves beneath a servile weight,
The dull laborious packhorse of the state ;
Drudges through tracks of infamy for pay,
And hackneys out his conscience by the day :
Yonder behold the busy peerless peer,
With aspect meagre and important air ;
His form how gothic, and his looks how sage !
He seems the living Plato of the age.
    Blest form !`in which alone thy merit's
      seen,
    Since all thy wisdom centers in thy mien !
  " Here Egmont, Albemarle, (for senates fit)
And W—— by the wise, in council sit :
Here looby G——n, Gr——m over dull,
By birth a senator, by fate a fool.
  " While these, Britannia, watchful o'er thy
    state,
Maintain thine honours, and direct thy fate,
How shall admiring nations round adore,
Behold thy greatness, tremble at thy pow'r ;
New Shebas come, invited by thy fame,
Revere thy wisdom, and extol thy name!
  " Lo ! to yon bench now, goddess, turn thine
And view thy sons in solemn dullness rise : [eyes,
All doating, wrinkled, grave, and gloomy, see
Each form confess thy dull divinity ;
True to thy cause behold each trencher'd sage
Increas'd in folly as advanc'd in age :
Here Ch——r, learn'd in mystic prophecy,
Confuting Collins, makes each prophet lie :
Poor Woolston by thy Smallbrook there assail'd;
Jails sure convinc'd him, though the prelate
    fail'd.
  " But chief Pastorius, ever grave and dull,
Devoid of sense, of zeal divinely full,
Retails his squibs of science o'er the town,
While charges, past'rals, through each street
    resound ;
These teach a heav'nly Jesus to obey,
While those maintain an earthly Appius' sway.
    Thy gospel truth, Pastorius, crost we see,
    While God and Mammon's serv'd at once by
      thee.
  " Who wou'd not trim, speak, vote, or consci-
    ence pawn,
To lord it o'er a see, and swell in lawn ?

  [1o] William Cheselden, an eminent surgeon.
VOL. XVI.

If arts like those, O Sherlock, honours claim,
Than thee none merits more the prelate's name:
Wond'ring behold him faithful to his fee,
Prove-parliaments dependent to be free ;
In senates blunder, flounder and dispute,
For ever reas'ning, never to confute.
Since courts for this their fated gifts decree,
Say, what is reputation to a see ?
  " Lo ! o'er yon flood Hare casts his low'ring
And wishful sees the rev'rend turrets rise. [eyes,
While Lambeth opens to thy longing view,
Hapless ! the mitre ne'er can bind thy brow :
Though courts should deign the gift, how won-
    d'rous hard
By thy own doctrines still to be debarr'd !
For, if from change [11] such mighty evil springs,
Translations sure, O Hare ! are sinful things.
  " These rulers see, and nameless numbers
O goddess, of thy train the choicest store, [more,
Who ignorance in gravity entrench,
And grace alike the pulpit and the bench.
  "Full plac'd and pension'd,see! Horatio stands;
Begrim'd his face, unpurify'd his hands :
To decency he scorns all nice pretence,
And reigns firm foe to cleanliness and sense.
How did Horatio Britain's cause advance !
How shine the sloven and buffoon of France !
In senates now, how scold, how rave, how roar,
Of treaties run the tedious train-trow o'er !
How blunder out whate'er should be conceal'd,
And how keep secret what should be reveal'd !
True child of Dullness ! see him, goddess, claim
Pow'r next myself, as next in birth and fame.
  " Silence ! ye senates, while enribbon'd Younge
Pours forth melodious nothings from his tongue !
How sweet the accents play around the ear,
Form'd of smooth periods, and of well-tun'd
    air !
Leave, gentle Younge, the senate's dry debate,
Nor labour 'midst the labyrinths of state ;
Suit thy soft genius to more tender themes,
And sing of cooling shades, and purling streams;
With modern sing-song murder ancient plays [12],
Or warble in sweet ode a Brunswick's praise:
So shall thy strains in purer dullness flow,
And laurels wither on a Cibber's brow.
Say, can the statesman wield the poet's quill,
And quit the senate for Parnassus' Hill ?
Since there no venal vote a pension shares,
Nor wants Apollo lords commissioners.
  " There W—— and P——, goddess, view,
Firm in thy cause, and to thy Appius true !
Lo ! from their labours what reward betides !
One pays my army, one my navy guides.
  "To dance, dress, sing, and serenade the fair,
' Conduct a finger, or reclaim a hair,'
O'er baleful tea with females taught to blame,
And spread a slander o'er a virgin's fame,
Form'd for these softer arts shall Hervey strain
With stubborn politics his tender brain !

  [11] A noted sermon preached on the 30th of
January, on this text, " Woe be unto them that
are given to change," &c.
  [12] This gentleman,with the assistance of Roome,
Concanen, and several others, altered the comedy of the Jovial Crew into a modern ballad
opera; which was scarce exhibited on the stage,
before it was thought necessary to be contracted
into one act.

For ministers laborious pamphlets write,
In senates prattle, and with patriots fight!
Thy fond ambition, pretty youth, give o'er,
Preside at balls, old fashions lost restore;
So shall each toilette in thy cause engage,
And H——ey shine a P——re of the age.
 " Behold a star emblazon C——n's coat!
Not that the knight has merit, but a vote.
And here, O goddess, num'rous wrongheads trace,
Lur'd by a pension, ribband, or a place.
 " To murder science, and my cause defend,
Now shoals of Grub-street garretteers descend;
From schools and desks the writing insects crawl,
Unlade their dullness, and for Appius bawl.
 " Lo! to thy darling Osborne turn thine eyes,
See him o'er politics superior rise;
While Caleb feels the venom of his quill;
And wond'ring ministers reward his skill:
Unlearn'd in logic, yet he writes by rule,
And proves himself in syllogism—a fool;
Now flies obedient, war with sense to wage,
And drags th' idea thro' the painful page:
Unread, unanswer'd, still he writes again,
Still spins the endless cobweb of his brain:
Charm'd with each line, reviewing what he writ,
Blesses his stars, and wonders at his wit.
 "Nor less, O Walsingham, thy worth appears!
Alike in merit, tho' unlike in years:
Ill-fated youth! what stars malignant shed
Their baneful influence o'er thy brainless head,
Doom'd to be ever writing, never read!
For bread to libel liberty and sense,
And damn thy patron weekly with defence.
Drench'd in the sable flood, O hadst thou still
O'er skins of parchment drove thy venal quill,
At Temple ale-house told an idle tale,
And pawn'd thy credit for a mug of ale;
Unknown to Appius then had been thy name,
Unlac'd thy coat, unsacrific'd his fame;
Nor vast unvended reams would Peele deplore,
As victims destin'd to the common-shore.
 " As dunce to dunce in endless numbers breed,
So to Concanen see a Ralph succeed;
A tiny witling of these writing days,     [plays.
Full-fam'd for tuneless rhimes, and short-liv'd
Write on, my luckless bard, still unasham'd,
Tho' burnt thy journals, and thy dramas damn'd;
'Tis bread inspires thy politics and lays,
Not thirst of immortality or praise.
 "These, goddess, view, the choicest of the train,
While yet unnumber'd dunces still remain;
Deans, critics, lawyers, bards, a motley crew,
To dullness faithful, as to Appius true."

 "Enough," the goddess cries, "enough I've seen;
While these support, secure my son shall reign;
Still shalt thou blund'ring rule Britannia's fate,
Still Grub-street hail thee minister of state.

## MANNERS:

### A SATIRE, 1738.

Paulus vel Cossus vel Drusus moribus esto.

                                    JUVENAL.

 " WELL—of all plagues which make mankind
        their sport,          [—a court.
Guard me, ye Heav'ns! from that worst plague

'Midst the mad mansions of Moorfields, I'd be
A straw-crown'd monarch, in mock majesty,
Rather than sovereign rule Britannia's fate,
Curs'd with the follies and the farce of state.
Rather in Newgate walls, O! let me dwell,
A doleful tenant of the darkling cell,
Than swell, in palaces, the mighty store
Of fortune's fools, and parasites of pow'r.
Than crowns, ye gods! be any state my doom,
Or any dungeon, but—a drawing-room.
 "Thrice happy patriot! whom no courts debase,
No titles lessen, and no stars disgrace.
Still nod the plumage o'er the brainless head;
Still o'er the faithless heart the ribband spread.
Such toys may serve to signalize the tool;
To gild the knave, or garnish out the fool;
While you, with Roman virtue arm'd, disdain
The tinsel trappings and the glitt'ring chain:
Fond of your freedom spurn the venal fee,
And prove he's only great—who dares be free."
Thus sung Philemon in his calm retreat,
Too wise for pow'r, too virtuous to be great.
 " But whence this rage at courts?" reply'd his
        grace,
" Say, is the mighty crime, to be in place?
Is that the deadly sin, mark'd out by Heav'n,
For which no mortal e'er can be forgiv'n?
Must all, all suffer, who in courts engage,
Down from lord steward, to the puny page?
Can courts and places be such sinful things,
The sacred gifts and palaces of kings?"
 A place may claim our rev'rence, sir, I own;
But then the man its dignity must crown:
'Tis not the truncheon, or the ermine's pride,
Can screen the coward, or the knave can hide.
Let Stair and *** head our arms and law,
The judge and gen'ral must be view'd with awe:
The villain then would shudder at the bar;
And Spain grow humble at the sound of war.
 What courts are sacred, when I tell your grace,
Manners alone must sanctify the place?
Hence only each its proper name receives;
Haywood's a brothel; White's¹ a den of thieves:
Bring whores and thieves to court, you change
        the scene,
St. James's turns the brothel, and the den.
Who would the courtly chapel holy call,
Tho' the whole bench should consecrate the wall?
While the trim chaplain, conscious of a fee,
Cries out, " My king, I have no God but thee;"
Lifts to the royal seat the asking eye,
And pays to George the tribute of the sky;
Proves sin alone from humble roofs must spring,
Nor can one earthly failing stain a king.
 Bishops and kings may consecrate, 'tis true;
Manners alone claim homage as their due.
Without, the court and church are both prophane,
Whatever prelate preach, or monarch reign;
Religion's rostrum virtue's scaffold grows,
And crowns and mitres are mere raree-shows.
In vain, behold yon rev'rend turrets rise,
And Sarum's sacred spire salute the skies!

———

 ¹ Dr. Swift says, " that the late earl of Oxford, in the time of his ministry, never passed by White's chocolate-house (the common rendezvous of infamous sharpers and noble cullies) without bestowing a curse upon that famous academy, as the bane of half the English nobility."

If the lawn'd Levite's earthly vote be sold,
And God's free gift retail'd for Mammon gold;
No rev'rence can the proud cathedral claim,
But Henley's shop, and Sherlock's, are the same.
  Whence have St. Stephen's walls so hallow'd
     been?
Whence? From the virtue of his sons within.
But should some guileful serpent, void of grace,
Glide in its bounds, and poison all the place;
Should e'er the sacred voice be set to sale,
And o'er the heart the golden fruit prevail;
The place is alter'd, sir; nor think it strange
To see the senate sink into a change.
  Or court, or church, or senate-house, or hall,
Manners alone beam dignity on all.
Without their influence, palaces are cells;
Crane-court², a magazine of cockle-shells;
The solemn bench no bosom strikes with awe,
But Westminster's a warehouse of the law.
  These honest truths, my lord, deny who can;
Since all allow that " Manners make the man."
Hence only glories to the great belong,
Or peers must mingle with the peasant throng.
  Though strung with ribbands, yet behold his
Shines but a lacquey in a higher place! [grace
Strip the gay liv'ry from the courtier's back,
What marks the diff'rence 'twixt my lord and Jack?
The same mean, supple, mercenary knave,
The tool of power, and of state the slave:
Alike the vassal heart in each prevails,
And all his lordship boasts is larger vales.
  Wealth, manors, titles, may descend, 'tis true;
But ev'ry heir must merit's claim renew.
Who blushes not to see a C—— heir
Turn slave to sound, and languish for a play'r³?
What piping, fidling, squeaking, quav'ring, brawl-
    ing!
What sing-song riot, and what eunuch-squawling!
C——, thy worth with all Italy shall own,
A statesman fit, where Nero⁴ fill'd the throne.
  See poor Lævinus, anxious for renown,
Through the long gallery trace his lineage down,
And claim each hero's visage for his own.
What though in each the self same features shine,
Unless some lineal virtue marks the line,
In vain, alas! he boasts his grandsire's name,
Or hopes to borrow lustre of his fame.
Who but must smile, to see the tim'rous peer
Point 'mong his race our bulwark in the war?
Or in sad English tell how senates hung
On the sweet music of his father's tongue?
Unconscious, though his sires were wise and brave,
Their virtues only find in him a grave.
  Not so with Stanhope⁵; see by him sustain'd
Each hoary honour which his sires had gain'd.
To him the virtues of his race appear
The precious portion of five hundred year;
Descended down, by him to be enjoy'd,
Yet holds the talent lost, if unemploy'd.
From hence behold his gen'rous ardour rise,
To swell the sacred stream with fresh supplies:

² The Royal Society.

³ That extraordinary instance of the folly, extravagance, and depravity of the English, Farinello.

⁴ A Roman emperor remarkable for his passion for music.

⁵ The right honourable the earl of Chesterfield.

Abroad, the guardian of his country's cause;
At home, a Tully to defend her laws.
Senates with awe the patriot sounds imbibe,
And bold corruption almost drops the bribe.
Thus added worth to worth, and grace to grace,
He beams new glories back upon his race.
  Ask ye, what's honour? I'll the truth impart.
Know, honour, then, is honesty of heart.
To the sweet scenes of social Stow⁶ repair,
And search the master's breast,—you'll find it
    there.
Too proud to grace the sycophant or slave,
It only harbours with the wise and brave;
Ungain'd by titles, places, wealth, or birth:
Learn this, and learn to blush, ye sons of Earth!
Blush to behold this ray of nature made
The victim of a ribband, or cockade.
  Ask the proud peer, what's honour? he dis-
    plays
A purchas'd patent, or the herald's blaze;
Or, if the royal smile his hopes has blest,
Points to the glitt'ring glory on his breast:
Yet, if beneath no real virtue reign,
On the gay coat the star is but a stain:
For I could whisper in his lordship's ear,
Worth only beams true radiance on the star.
  Hence see the garter'd glory dart its rays,
And shine round E—— with redoubled blaze:
Ask ye from whence this flood of lustre's seen?
Why E—— whispers, votes, and saw Turin.
  Long Milo reign'd the minion of renown;
Loud his eulogiums echo'd through the town:
Where'er he went, still crowds around him throng,
And hail'd the patriot as he pass'd along.
See the lost peer, unhonour'd now by all,
Steal through the street, or skulk along the Mall;
Applauding sounds no more salute his ear,
But the loud Pæan's sunk into a sneer.
Whence, you'll inquire, could spring a change so
Why, the poor man ran military mad; [sad?
By this mistaken maxim still misled,
That men of honour must be cloth'd in red.
My grandsire wore it, Milo cries—'tis good;
But know, the grandsire stain'd it red with blood.
First 'midst the deathful dangers of the field,
He shone his country's guardian, and its shield;
Taught Danube's stream with Gallic gore to flow;
Hence bloom'd the laurel on the grandsire's brow;
But shall the son expect the wreath to wear,
For the mock triumphs of an Hyde-park war?
Sooner shall Bunhill, Blenheim's glories claim,
Or Billers rival brave Eugene in fame;
Sooner a like reward their labours crown,
Who storm a dunghill, and who sack a town.
  Mark our bright youths, how gallant and how
    gay,
Fresh plum'd and powder'd in review array,
Unspoil'd each feature by the martial scar,
Lo! A—— assumes the god of war: [pay,
Yet vain, while prompt to arms by plume and
He claims the soldier's name from soldier's play.
This truth, my warrior, treasure in thy breast;
A standing soldier is a standing jest.
When bloody battles dwindle to reviews,
Armies must then descend to puppet-shews;
Where the lac'd log may strut the soldier's part,
Bedeck'd with feather, though unarm'd with heart

⁶ The seat of the right honourable the lord viscount Cobham.

There are who say, " You lash the sins of men!
Leave, leave to Pope the poignance of the pen ;
Hope not the bays shall wreath around thy head;
Fannius may write, but Flaccus will be read."
Shall only one have privilege to blame?
What then, are vice and folly royal game?
Must all be poachers who attempt to kill?
All, but the mighty sovereign of the quill?
Shall Pope, alone, the plenteous harvest have,
And I not glean one straggling fool, or knave?
Praise, 'tis allow'd, is free to all mankind ;
Say, why should honest satire be confin'd?
Though, like th' immortal bard's, my feeble dart
Stains not its feather in the culprit heart ;
Yet know, the smallest insect of the wing
The horse may tease, or elephant can sting :
Ev'n I, by chance, some lucky darts may show'r,
And gall some great leviathans of pow'r.
I name not Walpole; you the reason guess ;
Mark yon fell harpy hov'ring o'er the press.
Secure the Muse may sport with names of kings;
But ministers, my friend, are dang'rous things.
Who would have Paxton 7 answer what he writ ;
Or special juries, judges of his wit ?
Pope writes unhurt—but know, 'tis diff'rent
    quite
To beard the lion, and to crush the mite.
Safe may he dash the statesman in each line ;
Those dread his satire, who dare punish mine.
" Turn, turn your satire then," you cry, " to
    praise."
Why, praise is satire, in these sinful days.
Say, should I make a patriot of sir Bill,
Or swear that G——'s duke has wit at will ;
From the gull'd knight could I expect a place,
Or hope to lie a dinner from his grace,
Though a reward be graciously bestow'd
On the soft satire of each birth-day ode ?
The good and bad alike with praise are blest ;
Yet those who merit most, still want it least:
But conscious vice still courts the cheering ray,
While virtue shines, nor asks the glare of day.
Need I to any, Pult'ney's worth declare ?
Or tell him Carteret charms, who has an ear ?
Or, Pitt, can thy example be unknown,
While each fond father marks it to his son ?
I cannot truckle to a slave in state,
And praise a blockhead's wit, because he's great:
Down, down, ye hungry garretteers, descend,
Call Walpole 8 Burleigh, call him Britain's friend;
Behold the genial ray of gold appear,
And rouse, ye swarms of Grub-street and Rag-fair.
See with what zeal yon tiny insect 9 burns,
And follows queens from palaces to urns:
Though cruel death has clos'd the royal ear,
That flatt'ring fly still buzzes round the bier :
But what avails, since queens no longer live?
Why, kings can read, and kings, you know, may
    give.

7 A famous solicitor.
8 See these two characters compared in the
Gazetteers ; but, lest none of those papers should
have escaped their common fate, see the two characters distinguished in the Craftsman.
9 Dr. Alured Clarke, who wrote, or rather
stole, a character of the late queen from Dr.
Burnet's character of queen Mary. This pamphlet, however, has been ascribed to lord
Hervey.

A mitre may repay his heav'nly crown,
And, while he decks her brow, adorn his own.
    Let laureat Cibber birth-day sonnets sing,
Or Fanny crawl, an ear-wig on the king :.
While one is void of wit, and one of grace,
Why should I envy either song or place ?
I could not flatter, the rich butt to gain ;
Nor sink a slave, to rise vice chamberlain.
    Perish my verse ! whene'er one venal line
Bedaubs a duke, or makes a king divine.
First bid me swear, he's sound who has the
    plague,
Or Horace rivals Stanhope at the Hague.
What, shall I turn a pander to the throne,
And list with B—ll's 10 to roar for half-a-crown?
Sooner T—r—l shall with Tully vie,
Or W—n—n in senate scorn a lie;
Sooner Iberia tremble for her fate
From M——h's arms, or Ab——n's debate.
    Though fawning flatt'ry ne'er shall taint my
    lays,
Yet know, when virtue calls, I burst to praise.
Behold yon temple 11 rais'd by Cobham's hand,
Sacred to worthies of his native land :
Ages were ransack'd for the wise and great,
Till Barnard came, and made the groupe com-
    plete.
Be Barnard there—enliven'd by the voice,
Each busto bow'd, and sanctify'd the choice.
    Pointless all satire in these iron times ;
Too faint are colours, and too feeble rhymes.
Rise then, gay fancy, future glories bring,
And stretch o'er happier days thy healing wing.
    Rapt into thought, lo ! I Britannia see
Rising superior o'er the subject sea ;
View her gay pendents spread their silken wings,
Big with the fate of empires, and of kings:
The tow'ring barks dance lightly o'er the main,
And roll their thunder thro' the realms of Spain.
Peace, violated maid, they ask no more,
But waft her back triumphant to our shore ;
While buxom Plenty, laughing in her train,
Glads ev'ry heart, and crowns the warrior's pain.
On, fancy, on ! still stretch the pleasing scene,
And bring fair freedom with her golden reign ;
Cheer'd by whose beams ev'n meagre want can
    smile,
And the poor peasant whistle 'midst his toil.
    Such days, what Briton wishes not to see ?
And such each Briton, Frederic 12, hopes from
    thee.


10 A noted agent in a mob-regiment, who is employed to reward their venal vociferations, on certain occasions, with half-a-crown each man.

11 The Temple of British Worthies in the gardens at Stow, in which the lord Cobham has
lately erected the busto of sir John Barnard.

12 The father of George the Third.

## THE
### GYMNASIAD, OR BOXING MATCH;

A VERY SHORT, BUT VERY CURIOUS EPIC POEM,
WITH THE PROLEGOMENA OF SCRIBLERUS TERTIUS,
AND NOTES VARIORUM.

—— Nos hæc novimus esse nihil. MART.

TO THE MOST PUISSANT AND INVINCIBLE
Mr. JOHN BROUGHTON.

HAD this dedication been addressed to some reverend prelate, or female court-favourite, to some blundering statesman, or apostate patriot, I should doubtless have lanched into the highest encomiums on public spirit, policy, virtue, piety, &c. and, like the rest of my brother dedicators, had most successfully imposed on their vanity, by ascribing to them qualities they were utterly unacquainted with; by which means I had prudently reaped the reward of a panegyrist from my patron, and, at the same time, secured the reputation of a satirist with the public.

But scorning these base arts, I present the following poem to you, unswayed by either flattery or interest; since your modesty would defend you against the poison of the one, and your known economy prevent an author's expectations of the other. I shall therefore only tell you, what you really are, and leave those (whose patrons are of the higher class) to tell them what they really are not. But such is the depravity of human nature, that every compliment we bestow on another is too apt to be deemed a satire on ourselves; yet surely, while I am praising the strength of your arm, no politician can think it meant as a reflection on the weakness of his head; or, while I am justifying your title to the character of a man, will any modern petit-maitre think it an impeachment of his affinity to that of its mimic counterfeit, a monkey?

Were I to attempt a description of your qualifications, I might justly have recourse to the majesty of Agamemnon, the courage of Achilles, the strength of Ajax, and the wisdom of Ulysses; but, as your own heroic actions afford us the best mirror of your merits, I shall leave the reader to view in that the amazing lustre of a character, a few traits of which only, the following poem was intended to display; and in which, had the ability of the poet equalled the magnanimity of his hero, I doubt not but the Gymnasiad had, like the immortal Iliad, been handed down to the admiration of all posterity.

As your superior merits contributed towards raising you to the dignities you now enjoy, and placed you even as the safe-guard of royalty itself, so I cannot help thinking it happy for the prince, that he is now able to boast one real champion in his service: and what Frenchman would not tremble more at the puissant arm of a Broughton, than at the ceremonious gauntlet of a Dimmack?

I am,
with the most profound respect
to your heroic virtues,
your most devoted,
and most humble servant.

## SCRIBLERUS TERTIUS OF THE POEM.

IT is an old saying, that necessity is the mother of invention: it should seem then that poetry, which is a species of invention, must naturally derive its being from the same origin: hence it will be easy to account for the many flimsy ghost-like apparitions, that every day make their appearance among us; for if it be true, as naturalists observe, that the health and vigour of the mother is necessary to produce the like qualities in the child, what issue can be expected from the womb of so meagre a parent?

But there is another species of poetry, which, instead of owing its birth to the belly, like Minerva springs at once from the head: of this kind are those productions of wit, sense, and spirit, which once born, like the goddess herself, immediately become immortal. It is true, these are a sort of miraculous births, and therefore it is no wonder they should be found so rare among us.—As glory is the noble inspirer of the latter, so hunger is the natural incentive of the former: thus fame and food are the spurs with which every poet mounts his Pegasus; but, as the impetus of the belly is apt to be more cogent than that of the head, so you will ever see the one pricking and goading a tired jade to a hobbling trot, while the other only incites the foaming steed to a majestic capriol.

The gentle reader, it is apprehended, will not long be at a loss to determine, which species the following production ought to be ranked under: but as the parent most unnaturally cast it out as the spurious issue of his brain, and even cruelly denies it the common privilege of his name; struck with the delectable beauty of its features, I could not avoid adopting the little poetic orphan, and by dressing it up with a few notes, &c. present it to the public as perfect as possible.

Had I, in imitation of other great authors, only consulted my interest in the publication of this inimitable piece, (which doubtless will undergo numerous impressions) I might first have sent it into the world naked, then, by the addition of a commentary, notes variorum, prolegomena, and all that, levied a new tax upon the public; and after all, by a sort of modern poetical legerdemain, changing the name of the principal hero, and inserting a few hypercritics of a flattering friend's, have rendered the former editions incorrect, and cozened the curious reader out of a treble consideration for the same work; but however this may suit the tricking arts of a bookseller, it is certainly much below the sublime genius of an author.—I know it will be said, that a man has an equal right to make as much as he can of his wit, as well as of his money: but then it ought to be considered, whether there may not be such a thing as usury in both; and the law having only provided against it in one instance, is, I apprehend, no very moral plea for the practice of it in the other [1].

[1] As this may be thought to be particularly aimed at an author who was lately reported to be dead, and whose loss all lovers of the muses

The judicious reader will easily perceive, that the following poem in all its properties partakes of the epic; such as fighting, speeching, bullying, ranting, &c. (to say nothing of the moral) and, as many thousand verses are thought necessary to the construction of this kind of poem, it may be objected, that this is too short to be ranked under that class: to which I will only answer, that as conciseness is the last fault a writer is apt to commit, so it is generally the first a reader is willing to forgive; and though it may not be altogether so long, yet I dare say, it will not be found less replete with the true vis poetica, than (not to mention the Iliad, Æneid, &c.) even Leonidas itself.

It may farther be objected, that the characters of our principal heroes are too humble for the grandeur of the epic fable; but the candid reader will be pleased to observe, that they are not here celebrated in their mechanic, but in their heroic capacities, as boxers, who, by the ancients themselves, have ever been esteemed worthy to be immortalized in the noblest works of this nature; of which the Epëus and Euryalus of Homer, and the Entellus and Dares of Virgil, are incontestable authorities. And as those authors were ever careful, that their principal personages (however mean in themselves) should derive their pedigree from some deity, or illustrious hero, so our author has with equal propriety made his spring from Phaëton and Neptune; under which characters he beautifully allegorises their different occupations of watermen and coachmen.—But for my own part, I cannot conceive, that the dignity of the hero's profession is any ways essential to that of the action; for, if the greatest persons be guilty of the meanest actions, why may not the greatest actions be ascribed to the meanest persons?

As the main action of this poem is entirely supported by the principal heroes themselves, it has been maliciously insinuated to be designed, as an unmannerly reflection on a late glorious victory, where, it is pretended, the whole action was achieved without the interposition of the principal heroes at all.—But as the most innocent meanings may by ill minds be wrested to the most wicked purposes, if any such construction should be made, I will venture to affirm, that it must proceed from the factious venom of the reader, and not from any disloyal malignity in our author, who is too well acquainted with the power, ever to arraign the purity, of government:

would have the greatest reason to lament; it may not be improper to assure the reader, that it was written, and intended to have been published, before that report, and was only meant as an attack upon the general abuse of this kind. —As to our author himself, he has frequently given public testimonies of his veneration for that great man's genius; nor may it be unentertaining to the reader, to acquaint him with one private instance:—Immediately on hearing the report of Mr. Pope's death, he was heard to break forth in the following exclamation:

Pope dead!—Hush, hush, Report, the slander'ous lie;
Fame says he lives—immortals never die.

besides, the poignance of the sword is too prevalent for that of the pen; and who, when there are at present so many thousand unanswerable standing arguments ready to defend, would ever be Quixote enough to attack, either the omnipotence of a prince, or the omniscience of his ministers?

Were I to attempt an analysis of this poem, I could demonstrate that it contains (as much as a piece of so sublime a nature will admit of) all those true standards of wit, humour, raillery, satire, and ridicule, which a late writer has so marvellously discovered; and might, on the part of our author, say with that profound critic,—Jacta est Alea: but as the obscurity of a beauty too strongly argues the want of one, so an endeavour to elucidate the merits of the following performance, might be apt to give the reader a disadvantageous impression against it, as it might tacitly imply they were too mysterious to come within the compass of his comprehension, I shall therefore leave them to his more curious observation, and bid him heartily farewell— Lege & delectare.

SCRIBLERUS TERTIUS.

## THE GYMNASIAD.

### BOOK I.

#### ARGUMENT.

THE invocation, the proposition, the night before the battle described; the morning opens, and discovers the multitude hasting to the place of action; their various professions, dignities, &c. illustrated; the spectators being seated, the youthful combatants are first introduced; their manner of fighting displayed; to these succeed the champions of a higher degree; their superior abilities marked, some of the most eminent particularly celebrated; mean while, the principal heroes are represented sitting, and ruminating on the approaching combat, when the herald summons them to the lists.

SING, sing, O Muse, the dire contested fray,
And bloody honours of that dreadful day,
When Phaëton's bold son (tremendous name)
Dar'd Neptune's offspring to the lists of fame.
What fury fraught thee with ambition's fire,
Ambition, equal foe to son and sire?

V. 3, 4. *When Phaëton's bold son* } It is usual
*Dar'd Neptune's offspring* } for poets to
call the sons after the names of their fathers; as
Agamemnon the son of Atreus, and Achilles the
son of Peleus, are frequently termed Pelides and
Atrides. Our author would doubtless have followed this laudable example, but he found
Broughtonides and Stephensonides, or their contractions, too unmusical for metre, and therefore
with wonderful art adopts two poetical parents;
which obviates the difficulty, and at the same
time heightens the dignity of his heroes.

BENTLEIDES.

V. 6. *Ambition, equal foe to son and sire?*]
It has been maintained by some philosophers,
that the passions of the mind are in some measure hereditary, as well as the features of the

One, hapless fell by Jove's æthereal arms,
And one, the Triton's mighty pow'r disarms.
  Now all lay hush'd within the folds of night,
And saw in painted dreams th' important fight; 10
While hopes and fears alternate turn the scales,
And now this hero, and now that prevails;
Blows and imaginary blood survey,
Then waking, watch the slow approach of day;
When, lo! Aurora in her saffron vest
Darts a glad ray, and gilds the ruddy east.
  Forth issuing now all ardent seek the place
Sacred to fame, and the athletic race.
As from their hive the clust'ring squadrons pour
O'er fragrant meads, to sip the vernal flow'r; 20
So from each inn the legal swarms impel,
Of banded seers, and pupils of the quill.
Senates and shambles pour forth all their store,
Mindful of mutton, and of laws no more;
E'en money-bills, uncourtly, now must wait,
And the fat lamb has one more day to bleat.
The highway knight now draws his pistol's load,
Rests his faint steed, and this day franks the road.

body. According to this doctrine, our author
very beautifully represents the frailty of ambition descending from father to son;—and as original sin may in some sort be accounted for on
this system, it is very probable our author had a
theological, as well as physical, and moral meaning in this verse.
  For the latter part of this note we are obliged
to an eminent divine.
  V. 21. *legal swarms impel*,] An ingenious critic of my acquaintance objected to this simile,
and would by no means admit the comparison
between bees and lawyers to be just; one, he
said, was an industrious, harmless, and useful
species, none of which properties could be affirmed of the other; and therefore he thought the
drone, that lives on the plunder of the hive, a
more proper archetype. I must confess myself
in some measure inclined to subscribe my friend's
opinion; but then we must consider, that our
author did not intend to describe their qualities,
but their number; and in this respect no one,
I think, can have any objection to the propriety
of the comparison.
  V. 24. *and of laws no more*;] The original
MS. has it bribes; but, as this might seem to
cast an invidious aspersion on a certain assembly,
remarkable for their abhorrence of venality;
and, at the same time, might subject our publisher to some little inconveniences; I thought
it prudent to soften the expression; besides, I
think this reading renders our author's thought
more natural; for, though we see the most trifling avocations are able to draw off their attention from the public utility, yet nothing is sufficient to divert a steady pursuit of their private
emolument.
  V. 28. *this day franks the road.*] Our poet here
artfully insinuates the dignity of the combat he is
about to celebrate, by its being able to prevail on
a highwayman to lay aside his business, to become a spectator of it;—and as, on this occasion, he makes him forsake his daily bread, while
the senator only neglects the business of the nation, it may be observed, how satirically he gives
the preference, in point of disinterestedness, to
the highwayman.

Bailiffs, in crowds, neglect the dormant writ,
And give another Sunday to the wit:      30
He too would hie, but ah! his fortunes frown,
Alas! the fatal passport's—half-a-crown.
Shoals press on shoals, from palace and from
      cell;
Lords yield the court, and butchers Clerkenwell.
St Giles's natives, never known to fail,
All who have haply 'scap'd th' obdurate jail;
There many a martial son of Tott'nham lies,
Bound in Deveilian bands, a sacrifice
To angry justice, nor must view the prize.
  Assembled myriads crowd the circling seats,40
High for the combat every bosom beats,
Each bosom partial for its hero bold,
Partial through friendship—or depending gold.
  But first, the infant progeny of Mars
Join in the lists, and wage their pigmy wars;
Train'd to the manual fight, and bruiseful toil,
The stop defensive, and gymnastic foil,
With nimble fists their early prowess show,
And mark the future hero in each blow.
  To these, the hardy iron race succeed,      50
All sons of Hockley and fierce Brick-street breed:
Mature in valour, and inur'd to blood,
Dauntless each foe in form terrific stood;
Their callous bodies, frequent in the fray,
Mock'd the fell stroke, nor to its force gave
      way.
'Mongst these Gloverius, not the last in fame,
And he whose clog delights the beauteous dame;
Nor least thy praise, whose artificial light,
In Dian's absence, gilds the clouds of night.

  V. 37. *There many a martial son*, &c.] The
unwary reader may from this passage be apt to
conclude, that an amphitheatre is little better
than a nursery for the gallows, and that there is
a sort of physical connection between boxing and
thieving; but although boxing may be a useful
ingredient in a thief, yet it does not necessarily
make him one. Boxing is the effect, not the
cause; and men are not thieves because they
are boxers, but boxers because they are thieves.
Thus tricking, lying, evasion, with several other
such-like cardinal virtues, are a sort of properties
pertaining to the practice of the law, as well as
to the mercurial profession. But would any one
therefore infer, that every lawyer must be a
thief?                                SCHOLIAST.
  V. 44. *infant progeny of Mars*] Our author
in this description alludes to the Lusus Trojæ
of Virgil,

Incedunt pueri—————————
————————————Trojæ juventus
——Pugnæque ciunt simulachra sub armis.

  V. 51. *Hockley and fierce Brick-street breed*]
Two famous athletic seminaries.
  V. 57. *And he whose clog*, &c.] Here we are
presented with a laudable imitation of the ancient simplicity of manners; for, as Cincinnatus
disdained not the homely employment of a
ploughman, so we see our hero condescending to
the humble occupation of a clog-maker; and
this is the more to be admired, as it is one characteristic of modern heroism, to be either above
or below any occupation at all.
  V. 58. *whose artificial light*,] Various and
violent have been the controversies, whether our

While these the combat's direful arts display, 60
And share the bloody fortunes of the day,
Each hero sat, revolving in his soul
The various means that might his foe controul;
Conquest and glory each proud bosom warms,
When, lo! the herald summons them to arms.

---

### THE GYMNASIAD.

#### BOOK II.

###### ARGUMENT.

Stephenson enters the lists; a description of his
figure; an encomium on his abilities, with
respect to the character of a coachman.
Broughton advances; his reverend form described; his superior skill in the management
of the lighter and wherry displayed; his triumph of the badge celebrated; his speech;
his former victories recounted; the prepara-
tions for the combat, and the horrour of the
spectators.[1]

First, to the fight, advanc'd the charioteer:
High hopes of glory on his brow appear;
Terrour vindictive flashes from his eye,
(To one the fates the visual ray deny;)
Fierce glow'd his looks, which spoke his inward
                    rage;
He leaps the bar, and bounds upon the stage.
The roofs re-eccho with exulting cries,
And all behold him with admiring eyes.
Ill-fated youth! what rash desires could warm
Thy manly heart, to dare the Triton's arm ?  10
Ah! too unequal to these martial deeds,
Though none more skill'd to rule the foaming
The coursers, still obedient to thy rein,  [steeds.
Now urge their flight, or now their flight restrain.
Had mighty Diomed provok'd the race,
Thou far had'st left the Grecian in disgrace.
Where-e'er you drove, each inn confess'd your
                    sway,                    [hay.
Maids brought the dram, and ostlers flew with
But know, though skill'd to guide the rapid car,
None wages like thy foe the manual war.   20

author here intended to celebrate a lamp-lighter,
or a link-boy; but as there are heroes of both
capacities at present in the school of honour, it
is difficult to determine, whether the poet alludes to a Wells, or a Buckhorse.
  [1] Argument.]  It was doubtless in obedience
to custom, and the example of other great poets,
that our author has thought proper to prefix an
argument to each book, being minded that nothing should be wanting in the usual parapher-
nalia of works of this kind.—For my own part, I
am at a loss to account for the use of them, unless it be to swell a volume, or, like bills of fare,
to advertise the reader what he is to expect;
that, if it contains nothing likely to suit his taste,
he may preserve his appetite for the next course.
  V. 6, 7. He leaps the bar, &c. ⎫
        The roofs re-echo    ⎬  See the des-
riptions of Dares in Virgil. ⎭
Nec mora, continuo vastis cum viribus effert
Ora Dares, magnoque virum se murmure tollit.
  V. 19. But know, though skill'd]  Here our au-

Now Neptune's offspring dreadfully serene,
Of size gigantic, and tremendous mien,
Steps forth, and 'midst the fated lists appears;
Rev'rend his form, but yet not worn with years.
To him none equal, in his youthful day,
With feather'd oar to skim the liquid way;
Or through those straits whose waters stun the
The loaded lighter's bulky weight to steer.  [ear,
Soon as the ring their ancient warrior view'd,
Joy fill'd their hearts, and thund'ring shouts
                ensu'd;                        30
Loud as when o'er Thamesis' gentle flood,'
Superior with the Triton youths he row'd;
While far a-head his winged wherry flew,
Touch'd the glad shore, and claim'd the badge
                its due.
Then thus indignant he accosts the foe,
(While high disdain sat prideful on his brow:)
" Long has the laurel-wreath victorious spread
Its sacred honours round this hoary head;
The prize of conquest in each doubtful fray,
And dear reward of many a dire-fought day.  40
Now youth's cold wane the vig'rous pulse has
                chas'd,
Froze all my blood, and ev'ry nerve unbrac'd;
Now, from these temples shall the spoils be torn,
In scornful triumph by my foe be worn ?
What then avail my various deeds in arms,
If this proud crest thy feeble force disarms ?
Lost be my glories to recording fame,  [name!
When, foil'd by thee, the coward blasts my
I, who e'er manhood my young joints had knit,
First taught the fierce Grettonius to submit;  50
While, drench'd in blood, he prostrate press'd
                the floor,
And inly groan'd the fatal words—' no more.'
Allenius too, who ev'ry heart dismay'd,

thor inculcates a fine moral, by showing how
apt men are to mistake their talents; but were
men only to act in their proper spheres, how often should we see the parson in the pew of the
peasant, the author in the character of his
hawker, or a beau in the livery of his footman! &c.
  V. 34. the badge its due.]  A prize given by
Mr. Dogget, to be annually contested on the
first of August.—As among the ancients, games
and sports were celebrated on mournful as well
as joyful events, there has been some controversy, whether our loyal comedian meant the
compliment to the setting or rising monarch of
that day; but, as the plate has a horse for its
device, I am induced to impute it to the latter;
and, doubtless, he prudently considered, that,
as a living dog is better than a dead lion, the
living horse had, at least, an equal title to the
same preference.
  V. 42. Froze all my blood,]  See Virgil.
  ——Sed enim gelidus tardante senecta
Sanguis hebet, frigentque effœtæ in corpore
                vires.
  V. 50. Fierce Grettonius to submit ;]  Gretton,
the most famous Athleta in his days, over whom
our hero obtained his maiden prize.
  V. 53. Allenius too, &c.]  Vulgarly known by
the plebeian name of Pipes, which a learned critic
will have to be derived from the art and mystery
of pipe-making, in which it is affirmed this here

Whose blows, like hail, flew rattling round the head
Him oft the ring beheld with weeping eyes,
Stretch'd on the ground, reluctant yield the prize.
Then fell the swain, with whom none e'er could vie
Where Harrow's steeple darts into the sky.
Next the bold youth a bleeding victim lay,
Whose waving curls the barber's art display. 60
You too this arm's tremendous prowess know;
Rash man, to make this arm again thy foe!"
This said—the heroes for the fight prepare,
Brace their big limbs, and brawny bodies bare.
The sturdy sinews all aghast behold,
And ample shoulders of Atlean mould;
Like Titan's offspring, who 'gainst Heavens trove,
So each, though mortal, seem'd a match for Jove.
Now round the ring a silent horrour reigns,
Speechless each tongue, and bloodless all their
    veins; 70
When, lo! the champions give the dreadful sign,
And hand in hand in friendly token join;
Those iron hands, which soon upon the foe
With giant-force must deal the dreadful blow.

---

## THE GYMNASIAD.

### BOOK III.

#### ARGUMENT.

A description of the battle; Stephenson is vanquished; the manner of his body being carried off by his friends; Broughton claims the prize, and takes his final leave of the stage.

FULL in the centre now they fix in form,
Eye meeting eye, and arm oppos'd to arm;
With wily feints each other now provoke,
And cautious meditate th' impending stroke.
Th' impatient youth, inspir'd by hopes of fame,
First sped his arm, unfaithful to its aim;
The wary warrior, watchful of his foe,
Bends back, and 'scapes the death-designing blow;
With erring glance it sounded by his ear,

was an adept.—As he was the *delicium pugnacis generis*, our author, with marvellous judgment, represents the ring weeping at his defeat.

V. 54. *Whose blows, like hail*, &c.] Virgil.
    ———quam multa grandine nimbi
Culminibus crepitant.— ————

V. 57. *Then fell the swain*,] Jeoffrey Birch, who, in several encounters, served only to augment the number of our hero's triumphs.

V. 59. *Next the bold youth*] As this champion is still living, and even disputes the palm of manhood with our hero himself, I shall leave him to be the subject of immortality in some future Gymnasiad, should the superiority of his prowess ever justify his title to the *corona pugnea.*

V. 63. *This said*, &c,] Virgil.

Hæc fatus, duplicem ex humeris rejecit amictum:     [tosque
Et magnos membrorum artus, magna ossa lacer-
Exuit.

V. 7, 8. ———*watchful of his foe*⎫
  *Bends back and 'scapes the death-*⎬ Virgil.
  *designing blow*;⎭
———ille ictum venientem a vertice velox
Prævidit, celerique elapsus corpore cessit.

And whizzing, spent its idle force in air. 10
Then quick advancing on th' unguarded head,
A dreadful show'r of thunderbolts he shed :
As when a whirlwind, from some cavern broke,
With furious blasts assaults the monarch oak,
This way and that its lofty top it bends.
And the fierce storm the crackling branches
    rends ;
So wav'd the head, and now to left and right
Rebounding flies, and crash'd beneath the weight.
Like the young lion wounded by a dart,
Whose fury kindles at the galling smart; 20
The hero rouses with redoubled rage,
Flies on the foe, and foams upon the stage.
Now grappling, both in close contention join,
Legs lock in legs, and arms in arms entwine:
They sweat, they heave, each tugging nerve they
    strain;
Both, fix'd as oaks, their sturdy trunks sustain.
At length the chief his wily art display'd,
Pois'd on his hip the hapless youth he laid ;
Aloft in air his quiv'ring limbs he throw'd, [load.
Then on the ground down dash'd the pond'rous
So some vast ruin on a mountain's brow, ` 31
Which tott'ring hangs, and dreadful nods below,
When the fierce tempest the foundation rends,
Whirl'd though the air with horrid crush descends.

Bold and undaunted up the hero rose,
Fiercer his bosom for the combat glows;
Shame stung his manly heart, and fiery rage
New steel'd each nerve, redoubled war to wage.
Swift to revenge the dire disgrace he flies,
Again suspended on the hip he lies ; 40
Dash'd on the ground, again had fatal fell,
Haply the barrier caught his flying heel ;
There fast it hung, th' imprison'd head gave way,
And the strong arm defrauded of its prey.
Vain strove the chief to whirl the mountain o'er;
It slipt—he headlong rattles on the floor.

V. 10. *its idle force in air.*] Virgil
    ———vires in ventum effudit.———

V. 19. *Like the young lion*] It may be observed, that our author has treated the reader but with one simile throughout the two foregoing books ; but, in order to make him ample amends, has given him no less than six in this. Doubtless this was in imitation of Homer, and artfully intended to heighten the dignity of the main action, as well as our admiration, towards the conclusion of his work.—*Finis coronat opus.*

V. 24. *Arms in arms entwine* ;] Virgil.

Immiscentque manus manibus, pugnamque lacessunt.

V. 35. *Bold and undaunted*, &c.] Virgil.

At non tardatus casu, neque territus heros,
Acrior ad pugnam redit, & vim suscitat ira.
Tum pudor incendit vires————.

V. 42. *Haply the barrier*, &c.] Our author, like Homer himself, is no less to be admired in the character of an historian than in that of a poet : we see him here faithfully reciting the most minute incidents of the battle, and informing us, that the youthful hero, being on the lock, must again inevitably have come to the ground, had not his heel catched the bar ; and that his antagonist, by the violence of his straining, slipt

Around the ring loud peals of thunder rise,
And shouts exultant echo to the skies.
Uplifted now inanimate he seems,
Forth from his nostrils gush the purple streams;
Gasping for breath, and impotent of hand,      51
The youth beheld his rival stagg'ring stand:
But he, alas! had felt th' unnerving blow,
And gaz'd, unable to assault the foe.
As when two monarchs of the brindled breed
Dispute the proud dominion of the mead,
They fight, they foam, then weary'd in the fray,
Aloof retreat, and low'ring stand at bay;
So stood the heroes, and indignant glar'd,
While grim with blood their rueful fronts were
      smear'd;      60
Till with returning strength new rage returns,
Again their arms are steel'd, again each bosom
      burns.
Incessant now their hollow sides they pound,
Loud on each breast the bounding bangs re-
      sound;
Their flying fists around the temples glow,
And the jaws crackle with the massy blow.
The raging combat ev'ry eye appals,      [falls.
Strokes following strokes, and falls succeeding
Now droop'd the youth, yet, urging all his might,
With feeble arm still vindicates the fight,      70
Till on the part where heav'd the panting breath,
A fatal blow impress'd the seal of death.
Down dropt the hero, welt'ring in his gore,
And his stretch'd limbs lay quiv'ring on the floor.
So, when a falcon skims the airy way,
Stoops from the clouds, and pounces on his prey;
Dash'd on the earth the feather'd victim lies,
Expands its feeble wings, and, flutt'ring, dies.
His faithful friends their dying hero rear'd,
O'er his broad shoulders dangling hung his
      head;      80
his arm over his head, and by that means received
the fall he intended the enemy.—I thought it
incumbent on me as a commentator to say thus
much, to illustrate the meaning of our author,
which might seem a little obscure to those who
are unacquainted with conflicts of this kind.

V. 48. *echo to the skies,* &c.] Virgil.

It clamor cœlo————

The learned reader will perceive our author's
frequent allusions to Virgil; and whether he intended them as translations or imitations of the
Roman poet, must give us pause: but as, in our
modern productions, we find imitations are generally nothing more than bad translations, and
translations nothing more than bad imitations;
it would equally, I suppose, satisfy the gall of
the critic, should these unluckily fall within
either description.

V. 63. *Incessant now,* &c.] Virgil.

Multa viri nequicquam inter se vulnera jactant:
Multa cavo lateri ingeminant, & pectore vastos
Dant sonitus, erratque aures & tempora circum
Crebra manus: duro crepitant sub vulnere
      malæ.

V. 79. *His faithful friends*] Virgil.

At illum fidi æquales, genua ægra trahentem,
Jactantemque utroque caput, crassumque cruo-
      rem
Ore rejectantem, mistosque in sanguine dentes,
Ducunt ad naves.

Dragging its limbs, they bear the body forth,
Mash'd teeth and clotted blood came issuing
      from his mouth.
Thus then the victor—" O celestial pow'r!
Who gave this arm to boast one triumph more;
Now grey in glory, let my labours cease,
My blood-stain'd laurel wed the branch of peace;
Lur'd by the lustre of the golden prize,
No more in combat this proud crest shall rise;
To future heroes future deeds belong,
Be mine the theme of some immortal song."      90
This said—he seiz'd the prize, while round
      the ring,
High soar'd applause on acclamation's wing.

V. 88. *No more in combat,* &c.] Virgil.
——hic victor cæstus, artemque repono.

---

## HONOUR:

### A SATIRE, 1747.

Primores populi arripuit populumque tributim;
Scilicet uni æquus virtuti atque ejus amicis.
                                    HOR.

" Load, load the pallet, boy !" hark! Hogarth
      cries,
" Fast as I paint, fresh swarms of fools arise!
Groups rise on groups, and mock the pencil's
      pow'r,
To catch each new-blown folly of the hour."
While hum'rous Hogarth paints each folly
      dead,
Shall vice triumphant rear its hydra head?
At satire's sov'reign nod disdain to shrink?
New reams of paper, and fresh floods of ink!
On then, my Muse! Herculean labours dare,
And wage with virtue's foes eternal war;
Range through the town in search of ev'ry ill,
And cleanse th' Augean stable with thy quill.
" But what avails the poignance of the song,
Since all," you cry, " still persevere in wrong.
Would courtly crimes to Mulgrave's[1] muse sub-
      mit?
Or blush'd the monarch though a Wilmot[2] writ?
Still pandar peers disgrac'd the rooms of state,
Still Cæsar's bed sustain'd a foreign weight;
Slaves worshipp'd still the golden calf of pow'r,
And bishops, bowing, bless'd the scarlet whore.
Shall then thy verse the guilty great reclaim,
Though fraught with Dryden's heav'n-descended
      flame?
Will harpy Heathcote, from his mould'ring store,
Drag forth one cheering drachma to the poor?
Or Harrington, unfaithful to the seal,
Throw in one suffrage for the public weal?
Pointless all satire, and misplac'd its aim,
To wound the bosom, that's obdur'd to shame:
The callous heart ne'er feels the goad within;
Few dread the censure, who can dare the sin."
Though on the culprit's cheek no blush should
      glow,
Still let me mark him to mankind a foe:

[1] Translator of Horace's Art of Poetry, and
afterwards duke of Buckingham.
[2] Earl of Rochester.

Strike but the deer, however slight the wound,
It serves at least to drive him from the sound.
Shall reptile sinners frowning justice fear,
And pageant titles privilege the peer?
So falls the humbler game in common fields,
While the branch'd beast the royal forest shields.
On, Satire, then! pursue thy gen'rous plan,
And wind the vice, regardless of the man.
Rouse, rouse! th' ennobled herd for public sport,
And hunt them through the covert of a court.

Just as the play'r the mimic portrait draws,
All claim a right of censure or applause:
What guards the place-man from an equal fate,
Who mounts but actor on the stage of state?
Subject alike to each man's praise and blame,
Each critic voice the fiat of his fame;
Though to the private some respect we pay,
All public characters are public prey:
Pelham and Garrick, let the verse forbear
What sanctifies the treasurer or play'r.

Great in her laurel'd sages Athens see,
Free flow'd her satire while her sons were free:
Then purpled guilt was dragg'd to public shame,
And each offence 'tood fragrant with a name;
Polluted ermine n.. respect could win,
No hallow'd lawn could sanctify a sin;
'Till tyrant pow'r usurp'd a lawless rule:
Then sacred grew the titled knave and fool;
Then penal statutes aw'd the poignant song,
And slaves were taught, that kings could do no
wrong.
Guilt still is guilt, to me, in slave or king,
Fetter'd in cells, or garter'd in the ring:
And yet behold how various the reward,
Wild falls a felon, Walpole[3] mounts a lord!
The little knave the law's last tribute pays,
While crowns around the great one's chariot
blaze.
Blaze meteors, blaze! to me is still the same
The cart of justice, or the coach of shame.

Say, what's nobility, ye gilded train!
Does nature give it, or can guilt sustain?
Blooms the form fairer, if the birth be high?
Or takes the vital stream a richer dye;
What! though a long patrician line ye claim,
Are noble souls entail'd upon a name?
Anstis may ermine out the lordly earth,
Virtue's the herald that proclaims its worth.

Hence mark the radiance of a Stanhope's star,
And glow-worm glitter of thine, D***r:
Ignoble splendour! that but shines to all,
The humble badge of a court hospital.
Let lofty L**r wave his nodding plume,
Boast all the blushing honours of the loom,
Resplendent bondage no regard can bring,
'Tis Methuen's heart must dignify the string.

Vice levels all, however high or low;
And all the diff'rence but consists in show.
Who asks an alms, or supplicates a place,
Alike is beggar, though in rags or lace:
Alike his country's scandal and its curse,
Who vends a vote, or who purloins a purse;
Thy gamblers, Bridewell, and St James's bites,
The rooks of Mordington's, and sharks at White's.

3 Though the person here meant has indeed
paid the debt of nature, yet, as he has left that
of justice unsatisfied, the author apprehends that
the public are indisputably entitled to the assets
of his reputation.

" Why will you urge," Eugenio cries, "your
fate?
Affords the town no sins but sins of state?
Perches vice only on the court's high hill?'
Or yields life's vale no quarry for the quill?"
Manners, like fashions, still from courts descend,
And what the great begin, the vulgar end.
If vicious then the mode, correct it here;
He saves the peasant, who reforms the peer.
What Hounslow knight would stray from ho-
nour's path,
If guided by a brother of the Bath?
Honour's a mistress all mankind pursue;
Yet most mistake the false one for the true:
Lur'd by the trappings, dazzled by the paint,
We worship oft the idol for the saint.
Courted by all, by few the fair is won;
Those lose who seek her, and those gain who shun;
Naked she flies to merit in distress,
And leaves to courts the garnish of her dress.

The million'd merchant seeks her in his gold;
In schools the pedant, and in camps the bold:
The courtier views her, with admiring eyes,
Flutter in ribbons, or in titles rise:
Sir Epicene enjoys her in his plume;
Mead, in the learned wainscot of a room:
By various ways all woo the modest maid;
Yet lose the substance, grasping at the shade.
Who, smiling, sees not with what various
strife
Man blindly runs the giddy maze of life?
To the same end still diff'rent means employs;
This builds a church, a temple that destroys;
Both anxious to obtain a deathless name,
Yet, erring, both mistake report for fame.

Report, though vulture-like the name it bear,
Drags but the carrion carcass through the air;
While fame, Jove's nobler bird, superior flies,
And, soaring, mounts the mortal to the skies.
So Richard's[4] name to distant ages borne,
Unhappy Richard still is Britain's scorn:
Be Edward's wafted on fame's eagle wing,
Each patriot mourns the long-departed king;
Yet thine, O Edward! shall to George's[5] yield,
And Dettingen eclipse a Cressy's field.

Through life's wild ocean, who would safely
roam,
And bring the golden fleece of glory home,
Must, heedful, shun the barking Scylla's roar,
And fell Charybdis' all-devouring shore;
With steady helm an equal course support,
'Twixt faction's rocks, and quicksands of a court;
By virtue's beacon still direct his aim,
Through honour's channel, to the port of fame.

Yet, on this sea, how all mankind are tost!
For one that's sav'd, what multitudes are lost!
Misguided by ambition's treach'rous light,
Through want of skill, few make the harbour
right.
Hence mark what wrecks of virtue, friendship,
fame,
For four dead letters added to a name!
Whence dwells such Syren music in a word,
Or sounds not Brutus noble as my lord?
Though crownets, Pult'ney, blazon on thy plate,
Adds the base mark one scruple to its weight?
Though sounds patrician swell thy name, O
Stretches one acre thy plebeian lands? [Sandys!

4 Richard the Second.   5 George the Second.

Say, the proud title meant to plume the son,
Why gain by guilt, what virtue might have won?
Vain shall the son his herald honours trace,
Whose parent peer 's but patriot in disgrace.

Vain, on the solemn head of hoary age,
Totters the mitre, if ambition's rage
To mammon pow'r the hallow'd heart incline,
And titles only mark the priest divine.
Blest race! to whom the golden age remains,
Ease without care, and plenty without pains:
For you the earth unlabour'd treasure yields,
And the rich sheaves spontaneous crown the
　　fields;
No toilsome dews pollute the rev'rend brow,
Each holy hand unharden'd by the plough;
Still burst the sacred garners with their store,
And flails, unceasing, thunder on the floor.

O bounteous Heav'n! yet Heav'n how seldom
　　shares
The titheful tribute of the prelate's pray'rs! ,
Lost to the stall, in senates still they nod,
And all the monarch steals them from the God:
Thy praises, Brunswick, every breast inspire,
The throne their altar, and the court their choir;
Here earliest incense they devoutly bring,
Here everlasting hallelujah's sing:
Thou! only thou! almighty to—translate,
Thou their great golden deity of state.

Who seeks on merit's stock to graft success,
In vain invokes the ray of pow'r to bless;
The stem, too stubborn for the courtly soil,
With barren branches mocks the virtuous toil.
More pliant plants the royal regions suit,
Where knowledge still is held forbidden fruit;
'Tis these alone the kindly nurture share,
And all Hesperia's golden treasures bear.

Let folly still be fortune's fondling heir,
And science meet a step-dame in the fair.
Let courts, like fortune, disinherit sense,
And take the idiot charge from Providence.
The idiot head the cap and bells may fit,
But how disguise a Lyttelton and Pitt!

O !, once-lov'd youths! Britannia's blooming
　　hope,
Fair freedom's twins, and once the theme of Pope;
What wond'ring senates on your accents hung,
Ere flatt'ry's poison chill'd the patriot tongue!
Rome's sacred thunder awes no more the ear;
But Pelham smiles, who trembled once to hear.

Say, whence this change? less galling is the
　　chain,
Though Walpole, Carteret, or a Pelham reign?
If senates still the pois'nous bane imbibe,
And every palm grows callous with the bribe;
If sev'n long years mature the venal voice,
While freedom mourns her long-defrauded
　　choice;
If justice waves o'er fraud a lenient hand,
And the red locust rages through the land.

Sunk in these bonds, to Britain what avails,
Who wields her sword, or balances her scales?
Veer round the compass, change to change suc-
By every son the mother now must bleed :[ceed,
Vain all her hosts, on foreign shores array'd,
Though lost by Wentworth, or preserv'd by Wade.
Fleets, once which spread through distant worlds
　　her name!
Now ride inglorious trophies of her shame[6];

　6 Alluding to the ever-memorable no-fight in

While fading laurels shade her drooping head
And mark her Burleighs, Blakes, and Marlbro's
　　dead!
Such were thy sons, O happy isle! of old,
In counsel prudent, and in action bold:
Now view a Pelham puzzling o'er thy fate,
Lost in the maze of a perplex'd debate;
And sage Newcastle, with fraternal skill,
Guard the nice conduct of a nation's quill:
See truncheons trembling in the coward hand,
Though bold rebellion half subdue the land;
While ocean's god, indignant, wrests again
The long-deputed trident of the main[7].

Sleep our last heroes in the silent tomb?
Why springs no future worthies from the womb?
Not nature sure, since nature's still the same,
But education bars the road to fame.
Who hopes for wisdom's crop, must till the soul,
And virtue's early lesson should control:
To the young breast who valour would impart,-
Must plant it by example in the heart.

Ere Britain fell to mimic modes a prey,
And took the foreign polish of our day,
Train'd to the martial labours of the field,
Our youth were taught the massy spear to wield;
In halcyon peace, beneath whose downy wings
The merchant smiles, and lab'ring peasant sings,
With civil arts to guard their country's cause,
Direct her counsels, and defend her laws:
Hence a long race of ancient worthies rose,
Adorn'd the land, and triumph'd o'er our foes.

Ye sacred shades! who through th' Elysian
　　grove, ,
With Rome's fam'd chiefs, and Grecian sages rove,
Blush to behold what arts your offspring grace!
Each fopling heir now marks his sire's disgrace;
An embrio breed! of such a doubtful frame,
You scarce could know the sex but by the name:
Fraught with the native follies of his home,
Torn from the nurse, the babe of mirth must
　　roam;
Through foreign climes exotic vice explore,
And cull each weed, regardless of the flow'r,
Proud of thy spoils, O Italy and France!
The soft enervate strain, and cap'ring dance:
From Sequan's streams, winding banks of Po,
He comes, ye gods ! an all-accomplish'd beau!
Unhumaniz'd in dress, with cheeks so wan!
He mocks God's image in the mimic man;
Great judge of arts! o'er toilettes now presides,
Corrects our fashions, or an opera guides;
From tyrant Handel rends th'imperial bay,
And guards the Magna Charta of—Sol-fa.

Sick of a land where virtue dwells no more,
See Liberty prepar'd to quit our shore!
Pruning her pinions, on yon beacon'd height
The goddess stands, and meditates her flight;
Now spreads her wings, unwilling yet to fly,
Again o'er Britain casts a pitying eye;

the Mediterranean: as the nation was unluckily
the only victim on that occasion, the lenity of
our aquarian judicature has, I think, evidently
proved, that a court-martial and a martial-court
are by no means synonymous terms.
　7 The reader will readily conclude these lines
were written before our worthy admirals Anson
and Warren had so eminently distinguished
themselves in the service of their country.

Loath to depart, methinks I hear her say,
" Why urge me thus, ungrateful isle, away!
For you, I left Achaia's happy plains,
For you resign'd my Romans to their chains;
Here fondly fix'd my last lov'd favourite seat,
And 'midst the mighty nations made thee great:
Why urge me then, ungrateful isle, away!"
Again she, sighing, says, or seems to say.
 O Stanhope[8]! skill'd in ev'ry moving art,
That charms the ear, or captivates the heart !
Be your's the task, the goddess to retain,
And call her parent virtue back again;
Improve your pow'r a sinking land to save,
And vindicate the servant from the slave :
O ! teach the vassal courtier how to share
The royal favour with the public pray'r :
Like Latium's genius [9] stem thy country's doom,
And, though a Cæsar smile, remember Rome ;
With all the patriot dignify the place,
And prove at least one statesman may have
   grace.

   [8] Earl of Chesterfield.     [9] Brutus.

---

AN
## EPISTLE
### TO DOCTOR THOMSON, 1755.

Sed quia mente minus validus, quam corpore
  toto,
Nil audire velim, nil discere, quod levet ægrum,
Fidis offendar medicis.—————     Hor.

---

### PREFACE.

The reader will perceive, from two or three
passages in the following epistle, that it was
written some time since ; nor indeed would the
whole of it have now been thought interesting
enough to the public, to have passed the press,
had not the physical persecution, carried on
against the gentleman[1] to whom it is addressed, provoked the publication. When a body of
men, too proud to own their errours, and too prudent to part with their fees, shall (with their
legions of understrappers) enter into a conspiracy against a brother practitioner, only for ho-
nestly endeavouring to moderate the one, and
rectify the other; such a body, our author apprehends, becomes a justifiable object of satire ;
and only wishes his pen had, on this occasion, a
like killing efficacy with theirs.

---

Why do you ask, " that in this courtly dance,
Of in and out, it ne'er was yet my chance,
To bask beneath a statesman's fost'ring smile,
And share the plunder of the public spoil ? "
 E'er wants my table the health-chearing meal,
With Banstead mutton crown'd, or Essex veal?

 [1] Dr. Thompson was one of the physicians to
Frederick, prince of Wales, in that disorder
which ended his life. Upon that occasion, the
doctor differed from all the physicians that attended his highness, which brought upon him
their most virulent rage and indignation; for the

Smokes not from Lincoln meads the stately loin,
Or rosy gammon of Hantonian swine ?
From Darkin's roosts the feather'd victims bleed,
And Thames still wafts me ocean's scaly breed.
Though Gallia's vines their costly juice deny,
Still Tajo's [2] banks the jocund glass supply;
Still distant worlds nectareous treasures roll,
And either India sparkles in my bowl ;
Or Devon's boughs, or Dorset's bearded fields,
To Britain's arms a British beverage yields.
 Rich in these gifts, why should I wish for
   more ?
Why barter conscience for superfluous store ?
Or haunt the levee of a purse-proud peer,
To rob poor Fielding of the curule chair[3] ?
Let the lean bard, whose belly, void of bread,
Puffs up pierian vapours to his head,
In birth-day odes his flimsy fustian vent,
And torture truth into a compliment ;
Wear out the knocker of a great man's door,
Be pimp and poet, furnish rhyme or whore ;
Or fetch and carry for some foolish lord,
To sneak—a sitting footman at his board.
If such the arts that captivate the great,
Be yours, ye bards ! the sun-shine of a state ;
For place or pension prostitute each line ;
Make gods of kings, and ministers divine;
Swear St. John's self could neither read nor
   write,
And Cumberland [4] out-bravoes Mars in fight ;
Call Dorset patriot, Willes [5] a legal tool,
Horace [6] a wit, and Dodington a fool.

prince dying, the world was inclined to favour
doctor Thompson's recommendations. He was
an intimate friend of Mr. P. Whitehead, and
a favourite with him at the prince's-court. He
was a man of a peculiar character; but learned,
singular, and ingenious.
 [2] The Tagus—a principal river of Portugal,
famous for golden sands.
 Qua Tagus auriferis pallet turbatus arenis.
   Sil. xvi. 559.
 [3] It is reported, that during the time Mr.
Addison was secretary of state, when his old
friend and ally Ambrose Phillips applied to him
for some preferment, the great man very coolly
answered, that " he thought he had already
provided for him, by making him justice for
Westminster." To which the bard, with some
indignation, replied, " though poetry was a
trade he could not live by, yet he scorned to owe
his subsistence to another, which he ought not
to live by."—However great men, in our days,
may practise the secretary's prudence, certain
it is, the person here pointed at was very far
from making a precedent of his brother poet's
principles.
 [4] It is apprehended, our modern campaigns
cannot fail of furnishing the reader with a proper supply for this passage.
 [5] Lord high admiral Willes—a title, by
which this excellent chief magistrate is often distinguished among our marine, for his spirited
vindication of the supremacy of the civil flag,
and rectifying the martial mistakes of some late
naval tribunals.
 [6] A certain modern of that name, whose sole
pretension to this character (except a little arch

Such be your venal task; whilst, blest with ease,
'Tis mine, to scribble when, and what I please.
" Hold! what you please?" (sir Dudley cries)
" my friend,
Say, must my labours never, never end?
Still doom'd 'gainst wicked wit my pen to draw,
Correct each bard by critic rules of law;
'Twixt guilt and shame the legal buckler place,
And guard each courtly culprit from disgrace?
Hard task! should future jurymen inherit
The city-twelve's self-judging British spirit.7"
   While you, my Thompson! spite of med'cine
     save,
Mark how the college peoples every grave!
See Mead transfer estates from sire to son,
And·* * bar succession to a throne 8!
See Shaw scarce leave the passing-bell a fee,
And N**'s set the captive husband free!
Though widow'd Julia giggles in her weed,
Yet who arraigns the doctor for the deed?
O'er life and death all absolute his will,
Right the prescription, whether cure or kill.
   Not so,—whose practice is the mind's dis-
     ease;
His potion must not only cure, but please :·
Apply the caustic to the callous heart,
Undone's the doctor, if the patient smart;
Superior pow'rs his mental bill·control,
And law corrects the physic of the soul*.

buffoonery) consists in a truly poetical negligence of his person.

7 Alluding to the constitutional verdict given
on the trial of William Owen, for publishing
" The Case of the honourable Alexander Murray,
esq.''—a pamphlet written by P. Whitehead.

8 This line furnishes a melancholy memento
of the most fatal catastrophe that perhaps ever
befel this nation. Among the various tributary
verses which flowed on that occasion, our author
wrote the following; and which he here takes
the liberty to insert, being willing to seize every
opportunity, to perpetuate his sense of our public loss, in the death of that truly patriot prince,
Frederick.

When Jove, late revolving the state of mankind'
'Mong Britons no traces of virtue could find,
O'er the island, indignant, he stretch'd forth his
   rod;
Earth trembled, and Ocean acknowledg'd the
   God.*

   Still provok'd by our crimes, Heav'n's ven-
     geance to show,      [blow:
Ammon, grasping his bolts, aim'd at Britain the
But pausing—more dreadful, his wrath to evince,
Threw the thunder aside, and sent fate for the
   prince.

9 A like correction, with regard to the physic
of the body, might prove no bad security for
the life and property of the patient, as the faculty are at present accountable to no other
power but that of Heaven, for the rectitude of
their conduct.—And perhaps no civilized nation
can afford such an instance of physical anarchy
as ours, where the surgeon is permitted to usurp

   * Alluding to the preceding earthquakes, in
1750.

Shall Galen's sons with privilege destroy,
And I not one sound alt'rative employ,
To drive the rank distemper from within?
Or is man's life less precious than his sin?
   With palsied hand should justice hold the
     scale,
And o'er a judge court-complaisance prevail,
Satire's strong dose the malady requires :
I write—when, lo! the bench indignant fires;
Each hoary head erects its load of hair;
Their furs all bristle, and their eye-balls glare;
In rage they roar, " With rev'rend ermine sport!
Seize! seize him, tipstaff!—'Tis contempt of
     court."
   Led by the meteor of a mitre's ray,
If Sion's sons through paths unhallow'd stray,
For courtly rites neglect each rubric rule,
Quit all the saint, and truckle all the tool;
Their maker only in the monarch see,
Nor e'er omit, at Brunswick's name, the knee;
To cure this loyal lethargy of grace,
And rouse to Heav'n again its recreant race,
Say! should the Muse, with one irrev'rend line,
Probe but the mortal part of the divine;
'Tis blasphemy, by ev'ry priest decreed!
No benefit of clergy may I plead;
With every canon pointed at my head,
Alive I'm censur'd, and I'm damn'd when dead.
Lawyer and priest, like doctors, still agree;
'Tis theirs to give advice; 'tis ours, the fee :
To them alone all earthly rule is giv'n,
Diploma'd from St. James's, and from Heav'n.
   Yet ills there are, nor bench, nor pulpit reach;
In vain may Ryder charge, or Sherlock preach;
For law too mighty, and too proud for grace,
Lurk in the star, or lord it in a place;
Brood in the sacred circle of a crown,
While fashion wafts their poison through the
     town :
Hence o'er each village the contagion wings,
And peasants catch the maladies of kings.
   When purpled vice shall humble justice awe,
And fashion make it current, spite of law;
What sovereign med'cine can its course reclaim?
What, but the poet's panacea—shame!
Thus wit's great Esculapius 'o once prevail'd,
And satire triumph'd, where the fasces fail'd :
No consul's wreath could lurking folly hide,
No vestal looks secure the guilty bride:  [guise,
The poignant verse pierc'd through each fair dis-
And made Rome's matrons modest, statesmen
     wise.
   Search all your statutes, sergeant! where's the
     balm
Can cure the itching of a courtier's palm?
Where the chaste canon, say, thou hallow'd sage,
The virgin's glowing wishes can assuage?
Let but the star his longing lordship see,
What pow'r can set the captive conscience free?
Hang but the sparkling pendant at her ears,
What trembling maid the gen'rous lover fears?

the province of the physician, and the apothecary plumes himself in the perriwig and plunder
of both professions.—In a public spirited endeavour to cure this anarchy, and restore a proper
discipline in practice, consists a Thompson's em-
piricism.—Hinc illæ lachrymæ.—
   10 Horatius Flaccus.

When lawless passion seiz'd th' imperial
　　dame[11],
Brothels [12] were only found, to quench the flame ;
No routs, or balls, the kind convenience gave,
To lose her virtue, yet her honour save.
In Cupid's rites, now, so improv'd our skill,
Mode find the means, when nature finds the will.
Each rev'rend relict keeps a private pack,
And sturdy stallion with Atlean back ;
Where British dames to mystic rites repair,
Nor fail to meet a lurking Clodio there ;
In amorous stealths defraud the public stews,
And rob the Drury vestal of her dues ;　[gown,
Who hapless mourns her last, long-mortgag'd
While Douglass [13] damns the drums of lady
　　Brown.
By names celestial, mortal females call ;
Angels they are, but angels in their fall.
One royal phenix [14] yet redeems the race,
And proves, in Britain, beauty may have grace.
Vain shall the Muse the various symptoms find,
When every doctor 's of a diff'rent mind.
In **'s palm, be foul corruption found,
Each court-empiric holds, his grace is sound ;
In Sackville's [15] breast let public spirit reign,
Blisters ! (they cry) the cause is in his brain ;
So, Talbot's want of place is want of sense,
And Dashwood's [16] stubborn virtue, downright
　　insolence.
When ills are thus just what the doctors please,
And the soul's health is held the mind's disease ;
Not all thy art, O Horace ! had prevail'd ;
Here, all thy Roman recipes [17] had fail'd.
Had fate to Flaccus but our days decreed,
What Pollio would admire ? what Cæsar read ?
Great Maro's [18] self had dy'd an humble swain,
And Terence sought a Lælius now in vain.
Science no more employs the courtier's care,
No muse's voice can charm Northumberland's
　　ear.
The solid vote aërial verse outweighs,
And wins all courtly favour from the bays ;
Hence flow alone the sacred gifts of kings,
Staves, truncheons, feathers, mitres, stars, and
　　strings.
Hence cradles, see! with lisping statesmen
　　spawn,
And infant limbs beswaddled in the lawn ;
While honest Boyle [19], too impotent for place,
Sets, in meridian glory of disgrace :
Nor all the patriot music of Malone
Can charm a court, like Sackville, or like Stone ;
Blest twins of state ! whom love and pow'r con-
　　join,
Like Leda's offspring, made by Jove divine ;

[11] Pompeia, consort to Julius Cæsar, whom
the young Claudius took an opportunity of seducing at a solemn sacrifice of the Bona Dea.
[12] Intravit calidum veteri centone lupanar.
　　　　　　　　　　　　　　　　　Juv.
[13] An infamous, famous bawd.
[14] Princess of Wales, mother of his present
majesty George III.
[15] See a proposal for a militia, published by
lord Middlesex.
[16] Sir Francis Dashwood, afterwards lord Le
Despenser, the patron and protector of our author.
[17] Satires.　　　[18] Virgil.　　[19] Lord Orrery.

Fix'd in Hibernia's hemisphere to rule,
And shed your influence o'er each knave and
　　fool [20].
Whilst the sad summons of a mortar's knell
The rival deeds of each diploma tell ;
And death's increasing muster-rolls declare,
That health and Thompson are no longer here ;
How shall the Muse this salutation send ?
What place enjoys thee ? or what happier
　　friend ?
Say, if in Eastbury's [21] majestic towers,
Or wrapt in Ashley's [22] amarantine bowers,
By friendship favour'd, and unaw'd by state,
You barter science with the wise and great :
O'er Pelham's politics in judgment sit,
Reform the laws of nations, or of wit ;
With attic zest enrich the social bowl,
Crack joke on joke, and mingle soul with soul ;
On laughter's wanton wing now frolic sport,
Nor envy Fox [23] the closet of a court.
Lost in this darling luxury of ease,
Alike regardless both of fame and fees,
" Let Shaw" (you cry) " o'er physic sov'reign
Or W** boast his hecatombs of slain :　[reign,
Be mine, to stay some friend's departing breath,
And Child's [24] may take the drudgery of death."
Yet, Thompson ! say (whose gift it is to save,
Make sickness smile, and rescue from the grave)
Say, to what end this healing pow'r was meant ?
Nor hide the talent, which by Heav'n is lent.
Though envy all her hissing serpents raise,
And join with harpy fraud to blast thy bays :
Shall wan disease in vain demand thy skill,
While health but waits the summons of your
　　　quill ?
Shall Egypt's plague [25] the virgin cheek invade,
And beauty's wreck not win thee to its aid ?
O ! stretch a saving hand, and let the fair
Owe all her future triumphs to thy care :
Resume the pen ! and be thyself, once more,
What Ratcliff, Friend, and Syd'nham were
　　before
Yet, when reviving patients set you free,
Let Vaughan [26] yield one social hour to me.

[20] As our author lamented the occasion of these
lines, so no one more sincerely rejoices to find,
that the beam of public spirit is likely to dispel
the clouds which had interposed between loyalty and patriotism—A new political star in our
days, and which some more eastern magi would
do well to follow.
[21] A seat belonging to the right hon. George
Dodington.
[22] Another, belonging to lord Middlesex.
[23] Lord Holland.
[24] A coffee-house noted for the resort of our
modern Esculapics, where they ply for those
patients the apothecary is pleased to consign
over to them ; and where another appendage to
physic (called the undertakers) never fails to
attend the physical levee, in order to receive the
lucrative news of their joint endeavours.
[25] The small pox, said to have first appeared at
Alexandria. See the doctor's treatise on this
distemper.
[26] Owen Evan Vaughan, esq ; of Bodidris
castle ; a gentleman, in whose friendship the
doctor and our author more particularly pride

Come then, my friend ! if friendship's name
   can woo,
Come ! bring me all I want, that all in you.
If rural scenes have still the pow'r to please,
Flocks, vallies, hills, streams, villas, cots, and
   trees ;
Here all in one harmonious prospect blend,
And landscapes rise, scarce Lambert's [27] art
   can mend.
Thames, made immortal by her Denham's
   strains,          [plains ;
Meand'ring glides through Twick'nham's flow'ry
While royal Richmond's cloud-aspiring wood
Pours all its pendent pomp upon the flood.
By Rome's proud dames let storied Tiber flow,
And all Palladio grace the banks of Po ;
Here nature's charms in purer lustre rise,
Nor seek from wanton art her vain supplies.
Lo! Windsor, rev'rend in a length of years,
Like Cybele, her tow'r-crown'd summit rears;
And Hampton's turrets, with majestic pride,
Reflect their glories in the passing tide :
There British Henries gave to Gallia law;
Here bloom'd the laurels of a great Nassau [28].
O ! could these scenes one monarch more but
   please :
No frozen climates, no tempestuous seas,
For Brunswick's weal alarming fears shall bring,
Nor Britain envy meaner courts her king. [ see,
Here Campbell's [29] varied shades with wonder
Like Heaven's own Eden, stor'd with every tree ;
Each plant with plant in verdant glory vies ;
High-tow'ring pines, like Titans, scale the skies ;
And Lebanon's rich groves on Hounslow's deserts
   rise.
But chief—with awful step, O ! let us stray,
Where Britain's Orpheus tun'd his sacred lay,
Whose grove enchanted from his numbers grew,
And proves, what once was fabled, now is true.
Here oft the bard with Arbuthnot retir'd ;
Here flow'd the verse his healing art inspir'd[30] ;
Alike thy merit like thy fame should rise,
Could friendship give, what feeble art denies :
Though Pope's immortal verse the gods refuse,
Accept this off'ring from an humbler Muse.
Weak though her flight, yet honest still her
   strain,
And what no minister could ever gain ;
Pleas'd if the grateful tribute of her song,
Thy merit, Thompson ! shall one day prolong.
In marshal'd slaves let hungry princes trade,
And Britain's bullion bribe their venal aid[31] ;
Let brave Boscawen trophied honours gain,
And Anson wield the trident of the main.
Safe, in the harbour of my Twick'nam [32] bower,
From all the wrecks of state, or storms of power ;

themselves, as he has never polluted his ancient
British pedigree with any modern Anti-British
principles.

[27] A landscape-painter, much celebrated.

[28] William the Third.

[29] Duke of Argyle, celebrated as a warrior and
a statesman.

[30] Pope's Epistle to Arbuthnot.

[31] Alluding to a modern kind of military traffic,
which consists in the exchange of British gold
for German valour ; and by which means, it is
presumed, our politicians intend the native want
of either party shall be reciprocally supplied.

[32] He had a neat villa, in the style of a chateau,

No wreaths I court, no subsidies I claim,
Too rich for want, too indolent for fame.
Whilst here with vice a bloodless war I wage,
Or lash the follies of a trifling age,
Each gay-plum'd hour, upon its downy wings,
The Hybla freight of rich contentment brings;
Health, rosy handmaid, at my table waits,
And halcyon peace broods watchful o'er my
   gates.
Here oft, on contemplation's pinions bore,
To Heav'n I mount, and nature's works explore ;
Or, led by reason's intellectual clue,     [sue ;
Through errour's maze, truth's secret steps pur-
View ages past in story's mirror shown,     [own ;
And make time's mould'ring treasures all my
Or here the Muse now steals me from the throng,
And wraps me in th' enchantment of her song.
   Thus flow, and thus for ever flow ! my days,
Unaw'd by censure, or unbrib'd by praise ;
No friend to faction, and no dupe to zeal ;
Foe to all party, but the public weal.
Why then, from every venal bondage free,
Courts have no glitt'ring shackles left for me :
My reasons, Thompson ! prithee ask no more ;
Take them, as Oxford's Flaccus sung before [33].
   " My ease and freedom if for aught I vend,
Would not you cry, to Bedlam, Bedlam, friend !
But to speak out—shall what could ne'er engage
My frailer youth, now captivate in age ?
What cares can vex, what terrours frightful be,
To him whose shield is hoary sixty-three [34] ?
When life itself so little worth appears,
That ministers can give no hopes, or fears ;
Although grown grey within my humbler gate,
I ne'er kiss'd hands, or trod the rooms of state ;
Yet not unhonour'd have I liv'd, and blest
With rich convenience, careless of the rest ;
What boon more grateful can the gods bestow
On those avow'd their favourite sons below[35] ? "

on the north side of Twickenham Common,
sacred to the muses. It was afterwards inhabited by the lady Bridget Tallmach, daughter
of the late lord Northington.

[33] See conclusion of Dr. King's apology.

[34] Though the translator's virtue is not yet
secured by this palladium of his grand climac-
teric, yet he flatters himself he shall at least be
able to rival our truly Roman author, in the
practice of his heroic indifference, however short
he may fall of him in his elegant description
of it.

[35] Libera si pretio quantôvis otia vendam,
Cui non insanus videar : Sed apertius audi :
Quæ juvenem, infirmumque animi captare ne-
   quibant,
Illa senem capiant ? aut quæ terrere pericla
Posse putes hominem, cui climactericus annus
Præsidio est omni majus ? cui vita videtur
Haud equidem tanti esse, ut quid caveatve
   petatve
A regni satrapis, ullaque sit anxius horâ.
Si mihi non dextram tetigisse, aut limina regum
Contigit, & lare sub tenui mea canuit ætas :
Attamen æquo animo, non ullis rebus egenus,
Non inhonoratus vixi : neque gratius usquam
Dii munus dederunt, cui si favisse fatentur.

## AN
## OCCASIONAL SONG,

AS PERFORMED BY MR. BEARD, IN THE CHARACTER
OF A RECRUITING SERJEANT, AT THE THEATRE-
ROYAL IN COVENT-GARDEN, IN THE ENTER-
TAINMENT OF THE FAIR.

In story we're told
How our monarchs of old
O'er France spread their royal domain ;
But no annals shall show
Her pride laid so low,
As when brave George the Second did reign,
Brave boys !
As when brave, &c.

Of Roman and Greek
Let Fame no more speak ;
Though their arms did the Old world subdue,
Through the nations around
Let her trumpet now sound,
How Britons have conquer'd the New,
Brave boys !
How Britons have, &c.

East, west, north, and south,
Our cannon's loud mouth
Shall the rights of our monarch maintain ;
On America's strand
Amherst limits the land,
Boscawen gives law on the main,
Brave boys !
Boscawen gives, &c.

Each fort, and each town,
We still make our own,
Cape Breton, Crown Point, Niagar ;
Guardelupe, Senegal,
And Quebec's mighty fall,
Shall prove we've no equal in war,
Brave boys !
Shall prove we've, &c.

Though Conflans did boast
He wou'd conquer our coast,
Our thunder soon made monsieur mute ;
Brave Hawke wing'd his way,
Then pounc'd on his prey,
And gave him an English salute,
Brave boys !
And gave him, &c

At Minden you know
How we frighten'd the foe,
While homeward their army now steals,
" Though," they cry, " British bands
Are too hard for our hands,
Begar ! we can beat them in heels,"
Parbleu !
Begar ! we, &c.

Whilst our heroes from home
For laurels thus roam,
Should the flat-bottom'd boats but appear,
Our militia shall show
No wooden-shoed foe
Can with freemen in battle compare,
Brave boys !
Can with with freemen, &c.

VOL. XVI.

Your fortunes and lives,
Your children and wives,
To defend, 'tis the time now or never:
Then let each volunteer
To the drum-head repair—
King George and old England for ever !
Brave boys !
King George, &c.

---

## SONG,

SUNG BY MR. BEARD IN THE ENTERTAINMENT OF
APOLLO AND DAPHNE.

The Sun from the east tips the mountains with
gold ;
The meadows all spangled with dew-drops behold ! [day,
Hear ! the lark's early matin proclaims the new
And the horn's chearful summons rebukes our
delay.

### CHORUS.

With the sports of the field there's no pleasure
can vie,
While jocund we follow the hounds in full cry.

Let the drudge of the town make riches his sport;
The slave of the state hunt the smiles of a court;
No care and ambition our pastime annoy,
But innocence still gives a zest to our joy.
With the sports, &c.

Mankind are all hunters in various degree ;
The priest hunts a living—the lawyer a fee,
The doctor a patient—the courtier a place,
Though often, like us, he's flung out in the chase.
With the sports, &c.

The cit hunts a plumb—while the soldier hunts
The poet a dinner—the patriot a name ; [fame,
And the practis'd coquette, though she seems to
refuse,
In spite of her airs, still her lover pursues.
With the sports, &c.

Let the bold and the busy hunt glory and wealth;
All the blessing we ask is the blessing of health,
With hound and with horn through the wood-
lands to roam,
And, when tired abroad, find contentment at
home.
With the sports of the field there's no pleasure
can vie,
While jocund we follow our hounds in full cry.

---

## SONG,

SUNG BY MR. BEARD AT THE ANNUAL MEETING OF
THE PRESIDENT, VICE-PRESIDENTS, GOVERNORS,
&c. OF THE LONDON HOSPITAL.

Of trophies and laurels I mean not to sing,
Of Prussia's brave prince, or of Britain's good
king: [display,
Here the poor claim my song ; then the art I'll
How you all shall be gainers—by giving away.
Derry down.

The cruse of the widow, you very well know,
The more it was emptied, the fuller did flow :
So here with your purse the like wonder you'll
        find;
The more you draw out, still—the more left be-
        hind.
                        Derry down.

The prodigal here without danger may spend ;
That ne'er can be lavish'd, to Heaven we lend ;
And the miser his purse-strings may draw with
        out pain,
For what miser won't give—when giving is gain?
                        Derry down.

The gamester, who sits up whole days and whole
        nights,
To hazard his health and his fortune at White's;
Much more to advantage his bets he may make,
Here, set what he will, he will double his stake.
                        Derry down.

The fair-one, whose heart the four aces control,
Who sighs for sans-prendre, and dreams of a
        vole,                        [drille,
Let her here send a tithe of her gains at qua-
And she'll ne'er want a friend—in victorious
        spadille.
                        Derry down.

Let the merchant, who trades on the perilous sea,
Come here, and insure, if from loss he'd be free;
A policy here from all danger secures,
For safe is the venture—which Heaven insures.
                        Derry down.

The stock-jobber too may subscribe without fear,
In a fund which for ever a premium must bear ;
Where the stock must still rise, and where Scrip
        will prevail,
Though South-Sea, and India, and Omnium,
        should fail.
                        Derry down.

The churchman [1] likewise his advantage may
        draw,
And here buy a living, in spite of the law—
In Heaven, I mean; then, without any fear,
Let him purchase away—here's no simony here.
                        Derry down.

Ye rakes [2], who the joys of Hymen disclaim,
And seek, in the ruin of virtue, a fame ; [duty,
You may here boast a triumph consistent with
And keep, without guilt, a seraglio of beauty.
                        Derry down.

If from charity then such advantages flow,
That you still gain the more—the more you
        bestow ;                        [ease :
Here's the place will afford you rich profit with
When the bason comes round—be as rich as
        you please.
                        Derry down.

Then a health to that [3] patron, whose grandeur
        and store
Yield aid and defence to the sick and the poor;

[1] Additional stanza for the annual feast of the
sons of the Clergy
[2] Ditto for the Magdalen Hospital.
[3] The late duke of Devonshire.

Whom no courtier can flatter, no patriot can blame:
But, our president's here—or I'd tell you his
        name.
                        Derry down.

## FRAGMENT.

WHEN Bacchus, jolly God, invites
To revel in his ev'ning rites,
In vain his altars I surround,
Though with Burgundian incense crown'd:
No charm has wine without the lass ;
'Tis love gives relish to the glass.

Whilst all around, with jocund glee,
In brimmers toast their fav'rite she ;
Though ev'ry nymph my lips proclaim,
My heart still whispers Chloe's name ;
And thus with me, by am'rous stealth,
Still ev'ry glass is Chloe's health.

## VERSES

OCCASIONED BY LADY POMFRET'S PRESENT OF
SOME ANTIQUE STATUES TO OXFORD; THE
STREETS WHEREOF WERE FOOLISHLY SAID TO
BE PAVED WITH JACOBITES.

IF Oxford's stones, as Blaco writes,
And Pitt affirms, are Jacobites,
        That bid the court defiance ;
How must the danger now increase,
When stones are come from Rome and Greece,
        To form a grand alliance !

Yet, sprung from lands of liberty,
These stones can sure no Tories be,
        Or friends to the Pretender ;
And Pitt himself can ne'er devise,
That Whiggish stones should ever rise
        Against our faith's defender.

## TO DR. KING.

OFT have I heard, with clam'rous note,
A yelping cur exalt his throat
        At Cynthia's silver rays ;
So, with the blaze of learning's light,
When you, O King, offend his sight,
        The spaniel Blaco bays.

### THE

## BUTTERFLY AND BEE:

### TO FLAVIA.

SEE ! Flavia, see ! that flutt'ring thing,
Skim round yon flower with sportive wing,
        Yet ne'er its sweet explore ;
While, wiser, the industrious bee
Extracts the honey from the tree,
        And hives the precious store.

So you, with coy, coquettish art,
Play wanton round your lover's heart,

Insensible and free:
Love's balmy blessing would you try,
No longer sport a Butterfly,
But imitate the Bee.

## *VERSES*

DROPT IN MR. GARRICK'S TEMPLE OF SHAKE-
SPEARE.

While here to Shakespeare [1] Garrick pays
His tributary thanks and praise;
Invokes the animated stone,
To make the poet's mind his own;
That he each character may trace
With humour, dignity, and grace;
And mark, unerring mark, to men,
The rich creation of his pen;
  Preferr'd the pray'r—the marble god
Methinks I see, assenting, nod,
And, pointing to his laurell'd brow,
Cry—" Half this wreath to you I owe:
Lost to the stage, and lost to fame;
Murder'd my scenes, scarce known my name;
Sunk in oblivion and disgrace
Among the common, scribbling race,
Unnotic'd long thy Shakespeare lay,
To dulness and to time a prey:
But now I rise, I breathe, I live
In you—my representative!
Again the hero's breast I fire,
Again the tender sigh inspire;
Each side, again, with laughter shake,
And teach the villain-heart to quake;
All this, my son! again I do—
I?—No, my son!—'Tis I, and you."
  While thus the grateful statue speaks,
A blush o'erspreads the suppliant's cheeks—
" What!—Half this wreath, wit's mighty
          chief?—
O grant," he cries, " one single leaf;
That far o'erpays his humble merit,
Who's but the organ of thy spirit."
  Phœbus the gen'rous contest heard—
When thus the god address'd the bard:
" Here, take this laurel from my brow,
On him your mortal wreath bestow;—
Each matchless, each the palm shall bear,
In Heav'n the bard, on Earth the play'r.'

## CUPID BAFFLED.

Diana, hunting on a day,
Beheld where Cupid sleeping lay,
    His quiver by his head:
One of his darts she stole away,
And one of her's did close convey
    Into the other's stead.

When next the archer through the grove,
In search of prey, did wanton rove,
    Aurelia fair he 'spy'd;
Aurelia, who to Damon's pray'r
Disdain'd to lend a tender ear,
    And Cupid's pow'r defy'd.

[1] The statue of Shakespeare, in the temple dedicated to the bard by Mr. Garrick, in his delightful garden at Hampton, was the work of
that able and ingenious master, Roubiliac.

Soon as he ey'd the rebel maid;
" Now know my pow'r !" enrag'd, he said;
    Then levell'd at her heart:
Full to the head the shaft he drew;
But harmless to her breast it flew,
    For, lo!—'twas Dian's dart.

Exulting, then the fair-one cry'd,
" Fond urchin, lay your bow aside;
    Your quiver be unbound:
Would you Aurelia's heart subdue,
Thy play-thing arrows ne'er will do;
    Bid Damon give the wound."

## DEATH AND THE DOCTOR.

'Twixt Death and Schomberg, t'other day,
    A contest did arise;
Death swore his prize he'd bear away;
    The Doctor, Death defies.

Enrag'd to hear his pow'r defy'd,
    Death drew his keenest dart;
But wond'ring saw it glance aside,
    And miss the vital part.

AN
## OCCASIONAL PROLOGUE,

SPOKEN BY MR. POWELL, AT THE OPENING OF THE
THEATRE ROYAL IN COVENT-GARDEN, ON MON-
DAY, SEPTEMBER 14, 1767.

As when the merchant, to increase his store,
For dubious seas, advent'rous quits the shore;
Still anxious for his freight, he trembling sees
Rocks in each buoy, and tempests in each breeze;
The curling wave to mountain billows swells,
And ev'ry cloud a fancied storm foretells:
Thus rashly lanch'd on this theatric main,
Our all on board, each phantom gives us pain;
The catcall's note seems thunder in our ears,
And ev'ry hiss a hurricane appears;
In journal-squibs we lightning's blast espy,
And meteors blaze in every critic's eye.
  Spite of these terrours, still some hopes we view,
Hopes ne'er can fail us—since they're plac'd
          —in you,
Your breath the gale, our voyage is secure,
And safe the venture which your smiles insure;
Though weak his skill, th' advent'rer must suc-
          ceed,
Where candour takes th' endeavour for the deed.
For Brentford's state two kings could once suf-
          fice;
In our's, behold! four kings of Brentford se;
All smelling to one nosegay's od'rous savour,
The balmy nosegay of—the public favour.
From hence alone our royal funds we draw,
Your pleasure our support, your will our law.
While such our government, we hope you'll own
          us;
But should we ever tyrants prove—dethrone us.
Like brother monarchs, who to coax the nation,
Began their reign with some fair proclamation,
We too should talk at least—of reformation;
Declare, that during our imperial sway,
No bard shall mourn his long-neglected play;

But then the play must have some wit, some
    spirit,
And we allow'd sole umpires of its merit.
For those deep sages of the judging pit,
Whose taste is too refin'd for modern wit,
From Rome's great theatre we'll cull the piece,
And plant, on Britain's stage, the flow'rs of
    Greece.
If some there are our British bards can
    please,
Who taste the ancient wit of ancient days,
Be our's to save, from time's devouring womb,
Their works, and snatch their laurels from the
    tomb.
For you, ye fair, who sprightlier scenes may
    chuse,
Where music decks in all her airs the Muse,
Gay opera shall in all its charms dispense,
Yet boast no tuneful triumph over sense;
The nobler bard shall still assert his right,
Nor Handel rob a Shakespeare of his night.
To greet their mortal brethren of our skies,
Here all the gods of pantomime shall rise:
Yet 'midst the pomp and magic of machines,
Some plot may mark the meaning of our scenes;
Scenes which were held, in good king Rich's
    days,
By sages, no bad epilogues to plays.
If terms like these your suffrage can engage,
To fix our mimic empire of the stage;
Confirm our title in your fair opinions,
And croud each night to people our dominions.

---

### VERSES

ON CONVERTING THE CHAPEL TO A KITCHEN, AT
THE SEAT OF THE LORD DONNERAYLE, CALLED
THE GROVE, IN HERTFORDSHIRE.

By Ovid, among other wonders, we're told
What chanc'd to Philemon and Baucis of old;
How their cot to a temple was conjur'd by Jove,
So a chapel was chang'd to a kitchen at Grove.

The lord of the mansion most rightly conceiting,
His guests lov'd good prayers much less than good
    eating;
And possess'd by the devil, as some folks will tell
    [ye,
What was meant for the soul, he assign'd to the
    belly.

The word was scarce giv'n—when down dropp'd
    the clock,
And straight was seen fix'd in the form of a jack;
And, shameful to tell! pulpit, benches, and pews,
Form'd cupboards and shelves for plates, sauce-
    pans, and stews.

Pray'r-books turn'd into platters; nor think it a
    fable,
A dresser sprung out of the communion table;
Which, instead of the usual repast, bread and
    wine,
Is stor'd with rich soups, and good English sirloin.

No fire, but what pure devotion could raise,
'Till now, had been known in this temple to blaze:
But, good lord! how the neighbours around did
    admire,
When a chimney rose up in the room of a spire!

For a Jew many people the master mistook,
Whose Levites were scullions, his high-priest a
    cook;
And thought he design'd our religion to alter,
When they saw the burnt-offering smoke at the
    altar.

The bell's solemn sound, that was heard far and
    near,
And oft rous'd the chaplain unwilling to pray'r,
No more to good sermons now summons the sin-
    ner,
But blasphemous rings in—the country to dinner.

When my good lord the bishop had heard the
    strange story,     [G—'s glory;
How the place was profan'd, that was built to
Full of zeal he cried out, "Oh, how impious the
    deed,
To cram Christians with pudding, instead of the
    creed!"

Then away to the Grove hied the church's pro-
    tector,
Resolving to give his lay-brother a lecture;
But he scarce had begun, when he saw, plac'd
    before 'em,
A haunch piping hot from the *Sanctum Sancto-*
    *rum.*

"Troth!" quoth he, "I find no great sin in the
    plan,     [man:
What was useless to God—to make useful to
Besides, 'tis a true christian duty, we read,
The poor and the hungry with good things to
    feed."

Then again on the walls he bestowed consecration,
But reserv'd the full rights of a free visitation:
Thus, 'tis still the Lord's house—only varied the
    treat,
Now there's meat without grace—where was
    grace without meat.

---

### VERSES

ON THE DUKE OF CUMBERLAND'S VICTORY AT
CULLODEN, IN THE YEAR 1746.

As his worm-eaten volumes old Time tumbled
    o'er,     [yore,
To review the great actions that happen'd of
When the names of young Ammon and Cæsar
    he saw,
He to one oppos'd Churchill—to th' other Nassau;
Then said, with a sigh, "What! has Britain no
    friend?     end?"
"With these must her long race of heroes have
When straight a loud blast on her trumpet Fame
    blew,     [scarce knew;
Which so long had been silent, the sound he
But soon in his sight the swift goddess appear'd,
And, half out of breath, cry'd—"News, news!
    have you heard?—
I yet have one hero to add to your store,
Brave William has conquer'd—Rebellion's no
    more."     [name,
Well pleas'd, in his annals Time set down the
Made the record authentic,—and gave it to Fame.

## VERSES

INSCRIBED ON A MONUMENT CALLED THE TOMB OF CARE, IN THE GARDEN OF THE LATE JOHN RICH, ESQ. AT COWLEY, IN MIDDLESEX; WHERE-ON THREE BEAUTIFUL BOYS ARE COVERING A FUNERAL URN WITH A VEIL OF FLOWERS.

WHY, busy boys, why thus entwine
'The flowery veil around this shrine ?
As if, for halcyon days like these,
The sight too solemn were to please ;
Mistaken boys, what sight's so fair
To mortals, as the Tomb of Care ?
Here let the gloomy tyrant lie ;
His urn an altar shall supply,
Sacred to Ease, and social Mirth ;
For Care's decease—is Pleasure's birth.

## THE EPITAPH

(IN LETTERS OF BRASS, INSERTED BY A FEMALE FIGURE REPRESENTING HISTORY) ON A MARBLE PYRAMID OF THE MONUMENT OF JOHN, DUKE OF ARGYLE.

BRITON, behold, if patriot worth be dear,
A shrine that claims thy tributary tear !
Silent that tongue admiring senates heard,
Nerveless that arm opposing legions fear'd !
Nor less, O Campbell ! thine the pow'r to please,
And give to grandeur all the grace of ease.
Long. from thy life, let kindred heroes trace
Arts which ennoble still the noblest race.—
Others may owe their future fame to me;
I borrow immortality from thee.
Westminster Abbey.          P. WHITEHEAD.

## VERSES

ON THE NAME, P. WHITEHEAD, SUBSCRIBED TO THE ABOVE INSCRIPTION, BEING REMOVED THENCE SOME TIME AFTER THE MONUMENT WAS ERECT-ED.

O'ER the tombs as pale Envy was hov'ring around,
The manes of each hallow'd hero to wound ;
On Argyle's, when she saw only truth was related
Of him, whom alive she most mortally hated,
And finding the record adopted by Fame,
In revenge to the poet—she gnaw'd out his name'.

## VERSES,

TO MR. BROOKE, ON THE REFUSAL OF A LICENCE TO HIS PLAY OF GUSTAVUS VASA.
First published in the Gentleman's Magazine, 1739.

WHILE Athens glory'd in her free-born race,
And science flourish'd round her fav'rite place,

' These verses appeared first in captain Thom-son's Life of Whitehead, and perhaps were his own. The Epitaph was written at the request of the duchess. C.

The muse unfetter'd trod the Grecian stage ;
Free were her pinions, unrestrain'd her rage :
Bold and secure she aim'd the pointed dart,
And pour'd the precept poignant to the heart,
Till dire dominion stretch'd her lawless sway,
And Athens' sons were destin'd to obey :
Then first the stage a licens'd bondage knew,
And tyrants quash'd the scene they fear'd to view:
Fair Freedom's voice no more was heard to charm,
Or Liberty the Attic audience warm.
  Then fled the muse, indignant from the shore,
Nor deign'd to dwell where Freedom was no more:
Vain then, alas ! she sought Britannia's isle,
Charm'd with her voice, and cheer'd us with a smile.
If Gallic laws her gen'rous flight restrain,
And bind her captive with th' ignoble chain ;
Bold and unlicens'd, in Eliza's days,
Free flow'd her numbers, flourish'd fair her bays;
O'er Britain's stage majestic, unconfin'd,
She turn'd her patriot lessons to mankind ;
For mighty heroes ransack'd ev'ry age,
Then beam'd them glorious in her Shakespeare's page.
Shakespeare's no more !—lost was the poet's name,          [fame ;
Till thou, my friend, my genius, sprung to
Lur'd by his laurel's never-fading bloom,
You boldly snatch'd the trophy from his tomb,
Taught the declining muse again to soar,
And to Britannia give one poet more.
Pleas'd in thy lays we see Gustavus live ;
But, O Gustavus ! if thou can'st, forgive
Britons, more savage than the tyrant Dane,
Beneath whose yoke you drew the galling chain,
Degen'rate Briton's, by thy worth dismay'd,
Prophane thy glories, and proscribe thy shade.

## SONG.

As Granville's soft numbers tune Myra's just praise,
And Chloe shines lovely in Prior's sweet lays;
So, wou'd Daphne but smile, their example I'd follow,          [Apollo :
And, as she looks like Venus, I'd sing like
  But, alas ! while no smiles from the fair-one inspire,
  How languid my strains, and how tuneless my lyre !

Go, Zephyrs, salute in soft accents her ear,
And tell how I languish, sigh, pine, and despair ;
In gentlest murmurs my passion commend ;
But whisper it softly, for fear you offend, [pain ;
  For sure, O ye winds, ye may tell her my
  'Tis Strephon's to suffer, but not to complain.

Wherever I go, or whatever I do,          [view :
Still something presents the fair nymph to my
If I traverse the garden, the garden still shows
Me her neck in the lily, her lip in the rose :
  But with her neither lily nor rose can compare;
  Far sweeter's her lip, and her bosom more fair.

If, to vent my fond anguish, I steal to the grove,
The spring there presents the fresh bloom of my love;

The nightingale too, with impertinent noise,
Pours forth her sweet strains in my syren's sweet
    voice:          [brings;
  Thus the grove and its music her image still
  For, like spring she looks fair, like the night-
    ingale sings.

If, forsaking the groves, I fly to the court,
Where beauty and splendour united resort,
Some glimpse of my fair in each charmer I spy,
In Richmond's fair form, or in Brudenel's bright
    eye;        [appear?
  But, alas! what wou'd Brudenel or Richmond
  Unheeded they'd pass, were my Daphne but
    there.

If to books I retire, to drown my fond pain,
And dwell over Horace, or Ovid's sweet strain;
In Lydia, or Chloe, my Daphne I find;
But Chloe was courteous, and Lydia was kind:
  Like Lydia, or Chloe, wou'd Daphne but prove,
  Like Horace, or Ovid, I'd sing and I'd love.

## TO
## *DR. SCHOMBERG,*
### OF BATH.

To Schomberg quoth Death, " I your patient
    will have :"        [save."
To Death replied Schomberg, " My patient I'll
Then Death seiz'd his arrow, the doctor his pen,
And each wound the one gave, t'other heal'd it
    again;        [ance,
'Till Death swore he never had met such defi-
Since he and the college had been in alliance.

## *EPITAPH,*
BY MR. GARRICK, ON PAUL WHITEHEAD, ESQ.

Here lies a man misfortune could not bend,
Prais'd as a poet, honour'd as a friend :
Though his youth kindled with the love of fame,
Within his bosom glow'd a brighter flame :
Whene'er his friends with sharp afflictions bled,
And from the wounded deer the herd was fled,
Whitehead stood forth, the healing balm applied,
Nor quitted their distresses—till he died.
                     D. G.

THE

# POEMS

OF

## *EDWARD LOVIBOND, ESQ.*

# LIFE OF EDWARD LOVIBOND,

## *BY MR. CHALMERS.*

THE life of Mr. Lovibond appears to have afforded no subject for biography. Those who knew him best have declined the opportunity which the publication of his works afforded them to say something of the author. All they have been pleased to communicate is, that " he was a gentleman of fortune, who passed the greater part of his years in the neighbourhood of Hampton in Middlesex, where he lived greatly beloved by those who best knew him. He was an admirable scholar, of very amiable manners, and of universal benevolence, of which all his writings bear strong testimony. The little pieces which compose this volume were chiefly written on such incidents as occasionally arose in those societies of intimate acquaintance which he most frequented. After his death, which happened in 1775, his poems being dispersed in the hands of different friends, to whom they had been given by himself, many people expressed to his only brother, Anthony Lovibond Collins, esq. a wish to have them collected together, and preserved. This gentleman, equally zealous for the reputation of a brother he affectionately loved, hath put into the editor's hands those pieces he hath selected for that purpose."

Of a man of so many virtues, and so greatly beloved, the public might reasonably have expected a more detailed account. His father, I am told, was a director of the East India Company, and died in the year 1737, leaving him probably that fortune on which he was enabled to pass his days in the quiet enjoyment of the pleasures of rural life. He died September 27, 1775, at his house at Hampton, but the register of that parish is silent on his interment. I have been informed, also, that he was married, and not very happily.

When the World was began by Edward Moore, and his many noble and learned contributors, Mr. Lovibond furnished five papers; Nos. 93 and 94 contain some just remarks on the danger of extremes, and the impediments to conversation. In Nos. 132 and 134 he opposes the common erroneous notions on the subject of Providence with considerable force of argument, and concludes with some ironical remarks not ill applied. In No. 82 he first published the Tears of Old May Day, the most favourite of all his poems. The thoughts are peculiarly ingenious and happy, yet it may be questioned whether it is not exceeded by his Mulberry Tree, in which the distinguishing features of Johnson's and Garrick's characters are admirably hit off, the frivolous enthusiasm of the one, and the solid and steady veneration of the other for our immortal bard, are depicted with exquisite humour. Julia's printed letter appears to have been a favourite with the author. There are some bursts of genuine passion, and some tenderness displayed occasionally, but it wants simplicity. It was probably suggested by Pope's Eloisa, and must suffer in proportion as it reminds us of that inimitable effort. His lines on Rural Sports, are both poetical and moral, and contain some interesting pictures sweetly persuasive to a humane treatment of the brute creation.

His love verses, some of which are demi-platonic, are tender and sprightly. The Miss K— P— was Miss Kitty Phillips, a relation of a family now ennobled by the title of Milford.

The tale of the Hitchin Convent, the lines To a young Lady a very good Actress, the Verses to Mr. Wooddeson, and those on converting that gentleman's house into a poor-house, are all distinguished by original turns of thought. His pieces were generally circulated in private, as he had not the common ambition of an author, and was contented to please those whom he intended to please: yet he never attempted any subject which he did not illustrate by novelty of manner, and upon the whole may be considered as among the most successful of that class who are rather *amateurs*, than professional poets.

# POEMS

## OF

# EDWARD LOVIBOND.

## ON THE DEATH OF EDWARD LOVIBOND, ESQ.

BY MISS G————

AH ! what avails—that once the Muses crown'd
Thy head with laurels, and thy temples bound !
That in that polish'd mind bright genius shone,
That letter'd science mark'd it for her own!
Cold is that breast that breath'd celestial fire !
Mute is that tongue, and mute that tuneful
O could my Muse but emulate thy lays, [lyre !
Immortal numbers should record thy praise,
Redeem thy virtues from oblivion's sleep,
And o'er thy urn bid distant ages weep !—
Yet though no laureat flowers bestrew thy hearse,
Nor pompous sounds exalts the glowing verse,
Sublimer truth inspires this humbler strain,
Bids love lament, and friendship here complain ·
Bids o'er thy tomb the Muse her sorrows shed,
And weep her genius, number'd with the dead !—

## ADVERTISEMENT.

As the first poem in this collection was thirty-one years ago introduced to the public in a paper of The World, and written on a very remarkable event in our history, viz. the reforming our style or calendar to the general usage of the rest of Europe ; the paper explanatory of the subject being also written by Mr. Lovibond, it was judged proper to let it still precede it in this collection.

## THE WORLD.

### NUMBER LXXXII.

July 25th, 1754.

### TO MR. FITZ-ADAM.

SIR,

IT is a received opinion amongst politicians, that the spirit of liberty can never be too active under a constitution like ours. But though no lover of his country would desire to weaken this principle, which has more than once preserved the nation, yet he may lament the unfortunate application of it, when perverted to countenance party violence, and opposition to the most innocent measures of the legislature. The clamour against the alteration of the style seemed to be one of these instances. The alarm was given, and the most fatal consequences to our religion and government were immediately apprehended from it. This opinion gathered strength in its course, and received a tincture from the remains of superstition still prevailing in the counties most remote from town. I knew several worthy gentlemen in the west, who lived many months under the daily apprehension of some dreadful visitation from pestilence or famine. The vulgar were almost every where persuaded that Nature gave evident tokens of her disapproving these innovations. I do not indeed recollect that any blazing stars were seen to appear upon this occasion ; or that armies were observed to be encountering in the skies : people probably concluding that the great men who pretend to controul the Sun in his course, would assume equal authority over the inferior constellations, and not suffer any aerial militia to assemble themselves in opposition to ministerial proceedings.

The objection to this regulation, as favouring a custom established among papists, was not heard indeed with the same regard as formerly, when it actually prevented the legislature from passing a bill of the same nature : yet many a president of a corporation club very eloquently harangued upon it, as introductory to the doctrine of transubstantiation, making no doubt that fires would be kindled again in Smithfield before the conclusion of the year. This popular clamour has at last happily subsided, and shared the general fate of those opinions which derive their support from imagination, not reason.

In the present happy disposition of the nation the author of the following verses may venture to introduce the complaints of an ideal person- age, without seeming to strengthen the faction of real parties; without forfeiting his reputation as a good citizen; or bringing a scandal on the political character of Mr. Fitz-Adam, by making him the publisher of a libel against the state. This ideal personage is no other than Old May- day, the only apparent sufferer from the present regulation. Her situation is indeed a little mor- tifying, as every elderly lady will readily allow; since the train of her admirers is withdrawn from her at once, and their adoration transferred to a rival, younger than herself by at least eleven days.

I am, sir,
your most obedient servant,
E. L.

### THE TEARS OF OLD MAY-DAY.

Led by the jocund train of vernal hours
And vernal airs, uprose the gentle May;
Blushing she rose, and blushing rose the flow'rs
That sprung spontaneous in her genial ray.

Her locks with Heav'n's ambrosial dews were
      bright,
And am'rous Zephyrs flutter'd on her breast:
With ev'ry shifting gleam of morning light
The colours shifted of her rainbow vest.

Imperial ensigns grac'd her smiling form,
A golden key, and golden wand she bore;
This charms to peace each sullen eastern storm,
And that unlocks the summer's copious store.

Onward in conscious majesty she came.
The grateful honours of mankind to taste;
To gather fairest wreaths of future fame
And blend fresh triumphs with her glories
      past.

Vain hope! no more in choral bands unite
Her virgin vot'ries, and at early dawn.
Sacred to May and Love's mysterious rite,
Brush the light dew-drops [1] from the spangled
      lawn.

To her no more Augusta's [2] wealthy pride
Pours the full tribute from Potosi's mine;
Nor fresh blown garlands village maids provide,
A purer off'ring at her rustic shrine.

No more the May-pole's verdant height around
To valour's games th' ambitious youth ad-
      vance;
No merry bells and tabers' sprightlier sound
   Wake the loud carol, and the sportive dance.

Sudden in pensive sadness droop'd her head,
   Faint on her cheeks the blushing crimson dy'd—
" O! chaste victorious triumphs, whither fled?
My maiden honours, whither gone?" she cry'd.

" Ah! once to fame and bright dominion born,
The earth and smiling ocean saw me rise,
With time coeval and the star of morn,
   The first, the fairest daughter of the skies.

[1] Alluding to the country custom of gathering
May-dew.
[2] The plate garlands of London.

"Then, when at Heav'n's prolific mandate sprung
The radiant beam of new created day,
Celestial harps, to airs of triumph strung,
   Hail'd the glad dawn, and angel's call'd me
      May.

" Space in her empty regions heard the sound,
   And hills, and dales, and rocks, and vallies
The Sun exulted in his glorious round, [rung;
   And shouting planets in their courses sung.

" For ever then I led the constant year; [wiles;
   Saw Youth, and Joy, and Love's enchanting
Saw the mild Graces in my train appear,
   And infant Beauty brighten in my smiles.

" No Winter frown'd. In sweet embrace ally'd,
   Three sister Seasons danc'd th' eternal green;
And Spring's retiring softness gently vy'd
   With Autumn's blush, and Summer's lofty
      mien.

" Too soon, when man prophan'd the blessings
      giv'n,
   And vengeance arm'd to blot a guilty age,
With bright Astrea to my native Heav'n
   I fled, and flying saw the Deluge rage:

" Saw bursting clouds eclipse the noontide beams,
   While sounding billows from the mountains
      roll'd,
With bitter waves polluting all my streams,
   My nectar'd streams, that flow'd on sands of
      gold.

" Then vanish'd many a sea-girt isle and grove,
   Their forests floating on the watry plain:
Then, fam'd for arts and laws deriv'd from Jove,
   My Atalantis [3] sunk beneath the main.

" No longer bloom'd primeval Eden's bow'rs,
   Nor guardian dragons watch'd th' Hesperian
      steep:
With all their fountains, fragrant fruits and flow'rs,
   Torn from the continent to glut the deep.

" No more to dwell in sylvan scenes I deign'd
   Yet oft' descending to the languid Earth,
With quickning pow'rs the fainting mass sus-
      tain'd,
   And wak'd her slumb'ring atoms into birth.

" And ev'ry echo caught my raptur'd name,
   And ev'ry virgin breath'd her am'rous vows,
And precious wreaths of rich immortal fame,
   Show'r'd by the Muses, crown'd my lofty
      brows.

" But chief in Europe, and in Europe's pride,
   My Albion's favour'd realms, I rose ador'd;
And pour'd my wealth, to other climes deny'd,
   From Amalthea's horn with plenty stor'd.

" Ah me! for now a younger rival claims
   My ravish'd honours, and to her belong
My choral dances and vict'rious games,
   To her my garlands and triumphal song.

" O say what yet untasted bounties flow,
   What purer joys await her gentle reign?
Do lillies fairer, vi'lets sweeter blow?
   And warbles Philomel a softer strain?

[3] See Plato.

Do morning suns in ruddier glory rise ?
Does ev'ning fan her with serener gales ?
Do clouds drop fatness from the wealthier skies,
Or wantons plenty in her happier vales ?

" Ah ! no : the blunted beams of dawning light
Skirt the pale orient with uncertain day ;
And Cynthia, riding on the car of night,
Through clouds embattled faintly wins her
way.

" Pale, immature, the blighted verdure springs,
Nor mounting juices feed the swelling flow'r;
Mute all the groves, nor Philomela sings
When Silence listens at the midnight hour.

" Nor wonder, man, that Nature's bashful face,
And op'ning charms her rude embraces fear :
Is she not sprung of April's wayward race,
The sickly daughter of th' unripen'd year ?

" With show'rs and sunshine in her fickle eyes,
With hollow smiles proclaiming treach'rous
peace ;
With blushes, harb'ring in their thin disguise,
The blast that riots on the Spring's encrease.

" Is this the fair invested with my spoil
By Europe's laws, and senates' stern com-
mands ?
Ungen'rous Europe, let me fly the soil,
And waft my treasures to a grateful land :

" Again revive on Asia's drooping shore,
My Daphne's groves, or Lycia's ancient plain;
Again to Afric's sultry sands restore
Embow'ring shades, and Lybian Ammon's
fane :

" Or haste to northern Zembla's savage coast,
There hush to silence elemental strife;
Brood o'er the region of eternal frost,
And swell her barren womb with heat and life.

"Then Britain"—here she ceas'd. Indignant grief,
And parting pangs her fault'ring tongue sup-
prest :
Veil'd in an amber cloud, she sought relief,
And tears, and silent anguish told the rest.

---

### DEDICATION

TO THE REV. MR. WOODDESON, OF KINGSTON
UPON THAMES, AND THE LADIES OF HIS
NEIGHBOURHOOD.

O thou who sit'st in academic schools,
Less teaching than inspiring ancient art,
Thy own example nobler than your rules,
Thy blameless life best lesson for the heart.

And ye, who dwell in peaceful groves around,
Whose voice, whose verse enchants, harmoni-
ous maids !
Who mix the lyre with harps of Cambrian sound;
A mournful Muse, ah ! shelter in your shades!

Nor you she rivals nor such magic strain
As rescu'd Eloise from oblivion's sleep :
Enough, if one, the meekest of your train,
Poor Julia ! cries,—and turns aside to weep !—

### JULIA'S PRINTED LETTER

#### TO LORD ————.

—And dar'st thou then, insulting lord, demand
A friendly answer from this trembling hand ?
Perish the thought ! shall this unguarded pen
Still trust its frailties with the frauds of men.
To one, and one alone, again impart
The soft effusions of a melting heart !—
No more thy lips my tender page shall stain,
And print false kisses, dream't sincere in vain ;
No more thy eyes with sweet surprise pursue,
Love's secret mysteries there unveil'd to you.
Demand'st thou still an answer ?—let it be
An answer worthy vengeance, worthy me !—
Hear it in public characters relate
An ill starr'd passion, and capricious fate !
Yes, public let it stand ;—to warn the maid
From her that fell, less vanquish'd, than betray'd:
Guiltless, yet doom'd with guilty pangs to groan,
And expiate other's treasons, not her own:
A race of shame in honour's paths to run,
Still virtue's follower, yet by vice undone ;
Such free complaint to injur'd love belongs.
Yes, tyrant, read, and know me by my wrongs ;
Know thy own treacheries, bar'd to general view,
Yes, traitor, read, and reading tremble too !
What vice would perpetrate and fraud dis-
I come to blaze it to a nation's eyes; [guise,
I come—ah! wretch, thy swelling rage controul.
" Was he not once the idol of thy soul?—
True,—by his guilt thy tortur'd bosom bleeds,
Yet spare his blushes, for 'tis love that pleads !—
Respecting him, respect thy infant flame,
Proclaim the treason, hide the traitor's name !—
Enough to honour, and revenge be given,
This truth reserve for conscience and for Hea-
ven ! "
Talk'st thou,ingrate,of friendship's holy powers?
What binds the tiger and the lamb be ours !
This cold, this frozen bosom, can't thou dream
Senseless to love, will soften to esteem ?
What means thy proffer'd friendship?—but to
prove [love—
Thou wilt not hate her, whom thou can'st not
Remember thee !—repeat that sound again !—
My heart applauding echoes to the strain ;
Yes, till this heart forgets to beat, and grieve,
Live there thy image—but detested live !—
Still swell my rage—uncheck'd by time, or fate,
Nor waken memory but to kindle hate !—
Enter thy treacherous bosom, enter deep,
Hear conscience call, while flatt'ring passions
sleep !—
Impartial search, and tell thy boasted claim
To love's indulgence and to virtuous fame !
Where harbour Honour, Justice, Faith, and
Truth, [my youth :
Bright forms, whose dazzling semblance caught
How could I doubt what fairest seem'd and best
Should build its mansion in a noble breast ?
How doubt such generous virtues lodg'd in thine
That felt them glowing, tender maid, in mine ?
Boast not of trophies from my fall achiev'd,
Boast not, deceiver, in this soul deceiv'd ;
Easy the traitor wines an open heart,
Artless itself, and unsuspecting art :

Not by superiour wiles, successful proves,
But fond credulity in her that loves.—
   Blush, shameless grandeur, blush!—shall
    Britain's peer,
Daring all crimes, not dare to be sincere?—
His fraud in Virtue's fairest likeness paint,
And hide his nobleness in base constraint.
What charms were mine to tempt thy guilty
    fires!    [sires!
What wealth, what honours from illustrious
Can Virtue's simple spoils adorn thy race?
Shall annals mark a village-maid's disgrace?
Ev'n the sad secret, to thyself confin'd,
Sleeps, nor thou dar'st divulge it to mankind:
When bursting tears my inward anguish speak,
When paleness spreads my sometimes flushing
    cheek,
When my frame trembles with convulsive strife,
And spirits flutter on the verge of life,
When to my heart the ebbing pulse is driv'n,
And eyes throw faint accusing beams to Heav'n,
Still from the world those swelling sighs sup-
    prest,
Those sorrows streaming in one faithful breast;
Explain to her, from others hide my care,
Thought nature's weakness, and not love's de-
    spair,
The sprightly youth in gloomy languor pine,
My portion misery, yet not triumph thine—
Ah! whence derives thy sex its barbarous powers
To spoil the sweetness of our virgin hours?
Why leave me not, where first I met your eye,
A simple flower to bloom in shades, and die?—
Where sprightly morn on downy pinions rose,
And evening lull'd me to a deep repose?
Sharing pure joys, at least divine content,
The choicest treasure for mere mortals meant.
Ah! wherefore poisoning moments sweet as these,
Essay on me thy fatal arts to please?
Destin'd, if prosperous, for sublimer charms,
To court proud wealth, and greatness to thy
    arms!
How many a brighter, many a fairer dame,
Fond of her prize had fann'd thy fickle flame?
With livelier moments sooth'd thy vacant mind?
Easy possess'd thee, easy too resign'd—
Chang'd but her object, passion's willing slave,
Nor felt a wound to fester to the grave—
Oh! had I, conscious of thy fierce desires,
But half consenting, shar'd contagious fires,
But half reluctant, heard thy vows explain'd,
This vanquish'd heart had suffer'd, not com-
    plain'd—
But ah, with tears and crouded sighs to sue
False passion's dress in colours meant for true;
Artful assume confusion's sweet disguise,
Meet my coy virtues with dejected eyes,
Steal their sweet language that no words impart,
And give me back an image of my heart,
This, this was treachery, fated best to share
Hate from my bosom, and from thine despair—
Yet unrelenting still the tyrant cries,
Heedless of pity's voice and beauty's sighs,
" That pious frauds the wisest, best, approve,
And Heaven but smiles at perjuries in love.''—
No—'tis the villian's plea, his poor pretence,
To seize a trembling prey, that wants defence,
No—'tis the base sensation cowards feel;
The wretch that trembles at the brave man's
    steel,

Fierce and undaunted to a sex appears   [tears;
That breathes its vengeance but in sighs and
That helpless sex, by Nature's voice addrest
To lean its weakness on your firmer breast,
Protection pleads in vain—th' ungenerous slave
Insults the virtue he was born to save.—
   What! shall the lightest promise lips can feign
Bind man to man in honour's sacred chain?
And oaths to us not sanctify th' accord,
Not Heav'n attested, and Heav'n's awful Lord?
Why various laws for beings form'd the same?
Equal from one indulgent hand we came,
For mutual bliss that each assign'd its place,
With manly vigour temp'ring female grace.
Depriv'd our gentler intercourse, explain
Your solitary pleasures sullen reign;
What tender joys sit brooding o'er your store,
How sweet ambition slumbers gorg'd with gore!
'Tis our's th' unsocial passions to control,
Pour the glad balm that heals the wounded soul;
From wealth, from power's delusive, restless
    dreams
To lure your fancy to diviner themes.—
Confess at length your fancied rights you draw
From force superior, and not Nature's law,
Yet know, by us those boasted arms prevail,
By native gentleness, not man we fail;
With brave revenge a tyrant's blood to spill
Possessing all the power—we want the will.
Still if you glory in the lion's force,
Come, nobly emulate that lion's course!
From guarded herds he vindicates his prey,
Not lurks in fraudful thickets from the day;
While man, with snares to cheat, with wiles
    perplex,
Weakens already weak too soft a sex;
In law's, in custom's, fashion's fetters binds,
Relaxes all the nerves that brace our minds,
Then, lordly savage, rends the captive heart
First gain'd by treachery, then tam'd by art.—
   Are these reflections then that love inspires?
Is bitter grief the fruit of fair desires?
From whose example could I dream to find
A claim to curse, perhaps to wrong mankind?
Ah! long I strove to burst th' enchanting tie,
And form'd resolves, that ev'n in forming die;
Too long I linger'd on the shipwreck'd coast,
And ey'd the ocean where my wealth was lost!
In silence wept, scarce venturing to complain,
Still to my heart dissembled half my pain—
Ascrib'd my sufferings to its fears, not you;
Beheld you treacherous, and then wish'd you
    true;
Sooth'd by those wishes, by myself deceiv'd,
I fondly hop'd, and what I hop'd believ'd.—
Cruel! to whom? ah! whither should I flee,
Friends, fortune, fame, deserted all for thee!
On whom but you my fainting breast repose?
With whom but you deposit all its woes?
To whom but you explain its stifled groan?
And live for whom, but love and you alone?
What hand to probe my bleeding heart be found?
What hand to heal?—but his that gave the
    wound?—
   O dreadful chaos of the ruin'd mind!
Lost to itself, to virtue, human kind!   [wide,
From Earth, from Heaven, a meteor flaming
Link'd to no system, to no world allied;
A blank of Nature, vanish'd every thought
That Nature, reason, that experience taught,

Past, present, future trace, alike destroy'd,
Where love alone can fill the mighty void :
That love on unreturning pinions flown
We grasp a shade, the noble substance gone—
From one ador'd and once adoring, dream
Of friendship's tenderness—ev'n cold esteem
(Humble our vows) rejected with disdain,
Ask a last conference, but a parting strain,
More suppliant still, the wretched suit advance,
Plead for a look, a momentary glance,
A letter, token—on destru tion's brink
We catch the feeble plank of hope, and sink.—
  In those dread moments, when the hov'ring
    flame
Scarce languish'd into life, again you came,
Pursued again a too successful theme,
And dry'd my eyes, with your's again to stream ;
When treach'rous tears your venial faults con-
    fess'd,
And half dissembled, half excus'd the rest,
To kindred griefs taught pity from my own,
Sighs I return'd, and echoed groan for groan ;
Your self reproaches stifling mine, approv'd,
And much I credited, for much I lov'd.
  Not long the soul this doubtful dream pro-
    longs,
If prompt to pardon, nor forget its wrongs,
It scorns the traitor, and with conscious pride
Scorns a base self, deserting to his side ;
Great by misfortune, greater by despair,
Its Heaven once lost, rejects an humbler care ;
To drink the dregs of languid joys disdains,
And flies a passion but perceiv'd from pains ;
Too just the rights another claims to steal,
Too good its feelings to wish virtue feel,
Perhaps too tender or too fierce, my soul
Disclaiming half the heart, demands the whole.—
  I blame thee not, that, fickle as thy race,
New loves invite thee, and the old efface ;
That cold, insensible, thy soul appears
To virtue's smiles, to virtue's very tears ;
But ah ! an heart whose tenderness you knew,
That offer'd Heaven, but second vows to you,
In fond presumption that securely play'd.
Securely slumber'd in your friendly shade,
Whose every weakness, every sigh to share,
The powers that haunt the perjur'd, heard you
    swear ;
Was this an heart you wantonly resign'd
Victim to scorn, to ruin, and mankind ?
Was this an heart ?—O shame of honour, truth,
Of blushing candour, and ingenuous youth !
What means thy pity ? what can it restore ?·
The grave, that yawns till general doom's no
    more,
As soon shall quicken, as my torments cease,
Rock'd on the lap of innocence and peace,
As smiles and joy this pensive brow invade,
And smooth the traces by affliction made :
Flames, once extinguish'd, virtue's lamp divine,
And visits honour, a deserted shrine?
No, wretch, too long on passion's ocean tost,
Not Heaven itself restores the good you lost ;
The form exists not that thy fancy dream'd,
A fiend pursues thee that an angel seem'd ;
Impassive to the touch of reason's ray
His fairy phantom melts in clouds away ;
Yet take my pardon in my last farewell,
The wounds you gave, ah cruel ! never feel !

Fated like me to court and curse thy fate,
To blend in dreadful union love and hate ;
Chiding the present moment's slumb'ring haste,
To dread the future, and deplore the past ;
Like me condemn th' effect, the cause approve,
Renounce the lover, and retain the love.
Yes, Love ! ev'n now in this ill-fated hour,
An exile from thy joys, I feel thy power.
The Sun to me his noontide blaze that shrouds
In browner horrours than when veil'd in clouds,
The Moon, faint light that melancholy throws,
The streams that murmur, yet not court repose,
The breezes sickening with my mind's disease,
And vallies laughing to all eyes but these,
Proclaim thy absence, Love, whose beam alone
Lighted my morn with glories not its own.
O thou of generous passions purest, best !
Soon as thy flame shot rapture to my breast,
Each pulse expanding, trembled with delight,
And aching vision drank thy lovely light,
A new creation brightened to my view,
Nurs'd in thy smiles the social passions grew,
New strung, the thrilling nerves harmonious
And beat sweet unison to others' woes,   [rose,
Slumb'ring no more a Lethe's lazy flood,
In generous currents swell'd the sprightly blood,
No longer now to partial streams confin'd,
Spread like an ocean, and embrac'd mankind,
No more concentering in itself the blaze
The soul diffus'd benevolence's rays,
Kindled on Earth, pursued th' etherial road,
In hallow'd flames ascended to its God.—
  Yes, Love, thy star of generous influence cheers
Our gloomy dwelling in this vale of tears.
What ? if a tyrant's blasting hand destroys
Thy swelling blossoms of expected joys,
Converts to poison what for life was given,
Thy manna dropping from its native Heaven,
Still love victorious triumphs, still confest
The noblest transport that can warm the breast ;
Yes, traitor, yes, my heart to nature true,
Adores the passion and detests but you.

---

## ON REBUILDING COMBE-NEVILLE,

NEAR KINGSTON, SURREY, ONCE THE SEAT OF THE
FAMOUS KING-MAKING EARL OF WARWICK, AND
LATE IN THE POSSESSION OF THE FAMILY OF
HARVEY.

YE modern domes that rise elate
  O'er yonder prostrate walls,
In vain your hope to match the state
  Of Neville's ancient halls.

Dread mansion! on thy Gothic tower
  Were regal standards rais'd ;
The rose of York, white virgin flower,
  Or red Lancaster's blaz'd.

Warwick, high chief, whose awful word
  Or shook, or fix'd the throne,
Spread here his hospitable board,
  Or warr'd in tilts alone.

When Combe her garter'd knights beheld
  On barbed steeds advance,
Where ladies crown'd the tented field,
  And love inspir'd the lance.

U

Historic heralds here array'd
  Fair acts in gorgeous style,
But heroes toils were best repay'd
  By bashful beauty's smile.—

So flourish'd Combe, and flourish'd long
  With lords of bounteous soul ;
Her walls still echoed to the song,
  And mirth still drain'd her bowl.

And still her courts with footsteps meek
  The fainting traveller prest,
Still misery flush'd her faded cheek
  At Harvey's genial feast.—

Lov'd seat, how oft, in childish ease,
  Along thy woods I stray'd,
Now vent'rous climb'd embow'ring trees,
  Now sported in their shade.

Along thy hills the chase I led
  With echoing hounds and horns,
And left for thee my downy bed,
  Unplanted yet with thorns.

Now, languid with the noontide beams,
  Explor'd thy precious springs [1]
That proudly flow [2], like Susa's streams,
  To temper cups for kings.

But soon, inspir'd with nobler powers,
  I sought thy awful grove ;
There frequent sooth'd my evening hours,
  That best deceiver, love.

Each smiling joy was there, that springs
  In life's delicious prime ;
There young ambition plum'd his wings,
  And mock'd the flight of time.—

There patriot passions fir'd my breast
  With freedom's glowing themes,
And virtue's image rose confest
  In bright Platonic dreams.—

Ah me! my dreams of harmless youth
  No more thy walks invade,
The charm is broke by sober truth,
  Thy fairy visions fade.—

No more unstain'd with fear or guilt
  Such hours of rapture smile,
Each airy fabric fancy built
  Is vanish'd as thy pile!—

---

## ON LADY POMFRET'S

PRESENTING THE UNIVERSITY OF OXFORD WITH
HER COLLECTION OF STATUES.

WELCOME again the reign of ancient arts!
Welcome fair modern days from Gothic night,
Though late, emerging, sun of science hail!
Whose glorious rays enlightened Greece and
  Rome,

[1] Hampton-Court palace is supplied with water from the springs on Combe Hills.

[2] " There Susa by Choapes' amber stream,
  The drink of none but kings."
                        MILTON.

Illustrious nations ! Their's was empire's seat,
Their's virtue, freedom, each enchanting grace;
Sculpture with them to bright perfection rose,
Sculpture, whose bold Promethean hand inform'd
The stubborn mass with life—in fretted gold
Or yielding marble, to the raptur'd eye
Display'd the shining conclave of the skies,
And chiefs and sages gave the passions form,
And virtue shape corporeal : taught by her
The obedient brass dissolv'd ;
In love's soft fires thy winning charms she stole,
Thou mild retreating Medicean fair.
She mark'd the flowing Dryads lighter step,
The panting bosom, garments flowing loose,
And wanton tresses waving to the wind.—
Again by Pomfret's generous care, these stores
Of ancient fame revisit learning's seats,
Their old abode. O reverence learning's seats,
Ye beauteous arts! for know, by learning's
    smiles
Ye grew immortal—Know, however fair
Sculpture and Painting, fairer Poetry,
Your eldest sister, from the Aonian mount,
Imagination's fruitful realm, supply'd
The rich material of your lovely soil.
Her fairy forms, poetic fancy first
Peopled the hills, and vales, and fabled groves
With shapes celestial, and by fountain side
Saw fauns with wanton satyrs lead the dance
With meek-ey'd naïads; saw your Cyprian
Ascending from the ocean's wave;    [queen
Poetic fancy in Maonian song
Pictur'd immortal Jove, ere Phidias' hands
Sublime with all his thunders form'd the god.
Here then uniting with your kindred art,
Majestic Grecian sculpture deign to dwell,
Here shadss of Academe again invite,
Athenian philosophic shades, and here
Ye Roman forms, a nobler Tyber flows.
  Come, Pomfret, come, of rich munificence
Partake the fame, though candid blushes rise,
And modest virtues shun the blaze of day.
Pomfret, not all thy honours, splendid train,
Not the bright coronet that binds thy brow, .
Not all thy lovely offspring, radiant queens
On beauty's throne, shall consecrate thy praise
Like science, boasting in thy genial beam
Increasing stores: in these embowering shades
Stands the fair tablet of eternal fame ;
There memory's adamantine pen records
Her sons ; but each illustrious female's name
In golden characters engrav'd, defies
Envy and Time, superior to their rage.—
Pomfret shall live, the generous Pomfret join'd
With Caroline, and martial Edward's queen,
And great Eliza, regal names, like thee
Smiling on arts and learning's sons they reign'd.—
And see where Westmorland adorns the train
Of learning's princely patrons ! Lo, 1 see
A new pantheon rise as that of old
Famous, nor founded by ignobler hands;
Though thine, Agrippa, sway'd the helm of
I see enshrin'd majestic awful forms,   [Rome :
Chiefs, legislators, patriots, beauties, gods.
Not him by superstitious fears ador'd
With barbarous sacrifice and frantic zeal,
Yet not uncelebrated nor unsung, for oft
Thou, slumb'ring Cupid, with inverted torch
Betokening mildest fires, shall hear the sighs

Of virtuous, love-sick youths. You too shall
    reign,
Celestial Venus, though with chaster rites,
Addrest with vows from purer votaries heard.

---

## ON RURAL SPORTS.

The Sun wakes jocund—all of life, who breathe
  In air, or earth, and lawn, and thicket rove,
Who swim the surface, or the deep beneath,
  Swell the full chorus of delight and love.

But what are ye, who cheer the bay of hounds'
  Whose levell'd thunder frightens Morn's repose'
Who drag the net, whose hook insidious wounds
  A writhing reptile, type of mightier woes?

I see ye come, and havock loose the reins,
  A general groan the general anguish speaks,
The stately stag falls butcher'd on the plains,
  The dew of death hangs clammy on his cheeks.

Ah ! see the pheasant fluttering in the brake,
  Green, azure, gold, but undistinguish'd gore !
Yet spare the tenants of the silver lake !
  —I call in vain—they gasp upon the shore.

A yet ignobler band is guarded round
  With dogs of war—the spurning bull their
    prize ;
And now he bellows, humbled to the ground ;
And now they sprawl in howlings to the skies.

You too must feel their missile weapon's power,
  Whose clarion charms the midnight's sullen
    air ;
Thou the morn's harbinger, must mourn the hour
  Vigil to fasts, and penitence, and prayer'.

Must fatal wars of human avarice wage
  For milder conflicts, love their palm design'd ?
Now sheath'd in steel, must rival reason's rage
  Deal mutual death, and emulate mankind ?

Are these your sovereign joys, creation's lords ?
  Is death a banquet for a godlike soul ?
Have rigid hearts no sympathising chords
  For concord, order, for th' harmonious whole ?

Nor plead necessity, thou man of blood !
  Heaven tempers power with mercy—Heaven
    revere !
Yet slay the wolf for safety, lamb for food ;
  But shorten misery's pangs, and drop a tear !

Ah ! rather turn, and breath this evening gale'
  Uninjur'd and uninjuring nature's peace.
Come, draw best nectar from the foaming pail,
  Come, pen the fold, and count the stock's in-
    crease !

See pasturing heifers with the bull, who wields
  Yet budding horns, and wounds alone the soil!
Or see the panting spaniel try the fields
  While bursting coveys mock his wanton toil !

Now feel the steed with youth's elastic force
  Spontaneous bound, yet bear thy kind con-
    trol ;
Nor mangle all his sinews in the course,
  And fainting, staggering, lash him to the goal !

    ¹ Shrove Tuesday.

Now sweetly pensive, bending o'er the stream,
  Mark the gay floating myriads, nor molest
Their sports, their slumbers, but inglorious dream
  Of evil fled and all creation blest ?

Or else, beneath thy porch, in social joy
  Sit and approve thy infant's virtuous haste,
Humanity's sweet tones while all employ
  To lure the wing'd domestics to repast !

There smiling see a fop in swelling state,
  The turkey strut with valour's red pretence,
And duck row on with waddling honest gait,
  And goose mistake solemnity for sense !

While one with front erect in simple pride
  Full firmly treads, his consort waits his call,
Now deal the copious barley, waft it wide,
  That each may taste the bounty meant for all.

Yon bashful songsters with retorted eye
  Pursue the grain, yet wheel contracted flight,
While he, the bolder sparrow, scorns to fly,
  A son of freedom claiming nature's right.

Liberal to him ; yet still the wafted grain,
  Choicest for those of modest worth, dispense,
And blessing Heaven that wakes their grateful
    strain,
  Let Heaven's best joy be thine, Benevolence.

While flocks soft bleatings, echoing high and
    clear,
  The neigh of steeds, responsive o'er the heath,
Deep lowings sweeter melt upon thy ear
  Than screams of terrour and the groans of
    death.

Yet sounds of woe delight a giant brood :
  Fly then mankind, ye young, ye helpless old !
For not their fury, a consuming flood,
  Distinguishes the shepherd, drowns the fold.

But loosen once thy gripe, avenging law !
  Eager on man, a noble chase, they start ;
Now from a brother's side the dagger draw,
  Now sheath it deeper in a virgin's heart.

See as they reach ambition's purple fruits
  Their reeking hands in nation's carnage died !
No longer bathing in the blood of brutes,
  They swim to empire in a human tide.

But see him, see the fiend that others stung,
  With scorpion conscience lash himself the
    last !
See, festering in the bosom where they sprung,
  The fury passions that laid nature waste !

Behold the self-tormentor drag his chains,
  And weary Heaven with many a fruitless
    groan !
By pining fasts, by voluntary pains,
  Revenging nature's cause, he pleads his own.

Yet prostrate, suppliant to the throne above,
  He calls down Heaven in thunders to pursue
Heaven's fancied foes—O God of peace and love,
  The voice of thunder is no voice from you !

Mistaken mortal ! 'tis that God's decree
  To spare thy own, nor shed another's blood :
Heaven breathes benevolence, to all, to thee ;
  Each being's bliss consummates general good.

## ODE TO CAPTIVITY.

WRITTEN IN THE LAST WAR.

O STERN Captivity ! from Albion's land
Far, far, avert the terrours of thy rod !
O wave not o'er her fields thy flaming brand !
O crush not Freedom, fairest child of God !—
   Bring not from thy Gallic shore
   The galling fetters, groaning oar !
   Bring not hither Virtue's bane,
   Thy sister Superstition's train !
O spare from sanguine rites the silver floods !
Nor haunt with shapes obscene our unpolluted
   woods !—

Is yet too weak, rapacious power, thy throne ?
   While the chain'd continent thy vassal waits,
The Rhine, the Danube, and the sounding Rhone,
   Proclaim thy triumphs through an hundred
     states.
   See Valentia's smiling vales
   Courted for thee by ocean's gales !
   Through yawning vaults [1] on Tagus'
     streams,
   Thine revenge's dagger gleams :
Thy fury bursts on Rome's devoted head,
In vain the Scipios liv'd, the Decii, Cato bled !
Be these thy bounds—whose laws with monarchs
   reign,
To this fair isle how impotent thy hate !
Where Pitt, so righteous Heaven and George
   ordain,
In wisdom guides the thunder of the state.
   That thunder shook on Afric's shore,[2]
   The howling wild where lions roar ;
   In western worlds [3] its awful powers
   Sunk astonish'd Bourbon's towers;
That thunder sounding o'er the Celtic main,
Roll'd to Lutetia's walls along the affrighted
   Seine.

Daughters of Albion ! strew his paths with flowers,
O wake for him the lute's harmonious chord !
His name be echoed in your festal bowers,
   Happy fair, who seated far
   From haughty conquerors, barbarous war,
   Have heard alone in tragic songs
   Of cities storm'd and virgins' wrongs,
There felt the daughters, parents, consorts groan,
And wept historic woes, unpractis'd in your own !

Have you not heard how Sion's daughters mourn'd
   Their prostrate land ?—how Greece her victims
     tore
From flaming altars ?--captive queens they turn'd
   From Troy reluctant—on the sea-beat shore
   Their eyes to Heaven were roll'd in vain,
   Their eyes—for not the victor's chain
   Indulg'd thy privilege, Despair !
   Their hands to rend their flowing hair ;
Behind them Troy a smoking ruin lies,
Before lie unknown seas, and black incumbent
   skies.

[1] The late conspiracy against the Portuguese
government was planned amid the ruins of that
unfortunate capital.
   [2] Senegal.     [3] Louisbourg.

" Ye gales [4] !" they cried, " ye cruel eastern
    gales !
Adverse to Troy, conspiring with the foe,
That eager stretch the victor's swelling sails,
   To what unfriendly regions will ye blow ?
   Shall we serve on Doric plains ?
   Or where in Pithia Pyrrhus reigns ?
   Shall Echo catch our captive tales ?
   Joyless in the sprightly vales
Apidanus thy beauteous current laves,
Say, shall we sit and dream of Simois' fairer
    waves ?

" Shall Delos, sacred Delos, hear our woes ?
   Where when Latona's offspring sprung to birth,
The palm spontaneous, and the laurel rose,
   O Dian, Dian, on thy hallowed earth ;
   With Delian maids, a spotless band,
   At virtue's altar shall we stand
   And hail thy name with choral joy
   Invok'd in vain for falling Troy ?
Thy shafts victorious shall our songs proclaim,
When not an arrow fled to spare thy votaries
   shame.

" To Athens, art's fair empire, shall we rove ?
There for some haughty mistress ply the loom,
With daring fancy paint avenging Jove,
   His forked lightnings flaming through the
    gloom,
   To blast the bold Titanian race :
   Or deaf to nature, must we trace
   In mournful shades our hapless war ?
   What art, dread Pallas, to thy car,
Shall yoke th' immortal steeds ? what colours tell
By thine, by Pyrrhus' lance, how lofty Ilion fell ?

" Yes, cruel gods, our bleeding country falls,
   Her chiefs are slain—see brothers, sires expire !
Ah see, exulting o'er her prostrate walls,
   The victor's fury, and devouring fire !
   Asia's haughty genius broke,
   Bows the neck to Europe's yoke,
   Chains are all our portion now,
   No festal wreaths shall bind our brow,
Nor Hymen's torches light the bridal day :
O Death, and black Despair, behold your destin'd
    prey !"

---

## IMITATION FROM OSSIAN'S POEMS.

LATELY PUBLISHED BY THE TITLE OF FINGAL, &c.

BROWN Autumn nods upon the mountain's head,
   The dark mist gathers; howling winds assail
The blighted desert ; on its mineral bed
   Dark rolls the river through the sullen vale.
   On the hill's dejected scene
   The blasted ash alone is seen, [sleeps ;
   That marks the grave where Connal
   Gather'd into mould'ring heaps
   From the whirlwind's giddy round,
   Its leaves bestrew the hallowed ground.
Across the musing hunter's lonesome way
Flit melancholy ghosts, that chill the dawn of day.

[4] An imitation of the first chorus in the Hecu-
ba of Euripides.

Connal, thou slumber'st there, the great, the
        good !                    [trace ?
Thy long-fam'd ancestors what tongue can
Firm, as the oak on rocky heights, they stood ;
Planted as firm on glory's ample base.
        Rooted in their native clime,
        Brav'd alike devouring time,
        Full of honours, full of age,
        That lofty oak the winter's rage
        Rent from the promontory's brow,
        And death has laid the mighty low.
The mountains mourn their consecrated tree ;
His country Connal mourns :—what son shall
        rival thee ?

Here was the din of arms, and here o'erthrown
The valiant !—mournful are thy wars, Fingal ;
The caverns echo'd to the dying groan,
The fatal fields beheld the victor fall ;
        Tall amidst the host, as hills
        Above their vales and subject rills,
        His arm, a tempest lowering high,
        His sword, a beam of summers sky,
        His eyes, a fiery furnace, glare,
        His voice that shook th' astonish'd war,
Was thunder's sound : he smote the trembling
        foes,
As sportive infant's staff the bearded thistle mows.

Onward to meet this hero, like a storm,
A cloudy storm, the mighty Dargo came ;
As mountain caves, where dusky meteors form,
His hollow eye-balls flash'd a livid flame.
        And now they join'd, and now they wield
        Their clashing steel—resounds the field :
        Crimora heard the loud alarms,
        Rinval's daughter, bright in arms,
        Her hands the bow victorious bear,
        Luxuriant wav'd her auburn hair ;
Connal, her life, her love, in beauty's pride,
She follow'd to the war, and fought by Connal's
        side.

In wild despair, at Connal's foe she drew
The fatal string, impatient flew the dart ;
Ah hapless maid !—with erring course it flew ;
The shaft stood trembling in her lover's heart :
        He fell—so falls by thunder's shock
        From ocean's cliffs the rifted rock,
        That falls and ploughs the groaning strand
        He fell by love's unwilling hand,
        Hapless maid ! from eve to day,
        Connal, my love ; the breathless clay
My love, she calls—now rolls her frantic eyes—
—Now bends them sad to earth—she sinks, she
        faints, she dies.—

Together rest in Earth's parental womb,
        Her fairest offspring ; mournful in the vale
I sit, while, issuing from the moss-grown tomb,
        Your once-lov'd voices seem to swell the gale.—
        Pensive Memory wakes her powers,
        Oft recals your smiling hours
        Of fleeting life, that wont to move
        On downy wings of youth and love ;
        The smiling hours no more return ;
        —All is hush'd—your silent urn
The mountain covers with its awful shade,
Far from the haunts of men in pathless desert
        laid.

## ODE TO YOUTH.

Youth, ah stay, prolong delight,
Close thy pinions stretch'd for flight !
Youth, disdaining silver hairs,
Autumn's frowns and Winter's cares,
Dwell'st thou but in dimple sleek,
In vernal smiles and Summer's cheek ?
On Spring's ambrosial lap thy hands unfold,
They blossom fresh with hope, and all they touch
        is gold.

Graver years come sailing by :
Hark ! they call me as they fly ;
Quit, they cry, for nobler themes,
Statesman, quit thy boyish dreams !
Tune to crowds thy pliant voice,
Or flatter thrones, the nobler choice !
Deserting virtue, yet assume her state ;
Thy smiles, that dwell with love, ah ! wed them
        now to hate.

Or in victory's purple plain
Triumph thou on hills of slain !
While the virgin rends her hair,
Childless sires demand their heir,
Timid orphans kneel and weep :
Or, where the unsunn'd treasures sleep,
Sit brooding o'er thy cave in grim repose.
There mock at human joys, there mock at hu-
        man woes.

Years away ! too dear I prize
Fancy's haunts, her vales, her skies ;
Come, ye gales that swell the flowers,
Wake my soul's expanding powers ;
Come, by streams embow'r'd in wood,
Celestial forms, the fair, the good !
With moral charms associate vernal joys !
Pure nature's pleasures these—the rest are
        fashion's toys.

Come, while years reprove in vain,
Youth, with me, and rapture reign !
Sculpture, painting, meet my eyes,
Glowing still with young surprise !
Never to the virgin's lute
This ear be deaf, this voice be mute !
Come, beauty, cause of anguish, heal its smart,
—Now temperate measures beat, unalter'd else
        my heart.

Still my soul, for ever young,
Speak thyself divinely sprung !
Wing'd for Heaven, embracing Earth,
Link'd to all of mortal birth,
Brute or man, in social chain
Still link'd to all, who suffer pain.
Pursue the eternal law !—one power above
Connects, pervades the whole—that power di-
        vine is love.

## TO THE THAMES.

Nearer to my grove, O Thames !
Lead along thy sultry streams,
Summer fires the stagnant air,
Come and cool thy bosom there !
Trees shall shelter, Zephyrs play,
Odours court thy smiling stay ;

There the lily lifts her head,
Fairest child of Nature's bed.
  Oh! Thames, my promise all was vain:
Autumnal storms, autumnal rain
Have spoil'd that fragrance, strip those shades,
Hapless flower! that lily fades.—
What? if chance, sweet evening ray,
Or western gale of vernal day,
Momentary bloom renews,
Heavy with unfertile dews
It bends again, and seems to cry,
" Gale and sunshine, come not nigh!
Why reclaim from winter's power
This wither'd stalk, no more a flower !"
Such a flower, my youthful prime,
Chill'd by rigour, sapp'd by time,
Shrinks beneath the clouded storm :
What? if Beauty's beaming form,
And Cambrian virgin's vocal air
Expand to smiles my brow of care :
That beam withdrawn, that melting sound,
The dews of death hang heavier round,
No more to spring, to bloom, to be,
I bow to fate and Heaven's decree.
  Come then, Cambrian virgin, come,
With all thy music seek my tomb,
With all thy grace, thy modest state,
With all thy virtues, known too late!
Come, a little moment spare
From pious rites and filial care !
Give my tomb—no heart-felt sigh,
No tear convulsing pity's eye !
Gifts oft too endearing name
For you to grant, for me to claim ;
But bring the song—whose healing sounds
Were balm to all my festering wounds.
Bring the lyre—by music's power
My soul entranc'd shall wait the hour,
The dread majestic hour of doom,    [gloom,
When through the grave, and through the
Heaven shall burst in floods of day :
Dazzled with so fierce a ray,
My aching eyes shall turn to view
Its milder beams reflect from you.

## TO MISS K———— P————.

Gentle Kitty, take the lyre
Thy magic hands alone inspire !
But wake not once such swelling chords
As rouse ambition's stormy lords,
Nor airs that jocund tabors play
To dancing youth in shades of May,
Nor songs that shake old Picton's towers,
When feast and music blend their powers !
But notes of mildest accent call,
Of plaintive touch and dying fall ;
Notes, to which thy hand, thy tongue,
Thy every tender power is strung.—
Cambrian maid, repeat that strain !
Sooth my widow'd bosom's pain!
Its passions own thy melting tones ;
Sighs succeed to bursting groans ;
Soft and softer still they flow,
Breathing more of love than woe;
Glistening in my eye appears
A tenderer dew than bitter tears ;
Springing hope despair beguiles,
And sadness softens into smiles.

  I quit thy lyre—but still the train
Of sweet sensations warms my brain.
What? though social joy and love
Forget to haunt my sullen grove:
Though there my soul, a stagnant flood,
Nor flows its own, or others good,
Emblem of yon faded flower,
That, chill'd by frost, expands no more :
The dreary scene yet sometimes closes
When sleep inspires, on beds of roses,
Such dear delusions, fairy charms
As fancy dreams in virtue's arms.
For see, a gracious form is near !
She comes to dry my falling tear.
One pious hand in pity spread
Supports my else unshelter'd head ;
The other waves to chase away
The spectres haunting all my day :
She calls—above, below, around
Sweet fragrance breathes, sweet voices sound—
Such a balm to wounded minds,
Gentle Kitty, slumber finds ;
Such a change is misery's due—
—Who wakes to grief should dream of you.

## TO MISS K———— P————.

Ah! bow to music, bow my lays
To beauty's noblest art!
To reach the bosom mine the praise,
But thine to melt the heart.

'Tis mine to close affliction's wounds,
To brighten pleasure's eye :
But thine, by sweet dissolving sounds,
To make it bliss to die.

My notes but kindle cold desire,
Ah! what you feel for me !
Diviner passions thine inspire,
Ah! what I feel for thee !

Associate then thy voice, thy touch,
O wed to mine thy powers !
Be such at least, nor blush at such
Connubial union our's !

## TO MISS K———— P————.

Why, Kitty, with that tender air,
Those eyes to earth inclin'd,
Those timid blushes, why despair
Of empire o'er mankind ?

Ah! know, that beauty's surest arms
Are candour, softness, ease,
Your sweet distrust of pleasing charms
Is half the charm to please.—

Respect your own harmonious art !
For love securest wounds,
Securest takes th' imprison'd heart
Entranc'd by magic sounds !

If flowers of fiction's growth you call
This wreath that truth bestows ;
Survey around your attick wall
Each pencill'd form [1] that glows.

[1] Drawings from antique statues.

And ask the youths! why heavenly fair
Their tenderest vows inspires?
If Juno's more than regal air,
Or fierce Minerva's fires?
'Tis bashful Venus they prefer
Retiring from the view,
And, what their lips address to her,
Their bosoms feel for you.

---

## TO MISS K——— P———.

Your bosom's sweet treasures thus ever disclose!
For believe my ingenuous confession,
The veil meant to hide them but only bestows
A softness transcending expression.

" Good Heaven!" cries Kitty, " what language
I hear!
Have I trespass'd on chastity's laws?
Is my tucker's clear muslin indecently clear?
Is it no sattin apron, but gauze?"

Ah no!—not the least swelling charm is descried
Thro' the tucker, too bashfully decent;
And your apron hides all that short aprons can
hide,
From the fashion of Eve to the present.

The veil, too transparent to hinder the sight,
Is what modesty throws on your mind:
That veil only shades, with a tenderer light,
All the feminine graces behind.

---

## TO MISS K——— P———.

Si un arbre avoit du sentiment, il se plairoit à
voir celui qui le cultive se reposer sous son
ombrage, respirer le parfum de ses fleurs,
gouter la douceur de ses fruits: Je suis cet
arbre, cultivé par vous, & la Nature m' a
donné une ame.   MARMONTEL.

Amid thy native mountains, Cambrian fair,
Were some lone plant supported by thy care,
Sav'd from the blast, from winter's chilling powers,
In vernal suns, in vernal shades and showers,
By thee reviving: did the favoured tree
Exist, and blossom and mature by thee:
To that selected plant did Heaven dispense,
With vegetable life, a nobler sense:
Would it not bless thy virtues, gentle maid?
Would it not woo thy beauties to its shade?
Bid all its buds in rich luxuriance shoot,
To crown thy summer with autumnal fruit,
Spread all its leaves, a pillow to thy rest,
Give all its flowers to languish on thy breast,
Reject the tendrils of th' uxorious vine,  •
And stretch its longing arms to circle thine?
Yes; in creation's intellectual reign,
Where life, sense, reason, with progressive chain,
Dividing, blending, form th' harmonious whole:
—That plant am I, distinguish'd by a soul.

---

## TO MISS K——— P———,

WITH ANSON'S VOYAGE.

Raptur'd traveller, cease the tales
Of Tinian's lawns, Fernandes' vales;

Of isles, concentering Nature's charms,
Lapt in peaceful Ocean's arms;
Of that Hesperian world, which lies
Beneath the smile of southern skies,
Where Zephyr waves unflagging wings,
Where Albion's summers, Latian springs
Join thy autumns, smiling France,
And lead along th' eternal dance!
These enchanting scenes, and all
That wake to form at fancy's call,
And all the sportive pencil traces,
Are feeble types of living graces.
Of moral charms, that mental throne
Unclouded beauty calls her own.
Where all the Sun's meridian blaze
Is twilight gloom to virtue's ra.s.
There with richer blended sweets
Wedded Spring her Autumn meets;
There Fernandes' brighter shore,
There a purer Chili's ore,
Fruits and flowers are there combin'd
In fairer Tinian—Kitty's mind.

---

## THE COMPLAINT OF CAMBRIA.

TO MISS K——— P———, SETTING TO
MUSIC, AND SINGING ENGLISH
VERSES.

DONE INTO ENGLISH FROM THE WELCH ORIGINAL.

Degenerate maid, no longer ours!
Can Saxon ditties suit thy lyre?
Accents untun'd, that breathe no powers
To melt the soul, or kindle martial fire?
   It ill becomes thee to combine
   Such hostile airs with notes divine,
In Cambrian shades, the Druids' hallow'd bounds,
Whose infant voice has lisp'd the liquid Celtic
   sounds.

Revere thy Cambria's flowing tongue!
Though high-born Hoel's lips are dumb,
Cadwallo's harp no more is strung,
And silence sits on soft Lluellyn's tomb:
   Yet songs of British bards remain
   That, wedded to thy vocal strain,
Would swell melodious on the mountain breeze,
And roll on Milford's wave to distant echoing
   seas.——

O sing thy sires in genuine strains!
When Rome's resistless arm prevail'd,
When Edward delug'd all my plains¹,
And all the music of my mountains fail'd;
   When all her flames rebellion spread,
   Firmly they stood—O sing the dead!
The theme majestic to the lyre belongs,
To Picton's lofty walls, and Cambrian virgins
   songs.

¹ Edward I. put to death all the Welch bards.

## ON A PRESENT TO THE AUTHOR,

OF TWO IMPRESSIONS FROM A FINE ANTIQUE SEAL
OF THE HEAD OF ALEXANDER ;

THE ONE BY LADY P ——, ON PAPER ;
THE OTHER BY MISS J —— P ——, IN
WAX.

FAIR sculpture of Ammon's young graces!
    My lady with whim shall we tax?
On paper who marks thy faint traces,
    Which Stella stamps lively in wax?

Of their hearts they make mutual confession :
    That, cold to emotions once felt,
The mother's scarce yields to impression—
    —The daughter's can soften and melt.

ON THE SUBJECT OF THE

## MONUMENT IN ARCADIA.

O YOU, that dwell where shepherds reign,
    Arcadian youths, Arcadian maids,
To pastoral pipe who danc'd the plain,
    Why pensive now beneath the shades?

" Approach her virgin tomb," they cry,
    " Behold the verse inscrib'd above,
' Once too in Arcady was I,—'·
    Behold what dreams are life and love !"

## ON THE SAME.

SWEET Arcady, where shepherds reign,
    Your simple youths, your simple maids,
With pastoral dance still cheer the plain,
    Their pastoral pipe still charms the shades :

This only song still meets our ear,
    It swells the breeze, it fills the grove ;
What joys so sweet as Nature's here?
    What joy of Nature sweet as love?

## HITCHIN CONVENT.

### A TALE.

WHERE Hitch's gentle current glides,
    An ancient convent stands,
Sacred to prayer and holy rites
    Ordain'd by pious hands.

Here monks of saintly Benedict
    Their nightly vigils kept,
And lofty anthems shook the choir
    At hours when mortals slept.

But Harry's wide reforming hand
    That sacred order wounded ;
He spoke—from forth their hallow'd walls
    The friars fled confounded.

Then wicked laymen ent'ring in,
    Those cloisters fair prophan'd ;
Now riot loud usurps the seat
    Where bright devotion reign'd.

Ev'n to the chapel's sacred roof,
    Its echoing vaults along,
Resounds the flute, and sprightly dance,
    And hymeneal song.

Yet fame reports, that monkish shades
    At midnight never fail
To haunt the mansions once their own,
    And tread its cloisters pale.

One night, more prying than the rest,
    It chanc'd a friar came,
And enter'd where on beds of down
    Repos'd each gentle dame.

Here, softening midnight's raven gloom,
    Lay R——e, blushing maid ;
There, wrapt in folds of cypress lawn,
    Her virtuous aunt was laid.

He stopp'd, he gaz'd, to wild conceits
    His roving fancy run,
He took the aunt for prioress,
    And R——e for a nun,

It hap'd that R——'s capuchin,
    Across the couch display'd,
To deem her sister of the veil, |
    The holy sire betray'd.

Accosting then the youthful fair,
    His raptur'd accents broke ;
Amazement chill'd the waking nymph ;
    She trembled as he spoke.

" Hail halcyon days! Hail holy nun !
    This wondrous change explain :
Again religion lights her lamp,
    Reviews these walls again.

" For ever blest the power that checkt
    Reformists' wild disorders,
Restor'd again the church's lands.
    Reviv'd our sacred orders.

" To monks indeed, from Edward's days,
    Belong'd this chaste foundation ;
Yet sister nuns may answer too
    The founder's good donation.

" Ah ! well thy virgin vows are heard :
    For man were never given
Those charms, reserv'd to nobler ends,
    Thou spotless spouse of Heaven !

" Yet speak what cause from morning mass
    Thy ling'ring steps delays :
Haste to the deep-mouth'd organ's peal
    To join thy vocal praise.

" Awake thy abbess sisters all ;
    At Mary's holy shrine,
With bended knees and suppliant eyes
    Approach, thou nun divine !"—

" No Nun am I," recov'ring cried
    The nymph ; " No nun, I say,
Nor nun will be, unless this fright
    Should turn my locks to grey.

" 'Tis true, at church I seldom fail
    When aunt or uncle leads ;
Yet never rise by four o'clock
    To tell my morning beads.

" No mortal lover yet, I vow,
    My virgin heart has fixt,
But yet I bear the creatures talk
    Without a grate betwixt.

" To Heav'n my eyes are often cast
    (From Heav'n their light began)
Yet deign sometimes to view on Earth
    It's image stampt on man.

" Ah me ! I fear in borrow'd shape
   Thou com'st, a base deceiver ;
Perhaps the devil, to tempt the faith
   Of orthodox believer.

" For once my hand, at masquerade,
   A reverend friar prest ;
His form as thine, but holier sounds
   The ravish'd saint addrest.

" He told me vows no more were made
   To senseless stone and wood,
But adoration paid alone
   To saints of flesh and blood,

" That rosy cheeks, and radiant eyes,
   And tresses like the morn,
Were given to bless the present age,
   And light the age unborn:

" That maids, by whose obdurate pride
   The hapless lover fell,
Were doom'd to never-dying toils
   Of leading apes in Hell.

" ' Respect the first command,' (he cried,)
   ' It's sacred laws fulfil,
And well observe the precept given
   To Moses,—Do not kill.'

" Thus spoke, ah yet I hear him speak !
   My soul's sublime physician ;
Then get thee hence, thy doctrines vile
   Would sink me to perdition."

She ceas'd—the monk in shades of night
   Confus'dly fled away,
And superstition's clouds dissolv'd
   In sense, and beauty's ray.

---

## TO A YOUNG LADY,

### A VERY GOOD ACTRESS.

Powerful is beauty, when to mortal seats
   From Heaven descends the heaven-created
     good,
When fancy's glance the fairy phantom meets,
   Nymph of the shade, or Naiad of the flood.

So blooms Celena, daughter of the skies,
   Queen of the joys romantic rapture dreams,
Her cheeks are summer's damask rose, her eyes
   Steal their quick lustre from the morning's
     beams.

Her airy neck the shining tresses shade ;
   In every wanton curl a Cupid dwells :
To these, distrusting in the Graces' aid,
   She joins the mighty charms of magic spells.

Man, hapless man, in vain destruction flies,
   With wily arts th' enchantress nymph pursues;
To varying forms, as varying lovers rise,
   Shifts the bright Iris of a thousand hues.

Behold th' austere divine, opprest by years,
   Colics, and bulk, and tithes engend'red care ;
The sound of woman grates his aching ears,
   Of other woman than a scripture fair.

Sudden she comes a Deborah bright in arms,
   Or wears the pastoral Rachel's ancient mien ;
And now, as glow gay-flushing eastern charms,
   He sighs like David's son for Sheba's queen.

To Change the China trader speeds his pace,
   Nor heeds the chilly North's unripening dames;
'Tis her's, with twinkling eyes, and lengthen'd
     face,
   And pigmy foot, to wake forgotten flames.

She oft, in likeness of th' Egyptian Crone,
   Too well inform'd, relates to wand'ring swains
Their amorous plaints preferr'd to her alone :
   Her own relentless breast too well explains.

See, at the manor's hospitable board
   Enters a sire, by infant age rever'd ;
From shorten'd-tube exhaling fumes afford
   The incense bland that clouds his forky beard.

Conundrums quaint, and puns of jocund kind,
   With rural ditties, warm th' elated 'squire,
Yet oft sensations quicken in his mind,
   Other than ale and jocund puns inspire.

The forms where bloated Dropsy holds her seat,
   He views, unconscious of magicians' guiles,
Nor deems a jaundic'd visage lov'd retreat
   Of graces, young desires, and dimpled smiles.

Now o'er the portal of an antique hall
   A Grecian form the raptur'd patriot awes,
The hoary bust and brow severe recall
   Lycurgus, founder of majestic laws.

Awhile entranc'd, he dreams of old renown,
   And freedom's triumph in Platean fields,
Then turns—relaxing sees the furrow'd frown,
   To melting airs the soften'd marble yields.

I see the lips as breathing life, he cries,
   On icy cheeks carnation blooms display'd,
The pensive orbs are pleasure-beaming eyes
   And Sparta's lawgiver a blushing maid.

There, at the curtains of the shudd'ring youth,
   Stiff, melancholy, pale, a spectre stands,
Some love-lorn virgin's shade—O ! injur'd truth,
   Deserted phantom, and ye plighted hands,

He scarce had utter'd—from his frantic gaze
   The vision fades—succeeds a flood of light.
O friendly shadows, veil him, as the blaze
   Of beauty's sun emerging from the night.

Here end thy triumphs, nymph of potent charms,
   The laurel'd bard is Heaven's immortal care ;
Him nor illusion's spell nor philter harms,
   Nor music floating on the magic air.

The myrtle wand this arm imperial bears,
   Reluctant ghosts and stubborn elves obey :
Its virtuous touch the midnight fairy fears,
   And shapes that wanton in Aurora's ray.

I ceas'd ; the virgin came in native grace,
   With native smiles that strengthen beauty's
O vain the confidence of mortal race !   [chain:
   My laurel'd head and myrtle wand are vain.

Again wild raptures, kindling passions rise,
   As once in Andover's autumnal grove,
When looks that spoke, and eloquence of sighs,
   Told the soft mandate of another's love.

---

## TO AN ACCOMPLISHED LADY.

### IN THE MANNER OF WALLER.

O nymph ! than blest Pandora honour'd more,
What gods to grace thee lavish all their store !

We see thy form in awful beauty move,
At once repelling and inviting love ;
We see thy mind each bright perfection reach
That genius kindles, and the Graces teach :
Pallas to form that matchless mind, conspires
With wisdom's coolness, temp'ring fancy's fires ;
Here, as in Eden's blissful garden, shoot
The tree of knowledge and forbidden fruit.

## ADDRESS TO THE THAMES.

O THAMES ! thy clear majestic stream
Shall ever flow my raptur'd theme ;
Not because Augusta's pride
Builds her greatness on thy tide,
Courted by worlds in other oceans found :
Not because proud Cliefden laves
His pendent beeches in thy waves !
Not because thy limpid rills
Reflect on Hampton's towers, or Richmond's hills ;
Or Cooper's mountain, by the Muses crown'd,
Or catch the blaze from Windsor's beaming
    star,
Sacred to patriot chiefs, the boast of peace and
    war.

Nor yet because thy current loves
The haunt of academic groves ;
And still with ling'ring fond delay
Through Egham's vales delights to stray,
Once scene of freedom's claims, heroic cares :
But hail thee, Thames ! while o'er thy meads
Eliza with Louisa leads
Each winning grace of love and youth,
Ingenuous forms, fair candour and fair truth :
Oh ! fan their evening walk with mildest airs ;
So Gallic spoils shall crowd thy wealthy side,
And commerce swell her stores with each re-
    volving tide.

### TO MRS. B———,

READING JULIA WITH TEARS, DURING A HARD FROST

WHAT, though descending as the dews of morn,
On misery's sighs your tear of virtue waits ;
Forget the fallen Julia ! you were born
For heart-expanding joys and smiling fates.

To sooth with social pleasures human cares,
To call the Muse to Thames' frozen glades,
To wake the slumb'ring spring with vernal airs,
And plant an Eden in December's shades ;

To deck, like Eve [1], with soft officious haste,
Your banquet, worthiest of her angel guest ;
Amid the flowers that crown the fair repast
A flower yourself, the fairest of the feast.

There the great Giver for his bounties given
Your grateful consort blessing, blesses too
The sweet dispenser of the gifts of Heaven,
In wonder's silent prayer he blesses you :

Your infants there reflecting round the board,
Maternal graces while his eye approves ;
One tear to rapture give !—then sit ador'd
The gentle mother of the smiles and loves.

[1] See Milton's Paradise Lost, Book v. from
line 303.

### TO LADY F———,

ON HER MARRIAGE.

THOUGH to Hymen's gay season belong
Light airs, and the raptures of youth ;
Yet listen to one sober song ;
    O listen, fair Stella, to truth.

Farewell to the triumphs of beauty,
    To the soft serenade at your bower,
To the lover's idolatrous duty,
    To his vigils in midnight's still hour.

To your frowns darting amorous anguish,
    To your smiles chasing every care,
To the power of your eyes lively languish,
    To each glance waking hope or despair.

Farewell to soft bards, that in Heaven
    Dipt the pencil to picture your praise,
And blended the colours of even,
    With morning's gay opening rays :

They no longer on Thames shall proclaim you
    A Naiad new sprung from the flood,
Nor to Bushy's soft echoes shall name you
    Bright Dian, the queen of the wood.

Farewell to love's various season,
    Smiling days hung with tempests and night ;
But welcome the reign of fair reason,
    O ! welcome securer delight.

O ! welcome, in nature's own dress,
    Purest pleasures of gentler kind ;
O ! welcome the power to bless,
    To redeem fortune's wrongs on mankind.

Be a goddess indeed, while you borrow
    From plenty's unlimited store,
To gild the wan aspect of sorrow,
    To cheer the meek eyes of the poor.

When your virtues shall mix with the skies,
    When your beauty, bright phenix, decays ;
In your image new graces shall rise,
    And enlighten posterity's days.

Future ages shall trace every air ;
    Every virtue deriv'd to your blood
Shall remember that Stella was fair,
    Shall remember that Stella was good.

### SONG.

No gaudy Rubens ever dare
    With flaunting genius, rosy loves,
To crowd the scene, in sunshine's glare,
    Exposing her the Muse approves.

Let, chaste Poussin, thy shaded stream
    Reflect her pensive, tender air ;
Let evening veil with sober beam,
    In bashful night the bashful fair.

## VERSES

WRITTEN AFTER PASSING THROUGH FINDON, SUS-
SEX, 1768. ADDRESSED TO THE REV. MR. WOOD-
DESON,[1] OF KINGSTON UPON THAMES.

Wooddeson! these eyes have seen thy natal
    earth;
Thy Findon, sloping from the southern downs,
Have blest the roof ennobled by thy birth,
    And tufted valley, where no ocean frowns.

Thou wert not born to plough the neighbouring
    main,
Or plant thy greatness near ambition's throne,
Or count unnumber'd fleeces on thy plain:
—The Muses lov'd and nurs'd thee for their
    own!

And twin'd thy temples here with wreaths of
    worth,       [morn,
    And fenc'd thy childhood from the blights of
And taught enchanting song, and sent thee forth
    To stretch the blessing to an age unborn:

Best blessing!—what is pride's unwieldy state?
    What awkward wealth from Indian oceans
      given?
What monarchs nodding under empires' weight,
    If science smile not with a ray from Heaven?

Witness yon ruins, Arundel's high tower,
    And Bramber, now the bird of night's resort!
Your proud possessors reign'd in barbarous
    power;
    The war their business, and the chase their
      sport;

'Till there a minstrel, to the feast preferr'd,
    With Cambrian harp, in Gothic numbers
      charm'd,
Enlighten'd chiefs grew virtuous as they heard—
—The sun of science in its morning warm'd.—

How glorious, when it blaz'd in Milton's light,
    And Shakespear's flame, to full meridian day!
Yet smile, fair beam! though sloping from that
    height,
    Gild our mild evening with a setting ray.

## TO A LADY.

The simple swain, where Zembla's snows
    Are bound in frozen chains,
Where scarce a smile the Sun bestows
    To warm the sullen plains;

[1] The author of these poems had been educated under this gentleman, for whom he ever retained the most affectionate regard. Mr. Wooddeson was, in truth, one of those amiable beings
whom none could know without loving.—To the
abilities of an excellent scholar was united a
mind so candid, so patient, so replete with universal benevolence, that it glowed in every
action.—His life was an honour to himself, to
religion, to human nature.—He preserved to his
death such a simplicity of manners as is rarely to
be met with.—He judged of the world by the
standard of his own virtuous heart; and few men
who had seen such length of days ever left it so
little acquainted with it.

Not once conceives that Sun to rise
    With kinder, brighter ray,
Nor southern vales, Hesperian skies,
    To bask in smiling day.

As weak my thoughts respecting thee:
    Must thou, my better sun,
Because but smiling cold on me,
    Be therefore warm to none?

## STANZAS.

Where more is meant than meets the ear.
           MILTON.

The bird of midnight swell'd her throat,
    The virgins listen'd round
To sorrow's deeply-warbled note,
    To sweet but solemn sound:

When soon the lark ascending high,
    In sun-beams idly play'd;
As soon to greet him, see, they fly—
    One pensive virgin stay'd.

She stay'd to hear the mourner sing;
    The rest, to nature true,
The flutter of the gayer wing
    The vacant song pursue.

## TO A YOUNG LADY,

WHO OBJECTED TO SUP WITH A PARTY OF BOTH
SEXES THAT MET AT A COFFEE-HOUSE.

O far from Caroline, so soft a maid,
Be cruel coyness, pride, and cold disdain!
Who now of man, the monster man, afraid,
Flies the gay circle of the social train.

Away vain fears! away suspicious dreams,
From beauty, virtue, tenderness, and truth;
From eyes that dawn with wisdom's mildest
    beams,
From harmless smiles that wait on gentle youth.

Far other years and other nymphs befit
The prudish form, and high forbidding brow:
With others dwell, or frowns or scornful wit,
With nymphs less innocent, less fair than thou:

With her, whose youth, of virtue's mild control
Impatient, rush'd on wanton wild desires;
Now prayer or scandal cheers the gloomy soul
That pines in secret with forbidden fires:

Or her that triumph'd in her lover's sighs,
As round their brows the willow garlands bend;
She now dejected, now deserted lies,
Without a lover, and without a friend!

Another fate is youthful virtue's share:
Come with the graces, gentle maid, along;
Come, fairest thou among the young and fair,
To lead the dance, or join the virgins' song,

Come listen to the tale that youths complain,
To thousand vows, in amorous sighs address;
Propitious listen to the raptur'd strain,
When chaste majestic passions swell the breast.

Too long exterior charms of radiant eyes,
And blushing cheeks, the captive sense control;
Thy forms, fair harmony, too long we prize,
Forget the fairer, more harmonious soul.

Too long the lovers for an empty fair
At heedless ease inglorious arts advance;
Enough for them to deck the flowing hair,
Or flutter gaudy with the pride of France.

From worth with beauty nobler lessons taught,
Each youth that languishes, his flame shall prove
By generous action or heroic thought,
And merit fame by arts that merit love.

Shall once again the Grecian lyre be strung,
Restoring Hymen's mild Arcadian reign?
Shall patriot eloquence instruct the tongue,
And spoils be gather'd from the martial plain?

O! far unlike to such celestial flame
The passion kindled from impure desires;
Fatal to friends, to fortune, and to fame,
The momentary flash in night expires.

Love's lambent fire that beams from virtue's rays,
Each sordid passion as it burns, refin'd,
Still bright and brighter with benignant blaze
Embraces friends, a country, humankind.

## A DREAM.

With bridal cake beneath her head,
    As Jenny prest her pillow,
She dreamt that lovers, thick as hops,
    Hung pendent from the willow.

Around her spectres shook their chains,
    And goblins kept their station;
They pull'd, they pinch'd her, till she swore
    To spare the male creation.

Before her now the buck, the beau,
    The squire, the captain trips;
The modest seiz'd her hand to kiss,
    The forward seiz'd her lips.

For some she felt her bosom pant,
    For some she felt it smart;
To all she gave enchanting smiles,
    To one she gave her heart.

She dreamt—(for magic charms prevail'd,
    And fancy play'd her farce on)
That, soft reclin'd in elbow-chair,
    She kist a sleeping parson.

She dreamt—but, O rash Muse! forbear,
    Nor virgins dreams pursue;
Yet blest above the gods is he
    Who proves such visions true.

## THE MULBERRY TREE.

### A TALE.

For London's rich city, two Staffordshire swains,
Hight Johnson, hight Garrick, forsaking their
    plains,                    [by his tomb
Reach'd Shakespeare's own Stratford, where flows
An Avon, as proudly as Tyber by Rome.
Now Garrick, (sweet imp too of Nature was he,)
Would climb and would eat from his mulberry-
    tree;
Yet as Johnson, less frolic, was taller, was older,
He reach'd the first boughs by the help of his
    shoulder;                    [weather,
Where, shelter'd from famine, from bailiffs, and
Bards, critics, and players sat crowded together

Who devour'd in their reach, all the fruit they
    could meet,
The good, bad, indifferent, the bitter and sweet:
But Garrick climb'd high to a plentiful crop,
Then, Heavens! what vagaries he play'd on the
    top!                    [tight,
How, now on the loose twigs, and now on the
He stood on his head, and then bolted upright!
All features, all shapes, and all passions he tried;
He danc'd, and he strutted, he laugh'd, and he
    cried,                    [side!
He presented his face, and he show'd his back-
The noble, the vulgar, flock'd round him to see
What feats he perform'd in the mulberry-tree:
He repeated the pastime, then open'd to speak,
But Johnson below mutter'd strophes of Greek,
While Garrick proclaim'd—such a plant never
    grew,
So foster'd by sun-shine, by soil, and by dew,
The palm-trees of Delos, Phœnicia's sweet
    grove,
The oaks of Dodona, though hallow'd by Jove,
With all that antiquity shows to surpass us,
Compar'd to this tree, were mere shrubs of Par-
    nassus.                    [laid,
Not the beeches of Mantua, where Tityrus was
Not all Vallombrosa produc'd such a shade,
That the myrtles of France, like the birch of
    the schools,
Were fit only for rods to whip genius to rules;
That to Stratford's old mulberry, fairest and
    best,
The cedars of Eden must bow their proud crest:
Then the fruit—like the loaf in the Tub's plea-
    sant tale.                    [ale—
That was fish, flesh, and custard, good claret, and
It compris'd every flavour, was all, and was each,
Was grape, and was pine-apple, nectarine and
    peach;                    [told,
Nay, he swore, and his audience believ'd what he
That under his touch it grew apples of gold.——
Now he paus'd!—then recounted its virtues
    again—                    [grain:
'Twas a wood for all use, bottom, top, bark, and
It would saw into seats for an audience in full pits,
Into benches for judges, episcopal pulpits;
Into chairs for philosophers, thrones too for kings,
Serve the highest of purposes, lowest of things;
Make brooms to mount witches, make May-poles
    for May-days,
And boxes, and ink-stands, for wits and the la-
    dies.——
His speech pleas'd the vulgar, it pleas'd their
    superiors,                    [riors
By Johnson stopt short,—who his mighty poste-
Applied to the trunk—like a Sampson, his haun-
    ches                    [and shook branches!
Shook the roots, shook the summit, shook stem,
All was tremour and shock!—now descended in
    showers                    [blighted flowers!
Wither'd leaves, wither'd limbs, blighted fruits,
The fragments drew critics, bards, players along,
Who held by weak branches, and let go the strong;
E'en Garrick had dropt with a bough that was
    rotten,
But he leapt to a sound, and the slip was for-
    gotten.
Now the plant's close recesses lay open to day,
While Johnson exclaim'd, stalking stately away,

"Here's rubbish enough,till my homeward return,
For children to gather, old women to burn ;
Not practis'd to labour, my sides are too sore,
Till another fit season, to shake you down more.
What future materials for pruning, and cropping,
And cleaning, and gleaning, and lopping, and
    topping !       [tree,
Yet mistake me not, rabble! this tree's a good
Does honour, dame Nature, to Britain and thee;
And the fruit on the top,—take its merits in brief,
Makes a noble dessert, where the dinner's roast-
    beef!"

---

## TO A LADY.

Yes; wedlock's sweet bands were too blest, in
    her lover
If virtue her likeness could find,
What Plato [1] has fabled, could Julia recover
Her lost other half, from mankind.

What joy to receive all the good you impart,
Thy cares on another recline,
Another's fond bosom, and feel that his heart
Beats all the same measures with thine !

The features, the virtues of both, in your race,
How sweet the confusion, enjoy !
Yet more of thyself in the daughter still trace,
And more of thy lord in the boy.

Such bliss rivals Heaven—yet what grief, what
    disgrace,
Were riot's low follower thy lot,     [chase,
Were he whose loud pleasures are wine and the
All love's silent pleasures forgot !

What misery to hear, without daring reply,
All folly, all insolence speaks ;
Still calling the tear of reproach to thy eye,
The flush of disdain to thy cheeks !

Would soft macaronies have judgment to prize,
Whom arts and whom virtues adorn,
Who learnt every virtue and art to despise,
Where Catos and Scipios were born ?

Would wealth's drowsy heir, without spark of
    Heaven's fire,
Enshrin'd in his dulness completely,
Awake to the charmer, her voice and her lyre,
Ah ! charm they though ever so sweetly ?

But what with the gamester, ah ! what were thy
What fortune's caprices thy share !     [fate,
To sleep upon down under canopied state,
To wake on the straw of despair !

The timid free-thinker, that only defies
Those bolts which his Maker can throw ;
Would he, when blaspheming the Lord of the
    skies,
Yet rev'rence his image below ?

Would slaves to a court, or to faction's banditti,
Thy temperate spirits approve ;
So proud in their chains of the court and the city,
Disdaining no chains, but of love ?

  [1] Plato's fable is, that man and woman originally were one being, divided afterwards by Jupiter for their punishment ; that each part, in
perpetual search of the other, never recovers
happiness till their reunion.

O! mild as the Zephyr, like Zephyr that throws
    Its sweets on the sweet-breathing May ;
But not on the lap of cold winter bestows,
    What winter will never repay.

So turn thee from folly's cold aspect, ah ! turn
    From vice's hard bosom away ;
The wise and the virtuous thy sweets will return,
    As warm and as grateful as May.

---

## ON A VERY FINE LADY.

Fine B—— observes no other rules
    Than those the coterie prize ;
She thinks, whilst lords continue fools,
    'Tis vulgar to be wise :

Thinks rudeness wit in noble dames,
    Adultery, love polite ;
That ducal stars shoot brighter flames
    Than all the host of light.

Yet sages own that greatness throws
    A grace on Spencer's charms ;
On Hagley's verse, on Stanhope's prose,
    And gilded Marlborough's arms.

For titles here their rev'rence ends,
    In general wisdom thinks
The higher grandeur's scale ascends,
    The lower Nature's sinks.

---

## ON AN ASIATIC LADY.

O you who sail on India's wealthy wave,
    Of gems and gold who spoil the radiant east;
What oceans, say, what isles of fragrance gave
    This fairer treasure to the joyful west ?
What banks of Ganges, and what balmy skies
Saw the first infant dawn of those unclouded eyes?

By easy arts while Europe's beauties reign,
    Roll the blue languish of their humid eye ;
Rule willing slaves, who court and kiss the chain,
    Self-vanquish'd, helpless to resist or fly ;
Less yielding souls confess this eastern fair,
And lightning melts the heart that milder fires
    would spare.

Of gods, enamour'd with a mortal dame,
    Let Grecian story tell—the gifts display
That deck'd Cassandra, and each honoured name
    Lov'd by the god, who guides the golden day:
See! Asia triumphs in a brighter scene ;
A nobler Phœbus woos her summer's smiling
    queen.

Sublimer sense, and sprightlier wit to please,
    That Phœbus gave ; he gave the voice and lyre,
That warble sweeter than the spicy breeze,
    He gave what charms meridian suns inspire ;
What precious rays from light's pure fountain
    stream,
What warm the diamond's blaze and ruby's flam-
    ing beam.

## TO THE SAME,

### ON HER DRESS.

Ah envious robe! to frustrate Heaven's intent,
　Concealing beauty from the eye of day ;
Beauty to man by gracious Nature sent
　To cheer the wand'rer on his lonesome way.

One pow'r who wak'd Aurora's smiling light
　Gave skies their azure, and gave vales their
　　　　green,
Form'd the quick sense for wonder and delight,
　Made eyes to see, and Laura to be seen.

Curs'd be th' eclipse that plunges morn in night,
　And jealous clouds that shade the landscape's
On envious robes severer curses light,　[scene ;
　That veil the beauties of my summer's queen!

Ah Laura! cruel Laura! why constrain,
　In art's fantastic drapery, Nature's ease?
Why, form'd to empire, empire's arts disdain?
　Why, born for pleasure, still refuse to please?

Nor yet these folds on folds, this load of dress,
　Shall bar approaches to poetic love;
No—where the graces sport in sweet recess,
　'Tis fancy, bold intruder's joy to rove.

Fancy, pursuing where my Laura flies,
　With wanton gales forbidden charms reveals,
Betrays her slumbers, and with eager eyes
　The panting breast, devouring, dreams it feels.

Fancy indulgent to her votary's prayer,
　Shows where, sequester'd from the sultry beam,
The limpid wave but ill conceal'd the fair,
　With virgins sporting in her Ganges' stream.

---

## TO THE SAME.

Ah Laura! while graces and songs,
　While smiles, winning smiles you impart;
Indulgence but nurses desire,
　I sigh for that treasure, your heart.

Yes, take, too presumptuous, she cries,
　All that virtue can wish to receive ;
Yes, take all that virtue can grant,
　A heart I had never to give.

The maid of the north, like the lake,
　That sleeps by her peaceable cot,
Too languishing lives but for one,
　Forgetting the world, and forgot.

But born where my Ganges expands,
　To no partial channels confin'd,
Unfix'd to no object, I flow
　With innocent smiles on mankind.

Our Asia's bright dames, like their sun,
　Cheer all with benevolent reign,
Coy moons, Europe's daughters, but light
　A single disconsolate swain.

## ON READING THE FOREGOING
## VERSES.

### BY MISS G———.

Ah! Dorimant, victim to love,
　Too fatally caught in his wiles,
Can you in fair Laura approve
　Those diffusive, those general smiles?

If inconstancy dwells with that fire
　Which the Sun-beams of Asia impart
Can a daughter of Europe desire
　To change with your Laura a heart?

No!—happier the temp'rate mind,
　Which, fix'd to one object alone,
To one tender passion confin'd,
　Breathes no wishes, no sighs, but for one.—

Such bliss has the maid of the plain,
　Tho' secluded she lives in a cot;
Yet, rich in the love of her swain,
　She's contented, and blesses her lot.—

Ah! say, if deserving thy heart,
　The too undistinguishing fair,
Who to thousands can raptures impart,
　And the raptures of thousands can share?

Ah! say, does she merit those lays?
　Those lays which true passion define?—
No—unworthy the fair of thy praise,
　Who can listen to any but thine.

---

## REPLY TO MISS G———.

Sappho, while your Muse of fire,
　Listening to the vocal spheres,
Sits and tempers to her lyre
　Airs divine for mortal ears:

Viewing higher orbs that glow,
　Ever constant, ever true,
Still she dreams to find below
　Perfect forms, as Heaven and you.

Blame not Asia's fair, who glances
　Random smiles in heedless ease,
Shifts at will her wayward fancies,
　Pleasing all, whom all can please;

Blame her not—no envied treasure
　Is the tender, feeling heart,
Bosoms quick to keener pleasure
　Beat alas! as quick to smart.

Who with eyes that ever languish,
　Still to deserts sighs alone?
Who consumes her youth in anguish
　—She who keeps an heart for one.

Tender love repaid with treason,
　Fortune's frowns, parental power,
Blast her in the vernal season,
　Bend her, unsupported flower.

Happier she, with pliant nature
　Fleeting, fickle as the wind;
She, who proving one a traitor,
　Turns to meet another kind.

Blame her not—with Asian rovers
　What can Asia's fair pursue?
What? but lessons taught by lovers,
　Like the traitor, treacherous too.

Why should faith, obsequious duty,
. Sooth an eastern tyrant's scorn?
Who but rifles joyless beauty
Steals the honey, leaves the thorn.

Sadness sits by Ganges' fountains;
How can echo cheer the vale?
What repeat from fragrant mountains!
What but grief and horrour's tale?

What but shrieks of wild despair?
What but shouts that murder sleep?
There the struggling, fainting fair;
There—but see my Sappho weep!

Change the strain!—this mournful measure
Melts, oppresses virtuous hearts—
Sappho, wake thy lyre of pleasure!
Sing of Europe's happier arts!

Sing of all the mingled blessing
Reason, tempering passion, knows;
All the transport of possessing
Unpluck'd beauty's willing rose!

Sing of that refin'd sensation
Mutual melting bosoms prove,
Souls exchang'd, sweet emanation,
Separate being lost in love!

Rapture's tears, voluptuous stream!
Languor stealing sorrow's sighs!
Sing of love—thyself the theme!
Sing of love—thyself the prize!

## SONG.

Hang my lyre upon the willow,
Sigh to winds thy notes forlorn;
Or, along the foamy billow
Float the wrecking tempest's scorn.

Sprightly sounds no more it raises,
Such as Laura's smiles approve;
Laura scorns her poet's praises,
Calls his artless friendship love:

Calls it love, that spurning duty,
Spurning Nature's chastest ties,
Mocks thy tears, dejected beauty,
Sports with fallen virtue's sighs.

Call it love, no more profaning
Truth with dark suspicion's wound;
Or, my fair, the term retaining,
Change the sense, preserve the sound.

Yes, 'tis love—that name is given,
Angels, to your purest flames:
Such a love as merits Heaven,
Heaven's divinest image claims.

## LAURA'S ANSWER.

### BY MISS G———.

Soon be thy lyre to winds consign'd,
Or hurl'd beneath the raging deep,
For while such strains seduce my mind,
How shall my heart its purpose keep?

Thy artful lays, which artless seem,
With too much fondness I approve;
Ah! write no more on such a theme,
Or Laura's friendship—ends in love.

## TO MISS G———.

All leave, you cry, the harp unstrung,
For fortune shifts her fickle wind:
Resume thy lyre, on willows hung,
To sing the fair, no longer kind.

No—nearer view my alter'd state,
For fear too high, for hope too low;
Beneath the victor's joyful fate,
Yet far above the captive's woe.

The charms of sense no more beguile;
On reason's lap I lay me down:
If claiming now no beauties' smile,
Appears it just to meet their frown?

Light insects they, of gaudy hues,
Admire the glare of youthful day,
Still bathe in morn's, not evening's dews,
From shades of autumn fleet away.

Behold their train of captains, beaux!
Disdain my breast, disdain to sigh!
To these the fair, the rivals those,
The son of Jove's be my reply:

" Ah why desert th' Olympic games?
Aspire to victory!" Philip cries:
" I come," young Ammon fierce exclaims,
" If kings my rivals, thrones the prize."

Yes, letter'd maid! my soul approve,
The seat no more of vain desires:
Extinguish'd there the flame of love,
Extinguish'd there ambition's fires!

To save from vice, from folly save,
What aid can beauty, power afford?
Unworthy love to call thee slave,
Unworthy crowds to call thee lord!

Pure reason, yes; pure truth—but why,
Ah why! rebellious heart declare,
With flattering pulse and stifled sigh,
That other tenants harbour there?

Go—tranquil Hope, by turns to dwell,
Expelling reason pleasure's court,
Expelling passion wisdom's cell:
Go—reason's, passion's mutual sport.

Vain dreamer!—rather both revere,
But neither's sole dominion own:
When Heaven assign'd to each their sphere,
It never meant excluding one:

Excluding which?—objections wait
On vain pretensions either forms;
Alike to life's salubrious state
Ye both are fatal—calms and storms.

## TO LAURA,

### ON HER RECEIVING A MYSTERIOUS LETTER FROM A METHODIST DIVINE.

The doctor wakes early—half drest in his cassoc,
He steals from his consort to write;
She sleeps—and sweet Heaven is invok'd from
his hassoc,
To lengthen the trance of her night.

Now he writes to the fair, with what fervour he
  Heaven's glory concern'd in her fame; [paints
How he raves upon grace, and the union of
  Idolatry, raptures, and flame ?          [saints,

Equivocal priest, lay solemnity by,
  Deceiver thyself, or deceiv'd !
When you kneel to the idol of beauty, and sigh,
  Are your ardours for Heaven believ'd ?

' Will the heart that is kindled from passions
  Ascend in pure spirit above ?          [below
Ah ! analyse better, as blended they glow
  The flames of religion and love.—

Quit the teacher, my fair one, and listen to me,
  A doctor less grave and severe !
Who eternity's joys for the virtuous can see
  Consistent with happiness here.

Still reverence, I preach, those endearing relations
  Of daughter, of parent, of wife :
Yet I blame not your relish for slighter sensations
  That sweeten the medicine of life.

Know, the virtue it cherishes Heaven will reward,
  But attend to no blasphemous tales,
That the blaze of the Deity shines unimpair'd,
  Though human infirmity fails.

Know your God as he is, wise, good, beyond
  No tyrant in horrours array'd,          [measure,
But a father, who smiles on the innocent pleasure
  Of amiable creatures he made !—

Still please, and pursue his benevolent ends,
  Still enrapture the heart and the ear !
I can swear for myself, and believe for my friends,
  Our morals improve as we hear.

If the passions are waken'd by harmony's charm,
  Their breezes waft health to the mind,
What our reason but labours, vain toil ! to disarm,
  By virtue and song are refin'd.

Ah ! listen to me, in whose natural school
  Religion leads truth by the hand !—
Who regulates faith by a mystical rule,
  But builds his foundation on sand !

By the winds of unreconcil'd principles driven,
  Still fluctuates the methodist's plan ;
Now he wishes you chaste for the glory of Heaven,
  —Now frail—for the pleasure of man.

### TO THE SAME.

#### ON POLITICS.

From moments so precious to life,
  All politics, Laura, remove ;
Ruby lips must not animate strife,
  But breathe the sweet language of love.

What is party ?—a zeal without science,
  A bubble of popular fame,
In nature and virtue's defiance,
  'Tis reason enslav'd to a name.

'Tis the language of madness, or fashion,
  Where knaves only guess what they mean ;
'Tis a cloak to conceal private passion,
  To indulge, with applause, private spleen.

Can I, plac'd by my Laura, inquire,
  If poison or claret put out
Our Churchill's satyrical fire,
  If Wilkes lives with ears or without ?

When you vary your charms with your patches,
  To me 'tis a weightier affair,
Than who writes the northern dispatches,
  Or sits in the president's chair.

When, by nature and art form'd to please,
  You sing, and you talk, and you laugh,
Can I forfeit such raptures as these,
  To dream of the chamberlain's staff ?

Secure under Brunswick and Heaven,
  I trust the state vessel shall ride :
To Bute let the rudder be given,
  Or Pitt be permitted to guide.

At Almack's, when the turtle's well drest,
  Must I know the cook's country, or starve ?
And when George gives us liberty's feast,
  Not taste 'till Newcastle shall carve ?

Yet think not that wildly I range,
  With no sober system in view ;
My notions are fix'd, though they change,
  Applied to Great Britain and you.

There, I reverence our bright constitution,
  Not heeding what calumny raves,
Yet wish for a new revolution,
  Should rulers treat subjects as slaves.

Here, the doctrine of boundless dominion,
  Of boundless obedience is mine ;
Ah ! my fair, to cure schism in opinion,
  Confess non-resistance is thine.

### TO LAURA.

#### FAREWELL TO THE ROSE.

Go rose—in gaudy gardens wilt thou bloom,
  Far from the silent vale of peace and love ?
On fluttering insects lavish waste perfume,
  Or deck the fickle wreath that folly wove ?

And yet the fragrance of thy evening hour,
  Ambrosial odours, yet to me refuse ?
To me, who pay thy sweets, ungrateful flower !
  With rich returns of incense from the Muse ?—

Who but the Muse transplants thee, short-liv'd
  From mortal regions to celestial seats ? [rose !
By memory's fountain, where thy buds disclose
  Eternal beauties, with eternal sweets.

### SONG TO * * * *.

What ! bid me seek another fair
  In untry'd paths of female wiles ?
And posies weave of other hair,
  And bask secure in other smiles ?
Thy friendly stars no longer prize,
  And light my course by other eyes ?

Ah no ! my dying lips shall close,
  Unalter'd love, as faith professing ;
Nor praising him who life bestows,
  Forget who makes that gift a blessing,
My last address to Heav'n is due ;
  The last but one is all—to you.

### ON MEN BEING DEPRIVED, FROM CUSTOM AND DELICACY, OF ENJOYING SOCIAL FRIEND-SHIP WITH THE FAIR SEX.

Had soft Aspasia's sex been man,
  What friendship's holy chains
Had link'd our beings, fortune's plan,
  Our pleasures and our pains?

Alike our ruder, milder sports,
  Our studies too the same,
Companions both in shades and courts,
  In paths of love or fame.

By bright collision, patriot beams
  Had flush'd from soul to soul,
And war had seen, in union's streams,
  Our tide of glory roll.

There fate, that strikes the noblest breast,
  Had surely reverenc'd thine;
The thirsty lance I then had blest
  For only wounding mine.

But ah! my sweeter downy hours,
  Had I been chang'd, not you;
What tranquil joys, if kinder powers
  Had made me woman too!

Made each the other's softer care,
  One table then had fed,
One chamber lodg'd the faithful pair,
  Ah do not blush!—one bed.

Both sitting at one busy loom
  In nature's vernal bow'r,
Had rivall'd nature's vernal bloom,
  Creating both one flow'r.

Both screen'd from summer's sultry view,
  In shades by haunted stream,
Had own'd the moral vision true
  That youthful poets dream.

Sweet wisdom, couch'd in mystic rhyme,
  Yet bending o'er the brook,
Had gathered morals more sublime
  From great creation's book;

And felt our mixing souls refine
  In purer wisdom's ray,
The being virtue's friend and thine
  Had clear'd our mists away.

My morning incense, ev'ning pray'r,
  With thine, had soar'd above,
With thine ascending sweeter there
  On wings of song and love.

Vain dreams! for custom's laws, combin'd
  With virtue's stern decree,
Divide the beings nature join'd,
  Divide my fair from me.

---

### TO A YOUNG LADY,

#### FAINTING AT THE NEWS OF HER FRIEND'S MIS-FORTUNES.

Ah! maid too gentle, while thy tears deplore
The virtuous exile on a foreign shore,
Thy pulse forgets to beat, thy cheek to glow,
Dim the bright eye, fix'd monument of woe,

Lost every function, vanish'd every sense:
Is this thy lot, divine benevolence?
Approach no more, such bitter anguish, near
So soft a bosom; flow alone the tear,
That dew of Heaven, O maid! to Heaven allied,
Thy great Redeemer shed for man and died.
Good angels mourn creation's glories lost,
And mourning please, resemble him the most;
Flow then thy tear, ordain'd by Heaven's decree,
For bliss to others, sweeter bliss to thee!
With pity's pangs her dear sensations feel;
The shaft that wounds thee, drops a balm to heal.
Thy soul expanding, like a vernal flower,
Shall glow the brighter in affliction's shower
For every tear to suff'ring virtue given,
Itself approving, and approv'd by Heaven.
Weep then, but weep another's fate alone;
Let smiles be still attendant on thy own.

---

### ON THE DEATH OF AN INFANT.

How blest is he whom nature's gentle hand
Has snatch'd from human life and human woes,
Ev'n in his childish days, ere yet he knew
Or sin, or pain, or youthful passion's force!
In earth's soft lap, beneath the flowery turf,
His peaceful ashes sleep; to Heaven ascends
Th' unspotted soul, declar'd by voice divine
A guest well pleasing—Then no longer mourn,
Thou drooping parent, nor bewail him lost—
In life's first bloom, when infant reason dawn'd,
And the young mind, unfolding every power,
Gave promise fair of manhood, transport fill'd
The mother's bosom, pondering every word
And action there.   She now lamenting loud
Deplores him, from her vain embraces torn
By unrelenting fate, and fierce disease;
Like eastern storms that blast the opening year.

---

### TO MISS N——M,

#### WRITTEN AT BRIGHTHELMSTON.

Lovely N——m! rise, and see
Modest morn resemble thee!
Ocean smiles with your repose,
Come to seas, where Venus rose!
Bathing, Dr. Pool observes,
Braces all the optic nerves.
" Heavens," she cries, " what idle whim!
Youthful eyes are seldom dim;
Mine can mark the distant sail,
Or lowing herds in Sussex' vale;
Scarce a spire or cottage smoke,
Or cloud embracing mountain oak;
An object scarce of land or sea
Rises unperceiv'd by me."
True—but eyes that distant roam,
Frequent fail for scenes at home.
Let example make me clearer,
Place yourself at Shergold's mirror!
Every mild reflected grace,
That angel form, that angel face,
A world of wonders all can view,
Envy only blind and—you.

x

## TO THE MRS.'S R——S,

### WRITTEN AT BRIGHTHELMSTONE.

No, gentle ladies!—he on Brighton's flood,
  Who deck'd with N——'s name a feeble page;
For you, the guardians of the fair and good,
  Has arm'd no bitter stings of Satan's rage.

On impious necks the Muse of vengeance treads,
  For shameless folly dips her shafts in gall;
While, droping odours on your virtuous heads,
  The dews of praise, a precious ointment, fall.

Your N——m's mind in every virtue grew,
  In every grace, beneath your sweet control;
In genuine lustre were preserved by you
  Her polish'd form, reflecting all the soul.

Her candid smiles, unconscious of their worth;
  Her blush of nature without other dye!
You taught her modest eyes to love the Earth,
  Or soar in flaming rapture to the sky.

Her, the best gift of Heaven, its gracious love
  Permitted to your guidance—come and share
The joy of virtuous souls, whose toils improve
  The talents trusted to their fruitful care[1].

Come, faithful servants—hear a voice proclaim
  Your hymn of triumph—'tis no song of mine;
'Tis Heaven that calls you to partake your fame
  With God the giver, and this gift divine.

## VERSES

### WRITTEN AT BRIGHTHELMSTONE.

Here Charles lay shelter'd, from this desert
              shore                    [roar;
He lanch'd the bark, and brav'd the tempest's
He trusted here the faith of simple swains,
And ocean, friendlier than the Worcester plains[2].
No beauteous forms, as now adorn'd it then,
The downs were pathless, without haunt of men.
One shepherd wander'd on the lonely hill,
One village-maid explor'd the distant rill.
But mark the glittering scenes succeeding these;
See peopled all the shores, and healing seas;
Yet, friend to Britain, flows alike the wave
With India's treasures, and defrauds the grave.
Had fate now plac'd him on this fairy land,
The thoughtless Charles had linger'd on the
              strand,
Nor danger chill'd, nor high ambition fir'd
That wanton bosom, by the loves inspir'd:
His languid sails the monarch here had furl'd,
Had gain'd a N——n's smile, and lost the world.

## TO MISS G——.

### FROM BRIGHTHELMSTONE.

Come, Stella, let us climb the heights
  Where purer spirits flow,
And upward point our mental flights,
  And mock the scenes below.

[1] Matthew xxv.
[2] Charles the IId. after the battle of Worcester, escaped to France in a fishing-boat, from Brighthelmstone.

And turn no more the giddy rounds
  Of pleasure's wanton chace,
But range beyond material bounds,
  Eternity, and space!—

Come, read in ocean's ample page,
  Explain the cause that guides,
That bridles now, and now to rage
  Precipitates the tides.

In glory see the planets roll,
  Their laws, their measure, scan,
Nor there confin'd, explore the soul,
  And liberty, and man!

On soaring pinions let us shoot,
  Like him, the bird of Jove!
—"What waste," she cries, "in such pursuit,
  An age of life and love!

"With eagle flight and eagle view
  Let Newton sail the sky!
But what am I? or what are you,
  Philosopher?—a fly:

"Vain insect! now aloft he springs
  To drink the liquid light,
And quenches now his flagging wings
  In angry seas and night.

"Ah fool! to quit his reptile state
  Amid fresh dews and flowers!
Be his the justly purchas'd fate,
  The sober lesson ours.

"From clouds descending, let us try
  What humbler regions give!
Let others soar to fall and die!
  'Tis ours to creep, and live."

## ANSWER TO THE FOREGOING VERSES.

### BY MISS G——.

No more let science tempt thy searching eyes
  Beyond the bounds prescrib'd to mortal sight,
No more advent'rous mount the lofty skies,
  And daring, penetrate the realms of light.

With humble mind go trace thy Maker's hand
  In every smiling valley, fertile plain;
Adore his bounty in the cultur'd land,
  Revere his wisdom in the stormy main!

Nor thoughtless view the vast tremendous sea,
  Whose course impetuous power divine res-
            trains;                    [cree,
Whose rushing tide, control'd by Heaven's de-
  Forbears to violate the flow'ry plains.

Nor yet confine to these thy wand'ring sight,
  While splendid gems the face of Heav'n adorn;
Nor heedless view the radiant lamps of night,
  Nor heedless view the Sun that gilds the morn:

But turn with praise to Him who reigns above,
  Supreme o'er works that speak almighty
            power;
O! turn a grateful bosom breathing love,
  And learn the noblest lesson—to adore,

## ON THE DEATH OF A YOUNG GENTLEMAN.

Go, mournful spirit, wing thy dreary way,
Leave a lov'd mansion, leave the cheerful day;
A naked wanderer on the winter's wind,
Ah leave, reluctant, youth and strength behind!
Not long a wanderer, to that happier shore
Be Heaven thy guide, where mourning is no
In purer mansions, in a form divine, [more!
Immortal youth, immortal joy, be thine!

## INSCRIPTION FOR A FOUNTAIN.

'O you, who mark what flowrets gay,
    What gales, what odours breathing near,
What sheltering shades from summer's ray
    Allure my spring to linger here :

Yet see me quit this margin green,
    Yet see me deaf to pleasure's call,
Explore the thirsty haunts of men,
    Yet see my bounty flow for all.

O learn of me—no partial rill,
    No slumbering selfish pool be you;
But social laws alike fulfil ;
    O flow for all creation too!

### ON THE CONVERTING THE LATE MR. WOODDESON'S HOUSE, AT KINGSTON, INTO A POOR-HOUSE, AND CUTTING DOWN THE GREAT WALK OF HIGH TREES BEFORE IT.

Where the broad path-way fronts yon ancient
    seat,
Approach not, stranger, with unhallow'd feet,
Nor mock the spot, unshelter'd now, and bare!
The grove's old honours rose majestic there:
It's giant arms extending to defend
Thy reverend temples, man's and virtue's friend!
Secure thy walk that unpierc'd gloom along,
No storm approach'd to silence Homer's song;
No beam to wound thy Heav'n-directed eye :
The world's near tumult swept unheeded by.
Now, low as thine, these towering heads are laid,
No more embower the mansion in their shade,
Time-honour'd pile! that owning thee its lord,
Saw ancient manners, ancient faith, restor'd ;
In renovated youth beheld again
Saturnian days, the good Eliza's reign.
With thee too sheltering many an angel guest,
For what, but Heaven, serener than thy breast?—

Blest mansion then, simplicity's abode,
Where smiling innocence look'd up to God,
Where nature's genuine graces charm'd the heart,
Or nature, polish'd but by classic art. [beams,
There fancy, warm'd with brightest, chastest
The saint's high rapture, and the poet's dreams,
While virtue left, delighting there to dwell,
The pensive mountain, and the hermit's cell.—
There the good teacher held by turns to youth
The blaze of fiction and pure light of truth,
Who, less by precept than example fir'd,
Glow'd as he taught, inspiring and inspir'd.
    Nor think, gay revellers, this awful roof
Echoed no sounds but wisdom's harsh reproof;
The social board, attendant mirth, was there,
The smile unconscious of to morrow's care,
With every tranquil joy of wedded life,
The gracious children, and the faithful wife.
In dance, in song, in harmless sports approv'd,
There youth has frolick'd, there soft maids have
    lov'd.
There one, distinguish'd one—not sweeter blows
In simpler ornament attir'd, the rose,
The rose she cull'd to deck the nuptial bower,
Herself as fair—a transitory flower.—
    Thus a short hour—and woods and turrets
        fall ;
The good, the great, the beauteous, perish all.
Another age a gayer race supplies,
Less awful groves, and gaudier villas rise,
See wisdom's place usurp'd by folly's sons,
And scorners sit on virtue's vacant thrones.
See neighbouring Combe's old genius quit its
        bowers,                [towers;
Not Warwick's [1] name preserv'd his gothic
Nor distant see new royal domes [2] deride
What half remains of Wolsey's ancient pride!
While yet this humbler pile survives to prove
A mansion worthy of its master's love:
Like him, still welcomes to its liberal door
Whom most he honour'd, honouring most the
        poor ;
Like him, the lisping infant's blessing shares,
And age's gratitude in silent prayers.—
While such partake the couch, the frugal feast,
No regal chambers boast an equal guest ;
For, gracious Maker, by thy own decree,
Receiving mercy is receiving Thee !—

    [1] Combe-Neville, near Kingston, built by the
king-making earl of Warwick.
    [2] The new apartments at Hampton Court,
raised on the ruins of part of Wolsey's palace.

THE

# POEMS

OF

# *FRANCIS FAWKES, A. M.*

Die mihi quid melius desidiosus agam ?   MART.

# LIFE OF FRANCIS FAWKES,

## BY MR. CHALMERS.

MR. FAWKES was born in Yorkshire about the year 1721. He was educated at Leeds, under the care of the Rev. Mr. Cookson, vicar of that parish :
from whence he went to Jesus College, Cambridge, and took his bachelor's degree
in 1741, and his master's in 1745.

After being admitted into holy orders, he settled at Bramham in Yorkshire,
near the elegant seat of that name belonging to Robert Lane, esq. the beauties
of which afforded him the first subject for his muse. He published his Bramham
Park in 1745, but without his name. His next publications were the descriptions of May and Winter, from Gawen Douglas; the former in 1752, the latter
in 1754 : these brought him into considerable notice as a poetical antiquary,
and it was hoped that he would have been encouraged to modernise the whole
of that author's works.

About the year last mentioned, he removed to the curacy of Croydon in
Surrey, where he had an opportunity of courting the notice of archbishop Herring, who resided there at that time, and to whom, among other complimentary
verses, he addressed an ode on his grace's recovery, which was printed in Dodsley's
collection. These attentions, and his general merit as a scholar, induced the
archbishop to collate him, in 1755, to the vicarage of Orpington with St. Mary
Cray, in Kent. In 1757, he had occasion to lament his patron's death, in a
pathetic elegy styled Aurelius, printed with his grace's sermons in 1763, but previously in our author's volume of poems in 1761 ; about the same time he married
miss Purrier of Leeds.

In April 1774, by the late Dr. Plumptre's favour, he exchanged his vicarage
for the rectory of Hayes : this, except the office of chaplain to the princess
dowager of Wales, was the only ecclesiastical promotion he obtained.

In 1761, he published by subcription a volume of original poems and translations, by which he got more profit than fame. His subscribers amounted to
nearly eight hundred, but no second edition was called for. A few pieces are
now added from Mr. Nichols' collection; and from the Poetical Calendar, a periodical selection of fugitive poetry, which he published in conjunction with Mr.
Woty, an indifferent poet of that time. In 1767 he published an eclogue, entituled
Partridge Shooting, so inferior to his other productions that the omission of it
cannot be regretted. He was the editor also of a Family Bible, with notes, in 4to.
which is a work of very inconsiderable merit, but to which he probably contributed only his name, a common trick among the retailers of " Complete family
Bibles."

His translations of Anacreon, Sappho, Bion, Moschus and Musæus, appeared
in 1760; and his Theocritus, encouraged by another liberal subcription, in 1767.
His Apollonius Rhodius, a posthumous publication, completed by the Rev. Mr.
Meen of Emanuel College, Cambridge, made its appearance in 1780, when
Mr. Fawkes's widow was enabled, by the kindness of the editor, to avail herself
of the subscriptions, contributed as usual very liberally. Mr. Fawkes died
August 26, 1777.

These scanty materials are taken chiefly from Mr. Nichols's Life of Bowyer,
and little can now be added to them. Mr. Fawkes was a man of a social disposition, with much of the imprudence which adheres to it: although a profound classical scholar, and accounted an excellent translator, he was unable to publish any of his works without the previous aid of a subscription;
and his Bible was a paultry job, which necessity only could have induced him to
undertake. With all his failings, however, it appears that he was held in esteem
by many distinguished contemporaries, particularly by Drs. Pearce, Jortin,
Johnson, Warton, Plumptre and Askew, who contributed critical assistance to
his translation of Theocritus.

As an original poet, much cannot be said in his favour : his powers were confined to occasional slight and encomiastic verses, such as may be produced without great effort, and are supposed to answer every purpose when they have pleased
those to whom they were addressed. The Epithalamic ode may perhaps rank
higher, if we could forget an obvious endeavour to imitate Dryden and Pope. In
the elegy on the death of Dobbin, and one or two other pieces, there is a considerable portion of humour, which is a more legitimate proof of genius than
one species of poets are disposed to allow. His principal defects are want of
judgment and taste; these, however, are less discoverable in his translations;
and it was probably a consciousness of limitted powers which inclined him so
much to translation. In this he every where displays a critical knowledge of
his author, while his versification is smooth and elegant, and his expression remarkably clear. He was once esteemed the best translator since the days of
Pope; a praise which, if now disallowed, it is much that it could in his own time
have been bestowed with justice.

# POEMS

## OF

## *FRANCIS FAWKES.*

---

### *BRAMHAM PARK.*

#### TO ROBERT LANE, ESQ.

Quis caneret nymphas? quis humum floren-
tibus herbis
Spargeret? aut viridi fontes induceret umbrâ?
VIRG.

Written in May 1745.

---

### THE PREFACE.

I should think a preface to this volume absolutely unnecessary, except as it furnishes me
with an opportunity of returning my thanks
to those gentlemen who have favoured me with
their names ; and therefore to their candour
and indulgence I beg leave to inscribe the
following sheets.

Orpington, May 1, 1761.
F. FAWKES.

---

The themes of war to bolder bards belong,
Calm scenes of peace invite my humble song.
Lane, whom kind Heav'n has with mild man-
ners grac'd,
And bless'd with true hereditary taste,
Your blooming virtues these light lays demand,
Wrote in the gardens which your grandsire [2]
plan'd.
   When vernal breezes had the glebe unbound,
And universal verdure cloth'd the ground,
Profusely wild the flowers began to spring,
The trees to blossom, and the birds to sing :

---

A fine seat in Yorkshire, belonging to George
Fox-Lane, esq.
   Robert, lord Bingley.

---

As careless through those groves I took my way
Where Bramham gives new beauty to the day, [1]
(What time Aurora, rising from the main,
With rosy lustre spangled o'er the plain;)
The sylvan scenes a secret joy inspir'd,
And with soft rapture all my bosom fir'd ;
When, lo ! my eyes a lovely nymph survey'd,
With modest step advancing through the glade :
Her bloom divine, and sweet attractive grace,
Confess'd the guardian Dryad of the place :
The wind that gave her azure robe to flow,
Reveal'd a bosom white as Alpine snow ;
A flowery wreath around her neck she wore,
And in her hand a branch of olive bore [3] :
Adown her shoulders fell her auburn hair,
That loosely wanton'd with the buxom air,
The buxom air ambrosial odours shed,
And sweets immortal breath'd around her head [4].
My eager eyes o'er all her beauties ran,
When thus the guardian of the woods began.
   " Thrice happy ! whom the fates propitious
give
Secure in these sequester'd groves to live, [court,
Where Health, fair goddess, keeps her blooming
And all the nymphs, and all the graces sport :
How beautifully chang'd the scene appears
Within the compass of a thousand years !
Then fierce Bellona drench'd these plains in
blood,
Then virtue wander'd in the lonely wood—
But hear ! while I mysterious truths disclose,
Whose dire remembrance wakens all my woes.
In ancient days when Alfred [5], sacred name!
(Alfred the first in virtue as in fame)

---

[3] Paciferæque manu ramum prætendit olivæ.
Virg. Æn. viii. 116.
[4] Ambrosiæque comæ divinum vertice odorem
Spiravere.   Virg. Æn. 1. 403.
[5] Alfred. This most accomplished prince began his reign A.D. 872, at a time when the Danes

This barbarous isle with liberal arts refin'd,
Taught wholesome laws, and moraliz'd mankind ;
The ruthless Danes o'er all the county ran,
They levell'd cities, and they murder'd man :
Nor fields, nor fanes, nor sex, nor age, were free
From fire and sword, from lust and cruelty.
To tend my father's flock was then my care,
And country swains were wont to call me fair.
Not hence far distant I secur'd my charms,
Till rous'd from danger by the din of arms
To a lone cave, with nymphs a chosen few,
Secret I fled, conceal'd from human view;
Secret and safe, till (storm'd the country round)
Our close retreat the fierce barbarians found.
What could we do the furious foe to shun?—
To die seem'd better than to be undone.
Diana, huntress of the woodland shades,
Chaste guardian of the purity of maids,
With silver bows supplied the virgin train,
And manly courage to repel the Dane.
But what, alas ! avails the manly heart,
When female force emits the feeble dart ?
Though thrice three victims to our vengeance fell,
Though my keen shafts dispatch'd their chief to Hell ;
Too soon our fate with anguish we deplor'd,
Doom'd to the slaughter of the conquering sword :       [proves;
But happy they whose sufferings Heav'n ap-
Heav'n will reward that virtue which it loves.
The queen who makes bright chastity her care,
Thus to almighty Jove preferr'd her prayer ;
That we for ever in these shades might rove,
Nymphs of the wood, and guardians of the grove.
Well I remember, as I trembling lay,
Pale, breathless, cold, expiring on the clay,
How by degrees my mortal frame refin'd,
Nor left one earthly particle behind ;
In every nerve a pleasing change began,
And through my veins the streams immortal ran :
Soft on my mind ecstatic visions stole,
And heav'n-felt raptures dawn'd upon my soul.
E'er since I guard the groves, the woods, the plain,
Chief Dryad of the tutelary train ;
Supremely bless'd where all conspires to please;
War, civil war, alone disturbs my ease.
How did my soul recoil with secret dread,
When bold Northumberland [6] his army led,
Ill-fated Britons, whom he brought from far,
Against his sovereign waging horrid war !
I saw the combat on the neighbouring plain,
A knight victorious, and old Percy slain ;
I saw his visage, that with auguish frown'd,
And seem'd in rage to roll its eyes around.

after several invasions, had entirely over-run the kingdom, whom by his extraordinary valour and conduct he dispossessed of it. *Circa Eglerti tempora, anno Christi 800, nostra littora primùm in festarunt Dani. Postea mare cælo miscentes, multos annos per Angliam grassati, urbibus excisis, templis successis, & agris vastalis, omnia barbarâ immanitate egerunt, verterunt, rapuerunt.*

[6] In the year 1408, the old earl of Northumberland and his army was overthrown on Bram-ham-Moor by sir Thomas Rooksby, then high-

Borne in mock triumph from the fatal field;
The azure [7] lion on the golden shield
Wav'd vainly rampant.   But what horrors chill'd
My heaving heart, and through my bosom thrill'd,
When direful discord Britain's sons compell'd
To war on Towton's [8] memorable field.
I see the ranks embattled on the plain,
Torrents of blood, and mountains of the slain;
See kindred hosts with rival rage contend,
Deaf to the names of father, and of friend ;
The brother by a brother's sword expires,
And sons are slain by unrelenting sires.
The brook, that flow'd a scanty stream before,
Swell'd to a river red with human gore:
Verbeia [9] then in wild amazement stood,
To see her silver urn distain'd with blood;
Verbeia, erst her waters wont to lead
In peaceful murmurs through the flow'ry mead,
To purge her currents from the crimson stain,
Swift pour'd her waves to mingle with the main.
Oft, as with shining share he ploughs the field[10],
The swain astonish'd finds the massy shield,
On whose broad boss, sad source of various woes,
He views engrav'd the long-disputed rose.
Huge human bones the fruitful furrows hide
Of once-fam'd heroes that in battle died.
Now all dire feuds and curst contentions o'er,
They sleep in peace, and kindle wars no more :
The friend, the foe, the noble and the slave,
Rest undistinguish'd in one common grave.
" But let us now, since genial spring invites,
And lavish nature varies her delights,
Partake the general joy, and sweetly stray,
Where the birds warble, and the waters play ;

sheriff of Yorkshire, and the *posse comitatus* of the county, and slain in the battle.

The earl Northumberland and the lord Bardolph,
With a great pow'r of English and of Scots,
Are by the sh'riff of Yorkshire overthrown.
Shakespeare's Hen. IV.

[7] The arms of Percy are, Or, a lion rampant azure.

[8] A neighbouring village, near which, on the 29th day of March (being Palm Sunday) A. D. 1461, was fought a most remarkable and bloody battle between the houses of York and Lancaster : the number of the Yorkists, headed by Edward, earl of March, amounted to about 40,600 men, the Lancastrians were 60,000.   This battle proved decisive in favour of the house of York; and in consequence of it, Edward was, in June 1461, crowned king of England, &c.   There were killed in this engagement 36,776 men.   The rivulet Cock, adjoining to the field of battle, and the river Wharfe, were for several days, in a very extraordinary manner, discoloured with the blood of the slain.   For a circumstantial account of this battle, see *Drake's Eboracum.*

[9] *Verbeia* was the Roman name for the river Wharfe ; see an ancient inscription quoted by Camden.

[10] —————— ——————— ——————— finibus illis
Agricola, incurvo terram molitus aratro,
Exesa invenict scabrâ rubigine pila :
Aut gravibus rastris galeas pulsabit inanes,
Grandiaque effossis mirabitur ossa sepulcris.
Virg. Geor. 1.

Where Flora decks the dewy dale with flowers,
And beeches twine their branches into bowers,
The warbling birds, the gales that gently blow,
May tune thy reed, and teach the verse to flow."
    Thus spoke the nymph with soft alluring grace,
And led me round the flow'r-embroider'd place;
Through every variegated rural scene
Of shady forest, and of meadow green,
Of winding valleys, and of rising hills,
Of mossy fountains and translucent rills;
Where downs, or level lawns expanded wide,
The groves, the garden, and the wood divide;
Where walks by long-extended walks are crost,
And alleys in meandering alleys lost;
The dubious traces intricately run,
And end erroneous where they first begun:
Where Saxon fanes, that in fair order rise,
With elegant simplicity surprise.
Where'er the nymph directs my ravish'd sight,
New scenes appear that give a new delight:
Here spiry firs extend their lengthen'd ranks,
There violets blossom on the sunny banks;
Here horn-beam hedges regularly grow,
There hawthorns whiten, and wild roses blow.
Luxuriant Flora paints the purple plain,
And in the gardens waves the golden grain;
Curl'd round tall tufted trees the woodbine weaves
In fond embrace its tendrils with the leaves:
Sweet-scented shrubs a rich perfume exhale,
And health ambrosial floats on every gale.
From rushy-fringed founts rise sparkling rills
That glide in mazy windings down the hills:
Or under pendent shades of oziers flow,
Dispensing moisture to the plants below:
Now, hid beneath the flowery turf, they pass
Ingulph'd, now sport along the velvet grass,
With many an errour slowly-lingering stray,
And murmuring in their course reluctant roll away;
Thence into lucid lakes profusely fall
Foaming, or form the beautiful canal,
So smooth, so level, that it well might pass
For Cytherea's face-reflecting glass,
(Save when mild zephyrs o'er the surface stray,
Curl the light waves, and on its bosom play)
Yet to the bottom so distinctly clear,
The eye might number every pebble there;
And every fish that quickly-glancing glides,
Sports in the stream, and shows his silver sides.
    If through the glades I turn my raptur'd eyes,
What various views, what lovely landscapes rise?
Here a once-hospitable mansion stands
'Midst fruitful plains, and cultivated lands;
There russet heaths, with fields of corn between,
And peaceful cots, and hamlets intervene:
These far-stretch'd views direct me to admire
A tower dismantled, or a lofty spire,
Or farm imbosom'd in some aged wood,
Or lowing herds that crop the flowery food;
Through these, irriguous vales, and lawns appear,
And fleecy flocks, and nimble-footed deer:
Sun-glittering villas, and bright streams are seen,
Gay meads, rough rocks, hoar hills, and forests green:
As when Belinda works, with art divine,
In the rich screen some curious, gay design;
Quick as the fair the nimble needle plies,
Cots, churches, towers, or villages arise;

A varied group of flocks, and herds, and swains,
Groves, fountains, fields, and daisy-painted plains;
At Bramham thus with ravish'd eyes we see
How order strives with sweet variety:
Nature, kind goddess, joins the aid of art
To plan, to form, and finish every part.
    But now beneath the beechen shade reclin'd,
Whose tall top trembling dances in the wind,
Fast by the falling of a hoarse cascade,
What glowing transports all my breast invade!
Down channel'd stone collected currents flow,
And steal obliquely through the vale below;
The feather'd songsters on the trees above
Attune their voices to the notes of love,
Notes so melodiously distinct and clear,
They charm my soul, and make it Heav'n to hear.
    O! what descriptive eloquence can tell
The woods, and winding walks of Boscobell[1]?
The various vistas, and the grassy glades,
The bowery coverts in sequester'd shades?
Or where the wandering eye with pleasure sees
A spacious amphitheatre of trees?
Or where the differing avenues unite,
Conducting to more pompous scenes the sight?
Lo! what high mounds immense divide the moor,      [shore!
Stretch'd from the southern to the northern
These are but relics of the Roman way,
Where the firm legions march'd in dread array,
Where rode the hero in his iron car,
And big with vengeance roll'd the mighty war:
Here oft the curious coins and urns explore,
Which future Meads and Pembrokes shall adore;
To me more pleasing far yon tranquil dell,
Where Labour, Health, and sweet Contentment dwell;
More pleasing far beside yon aged oaks,
Grotesque and wild, the cottage chimney smokes.
Fair to the view old Ebor's temple stands,
The work of ages, rais'd by holy hands;
How firm the venerable pile appears!
Reverend with age, but not impair'd by years.
O! could I build the Heav'n-directed rhyme,
Strong as thy fabric, as thy tow'rs sublime,
Then would the Muse on bolder pinions rise,
And make thy turrets emulate the skies.
    Such are the scenes where woodland nymphs resort,
And such the gardens where the Graces sport:
Would fate this verse to future times prolong,
These scenes should bloom for ever in my song.
Not Tempe's plains so beautiful appear,
Nor flow Castalia's sacred springs so clear;
The Muses, had they known this lov'd retreat,
Had left Parnassus for a nobler seat.
    Well may these groves in elegance excel,
When Lane completes what Bingley plann'd so well;
Bids crystal currents sweetly-murmuring flow,
Fair temples rise, and future navies grow.
Here D——n might an idle hour employ,
And those diversions, which he loves, enjoy;

[1] *Boscobell*.  A beautiful wood, disposed in an elegant taste, and separated from the gardens by the park.

With wary spaniels furrow'd fields beset,
And close the partridge in the silken net :
Or search the woods, and with unerring aim
With leaden wounds transfix the flying game :
Or with stanch hounds the wily fox pursue,
And trace his footsteps o'er the tainted dew.
With what delight would friendly N—y change
Don's [1] fertile valleys for this ampler range ?
And with the music of th' enlivening horn
Cheer the fleet pack, and wake the lingering
   morn.
But lo ! faint Phœbus darts a languid ray,
And gold-edg'd clouds foretel the close of day;
The nymph observant took her airy flight,
And, like a vision, vanish'd from my sight.

[1] *Don.* The river that runs by Doncaster.

---

A DESCRIPTION OF

## CALYPSO AND HER GROTTO.

### FROM TELEMACHUS, BOOK I.

The queen he follow'd as she mov'd along,
Surrounded by her nymphs, a beauteous throng;
But far the fairest, and supremely tall,
She walk'd majestic, and outshone them all :
Thus 'midst a grove the princely oak appears,
And high in air his branching honours rears.
Her radiant beauty charm'd his youthful mind,
Her purple robe that floated in the wind,
And locks bound graceful with a clasp behind :
But her bright eyes, instilling fond desire,
Beam'd sweetness temper'd with celestial fire.
Sage Mentor follow'd, as in thought profound,
And silent fix'd his eyes upon the ground.
And now, conducted by the royal dame,
Soon to the entrance of her grott [1] they came,

[1] Perhaps the reader will not be displeased to
see Homer's description of this famous grotto, as
it is translated by Mr. Pope from the fifth book
of the Odyssey.

Large was the grott, in which the nymph he
   found,
(The fair-hair'd nymph with every beauty crown'd)
She sat and sung; the rocks resound her lays :
The cave was brighten'd with a rising blaze:
Cedar and frankincense, an odorous pile,
Flam'd on the hearth, and wide perfum'd the isle;
While she with work and song the time divides,
And through the loom the golden shuttle guides.
Without the grott, a various sylvan scene
Appear'd around, and groves of living green ;
Poplars and alders ever quivering play'd,
And nodding cypress form'd a fragrant shade ;
On whose high branches, waving with the storm,
The birds of broadest wing their mansion form ;
The chough, the sea-mew, the loquacious crow,
And scream aloft, and skim the deeps below.
Depending vines the shelving cavern screen,
With purple clusters blushing through the green.
Four limpid fountains from the clefts distil,
And every fountain pours a several rill,
In mazy windings wandering down the hill :
Where bloomy meads with vivid greens were
   crown'd,
And glowing violets threw odours round.

Amaz'd to find within this lonely cell
Nature with all her rural graces dwell.
There no high-polish'd marble they behold,
No storied columns, and no sculptur'd gold;
No speaking busts, no silver richly wrought,
No breathing pictures seem'd inform'd with
   thought.
The grott, divided into various cells,
Was deck'd with spar, and variegated shells;
The place of tap'stry a young vine supply'd,
And spread her pliant arms on ev'ry side:
Cool zephyrs, though the Sun intensely glow'd,
Breath'd through the place sweet freshness as
   they flow'd.
O'er amaranthine beds fair fountains stray'd,
And, softly murmuring, in the meadows play'd,
Or in broad basons pour'd the crystal wave,
Where oft the goddess wont her limbs to lave.
Fast by the grott sweet flowers of every hue,
Purpling the lawn, in gay confusion grew.
Here wav'd a wood, all glorious to behold;
Of trees that bloom with vegetable gold;
Whose branches, in eternal blossom, yield
Fragrance delicious as the flowery field,
This wood, impervious to the solar ray,
Crown'd the fair spot, and guarded it from day.
Here birds melodious pour'd the sprightly song;
There torrents thunder'd the rough rocks among,
Down dash'd precipitately from the hills,
Then o'er the level lawn diffus'd their curling
   rills.
  Calypso's grotto crown'd the breezy steep,
From whence appear'd the party-colour'd deep ;
Now smooth and even as a mirror seen,
Now vainly wreaking on the rocks its spleen,
Indignant, foaming with tremendous roar,
And in huge mountains rolling to the shore.
More pleasing was the prospect to the plain ;
A river, winding through the rich champaign,
Form'd various isles with lines sweet-flowering
   crown'd,
And cloud-aspiring poplars border'd round.
Among the banks the sportive waters play'd,
And woo'd the lovely islands which they made :
Some swiftly pour'd their crystal currents strong;
Some led their waves with liquid lapse along ;
With many an errour lingering seem'd to stray,
As if they wish'd for ever here to stay,
And murmuring in their course reluctant roll'd
   away.
The distant mountains their hoar heads on high
Upheav'd, and lost their summits in the sky :
Their airy forms fantastic pleas'd the sight,
And fill'd the mind with wonder and delight.
The neighb'ring hills were spread by nature's
   boon
With vines that hung in many a fair festoon ;
Whose swelling grapes in richest purple dy'd,
The leaves attempted, but in vain, to hide :
So lov'd the generous vine to flourish here,
It bent beneath the plenty of the year.
Here purple figs with luscious juice overflow'd,
With deepen'd red the full pomegranate glow'd ;
The peaceful olive spread her branches round,
And every tree, with verdant honours crown'd,
Whose fruit the taste, whose flower the eye
   might cheer,
And seem'd to make a new Elysium here.
  Cambridge, 1738.

AN

*EPITHALAMIC ODE.*

INTENDED FOR MUSIC.

Felices ter & amplius
Quos irrupta tenet copula.          Hor.

Clad in flow'r-embroider'd veil,
Hail, auspicious morning, hail!
    When in Hymen's holy bands,
Blooming Emily, the fair,
And Eugenio, happy pair!
Chang'd their hearts, and join'd their hands.
Virgin coldness then relented,
    Like the snow before the Sun,
Then sweet Emily consented,
    Not unwilling, to be won.

AIR.

Ye sons of harmony, prepare
Your hymns to greet this happy pair:
Let the sweet notes, distinctly clear,
In soft divisions melt upon the ear,
Such as may all the tender passions move,
Sooth the rapt soul, and be the food of love.

RECITATIVE.

Hark! the mighty queen of sound
Wakes each instrument around,
The merry pipe, the mellow-breathing lute,
The warbling lyre, the love-lamenting lute:
    Now the light fantastic measure
    Ravishes our ears with pleasure;
    Now the trumpets loud and shrill,
    From yon river-circled hill,
    With manly notes our hearts inspire,
    And emulate the golden lyre;
While the majestic, deep-mouth'd organs blow
In lengthen'd strains magnificently slow,
Divinely sweet, and delicately strong;
    Till gently dying by degrees,
    Like the last murmurs of the breeze,
Expires the soft-attenuated song:
And at the close of each mellifluous lay,
This verse is sung in honour of the day.

CHORUS.

Happy they as gods above
Whom Hymen binds in wreaths of love!
Love's pure flame itself endears,
And brightens with the length of years:
Love contents the humble state,
And show'rs down blessings on the great,
Sooths desires that wildly roll,
And calms the tempests of the soul.

RECITATIVE.

But, lo! sweet Emily, the fair,
And Eugenio, happy pair!
With placid look and graceful mien,
Appear advancing o'er the green:
Mark well the youth's love-darting eye,
Soft-beaming with expressive joy,
To view the object of his wishes near,
Mild as the gentlest season of the year,
Blooming as health, and fresh as early day,
Fair, sweet, and bright as all the flowers of May.

And as, intent upon her charms,
Eugenio woos the damsel to his arms,
Her cheeks vermilion'd with a lovely blush,
Glow like twin roses on the verdant bush
    While thus, methinks, I hear him say,
    " Come; my fair one, come away;
    Let us fleeting time improve
    In the chaste joys of wedded love :
    I see propitious Hymen stand,
    His torch bright-blazing in his hand,
    To light us to the genial bed
    By the decent Graces spread,
    Where the rosy-finger'd Hours
    Scatter never-fading flowers.
    Love admits not of delay,
    Haste, my fair one, haste away.''
And you, Heav'n-favour'd pair,
Who now the purest pleasures share,
In happy union may you long enjoy
Those heart-felt blandishments that never cloy;
And may kind Heav'n the full abundance pour
Of nuptial blessings in a fruitful shower ;
Crown all our wishes with a beauteous race,
    That may your bright accomplishments in-
        herit,
The mother's mildness, loveliness, and grace,
    The father's honest heart, and sense, and ge-
        nerous spirit.
Like two pure springs whose gentle rills unite,
Long may your stream of life serenely glide,
    Through verdant vales, and meadows of delight,
Where flow'rs unnumber'd, deck'd in beauty's
        pride,                           [side.
Blow on the blissful banks, and bloom on either
    May no rude tempest discompose
    Your course of quiet as it flows,
    No clouded care, no chilling fear,
    Nor anxious murmur hover there ;
But mildest zephyrs on the surface play,
And waft each light disquietude away :
Till after all the winding journey past,
You mingle with eternity at last.
That tranquil sea, where sorrows are no more,
No storm-vext billows lash the peaceful shore :
There in Heav'n's bliss embosom'd, may you
        prove
The height of endless happiness and love.

---

*THE DEATH OF THE LARK.*

1738.

The golden Sun, emerging from the main,
Beams a blue lustre on the dewy plain ;
Elate with joy all creatures hail his rise,
That haunt the forest, or that skim the skies,
Gay-blooming flow'rs their various charms
        renew,
A breathing fragrance, or a lovely hue :
Sweet pipes the shepherd, the fair morn to greet,
To his stout team the ploughman whistles sweet.
All nature smiles around. On airy wing
The lark, harmonious herald of the spring,
Rises aloft to breath his mattius loud
On the bright bosom of some fleecy cloud.
Ah! little conscious that he dies to day,
He sports his hour in innocence away,
And from the treble of his tuneful throat
Pours the soft strain, or trills the sprightly note;

Or calls his mate, and as he sweetly sings,
Soars in the sun-beam, wavering on his wings.
The ruthless fowler, with unerring aim,
Points the dire tube—forth streams the sudden
    flame:
Swift in hoarse thunder flies the leaden wound,
The rigid rocks return the murdering sound ;
The strains unfinish'd with the warbler die,
Float into air, and vanish in the sky.
    Thus oft, fond man, rejoicing in his might,
Sports in the sunshine of serene delight;
Fate comes unseen, and snaps the thin spun
    thread,
He dies, and sleeps forgotten with the dead.

## THE SPARROW.

FROM CATULLUS.  1738.

ALL ye gentle powers above,
Venus, and thou god of love ;
All ye gentle souls below,
That can melt at others woe ;
Lesbia's loss with tears deplore,
Lesbia's sparrow is no more ;
Late she wont her bird to prize
Dearer than her own bright eyes.
Sweet it was and lovely too,
And its mistress well it knew.
Nectar from her lips it sipt,
Here it hopt, and there it skipt:
Oft it wanton'd in the air,
Chirping only to the fair :
Oft it lull'd its head to rest
On the pillow of her breast.
Now, alas ! it chirps no more:
All its blandishments are o'er ;
Death has summon'd it to go
Pensive to the shades below ;
Dismal regions ! from whose bourn
No pale travellers return.
Death ! relentless to destroy
All that's form'd for love or joy !
Joy is vanish'd, love is fled,
For my Lesbia's sparrow's dead.
Lo, the beauteous nymph appears
Languishingly drown'd in tears !

ON THE

## DEATH OF A YOUNG GENTLEMAN.

September, 1739.

Man cometh forth like a flower, and is cut down.
                                        JOB, xiv. 2.

SHORT and precarious is the life of man ;
The line seems fathomless, but proves a span;
A youth of follies, an old-age of sorrow ;
Like flowers to day we bloom, we die to morrow.
Say then, what specious reasons can we give,
And why this longing, fond desire to live ?
Blind as we are to what the Lord ordains,
We stretch our troubles, and prolong our pains.
    But you, blest genius, dear departed shade,
Now wear a chaplet that shall never fade ;

Now sit exalted in those realms of rest
Where virtue reigns, and innocence is blest,
Relentless death's inevitable doom
Untimely wrapt you in the silent tomb,
Ere the first tender down o'erspread your chin,
A stranger yet to sorrow, and to sin.
    As some sweet rose-bud, that has just begun
To ope its damask beauties in the sun,
Cropt by a virgin's hand, remains confest
A sweeter rose-bud in her balmy breast :
    Thus the fair youth, when Heav'n requir'd his
        breath,
Sunk, sweetly smiling, in the arms of death;
For endless joys exchanging endless strife,
And bloom'd renew'd in everlasting life.

AN

## EPISTLE

TO A FRIEND IN YORKSHIRE.

HAPPY the Briton, whom indulgent fate
Has fix'd securely in the middle state,
The golden mean, where joys for ever flow,
Nor riches raise too high, nor wants depress too
    low ;
Stranger to faction, in his calm retreat,
Far from the noise of cities, and the great,
His days, like streams that feed the vivid grass,
And give fair flowers to flourish as they pass,
Waving their way, in sacred silence flow,
And scarcely breath a murmur as they go.
No hopes, nor fears his steady mind can vex,
No schemes of state, or politics perplex:
Whate'er propitious Providence has sent
He holds sufficient, and himself content.
Though no proud columns grace his marble hall,
Nor Claude nor Guido animate the wall ;
Blest who with sweet security can find,
In health of body, and in peace of mind,
His easy moments pass without offence
In the still joys of rural innocence.
Such was the life our ancestors admir'd,
And thus illustrious from the world retir'd :
Thus to the woodland shades my friend repairs
With the lov'd partner of his joys and cares,
Whose social temper can his griefs allay,
And smile each light anxiety away :
In cheerful converse sweetly form'd to please,
With wit goodnatur'd, and polite with ease :
Blest with plain prudence, ignorant of art,
Her native goodness wins upon your heart.
Not fond of state, nor eager of control,
Her face reflects the beauties of her soul,
Such charms still bloom when youth shall fade
        away,
And the brief roses of the face decay.
    O ! would propitious Heav'n fulfil my prayer,
(The bliss of man is Providence's care)
Such be the tranquil tenour of my life,
And such the virtues of my future wife ;
With her in calm, domestic leisure free,
Let me possess serene obscurity ;
In acts of meek benevolence delight,
And to the widow recompense her mite.    [end,
Thus far from the crowds, not thoughtless of my
With reading, musing, writing, and a friend,

May silent pleasures every hour delude
In sweet oblivion of solicitude.

Cambridge, 1741.

---

## ON A LADY'S SINGING, AND PLAYING UPON THE HARPSICHORD.

" Say, Zephyr, what music enchants the gay
    plains ?
As soft and as sweet as the nightingale's strains;
My heart it goes pitapatee with a bound,
And gently transported beats time to the sound.

" O say, is it Sappho that touches the strings ?
And some song of the Syrens' you bear on your
    wings ? "
Said Zephyr, and whisper'd distinctly the lays,
" 'Tis Belinda that sings, and Belinda that
    plays."

Ah ! swains, if you value your freedom, be-
    ware,                                [fair ;
You hear her sweet voice, and [I know that she's
She's fair and inconstant ; and thus with her art,
She will ravish your ears to inveigle your heart.

---

## ON THE DEATH OF THE RIGHT HON. THE EARL OF UXBRIDGE.

Obiit 30° Aug. A. D. 1743. Ætat. 83.

Quem tu, Dea, tempore in omni
Omnibus ornatum voluisti excellere rebus.
                                        Lucr.

As 'midst the stars the cheering lamp of light,
In Heav'n's high concave eminently bright,
First tips the mountains with a golden ray,
Then gradual streams effulgency of day,
Till more serenely, with a mild decline,
Regretted sinks, in other worlds to shine :
    Thus from the world, an age of honour past,
Pride of the present, glory of the last,
Retir'd great Uxbridge to the blest abode,
To live for ever with the saints of God ;
There in celestial lustre to appear,
And share the wages of his labours here.
When the last trump shall rouse the dead that
    sleep
Entomb'd in earth, or buried in the deep;
When worlds dissolving on that awful day,
And all the elements shall melt away;
When every word shall be in judgment brought,
Weigh'd every action, canvass'd every thought,
Then shall thy alms in sweet memorial rise,
More grateful than the incens'd sacrifice :
The gladden'd widow's blessing shall be heard,
And prayers in fervency of soul preferr'd.    [vcy
The Lord shall bless thee, and well pleas'd sur-
The tears of orphans ¹ wip'd by thee away.
    What ! but a virtue resolutely just,
Firm to its purpose, steady to its trust,

¹ His lordship gave 2000 l. to the Foundling
Hospital; 1000 l. to St. George's, Hyde-Park
Corner; and near another 1000 l. to the neigh-
bouring parishes where he lived,

The full persuasion, and the true delight
Of having acted by the rules of right,
Could to thy soul a conscious calm impart,
When Death severe approach'd, and shook his
    dreadful dart,
'Twas this thy faith confirm'd, thy joy refin'd,
And spoke sweet solace to thy troubled mind;
This turn'd to silent peace each rising dread,
And sooth'd the terrours of the dying bed.
    May we like thee in piety excel,
Believe as stedfastly, and act as well ;
Cleave to the good and from the bad depart,
And wear the scriptures written in our heart ;²
Then shall we live, like thee, serenely gay,
And every moment calmly pass away :
And when this transitory life is o'er,
And all these earthly vanities no more,
Shall go where perfect peace is only found,
And streams of pleasure flow, an everlasting
    round.

September 3, 1743.

---

## TO THE RIGHT HONOURABLE THE COUNTESS OF UXBRIDGE,

OCCASIONED BY THE DEATH OF THE EARL, HER
HUSBAND.

Cease, cease illustrious partner of his bed,
O ! cease the tributary tear to shed:
Mourn not for him whom God has given to die
From earthly vanities to heavenly joy ;
These are the greatest honours we can give,
To mark his ways, and as he liv'd to live.
Still bloom in goodness as you bloom'd before ;
Heaven asks but this, and saints can do no more:
Exert each virtue of the Christian mind,
And still continue friend of human kind.
Be this your chief delight, for 'tis the best,
With ready alms to succour the distress'd ;
To clothe the naked and the hungry feed,
Nor pass a day without some gracious deed.
These acts are grateful to Jehovah's eye,
For these the poor shall bless you ere they die :
These hide our sins, these purchase solid gain,
And these shall bring you to your Lord again.

September 6, 1743.

---

## TO LAURA, 1742.

With generous wishes let me greet your ear,
Wishes which Laura may with safety hear.
    May all the blessings to your portion fall,
The wise can want, for you deserve them all :
Soft joy, sweet ease, and ever-blooming health,
Calmness of mind, and competence of wealth;
Whate'er th' Almighty Father can bestow,
To crown the happiness of man below,
And when with all those virtues, all those charms,
You deign to bless some happy husband's arms;

² It is remarkable that his lordship could repeat, *memoriter*, all the Gospels, the Psalms,
and other considerable parts of the Old and New
Testament.

R

388 FAWKES' POEMS.

May he in every manly grace excel,
To glad the virgin who deserves so well :
Bless'd with plain sense, with native humour gay,
To rule with prudence, and with pride obey ;
To kindness fashion'd, with mild temper fraught,
And form'd, if possible, without a fault.
Long may ye live, of mutual love possess'd,
Like streams uniting, in each other bless'd ;
Till Death shall gently call you hence away
From life's vain business to the realms of day ;
May Death unfelt the common summons give,
And both, like righteous Enoch, cease to live ;
Cease from a life beset with cares and pain,
And in eternal glories meet again.

## SONG TO LAURA, ABSENT.

January, 1745.

Come, Laura, joy of rural swains,
O! come, and bless our cheerless plains;
The skies still drooping mourn in showers,
No meadows bloom with bright-ey'd flowers,
No daisies spring, no beeches bud,
No linnets warble in the wood ;
Cold winter checks with blasts severe
The early-dawning of the year. •
  Come, lovely Laura, haste away,
Your smiles will make the village gay ;
When you return, the vernal breeze
Will wake the buds, and fan the trees ;
Where-e'er you walk the daisies spring,
The meadows laugh, the linnets sing ;
Your eyes our joyless hearts can cheer ;
O! haste, and make us happy here.

## A NOSEGAY FOR LAURA.

July 1745.

Come, ye fair, ambrosial flowers,
Leave your beds, and leave your bowers,
Blooming, beautiful, and rare,
Form a posy for my fair ;
Fair, and bright, and blooming be,
Meet for such a nymph as she.
Let the young vermilion rose
A becoming blush disclose ;
Such as Laura's cheeks display,
When she steals my heart away.
Add carnation's varied hue,
Moisten'd with the morning dew:
To the woodbine's fragrance join
Sprigs of snow-white jessamine.
  Add no more; already I
Shall, alas ! with envy die,
Thus to see my rival blest,
Sweetly dying on her breast.

## TO LAURA, ABSENT.

November 1745.

If you ever heard my prayer,
Hear it now, indulgent fair ;
Let your swain no longer mourn,
But return, my fair, return.

Lo! tempestuous winter near
Stains the evening of the year ;
Gloomy clouds obscure the day,
Nature ceases to be gay ;
The sweet tenants of the grove
Warble no soft tales of love :
Rise, my fair, and bring with thee
Joy for all, but love for me.
Where are all those blooming flowers
That adorn'd my rural bowers ?
Dappled pinks, and violets blue,
And the tulip's gaudy hue,
Lillies white, and roses red ?
All are wither'd, all are dead :
Yes—they hasten'd to decay,
When my Laura went away ;
When she comes, again they'll rise,
Blooming where she points her eyes.
  Hark ! I hear a sound from far,
Clanking arms, the din of war,
Dreadful music to my ear !
All was peace when you was here.
Now rebellion shakes the land,
Murder waves her bloody hand ;
High in air their banners fly,
Dreadful tumults rend the sky:
Rise, my fair, and bring with thee
Softer, sweeter, harmony;
All my doubts and fears remove,
Give me freedom, give me love ;
Discord when you come will cease,
And in my bosom all be peace.

TO HIS GRACE

## DR. THOMAS HERRING,

LORD ARCHBISHOP OF CANTERBURY, ON HIS SICK-
NESS AND RECOVERY.

June 25, 1753.

Serus in cœlum redeas, diuque
Lætus intersis populo Britanno.    Hor.

While rosy health abounds in every breeze,
Smiles in the flowers, and blossoms in the trees,
Matures the fields, and in the fountain flows,
Breathes through all life, and in all nature
    glows ;
Why droops Aurelius by sharp pains opprest,
Whose danger saddens every virtuous breast ?
Enough, enough has Heav'n's afflicting hand
With arms and earthquakes terrified the land :
On foreign plains has stream'd the British
    blood,
And British heroes perish'd in the flood :
Frederick, alas ! the kingdom's justest pride,
Fair in the bloom of all his virtues, died.
Ah ! generous master of the candid mind,
Light of the world, and friend of human kind,
Leave us not cause our sorrows to renew,
Nor fear the falling of the state in you.
  I see, I see conspicious how you stood,
And dauntless crush'd rebellion in the bud ;
With Ciceronian energy divine,
Dashing the plots of fraudful Catiline.

Your righteous zeal the brave Brigantes warm'd,
Silent they heard, approv'd, united, arm'd.
Ye gales, that on the downs of Surry stray,
Sleep on the Mole[1], or on the Vandal[1] play,
From every flower medicinal that springs,
Waft balmy fragrance with your temperate
    wings,
The grace, the glory of the church restore,
And save the friend, the father of the poor.
And lo ! our prayers, with fervency preferr'd,
Rise sweet as incense, and by Heav'n are heard :
The genial season, with refreshing rains,
Bright-beaming mornings, health-exhaling plains,
And pure etherial gales, conspire to heal
Our public father, for the public weal.
Oh ! by kind Providence to Britain given,
Long may you live, and late revisit Heaven ;
Continue still to bless us with your stay,
Nor wish for Heav'n till we have learnt the way.
So by your pattern shall our years be spent
In sweet tranquillity, and gay content ;
So shall we rise immortal from the dust,
And gain the blissful kingdoms of the just.

---

## TO MRS. HERRING.

WITH FOUR ODES ON THE SEASONS.

Since your goodness poetical tribute demands,
Permit the four seasons to kiss your fair hands :
And if in right colours your virtues I view,
The seasons, dear madam, are emblems of you.
In the gentle Spring's delicate flow'rets I trace
The beams of your eyes, and the bloom of your
    face :
The bright glowing ardour of Summer I find
Express'd in your friendly, benevolent mind :
As bountiful Autumn with plenty is crown'd,
Thus calm you distribute your blessings around :
But with you how shall I cold Winter compare ?
Your wit is as piercing and keen as the air:
Thus you furnish with emblems whenever I sing
Of Winter, or Autumn, or Summer, or Spring.

---

## A VERNAL ODE,

SENT TO HIS GRACE THE LORD ARCHBISHOP OF CAN-
TERBURY.

### March 12, 1754.

Bright god of day, whose genial power
  Revives the buried seed ;
That spreads with foilage every bower,
  With verdure every mead ;
Bid all thy vernal breezes fly,
Diffusing mildness through the sky ;
Give the soft season to our drooping plains,
Sprinkled with rosy dews, and salutary rains.

  [1] Two rivers in Surry, thus described by Mr.
Pope :
  The blue, transparent Vandalis appears,
  And sullen Mole, that hides his diving flood.

Enough has Winter's hand severe
  Chastis'd this dreary coast,
And chill'd the tender dawning year
  With desolating frost :
Give but thy vital beams to play,
These ice-wrought scenes will melt away ;
And, mix'd in sprightly dance, the blooming
    hours
Will wake the drowsy Spring, the Spring awake
  the flowers.

Let Health, gay daughter of the skies,
  On Zephyr's wings descend,
And scatter pleasures, as she flies,
  Where Surry's downs extend :
There, Herring wooes her friendly power ;
There may she all her roses shower ;
To heal that shepherd all her balms employ,
So will she sooth our fears, and give a nation joy.

The grateful seasons, circling fast,
  Reviving suns restore,
But life's short spring is quickly past,
  And blooms, alas ! no more ;
Then let us, ere by sure decays
We reach the winter of our days,
In virtue emulate the bless'd above,
And like the Spring display benevolence and love.

---

## ODE TO SUMMER.

BY A GENTLEMAN OF CAMBRIDGE.

Hail, gentle Summer, to this isle !
Where Nature's fairest beauties smile,
  And breathe in every plain ;
'Tis thine to bid each flower display,
And open to the eye of day
  The glories of its reign.

While yon few sheep enjoy the breeze,
That softly dies upon the trees,
  And rest beneath the shade ;
This pipe, which Damon gave, shall raise
Its rural notes to sing thy praise,
  And ask the Muse's aid.

Diana's ear shall catch the sound,
And all the nymphs that sport around
  The vale, or upland lawn ;
The nymphs, that o'er the mountain's brow
Pursue the lightly-bounding roe,
  Or chase the flying fawn.

Ev'n now, perchance, some cool retreat
Defends the lovely train from heat,
  And Phœbus' noontide beam ;
Perchance they twine the flowery crown
On beds of roses, soft as down,
  Beside the winding stream.

Delightful season ! every mead
With thy fair robe of plenty spread,
  To thee that plenty owes ;
The laughing fields with joy declare,
And whisper all in reason's ear,
  From whence that plenty flows.

Happy the man whose vessel glides
Safe and unhurt by passion's tides,
　Nor courts the gusts of praise !
He sails with even, steady pace,
While virtue's full-blown beauties grace
　The summer of his days.

---

## AN AUTUMNAL ODE.

### TO MR. HAYMAN, THE PAINTER.

#### October 1754.

Yet once more, glorious god of day,
　While beams thine orb serene,
O let me warbling court thy stay
　To gild the fading scene !
Thy rays invigorate the Spring,
Bright Summer to perfection bring,
The cold inclemency of Winter cheer,
And make th' Autumnal months the mildest of
　the year.

Ere yet the russet foliage fall,
　I'll climb the mountain's brow,
My friend, my Hayman, at thy call,
　To view the scene below:
How sweetly pleasing to behold
Forests of vegetable gold! 　　　　[tween
How mix'd the many chequer'd shades be-
The tawny, mellowing hue, and the gay vivid
　green!

How splendid all the sky! how still !
　How mild the dying gale !
How soft the whispers of the rill
　That winds along the vale!
So tranquil Nature's works appear,
It seems the Sabbath of the year :
As if, the Summer's labour past, she chose
This season's sober calm for blandishing repose.

Such is of well-spent life the time,
　When busy days are past;
Man, verging gradual from his prime,
　Meets sacred peace at last :
His flowery Spring of pleasures o'er,
And Summer's full-blown pride no more,
I'e gains pacific Autumn, mild and bland,
And dauntless braves the stroke of Winter's pal-
　sy'd hand.

For yet a while, a little while,
　Involv'd in wintry gloom,
And lo! another spring shall smile,
　A spring eternal bloom :
Then shall he shine, a glorious guest,
In the bright mansions of the blest,
Where due rewards on virtue are bestow'd,
And reap the golden fruits of what his autumn
　sow'd.

---

## ODE ON WINTER.

### BY A GENTLEMAN OF CAMBRIDGE.

From mountains of eternal snow,
　And Zembla's dreary plains ;
Where the bleak winds for ever blow,
　And frost for ever reigns ;

Lo ! Winter comes, in fogs array'd,
　With ice and spangled dews ;
To dews, and fogs, and storms, be paid
　The tribute of the Muse.

Each flowery carpet Nature spread
　Is vanish'd from the eye ;
Where'er unhappy lovers tread,
　No Philomel is nigh.

(For well I ween her plaintive note
　Can soothing ease impart ;
The little warblings of her throat
　Relieve the wounded heart.)

No blushing rose unfolds its bloom,
　No tender lilies blow,
To scent the air with rich perfume,
　Or grace Lucinda's brow.

Th' indulgent Father who protects
　The wretched and the poor ;
With the same gracious care directs
　The sparrow to our door.

Dark, scowling tempests rend the skies
　And clouds obscure the day ;
His genial warmth the Sun denies,
　And sheds a fainter ray.

Yet blame we not the troubled air,
　Or seek defects to find ;
For Power Omnipotent is there,
　And walks upon the wind.

Hail every pair whom love unites
　In wedlock's pleasing ties ;
That endless source of pure delights,
　That blessing to the wise !

Though yon pale orb no warmth bestows,
　And storms united meet ;
The flame of love and friendship glows
　With unextinguish'd heat.

---

## AN ODE

### TO HIS GRACE THE LORD ARCHBISHOP OF CANTERBURY.

Thanks to the generous hand that plac'd me
　here,
　Fast by the fountains of the silver Cray,
Who leading to the Thames his tribute clear,
　Through the still valley winds his secret way.

Yet from his lowly bed with transport sees
　In fair exposure noblest villas rise,
Hamlets embosom'd deep in antient trees,
　And spires that point with reverence to the
　　skies.

O lovely dale ! luxuriant with delight!
O woodland hills ! that gently rising swell ;
O streams ! whose murmurs soft repose invite;
　Where peace and joy and rich abundance
　　dwell :

How shall my slender reed your praise resound
　In numbers worthy of the polish'd ear ?
What powers of strong expression can be found
　To thank the generous hand that plac'd me
　　here :

That gave each requisite of blissful life;
. Sweet leisure in sequester'd shades of Kent,
The softening virtues of a faithful wife,
And competence well sorted with content ?'

For these, if I forget my patron's praise,
  While bright ideas dance upon my mind,
Ne'er may these eyes behold auspicious days,
  May friends prove faithless, and the Muse
    unkind.

May 1756.

AURELIUS:

AN ELEGY.

SACRED TO THE MEMORY OF THOMAS HERRING, D D.
LATE LORD ARCHBISHOP OF CANTERBURY.

Quicquid ex illo amavimus, quicquid mirati sumus, manet mansurumque est in animis ho-
  minum, in æternitate temporum, famâ rerum.                    TACIT. Vit. Agric.

FAST by the fountains of the silver Cray[1]
  Encircled deep with weeping willows round,
O! let me sorrowing pass the pensive day,
  And wake my reed to many a plaintive sound.

For good Aurelius (now alas ! no more)
  Sighs follow sighs, and tears to tears succeed ;
Him shall the Muse in tenderest notes deplore,
  For oft he tun'd to melody my reed.

How was I late by his indulgence blest,
  Cheer'd with his smiles, and by his precepts
    taught !
My fancy deem'd him some angelic guest,
  Some Heaven-sent guide, with blissful tidings
    fraught.

Mild was his aspect, full of truth and grace,
  Temper'd with dignity and lively sense ;
Sweetness and candour beam'd upon his face,
  Emblems of love and large benevolence.

Yet never useless slept those virtues fair,
  Nor languish'd unexerted in the mind ;
Secret as thought, yet unconfin'd as air,
  He dealt his bounties out to all mankind.

How will the poor, alas ! now truly poor,
  Bewail their generous benefactor dead ?
Who daily, from his hospitable door,
  The naked cloth'd, and gave the hungry
    bread.

To sick and orphans duly sent relief,
  Was feet and eyes to cripples and the blind,
Sooth'd all the suffering family of grief,
  And pour'd sweet balsam on the wounded mind.

How will the nation their lost guardian mourn ?
  Lo ! pale-ey'd Science fix'd in grief appears;
The drooping Arts, reclining on his urn,
  Lament, and every Muse dissolves in tears.

Genius of Britain ! search the kingdom round,
  Ere yet the strict inquiry be too late ;
What bold, unblemish'd patriot can be found[*],
  To rouse the virtues of a languid state?

[1] A river in Kent.
[*] This poem was wrote in 1757.

With freedom's voice to wake the slumbering
    age,
To cheer fair merit, prowess to advance,
Dauntless to rise, and scourge with generous rage
  The high-plum'd pride and perfidy of France.

Alas ! no longer burns the glorious flame :
  The patriot passion animates no more ;
But, like the whirling eddy, some low aim
  Absorbs alike the great, the rich, the poor.

Not so, when wise Aurelius o'er the north
  Shed the mild influence of his pastoral care,
The madness of rebellion issuing forth,
  He stemm'd the torrent of the rising war.

Behold him ! with his country's weal inspir'd,
  Before the martial sons of Ebor stand,
Fair in the robe of eloquence attir'd,
  In act to speak, he waves the graceful hand :

Silent as evening, lo ! the listening throng,
  While from his lips the glowing periods fall,
Drink sweet persuasion streaming from his
    tongue,
  And the firm chain of concord binds them all

As some large river, gentle, strong, and deep,
  Winds his smooth volumes o'er the wide cam-
    paign,
Then forceful flows, and with resistless sweep,
  Rolls, in his strength collected, to the main :

Thus the good prelate, in his country's cause,
  Pour'd the full tide of eloquence along ;
As erst Tyrtæus gain'd divine applause,
  Who fir'd the Spartans with heroic song.

But when religious truths his bosom warm'd,
  Faith, hope, repentance, and eternal love,
With such pathetic energy he charm'd,
  He rais'd our souls to Paradise above.

The holy city's adamantine gate
  On golden hinge he open'd to our view;
Unravell'd every path, perplex'd and strait,
  And gave to willing minds the safe-conducting
    clew.

For God's Messiah was his chosen guide ;
  And well the sacred lore he understood,
And well the precept, sent from Heaven, apply'd,
  " For evil meekly recompensing good."

Thus mild, thus humble, in the highest state,
  The " one thing needful" was his sole regard .
Belov'd, and blamelesss he prolong'd his date '
  By acts of goodness, which themselves reward.

To him the bed of sickness gave no pain;
  For, trusting only in th' Almighty King,
He look'd on dissolution as his gain;
  No terrours had the grave, and death no sting.

Ah ! Muse, forbear that last sad scene to draw—
  This homage, due to virtue, let me pay,
These heart-sprung tears, inspir'd by filial awe,
  These numbers warbled to the silver Cray.

May, 1757.

ON THE DEATH OF HIS MOST SACRED MAJESTY

## KING GEORGE THE SECOND.

Ah, fatal hour!—we must at last resign—
Farewel, great hero of the Brunswick line!
For valour much, for virtue more renown'd,
With wisdom honour'd, and with glory crown'd.
'Twas thy bless'd lot a happy reign to close,
And die serene, triumphant o'er thy foes;
To see the faithless, vain insulting Gaul,
Like proud Goliath, nodding to his fall;
In chains the sons of tyranny to bind,
And vindicate the rights of human kind.
　No brighter crown than Britain's God could
　　　give
To grace the monarch, till he ceas'd to live;
Then gave him, to reward his virtuous strife,
A heavenly kingdom, and a crown of life.

October 26, 1760.

## TO HIS MOST SACRED MAJESTY ON HIS ACCESSION.

Jam nova progenies cœlo dimittitur alto.　Virg.

When now the sad solemnity is o'er,
And death-denouncing bells are heard no more,
Nor pausing cannon in loud notes declare
A nation's grief, and rend the troubled air;
Deign,. mighty prince, these gentler sounds to
　　　hear:
Oh! were they worthy of the sovereign's ear,
The Muse should greet Britannia's blissful isle,
Where crown'd with liberty the graces smile;
Where the pleas'd halcyon builds her tranquil
　　　nest,
No storms disturb her, and no wars molest:
For still fair peace and plenty here remain'd,
While George, the venerable monarch, reign'd.
One generation pass'd secure away,
" Wise by his rules, and happy by his sway;"
Now cold in death the much-lov'd hero lies,
His soul unbodied seeks her native skies:
The living laurels which his temples crown'd
Strike root, and shade his funeral pile around.
　As when the Sun, bright ruler of the year,
Through glowing Cancer rolls his golden sphere,
He gains new vigour as his orb declines,
And at the goal with double lustre shines:
In splendour thus great George's reign surpast,
Bright beam'd each year, but brightest far the
　　　last:
Where-ever waves could roll, or breezes blow,
His fleet pour'd ruin on the faithless foe: [hurl'd,
France saw, appall'd, the dreadful vengeance
And own'd him monarch of her western world.
But now, alas! see pale Britannia mourn,
And all her sons lamenting o'er his urn.
　Thus when Vespasian died, imperial Rome
With copious tears bedew'd the patriot's tomb;
But soon o'er sorrow bright-ey'd joy prevail'd,
When Titus her lov'd emperor she hail'd;
Titus, a blessing to the world design'd,
The darling and delight of human-kind.

With joy, great prince, your happy subjects
A better Titus now reviv'd in you;　　[view
Of gentler nature, and of nobler blood,
Whose only study is your people's good:
For you (so truly is your heart benign)
To heathen virtues christian graces join.
　O may Heaven's providence around you wait,
And bless you with a longer, happier date;
Then will your virtue all its powers display,
And noble deeds distinguish every day;
Joys unallay'd will sweetly fill your breast,
Your people blessing, by your people blest;
Then will the rage of rancorous discord cease,
The drooping arts revive, and all the world have
　　　peace.

November 15, 1760.

## A PARODY ON A PASSAGE IN MILTON'S PARADISE LOST.

### BOOK IV.

Beneath a beech's bowery shade
Damon in musing mood was laid,
A brook soft-dimpling by his side,
Thus echo, as he sung, reply'd:

" Sweet is the breath of rosy morn,
　Soft melody the sky-lark trills,
Bright are the dew-drops on the thorn,
　Fresh are the zephyrs on the hills,
Pure are the fountains in the vale below,
And fair the flowers that on their borders blow:
　Yet neither breath of roseate morn,
　　Nor wild notes which the sky-lark trills,
　Nor dew-drops glittering on the thorn,
　　Nor the fresh zephyrs of the hills,
Nor streams that musically-murmuring flow,
Nor flowers that on their mossy margins grow,
　　Can any joy suggest
　　But to the temper'd breast,
　　Where virtue's animating ray
　　Illumines every golden day,
Beams on the mind, and makes all nature gay."

## THE LORD'S PRAYER.

Father of all, whose throne illumines Heaven,
All honour to thy holy name be given.
Thy gracious kingdom come: thy righteous will
Let men on Earth as saints in Heaven fulfil.
Give us this day the bread by which we live:
As we our debtors, thou our debts forgive.
Let not temptation lead us into woe:
Keep us from sin, and our infernal foe.
For thy supreme dominion we adore;
Thy power, thy glory, is for evermore.
　　　　　　　　　　　　　　Amen.

## DAVID'S LAMENTATION OVER SAUL AND JONATHAN.

### SAMUEL, BOOK II. CHAPTER I.

The flow'r of Israel withers on the plain;
How are the mighty on the mountains slain!

In Gath, ah! never this dishonour name,
Nor in the streets of Askelon proclaim;
Lest the sad tidings of our country's woe
Cause triumph to the daughters of the foe.
May Heav'n, Gilboa, on thy heights ne'er pour
The dew refreshing, or the fruitful shower;
Ne'er may thy furrows give the golden seed,
Nor from thy folds the fleecy victims bleed:
There mighty men through fear their shields re-
      sign'd,
The shield of Saul was basely left behind.
Thy bow, O Jonathan, oft strew'd the plain
With carcasses of valiant heroes slain;
Thy sword, O Saul, ne'er left its sheath in vain.
Blest pair! whom love with sweetest concord tied,
Whom glory join'd, and death cou'd not divide.
Dreadful through all the war they mov'd along,
Swift as the eagle, as the lion strong.    [drest
Weep, weep for Saul, ye maids, whose bounty
Israel's fair daughters in the scarlet vest;
Who gave you gold and pearls your robes to
      deck,
And rings and jewels for your hands and neck.
Thy prowess, much lov'd Jonathan, prov'd vain;
How are the mighty on the mountains slain!
To me, O Jonathan, for ever dear,
Thy fate, alas! demands th' eternal tear:
Where can such faith, such piety be found?
Such pleasing converse with firm friendship
      bound?
Thy love was wondrous, soothing all my care,
Passing the fond affection of the fair.
How are the mighty on the mountains slain!
And all the instruments of battle vain!

---

## THE PICTURE OF OLD-AGE,

PARAPHRASED FROM THE SEVEN FIRST VERSES OF
THE TWELFTH CHAPTER OF ECCLESIASTES.

My son, attentive hear the voice of truth;
Remember thy Creator in thy youth,
Ere days of pale adversity appear,
And age and sorrow fill the gloomy year,
When wearied with vexation thou shalt say,
" No rest by night I know, no joy by day;"
Ere the bright soul's enlighten'd pow'rs wax frail,
Ere reason, memory, and fancy fail,
But care succeeds to care, and pain to pain,
As clouds urge clouds, returning after rain:
Ere yet the arms unnerv'd and feeble grow,
The weak legs tremble, and the loose knees bow;
Ere yet the grinding of the teeth is o'er,
And the dim eyes behold the Sun no more;
Ere yet the pallid lips forget to speak,
The gums are toothless, and the voice is weak;
Restless he rises when the lark he hears,
Yet sweetest music fails to charm his ears.
A stone, or hillock, turns his giddy brain,
Appall'd with fear he totters o'er the plain;
And as the almond-tree white flow'rs displays,
His head grows hoary with the length of days;
As leanness in the grasshopper prevails,
So shrinks his body, and his stomach fails;
Doom'd to the grave his last long home to go,
The mourners march along with solemn woe:
Ere yet life's silver cord be snapt in twain,
Ere broke the golden bowl that holds the brain,

Ere broke the pitcher at the fountful heart,
Or life's wheel shiver'd, and the soul depart,
Then shall the dust to native earth be given,
The soul shall soar sublime, and wing its way to
    Heaven.

---

## A GOOD WIFE.

FROM PROVERBS, Chapter xxxi.

More precious far than rubies, who can find
A wife embellished with a virtuous mind:
In her securely, as his better part,
Her happy husband cheerful rests his heart:
With such a lovely partner of his toil
His goods increase without the need of spoil.
Bless'd in the friendship of his faithful wife,
He steers through all vicissitudes of life.
Well pleas'd she labours, nor disdains to cull
The textile flax, or weave the twisted wool.
Rich as the merchant ships that crowd the
    strands,
She reaps the harvest of remotest lands.
Early she rises ere bright Phœbus shines,
And to her damsels separate tasks assigns:
Refresh'd with food her hinds renew their toil,
And cheerful haste to cultivate the soil.
If to her farm some field contiguous lies,
With care she views it, and with prudence buys;
And with the gains which Heaven to wisdom
    grants,
A vineyard of delicious grapes she plants.
Inur'd to toils she strength and sweetness joins,
Strength is the graceful girdle of her loins.
With joy her goodly merchandise she views,
And oft till morn her pleasing work pursues.
The spindle twirls obedient to her tread,
Round rolls the wheel, and spins the ductile
Benignant from her ever-open door     [thread.
She feeds the hungry, and relieves the poor.
Nor frost nor snow her family molest,
For all her household are in scarlet drest.
Resplendent robes are by her husband worn,
Her limbs fine purple and rich silks adorn:
For wisdom fam'd, for probity renown'd,
He sits in council with bright honour crown'd.
To weave rich girdles is her softer care,    [wear.
Which merchants buy, and mighty monarchs
With strength and honour she herself arrays,
And joy will bless her in the latter days.
Wise are her words, her sense divinely strong,
For kindness is the tenour of her tongue.
Fair rule and order in her mansion dwell,
She eats with temperance what she earns so well.
Rich in good works her children call her blest,
And thus her husband speaks his inmost breast:
" To Eve's fair daughters various virtues fall,
But thou, lov'd charmer, hast excell'd them all."
Smiles oft are fraudful, beauty soon decays,
But the good woman shall inherit praise.
To her, O grateful, sweet requital give!
Her name, her honour shall for ever live.

## NATHAN'S PARABLE.

### II. SAMUEL, Chap. xii.

To Israel's king thus spoke the holy seer:
" O mighty monarch, fam'd for wisdom, hear
While to my lord a tale of woe I tell:
Two men, O king, in one fair city dwell;
The one is friendless, and exceeding poor,
The other rich, and boastful of his store:
Large herds of oxen in his pastures feed,
And flocks unnumber'd whiten every mead.
The poor man's stock was only one ewe-lamb
Of snowy fleece, wean'd lately from its dam;
He bought it with what treasure he could spare,
Ev'n all his wealth, and 'twas his only care;
Nurs'd by his hand, and with his children bred,
With them it wanton'd, and with them it fed;
Of his own mess it eat without control,
And drank the beverage of his milky bowl;
Then lightly-sportful skipt, and, tir'd with play,
Dear as a daughter in his bosom lay.
A traveller of no ignoble fame,
By chance conducted, to the rich man came;
Yet from his herds he could not spare an ox
To treat him, nor a wether from his flocks,
But took by cruel force, and kill'd and drest
The poor man's lamb to feed his pamper'd guest."
    The monarch paus'd—then made this stern
            reply
Incens'd: " I swear by God that rules the sky,
The man that did this thing shall surely die:
The lamb fourfold he likewise shall restore,
To recompense the friendless and the poor:
Because his heart no soft compassion felt,
At other's woe unknowing how to melt."
    " Thou art the man," reply'd the holy seer,
' Thus saith the Lord, the God of Israel, hear:
A king thou art, anointed at my call,
O'er Israel; and I rescued thee from Saul;
And gave thee all thy master's servants lives,
His large possessions, and his numerous wives:
Was that too little? Could'st thou more require?
I would have given thee all thy heart's desire.
Then wherefore didst thou God's commandment
Committing this great evil in his sight?    [slight,
Lo! thou hast robb'd Uriah of his wife,
Defil'd his bed, and then destroy'd his life,
Hast slain him with the adversary's sword:
Now therefore hear the judgment of the Lord,
And lock this awful sentence in thy heart;
' The sword shall never from thy house depart,
For thou hast robb'd Uriah of his wife,
Defil'd his bed, and then destroy'd his life.'
Thus saith the Lord, nor thou his words despise,
The power of evil in thy house shall rise,
Lo! I will take thy wives before thine eyes;
Thy concubines shall be in triumph led,
The Sun shall see them in thy neighbour's bed:
Thou didst it secret—this thing shall be done
Before all Israel, and before the Sun."
    Aghast, convict the mighty monarch stood,
And from his eyes stream'd sorrow in a flood;
And while a sigh repentant heav'd his breast,
He thus the anguish of his soul exprest:    [sword,
" Thy words are sharper than the two-edg'd
For I, alas! have sinn'd against the Lord."
    Stung with remorse he mourn'd his past of-
            fence
With bitter tears, and heart-sprung penitence.

The seer then sooth'd him with this calm reply;
" Thy sin is pardon'd, and thou shall not die."
Thus may we clearly see each secret sin,
Warn'd by the faithful monitor within:
Thus may we, blest with bounteous grace from
            Heaven,
Like Judah's king repent, and be forgiven.

---

## THE SONG OF DEBORAH.

Lend, O ye princes, to my song an ear,
Ye mighty rulers of the nations, hear,
While to the Lord the notes of praise I sing,
To Israel's God, the everlasting king.
    When from aerial Seir, in dread array,
From Edom when th' Almighty took his way,
" On Cherub, and on Cherubim he rode," [God:
The trembling Earth proclaim'd th' approach of
The heavens dissolv'd, the clouds in copious
            rains                [plains:
Pour'd their black stores, and delug'd all the
The rent rocks shiver'd on that awful day,
And mountains melted like soft wax away.
    In Shamgar's days, in Jael's hapless reign,
How were the princes, and the people slain?
When Sisera, terrific with his hosts,
Pour'd dire destruction on pale Judah's coasts,
The cities no inhabitants contain'd;
The public ways unoccupied remain'd;
The travellers through dreary deserts stray'd,
Or pensive wander'd in the lonely glade,
Till, sent by Heaven, I, Deborah, arose
To rule and rescue Israel from their foes.
    Those patriot warriors of immortal fame,
Who sav'd their country all my favour claim:
Ye judges, speak, ye shepherd swains, rehearse
Jehovah's praise in never-dying verse.
Awake, awake; raise, Deborah, thy voice,
And in loud numbers bid the lyre rejoice:
Raise to the Lord of Heaven thy grateful song,
Who gave the weak dominion o'er the strong.
    The tribes of Israel sent their mighty men,
That wield the falchion, or that guide the pen.
Gilead, Oh shame! by fountful Jordan lay,
Dan in his ships, and Asher in his bay:
Their bleating flocks (ignoble care!) withheld
The tribes of Reuben from the tented field:
But chiefs intrepid to the conflict came,
Heroes that fought for empire and for fame:
In Taanach where Megiddo's streams are roll'd,
There fought the monarchs resolutely bold.
Heav'n's thunders to our foes destruction
            wrought,
The stars 'gainst Sisera conspiring fought.
The river Kishon swept away the slain,
Kishon, that antient river, to the main.
For ever bless'd be Jael's honour'd name!
For ever written in the rolls of fame!
He ask'd refreshment from the limpid wave,
The milky beverage to the chief she gave:
He drank, he slept extended on the floor,
She smote the warrior, and he wak'd no more:
Low at her feet he bow'd his nail-pierc'd head;
Low at her feet he bow'd, he fell, he lay down
            dead.
    The hero's mother, anxious for his stay,
Thus, fondly sighing, chid his long delay:

" What hopes, what fears my tortur'd bosom
    feels!
Alas! why linger thus his chariot-wheels?
Some captive maid, distinguish'd for her charms,
Perchance detains the conqueror in her arms :
Perchance his mules, rich laden from afar,
Move slowly with the plunder of the war."
    Ah, wretched mother! all thy hopes are vain,
Thy son, alas! lies breathless on the plain,
Vanquish'd by Israel's sons, and by a woman
    slain.

## EPITAPHS.

Oh let your once-lov'd friend inscribe the stone,
And, with domestic sorrows, mix his own !
                                    POPE.

## ON A VERY GOOD WOMAN.

COULD marble know what virtue's buried here,
This monument would scarce refuse a tear,
But mourn, so early snatch'd from mortal life,
The tenderest parent, and the dearest wife,
Bless'd with sweet temper, and of soul so even,
She seem'd a copy of the saints in Heaven.

## ON A YOUNG GENTLEMAN
### WHO DIED A. D. 1743, ÆTAT. 15.
### IN A CHURCH IN CHESHIRE.

WHEN age, all patient, and without regret,
Lies down in peace, and pays the general debt,
'Tis weakness most unmanly to deplore
The death of those who relish life no more.
But when fair youth, that every promise gave,
Sheds his sweet blossom in the blasting grave,
All eyes o'erflow with many a streaming tear,
And each sad bosom heaves the sigh sincere.

## ON A WORTHY FRIEND
### WHO WAS ACCOMPLISHED IN THE SISTER ARTS OF MUSIC AND PAINTING.

OH born in liberal studies to excel,
Thou friendly, candid, virtuous mind, farewell !
To speak thy praise all eloquence is faint,
Except the style's expressive as thy paint :
Unless th' enliven'd numbers sweetly flow,
As when thy music gave the soul to glow :
Unless the Muses polish every line,
And draw the good man with a warmth divine,
Serenely pious, with the gentlest mind,
Through life contented, and in death resign'd.

## ON THE REV. MR. COOKSON,
### VICAR OF LEEDS.

WRAPT in cold clay beneath this marble lies
What once was generous, eloquent, and wise;

A genius form'd in every light to shine,
A well bred scholar, and a sage divine;
An orator in every art refin'd,
To teach, to animate and mend mankind :
The wise and good approv'd the life he led,
And, as they lov'd him living, mourn him dead.
                                    1747.

## ON MRS. FOUNTAYNE,
### DAUGHTER OF THOMAS WHICHCOT. ESQ. AND WIFE TO THE DEAN OF YORK; WHO DIED IN CHILD-BED, JULY 1750. ÆTAT. 19.

IF e'er thy bosom swell'd with grief sincere,
View this sad shrine, and pour the pitying tear:
Here Fountayne lies, in whom all charms com-
    bin'd,
All that e'er grac'd, or dignified her kind.
    Farewel, bright pattern of unblemish'd youth,
Of mildest merit, modesty, and truth !
Death snatch'd thy sweetness in the genial hour,
Just when thy stem put forth its infant flower:
Still blooms the tender flower; as oft we see
Fair branches budding from the lifeless tree.

## ON A YOUNG GENTLEMAN,
### WHO DIED FOR LOVE.

IF modest merit ever claim'd thy tear,
Behold this monument, and shed it here:
Here every blooming virtue beam'd in one,
The friend, the lover, and the duteous son.
    Bless'd youth ! whose bosom nature form'd to
        glow
With purest flame the heart of man can know,
Go, where bright angels heavenly raptures
        prove,
And melt in visions of seraphic love.
                                    1751.

## ON JAMES FOX, ESQ.
### 1754.

PEACE to the noblest, most ingenuous mind,
In wisdom's philosophic school refin'd,
The friend of man ; to pride alone a foe ;
Whose heart humane would melt at others woe.
Oft has he made the breast of anguish gay,
And sigh'd, like Titus, when he lost a day.
All vice he lash'd, or in the rich or great,
But prais'd mild merit in the meanest state.
Calm and serene in virtue's paths he trod,
Lov'd-mercy, and walk'd humbly with his God.

## TO A YOUNG LADY,
### WITH A PRESENT OF BOOKS, PARTRIDGES, AND SNUFF.

I'VE sent you, dear Nanny, a basket of stuff,
Some books, and some birds, with a paper of
    snuff:

The present is trifling, yet still you will find
Some food for the body as well as the mind.
To tell you their uses there is not much need—
The birds you will roast, and the books you may
    read,
And as for the paper of snuff, I suppose
You are very well satisfied that's for your nose.
My respects to all friends, as a favour I ask it,
And I hope you'll remember to send back the
    basket.
                        September 1744.

---

## AN ELEGY

### ON THE DEATH OF DOBBIN, THE BUTTERWOMAN'S HORSE.

THE death of faithful Dobbin I deplore ;
Dame Jolt's brown horse, old Dobbin, is no
    more.
The cruel Fates have snapt his vital thread,
And gammer Jolt bewails old Dobbin dead.
From stony Cudham down to watery Cray,
This honest horse brought butter every day;
Fresh butter meet to mix with nicest rolls,
And sometimes eggs, and sometimes geese and
    fowls ;
And though this horse to stand had ne'er a leg,
He never dropt a goose, or broke an egg.
  Ye maids of Cray, your butter'd rolls deplore,
  Dame Jolt's brown horse, old Dobbin, is no
    more.

Oft did the 'squire that keeps the great hall-
    house,
Invite the willing vicar to a goose ;
For goose could make his kindred Muse aspire
From earth to air, from water to the fire ;
But now, alas ! his towering spirit's fled,
His muse is founder'd, for poor Dobbin's dead,
Last Friday was a luckless day, I wot,
For Friday last lean Dobbin went to pot ;
No drinks could cherish, no prescriptions save ;
In C———n's hounds he found a living grave:
  Weep all, and all (except sad dogs) deplore,
  Dame Jolt's brown horse, old Dobbin, is no
    more.

Sculk, Reynard, sculk in the securest grounds,
Now Dobbin hunts thee in the shape of hounds :
Late sure but slow he march'd as foot could fall,
Sure to march slow whene'er he march'd at all ;
Now fleeter than the pinions of the wind,
He leaves the huntsmen, and the hunt behind,
Pursues thee o'er the hills, and down the steep,
Through the rough copse, wide woods, and waters
    deep,
Along th' unbounded plain, along the lea,
But has no pullet, and no goose for thee.
Ye dogs, ye foxes, howl for Dobbin dead,
Nor thou, O Muse, disdain the tear to shed ;
  Ye maids of Cray, your butter'd rolls deplore,
  Dame Jolt's brown horse, old Dobbin. is no
    more.

---

## EPITHALAMIUM

### ON THE MARRIAGE OF A COBLER AND A CHIMNEY-SWEEPER.

YE sable sweepers, and ye coblers all,
Sons of the chimney, masters of the stall,
Whether ye deal in smearing soot, or leather,
Hail to the day that joins your trades together.
  Huzza, my jolly coblers ! and huzza,
  My sable sweepers ! Hail the joyous day.

Immortal fame, O coblers, ye derive
From Crispin, a good cobler when alive,
Who kept his stall at Hockley in the Hole,
With nut-brown beer encouraging his soul :
A bonnet blue he wore upon his head,
His nose was copper, and his jerkin red ;
For conjurer and astrologer he past,
And mended understandings to his last.
  Huzza, my jolly coblers ! and huzza,
  My sable sweepers ! Hail the joyous day.

Sly Jobson, though he never learn'd in France,
Not only mended shoes, but taught to dance;
So when he'd worn his pupils' soles quite out,
With leading of the booby bears about,
He soon repair'd the damage with his awl,
And brought convenient custom to his stall.
  Huzza, my jolly coblers ! and huzza,
  My sable sweepers! Hail the joyous day.

Nor less distinguish'd is your noble line,
Ye sweepers, sprung from pedigree divine !
Your ancient ancestor, whose name was Smut,
Work'd at the forge, with Vulcan, in his hut.
Once as the limping god was hammering out
Those tongs that pinch'd the Devil by the snout,
Smut chanc'd to jest upon his awkward frame,
Which chaf'd the bickering blacksmith into
    flame ;
He hurl'd his hammer at the joker's head,
Which sure had left him on the pavement dead,
But Smut was nimble, and, to shun the stroke,
Sheer up the chimney went, like wreaths of
    smoke;
Happy to find so snug a hole to creep in,
And since that time he took to chimney-sweeping.
  Huzza, my jolly sweepers ! hail the day !
  My jolly coblers'! roar aloud huzza.

And you, meet couple, memorable match,
May live with comfort in your cot of thatch ;
While venal members sell their venal friends,
The cobler brings all soles to serve his ends.
And as the fair miss Danae sate smiling,
To see the gold come pattering through the tiling,
Our sweeper joys to see the chimney drop her
Meat, drink, and clothing, in a shower of copper.
  Huzza, my jolly coblers ! and huzza,
  My sable sweepers ! Hail the joyous day.

---

## THE SMOKING DOCTOR'S SOLILO-QUY OVER HIS PIPE.

Dulce tubo, genitos haurire & reddere fumos.

EMERGING awful through a cloud of smoke,
The tall lean doctor snapt his box and spoke :

" Though scorn'd by fribbles all bedaub'd with
I value not their censures of a puff,        [snuff,'
Who, if kind Heav'n had furnish'd 'em with brains,
Would into pipes convert their taper canes,
Be sick that nauseous nostril-dust to see,
And substitute tobacco for rappee.
I less regard the rage of female railings—
Some ladies have their waters, and their failings:
Though when grey prudence comes, and youth
                              is past,
They'll learn to smoke (or I am deceiv'd) at last!
Peace to the beaux, and every scented belle,
Who cry ' Tobacco has an odious smell :'
To men of sense I speak, and own with pleasure,
That smoking sooths my studies and my leisure;
It aids my eyes, inspires my mind to think,
And is a calm companion when I drink.
At home how sweetly does a pipe engage
My sense to relish Tully's moral page !
Or Homer's Heaven-aspiring Muse divine,
And puffing measure each sonorous line !
But if to Tom's I stray to read the Daily,
Or at the tavern spend my evening gaily,
My pipe still adds, as the mild minutes pass,
Charms to the toast, and flavour to the glass.
Blest Indian leaf! what raptures I inhale
From each light breath of thy ambrosial gale !
Thou giv'st the soldier courage, to the hind
Repose, to captives sacred peace of mind ;
Can'st wealth on merchants, state on kings be-
And to physicians only art a foe.        [stow,
Thou sav'st, when pestilence spreads far and wide,
From that dread plague, and every plague be-
                              side.
Though by thy fumes the teeth are blacken'd o'er,
Thy ashes scour them whiter than before
O with abundant riches amply blest,
He, who can buy one ounce of Freeman's best !
If in this fob my well-fill'd box I feel,        [steel,
In that my short pipe, touchwood, flint, and
Gold I regard not, I can live without;
I carry every requisite about.
Whether my stomach calls for drink or meat,
Whether the cold affects me, or the heat,
The weed of India answers the demand,
And is the pleasing remedy at hand.
O noblest proof of nature's genial power !
O weed more precious than the choicest flower !
Thy vapours bland through every state engage,
¹ Charm us when young, and solace us in age ;
Adorn when fortune showers her golden store,
And breathe kind comfort when she smiles no
                      more:
Tranquil at home they lull with sweet content,
Abroad they give us no impediment ;
But, mild associates, tend us night and day,
And if we travel cheer us on our way ;
In town or country soft repose incite,
And puff us up with exquisite delight."


¹ In allusion to that fine passage in Tully.
Hæc studia adolescentiam alunt, senectutem
oblectant ; secundas res ornant, adversis perfu-
gium et solatium præbent; delectant domi, non
impediunt foris ; pernoctant nobiscum, peregri-
nantur, rusticantur.

## WOMAN :

### A BALLAD.

BEING A CONTRAST TO " THE WOMEN ALL TELL
ME I'M FALSE TO MY LASS."

No longer let whimsical songsters compare
The merits of wine with the charms of the fair ;
I appeal to the men to determine between
A tun-bellied Bacchus, and beauty's fair queen.

The pleasures of drinking henceforth I resign,
For though there is mirth, yet there's madness
                      in wine ;
Then let not false sparkles our senses beguile,
'Tis the mention of Chloe that makes the glass
                      smile.

Her beauties with rapture my fancy inspire,
And the more I behold her, the more I admire ;
But the charms of her temper and mind I adore;
These virtues shall bless me when beauty's no
                      more.

How happy our days when with love we engage,
'Tis the transport of youth, 'tis the comfort of
                      age ;
But what are the joys of the bottle or bowl ?
Wine tickles the taste, love enraptures the soul.

Let the men of all nations, but Italy, prove
The blessings that wait upon beauty and love:
But in boosing, alas! one unfortunate bout
Will rob us of vigour, and leave us the gout.

A sot, as he riots in liquor, will cry,
" The longer I drink, the more thirsty am I,"
From this fair confession, 'tis plain, my good
                      friend,
You're a toper eternal, and drink to no end.

Your big-bellied bottle may ravish your eye,
But how foolish you'll look when your bottle is
                      dry !        [spring,
Sweet pleasure from woman still flows like a
Nay the Stoics must own it—She is the best
                      thing.

Yet some praises to wine we may justly afford,
For a time it will make one as great as a lord ;
But woman for ever gives transport to man,
And I'll stand by the ladies as long as I can.

## THE BROWN JUG :

### A SONG.

IMITATED FROM THE LATIN OF HIERONYMUS
AMALTHEUS.

DEAR Tom, this brown jug that now foams with
                      mild ale,
(In which I will drink to sweet Nan of the Vale)
Was once Toby Fillpot, a thirsty old soul
As e'er drank a bottle, or fathom'd a bowl ;
In boosing about 'twas his praise to excel,
And among jolly topers he bore off the bell.,
It chanc'd as in dog-days he sat at his ease
In his flow'r-woven arbour as gay as you please,
With a friend and a pipe puffing sorrows away,
And with honest old stingo was soaking his clay,

His breath-doors of life on a sudden were shut,
And he died full as big as a Dorchester butt.

His body, when long in the ground it had lain,
And time into clay had resolv'd it again,
A potter found out in its covert so snug,
And with part of fat Toby he form'd this brown
              jug,                    [ale,
Now sacred to friendship, and mirth, and mild
So here's to my lovely sweet Nan of the Vale.

## A PAIR OF SPECTACLES.

### FROM BOURNE.

Of all the spectacles to mend the sight
Devis'd by art for viewing objects right,
Those are most useful, which the prudent place
High on the handle of the human face.
Some on the temples fix 'em, I suppose,
Lest they should seem to snuffle through the nose:
Some in one hand the single-convex hold,
But these are prigs asham'd of being old,
None are in news or polities so wise,
As he whose nose is saddled with his eyes;
And if the taper tube regale his snout,
There's nought so secret but he'll smell it out.
Should gammer Gurton leave these helps at home,
To church with Bible 'tis in vain to come;
The plainest sermon is the most perplext,
Unless with care she double down the text.
Lo! how the parish clerk, with many a hum,
By turns now fits 'em to his nose or thumb,
Methodically regular, as need
By turns requires him, or to sing, or read:
His thumb then held them, if report says true,
When on the lovely lass he leer'd askew;
With snow-white bosom bare, sweet-slumbering
              in her pew. [2]
Those who see dimly may their eyes restore
By adding two to what they had before;
And he who would be deem'd profoundly wise
Must carry in his head, and in his pocket—eyes.

## THE STAGE COACH.

### FROM THE SAME.

To pay my duty to sweet Mrs. Page,
A place was taken in the Stamford stage.
Our coachman Dick, the shades of night to shun,
Had yok'd his horses long before the Sun:
Disturb'd I start; and drowsy all the while,
Rise to be jolted may a weary mile;
On both sides squeez'd, how highly was I bless'd!
Between two plump old women to be press'd!
A corporal fierce, a nurse and child that cried,
And a fat landlord fill'd the other side.      [load
Scarce dawns the morning, ere the cumberous
Rolls roughly-rumbling o'er the rugged road.
One old wife coughs, and wheezes in my ears,
Loud scolds the other, and the corporal swears;

 [2] Alluding to a picture of Hogarth's, which
very humourously describes a slumbering congregation.

Sour, unconcocted breath escapes my host,
The squawling child returns his milk and toast:
Ye gods! if such the pleasures of the stage,
I chuse to walk and visit Mrs. Page.

## ΔΩΡΟΝ ΑΔΩΡΟΝ.
## THANK YOU FOR NOTHING.

### FROM THE SAME.

When cloudless skies, or Spring's soft season
Calls forth the citizens to take the air;      [fair,
The landlord kindly asks his guests to dine
On well-corn'd beef, or pork's high-relish'd chine:
The season'd fraud succeeds, and soon or late
A shoal of gudgeons gobble up the bait.
The savoury viands make them thirst the more,
Creating drought, and swelling out the score.
My landlord, faith! is not so kind, I think;
He gives his victuals, but he sells his drink.

## AN EULOGY

## ON SIR ISAAC NEWTON.

### TRANSLATED FROM THE LATIN OF DR. HALLEY.

Behold the regions of the Heavens survey'd!
And this fair system in the balance weigh'd;
Behold the law which (when in ruin hurl'd
God out of Chaos call'd the beauteous world)
Th' Almighty fix'd, when all things good he saw!
Behold the chaste, inviolable law!
Before us now new scenes unfolded lie,
And Heav'n appears expanded to the eye;
Th' illumin'd mind now sees distinctly clear
What power impels each planetary sphere.
Thron'd in the centre glows the king of day,
And rules all nature with unbounded sway;
Through the vast void his subject planets run,
Whirl'd in their orbits by the regal Sun.
What course the dire tremendous comets steer
We know, nor wonder at their prone career;
Why silver Phœbe, meek-ey'd queen of night,
Now slackens, now precipitates her flight;
Why, scan'd by no astronomers of yore,
She yielded not to calculation's power;
Why the nodes' motions retrograde we call,
And why the apsides progressional.
Hence too we learn, with what proportion'd force
The Moon impels, erroneous in her course,
The refluent main: as waves on waves succeed,
On the bleak beach they toss the sea-green weed,
Now bare the dangers of th' engulphing sand,
Now swelling high roll foaming on the strand.
What puzzling schoolmen sought so long in vain,
See cloud-dispelling Mathesis explain!
O highly blest, to whom kind fate has given
Minds to expatiate in the fields of Heaven!
All doubts are clear'd, all errours done away,
And truth breaks on them in a blaze of day.
Awake, ye sons of men, arise! exclude
Far from your breasts all low solicitude;
Learn hence the mind's etherial powers to trace,
Exalted high above the brutal race.
Ev'n those fam'd chiefs who human life refin'd
By wholesome laws, the fathers of mankind;

Or they who first societies immur'd
In cities, and from violence secur'd;
They who with Ceres' gifts the nations blest,
Or from the grape delicious nectar prest;
They who first taught the hieroglyphic style
On smooth papyrus [1], native plant of Nile,
(For literary elements renown'd)
And made the eye an arbiter of sound :
All these, though men of deathless fame, we find
Have less advanc'd the good of human-kind :
Their schemes were founded on a narrower plan,
Replete with few emoluments to man.
But now, admitted guests in Heav'n, we rove
Free and familiar in the realms above;
The wonders hidden deep in Earth below,
And nature's laws, before conceal'd, we know.
Lend, lend your aid, ye bright superior powers,
That live embosom'd in Elysian bowers,
Lend your sweet voice to warble Newton's praise,
Who search'd out truth through all her mystic
    maze,
Newton, by every favouring Muse inspir'd,
With all Apollo's radiations fir'd :
Newton, that reach'd th' insuperable line,
The nice barrier 'twixt human and divine.

---

## CLAUDIAN'S OLD MAN,

WHO NEVER WENT OUT OF THE SUBURBS OF
VERONA.

BLEST who, content with what the country
    yields,
Lives in his own hereditary fields;
Who can with pleasure his past life behold ;
Whose roof paternal saw him young and old ;
And as he tells his long adventures o'er,
A stick supports him where he crawl'd before ;
Who ne'er was tempted from his farm to fly,
And drink new streams beneath a foreign sky :
No merchant, he, solicitous of gain,    [main :
Dreads not the storms that lash the sounding
Nor soldier, fears the summons to the war ;
Nor the hoarse clamours of the noisy bar.
Unskill'd in business, to the world unknown,
He ne'er beheld the next contiguous town ;
Yet nobler objects to his views are given,
Fair flowery fields, and star-embellish'd Heaven.
He marks no change of consuls, but computes
Alternate seasons by alternate fruits;
Maturing autumns store of apples bring,
And flowerets are the luxury of spring.
His farm that catches first the Sun's bright ray,
Sees the last lustre of his beams decay :
The passing hours erected columns show,
And are his landmarks and his dials too.
Yon spreading oak a little twig he knew,
And the whole grove in his remembrance grew.
Verona's walls remote as India seem ;
Benacus is th' Arabian Gulph to him.
Yet health three ages lengthens out his span,
And grandsons hail the vigorous old man.
Let others vainly sail from shore to shore,
Their joys are fewer, and their labours more.

    [1] An Egyptian plant, growing in the marshy
places near the banks of the Nile, on the leaves
of which the antients used to write.

---

## ARCHIMEDES'S SPHERE :

FROM CLAUDIAN.

JOVE saw the Heav'ns in glassy sphere exprest,
And smiling, thus the pow'rs above addrest :
"At what bold tasks will man's presumption aim!
In this small globe he mocks the worldly frame.
Lo! from my work the rival artist draws
The heavenly motions, and great Nature's laws.
Each star includes an animating soul,
And beauteous order regulates the whole.
Through the bright zodiac yearly rolls the Sun,
And mimic moons each month their courses run.
Audacious Art thus lifts her crest on high,
And deems she sways the empire of the sky.
Salmoneus once fictitious lightning hurl'd :
But here behold a counterfeited world!"

---

## ON MENANDER.

IMITATED FROM A GREEK EPIGRAM IN THE
ANTHOLOGIA.

ON thy sweet lips the bees in clusters hung,
And dropp'd Hyblæan honey on thy tongue :
For thee the Muses pluck'd Pierian flowers ;
The Graces woo'd thee in sequester'd bowers.
Ages to come shall celebrate thy name,
And Athens gather glory from thy fame.

---

## FRAGMENTS OF MENANDER :

TRANSLATED FROM THE GREEK.

Thou, whom the Nine with Plautus' wit inspire,
The art of Terence, with Menander's fire.

POPE.

---

## SOME ACCOUNT OF MENANDER.

MENANDER was born at Athens, the third year of
the 109th Olympiad, 344 years before Christ,
and exhibited his first comedy, according to
Meursius, the third of the 114th Olympiad, that is
324 years before our Saviour's time, being then
only twenty years of age. His introduction of
the new comedy in a short time spread his fame
over the world; and his friendship was courted
by the kings of Egypt and Macedon. Of his
works, which amounted to upwards of an hundred
comedies, only a few fragments now remain.
Terence borrowed several plays from him ; and
it is from the character of the Roman, that most
men now judge of the merit of the Grecian author.
We find the old masters of rhetoric recommending his works as the true standard of beauty,
containing every grace of public speaking. Quintilian declares, that a careful imitation of Menander only will satisfy all the rules he has laid
down in his institutions. It is in Menander that
he would have his orator search for a copiousness
of invention, for a happy elegance of expression,
and especially for an universal genius, able to
accommodate itself naturally to all persons,
things, and affections.

His wonderful talent at expressing nature, in every condition, and under every circumstance of life, has always made the noblest part of his character, which gave occasion to Aristophanes the grammarian to ask this genteel question; Ω Μενανδρε, και Βιε, Ποτερος αρ υμων ποτερον επιμιμησατο? O Menander and Nature, which of you have imitated the other? Julius Cæsar has left us the noblest, as well as the justest praise of Menander's works, when addressing himself in a compliment to Terence, he calls him, Dimidiate Menander, Half-Menander. He died in the third year of the 122nd Olympiad, 292 years before Christ, being fifty-two years of age.

---

### WORSHIP DUE TO THE DEITY.

SERVE then the great first cause whence nature springs,
Th' almighty Sire, th' eternal King of kings;
Who gave us being, and who gives us food,
Lord of all life, and author of all good.

Page 48.

---

### SUBMISSION.

FIGHT not with God, nor thwart his wiser will,
(Contending serves to aggravate an ill,)
But bravely bear those ills he's pleas'd to send;
Why should we blame the laws we cannot mend?

Page 70.

---

### THE ACCEPTABLE SACRIFICE.

WHOE'ER approaches to the Lord of all,
And with his offerings desolates the stall;
Who brings an hundred bulls with garlands drest,
The purple mantle, or the golden vest,
Or ivory figures richly wrought around,
Or curious images with emeralds crown'd;
And hopes with these God's favour to obtain,
His thoughts are foolish, and his hopes are vain,
He, only he may trust his pray'rs will rise,
And Heav'n accept his grateful sacrifice,
Who leads beneficent a virtuous life,
Who wrongs no virgin, who corrupts no wife;
No robber he, no murderer of mankind,
No miser, servant to the sordid mind.
Dare to be just, my Pamphilus, disdain
The smallest trifle for the greatest gain:
For God is nigh thee, and his purer sight
In acts of goodness only takes delight:
He feeds the labourer for his honest toil,
And heaps his substance as he turns the soil.
To him then humbly pay the rites divine,
And not in garments, but in goodness shine.
Guiltless of conscience thou may'st safely sleep,
Though thunder bellow through the boundless deep.

Page 268.

*⁎* The figures at the bottom of each fragment refer to the page in Le-Clerc's edition, where the original is to be found.

---

### THE MISERIES OF OLD-AGE.[1]

HIM, Parmeno, I deem the happiest man,
Who having once survey'd great Nature's plan,
This beauteous system, this stupendous frame,
Soon to that place retires from whence he came.
This common Sun, the stars, the streams that flow,
The clouds that darken, and the fires that glow;
These shall be always present to thy view,
Whether thou liv'st an hundred years, or few;
And nobler works, or wrought with better skill,
None ever yet beheld, or ever will.
This life on Earth, these scenes to man assign'd,
Suppose a mighty concourse of mankind,
Where all contrive to trifle time away
In business, bustle, villany, or play:
If first this inn you quit, a transient guest,
You'll pay but little, and you'll fare the best:
Go then equipt, nor fear the stroke of fate,
You'll travel free from envy and from hate.
But lingering guests, who longer being crave,
Must sink at last with sorrow to the grave:
For antient men experience wants and woes
From friends departing or surviving foes.

[1] The late ingenious and learned I. Hawkins Browne, esq. has translated and interwoven this fine fragment into his excellent poem De Animi Immortalitate, book the first.

Quocirca ille mihi felix vixisse videtur,
Qui pòstquam aspexit mundi solenne theatrum
Æquo animo, hunc solem, et terras, mare, nubila,
et ignem;
Protinus unde abiit, satur ut conviva remigrat.
Nempe hæc, seu centum vivendo conteris annos,
Seu paucos numeras, eadem redeuntia cernes;
Hisque nihil melius, nihil atque recentius unquam
Omne adeo in terris agitur quod tempus, habeto
Ut commune forum; peregre vel euntibus amplum
Hospitium, temerè fluitans ubi vita moratur,
Mille inter nugas jactata, negotia mille.
Qui prior abscedit, portum prior occupat; Eja!
Collige vela citus, ne fortè viatica desint.
Quid cessas? subeunt morbique et acerba tuorum
Funera, et insidiis circùm undique septa senectus.

Perhaps the reader will not be displeased to see Mr. Soame Jennyn's translation of the above passage quoted from Mr. Browne's Immortality.

To me most happy therefore he appears,
Who having once, unmov'd by hopes or fears,
Survey'd this sun, earth, ocean, clouds, and flame,
Well satisfy'd returns from whence he came.
Is life a hundred years, or e'er so few,
'Tis repetition all, and nothing new:
A fair, where thousands meet, but none can stay,
An inn, where travellers bait, then post away:
A sea, where man perpetually is tost,
Now plung'd in business, now in trifles lost:
Who leave it first, the peaceful port first gain;
Hold then! no farther lanch into the main:
Contract your sails; life nothing can bestow
By long continuance, but continued woe:
The wretched privilege daily to deplore
The funerals of our friends, who go before:
Diseases, pains, anxieties, and cares,
And age surrounded with a thousand snares.

Dodsley's Collection, vol. vi.

He dies not well, who bending into age,
Droops under years, and tottering quits the
stage.
Page 184.

---

### VIRTUE ONLY IS NOBILITY.

CEASE, if you love me, mother, cease to trace
Our long extraction to an antient race ;
'Tis theirs alone who boast no inbred worth
To found their claim of honour on their birth,
And strive their want of virtue to supply
With glory borrow'd from old ancestry.
That all had ancestors the proof you give,
When you admit, that all have liv'd, or live :
If thousands find it difficult to trace       [place)
(Through lack of friends, or luckless change of
In whose pure veins their streams of kindred ran,
Are they less noble than the few that can?
The poorest tenant of the Libyan wild,
Whose life is pure, whose thoughts are undefil'd,
In titled ranks may claim the first degree,
For virtue only is nobility.
Page 240.

---

### THE OMNIPOTENCE OF GOLD.

An ancient sage[1], which some perhaps think odd,
Asserts that every element's a god ;
A god this earth, where vivid verdure grows ;
A god the fire that burns, the breeze that
blows ;
The silver streams that thro' the vallies stray,
The stars that shine by night, the Sun by day.
But I this plain, this certain maxim hold,
" There's no propitious deity but gold :"
Safe in thy house this splendid god inshrine,
And all the blessings of the world are thine ;
The grand retinue, and the burnish'd plate,
The pompous villa, and the menial great ;
Gold can buy friends, or soften rigid laws,
And bias every witness to your cause :
Spare not expense—give largely, and 'tis odds
But mighty gold will bribe the very gods.
Page 249.

---

### THE MISERY AND FOLLY OF MAN.

LORD of creation, man—come, all things see
Exceed in happiness and wisdom thee.
Behold yon ass, to whom thy partial race
Gives in the world of life the lowest place :
Thou call'st him wretched, and I grant him so,
But not from self his pitied sufferings flow ;
Beneath stern nature's load the wretch may
groan,
Yet wisely still adds nothing of his own :
But man, alas ! besides his natural share,
Makes half those evils he repines to bear.
Does any sneeze[2]? grief turns the hearers pale ;
We burn with anger if the world should rail :
Unlucky dreams with terrour fill the soul ;
We tremble at the hooting of an owl :
By contests, prejudices, pride, and law,
Unnumber'd evils on ourselves we draw.
Page 244.

[1] Epicharmus.
[2] Sneezing was sometimes reckoned an ill
omen.

---

### MAN UNHAPPY, COMPARED WITH OTHER CREATURES.

IF to my choice indulgent Heav'n would give,
This life worn out, another life to life,
And say, "Partake what form delights thee best,
Be man again, again with reason blest ;
Assume the horse's strength, the sheep's warm
coat,
Bark in the dog, or wanton in the goat ;
For this is fate's immutable decree,
And one more being is reserv'd for thee :"
To bounteous Heav'n I'd thus prefer my prayer ;
" O let not reason's lamp be lighted here !
Make me not man ; his only-partial race
Holds vice in credit, virtue in disgrace.
The steed victorious in the rapid course
Eats food more dainty than the sluggish horse :
Is there a dog, distinguish'd for his smell ?
No common dog will ever fare so well :
The gallant cock that boasts heroic blood,
Rakes not in dirty dunghills for his food ;
And should he strut among the feather'd crew,
Each conscious brother pays him honour due.
Man, tho' of each accomplishment possest,
Renown'd for valour, and with virtue blest,
Gains from the heedless world no due regard,
His worth no praise, his valour no reward :
While fawning flatterers bask in fortune's ray,
Knaves that detract, and villains that betray.
'Tis better far thro' any form to pass,
To crawl a reptile, or to drudge an ass,
Than see base miscreants, guilt's abandon'd crew,
Enjoy those honours that are virtue's due."
Page 248.

---

### THE ORIGIN OF MAN.

To know the origin from whence you came,
And the frail fashion of this human frame,
Pause o'er those monuments with pensive eye,
Where purpled tyrants, proud oppressors lie ;
All who could boast wealth,wisdom,beauty,birth,
Here meet, and mingle with one common earth :
Yet these no bright accomplishments could save
From fate's dread sentence to the gloomy
grave :
There while you read the frailty of your frame,
Learn from what vile original you came.
Page 276.

---

### THE PLEASURES OF SOLITUDE.

How sweet and pleasant to a man endued
With moral goodness, is deep solitude ?
Pensive to rove, not meditating harm,
And live in affluence at his country farm.]
For in large cities where the many bide,
Self-cankering envy dwells,and high-blown pride:
There lull'd in all the luxury of ease,
They live at large, licentious as they please ;
Yet soon these pleasures pall, and quick decay,
Like the light blaze that crackling dies away.
Page 178.

---

### SORROW FAMILIAR TO ALL MEN.

SURE sorrows are to human-kind ally'd :
They reign where Fortune pours her golden tide ;

Besiege the son of glory's splendid door,
Grow grey and old together with the poor.
Page 104.

### GOOD AND EVIL BLENDED.

No good in life the race of men can see,
Spring from one root, as branches from the tree;
But near the good we find the evil still,
And frequent good arises out of ill.
Page 156.

### CONTENT.

Mixt with all good full many ills we find,
But no one bliss to gratify the mind;
If more of good than ill the gods have given,
Pleas'd let us bless the bounteous hand of Heaven.
Page 30.

### BANISH CARE.

Whate'er offends thee, care, or grief, or strife,
Drive far away beyond the verge of life:
For here, alas! we little time posses,
And every sorrow makes that little less.
Page 158.

### TEMPLE OF REASON.

Where'er the sacred rays of reason shine,
There dwells the god that utters truths divine.
Page 22.

### THE MAN OF REASON.

In human nature nothing can excel
The man that regulates and reasons well;
To show good sense and order in a thing,
Denotes the chief, the counsellor, the king:
These noble virtues nothing can exceed,
The man of reason is a man indeed.
Page 90.

### GOODSENSE.

Blest are the wealthy who abound in sense,
Which gives a noble sanction to expense:
This, this should be the son of fortune's care,
The weight of wealth with equal mind to bear;
For riches oft deprave the human will,
And turn the bias of the mind to ill.
Page 120.

### A GOOD NAME.

In every state the good protection claim,
For the best passport is an honest name.
Page 134.

### PATIENCE.

Him I esteem most virtuous of mankind,
Who bears offences with a patient mind.
Page 32.

### MAN BLIND TO FUTURE EVENTS.

Say not, O man! for it becomes thee not,
This evil shall not happen to my lot.
Page 56.

### FRIENDSHIP.

As gold more splendid from the fire appears,
Thus friendship brightens by the length of years.
Page 272.

### TYRANTS UNHAPPY.

Ah! dreadful state of soul-consuming woe,
Which tyrants, proud oppressors, undergo!
Not all their power, nor riches, can bestow
One heart-felt pleasure which the meanest know.
What torments then must curse their guilty hours
Who live immur'd in citadels and towers?
Who think, mistrustful of their menial band,
Each slave conceals a dagger in his hand!
Such chastisements the gods for those ordain
Who uncontrol'd despotically reign.
Page 24.

### THE POOR SHOULD NOT BE OPPRESSED.

Who dares with wrongs the needy to pursue,
Is base, nor base alone, but foolish too.
What thoughtless pride to spurn that humble state,
Which chance may make his own unpitied fate?
Though now he boasts his heaps of golden store,
Soon may those fail, and he be rich no more;
The streams of fortune, never at a stay,
Oft change their course, and quickly glide away.
Page 34.

### RICHES.

What can be weigh'd with riches in the scale?
They screen all vices with a golden veil.
Page 30.

### RICH AND POOR EQUALLY UNHAPPY.

The rich all happy I was wont to hold,
Who never paid large usury for gold.
" Those sons of fortune never sigh" (I said)
" Nor toss with anguish on their weary bed
But soft dissolving into balmy sleep,
Indulge sweet slumbers, while the needy weep:"
But now the great and opulent, I see,
Lament their lots, and mourn as well as we.
Page 104.

### FORTUNE BLIND.

This sacred truth print deeply on thy mind;
Fortune, and Fortune's votaries are blind.
Page 28.

# FRAGMENTS OF MENANDER.

403

### EVIL COMPANY CONTAGIOUS.

Let not false arguments thy reason blind,
For evil converse taints the virtuous mind[1].

Page 78.

### IMPUDENCE.

He stands in impudence without a peer,
Who scorns to blush, and knows not how to fear.

Page 6.

### IMPORTUNATE ADVICE.

When well ourselves, we boast the doctor's skill,
And give advice to others that are ill[2].

Page 16.

### THE DANGERS OF MATRIMONY.

A. While prudence guides, change not, at any rate,
A life of freedom for the married state:
I ventur'd once to play that desperate game,
And therefore warn you, not to do the same.
B. The counsel may be sage which you advance;
But I'm resolv'd to take the common chance.
A. Mild gales attend that voyage of your life,
And waft you safely thro' the sea of strife:
Not the dire Libyan, or Ægæan sea,
Where out of thirty ships scarce perish three;
But that, where daring fools most dearly pay,
Where all that sail are surely cast away.

Page 22.

### THE COMFORTS OF MATRIMONY.

You judge quite wrong to think your fortune hard;
Life's troubles, not its blessings, you regard:
Believe me, friend; the race of man can know
No earthly comfort, unallay'd with woe.
Much plague, no doubt, attends a sumptuous wife,
She's the sure torment of her husband's life.
Yet ev'n from her some benefits accrue. [too:
She brings him sons, she brings him daughters
When ill, her care administers relief,
When fortune frowns, she solaces his grief:
When age or sickness, brings him to his end,
She decently inters him, like a friend.
Think, think on this when slight vexations tease;
The mighty charm will set your heart at ease:
But if you let wild sorrow thus prevail,
And place no comforts in the other scale;
Not weighing gain with loss, nor good with ill,
Still you must murmur, and be wretched still.

Page 122.

### THE RICH AND YOUNG SHOULD MARRY.

Those that are rich, and in the bloom of life,
May wed and prove the comforts of a wife;

1 St. Paul has copied this sentence from Menander, Φθειρουσιν ηθη χρησθ' ομιλιαι κακαι, which
are the very words of our author.—Evil commu-
nications corrupt good manners. 1 Cor. 15. 33.
2 Facile omnes cum valemus ægrotis consilia
damus. Ter.

VOL. XVI.

But who postpone the bliss till past their prime,
Must pay large interest for neglect of time.

Page 84.

### MATERNAL AFFECTION.

Why for her children should the wife express
More fond affection, and the husband less?
The reason, if I rightly judge, is this,
She knows them her's, and he but thinks them his.

Page 236.

### NURSE MYRTILA.

Rouse but old Myrtila, the nurse, and give her
The least occasion, and she'll talk for ever:
With far less art and ease you may restrain
The sounding cymbals of Dodona's fane,
(Which, if but touch'd, the holy augur hears
The live-long day remurmur'd in his ears)
Than still this chattering crone who with her tales
Torments the weary night as soon as evening fails.

The learned reader will find the original of this fragment in Dr. Bentley's Emendations of Menander, page 16, printed at Cambridge, in the year 1713.

### POWER OF MUSIC.

Music has charms the savage breast to move,
And songs are Syrens that invite to love.

Page 84.

### THE STRICTLY-RIGHTEOUS FIELD.

Sure never swain with anxious labour till'd
A more religious, or a juster field:
Abundant tribute to the gods it pays
In ivy, flowers, and honorary bays:
If I sow barely, to a single grain,
It justly brings the quantity again.

Page 32.

### LOVE OMNIPOTENT.

'Gainst love's unerring arts there's no defence,
They wound the blockhead, and the man of sense.

Page 14.

### KNOW OTHERS.

"Know thou thyself," was always said of old,
A maxim not quite absolute I hold;
It had been better far, you must allow,
And more our interest, "Other men to know,"

Page 86.

## IGNIS FATUUS[1]:

GRAMINEOS infra campos, penetralia Floræ
Purpureis opibus redolentia, fumeus aër
Caligat; varios hîc tellus ubere partu
Flammarum ponit fœtus, et pinguia venis
Nutrimenta fovet, genitalia semina rerum.
Quæ postquam matris dudum sopita silenti
Incubûere sinu, quoties Titanius ardor
Sævit in æstivas luces, patefacta sub auras
Reddit humus; pars æthereâ regione viarum
Expatiatur ovans; levitas sua sufficit alas.
Pars ignava tenet terræ confinia, sese
Insinuans inter nocturnos undique rores.
Et jam, seu calidis pugnent humentia, vires
Sive bitumineæ rapiant incendia, flamma
Exilit, et vivos imitatur ludicra motus.
  Aspice! cùm rebus nox abstulit atra colorem,
Fusus ad irriguas ripas, micat igneus humor,
Mobilitate vigens, et eundo flumina verrit
Summa levis, liquidisque sororibus oscula libat.
  Jam varios meditans excursus ocyus Euro
Ardet abire fugâ per inane volatile lumen.
Stare loco nescit, saliensque per omnia puncto
Temporis itque reditque vagans sine corpore vita.
  Hinc sæpe, obscœnos iterat dum noctua cantus,
Nigrantes inter tenebras prope limina Divûm
Tristibus insultat lux importuna sepulchris.
Ægros huc gressus si fortè advertat anus quæ,
Igneolos cernit lemures, simulachraque mille
Horret inops animi, stolidi figmenta timoris.
Jamque adeo latè fabellam spargit anilem
Fama volans, trepidat mentes ignobile vulgus.
Scilicet hîc animæ tenues, defunctaque vitâ
Corpora, subsiliunt obscurâ nocte per umbram.
Seu Libitina fero visu sua regna pererrat,
Et tumulos numerans lugubres, horrida quassat
Funebres tædas & formidabile lumen.
  Quin & mille dolos volvens sub pectore flamma
Avia pervolitat, quam cæcâ nocte viator
Deprensus sectatur ovans; quid cogitet ignis
Nescius heu! Fax ante volans per opaca locorum
Errabunda regit vestigia, perfida tandem
Deferit immersum stagno squalente colonum
Eructantem iras, hirsutaque colla madentem.
  Talem flumineæ quondam risêre sorores
Pana Deum Arcadiæ, taciti Ladonis ad amnem;
Scilicet hic nympham captans juvenile micantem,
Oscula dum peteret, mediis effusus in undis
Virgine pro tenerâ fœdam complectitur ulvam.
  Ast ubi jam Phœbi radiis Aurora rubescit
Pulchrior, & stellis acies obtusa videtur,
Purpureo superata die, caput abdit imago,
Et procul in tenues it vita minutula ventos.
Haud secus ignaros duxit Cartesius olim
Philosophos, rapiens deserta per ardua cœcæ
Naturæ; demum Newtonus luce coruscans
Eoâ, mundique sagax arcana tueri,
Materiam pepulit subtilem, egitque sub umbras.
  Cantabr. in comitiis prioribus, 1730-1.

[1] This elegant copy of verses was written, as
an academical exercise, by my worthy friend,
and former tutor, the rev. Richard Oakley,
M. A. late fellow of Jesus College, Cambridge.

## WILL WITH A WISP.

DEEP in the silence of the grassy plains,
Where Flora, drest in purple beauty reigns,
Ambrosial queen of flowerets sweet and fair;
Impregnated with vapours the thick air
Grows stagnant: here at frequent births trans-
Profuse, the living particles of fire, [pire,
Which, from her lap, the Earth prolific flings,
The genial seeds, and origin of things:
These, long time ripening, oft as Titan's ray
Bright-burning blazes on the summer's day,
At length, emerging from the soil, repair,
And sport, capricious, in the fields of air:
Some, lightly mounting in th' etherial sky,
Expatiate freely, and in meteors fly: [sue,
Some, near the ground their vagrant course pur-
And blend delusion with the nightly dew:
For whether from the strife of moist and dry,
Or from bitumen fiery sparkles fly,
A sudden flame the mingling vapours give,
Which seems, to mortal eyes, to move and live.
Lo! when the beauteous landscape fades in night,
In some irriguous valley, glimmering bright,
The false flame dances, or with quivering gleam,
Skims on the bosom of the winding stream,
Sports with the Naiads, and in wanton play,
Kisses the sisters of the watery way.
Now through the void the vain excursive light,
Fleet as the wind, precipitates its flight,
Unfix'd and volatile with instant bound
'Tis here, 'tis there, and roves the country round.
Oft as the darkling owl renews her song,
In lone church-yards it gleams, the mournful
  graves among,
Should some old hag slow hobbling hither tend,
She spies, no doubt, the fiery-flaming fiend;
To her mind's eye a thousand ghosts appear,
The foolish apparitions of her fear.
Then all around tremendous tales are spread,
And the weak vulgar stand appall'd with dread;
For here they deem, depriv'd the golden light,
That spirits wander in the gloom of night;
Or that pale Proserpine, fierce-visag'd, comes
To number all the melancholy tombs,
And dreadful, as she frowns, the deadly dame
Shakes her dire torches tipt with livid flame.
  Oft o'er the dreary waste, or boundless plain,
This bright deception leads the nightly swain;
Thoughtless of harm he plods the forest o'er,
Where never wanderer bent his way before,
At length, deluded by the fickle fire,
He sinks absorpt in bogs, and flounces in the
  mire.
  Thus once, where Ladon rolls his silent flood,
Laugh'd the fair Naiads at th' Arcadian god;
A blooming nymph he saw, admir'd, carest,
And when he strove to clasp her to his breast,
Plung'd in the waves among the watery weeds
He lost the virgin, and embrac'd the reeds.
  But when the rosy morn her blush displays,
And all the splendour of the stars decays,
The light fantastic phantoms cease to glare,
Lost in the day, and flit in empty air.
  Descartes thus, great Nature's wandering
Fallacious led philosophy aside, [guide,
'Till Newton rose, in orient beauty bright, [light,
He rose, and brought the world's dark laws to
Then subtile matter saw, and vanished at his
  sight.

## DATUR MUNDORUM PLURALITAS.

### BY CHRISTOPHER SMART, M. A.

Unde labor novus hic menti? Quæ cura quie-
Sollicitat, rapiensque extra confinia terræ, [tam
Cœlestes sine more jubet volitare per ignes?
Scilicet impatiens angusto hoc orbe teneri,
Fontenelle, tuos audax imitarier ausus
Gestio, & insolitas spirant præcordia flammas.

Fallor, an ipse venit? Delapsus ab æthere
    summo
Pegason urget eques, laterique flagellifer instat:
Me vocat; & duris desiste laboribus, inquit,
" Me duce, carpe viam facilem, tibi singula clarè
Expediam, tibi cernere erit, quos sidera nôrunt,
Indigenas, cultusque virûm, moresque docebo."
Nec mora, pennipedem conscendo jussus, ovans-
    que    [orum
(Quanquam animus secum volvens exempla pri-
Bellerophonteæ pallet dispendia famæ)
Post equitem sedeo, liquidumque per aëra labor.
—Mercurium petimus primùm: dux talibus in-
" Aspicias vanæ malesana negotia gentis, [fit:
Quam mens destituit Titane exusta propinquo.
Stramineis viden'? Hic velatus tempora sertis
Emicat, & solos reges crepat atque tetrarchas.
Ille suam carbone Chloen depingit amator
Infelix, ægram rudia indigestaque mentem
Carmina demulcent, indoctaque tibia musas.
En! sedet incomptus crines barbataque menta
Astrologus, nova qui venatur sidera, solus
Semper in obscuro penetrali; multaque muros
Linea nigrantes, & multa triangula pingunt.
Ecce! sed interea curru flammante propinquat
Titan.—Clamo, O me! gelidâ sub rupe, sub
    umbâ
Siste precor: tantos nequeo perferre calores."


Pegason inde tuo genius felicior astro
Appulit, alma Venus. Spirant quam molliter
    auræ!
Ridet ager, frugum facilis, lascivaque florum
Nutrix; non Eûri ruit hic per dulcia Tempe
Vis fera, non Boreæ: sed blandior aura Favonî,
Lenis agens tremulo nutantes vertice sylvas,
Usque fovet teneros, quos usque resuscitat, ig-
Hic lætis animata sonis saltatio vivit: [nes.
Hic jam voce ciet cantum, jam pectine, dulces
Musica docta modos: pulchræ longo ordine
    nymphæ
Cestivas ducunt choreas, dilecta juventus
Fertatim stipant comites: latè halat amomo
Omne nemus, varioque æterni veris odore:
Cura procul: circumvolitant risusque jocique:
Atque amor est, quodcunque vides. Venus ipsa
    volentes
Imperio regit indigenas, hic innuba Phœbe,
Innuba Pallas amet, cupiant servire Catones.

## A VOYAGE TO THE PLANETS.

Whence this new ardor? whence this rage to
    trace    [space?
New worlds that roll through ether's boundless
Snatch'd from the confines of this orb of clay,
With emulation fir'd I wing my way,
Where Fontenelle first saw the planets roll,
And all the god tumultuous shakes my soul.
  Yes, yes, he comes! and through the sun-
    bright skies    [cries.
Drives foaming Pegasus; " Cease, cease," he
" All meaner tasks; 'tis thine with me to soar,
And visit kingdoms unexplor'd before;
While I succinctly show each various race,
The manners, and the genius of the place."
I (though my mind with lively horrour fraught,
Thinks on Bellerophon, and dreads the thought)
Mount quick behind; the winged courser flies,
And cleaves the azure of the liquid skies.
  First Mercury, swift circling round the Sun,
We reach, when thus my friendly guide begun:
" Mark well the genius of this fiery place,
The wild amusements of the brainsick race,
Whose minds the beams of Titan, too intense,
Affect with frenzy, and distract the sense.
A monarch here gives subject princes law
A mighty monarch, with a crown of straw.
Here the lone lover, on the cieling bare,
With charcoal paints his Chloe heav'nly fair;
In sadly soothing strain rude notes he sings,
Or grates harsh discord from the jarring strings.
Lo; an astrologer, with filth besmear'd,
Rough and neglected, with a length of beard;
Pores round his cell for undiscover'd stars,
And decks the wall with triangles and squares.
Lo!—But the radiant car of Phœbus nigh
Glows with red ardour, and inflames the sky—
Oh! waft me, hide me in some cool retreat;
I droop, I sicken with the fervent heat,"
  Thence to that milder orb we wing our way,
Where Venus governs with an easy sway.
Soft breathes the air; fair Flora paints the ground,
And fruitful Ceres deals her gifts around.
This blissful Tempe no rough blasts molest;
Of blustering Boreas, or the baleful east;
But gentle Zephyrs o'er the woodlands stray,
Court the tall trees, and round the branches play,
Their genial gales dispensing as they flow,
To fan those passions which they teach to glow.
Here the gay youth in measur'd steps advance,
While sprightly music animates the dance;
Here the soft sounds of melody inspire
Sighs to the song, and languors to the lyre:
Fair nymphs and amorous swains, a lovely band,
Blend in the dance, light-bounding hand in
    hand.
From every grove the buxom Zephyrs bring
The rich ambrosia of eternal spring.
Care dwells not here, their pleasures to destroy,
But laughter, jest, and universal joy:
All, all is love; for Venus reigns confest
The sole sultana of each captive breast:
Cold Cynthia here would Cupid's victim prove,
Or the chaste daughter of imperial Jove,
And rigid Cato be the slave of love.

Jamque datum molimur iter, sedesque beatas
Multa gemens linquo; & lugubre rubentia
    Martis
Arva, ubi sanguineæ dominantur in omnia rixæ,
Advehimur, ferro riget horrida turba, geritque
Spiculaque, gladiosque, ferosque in bella dolones.
Pro choreâ, & dulci modulamine, Pyrrhicus illis
Saltus, & horribiles placet ære ciere sonores.
Hic conjux viduata viro longo effera luctu
Flet noctum, solumque torum sterilesque Hyme-
    næos
Deplorans, lacerat crines, & pectora plangit:
Necquicquam—sponsus ni fortè appareat, hospes
Heu! brevis, in somnis, & ludicra fallat imago.
Immemor ille tori interea ruit acer in hostem:
Horrendum strepit armorum fragor undique
    campis;
Atque immortales durant in sæcula pugnæ.


Hinc Jovis immensum delati accedimus or-
Illic mille locis exercet sæva tyrannus   [bem.
Imperia in totidem servos, totidemque rebelles:
Sed brevis exercet: parat illi fata veneno
Perjurus, populosque premit novus ipse tyrannus.
Hi decies pacem figunt pretio atque refigunt:
Tum demum arma parant: longe lateque co-
    hortes
Extenduntur agris; simul æquora tota teguntur
Classibus, & ficti celebrantur utrinque triumphi.
Fœdera mox ineunt nunquam violanda: brevique
Belli iterum simulacra cient! referuntur in al-
Classes, pacificoque replentur milite campi. [tum
Filius hic patri meditatur, sponsa marito,
Servus hero insidias. Has leges scilicet illis
Imposuit natura locis, quo tempore patrem
Jupiter ipse suum solio detrusit avito.
Inde venena viris, perjuria, munera, fraudes,
Suadet opum sitis, & regnandi dira cupido.


Saturni tandem nos illætabilis ora
Accipit: ignavum pecus hic per opaca locorum
Pinguescunt de more, gravi torpentque veterno.
Vivitur in specubus: quis enim tam sedulus,
    arces
Qui struat ingentes, operosaque mænia condat?
Idem omnes stupor altus habet, sub pectore fixus.
Non studia ambitiosa Jovis, variosve labores
Mercurii, non Martis opus, non Cyprida nôrunt.
Post obitum, ut perhibent, sedes glomerantur in
    istas
Qui longam nullas vitam excoluêre per artes;
Sed Cerere & Baccho pleni, somnoque sepulti
Cunctarum duxêre æterna oblivia rerum. [rum,
Non avium auditur cantus, non murmur aqua-
Mugitusve boum, aut pecorum balatus in agris:
Nudos non decorant segetes, non gramina cam-
    pos.
Sylva, usquam si sylva, latet sub monte nivali,
Et canet viduata comis: hic noctua tantùm
Glisque habitat, bufoque & cum testudine, talpa.
Flumina dum tardè subterlabentia terras

Now through the destin'd fields of air we fly,
And leave those happy mansions with a sigh:
Thence the dire coast we reach, the dreary
    plains,    [reigns:
Where Mars, grim god, and bloody Discord
The host in arms embattled sternly stands,
The sword, the dart, the dagger in their hands.
Here no fair nymphs to silver sounds advance,
But buskin'd heroes form the Pyrrhic dance.
And brazen trumpets, terrible from far,
With martial music fire the soul to war.
Here mourns the lovely bride her husband fled,
The sterile nuptials, the deserted bed,
Sighs the long nights, and, frantic with despair,
Beats her soft breast, and rends her flowing hair:
In vain she sighs, in vain dissolves in tears—
In sleep, perchance, the warrior lord appears,
A fleeting form that glides before her sight,
A momentary vision of the night.
Mean while, regardless of her tender woe,
The hardy husband rushes on the foe:
Harsh sounds of war through regions distant rage,
And fights immortal last from age to age.
  Hence through the boundless void we nimbly
    move,
And reach the wide-extended plains of Jove.
Here the stern tyrant sways an iron rod;
A thousand vassals tremble at his nod.
How short the period of a tyrant's date!
The poisonous phial speeds the work of fate:
Scarce is the proud, imperious tyrant dead,
But, lo! a second lords it in his stead.
Here peace, as common merchandize is sold,
Heav'n's first, best blessing, for pernicious gold:
War soon succeeds, the sturdy squadrons stand
Wide o'er the fields, a formidable band:
With numerous fleets they crowd the groaning
    main,
And triumph for the victories they feign:
Again in strict alliances unite,
Till Discord raise the phantom of a fight;
Again they sail; again the troops prepare
Their falchions for the mockery of war.
The son inhuman seeks his father's life,
The slave his master's, and her lord's the wife.
With vengeance thus their kindling bosoms fire,
Since Jove usurp'd the sceptre of his sire.
Hence poisons, bribes, frauds, perjuries, betray;
And thirst of gold, and avarice of sway.
  At length we land, vast fields of ether crost,
On Saturn's cold, uncomfortable coast;
In dismal gloom here drones inactive lull
The lazy hours, lethargically dull.
In caves they live; were sluggards ever known
To raise a citadel, or build a town?
The same deep stupor, through the lifeless whole,
Chills in the breast, and freezes in the soul.
These never know th' ambitious schemes of Jove,
Their breasts not fire-fraught Mercury can move,
Mars cannot spur to war, nor Venus woo to love.
Here rove those souls, 'tis said, when life departs,
Who left uncultivated useful arts;
But stupify'd with plenty and repose,
Dreamt out long life in one continued doze!
No feather'd songsters, with sweet-warbled
Attune to melting melody the plains,    [strains
No flocks, no herds here feed in pastures wide,
No fountains musically-murmuring glide;
Th' ungenial waste no tender herbage yields,
No harvests wave luxuriant in the fields.

Pigram undam volvunt, & sola papavera pascunt:
Quorum lentus odor, lethæaque pocula somnos
Suadent perpentus, circumfusæque tenebræ.

Horrendo visu obstupui: quin Pegason ipsum
Defecêre animi; sensit dux, terque flagello
Insonuit clarùm, terque alta voce morantem
Increpuit: secat ille cito pede lævia campi
Ætherei, terræque secundâ allabitur aurâ.

Cantabr. in Comitiis prioribus, 1740-1.

## MATERIES GAUDET VI INERTIÆ.
### BY CHRISTOPHER SMART, M. A.

VERVECUM in patria, quà latè Belgica squalent
Arva inarata, palus horrenda voragine crebrâ
Ante oculos jacet; haud illic impune viator,
Per tenebras iter instituat; tremit undique tellus
Sub pedibus malefida, vapores undique densos
Sudat humus,nebulisque amicitur tristibus herba.

Huc fato infelix si quando agiteris iniquo,
Et tutò in medium liceat penetrare, videbis
Attonitus, nigrâ de nube emergere templum,
Templum ingens, immane, altum penetrale
Stuporis.
Plumbea stat turris, plumbum sinuatur in arcus,
Et solido limosa tument fundamina plumbo.
Hanc pia Materies Divo ædem extruxit inerti,
Stultitiæ impulsu—quid enim? Lethargica sem-
per
Sponte suâ nihil aggreditur, dormitat in horas,
Et, sine vi, nullo gaudet Dea languida motu.
Hìc ea monstra habitant, quæ olim sub lumi-
nis auras
Materies peperit somno patre, lividus iste
Zoilus, & Bavio non impar Mævius; audax
Spinoza, & Pyrrho, cumque Hobbesio Epicurus.
Ast omnes valeat quæ musa referre! frequentes
Usque adeo videas hebetes properare?—nec
adfert
Quidquam opis Anglorum doctæ vicinia gentis.
Sic quondam, ut perhibent, stupuit Bæotica tel-
Vicinâ licet Antycirâ, nihil inde salutis, [lus
Nil tulit hellebori Zephyrus, cum sæpe per
æquor
Felicem ad Lesbon levibus volitaverit alis,
Indigenæ mellita ferens suspiria Floræ.

Porticus illa vides? Gothicis suffulta columnis,
Templi aditus, quàm laxa patet! custodia qualis
Ante fores! quatuor formæ sua tollere miris
Ora modis! en! torva tuens stat limine in ipso,
Personam Logices induta, Sophistica, denis
Cincta Categoriis; matrem quæ maxima natu
Filia Materiem agnoscit—quantum instar in
ipsâ est!

The woods, if woods there be, lie leafless, low
Beneath bleak mountains of eternal snow.
Dull animals inhabit this abode,
The owl, mole, dormouse, tortoise, and the toad.
Dull rivers roll within their channels deep,
And only feed the poppy as they creep: [vite
Whose stagnant fumes, and dozing draughts in-
Perpetual slumbers in perpetual night.
Aghast I stood, the drowsy vapours lull
My soul in gloom, ev'n Pegasus grew dull.
My guide observ'd, and thrice he urg'd his speed,
Thrice the loud lash resounded from the steed,
Fir'd at the strokes, he flies with slacken'd rein
Swift o'er the level of the liquid plain,
Glides with the gentle gale, and lights on earth
again.

## THE TEMPLE OF DULNESS.

DEEP in the bosom of Batavian plains,
Where wethers fatten, and where dulness
reigns,
Full many a fen infests the putrid shore,
And many a gulph the melancholy moor.
Let not the stranger in these regions stay,
Dark is the sky and perilous the way;
Beneath his steps the quivering turfs resound,
Dense fogs exhale, and dwell upon the ground.
Here should you rove, by Fate's severe com-
mand,
You'll see, within the centre of the land,
The fane of Dulness, of prodigious size,
Emerging from a sable cloud arise.
A leaden tower upheaves its heavy head,
Large leaden arches press the slimy bed,
The soft soil swells beneath the load of lead,
Old Matter here erected this abode,
At Folly's impulse, to the slothful god.
Here the majestic drone delights to stay,
Slumbering the dull, inactive hours away;
Here still, unless by foreign force imprest,
She holds the sceptre of eternal rest.
Their habitation here those monsters keep,
Whom Matter father'd on the god of Sleep:
Here Zoilus, with cankering envy pale,
Here Mævius bids his brother Bavius, hail;
Bold atheist leaders head their senseless mobs,
Spinoza, Pyro, Epicurus, Hobbes.
How can the Muse recount the numerous crew
Of frequent dunces crowding on the view?
Nor can learn'd Albion's sun that burns so bright,
Illuminate the realms involv'd in night.
Bœotia thus remain'd, in days of yore,
Senseless and stupid, tho' the neighbouring shore
Afforded salutary hellebore:
No cure exhal'd from Zephyr's buxom breeze,
That gently brush'd the bosom of the seas,
As oft to Lesbian fields he wing'd his way,
Fanning fair Flora, and in airy play
Breath'd balmy sighs, that melt the soul away.
Behold that portico! how vast, how wide!
The pillars Gothic, wrought with barbarous pride:
Four monstrous shapes before the portal wait,
Of horrid aspect, centries to the gate:
Lo! in the entrance, with disdainful eye,
In Logick's dark disguise, stands Sophistry:
Her very front would common sense confound,
Encompass'd with ten categories round:

Grande caput, tenues oculi, cutis arida produnt
Fallacem : rete una manus tenet, altera fustem.
Vestis arachneis sordet circumdata telis,
Queis gaudet labyrinthæos Dea callida nodos.
Aspicias jam funereo gradientem incessu—
Quàm lentè cœlo Saturni volvitur astrum :
Quàm lentè saltaverunt post Orphea montes:
Quàm lentè, Oxonii, solennis pondera cænæ
Gestant tergeminorum abdomina bedellorum.

She from Old Matter, the great mother came,
By birth the eldest—and how like the dame !
Her shrivel'd skin, small eyes, enormous pate,
Denote her shrewd, and subtle in debate :
This hand a net, and that sustains a club,
T'entangle her antagonist, or drub.
The spider's toils, all o'er her garment spread,
Imply the mazy errours of her head.
Behold her marching with funereal pace,
Slow as old Saturn through prodigious space,
Slow as the mighty mountains mov'd along,
When Orpheus rais'd the lyre-attended song :
Slow as at Oxford, on some gaudy day,
Fat beadles, in magnificent array,
With big round bellies bear the ponderous treat
And heavily lag on, with the vast load of meat.

Proxima deinde tenet loca sorte insana Ma-
   thesis,         [capillos,
Nuda pedes, chlamydem discincta, incompta
Immemor externi, punctoque innixa reclinat.
Ante pedes vario insriptam diagrammate arenam
Cernas, rectis curva, atque intertexta rotunda
Schemata quadratis—queis scilicet abdita rerum
Pandere se jactat solam, doctasque sorores
Fastidit, propriæque nihil non arrogat arti.
Illam olim, duce Neutono, dum tendit ad astra,
Ætheriasque domos superûm, indignata volan-
   tem           [scens
Turba mathematicûm retrahit, pœnasque repo-
Detinet in terris, nugisque exercet ineptis.

Next her, mad Mathesis; her feet all bare,
Ungirt, untrimm'd, with loose neglected hair:
No foreign object can her thoughts disjoint;
Reclin'd she sits, and ponders o'er a point
Before her, lo ! inscrib'd upon the ground
Strange diagrams th' astonish'd sight confound,
Right lines and curves, with figures square and
   round.
With these the monster, arrogant and vain,
Boasts that she can all mysteries explain,
And treats the sacred sisters with disdain,
She, when great Newton sought his kindred skies,
Sprung high in air, and strove with him to rise,
In vain—the mathematic mob restrains
Her flight, indignant, and on Earth detains ;
E'er since she dwells intent on useless schemes,
Unmeaning problems, and deliberate dreams.

Tertia Microphile, proles furtiva parentis
Divinæ ! produxit enim commixta furenti
Diva viro Physice—muscas & papiliones
Lustrat inexpletùm, collumque & tempora rident
Floribus, & fungis, totàque propagine veris.
Rara oculis nugarum avidis animalia quærit
Omne genus, seu serpit humi, seu ludit in undis,
Seu volitans tremulis liquidum secat aëra pennis.
O ! ubi littoribus nostris felicior aura
Polypon appulerit, quanto cava templa Stuporis
Mugitu concussa trement, reboabit & ingens
Pulsa palus ! Plausu excipiet Dea blanda secundo
Microphile ante omnes; jam non crocodilon ado-
   rat !         [ardet,
Non bombyx, chonchæve juvant : sed Polypon
Solum Polypon ardet,—& ecce ! faceta feraci
Falce novos creat assiduè, pascitque creatos,
Ah ! modo dilectis pascit nova gaudia muscis.

Microphile is station'd next in place,
The spurious issue of celestial race ;
From heavenly Physice she took her birth,
Her sire a madman of the sons of Earth ;
On flies she pores with keen, unwearied sight,
And moths and butterflies, her dear delight;
Around her neck hang dangling on a string
The fungous tribe, with all the flowers of spring,
With greedy eyes she'll search the world to find
Insects and reptiles rare of every kind ;
Whether along the lap of Earth they stray,
Or nimbly sportive in the waters play,
Or through the light expanse of ether fly,
And on light wing float wavering in the sky.
Ye gales, that gently breathe upon our shore,
O ! let the polypus be wafted o'er ;
How will the hollow dome of Dulness ring ?
With what loud joy receive the wonderous thing ?
Applause will rend the skies, and all around
The quivering quagmires bellow back the sound ?
How will Microphile her joy attest,
And glow with warmer raptures than the rest ?
No longer shall the crocodile excel,
Nor weaving worm, nor variegated shell ;
The polypus shall novelties inspire,
The polypus, her only fond desire.
Lo ! by the wounds of her creating knife,
New polypusses wriggle into life,
Fast as the reptiles rise, she feeds with store
Of once rare flies, but now esteem'd no more.

Quartam Materies peperit conjuncta Stupori,
Nomen Atheia illi, monstrum cui lumen ademp-
   tum,
Atque aures; cui sensus abest, sed mille trisulcæ
Ore micant linguæ, refugas quibus inficit auras.

The fourth dire shape from mother Matter
Dulness her sire, and Atheism her name ; [came,
In her no glimpse of sacred Sense appears,
Depriv'd of eyes, and destitute of ears :
And yet she brandishes a thousand tongues,
And blasts the world with air-infecting lungs.

Hanc stupor ipse parens odit, vicina nefandos
Horret sylva sonos, neque surda repercutit Echo.
Mendacem natura redarguit ipsa, Deumque
Et cœlum, & terræ, veraciaque Astra fatentur.
Se simul agglomerans surgit chorus omnis aqua-
    rum,
Et puro sublimè sonat grave fulmen olympo.


Fonte ortus Lethæo, ipsus ad ostia templi,
Ire soporifero tendit cum murmure rivus,
Huc potum Stolidos Deus evocat agmine magno:
Crebri adsunt, largisque sitim restinguere gau-
    dent             [stupendo.
Haustibus, atque iterant calices, certantque
"Me, me etiam," clamo, occurrens;—sed vellicat
    aurem
Calliope, nocuasque vetat contingere lymphas

---

Curs'd by her sire, her very words are wounds,
No grove re-echoes the detested sounds.
Whate'er she speaks all nature proves a lye,
Earth, Heaven, and stars proclaim a Deity :
The congregated waves in mountains driven
Roar in grand chorus to the lord of Heaven ;
Through skies serene the pealing thunders roll,
Loudly pronounce the god, and shake the
    sounding pole.
A river, murmuring from Lethæan source,
Full to the fane directs its sleepy course ;
The Power of Dulness, leaning on the brink,
Here calls the multitude of fools to drink.
Swarming they crowd to stupify the skull,
With frequent cups contending to be dull.
"Me, let me taste the sacred stream," (I cry'd),
With out-stretch'd arm—the Muse my boon
    deny'd,
And sav'd me from the sense-intoxicating tide.

---

## MUTUA OSCITATIONUM PROPAGA-
## TIO SOLVI POTEST MECHANICE
### BY CHRISTOPHER SMART, M. A.

Momus, scurra procax superûm, quo tempora
    Pallas
Exiluit cerebro Jovis, est pro more jocatus
Nescio quid stultum de partu: excanduit irâ
Jupiter, asper, acerba tuens; "et tu quoque,
    dixit,
Garrule, concipies, fœtumque ex ore profundes:"
Haud mora, jamque supinus in aulâ extenditur
    ingens
Derisor; dubiâ velantur lumina nocte ;
Stertit hians immane;—e naso Gallica clangunt
Classica, Germanique simul sermonis amaror,


Edita vix tandem est monstrum Polychasmia,
    proles
Tanto digna parente, aviæque simillima Nocti.
Illa oculos tentat nequicquam aperire, veterno
Torpida, &`horrendo vultum distorta cachinno.
Æmulus hanc Jovis aspiciens, qui fictile vulgus
Fecerat infelix, imitarier arte Prometheus
Audet—nec flammis opus est cœlestibus: auræ
Tres Stygiæ flatus, nigræ tria pocula Lethes
Miscet, & innuptæ suspiria longa puellæ,
His adipem suis & guttur conjungit aselli,
Tensaque cum gemitu somnisque sequacibus ora.
Sic etiam in terris dea, quæ mortalibus ægris
Ferret opem, inque hebetes dominarier apta,
    creata est.
Nonne vides, ut præcipiti petit oppida cursu
Rustica plebs, stipatque forum ? sublime tribunal
Armigerique equitesque premunt, de more parati
Justitiæ lances proferre fideliter æquas,
Grande capillitium induti, frontemque minacem,
Non temerè attoniti caupones, turbaque furum
Aufugiunt, gravidæque timent trucia ora puellæ.
At mox fida comes Polychasmia, matutinis
Quæ se miscuerat poc'lis Cerealibus, ipsum
Judicus in cerebrum scandit—jamque unus &
Cœperunt longas in hiatum ducere voces : [alter
Donec per cunctos dea jam solenne, profundum
Sparserit Hum—nutant taciti, tum brachia
    magno
Extendunt nisu, patulis & faucibus hiscunt.

---

### MECHANICAL SOLUTION OF THE
## PROPAGATION OF YAWNING.

When Pallas issued from the brain of Jove,
Momus, the mimic of the gods above,
In his mock mood impertinently spoke,
About the birth, some low, ridiculous joke :
Jove, sternly frowning, glow'd with vengeful ire,
And thus indignant said th' almighty sire;
"Loquacious slave, that laugh'st without a cause,
Thou shalt conceive, and bring forth at thy jaws."
He spoke—stretch'd in the hall the mimic lies,
Supinely dull, thick vapours dim his eyes :
And as his jaws a horrid-chasm disclose,
The Gallic trumpet sounded from his nose ;
Harsh was the strain, and horrible to hear,
Like German jargon grating on the ear.
At length was Polychasmia brought to light,
Like her strange sire, and grandmother, Old
    Night.
Her eyes to open oft in vain she try'd,
Lock'd were the lids, her mouth distended wide.
Her when Prometheus happen'd to survey
(Rival of Jove, that made mankind of clay)
He dar'd to emulate the wonderous frame,
Nor sought assistance from celestial flame.
To three Lethæan cups he learn'd to mix
Deep sighs of virgins, with three blasts from Styx,
The bray of asses, with the grunt of boar,
The sleep-preceding groan, and hideous snore.
Thus took the goddess her mirac'lous birth,
Helpful to all the muzzy sons of Earth.
Behold! the motley multitude from far
Haste to the town, and crowd the clam'rous bar.
The prest bench groans with many a squire and
    knight,
Who weigh out justice, and distribute right:
Severe they seem, and formidably big,
With awful aspect and tremendous wig.
The pale delinquent pays averse his fine,
And the fat landlord trembles for his sign.
Poor, pilfering villains skulk aloof dismay'd,
And conscious terrours seize the pregnant maid.
Soon Polychasmia, who was always near,
Full fraught with morning cups of humming beer,
Steals to his worship's brain; thence quickly ran
Prodigious yawnings, catch'd from man to man :

Intereà legum caupones jurgia miscent,
Queis nil rhetoricè est, nisi copia major hiandi :
Vocibus ambiguis certant, nugasque strophasque
Alternis jaculantur, & irascuntur amicè,
Donantque accipiumtque stuporis missile plum-
     bum.
   Vos, Fanatica turba, nequit pia Musa tacere.
Majoremne aliunde potest diducere rictum ?
Ascendit gravis Orator, miseràque loquelâ
Expromit thesin ; in partes quam deinde minutas
Distrahit, ut connectat, & explicat obscurando :
Spargitur hue! pigris verborum somnus ab alis,
Grex circùm gemit, & plausum declarat hiando.


Nec vos, qui falsò matrem jactatis Hygeian,
Patremque Hippocratem,taceam—Polychasmia,
     vestros
Agnosco natos : tumidas sine pondere voces
In vulgum eructant ; emuncto quisque bacillum
Applicat auratum naso, graviterque facetus
Totum se in vultum cogit,medicamina pandens—
Rusticus haurit amara, atque insanabile dormit;
Nec sensus revocare queant fomenta, nec herbæ,
Non ars, non miræ magicus sonus Abracadabræ.


Ante alios summa es, Polychasmia, cura so-
     phistæ :
Ille Tui cæcas vires, causamque latentem
Sedulus exquirit—quo scilicet impete fauces
Invitæ disjunguntur ; quo vortice aquosæ
Particulæ fluitent, comitesque ut fulminis im-
     bres,
Cum strepitu erumpant; ut deinde vaporet
     ocellos
Materies subtilis ; ut in cutis insinuet se
Retia ; tum, si forte datur contingere nervos
Concordes, cunctorum ora expanduntur hiulca.
Sic ubi, Phœbe pater, sumis chelyn, harmoniam-
     que
Abstrusam in chordis simul elicis, altera, siquam
Æqualis tenor aptavit, tremit æmula cantûs,
Memnoniamque imitata lyram sine pollicis ictu
Divinum resonat proprio modulamine carmen.
   Me quoque, mene tuum tetigisti, ingrata,
     poetam ?
Hei mihi ! totus hio tibi jam stupefactus, in ipso
Parnasso captus longè longèque remotas
Prospecto Musas, sitioque, ut Tantalus alter,
Castalias situs inter aquas, inhiantis ab ore
Nectarei fugiunt latices—hos Popius urnâ
Excipit undanti, & fontem sibe vendicat omnem.


Haud aliter Socium esuriens Sizator edacem
Dum videt, appositusque cibus frustratur hian-
     tem,
Dentibus infrendens nequicquam lumine torvo
Sæpius exprobrat ; nequicquam brachia tendit
Sedulis officiosa, dapes removere paratus.
Olli nunquam exempta fames, quin frusta su-
     prema
Devoret, & peritura immani ingurgitet ore :
Tum demum jubet auferri ; nudata capaci
Ossa sonant, lugubre sonant catino.


Silent they nod, and with laborious strain
Stretch out their arms, then listless yawn again :
For all the flowers of rhetoric they can boast,
Amidst their wranglings, is to gape the most ;
Ambiguous quirks, and friendly wrath they vent,
And give and take the leaden argument.
   Ye too, Fanatics, never shall escape
The faithful Muse ; for who so widely gape ?
Mounted on high, with serious care perplext,
The miserable preacher takes his text ;
Then into parts minute, with wondrous pains,
Divides, connects, disjoints, obscures, explains :
While from his lips lean periods lingering creep,
And not one meaning interrupts their sleep,
The drowsy hearers stretch their weary jaws,
Add groan to groan, and yawn a loud applause.
   The quacks of physic next provoke my ire,
Who falsely boast Hippocrates their sire :
Goddess ! thy sons I ken—verbose and loud,
They feed with windy puffs the gaping crowd.
With look important, critical, and vain,
Each to his nose applies the gilded cane ;
Each as he nods, and ponders o'er the case,
Gravely collects himself into his face,
Explains his med'cines—which the rustic buys,
Drinks the dire draught, and of the doctor dies ;
No pills, no potions can to life restore ;
Abracadabra, necromantic power !
Can charm, and conjure up from death no more.
   The Sophs, great goddess, are thy darling
     care,
Who hunt out questions intricately rare ;
Explore what secret spring, what hidden cause,
Distends with hideous chasm th' unwilling jaws,
How watery particles with wonderous power
Burst into sound, like thunder with a shower :
How subtile matter, exquisitely thin,
Pervades the curious net-work of the skin,
Affects th' accordant nerves—all eyes are
     drown'd
In drowsy vapours, and the yawn goes round.
When Phœbus thus his flying fingers flings
Across the chords, and sweeps the quiverings
If e'er a lyre at unison remain,     [strings ;
Trembling it swells, and emulates the strain :
Thus Memnon's harp, in ancient times renown'd,
Express'd, untouch'd, sweet-modulated sound.
   But oh ! ungrateful ! to thy own true bard,
Is this, O goddess ! this my just reward ?
Thy drowsy dews upon my head distil,
Just at the entrance of th' Aonian hill ;
Listless I yawn, unactive, and supine,
And at vast distance view the sacred Nine :
Wishful I view Castalia's streams, accurst,
Like Tantalus, with unextinguish'd thirst ;
The waters fly my lips, my claim disown—
Pope drinks them deeply, they are all his own.
   Thus the lank Sizar views, with gaze aghast,
The harpy tutor at his noon's repast ;
In vain his teeth he grinds—oft checks a sigh,
And darts a silent censure from his eye :
Now he prepares, officious, to convey
The lessening relics of the meal away—
In vain, no morsel 'scapes the greedy jaw,
All. all is gorg'd in magisterial maw ;
Till at the last observant of his word,
The lamentable waiter clears the board,
And inly-murmuring miserably groans,
To see the empty dish, and hear the rattling
     bones.

# A DESCRIPTION OF MAY,

FROM GAWIN DOUGLAS, BISHOP OF DUNKELD.

Hic ver purpureum; varios hoc flumina circum
Fundit humus flores.                    VIRG.

### TO WILLIAM DIXON, ESQ.

WHILE at your Loversal, secure retreat,
Far from the vain, the busy, and the great,
Retirement's calm, yet useful arts you know,
Bid buildings rise, and future navies grow ;
Or, by the sacred thirst of learning led,
Converse familiar with th' illustrious dead,
Worthies of old, who life by arts refin'd,
Taught wholesome laws, and humaniz'd man-
    kind :
Can my friend listen to this flowery lay,
Where splendid Douglas paints the blooming
    May ?
If aught these lines thy candid ear engage,
The Muse shall learn to moralise the page,
Give modest merit the reward that's due,
And place the interests of mankind in view,
Form tender minds by virtue's better lore,
And teach old infidels to doubt no more.
To thee this verse belongs ; and may it prove
An earnest of my gratitude and love.

----

### THE PREFACE.

THE following poem of Gawin Douglas is prefixed to the XIIth book of his translation of Virgil's Æneis, and entitled, " Ane singular lernit
Proloug of the discription of May ;" and is now
publish'd, as a proof, that the muses had visited
Great Britain, and the flowers of poetry began
to bloom 250 years ago. It may also serve as an
instance, that the lowland Scotch language and
the English, at that time were nearly the same.
Chaucer and Douglas may be look'd upon as the
two bright stars that illumined England and
Scotland, after a dark interval of dulness, a long
night of ignorance and superstition, and foretold
the return of day, and the revival of learning.
    This description of May is extremely pictu-
resque and elegant, and esteemed to be one of
the most splendid descriptions of that month
that has appeared in print ; which is all the apology I shall make for having given it a more
modern dress.
    The old Scotch is printed exactly after the
Edinburgh edition, which was published in the
year 1710.

----

### SOME ACCOUNT OF GAWIN DOUG-
LAS.

GAWIN DOUGLAS, bishop of Dunkeld, was nobly
descended, being a son of the illustrious family

of Angus. His father was Archibald, the sixth
earl of Angus : he married Elizabeth, daughter
to Robert Boyd, (who was chancellor and one
of the governors of the kingdom of Scotland,
A. D. 1468) by whom he had issue four sons,
George, William, Gawin, and Archibald. The
two eldest, with two hundred gentleman of the
name of Douglas, were killed in the battle of
Flodden.
    Our author was born the latter end of the year
1474, or the beginning of 1475. Great care was
taken of his education, and he was early instructed in the liberal arts and sciences. When he had
completed his studies in his own country, he
went abroad, that he might farther improve
himself by conversation with great and learned
men, and observations on the laws and customs
of other countries. Upon his return to Scotland,
he was advanced to be provost of the collegiate
church of St. Giles in Edinburgh, and rector of
Heriot church, some few miles distant from it.
In this station he continued several years, be-
having himself as became his holy character,
noble birth, and liberal education. After the
battle of Flodden many ecclesiastical dignities
became vacant ; among which was the abbacy
of Aberbrothock, one of the most considerable in
the kingdom. The queen mother, who was then
regent, and shortly after married to the earl of
Angus, our author's nephew, presented him to it ;
and soon after to the archbishopric of St. Andrews. But he met with so great opposition in
this affair, that neither the royal authority, nor
the influence of his noble relations, nor his own
unexceptionable merit, were able to procure him
peaceable possession : for Andrew Forman (bishop of Murray, and archbishop of Bourges in
France) by the interest he had in the court of
Rome, and the duke of Albany, obtained a bull
from the pope for that dignity, and was accordingly acknowledged as archbishop by most of the
clergy of the see. Mr. Douglas, reflecting on
the scandals which arose from such unworthy
contests, and preferring the honour of a Christian, and peaceable disposition to his temporal
interest and greatness, wholly laid aside his
pretensions to that see. But the bishopric of
Dunkeld becoming vacant, in January 1515, the
queen advanced him to it ; and afterwards, by the
intercession of Henry III. king of England,
obtained a bull in his favour from pope Leo X.
Notwithstanding his right was founded on the
royal and papal authority, yet he could not
obtain consecration for a considerable time,
because of a powerful competitor ; for Andrew
Stuart, prebendary of Craig, and brother
to the earl of Athole, had got himself nomi-
nated bishop by such of the chapter as were
present ; and his title was supported by all the
enemies of the queen and her husband the earl
of Angus, particularly the duke of Albany, who,
returning to Scotland in May 1515, was declared
regent. In the first session of parliament after
the governor's arrival, Mr. Douglas was accused,
on some groundless pretext or other, of acting
contrary to the laws of the nation, was pronounced guilty, and committed to the castle of St.
Andrews, and imprisoned upwards of a year, till
the governor was reconciled to the queen and the

earl of Angus : then he was set at liberty, received into the favour of the regent, and consecrated bishop at Glasgow. Notwithstanding, his troubles were not yet at an end ; for his old antagonist, Andrew Stuart, had possessed himself of the palace of Dunkeld, and seemed resolved to defend it against the bishop by force of arms : however, at last it was yielded up, without any bloodshed; which was very acceptable to the good bishop, who was of a gentle and merciful disposition, and always regulated himself by the excellent laws of the Christian religion.

Being at last put in peaceable possession of his office, he resolved to give himself wholly to the faithful discharge of his duty : but the interest of his country would not permit him long to satisfy his own inclinations ; for he was pitched upon to attend the duke of Albany into France, to renew the antient league between the two nations : however, he soon returned to Edinburgh, with a joyful account of the confirmation of the league ; and thence repaired to his diocese, and applied himself to the duties of his function.

But several unhappy divisions being soon after fomented in Scotland, and the bishop of Dunkeld perceiving the violent aversion which the court had conceived against the family of Angus, and the danger he was exposed to on that account, resolved to retire into England till the storm was blown over. This happened a a time when the king of England had just declared war against the Scots : which gave his enemies at home, who were the prevailing party at court, an opportunity to endeavour his ruin. A proclamation wa soon issued out against him, he was declared an enemy to his country, the revenues of his bishopric were sequestered, and all corespondence with him was forbid.

Soon after his coming to London, it pleased God to put an end to the persecutions of his enemies, by taking him to himself. Most authors agree that he died of the plague, which then raged in the city, in April 1522, about the forty-eighth year of his age. He was buried in the hospital-church of the Savoy, on the left side of the tomb-stone of Thomas Halsay, bishop of Leighlin in Ireland, In Weever's antient monuments, we find this inscription for them both. Hic jacet Tho. Halsay Leighlinen. Episcopus, in Basilica St. Petri Romæ nationis Anglicorum Pænitentiarius, summæ probitatis vir, qui hoc solum post se reliquit ; vixit, dum vixit, bene. Cui. lævus. conditur. Gawinus. Douglas Scotus. Dunkelden. Præsul. Patria. sua. exul. 1552.

Such was the fate of this great genius and good man ; for whose elogy, as a poet, I shall refer the reader to his works, which are very eloquent in his praise ; and out of several testimonies of eminent men that might be produced in his favour, shall only transcribe this passage from Hume's History of the Douglasses, p. 220.

" G. Douglas left behind him great approbation of his virtues, and love of his person, in the hearts of all good men ; for besides the nobility of his birth, the dignity and comeliness of his personage, he was learned, temperate, and of singular moderation of mind ; and in those turbulent times had always carried himself among the factions of the nobility equally, and with a mind to make peace, and not to stir up parties."

His chief works are, his translation of Virgil's Æneis,, the Palace of Honour, a Poem, Aureæ narrationes, Comœdiæ aliquot sacræ, & de rebus Scoticis Liber.

---

## GAWIN DOUGLAS

### HIS SINGULAR LERNIT PROLOUG OF THE DESCRIPTION OF MAY.

Dionea, nycht hird, and wache of day,
The sternes chasit of the heuin away,
Dame Cynthia doun rolling in the seye,
And Venus loist the bewte of hir eye,
Fleand eschamet within Cyllenius caue,
Mars umbedrew from all his grundin glaue,
Nor frawart Saturne from his mortall spere
Durst langare in the firmament appere,
Bot stal abak zound in his regioun far,
Behind the circulate warld of Jupiter;
Nyctimene effrayit of the lycht
Went under couert, for gone was the nycht ;
As fresche Aurora, to mychty Tithone spous,
Ischit of her safferon bed and euyr hous,
In crammesy clede and granit violate,
With sanguyne cape, and seluage purpurate,
Unschet the wyndois of hir large hall,
Spred all with rosis, and full of balme riall,

---

## A DESCRIPTION OF MAY.

### BY GAWIN DOUGLAS, BISHOP OF DUNKELD.

### MODERNIZED.

Venus, bright beam of night, and watch of
     day
Had chas'd the lingering stars of Heaven away,
Driven to the deep pale Cynthia from the sky,
And lost herself the beauty of her eye;
With Mercury she sought the secret shade,
And Mars withdrew, for all his burning blade ;
Nor gloomy Saturn, rolling in his sphere,
Durst longer in the firmament appear,
But vanish'd far from ken of mortals, far
Beyond great Jupiter's imperial star.
The screech-owl, startled at the dawning light,
Wing'd to her bower her solitary flight :
For fresh Aurora, Tithon's splendid spouse,
Rose from her saffron bed, and left her ivory
     house ;
Her violet robe was stain'd with crimson hue,
The cape vermilion, and the border blue ;
Her hands the windows of her hall unbarr'd,
Spread all with roses, and perfum'd with nard:

And eik the heuinly portis christallyne
Upwarpis brade, the warlde till illumyne;
The twynkling stremouris of the orient
Sched pourpour sprayngis with gold and asure
Persand the sabil barmkin nocturnall, [ment,
Bet down the skyes cloudy mantil wall;
Eous the stede, with ruby hammys rede,
Abufe the seyis liftis furth his hede,
Of culloure sore, and sume dele broune as bery,
For to alichtin and glad our emispery,
The flambe out brastin at the neiss thirlis,
So fast Phaeton ¹ with the quihip him quhirlis,
To roll Apollo his faderis goldin chare,
That schroudith all the heuynnys and the are;
Quhil schortlie with the blesand torche of day,
Abulzeit in his lemand freche array,
Furth of his palice riall ischit Phebus,
With goldin croun and visage glorius,
Crisp haris, bricht as chrissolite or thopas,
For quhais hew mycht nane behald his face
The fyrie sparkis brasting from his ene,
To purge the are, and gilt the tendir grene,
Defoundand from his sege etheriall
Glade influent aspectis celicall,
Before his regal hie magnificence
Mysty vapoure vpspringand sweet as sence,
In smoky soppis of donk dewis wak,
With hailsum stous ouerheiland the slak,
The auriate phanis of his trone souerane
With glitterand glance ouerspred the octiane,
The large fludis lemand all of licht,
Bot with ene blenk of his supernale sicht ;
For to behald it was ane glore to se,
The stabyllyt wyndys, and the calmyt se,
The soft sessoun, the firmament serene,
The loune illuminate are, and firth amene,
The siluer scalit fyschis on the grete, [hete,
Ouer thowrt clere stremes sprinkilland for the
With fynnys schinand broun as synopare,
And chesal talis, stourand here and thare;
The new cullour alichting all the landis
Forgane the stanryis schene, and berial strandis:
Quhil the reflex of the diurnal bemes
The bene bonkis kest full of variant glemes:
And lusty Flora did hir blomes sprede
Under the fete of Phebus sulzeart stede:
The swardit soyll enbrode with selkouth hewis,
Wod and forest obumbrate with the bewis,
Quhais blysful branchis porturate on the ground
With schaddois schene shew rochis rubicund,
Towris, turettis, kirnalis, and pynnakillis hie
Of kirkis, castellis, and ilk faire ciete,
Stude payntit, euery fane, phioll and stage
Apoun the plane ground, by their awin umbrage:
Of Eolus north blastis hauand na drede,
The sulze spred hir brade bosum on brede,
Zephyrus confortabill inspiratioun
For tyll ressaue law in hir barne adoun :
The cornis croppis, and the bere new brerde
Wyth gladesum garmont reuesting the erd ;
So thyk the plantis sprang in euery pete,
The feildis ferlyis of their fructuous flete :
Byssy dame Ceres, and proude Priapus
Reiosing of the planis plentuous,

¹ This confusion of Phœbus and Phaeton is an errour which several old English writers have fallen into.

The crystal gates of Heaven expanded wide
Pour'd streams of splendour in an amplé tide :
The beaming orient beauteous to behold,
Shed purple rays, and azure mix'd with gold,
Dispersing with all-penetrating light
The solid gloom of cloud-envelop'd night.
The Sun's gay coursers, in their harness red,
Above the billowy ocean's boundless bed
Rais'd high their heads, impetuous in career,
To give the light, and glad our hemisphere.
So fast they scour'd, that from their nostrils came
A cloud of smoke, and streams of living flame.
Fir'd by the whirling whip their round to run,
And roll the golden chariot of the Sun.
While shortly with the blazing torch of day,
Forth from his royal hall in fresh array,
Sprung Phœbus, by his flaming mantle known;
His glorious visage, and his golden crown;
His glossy locks were as the topaz bright,
His radiance beam'd intolerable light;
His eye-balls sparkled with celestial sheen,
To purge the air, and gild the tender green,
Diffusing from the brightness of his brow,
Etherial mildness on the world below.
Before the king of day thin vapours rose.
Like clouds of incense, and as sweet as those,
(The dewy tribute which the meads exhale)
Curling they rose, and hover'd o'er the vale.
The golden splendour of his glorious beams
Glanc'd on the floods, and glitter'd in the streams,
And all the ocean shone serenely bright,
With the first glimpse of his supernal sight.
How calm ! how still ! how pleasing to behold
The sea's broad bosom where no billows roll'd !
The season soft, the firmament serene,
Th' illumin'd landscape, and the watry scene !
Where sportive fish display'd their silver pride,
Quick glancing on the surface of the tide,
By russet fins impell'd from shore to shore,
Their tail the rudder, and their fin the oar.
New lustre gilded all the rising lands,
The stony hillocks, and the beryl strands ;
While the reflection of the glowing beams
Play'd on the banks in variegated gleams.
Where-e'er Apollo's radiant coursers went,
Sprung flowers unnumber'd of delicious scent ;
Earth's flourish'd carpet various hues display'd,
And wood and forest wore a fuller shade. [green,
Whose beauteous branches, chequer'd on the
Imbrown'd the rigid rocks that rose between :
Tow'rs, battlements, and castles huge and high,
Turrets, and spires that mingle with the sky,
And every dome, and pinnacle, and fane,
By their own shade stood figur'd on the plain.
The glebe, now fearless of the north's keen air,
To buxom Zephyr spread her bosom bare,
With genial warmth her fertile lap to cheer,
And fill her with the plenty of the year.
Fresh springing corn enlivened all the scene,
And cloth'd the country with a robe of green:
And plants so numerous opened to the view,
The fields rejoicing wonder'd how they grew.
With joy the goddess of the golden grain,
And proud Priapus ey'd the pregnant plain ;

Plennyst so plesand, and maist propirly,
By nature nurissit wounder tendirly,
Plennast so plesand, and maist propirly
By nature nurissit wounder tendirly,
On the fertyl skyrt lappis of the ground
Strekand on brede under the cyrkil round:
The varyant vesture of the venust vale
Schrowdis the scherand fur, and euery fale
² Ouerfrett with fulzeis and fyguris ful dyuers,
The pray bysprent with spryng and sproutis dy-
    spers,
For callour humours on the dewy nycht,
Rendryng sum place the gyrs pylis thare licht,
Als fer as catal the lang somerys day
Had in thare pasture ete and gnyp away:
And blyssfull blossomys in the blomyt zard
Submittis thare hedys in the zoung sonnys saf-
    gard:
Iue leius rank ouerspred the barmkyn wall,
The blomit hauthorne cled his pykis all,
Furth of fresche burgeouns the·wyne grapis zing
Endlang the trazileys dyd on twistis hing,
The loukit buttouns on the gemyt treis
Ouerspredand leuis of naturis tapestryis.
Soft gresy verdoure eftir balmy schouris.
On curland stalkis smyland to thare flowris:
Behaldand thame sa mony divers hew
Sum piers, sum pale, sum burnet, and sum blew,
Sum gres, sum gowlis, sum purpure, sum san-
    guane,
Blanchis or broun, fauch zallow mony ane,
Sum heuinly colourit in celestial gre,
Sum watty hewit as the haw wally se,
And sum departe in freklis rede and quhyte,
Sum bricht as gold with aureate leuis lyte.
The dasy did on brede hir crowned smale,
And euery flour unlappit in the dale,
In battil gers burgeouns, the banwart wyld,
The clauir, catcluke, and the cammomylde;
The flourdelyce furth sprede his heuynly hew,
Floure damas, and columbe blak and blew,
Sere downis smal on dentilioun sprang,
The zoung grene blomit strabery leus amang,
Gimp jereflouris ³ thareon leuis unschet,
Fresche prymrois, and the pourpour violet,
The rois knoppis, tetand furth thare hede,
Gan chyp, and kyth thare vernale lippis rede.
Crysp skarlet leuis sum scheddand baith attanis,
⁴ Kest fragrant smelamyd fra goldin granis,
Heuinlie lyllyis, with lokkerand toppis quhyte,
Opynnit and schew thare istis redemyte,

---

² It is evident our author intends to describe
two distinct things, viz. cornfields, and meadows or pasture-lands, the former in the three
first lines, *the varyant vesture, &c.*———— is
plainly arable, and the *fulzeis and fyguris full
dyuers*, are the various leaves and flowers of the
weeds growing among the corn, and making a
piece of embroidery. And here the description
of cornfields ends, and that of pasture-lands begins at, *the pray bysprent*, &c. *pray*, not as the
glossary to G. Douglas says, *corruptedly for spray*,
but formed from the Lat. *pratum* and *spryng and
sproutis*, rising springs, from the Ital. *spruzzare,
spruzzolare aspergere.*

³ Probably Gawin Douglas wrote *thare awin.*
Vide ver. 72. *thare awin umbrage.*

⁴ It is observable, that Gawin Douglas never

---

Where fruitful Nature wak'd her genial power,
And rear'd, and foster'd every herb and flower:
The fair creation swell'd upon the eye;
Earth was their bed, their canopy the sky.
A varied verdure rob'd the vales around,
And spread luxuriant o'er the furrow'd ground:
And flowery weeds, that grew profuse between
The barley-lands, diversified the scene.
The silver springs, that thro' the meadows flow'd
In many a rill, fertility bestow'd;
And where the humid night's restoring dew
Dropt on the ground the bladed herbage grew,
As fast as cattle the long summer's day
Had cropt the grassy sustenance away.
A bloom diffusive o'er the gardens run,
Confiding in the safeguard of the Sun:
Wreath'd ivy mantled round the lofty tower;
And hawthorn-hedges whiten'd into flower.
The fresh-form'd grapes in little clusters hung;
Close to their props the curling tendrils clung.
The buds, that swell'd in gems on every tree,
Burst into foliage, nature's tapestry.
Lo! by soft zephyrs wak'd, and gentle showers,
On bending stalks smile voluntary flowers,
Trick'd off in vast variety of hue,
Some red, pale, purple, yellow, brown or blue;
Some brightly ting'd in Heaven's etherial stain,
And some cerulean like the watry main,
Some crimson-colour'd fairly fleckt with white,
Some gold that gaily glitter'd in the light.
The daisy did its coronet unveil,
And every flower unfolded in the dale;
Rank sprung salubrious herbs, and every weed,
And clover bloom'd luxuriant in the mead:
The flow'r-de-luce abroad its beauty spread,
And columbine advanc'd his purple head:
From dandelion flew the seeded down, [own.
And strawb'ry beds bore wild weeds, not their
Carnations glow'd in gaily-mingled hue;
Pale was the primrose, and the violet blue.
Its velvet lips the bashful rose begun
To show, and catch the kisses of the Sun;
Some fuller blown their crimson honours shed;
Sweet smelt the golden chives that grac'd their
    head.
Queen of the field, in milkwhite mantle drest,
The lovely lilly wav'd her curling crest.

---

once mentions the scent of flowers till he comes
to the rose, and never at all the scent of any particular flower, except the rose, not even of the
lilly; for I take it, the words, from *thare sylkyn
croppis*, are meant to describe the flowers in general; and the balmy vapour to be the same
with the *fresche liquor*, and the *dulce humouris
Quhareof the beis wrocht thare heny swete*, an
exhalation distinct from that which causes the
scent; and *redolent odour*, is general; for he
certainly means to close his description of the vegetable world, (and he does it nobly) by one universal cloud of fragrance from all nature.

The balmy vapour from thare sylkyn croppis
Distilland halesum sugurat hony droppis,
And sylver schakeris gan fra leuis hing,
With chrystal sprayngis on the verdure zing:
The plane pouderit with semelie seitis sound,
Bedyit ful of dewy peirlys round;
So that ilk burgeon, syon, herbe, or floure,
Wox all embalmit of the fresche liquour,
And baithit hait did in dulce humouris flete,
Quhareof the beis wrocht thare hony swete,
Be mychty Phebus operatiouns,
In sappy subtell exhalatiouns,
Forgane the cummyn of this prynce potent,
Redolent odour up from the rutis sprent,
Halesum of smel as ony fyne potioun,
Must, myr, aloyes, or confectioun.
Ane paradise it semyt to draw nere
Their galzeard gardingis, and eik grene herbere:
Mayst amyabil waxis the emerant medis.
Swannis souchis throw out the respand redis,
Ouer all the lochis and the fludis gray,
Sersand by kynd ane place quhare they suld lay
Phebus [5] rede foule his curale creist can stere,
Oft strekand furth his hekkil crawand clere
Amyd the wortis, and the rutis gent.
Pickland hys mete in alayis quhare he went,
His wyffis Toppa and Partolet hym by,
As bird al tyme that hantis bygamy ;
The payntit powne paysand with plumys gym,
Kest up his tale and proud plesand quhiie rym,
Ischrowdit in his fedderane bricht and schene,
Schapand the prent of Argois hundreth ene;
Amang the bronys of the olyue twistis,
Sere smale floulis, wirkand crafty nestis,
Endlang the hedgeis thik, and on rank akis
Ilk bird reiosand with thare mirthful makis :
In corneris and clere fenesteris of glas
Full besely Arachne weuand was,
To knyt hyr nettisand hyr wobbis sle,
Tharewith to cauch the litil mige or fle :
Under the bewis bene in lufely valis,
Within fermance and parkis clois of palis,
The bustuous bukkis rakis furth on raw,
Heirdis of hertis throw the thyck wod schaw,
The zoung fownys followand the dun days,
Kiddis skippand throw ronnys eftir rais,
In lesuris and on leyis litill lammes
Full tait and trig socht bletand to thare dammes.


On salt stremes wolk Dorida and Thetis,
By rynnand strandis, nymphs and naiades,
Sic as we clepe wenschis and damyssellis,
Iu gersy grauis wanderand by spring wellis,
Of blomed branchis and flouris quhyte and rede
Plettand their lusty chaplettis for thare hede :
Sum sang ring sangis, dancis, ledis, and roundis,
With vocis schil, quhil all the dale resoundis ;
And thochtful luffaris rownyis to and fro,
To leis thare pane, and plene thare joly wo,

From every flower ambrosial sweets distill'd,
Ambrosial sweets the ambient ether fill'd.
Dew-drops like diamonds hung on every tree,
And sprinkled silvery lustre o'er the lea,
And all the verdurous herbage of the ground
Was deck'd with pearls which cast a splendour
　　round.
The flowers, the buds, and every plant that grew,
Sipt the fresh fragrance of the morning dew :
In every plant the liquid nectar flow'd,
In every bud, and every flower that blow'd ;
Here rov'd the busy bees without control,
Robb'd the sweet bloom, and suck'd its balmy soul.
To greet the god, from Earth's fair bosom flow'd
All nature's incense in a fragrant cloud,
More grateful far than those gross fumes impart
Which torturing fires extract by chemic art.
Like Paradise appear'd each blissful scene
Of purple gardens, and enclosures green,
Of bloomy hedges, and of waving woods,
Of flowery meads, and rushy-fringed floods :
Where silver swans, with snowy pride elate,
Their tall necks mantling, sail'd along in state,
By instinct taught their ozier nests to make
On the dank margin of the lucid lake.
Brisk chanticleer wav'd high his coral crest,
And crowing clapt his pinions to his breast ;
With orient heel he lightly spurn'd the ground,
And chuck'd for joy at every corn he found ;
And as he strutted on in gallant pride,
Two wives obsequious waited at his side ;
For cocks, that couple with their nearest kin,
Hold bygamy a pardonable sin.
The peacock proudly pac'd upon the plain,
And like a circle bent his gaudy train,
Where vivid colours brightly-beaming strove ;
He seem'd beneath a canopy to move :
His starry plumes reflected various dyes,
Resembling Argus with his hundred eyes.
Where leafy branches form'd a secret shade
The painted birds their cunning fabrics made,
Or on the oak, or implicated thorn,
And wanton'd in the beauty of the morn.
Her wary stand the watchful spider took
In the glass window, or some gloomy nook,
There wove her web, in filmy texture sly,
To captivate the little gnat, or fly,
Beneath the trees that screen the lovely vale,
Within the limits of the fencing pale,
March nimble-footed deer in rank array'd,
Or seek the shelter of the green-wood shade :
Young kids, light skipping, and the timorous fawns
Brush thro' the copse, and bound along the lawns :
While in fresh pastures or on fallows gray
Lambs nibble in the wantonness of play.
　　Emerging from their coral-paven cave
Thetis and Doris walk upon the wave,
But stream presiding nymphs, and naiads trim,
By the clear current, or the fountain's brim,
Such as we name our gentle maids that rove
By water swelling in the grassy grove,
Culling green boughs, and bells, and flowerets fair,
And weaving garlands for their golden hair ;
Some sweetly sing, some lead the festive round ;
The distant dales re-echoe to the sound :

[5] That Milton had his eye upon this passage,
is plain from his describing the swan, the cock,
and peacock, in the order and with several of the

attributes, that our author has given them.
Vid. b. 7. v. 438, &c.

Eftir thare gise, now singand, now in sorrow,
With hertis pensiue, the lang someris morrow :
Sum balfettis list endite of his lady,
Sum leuis in hope, and sum alluterly
Disparit is, and sa quyte out of grace,
Hys purgarory he fyndis in euery place.


\*\*\* new curage kitillis all gentil hertis,
Seand throw kynd ilk thing spryngis and reuertis:
Dame naturis menstralis on that uthyr parte,
Thare blissful bay intonyng euery arte,
To bete thare amouris of thare nychtis bale,
The merle, the mauys, and the nychtingale,
With mirry notis myrthfully furth brist,
Enforsing thaym quha micht do clink it best :
The kowschot croudis and pykkis on the ryse,
The stirling changis diuers steuynnys nyse,
The sparrow chirmis in the wallis clyft,
Goldspink and lintquhite fordynnand the lyft,
The gukkow galis, and so quhitteris the quale,
Quhil ryveris reirdit, schawis, and euery dale,
And tendir twistis trymblit on the treis,
For birdis sang, and bemyng of the beis,
In werblis dulce of heuinlie armonyis,
The larkis loude releischand in the skyis,
Louis thare lege with tonys curious ;
Bayth to dame Natur, and the fresche Venus,
Rendring hie laudis in thare obseruance,
Quhais suggourit throttis made glade hartis dance
And al smal foulis singis on the spray ;
  Welcum the lord of licht, and lampe of day,
Welcum fosterare of tendir herbis grene,
Welcum quhikkynnar of flurist flouris schene,
Welcum support of euery rute and vane,
Welcum confort of al kind frute and grane,
Welcum the birdis beild apoun the brere,
Welcum maister and reulare of the zere,
Welcum welefare of husbandis at the plewis,
Welcum reparare of woddis, treis, and bewis,
Welcum depaynter of the blomyt medis,
Welcum the lyffe of eury thing that spredis,
Welcum storare of all kynd bestial,
Welcum be thy bricht bemes gladand al.

And thoughtful lovers to the winds complain,
To mitigate the madness of their pain;
Now warbling madrigals so light and gay,
Now pale and pensive the long summer's day ;
Some write in high heroics to the fair,
Some live in hope, and some thro' sad despair
In every place a purgatory find ;
Such is the moody genius of their mind.
  All gentle hearts confess the quickening spring,
For May invigorates every living thing.
Hark ! how the merry minstrels of the grove
Devote the day to melody and love ;
The ouzle shrill, that haunts the thorny dale,
The mellow thrush, the love-lorn nightingale;
Their little breasts with emulation swell,
And sweetly strive in singing to excell.
In the thick forest feeds the cooing dove ;
The starling whistles various notes of love :
The sparrow chirps, the clefted walls among;
To the sweet wildness of the linnet's song,
To the harsh cuckoo, and the twittering quail
Resounds the wood, the river, and the vale ;
And tender twigs, all trembling on the trees,
Dance to the murmuring music of the bees.
Upspring the airy larks, shrill voic'd and loud,
And breathe their mattins from a morning cloud.
To greet glad Nature, and the god of day,
And flowery Venus, blooming queen of May ;
The songs of praise their tuneful breasts employ,
Charm every ear, and wrap the soul in joy.
Thus sung the sweet musicians on the spray ;
  " Welcome, thou lord of light, and lamp of day;
Welcome to tender herbs, and myrtle bowers,
Welcome to plants, and odour-breathing flowers ;
Welcome to every root upon the plain,
Welcome to gardens, and the golden grain:
Welcome to birds that build upon the breere,
Welcome, great lord and ruler of the year :
Welcome, thou source of universal good,
Of buds to boughs, and beauty to the wood:
Welcome, bright Phœbus, whose prolific power
In every meadow spreads out every flower ;
Where-e'er thy beams in mild effulgence play,
Kind Nature smiles, and all the world is gay."

*GAWIN DOUGLAS,*

HIS ELOQUENT DISCRIPTION OF WYNTER, WYTH HYS
GRETE STORMES AND TEMPESTIS.

A DESCRIPTION OF WINTER

FROM GAWIN DOUGLAS, BISHOP OF
DUNKELD,

Bruma recurrit iners.                        HOR.

To the Memory of my late ingenious and learned
  Friend, and Schoolmaster, the Rev. John
  Lister, A. M.  The following Poem is, with a
  just Sense of Gratitude, inscribed.

As bricht Phebus schene souerane heuinnis E
The opposit held of his chymes hie,
Clere schynand bemes, and goldin suneris hew
In lattoun cullour altering all of new,
Kything no signe of heit be his vissage,
So nere approchit he his wynter stage
Reddy he was to enter the thrid morne
In cludy sykes under Capricorne :
All thoucht he be the lampe and hert of heuin,
Forfeblit wox his lemand gilty leuin,

Now had fair Phœbus, Heav'n's illustrious eye
Enter'd the wintery regions of the sky ;
Like burnish'd gold no longer beam'd his sphere,
So faded was the colour of the year :
Just at the period of his annual course,
All faint and feeble grew his vital force,
Prepar'd to enter, the succeeding morn,
The dark domain of clouded Capricorn:
For tho' he sheds sweet influence from on high,
Lamp of the world, and glory of the sky,

Throw the declynying of his large round spere.

The frosty regioun ryngis of the zere,

The tyme and sessoun bitter, cauld and pale,
The schort dayis, that clerkis clepe Brumale:
Quhen brym blastis of the northyn art
Ouerquhelmythad Neptunus in his cart,
And all to schaik the leuys of the treis,
The rageand stormes ourwelterand wally seis,
Ryueris ran rede on spate with wattir broun,
And burnis harlis all thare bankis doun,
And landbirst rumbland rudely with sic bere,
Sa loud neuir rummyst wyld lyoun nor bere ;
Fludis monstouris, sic as mereswynis and quhalis
For the tempest law in the deep deualis :
Mars occident retrogade in his spere,
Prouocand stryffe, regnit as lord that zere.
Rany Orioun with his stormy face
Bywauit oft the schipman by hys race:
Frawart Saturne, chil of complexioun,
Throw quhais aspect darth and infectioun
Bene causit oft and mortall pestilence,
When progressiue the greis of his ascence :
And lusty Hebe Junois dochter gay,
Stude spulzete of hir office and array:
The sole ysowpit in to wattir wak,
The firmament ouercast with cludis blak :
The ground fadit, and fauch wox al the feildis,
Mountane toppis slekit with snaw ouer heildis :
On raggit rolkis of hard hask quhyn stane,
With frosyn frontis cald clynty clewis schane :
Bewty was loist, and barrand schew the landis,
With frostis hare ouerfret the feildis standis.
Sere birtir bubbis and the schoutis snell
Semyt on the swarde in similitude of hell,
Reducing to our mynde in euery stede
Gousty schaddois of eild and grisly dede :
Thik drumly skuggis dirkinnit so the heuin,
Dym skyis oft furth warpit fereful leuin,
Flaggis of fyre, and mony felloun flaw,
Scharp soppis of sleit, and of the synppand snaw:
The dolly dikis war al donk and wak,
The law valis flodderit all wyth spate,
The plane stretis and eury hie way
Full of fluschis, dubbis, myre and clay,
Laggerit leyis wallowit fernis schew,
Broun muris kythit thare wyssinyt mossy hew,
Bank, bray and boddum blanschit wox and bare;
For gourl weddir growit beistis hare,
The wynd maid waif the rede wede on the dyk.
Bedowin in bonkis depe was euery sike :
Ouer craggis and the frontis of rochis sere
Hang grete yse schokkillis lang as ony spere :
The grund stude barrane widderit, dosk, and gray,
Herbis, flouris, and gerssis wallowit away:
Woddis, forestis with naket bewis blout
Stude stripit of thare wede in euery hout :
Sa bustouslie Boreas his bugill blew,
The dere full derne doun in the dalis drew :
Small birdis flokand throw thik ronnys thrang,
In chirmynge, and with cheping changit thare
      sang,
Sekand hidlis and hirnys thame to hyde
Fra fereful thuddis of the tempestuus tyde :
The wattir lynnys rowtis, and euery lynd
Quhislit and brayit of the souchand wynd :

Pure labouraris and byssy husband men
Went weet and wery draglit in the fen;

In weeping Winter, when his orb declines,
Languid he looks, and wan and watry shines.
Now reign'd the power of keen congealing frost,
When all the beauty of the year is lost ;
The Brumal season, bitter, cold, and pale, [vail.
When short dull days, and sounding storms pre-
The wild north wind, tremendous from afar,
O'erwhelm'd imperial Neptune in his carr,
Their scatter'd honours from the forests tore,
And dash'd the mad waves headlong on the shore.
Fierce, foaming rivers, swell'd with torrents brown,
Hurl'd all their banks precipitately down ;
Loud roar'd the thunder of the raging floods,
Loud as gaunt lions bellowing shake the woods.
Th' unwieldy monsters which the deeps contain,
Sought safety at the bottom of the main.
Strife-stirring Mars, regressive in his sphere,
Sustain'd the cold dominions of the year ;
And black Orion dimm'd the face of day,
Leading the luckless mariner astray.
Saturn, whose boding aspect, chill and wan,
Frowns in dread vengeance on the race of man,
Denouncing dearth, and desolating pest,
Held high his course progressive in the east ;
And blooming Hebe, Juno's daughter gay,
Was ravish'd of her beautiful array.
Incessant rains had drench'd the floated ground,
And clouds o'ercast the firmament around :
White shone the hills involv'd in silver snow,
But brown and barren were the vales below:
On firm foundations of eternal stone
High rugged rocks in frosty splendour shone ;
The hoary fields no vivid verdure wore,
Frost warpt the world, and beauty was no more.
Wide-wasting winds that chill'd the dreary day,
And seemed to threaten Nature with decay,
Reminded man, at every baleful breath,
Of wintry age, and all-subduing death.
Horrific gloom deform'd the turbid air,
And livid lightning shot a dismal glare :
Above pale meteors gleam'd, and all below
Was one bleak scene of drizzling sleet and snow.
The hollow ditches, swell'd with sudden rains,
Pour'd a black deluge on the lowland plains,
And every road receiv'd the sordid flood,
Swam with the swell, or stiffen'd into mud.
Fern on the fallows wither'd as it grew,
And brown heaths bore a mossy-colour'd hue ;
Bare were the bottoms, and the high hills hoar;
The drooping cattle moan'd upon the moor;
The red weed waver'd on the breezy dike ;
Rills in deep channels murmuring roll'd oblique.
From horrid rocks, that lour'd upon the coast,
Hung icy spears, the beauteous work of frost.
Dun was the soil and steril, and decay'd
Was every flower, and every tender blade;
And every wood and wilderness around
Diffus'd their wither'd honours on the ground.
So stoutly Boreas his loud bugle blew,
Down to the dales the trembling deer withdrew :
To thorny thickets flock'd the feather'd throng,
And pensive plied their melancholy song,
Or to the shelter of the forest driven,
Escap'd the windy turbulence of Heaven.
Down the rough rock dash'd torrents with harsh
      sound
Rush'd, and impetuous shook the country round,
The trees, that o'er the mountain's top reclin'd :
Wav'd their high heads, and murmur'd to the
      wind.

The cilly schepe and thare litill hird gromes
Lurkis vnder lye of bankis, woddis and bromes:
Ann vtheris dantit greter beistial,
Within thare stabill sesit in the stall,
Sic as mulis, hors, oxin or ky,
Fed tuskit baris, and fat swyne in sty,
Sustenit war be mannis gouernance
On hervist, and on someris puruiance:
Widequhare with sors so Eolus schoutis schill
In this congelit sesoun scharp and chill,
The callour are penetratiue and pure
Dasing the blude in euery creature,
Maid seik warme stouis and bene fyris hote,
In doubil garmont cled and wylecote,
With mychty drink, and metis confortiue,
Aganis the sterne wynter for to striue.
Recreate wele and by the chymnay bekit,
At euin be tyme doun in ane bed me strekit,
Warpit my hede, kest on claithis thyrnfald
For to expell the perrellus persand cald:
I crosit me, syne bownit for to slepe:
Quhare lemand throw the glas I did take kepe
Latonia the lang irksum nycht
Hir subtell bleukis sched and watry lycht,
Full hie vp quhirlit in hir regioun,
Till Phebus right in opposicioun,
Into the crab hir propir mansioun draw,
Haldand the hicht althocht the son went law:
The hornyt byrd quhilk we clepe the nicht oule,
Within hir cauerne hard I schout and zoule,
Laithely of forme, with crukit camscho beik,
Ugsum to here was hir wylde Irische skreik.
The wyld geis eik claking by nychtis tyde
Attour the ciete fleand hard I glyde.
On slummer I slade full sone, and slepyt sound,
Quhill the horisont upwart can rebound:
Phebus crounit bird, the nychtis orlagere,
Clappin his wingis thryis had crawin clere:
Approching nere the greking of the day,
Within my bed I walkynyt quhare I lay,
Sa fast declynnys Cynthia the mone,
And kayis keklys on the rufe abone:
Palamedes birdis crowpand in the sky,
Fleand on randoun, schapin lyk ane Y;
And as ane trumpit rang thare vocis soun,
Quhais cryis bene pronosticacioun
Of wyndy blastis and ventositeis.
Fast by my chalmer on hie wisnit treis
The sary gled quhissllis with mony ane pew,
Quharby the day was dawing wele I knew;
Bad bete the fyre, and the candyll alicht,
Syne blissit me, and in my wedis dicht;
Ane schot wyndo unschet ane litel on char,
Persauyt the mornyng bla, wan and har,
Wyth cloudy gum and rak ouerquhelmyt the are,
The sulze stiche, hasard, rouch and hare;
Branchis brattlyng, and blaiknyt schew the brayis,
With hirstis harsk of waggand wyndil strayis,
The dew droppis congelit on stibbil and rynd,
And scharp hailstanys mortfundyit of kynd,
Hoppand on the thak and on the causay by:
The schote I closit, and drew inwart in hy,
Cheuerand for cald, the sessoun was sa snell,
Schupe with nait flambis to fleme the fresing fell.

Industrious peasants, toil-enduring men,
Went wet and weary, draggled in the fen:
Beneath the wild broom, or the shelving steep,
Securely skulk'd the shepherd and his sheep;
But household animals which man had bred,
Enjoy'd warm cover, or in stables fed:
The mule, the horse, the ox, and brindled boar,
And liv'd at large on summer's golden store.
The hollow-howling winds, and frost intense,
Benumb'd man's vigour, and congeal'd the sense;
And loudly told him what his wants require,
A double garment, and bright-burning fire,
And generous wine, and comfortable cheer,
To guard against the rigour of the year.
Warm from the hearth, and plentifully fed,
With early eve I press'd my downy bed,
And of soft covering added many a fold
To dissipate the penetrating cold;
Then, duly cross'd, prepar'd for balmy sleep,
When through the glass I saw pale Cynthia peep:
Her silver orb display'd a watery light,
And faintly glimmer'd all the livelong night;
She calmly sailing through th' etherial way,
Full orb'd, oppos'd the glorious lamp of day,
And reach'd the sign where Cancer's kingdoms
    glow,
Thron'd in her zenith, tho' the Sun was low.
In boding note, within her darksome bower,
Where crawling ivy clasps yon antient tower,
I heard the solitary owl complain,   [strain:
Saddening dread midnight with her hideous
While clamourous wild-geese in long trains on
With lazy pinions fann'd the liquid sky; [high,
Lull'd by the drowsy din in sleep I lay,
Till from the east pale gleam'd the dubious day;
Till chanticleer his merry notes begun, [Sun.
Thrice clapt his wings, and call'd the lingering
Rous'd by his orisons from sweet repose,
I shook off slumbers as the morning rose;
The morning rose, but shed a languid light,
And down in ocean sunk the queen of night.
Then jack-daws chatter'd on the chimney high;
And cranes renewed their voyage thro' the sky:
Whose piercing clamours sounded in my ear,
Presage of wintery winds and tempests gathering
    near.
Perch'd on a tree that nigh my chamber grew,
The kite began her lamentable pew,
Whereby the dawning of the day I knew; [drest,
Then call'd for lights, and Heav'n with pray'r ad-
And wrapt my cold limbs in the warmest vest,
And thro' the window half-way opening saw
The melancholy morning bleak and raw;
Thick clouds envelop'd all the mountains round,
And rough and rigid was the hoary ground;
The bare boughs clashing rattled to the blast,
And tall grass trembled as the wild wind past.
Like pendent pearls, on every shrub that grew
And every stubble, hung the frozen dew;
And hail-stones pattering from the chilling sky
Hopt on the thatch, and on the causeway by.
Aghast, the joyless season to behold,
My teeth all chattering with the piercing cold,
I clos'd the casement, and retir'd in haste
To quell with cheering blaze the horrour-breath-
    ing blast.

## GLOSSARY TO

### MAY AND WINTER.

*ABAK*, back, behind
*Abulzeit*, dressed, cloathed.
*Affrayit*, afraid,
*Akis*, oaks.
*Als*, as.
*Amene*, pleasant, [Lat. *amœnus*.]
*Art*, the northern constellation, from *arctos*, *ursa*.
*Attanis*, at once.
*Attour*, *q. d.* out over, beyond.
*Awin*, own.
*Baris*, boars.
*Barmkin*, rampart, fortification.
*Batil*, thick, rank.
*Bekit*, basked, warmed.
*Bene*, pleasant, from the Latin, *bonus*,
*Bere*, barley; also roar, noise.
*Bla*, livid.
*Blaiknyt*, blacken'd.
*Blanschit*, blanched, bleached.
*Blenk*, a blink, a view.
*Blout*, bare.
*Bot*, but.
*Bownit*, prepared.
*Brade*, broad. *Brede* ibid. *On brede*, abroad.
*Brattlyng*, clashing.
*Bray*, side of a hill, bank of a river.
*Brerde*, new sprung.
*Bronys*, branches.
*Brym*, fierce.
*Bubbis*, blasts,
*Burgeouns*, buds, young sprigs.
*Burnis*, brooks.
*Bustuous*, huge, fierce.
*Bysprent*, besprinkled.
*Bywauit*, made to wander.
*Callour*, fresh, cool.
*Camscho*, crooked, distorted, [Lat. *camurus*.]
*Catcluke*, the name of an herb.
*Chesal*, chisel, or shaped like a chisel.
*Chirmyng*, chirping.
*Chymes*, buildings or houses.
*Clewis*, cliffs, rocks.
*Clois*, cloyster.
*Clynty*, flinty.
*Crammesy*, crimson, [Fr. *cramoisi*]
*Croude*, to coo like a dove.
*Crowping*, the noise made by cranes.
*Dantit*, subdued, tamed.
*Dasing*, congealing, benumming.
*Days*, does.
*Dede*, death.
*Defoundand*, pouring down, diffusing.
*Derne*, lonely, solitary
*Deualis*, descended.
*Dolly*, doleful, [Lat. *dolor*.]
*Drumly*, foggy.
*Dubbis*, pools of water.
*Eild*, old-age.
*Elrische*, hideous.
*Emerant*, green, verdant.
*Embrode*, embroidered.
*Endlang*, along.
*Erd*, the earth.
*Eschamet*, ashamed.
*Fale*, turf.

*Fauch*, grey coloured, or rather reddish, fallow.
*Fenesteris*, windows, [Lat. *fenestra*.]
*Ferlie*, to wonder.
*Flaggis*, flashes.
*Flaw*, blast, wind, [Lat. *flatus*.]
*Fleand*, flying, fleeing.
*Fleme*, to drive away.
*Flete*, flow, product.
*Flodderit*, overflowed.
*Fludis*, floods.
*Fordynnand*, echoing, resounding.
*Forgane*, against, also over against.
*Frawart*, froward.
*Fructuous*, fruitful.
*Fulzeis*, leaves, [Fr. *Feuille*, Lat. *Folium*].
*Galis*, makes a noise like a cuckow.
*Galzeard*, cheerful, pretty.
*Gent*, genteel, spruce.
*Gers*, grass, gyrs, ibid.
*Gilty*, gilded, golden.
*Glave*, a sword, [Fr. *glaive*, Lat. *gladium*.]
*Gled*. a glead, kite.
*Gnyp*, to crop or browze.
*Gousty*, ghastly.
*Gowlis*, red *gules* from the Fr.
*Granit*, having grains, forked, scarlet, or crimson,
*Gravis*, groves.
*Gre*, degree. *Gres*, gray.
*Greking*, peep of day.
*Grete*, sand, or gravel in rivers.
*Grundin*, grinded, sharpened.
*Gum*, vapour.
*Hammys*, a collar for horses.
*Hant*, to frequent, use. [Fr. *hanter*]
*Har*, sharp, nipping, *Hare*, hoary.
*Harsk*, harsh, rough.
*Hasard*, grey.
*Haw*, blueish, cerulean.
*Hekkil*, a heckle, comb.
*Hidlis*, hiding places.
*Hird*, shepherd, Ang. Sax.
*Hirnys*, holes, corners.
*Hirstis*, bare and hard parts of hills.
*Hout*, a holt, wood.
*Hy*, haste.
*Ischit*, issued, came out.
*Kayis*, jackdaws.
*Keklys*, cackled, giggled.
*Kepe*, notice.
*Kirnailis*, battlements, parapets.
*Kitillis*, tickles, moves. [Lat. *titillare*.]
*Kowschot*, a ring-dove, or wild pigeon.
*Kyth*, to show, make appear.
*Laggerit*, bemired.
*Laithely*, loathsome.
*Landbirst*, the breaking down of banks by the violence of floods.
*Lattoun*, a mixt metal, here sig. pallid.
*Law*, low.
*Leis*, to lose; *Leese*, 1 Kings, Ch. xviii. ver. 5. in the same sense.
*Lemand*, blazing, shining.
*Lesuris*, pastures, glades.
*Leuin*, lightning, light.
*Leuys*, leaves.
*Leyis*, leas, untilled ground,
*Lochis*, lakes.
*Lockkerand*, curling.
*Louis*, praise,

T

*Loukit*, locked up, enclosed.
*Loune*, calm.
*Lusty*, vigorous.
*Lye*, or *Le*, a shelter.
*Lyft*, the firmament.
*Lynd*, the linden-tree.
*Lynnys*, cataracts.
*Mavys*, a thrush.
*Ment*, mixed, mingled together.
*Merle*, an ouzle, blackbird. [Lat. *merula*.]
*Mereswynis*, sea-swine, porci marini.
*Mortfundyit*, deadly, cold.
*Neis thirlis*, nostrils.
*Obumbrate*, shaded over.
*Octiane*, the ocean.
*Orlagere*, a clock, [Lat. *horologium*.]
*Ouerfrett*, overspread, embellished.
*Ouerheidland*, covering over.
*Ouerwelterand*, overturning.
*Peirs*, sky-coloured.
*Pete*, a clod, or clod of earth.
*Phanis*, not *fanes* or *ensigns*, (as the *Glossary* interprets it) but appearance or splendour, from the Gr. φαινω ostendo, splendeo.
*Phioll*, a cupola.
*Plene*, to complain.
*Powne*, a peacock.
*Play*, a meadow. [Lat. *pratum*.]
*Pure*, poor.
*Puruiance*, provision.
*Pylis*, hairs, or tops of grass.
*Quha*, who—*Quhais*, whose.
*Quhalis*, whales.
*Quhile*, a wheel.
*Quhin*, stone, hard stone.
*Quhip*, a whip.
*Rais*, roes.
*Rak*, fog, mist.
*Rakis on raw*, march in order.
*Redemyte*, decked, beautiful.
*Reirdit*, resounded-
*Releischand*, mounting up.
*Rendrying*, restoring.
*Respand*, the rustling of reeds.
*Ressaue*, to receive.
*Revertis*, returns.
*Revesting*, clothing.
*Ronnys*, brambles, briars.
*Rumnyst*, rumbled, roared.
*Rym*, the circle of a wheel.
*Ryng*, reign.
*Ryse*, bulrushes, may signify shrubs or bushes.
*Sary*, sorry, sad.
*Schaik*, to shake.
*Schaw*, a wood, forest, or grove.
*Schene*, shining.
*Scherand*, cleaving.
*Schill*, shrill.
*Schote*, shutter of a window.
*Schoutis*, shouts.
*Schroudith*, covers over.
*Schupe*, prepar'd.
*Sege*, seat. [Fr. *siege*.]
*Selkouth*, strange, uncommon.
*Semelie*, seemly.
*Sence*, incense.
*Sere*, several, likewise sore, violent.
*Sesit*, rested.
*Seye*, sea.
*Sic*, such.

*Sike*, a rivulet.
*Skuggis*, shades.
*Slak*, a bottom or valley.
*Slekit*, smooth.
*Snell*, piercing, sharp.
*Snyppand*, nipping.
*Sole*, soil. [Lat. *solum*.]
*Soppis*, showers, clouds.
*Sore*, sorrel, chesnut.
*Souch*, to make a noise.
*Spate*, foam, froth.
*Sprayngis*, rays, streaks of different colours.
*Sprinkilland*, gliding swiftly.
*Spulzeit*, spoiled, robbed.
*Stabyillt*, settled, calm
*Stanryis*, the shore.
*Stede*, place.
*Sternes*, stars.
*Steuynnis*, notes, sounds.
*Storare*, restorer.
*Stouis*, vapours, exhalations.
*Stourand*, stirring.
*Strandis*, strands,——sometimes signifies rivulets.
*Strekit*, stretched.
*Sulze*, the soil, ground.
*Sulzeart*, bright, glittering,
*Sum dele*, somewhat, a little.
*Swarde*, the surface of the ground.
*Syne*, then, afterwards.
*Syon*, a scion, or young shoot.
*Tait*, tight.
*Tetand*, putting forth.
*Thareon*, their own.
*Thoucht*, though.
*Thrang*, in crowds.
*Thrid*, third.
*Thuddis*, blasts.
*Till*, to, unto.
*Trazileys*, props, or supporters of vines.
*Umbedrew*, withdrew.
*Unschet*, opened.
*Upwarpis*, thrown up.
*Uthyr*, other.
*Wak*, moist, watry.
*Wallowit*, withered.
*Wally*, wavy, billowy.
*Warpit*, threw.
*Widequhare*, far and near.
*Wissinyt*, decayed, dried.
*Wobbis*, webbs.
*Wortis*, herbs, plants.
*Wylecote*, a jacket next the shirt, a fly coat,
*Wyndilstrayis*, windlestraws, tall grass.
*Yseschokkillis*, icicles.
*Ysowpit*, drenched, sopt.
*Zallow*, yellow.
*Zard*, yard, garden.
*Zere*, year.
*Zing*, young.
*Zoule*, howl.
*Zound*, yonder, farther off.

## PART OF SAT. VI. BOOK II. OF HO-RACE, TRANSLATED.

BEGINNING AT, PERDITUR HÆC INTER MISERO LUX, NON SINE VOTIS, &c.

Consum'd in trifles, thus the golden day
Steals, not without this ardent wish, away;
When shall I see my peaceful country farm,
My fancy when with antient authors charm?
Or, lull'd to sleep, the cares of life elude
In sweet oblivion of solicitude?
O, for those beans which my own fields provide!
Deem'd by Pythagoras to man allied;
The savoury pulse serv'd up in platters nice,
And herbs high-relish'd with the bacon slice?
O, tranquil nights in pleasing converse spent,
Ambrosial suppers that might gods content!
When with my chosen friends (delicious treat!)
Before the household deities we eat;
The slaves themselves regale on choicest meat.
Free from mad laws we sit reclin'd at ease,
And drink as much, or little, as we please.
Some quaff large bumpers that expand the soul,
And some grow mellow with a moderate bowl.
We never talk of this man's house or vill,
Or whether Lepos dances well or ill:
But of those duties which ourselves we owe,
And which 'tis quite a scandal not to know:
As whether wealth or virtue can impart
The truest pleasure to the human heart:
What should direct us in our choice of friends,
Their own pure merit, or our private ends:
What we may deem, if rightly understood,
Man's sovereign bliss, his chief, his only good.
Mean-time my friend, old Cervius, never fails
To cheer our converse with his pithy tales:
Praise but Arellius, or his ill-got store,
His fable thus begins: " In days of yore
A country mouse within his homely cave
A treat to one of note, a courtier, gave;
A good plain mouse our host, who lov'd to spare
Those heaps of forage he had glean'd with care;
Yet on occasion would his soul unbend,
And feast with hospitality his friend:
He brought wild oats and vetches from his hoard;
Dried grapes and scraps of bacon grac'd the
board:
In hopes, no doubt, by such a various treat,
To tempt the dainty traveller to eat.
Squat on fresh chaff, the master of the feast
Left all the choicest viands for his guest,
Nor one nice morsel for himself would spare,
But gnaw'd coarse grain, or nibbled at a tare.
At length their slender dinner finish'd quite,
Thus to the rustic spoke the mouse polite:
" ' How can my friend a wretched being drag
On the bleak summit of this airy crag?
Say, do you still prefer this barbarous den
To polish'd cities, savages to men?
Come, come with me, nor longer here abide,
I'll be your friend, your comrade, and your
guide.
Since all must die that draw this vital breath,
Nor great nor small can shun the shafts of death,
'Tis ours to sport in pleasures while we may:
For ever mindful of life's little day.'     [mouse,
" These weighty reasons sway'd the country
And light of heart he sallied from his house.

Resolv'd to travel with this courtly spark,
And gain the city when securely dark.
" Now midnight hover'd o'er this earthly ball,
When our small gentry reach'd a stately hall,
Where brightly glowing, stain'd with Tyrian
dye,
On ivory couches richest carpets lie;
And in large baskets, rang'd along the floor,
The rich collation of the night before.
On purple bed the courtier plac'd his guest,
And with choice cates prolong'd the grateful
feast;
He carv'd, he serv'd, as much as mouse could do,
And was his waiter, and his taster too.
Joy seiz'd the rustic as at ease he lay:
This happy change had made him wondrous gay—
When lo! the doors burst open in a trice,
And at their banquet terrified the mice:
They start, they tremble, in a deadly fright,
And round the room precipitate their flight;
The high-roof'd room with hideous cries resound:
Of baying mastiffs, and loud-bellowing hounds
Then thus the rustic in the courtier's ear;
' Adieu! kind sir! I thank you for your cheer:
Safe in my cell your state I envy not;
Tares be my food, and liberty my lot!'"

---

## A PARODY ON THE CITY AND COUN-TRY MOUSE.

A country vicar in his homely house,
Pleas'd with his lot, and happy in his spouse,
With simple diet, at his humble board,
Once entertain'd the chaplain of a lord;—
He gave him (all he could) a little fish,
With sauce of oysters, in no silver dish;
And, for the craving stomach's sure relief,
The glory of Old England, rare roast-beef,
Horse-raddish and potatoes, Ireland's pride;
A pudding too the prudent dame supplied:
Their cheering beverage was a pint of port
(Tho' small the quantum) of the better sort;
But plenty of good beer, both small and stout,
With wine of elder to prevent the gout.
The vicar hop'd, by such a various treat,
To tempt his scarf-embellish'd friend to eat;
With nicest bits provok'd his guest to dine,
He carv'd the haddock, and he serv'd the wine:
Content his own sharp stomach to regale
With plain, substantial roast meat, and mild ale.
Our courtly chaplain, as we may suppose,
At such old-fashion'd commons curl'd his nose;
He tried in vain to piddle, and, in brief,
Pish'd at the pudding, and declin'd the beef;—
At length, their homely dinner finish'd quite,
Thus to the vicar spoke the priest polite:
" How can my brother in this paltry town
Live undistinguish'd, to the world unknown?
And not exalt your towering genius higher,
Than here to herd with country clown—or squire;
Stunn'd with the discord of hoarse cawing rooks,
The roar of winds, the dissonance of brooks,
Which discontented through the valley stray,
Plaintive and murmuring at their long delay.
Come, come with me, nor longer here abide;
You've friends in town, and I will be your guide:
Soon great preferment to your share will fall,
A good fat living, or perhaps—a stall."

These weighty reasons sway'd the vicar's mind—
To town he hied, but left his wife behind:—
Next levee-day he waited on his grace,
With hundreds more, who bow'd to get a place;
Shov'd in the crowd, he stood amaz'd to see
Lords who to Baal bent the supple knee,
And doctors sage he could not but admire,
Who stoop'd profoundly low—to rise the higher.
So much of ermine, lace, beaus, bishops, young
   and old,
'Twas like a cloud of sable edg'd with gold:
By turns his grace the servile train address,
Pleas'd with a smile, or in a whisper blest.
Sick of the scene, the vicar sought the door,
Determin'd never to see London more;
But, as his friend had pleas'd the hour to fix,
First went to dinner to my lord's at six;—
He knock'd—was usher'd to the room of state,
(My lord abroad) and dinner serv'd in plate;
Which, though it seem'd but common soup and
Was really callipee and callipash,    [hash,
(The relics of the gaudy day before)
What Indians eat, and Englishmen adore;
With bright champaign the courtier crown'd the
   feast,
Sooth'd his own pride, and gratified his guest
All this conspir'd our Stoic to controul,
And warpt the steady purpose of his soul—
When lo! the cry of fire creates amaze—
" The next house, Lady Riot's, in a blaze"—
Aghast the vicar stood, in wild affright,
Then briefly thus addres'd the priest polite:
" Adieu, my friend—your state I envy not—
Beef, liberty, and safety be my lot".

---

## HORACE, EPIST. V. BOOK I. IMI-
## TATED.

### TO JOHN HAWKESWORTH, ESQ.

If you dear sir, will deign to pass a day
In the fair vale of Orpington and Cray,
And live for once as humble vicars do;
On Thursday let me see you here by two.
Expect no niceties my plates to foul,
But Bansted mutton, and a barn-door fowl,
My friends with generous liquors I regale,
Good port, old hock, or, if they like it, ale;
But if of richer wine you chuse a quart,
Why bring, and drink it here—with all my heart.
Plain is my furniture, as is my treat,
For 'tis my best ambition, to be neat.
Leave then all sordid views, and hopes of gain,
To mortals miserable, mad, or vain;
Put the last polish to th' historic page,
And cease awhile to moralize the age.
By your sweet converse cheer'd, the live-long day
Will pass unnotic'd like the stream, away.
Why should kind Providence abundance give,
If we, like niggards, can't afford to live?
The wretched miser, poor 'midst heaps of pelf,
To cram his heir, most madly starves himself—
So will not I—give me good wine and ease,
And let all misers call me fool that please.
What cannot wine?—it opens all the soul;
Faint hope grows brilliant o'er the sparkling bowl:
Wine's generous spirit makes the coward brave,
Gives ease to kings, and freedom to the slave:

Bemus'd in wine the bard his duns forgets,
And drinks serene oblivion to his debts:
Wine drives all cares, and anguish from the heart,
And dubs us connoisseurs of every art:
Whom does not wine with eloquence inspire?
The bousey beggar struts into a squire.
This you well know —— to me belongs to mind,
That neatness with frugality be join'd;
That no intruding blab, with itching ears,
Darken my doors, who tells whate'er he hears;
Two D—s, each a poet, with me dine,
Your friends, and decent C—n, a divine:
There's room for more—so to complete the band,
Your wife will bring fair Innocence [1] in hand.
Should Cave want copy, let the teaser wait,
While you steal secret through the garden gate.

---

## A PASSAGE FROM PETRONIUS,

### TRANSLATED.

Fallen are thy locks! for woeful winter hoar
Has stolen thy bloom, and beauty is no more!
Thy temples mourn their shady honours shorn,
Parch'd like the fallow destitute of corn.
Fallacious gods! whose blessings thus betray;
What first ye give us, first ye take away.
Thou, late exulting in thy golden hair,
As bright as Phœbus, or as Cynthia fair,
Now view'st, alas! thy forehead smooth and plain
As the round fungus, daughter of the rain:
Smooth as the surface of well polish'd brass,
And fly'st with fear each laughter-loving lass:
Death hastes amain—thy wretched fate deplore—
Fallen are thy locks, and beauty is no more.

---

## AGAINST LIFE.

### FROM THE GREEK OF POSIDIPPUS.

What tranquil road, unvex'd by strife,
Can mortals chuse through human life?
Attend the courts, attend the bar—
There discord reigns, and endless jar:
At home the weary wretches find
Severe disquietude of mind;
To till the fields, gives toil and pain;
Eternal terrours sweep the main:
If rich, we fear to lose our store,
Need and distress await the poor:
Sad cares the bands of hymen give;
Friendless, forlorn, th' unmarried live:
Are children born? we anxious groan;
Childless, our lack of heirs we moan:
Wild, giddy schemes our youth engage;
Weakness and wants depress old age.
Would fate then with my wish comply,
I'd never live, or quickly die.

---

## FOR LIFE

### FROM THE GREEK OF METRODORUS.

Mankind may rove, unvex'd by strife,
Through every road of human life.
Fair wisdom regulates the bar,
And peace concludes the wordy war:

[1] The name of a very agreeable young lady.

At home auspicious mortals find
Serene tranquillity of mind;
All-beauteous nature decks the plain,
And merchants plough for gold the main:
Respect arises from our store,
Security from being poor:
More joys the bands of Hymen give;
Th' unmarried with more freedom live:
If parents, our blest lot we own;
Childless, we have no cause to moan:
Firm vigour crowns our youthful stage,
And venerable hairs old-age.
Since all is good, then who would cry,
"I'd never live, or quickly die?"

## ON OCCASION OF THE PEACE.

Peace o'er the world her olive wand extends,
And white-rob'd Innocence from Heaven de-
    scends.           POPE.

ADIEU the horrours of destructive war,
And mad Bellona in her iron car!
But welcome to our smiling fields again,
Sweet Peace! attended with thy jocund train,
Truth, Virtue, Freedom, that can never cloy,
And all the pleasing family of Joy.    [plan'd,
Those schemes pursued, which Pitt so wisely
Conquest has shower'd her blessings on the land;
And Britain's sons more laurels have obtain'd,
Than all her Henries, or her Edwards gain'd:
George saw with joy the peaceful period given,
And bow'd obedient to the will of Heaven:
Awful he rose to bid dissention cease,
And all the warring world was calm'd to peace;
"Thus did the roaring waves their rage compose.
When the great father of the floods arose."
Then came Astrea mild, our isle to bless,
Fair queen of virtue, and of happiness!
Then came our troops in fighting fields renown'd,
And mark'd with many an honourable wound.
The tender fair one, long by fears opprest,
Now feels soft raptures rising in her breast,
The blooming hero of her heart to view,
And hear him bid the dangerous camp adieu.
The widow'd bride, that long on grief had fed,
And bath'd with weeping the deserted bed,
Glad that the tumults of the war are o'er,
That terrour, rage, and rapine are no more,
Greets her rough lord, secure from hostile harms,
And hopes an age of pleasure in his arms:
While he, with pompous eloquence, recites
Dire scenes of castles, storm'd and desperate
    fights;
Or tells how Wolfe the free-born Britons led,
How Granby conquer'd and the household fled;
She, to the pleasing dreadful tale intent,
Now smiles, now trembles, for the great event.
O curst Ambition, foe to human good,
Pregnant with woe, and prodigal of blood!
Thou fruitful source, whence streams of sorrow
What devastations to thy guilt we owe!   [flow,
Where-e'er thy fury riots, all around
Confusion, havoc, and dread deaths abound:
Where Ceres flourish'd, and gay Flora smil'd,
Behold a barren, solitary wild!
To stately cedars thorns and briars succeed,
And in the garden spreads the noxious weed;

Where cattle pastured late, the purple plain,
Sad scene of horrour! teems with heroes slain;
Where the proud palace rear'd its haughty head,
Deep in the dust, see! crumbling columns
    spread;
See gallant Britons in the field expire,
Towns turn'd to ashes, fanes involv'd in fire!
These deeds the guilt of rash Ambition tell,
And bloody Discord, furious fiend of Hell!
Ye baneful sisters, with your frantic crew,
Hence speed your flight, and take your last adieu,
Eternal wars in barbarous worlds to wage;
There vent your inextinguishable rage.
But come, fair Peace, and be the nation's bride,
And let thy sister Plenty grace thy side,
O come! and with thy placid presence cheer
Our drooping hearts, and stay for ever here.
Now be the shrill, strife-stirring trumpet mute;
Now let us listen to the softer lute:
The shepherd now his numerous flocks shall feed,
Where war relentless doom'd the brave to bleed;
On ruin'd ramparts shall the hawthorn flower,
And mantling ivy clasp the nodding tower,
Unusual harvests wave along the dale,
And the bent sickle o'er the sword prevail.
No more shall states with rival rage contend,
But arts their empire o'er the world extend;
Ingenious arts, that humanize the mind,
And give the brightest polish to mankind!
Then shall our chiefs in breathing marble stand,
And life seem starting from the sculptor's hand;
Then lovely nymphs in living picture rise,
The fairest faces, and the brightest eyes:
There polish'd Lane [1] no loss of beauty fears;
Her charms, still mellowing with revolving years,
Shall, ev'n on canvas, youthful hearts engage,
And warm the cold indifference of age:
Then the firm arch shall stem the roaring tide,
And join those countries which the streams di-
Then villas rise of true palladian proof,   [vide;
And the proud palace rear its ample roof;
Then statelier temples to the skies ascend,
Where mix'd with nobles mighty kings may bend,
Where poverty may send her sighs to Heaven,
And guilt return, repent, and be forgiven.
Such are the fruits which sacred peace imparts,
Sweet nurse of liberty and learned arts!
These she restores—O! that she could restore
Life to those Britons who now breathe no more,
Who in th' embattled field undaunted stood,
And greatly perish'd in their country's good;
Or who, by rage of angry tempests tost,
In whirlpools of the whelming main were lost.
Ye honour'd shades of chiefs untimely slain!
Whose bones lie scatter'd on some foreign plain;
That now perchance by lonely hind are seen
In glittering armour gliding o'er the green;
Ye! that beneath the cold cerulean wave
Have made the watery element your grave,
Whose wandering spirits haunt the winding shore,
Or ride on whirlwinds while the billows roar,
With kind protection still our isle defend,
(If souls unbodied can protection lend)
Still o'er the king your shadowy pinions spread,
And in the day of danger shield his head;

[1] The hon. Mrs. Lane, daughter of the right hon. lord chancellor Henley, and wife to the hon. Mr. Lane.

Your bright examples shall our pattern be,
To make us valiant, and to keep us free.

Dec. 1762.

---

## ON A COUNTRY VICAR

CARRYING HIS WIFE BEHIND HIM, TO VISIT HIS
PARISHIONERS. BY MR. ——, OF BRAZEN
NOSE COLLEGE, OXFORD.

In southern climes there lies a village,
Where oft the vicar, fond to pillage,
Sallies with gun aloft on shoulder,
(Orlando's self could ne'er look bolder)
With which, well ramm'd with proper cartridge,
He knocks down apples, or a partridge;
And whilst o'er all his neighbours' ground,
Striding, he throws his eyes around,
Surveying, with a look most blithe,
The growing riches of his tithe,
Minds not the game for which he's beating;
But, to prevent his flock from cheating,
Looks in each yard with jealous eye,
With care examines every stye,
Numbers the cows, observes their udders,
And at the dread of losing shudders.
" His composition's low; the butter
From so much milk"—he can but mutter.
He counts the poultry, large and fine,
" Forty and five, then four are mine."
But when the vernal season came,
And took him from pursuit of game,
A sudden thought of his condition
Induc'd him to an expedition;
An expedition of great moment,
Which sing I must, let what will come on 't.
Scratching his head one day in strong sort,
Then turning short upon his consort,
" My joy," quoth he, " now things are dearish,
To make some visits in the parish
I think can never be amiss;
As for my reason, it is this:
Some farms, you know, lie very distant,
At which I seldom am a vist'ant;
And, now the shooting season's over,
Cannot so readily discover
If any sharp or filching wight
Should cheat us of our lawful right;
Nor have we any means to hear how
Soon they expect a sow to farrow.
Besides, my dearest, should they cheat us,
We shall get something when they treat us;
And save at home the spit and pot;
A penny sav'd 's a penny got."
While thus, with all his oratory,
He labour'd through the pleasing story;
Ma'am by his side was all attention,
Delighted with his good invention;
Admir'd, and prais'd, then seal'd his bliss
With joyous matrimonial kiss.
And soon the loving pair agreed
By this same system to proceed;
And through the parish, with their how d'ye,
Go to each gaffer and each goody.
'Twas then resolv'd, that first of all
They pay a visit at E—t hall;
And William 's order'd, to save trouble,
To get a steed that carries double.

A neighbour's palfry, small and pretty,
Is borrow'd for the use of Kitty.
All things provided, out they stalk;
Poor Dobbin wishes them at York;
Then mount and sally in great state,
William before, behind them Kate;
When thus he entertains his spouse
With observations on each house,
Each field and orchard, as they ride,
Looking and pointing on each side;
Remarking whence his profits rise,
And where he gets the best supplies.
" That house is manag'd ill, my dear,
It scarce affords a pig a year:
This orchard 's good, but, were it wider,
'Twould yield a hogshead of good cider."
With joy he shows where turnips grew,
And tells what profits thence accrue;
But looks with envy on each stubble,
That nothing pays for vicar's trouble.
Pleas'd, she admires the lambkins play,
And loves them—when she 's told they pay.
Suppose them now arriv'd; my dame
Runs out, inquiring how they came;
Welcomes them in, and after all her
Forms are gone through, she shews her parlour.
" Pray, madam, take a dram; the weather,
Is cold and damp, and I have either
Good rum or brandy, plain or cherry;
A glass will make you warm and merry."
Next on the board the tea-things rattle,
And introduce a world of prattle.
" Your china's pretty, I declare;
'Tis pity 'tis such brittle ware."—
" Your tea is to your mind, I hope"—
" Exceeding good"—" Pray one more cup."
" Your toast is very nice; I've eat
Till I'm asham'd."—" Another bit:
The butter, ma'am, is fresh and sweet,
Although I say 't, that should not say 't."
After removing all the clutter
Of china, tea, and toast and butter,
Pipes and tobacco come, and beer
Preserv'd through many a rolling year;
And currant-wine, and punch, fit liquor
To elevate the heart of vicar.
At loo the ladies take a game,
All but my notable old dame;
She has no time to seat her crupper,
She 's so intent on getting supper.
At length it comes, a spare-rib, large
Enough to cover a small barge;
Or for (the simile to drag on)
A tilt for any carrier's waggon:
Attended by a brace of chicken,
But twelve months old, for lady's picking:
A link of sausages, that seem
A boom design'd for some strong stream.
" Your chicks are very fine,"—" You flatter;
I wish they were a little fatter.
But I have two shut up, design'd
For you ma'am."—"You're extremely kind."—
" And soon (my sow is very big)
I hope to send you a fat pig."
(The vicar inward smil'd, to see
His scheme succeed so happily.)
And last an apple-pye appear'd,
In earthen bowl, with custard smear'd.
The cloth remov'd, the chearful glass
Begins to circulate apace:

·The landlord, waxing brisk and mellow,
Becomes a hearty jovial fellow;
And now with liquor grown full ripe,
" Parson, you shall take t' other pipe."—
" We must not stay; 'tis late, Sir."—" No"—
" Well, one half pipe, and then wo go."
The pipe and liquor out, they start,
And homeward speed, with joyful heart.
He triumphs in his good success;
And she applauds his nice finesse.

---

## THE VICAR'S REPLY.

### BY FRANCIS FAWKES, M. A.

RHYMES! bless me! doggrel, I suppose,
Penn'd by some son of Brazen Nose;
Some starveling bard, or curate thin,
Whose bones have elbow'd out his skin;
And jogg'd him to provoke his Muse
An honest vicar to abuse,
Because he looks a little sleek,
With belly fair, and rosy cheek,
Which never but in men abound
Of easy minds, and bodies sound.
This vicar lives so blithe and happy,
With daily roast-meat, and ale nappy;
With dogs to hunt, and steeds to ride,
And wife that ambles at his side;
Who loves no hurries, routs, nor din,
But gently chucks her husband's chin.
These blessings, altogether met,
Have put lean curate in a pet,
As meagre wine is apt to fret.
And so this bard ecclesiastic
One day presum'd in Hudibrastic,
One day in Lent, un-eating time,
To prick his genius into rhyme;
The wind fresh blowing from the south,
And Indian vapours from his mouth:
For smoking aids this dry divine;
Puff follows puff, and line succeeds on line.
His lines by puffs he's wont to measure;
He rhymes for drink, and puffs for pleasure.
And as he labours for a joke,
Out comes a puff, that ends in smoke.
Lo! swelling into thought he sits;
Wrapt in the rage of rhyming fits;
Fits which are seldom known to fail,
When full blown up with bottled ale.
But puffy cider's better still,
It always works his doggrel mill;

By which, 'tis plain to all mankind,
His mill for verses goes by wind.
Encourag'd thus with bouncing liquor,
He points his wit against the vicar;
Then grows satiric on his wife,
The very meekest thing in life;
And next on cunning-looking Kitty,
And calls her palfry, not her,—pretty.
But why, sad poet, should you fall
On the good woman of E.—t Hall?
Because you did not taste her supper,
You hit her hard upon her crupper.
Next time that I and spouse ride double,
To save your Muse, and you too, trouble;
And keep my horse from being hit
With any of your waggish wit;
I'll take you in my hand along,
And thus prevent some idle song;
Cram you with custard till you choke:
And fill with punch, and not with smoke.
Mean while, to prove my honest heart,
Step down direct, and take a quart.

---

## TO DR. REDMAN,

WHO SENT THE AUTHOR A HARE, AND PROMISED
TO SUP WITH HIM. BY THE REV. DR. COWPER[1].

QUI leporem mittis contingis cuncta lepore;
  Condiat O leporem, te veniente, lepos!
Digna etenim, Redmanne, Jove est lepidissima
    coena,
  Quæ sic tota tua est et lepus atque lepos.

---

### IMITATED BY MR. FAWKES.

A HARE you in season presented to us, [puss:
And with fine Attic salt you will season your
'Tis a jovial treat—worthy Jove, I declare,
For the sauce and the supper will suit to a
    hair.

[1] John, eldest son of judge Cowper, rector of
Berkhamsted, Herts, patentee for making out
commissions of bankruptcy, one of K. George
the Second's chaplains, and afterwards dean of
Durham.

THE

# POEMS

OF

*JOHN ARMSTRONG, M. D.*

# LIFE OF ARMSTRONG,

## *BY MR. CHALMERS.*

THESE scanty materials are taken principally from Mr. Nichols's Life of Bowyer, and the Biographical Dictionary. To the former they were communicated, however sparingly, by the friends of Dr. Armstrong.

He was born in the parish of Castleton in Roxburghshire, where his father and brother were clergymen : and having compleated his education at the university of Edinburgh, took his degree in physic, Feb. 4, 1732 [1], with much reputation. His thesis *De Tabe purulente* was published as usual.

He appears to have courted the Muses while a student : his descriptive sketch in imitation of Shakespeare was one of his first attempts, and received the cordial approbation of Thomson, Mallet, and Young. Mallet, he informs us, intended to have published it, but altered his mind. His other imitations of Shakespeare were part of an unfinished tragedy written at a very early age. Much of his time, if we may judge from his writings, was devoted to the study of polite literature, and although he cannot be said to have entered deeply into any particular branch, he was more than a superficial connoisseur in painting, statuary, and music.

At what time he came to London is uncertain, but in 1735, he published an octavo pamphlet, without his name, entitled An Essay for abridging the Study of Physic : to which is added a Dialogue between Hygeia, Mercury, and Pluto, relating to the Practice of Physic, as it is managed by a certain illustrious Society. As also an Epistle from Usbeck the Persian, to Joshua Ward, esq. It is dedicated to the "Antacademic Philosophers, to the generous despisers of the schools, to the deservedly-celebrated Joshua Ward, John Moor, and the rest of the numerous sect of inspired physicians." The Essay, which has been lately reprinted in Dilly's Repository, is an humourous attack on quacks and quackery, with allusions to the neglect of medical education among the practising apothecaries :

---

[1] Three days after he sent a copy of his thesis to sir Hans Sloane, accompanied by a handsome Latin letter, now in the British Museum. I find in the same repository a paper written by him in 1744 on the alcalescent disposition of animal fluids, which appears to have been read in the Royal Society, but not published. C.

but the author had exhausted his wit in it, and the Dialogue and Epistle are consequently flat and insipid.

In 1737, he published A Synopsis of the History and Cure of the Venereal Disease, probably as an introduction to practice in that lucrative branch: but it was unfortunately followed by his poem, The Economy of Love, which, although it enjoyed a rapid sale, has been very properly excluded from every collection of poetry, and is supposed to have impeded his professional career. In 1741, we find him soliciting Dr. Birch's recommendation to Dr. Mead, that he might be appointed physician to the forces then going to the West Indies.

His celebrated poem, The Art of Preserving Health, appeared in 1744, and contributed highly to his fame as a poet. Dr. Warton, in his Reflections on Didactic Poetry, annexed to his edition of Virgil, observed that " To describe so difficult a thing, gracefully and poetically, as the effects of distemper on the human body, was reserved for Dr. Armstrong, who accordingly hath nobly executed it at the end of the third book of his Art of Preserving Health, where he hath given us that pathetic account of the sweating sickness. There is a classical correctness and closeness of style in this poem that are truly admirable, and the subject is raised and adorned by numberless poetical images." Dr. Mackenzie, in his History of Health, bestowed similar praises on this poem, which was indeed every where read and admired.

In 1746, he was appointed one of the physicians to the hospital for lame and sick soldiers behind Buckingham-house. In 1751, he published his poem on Benevolence, in folio, a production which seems to come from the heart, and contains sentiments which could have been expressed with equal ardour only by one who felt them. His Taste, an Epistle to a young critic, 1753, is a lively and spirited imitation of Pope, and the first production in which our author began to view men and manners with a splenetic eye. In 1758, he published Sketches, or Essays on Various Subjects, under the fictitious name of Lancelot Temple, esq. In some of these he is supposed to have been assisted by the celebrated John Wilkes, with whom he lived in habits of intimacy. What Mr. Wilkes contributed we are not told, but this gentleman, with all his moral failings had a more chaste classical taste and a purer vein of humour than we find in these Sketches, which are deformed by a perpetual flow of affectation, a struggle to say smart things, and above all a most disgusting repetition of vulgar oaths and exclamations. This practice, so unworthy of a gentleman or a scholar, seems to have predominated in Dr. Armstrong's conversation, and is not unsparingly scattered through all his works, with the exception of his Art of Preserving Health. It incurred the just censure of the critics of his day, with whom, for this reason, he could never be reconciled.

In 1760, he was appointed physician to the army in Germany, where in 1761 he wrote a poem called Day, addressed to Mr. Wilkes. It was published in the same year, probably by some person to whom Mr. Wilkes had lent it. The editor, in his prefatory advertisement, professes to lament that it is not in his power to present the public with a more perfect copy of this spirited letter. He ventures to publish it exactly as it came into his hands, without the knowledge or consent of the author, or of the gentleman to whom it is addressed. His sole motive is to communicate to others the pleasure he has received from a work of taste and genius. He thinks himself secure of the thanks of the public, and hopes this farther advantage will attend the present publication, that it will soon be followed by a correct and compleat edition from the author's own manuscript.

All this is somewhat mysterious, but there will not, however, be much injustice in supposing that Mr. Wilkes conveyed to the press as much of this Epistle as he thought would do credit to the author and to himself. It is certain the poem was published by Andrew Miller who was well acquainted with Dr. Armstrong, and would not have joined in any attempt to injure his fame or property. The poem contains many striking allusions to manners and objects of taste, but the versification is frequently careless: the author did not think proper to add it to his collected works, nor was it ever published in a more correct form.

In this poem he was supposed to reflect on Churchill, but in a manner so distant that few except of Churchill's irascible temper could have laid hold of any cause of offence. This libeller, however, retorted on our author in The Journey, with an accusation of ingratitude, the meaning of which is said to have been, that Dr. Armstrong forgot certain pecuniary obligations he owed to Mr. Wilkes. About the same time a coolness took between place Dr. Armstrong and Mr. Wilkes on political grounds. Armstrong not only serving under government as an army-physician, but he was also a Scotchman, and could not help resenting the indignity which Wilkes was perpetually attempting to throw on that nation in his North Briton. On this account they appear to have continued at variance as late as the year 1773, when our author called Wilkes to account for some reflections on his character which he suspected he had written in his favourite vehicle, the Public Advertiser. The conversation which passed on this occasion was lately published in the Gentleman's Magazine (1792), and is said to have been copied from minutes taken the same afternoon, April 7, 1773, and sent to a friend: but as the doctor makes by far the worst figure in the dialogue, it can be no secret by whom the minutes were taken, and afterwards published. The contests, however, of Wilkes and his friends are of very little moment: there appears to have been no sound principle of friendship among them, and no ties which they did not think themselves at liberty to violate when it suited their interest.

After the peace, Dr. Armstrong resided some years in London, where his practice was confined to a small circle, but where he was respected as a man of general knowledge and taste, and an agreeable companion. In 1770, he published two volumes of Miscellanies, containing the articles already mentioned, except the Economy of Love (an edition of which he corrected for separate publication in 1768) and his Epistle to Mr. Wilkes. The new articles were, the Imitations of Shakespeare and Spenser, the Universal Almanac, and the Forced Marriage, a tragedy, which was offered to Garrick about the year 1754, and rejected. A second part of his Sketches was likewise added to these volumes, and appeared to every delicate and judicious mind, as rambling and improper as the first. "I know not," says Dr. Beattie to his friend sir William Forbes, "what is the matter with Armstrong, but he seems to have conceived a rooted aversion at the whole human race, except a few friends, who, it seems, are dead. He sets the public opinion at defiance: a piece of boldness, which neither Virgil nor Horace

were ever so shameless as to acknowledge. I do not think that Dr. Armstrong
has any cause to complain of the public : his Art of Health is not indeed a popular poem, but it is very much liked, and has often been printed. It will make him
known and esteemed by posterity : and I presume he will be more esteemed if
all his other works perish with him. In his Sketches, indeed, are many sensible
and some striking remarks : but they breathe such a rancorous and contemptuous
spirit, and abound so much in odious vulgarisms and colloquial execrations, that
in reading we are as often disgusted as pleased. I know not what to say of his
Univeral Almanac ; it seems to me an attempt at humour, but such humour is
either too high or too low for my comprehension. The plan of his tragedy, called
The Forced Marriage, is both obscure and improbable : yet there are good strokes
in it, particularly in the last scene."

In 1771, he published another extraordinary effusion of spleen, under the title
of A short Ramble through some parts of France and Italy, and with his assumed name of Lancelot Temple. This ramble he took in company with Mr.
Fuseli, the celebrated painter, who speaks highly in favour of the general benevolence of his character[2]. In 1773, under his own name, and unfortunately for
his reputation, appeared a quarto pamphlet of Medical Essays, in which, while
he condemns theory, he plunges into all the uncertainties of theoretical conjectures. He complains, likewise, in a very coarse style, of the neglect he met with
as a physician, and the severity with which he was treated as an author, and appears to write with a temper soured by disappointment in all his pursuits.

He died at his house in Russell-street, Covent Garden, on Sept. 7, 1779. His
death was attributed to an accidental contusion in his thigh, while getting into
the carriage which brought him to town from a visit in Lincolnshire. To the
surprise of his friends, who thought that poverty was the foundation of his
frequent complaints, he left behind him more than three thousand pounds, saved
out of a very moderate income arising principally from his half-pay.

His character is said to have been that of a man of learning and genius, of considerable abilities in his profession, of great benevolence and goodness of heart,
fond of associating with men of parts and genius, but indolent and inactive, and
therefore totally unqualified to employ the means that usually lead to medical employment, or to make his way through a crowd of competitors. An intimate
friendship always subsisted between him and Thomson the poet ; as well as with
other gentlemen of learning and genius ; and he was intimate with, and respected
by sir John Pringle, at the time of his death[3]. In 1753, Dr. Theobald addressed
two Latin Odes, Ad ingenuum virum, tum medicis, tum poeticis facultatibus
præstantem, Johannem Armstrong, M. D[4].

Dr. Armstrong's fame as a poet must depend entirely on his Art of Preserving

---

[2] He had been acquainted with Mr. Fuseli for many years ; and Mr. Isaac Reed informed me that
it is to this gentleman he alludes in the following passage in one of his Sketches, published in 1770,
On the Influence of Climate upon Genius.—"As to history (painting) itself, besides some promising specimens of it at home, perhaps even this barren age has produced a genius, not indeed of
British growth; unpatronized, and at present almost unknown ; who may live to astonish, to terrify,
and delight all Europe." C.

[3] Nichols' Life of Bowyer, p. 281, 282, 4to. edit. I am happy to inform my readers, that they
may soon expect an enlarged edition of this valuable collection of literary history, in four volumes
8vo. C.

[4] Ibid. p. 583.

Health, which, although liable to some of the objections usually offered against didactic poetry, is yet free from the weightiest ; and in this respect he may be
deemed more fortunate, as he certainly is superior to Philips, Dyer, and Grainger.
The Art of Preserving Health is 'so different from those which are mechanical,
that his Muse is seldom invited to an employment beneath her dignity. The means
of preserving health are so intimately connected with the mind, and depend so
much on philosophy, reflection, and observation, that the author has full scope
for the powers of fancy, and for many of those ornamental flights which are not
only pleasing, but constitute genuine poetry. In considering the varieties of air
and exercise, he has seized many happy occasions for picturesque description ; and
when treating on the passions, he has many striking passages of moral sentiment,
which are vigorous, just, and impressive. In Book II. on Diet, we discover more
judgment than poetical inspiration, and he seems to be aware that the subject had
a natural tendency to lower his tone. He seems therefore intent in this book
principally to render useful precepts familiar, and if possible to make them take
hold of the imagination. There are however descriptive passages even here that
are very grand. It would perhaps be difficult to select from these volumes an
image more finely conceived and uniformly preserved, than where he inculcates the
simple precept, that persons who have been exhausted for want of food ought not
to indulge when plenty presents itself :

———————————While the vital fire
Burns feebly, heap not the green fuel on ;
But prudently foment the wandering spark
With what the soonest feeds its kindred touch:
Be frugal ev'n of that : a little give
At first : that kindled, add a little more :
Till, by deliberate nourishing, the flame
Reviv'd, with all its wonted vigour glows 5.

5 I have great pleasure in referring the reader to an elaborate criticism on this poem, by Dr. Aikin,
prefixed to an ornamented edition, published by Messrs. Cadell and Davies in 1803.

# POEMS

OF

# DR. ARMSTRONG.

## THE ART OF PRESERVING HEALTH.

### BOOK I.—AIR.

Daughter of Pæon, queen of every joy,
Hygeia [1]; whose indulgent smile sustains
The various race luxuriant Nature pours,
And on th' immortal essences bestows
Immortal youth; auspicious, O descend!
Thou cheerful guardian of the rolling year,
Whether thou wanton'st on the western gale,
Or shak'st the rigid pinions of the North,
Diffusest life and vigour through the tracts
Of air, thro' earth, and ocean's deep domain.
When thro' the blue serenity of Heaven
Thy power approaches, all the wasteful host
Of Pain and Sickness, squalid and deform'd,
Confounded sink into the loathsome gloom,
Where in deep Erebus involv'd the Fiends
Grow more profane.   Whatever shapes of death,
Shook from the hideous chambers of the globe,
Swarm thro' the shuddering air: whatever
          plagues
Or meagre famine breeds, or with slow wings
Rise from the putrid wat'ry element,
The damp waste forest, motionless and rank,
That smothers earth, and all the breathless
          winds,
Or the vile carnage of th' inhuman field;
Whatever baneful breathes the rotten South;
Whatever ills th' extremes or sudden change
Of cold and hot, or moist and dry produce;
They fly thy pure effulgence: they and all
The secret poisons of avenging Heaven,
And all the pale tribes halting in the train
Of Vice and heedless Pleasure: or if aught
The comet's glare amid the burning sky,

[1] Hygeia, the goddess of health, was, according to the genealogy of the heathen deities, the daughter of Æsculapius; who, as well as Apollo, was distinguished by the name of Pæon.

Mournful eclipse, or planets ill combin'd,
Portend disastrous to the vital world;
Thy salutary power averts their rage,
Averts the general bane: and but for thee
Nature would sicken, nature soon would die.
    Without thy cheerful active energy
No rapture swells the breast, no poet sings,
No more the maids of Helicon delight.
Come then with me, O goddess, heav'nly gay!
Begin the song; and let it sweetly flow,
And let it wisely teach thy wholesome laws:
" How best the fickle fabric to support
Of mortal man; in healthful body how
A healthful mind the longest to maintain."
'Tis hard, in such a strife of rules, to choose
The best, and those of most extensive use;
Harder in clear and animated song
Dry philosophic precepts to convey.
Yet with thy aid the secret wilds I trace
Of Nature, and with daring steps proceed
Thro' paths the Muses never trod before.
    Nor should I wander doubtful of my way,
Had I the lights of that sagacious mind
Which taught to check the pestilential fire,
And quell the deadly Python of the Nile.
O thou belov'd by all the graceful arts,
Thou long the fav'rite of the healing powers,
Indulge, O Mead! a well-design'd essay,
Howe'er imperfect: and permit that I
My little knowledge with my country share,
Till you the rich Asclepian stores unlock,
And with new graces dignify the theme.
    Ye who amid this feverish world would wear
A body free of pain, of cares a mind;
Fly the rank city, shun its turbid air;
Breathe not the chaos of eternal smoke
And volatile corruption, from the dead,
The dying, sick'ning, and the living world
Exhal'd, to sully Heaven's transparent dom
With dim mortality.   It is not air
That from a thousand lungs reeks back to thine,
Sated with exhalations rank and fell,
The spoil of dunghills, and the putrid thaw
Of nature; when from shape and texture she

Relapses into fighting elements:
It is not air, but floats a nauseous mass
Of all obscene, corrupt, offensive things.
Much moisture hurts; but here a sordid bath,
With oily rancour fraught, relaxes more
The solid frame than simple moisture can.
Besides, immur'd in many a sullen bay
That never felt the freshness of the breeze,
This slumb'ring deep remains, and ranker grows
With sickly rest: and (tho' the lungs abhor
To drink the dun fuliginous abyss)
Did not the acid vigour of the mine,
Roll'd from so many thundering chimnies, tame
The putrid steams that overswarm the sky;
This caustic venom would perhaps corrode
Those tender cells that draw the vital air,
In vain with all the unctuous rills bedew'd;
Or by the drunken venous tubes, that yawn
In countless pores o'er all the pervious skin
Imbib'd, would poison all the balsamic blood,
And rouse the heart to every fever's rage.
While yet you breathe, away; the rural wilds
Invite.; the mountains call you, and the vales;
The woods, the streams, and each ambrosial
                                    breeze
That fans the ever-undulating sky;
A kindly sky! whose fost'ring power regales
Man, beast, and all the vegetable reign.
Find then some woodland scene where Nature
    smiles
Benign, where all her honest children thrive.
To us there wants not many a happy seat!
Look round the smiling land, such numbers rise
We hardly fix, bewilder'd in our choice.
See where enthron'd in adamantine state,
Proud of her bards, imperial Windsor sits;
Where choose thy seat in some aspiring grove
Fast by the slowly-winding Thames; or where
Broader she laves fair Richmond's green retreats,
(Richmond that sees an hundred villas rise
Rural or gay.) O! from the summer's rage
O! wrap me in the friendly gloom that hides
Unbrageous Ham!—But if the busy town
Attract thee still to toil for power of gold,
Sweetly thou may'st thy vacant hours possess
In Hampstead, courted by the western wind;
Or Greenwich, waving o'er the winding flood;
Or lose the world amid the sylvan wilds
Of Dulwich, yet by barbarous arts unspoil'd.
Green rise the Kentish hills in cheerful air;
But on the marshy plains that Lincoln spreads
Build not, nor rest too long thy wandering feet.
For on a rustic throne of dewy turf,
With baneful fogs her aching temples bound,
Quartana there presides; a meagre fiend
Begot by Eurus, when his brutal force
Compress'd the slothful Naiad of the fens.
From such a mixture sprung, this fitful pest
With fev'rish blasts subdues the sick'ning land:
Cold tremours come, with mighty love of rest,
Convulsive yawnings, lassitude, and pains
That sting the burden'd brows, fatigue the loins,
And rack the joints, and every torpid limb;
Then parching heat succeeds, till copious sweats
O'erflow: a short relief from former ills
Beneath repeated shocks the wretches pine,
The vigour sinks, the habit melts away:
The cheerful, pure, and animated bloom
Dies from the face, with squalid atrophy

Devour'd, in sallow melancholy clad.
And oft the sorceress, in her'sated wrath,
Resigns them to the furies of her train:
The bloated Hydrops, and the yellow Fiend
Ting'd with her own accumulated gall.
    In quest of sites, avoid the mournful plain
Where osiers thrive, and trees that love the
    lake;
Where many lazy muddy rivers flow:
Nor for the wealth that all the Indies roll
Fix near the marshy margin of the main.
For from the humid soil and wat'ry reign
Eternal vapours rise; the spongy air
For ever weeps: or, turgid with the weight
Of waters, pours a sounding deluge down.
Skies such as these let every mortal shun
Who dreads the dropsy, palsy, or the gout,
Tertian, corrosive scurvy, or moist catarrh;
Or any other injury that grows
From raw-spun fibres idle and unstrung,
Skin ill-perspiring, and the purple flood
In languid eddies loitering into phlegm.
    Yet not alone from humid skies we pine;
For air may be too dry. The subtle Heaven,
That winnows into dust the blasted downs,
Bare and extended wide without a stream,
Too fast imbibes th' attenuated lymph
Which, by the surface, from the blood exhales
The lungs grow rigid, and with toil essay
Their flexible vibrations! or inflam'd,
Their tender ever-moving structure thaws,
Spoil'd of its limpid vehicle, the blood
A mass of lees remains, a drossy tide
That slow as Lethe wanders thro' the veins;
Unactive in the services of life,
Unfit to lead its pitchy current thro'
The secret mazy channels of the brain.
The melancholic fiend (that worst despair
Of physic) hence the rust-complexion'd man
Pursues, whose blood is dry, whose fibres gain
Too stretch'd a tone; and hence in climes adust
So sudden tumults seize the trembling nerves,
And burning fevers glow with double rage.
    Fly, if you can, these violent extremes
Of air; the wholesome is nor moist nor dry.
But as the power of choosing is deny'd
To half mankind, a further task ensues;
How best to mitigate these fell extremes,
How breathe unhurt the withering element,
Or hazy atmosphere: though custom moulds
To every clime the soft Promethean clay;
And he who first the fogs of Essex breath'd
(So kind is native air) may in the fens
Of Essex from inveterate ills revive
At pure Montpelier or Bermuda caught.
But if the raw and oozy heaven offend;
Correct the soil, and dry the sources up
Of wat'ry exhalation: wide and deep
Conduct your trenches through the quaking
    bog;
Solicitous, with all your winding arts,
Betray the unwilling lake into the stream;
And weed the forest, and invoke the winds
To break the toils where strangled vapours lie;
Or through the thickets send the crackling
    flames.
Meantime at home with cheerful fires dispel
The humid air: and let your table smoke
With solid roast or bak'd; or what the herds

Of tamer breed supply; or what the wilds
Yield to the toilsome pleasures of the chase.
Generous your wine, the boast of ripening
    years;
But frugal be your cups: the languid frame,
Vapid and sunk from yesterday's debauch,
Shrinks from the cold embrace of wat'ry Heavens.
But neither these nor all Apollo's arts,
Disarm the dangers of the dropping sky,
Unless with exercise and manly toil    [blood.
You brace your nerves, and spur the lagging
The fat'ning clime let all the sons of ease
Avoid; if indolence would wish to live,
Go, yawn and loiter out the long slow year
In fairer skies. If droughty regions parch
The skin and lungs, and bake the thickening
    blood;
Deep in the waving forest choose your seat,
Where fuming trees refresh the thirsty air;
And wake the fountains from their secret beds,
And into lakes dilate their rapid stream.
Here spread your gardens wide; and let the cool,
The moist relaxing vegetable store
Prevail in each repast: your food supply'd
By bleeding life, be gently wasted down,
By soft decoction and a mellowing heat,
To liquid balm; or, if the solid mass
You choose, tormented in the boiling wave:
That through the thirsty channels of the blood
A smooth diluted chyle may ever flow.
The fragrant dairy from its cool recess
Its nectar acid or benign will pour
To drown your thirst; or let the mantling bowl
Of keen sherbet the fickle taste relieve.
For with the viscous blood the simple stream
Will hardly mingle; and fermented cups
Oft dissipate more moisture than they give.
Yet when pale seasons rise, or Winter rolls
His horrours o'er the world, thou may'st indulge
In feasts more genial, and impatient broach
The mellow cask. Then too the scourging air
Provokes to keener toils than sultry droughts
Allow. But rarely we such skies blaspheme.
Steep'd in continual rains, or with raw fogs
Bedew'd, our seasons droop: incumbent still
A ponderous Heaven o'erwhelms the sinking soul.
Lab'ring with storms in heapy mountains rise
Th' imbattled clouds, as if the Stygian shades
Had left the dungeon of eternal night,
Till black with thunder and the South descends.
Scarce in a showerless day the Heavens indulge
Our melting clime; except the baleful East
Withers the tender spring, and sourly checks
The fancy of the year. Our fathers talk
Of summers, balmy air, and skies serene.
Good Heaven! for what unexpiated crimes
This dismal change! the brooding elements,
Do they, your powerful ministers of wrath,
Prepare some fierce exterminating plague?
Or is it fix'd in the decrees above
That lofty Albion melt into the main?
Indulgent Nature! O dissolve this gloom!
Bind in eternal adamant the winds
That drown or wither: give the genial West
To breathe, and in its turn the sprightly North:
And may once more the circling seasons rule
The year; not mix in every monstrous day.
    Meantime, the moist malignity to shun [paign
Of burthen'd skies; mark where the dry cham-

Swells into cheerful hills: where marjoram
And thyme, the love of bees, perfume the air;
And where the cynorrhodon [2] with the rose
For fragrance vies; for in the thirsty soil
Most fragrant breathe the aromatic tribes.
There bid thy roofs high on the basking steep
Ascend, there light thy hospitable fires.
And let them see the winter morn arise,
The summer evening blushing in the West:
While with umbrageous oaks the ridge behind
O'erhung, defends you from the blust'ring North,
And bleak affliction of the peevish East.
Oh! when the growling winds contend, and all
The sounding forest fluctuates in the storm;
To sink in warm repose, and hear the din
Howl o'er the steady battlements, delights
Above the luxury of vulgar sleep.
The murmuring rivulet, and the hoarser strain
Of waters rushing o'r the slippery rocks,
Will nightly lull you to ambrosial rest.
To please the fancy is no trifling good,
Where health is studied; for whatever moves
The mind with calm delight, promotes the just
And natural movements of th' harmonious
    frame.
Besides, the sportive brook for ever shakes
The trembling air, that floats from hill to hill
From vale to mountain, with incessant change
Of purest element, refreshing still
Your airy seat, and uninfected gods.
Chiefly for this I praise the man who builds
High on the breezy ridge, whose lofty sides
Th' ethereal deep with endless billows chafes.
His purer mansion nor contagious years
Shall reach, nor deadly putrid airs annoy.
    But may no fogs, from lake or fenny plain,
Involve my hill! and whereso'er you build,
Whether on sun-burnt Epsom, or the plains
Wash'd by the silent Lee; in Chelsea low,
Or high Blackheath with wintry winds assail'd;
Dry be your house: but airy more than warm.
Else every breath of ruder wind will strike
Your tender body through with rapid pains;
Fierce coughs will tease you, hoarseness bind your
    voice,
Or moist gravedo load your aching brows.
These to defy, and all the fates that dwell
In cloister'd air tainted with steaming life,
Let lofty ceilings grace your ample rooms;
And still at azure noontide may your dome
At every window drink the liquid sky.
    Need we the sunny situation here,
And theatres open to the South, commend?
Here, where the morning's misty breath infests
More than the torrid noon? How sickly grow,
How pale, the plants in those ill-fated vales,
That, circled round with the gigantic heap
Of mountains, never felt, nor ever hope
To feel, the genial vigour of the Sun!
While on the neighbouring hill the rose in-
    flames
The verdant spring; in virgin beauty blows
The tender lily, languishingly sweet;
O'er every hedge the wanton woodbine roves,
And autumn ripens in the summer's ray.
Nor less the warmer living tribes demand
The fost'ring Sun, whose energy divine

    [2] The wild rose, or that which grows on the
common briar.

Dwells not in mortal fire; whose gen'rous heat
Glows thro' the mass of grosser elements,
And kindles into life the ponderous spheres.
Cheer'd by thy kind invigorating warmth,
We court thy beams, great majesty of day !
If not the soul, the regent of this world,
First-born of Heaven, and only less than God !

## THE ART OF PRESERVING HEALTH.

### BOOK II.—DIET.

Enough of air. A desert subject now,
Rougher and wilder, rises to my sight.
A barren waste, where not a garland grows
To bind the Muse's brow ; not ev'n a proud
Stupendous solitude frowns o'er the heath,
To rouse a noble horrour in the soul :
But rugged paths fatigue, and errour leads
Thro' endless labyrinths the devious feet.
Farewell, ethereal fields ! the humbler arts
Of life ; the table and the homely gods
Demand my song. Elysian gales, adieu !
The blood, the fountain whence the spirits flow,
The generous stream that waters every part,
And motion, vigour, and warm life conveys
To every particle that moves or lives ;
This vital fluid, through unnumber'd tubes
Pour'd by the heart, and to the heart again
Refunded ; scourg'd for ever round and round ;
Enrag'd with heat and toil, at lasts forgets
Its balmy nature; virulent and thin
It grows ; and now, but that a thousand gates
Are open to its flight, it would destroy
The parts it cherish'd and repair'd before.
Besides, the flexible and tender tubes
Melt in the mildest most nectareous tide
That ripening Nature rolls; as in the stream
Its crumbling banks ; but what the force
Of plastic fluids hourly batters down,
That very force, those plastic particles
Rebuild : so mutable the state of man.
For this the watchful appetite was given,
Daily with fresh materials to repair
This unavoidable expense of life,
This necessary waste of flesh and blood.
Hence, the concoctive powers, with various art,
Subdue the cruder aliments to chyle ;
The chyle to blood; the foamy purple tide
To liquors, which thro' finer arteries
To different parts their winding course pursue ;
To try new changes, and new forms put on,
Or for the public, or some private use,
Nothing so foreign but th' athletic hind
Can labour into blood. The hungry meal
Alone he fears, or aliments too thin ;
By violent powers too easily subu'd,
Too soon expell'd. His daily labour thaws,
To friendly chyle, the most rebellious mass
That salt can harden, or the smoke of years ;
Nor does his gorge the luscious bacon rue,
Nor that which Cestria sends, tenacious paste
Of solid milk. But ye of softer clay,
Infirm and delicate ! and ye who waste
With pale and bloated sloth the tedious day !
Avoid the stubborn aliment, avoid

The full repast ; and let sagacious age
Grow wiser, lesson'd by the dropping teeth.
Half subtiliz'd to chyle, the liquid food
Readiest obeys th' assimilating powers ;
And soon the tender vegetable mass
Relents ; and soon the young of those that tread
The stedfast earth, or cleave the green abyss,
Or pathless sky. And if the steer must fall,
In youth and sanguine vigour let him die ;
Nor stay till rigid age, or heavy ails,
Absolve him ill-requited from the yoke.
Some with high forage; and luxuriant ease,
Indulge the veteran ox ; but wiser thou,
From the bald mountain or the barren downs,
Expect the flocks by frugal Nature fed ;
A race of purer blood, with exercise
Refin'd and scanty fare : for, old or young,
The stall'd are never healthy ; nor the cramm'd.
Not all the culinary arts can tame
To wholesome food, the abominable growth
Of rest and gluttony ; the prudent taste
Rejects like bane such loathsome lusciousness.
The languid stomach curses even the pure
Delicious fat, and all the race of oil :
For more the oily aliments relax
Its feeble tone ; and with the eager lymph
(Fond to incorporate with all it meets)
Coyly they mix, and shun with slippery wiles
The woo'd embrace. Th' irresoluble oil,
So gentle late and blandishing, in floods
Of rancid bile o'erflows : what tumults hence,
What horrors rise, were nauseous to relate.
Choose leaner viands, ye whose jovial make
Too fast the gummy nutriment imbibes :
Choose sober meals ; and rouse to active life
Your cumbrous clay ; nor on the enfeebling down,
Irresolute, protract the morning hours.
But let the man whose bones are thinly clad,
With cheerful ease and succulent repast
Improve his habit if he can ; for each
Extreme departs from perfect sanity.
I could relate what table this demands,
Or that complexion ; what the various powers
Of various foods : but fifty years would roll,
And fifty more before the tale were done.
Besides, there often lurks some nameless, strange,
Peculiar thing ; nor on the skin display'd,
Felt in the pulse, nor in the habit seen ;
Which finds a poison in the food that most
The temp'rature affects. There are, whose blood
Impetuous rages thro' the turgid veins,
Who better bear the fiery fruits of India
Than the moist melon, or pale cucumber.
Of chilly nature others fly the board
Supply'd with slaughter, and the vernal powers
For cooler, kinder sustenance implore.
Some even the generous nutriment detest
Which, in the shell, the sleeping embryo rears.
Some, more unhappy still, repent the gifts
Of Pales ; soft, delicious and benign :
The balmy quintessence of every flower,
And every grateful herb that decks the spring ;
The fost'ring dew of tender sprouting life ;
The best refection of declining age ;
The kind restorative of those who lie
Half dead and panting, from the doubtful strife
Of nature struggling in the grasp of death.
Try all the bounties of this fertile globe,
There is not such a salutary food

As suits with every stomach. But (except,
Amid the mingled mass of fish and fowl,
And boil'd and bak'd, you hesitate by which
You sunk oppress'd, or whether not by all)
Taught by experience soon you may discern
What pleases, what offends. Avoid the cates
That lull the sicken'd appetite too long;
Or heave with fev'rish flushings all the face,
Burn in the palms, and parch the rough'ning
tongue;
Or much diminish or too much increase
Th' expense, which Nature's wise economy,
Without or waste or avarice, maintains.
Such cates abjur'd, let prowling hunger loose,
And bid the curious palate roam at will;
They scarce can err amid the various stores
That burst the teeming entrails of the world.
Led by sagacious taste, the ruthless king
Of beasts on blood and slaughter only lives;
The tiger, form'd alike to cruel meals,
Would at the manger starve: of milder seeds
The generous horse to herbage and to grain
Confines his wish; tho' fabling Greece resound
The Thracian steeds with human carnage wild.
Prompted by instinct's never-erring power,
Each creature knows its proper aliment;
But man, th' inhabitant of every clime,
With all the commoners of Nature feeds.
Directed, bounded, by this power within,
Their cravings are well-aim'd: voluptuous man
Is by superior faculties misled;
Misled from pleasure even in quest of joy,
Sated with Nature's boons, what thousands seek,
With dishes tortur'd from their native taste,
And mad variety, to spur beyond
Its wiser will the jaded appetite!
Is this for pleasure? Learn a juster taste;
And know that temperance is true luxury.
Or is it pride? Pursue some nobler aim,
Dismiss your parasites who praise for hire;
And earn the fair esteem of honest men, [yours,
Whose praise is fame. Form'd of such clay as
The sick, the needy, shiver at your gates.
Even modest want may bless your hand unseen,
Tho' hush'd in patient wretchedness at home.
Is there no virgin, grac'd with ev'ry charm
But that which binds the mercenary vow?
No youth of genius, whose neglected bloom
Unfoster'd sickens in the barren shade?
No worthy man by fortune's random blows,
Or by a heart too generous and humane,
Constrain'd to leave his happy natal seat,
And sigh for wants more bitter than his own?
There are, while human miseries abound,
A thousand ways to waste superfluous wealth,
Without one fool or flatterer at your board,
Without one hour of sickness or disgust.
But other ills th' ambiguous feast pursue,
Besides provoking the lascivious taste.
Such various foods, tho' harmless each alone,
Each other violate; and oft we see
What strife is brew'd, and what pernicious bane,
From combinations of obnoxious things.
Th' unbounded taste I mean not to confine
To hermit's diet needlessly severe.
But would you long the sweets of health enjoy,
Or husband pleasure; at one impious meal
Exhaust not half the bounties of the year,
Of every realm. It matters not meanwhile

How much to morrow differ from to day;
So far indulge; 'tis fit, besides, that man,
To change obnoxious, be to change inur'd.
But stay the curious appetite, and taste
With caution fruits you never tried before.
For want of use the kindest aliment
Sometimes offends; while custom tames the
rage
Of poison to mild amity with life.
So Heaven has form'd us to the general taste
Of all its gifts: so custom has improv'd
This bent of nature; that few simple foods,
Of all that earth, or air, or ocean yield,
But by excess offend. Beyond the sense
Of light refection, at the genial board
Indulge not often; nor protract the feast
To dull satiety; till soft and slow
A drowsy death creeps on, th' expansive soul
Oppress'd, and smother'd the celestial fire.
The stomach, urg'd beyond its active tone,
Hardly to nutrimental chyle subdues
The softest food: unfinish'd and deprav'd,
The chyle, in all its future wanderings, owns
Its turbid fountain; not by purer streams
So to be clear'd, but foulness will remain.
To sparkling wine what ferment can exalt
Th' unripen'd grape? or what mechanic skill
From the crude ore can spin the ductile gold?
Gross riot treasures up a wealthy fund
Of plagues: but more immedicable ills
Attend the lean extreme. For physic knows
How to disburthen the too tumid veins,
Even how to ripen the half-labour'd blood:
But to unlock the elemental tubes,
Collaps'd and shrunk with long inanity,
And with balsamic nutriment repair
The dried and worn-out habit, were to bid
Old age grow green, and wear a second spring;
Or the tall ash, long ravish'd from the soil,
Thro' wither'd veins imbibe the vernal dew.
When hunger calls, obey; not often wait
Till hunger sharpen to corrosive pain:
For the keen appetite will feast beyond
What nature well can bear: and one extreme
Ne'er without danger meets its own reverse.
Too greedily th' exhausted veins absorb
The recent chyle, and load enfeebled powers
Oft to th' extinction of the vital flame.
To the pale cities, by the firm-set siege
And famine humbled, may this verse be borne;
And hear, ye hardiest sons that Albion breeds,
Long toss'd and famish'd on the wintry main;
The war shook off, or hospitable shore
Attain'd, with temperance bear the shock of joy;
Nor crown with festive rites th' auspicious day:
Such feasts might prove more fatal than the
waves,
Than war or famine. While the vital fire
Burns feebly, heap not the green fuel on;
But prudently foment the wandering spark
With what the soonest feeds its kindest touch
Be frugal ev'n of that: a little give
At first; that kindled, add a little more;
Till, by deliberate nourishing, the flame
Reviv'd, with all its wonted vigour glows.
But tho' the two (the full and the jejune)
Extremes have each their vice; it much avails
Ever with gentle tide to ebb and flow
From this to that: so nature learns to bear

Whatever chance or headlong appetite
May bring. Besides, a meagre day subdues
The cruder clods by sloth or luxury
Collected, and unloads the wheels of life.
Sometimes a coy aversion to the feast
Comes on, while yet no blacker omen lours;
Then is the time to shun the tempting board
Were it your natal or your nuptial day.
Perhaps a fast so seasonable starves
The latent seeds of woe, which rooted once
Might cost you labour. But the day return'd
Of festal luxury, the wise indulge
Most in the tender vegetable breed :
Then chiefly when the summer beams inflame
The brazen Heavens; or angry Sirius sheds
A feverish taint thro' the still gulph of air.
The moist cool viands then, and flowing cup
From the fresh dairy-virgin's liberal hand,
Will save your head from harm, tho'. round the
                world
The dreaded causos³ roll his wasteful fires.
Pale humid Winter loves the generous board,
The meal more copious, and the warmer fare ;
And longs with old wood and old wine to cheer
His quaking heart. The seasons which divide
Th' empires of heat and cold ; by neither
                claim'd,
Influenc'd by both ; a middle regimen
Impose. Thro' Autumn's languishing domain
Descending, Nature by degrees invites
To glowing luxury. But from the depth
Of Winter when th' invigorated year
Emerges ; when Favonius, flush'd with love,
Toyful and young, in every breeze descends
More warm and wanton on his kindling bride ;
Then, shepherds, then begin to spare your
                flocks ;
And learn, with wise humanity, to check
The lust of blood. Now pregnant earth commits
A various offspring to the indulgent sky :
Now bounteous Nature feeds with lavish hand
The prone creation ; yields what once suffic'd
Their dainty sovereign, when the world was
                young ;
Ere yet the barbarous thirst of blood had seiz'd
The human breast.— Each rolling month matures
The food that suits it most ; so does each clime.

    Far in the horrid realms of Winter, where
Th' establish'd ocean heaps a monstrous waste
Of shining rocks and mountains to the pole,
There lives a hardy race, whose plainest wants
Relentless Earth, their cruel step-mother,
Regards not. On the waste of iron fields,
Untam'd, intractable, no harvests wave :
Pomona hates them, and the clownish god
Who tends the garden. In this frozen world
Such cooling gifts were vain : a fitter meal
Is earn'd with ease ; for here the fruitful spawn
Of ocean swarms, and heaps their genial board
With generous fare and luxury profuse.
These are their bread, the only bread they know :
These, and their willing slave the deer that crops
The shrubby herbage on their meagre hills.
Girt by the burning zone, not thus the South
Her swarthy sons in either Ind maintains :
Or thirsty Libya ; from whose fervid loins
The lion bursts, and every fiend that roams
Th' affrighted wilderness. The mountain herd,

    ³ The burning fever.

Adust and dry, no sweet repast affords ;
Nor does the tepid main such kinds produce,
So perfect, so delicious, as the shoals
Of icy Zembla. Rashly where the blood
Brews feverish frays ; where scarce the tubes
                sustain
Its tumid fervour, and tempestuous course;
Kind Nature tempts not to such gifts as these.
But here in livid ripeness melts the grape :
Here, finish'd by invigorating suns,
Thro' the green shade the golden orange glows :
Spontaneous here the turgid melon yields
A generous pulp : the cocoa swells on high
With milky riches ; and in horrid mail
The crisp ananas wraps its poignant sweets.
Earth's vaunted progeny : in ruder air
Too coy to flourish, even too proud to live ;
Or hardly rais'd by artificial fire
To vapid life. Here with a mother's smile
Glad Amalthea pours her copious horn.
Here buxom Ceres reigns : the autumnal sea
In boundless billows fluctuates o'er their plains.
What suits the climate best, what suits the men,
Nature profuses most, and most the taste
Demands. The fountain, edg'd with racy wine
Or acid fruit, bedews their thirsty souls.
The breeze eternal breathing round their limbs
Supports in else intolerable air :
While the cool palm, the plantain, and the grove
That waves on gloomy Lebanon, assuage
The torrid Hell that beams upon their heads.

    Now come ye Naiads, to the fountains lead ;
Now let me wander thro' your gelid reign.
I burn to view th' enthusiastic wilds
By mortal else untrod. I hear the din
Of waters thund'ring o'er the ruin'd cliffs.
With holy reverence I approach the rocks [song.
Whence glide the streams renown'd in ancient
Here from the desert down the rumbling steep
First springs the Nile ; here bursts the sounding
In angry waves ; Euphrates hence devolves [Po
A mighty flood to water half the East ;
And there in Gothic solitude reclin'd,
The cheerless Tanais pours his hoary urn.
What solemn twilight ! what stupendous shades
Enwrap these infant floods ! thro' every nerve
A sacred horrour thrills, a pleasing fear
Glides o'er my frame. The forest deepens round ;
And more gigantic still th' impending trees
Stretch their extravagant arms athwart the gloom.
Are these the confines of some fairy world ?
A land of genii ? Say, beyond these wilds
What unknown nations ? If indeed beyond
Aught habitable lies. And whither leads,
To what strange regions, or of bliss or pain,
That subterraneous way ! Propitious maids,
Conduct me, while with fearful steps I tread
This trembling ground. The task remains to sing
Your gifts (so Pæon, so the powers of health
Command) to praise your chrystal element :
The chief ingredient in Heaven's various works :
Whose flexile genius sparkles in the gem,
Grows firm in oak, and fugitive in wine ;
The vehicle, the source, of nutriment
And life, to all that vegetate or live.

    O comfortable streams ? with eager lips
And trembling hand the languid thirsty quaff
New life in you ; fresh vigour fills their veins.
No warmer cups the rural ages knew ;

None warmer sought the sires of human kind.
Happy in temperate peace ! their equal days
Felt not th' alternate fits of feverish mirth,
And sick dejection. Still serene and pleas'd
They knew no pains but what the tender soul
With pleasure yields to, and would ne'er forget.
Blest with divine immunity from ails,
Long centuries they liv'd; their only fate
Was ripe old age, and rather sleep than death.
Oh ! could those worthies from the world of Gods
Return to visit their degenerate sons,
How would they scorn the joys of modern time,
With all our art and toil improv'd to pain!
Too happy they ! but wealth brought luxury,
And luxury on sloth begot disease.
Learn temperance, friends ; and hear without
    disdain
The choice of water. Thus the Coan sage [4]
Opin'd, and thus the learn'd of every school.
What least of foreign principles partakes
Is best : the lightest then ; what bears the touch
Of fire the least, and soonest mounts in air ;
The most insipid ; the most void of smell.
Such the rude mountain from his horrid sides
Pours down ; such waters in the 'sandy vale
For ever boil, alike of winter frosts
And summers heat secure. The crystal stream,
Thro' rocks resounding, or for many a mile
O'er the chaf'd pebbles hurl'd, yields wholesome,
    pure,
And mellow draughts ; except'when winter thaws,
And half the mountains melt into the tide.
Tho' thirst were e'er so resolute, avoid
The sordid lake, and all such drowsy floods
As fill from Lethe Belgia's slow canals ;
(With rest corrupt, with vegetation green ;
Squalid with generation, and the birth
Of little monsters ;) till the power of fire
Has from profane embraces disengag'd
The violated lymph. The virgin stream
In boiling wastes its finer soul in air.
    Nothing like simple element dilutes
The food, or gives the chyle so soon to flow.
But where the stomach indolent and cold
Toys with its duty, animate with wine
Th' insipid stream : tho' golden Ceres yields
A more voluptuous, a more sprightly draught ;
Perhaps more active. Wine unmix'd, and all
The gluey floods that from the vex'd abyss
Of fermentation spring ; with spirit fraught,
And furious with intoxicating fire ;
Retard concoction, and preserve unthaw'd
Th' embodied mass. You see what countless
Embalm'd in fiery quintessence of wine, [years,
The puny wonders of the reptile world,
The tender rudiments of life, the slim
Unravellings of minute anatomy,
Maintain their texture, and unchang'd remain.
    We curse not wine : the vile excess we blame ;
More fruitful than th' accumulated board,
Of pain and misery. For the subtle draught
Faster and surer swells the vital tide ;
And with more active poison than the floods
Of grosser crudity convey, pervades
The far remote meanders of our frame.
Ah ! sly deceiver ! branded o'er and o'er,
Yet still believ'd ! exulting o'er the wreck
Of sober vows !—But the Parnassian maids

[4] Hippocrates.

Another time perhaps shall sing the joys [5],
The fatal charms, the many woes of wine ;
Perhaps its various tribes and various powers.
    Meantime, I would not always dread the
        bowl,
Nor every trespass shun. The feverish strife,
Rous'd by the rare debauch, subdues, expels
The loitering crudities that burden life ;
And, like a torrent full and rapid, clears
Th' obstructed tubes. Besides, this restless world
Is full of chances, which, by habit's power,
To learn to bear is easier than to shun.
Ah ! when ambition, meagre love of gold,
Or sacred country calls, with mellowing wine
To moisten well the thirsty suffrages ;
Say how, unseason'd to the midnight frays
Of Comus and his rout, wilt thou contend
With Centaurs long to hardy deeds inur'd ?
Then learn to revel ; but by slow degrees :
By slow degrees the liberal arts are won ;
And Hercules grew strong. But when you smooth
The brows of care, indulge your festive vein
In cups by well-inform'd experience found
The least your bane : and only with your friends.
There are sweet follies ; frailties to be seen
By friends alone, and men of generous minds.
    Oh ! seldom may the fated hours return
Of drinking deep ! I would not daily taste,
Except when life declines, even sober cups.
Weak withering age no rigid law forbids,
With frugal nectar, smooth and slow with balm,
The sapless habit daily to bedew,
And give the hesitating wheels of life
Gliblier to play. But youth has better joys ;
And is it wise when youth with pleasure flows,
To squander the reliefs of age and pain !
    What dextrous thousands just within the goal
Of wild debauch direct their nightly course !
Perhaps no sickly qualms bedim their days,
No morning admonitions shock the head.
But, ah ! what woes remain ! life rolls apace
And that incurable disease, old age,
In youthful bodies more severely felt,
More sternly active, shakes their blasted prime ;
Except kind Nature by some hasty blow
Prevent the lingering fates. For know, whate'er
Beyond its natural fervour hurries on
The sanguine tide ; whether the frequent bowl,
High-season'd fare, or exercise to toil
Protracted ; spurs to its last stage tir'd life,
And sows the temples with untimely snow.
When life is new the ductile fibres feel
The heart's increasing force ; and, day by day,
The growth advances : 'till the larger tubes
Acquiring (from their elemental veins [6],

[5] See Book IV.

[6] In the human body, as well as in those of other animals, the larger blood-vessels are composed of smaller ones ; which, by the violent motion and pressure of the fluids in the large vessels, lose their cavities by degrees, and degenerate into impervious chords or fibres. In proportion as these small vessels become solid, the larger must of course become less extensile, more rigid, and make a stronger resistance to the action of the heart, and force of the blood. From this gradual condensation of the smaller vessels, and consequent rigidity of the larger ones, the progress of

Condens'd to solid chords) a firmer tone,
Sustain, and just sustain, th' impetuous blood.
Here stops the growth.   With overbearing pulse
And pressure, still the great destroy the small;
Still with the ruins of the small grow strong.
Life glows meantime, amid the grinding force
Of viscous fluids and elastic tubes;
Its various functions vigorously are plied
By strong machinery ; and in solid health
The man confirm'd long triumphs o'er disease.
But the full ocean ebbs : there is a point,
By Nature fix'd, when life must downward tend.
For still the beating tide consolidates
The stubborn vessels, more reluctant still
To the weak throbs of th' ill supported heart.
This languishing, these strength'ning by degrees
To hard unyielding unelastic bone,
Thro' tedious channels the congealing flood
Crawls lazily, and hardly wanders on ;
It loiters still ;  and now it stirs no more.
This is the period few attain ;  the death
Of Nature; thus (so Heaven ordain'd it) life
Destroys itself;  and could these laws have
              chang'd
Nestor might now  the fates of Troy relate;
And Homer live immortal as his song.
      What does not fade ?  the tower that long had
              stood
The crush of thunder and the warring winds,
Shook by the slow, but sure destroyer, Time,
Now hangs in doubtful ruins o'er its base.
And flinty pyramids, and walls of brass,
Descend :  the Babylonian spires are sunk;
Achaia, Rome, and Egypt moulder down.
Time shakes the stable tyranny of thrones,
And tottering empires crush by their own weight.
This huge rotundity we tread grows old ;
And all those worlds that roll around the Sun,
The Sun himself, shall die ;  and ancient Night
Again involve the desolate abyss :
'Till the Great FATHER thro' the lifeless gloom
Extend his arm to light another world,
And bid new planets roll by other laws.
For through the regions of unbounded space,
Where unconfin'd Omnipotence has room,
Being, in various systems, fluctuates still
Between creation and abhorr'd decay :
It ever did, perhaps and ever will.
New worlds are still emerging from the deep ;
The old descending, in their turns to rise.

---

### THE ART OF PRESERVING HEALTH.

#### BOOK III.—EXERCISE.

THRO' various toils th' adventurous Muse has
      past ;
But half the toil, and more than half, remains.
Rude is her theme, and hardly fit for song;
Plain, and of little ornament ; and I
But little practis'd in th' Aonian arts.
Yet not in vain such labours have we tried,

the human body from infancy to old age is accounted for.

If aught these lays the fickle health confirm.
To you, ye delicate, I write; for you
I tame my youth to philosophic cares,
And grow still paler by the midnight lamps.
Not to debilitate with timorous rules
A hardy frame: nor needlessly to brave
Inglorious dangers, proud of mortal strength,
Is all the lesson that in wholesome years
Concerns the strong.  His care were ill bestow'd
Who would with warm effeminacy nurse
The thriving oak which on the mountain's brow
Bears all the blasts that sweep the wint'ry Hea-
              ven.
      Behold the labourer of the glebe, who toils
In dust, in rain, in cold and sultry skies!
Save but the grain from mildews and the flood,
Nought anxious he what sickly stars ascend.
He knows no laws by Esculapius given;
He studies none.  Yet him nor midnight fogs
Infest, nor those envenom'd shafts that fly
When rabid Sirius fires th' autumnal noon.
His habit pure with plain and temperate meals,
Robust with labour, and by custom steel'd
To every casualty of varied life ;
Serene he bears the peevish eastern blast,
And uninfected breathes the mortal south.
      Such the reward of rude and sober life ;
Of labour such.  By health the peasant's toil
Is well repaid ; if exercise were pain
Indeed, and temperance pain.  By arts like these
Laconia nurs'd of old her hardy sons;     [way,
And Rome's unconquer'd legions urg'd their
Unhurt, through every toil in every clime.
      Toil, and be strong.  By toil the flaccid nerves
Grow firm, and gain a more compacted tone ;
The greener juices are by toil subdu'd,
Mellow'd and subtiliz'd ; the vapid old
Expell'd, and all the rancour of the blood.
Come, my companions,' ye who feel the charms
Of Nature and the year ; come, let us stray
Where chance or fancy leads our roving walk :
Come, while the soft voluptuous breezes fan
The fleecy Heavens, enwrap the limbs in balm,
And shed a charming languour o'er the soul.
Nor when bright Winter sows with prickly frost
The vigorous ether, in unmanly warmth
Indulge at home ; nor even when Eurus' blasts
This way and that convolve the lab'ring woods.
My liberal walks, save when the skies in rain
Or fogs relent, no season should confine
Or to the cloister'd gallery or arcade.
Go, climb the mountain; from th' ethereal source
Imbibe the recent gale.  The cheerful morn
Beams o'er the hills; go, mount th' exulting
              steed.
Already, see, the deep-mouth'd beagles catch
The tainted mazes; and, on eager sport
Intent, with emulous impatience try
Each doubtful trace.  Or, if a nobler prey
Delight you more, go chase the desperate deer;
And through its deepest solitudes awake
The vocal forest with the jovial horn.
      But if the breathless chase o'er hill and dale
Exceed your strength, a sport of less fatigue,
Not less delightful, the prolific stream
Affords.  The crystal rivulet, that o'er
A stony channel rolls its rapid maze,
Swarms with the silver fry.  Such, through the
              bounds

Of pastoral Stafford, runs the brawling Trent;
Such Eden, sprung from Cumbrian mountains;
 such     [stream
The Esk, o'erhung with woods; and such the
On whose Arcadian banks I first drew air,
Liddel; till now, except in Doric lays
Tun'd to her murmurs by her love-sick swains,
Unknown in song; though not a purer stream,
Through meads more flowery, more romantic
 groves,      [flood!
Rolls toward the western main. Hail, sacred
May still thy hospitable swains be blest
In rural innocence; thy mountains still
Teem with the fleecy race; thy tuneful woods
For ever flourish; and thy vales look gay
With painted meadows, and the golden grain!
Oft, with thy blooming sons, when life was new,
Sportive and petulant, and charm'd with toys,
In thy transparent eddies have I lav'd:
Oft trac'd with patient steps thy fairy banks,
With the well-imitated fly to hook
The eager trout, and with the slender line
And yielding rod solicit to the shore
The struggling panting prey; while vernal clouds
And tepid gales obscur'd the ruffled pool,
And from the deeps call'd forth the wanton
 swarms.
 Form'd on the Samian school, or those of Ind,
There are who think these pastimes scarce hu-
 mane.
Yet in my mind (and not relentless I)
His life is pure that wears no fouler stains.
But if through genuine tenderness of heart,
Or secret want of relish for the game,
You shun the glories of the chase, nor care
To haunt the peopled stream; the garden yields
A soft amusement, an humane delight.
To raise th' insipid nature of the ground;
Or tame its savage genius to the grace
Of careless sweet rusticity, that seems
The amiable result of happy chance,
Is to create; and gives a god-like joy,
Which every year improves. Nor thou disdain
To check the lawless riot of the trees,
To plant the grove, or turn the barren mould.
O happy he! whom, when his years decline,
(His fortune and his fame by worthy means
Attain'd, and equal to his moderate mind;
His life approv'd by all the wise and good,
Even envied by the vain) the peaceful groves
Of Epicurus, from this stormy world,
Receive to rest; of all ungrateful cares
Absolv'd, and sacred from the selfish crowd.
Happiest of men! if the same soil invites
A chosen few, companions of his youth,
Once fellow-rakes perhaps, now rural friends;
With whom in easy commerce to pursue
Nature's free charms, and vie for sylvan fame:
A fair ambition; void of strife or guile,
Or jealousy, or pain to be outdone.
Who plans th' enchanted garden, who directs
The visto best, and best conducts the stream:
Whose groves the fastest thicken and ascend;
Whom first the welcome Spring salutes; who
 shows
The earliest bloom, the sweetest proudest charms
Of Flora; who best gives Pomona's juice
To match the sprightly genius of champagne.
Thrice happy days! in rural business past:

Blest winter nights! when as the genial fire
Cheers the wide hall, his cordial family
With soft domestic arts the hours beguile,
And pleasing talk that starts no timorous fame,
With witless wantonness to hunt it down:
Or through the fairy-land of tale or song
Delighted wander, in fictitious fates
Engag'd, and all that strikes humanity:
Till lost in fable, they the stealing hour
Of timely rest forget. Sometimes, at eve
His neighbours lift the latch, and bless unbid
His festal roof; while, o'er the light repast,
And sprightly cups, they mix in social joy;
And, through the maze of conversation, trace
Whate'er amuses or improves the mind.
Sometimes at eve (for I delight to taste
The native zest and flavour of the fruit,
Where sense grows wild and tastes of no manure)
The decent, honest, cheerful husbandman
Should drown his labour in my friendly bowl;
And at my table find himself at home.
 Whate'er you study, in whate'er you sweat,
Indulge your taste. Some love the manly foils;
The tennis some; and some the graceful dance.
Others more hardy, range the purple heath,
Or naked stubble; where, from field to field,
The sounding coveys urge their labouring flight;
Eager amid the rising cloud to pour
The gun's unerring thunder: and there are
Whom still the meed [1] of the green archer
 charms.
He chooses best, whose labour entertains
His vacant fancy most: the toil you hate
Fatigues you soon, and scarce improves your
 limbs.
 As beauty still has blemish, and the mind
The most accomplish'd its imperfect side,
Few bodies are there of that happy mould
But some one part is weaker than the rest:
The legs, perhaps, or arms refuse their load,
Or the chest labours. These assiduously,
But gently, in their proper arts employ'd,
Acquire a vigour and springy activity,
To which they were not born. But weaker parts
Abhor fatigue and violent discipline.
 Begin with gentle toils; and as your nerves
Grow firm, to hardier by just steps aspire;
The prudent, even in every moderate walk,
At first but saunter, and by slow degrees
Increase their pace. This doctrine of the wise
Well knows the master of the flying steed.
First from the goal the manag'd coursers play
On bended reins; as yet the skilful youth
Repress their foamy pride; but every breath
The race grows warmer, and the tempest swells,
Till all the fiery mettle has its way,
And the thick thunder hurries o'er the plain.
When all at once from indolence to toil
You spring, the fibres by the hasty shock
Are tir'd and crack'd, before their unctuous
 coats,
Compress'd, can pour the lubricating balm.
Besides, collected in the passive veins,
The purple mass a sudden torrent rolls,
O'erpowers the heart, and deluges the lungs
With dangerous inundation: oft the source

[1] This word is much used by some of the old
English poets, and signifies reward or prize.

Of fatal woes; a cough that foams with blood,
Asthma, and feller peripneumony *,
Or the slow minings of the hectic fire.
　Th' athletic fool, to whom what Heaven deny'd
Of soul is well compensated in limbs,
Oft from his rage, or brainless frolic, feels
His vegetation and brute force decay.
The men of better clay and finer mould
Know nature, feel the human dignity,
And scorn to vie with oxen or with apes.
Pursu'd prolixly, even the gentlest toil
Is waste of health : repose by small fatigue
Is earn'd, and (where your habit is not prone
To thaw)' by the first moisture of the brows.
The fine and subtle spirits cost too much
To be profus'd, too much the roscid balm.
But when the hard varieties of life
You toil to learn, or try the dusty chase,
Or the warm deeds of some important day:
Hot from the field, indulge not yet your limbs
In wish'd repose; nor court the fanning gale,
Nor taste the spring.　O! by the sacred tears
Of widows, orphans, mothers, sisters, sires,
Forbear! no other pestilence has driven
Such myriads o'er th' irremeable deep.
Why this so fatal, the sagacious Muse
Thro' nature's cunning labyrinths could trace :
But there are secrets which who knows not now,
Must, ere he reach them, climb the heapy Alps
Of science; and devote seven years to toil.
Besides, I would not stun your patient ears
With what it little boots you to attain.
He knows enough, the mariner, who knows
Where lurk the shelves, and where the whirlpools
　　boil,
What signs portend the storm : to subtler minds
He leaves to scan, from what mysterious cause
Charybdis rages in th' Ionian wave;
Whence those impetuous currents in the main
Which neither oar nor sail can stem ; and why
The roughening deep expects the storm, as sure
As red Orion mounts the shrouded Heaven
　In ancient times, when Rome with Athens vied
For polish'd luxury and useful arts ;
All hot and reeking from th' Olympic strife,
And warm Palestra, in the tepid bath
Th' athletic youth relax'd their weary limbs.
Soft oils bedew'd them, with the grateful pow'rs
Of nard and cassia fraught, to sooth and heal
The cherish'd nerves.　Our less voluptuous
　　clime
Not much invites us to such arts as these.
'Tis not for those whom gelid skies embrace,
And chilling fogs; whose perspiration feels
Such frequent bars from Eurus and the North ;
'Tis not for those to cultivate a skin
Too soft : or teach the recremental fume
Too fast to crowd thro' such precarious ways.
For through the small arterial mouths, that pierce
In endless millions the close-woven skin,
The baser fluids in a constant stream
Escape, and viewless melt into the winds.
While this eternal, this most copious waste
Of blood, degenerate into vapid brine,
Maintains its wonted measure, all the powers
Of health befriend you, all the wheels of life
With ease and pleasure move : but this restrain'd

　　　* The inflammation of the lungs.

Or more or less, so more or less you feel
The functions labour : from this fatal source
What woes descend is never to be sung.
To take their numbers were to count the sands
That ride in whirlwind the parch'd Libyan air ;
Or waves that, when the blustering North em-
　　broils
The Baltic, thunder on the German shore.
Subject not then, by soft emollient arts,
This grand expense, on which your fates depend,
To every caprice of the sky ; nor thwart
The genius of your clime: for from the blood
Least fickle rise the recremental steams,
And least obnoxious to the styptic air,
Which breathe through straiter and more callous
　　pores.
The temper'd Scythian hence, half-naked treads
His boundless snows, nor rues th' inclement
　　Heaven ;
And hence our painted ancestors defied
The east: nor curs'd, like us, their fickle sky.
　The body, moulded by the clime, endures
The equator heats or hyperborean frost :
Except by habits foreign to its turn,
Unwise you counteract its forming pow'r.
Rude at the first, the winter shocks you less
By long acquaintance : study then your sky,
Form to its manners your obsequious frame,
And learn to suffer what you cannot shun.
Against the rigors of a damp cold heav'n
To fortify their bodies, some frequent
The gelid cistern; and, where nought forbids,
I praise their dauntless heart : a frame so steel'd
Dreads not the cough, nor those ungenial blasts
That breathe the tertian or fell rheumatism ;
The nerves so temper'd never quit their tone,
No chronic languors haunt such hardy breasts.
But all things have their bounds: and he who
By daily use the kindest regimen　　[makes
Essential to his health, should never mix
With human kind, nor art nor trade pursue.
He not the safe vicissitudes of life
Without some shock endures; ill-fitted he
To want the known, or bear unusual things
Besides, the powerful remedies of pain
(Since pain in spite of all our care will come)
Should never with your prosperous days of health
Grow too familiar : for by frequent use
The strongest medicines lose their healing power,
And even the surest poisons theirs to kill.
　Let those who from the frozen Arctos reach
Parch'd Mauritania, or the sultry west,
Or the wide flood that laves rich Indostan,
Plunge thrice a day, and in the tepid wave
Untwist their stubborn pores; that full and free
Th' evaporation through the soften'd skin
May bear proportion to the swelling blood.
So may they 'scape the fever's rapid flames;
So feel untainted the hot breath of Hell.
With us, the man of no complaint demands
The warm ablution just enough to clear
The sluices of the skin, enough to keep
The body sacred from indecent soil.
Still to be pure, ev'n did it not conduce
(As much it does) to health, were greatly worth
Your daily pains.　'Tis this adorns the rich ;
The want of this is poverty's worst woe ;
With this external virtue age maintains
A decent grace ; without it youth and charms

Are loathsome.  This the venal graces know;
So doubtless do your wives: for married sires,
As well as lovers, still pretend to taste;
Nor is it less (all prudent wives can tell)
To lose a husband's than a lover's heart.
But now the hours and seasons when to toil
From foreign themes recal my wandering song.
Some labour fasting, or but slightly fed
To lull the grinding stomach's hungry rage.
Where nature feeds too corpulent a frame
'Tis wisely done: for while the thirsty veins,
Impatient of lean penury, devour
The treasur'd oil, then is the happiest time
To shake the lazy balsam from its cells.
Now while the stomach from the full repast
Subsides, but ere returning hunger gnaws,
Ye leaner habits, give an hour to toil:
And ye,whom no luxuriancy of growth
Oppresses yet, or threatens to oppress.
But from the recent meal no labours please,
Of limbs or mind.  For now the cordial powers
Claim all the wandering spirits to a work
Of strong and subtle toil, and great event:
A work of time: and you may rue the day
You hurried, with untimely exercise,
A half-concocted chyle into the blood.
The body overcharged with unctuous phlegm
Much toil demands: the lean elastic less.
While winter, chills the blood and binds the
    veins,
No labours are too hard: by those you 'scape
The slow diseases of the torpid year;
Endless to name; to one of which alone,
To that which tears the nerves, the toil of slaves
Is pleasure: Oh! from such inhuman pains
May all be free who merit not the wheel!
But from the burning Lion when the Sun
Pours down his sultry wrath; now while the
    blood
Too much already maddens in the veins,
And all the finer fluids through the skin
Explore their flight; me, near the cool cascade
Reclin'd, or saunt'ring in the lofty grove,
No needless slight occasion should engage
To pant and sweat beneath the fiery noon.
Now the fresh morn alone and mellow eve
To shady walks and active rural sports
Invite.  But, while the chilling dews descend,
May nothing tempt you to the cold embrace
Of humid skies; though 'tis no vulgar joy
To trace the horrours of the solemn wood
While the soft evening saddens into night:
Though the sweet poet of the vernal groves
Melts all the night in strains of am'rous woe.
    The shades descend, and midnight o'er the
        world
Expands her sable wings.  Great nature droops
Thro' all her works.  Now happy he whose toil
Has o'er his languid powerless limbs diffus'd
A pleasing lassitude: he not in vain
Invokes the gentle deity of dreams.
His powers the most voluptuously dissolve
In soft repose: on him the balmy dews
Of sleep with double nutriment descend.
But would you sweetly waste the blank of night
In deep oblivion; or on Fancy's wings
Visit the paradise of happy dreams,
And waken cheerful as the lively morn;
Oppress not nature sinking down to rest

With feasts too late, too sordid, or too full:
But be the first concoction half-matur'd
Ere you to mighty indolence resign
Your passive faculties.  He from the toils
And troubles of the day to heavier toil    [rocks
Retires, whom trembling from the tower that
Amid the clouds, or Calpe's hideous height,
The busy demons hurl; or in the main
O'erwhelm; or bury struggling under ground.
Not all a monarch's luxury the woes
Can counterpoise of that most wretched man,
Whose nights are shaken with the frantic fits
Of wild Orestes; whose delirious brain,
Stung by the furies, works with poison'd thought;
While pale and monstrous painting shocks the
    soul;
And mangled consciousness bemoans itself
For ever torn; and chaos floating round.
What dreams presage, what dangers these or
    those
Portend to sanity, tho' prudent seers
Reveal'd of old, and men of deathless fame,
We would not to the superstitious mind
Suggest new throbs, new vanities of fear.
'Tis ours to teach you from the peaceful night
To banish omens and all restless woes.
    In study some protract the silent hours,
Which others consecrate to mirth and wine;
And sleep till noon, and hardly live till night.
But surely this redeems not from the shades
One hour of life.  Nor does it naught avail
What season you to drowsy Morpheus give
Of th' ever-varying circle of the day;
Or whether, through the tedious winter gloom,
You tempt the midnight or the morning damps.
The body, fresh and vigorous from repose,
Defies the early fogs: but, by the toils
Of wakeful day exhausted and unstrung,
Weakly resists the night's unwholesome breath.
The grand discharge, th' effusion of the skin,
Slowly impair'd, the languid maladies    [steal.
Creep on, and through the sick'ning functions
As, when the chilling east invades the Spring,
The delicate narcissus pines away
In hectic languor, and a slow disease
Taints all the family of flowers, condemn'd
To cruel heav'ns.  But why, already prone
To fade, should beauty cherish its own bane?
O shame! O pity! nipt with pale quadrille,
And midnight cares, the bloom of Albion dies!
    By toil subdu'd, the warrior and the hind
Sleep fast and deep: their active functions soon
With generous streams the subtle tubes supply:
And soon the tonic irritable nerves
Feel the fresh impulse and awake the soul.
The sons of indolence with long repose
Grow torpid; and, with slowest Lethe drunk,
Feebly and ling'ringly return to life,
Blunt every sense and pow'rless every limb.
Ye, prone to sleep (whom sleeping most an-
On the hard matrass or elastic couch    [noys)
Extend your limbs, and wean yourselves from
    sloth;
Nor grudge the lean projector, of dry brain
And springy nerves, the blandishments of down:
Nor envy while the buried Bacchanal
Exhales his surfeit in prolixer dreams.
    He without riot, in the balmy feast
Of life, the wants of nature has supply'd,

Who rises, cool, serene, and full of soul.
But pliant nature more or less demands,
As custom forms her; and all sudden change
She hates of habit, even from bad to good.
If faults in life, or new emergencies,
From habits urge you by long time confirm'd,
Slow may the change arrive, and stage by stage;
Slow as the shadow o'er the dial moves,
Slow as the stealing progress of the year.
  Observe the circling year. How unperceiv'd
Her seasons change! Behold! by slow degrees,
Stern Winter tam'd into a ruder Spring;
The ripen'd Spring a milder Summer's glows;
The parting Summer sheds Pomona's store,
And aged Autumn brews the winter storm.
Slow as they come, these changes come not void
Of mortal shocks: the cold and torrid reigns,
The two great periods of the important year,
Are in their first approaches seldom safe;
Funeral Autumn all the sickly dread;
And the black fates deform the lovely Spring.
He well advis'd who taught our wiser sires
Early to borrow Muscovy's warm spoils,
Ere the first frost has touch'd the tender blade;
And late resign them, though the wanton Spring
Should deck her charms with all her sister's
  rays.
For while the effluence of the skin maintains
Its native measure, the pleuritic Spring
Glides harmless by; and Autumn, sick to death
With sallow quartans, no contagion breathes.
  I in prophetic numbers could unfold
The omens of the year: what seasons teem
With what diseases; what the humid South
Prepares, and what the demon of the East:
But you perhaps refuse the tedious song,
Besides, whatever plagues in heat, or cold,
Or drought, or moisture dwell, they hurt not you,
Skill'd to correct the vices of the sky,
And taught already how to each extreme
To bend your life. But should the public bane
Infect you; or some trespass of your own,
Or flaw of nature, hint mortality;
Soon as a not unpleasing horrour glides
Along the spine, through all your torpid limbs;
When first the head throbs, or the stomach feels
A sickly load, a weary pain the loins;
Be Celsus call'd: the fates come rushing on;
The rapid fates admit of no delay.
While wilful you, and fatally secure,
Expect to morrow's more auspicious sun,
The growing pest, whose infancy was weak
And easy vanquish'd, with triumphant sway
O'erpow'rs your life. For want of timely care,
Millions have died of medicable wounds.
  Ah! in what perils is vain life engag'd!
What slight neglects, what trivial faults destroy
The hardiest frame! of indolence, of toil,
We die; of want, of superfluity:
The all-surrounding Heaven, the vital air,
Is big with death. And, though the putrid
Be shut; though no convulsive agony   [South
Shake, from the deep foundations of the world,
Th' imprison'd plagues; a secret venom oft
Corrupts the air, the water, and the land.
What livid deaths has sad Byzantium seen!
How oft has Cairo, with a mother's woe,
Wept o'er her slaughter'd sons and lonely streets!
Even Albion, girt with less malignant skies,

Albion the poison of the gods has drank,
And felt the sting of monsters all her own.
  Ere yet the fell Plantagenets had spent
Their ancient rage, at Bosworth's purple field;
While, for which tyrant England should receive,
Her legions in incestuous murders mix'd,
And daily horrours; till the fates were drunk
With kindred blood by kindred hands profus'd:
Another plague of more gigantic arm
Arose, a monster, never known before,
Rear'd from Cocytus its portentous head.
This rapid fury not, like other pests,
Pursu'd a gradual course, but in a day
Rush'd as a storm o'er half the astonish'd isle,
And strew'd with sudden carcases the land.
  First, through the shoulders, or whatever part
Was seiz'd the first, a fervid vapour sprung.
With rash combustion thence, the quivering
Shot to the heart, and kindled all within; [spark
And soon the surface caught the spreading fires.
Through all the yielded pores, the melted blood
Gush'd out in smoky sweats; but nought as-
    suag'd
The torrid heat within, nor ought reliev'd
The stomach's anguish. With incessant toil,
Desperate of ease, impatient of their pain,
They toss'd from side to side. In vain the stream
Ran full and clear, they burnt and thirsted still.
The restless arteries with rapid blood
Beat strong and frequent. Thick and pantingly
The breath was fetch'd, and with huge lab'rings
    heav'd.
At last a heavy pain oppress'd the head,
A wild delirium came; their weeping friends
Were strangers now, and this no home of theirs.
Harass'd with toil on toil, the sinking powers
Lay prostrate and o'erthrown; a ponderous sleep
Wrapt all the senses up: they slept and died.
  In some a gentle horrour crept at first
O'er all the limbs; the sluices of the skin
Withheld their moisture, till by art provok'd
The sweats o'erflow'd; but in a clammy tide:
Now free and copious, now restrain'd and slow;
Of tinctures various, as the temperature
Had mix'd the blood; and rank with fetid steams:
As if the pent-up humours by delay
Were grown more fell, more putrid, and malign.
Here lay their hopes (tho' little hope remain'd)
With full effusion of perpetual sweats
To drive the venom out. And here the fates
Were kind, that long they linger'd not in pain;
For who surviv'd the Sun's diurnal race
Rose from the dreary gates of Hell redeem'd:
Some the sixth hour oppress'd, and some the
    third.
  Of many thousands few untainted 'scap'd;
Of those infected fewer 'scap'd alive:
Of those who liv'd some felt a second blow;
And whom the second spar'd a third destroy'd.
Frantic with fear, they sought by flight to shun
The fierce contagion. O'er the mournful land
Th' infected city pour'd her hurrying swarms:
Rous'd by the flames that fir'd her seats around,
Th' infected country rush'd into the town.
Some, sad at home, and in the desert some,
Abjur'd the fatal commerce of mankind:
In vain: where'er they fled, the fates pursu'd.
Others, with hopes more specious, cross'd the
    main,

To seek protection in far distant skies;
But none they found. It seem'd the general air,
From pole to pole, from Atlas to the east,
Was then at enmity with English blood.
For, but the race of England, all were safe
In foreign climes; nor did this fury taste
The foreign blood which England then contain'd.
Where should they fly? The circumambient
　　　　Heaven
Involv'd them still; and every breeze was bane.
Where find relief? The salutary air
Was mute; and, startled at the new disease,
In fearful whispers hopeless omens gave.
To Heaven with suppliant rites they sent their
　　　　pray'rs;
Heav'n heard them not. Of every hope depriv'd;
Fatigued with vain resources; and subdued
With woes resistless and enfeebling fear;
Passive they sunk beneath the weighty blow.
Nothing but lamentable sounds was heard,
Nor aught was seen but ghastly views of death.
Infectious horrour ran from face to face,
And pale despair. 'Twas all the business then
To tend the sick, and in their turns to die.
In heaps they fell: and oft one bed, they say,
The sick'ning, dying, and the dead contain'd.
Ye guardian gods, on whom the fates depend
Of tottering Albion! ye eternal fires
That lead thro' Heav'n the wandering year! ye
　　　　powers
That o'er th' encircling elements preside!
May nothing worse than what this age has seen
Arrive! Enough abroad, enough at home
Has Albion bled. Here a distemper'd heaven
Has thin'd her cities, from those lofty cliffs
That awe proud Gaul, to Thulé's wintry reign;
While in the west, beyond the Atlantic foam,
Her bravest sons, keen for the fight, have dy'd
The death of cowards and of common men:
Sunk void of wounds, and fall'n without renown.
　　But from these views the weeping Muses turn,
And other themes invite my wandering song.

---

## THE ART OF PRESERVING HEALTH.

### BOOK IV.—THE PASSIONS.

The choice of aliment, the choice of air,
The use of toil, and all external things,
Already sung; it now remains to trace
What good, what evil, from ourselves proceeds:
And how the subtle principle within
Inspires with health, or mines with strange decay
The passive body. Ye poetic shades
Who know the secrets of the world unseen,
Assist my song! for, in a doubtful theme
Engag'd, I wander thro' mysterious ways.
　　There is, they say, (and I believe there is)
A spark within us of th' immortal fire,
That animates and moulds the grosser frame;
And when the body sinks, escapes to Heaven,
Its native seat, and mixes with the gods.
Meanwhile this heavenly particle pervades
The mortal elements; in every nerve
It thrills with pleasure, or grows mad with pain.
And, in its secret conclave, as it feels
The body's woes and joys, this ruling power

Wields at its will the dull material world,
And is the body's health or malady.
By its own toil the gross corporeal frame
Fatigues, extenuates, or destroys itself.
Nor less the labours of the mind corrode
The solid fabric: for by subtle parts
And viewless atoms, secret Nature moves
The mighty wheels of this stupendous world.
By subtle fluids pour'd through subtle tubes
The natural vital functions are perform'd.
By these the stubborn aliments are tam'd;
The toiling heart distributes life and strength;
These the still-crumbling frame rebuild; and
　　　　these
Are lost in thinking, and dissolve in air.
　　But 'tis not thought, (for still the soul's em-
　　　　ploy'd)
'Tis painful thinking that corrodes our clay.
All day the vacant eye without fatigue
Strays o'er the Heaven and Earth; but long in-
　　　　tent
On microscopic arts, its vigour fails.
Just so the mind, with various thought amus'd,
Nor aches itself, nor gives the body pain.
But anxious study, discontent, and care,
Love without hope, and hate without revenge,
And fear, and jealousy, fatigue the soul,
Engross the subtle ministers of life,
And spoil the lab'ring functions of their share.
Hence the lean gloom that melancholy wears;
The lover's paleness; and the sallow hue
Of envy, jealousy; the meagre stare
Of sore revenge: the canker'd body hence
Betrays each fretful motion of the mind.
　　The strong-built pedant, who both night and
　　　　day
Feeds on the coarsest fare the schools bestow,
And crudely fattens at gross Burman's stall;
O'erwhelm'd with phlegm lies in a dropsy drown'd,
Or sinks in lethargy before his time.
With useful studies you, and arts that please
Employ your mind; amuse, but not fatigue.
Peace to each drowsy metaphysic sage!
And ever may all heavy systems rest!
Yet some there are, even of elastic parts,
Whom strong and obstinate ambition leads
Thro' all the rugged roads of barren lore,
And gives to relish what their generous taste
Would else refuse. But may not thirst of fame,
Nor love of knowledge, urge you to fatigue
With constant drudgery the liberal soul.
Toy with your books: and, as the various fits
Of humour seize you, from philosophy
To fable shift: from serious Antonine
To Rabelais' ravings, and from prose to song.
　　While reading pleases, but no longer, read;
And read aloud resounding Homer's strain,
And wield the thunder of Demosthenes.
The chest so exercis'd improves its strength;
And quick vibrations through the bowels drive
The restless blood, which in unactive days
Would loiter else thro' unelastic tubes.
Deem it not trifling while I recommend
What posture suits: to stand and sit by turns,
As nature prompts, is best. But o'er your
　　　　leaves
To lean for ever, cramps the vital parts,
And robs the fine machinery of its play.
　　'Tis the great art of life to manage well
The restless mind. For ever on pursuit

Of knowledge bent, it starves the grosser powers:
Quite unemployed, against its own repose
It turns its fatal edge, and sharper pangs
Than what the body knows embitter life.
Chiefly where solitude, sad nurse of care,
To sickly musing gives the pensive mind,
There madness enters; and the dim-ey'd fiend,
Sour Melancholy, night and day provokes
Her own eternal wound. The Sun grows pale;
A mournful visionary light o'erspreads
The cheerful face of Nature: Earth becomes
A dreary desert, and Heaven frowns above.
Then various shapes of curs'd illusion rise:
Whate'er the wretched fears, creating fear
Forms out of nothing, and with monsters teems
Unknown in Hell. The prostrate soul beneath
A load of huge imagination heaves;
And all the horrours that the murderer feels
With anxious flutterings wake the guiltless
    breast.
    Such phantoms pride in solitary scenes,
Or fear, or delicate self-love creates.
From other cares absolv'd, the busy mind
Finds in yourself a theme to pore upon;
It finds you miserable, or makes you so.
For while yourself you anxiously explore,
Timorous self-love, with sick'ning fancy's aid,
Presents the danger that you dread the most,
And ever galls you in your tender part.
Hence some for love, and some for jealousy,
For grim religion some, and some for pride,
Have lost their reason: some for fear of want
Want all their lives; and others every day
For fear of dying suffer worse than death.
Ah! from your bosoms banish if you can
Those fatal guests; and first the demon Fear,
That trembles at impossible events;
Lest aged Atlas should resign his load,
And Heaven's eternal battlements rush down.
Is there an evil worse than fear itself?
And what avails it that indulgent Heaven
From mortal eyes has wrapt the woes to come,
If we, ingenious to torment ourselves,
Grow pale at hideous fictions of our own?
Enjoy the present: nor with needless cares,
Of what may spring from blind misfortune's
    womb,
Appal the surest hour that life bestows.
Serene, and master of yourself, prepare
For what may come; and leave the rest to Hea-
    ven.
    Oft from the body, by long ails mis-tun'd,
These evils sprung, the most important health,
That of the mind, destroy: and when the mind
They first invade, the conscious body soon
In sympathetic languishment declines.
These chronic passions, while from real woes
They rise, and yet without the body's fault
Infest the soul, admit one only cure;
Diversion, hurry, and a restless life.
Vain are the consolations of the wise;
In vain your friends would reason down your
    pain.
O ye, whose souls relentless love has tam'd
To soft distress, or friends untimely fall'n!
Court not the luxury of tender thought;
Nor deem it impious to forget those pains
That hurt the living, nought avail the dead.
Go, soft enthusiast! quit the cypress groves,
Nor to the rivulet's lonely moanings tune

Your sad complaint. Go, seek the cheerful haunts
Of men, and mingle with the bustling crowd;
Lay schemes for wealth, or power, or fame, the
    wish
Of nobler minds, and push them night and day.
Or join the caravan in quest of scenes.
New to your eyes, and shifting every hour,
Beyond the Alps, beyond the Appennines.
Or more advent'rous, rush into the field
Where war grows hot; and, raging thro' the sky,
The lofty trumpet swells the madd'ning soul:
And in the hardy camp and toilsome march
Forget all softer and less manly cares.
    But most, too passive when the blood runs
    low,
Too weakly indolent to strive with pain,
And bravely by resisting conquer fate,
Try Circe's arts; and in the tempting bowl
Of poison'd nectar sweet oblivion swill.   [solves
Struck by the powerful charm, the gloom dis-
In empty air, Elysium opens round,
A pleasing phrenzy buoys the lighten'd soul,
And sanguine hopes dispel your fleeting care;
And what was difficult, and what was dire,
Yields to your prowess and superior stars:
The happiest you of all that e'er were mad,
Or are, or shall be, could this folly last.
But soon your Heaven is gone; a heavier gloom
Shuts o'er your head: and as the thund'ring
    stream,
Swoln o'er its banks with sudden mountain rain,
Sinks from its tumult to a silent brook;
So, when the frantic raptures in your breast
Subside, you languish into mortal man;
You sleep, and waking find yourself undone.
For, prodigal of life, in one rash night
You lavish'd more than might support three days.
A heavy morning comes; your cares return
With tenfold rage. An anxious stomach well
May be endur'd; so may the throbbing head:
But such a dim delirium, such a dream,
Involves you; such a dastardly despair
Unmans your soul, as madd'ning Pentheus felt,
When, baited round Cythæron's cruel sides
He saw two suns, and double Thebes ascend.
You curse the sluggish port; you curse the
    wretch,
The felon, with unnatural mixture first
Who dar'd to violate the virgin wine.
Or on the fugitive champaign you pour
A thousand curses; for to Heav'n it wrapt,
Your soul, to plunge you deeper in despair.
Perhaps you rue even that diviner gift,
The gay, serene, good-natur'd Burgundy,
Or the fresh fragrant vintage of the Rhine:
And wish that Heaven from mortals had withheld
The grape, and all intoxicating bowls.
    Besides, it wounds you sore to recollect
What follies in your loose unguarded hour
Escap'd. For one irrevocable word,
Perhaps that meant no harm, you lose a friend.
Or in the rage of wine your hasty hand
Performs a deed to haunt you to the grave.
Add that your means, your health, your parts,
    decay;
Your friends avoid you; brutishly transform'd,
They hardly know you; or if one remains
To wish you well, he wishes you in Heaven.
Despis'd, unwept you fall; who might have left
A sacred cherish'd, sadly-pleasing name;

A name still to be utter'd with a sigh.
Your last ungraceful scene has quite effac'd
All sense and memory of your former worth.
  How to live happiest ? how avoid the pains,
The disappointments, and disgusts of those
Who would in pleasure all their hours employ;
The precepts here of a divine old man
I could recite. Tho' old, he still retain'd
His manly sense, and energy of mind.
Virtuous and wise he was, but not severe;
He still remember'd that he once was young;
His easy presence check'd no decent joy.
Him even the dissolute admir'd ; for he
A graceful looseness when he pleas'd put on,
And laughing could instruct. Much had he read,
Much more had seen : he studied from the life,
And in th' original perus'd mankind.
  Vers'd in the woes and vanities of life,
He pitied man : and much he pitied those
Whom falsely-smiling fate has curs'd with
    means
To dissipate their days in quest of joy.
" Our aim is happiness; 'tis yours, 'tis mine,"
He said, " 'tis the pursuit of all that live :
Yet few attain it, if 'twas ere attain'd.
But they the widest wander from the mark,
Who thro' the flowery paths of sauntering joy
Seek this coy goddess : that from stage to stage
Invites us still, but shifts as we pursue.
For, not to name the pains that pleasure brings
To counterpoise itself, relentless fate
Forbids that we thro' gay voluptuous wilds
Should ever roam : and were the fates more kind,
Our narrow luxuries would soon grow stale :
Were these exhaustless, nature would grow sick,
And, cloy'd with pleasure, squeamishly complain
That all is vanity, and life a dream.
Let nature rest : be busy for yourself,
And for your friend; be busy even in vain,
Rather than tease her sated appetites.
Who never fasts, no banquet e'er enjoys;
Who never toils or watches, never sleeps.
Let nature rest : and when the taste of joy
Grows keen, indulge ; but shun satiety.
  " 'Tis not for mortals always to be blest.
But him the least the dull or painful hours
Of life oppress, whom sober sense conducts,
And virtue, thro' this labyrinth we tread.
Virtue and sense I mean not to disjoin ;
Virtue and sense are one : and, trust me, still
A faithless heart betrays the head unsound.
Virtue (for mere good-nature is a fool)
Is sense and spirit with humanity :
'Tis sometimes angry, and its frown confounds ;
'Tis even vindictive, but in vengeance just.
Knaves fain would laugh at it; some great ones
    dare;
But at his heart the most undaunted son
Of fortune dreads its name and awful charms.
To noblest uses this determines wealth ;
This is the solid pomp of prosperous days;
The peace and shelter of adversity.
And if you pant for glory, build your fame
On this foundation, which the secret shock
Defies of envy and all-sapping time.
The gawdy gloss of fortune only strikes
The vulgar eye ; the suffrage of the wise
The praise that's worth ambition, is attain'd
By sense alone, and dignity of mind.

  " Virtue, the strength and beauty of the soul,
Is the best gift of Heaven : a happiness
That even above the smiles and frowns of fate
Exalts great Nature's favourites ; a wealth
That ne'er encumbers, nor can be transferr'd.
Riches are oft by guilt and baseness earn'd ;
Or dealt by chance to shield a lucky knave,
Or throw a cruel sunshine on a fool.
But for one end, one much-neglected use,
Are riches worth your care ; (for nature's wants
Are few, and without opulence supply'd ;)
This noble end is, to produce the soul ;
To show the virtues in their fairest light ;
To make humanity the minister
Of bounteous Providence ; and teach the breast
That generous luxury the gods enjoy."
  Thus, in his graver vein, the friendly sage
Sometimes declaim'd. Of right and wrong he
    taught
Truths as refin'd as ever Athens heard ;
And (strange to tell!) he practis'd what he
    preach'd.
Skill'd in the passions, how to check their sway,
He knew, as far as reason can control
The lawless powers. But other cares are mine ;
Form'd in the school of Pæon, I relate
What passions hurt the body, what improve :
Avoid them, or invite them as you may.
Know then, whatever cheerful and serene
Supports the mind, supports the body too.
Hence, the most vital movement mortals feel
Is hope : the balm and life-blood of the soul.
It pleases, and it lasts. Indulgent Heaven
Sent down the kind delusion, through the paths
Of rugged life to lead us patient on ;
And make our happiest state no tedious thing,
Our greatest good, and what we least can spare,
Is hope : the last of all our evils, fear.
  But there are passions grateful to the breast,
And yet no friends to life : perhaps they please
Or to excess, and dissipate the soul ;
Or while they please, torment. The stubborn
    clown,
The ill-tam'd ruffian, and pale usurer,
(If love's omnipotence such hearts can mould)
May safely mellow into love ; and grow
Refin'd, humane, and generous, if they can.
Love in such bosoms never to a fault
Or pains or pleases. But ye finer souls,
Form'd to soft luxury, and prompt to thrill
With all the tumults, all the joys and pains,
That beauty gives; with caution and reserve
Indulge the sweet destroyer of repose,
Nor court too much the queen of charming cares.
For, while the cherish'd poison in your breast
Ferments and maddens ; sick with jealousy,
Absence, distrust, or even with anxious joy,
The wholesome appetites and powers of life
Dissolve in languor. The coy stomach loathes
The genial board : your cheerful days are gone ;
The generous bloom that flush'd your cheeks is
    fled.
To sighs devoted and to tender pains,
Pensive you sit, or solitary stray,
And waste your youth in musing. Musing first
Toy'd into care your unsuspecting heart :
It found a liking there, a sportful fire,
And that fomented into serious love ;
Which musing daily strengthens and improves

Thro' all the heights of fondness and romance :
And you're undone, the fatal shaft has sped,
If once you doubt whether you love or no.
The body wastes away ; th' infected mind,
Dissolv'd in female tenderness, forgets
Each manly virtue, and grows dead to fame.
Sweet Heaven, from such intoxicating charms
Defend all worthy breasts ! not that I deem
Love always dangerous, always to be shunn'd.
Love well repaid, and not too weakly sunk
In wanton and unmanly tenderness,
Adds bloom to health ; o'er ev'ry virtue sheds
A gay, humane, a sweet, and generous grace,
And brightens all the ornaments of man.
But fruitless, hopeless, disappointed, rack'd
With jealousy, fatigu'd with hope and fear,
Too serious, or too languishingly fond,
Unnerves the body and unmans the soul.
And some have died for love; and some run
　　mad ;
And some with desperate hands themselves have
　　slain.
　　Some to extinguish, others to prevent,
A mad devotion to one dangerous fair,
Court all they meet ; in hopes to dissipate
The cares of love amongst an hundred brides.
Th' event is doubtful : for there are who find
A cure in this ; there are who find it not.
'Tis no relief, alas ! it rather galls
The wound, to those who are sincerely sick.
For while from feverish and tumultuous joys
The nerves grow languid and the soul subsides,
The tender fancy smarts with every sting,
And what was love before is madness now.
Is health your care, or luxury your aim,
Be temperate still : when Nature bids, obey ;
Her wild impatient sallies bear no curb :
But when the prurient habit of delight,
Or loose imagination spurs you on
To deeds whose your strength, impute it not
To Nature : Nature all compulsion hates.
Ah ! let not luxury nor vain renown
Urge you to feats you well might sleep without;
To make what should be rapture a fatigue,
A tedious task ; nor in the wanton arms
Of twining Lais melt your manhood down.
For from the colliquation of soft joys　　[was !
How chang'd you rise ! the ghost of what you
Languid, and melancholy, and gaunt, and wan;
Your veins exhausted, and your nerves unstrung.
Spoil'd of its balm and sprightly zest, the blood
Grows vapid phlegm ; along the tender nerves
(To each slight impulse tremblingly awake)
A subtle fiend that mimics all the plagues,
Rapid and restless springs from part to part.
The blooming honours of your youth are fallen ;
Your vigour pines ; your vital powers decay ;
Diseases haunt you ; and untimely age
Creeps on ; unsocial, impotent, and lewd.
Infatuate, impious epicure ! to waste
The stores of pleasure, cheerfulness, and health !
Infatuate all who make delight their trade,
And coy perdition every hour pursue.
　　Who pines with love, or in lascivious flames
Consumes, is with his own consent undone ;
He chooses to be wretched, to be mad ;
And warn'd, proceeds, and wilful to his fate.
But there's a passion, whose tempestuous sway,
Tears up each virtue planted in his breast,

And shakes to ruins proud philosophy.
For pale and trembling anger rushes in, [stare ;
With fault'ring speech, and eyes that wildly
Fierce as the tiger, madder than the seas,
Desperate, and arm'd with more than human
　　strength.
How soon the calm, humane, and polish'd man
Forgets compunction, and starts up a fiend !
Who pines in love, or wastes with silent cares,
Envy, or ignominy, or tender grief,
Slowly descends, and ling'ring, to the shades :
But he whom anger stings, drops, if he dies,
At once, and rushes apoplectic down ;
Or a fierce fever hurries him to Hell.
For, as the body thro' unnumber'd strings
Reverberates each vibration of the soul ;
As is the passion, such is still the pain
The body feels : or chronic, or acute.
And oft a sudden storm at once o'erpowers
The life, or gives your reason to the winds.
Such fates attend the rash alarm of fear,
And sudden grief, and rage, and sudden joy.
　　There are, meantime, to whom the boist'rous
Is health, and only fills the sails of life. 　[fit
For where the mind a torpid winter leads,
Wrapt in a body corpulent and cold,
And each clogg'd function lazily moves on ;
A generous sally spurns th' incumbent load,
Unlocks the breast, and gives a cordial glow.
But if your wrathful blood is apt to boil,
Or are your nerves too irritably strung,
Wave all dispute ; be cautious, if you joke ;
Keep Lent for ever, and forswear the bowl.
For one rash moment sends you to the shades,
Or shatters ev'ry hopeful scheme of life,
And gives to horrour all your days to come.
Fate, arm'd with thunder, fire, and ev'ry plague,
That ruins, tortures, or distracts mankind,
And makes the happy wretched in an hour,
O'erwhelms you not with woes so horrible
As your own wrath, nor gives more sudden blows.
　　While choler works, good friend, you may
　　　　be wrong.
Distrust yourself, and sleep before you fight,
'Tis not too late to morrow to be brave ;
If honour bids, to morrow kill or die.
But calm advice against a raging fit
Avails too little ; and it braves the power
Of all that ever taught in prose or song,
To tame the fiend, that sleeps a gentle lamb,
And wakes a lion. Unprovok'd and calm,
You reason well ; see as you ought to see,
And wonder at the madness of mankind :
Seiz'd with the common rage, you soon forget
The speculations of your wiser hours.
Beset with furies of all deadly shapes,
Fierce and insidious, violent and slow :
With all that urge or lure us on to fate :
What refuge shall we seek ? what arms prepare ?
Where reason proves too weak, or void of wiles
To cope with subtle or impetuous powers,
I would invoke new passions to your aid :
With indignation would extinguish fear ;
With fear, or generous pity, vanquish rage ;
And love with pride ; and force to force oppose.
　　There is a charm, a power, that sways the
Bids every passion revel or be still ; 　[breast ;
Inspires with rage, or all your cares dissolves ;
Can sooth distraction, and almost despair.

That power is music : far beyond the stretch
Of those unmeaning warblers on our stage ;
Those clumsy heroes, those fat-headed gods,
Who move no passion justly but contempt :
Who, like our dancers, (light indeed and strong!)
Do wond'rous feats, but never heard of grace.
The fault is ours; we beat those monstrous
    arts ;
Good Heaven! we praise them : we, with loud-
    est peals
Applaud the fool tnat highest lifts his heels ;
And with insipid show of rapture, die
Of ideot notes impertinently long.
But he the Muse's laurel justly shares,
A poet he, and touch'd with Heaven's own fire,
Who, with bold rage or solemn pomp of sound,
Inflames, exalts, and ravishes the soul ;
Now tender, plaintive, sweet almost to pain,
In love dissolves you; now in sprightly strains
Breathes a gay rapture thro' your thrilling
    breasts;
Or melts the hearts with airs divinely sad ;
Or wakes to horrour the tremendous strings.
Such was the bard, whose heavenly strains of old
Appeas'd the fiend of melancholy Saul.
Such was, if old and heathen fame say true,
The man who bade the Theban domes ascend,
And tam'd the savage nations with his song ;
And such the Thracian, whose melodious lyre,
Tun'd to scft woe, made all the mountains weep ;
Sooth'd even th' inexorable powers of Hell,
And half redeem'd his lost Eurydice.
Music exalts each joy, allays each grief,
Expels diseases, softens every pain,
Subdues the rage of poison and of plague ;
And hence the wise of ancient days ador'd
One power of physic, melody, and song.

---

## OF BENEVOLENCE.

### AN EPISTLE TO EUMENES. [1]

#### 1751.

KIND to my frailties still, Eumenes, hear ;
Once more I try the patience of your ear.
Not oft I sing : the happier for the town,
So stunn'd already they're quite stupid grown
With monthly, daily—charming things I own.
Happy for them, l seldom court the Nine ;
Another art, a serious art is mine.
Of nauseous verses offer'd once a week,
" You cannot say I did it," if you're sick.
'Twas ne'er my pride to shine by flashy fits
Amongst the daily, weekly, monthly wits.
Content if some few friends indulge my name,
So slightly am I stung with love of fame,
I would not scrawl one hundred idle lines—
Not for the praise of all the magazines.
    Yet once a moon, perhaps, l steal a night ;
And, if our sire Apollo pleases, write. [follow,
You smile : but all the train the Muse that
Christians and dunces, still we quote Apollo.

[1] This little piece was addressed to a worthy
gentleman, as an expression of gratitude for his
kind endeavours to do the author a great piece
of service.

Unhappy still our poets will rehearse
To Goths, that stare astonish'd at their verse ;
To the rank tribes submit their virgin lays :
So gross, so bestial, is the lust of praise !
    I to sound judges from the mob appeal,
And write to those who most my subject feel.
Eumenes, these dry moral lines I trust [disgust.
With you, whom nought that's moral can
With you I venture, in plain home-spun sense,
What I imagine of Benevolence.
    Of all the monsters of the human kind,
What strikes you most is the low selfish mind.
You wonder how, without one liberal joy,
The steady miser can his years employ ;
Without one friend, howe'er his fortunes thrive,
Despis'd and hated, how he bears to live.
With honest warmth of heart, with some degree
Of pity that such wretched things should be,
You scorn the sordid knave—He grins at you,
And deems himself the wiser of the two.—
'Tis all but taste, howe'er we sift the case ;
He has his joy, as every creature has.
'Tis true, he cannot boast an angel's share,
Yet has what happiness his organs bear.
Thou likewise mad'st the high seraphic soul,
Maker Omnipotent ! and thou the owl.
Heav'n form'd him too, and doubtless for some use :
But Crane-court knows not yet all Nature's views.
    'Tis chiefly taste, or blunt, or gross, or fine,
Makes life insipid, bestial, or divine.
Better be born with taste to little rent,
Than the dull monarch of a continent.
Without this bounty which the Gods bestow,
Can Fortune make one favourite happy ?—No.
As well might Fortune in her frolic vein,
Proclaim an oyster sovereign of the main.
Without fine nerves, and bosom justly warm'd,
An eye, an ear, a fancy to be charm'd,
In vain majestic Wren expands the dome ;
Blank as pale stucco Rubens lines the room :
Lost are the raptures of bold Handel's strain ;
Great Tully storms, sweet Virgil sings, in vain.
The beauteous forms of Nature are effac'd ;
Tempe's soft charms, the raging wat'ry waste ;
Each greatly-wild, each sweet romantic scene,
Unheeded rises, and almost unseen.
    Yet these are joys, with some of better clay,
To sooth the toils of life's embarrass'd way.
These the fine frame with charming horrours chill,
And give the nerves delightfully to thrill.
But of all taste the noblest and the best,
The first enjoyment of the generous breast,
Is to behold in man's obnoxious state
Scenes of content, and happy turns of fate.
Fair views of Nature, shining works of art,
Amuse the fancy : but those touch the heart.
Chiefly for this proud epic song delights,
For this some riot on th' Arabian Nights.
Each case is ours : and for the human mind
'Tis monstrous not to feel for all mankind.
Were all mankind unhappy, who could taste
Elysium ? or be solitarily blest ?
Shock'd with surrounding shapes of human woe,
All that or sense or fancy could bestow,
You would reject with sick and coy disdain,
And pant to see one cheerful face again.
    But if life's better prospects to behold
So much delight the man of generous mould ;
How happy they, the great, the godlike few,
Who daily cultivate this pleasing view !

This is a joy possess'd by few indeed !
Dame Fortune has so many fools to feed,
She cannot oft afford, with all her store,
To yield her smiles where Nature smil'd before.
To sinking worth a cordial hand to lend ;
With better fortune to surprize a friend ;
To cheer the modest stranger's lonely state ;
Or snatch an orphan family from fate ;
To do, possess'd with virtue's noblest fire,
Such generous deeds as we with tears admire ;
Deeds that, above ambition's vulgar aim,
Secure an amiable, a solid fame :          [seize;
These are such joys as Heaven's first favourites
These please you now, and will for ever please.
    Too seldom we great moral deeds admire ;
The will, the power, th' occasion must conspire.
Yet few there are so impotent and low,
But can some small good offices bestow.
Small as they are, however cheap they come,
They add still something to the general sum :
And him who gives the little in his power,
The world acquits; and Heaven demands no more.
    Unhappy he ! who feels each neighbour's woe,
Yet no relief, no comfort can bestow.
Unhappy too, who feels each kind essay,
And for great favours has but words to pay ;
Who, scornful of the flatterer's fawning art,
Dreads even to pour his gratitude of heart ;
And with a distant lover's silent pain
Must the best movements of his soul restrain.
But men sagacious to explore mankind
Trace even the coyest passions of the mind.
    Not only to the good we owe good-will ;
In good and bad distress demands it still.
This with the generous lays distinction low,
Endears a friend, and recommends a foe.
Not that resentment ever ought to rise ;
For even excess of virtue ranks with vice :
And there are villanies no bench can awe,
That sport without the limits of the law.
No laws th' ungenerous crime would reprehend
Could I forget Eumenes was my friend :
In vain the gibbet or the pillory claim
The wretch who blasts a helpless virgin's fame.
Where laws are dup'd, 'tis nor unjust nor mean
To seize the proper time for honest spleen.
An open candid foe I could not hate,
Nor even insult the base in humbled state ;
But thriving malice tamely to forgive—
'Tis somewhat late to be so primitive.
    But I detain you with these tedious lays,
Which few perhaps would read, but fewer praise.
No matter : could I please the polish'd few
Who taste the serious or the gay like you,
The squeamish mob may find my verses bare
Of every grace—but curse me if I care.
Besides, I little court Parnassian fame ;
There's yet a better than a poet's name.
'Twould more indulge my pride to hear it said,
That I with you the paths of honour tread,
Than that amongst the proud poetic train
No modern boasted a more classic vein ;
Or that in numbers I let loose my song,
Smooth as the Tweed, and as the Severn strong.

## TASTE.

AN EPISTLE TO A YOUNG CRITIC. 1753.

Proferre quæ sentiat cur quisquam liber dubi-
tet?—Malim, me hercule, solus insanire, quam
sobrius aut plebis aut patrum delirationibus ig-
naviter assentari.——
                        Autor anonym. Fragm.

RANGE from Tower-hill all London to the Fleet,
Thence round the Temple t' utmost Grosvenor-
        street :
Take in your route both Gray's and Lincoln's Inn ;
Miss not, be sure, my lords and gentlemen ;
You'll hardly raise, as I with Petty [1] guess,
Above twelve thousand men of taste ; unless
In desperate times a connoisseur may pass.
    " A connoisseur ! what's that ?"   'Tis hard `
But you must oft amidst the fair and gay [to say :
Have seen a wou'd-be rake, a fluttering fool,
Who swears he loves the sex with all his soul.
Alas, vain youth ! dost thou admire sweet Jones ?
Thou be gallant without or blood or bones !
You'd split to hear th' insipid coxcomb cry
" Ah, charming Nancy ! 'tis too much ! I die !"
"Die and be d—n'd," says one; " but let me tell ye
I'll pay the loss if ever rapture kill ye."
    'Tis easy learnt the art to talk by rote :
At Nando's 'twill but cost you half a groat ; [sir ;
The Bedford school at three pence is not dear,
At White's—the stars instruct you for a tester.
But he, whom Nature never meant to share
One spark of taste, will never catch it there :—
Nor no where else ; howe'er the booby beau
Grows great with Pope, and Horace, and Boileau.
    Good native taste, though rude, is seldom
Be it in music, painting, or in song.   [wrong,
But this, as well as other faculties,
Improves with age and ripens by degrees.
I know, my dear, 'tis needless to deny't,
You like Voiture, you think him wondrous bright :
But seven years hence, your relish more matur'd,
What now delights will hardly be endur'd.
The boy may live to taste Racine's fine charms,
Whom Lee's bald orb or Rowe's dry rapture
        warms :
But he, enfranchis'd from his tutor's care,
Who places Butler near Cervantes' chair ;
Or with Erasmus can admit to vie
Brown of Squab-hall of merry memory ;
Will die a Goth : and nod at Woden's feast [2],
Th' eternal winter long, on Gregory's breast [3].
    Long may he swill, this patriarch of the dull,
The drowsy mum—But touch not Maro's skull !
His holy barbarous dotage sought to doom,
Good Heaven ! th' immortal classics to the
        tomb !—
Those sacred lights shall bid new genius rise
When all Rome's saints have rotted from the skies.

[1] Sir William Petty, author of the Political
Arithmetic.
[2] Alluding to the Gothic Heaven, Woden's hall ;
where the happy are for ever employed in drinking beer, mum, and other comfortable liquors out
of the skulls of those whom they had slain in battle.
[3] Pope Gregory the VIth, distinguished by the
name of St. Gregory; whose pious zeal in the
cause of barbarous ignorance and priestly tyranny, exerted itself in demolishing, to the utmost of his power, all the remains of heathen
genius.

Be these your guides, if at the ivy crown
You aim ; each country's classics, and your own.
But chiefly with the ancients pass your prime
And drink Castalia at the fountain's brim.
The man to genuine Burgundy bred up,
Soon starts, the dash of Methuen in his cup.

Those sovereign masters of the Muses skill
Are the true patterns of good writing still.
Their ore was rich and seven times purg'd of lead.
Their art seem'd nature, 'twas so finely hid.
Though born with all the powers of writing well,
What pains it cost they did not blush to tell.
Their ease (my lords !) ne'er loung'd for want of
Nor did their rage through affectation tire,[fire,
Free from all tawdry and imposing glare
They trusted to their native grace of air.
Rapt'rous and wild the trembling soul they seize,
Or sly coy beauties steal it by degrees ;
The more you view them still the more they
      please.
Yet there are thousands of scholastic merit
Who worm their sense out but ne'er taste their
      spirit.
Witness each pedant under Bentely bred ;
Each commentator that e'er commented.
(You scarce can seize a spot of classic ground,
With leagues of Dutch morass so floated round.)
Witness—but sir, I hold a cautious pen,
Lest I should wrong some " honourable men."
They grow enthusiasts too—" 'Tis true! 'tis pity !"
But 'tis not every lunatic that's witty.
Some have run Maro—and some Milton—mad,
Ashley once turn'd a solid barber's head :
Hear all that's said or printed if you can,
Ashley has turn'd more solid heads than one.

Let such admire each great or specious name ;
For right or wrong the joy to them's the same.
" Right !" Yes, a thousand times.—Each fool
      has heard
That Homer was a wonder of a bard.
Despise them civilly with all my heart—
But to convince them is a desperate part.
Why should you tease one for what secret cause
One doats on Horace, or on Hudibras ?
'Tis cruel, sir, 'tis needless, to endeavour
To teach a sot of taste he knows no flavour.
To disunite I neither wish nor hope
A stubborn blockhead from his fav'rite fop.
Yes—fop I say, were Maro's self before 'em :
For Maro's self grows dull as they pore o'er him.
      But hear their raptures o'er some specious
      rhyme
Dubb'd by the musk'd and greasy mob sublime.
For spleen's dear sake hear how a coxcomb prates
As clam'rous o'er his joys as fifty cats ;
" Music has charms to sooth a savage breast,
To soften rocks, and oaks,"—and all the rest :
"I've heard"—Bless these long ears !—"Heav'ns
      what a strain !
Good God ! what thunders burst in this Campaign!
Hark ! Waller warbles ! ah ! how sweetly killing !
Then that inimitable Splendid Shilling !
Rowe breathes all Shakespeare here !—That ode
      of Prior
Is Spenser quite ! egad his very fire !—
As like "—Yes faith ! as gum-flowers to the rose,
Or as to claret flat Minorca's dose ;
As like as (if I am not grossly wrong)
Erle Robert's Mice to aught e'er Chaucer sung.

Read boldly, and unprejudic'd peruse
Each fav'rite modern, ev'n each ancient muse.
With all his comic salt and tragic rage,
The great stupendous genius of our stage,
Boast of our island, pride of human-kind,
Had faults to which the boxes are not blind.
His frailties are to ev'ry gossip known :
Yet Milton's pedantries not shock the town.
Ne'er be the dupe of names, however high ;
For some outlive good parts, some misapply.
Each elegant Spectator you admire ;
But must you therefore swear by Cato's fire ?
Masques for the court, and oft a clumsey jest,
Disgrac'd the Muse that wrought the Alchemist.
" But to the ancients."—Faith ! I am not clear,
For all the smooth round type of Elzevir,
That every work which lasts in prose or song
Two thousand years, deserves to last so long.
For not to mention some eternal blades
Known only now in th' academic shades,
(Those sacred groves where raptur'd spirits stray,
And in word-hunting waste the live-long day)
Ancients whom none but curious critics scan,
Do read Messalas' [4] praises if you can.
Ah ! who but feels the sweet contagious smart
While soft Tibullus pours his tender heart ?
With him the Loves and Muses melt in tears ;
But not a word of some hexameters.
" You grow so squeamish and so dev'lish dry,
You'll call Lucretius vapid next." Not I.
Some find him tedious, others think him lame :
But if he lags, his subject is to blame. [tried,
Rough weary roads through barren wilds he
Yet still he marches with true Roman pride :
Sometimes a meteor, gorgeous, rapid, bright,
He streams athwart the philosophic night.
Find you in Horace no insipid odes ?—
He dar'd to tell us Homer sometimes nods ;
And but for such a critic's hardy skill
Homer might slumber unsuspected still.
Tasteless, implicit, indolent, and tame,
At second-hand we chiefly praise or blame.
Hence 'tis, for else one knows not why or how,
Some authors flourish for a year or two :
For many some, more wond'rous still to tell ;
Farquhar yet lingers on the brink of Hell.
Of solid merit others pine unknown ;
At first, though Carlos [5] swimmingly went down,
Poor Belvidera fail'd to melt the town.
Sunk in dead night the giant Milton lay,
'Till Sommer's hand produc'd him to the day.
But, thanks to Heav'n and Addison's good grace,
Now ev'ry fop is charm'd with Chevy Chace.

Specious and sage, the sovereign of the flock
Led to the downs, or from the wave-worn rock
Reluctant hurl'd, the tame implicit train
Or crop the downs, or headlong seek the main.
As blindly we our solemn leaders follow,
And good, and bad, and execrable swallow.

[4] A poem of Tibullus's in hexameter verse ;
as yawning and insipid as his elegies are tender
and natural.

[5] Don Carlos, a tragedy of Otway's, now long
and justly forgotten, went off with great applause;
while his Orphan, a somewhat better performance,
and what is yet more strange, his Venice Preserved, according to the theatrical anecdotes of
those times, met with a very cold reception.

Pray, on the first throng'd evening of a play
That wears the facies hippocratica [6],
Strong lines of death, signs dire of reprobation;
Have you not seen the angel of salvation
Appear sublime; with wise and solemn rap
To teach the doubtful rabble where to clap?—
The rabble knows not where our dramas shine;
But where the cane goes pat—"By G— that's
    fine!"
    Judge for yourself; nor wait with timid
        phlegm
'Till some illustrious pedant hum or hem.
The lords who starv'd old Ben were learn'dly fond
Of Chaucer, whom with bungling toil they comm'd.
Their sons, whose ears bold Milton could not seize,
Would laugh o'er Ben like mad, and snuff and
    sneeze,
And swear, and seem as tickled as you please.
Their spawn, the pride of this sublimer age,
Feel to the toes and horns grave Milton's rage.
Though liv'd he now he might appeal with scorn
To lords, knights, 'squires, and doctors, yet un-
Or justly mad, to Moloch's burning fane [born;
Devote the choicest children of his brain.
Judge for yourself; and, as you find, report
Of wit, as freely as of beef or port.
Zounds! shall a pert or bluff important wight,
Whose brain is fanciless, whose blood is white;
A mumbling ape of taste; prescribe us laws
To try the poets, for no better cause
Than that he boasts per ann. ten thousand clear,
Yelps in the house, or barely sits a peer?
For shame! for shame! the liberal British soul
To stoop to any stale dictator's rule!
I may be wrong, and often am no doubt,
But right or wrong with friends, with foes 'twill
Thus 'tis perhaps my fault if I complain    [ont.
Of trite invention and a flimsy vein,
Tame characters, uninteresting, jejune,
And passions drily copied from Le Brun [7].
For I would rather never judge than wrong
That frien[d] of all men, generous Fenelon.
But in the name of goodness, must I be
The dupe of charms I never yet could see?

[6] The appearance of the face in the last stage
of a consumption, as it is described by Hippocrates.

[7] First painter to Lewis XIV. who, to speak in
fashionable French English, called himself Lewis
the Great. Our sovereign lords the passions,
Love, Rage, Despair, &c. were graciously pleased to sit to him in their turns for their portraits;
which he was generous enough to communicate
to the public; to the great improvement, no
doubt, of history-painting. It was he who they
say poisoned Le Sueur; who, without half his
advantages in many other respects, was so un-
reasonable and provoking as to display a genius
with which his own could stand no comparison.
It was he and his Gothic disciples, who, with sly
scratches, defaced the most masterly of this Le
Sueur's performances, as often as their barbarous
envy could snugly reach them. Yet after all
these achievements he died in his bed! A catastrophe which could not have happened to him in
a country like this, where the fine arts are as
zealously and judiciously patronised as they are
well understood.

And then to flatter where there's no reward—
Better be any patron-hunting bard,
Who half our lords with filthy praise besmears,
And sing an anthem to all ministers:
Taste th' Attic salt in ev'ry peer's poor rebus,
And crown each Gothic idol for a Phœbus.
    Alas! so far from free, so far from brave,
We dare not show the little taste we have.
With us you'll see ev'n vanity control
The most refin'd sensations of the soul.
Sad Otway's scenes, great Shakespeare's we defy:
"Lard, madam! 'tis so unpolite to cry!—
For shame, my dear! d'ye credit all this stuff?—
I vow—well, this is innocent enough."
At Athens long ago, the ladies—(married)
Dreamt not they misbehav'd though they mis-
    carried,
When a wild poet with licentious rage
Turn'd fifty furies loose upon the stage.
    They were so tender and so easy mov'd,
Heav'ns! how the Grecian ladies must have
    lov'd!
For all the fine sensations still have dwelt,
Perhaps, where one was exquisitely felt.
Thus he who heavenly Maro truly feels,
Stands fix'd on Raphael, and at Handel thrills.
The grosser senses too, the taste, the smell,
Are likely truest where the fine prevail:
Who doubts that Horace must have cater'd well?
Friend, I'm a shrewd observer, and will guess
What books you doat on from your fav'rite mess.
Brown and L'Estrange will surely charm whom-
    e'er
The frothy pertness strikes of weak small-beer.
Who steeps the calf's fat loin in greasy sauce
Will hardly loathe the praise that bastes an ass.
Who riots on scotcht collops scorns not any
Insipid, fulsome, trashy miscellany;
And who devours whate'er the cook can dish up,
Will for a classic consecrate each bishop [8].
    But I am sick of pen and ink; and you
Will find this letter long enough.    Adieu!

---

## IMITATIONS OF SHAKESPEARE AND SPENSER.

ADVERTISEMENT FROM THE PUBLISHER.

The following imitation of Shakespeare was one
of our author's first attempts in poetry, made
when he was very young. It helped to amuse
the solitude of a winter passed in a wild romantic country; and, what is rather particular, was just finished when Mr. Thomson's
celebrated poem upon the same subject appeared. Mr. Thomson, soon hearing of it,
had the curiosity to procure a copy by the
means of a common acquaintance. He showed
it to his poetical friends, Mr. Mallet, Mr.
Aaron Hill, and Dr. Young, who, it seems,
did great honour to it; and the first-mention-
ed gentleman wrote to one of his friends at
Edinburgh, desiring the author's leave to
publish it; a request too flattering to youthful
vanity to be resisted. But Mr. Mallet altered
his mind; and this little piece has hitherto
remained unpublished.

[8] See Felton's Classics.

The other imitations of Shakespeare happen to have been saved out of the ruins of an unfinished tragedy on the story of Tereus and Philomela; attempted upon an irregular and extravagant plan, at an age much too early for such achievements. However, they are here exhibited for the sake of such guests as may like a little repast of scraps.

Now Summer with her wanton court is gone
To revel on the south-side of the world,
And flaunt and frolic out the live-long day.
While Winter rising pale from northern seas
Shakes from his hoary locks the drizzling rheum.
A blast so shrewd makes the tall-bodied pines
Unsinew'd bend, and heavy-paced bears
Sends growling to their savage tenements.
  Now blows the surly north, and chills throughout
The stiffening regions; while, by stronger charms
Than Circe e'er or fell Medea brew'd,
Each brook that wont to prattle to its banks,
Lies all bestill'd and wedg'd betwixt its banks,
Nor moves the wither'd reeds: and the rash flood
That from the mountains held its headstrong course,
Buried in livid sheets of vaulting ice,          [course,
Seen through the shameful breaches, idly creeps
To pay a scanty tribute to the ocean.
What wonder? when the floating wilderness
That scorns our miles, and calls geography
A shallow pryer; from whose unsteady mirror
The high-hung pole surveys his dancing locks;
When this still-raving deep lies mute and dead,
Nor heaves its swelling bosom to the winds.
The surges, baited by the fierce north-east,
Tossing with fretful spleen their angry heads
To roar and rush together,
Even in the foam of all their madness struck
To monumental ice, stand all astride
The rocks they washed so late.  Such execution,
So stern, so sudden, wrought the grisly aspect
Of terrible Medusa, ere young Perseus
With his keen sabre cropt her horrid head,
And laid her serpents rowling on the dust; [stone
When wandering thro' the woods she frown'd to
Their savage tenants: just as the foaming lion
Sprung furious on his prey, her speedier power
Outrun his haste; no time to languish in,
But fix'd in that fierce attitude he stands
Like Rage in marble.—Now portly Argoses
Lie wedg'd 'twixt Neptune's ribs.  The bridg'd
          abysm
Has chang'd our ships to horses; the swift bark
Yields to the heavy waggon and the cart,
That now from isle to isle maintain the trade;
And where the surface-haunting dolphin led
Her sportive young, is now an area fit
For the wild school-boy's pastime.
  Meantime the evening skies, crusted with ice,
Shifting from red to black their weighty skirts,
Hang mournful o'er the hills; and stealing night
Rides the bleak puffing winds, that seem to spit
Their foam sparse thro' the welkin, which is nothing
          thing
If not beheld.  Anon the burden'd Heaven
Shakes from its ample sieve the boulted snow;
That fluttering down besprinkles the sad trees
In mockery of leaves; piles up the hills
To monstrous altitude, and chokes to the lips

The deep impervious vales that yawn as low
As to the centre, Nature's vasty breaches.
While all the pride of men and mortal things
Lies whelm'd in Heaven's white ruins.—
  The shivering clown digs his obstructed way
Through the snow-barricadoed cottage door;
And muffled in his home-spun plaid encounters
With livid cheeks and rheum-distilling nose
The morning's sharp and scourging breath; to
          count
His starving flock whose number's all too short
To make the goodly sum of yester-night:
Part deep ingurgitated, part yet struggling
With their last pantings melt themselves a grave
In Winter's bosom; which yields not to the
Of the pale languid crescet of this world, [touch
That now with lean and churlish husbandry
Yields heartlessly the remnants of his prime;
And, like most spendthrifts, starves his latter days
For former rankness.  He with bleary eye
Blazons his own disgrace; the harness'd waste
Rebellious to his blunt defeated shafts;
And idly strikes the chalky mountains' tops
That rise to kiss the welkin's ruddy lips;
Where all the rash young bullies of the air
Mount their quick slender penetrating wings,
Whipping the frost-burnt villagers to the bones;
And growing with their motion mad and furious,
'Till swoln to tempests they out-rage the thunder;
Winnow the chaffy snow, and mock the skies
Even with their own artillery retorted;
Tear up and throw th' accumulated hills
Into the vallies.  And as rude hurricanes,
Discharg'd from the wind-swoln cheeks of Hea-
Buoy up the swilling skirts of Araby's     [ven,
Inhospitable wilds,
And roll the dusty desert through the skies,
Choaking the liberal air, and smothering
Whole caravans at once; such havoc spreads
This war of Heaven and Earth, such sudden ruin
Visits their houseless citizens, that shrink
In the false shelter of the hills together,
And hear the tempest howling o'er their heads
That by and by o'erwhelms them.  The very
          birds,
Those few that troop'd not with the chiming tribe
Of amorous Summer, quit their ruffian element;
And with domestic tameness hop and flutter
Within the roofs of persecuting man,
(Grown hospitable by like sense of sufferance;)
Whither the hinds, the debt o' the day discharg'd,
From kiln or barn repairing, shut the door
On surly Winter; crowd the clean-swept hearth
And cheerful shining fire; and doff the time,
The whilst the maids their twirling spindles ply,
With musty legends, and ear-pathing tales,
Of giants, and black necromantic deeds,
Of air-built castles, feats of madcap knights,
And every hollow fiction of romance.
And, as their rambling-humour leads them, talk
Of prodigies, and things of dreadful utterance,
That set them all agape, rouse up their hair,
And make the ideot drops start from their eyes;
Of church-yards belching flames at dead of night,
Of walking statues, ghosts unaffable,
Haunting the dark waste tower or airless dungeon;
Then of the elves that deftly trip the green,
Drinking the summer's moonlight from the
          flowers;

And all the toys that phantasy pranks up
T' amuse her fools withal.—Thus they lash on
The snail-pac'd hyperborean nights, till Heaven
Hangs with a juster poize: when the murk clouds
Roll'd up in heavy wreathes low-bellying, seem
To kiss the ground, and all the waste of snow
Looks blue beneath 'em; till plump'd with
    bloating dropsy,
Beyond the bounds and stretch of continence,
They burst at once ; down pours the hoarded
    rain,
Washing the slippery winter from the hills,
And floating all the vallies.   The fading scene
Melts like a lost enchantment or vain phantasm
That can no more abuse.   Nature resumes
Her old substantial shape ; while from the waste
Of undistinguishing calamity,
Forests, and by their sides wide-skirted plains,
Houses and trees arise ; and waters flow,
That from their dark confinements bursting,
    spurn
Their brittle chains ; huge sheets of loosen'd ice
Float on their bosoms to the deep, and jarr
And clatter as they pass; th' o'erjutting banks,
As long unpractis'd to so steep a view,
Seem to look dizzy on the moving pomp.
Now ev'ry petty brook that crawl'd along,
Railing its pebbles, mocks the river's rage,
Like the proud frog i' the fable.    The huge
    Danube,
While melting mountains rush into its tide,
Rolls with such headstrong and unreined course,
As it would choke the Euxine's gulphy maw,
Bursting its crystal cerements.   The breathing
    time
Of peace expir'd, that hush'd the deafning scenes
Of clam'rous indignation, ruffian war
Rebels, and Nature stands at odds again :
When the rous'd furies of the fighting winds
Torment the main; that swells its angry sides,
And churns the foam betwixt its flinty jaws ;
While through the savage dungeon of the night
The horrid thunder growls.   Th' ambitious waves
Assault the skies, and from the bursting clouds
Drink the glib lightening ; as if the seas
Would quench the ever-burning fires of Heaven.
Straight from their slipp'ry pomp they madly
    plunge
And kiss the lowest pebbles.   Wretched they
That 'midst such rude vexation of the deep
Guide a frail vessel!  Better ice-bound still,
Than mock'd with liberty thus be resign'd
To the rough fortune of the froward time;
When Navigation all a-tiptoe stands
On such unsteady footing.   Now they mount
On the tall billow's top, and seem to jowl
Against the stars; whence (dreadful eminence!)
They see with swimming eyes (enough to hurry
    round
In endless vertigo the dizzy brain)
A gulph that swallows vision, with wide mouth
Steep-yawning to receive them ; down they duck
To the rugged bottom of the main, and view
The adamantine gates of vaulted Hell :
Thence toss'd to light again: till borne adrift
Against some icy mountain's bulging sides
They reel, and are no more.—Nor less by land
Ravage the winds, that in their wayward rage
Howl through the wide unhospitable glens ;

That rock the stable-planted towers, and shake
The hoary monuments of ancient time
Down to their flinty bases ; that engage
As they would tear the mountains from their
    roots,                              [heads ;
And brush th' high Heavens with their woody
Making the stout oaks bow.—But I forget
That sprightly Ver trips on old Winter's heel:
Cease we these notes too tragic for the time,
Nor jar against great Nature's symphony;
When even the blustrous elements grow tuneful,
Or listen to the concert.  Hark ! how loud
The cuckoo wakes the solitary wood!
Soft sigh the winds as o'er the greens they stray,
And murmuring brooks within their channels
    play.

---

## PROGNE'S DREAM:

DARKLY EXPRESSIVE OF SOME PAST EVENTS THAT
    WERE SOON TO BE REVEALED TO HER.

— — — LAST night I dreamt,
Whate'er it may forebode it moves me strangely,
That I was rapt into the raving deep;
An old and reverend sire conducted me:
He plung'd into the bosom of the main,
And bade me not to fear but follow him.
I followed : with impetuous speed we div'd,
And heard the dashing thunder o'er our heads.
Many a slippery fathom down we sunk,
Beneath all plummet's sound, and reach'd the
    bottom.
When there, I ask'd my venerable guide
If he could tell me where my sister was ;
He told me that she lay not far from thence
Within the bosom of a flinty rock,
Where Neptune kept her for his paramour,
Hid from the jealous Amphitrite's sight:
And said he could conduct me to the place.
I beg'd he would.  Through dreadful ways we
    past,                                [side,
'Twixt rocks that frightfully lower'd on either
Whence here and there the branching coral
    sprung ;                      [gold and gems,
O'er dead men's bones we walk'd, o'er heaps of
Into a hideous kind of wilderness,
Where stood a stern and prison-looking rock,
Daub'd with a mossy verdure all around,
The mockery of paint.   As we drew near,
Out sprung a hydra from a den below,
A speckl'd fury ; fearfully it hiss'd,
And roll'd its sea-green eyes so angrily
As it would kill with looking.   My old guide
Against its sharp head hurl'd a rugged stone—
The curling monster rais'd a brazen shriek,
Wallow'd and died in fitful agonies.
We gain'd the cave.  Through woven adamant!
I look'd, and saw my sister all alone.
Employ'd she seem'd in writing something sad;
So sad she look'd : her cheek was wond'rous wan,
Her mournful locks like weary sedges hung.
I call'd—she, turning, started when she saw me,
And threw her head aside as if asham'd :
She wept, but would not speak—I call'd again;
Still she was mute.—Then madly I address,
With all the lion-sinews of despair,
To break the flinty ribs that held me out ;
And with the struggling wak'd.—

### A STORM.;

RAISED TO ACCOUNT FOR THE LATE RETURN OF A MESSENGER

— — — THE Sun went down in wrath ;
The skies foam'd brass, and soon th' unchained
   winds
Burst from the howling dungeon of the north :
And rais'd such high delirium on the main,
Such angry clamour ; while such boiling waves
Flash'd on the peevish eye of moody night,
It look'd as if the seas would scald the Heavens.
Still louder chid the winds, th' enchafed surge
Still answer'd louder ; and when the sickly morn
Peep'd ruefully through the blotted thick-brow'd
   east
To view the ruinous havoc of the dark,
The stately towers of Athens seem'd to stand
On hollow foam tide-whipt ; the ships that lay
Scorning the blast within the marble arms
Of the sea-chid Portumnus, danc'd like corks
Upon th' enraged deep, kicking each other ;
And some were dash'd to fragments in this fray
Against the harbour's rocky chest. The sea
So roar'd, so madly rag'd, so proudly swell'd,
As it would thunder full into the streets,
And steep the tall Cecropian battlements
In foaming brine. The airy citadel,
Perch'd like an eagle on a high-brow'd rock,
Shook the salt water from its stubborn sides
With eager quaking; the Cyclades appear'd
Like ducking cormorants—Such a mutiny
Out-clamour'd all tradition, and gain'd belief
To ranting prodigies of heretofore.
Seven days it storm'd, &c.

---

### AN IMITATION OF SPENSER.

WRITTEN AT MR. THOMSON'S DESIRE, TO BE IN-SERTED INTO THE CASTLE OF INDOLENCE.

FULL many a fiend did haunt this house of rest,
   And made of passive wights an easy prey.
Here Lethargy with deadly sleep opprest,
   Stretch'd on his back, a mighty lubbard lay,
   Heaving his sides ; and snored night and day.
To stir him from his traunce it was not eath,
And his half-open'd eye he shut straightway :
   He led I ween the softest way to death,
And taught withouten pain or strife to yield the
   breath.

Of limbs enormous, but withal unsound,
   Soft-swoln and pale, here lay the Hydropsie;
Unwieldly man, with belly monstrous round
   For ever fed with watery supply ;
For still he drank, and yet he still was dry.
   And here a moping mystery did sit,
Mother of Spleen, in robes of various dye :
   She call'd herself the Hypochondriac Fit,
And frantic seem'd to some, to others seem'd a
   wit :

A lady was she whimsical and proud,
   Yet oft thro' fear her pride would crouchen
   low.
She felt or fancied in her fluttering mood
All the diseases that the spitals know,

And sought all physic that the shops bestow ;
And still new leaches and new drugs would
   try.
'Twas hard to hit her humour high or low,
   For sometimes she would laugh and some-
   times cry,
Sometimes would waxen wroth; and all she
   knew not why.

Fast by her side a listless virgin pin'd,
   With aching head and squeamish heart-
   burnings ;         [kind,
Pale, bloated, cold, she seem'd to hate man-
   But lov'd in secret all forbidden things.
And here the Tertian shook his chilling wings.
   And here the Gout, half tiger half a snake,
Rag'd with an hundred teeth, an hundred
   stings.
   These and a thousand furies more did shake
Those weary realms, and kept ease-loving men
   awake.

---

### A DAY :

AN EPISTLE TO JOHN WILKES, OF AYLESBURY, ESQ.

ESCAP'D from London now four moons, and
   more,
I greet gay Wilkes from Fulda's wasted shore,
Where cloth'd with wood a hundred hills ascend,
Where Nature many a paradise has plann'd :
   A land that, e'en amid contending arms,
Late smil'd with culture, and luxuriant charms ;
But now the hostile scythe has bar'd her soil,
And her sad peasants starve for all their toil.
   What news to day ?—I ask you not what
      rogue,
What paltry imp of fortune 's now in vogue ;
What forward blundering fool was last preferr'd,
By mere pretence distinguish'd from the herd ;
With what new cheat the gaping town was smit ;
What crazy scribbler reigns the present wit ;
What stuff for winter the two Booths have mixt ;
What bouncing mimic grows a Roscius next.
Wave all such news : I've seen too much, my
   friend,
To stare at any wonders of that kind.
   News, none have I: you know I never had ;
I never long'd the day's dull lye to spread ;
I left to gossips that sweet luxury,
More in the secrets of the great than I ;
To nurses, midwives, all the slippery train,
That swallow all, and bring up all again :
Or did I e'er a brief event relate,
You found it soon at length in the Gazette.
   Now for the weather—This is England still
For aught I find, as good, and quite as ill.
Even now the pond'rous rain perpetual falls,
Drowns every camp, and crowds our hospitals.
This soaking deluge all unstrings my frame,
Dilutes my sense, and suffocates my flame—
'Tis that which makes these present lines so tame.
The parching east wind still pursues me too—
Is there no climate where this fiend ne'er
   flew ?—
By Heaven, it slays Japan, perhaps Peru !
It blasts all Earth with its envenom'd breath,
That scatters discord, rage, diseases, death.

'Twas the first plague that burst Pandora's chest,
And with a livid smile sow'd all around the rest.
  Heaven guard my friend from every plague
      that flies,
Still grant him health, whence all the pleasures
But oft diseases from slow causes creep,   [rise.
And in this doctrine as (thank Heaven) I'm deep,

   *     *     *     *     *
   *     *     *     *     *
   *     *     *     *     *

Mean time excuse me that I slily snatch
The only theme in which I shine your match.
  You study early : some indulge at night,
Their prudish Muse steals in by candle-light ;
Shy as the Athenian bard, she shuns the day,
And finds December genial more than May.
But happier you who court the early Sun,
For morning visits no debauch draw on,
Nor so the spirits, health, or sight impair,
As those that pass in the raw midnight air.
  The task of breakfast o'er ; that peevish, pale,
That lounging, yawning, most ungenial meal ;
Rush out, before these fools rush in to worry ye,
Whose business is to be idle in a hurry,
Who kill your time as frankly as their own,
And feel no civil hints e'er to be gone.
These flies all fairly flung, whene'er the house,
Your country's business, or your friend's, al-
    lows,
Rush out, enjoy the fields and the fresh air ;
Ride, walk, or drive, the weather foul or fair.
Yet in the torrid months I would reverse
This method, leave behind both prose and verse;
With the grey dawn the hills and forest roam,
And wait the sultry noon embower'd at home,
While every rural sound improves the breeze,
The railing stream, the busy rooks, and murmur
    of the bees.
You'll hardly choose these cheerful jaunts
    alone—
Except when some deep scheme is carrying on.
With you at Chelsea oft may I behold
The hopeful bud of sense her bloom unfold,
With you I'd walk to *  *  *  *  *  *
To rich, insipid Hackney, if you will :
With you no matter where, while we're together,
I scorn no spot on Earth, and curse no weather.
  When dinner comes, amid the various feast,
That crowns your genial board, where every
    guest,
Or grave, or gay, is happy, and at home,
And none e'er sigh'd for the mind's elbow-room ;
I warn you still to make your chief repast
On one plain dish, and trifle with the rest.

   *     *     *     *     *
   *     *     *     *     *

Beef, in a fever, if your stomach crave it,
Ox-cheek, or mawkish cod, be sure you have it.
For still the constitution, even the case,
Directs the stomach ; this informs the taste ;
And what the taste in her capricious fits
Coyly, or even indifferently admits,
The peevish stomach, or disdains to toil,
Or indolently works to vapid chyle.
This instinct of the taste so seldom errs,
That if you love, yet smart for cucumbers,
Or plumbs of bad repute, you'll likely find
'Twas for you separated what Nature join'd,
The spicy kernel here, and there the rind.

  *     *     *     *     *
  *     *     *     *     *

'Tis strange how blindly we from Nature
    stray !
The only creatures we that miss their way !
" To err is human," man's prerogative,
Who 'as too much sense by Nature's laws to live :
Wiser than Nature he must thwart her plan,
And ever will be spoiling, where he can.
'Tis well he cannot ocean change to cream,
Nor earth to a gilded cake ; not e'en could tame
Niagara's steep abyss to crawl down stairs [1],
Or dress in roses the dire Cordelliers [2] :
But what he can he does : well can he trim
A charming spot into a childish whim ;
Can every generous gift of Nature spoil,
And rates their merits by his cost and toil.
Whate'er the land, whate'er the seas produce,
Of perfect texture, and exalted juice,
He pampers, or to fulsome fat, or drains,
Refines and bleaches, till no taste remains.

  *     *     *     *     *
  *     *     *     *     *

Enough to fatten fools, or drive the dray,
But plagues and death to those of finer clay.
No corner else, 'tis not to be denied,
Of all our isle so rankly is supplied
With gross productions, and adulterate fare,
As our renown'd abode, whose name I spare.
They cram all poultry, that the hungry fox
Would loathe to touch them ; e'en their boasted
    ox
Sometimes is glutted so with unctuous spoil,
That what seems beef is rather rape-seed oil.
D'ye ye know what brawn is ?—O th' unhappy
    beast ! '
He stands eternal, and is doom'd to feast
Till—but the nauseous process I forbear—
Only, beware of brawn—besure, beware !
Yet brawn has taste—it has ; their veal has none,
Save what the butcher's breath inspires alone ;
Just Heaven one day may send them hail for
    wheat,
Who spoil all veal because it should be white.
'Tis hard to say of what compounded paste
Their bread is wrought, for it betrays no taste,
Whether 'tis flour and chalk, or chalk and flour,
Shell'd and refin'd till it has taste no more ;
But if the lump be white, and white enough,
No matter how insipid, dry or tough.
In salt itself the sapid savour fails,
Burnt alum for the love of white prevails :
While tasteless cole-seed we for mustard swal-
    low,
'Tis void of zest indeed—but still 'tis yellow.
Parsnip, or parsley-root, the rogues will soon
Scrape for horse-radish, and 'twill pass unknown,
For by the colour, not the taste, we prove all,
As hens will sit on chalk, if 'tis but oval.
  I must with caution the cook's reign invade,
Hot as the fire, and hasty from his trade,

  *     *     *     *     *
  *     *     *     *     *
  *     *     *     *     *

---

[1] Vide Chatsworth, 1753.
[2] Les Cordelleiras des Andes are a chain of
hills which run through South-America.

A cook of genius, bid him roast a hare,
By all that's hot and horrible would swear,
Parch native dryness! zounds, that's not the
   thing—
But stew him, and he might half dine a king.
His gen'rous broth I should almost prefer
To turtle soup, though turtle travels far.
   You think me nice perhaps: yet I could dine
On roasted rabbit; or fat turkey and chine;
Or fulsome haslet; or most drily cram
My throat with tasteless fillet and wet ham:
But let me ne'er of mutton-saddle eat,
That solid phantom, that most specious cheat;
Yet loin is passable, he was no fool
Who said the half is better than the whole:

   But I have cook'd and carv'd enough and
   more,
We come to drinking next. 'Till dinner's o'er,
I would all claret, even champaign forbear;
Give me fresh water—bless me with small-beer.
But still whate'er you drink with cautious lip
Approach, survey, and e'er you swallow, sip;
For often, O defend all honest throats!
The reeling wasp on the drench'd borage floats.
I've known a dame, sage else as a divine,
For brandy whip off ipecacuan wine;
And I'm as sure amid your careless glee,
You'll swallow port one time for cote-rotie.
But you aware of that Lethean flood,
Will scarce repeat the dose—forbid you should!
'Tis such a deadly foe to all that's bright,
'Twould soon encumber e'en your fancy's flight:
And if 'tis true what some wise preacher says,
That we our gen'rous ancestors disgrace,
The fault from this pernicious fountain flows,
Hence half our follies, half our crimes and woes;
And ere our maudlin genius mounts again,
'Twill cause a sea of claret and champaign
Of this retarding glue to rinse the nation's
   brain.
The mud-fed carp refines amid the springs,
And time and burgundy might do great things:
But health and pleasure we for trade despise,
For Portugal's grudg'd gold our genius dies.
O hapless race! O land to be bewail'd!
With murders, treasons, horrid deaths appal'd;
Where dark-red skies with livid thunders frown,
While Earth convulsive shakes her cities down;

Where Hell in Heaven's name holds her impious
   court,
And the grape bleeds out that black poison, port;
Sad poison to themselves, to us still worse,
Brew'd and rebrew'd, a double, treble, curse.
   Toss'd in the crowd of various rules, I find
Still some material business left behind:

  *   *   *   *   *
  *   *   *   *   *

The fig, the gooseberry, beyond all grapes,
Mellower to eat, as rich to drink perhaps.
But pleasures of this kind are best enjoy'd,
Beneath the tree, or by the fountain side,
Ere the quick soul, and dewy bloom exhale,
And vainly melt into the thankless gale.

  *   *   *   *   *
  *   *   *   *   *

Who from the full meal yield to natural rest,
A short repose; 'tis strange how soon you'll
   find
A second morn rise cheerful on your mind:
Besides it softly, kindly, sooths away
The saddest hour to some that damps the day.
But if you're coy to sleep, before you spread
Some easy-trotting poet's lines—you're dead
At once : even these may hasten your repose,
Now rapid verse, now halting nearer prose;
There smooth, here rough, what I suppose you'd
   chuse,
As men of taste hate sameness in the Muse:
Yes, I'd adjourn all drinking till 'tis late,
And then indulge, but at a moderate rate.
By Heaven not * * * with all his genial wit,
Should ever tempt me after twelve to sit—
You laugh—at noon you say : I mean at night.
   I long to read your name once more again,
But while at Cassel, all such longing's vain.
Yet Cassel else no sad retreat I find,
While good and amiable Gayot[3] is my friend,
Generous and plain, the friend of human-kind;
Who scorns the little-minded's partial view;
One you would love, one that would relish you.
With him sometimes I sup, and often dine,
And find his presence cordial more than wine.
There lively, genial, friendly, Goy and I
Touch glasses oft to one whose company
Would—but what's this?—Farewell—within two
   hours
We march for Hoxter—ever, ever yours.

   [3] Mons. de Gayot, fils, conseiller d'estat, et
intendant de l'armée Françoise en Allemagne.

THE

# POEMS

OF

*JOHN LANGHORNE, DD.*

# LIFE OF LANGHORNE,

## BY MR. CHALMERS.

JOHN LANGHORNE, the son of a clergyman beneficed in Lincolnshire, was born at Kirkby-Steven, in Westmoreland, in the month of March 1735. His father dying when he was only four years of age, the care of his education devolved on his mother, who initiated him in the first principles of knowledge with such tender anxiety as left a pleasing and indelible impression on his memory. He celebrated her virtues on her tomb, and more particularly by a beautiful Monody inserted among his poems.

When of sufficient age, he was placed at a school at Winton, and afterwards at Appleby, where he recommended himself to the good opinion of Mr. Yates, his master, not only by speedily dispatching the usual school tasks, but by performing voluntary exercises which he submitted to his revisal. By this employment of his leisure hours, he probably excelled his companions, and we are told that at the age of thirteen he was able to read and construe the Greek Testament.

He did not leave this school until his eighteenth year, when having no means of defraying the expenses of an university education, he engaged himself as private tutor in a family near Ripon. He had attained a thorough knowledge of the classical languages, and during his residence in this neighbourhood, began to write verses, the greater part of which his more mature judgment led him to destroy. One of these pieces, however, Studley Park, has been very properly snatched from oblivion by his biographer, and now stands at the head of this collection, not indeed as the best, but as the earliest specimen of his powers. It appears that he had some expectations from the possessor of this beautiful place, which were not gratified, and he therefore thought proper to omit it in the subsequent editions of his poems.

His next occupation was that of an assistant at the free-school of Wakefield, then superintended by Mr. Clarke, and while here he took deacon's orders, and became, it is said, "a popular preacher." In the year 1759, Mr. Clarke recommended him as preceptor to the sons of Robert Cracroft, esq. of Hackthorn, near Lincoln. Mr. Cracroft had nine sons, and Mr. Langhorne must have been fully employed in the family, yet he added to theirs the tuition of Mr. Edmund

Cartwright, a young gentleman of a poetical turn, who afterwards wrote an elegy, entitled Constantia, on the death of his preceptor's wife.

During his residence at Hackthorn, our author published a volume of his poems for the relief of a gentleman in distress, most of which are included in the present edition: and in the same year a poem entitled The Death of Adonis, from the Greek of Bion. Public opinion gave him no encouragement to reprint this last, but he derived from it the advantage of being noticed as a critic of considerable acumen in Greek poetry.

In 1760, he entered his name at Clarehall, Cambridge, in order to take the degree of bachelor of divinity, which he supposed, by the statutes of the university, any person in orders is impowered to do without residence, but in this it is probable he did not succeed, as his name is not to be found among the Cambridge graduates. His being included in Mr. Cole's list, is, however, a proof that he entered of Clarehall.; and while here, he wrote a poem on the King's Accession, and another on the Royal Nuptials which he afterwards inserted in Solyman and Almena. In the same year, he published The Tears of the Muses, a poem to the memory of Handel, with an Ode to the River Eden, 4to.

While employed in the education of the sons of Mr. Cracraft, he became enamoured of the amiable disposition and personal charms of Miss Anne Cracraft, one of that gentleman's daughters. He had given her some instructions in the Italian language, and was often delighted by her skill in music, for which he had a very correct ear. A mutual attachment was the consequence of these many opportunities and coincidences in polite accomplishments, which Mr. Langhorne was eager to terminate in marriage. But the lady, who knew that a match so disproportioned as to fortune, would be opposed by her family, gave him a denial as firm and as gentle as her good sense and secret attachment would permit.

For this, however, Mr. Langhorne was not prepared, and immediately left his situation in hopes of recovering a more tranquil tone of mind in distant scenes and different employment. In 1761, he officiated as curate to the rev. Abraham Blackburn of Dagenham, and obtained the friendship of the Gilmans, a very amiable family in that place. While endeavouring to forget his heart's disappointment, he found some relief in penning a Hymn to Hope [1], which he published this year in London, 4to.; and in the course of the next, he gave farther vent to his thoughts in The Visions of Fancy, four elegies 4to.; Letters on Religious Retirement, 8vo; and Solyman and Almena, a fiction, in the manner of the eastern tales, but not much to be praised for invention. The letters are of a sentimental, melancholy cast, with a considerable mixture of lighter and more entertaining matter.—In the same year he published the Viceroy, a poem in honour of lord Halifax, then lord lieutenant of Ireland. Here, as in the case of Studley Park, our author appears to have expected to find a patron, but lord Halifax did not condescend to notice what, it must be confessed, flatters him with too much artifice; and Langhorne, when he collected his poems, retained only a favourite fragment of this unlucky piece, omitting altogether the name of Halifax, or Viceroy. The whole, however, is given in the present edition as originally written.

---

[1] This piece was much admired by lord Lyttelton, whom our author had the honour to rank among his friends and correspondents. C.

His Letters on Religious Retirement were dedicated with rather more success to bishop Warburton, who returned a complimentary letter, in which he encouraged our author to make some attempt in the cause of religion. This is supposed to have produced, in 1763, the letters that passed between Theodosius and Constantia, a fiction founded on a well-known story in the Spectator. The style of these letters is in general elegant, but in some parts too florid. The letter on Prayer is very equivocal in its tendency. This year also gave birth to a poem, meant to be philosophical, entitled The Enlargement of the Mind, (part first), in which we find some noble sentiments expressed in glowing and elevated language. His next publication, about the same time, called Effusions of Friendship and Fancy, 2 vols. 12mo. was a work of considerable popularity : it is indeed a very pleasing miscellany of humour, fancy, and criticism; but the style is often flippant and irregular, and made him be classed among the imitators of Sterne, whom it was the fashion at that time to read and to admire.

In the year 1764, having obtained the curacy and lectureship of St. John's, Clerkenwell, he was enabled to reside in London, where only literary talents meet with ready encouragement, and where he was already ranked among the elegant and pleasing poets of the day, and had given ample proof of ease and versatility in the choice and management of his subjects. His first publication this year was the continuation of Theodosius and Constantia, of much the same character as the former work, but enlivened by more variety. As he appears to have aspired to promotion through the popularity of his talents in the pulpit, he now gave a specimen of what had pleased his congregation, in two volumes of Sermons. His biographer has taken some pains to defend these against the censure of the late Mr. Mainwaring, of St. John's, Cambridge, in his dissertation prefixed to his Sermons (1780). But it appears to me that they abound in the false pathos, and that the reasoning, where any occurs, is very superficial. They have, however, this advantage to those who dislike sermons of every kind, that they are perhaps the shortest ever published.

About this time, his son informs us, that he engaged with Mr. Griffiths as a writer in the Monthly Review, and that this engagement, with scarcely any intermission, continued to his death. I suspect there is some mistake in this account, although the secrecy which very properly prevails in the management of a review, will not allow me to rectify it. That Mr. Langhorne was a writer in the Monthly Review, has been repeated from so many quarters, that there seems no reason to doubt it, but a dispute relating to a work hereafter mentioned which took place between Mr. Langhorne and the editor of the Review, affords some ground to think that his connection with it had ceased about the year 1769.

But whatever may be in this, his employment as a critic, we are told, procured him many acquaintances among literary men, while the vein of ridicule which he indulged in treating several of the subjects that fell under his consideration, created him many enemies, who, in their turn, endeavoured to depreciate his performances. As no judgment can now be pronounced on the articles which he wrote, it is impossible to say whether this vein of ridicule was employed as the just chastisement of arrogance and immorality, or substituted for fair and legitimate criticism. Illiberality has not often been imputed to the journal in which he wrote ;

and as to his enemies, I know of none more formidable than Churchill, Kelly, and Kenrick, two of whom were libellers by profession. Smollet, whose jealousy of the Monthly Review led him often to disgrace his talents by invidious attacks on the supposed writers belonging to it, bestows almost uniform praise on Langhorne's various works.

In 1765, his productions were, The second Epistle on the Enlargement of the Mind ; an edition of the poems of the elegant and tender Collins, with a criticism and some memoirs ; and letters on that difficult subject, The Eloquence of the Pulpit. He had now occasion to exert his own talents before a more enlightened auditory than he had ever yet addressed, having been appointed by Dr. Hurd (the venerable bishop of Winchester) to the office of assistant preacher at Lincoln's-Inn Chapel.

In the following year, we do not find that any thing original came from his pen ; he prepared for the press, however, an enlarged edition of his Effusions of Friendship and Fancy, and a collection of his poems, in two vols. 12mo. The principal article of these, not before published, is a dramatic poem, or Tragedy, entitled: The Fatal Prophecy. This was his only attempt in this species of poetry, and was universally accounted unsuccessful. He had the good sense to acquiesce in the decision, and neither attempted the drama again, nor reprinted this specimen.

During Churchill's career, our author endeavoured to counteract the scurrility he had thrown out against Scotland in his Prophecy of Famine, by an elegant poem entitled Genius and Valour. This provoked Churchill to introduce his name once or twice with his usual epithets of contempt, which Langhorne disregarded, and disregarded his own interest at the same time, by dedicating this poem to lord Bute, a minister going out of place! It produced him, however, a very flattering letter in the year 1766, from Dr. Robertson, the celebrated historian, and principal of the university of Edinburgh, requesting him to accept a diploma for the degree of doctor in divinity. He was farther consoled by the approbation of every wise and loyal man who contemplated the miseries of disunion, and the glaring absurdity of perpetuating national prejudices.

In 1767, after a courtship of five years, Dr. Langhorne obtained the hand of Miss Cracraft, to whom he had ever been tenderly attached, and with whom he had kept up a correspondence [2] since his departure from Hackthorn. By what means her family were reconciled to the match, we are not told ; but some fortune accompanied it, as the living of Blagden in Somersetshire was purchased for him, and there he went immediately to reside. His happiness, however, with this lady was of short duration, as she died in childbirth of a son, May 4, 1768. She was interred in the chancel of Blagden church, with the following lines on her monument, written by her husband :

> With Sappho's taste, with Arria's tender heart,
> Lucretia's honour, and Cecilia's art,
> That such a woman died surprise can't give,
> 'Tis only strange that such a one should live.

[2] This correspondence, his son informs us, he published after her death, under the title of Letters to Eleanora, from a sacred compliance with her request. This publication I have not seen, but the accounts of it in the critical journals are very unfavourable. The Monthly Reviewer says, that the author "has preposterously ventured to impress his reader with sensations and emotions which he himself did not feel." This, perhaps, may strengthen my conjecture on the termination of his connexion with this Review. C.

He afterwards composed a more elegant and pathetic tribute to her virtues, which may be found among his poems. The allusion to the cause of her death is an original thought introduced with great skill and tenderness.

During Mrs. Langhorne's life, he produced one poem only, entitled Precepts of Conjugal Happiness, addressed to Mrs. Nelthorpe, a sister of his wife. To this lady he committed the care of his infant child, who has lived to acknowledge her friendship, and to discharge the duties of an affectionate son, by the late Memoirs of his father, prefixed to an elegant edition of his poems.—In the Precepts of Conjugal Happiness, there is more good sense than poetry. It appears to have been a temporary effusion on which he bestowed no extraordinary pains.

Not long after Mrs. Langhorne's death, our author went to reside at Folkestone in Kent where his brother, the rev. William Langhorne, then officiated as minister, a man of a very amiable character. He was born in the year 1721, and presented by the archbishop of Canterbury to the rectory of Hakinge, with the perpetual curacy of Folkestone, in 1754, and on this preferment he passed the remainder of his life. He published Job, a poem ; and a poetical paraphrase on a part of Isaiah ; neither of which raised him to the fame of a poet, although they are not without the merit of correctness and spirit. He died Feb. 17, 1772, and his brother wrote some elegant lines to his memory, which are inscribed on a tablet in the chancel of Folkestone church [3].

Between these brothers the closest affection subsisted; each was to other " more the friend than brother of his heart." During their residence together at Folkestone, they were employed in preparing a new translation of Plutarch's lives: and our poet, who became about this time intimate with Scott, the poet of Amwell (who likewise had just lost a beloved wife from a similar cause), paid him a visit at Amwell, where he wrote the Monody inscribed to Mr. Scott.

Amidst these engagements he found leisure to give to the world two productions strongly marked by the peculiarities of his style and turn of thinking: the one entitled Frederick and Pharamond, or the Consolations of Human Life, 8vo.; the other, Letters supposed to have passed between M. de St. Evremond and Waller. In this last, while he was allowed to have preserved their characters tolerably, he was at the same time accused by the critic in the Monthly Review, of taking frequent opportunities to compliment himself on the merit of the letters he had written for St. Evremond and Waller. This produced a complaint from Langhorne, which was answered by the reviewer, respectfully indeed, but not in the manner that might have been expected from an associate. It is from this circumstance that I have been led to conjecture that his connexion with the Review ceased when he left London in consequence of his obtaining the living of Blagden.—Frederick and Pharamond was begun with a view to alleviate the afflictions of a friend, and pursued perhaps to alleviate his own. It attempts that by argument which is rarely accomplished but by time.

The translation of Plutarch, by the brothers, appeared in 1770, and soon became a very popular book. In 1771, Dr. Langhorne gave another proof of the variety on which he exercised his fancy, in a favourite little volume, entitled the

[3] Gent. Mag. vol. 74. p. 1001. C.

Fables of Flora. In this, although he claimed too hastily the merit of combining for the first time imagery, description, and sentiment, yet he has certainly enlarged the province of fable, and given proof of a wide range of imagination. It cannot however be denied, that the moral is not always sufficiently pointed, that the style is too much ornamented, and the general cast of sentiment too obscure, for the persons in whose hands fables are usually placed. In answer to the objection made to the language of flowers, his son very justly remarks, that "impersonation may certainly be applied with as much reason to the vegetable as to the animal creation, if the characteristic attributes of each plant or flower are faithfully marked, and the unity of the fable is maintained."

Towards the latter end of the year 1771, Dr. Langhorne went to reside for a few months at Potton in Bedfordshire, where he wrote his Origin of the Veil, which, however, was not published for some time after. In 1772, he paid a visit to his native country, and married a second wife, the daughter of —— Thomson, esq. a magistrate near Brough, and soon after took her with him on a tour through part of France and Flanders, the scenery of which afforded new topics for his muse.

Late in the spring he returned to Blagden, where he was put into the commission of the peace; and having considered the usual practice of the duties of that office, he imparted his sentiments on the subject in a species of didactic and satirical poem, entitled The Country Justice, in three parts, published in 1774, 1775, and 1777. This humane endeavour to plead the cause of the poor and wretched against oppression and neglect, does great honour to his feelings, which, indeed, in all his works, are on the side of benevolence and virtue. It is said to have been written in consequence of the suggestion, and as to facts, probably with the assistance, of Dr. Burn, the well-known author of a Digest of the Laws relating to Justices of the Peace.—In 1773, Dr. Langhorne presented the public with a liberal translation of that part of Denina on the Ancient Republics of Italy, which contains the author's reflections on the admission of the Italian states to the franchises of Rome [4].

In 1776, he lost his second wife, who died like the former, in child-bed, five years after her marriage, and left a daughter whom he consigned by his will to the protection of his friend, Mrs. Gillman. What impression this second interruption to domestic happiness produced on his mind, we are not told. In this year, however, we find him again employing the press in a Translation of Milton's Italian Sonnets, and on two occasional sermons. In 1777, at the request of the Bouverie family (who highly respected Dr. Langhorne), Dr. Moss, bishop of Bath and Wells, presented him with a prebend in the cathedral of Wells.

His last production was the tale of Owen of Carron, which, with some beauties, has less of his usual energy and vigour: it is uncertain whether this was owing to the nature of the poem, in which he conceived it necessary to imitate the ballad simplicity, or to a languor of body and mind. The death of the right hon. Charles Yorke, from whom he had great expectations, is said to have made a

---

[4] The author's object in this publication is not very obvious. In our days it might be of more importance to discuss the question, by what means the Romans acquired their superiority and were enabled to extend their conquests ?    C.

lasting impression on him, but as Mr. Yorke died in 1770, this seems wholly improbable.

His biographer passes over his last days without notice of his situation or employments. We are merely told that he died on April 1, 1779, in the forty-fifth year of his age.

In 1804, his son published an edition of his poems, in two elegant volumes 12mo. with memoirs of the Author. To these I am indebted for the principal part of this sketch.

If we may judge from his writings, Dr. Langhorne was a man of an amiable disposition, a friend to religion and morals, and though a wit, he never descends to grossness or indelicacy. His memory has not been followed by any worse objection than that he was of a social turn, and during the latter part of his life more addicted to convivial indulgences than is consistent with health. This, however, is a serious objection, and not much lessened by the supposition that he was driven to this unhappy species of relief by having twice lost the chief source of domestic happiness.

Incidental notice having been already taken of many of his pieces, it will not be necessary to enlarge on the subject in this place. Ease, elegance, and tenderness, are the most striking features of his poetry: nor is he deficient in invention ; an attentive perusal will discover many original sentiments, and spirited flights, which the critics of his day pointed out with high praise. He is very seldom a copyist; his style and his sentiments, whatever their merit, are his own.

His prose works are various enough to convince us that he was either a laborious writer, or possessed of great fertility of imagination, and the latter will probably be the safest conjecture. But, although a scholar of high attainments, he has rarely brought learning to his aid. His mind was stored with remarks on men and manners, which he expressed in various and desultory modes, so as to give an air of novelty to every thing he wrote, but we find nothing very profound. He appeared so frequently before the public as to secure a considerable degree of fame ; what he announced was expected with eagerness, and what he published was read with pleasure ; but as his abilities were confined to the lighter provinces of literature, there are few of his productions which will be honoured by permanent popularity.

# POEMS

OF

# DR. JOHN LANGHORNE.

TO THE REV. MR. J. LANGHORNE, ON READING HIS VISIONS OF FANCY, &c.

### BY MISS WHATELEY.

Fraught with each wish the friendly breast can
  form,
  A simple Muse, O! Langhorne, would intrude;
Her lays are languid, but her heart is warm,
  Though not with Fancy's potent powers endu'd.

Fancy, though erst she shed a glimmering ray,
  And op'd to fairy scenes my infant eye,
From Pain and Care, has wing'd her cheerful
  way,
  And with Hygeia sought a milder sky.

No more my trembling hand attempts the lyre,
  Which Shenstone oft (sweet bard) has deign'd
  to praise;
Even tuneful Langhorne's friendship fails t' inspire
  The glow that warm'd my breast in happier
  days.

Yet not this cold heart can remain unmov'd,
  When thy sweet numbers strike my raptur'd
  ear,
The silver sounds, by ev'ry Muse approv'd,
  Suspend a while the melancholy tear.

What time, on Arrowe's osier'd banks reclin'd,
  I to the pale Moon pour'd thy plaintive lay;
Smooth roll'd the waves, more gently sigh'd the
  wind,
  And Echo stole the tender notes away.

Sweet Elves and Fays, that o'er the shadowy
  plains
  Their mystic rites and mazy dance pursue,
Tun'd their light minstrelsy to softer strains,
  And from thy lays their melting music drew.

Sweet son of Fancy! may the white-rob'd Hours
  Shed their kind influence on thy gentle breast;
May Hebe strew thy vernal path with flow'rs,
  Blest in thy love, and in thy friendship blest.

Smooth as thy numbers may thy years advance,
  Pale Care and Pain their speeding darts sus-
  pend;
May Health, and Fancy, lead the cheerful dance,
  And Hope for ever her fair torch extend.

For thee may Fame her fairest chaplets twine;
  Each fragrant bloom that paints Aonia's
  brow,
Each flow'r, that blows by Alcidale, be thine.;
  With the chaste laurel's never-fading bough.

On thee may faithful friendship's cordial smile,
  Attendant wait to sooth each rising care;
The nymph thou lov'st be thine devoid of guile,
  Mild, virtuous, kind, compassionate, and fair.

May thy sweet lyre still charm the generous
  mind,
  Thy liberal Muse the patriot spirit raise;
While, in thy page to latest time consign'd,
  Virtue receives the meed of polish'd praise.

---

## SONNET TO MR. LANGHORNE.

### BY JOHN SCOTT, ESQ.

Langhorne, unknown to me (sequester'd swain!)
  Save by the Muse's soul-enchanting lay,
To kindred spirits never sung in vain,
  Accept the tribute of this light essay;

Due for thy sweet songs that amus'd my day!
  Where Fancy held her visionary reign, [strain
  Or Scotland's honours claim'd the pastoral
Or Music came o'er Handel tears to pay:

For all thy Irwan's flow'ry banks display
  Thy Persian lover and his Indian fair;
All Theodosius' mournful lines convey,
  Where Pride and Av'rice part a matchless
  pair;

Receive just praise and wreaths that ne'er decay,
  By Fame and Virtue twin'd for thee to wear.

Amwell, near Ware,
  16 March, 1766.

---

## TO THE HON. CHARLES YORKE.

A Muse that lov'd in Nature's walks to stray,
And gather'd many a wild flower in her way,

To Nature's friend her genuine gifts would bring,
The light amusements of life's vacant spring;
Nor shalt thou, Yorke, her humble offering
    blame,
If pure her incense, and unmixt her flame.
She pours no flattery into Folly's ear,
No shameless hireling of a shameless peer,
The friends of Pope indulge her native lays,
And Gloucester joins with Lyttelton to praise.
Each judge of art her strain, though artless,
    loves;      [proves.
And Shenstone smil'd, and polish'd Hurd ap-
O may such spirits long protect my page,
Surviving lights of wit's departed age!
Long may I in their kind opinion live!
All meaner praise, all envy, I forgive.—
   Yet fairly be my future laurels won!
Nor let me bear a bribe to Hardwicke's son!
Should his free suffrage own the favour'd strain,
Though vain the toil, the glory were not vain.

## PROEMIUM.

### WRITTEN IN 1766.

In Eden's[1] vale, where early fancy wrought
Her wild embroidery on the ground of thought,
Where Pembroke's[2] grottos, strew'd with Sidney's
    bays,
Recall'd the dreams of visionary days,   [youth,
Thus the fond Muse, that sooth'd my vacant
Prophetic sung, and what she sung was truth.
  " Boy, break thy lyre, and cast thy reed
    away;
Vain are the honours of the fruitless bay.
Though with each charm thy polish'd lay should
    please,
Glow into strength, yet soften into ease;
Should Attic fancy brighten ev'ry line,
And all Aonia's harmony be thine;
Say would thy cares a grateful age repay,
Fame wreathe thy brows, or Fortune gild thy
    way?
Ev'n her own fools, if Fortune smile, shall blame;
And Envy lurks beneath the flowers of Fame.
  " Yet, if resolv'd, secure of future praise,
To tune sweet songs, and live melodious days,
Let not the hand, that decks my holy shrine,
Round Folly's head the blasted laurel twine.
Just to thyself, dishonest grandeur scorn;
Nor gild the bust of meanness nobly born.
Let truth, let freedom still thy lays approve!
Respect my precepts, and retain my love!"

## STUDLEY PARK.

### TO THE REV. MR. FARRAR.

Farrar! to thee these early lays I owe:
Thy friendship warms the heart from whence
    they flow.

[1] The river Eden, in Westmorland.
[2] The countess of Pembroke, to whom sir
Philip Sidney dedicated his Arcadia, resided at
Appleby, a small but beautiful town in Westmorland, situated upon the Eden.

Thee, thee I find, in all I find to please;
In this thy elegance, in that thy ease.
Come then with Fancy to thy fav'rite scene,
Where Studley triumphs in her wreaths of
    green,
And pleas'd for once, while Eden smiles again,
Forget that life's inheritance is pain.
  Say, shall we muse along yon arching shades,
Whose awful gloom no brightening ray pervades;
Or down these vales where vernal flowers display
Their golden bosoms to the smiles of day;
Where the fond eye in sweet distraction strays.
Most pleas'd, when most it knows not where to
    gaze?
  Here groves arrang'd in various order rise,
And blend their quiv'ring summits in the skies.
The regal oak high o'er the circling shade,
Exalts the hoary honours of his head.
The spreading ash a diff'ring green displays,
And the smooth asp in soothing whispers plays.
The fir that blooms in Spring's eternal prime,
The spiry poplar, and the stately lime.
  Here moss-clad walks, there lawns of lively
    green,
United, form one nicely-varying scene:
The varying scene still charms th' attentive sight,
Or brown with shades, or op'ning into light.
  Here the gay tenants of the tuneful grove,
Harmonious breathe the raptures of their love:
Each warbler sweet that hails the genial Spring,
Tunes the glad song, and plies th' expanded
    wing:
The love-suggested notes in varied strains,
Fly round the vocal hills and list'ning plains:
The vocal hills and list'ning plains prolong
In varied strains the love-suggested song.
To thee, all-bounteous Nature! thee they pay
The welcome tribute of their grateful lay!
To thee, whose kindly-studious hand prepares
The fresh'ning fields and softly-breathing airs;
Whose parent-bounty annual still provides
Of foodful insects such unbounded tides.
Beneath some friendly leaf supremely blest,
Each pours at large the raptures of his breast:
Nor changeful seasons mourn, nor storms unkind,
With those contented, and to these resign'd.
  Here sprightly range the grove, or skim the
    plain,
The sportive deer, a nicely-checker'd train.
Oft near their haunt, on him who curious strays,
All throng'd abreast in fix'd attention gaze;
Th' intruding spy suspiciously survey,
Then butting limp along, and lightly frisk away.
  Not so, when raves the pack's approaching
    roar,
Then loves endear, then Nature smiles no more:
In wild amaze, all tremblingly-dismay'd,
Burst through the groves, and bound along the
    glade;
'Till now some destin'd stag, prepar'd to fly,
Fires all the malice of the murd'ring cry:
Forc'd from his helpless mates the fated prey
Bears on the wings of quiv'ring fear away:
In flight (ah! could his matchless flight avail!)
Scorns the fierce steed, and leaves the flying gale.
Now trembling stops—and listens from afar,
In long, long deep'ning howls, the madd'ning war;
While loud-exulting triumphs thunder round,
Tremble the mountains, and the rocks rebound.

In vain, yet vig'rous, he renews his race,
In vain dark mazes oft perplex the chase :
With speed inspir'd by grief, he springs again
Through vaulted woods, and devious wilds in
    vain.
Th' unrav'lling pack, still onward pouring, trace
The various mazes of his circling race.
Breathless at last with long-repeated toil,
Sick'ning he stands—he yields—he falls the spoil.
    From all the various blooms of painted bow'rs,
Fair banky wilds, and vallies fring'd with flow'rs,
Where Nature in profusion smiles delight,
With pleasure sated turns the roving sight.
    Come then, bright vision! child of heav'nly
      day!
From this fair summit ampler scenes survey:
One spacious field in circling order eye,
And active round the far horizon fly,
Where dales descend, or ridgy mountains rise,
And lose their aspect in the falling skies.
    What pleasing scenes the landscape wide dis-
      plays!
Th' enchanting prospect bids for ever gaze.
Hail charming fields, of happy swains the care!
Hail happy swains, possest of fields so fair!
In peace your plenteous labours long enjoy;
No murd'ring wars shall waste, nor foes destroy;
While western gales Earth's teeming womb un-
    bind,
The seasons change, and bounteous suns are kind.
To social towns, see! wealthy Commerce brings
Rejoicing affluence on his silver wings.
On verdant hills, see! flocks innum'rous feed,
Or thoughtful listen to the lively reed.
See! golden harvests sweep the bending plains;
" And peace and plenty own a Brunswick reigns."
    The wand'ring eye from Nature's wild domain
Attracted, turns to fairer scenes again.
Scenes, which to thee, refining Art! belong,
Invite the poet, and inspire the song.
    Sweet, philosophic Muse! that lov'st to stray
In woody-curtain'd walks and dim-seen day,
Lead me, where lonely Contemplation roves,
Through silent shades and solitary groves
Stop, daring foot! the sacred maid is here!
These awful glooms confess the goddess near.
Low in these woods her fav'rite scene is laid,
The fence umbrageous, and the dark'ning shade,
Whose bow'ry branches bar the vagrant eye,
Assailing storms and parching suns defy.
A gentle current calmly steals serene,
In silv'ry mazes, o'er the weeping green,
Till op'ning bright, its bursting waters spread,
And fall fast-flashing down a wide cascade.
A spacious lake below expanded lies,
And lends a mirror to the quiv'ring skies.
Here pendent domes, there dancing forests seem
To float and tremble in the waving gleam.
    While gaily musing o'er it's verdant side,
Pleas'd I behold the glassy riv'let glide:
Bright in the verdure of the blooming year,
Where circling groves their full-blown honours
    wear;
Ambrosial daughter of the spicy Spring, [wing;
While fragrant woodbine scents each Zephyr's
While nectar-footed Morn, approaching, dyes,
In radiant blush, the rosy-checker'd skies;
The first fair Eden, o'er th' enchanted plain
Reviving, smiles, or seems to smile again.

Hail, blissful scene! divine Elysium hail!
Ye flow'ry blooms eternal sweets exhale :
The blest asylum's here, the sacred shore,
Where toils tumultuous tear the breast no more.
    From wild ambition free, from dire despair,
Appalling terrour, and perplexing care,
Happy the man who in these shades can find
That angel-bliss, serenity of mind;
Walk the fair green, or in the grotto lie,
With hope-strung breast, and heav'n-erected eye!
While cheated worlds, by pleasure's lure be-
    tray'd,
Through rocks and sands pursue the siren maid;
And, long-bewilder'd, urge the weary chase,
Though still the phantom slips their vain em-
    brace :
'Tis his with pitying eye to see—to know
Whence purest joy's perennial fountains flow.
With this exalting charm divinely blest,
The dear reflection of a blameless breast:
Where sweet-ey'd Love still smiles serenely gay,
And heav'nly Virtue beams a brighter ray.
Soft, smoothly-pacing slide his peaceful days,
His own his censure, and his own his praise:
Alike to him, both subjects of the grave,
The scepter'd monarch, and the menial slave.
Thrice happy he who life's poor pains has laid
In the lone tomb of some sequester'd shade!
More amply blest, if gloriously retir'd, [fir'd;
With learning charm'd, and with the Muses
Who nobly dares with philosophic eye,
Through full creation's bounded orbs to fly;
Pleas'd, in their well-form'd systems still to find
The matchless wisdom of th' immortal mind.
Still charm'd, in Nature's various plan, to trace
His boundless love and all-supporting grace.
    Ye pompous great! whose dream of glory
      springs
From sounding titles or the smiles of kings :
Ye, laurel'd in the bleeding wreathes of war!
And ye, whose hearts are center'd in a star!
Say, all ye sons of power and splendour, say,
E'er could ye boast one unembitter'd day ?
Cease the vain hope in dazzling pomp to find
Divine content, to humbler lots assign'd;
The modest fair frequents the lowly cell,
Where smiling Peace and conscious Virtue dwell.
    While through the maze of winding bow'rs I
      stray,
The shade's dim gloom, or vista's op'ning day;
Soft-sighing groves, where silky breezes fill,
Kiss the smooth plain, and glassy-dimpling rill;
In silent vales, by sadly-mourning streams,
Where swift-ey'd Fancy wings her waving dreams;
What sacred awe the lonely scenes inspire!
What joys transport me, and what raptures fire!
Visions divine, enchanted I behold,
And all the Muses all their charms unfold.
    Ye, woods of Pindus, and Ætolian plains,
No more shall listen to immortal strains :
Flow unconcern'd, no Muse celestial sings,
Ye Thracian fountains, and Aonian springs!
No more your shades shall leave their nat've
    shore,
Nor songs arrest your raptur'd currents more.
    And thou, Parnassus, wrapt in deep alcoves,
Mourn, in sad silence, thy forsaken groves :
No more thy warblers rival notes admire,
Nor choral zephyrs fill the breathing lyre.

Each drooping laurel bends its languid head ;
The strains are vanish'd, and the Muses fled.

To nobler hills, where fairer forests grow,
To vales, where streams in sweeter accents flow ;
To blooming Studley's more delightful shades
Welcome, ye sacred, ye celestial maids !
Wake the soft lute, here strike the sounding
    string,
Make the groves echo, and the vallies ring ;
Harmonious lead, through rosy-smiling bow'rs,
The soft-ey'd Graces and the dancing Hours.

In awful scenes retir'd, where gloomy Night
Still broods, unbanish'd by returning light ;
Where Silence, fix'd in meditation deep,
Folds in her arms her fav'rite offspring, Sleep ;
Musing along the lonely shades I roam
'Till beauteous rises a devoted dome :
Thy fane, seraphic Piety ! low plac'd
In sable glooms, by deep'ning woods embrac'd.
Nor radiant here the prince of day displays
His morning blushes, nor meridian blaze :
Rolls o'er the world the splendid orb unseen,
'Till his last glories gild the streaming green ;
Then sportive gleams through parting columns
    play,
Here waves a shadow, and there smiles a ray.
Just emblem of the man who, free from strife,
Th' uneasy pains that vex the noon of life,
Not dazzled with the diamond-beaming zone,
Flash of a lace, or brilliance of a stone,
Courts the last smiles of life's declining ray,
Where Hope exulting reaps eternal day.
The sacred solitude, the lone recess,
An awful pleasure on my soul impress.
Raptures divine through all my bosom glow,
The bliss alone immortal beings know.
Ah, knew that sovereign bliss no base alloy,
Wer't thou, my Farrer ! witness to my joy ;
What nobler pleasure could we boast below !
What joy sublimer Heav'n itself bestow !
Haste, my gay friend ! my dear associate, haste!
Life of my soul, and partner of my breast !
Quick to these shades, these magic shades retire :
Here light thy graces, and thy virtue fire :
Here sheds sweet Piety her beams divine,
And all the goddess fills her heav'nly shrine.
Celestial maids before her altar move :
White handed Innocence, and weeping Love.

Her tow'ring domes let Richmond boast alone ;
The sculptur'd statue and the breathing stone :
Alone distinguish'd on the plains of Stowe,
From Jones's hand the featur'd marble glow :
Though there unnumber'd columns front the
    skies,
To fancied gods forbidden temples rise ;
Unenvied, Studley, be this pomp of art,
'Tis thine the pow'r to please a virtuous heart.

From this lov'd scene with anxious st ps I
    trace
Each devious winding of the banky maze;
To the tall summit of the steep repair,
And view the gay surrounding prospect there.
What joys expand my breast! what rapture
    warms !
While all the landscape opens all its charms :
While pleas'd I see, the parting shades between,
The lake fair-gleaming and the smoother green ;
Through lowly grots where wand'ring shadows
    stray,
Groves gently wave, and glist'ning waters play.

On thee, fair Hackfall ! Fancy bends her eye,
Longs o'er the cliffs and deep'ning lawns to fly.
Enchanted sees each silv'ry-floating wave
Beat thy green banks, thy lovely vallies lave :
And now delighted, now she joys to hear
Thy deep, slow falls, long-lab'ring through her
    ear.[1]

All-beauteous Nature ! object of my song,
To thee my first, my latest strains belong :
To thee my lays I tune, while envious Art
In rival charms here courts the raptur'd heart.
Like thee to please, she decks the painted bow'r,
Spreads the smooth lawn, and rears the velvet
    flow'r :
With winding arbours crowns the sylvan dale,
And bends the forest o'er the lowly vale :
Bids the loud cataract deep-thund'ring roar,
Or winds the rivlet round a mazy shore.
Ambitious still, like thee, when she beguiles,
Wins with thy grace, and in thy beauty smiles.
In this gay dome [2] where sportive Fancy plays,
And imag'd life the pictur'd roof arrays ;
Proud in thy charms the mimic shines confest,
Beams the soft eye, and heaves the panting
    breast.
From thee, prime source ! kind-handed god-
    dess ! flow
The purest blessings that we boast below :
To thee its beauty owes this charming scene,
These groves their fragrance, and those plains
    their green :
For thee the Muses wreaths eternal twine,
Immortal maid ! for every Muse is thine.

Oh, wou'd'st thou lead me through the bound-
    less sky !
Regions untravell'd by a mortal eye ;
Or kindly aid, while studious I explore
Those arduous paths thy Newton trod before !
There wand'ring should my ravish't eye survey
New worlds of being, and new scenes of day.
But if for my weak wing and trembling sight,
Too vast the journey, and too full the light ;
Inglorious here I'll tune the lowly reed,
How rolls the fountain, and how springs the mead.
Or, bear me to the banks, ye sacred Nine !
Of beauteous Isis, or the silver Tine ;
To Tine's delightful banks, where, ever gay,
The generous F—— lives the peaceful day :
F—— still free from passion's fretful train,
Ne'er felt the thorn of anguish nor of pain ;
His heart-felt joys still Nature's charms improve,
Her voice is music, and her visage love :
Pleas'd with the change each various season
    brings,
Imbrowning autumns, and impurpled springs:
For him kind Nature all her treasures yields,
She decks the forest, and she paints the fields.
O say ! where bloom those time-surviving
    groves,
Where ancient bards first sung their sacred loves:
Those sadly-solemn bow'rs, ye Muses ! say,
Where once the melancholy Cowley lay ?
When long perplext with life's deluding snares,
Her flatt'ring pleasures, and her fruitless cares ;

---

[1] Who would not perceive the imitative harmony of this line, and realize to his imagination
the falling of the water ?—Editor.

[2] Upon an eminence, east of the gardens,
stands a house of Chinese structure.

Obscure he fled to sylvan shades alone,
And left mankind to be for ever known.
  Such were the scenes where Spenser once re-
    tir'd,
When great Eliza's fame the Muse inspir'd ;
When Gloriana led her poet's dreams,
O'er flow'ry meadows, and by murm'ring streams.
  Immortal bards! whose death-contemning
    lays
Shall shine distinguish'd with eternal praise.
Knew my poor Muse, like these to soar sublime,
And spurn the ruins of insulting Time ;
Where'er I stray, where blooming Flora leads,
O'er sunny mountains, and through purple
    meads ;
Or careless in the sylvan covert laid,
Where falling rills amuse the mournful shade ;
Ye, rural fields, should still resound my lay,
And thou, fair Studley ! smile for ever gay.

---

## GENIUS AND VALOUR:
### A PASTORAL POEM.

WRITTEN IN HONOUR OF A SISTER KINGDOM.
MDCCLXIII.

AMYNTOR, CHORUS OF SHEPHERDS.

Where Tweed's fair plains in liberal beauty
And Flora laughs beneath a lucid sky ;      [lie,
Long-winding vales where crystal waters lave,
Where blythe birds warble, and where green
    woods wave,                     [bloom,
A bright-hair'd shepherd, in young beauty's
Tun'd his sweet pipe behind the yellow broom.
  Free to the gale his waving ringlets lay,
And his blue eyes diffus'd an azure day.
Light o'er his limbs a careless robe he flung ;
Health rais'd his heart, and strength his firm
    nerves strung ;
  His native plains poetic charms inspir'd,
Wild scenes, where ancient Fancy oft retir'd !
Oft led her Faeries to the Shepherd's lay,
By Yarrow's banks, or groves of Endermay.
  Nor only his those images that rise
Fair to the glance of Fancy's plastic eyes ;
His country's love his patriot soul possess'd,
His country's honour fir'd his filial breast.
Her lofty genius, piercing, bright, and bold,
Her valour witness'd by the world of old,
Witness'd once more by recent heaps of slain
On Canada's wild hills, and Minden's plain,
To sound sublimer wak'd his pastoral reed—
Peace, Mountain-echoes ! while the strains pro-
    ceed.

AMYNTOR.

  No more of Tiviot, nor the flowery braes,
Where the blythe shepherd tunes his lightsome
    lays ;
No more of Leader's faery-haunted-shore,
Of Athol's lawns, and Gledswood banks no more;
Unheeded smile my country's native charms,
Lost in the glory of her arts and arms.
These, shepherds, these demand sublimer strains
Than Clyde's clear fountains, or than Athol's
    plains.

CHORUS OF SHEPHERDS.

  Shepherd, to thee sublimer lays belong,
The force divine of soul-commanding song.
These humble reeds have little learnt to play,
Save the light airs that cheer the pastoral day.
Of the clear fountain, and the fruitful plain
We sing, as fancy guides the simple strain.
If then thy country's sacred fame demand
The high-ton'd music of a happier hand—
Shepherd, to thee sublimer lays belong,
The force divine of soul-commanding song.

AMYNTOR.

  In spite of faction's blind, unmanner'd rage,
Of various fortune and destructive age,
Fair Scotland's honours yet unchang'd are seen.
Her palms still blooming, and her laurels green.
  Freed from the confines of her Gothic grave,
When her first light reviving Science gave,
Alike o'er Britain shone the liberal ray,
From Enswith's [1] mountains to the banks of Tay.
For James [2] the Muses tun'd their sportive
    lays,                              [bays.
And bound the monarch's brow with Chaucer's
Arch Humour smil'd to hear his mimic strain,
And plausive Laughter thrill'd thro' every vein.
When taste and genius form the royal mind,
The favour'd arts a happier era find.
By James belov'd the Muses tun'd their lyres
To nobler strains, and breath'd diviner fires.
But the dark mantle of involving time
Has veil'd their beauties, and obscur'd their
    rhyme.
  Yet still some pleasing monuments remain,
Some marks of genius in each later reign.
In nervous strains Dunbar's bold music flows,
And Time yet spares the Thistle and the Rose [3].
  O, while his course the hoary warrior steers
Thro' the long range of life-dissolving years,
Thro' all the evils of each changeful age,
Hate, envy, faction, jealousy, and rage,
Ne'er may his scythe these sacred plants divide,
These plants by Heaven in native union tied !
Still may the flower its social sweets disclose,
The hardy Thistle still defend the Rose !
  Hail, happy days ! appeas'd by Margaret's
    charms,
When rival Valour sheath'd his fatal arms ; [1]
When kindred realms unnatural war supprest,
Nor aim'd their arrows at a sister's breast.
Kind to the Muse is quiet's genial day ;
Her olive loves the foliage of the bay.
  With bold Dunbar arose a numerous choir
Of rival bards that strung the Dorian lyre.
In gentle Henryson's [4] unlabour'd strain
Sweet Arethusa's shepherd breath'd again.

[1] A chain of mountains near Folkstone in
Kent.
[2] James the First, king of Scotland, author of
the famous old song, entitled Christ's Kirk on the
Green.
[3] A poem so called, written in honour of Margaret, daughter of Henry VII. on her marriage
to James IV. king of Scots. By Mr. William
Dunbar.
[4] Mr. Robertson Henryson, an ingenious pastoral poet.

Nor shall your tuneful visions be forgot,
Sage Bellentyne [5], and fancy-painting Scott[6].
But, O my country ! how shall memory trace
Thy bleeding anguish, and thy dire disgrace ?
Weep o'er the ruins of thy blasted bays,
Thy glories lost in either Charles's days ?
When thro' thy fields destructive rapine spread,
Nor sparing infant's tears, nor hoary head.
In those dread days the unprotected swain
Mourn'd on the mountains o'er his wasted plain.
Nor longer vocal with the shepherd's lay
Were Yarrow's banks, or groves of Endermay.

### CHORUS OF SHEPHERDS.

Amyntor, cease ! the painful scene forbear,
Nor the fond breast of filial duty tear.
Yet in our eyes our father's sorrows flow,
Yet in our bosoms lives their lasting woe.
At eve returning from their scanty fold,
When the long sufferings of their sires they told,
Oft we have sigh'd the piteous tale to hear,
And infant wonder dropt the mimic tear.

### AMYNTOR.

Shepherds, no longer need your sorrows flow,
Nor pious duty cherish endless woe.
Yet should Remembrance, led by filial love,
Through the dark vale of old afflictions rove,
The mournful shades of sorrows past explore,
And think of miseries that are no more ;
Let those sad scenes that ask the duteous tear,
The kind return of happier days endear.
Hail, Anna, hail ! O may each Muse divine
With wreaths eternal grace thy holy shrine !
Grav'd on thy tomb this sacred verse remain,
This verse more sweet than conquest's sounding
    strain:
" She bade the rage of hostile nations cease,
The glorious arbitress of Europe's peace.''
She, thro' whose bosom roll'd the vital tide
Of Britain's monarchs in one stream allied,
Clos'd the long jealousies of different sway,
And saw united sister-realms obey.
Auspicious days ! when Tyranny no more
Rais'd his red arm, nor drench'd his darts in
    gore;
When, long an exile from his native plain,
Safe to his fold return'd the weary swain.
Return'd, and, many a painful summer past,
Beheld the green bench by his door at last.
Auspicious days ! when Scots, no more opprest,
On their free mountains bar'd the fearless breast;
With pleasure saw their flocks unbounded feed,
And tun'd to strains of ancient joy the reed.
Then, shepherds, did your wondering sires
    behold
A form divine, whose vesture flam'd with gold ;
His radiant eyes a starry lustre shed,
And solar glories beam'd around his head.

[5] Mr. John Bellentyne, archdean of Murray,
author of a beautiful allegorical poem, entitled,
Virtue and Vice.
  [6] Mr. Archibald Scott, in the year 1524, translated the Vision, a poem, said to have been written in the year 1360. He was the author of the
Eagle and the Redbreast also, and several other
pieces written with uncommon elegance for their
day.

Like that strange power by fabling poets feign'd,
From east to west his mighty arms he strain'd.
A rooted olive in one hand he bore,
In one a globe, inscrib'd with sea and shore.
From Thames's banks, to Tweed,to Tay he came,
Wealth in his rear, and Commerce was his name.
  Glad Industry the glorious stranger hails,
Rears the tall masts, and spreads the swelling
    sails ;
Regions remote with active hope explores,
Wild Zembla's hills, and Afric's burning shores.
But chief, Columbus, of thy various coast,
Child of the Union, Commerce bears his boast.
To seek thy new-found worlds, the vent'rous
His lass forsaking, left the lowland plain; [swain,
Aside his crook, his idle pipe he threw,
And bade to Music, and to Love adieu.
  Hence, Glasgow fair, thy wealth-diffusing
    hand,
Thy groves of vessels, and thy crowded strand.
Hence, round his folds the moorland shepherd
    spies
New social towns, and happy hamlets rise.
But me not splendour, nor the hopes of gain
Should ever tempt to quit the peaceful plain.
Shall I, possest of all that life requires,
With tutor'd hopes, and limited desires,   [ease,
Change these sweet fields, these native scenes of
For climes uncertain, and uncertain seas ?
  Nor yet, fair Commerce, do I thee disdain,
Though Guilt and Death and Riot swell thy train.
Cheer'd by the influence of thy gladd'ning ray,
The liberal arts sublimer works essay.
Genius for thee relumes his sacred fires,
And Science nearer to her Heaven aspires.
  The sanguine eye of Tyranny long clos'd,
By Commerce foster'd, and in peace repos'd,
No more her miseries when my country mourn'd,
With brighter flames her glowing genius burn'd.
Soon wandering fearless many a Muse was seen
O'er the dun mountain, and the wild wood green.
Soon, to the warblings of the pastoral reed,
Started sweet Echo from the shores of Tweed.
  O favour'd stream ! where thy fair current
    flows,
The child of Nature, gentle Thomson, rose.
Young as he wander'd on thy flowery side,
With simple joy to see thy bright waves glide,
Thither, in all thy native charms array'd,
From climes remote the sister Seasons stray'd.
  Long each in beauty boasted to excel,
(For jealousies in sister-bosoms dwell)
But now, delighted with the liberal boy,
Like Heaven's fair rivals in the groves of Troy,
Yield to an humble swain their high debate,
And from his voice the palm of beauty wait.
  Her naked charms, like Venus, to disclose,
Spring from her bosom threw the shadowing rose,
Bar'd the pure snow that feeds the lover's fire,
The breast that thrills with exquisite desire ;
Assum'd the tender smile, the melting eye,
The breath favonian, and the yielding sigh.
One beauteous hand a wilding's blossom grac'd,
And one fell careless o'er her zoneless waist.
  Majestic Summer, in gay pride adorn'd,
Her rival sister's simple beauty scorn'd.
With purple wreathes her lofty brows were
    bound,
With glowing flowers her rising bosom crown'd.

In her gay zone, by artful Fancy fram'd,
The bright rose blush'd, the full carnation flam'd.
Her cheeks the glow of splendid clouds display,
And her eyes flash insufferable day.
With milder air the gentle Autumn came,
But seem'd to languish at her sister's flame.
Yet, conscious of her boundless wealth, she bore
On high the emblems of her golden store.
Yet could she boast the plenty-pouring hand,
The liberal smile, benevolent and bland.
Nor might she fear in beauty to excel,
From whose fair head such golden tresses fell;
Nor might she envy Summer's flowery zone,
In whose sweet eye the star of evening shone.
    Next, the pale power that blots the golden
        sky,
Wreath'd her grim brows, and roll'd her stormy
        eye;
"Behold," she cried, with voice that shook the
        ground,
(The bard, the sisters, trembled at the sound)
"Ye weak admirers of a grape, or rose,
Behold my wild magnificence of snows!
See my keen frost her glassy bosom bare!
Mock the faint Sun, and bind the fluid air!
Nature to you may lend a painted hour,
With you may sport, when I suspend my power.
But you and Nature, who that power obey,
Shall own my beauty, or shall dread my sway."
    She spoke: the bard, whose gentle heart ne'er
        gave
One pain or trouble that he knew to save,
No favour'd nymph extols with partial lays,
But gives to each her picture for her praise.
Mute lies his lyre in death's uncheerful gloom,
And Truth and Genius weep at Thomson's tomb.
Yet still the Muse's living sounds pervade
Her ancient scenes of Caledonian shade.
Still Nature listens to the tuneful lay,
On Kilda's mountains and in Endermay.
    Th' ethereal brilliance of poetic fire,
The mighty hand that smites the sounding lyre,
Strains that on Fancy's strongest pinion rise,
Conceptions vast, and thoughts that grasp the
        skies,

To the rapt youth that mus'd on Shakespear's
To Ogilvie the Muse of Pindar gave.    [grave[7],
Time [8], as he sung, a moment ceas'd to fly,
And lazy Sleep [9] unfolded half his eye.
    O wake, sweet bard, the Theban lyre again;
With ancient valour swell the sounding strain;
Hail the high trophies by thy country won,
The wreaths that flourish for each valiant son.
    While Hardyknute frowns red with Norway's
        gore,
Paint her pale matrons weeping on the shore.
Hark! the green clarion pouring floods of breath
Voluminously loud; high scorn of death
Each gallant spirit elates; see Rothsay's thane
With arm of mountain oak his firm bow strain!
Hark! the string twangs—the whizzing arrow
        flies:
The fierce horse falls—indignant falls—and dies.
O'er the dear urn, where glorious Wallace [10]
        sleeps,
True valour bleeds, and patriot virtue weeps.
Son of the lyre, what high ennobling strain,
What meed from these shall generous Wallace
Who greatly scorning an usurper's pride, [gain?
Bar'd his brave breast for liberty, and died.
    Boast, Scotland, boast thy sons of mighty name,
Thine ancient chiefs of high heroic fame,
Souls that to death their country's foes oppos'd,
And life in freedom, glorious freedom, clos'd.
    Where, yet bewail'd, Argyle's warm ashes lie,
Let Music breathe her most persuasive sigh.
To him, what Heaven to man could give, it gave,
Wise, generous, honest, eloquent and brave,
Genius and Valour for Argyle shall mourn,
And his own laurels flourish round his urn.
O, may they bloom beneath a fav'ring sky,
And in their shade Reproach and Envy die!

    [7] See Mr. Ogilvie's Ode to the Genius of
Shakespear.
    [3] Ode to Time.  Ibid.
    [9] Ode to Sleep.  Ibid.
    [10] William Wallace, who, after bravely defend-
ing his country against the arms of Edward I.
was executed as a rebel, though he had taken no
oath of allegiance.

THE

# VISIONS OF FANCY.

## IN FOUR ELEGIES.

La raison sçait que c'est un songe,
Mais elle en saisit les douceurs :
Elle a besoin de ces fantômes,
Presque tous les plaisirs des hommes
Ne sont que de douces erreurs.          GRESSET.

WRITTEN IN 1762.

### ELEGY I.

CHILDREN of Fancy, whither are ye fled?
  Where have ye borne those hope-enliven'd
    hours,
That once with myrtle garlands bound my head,
  That once bestrew'd my vernal path with
    flowers?

In yon fair vale, where blooms the beechen grove,
  Where winds the slow wave thro' the flowery
    plain,
To these fond arms you led the tyrant, Love,
  With Fear and Hope and Folly in his train.

My lyre, that, left at careless distance, hung
  Light on some pale branch of the osier shade,
To lays of amorous blandishment you strung,
  And o'er my sleep the lulling music play'd.

" Rest, gentle youth ! while on the quivering
    breeze
  Slides to thine ear this softly-breathing strain ;
Sounds that move smoother than the steps of ease,
  And pour oblivion in the ear of pain.

" In this fair vale eternal Spring shall smile,
  And Time unenvious crown each roseate hour ;
Eternal joy shall every care beguile,
  Breathe in each gale, and bloom in every
    flower.

" This silver stream, that down its crystal way
  Frequent has led thy musing steps along,
Shall, still the same, in sunny mazes play,
  And with its murmurs melodise thy song.

" Unfading green shall these fair groves adorn ;
  Those living meads immortal flowers unfold ;
In rosy smiles shall rise each blushing morn,
  And every evening close in clouds of gold.

"The tender Loves that watch thy slumbering rest,
  And round thee flowers and balmy myrtles strew,
Shall charm, thro' all approaching life, thy breast,
  With joys for ever pure, for ever new.

" The genial power that speeds the golden dart,
  Each charm of tender passion shall inspire ;
With fond affection fill the mutual heart,
  And feed the flame of ever—young desire.

" Come, gentle Loves ! your myrtle garlands
    bring ;
  The smiling bower with cluster'd roses spread ;
Come, gentle airs ! with incense-dropping wing
  The breathing sweets of vernal odour shed.

" Hark, as the strains of swelling music rise,
  How the notes vibrate on the far'ring gale !
Auspicious glories beam along the skies,
  And powers unseen the happy moments
    hail !

" Extatic hours ! so every distant day
  Like this serene on downy wings shall move ;
Rise crown'd with joys that triumph o'er decay,
  The faithful joys of Fancy and of Love."

---

### ELEGY II.

AND were they vain, those soothing lays ye
    sung ?
  Children of Fancy ! yes, your song was vain ;
On each soft air though rapt Attention hung,
  And Silence listen'd on the sleeping plain.

The strains yet vibrate on my ravish'd ear,
  And still to smile the mimic beauties seem,
Though now the visionary scenes appear
  Like the faint traces of a vanish'd dream.

Mirror of life ! the glories thus depart
  Of all that youth and love and fancy frame,
When painful Anguish speeds the piercing dart,
  Or Envy blasts the blooming flowers of fame.

Nurse of wild wishes, and of fond desires,
  The prophetess of Fortune, false and vain,
To scenes where Peace in Ruin's arms expires
  Fallacious Hope deludes her hapless train.

Go, Siren, go—thy charms on others try;
  My beaten bark at length has reach'd the shore:
Yet on the rock my dropping garments lie;
  And let me perish if I trust thee more.

Come, gentle Quiet! long-neglected maid!
  O come, and lead me to thy mossy cell;
There unregarded in the peaceful shade,
  With calm Repose and Silence let me dwell.

Come happier hours of sweet unanxious rest,
  When all the struggling passions shall sub-
      side;
When Peace shall clasp me to her plumy breast,
  And smooth my silent minutes as they glide.

But chief, thou goddess of the thoughtless eye,
  Whom never cares or passions discompose,
O, blest Insensibility, be nigh,
  And with thy soothing hand my weary eyelids
      close.

Then shall the cares of love and glory cease,
  And all the fond anxieties of fame;
Alike regardless in the arms of Peace,
  If these extol, or those debase a name.

In Lyttelton though all the Muses praise,
  His generous praise shall then delight no more,
Nor the sweet magic of his tender lays
  Shall touch the bosom which it charm'd be-
      fore.

Nor then, though Malice, with insidious guise
  Of Friendship, ope the unsuspecting breast;
Nor then, tho' Envy broach her blackening lies,
  Shall these deprive me of a moment's rest.

O state to be desir'd! when hostile rage
  Prevails in human more than savage haunts;
When man with man eternal war will wage,
  And never yield that mercy which he wants.

When dark Design invades the cheerful hour,
  And draws the heart with social freedom warm,
Its cares, its wishes, and its thoughts to pour,
  Smiling insidious with the hopes of harm.

Vain man, to other's failings still severe,
  Yet not one foible in himself can find;
Another's faults to Folly's eye are clear,
  But to her own e'en Wisdom's self is blind.

O let me still, from these low follies free,
  This sordid malice, and inglorious strife,
Myself the subject of my censure be,
  And teach my heart to comment on my life.

With thee, Philosophy, still let me dwell,
  My tutor'd mind from vulgar meanness save;
Bring Peace, bring Quiet to my humble cell,
  And bid them lay the green turf on my grave.

### ELEGY III.

Bright o'er the green hills rose the morning ray,
  The wood-lark's song resounded on the plain;
Fair Nature felt the warm embrace of day,
  And smil'd thro' all her animated reign.

When young Delight, of Hope and Fancy-born,
  His head on tufted wild thyme half-reclin'd,
Caught the gay colours of the orient morn,
  And thence of life this picture vain design'd.

" O born to thoughts, to pleasures more sublime
  Than beings of inferior nature prove!
To triumph in the golden hours of time,
  And feel the charms of fancy and of love!

" High-favour'd man! for him unfolding fair
  In orient light this native landscape smiles;
For him sweet Hope disarms the hand of Care,
  Exalts his pleasures, and his grief beguiles.

" Blows not a blossom on the breast of Spring,
  Breathes not a gale along the bending mead,
Trills not a songster of the soaring wing,
  But fragrance, health, and melody succeed.

" O let me still with simple Nature live,
  My lowly field-flowers on her altar lay,
Enjoy the blessings that she meant to give,
  And calmly waste my inoffensive day!

" No titled name, no envy-teasing dome,
  No glittering wealth my tutor'd wishes crave;
So Health and Peace be near my humble home,
  A cool stream murmur, and a green tree wave:

" So may the sweet Euterpe not disdain
  At Eve's chaste hour her silver lyre to bring;
The Muse of pity wake her soothing strain,
  And tune to sympathy the trembling string.

" Thus glide the pensive moments, o'er the vale
  While floating shades of dusky night descend:
Not left untold the lover's tender tale,
  Nor unenjoyed the heart-enlarging friend.

" To love and friendship flow the social bowl!
  To attic wit and elegance of mind;
To all the native beauties of the soul,
  The simple charms of truth, and sense refin'd.

" Then to explore whatever ancient sage
  Studious from Nature's early volume drew,
To chase sweet Fiction through her golden age,
  And mark how fair the sun-flower, Science,
      blew!

" Haply to catch some spark of eastern fire,
  Hesperian fancy, or Aonian ease;
Some melting note from Sappho's tender lyre,
  Some strain that Love and Phoebus taught to
      please.

" When waves the grey light o'er the mountain's
      head,              [ray;
Then let me meet the morn's first beauteous
Carelessly wander from my sylvan shed,
  And catch the sweet breath of the rising day.

" Nor seldom, loitering as I muse along, [bore;
  Mark from what flower the breeze its sweetness
Or listen to the labour-soothing song
  Of bees that range the thymy uplands o'er.

" Slow let me climb the mountain's airy brow,
  The green height gain'd, in museful rapture
Sleep to the murmur of the woods below, [lie,
  Or look on Nature with a lover's eye.

" Delightful hours! O, thus for ever flow;
  Led by fair Fancy round the varied year:
So shall my breast with native raptures glow,
  Nor feel one pang from folly, pride, or fear.

" Firm be my heart to Nature and to Truth,
  Nor vainly wander from their dictates sage:
So Joy shall triumph on the brows of youth,
  So Hope shall smooth the dreary paths of age."

### ELEGY IV.

Oh! yet, ye dear, deluding visions stay !
Fond hopes, of Innocence and Fancy born !
For you I'll cast these waking thoughts away,
    For one wild dream of life's romantic morn.

Ah ! no : the sunshine o'er each object spread
    By flattering Hope, the flowers that blew so
Like the gay gardens of Armida, fled,      [fair,
    And vanish'd from the powerful rod of Care.

So the poor pilgrim, who in rapturous thought
    Plans his dear journey to Loretto's shrine,
Seems on his way by guardian seraphs brought,
    Sees aiding angels favour his design.

Ambrosial blossoms, such of old as blew
    By those fresh founts on Eden's happy plain,
And Sharon's roses all his passage strew:
    So Fancy dreams ; but Fancy's dreams are
        vain.

Wasted and weary on the mountain's side,
    His way unknown, the hapless pilgrim lies,
Or takes some ruthless robber for his guide,
    And prone beneath his cruel sabre dies.

Life's morning-landscape gilt with orient light,
    Where Hope and Joy and Fancy hold their
        reign,                          [bright,
The grove's green wave, the blue stream sparkling
    The blythe Hours dancing round Hyperion's
        wain,,

In radiant colours youth's free hand pourtrays,
    Then holds the flattering tablet to his eye ;
Nor thinks how soon the vernal grove decays,
    Nor sees the dark cloud gathering o'er the sky.

Hence Fancy conquer'd by the dart of Pain,
    And wandering far from her Platonic shade,
Mourns o'er the ruins of her transient reign,
    Nor unrepining sees her visions fade.

Their parent banish'd, hence her children fly,
    The fairy race that fill'd her festive train ;
Joy tears his wreath, and Hope inverts her eye,
    And Folly wonders that her dream was vain.

---

### A POEM TO THE MEMORY OF MR. HANDEL.

#### WRITTEN IN 1760.

Spirits of music, and ye powers of song,
That wak'd to painful melody the lyre
Of young Jessides, when, in Sion's vale
He wept o'er bleeding friendship ; ye that
        mourn'd,
While Freedom, drooping o'er Euphrates' stream,
Her pensive harp on the pale osier hung,
Begin once more the sorrow soothing-lay.
    Ah ! where shall now the Muse fit numbers
        find ?
What accents pure to greet thy tuneful shade,
Sweet harmonist ? 'twas thine, the tender fall
Of pity's plaintive lay ; for thee the stream
Of silver-winding music sweeter play'd,
And purer flow'd for thee—all silent now

Those airs [1] that, breathing o'er the breast o
        Thames,
Led amorous Echo down the long, long vale,
Delighted ; studious from thy sweeter strain
To melodise her own ; when fancy-lorn,
She mourns in anguish o'er the drooping breast
Of young Narcissus. From their amber urns,
Parting their green locks streaming in the sun [2],
The Naiads rose and smil'd : nor since the day,
When first by music, and by freedom led
From Grecian Acidale ; nor since the day,
When last from Arno's weeping fount they came,
To smooth the ringlets of Sabrina's hair,
Heard they like minstrelsy—fountains and shades
Of Twit'nam, and of Windsor fam'd in song !
Ye heights of Clermont, and ye bowers of Ham !
That heard the fine strain vibrate through your
        groves,
Ah ! where were then your long-lov'd Muses fled
When Handel breath'd no more ?—and thou,
        sweet queen,
That nightly wrapt thy Milton's hallow'd ear
In the soft ecstacies of Lydian airs ;
That since attun'd to Handel's high-wound lyre [3]
The lay by thee suggested ; could'st not thou
Soothe with thy sweet song the grim fury's
        breast [4]?
    Cold-hearted Death ! his wanly-glaring eye
Nor Virtue's smile attracts, nor Fame's loud
        trump
Can pierce his iron ear, for ever barr'd
To gentle sounds : the golden voice of song,
That charms the gloomy partner of his birth,
That soothes despair and pain, he hears no more,
Than rude winds, blust'ring from the Cambrian
        cliffs,
The traveller's feeble lay. To court fair Fame,
To toil with slow steps up the star-crown'd hill,
Where Science, leaning on her sculptur'd urn,
Looks conscious on the secret-working hand
Of Nature ; on the wings of Genius borne,
To soar above the beaten walks of life,
Is, like the paintings of an evening cloud,
Th' amusement of an hour. Night, gloomy Night,
Spreads her black wings, and all the vision dies.
    Ere long, the heart, that heaves this sigh to
        thee,
Shall beat no more ! ere long, on this fond lay
Which mourns at Handel's tomb, insulting Time
Shall strew his cankering rust. Thy strain per-
        chance,
Thy sacred strain, shall the hoar warrior spare ;
For sounds like thine, at Nature's early birth,
Arous'd him slumbering on the dead profound
Of dusky chaos ; by the golden harps
Of choral angels summon'd to his race :
And sounds like thine, when Nature is no more,
Shall call him weary from the lengthen'd toils
Of twice ten thousand years. O would his hand
Yet spare some portion of this vital flame,
The trembling Muse that now faint effort makes
On young and artless wing, should bear thy
        praise

[1] The water-music.
[2] Rorantesque comas a fronte removit ad
        aures.          Ovid. Met.
[3] L'Allegro and Il Penseroso, set to music by
Mr. Handel.
[4] See Milton's Lycidas.

Sublime, above the mortal bounds of Earth,
With heavenly fire relume her feeble ray,
And, taught by seraphs, frame her song for thee.
    I feel, I feel the sacred impulse—hark !
Wak'd from according lyres the sweet strains flow
In symphony divine : from air to air
The trembling numbers fly : swift bursts away
The flow of joy—now swells the flight of praise
Springs the shrill trump aloft ; the toiling chords
Melodious labour through the flying maze ;
And the deep base his strong sound rolls away,
Majestically sweet—Yet, Handel, raise,
Yet wake to higher strains thy sacred lyre :
The Name of ages, the Supreme of things,
The great Messiah asks it : He whose hand
Led into form yon everlasting orbs,
The harmony of Nature—He whose hand
Stretch'd o'er the wilds of space this beauteous
        ball,
Whose spirit breathes through all his smiling
        works
Music and love—yet, Handel, raise the strain.
    Hark ! what angelic sounds, what voice divine
Breathes through the ravisht air ! my rapt ear
        feels
The harmony of Heaven.  Hail sacred choir !
Immortal spirits, hail ! If haply those
That erst in favour'd Palestine proclaim'd
Glory and peace : her angel-haunted groves,
Her piny mountains, and her golden vales
Re-echo'd peace—But, Oh, suspend the strain—
The swelling joy's too much for mortal bounds !
'Tis transport even to pain.
    Yet, hark ! what pleasing sounds invite mine
So venerably sweet ?  'Tis Sion's lute.    [ear
Behold her hero⁵! from his valiant brow
Looks Judah's lion, on his thigh the sword
Of vanquish'd Apollonius—The shrill trump

⁵ Judas Maccabeus.

Through Bethoron proclaims the approaching
        fight,
I see the brave youth lead his little band,
With toil and hunger faint ;  yet from his arm
The rapid Syrian flies.  Thus Henry once,
The British Henry, with his way-worn troop,
Subdu'd the pride of France—Now louder blows
The martial clangor : lo Nicanor's host !
With threat'ning turrets crown'd, slowly advance
The ponderous elephants——
The blazing Sun, from many a golden shield
Reflected gleams afar.  Judean chief !
How shall thy force, thy little force, sustain
The dreadful shock !
The hero comes⁶—'Tis boundless mirth and song,
And dance and triumph ; every labouring string,
And voice, and breathing shell in concert strain
To swell the raptures of tumultuous joy.
    O master of the passions and the soul,
Seraphic Handel !  how shall words describe
Thy music's countless graces, nameless powers !
    When he of Gaza⁷, blind and sunk in chains,
On female treachery looks greatly down,
How the breast burns indignant ! in thy strain,
When sweet-voic'd piety resigns to Heaven,
Glows not each bosom with the flame of virtue ?
    O'er Jeptha's votive maid when the soft lute
Sounds the slow symphony of funeral grief,
What youthful breast but melts with tender pity?
What parent bleeds not with a parent's woe ?
    O, longer than this worthless lay can live !
While fame and music soothe the human ear ;
Be this thy praise : to lead the polish'd mind
To virtue's noblest heights ; to light the flame
Of British freedom, rouse the generous thought,
Refine the passions, and exalt the soul
To love, to Heaven, to harmony and thee.

⁶ Chorus of youths, in Judas Maccabæus.
⁷ See the Oratorio of Samson.

# THE ENLARGEMENT OF THE MIND.

## TO GENERAL CRAUFURD.

WRITTEN AT BELVIDERE.  1763.

### EPISTLE I.

WHERE is the man, who, prodigal of mind,
In one wide wish embraces human kind ?
All pride of sects, all party zeal above,
Whose priest is Reason, and whose god is Love ;
Fair Nature's friend, a foe to fraud and art—
Where is the man so welcome to my heart ?
    The sightless herd sequacious, who pursue
Dull folly's path, and do as others do,
Who look with purblind prejudice and scorn,
On different sects, in different nations born,
Let us, my Craufurd, with compassion view,
Pity their pride, but shun their errour too.

From Belvidere's fair groves, and mountains
Which Nature rais'd, rejoicing to be seen,[green,
Let us, while raptur'd on her works we gaze,
And the heart riots on luxurious praise,
Th' expanded thought, the boundless wish retain,
And let not Nature moralize in vain.
    O sacred guide ! preceptress more sublime
Than sages boasting o'er the wrecks of time !
See on each page her beauteous volume bear
The golden characters of good and fair.
All human knowledge (blush collegiate pride !)
Flows from her works, to none that reads denied.
    Shall the dull inmate of pedantic walls,
On whose old walk the sun-beam seldom falls,

Who knows of Nature, and of man no more
Than fills some page of antiquated lore—
Shall he, in words and terms profoundly wise,
The better knowledge of the world despise,
Think wisdom center'd in a false degree.
And scorn the scholar of humanity?
  Something of men these sapient drones may
    know,
Of men that liv'd two thousand years ago.
Such human monsters if the world e'er knew,
As ancient verse, and ancient story drew!
  If to one object, system, scene confin'd,
The sure effect is narrowness of mind.
'Twas thus St. Robert, in his lonely wood,
Forsook each social duty—to be good.
Thus Hobbes on one dear system fix'd his eyes,
And prov'd his nature wretched—to be wise.
Each zealot thus, elate with ghostly pride,
Adores his God, and hates the world beside.
  Though form'd with powers to grasp this va-
    rious ball,
Gods! to what meanness may the spirit fall!
Powers that should spread in reason's orient ray,
How are they darken'd, and debarr'd the day!
  When late, where Tajo rolls his ancient tide,
Reflecting clear the mountain's purple side,
Thy genius,Craufurd, Britain's legions led,
And fear's chill cloud forsook each brightening
    head,
By nature brave, and generous as thou art,
Say did not human follies vex thy heart?
Glow'd not thy breast indignant, when you saw
The dome of murder consecrate by law?
Where fiends, commission'd with the legal rod,
In pure devotion, burn the works of God.
O change me, powers of Nature, if ye can,
Transform me, make me any thing but man.
Yet why? This heart all human kind forgives,
While Gillman loves me, and while Craufurd
    lives.
Is Nature, all benevolent, to blame
That half her offspring are their mother's shame?
Did she ordain o'er this fair scene of things
The cruelty of priests, or pride of kings?
Tho' worlds lie murder'd for their wealth or fame,
Is Nature all benevolent to blame?
  O that the world were emptied of its slaves!
That all the fools were gone, and all the knaves!
Then might we, Craufurd, with delight embrace,
In boundless love, the rest of human race.
But let not knaves misanthropy create,
Nor feed the gall of universal hate.
Wherever Genius, Truth, and Virtue dwell,
Polish'd in courts, or simple in a cell,
All views of country, sects, and creeds apart,
These, these I love, and hold them to my heart.
  Vain of our beauteous isle, and justly vain,
For Freedom here, and Health, and Plenty reign,
We different lots contemptuously compare,
And boast, like children, of a fav'rite's share.
Yet though each vale a deeper verdure yields
Than Arno's banks, or Andalusia's fields,
Though many a tree-crown'd mountain teems
    with ore,
Though flocks innumerous whiten every shore,
Why should we, thus with Nature's wealth elate,
Behold her different families with hate?
Look on her works—on every page you'll find
Inscrib'd the doctrine of the social mind.

  See countless worlds of insect beings share
Th' unenvied regions of the liberal air!
In the same grove what music void of strife!
Heirs of one stream what tribes of scaly life!
See earth, and air, and fire, and flood combine,
Of general good to aid the great design!
  Where Anton drags o'er Lincoln's lurid plain,
Like a slow snake, his dirty-winding train,
Where fogs eternal blot the face of day,
And the lost bittern moans his gloomy way;
As well we might, for unpropitious skies,
The blameless native with his clime despise,
As him who still the poorer lot partakes
Of Biscay's mountains, or Batavia's lakes.
  Yet look once more on Nature's various plan!
Behold, and love her noblest creature man!
She, never partial, on each various zone,
Bestow'd some portion to the rest unknown,
By mutual interest meaning thence to bind
In one vast chain the commerce of mankind.
  Behold, ye vain disturbers of an hour!
Ye dupes of faction! and ye tools of power!
Poor rioters on life's contracted stage!
Behold, and lose your littleness of rage!
Throw envy, folly, prejudice behind!
And yield to Truth the empire of the mind.
  Immortal Truth! O from thy radiant shrine
Where light created first essay'd to shine;
Where clustering stars eternal beams display,
And gems ethereal drink the golden day;
To chase this moral, clear this sensual night,
O shed one ray of thy celestial light!
Teach us, while wandering thro' this vale below
We know but little, that we little know.
One beam to mole-ey'd Prejudice convey,
Let Pride perceive one mortifying ray.
Thy glass to fools, to infidels apply,
And all the dimness of the mental eye.
  Plac'd on this shore of Time's far-stretching
    bourn,
With leave to look at Nature and return;
While wave on wave impels the human tide,
And ages sink, forgotten as they glide;
Can life's short duties better be discharg'd,
Than when we leave it with a mind enlarg'd?
  Judg'd not the old philosopher aright,
When thus he preach'd, his pupils in his sight?
" It matters not, my friends, how low or high
Your little walk of transient life may lie.
Soon will the reign of hope and fear be o'er,
And warring passions militate no more.
And trust me, he who, having once survey'd
The good and fair which Nature's wisdom made,
The soonest to his former state retires,
And feels the peace of satisfied desires,
(Let others deem more wisely if they can),
I look on him to be the happiest man."
  So thought the sacred sage, in whom I trust,
Because I feel his sentiments are just.
'Twas not in lustrums of long counted years
That swell'd th' alternate reign of hopes and fears;
Not in the splendid scenes of pain and strife,
That Wisdom plac'd the dignity of life:
To study Nature was the task design'd,
And learn from her th' enlargement of the mind.
Learn from her works whatever Truth admires,
And sleep in death with satisfied desires.

EPISTLE II.

TO WILLIAM LANGHORNE, M. A. WRITTEN IN
1765.

Light heard his voice, and, eager to obey,
From all her orient fountains burst away.
At Nature's birth, O! had the power divine
Commanded thus the moral sun to shine,
Beam'd on the mind all reason's influence bright,
And the full day of intellectual light,
Then the free soul, on truth's strong pinion born,
Had never languish'd in this shade forlorn.
  Yet thus imperfect form'd, thus blind and
    vain,
Doom'd by long toil a glimpse of truth to gain;
Beyond its sphere shall human wisdom go,
And boldly censure what it cannot know?
For what Heaven gave let us the donor bless;
Nor than their merits rank our mercies less.
'Tis ours to cherish what Heav'n deign'd to give,
And thankful for the gift of being to live.
  Progressive powers, and faculties that rise,
From Earth's low vale, to grasp the golden skies,
Though distant far from perfect, good, or fair,
Claim the due thought, and ask the grateful care.
Come then, thou partner of my life and name,
From one dear source, whom Nature form'd the
    same,
Ally'd more nearly in each nobler part,
And more the friend, than brother, of my heart!
Let us, unlike the lucid twins that rise
At different times, and shine in distant skies,
With mutual eye this mental world survey,
Mark the slow rise of intellectual day,
View reason's source, if man the source may find,
And trace each science that exalts the mind.
  " Thou self-appointed lord of all below!
Ambitious man, how little dost thou know?
For once let Fancy's towering thoughts subside;
Look on thy birth, and mortify thy pride!
A plaintive wretch, so blind, so helpless born,
The brute sagacious might behold with scorn.
How soon, when Nature gives him to the day,
In strength exulting, does he bound away!
By instinct led, the fostering teat he finds,
Sports in the ray, and shuns the searching winds:
No grief he knows, he feels no groundless fear,
Feeds without cries, and sleeps without a tear.
Did he but know to reason and compare,
See here the vassal, and the master there :
What strange reflections must the scene afford,
That show'd the weakness of his puling lord!"
  Thus Sophistry unfolds her specious plan,
Form'd not to humble, but depreciate man.
Unjust the censure, if unjust to rate
His pow'rs and merits from his infant-state.
For, grant the children of the flow'ry vale
By instinct wiser, and of limbs more hale,
With equal eye their perfect state explore,
And all the vain comparison's no more.
  " But why should life, so short by Heav'n or-
    dain'd,
Be long to thoughtless infancy restrain'd—
To thoughtless infancy, or vainly sage,
Mourn through the languors of declining age?"
  O blind to truth! to Nature's wisdom blind!
And all that she directs, or Heav'n design'd!
Behold her works in cities, plains, and groves,
All life that vegetates, and life that moves!

In due proportion, as each being stays
In perfect life, it rises and decays.
Is man long helpless? Through each tender
    hour,
See love parental watch the blooming flower!
By op'ning charms, by beauties fresh display'd,
And sweets unfolding, see that love repaid!
Has age its pains? For luxury it may—
The temp'rate wear insensibly away.
While sage experience, and reflection clear
Beam a gay sunshine on life's fading year.
But see from age, from infant weakness see,
That man was destin'd for society;
There from those ills a safe retreat behold,
Which young might vanquish, or afflict him old.
  " That, in proportion as each being stays
In perfect life, it rises and decays—
Is Nature's law—to forms alone confin'd;
The laws of matter act not on the mind!
Too feebly, sure, its faculties must grow,
And Reason brings her borrow'd light too slow."
  O! still censorious? Art thou then possess'd
Of Reason's power, and does she rule thy breast?
Say what the use had Providence assign'd
To infant years maturity of mind? •
That thy pert offspring, as their father wise,
Might scorn thy precepts, and thy pow'r des-
    pise?
Or mourn, with ill-match'd faculties at strife,
O'er limbs unequal to the task of life?
To feel more sensibly the woes that wait
On every period, as on every state ;
And slight, sad convicts of each painful truth,
The happier trifles of unthinking youth?
  Conclude we then the progress of the mind
Ordain'd by wisdom infinitely kind :
No innate knowledge on the soul imprest,
No birth-right instinct acting in the breast,
No natal light, no beams from Heav'n display'd,
Dart through the darkness of the mental shade.
Perceptive powers we hold from Heaven's de-
Alike to knowledge as to virtue free,      [cree,
In both a lib'ral agency we bear,
The moral here, the intellectul there ;
And hence in both an equal joy is known,
The conscious pleasure of an act our own.
  When first the trembling eye receives the day,
External forms on young perception play ;
External forms affect the mind alone,
Their diff'rent pow'rs and properties unknown.
See the pleas'd infant court the flaming brand,
Eager to grasp the glory in its hand !
The crystal wave as eager to pervade,
Stretch its fond arms to meet the smiling shade !
When Memory's call the mimic words obey,
And wing the thought that faulters on its way ;
When wise Experience her slow verdict draws,
The sure effect exploring in the cause,
In Nature's rude, but not unfruitful wild,
Reflection springs, and Reason is her child :
On her fair stock the blooming scyon grows,
And brighter through revolving seasons blows.
  All beauteous flow'r! immortal shalt thou
    shine,
When dim with age yon golden orbs decline ;
Thy orient bloom, unconscious of decay,
Shall spread and flourish in eternal day.
  O! with what art, my friend, what early care,
Should Wisdom cultivate a plant so fair !

How should her eye the rip'ning mind revise,
And blast the buds of folly as they rise !
How should her hand with industry restrain,
The thriving growth of passion's fruitful train,
Aspiring weeds, whose lofty arms would tower
With fatal shade o'er Reason's tender flow'r.

From low pursuits the ductile mind to save,
Creeds that contract, and vices that enslave ;
O'er life's rough seas its doubtful course to steer,
Unbroke by av'rice, bigotry, or fear !
For this fair Science spreads her light afar,
And fills the bright urn of her eastern star.
The liberal power in no sequester'd cells,
No moonshine courts of dreaming schoolmen
        dwells,
Distinguish'd far her lofty temple stands,
Where the tall mountain looks o'er distant lands ;
All round her throne the graceful Arts appear,
That boast the empire of the eye or ear.

See favour'd first and nearest to the throne,
By the rapt mien of musing Silence known.
Pled from herself, the Pow'r of Numbers plac'd
Her wild thoughts watch'd by Harmony and Taste.

There (but at distance never meant to vie)
The full-form'd image glancing on her eye,
See lively Painting ! On her various face
Quick-gliding forms a moment find a place ;
She looks, she acts the characters she gives,
And a new feature in each feature lives.

See attic ease in Sculpture's graceful air,
Half loose her robe, and half unbound her hair ;
To life, to life, she smiling seems to call,
And down her fair hands negligently fall.

Last, but not meanest, of the glorious choir,
See Music, list'ning to an angel's lyre.
Simplicity, their beauteous handmaid, drest
By Nature, bears a field-flower on her breast.

O arts divine ! O magic powers that move
The springs of truth, enlarging truth and
love !        [ends,
Lost in their charms each mean attachment
And taste and knowledge thus are virtue's friends.

Thus Nature deigns to sympathize with art,
And leads the moral beauty to the heart ;
There, only there, that strong attraction lies,
Which wakes the soul, and bids her graces rise ;
Lives in those powers of harmony that bind
Congenial hearts, and stretch from mind to mind :
Glow'd in that warmth, that social kindness gave,
Which once—the rest is silence and the grave.

    O tears, that warm from wounded friendship
       flow !
O thoughts that wake to monuments of woe !
Reflection keen, that points the painful dart ;
Mem'ry, that speeds its passage to the heart ;
Sad monitors, your cruel power suspend,
And hide, for ever hide, the buried friend :
—In vain—confest I see my Craufurd stand,
And the pen falls—falls from my trembling hand.
E'en Death's dim shadow seeks to hide, in
       vain,
That lib'ral aspect, and that smile humane ;
E'en Death's dim shadow wears a languid light,
And his eye beams through everlasting night.

'Till the last sigh of genius shall expire,
His keen eye faded, and extinct his fire,
'Till Time, in league with Envy and with Death,
Blast the skill'd hand, and stop the tuneful breath,
My Craufurd still shall claim the mournful song,
So long remembered and bewail'd so long.

## AN ODE TO THE RIVER EDEN.

### WRITTEN IN 1759.

Delightful Eden ! parent stream,
   Yet shall the maids of Memory say,
(When led by Fancy's fairy dream,
   My young steps trac'd thy winding way)
How oft along thy mazy shore,
That many a gloomy alder bore,
   In pensive thought their poet stray'd ;
Or, careless thrown thy bank beside,
Beheld thy dimply waters glide,
   Bright thro' the trembling shade.

Yet shall they paint those scenes again,
   Where once with infant-joy he play'd,
And bending o'er thy liquid plain,
   The azure worlds below survey'd :
Led by the rosy-handed Hours,
When Time trip'd o'er that bank of flowers,
   Which in thy crystal bosom smil'd :
Tho' old the god, yet light and gay,
He flung his glass, his scythe away,
   And seem'd himself a child.

The poplar tall, that waving near
   Would whisper to thy murmurs free ;
Yet rustling seems to soothe mine ear,
   And trembles when I sigh for thee.
Yet seated on thy shelving brim,
Can Fancy see the Naiads trim
   Burnish their green locks in the Sun ;
Or at the last lone hour of day,
To chase the lightly glancing fay,
   In airy circles run.

But, Fancy, can thy mimic power
   Again those happy moments bring ?
Can'st thou restore that golden hour,
   When young Joy wav'd his laughing wing ?
When first in Eden's rosy vale,
My full heart pour'd the lover's tale,
   The vow sincere, devoid of guile !
While Delia in her panting breast,
With sighs, the tender thought supprest,
   And look'd as angels smile.

O goddess of the crystal bow,
   That dwell'st the golden meads among ;
Whose streams still fair in memory flow,
   Whose murmurs melodise my song !
Oh ! yet those gleams of joy display,
Which bright'ning glow'd in fancy's ray,
   When, near thy lucid urn reclin'd,
The dryad, Nature, bar'd her breast,
And left, in naked charms imprest,
   Her image on my mind.

In vain—the maids of Memory fair
   No more in golden visions play ;
No friendship smoothes the brow of Care,
   No Delia's smile approves my lay.
Yet, love and friendship lost to me,
'Tis yet some joy to think of thee,
   And in thy breast this moral find ;
That life, though stain'd with sorrow's showers,
Shall flow serene, while Virtue pours
   Her sunshine on the mind.

## AUTUMNAL ELEGY.

TO MISS CRACROFT. 1763.

WHILE yet my poplar yields a doubtful shade,
　Its last leaves trembling to the Zephyr's sigh;
On this fair plain ere every verdure fade,
　Or the last smiles of golden Autumn die;

Wilt thou, my Nancy, at this pensive hour,
　O'er Nature's ruin hear thy friend complain :
While his heart labours with th' inspiring power,
　And from his pen spontaneous flows the strain ?

Thy gentle breast shall melt with kindred sighs,
　Yet haply grieving o'er a parent's bier;
Poets are Nature's children ; when she dies,
　Affection mourns, and Duty drops a tear.

Why are ye silent, brethren of the grove,
　Fond Philomel, thy many-chorded lyre
So sweetly tun'd to tenderness and love,
　Shall love no more, or tenderness inspire ?

O mix once more thy gentle lays with mine ;
　For well our passions, well our notes agree:
An absent love, sweet bird, may soften thine :
　An absent love demands a tear from me.

Yet, ere ye slumber, songsters of the sky,
　Thro' the long night of winter wild and drear :
O let us tune, ere Love and Fancy die,
　One tender farewell to the fading year.

Farewell ye wild hills, scatter'd o'er with spring !
　Sweet solitudes, where Flora smil'd unseen !
Farewell each breeze of balmy-burthen'd wing !
　The violet's blue bank, and the tall wood green !

Ye tuneful groves of Belvidere, adieu !
　Kind shades that whisper o'er my Craufurd's
　　rest !
From courts, from senates, and from camps to you,
　When Fancy leads him, no inglorious gues. !

Dear shades adieu ! where late the moral Muse
　Led by the dryad, Silence, oft reclin'd,
Taught Meanness to extend her little views,
　And look on Nature to enlarge her mind.

Farewell the walk along the woodland-vale ;
　Flower-feeding rills in murmurs drawn away !
Farewell the sweet breath of the early gale !
　And the dear glories of the closing day !

The nameless charms of high poetic thought,
　That Spring's green hours to Fancy's children
The words divine, Imagination wrote　　[bore ;
　On Slumber's light leaf by the murmuring
　　shore—

All, all adieu ! from Autumn's sober power
　Fly the dear dreams of Spring's delightful reign;
Gay Summer strips her rosy-mantled bower,
　And rude winds waste the glories of her train.

Yet Autumn yields her joys of humbler kind ;
　Sad o'er her golden ruins as we stray,
Sweet Melancholy soothes the musing mind,
　And Nature charms, delightful in decay.

All-bounteous power, whom happy worlds adore !
　With every scene some grateful change she
　　brings—
In Winter's wild snows, Autumn's golden store,
　In glowing summers and in blooming springs !

O most belov'd ! the fairest and the best
　Of all her works ! may still thy bosom find
Fair Nature's frankness in thy gentle breast ;
　Like her be various, but like her be kind.

Then, when the Spring of smiling youth is o'er;
　When Summer's glories yield to Autumn's sway ;
When golden Autumn sinks in Winter hoar,
　And life declining yields its last weak ray :

In thy lov'd arms my fainting age shall close,
　On thee my fond eye bend its trembling light :
Rememb'rance sweet shall soothe my last repose,
　And my soul bless thee in eternal night.

## TO MISS CRACROFT.

1763.

WHEN pale beneath the frowning shade of death,
　No soothing voice of love, or friendship nigh,
While strong convulsions seiz'd the lab'ring
　　breath,
　And life suspended left each vacant eye ;

Where, in that moment, fled th' immortal mind ?
　To what new region did the spirit stray ?
Found it some bosom hospitably kind,
　Some breast that took the wanderer in its way ?

To thee, my Nancy, in that deathful hour,
　To thy dear bosom it once more return'd ;
And wrapt in Hackthorn's solitary bower,
　The ruins of its former mansion mourn'd.

But, didst thou, kind and gentle as thou art,
　O'er thy pale lover shed the generous tear ?
From those sweet eyes did Pity's softness start,
　When Fancy laid him on the lowly bier ?

Didst thou to Heaven address the forceful prayer,
　Fold thy fair hands, and raise the mournful eye,
Implore each power benevolent to spare,
　And call down Pity from the golden sky?

O born at once to bless me and to save,
　Exalt my life, and dignify my lay !
Thou too shalt triumph o'er the mouldering grave,
　And on thy brow shall bloom the deathless bay.

Dear shades of genius ! heirs of endless fame !
　That in your laureate crowns the myrtle wove,
Snatch'd from oblivion Beauty's sacred name,
　And grew immortal in the arms of Love !

O may we meet you in some happier clime,
　Some safer vale beneath a genial sky ;
Whence all the woes that load the wing of Time,
　Disease, and death, and fear, and frailty fly !

## TO MISS CRACROFT.

THE COMPLAINT OF HER RING-DOVE. 1759.

FAR from the smiles of blue hesperian skies,
　Far from those vales, where flowery pleasures
　　dwell,
(Dear scenes of freedom lost to these sad eyes !)
　How hard to languish in this lonely cell !

When genial gales relume the fires of love,
　When laughing Spring leads round the jocund
　　year ;
Ah ! view with pity, gentle maid, your dove,
　From every heart-felt joy secluded here !

To me no more the laughing Spring looks gay ;
  Nor annual loves relume my languid breast ;
Time slowly drags the long, delightless day,
  Thro' one dull scene of solitary rest.

Ah ! what avails that dreaming Fancy roves
  Thro' the wild beauties of her native reign !
Breathes in green fields, and feeds in freshening
      groves,
  To wake to anguish in this hopeless chain ?

Tho' fondly sooth'd with Pity's tenderest care,
  Tho' still by Nancy's gentle hand carest,
For the free forest, and the boundless air,
  The rebel, Nature, murmurs in my breast.

Ah let not Nature, Nancy, plead in vain !
  For kindness sure should grace a form so fair :
Restore me to my native wilds again,
  To the free forest, and the boundless air.

---

### SONNET

#### IN THE MANNER OF PETRARCH.

##### TO MISS CRACROFT. 1765.

On thy fair morn, O hope-inspiring May !
  The sweetest twins that ever Nature bore,
  Where Hackthorn's vale her field-flower-gar-
      land wore,
Young Love and Fancy met the genial day.
And, all as on the thyme-green bank I lay,
  A nymph of gentlest mien their train before,
  Came with a smile ; and " Swain," she cried,
    " no more
To pensive sorrow tune thy hopeless lay.
Friends of thy heart, see Love and Fancy bring
  Each joy that youth's enchanted bosom warms ;
Delight that rifles all the fragrant spring !
  Fair-handed Hope, that paints unfading charms !
And dove-like Faith, that waves her silver
    wing.—
These, swain, are thine ; for Nancy meets thy
    arms."

---

### TO MISS CRACROFT.

##### WRAPPED ROUND A NOSEGAY OF VIOLETS.
##### 1761.

Dear object of my late and early prayer !
Source of my joy ! and solace of my care !
Whose gentle friendship such a charm can give,
As makes me wish, and tells me how to live.
To thee the Muse with grateful hand would bring
These first fair children of the doubtful Spring.
O may they, fearless of a varying sky,
Bloom on thy breast, and smile beneath thine eye !
In fairer lights their vivid blue display,
And sweeter breathe their little lives away !

---

### TO MISS CRACROFT.

##### ON THE MORAL REFLECTIONS
##### CONTAINED IN HER ANSWER TO THE ABOVE VERSES.
##### 1761.

Sweet moralist ! whose moving truths impart
At once delight and anguish to my heart !
Tho' human joys their short-liv'd sweets exhale,
Like the wan beauties of the wasted vale ;

Yet, trust the Muse, fair friendship's flower shall
    last ;
When life's short sunshine, like its storms is past ;
Bloom in the fields of some ambrosial shore,
Where Time, and Death, and Sickness are no
    more.

---

### WRITTEN IN A COLLECTION OF MAPS.

#### 1765.

Realms of this globe, that ever-circling run,
And rise alternate to embrace the Sun ;
Shall I with envy at my lot repine,
Because I boast so small a portion mine ?
If e'er in thought of Andalusia's vines,
Golconda's jewels, or Potosi's mines ;
In these, or those, if vanity forgot
The humbler blessings of my little lot ;
Then may the stream that murmurs near my door,
The waving grove that loves its mazy shore,
Withhold each soothing pleasure that they gave,
No longer murmur, and no longer wave !

---

### THEODOSIUS TO CONSTANTIA.

#### 1760.

Let others seek the lying aids of art,
And bribe the passions to betray the heart ;
Truth, sacred truth, and faith unskill'd to feign,
Fill my fond breast, and prompt my artless strain,
Say, did thy lover, in some happier hour,
Each ardent thought, in wild profusion pour ;
With eager fondness on thy beauty gaze,
And talk with all the ecstacy of praise ?
The heart sincere its pleasing tumult prov'd ;
All, all declar'd that Theodosius lov'd.
Let raptur'd fancy on that moment dwell,
When thy dear vows in trembling accents fell ;
When love acknowledg'd wak'd the tender sigh,
Swell'd thy full breast, and fill'd thy melting eye.

O ! blest for ever be th' auspicious day,
Dance all its hours in pleasure's golden ray !
Pale sorrow's gloom from every eye depart !
And laughing joy glide lightly thro' the heart !
Let village-maids their festive brows adorn,
And with fresh garlands meet the smiling morn ;
Each happy swain, by faithful love repaid,
Pour his warm vows, and court his village maid.

Yet shall the scene to ravish'd memory rise ;
Constantia present yet shall meet these eyes ;
On her fair arm her beauteous head reclin'd,
Her locks flung careless to the sportful wind.
While love, and fear, contending in her face,
Flush every rose, and heighten every grace.

O, never, while of life and hope possest,
May this dear image quit my faithful breast !
The painful hours of absence to beguile,
May thus Constantia look, Constantia smile !

---

### ELEGY.

#### 1760.

The eye of Nature never rests from care ;
  She guards her children with a parent's love :
And not a mischief reigns in earth or air,
  But time destroys, or remedies remove.

In vain no ill shall haunt the walks of life,
No vice in vain the human heart deprave.
The pois'nous flower, the tempest's raging strife
From greater pain, from greater ruin save.

Lavinia, form'd with every powerful grace,
With all that lights the flame of young desire;
Pure ease of wit, and elegance of face,
A soul all fancy, and an eye all fire.

Lavinia !— Peace, my busy fluttering breast !
Nor fear to languish in thy former pain :
At length she yields—she yields the needful rest;
And frees her lover from his galling chain.

The golden star, that leads the radiant morn,
Looks not so fair, fresh-rising from the main ;
But her bent eye-brow bears forbidding scorn,—
But Pride's fell furies every heart-string strain.

Lavinia, thanks to thy ungentle mind ;
I now behold thee with indifferent eyes ;
And Reason dares, tho' Love as Death be blind,
Thy gay, thy worthless being to despise.

Beauty may charm without one inward grace,
And fair proportions win the captive heart,—
But let rank pride the pleasing form debase,
And Love disgusted breaks his erring dart.

The youth that once the sculptur'd nymph admir'd,
Had look'd with scornful laughter on her charms,
If the vain form, with recent life inspir'd,
Had turn'd disdainful from his offer'd arms.

Go, thoughtless maid ! of transient beauty vain,
Feed the high thought, the towering hope extend ;
Still may'st thou dream of splendour in thy train,
And smile superb, while love and flattery bend.

For me, sweet peace shall soothe my troubled mind,
And easy slumbers close my weary eyes ;
Since Reason dares, tho' Love as Death be blind,
Thy gay, thy worthless being to despise.

---

## INSCRIPTION

### ON THE DOOR OF A STUDY.

O THOU that shalt presume to tread
This mansion of the mighty dead,
Come with the free, untainted mind ;
The nurse, the pedant leave behind ;
And all that superstition, fraught
With folly's lore, thy youth has taught—
Each thought that reason can't retain,—
Leave it, and learn to think again.
Yet, while thy studious eyes explore,
And range these various volumes o'er,
Trust blindly to no fav'rite pen,
Rememb'ring authors are but men.
Has fair Philosophy thy love ?
Away ! she lives in yonder grove.
If the sweet Muse thy pleasure gives ;—
With her in yonder grove she lives :
And if Religion claims thy care ;
Religion, fled from books, is there.
For first from Nature's works we drew
Our knowledge, and our virtue too.

## TO LORD GRANBY.

IN spite of all the rusty fools
That glean old nonsense in the schools ;
Nature, a mistress never coy,
Has wrote on all her works—Enjoy.
Shall we then starve, like Gideon's wife,
And die to save a makeweight's life ?
No, friend of Nature, you disdain
So fair a hand shou'd work in vain.

But, my good lord, make her your guide,
And err not on the other side :
Like her, in all you deign to do,
Be liberal, but be sparing too.
When sly sir Toby, night by night,
With his dear bags regales his sight ;
And conscience, reason, pity sleep,
Tho' virtue pine, tho' merit weep ;
I see the keen reproaches fly
Indignant from your honest eye ;
Each bounteous wish glows unconfin'd,
And your breast labours to be kind.

At this warm hour, my lord, beware
The servile flatterer's specious snare,
The fawning sycophant, whose art
Marks the kind motions of the heart :
Each idle, each insidious knave,
That acts the graceful, wise, or brave.

With festive board, and social eye,
You've seen old Hospitality ;
Mounted astride the moss-grown wall,
The genius of the ancient hall.
So reverend, with such courtly glee,
He serv'd your noble ancestry ;
And turn'd the hinge of many a gate,
For Russel, Rous, Plantagenet.
No lying porter levied there
His dues on all imported ware ;
There, rang'd in rows, no liveried train
E'er begg'd their master's beef again ;
No flatterer's planetary face
Plied for a bottle, or a place ;
Toad-eating France, and fiddling Rome,
Kept their lean rascals starv'd at home.
" Thrice happy days !"
        In this, 'tis true,
Old times were better than the new ;
Yet some egregious faults you'll see
In ancient Hospitality.
See motley crowds, his roof beneath,
Put poor Society to death !
Priests, knights, and 'squires, debating wild,
On themes unworthy of a child ;
'Till the strange compliment commences,
To praise their host, and lose their senses.
Go then, my lord ! keep open hall ;
Proclaim your table free for all ;
Go, sacrifice your time, your wealth,
Your patience, liberty, and health,
To such a thought-renouncing crew,
Such foes to care—e'en care for you.
" Heav'ns ! and are these the plagues that wait
Around the hospitable gate ?—
Let tenfold iron bolt my door,
And the gaunt mastiff growl before ;
There, not one human creature nigh,
Save, dear sir Toby, you and I,
In cynic silence let us dwell ;
Ye plagues of social life, farewell !"

Displeases this?—The modern way,
Perhaps, may please—a public day.
" A public day ! detested name !
The farce of friendship and the shame.
Did ever social freedom come
Within the pale of drawing-room ?
See pictur'd round the formal crowd !
How nice, how just each attitude :
My lord approaches—what surprise !
The pictures speak, the pictures rise !
Thrice ten times told the same salute,
Once more the mimic forms are mute.
Meanwhile the envious rows between,
Distrust and Scandal walk unseen ;
Their poisons silently infuse,
'Till these suspect, and those abuse.
    " Far, far from these, in some lone shade,
Let me, in easy silence laid,
Where never fools, or slaves intrude,
Enjoy the sweets of solitude !"
    What ! quit the commerce of mankind !
Leave virtue, fame, and worth behind !
Who fly to solitary rest,
Are reason's savages at best.
    Though human life's extensive field
Wild weeds and vexing brambles yield ;
Behold her smiling vallies bear
Mellifluous fruits, and flowrets fair !
The crowds of folly you despise—
Associate with the good and wise ;
For virtue, rightly understood,
Is to be wise, and to be good.

## MONODY.
### 1759.

All scenes belov'd ! ah conscious shades,
    That wave these parent-vales along !
Ye bowers, where Fancy met the tuneful maids,
    Ye mountains, vocal with my Doric song,
    Teach your wild echoes to complain
In sighs of solemn woe, in broken sounds of pain.

    For her I mourn,
Now the cold tenant of the thoughtless urn—
    For her bewail these strains of woe,
    For her these filial sorrows flow,
Source of my life, that led my tender years,
    With all a parent's pious fears,
That nurs'd my infant thought, and taught my
    mind to grow.

    Careful, she mark'd each dangerous way,
    Where youth's unwary footsteps stray.
She taught the struggling passions to subside,
    Where sacred truth, and reason guide,
In virtue's glorious path to seek the realms of day.
    Lamented goodness ! yet I see
The fond affections melting in her eye :
    She bends its tearful orb on me,
And heaves the tender sigh:
    As thoughtful, she the toils surveys,
That crowd in life's perplexing maze,
    And for her children feels again
All, all that love can fear, and all that fear can
    feign.

    O best of parents ! let me pour
My sorrows o'er thy silent bed ;
    There early strew the vernal flower,
The parting tear at evening shed—

Alas ! are these the only meed
Of each kind thought, each virtuous deed,
These fruitless offerings that embalm the dead ?
Then, fairy-featur'd Hope, forbear—
    No more thy fond illusions spread :
Thy shadowy scenes dissolv'd in air,
    Thy visionary prospects fled ;
With her they fled, at whose lamented shrine
    Love, gratitude, and duty mingled tears,
Condemn'd each filial office to resign,
    Nor hopeful more to sooth her long declining
        years.

## TO MRS. ******,
IN TEARS FOR THE DEATH OF A FRIEND.    1762.

So feeble Nature weeps o'er Friendship's grave,
And mourns the rigour of that law she gave :
Yet, why not weep ? When in that grave expire
All Pembroke's elegance, all Waldegrave's fire.
No more those eyes in soft effulgence move,
No more that bosom feels the spark of love.
O'er those pale cheeks the drooping Graces
    mourn,
And Fancy tears her wild wreath o'er that urn.
There Hope at Heaven once cast a doubtful eye,
Content repin'd, and Patience stole a sigh.
Fair Friendship griev'd o'er ——'s sacred bier,
And Virtue wept, for **** dropt a tear.

## TO MRS. GILLMAN.

With sense enough for half your sex beside,
With just no more than necessary pride ;
With knowledge caught from Nature's living page,
Politely learn'd, and elegantly sage—
Alas ! how piteous, that in such a mind
So many foibles free reception find !
Can such a mind, ye gods ! admit disdain ?
Be partial, envious, covetous, and vain ?
Unwelcome truth ! to love, to blindness clear !
Yet, Gillman, hear it ;—while you blush to hear :
    That in your gentle breast disdain can dwell,
Let knavery, meanness, pride that feel it, tell !
With partial eye a friend's defects you see,
And look with kindness on my faults and me.
And does no envy that fair mind o'ershade ?
Does no short sigh for greater wealth invade ;
When silent merit wants the fostering meed,
And the warm wish suggests the virtuous deed ?
Fairly the charge of vanity you prove,
Vain of each virtue of the friends you love,
    What charms, what art of magic have conspir'd
Of power to make so many faults admir'd ?

## FRAGMENT OF A POEM WRITTEN AT CLARE-HALL ON THE KING'S ACCESSION.
### 1760.
* * * * * * * *

While every gale the voice of triumph brings,
And smiling Victory waves her purple wings ;

While earth and ocean yield their subject powers,
Neptune his waves and Cybele her towers ;
Yet will you deign the Muse's voice to hear,
And let her welcome greet a monarch's ear ?
Yes ; midst the toils of glory ill-repaid,
Oft has the monarch sought her soothing aid.
See Frederic court her in the rage of war,
Though rapid Vengeance urge his hostile car :
With her repos'd in philosophic rest,
The sage's sunshine smooths the warrior's breast.
  Whate'er Arcadian fancy feign'd of old
Of halcyon days, and minutes plum'd with gold ;
Whate'er adorn'd the wisest, gentlest reign,
From you she hopes—let not her hopes be vain!
Rise, ancient suns! advance, Pierian days!
Flow, Attic streams! and spring, Aonian bays :
Cam, down thy wave in brisker mazes glide,
And see new honours crown thy hoary side !
Thy osiers old see myrtle groves succeed !
And the green laurel meet the waving reed!
          * * * * * * *

### CÆSAR'S DREAM,

BEFORE HIS INVASION OF BRITAIN.

1758.

WHEN rough Helvetia's hardy sons obey,
And vanquish'd Belgia bows to Cæsar's sway
When, scarce-beheld, embattled nations fall,
The fierce Sicambrian, and the faithless Gaul ;
Tir'd Freedom leads her savage sons no more,
But flies, subdued, to Albion's utmost shore.
'Twas then, while stillness grasp'd the sleeping
        air,
And dewy slumbers seal'd the eye of care ;
Divine Ambition to her votary came :
Her left hand waving, bore the trump of Fame ;
Her right a regal sceptre seem'd to hold,
With gems far-blazing from the burnish'd gold.
And thus, " My son," the queen of glory said ;
" Immortal Cæsar, raise thy languid head.
Shall Night's dull chains the man of counsels
        bind ?
Or Morpheus rule the monarch of mankind ?
See worlds unvanquish'd yet await thy sword !
Barbaric lands, that scorn a Latian lord.   [sky,
See yon proud isle, whose mountains meet the
Thy foes encourage and thy power defy !
What, tho' by Nature's firmest bars secur'd,
By seas encircled, and with rocks immur'd,
Shall Cæsar shrink the greatest toils to brave,
Scale the high rock, or beat the maddening
        wave ?"
She spoke—her words the warrior's breast in-
flame
With rage indignant, and with conscious shame ;
Already beat, the swelling floods give way,
And the fell genii of the rocks obey :
Already shouts of triumph rend the skies,
And the thin rear of barbarous nations flies.
    Quick round their chief his active legions
        stand,
Dwell on his eye, and wait the waving hand.
The hero rose, majestically slow,
And look'd attention to the crowds below.
  " Romans and friends ! is there who seeks for
        rest,
By labours vanquish'd, and with wounds opprest?
VOL. XVI.

That respite Cæsar shall with pleasure yield,
Due to the toils of many a well-fought field.
Is there who shrinks at thought of dangers past,
The ragged mountain, or the pathless waste—
While savage hosts, or savage floods oppose,
Or shivering fancy pines in Alpine snows ?
Let him retire to Latium's peaceful shore ;
He once has toil'd, and Cæsar asks no more.
Is there a Roman, whose unshaken breast
No pains have conquer'd, and no fears deprest ?
Who, doom'd through Death's dread ministers
        to go,
Dares to chastise the insults of a foe ;
Let him, his country's glory and her stay,
With reverence hear her, and with pride obey.
A form divine, in heavenly splendour bright,
Whose look threw radiance round the pall of
        night,
With calm severity approach'd and said,
Wake thy dull ear, and lift thy languid head.
What ! shall a Roman sink in soft repose,
And tamely see the Britons aid his foes ?
See them secure the rebel Gaul supply ;
Spurn his vain eagles and his power defy ?
Go ! burst their barriers, obstinately brave ;
Scale the wild rock, and beat the maddening
        wave."
  Here paus'd the chief ; but waited no reply,
The voice assenting spoke from every eye :
Nor, as the kindness that reproach'd with fear,
Were dangers dreadful, or were toils severe.

### INSCRIPTION IN A TEMPLE OF SOCIETY.

SACRED rise these walls to thee,
Blithe-eyed nymph, Society !
In whose dwelling, free and fair,
Converse smoothes the brow of Care.
Who, when waggish Wit betray'd
To his arms a sylvan maid,
All beneath a myrtle tree,
In some vale of Arcady,
Sprung, I ween, from such embrace,
The lovely contrast in her face.
  Perchance, the Muses as they stray'd,
Seeking other spring, or shade,
On the sweet child cast an eye
In some vale of Arcady ;
And blithest of the sisters three,
Gave her to Euphrosyne.
  The Grace, delighted, taught her care
The cordial smile, the placid air ;
How to chase, and how restrain
All the fleet, ideal train ;
How with apt words well-combin'd,
To dress each image of the mind—
Taught her how they disagree,
Awkward fear and modesty,
And freedom and rusticity.
True politeness how to know
From the superficial show ;
From the coxcomb's shallow grace,
And the many-modell'd face.
That Nature's unaffected ease
More than studied forms would please—
When to check the sportive vein ;
When to Fancy yield the rein ;
                                F f

On the subject when to be
Grave or gay, reserv'd or free :
The speaking air, th' impassion'd eye,
The living soul of symmetry ;
And that soft sympathy which binds
In magic chains congenial minds.

## INSCRIPTION IN A SEQUESTERED GROTTO.

### 1763.

Sweet Peace, that lov'st the silent hour,
　The still retreat of leisure free ;
Associate of each gentle power,
　And eldest born of Harmony !

O, if thou own'st this mossy cell,
　If thine this mansion of repose ;
Permit me, nymph, with thee to dwell,
　With thee my wakeful eye to close.

And tho' those glittering scenes should fade,
　That Pleasure's rosy train prepares;
What vot'ry have they not betray'd ?
　What are they more than splendid cares ?

But smiling days, exempt from care,
　But nights, when sleep, and silence reign ;
Serenity, with aspect fair,
　And love and joy are in thy train.

### ANOTHER INSCRIPTION IN THE SAME GROTTO.

### 1756.

O fairest of the village-born,
　Content, inspire my careless lay !
Let no vain wish, no thought forlorn
　Throw darkness o'er the smiling day.

Forget'st thou, when we wander'd o'er
　The sylvan Beleau's[1] sedgy shore,
Or rang'd the woodland wilds along ;
　How oft on Herclay's[2] mountains high
We've met the Morning's purple eye,
　Delay'd by many a song ?

From thee, from those by fortune led ;
　To all the farce of life confin'd ;
At once each native pleasure fled,
　For thou, sweet nymph, wast left behind.

Yet could I once, once more survey
Thy comely form in mantle grey,
　Thy polish'd brow, thy peaceful eye ;
Where e'er, forsaken fair, you dwell,
Though e'er in this dim sequester'd cell,
　With thee I'd live and die.

### LEFT WITH THE MINISTER OF RIPONDEN, A RO-MANTIC VILLAGE IN YORKSHIRE. 1758.

Thrice happy you, whoe'er you are,
From life's low cares secluded far,
　In this sequester'd vale !—
Ye rocks on precipices pil'd !
Ye ragged desarts, waste and wild !
　Delightful horrours, hail !

What joy within these sunless groves,
Where lonely Contemplation roves,

[1] A small river in Westmorland.

[2] A romantic village in the above mentioned county, formerly the seat of the Herclays, earls of Carlisle.

To rest in fearless ease !
Save weeping rills, to see no tear,
Save dying gales, no sigh to hear,
　No murmur, but the breeze.

Say, would you change that peaceful cell,
Where Sanctity and Silence dwell,
　For Splendor's dazzling blaze ?
For all those gilded toys that glare
Round high-born Power's imperial chair,
　Inviting fools to gaze ?

Ah friend ! Ambition's prospects close,
And, studious of your own repose,
　Be thankful here to live:
For, trust me, one protecting shed,
And nightly peace, and daily bread
　Is all that life can give.

## WRITTEN AMONG THE RUINS OF PONTEFRACT CASTLE.

### 1756.

Right sung the bard, that all-involving age
　With hand impartial deals the ruthless blow ;
That war, wide-wasting with impetuous rage,
　Lays the tall spire and sky-crown'd turret low.

A pile stupendous, once of fair renown,
　This mould'ring mass of shapeless ruin rose,
Where nodding heights of fractur'd columns frown,
　And birds obscene in ivy-bow'rs repose :

Oft the pale matron from the threat'ning wall,
　Suspicious, bids her heedless children fly ;
Oft, as he views the meditated fall,
　Full swiftly steps the frighted peasant by.

But more respectful views th' historic sage,
　Musing, these awful relics of decay,
That once a refuge form'd from hostile rage,
　In Henry's and in Edward's dubious day.

He pensive oft reviews the mighty dead,
　That erst have trod this desolated ground;
Reflects how here unhappy Sal'sbury bled,
　When Faction aim'd the death-dispensing wound.

Rest, gentle Rivers ! and ill-fated Gray !
　A flow'r or tear oft strews your humble grave,
Whom Envy slew, to pave Ambition's way,
　And whom a monarch wept in vain to save.

Ah ! what avail'd th' alliance of a throne ?
　The pomp of titles what, or pow'r rever'd ?
Happier to these the humble life unknown,
　With virtue honour'd, and by peace endear'd.

Had thus the sons of bleeding Britain thought,
　When hapless here inglorious Richard lay,
Yet many a prince, whose blood full dearly bought
　The shameful triumph of the long-fought day ;

Yet many a hero, whose defeated hand
　In death resign'd the well-contested field,
Had in his offspring sav'd a sinking land,
　The tyrant's terrour, and the nation's shield.

Ill could the Muse indignant grief forbear,
　Should Mem'ry trace her bleeding country's woes,
Ill could she count, without a bursting tear, [woes,
　Th' inglorious triumphs of the vary'd Rose !

While York, with conquest and revenge elate,
Insulting, triumphs on St. Alban's plain,
Who views, nor pities Henry's hapless fate,
Himself a captive, and his leaders slain?

Ah prince! unequal to the toils of war,
To stem ambition, faction's rage to quell;
Happier, from these had Fortune plac'd thee far,
In some lone convent, or some peaceful cell.

For what avail'd that thy victorious queen
Repair'd the ruins of that dreadful day; [green,
That vanquish'd York, on Wakefield's purple
Prostrate amidst the common slaughter lay:

In vain fair Vict'ry beam'd the gladd'ning eye,
And, waving oft her golden pinions, smil'd;
Full soon the flatt'ring goddess meant to fly,
Full rightly deem'd unsteady Fortune's child.

Let Towton's field—but cease the dismal tale:
For much its horrours would the Muse appal,
In softer strains suffice it to bewail
The patriot's exile, or the hero's fall.

Thus, silver Wharf[1], whose crystal-sparkling urn
Reflects the brilliance of his blooming shore,
Still, melancholy-mazing, seems to mourn,
But rolls, confus'd, a crimson wave no more.

## THE VICEROY:

ADDRESSED TO THE EARL OF HALIFAX[2].

FIRST PUBLISHED IN 1762.

'Twas on Time's birth-day, when the voice divine
Wak'd sleeping Nature, while her infant eye,
Yet trembling, struggl'd with created light;
The heaven-born Muse, sprung from the source
sublime

[1] A river near the field of battle, in which were slain 35,000 men.

[2] The following resolution of the Irish house of commons respecting the revenue of the lord lieutenant, and his excellency's speech in consequence thereof, will both illustrate this poem and show the occasion of it.

Copy of a resolution of the Irish parliament, respecting the revenue of the lord lieutenant.

Veneris, 26 Feb. 1762.

" Resolved, _nemine contradicente_, That an address be presented to his excellency the lord lieutenant, that he will represent to his majesty the sense of this house, that the entertainments and appointments of the lord lieutenant of Ireland are become inadequate to the dignity of that high office, and to the expense with which it is, and ought to be supported; and that it is the humble desire of this house, that his majesty will be graciously pleased to grant such an augmentation to the entertainment of the lord lieutenant for the time being, as, with the present allowances, will in the whole amount to the annual sum of sixteen thousand pounds. And to express that satisfaction which we feel at the pleasing hope, that this just and necessary augmentation should take place during the administration of a chief governor, whose many great and amiable qualities, whose wise and happy administration in the government of this kingdom, have universally endeared him to the people of Ireland. "

E. STERLING, }
H. ALCOCK, } Cler. Dom. Com.

Of Harmony immortal, first receiv'd
Her sacred mandate. " Go, seraphic maid,
Companion still to Nature; from her works
Derive thy lay melodious, great, like those,

Copy of the answer of the lord lieutenant to the address of the house of commons, Feb. 27, 1762.

" I shall take the first opportunity of laying before his majesty the sense of the house of commons contained in this address. I enter fully into the truly liberal motives which have influenced your conduct in this unanimous resolution. That you are solicitous not only to support his majesty's government, but to support it with becoming grandeur and magnificence, reflects the highest honour on yourselves : that you have chosen the time of my administration; that you have distinguish'd my person as the object of your favour, reflects the highest honour on me ; and I must ever consider this event as one of the most fortunate and honourable circumstances of my life. Whatever merit you ascribe to me in the government of this kingdom, in reality arises from your own conduct, though your partiality would transfer it to mine. Your unanimity has first created this merit, and your liberality would now reward it.

" I am sensible of the obligation you confer ; and I can in no way properly demonstrate my sense of it, but by being, as I am, unalterably determined to implore his majesty, that I may be permitted to enjoy it pure and unmixed with the lucrative advantages which you propose should attend it. This affectionate address is intended as an honour to me; that intention has, on your part, been fully answered: to make it truly honourable, something is still necessary on mine : it becomes me to vie with the generosity of parliament, and to keep up an emulation of sentiment. It has been my duty, in the course of this session, to propose large plans of public expense, and to promise an attention to public economy ; and I could not without pain submit, that the establishment, already burthened at my recommendation, should be still further charged for my own particular profit.

" But while I consider myself at liberty to sacrifice my private interests to my private feelings, I must consider myself as bound likewise to consult, in compliance with your enlarged and liberal sentiments, the future support of the station in which I am placed, to the dignity of which the emoluments are, as you represent them, inadequate. I shall transmit therefore the sense of the house of commons, that the augmentation which your generosity has proposed, may, if his majesty shall think fit, be made the establishment of my successor, when he shall enter on the government of this kingdom; and when it is probable the circumstances of this country may be better able to support such additional burthen. But while I must decline accepting any part of the profits, I rejoice to charge myself with the whole of the obligation; abundantly happy, if, when I shall hereafter be removed from this high, and, through your favour, desireable situation, I should leave it, through your liberality, augmented in its emoluments, and by my inability not diminished in its reputation,"

And elegantly simple. In thy train,
Glory, and fair Renown, and deathless Fame
Attendant ever, each immortal name,
By thee deem'd sacred, to yon starry vault
Shall bear, and stamp in characters of gold.
Be thine the care, alone where truth directs
The firm heart, where the love of human kind
Inflames the patriot spirit, there to soothe
The toils of Virtue with melodious praise :
For those, that smiling seraph bids thee wake
His golden lyre ; for those, the young-ey'd Sun
Gilds this fair-form'd world ; and genial Spring
Throws many a green wreath liberal from his
    bosom."
So spake the voice divine, whose last sweet sound
Gave birth to Echo, tuneful nymph, that loves
The Muse's haunt, dim grove, or lonely dale,
Or high wood old ; and, listening while she sings,
Dwells in long rapture on each falling strain.
   O Halifax! an humble Muse, that dwells
In scenes like these, a stranger to the world,
To thee a stranger, late has learnt thy fame,
Even in this vale of silence ; from the voice
Of Echo learnt it, and, like her, delights,
With thy lov'd name, to make these wild woods
    vocal.
   Spirits of ancient time, to high renown
By martial glory rais'd, and deeds august,
Achiev'd for Britain's freedom ! patriot hearts,
That, fearless of a tyrant's threatening arm,
Embrac'd your bleeding country ! o'er the page,
Where History triumphs in your holy names,
O'er the dim monuments that mark your graves,
Why streams my eye with pleasure ? 'Tis the joy
The soft delight that through the full breast flows,
From sweet rememb'rance of departed virtue !
   O Britain, parent of illustrious names,
While o'er thy annals Memory shoots her eye,
How the heart glows, rapt with high-wondering
    love,
And emulous esteem!—Hail, Sydney, hail !
Whether Arcadian blythe, by fountain clear,
Piping thy love-lays wild, or Spartan bold,
In Freedom's van distinguish'd, Sydney hail !
Oft o'er thy laurell'd tomb from hands unseen
Fall flowers ; oft in the vales of Penshurst fair,
Menalca, stepping from his evening fold,
Listeneth strange music, from the tiny breath
Of fairy minstrels warbled, which of old,
Dancing to thy sweet lays, they learned well.
   On Raleigh's grave, O strew the sweetest
    flowers
That on the bosom of the green vale blow !
There hang your vernal wreaths, ye village-
    maids !              [bring
Ye mountain nymphs, your crowns of wild thyme
To Raleigh's honour'd grave ! There bloom the
The virgin rose, that, blushing to be seen, [bay,
Folds its fair leaves ; for modest worth was his;
A mind where Truth, Philosophy's first born,
Held her harmonious reign : a Britain's breast,
That, careful still of Freedom's holy pledge,
Disdain'd the mean arts of a tyrant's court,
Disdain'd and died ! Where was thy spirit then,
Queen of sea-crowning isles, when Raleigh bled ?
How well he serv'd thee, let Iberia tell !
Ask prostrate Cales, yet trembling at his name,
How well he serv'd thee: when her vanquish'd
    hand

Held forth the base bribe, how he spurn'd it from
And cried, I fight for Britain ! History rise,[him
And blast the reigns that redden with the blood
Of those that gave them glory ! Happier days,
Gilt with a Brunswick's parent smile, await,
The honour'd Viceroy. More auspicious hours
Shall Halifax behold, nor grieve to find
A favour'd land ungrateful to his care.
   O for the Muse of Milton, to record
The honours of that day, when full conven'd
Hibernia's senate with one voice proclaim'd
A nation's high applause ; when, long opprest
With wealth-consuming war, their eager love
Advanc'd the princely dignity's support,
While Halifax presided ! O, belov'd
By every Muse, grace of the polish'd court,
The peasant's guardian, then what pleasure felt
Thy liberal bosom ! not the low delight
Of Fortune's added gifts, greatly declin'd ;
No, 'twas the supreme bliss that fills the breast
Of conscious Virtue, happy to behold
Her cares successful in a nation's joy.
   But O, ye sisters of the sacred spring,
To sweetest accents tune the polish'd lay,
The music of persuasion ! You alone
Can paint that easy eloquence that flow'd
In Attic streams, from Halifax that flow'd,
When all Ierne listen'd. Albion heard,
And felt a parent's joy : " No more," she cried,
" No more shall Greece the man of Athens boast,
Whose magic periods smooth'd the listening
    wave
Of rapt Ilyssus. Rome shall claim no more
The flowery path of eloquence alone
To grace her consul's brow; for never spoke
Himeria's Viceroy words of fairer phrase,
Forgetful of Alpheus' hastening stream,
When Arethusa stop'd her golden tide, [swains,
Aud call'd her nymphs, and call'd her shepherd
To leave their sweet pipes silent. Silent lay
Your pipes, Hibernian Shepherds." Liffey smil'd.
And on his soft hand lean'd his dimply cheek,
Attentive : " Once so Wharton spoke," he
    cried,
" Unhappy Wharton, whose young eloquence
Yet vibrates on mine ear." Whatever powers,
Whatever genii old, of vale or grove
The high inhabitants, all throng'd to hear.
Sylvanus came, and from his temples grey
His oaken chapled flung, lest haply leaf
Or interposing bough should meet the sound,
And bar its soft approaches to his ear,
Pan ceas'd to pipe—a moment ceas'd—for then
Suspicion grew, that Phoebus in disguise
His ancient reign invaded : down he cast,
In petulance, his reed ; but seiz'd it anon
And fill'd the woods with clangour. Measures wild
The wanton Satyrs danc'd, then listening stood,
And gaz'd with uncouth joy.
   But hark ! wild riots shake the peaceful plain,
The gathering tumult rears, and Faction opes
Her blood-requesting eye. The frighted swain
Mourns o'er his wasted labours, and implores
His country's guardian. Previous to his wish
That guardian's care he found. The tumult
    ceas'd,
And Faction clos'd her blood-requesting eye.
   Be these thy honours, Halifax ! and these
The liberal Muse, that never stain'd her page

With flattery, shall record : from each low view,
Each mean connection free, her praise is fame.
O, could her hand in future times obtain
One humble garland from th' Aonian tree,
With joy she'd bind it on thy favour'd head,
And greet thy judging ear with sweeter strains!
  Mean while pursue, in public virtue's path,
The palm of glory: only there will bloom
Pierian laurels. Should'st thou deviate thence,
Perish the blossoms of fair folding fame!
Ev'n this poor wreath, that now affects thy brow,
Would lose its little bloom, the Muse repine,
And blush that Halifax had stole her praise.

---

## PRECEPTS OF CONJUGAL HAPPI-NESS.

Friend, sister, partner of that gentle heart
Where my soul lives, and holds her dearest part ;
While love's soft raptures these gay hours em-
  ploy,
And Time puts on the yellow robe of Joy ;
Will you, Maria, mark with patient ear
The moral Muse, nor deem her song severe ?
  Through the long course of life's unclouded
  day,
Where sweet Contentment smiles on Virtue's way;
Where Fancy opes her ever-varying views,
And Hope strews flowers, and leads you as she
  strews ;
May each fair pleasure court thy favour'd breast,
By truth protected, and by love caress'd !
  So Friendship vows, nor shall her vows be vain;
For every pleasure comes in Virtue's train ;
Each charm that tender sympathies impart,
The glow of soul, the transports of the heart,
Sweet meanings, that in silent truth convey
'Mind into mind, and steal the soul away;
These gifts, O Virtue, these are all thy own ;
Lost to the vicious, to the vain unknown !
  Yet blest with these, and happier charms than
  these,
By Nature form'd, by genius taught to please,
E'en you, to prove that mortal gifts are vain,
Must yield your human sacrifice to pain ;
The wizard Care shall dim those brilliant eyes,
Smite the fair urns, and bid the waters rise.
  With mind unbroke that darker hour to bear,
Nor, once his captive, drag the chains of Care,
Hope's radiant sun-shine o'er the scene to pour,
Nor future joys in present ills devour,
These arts your philosophic friend may show,
Too well experienced in the school of woe.
  In some sad hour, by transient grief opprest,
Ah ! let not vain reflection wound your breast ;
For Memory then, to happier objects blind,
Though once the friend, the traitor of the mind,
Life's varied sorrows studious to explore,
Turns the sad volume of its sufferings o'er.
  Still to the distant prospect stretch your eye,
Pass the dim cloud, and view the brightening sky,
On Hope's kind wing, more genial climes survey,
Let Fancy join, but Reason guide your way ;
For Fancy, still to tender woes inclin'd
May sooth the heart, but misdirects the mind.
  The source of half our anguish, half our tears,
Is the wrong conduct of our hopes and fears ;

Like ill-train'd children, still their treatment such,
Restrain'd too rashly, or indulg'd too much.
Hence Hope, projecting more than life can give,
Would live with angels, or refuse to live ;
Hence spleen-ey'd Fear, o'er-acting Caution's
  part,
Betrays those succours Reason lends the heart.
Yet these, submitted to fair Truth's coutroul,
These tyrants are the servants of the soul ;
Through vales of peace the dove-like Hope shall
  stray
And bear at eve her olive branch away,
In every scene some distant charm descry,
And hold it forward to the brightening eye ;
While watchful Fear, if Fortitude maintain
Her trembling steps, shall ward the distant pain.
  Should erring Nature casual faults disclose,
Wound not the breast that harbours your repose :
For every grief that breast from you shall prove,
Is one link broken in the chain of love.
Soon, with their objects, other woes are past,
But pains from those we love are pains that last.
Though faults or follies from reproach may fly,
Yet in its shade the tender passions die.
  Love, like the flower that courts the Sun's
  kind ray,
Will flourish only in the smiles of day ;
Distrust's cold air the generous plant annoys,
And one chill blight of dire contempt destroys.
O shun, my friend, avoid that dangerous coast,
Where peace expires; and fair affection's lost ;
By wit, by grief, by anger urg'd, forbear
The speech contemptuous, and the scornful air.
  If heart-felt quiet, thoughts unmix'd with pain,
While Peace weaves flowers o'er Hymen's golden
  chain,
If tranquil days, if hours of smiling ease,
The sense of pleasure, and the power to please,
If charms like these deserve your serious care,
Of one dark foe, one dangerous foe beware !
Like Hecla's mountain, while his heart's in flame,
His aspect's cold,—and Jealousy's his name.
His hideous birth his wild disorders prove,
Begot by Hatred on despairing Love !
Her throes in rage the frantic mother bore,
And the fell sire with angry curses tore
His sable hair.—Distrust beholding smil'd,
And lov'd her image in her future child.
With cruel care, industrious to impart
Each painful sense, each soul-tormenting art,
To Doubt's dim shrine her hapless charge she led,
Where never sleep reliev'd the burning head,
Where never grateful fancy sooth'd suspense,
Or the sweet charm of easy confidence.
Hence fears eternal, ever-restless care,
And all the dire associates of despair.
Hence all the woes he found that peace destroy,
And dash with pain the sparkling stream of joy.
  When love's warm breast, from rapture's
  trembling height,
Falls to the temperate measures of delight ;
When calm delight to easy friendship turns,
Grieve not that Hymen's torch more gently burns.
Unerring Nature, in each purpose kind,
Forbids long transports to usurp the mind :
For, oft dissolv'd in joy's oppressive ray,
Soon would the finer faculties decay.
  True tender love one even tenour keeps ;
'Tis reason's flame, and burns when passion sleeps.

The charm connubial, like a stream that glides
Through life's fair vale, with no unequal tides,
With many a plant along its genial side,
With many a flower that blows in beauteous pride,
With many a shade, where Peace in rapturous
Holds sweet Affiance to her fearless breast, [rest
Pure in its source, and temperate in its way,
Still flows the same, nor find its urn decay.
  O bliss beyond what lonely life can know,
The soul-felt sympathy of joy and woe!
That magic charm which makes e'en sorrow dear,
And turns to pleasure the partaken tear!
  Long, beauteous friend, to you may Heaven im-
The soft endearments of the social heart! [part
Long to your lot may every blessing flow,
That sense, or taste, or virtue can bestow!
And oh, forgive the zeal your peace inspires,
To teach that prudence which itself admires.

## OWEN OF CARRON.

There is something romantic in the story of the following poem; but the author has his reasons for believing that there is something likewise authentic. On the simple circumstances of the ancient narrative, from which he first borrowed his idea, those reasons are principally founded; and they are supported by others, with which, in a work of this kind, to trouble his readers would be superfluous.

This poem is inscribed to a lady, whose elegant taste, whose amiable sensibility, and whose unaffected friendship, have long contributed to the pleasure and happiness of

THE AUTHOR.

On Carron's side the primrose pale,
  Why does it wear a purple hue?
Ye maidens fair of Marlivale,
  Why stream your eyes with pity's dew?

'Tis all with gentle Owen's blood
  That purple grows the primrose pale;
That pity pours the tender flood
  From each fair eye in Marlivale.

The evening star sate in his eye,
  The Sun his golden tresses gave,
The North's pure morn her orient dye,
  To him who rests in yonder grave!

Beneath no high, historic stone,
  Tho' nobly born, is Owen laid,
Stretch'd on the green wood's lap alone,
  He sleeps beneath the waving shade.

There many a flowery race hath sprung,
  And fled before the mountain gale,
Since first his simple dirge ye sung,
  Ye maidens fair of Marlivale!

Yet still, when May with fragrant feet
  Hath wander'd o'er your meads of gold,
That dirge I hear so simply sweet
  Far echoed from each evening fold.

'Twas in the pride of William's [1] day,
  When Scotland's honours flourish'd still,
The Moray's earl, with mighty sway,
  Bore rule o'er many a Highland hill.

[1] William the Lion, king of Scotland.

And far for him their fruitful store
  The fairer plains of Carron spread;
In fortune rich, in offspring poor,
  An only daughter crown'd his bed.

Oh! write not poor—the wealth that flows,
  In waves of gold round India's throne,
All in her shining breast that glows,
  To Ellen's [2] charms, were earth and stone.

For her the youth of Scotland sigh'd,
  The Frenchman gay, the Spaniard grave,
And smoother Italy apply'd,
  And many an English baron brave.

In vain by foreign arts assail'd,
  No foreign loves her breast beguile,
And England's honest valour fail'd,
  Paid with a cold, but courteous smile.

"Ah! woe to thee, young Nithisdale,
  That o'er thy cheek those roses stray'd,
Thy breath, the violet of the vale,
  Thy voice, the music of the shade!

"Ah! woe to thee, that Ellen's love
  Alone to thy soft tale would yield!
For soon those gentle arms shall prove
  The conflict of a ruder field."

'Twas thus a wayward sister spoke,
  And cast a rueful glance behind,
As from her dim wood glen she broke,
  And mounted on the moaning wind.

She spoke and vanish'd—more unmov'd
  Than Moray's rocks, when storms invest,
The valiant youth, by Ellen lov'd,
  With aught that fear or fate suggest.

For Love, methinks, hath power to raise
  The soul beyond a vulgar state;
Th' unconquer'd banners he displays
  Control our fears, and fix our fate.

'Twas when, on summer's softest eve,
  Of clouds that wander'd west away,
Twilight with gentle hand did weave
  Her fairy robe of night and day;

When all the mountain gales were still,
  And the wave slept against the shore,
And the Sun, sunk beneath the hill,
  Left his last smile on Lemmermore [3];

Led by those waking dreams of thought
  That warm the young unpractis'd breast,
Her wonted bower sweet Ellen sought,
  And Carron murmur'd near, and sooth'd her
    into rest.

There is some kind and courtly sprite
  That o'er the realm of Fancy reigns,
Throws sunshine on the mask of night,
  And smiles at slumber's powerless chains;

[2] The lady Ellen, only daughter of John earl of Moray, betrothed to the earl of Nithisdale, and afterwards to the earl Barnard, was esteemed one of the finest women in Europe, insomuch that she had several suitors and admirers from foreign courts.

[3] A chain of mountains running through Scotland from east to west.

'Tis told, and I believe the tale,
  At this soft hour that sprite was there,
And spread with fairer flowers the vale,
  And fill'd with sweeter sounds the air.

A bower he fram'd (for he could frame
  What long might weary mortal wight:
Swift as the lightning's rapid flame
  Darts on the unsuspecting sight);

Such bower he fram'd with magic hand,
  As well that wizard bard hath wove,
In scenes where fair Armida's wand
  Wav'd all the witcheries of love:

Yet it was wrought in simple show;
  Nor Indian mines nor orient shores
Had lent their glories here to glow,
  Or yielded here their shining stores.

All round a poplar's trembling arms
  The wild rose wound her damask flower;
The woodbine lent her spicy charms,
  That loves to weave the lover's bower.

The ash, that courts the mountain-air,
  In all her painted blooms array'd,
The wilding's blossom blushing fair,
  Combin'd to form the flowery shade.

With thyme that loves the brown hill's breast,
  The cowslip's sweet reclining head,
The violet of sky-woven vest,
  Was all the fairy ground bespread.

But who is he, whose locks so fair
  Adown his manly shoulders flow?
Beside him lies the hunter's spear,
  Beside him sleeps the warrior's bow.

He bends to Ellen—(gentle sprite,
  Thy sweet seductive arts forbear)—
He courts her arms with fond delight,
  And instant vanishes in air.

Hast thou not found at early dawn
  Some soft ideas melt away,
If o'er sweet vale, or flowery lawn,
  The sprite of dreams hath bid thee stray?

Hast thou not some fair object seen,
  And, when the fleeting form was past,
Still on thy memory found its mien,
  And felt the fond idea last?

Thou hast—and oft the pictur'd view,
  Seen in some vision counted vain,
Hast struck thy wondering eye anew,
  And brought the long-lost dream again.

With warrior-bow, with hunter's spear,
  With locks adown his shoulders spread,
Young Nithisdale is ranging near—
  He's ranging near yon mountain's head.

Scarce had one pale Moon pass'd away,
  And fill'd her silver urn again,
When in the devious chase to stray,
  Afar from all his woodland train,

To Carron's banks his fate consign'd;
  And, all to shun the fervid hour,
He sought some friendly shade to find,
  And found the visionary bower.

Led by the golden star of love,
  Sweet Ellen took her wonted way,
And in the deep-defending grove
  Sought refuge from the fervid day—

Oh!—who is he whose ringlets fair
  Disorder'd o'er his green vest flow,
Reclin'd in rest—whose sunny hair
  Half hides the fair cheek's ardent glow?

'Tis he, that sprite's illusive guest,
  (Ah me! that sprites can fate control!)
That lives still imag'd on her breast,
  That lives still pictur'd in her soul.

As when some gentle spirit fled
  From Earth to breathe elysian air,
And, in the train whom we call dead,
  Perceives its long-lov'd partner there;

Soft, sudden pleasure rushes o'er,
  Resistless, o'er its airy frame,
To find its future fate restore
  The object of its former flame:

So Ellen stood—less power to move
  Had he, who, bound in Slumber's chain,
Seem'd hap'ly o'er his hills to rove,
  And wind his woodland chase again.

She stood, but trembled—mingled fear,
  And fond delight, and melting love,
Seiz'd all her soul—she came not near,
  She came not near that fated grove.

She strives to fly—from wizzard's wand
  As well might powerless captive fly—
The new-cropt flower falls from her hand—
  Ah! fall not with that flower to die!

Hast thou not seen some azure gleam
  Smile in the Morning's orient eye,
And skirt the reddening cloud's soft beam,
  What time the Sun was hasting nigh?

Thou hast—and thou canst fancy well
  As any Muse that meets thine ear,
The soul-set eye of Nithisdale,
  When, wak'd, it fix'd on Ellen near.

Silent they gaz'd—that silence broke;
  " Hail goddess of these groves," he cry'd,
" O let me wear thy gentle yoke!
  O let me in thy service bide!

" For thee I'll climb the mountain steep,
  Unwearied chase the destin'd prey;
For thee I'll pierce the wild-wood deep,
  And part the sprays that vex thy way.

" For thee"—" O stranger, cease," she said,
  And swift away, like Daphne, flew;
But Daphne's flight was not delay'd
  By aught that to her bosom grew.

'Twas Atalanta's golden fruit,
  The fond idea that confin'd
Fair Ellen's steps, and bless'd his suit,
  Who was not far, not far behind.

O Love! within those golden vales,
  Those genial airs where thou wast born,
Where Nature, listening thy soft tales,
  Leans on the rosy breast of Morn;

Where the sweet Smiles, the Graces dwell,
  And tender sighs the heart remove,
In silent eloquence to tell
  Thy tale, O soul-subduing Love!

Ah! wherefore should grim Rage be nigh,
  And dark Distrust, with changeful face,
And Jealousy's reverted eye
  Be near thy fair, thy favour'd place?

Earl Barnard was of high degree,
  And lord of many a lowland hind,
And long for Ellen love had he,
  Had love, but not of gentle kind.

From Moray's halls her absent hour
  He watch'd with all a miser's care ;
The wide domain, the princely dower
  Made Ellen more than Ellen fair.

Ah wretch ! to think the liberal soul
  May thus with fair affection part !
Though Lothian's vales thy sway control,
  Know, Lothian is not worth one heart.

Studious he marks her absent hour,
  And, winding far where Carron flows,
Sudden he sees the fated bower,
  And red rage on his dark brow glows.

For who is he ?—'Tis Nithisdale !
  And that fair form with arm reclin'd
On his ?—'Tis Ellen of the vale,
  'Tis she (O powers of vengeance !) kind.

Should he that vengeance swift pursue ?
  No—that would all his hopes destroy ;
Moray would vanish from his view,
  And rob him of a miser's joy.

Unseen to Moray's halls he hies—
  He calls his slaves, his ruffian band,
And, " Haste to yonder groves," he cries,
  " And ambush'd lie by Carron's strand.

" What time ye mark from bower or glen
  A gentle lady take her way,
To distance due, and far from ken,
  Allow her length of time to stray.

" Then ransack straight that range of groves,—
  With hunter's spear, and vest of green,
If chance, a rosy stripling roves,—
  Ye well can aim your arrows keen. "

And now the ruffian slaves are nigh,
  And Ellen takes her homeward way :
Though stay'd by many a tender sigh,
  She can no longer, longer stay.

Pensive, against yon poplar pale
  The lover leans his gentle heart,
Revolving many a tender tale,
  And wondering still how they could part.

Three arrows pierc'd the desert air,
  Ere yet his tender dreams depart ;
And one struck deep his forehead fair,
  And one went through his gentle heart.

Love's waking dream is lost in sleep—
  He lies beneath yon poplar pale ;
Ah ! could we marvel ye should weep,
  Ye maidens fair of Marlivale !

When all the mountain gales were still,
  And the wave slept against the shore,
And the Sun, sunk beneath the hill,
  Left his last smile on Lemmermore ;

Sweet Ellen takes her wonted way
  Along the fairy-featur'd vale ;
Bright o'er his wave does Carron play,
  And soon she'll meet her Nithisdale.

She'll meet him soon—for at her sight
  Swift as the mountain deer he sped ;
The evening shades will sink in night,—
  Where art thou, loitering lover, fled ?

O ! she will chide thy trifling stay,
  E'en now the soft reproach she frames :
" Can lovers brook such long delay ?
  Lovers that boast of ardent flames ! ' "

He comes not—weary with the chase,
  Soft Slumber o'er his eyelids throws
Her veil—we'll steal one dear embrace,
  We'll gently steal on his repose.

This is the bower—we'll softly tread—
  He sleeps beneath yon poplar pale—
Lover, if e'er thy heart has bled,
  Thy heart will far forego my tale !

Ellen is not in princely bower,
  She's not in Moray's splendid train ;
Their mistress dear, at midnight hour,
  Her weeping maidens seek in vain.

Her pillow swells not deep with down ;
  For her no balms their sweets exhale :
Her limbs are on the pale turf thrown,
  Press'd by her lovely cheek as pale.

On that fair cheek, that flowing hair,
  The broom its yellow leaf hath shed,
And the chill mountain's early air
  Blows wildly o'er her beauteous head.

As the soft star of orient day,
  When clouds involve his rosy light,
Darts thro' the gloom a transient ray,
  And leaves the world once more to night ;

Returning life illumes her eye,
  And slow its languid orb unfolds—
What are those bloody arrows nigh ?
  Sure, bloody arrows she beholds !

What was that form so ghastly pale,
  That low beneath the poplar lay ?—
'Twas some poor youth—" ah Nithisdale !"
  She said, and silent sunk away.

The morn is on the mountains spread,
  The wood-lark trills his liquid strain—
Can morn's sweet music rouse the dead,
  Give the set eye its soul again ?

A shepherd of that gentler mind
  Which Nature not profusely yields,
Seeks in these lonely shades to find
  Some wanderer from his little fields.

Aghast he stands—and simple fear
  O'er all his paly visage glides—
" Ah me ! what means this misery here,
  What fate this lady fair betides ?"

He bears her to his friendly home,
  When life, he finds, has but retir'd ;—
With haste he frames the lover's tomb,
  For his is quite, is quite expir'd !

" O hide me in my humble bower,"
  Returning late to life she said ;
" I'll bind thy crook with many a flower ;
  With many a rosy wreath thy head.

" Good shepherd, haste to yonder grove,
  And, if my love asleep is laid,
Oh ! wake him not ; but softly move
  Some pillow to that gentle head.

" Sure, thou wilt know him, shepherd swain,
  Thou know'st the sun-rise o'er the sea—
But oh ! no lamb in all thy train
  Was e'er so mild, so mild as he."

" His head is on the wood-moss laid ;
  I did not wake his slumber deep—
Sweet sings the redbreast o'er the shade—
  Why, gentle lady, would you weep ?"

As flowers that fade in burning day,
  At evening find the dew-drop dear,
But fiercer feel the noon-tide ray,
  When soften'd by the nightly tear ;

Returning in the flowing tear,
  This lovely flower, more sweet than they,
Found her fair soul, and, wandering near,
  The stranger, Reason, cross'd her way.

Found her fair soul—Ah ! so to find
  Was but more dreadful grief to know !
Ah ! sure the privilege of mind
  Can not be worth the wish of woe.

On melancholy's silent urn
  A softer shade of sorrow falls,
But Ellen can no more return,
  No more return to Moray's halls.

Beneath the low and lonely shade
  The slow, consuming hour she'll weep,
Till Nature seeks her last-left aid,
  In the sad, sombrous arms of Sleep.

" These jewels, all unmeet for me,
  Shalt thou," she said, " good shepherd, take ;
These gems will purchase gold for thee,
  And these be thine for Ellen's sake,

" So fail thou not, at eve and morn,
  The rosemary's pale bough to bring—
Thou know'st where I was found forlorn—
  Where thou hast heard the redbreast sing.

" Heedful I'll tend thy flocks the while,
  Or aid thy shepherdess's care,
For I will share her humble toil,
  And I her friendly roof will share. "

And now two longsome years are past
  In luxury of lonely pain—
The lovely mourner, found at last,
  To Moray's halls is borne again.

Yet has she left one object dear,
  That wears Love's sunny eye of joy—
Is Nithisdale reviving here ?
  Or is it but a shepherd's boy ?

By Carron's side, a shepherd's boy,
  He binds his vale-flowers with the reed ;
He wears Love's sunny eye of joy,
  And birth he little seems to heed.

But ah ! no more his infant sleep
  Closes beneath a mother's smile,
Who, only when it clos'd, would weep,
  And yield to tender woe the while.

No more, with fond attention dear,
  She seeks th' unspoken wish to find ;
No more shall she, with pleasure's tear,
  See the soul waxing into mind.

Does Nature bear a tyrant's breast ?
  Is she the friend of stern Controul ?
Wears she the despot's purple vest ?
  Or fetters she the free-born soul ?

Where, worst of tyrants, is thy claim
  In chains thy children's breasts to bind ?
Gav'st thou the Promethéan flame ?
  The incommunicable mind ?

Thy offspring are great Nature's—free,
  And of her fair dominion heirs ;
Each privilege she gives to thee ;
  Know, that each privilege is theirs.

They have thy feature, wear thine eye,
  Perhaps some feelings of thy heart ;
And wilt thou their lov'd hearts deny
  To act their fair, their proper part ?

The lord of Lothian's fertile vale,
  Ill-fated Ellen, claims thy hand ;
Thou know'st not that thy Nithisdale
  Was low laid by his ruffian-band.

And Moray, with unfather'd eyes,
  Fix'd on fair Lothian's fertile dale,
Attends his human sacrifice,
  Without the Grecian painter's veil.

O married Love ! thy bard shall own,
  Where two congenial souls unite,
Thy golden chain inlaid with down,
  Thy lamp with Heaven's own splendour bright ;

But if no radiant star of love,
  O Hymen ! smile on thy fair rite,
Thy chain a wretched weight shall prove,
  Thy lamp a sad sepulchral light.

And now has Time's slow wandering wing
  Borne many a year unmark'd with speed—
Where is the boy by Carron's spring,
  Who bound his vale-flowers with the reed ?

Ah me ! those flowers he binds no more ;
  No early charm returns again ;
The parent, Nature, keeps in store
  Her best joys for her little train.

No longer heed the sun-beam bright
  That plays on Carron's breast he can,
Reason has lent her quivering light,
  And shown the chequer'd field of man.

As the first human heir of Earth
  With pensive eye himself survey'd,
And, all unconscious of his birth,
  Sate thoughtful oft in Eden's shade ;

In pensive thought so Owen stray'd
  Wild Carron's lonely woods among,
And once, within their greenest glade,
  He fondly fram'd this simple song :

" Why is this crook adorn'd with gold ?
  Why am I tales of ladies told ?
Why does no labour me employ,
  If I am but a shepherd's boy ?

" A silken vest like mine so green
  In shepherd's hut I have not seen—
Why should I in such vesture joy,
  If I am but a shepherd's boy ?

" I know it is no shepherd's art
  His written meaning to impart—
They teach me, sure, an idle toy,
  If I am but a shepherd's boy.

" This bracelet bright that binds my arm—
  It could not come from sheperd's farm ;
It only would that arm annoy,
  If I were but a shepherd's boy.

" And O thou silent picture fair,
  That lov'st to smile upon me there,
O say, and fill my heart with joy,
  That I am not a shepherd's boy "

Ah, lovely youth! thy tender lay
  May not thy gentle life prolong:
See'st thou yon nightingale a prey?
  The fierce hawk hovering o'er his song?

His little heart is large with love:
  He sweetly hails his evening star,
And fate's more pointed arrows move,
  Insidious, from his eye afar.

The shepherdess, whose kindly care
  Had watch'd o'er Owen's infant breath,
Must now their silent mansions share,
  Whom time leads calmly down to death.

" O tell me, parent if thou art,
  What is this lovely picture dear?
Why wounds its mournful eye my heart?
  Why flows from mine th' unbidden tear?"

" Ah! youth! to leave thee loth am I,
  Tho' I be not thy parent dear;
And would'st thou wish, or ere I die,
  The story of thy birth to hear?

" But it will make thee much bewail,
  And it will make thy fair eye swell:"—
She said, and told the woesome tale,
  As sooth as sheperdess might tell.

The heart, that sorrow doom'd to share,
  Has worn the frequent seal of woe,
Its sad impressions learns to bear,
  And finds full oft its ruin slow.

But when that seal is first imprest,
  When the young heart its pain shall try,
From the soft, yielding, trembling breast,
  Oft seems the startled soul to fly:

Yet fled not Owen's—wild amaze
  In paleness cloth'd, and lifted hands,
And horrour's dread, unmeaning gaze,
  Mark the poor statue, as it stands.

The simple guardian of his life
  Look'd wistful for the tear to glide;
But when she saw his tearless strife,
  Silent, she lent him one,— and died.

" No, I am not a shepherd's boy,"
  Awaking from his dream, he said:
" Ah, where is now the promis'd joy
  Of this?—for ever, ever fled!

" O picture dear!—for her lov'd sake
  How fondly could my heart bewail!
My friendly shepherdess, O wake,
  And tell me more of this sad tale:

" O tell me more of this sad tale—
  No; thou enjoy thy gentle sleep!
And I will go to Lothian's vale,
  And more than all her waters weep. "

Owen to Lothian's vale is fled—
  Earl Barnard's lofty towers appear—
" O! art thou there," the full heart said,
  " O art thou there, my parent dear?"

Yes, she is there; from idle state
  Oft has she stole her hour to weep;
Think how she ' by thy cradle sate, '
  And how she ' fondly saw thee sleep'. '

Now tries his trembling hand to frame
  Full many a tender line of love;
And still he blots the parent's name,
  For that, he fears, might fatal prove.

O'er a fair fountain's smiling side
  Reclin'd a dim tower, clad with moss,
Where every bird was wont to bide,
  That languish'd for its partner's loss.

This scene he chose, this scene assign'd
  A parent's first embrace to wait,
And many a soft fear fill'd his mind,
  Anxious for his fond letter's fate.

The hand that bore those lines of love,
  The well-informing bracelet bore—
Ah! may they not unprosperous prove!
  Ah! safely pass yon dangerous door!

" She comes not ;—can she then delay! "
  Cried the fair youth, and dropt a tear—
" Whatever filial love could say,
  To her I said, and call'd her dear."

" She comes—Oh! no—encircled round
  'Tis some rude chief with many a spear,
My hapless tale that earl has found—
  Ah me! my heart!—for her I fear."

His tender tale that earl had read,
  Or ere it reach'd his lady's eye,
His dark brow wears a cloud of red,
  In rage he deems a rival nigh.

'Tis o'er—those locks that wav'd in gold,
  That wav'd adown those cheeks so fair,
Wreath'd in the gloomy tyrant's hold,
  Hang from the sever'd head in air!

That streaming head he joys to bear
  In horrid guise to Lothian's halls;
Bids his grim ruffians place it there,
  Erect upon the frowning walls.

The fatal tokens forth he drew—
  " Know'st thou these—Ellen of the vale?"
The pictur'd bracelet soon she knew,
  And soon her lovely cheek grew pale.

The trembling victim straight he led,
  Ere yet her soul's first fear was o'er:
He pointed to the ghastly head—
  She saw—and sunk to rise no more.

[1] See the ancient Scottish ballad, called Gill Morrice.

THE

# FABLES OF FLORA.

————Sylvas, saltusque sequamur
Intactos ————              Virg.

## FABLE I.

### THE SUN-FLOWER AND THE IVY.

As duteous to the place of prayer,
  Within the convent's lonely walls,
The holy sisters still repair,
  What time the rosy morning calls:

So fair, each morn, so full of grace,
  Within their little garden rear'd,
The flower of Phœbus turn'd her face
  To meet the power she lov'd and fear'd.

And where, along the rising sky,
  Her god in brighter glory burn'd,
Still there her fond observant eye,
  And there her golden breast she turn'd.

When calling from their weary height
  On western waves his beams to rest,
Still there she sought the parting sight,
  And there she turn'd her golden breast.

But soon as night's invidious shade
  Afar his lovely looks had borne,
With folded leaves and drooping head,
  Full sore she griev'd, as one forlorn.

Such duty in a flower display'd
  The holy sisters smil'd to see,
Forgave the pagan rites it paid,
  And lov'd its fond idolatry.

But painful still, though meant for kind,
  The praise that falls on Envy's ear,
O'er the dim window's arch entwin'd,
  The canker'd Ivy chanc'd to hear.

And "See," she cried, "that specious flower,
  Whose flattering bosom courts the Sun,
The pageant of a gilded hour,
  The convent's simple hearts hath won!

"Obsequious meanness! ever prone
  To watch the patron's turning eye;
No will, no motion of its own!
  'Tis this they love, for this they sigh:

"Go, splendid sycophant! no more
  Display thy soft seductive arts,
The flattering clime of courts explore,
  Nor spoil the convent's simple hearts.

"To me their praise more justly due,
  Of longer bloom, and happier grace!
Whom changing months unalter'd view,
  And find them in my fond embrace."

"How well," the modest flower replied,
  "Can Envy's wrested eye elude
The obvious bounds that still divide
  Foul Flattery from fair Gratitude.

"My duteous praise each hour I pay,
  For few the hours that I must live,
And give to him my little day,
  Whose grace another day may give.

"When low this golden form shall fall
  And spread with dust its parent plain;
That dust shall hear his genial call,
  And rise, to glory rise again.

"To thee, my gracious power, to thee
  My love, my heart, my life are due!
Thy goodness gave that life to be;
  Thy goodness shall that life renew.

"Ah me! one moment from thy sight
  That thus my truant-eye should stray!
The god of glory sets in night!
  His faithless flower has lost a day."

Sore griev'd the flower, and droop'd her head;
  And sudden tears her breast bedew'd:
Consenting tears the sisters shed,
  And, wrapt in holy wonder, view'd.

With joy, with pious pride elate,
  "Behold," the aged abbess cries,
"An emblem of that happier fate
  Which Heaven to all but us denies.

"Our hearts no fears but duteous fears,
  No charm but duty's charm can move?
We shed no tears but holy tears
  Of tender penitence and love.

"See there the envious world pourtray'd
  In that dark look, that creeping pace!
No flower can bear the Ivy's shade;
  No tree support its cold embrace.

"The oak that rears it from the ground,
  And bears its tendrils to the skies,
Feels at his heart the rankling wound,
  And in its poisonous arms he dies."

Her moral thus the matron read,
  Studious to teach her children dear,
And they by love, or duty led,
  With pleasure heard, or seem'd to hear.

Yet one less duteous, not less fair,
  (In convents still the tale is known)
The fable heard with silent care,
  But found a moral of her own.

The flower that smil'd along the day,
  And droop'd in tears at evening's fall;
Too well she found her life display,
  Too well her fatal lot recall.

The treacherous Ivy's gloomy shade,
  That murder'd what it most embrac'd,
Too well that cruel scene convey'd
  Which all her fairer hopes effac'd.

Her heart with silent horrour shook;
    With sighs she sought her lonely cell:
To the dim light she cast one look;
    And bade once more the world farewell.

---

## FABLE II.

### THE EVENING PRIMROSE.

THERE are that love the shades of life,
    And shun the splendid walks of fame;
There are that hold it rueful strife
    To risk ambition's losing game;

That far from Envy's lurid eye
    The fairest fruits of genius rear,
Content to see them bloom and die,
    In Friendship's small but kindly sphere.

Than vainer flowers tho' sweeter far,
    The evening Primrose shuns the day;
Blooms only to the western star,
    And loves its solitary ray.

In Eden's vale an aged hind,
    At the dim twilight's closing hour,
On his time-smoothed staff reclin'd,
    With wonder view'd the opening flower.

" Ill-fated flower, at eve to blow,"
    In pity's simple thought he cries,
"Thy bosom must not feel the glow
    Of splendid suns, or smiling skies.

" Nor thee, the vagrants of the field,
    The hamlet's little train behold;
Their eyes to sweet oppression yield,
    When thine the falling shades unfold.

" Nor thee the hasty shepherd heeds,
    When love has fill'd his heart with cares,
For flowers he rifles all the meads,
    For waking flowers—but thine forbears.

" Ah! waste no more that beauteous bloom
    On night's chill shade, that fragrant breath:
Let smiling suns those gems illume!
    Fair flower, to live unseen is death."

Soft as the voice of vernal gales
    That o'er the bending meadow blow,
Or streams that steal thro' even vales,
    And murmur that they move so slow:

Deep in her unfrequented bower,
    Sweet Philomela pour'd her strain;
The bird of eve approv'd her flower,
    And answered thus the anxious swain.

            " Live unseen!
By moonlight shades, in valleys green,
    Lovely flower, we'll live unseen.
Of our pleasures deem not lightly,
Laughing Day may look more sprightly,
    But I love the modest mien,
    Still I love the modest mien
Of gentle Evening. fair, and her star-train'd
        queen.

" Didst thou, shepherd, never find,
    Pleasure is of pensive kind?
Hast thy cottage never known
That she loves to live alone?
Dost thou not at evening hour
Feel some soft and secret power,

Gliding o'er thy yielding mind,
Leave sweet serenity behind,
While all disarm'd, the cares of day
Steal thro' the falling gloom away?
Love to think thy lot was laid
In this undistinguish'd shade.
Far from the world's infectious view,
Thy little virtues safely blew.
Go, and in day's more dangerous hour,
Guard thy emblematic flower."

---

## FABLE III.

### THE LAUREL AND THE REED.

THE reed [1] that once the shepherd blew
    On old Cephisus' hallow'd side,
To Sylla's cruel bow apply'd,
    Its inoffensive master slew.

Stay, bloody soldier, stay thy hand,
    Nor take the shepherd's gentle breath:
Thy rage let innocence withstand;
    Let music soothe the thirst of death.

He frown'd—he bade the arrow fly—
    The arrow smote the tuneful swain;
No more its tone his lip shall try,
    Nor wake its vocal soul again.

Cephisus, from his sedgy urn,
    With woe beheld the sanguine deed;
He mourn'd, and, as they heard him mourn,
    Assenting sigh'd each trembling reed.

" Fair offspring of my waves," he cried;
    " That bind my brows, my banks adorn,
Pride of the plains, the river's pride,
    For music, peace, and beauty born!

" Ah! what, unheedful have we done?
    What demons here in death delight?
What fiends that curse the social Sun?
    What furies of infernal night?

" See, see my peaceful shepherds bleed!
    Each heart in harmony that vy'd,
Smote by its own melodious reed,
    Lies cold, along my blushing side.

" Back to your urn, my waters, fly;
    Or find in earth some secret way;
For horrour dims yon conscious sky,
    And Hell has issu'd into day."

Thro' Delphi's holy depth of shade
    The sympathetic sorrows ran;
While in his dim and mournful glade
    The Genius of her groves began:

" In vain Cephisus sighs to save
    The swain that loves his watry mead,
And weeps to see his reddening wave,
    And mourns for his perverted reed:

" In vain my violated groves
    Must I with equal grief bewail,
While desolation sternly roves,
    And bids the sanguine hand assail.

---

[1] The reeds on the banks of the Cephisus, of
which the shepherds made their pipes, Sylla's
soldiers used for arrows.

" God of the genial stream, behold
My laurel shades of leaves so bare !
Those leaves no poet's brows enfold,
Nor bind Apollo's golden hair.

Like thy fair offspring, misapply'd,
Far other purpose they supply ;
The murderer's burning cheek to hide,
And on his frownful temples die.

" Yet deem not these of Pluto's race,
Whom wounded Nature sues in vain ;
Pluto disclaims the dire disgrace,
And cries, indignant, They are men."

---

## FABLE IV.

### THE GARDEN ROSE AND THE WILD ROSE.

" As Dee, whose current, free from stain,
Glides fair o'er Merioneth's plain,
By mountains forc'd his way to steer,
Along the lake of Pimble Mere,
Darts swiftly thro' the stagnant mass,
His waters trembling as they pass,
And leads his lucid waves below,
Unmix'd, unsullied as they flow—
So clear thro' life's tumultuous tide,
So free could Thought and Fancy glide;
Could Hope as sprightly hold her course,
As first she left her native source,
Unsought in her romantic cell
The keeper of her dreams might dwell.
    " But ah ! they will not, will not last—
When life's first fairy stage is past,
The glowing hand of Hope is cold ;
And Fancy lives not to be old.
Darker, and darker all before ;
We turn the former prospect o'er ;
And find in Memory's faithful eye
Our little stock of pleasures lie.
    " Come, then; thy kind recesses ope !
Fair keeper of the dreams of Hope !
Come with thy visionary train,
And bring my morning scenes again !
To Enon's wild and silent shade,
Where oft my lonely youth was laid ;
What time the woodland Genius came,
And touch'd me with his holy flame.—
    " Or, where the hermit, Bela,' leads
Her waves thro' solitary meads ;
And only feeds the desert-flower,
Where once she sooth'd my slumbering hour :
Or rous'd by Stainmore's wintry sky,
She wearies Echo with her cry ;
And oft, what storms her bosom tear,
Her deeply-wounded banks declare.—
    " Where Eden's fairer waters flow,
By Milton's bower, or Osty's brow,
Or Brockley's alder-shaded cave,
Or, winding round the Druid's grave,
Silently glide, with pious fear
To sound his holy slumbers near.—

    " To these fair scenes of Fancy's reign,
O Memory ! bear me once again :
For, when life's varied scenes are past,
'Tis simple Nature charms at last "

'Twas thus of old a poet pray'd ;
Th' indulgent power his pray'r approv'd,
And, ere the gather'd rose could fade,
Restor'd him to the scenes he lov'd.

A rose, the poet's favourite flower,
From Flora's cultur'd walks he bore ;
No fairer bloom'd in Esher's bower,
Nor Prior's charming Chloe wore.

No fairer flowers could Fancy twine
To hide Anacreon's snowy hair ;
For there Almeria's bloom divine,
And Elliot's sweetest blush was there.

When she, the pride of courts, retires,
    And leaves for shades a nation's love,
With awe the village maid admires,
    How Waldegrave looks, how Waldegrave
moves.

So marvell'd much in Enon's shade
    The flowers that all uncultur'd grew,
When there the splendid Rose display'd
    Her swelling breast and shining hue.

Yet one, that oft adorn'd the place
    Where now her gaudy rival reign'd,
Of simpler bloom, but kindred race,
    The pensive Eglantine complain'd.—

" Mistaken youth," with sighs she said,
    " From Nature and from me to stray !
The bard, by splendid forms betray'd,
    No more shall frame the purer lay.

" Luxuriant, like the flaunting Rose,
    And gay the brilliant strains may be,
But far, in beauty, far from those,
    That flow'd to Nature and to me."

The poet felt, with fond surprise,
    The truths the sylvan critic told ;
And, "Though this courtly Rose," he cries,
    " Is gay, is beauteous to behold ;

" Yet, lovely flower, I find in thee
    Wild sweetness which no words express,
And charms in thy simplicity,
    That dwell not in the pride of dress."

---

## FABLE V.

### THE VIOLET AND THE PANSY.

Shepherd, if near thy artless breast
    The god of fond desires repair ;
Implore him for a gentle guest,
    Implore him with unwearied prayer.

Should beauty's soul-enchanting smile,
    Love-kindling looks, and features gay,
Should these thy wandering eye beguile,
    And steal thy wareless heart away ;

That heart shall soon with sorrow swell,
    And soon the erring eye deplore,
If in the beauteous bosom dwell
    No gentle virtue's genial store.

Far from his hive one summer-day,
    A young and yet unpractis'd bee,
Borne on his tender wings away,
    Went forth the flowery world to see.

The morn, the noon in play he pass'd,
But when the shades of evening came,
No parent brought the due repast,
And faintness seiz'd his little frame.

By nature urg'd, by instinct led,
The bosom of a flower he sought,
Where streams mourn'd round a mossy bed,
And violets all the bank enwrought.

Of kindred race, but brighter dies,
On that fair bank a Pansy grew,
That borrow'd from indulgent skies
A velvet shade and purple hue.

The tints that stream'd with glossy gold,
The velvet shade, the purple hue,
The stranger wonder'd to behold,
And to its bounteous bosom flew.

Not fonder haste the lover speeds,
At evening's fall, his fair to meet;
When o'er the hardly-bending meads
He springs on more than mortal feet.

Nor glows his eyes with brighter glee,
When stealing near her orient breast,
Than felt the fond enamour'd bee,
When first the golden bloom he prest.

Ah! pity much his youth untry'd,
His heart in beauty's magic spell!
So never passion thee betide,
But where the genial virtues dwell.

In vain he seeks those virtues there;
No soul-sustaining charms abound:
No honey'd sweetness to repair
The languid waste of life is found.

An aged bee, whose labours led
Thro' those fair springs, and meads of gold,
His feeble wing, his drooping head
Beheld, and pitied to behold.

" Fly, fond adventurer, fly the art
That courts thine eye with fair attire;
Who smiles to win the heedless heart,
Will smile to see that heart expire.

" This modest flower of humbler hue,
That boasts no depth of glowing dyes,
Array'd in unbespangled blue,
The simple clothing of the skies—

" This flower, with balmy sweetness blest,
May yet thy languid life renew:"
He said, and to the Violet's breast
The little vagrant faintly flew.

----

FABLE VI.

### THE QUEEN OF THE MEADOW AND THE CROWN IMPERIAL

From Bactria's vales, where beauty blows
Luxuriant in the genial ray;
Where flowers a bolder gem disclose,
And deeper drink the golden day.

From Bactria's vales to Britain's shore
What time the Crown Imperial came,
Full high the stately stranger bore
The honours of his birth and name.

In all the pomp of eastern state,
In all the eastern glory gay,
He bade, with native pride elate,
Each flower of humbler birth obey.

O, that the child unborn might hear,
Nor hold it strange in distant time,
That freedom e'en to flowers was dear,
To flowers that bloom'd in Britain's clime!

Through purple meads, and spicy gales,
' Where Strymon's[1] silver waters play,
While far from hence their goddess dwells,
She rules with delegated sway.

That sway the Crown Imperial sought,
With high demand and haughty mien:
But equal claim a rival brought,
A rival call'd the Meadow's Queen.

" In climes of orient glory born,
Where beauty first and empire grew;
Where first unfolds the golden morn,
Where richer falls the fragrant dew:

" In light's ethereal beauty drest,
Behold," he cried, " the favour'd flower,
Which Flora's high commands invest
With ensigns of imperial power!

" Where prostrate vales, and blushing meads,
And bending mountains own his sway,
While Persia's lord his empire leads,
And bids the trembling world obey;

" While blood bedews the straining bow,
And conquest rends the scatter'd air,
'Tis mine to bind the victor's brow,
And reign in envy'd glory there.

" Then lowly bow, ye British flowers!
Confess your monarch's mighty sway,
And own the only glory yours,
When fear flies trembling to obey."

He said, and sudden o'er the plain,
From flower to flower a murmur ran,
With modest air, and milder strain,
When thus the Meadow's Queen began :

" If vain of birth, of glory vain,
Or fond to bear a regal name,
The pride of folly brings disdain,
And bids me urge a tyrant's claim .

" If war my peaceful realms assail,
And then, unmov'd by pity's call,
I smile to see the bleeding vale,
Or feel one joy in Nature's fall,

" Then may each justly vengeful flower
Pursue her queen with gen'rous strife,
Nor leave the hand of lawless power
Such compass on the scale of life.

" One simple virtue all my pride!
The wish that flies to mis'ry's aid;
The balm that stops the crimson tide*,
And heals the wounds that war has made."

Their free consent by zephyrs borne,
The flowers their Meadow's Queen obey;
And fairer blushes crown'd the morn,
And sweeter fragrance fill'd the day.

! The Ionian Strymon.
2 The property of that flower.

## FABLE VII.

### THE WALL-FLOWER.

" Why loves my flower, the sweetest flower
That swells the golden breast of May,
Thrown rudely o'er this ruin'd tower,
To waste her solitary day ?

" Why, when the mead, the spicy vale,
The grove and genial garden call,
Will she her fragrant soul exhale,
Unheeded on the lonely wall ?

" For never sure was beauty born
To live in death's deserted shade !
Come, lovely flower, my banks adorn,
My banks for life and beauty made."

Thus Pity wak'd the tender thought,
And by her sweet persuasion led,
To seize the hermit-flower I sought,
And bear her from her stony bed.

I sought—but sudden on mine ear
A voice in hollow murmurs broke,
And smote my heart with holy fear—
The Genius of the Ruin spoke.

" From thee be far th' ungentle deed,
The honours of the dead to spoil,
Or take the sole remaining meed,
The flower that crowns their former toil !

" Nor deem that flower the garden's foe,
Or fond to grace this barren shade ;
'Tis Nature tells her to bestow
Her honours on the lonely dead.

" For this, obedient zephyrs bear
Her light seeds round yon turret's mould,
And undispers'd by tempests there,
They rise in vegetable gold.

" Nor shall thy wonder wake to see
Such desert scenes distinction crave ;
Oft have they been, and oft shall be
Truth's, Honour's, Valour's, Beauty's grave.

" Where longs to fall that rifted spire,
As weary of th' insulting air;
The poet's thought, the warrior's fire,
The lover's sighs are sleeping there.

" When that too shakes the trembling ground,
Borne down by some tempestuous sky,
And many a slumbering cottage round
Startles—how still their hearts will lie !

" Of them who, wrapt in earth so cold,
No more the smiling day shall view,
Should many a tender tale be told ;
For many a tender thought is due.

" Hast thou not seen some lover pale,
When evening brought the pensive hour,
Step slowly o'er the shadowy vale,
And stop to pluck the frequent flower ?

" Those flowers he surely meant to strew
On lost affection's lowly cell ;
Tho' there, as fond remembrance grew,
Forgotten, from his hand they fell.

" Has not for thee the fragrant thorn
Been taught her first rose to resign ?
With vain but pious fondness borne
To deck thy Nancy's honour'd shrine !

" 'Tis Nature pleading in the breast,
Fair memory of her works to find ;
And when to fate she yields the rest,
She claims the monumental mind.

" Why, else, the o'ergrown paths of time
Would thus the letter'd sage explore,
With pain these crumbling ruins climb,
And on the doubtful sculpture pore ?

" Why seeks he with unwearied toil
Through death's dim walks to urge his way,
Reclaim his long-asserted spoil,
And lead oblivion into day ?

" 'Tis Nature prompts, by toil or fear
Unmov'd, to range through death's domain:
The tender parent loves to hear
Her children's story told again.

" Treat not with scorn his thoughtful hours,
If haply near these haunts he stray;
Nor take the fair enlivening flowers
That bloom to cheer his lonely way."

---

## FABLE VIII.

### THE TULIP AND THE MYRTLE.

'Twas on the border of a stream
A gaily-painted Tulip stood,
And, gilded by the morning beam,
Survey'd her beauties in the flood.

And sure, more lovely to behold,
Might nothing meet the wistful eye,
Than crimson fading into gold,
In streaks of fairest symmetry.

The beauteous flower, with pride elate,
Ah me ! that pride with beauty dwells !
Vainly affects superior state,
And thus in empty fancy swells :

" O lustre of unrivall'd bloom !
Fair painting of a hand divine !
Superior far to mortal doom,
The hues of Heav'n alone are mine !

" Away, ye worthless, formless race !
Ye weeds, that boast the name of flowers ?
No more my native bed disgrace,
Unmeet for tribes so mean as yours !

" Shall the bright daughter of the Sun
Associate with the shrubs of Earth ?
Ye slaves, your sovereign's presence shun !
Respect her beauties and her birth.

" And thou, dull, sullen ever-green !
Shalt thou my shining sphere invade ?
My noon-day beauties beam unseen,
Obscur'd beneath thy dusky shade !"

" Deluded flower !" the Myrtle cries,
Shall we thy moment's bloom adore ?
The mean'st shrub that you despise,
The meanest flower has merit more.

" That daisy, in its simple bloom,
Shall last along the changing year;
Blush on the snow of Winter's gloom,
And bid the smiling Spring appear.

"The violet, that, those banks beneath,
  Hides from thy scorn its modest head,
Shall fill the air with fragrant breath,
  When thou art in thy dusty bed.

"E'en I, who boast no golden shade,
  Am of no shining tints possess'd,
When low thy lucid form is laid,
  Shall bloom on many a lovely breast.

"And he, whose kind and fostering care
  To thee, to me, our beings gave,
Shall near his breast my flowrets wear,
  And walk regardless o'er thy grave.

"Deluded flower, the friendly screen
  That hides thee from the noon-tide ray,
And mocks thy passion to be seen,
  Prolongs thy transitory day.

"But kindly deeds with scorn repaid,
  No more by virtue need be done :
I now withdraw my dusky shade.
  And yield thee to thy darling Sun."

Fierce on the flower the scorching beam
  With all its weight of glory fell ;
The flower exulting caught the gleam,
  And lent its leaves a bolder swell.

Expanded by the searching fire,
  The curling leaves the breast disclos'd ;
The mantling bloom was painted higher,
  And every latent charm expos'd.

But when the Sun was sliding low
  And ev'ning came, with dews so cold ;
The wanton beauty ceas'd to blow,
  And sought her bending leaves to fold.

Those leaves, alas ! no more would close ;
  Relax'd, exhausted, sick'ning, pale,
They left her to a parent's woes,
  And fled before the rising gale.

---

### FABLE IX.

### THE BEE FLOWER[1].

Come, let us leave this painted plain;
  This waste of flowers that palls the eye :
The walks of Nature's wilder reign
  Shall please in plainer majesty.

Through those fair scenes, where yet she owes
  Superior charms to Brockman's art,
Where, crown'd with elegant repose,
  He cherishes the social heart—

[1] This is a species of the orchis, which is found in the barren and mountainous parts of Lincolnshire, Worcestershire, Kent, and Herefordshire. Nature has formed a bee apparently feeding on the breast of a flower with so much exactness, that it is impossible at a very small distance to distinguish the imposition. For this purpose she has observed an economy different from what is found in most other flowers, and has laid the petals horizontally. The genius of the orchis, or satyrion, she seems professedly to have made use of for her paintings, and on the different species has drawn the perfect forms of different insects, such as bees, flies, butterflies, &c.

Through those fair scenes we'll wander wild,
  And on yon pastur'd mountains rest ;
Come, brother dear ! come, Nature's child !
  With all her simple virtues blest.

The Sun far-seen on distant towers,
  And clouding groves and peopled seas,
And ruins pale of princely bowers
  On Beachb'rough's airy heights shall please.

Nor lifeless there the lonely scene;
  The little labourer of the hive,
From flower to flower, from green to green,
  Murmurs and makes the wild alive.

See, on that flowret's velvet breast
  How close the busy vagrant lies !
His thin-wrought plume, his downy breast,
  Th' ambrosial gold that swells his thighs !

Regardless, while we wander near,
  Thrifty of time, his task he plies ;
Or sees he no intruder near ?
  And rest in sleep his weary eyes ?

Perhaps his fragrant load may bind
  His limbs ;—we'll set the captive free—
I sought the living Bee to bind,
  And found the picture of a Bee.

Attentive to our trifling selves,
  From thence we plan the rule of all ;
Thus Nature with the fabled elves,
  We rank, and these her sports we call.

Be far, my friend, from you, from me,
  Th' unhallow'd term, the thought profane,
That life's majestic source may be
  In idle fancy's trifling vein.

Remember still, 'tis Nature's plan
  Religion in your love to find ;
And know, for this, she first in man
  Inspir'd the imitative mind.

As conscious that affection grows,
  Pleas'd with the pencil's mimic power ;
That power with leading hand she shows,
  And paints a Bee upon a flower.

Mark, how that rooted mandrake wears
  His human feet, his human hands !
Oft, as his shapely form he rears,
  Aghast the frighted ploughman stands.

See where, in yonder orient stone,
  She seems e'en with herself at strife,
While fairer from her hand is shown
  The pictur'd, than the native life.

Helvetia's rocks, Sabrina's waves,
  Still many a shining pebble bear,
Where oft her studious hand engraves
  The perfect form, and leaves it there.

O long, my Paxton[3], boast her art ;
  And long her laws of love fulfil :
To thee she gave her hand and heart,
  To thee, her kindness and her skill !

[2] The well-known fables of the Painter and the Statuary that fell in love with objects of their own creation, plainly arose from the idea of that attachment, which follows the imitation of agreeable objects, to the objects imitated.

[3] An ingenious portrait-painter in Rathbone Place.

## FABLE X.
### THE WILDING AND THE BROOM.

In yonder green wood blows the broom;
　Shepherds we'll trust our flocks to stray.
Court Nature in her sweetest bloom,
　And steal from care one summer-day.

From him [1] whose gay and graceful brow
　Fair-handed Hume with roses binds,
We'll learn to breathe the tender vow,
　Where slow the fairy Fortha winds.

And oh! that he [2] whose gentle breast
　In Nature's softest mould was made,
Who left her smiling works imprest
　In characters that cannot fade;

That he might leave his lowly shrine,
　Tho' softer there the seasons fall—
They come, the sons of verse divine,
　They come to Fancy's magic call.

———————"What airy sounds invite
My steps not unreluctant, from the depth
Of Shene's delightful groves? Reposing there
No mo~ : I hear the busy voice of men
Far-toiling o'er the globe—save to the call
Of soul-exalting poetry, the ear
Of death denies attention. Rous'd by her,
The genius of sepulchral silence opes
His drowsy cells, and yields us to the day.
For thee, whose hand, whatever paints the
　　　　　　Spring,
Or swells on Summer's breast, or loads the lap
Of Autumn, gathers heedful—Thee whose rites
At Nature's shrine with holy care are paid
Daily and nightly, boughs of brightest green,
And every fairest rose, the good of groves,
The queen of flowers, shall sweeter save for thee.
Yet not if beauty only claim thy lay,
Tunefully trifling. Fair philosophy,
And Nature's love, and every mortal charm
That leads in sweet captivity the mind
To virtue—ever in thy nearest cares
Be these, and animate thy living page
With truth resistless, beaming from the source
Of perfect light immortal—Vainly boasts
That golden Broom its sunny robe of flowers:
Fair are the sunny flowers; but, fading soon
And fruitless, yield the forester's regard
To the well-loaded wilding—Shepherd, there
Behold the fate of song, and lightly deem
Of all but moral beauty."

———————"Not in vain?"—
I hear my Hamilton reply.
(The torch of fancy in his eye)
" 'Tis not in vain," I hear him say,
" That Nature paints her works so gay;
For, fruitless though that fairy broom,
Yet still we love her lavish bloom.
Cheer'd with that bloom, yon desert wild
Its native horrours lost, and smil'd;
And oft we mark her golden ray
Along the dark wood scatter day.
　" Of moral uses take the strife;
Leave me the elegance of life.

[1] William Hamilton of Bangour.
[2] Thomson.

Whatever charms the ear or eye,
All beauty and all harmony;
If sweet sensations these produce,
I know they have their moral use;
I know that Nature's charms can move
The springs that strike to virtue's love."

———

## FABLE XI.
### THE MISLETOE AND THE PASSION-FLOWER.

In this dim cave a druid sleeps,
　Where stops the passing gale to moan;
The rock he hollow'd o'er him weeps,
　And cold drops wear the fretted stone.

In this dim cave, of diff'rent creed,
　An hermit's holy ashes rest:
The school-boy finds the frequent bead,
　Which many a formal matin blest.

That truant-time full well I know,
　When here I brought, in stolen hour,
The druid's magic misletoe,
　The holy hermit's passion-flower.

The off'rings on the mystic stone
　Pensive I laid, in thought profound.
When from the cave a deep'ning groan
　Issued, and froze me to the ground.

I hear it still—dost thou not hear?
　Does not thy haunted fancy start?
The sound still vibrates through mine ear,
　The horrour rushes on my heart.

Unlike to living sounds it came,
　Unmix'd, unmelodis'd with breath;
But, grinding through some scrannel frame,
　Creak'd from the bony lungs of death.

I hear it still—" Depart," it cries;
　" No tribute bear to shades unblest:
Know, here a bloody druid lies,
　Who was not nurs'd at Nature's breast.

" Associate he with demons dire,
　O'er human victims held the knife,
And pleas'd to see the babe expire,
　Smil'd grimly o'er its quiv'ring life.

"Behold his crimson-streaming hand
　Erect!—his dark, fix'd, murd'rous eye!"
In the dim cave I saw him stand;
　And my heart died—I felt it die.

I see him still—Dost thou not see
　The haggard eye-ball's hallow glare?
And gleams of wild ferocity
　Dart through the sable shade of hair?

What meagre form behind him moves,
　With eye that rues th' invading day;
And wrinkled aspect wan, that proves
　The mind to pale remorse a prey?

What wretched—Hark—the voice replies,
　" Boy, bear these idle honours hence!
For, here a guilty hermit lies,
　Untrue to Nature, Virtue, Sense.

" Though Nature lent him powers to aid
　The moral cause, the mutual weal;
Those powers he sunk in this dim shade,
　The desp'rate suicide of zeal.

G g

" Go, teach the drone of saintly haunts,
Whose cell's the sepulchre of time;
Though many a holy hymn he chants,
His life is one continu'd crime.

" And bear them hence, the plant, the flower
No symbols those of systems vain !
They have the duties of their hour;
Some bird, some insect to sustain."

## THE COUNTRY JUSTICE.

BY ONE OF HIS MAJESTY'S JUSTICES OF THE PEACE
FOR THE COUNTY OF SOMERSET.

### PART THE FIRST.

### TO RICHARD BURN, LL. D.

ONE OF HIS MAJESTY'S JUSTICES OF THE PEACE FOR
THE COUNTIES OF WESTMORLAND AND CUMBERLAND.

DEAR SIR,
    A POEM written professedly at
your request, naturally addresses itself to you.
The distinction you have acquired on the subject,
and your taste for the arts, give that address
every kind of propriety. If I have any particular satisfaction in this publication, beside what
arises from my compliance with your commands,
it must be in the idea of that testimony it bears
to our friendship. If you believe that I am more
concerned for the duration of that than of the
Poem itself, you will not be mistaken; for I am,
DEAR SIR,

your truly affectionate brother

and faithful humble servant,

THE AUTHOR.

Somersetshire,
April 25, 1774.

## THE COUNTRY JUSTICE.

### INTRODUCTION.

In Richard's days, when lost his pastur'd plain,
The wand'ring Briton sought the wild wood's
With great disdain beheld the feudal hord,[reign,
Poor life-let vassals of a Norman lord;
And, what no brave man ever lost, possess'd
Himself—for Freedom bound him to her breast.
Lov'st thou that Freedom ? By her holy shrine,
If yet one drop of British blood be thine,
See, I conjure thee, in the desert shade,
His bow unstrung, his little household laid,
Some brave forefather; while his fields they
    share,
By Saxon, Dane, or Norman, banish'd there !
And think he tells thee, as his soul withdraws,
As his heart swells against a tyrant's laws,
The war with fate, though fruitless to maintain,
To guard that liberty he lov'd in vain.
Were thoughts like these the dreams of ancient
Peculiar only to some age, or clime?   [time ?
And does not Nature thoughts like these impart,
Breathe in the soul, and write upon the heart ?
    Ask on their mountain yon deserted band,
That point to Paoli with no plausive hand ;

Despising still, their freeborn souls unbroke,
Alike the Gallic and Ligurian yoke.
    Yet while the patriot's gen'rous rage we share,
Still civil safety calls us back to care ;—
To Britain lost in either Henry's day,
Her woods her mountains one wild scene of prey !
Fair Peace from all her bounteous vallies fled,
And Law beneath the barbed arrow bled.
    In happier days, with more auspicious fate,
The far-fam'd Edward heal'd his wounded state ;
Dread of his foes, but to his subjects dear,
These learn'd to love, as those are taught to fear,
Their laurell'd prince with British pride obey,
His glory shone their discontent away.
    With care the tender flower of love to save,
And plant the olive on Disorder's grave,
For civil storms fresh barriers to provide,
He caught the fav'ring calm and falling tide.

### THE APPOINTMENT, AND ITS PURPOSES.

The social laws from insult to protect ;
To cherish peace, to cultivate respect ;
The rich from wanton cruelty restrain,
To smooth the bed of penury and pain ;
The hapless vagrant to his rest restore,
The maze of fraud, the haunts of theft explore ;
The thoughtless maiden, when subdu'd by art,
To aid, and bring her rover to her heart ;
Wild riot's voice with dignity to quell,
Forbid unpeaceful passions to rebel;
Wrest from revenge the meditated harm,
For this fair Justice rais'd her sacred arm;
For this the rural magistrate, of yore,
Thy honours, Edward, to his mansion bore.

### ANCIENT JUSTICE'S HALL.

Oft, where old Air in conscious glory sails,
On silver waves that flow thro' smiling vales,
In Harewood's groves, where long my youth was
    laid,
Unseen beneath their ancient world of shade,
With many a groupe of antique columns crown'd,
In Gothic guise such mansion have I found.
    Nor lightly deem, ye apes of modern race,
Ye cits that sore bedizen Nature's face,
Of the more manly structures here ye view ;
They rose for greatness that ye never knew !
Ye reptile cits, that oft have mov'd my spleen,
With Venus, and the Graces on your green !
Let Plutus, growling o'er his ill-got wealth,
Let Mercury, the thriving god of stealth,
The shopman, Janus, with his double looks,
Rise on your mounts, and perch upon your books !
But, spare my Venus, spare each sister Grace,
Ye cits, that sore bedizen Nature's face.
    Ye royal architects, whose antic taste,
Would lay the realms of Sense and Nature
    waste ;
Forgot, whenever from her steps ye stray,
That folly only points each other way ;
Here, tho' your eye no courtly creature sees ;
Snakes on the ground, or monkies in the trees ;
Yet let not too severe a censure fall,
On the plain precincts of the ancient hall.
    For tho' no sight your childish fancy meets,
Of Thibet's dogs, or China's perroquets ;
Tho' apes, asps, lizards, things without a tail,
And all the tribes of foreign monsters fail ;

Here shall ye sigh to see, with rust o'ergrown,
The iron griffin and the sphynx of stone;
And mourn, neglected in their waste abodes.
Fire-breathing drakes, and water-spouting gods.
  Long have these mighty monsters known dis-
        grace,
Yet still some trophies hold their ancient place;
Where, round the hall, the oak's high surbase
        rears
The field-day triumphs of two hundred years.
  Th' enormous antlers here recall the day
That saw the forest-monarch forc'd away;
Who, many a flood, and many a mountain past,
Nor finding those, nor deeming these the last,
O'er floods, o'er mountains yet prepar'd to fly,
Long ere the death-drop fill'd his failing eye!
  Here, fam'd for cunning, and in crimes grown
        old,
Hangs his grey brush, the felon of the fold.
Oft, as the rent feast swells the midnight cheer,
The maudling farmer kens him o'er his beer,
And tells his old, traditionary tale,
Tho' known to every tenant of the vale.
  Here, where, of old, the festal ox has fed,
Mark'd with his weight, the mighty horns are
        spread:
Some ox, O Marshall, for a board like thine,
Where the vast master with the vast sirloin
Vied in round magnitude—Respect I bear
To thee, tho' oft the ruin of the chair.
  These, and such antique tokens, that record
The manly spirit, and the bounteous board,
Me more delight than all the gew-gaw train,
The whims and zigzag of a modern brain,
More than all Asia's marmosets to view
Grin, frisk, and water, in the walks of Kew.

### CHARACTER OF A COUNTRY JUSTICE.

  Thro' these fair vallies, stranger, hast thou
        stray'd,
By any chance to visit Harewood's shade,
And seen with honest, antiquated air,
In the plain hall the magistratial chair?
There Herbert sate—the love of human kind,
Pure light of truth, and temperance of mind,
In the free eye the featur'd soul display'd,
Honour's strong beam, and Mercy's melting
        shade;
Justice, that, in the rigid paths of law,
Would still some drops from Pity's fountain draw,
Bend o'er her urn with many a gen'rous fear,
Ere his firm seal should force one orphan's tear;
Fair Equity, and Reason, scorning art,
And all the sober virtues of the heart—
These sate with Herbert, these shall best avail,
Where statutes order, or where statutes fail.

### GENERAL MOTIVES FOR LENITY.

  Be this, ye rural Magistrates, your plan:
Firm be your justice, but be friends to man.
  He whom the mighty master of this ball,
We fondly deem, or farcically call,
To own the patriarch's truth however loth,
Holds but a mansion crush'd before the moth.
  Frail in his genius, in his heart, too, frail,
Born but to err, and erring to bewail;
Shalt thou his faults with eye severe explore,
And give to life one human weakness more?

Still mark if vice or nature prompts the deed;
Still mark the strong temptation and the need:
On pressing want, on famine's powerful call,
At least more lenient let thy justice fall.

### APOLOGY FOR VAGRANTS.

  For him, who, lost to ev'ry hope of life,
Has long with fortune held unequal strife,
Known to no human love, no human care,
The friendless, homeless object of despair;
For the poor vagrant, feel, while he complains,
Nor from sad freedom send to sadder chains.
Alike, if folly or misfortune brought
Those last of woes his evil days have wrought;
Believe with social mercy and with me,
Folly's misfortune in the first degree.
  Perhaps on some inhospitable shore
The houseless wretch a widow'd parent bore,
Who, then, no more by golden prospects led,
Of the poor Indian begg'd a leafy bed,
Cold on Canadian hills, or Minden's plain,
Perhaps that parent mourn'd her soldier slain;
Bent o'er her babe, her eye dissolv'd in dew,
The big drops mingling with the milk he drew,
Gave the sad presage of his future years,
The child of misery, baptiz'd in tears!

### APOSTROPHE TO EDWARD THE THIRD.

  O Edward, here thy fairest laurels fade!
And thy long glories darken into shade;
While yet the palms thy hardy veterans won,
The deeds of valour that for thee were done,
While yet the wreaths for which they bravely bled,
Fir'd thy high soul, and flourish'd on thy head,
Those veterans to their native shores return'd,
Like exiles wander'd and like exiles mourn'd;
Or, left at large no longer to bewail,
Were vagrants deem'd and destin'd to a jail!
  Were there no royal, yet uncultur'd lands,
No wastes that wanted such subduing hands?
Were Cressy's heroes such abandon'd things?
O fate of war and gratitude of kings!

### THE GYPSEY-LIFE.

  The gypsey-race my pity rarely move;
Yet their strong thirst of liberty I love.
Not Wilkes, our freedom's holy martyr, more;
Nor his firm phalanx, of the common shore.
  For this in Norwood's patrimonial groves,
The tawny father with his offspring roves,
When summer suns lead slow the sultry day,
In mossy caves, where welling waters play,
Fann'd by each gale that cools the fervid sky,
With this in ragged luxury they lie.
Oft at the sun the dusky elfins strain
The sable eye, then, snugging, sleep again;
Oft, as the dews of cooler evening fall,
For their prophetic mother's mantle call.
  Far other cares that wandering mother wait,
The mouth, and oft the minister of Fate!
From her to hear, in evening's friendly shade,
Of future fortune, flies the village-maid,
Draws her long-hoarded copper from its hold;
And rusty halfpence purchase hopes of gold.
  But, ah! ye maids, beware the gypsey's lures!
She opens not the womb of Time, but yours.
Oft has her hands the hapless Marian wrung,
Marian, whom Gay in sweetest strains has sung!

The parson's maid—sore cáuse had she to rue
The gypsey's tongue ; the parson's daughter too,
Long had that anxious daughter sighed to know
What Vellum'ssprucy clerk, the valley's beau,
Meant by those glances, which at church he stole,
Her father nodding to the psalms slow drawl ;
Long had she sigh'd, at length a prophet came,
By many a sure prediction kuown to fame,
To Marian known, and all she told, for true :
She knew the future, for the past she knew.
　　Where, in the darkling shed, the Moon's dim
　　　　rays
Beam'd on the ruins of a one-horse chaise,
Villaria sate, while faithful Marian brought
The wayward prophet of the woe she sought.
Twice did her hands, the income of the week,
On either side, the crooked sixpence seek ;
Twice were those hands withdrawn from either
　　side,
To stop the titt'ring laugh, the blush to hide.
The wayward prophet made no long delay,
No novice she in Fortune's devious way !
"Ere yet," she cried, " ten rolling months are
　　o'er,
Must ye be mothers ; maids at least no more.
With you shall soon, O lady fair, prevail
A gentle youth, the flow'r of this fair vale.
To Marian, once of Colin Clout the scorn,
Shall bumpkin come, and bumpkinets be born "
　　Smote to the heart, the maidens marvell'd
　　　　sore,
Than ten short months had such events in store ;
But holding firm, what village-maids believe,
" That strife with fate is milking in a sieve ;"
To prove their prophet true, tho' to their cost,
They justly thought no time was to be lost.
　　These foes to youth, that seek, with dang'rous
To aid the native weakness of the heart ;　[art,
These miscreants from thy harmless village drive,
As wasps felonious from the lab'ring hive.

---

### THE COUNTRY JUSTICE.

#### PART II.

##### TO ROBERT WILSON CRACROFT, ESQ.

Born with a gentle heart, and born to please
　　With native goodness, of no fortune vain,
The social aspect of inviting ease,
　　The kind opinion, and the sense humane ;

To thee, my Cracroft, whom, in early youth,
　　With lenient hand, and anxious love I led
Thro' paths where science points to manly truth :
　　And glory gilds the mansions of the dead :

To thee this offering of maturer thought,
　　That since wild Fancy flung the lyre aside,
With heedful hand the moral Muse hath wrought,
　　That Muse devotes, and bears with honest
　　　　pride.

Yet not that period of the human year,
　　When Fancy reign'd, shall we with pain review,
All Nature's seasons different aspects wear,
　　And now her flowers, and now her fruits are due:

Not that in youth we rang'd the smiling meads,
　　On Essex' shores the trembling angle play'd,
Urging at noon the slow boat in the reeds,
　　That wav'd their green uncertainty of shade ;

Nor yet the days consum'd in Hackthorn's vale,
　　That lonely on the heath's wide bosom lies,
Should we with stern severity bewail,
　　And all the lighter hours of life despise.

For Nature's seasons different aspects wear,
　　And now her flowers, and now her fruits are due ;
Awhile she freed us from the scourge of Care,
　　But told us then—for social ends we grew.

To find some virtue trac'd on life's short page,
　　Some mark of service paid to human kind,
Alone can cheer the wintry paths of age,
　　Alone support the far-reflecting mind.

Oh ! often thought—when Smith's discerning care
　　To further days prolong'd this failing frame !
To die, was little—But what heart could bear
　　To die, and leave an undistinguish'd name
Blagdon- House,
　　Feb. 22, 1775.

---

##### PROTECTION OF THE POOR.

Yet [1], while thy rod restrains the needy crew,
Remember that thou art their monarch too.
King of the beggars!—Lov'st thou not the name?
O, great from Ganges to the golden Tame !
Far-ruling sovereign of this begging ball,
Low at thy footstool other thrones shall fall.
His alms to thee the whisker'd Moor convey [2],
And Prussia's sturdy beggar own thy sway ;
Courts, senates—all to Baal that bend the knee [3],
King of the beggars, these are fiefs to thee !
But still, forgot the grandeur of thy reign,
Descend to duties meaner crowns disdain ;
That worst excrescency of power forego,
That pride of kings, humanity's first foe.
Let age no longer toil with feeble strife,
Worn by long service in the war of life ;
Nor leave the head, that time hath whiten'd, bare
To the rude insults of the searching air ;
Nor bid the knee, by labour harden'd, bend,
O thou, the poor man's hope, the poor man's
　　friend !
If, when from Heav'n severer seasons fall,
Fled from the frozen roof, and mouldering wall,
Each face the picture of a winter-day, 　[tray ;—
More strong than Teniers' pencil could pour-
If then to thee resort the shivering train,
Of cruel days, and cruel man complain,
Say to thy heart (remembering him who said)
" These people come from far, and have no
　　bread."
Nor leave thy venal clerk empower'd to hear ;
The voice of want is sacred to thy ear.
He, where no fees his sordid pen invite,
Sports with their tears, too indolent to write ;
Like the fed monkey in the fable, vain
To hear more helpless animals complain.
But chief thy notice shall one monster claim,
A monster furnish'd with a human frame,

[1] Refers to the conclusion of the first part.
[2] The Mahometan princes seem to have a regular system of begging. Nothing so common
as to hear that the dey of Algiers, &c. &c. are
dissatisfied with their presents. It must be
owned, it would be for the welfare of the world,
if princes in general would adhere to the maxim,
that " it is better to beg than to steal."
[3] ——— Tu poscis vilia rerum,
　　Quamvis fers te nullius egentem.

The parish-officer !—tho' verse disdain
Terms that deform the splendour of the strain;
It stoops to bid thee bend the brow severe
On the sly, pilfering, cruel overseer;
The shuffling farmer, faithful to no trust,
Ruthless as rocks, insatiate as the dust!
  When the poor hind, with length of years de-
    cay'd,
Leans feebly on his once subduing spade,
Forgòt the service of his abler days,
His profitable toil, and honest praise,
Shall this low wretch abridge his scanty bread,
This slave,- whose board his former labours
    spread?
  When harvest's burning suns and sick'ning air
From labour's unbrac'd hand the grasp'd hook
    tear,
Where shall the hapless family be fed,
That vainly languish for a father's bread ?
See the pale mother, sunk with grief and care,
To the proud farmer fearfully repair ;
Soon to be sent with insolence away,
Referr'd to vestries, and a distant day !
Referr'd—to perish !—Is my verse severe?
Unfriendly to the human character ?
Ah ! to this sigh of sad experience trust:
The truth is rigid, but the tale is just.
If in thy courts this caitiff wretch appear,
Think not that patience were a virtue here.
His low-born pride with honest rage control,
Smite his hard heart, and shake his reptile soul.
  But, hapless ! oft thro' fear of future woe,
And certain vengeance of th' insulting foe,
Oft, ere to thee the poor prefer their pray'r,
The last extremes of penury they bear.
  Wouldst thou then raise thy patriot office
    higher,
To something more than magistrate aspire ?
And, left each poorer, pettier chace behind,
Step nobly forth, the friend of human kind ?
The game I start courageously pursue !
Adieu to fear ! to indolence adieu !
And, first we'll range this mountain's stormy
    side,         [ride,
Where the rude winds the shepherd's roof de-
As meet no more the wintry blast to bear,
And all the wild hostilities of air.
  —That roof have I remember'd many a year ;
It once gave refuge to a hunted deer—
Here, in those days, we found an aged pair;—
But Time untenants—Hah! what seest thou
    there ?—
" Horrour!—By Heav'n, extended on a bed
Of naked fearn, two human creatures dead !
Embracing as alive !—ah, no !—no life !
Cold, breathless !"—
         'Tis the shepherd and his wife.
I knew the scene, and brought thee to behold
What speaks more strongly than the story told.
They died thro' want—
        " By every power I swear,
If the wretch treads the earth, or breathes the
Thro' whose default of duty, or design,   [air,
These victims fell, he dies."—
           They fell by thine.
" Infernal !—Mine!—by—"
        Swear on no pretence :
A swearing justice wants both grace and sense.
  When thy good father held this wide domain,
The voice of sorrow never mourn'd in vain.

Sooth'd by his pity, by his bounty fed,
The sick found med'cine, and the aged bread.
He left their interest to no parish-care,
No bailiff urg'd his little empire there :
No village-tyrant starv'd them, or oppress'd ;
He learnt their wants, and he those wants re-
    dress'd.
E'en these, unhappy ! who, beheld too late,
Smote thy young heart with horrour at their fate,
His bounty found, and destin'd here to keep
A small detachment of his mountain sheep.
Still pleas'd to see them from the annual fair
Th' unwritten history of their profits bear ;
More nobly pleas'd those profits to restore,
And, if their fortune fail'd them, make it more.
  When Nature gave her precept to remove
His kindred spirit to the realms of love,
Afar their anguish from thy distant ear,
No arm to save, and no protection near,
Led by the lure of unaccounted gold,
Thy bailiff seiz'd their little flock, and sold.
  Their want contending parishes survey'd,
And this disown'd, and that refus'd to aid:
A while, who should not succour them, they tried,
And in that while the wretched victims died.
  " I'll scalp that bailiff—sacrifice—"
              In vain
To rave at mischief, if the cause remain.
  O days long lost to man in each degree !
The golden days of hospitality !
When liberal fortunes vied with liberal strife
To fill the noblest offices of life ;    [gate
When Wealth was Virtue's handmaid, and her
Gave a free refuge from the wrongs of fate ;
The poor at hand their natural patrons saw,
And lawgivers were supplements of law.
  Lost are those days, and Fashion's boundless
Has borne the guardian magistrate away: [sway
Save in Augusta's streets, on Gallia's shore,
The rural patron is beheld no more.
No more the poor his kind protection share,
Unknown their wants, and unreceiv'd their
    pray'r.
  Yet has that Fashion, long so light and vain,
Reform'd at last, and led the moral train ?
Have her gay vot'ries nobler worth to boast
For Nature's love, for Nature's virtue lost ?
No—fled from these, the sons of fortune find
What poor respect to wealth remains behind.
The mock regard alone of menial slaves,
The worship'd calves of their outwitting knaves !
  Foregone the social, hospitable days,
When wide vales echo'd with their owner's
Of all that ancient consequence bereft,  [praise,
What has the modern man of fashion left ?
  Does he, perchance, to rural scenes repair,
And " waste his sweetness" on the essenc'd air ?
Ah ! gently lave the feeble frame he brings,
Ye scouring seas ! and ye sulphureous springs !
  And thou, Brightelmstone, where no cits annoy
(All borne to Margate, in the Margate-hoy,)
Where, if the hasty creditor advance,
Lies the light skiff, and ever-bailing France,
Do thou defend him in the dog-day suns ;
Secure in winter from the rage of duns !
  While the grim catchpole, the grim porter
    swear,
One that he is, and one, he is not there,
The tortur'd us'rer, as he murmurs by,
Eyes the Venetian blinds, and heaves a sigh.

O, from each title folly ever took,
Blood! Maccarone! Cicisbeo! or Rook!
From each low passion, from each low resort,
The thieving alley, nay, the righteous court,
From Bertie's, Almack's, Arthur's, and the nest
Where Judah's ferrets earth with Charles un-
        blest!
From these and all the garbage of the great,
At Honour's, Freedom's, Virtue's call—retreat!
Has the fair vale, where rest, conceal'd in
        flowers,
Lies in sweet ambush for thy careless hours ;
The breeze, that, balmy fragrance to infuse,
Bathes its soft wing in aromatic dews ; [breast,
The stream, to soothe thine ear, to cool thy
That mildly murmurs from its crystal rest ;—
Have these less charms to win, less power to
        please,
Than haunts of rapine, harbours of disease ?
Will no kind slumbers o'er thine eyelids creep,
Save where the sullen watchman growls at sleep?
Does morn no sweeter, purer breath diffuse,
Than streams thro' alleys from the lungs of Jews?
And is thy water, pent in putrid wood,
Bethesda-like, when troubled only good ?
Is it thy passion Linley's voice to hear,
And has no mountain-lark detain'd thine ear?
Song marks alone the tribes of airy wing;
For, trust me, man was never meant to sing:
And all his mimic organs e'er exprest
Was but an imitative howl at best.
Is it on Garrick's attitude you doat;
See on the pointed cliff yon lordly goat!
Like Lear's, his beard descends in graceful snow,
And wild he looks upon the world below.
Superior here the scene in every part!
Here reigns great Nature, and there little art!
Here let thy life assume a nobler plan,
To Nature faithful, and the friend of man!
Unnumber'd objects ask thy honest care,
Beside the orphan's tear, the widow's pray'r.
Far as thy power can save, thy bounty bless,
Unnumber'd evils call for thy redress.
Seest thou afar yon solitary thorn,   [torn?
Whose aged limbs the heath's wild winds have
While yet to cheer the homeward shepherd's eye,
A few seem straggling in the ev'ning sky !
Not many suns have hasten'd down the day,
Or blushing moons immers'd in clouds their way,
Since there a scene, that stain'd their sacred
        light,
With horrour stopp'd a felon in his flight ;
A babe just born that signs of life exprest,
Lay naked o'er the mother's lifeless breast.
The pitying robber, conscious that, pursu'd,
He had no time to waste, yet stood and view'd ;
To the next cot the trembling infant bore;
And gave a part of what he stole before ;
Nor known to him the wretches were, nor dear ;
He felt as man, and dropp'd a human tear.
Far other treatment she who breathless lay
Found from a viler animal of prey.
Worn with long toil on many a painful road,
That toil increas'd by nature's growing load,
When ev'ning brought the friendly hour of rest,
And all the mother throng'd about her breast,
The ruffian officer oppos'd her stay,
And, cruel, bore her in her pangs away ;
So far beyond the town's last limits drove,
That to return were hopeless, bad she strove.

Abandon'd there—with famine, pain and cold,
And anguish, she expir'd—the rest I've told.
  " Now let me swear—For, by my soul's last
        sigh,
That thief shall live, that overseer shall die."
Too late !—His life the gen'rous robber paid,
Lost by that pity which his steps delay'd !
No soul-discerning Mansfield sate to hear,
No Hertford bore his prayer to mercy's ear ;
No lib'ral justice first assign'd the jail,
Or urg'd, as Camplin would have urg'd, his tale.
The living object of thy honest rage,
Old in parochial crimes, and steel'd with age,
The grave church-warden ! unabash'd he bears
Weekly to church his book of wicked prayers,
And pours, with all the blasphemy of praise,
His creeping soul in Sternhold's creeping lays !

## THE COUNTRY JUSTICE.

### PART THE THIRD.

To Thomas Smith, M. D. of Wrington, in the
county of Somerset, this last of the little
poems, intended to cultivate, in the provincial administration of justice, that humanity
by which he is so amiably distinguished, is
gratefully inscribed by his most obliged, most
affectionate, and most faithful servant,

                                THE AUTHOR.

#### DEPREDATION.

O, No !—sir John—the Muse's gentle art
Lives not to blemish, but to mend the heart.
While Gay's brave robber grieves us for his fate,
We hold the harpies of his life in hate.
Ingenuous youth, by Nature's voice addrest,
Finds not the harden'd, but the feeling breast;
Can form no wish the dire effects to prove
Of lawless valour, or of venal love,
Approves the fondness of the faithful maid,
And mourns a gen'rous passion unrepaid.
Yet would I praise the pious zeal that saves
Imperial London from her world of knaves ;
Yet would I count it no inglorious strife
To scourge the pests of property and life.
Come then, long skill'd in theft's illusive ways,
Lord of the clue that threds her mighty maze!
Together let us beat all Giles's fields,
Try what the night-house, what the round-house
        yields,
Hang when we must, be candid when we please,
But leave no bawd, unlicens'd, at her ease.
Say first, of thieves above, or thieves below,
What can we order till their haunts we know ?
Far from St. James's let your Nimrods stray,
But stop and call at Stephen's in their way.
That ancient victualler, we've been told, of late,
Has kept bad hours, encourag'd high debate ?
That those without still pelting those within,
Have stunn'd the peaceful neighbours with their
That if you close his private walls invest,  [din;
'Tis odds, you meet with some unruly guest—
Good Lord, sir John, how would the people stare,
To see the present and the late lord mayor [1],
Bow to the majesty of Bow-street chair!

----
[1] This was written about the year 1776.

Illustrious chiefs ! can I your haunts pass by,
Nor give my long-lov'd liberty a sigh ?
That heav'nly plant which long unblemish'd
Dishonour'd only, only hurt by you !   [blew,
Dishonour'd, when with harden'd front you claim
To deeds of darkness her diviner name !
For you grim Licence strove with hydra breath
To spread the blasts of pestilence and death :
Here for poor vice, for dark ambition there ,
She scatter'd poison thro' the social air.
    Yet here, in vain—Oh, had her toil been vain,
When with black wing she swept the western
When with low labour, and insidious art, [main ;
She tore a daughter from her parent's heart !
Oh, patriots, ever patriots out of place,
Fair honour's foil, and liberty's disgrace !
With spleen I see your wild illusions spread
Thro' the long region of a land misled ;
See commerce sink, see cultivation's charms
Lost in the rage of anarchy and arms !
    And thou, O Ch——m, once a nation's pride,
Borne on the brightest wave of glory's tide !
Hast thou the parent spurn'd, the erring child
With prospects vain to ruin's arms beguil'd ?
Hast thou the plans of dire defection prais'd
For the poor pleasure of a statue rais'd ?
    Oh, patriots, ever patriots out of place,
From Charles quite graceless, up to Grafton's
    grace !
Where forty-five once mark'd the dirty door,
And the chain'd knife [1] invites the paltry whore;
Tho' far, methinks, the choicest guests are fled,
And Wilkes and Humphrey number'd with the
    dead,
Wilkes, who in death would friendship's vows
    fulfil,
True to his cause, and dines with Humphrey
    still—
Where sculks each dark, where roams each
    desp'rate wight,
Owls of the day and vultures of the night,—
Shall we, O Knight, with cruel pains explore,
Clear these low walks, and think the bus'ness
    o'er ?
No—much, alas ! for you, for me remains,
Where Justice sleeps, and Depredation reigns.
    Wrapt in kind darkness, you no spleen betray,
When the gilt Nabob lacqueys all the way :
Harmless to you his towers, his forests rise,
That swell with anguish my indignant eyes;
While in those towers raz'd villages I see,
And tears of orphans watering every tree.
Are these mock-ruins that invade my view ?
These are the entrails of the poor Gentoo.
That column's trophied base his bones supply ;
That lake the tears that swell'd his sable eye !
Let here, O Knight, their steps terrific steer
Thy hue and cry, and loose thy bloodhounds here.
    Oh, Mercy ! thron'd on His eternal breast,
Who breath'd the savage waters into rest;
By each soft pleasure that thy bosom smote,
When first creation started from his thought ;
By each warm tear that melted o'er thine eye,
When on his works was written " These must die;"
If secret slaughter yet, nor cruel war
Have from these mortal regions forc'd thee far,
Still to our follies, to our frailties blind,
Oh, stretch thy healing wings o'er human kind !

[1] Chain'd to the table, to prevent depredations.

—For them I ask not, hostile to thy sway,
Who calmly on a brother's vitals prey;
For them I plead not, who, in blood embru'd,
Have ev'ry softer sentiment subdu'd.

### PRISONS.

    Yet, gentle power, thy absence I bewail,
When seen the dank, dark regions of a jail ;
When found alike in chains and night enclos'd,
The thief detected, and the thief suppos'd !
Sure, the fair light and the salubrious air
Each yet-suspected prisoner might share.
—To lie, to languish in some dreary cell,
Some loathed hold, where guilt and horrour dwell,
Ere yet the truth of seeming facts be tried,
Ere yet their country's sacred voice decide
Britain, behold thy citizens expos'd,
And blush to think the Gothic age unclos'd !

### FILIATION.

    Oh, more than Goths, who yet decline to raze
That pest of James' puritanic days,
The savage law [1] that barb'rously ordains
For female virtue lost a felon's pains !
Dooms the poor maiden, as her fate severe,
To toil and chains a long-enduring year.
Th' unnatural monarch, to the sex unkind,
An owl obscene, in learning's sunshine blind !
Councils of pathics, cabinets of tools,
Benches of knaves, and parliaments of fools,
Fanatic fools, that, in those twilight times,
With wild religion cloak'd the worst of crimes!—
Hope we from such a crew, in such a reign,
For equal laws, or policy humane ?
    Here, then, O Justice ! thy own power forbear;
The sole protector of th' unpitied fair.
Tho' long entreat the ruthless overseer;
Tho' the loud vestry tease thy tortur'd ear;
Tho' all to acts, to precedents appeal,
Mute by her pen, and vacant rest thy seal.
    Yet shalt thou know, nor is the diff'rence nice,
The casual fall, from impudence of vice.
Abandon'd guilt by active laws restrain,
But pause .. ... if virtue's slightest spark re-
    main.
Left to the shameless lash, the hardning jail,
The fairest thoughts of modesty would fail.
The down-cast eye, the tear that flows amain,
As if to ask her innocence again ;
The plaintive babe, that slumb'ring seem'd to lie
On her soft breast, and wakes at the heav'd sigh ;
The cheek that wears the beauteous robe of
    shame;
How loth they leave a gentle breast to blame !
    Here, then, O Justice ! thy own power for-
    bear ;—
The sole protector of th' unpitied fair !

---

## THE ORIGIN OF THE VEIL.

Warm from this heart while flows the faithful line,
The meanest friend of beauty shall be mine.
What Love, or Fame, or Fortune could bestow,
The charm of praise, the ease of life, I owe.
To beauty present, or to beauty fled,
To Hertford living, or Caernarvon dead,

1 7 Jac. c. 4.

To  Tweedale's  taste,  to  Edgecumbe's  sense
    serene,
And (Envy spare this boast) to Britain's queen ;
Kind to the lay that all unlabour'd flow'd,
What Fancy caught, where Nature's pencil
    glow'd [1],
She saw the path to new, tho' humble fame,
Gave me her praise, and left me fools to blame.
    Strong in their weakness are each woman's
        charms,
Dread that endears, and softness that disarms.
The tim'rous eye retiring from applause,
And the mild air that fearfully withdraws,
Marks of our power these humble graces prove,
And, dash'd with pride, we deeper drink of love.
    Chief of those charms that hold the heart in
At thy fair shrine, O Modesty, we fall.  [thrall,
Not Cynthia rising o'er the wat'ry way,
When on the dim wave falls her friendly ray ;
Not the pure ether of Æolian skies,
That drinks the day's first glories as they rise ;
Not all the tints from evening-clouds that break,
Burn in the beauties of the virgin's cheek ;
When o'er that cheek, undisciplin'd by art,
The sweet suffusion rushes from the heart.
    Yet the soft blush, untutor'd to control,
The glow that speaks the susceptible soul,
Led by nice honour, and by decent pride,
The voice of ancient virtue taught to hide ;
Taught beauty's bloom the searching eye to shun,
As early flowers blow fearful of the Sun.
    Far as the long records of time we trace [2]
Still flow'd the veil o'er modesty's fair face :
The guard of beauty, in whose friendly shade,
Safe from each eye the featur'd soul is laid,—
The pensive thought that paler looks betray,
The tender grief that steals in tears away,
The hopeless wish that prompts the frequent sigh
Bleeds in the blush, or melts upon the eye.
    The man of faith thro' Gerar doom'd to stray,
A nation waiting his eventful way,
His fortune's fair companion at his side,
The world his promise, Providence his guide ;
Once, more than virtue dar'd to value life,
And call'd a sister whom he own'd a wife.
Mistaken father of the faithful race,
Thy fears alone could purchase thy disgrace.
" Go" to the fair, when conscious of the tale,
Said Gerar's prince, "thy husband is thy veil [3]."
O ancient faith ! O virtue mourn'd in vain !
When Hymen's altar never held a stain;
When his pure torch shed undiminish'd rays,
And fires unholy died beneath the blaze!
For faith like this fair Greece was early known,
And claim'd the veil's first honours as her own.

[1] The Fables of Flora.

[2] Plato mentions two provinces in Persia, one
of which was called the Queen's Girdle, the other
the Queen's Veil, the revenues of which, no
doubt, were employed in purchasing those parts
of her majesty's dress.  It was about the middle
of the third century, that the eastern women, on
taking the vow of virginity, assumed that veil
which had before been worn by the Pagan
priestesses, and which is used by the religious
among the Romanists now.

[3] " He is the veil of thine eyes to all that are
with thee, and to all others."—Gen. xx. 16. Vet.
Trans.

Ere half her sons, o'er Asia's trembling coast,
Arm'd to revenge one woman's virtue lost ;
Ere he, whom Circe sought to charm in vain,
Follow'd wild fortune o'er the various main,
In youth's gay bloom he plied th' exulting oar,
From Ithaca's white rocks to Sparta's shore :
Free to Nerician gales [4] the vessel glides,
And wild Eurotas [5] smoothes his warrior tides ;
For am'rous Greece, when Love conducts the way,
Beholds her waters, and her winds obey.
No object hers but Love's impression knows,
No wave that wanders, and no breeze that blows,
Her groves [6], her mountains have his power con-
    fest,
And Zephyr sigh'd not but for Flora's breast.
'Twas when his sighs in sweetest whispers
    stray'd
Far o'er Laconia's plains from Eva's [7] shade !
When soft-ey'd Spring resum'd his mantle gay,
And lean'd luxurious on the breast of May,
Love's genial banners young Ulysses bore
From Ithaca's white rocks to Sparta's shore.
    With all that soothes the heart, that wins, or
        warms,
All princely virtues, and all manly charms,
All love can urge, or eloquence persuade,
The future hero woo'd his Spartan maid.
Yet long he woo'd—in Sparta, slow to yield,
Beauty, like valour, long maintain'd the field.
    " No bloom so fair Messene's banks disclose,
No breath so pure o'er Tempe's bosom blows ;
No smile so radiant throws the genial ray
Thro' the fair eye-lids of the op'ning day ;
But deaf to vows with fondest passion prest,
Cold as the wave of Hebrus' wint'ry breast,
Penelope regards her lover's pain,
And owns Ulysses eloquent in vain.
    " To vows that vainly waste their warmth in
        air,
Insidious hopes that lead but to despair,
Affections lost, desires the heart must rue,
And love, and Sparta's joyless plains, adieu !
    " Yet still this bosom shall one passion share,
Still shall my country find a father there.
Ev'n now the children of my little reign
Demand that father of the faithless main,
Ev'n now, their prince solicitous to save,
Climb the tall cliff, and watch the changeful
    wave.
    " But not for him their hopes or fears alone !
They seek the promis'd partner of his throne ;
For her their incense breathes, their altars blaze,
For her to Heaven the suppliant eye they raise.
Ah ! shall they know their prince implor'd in
    vain ?
Can my heart live beneath a nation's pain ?"
    There spoke the virtue that her soul admir'd,
The Spartan soul, with patriot ardour fir'd.
" Enough !" she cried—" Be mine to boast a
    part
In him, who holds his country to his heart.
Worth, honour, faith, that fair affection gives,
And with that virtue, ev'ry virtue lives.[8]"

[4] From the mountain Neritos in Ithaca, now
called Nericia.

[5] The Spartan river.

[6] E merite d'Alberghe amore.—Tasso.

[7] A mountain in Peloponnesus.

[8] Omnes omnium caritates, &c.—Cic.

Pleas'd that the nobler principles could move
His daughter's heart, and soften it to love,
Icarius own'd the auspices divine,
Wove the fair crown 9, and bless'd the holy
    shrine.
But ah ! the dreaded parting hour to brave !
Then strong affection griev'd for what it gave.
Should he the comfort of his life's decline,
His life's last charm to Ithaca resign ?
Or, wand'ring with her to a distant shore,
Behold Eurotas' long-lov'd banks no more ?
Expose his grey hairs to an alien sky,
Nor on his country's parent bosom die 10 ?
  " No, prince," he cried ; " for Sparta's hap-
    pier plain
Leave the lov'd honours of thy little reign.
The grateful change shall equal honours bring.
—Lord of himself, a Spartan is a king."
  When thus the prince, with obvious grief
    opprest,
" Canst thou not force the father from thy breast?
Not without pain behold one child depart,
Yet bid me tear a nation from my heart ?
—Not for all Sparta's, all Euboea's plains"—
He said, and to his coursers gave the reins.
  Still the fond sire pursues with suppliant voice;
'Till, mov'd, the monarch yields her to her
    choice.
" Tho' mine by vows, by fair affection mine,
And holy truth, and auspices divine,
This suit let fair Penelope decide,
Remain the daughter, or proceed the bride."
  O'er the quick blush her friendly mantle fell,
And told him all that modesty could tell.
No longer now the father's fondness strove
With patriot virtue or acknowledg'd love,
But on the scene that parting sighs endear'd,
Fair Modesty's 11 first honour'd fane he rear'd.
  The daughter's form the pictur'd goddess
    wore,
The daughter's veil 12 before her blushes bore,

9 The women of ancient Greece, at the marriage ceremony, wore garlands of flowers, probably as emblems of purity, fertility, and beauty.
Thus Euripides,

      —— αλλ' ὅμως
Σοι κατασεψατ' ἐγωνιν ἡνεν, ὡς γαμουμενην·   IPH.

The modern Greek ladies wear these garlands in
various forms, whenever they appear dressed ;
and frequently adorn themselves thus for their
own amusement, and when they do not expect to
be seen by any but their domestics.
           Voyage Litteraire de la Grece.
  10 The ancients esteemed this one of the
greatest misfortunes that could befall them. The
Trojans thought it the most lamentable circumstance attending the loss of their pilot Palinurus,
that his body should lie in a foreign country.
    —— Ignotâ, Palinure, jacebis arenâ.
  11 Pausanias, who has recorded the story on
which this little poem is founded, tells us that
this was the first temple erected to Modesty in
Greece.
  12 See the Veil of Modesty in the Musum
Capitolinum, vol. iii.; and for further proofs
of its high antiquity, see Hom. Odyss. lib. vi.
Claud. Epithal. Honor. where he says,

Et crines festina ligat, peplumque fluentem
Allevat—

And taught the maids of Greece this sovereign
    law—
She most shall conquer, who shall most with-
    draw.

## VERSES IN MEMORY OF A LADY.

WRITTEN AT SANDGATE CASTLE, 1768.

Nec tantum ingenio, quantum servire dolori.
                    PROPERT.

LET others boast the base and faithless pride,
No nuptial charm to known, or known, to hide,
With vain disguise from Nature's dictates part,
For the poor triumph of a vacant heart ;
My verse the god of tender vows inspires,
Dwells on my soul, and wakens all her fires.
  Dear, silent partner of those happier hours,
That pass'd in Hackthorn's vales, in Blagdon's
    bowers !
If yet thy gentle spirit wanders here,
Borne by its virtues to no nobler sphere ;
If yet that pity which, of life possest,
Fill'd thy fair eye, and lighten'd thro' thy breast;
If yet that tender thought, that gen'rous care,
The gloomy power of endl ess night may spare ;
Oh ! while my soul for thee, for thee complains,
Catch her warm sighs, and kiss her bleeding
    strains.             [breath,
Wild, wretched wish ! Can pray'r with feeble
Pierce the pale ear, the statu'd ear of death ?
Let patience pray, let hope aspire to prayer !
And leave me the strong language of despair !
Hence, ye vain painters of ingenious woe,
Ye Lytteltons, ye shining Petrarchs, go !
I hate the languor of your lenient strain,
Your flow'ry grief, your impotence of pain.
Oh ! had ye known what I have known, to
    prove
The searching flame, the agonies of love !
Oh ! had ye known how souls to souls impart
Their fire, or mix the life-props of the heart !
Not like the streams that down the mountain
    side
Tunefully mourn, and sparkle as thy glide ;
Not like the breeze, that sighs at ev'ning-hour,
On the soft bosom of some folding flower ;
Your stronger grief, in stronger accents borne,
Had sooth'd the breast with burning anguish
    torn.
The voice of seas, the winds that rouse the deep,
Far-sounding floods that tear the mountain's
    steep ;
Each wild and melancholy blast that raves
Round these dim towers, and smites the beating
    waves—           [breath,
This soothes my soul—'Tis Nature's mournful
'Tis Nature struggling in the arms of death !
See, the last aid of her expiring state,
See Love, e'en Love, has lent his darts to fate ! 1

Iphig. in Taur. Act. iv.; and Colut. Rapt. Helen.
lib. i. v. 381, where Hermione tears her gold-
embroidered veil on the disappearance of Helen :

  —— Aureum quoque rupit capitis tegmen.
    1 The lady died in child-bed.

Oh! when beneath his golden shafts I bled,
And vainly bound his trophies round my head:
When crown'd with flowers, he led the rosy day,
Liv'd to my eye, and drew my soul away—
Could fear, could fancy, at that tender hour,
See the dim grave demand the nuptial flower?
There, there his wreathes dejected Hymen
        strew'd;
And mourn'd their bloom unfaded as he view'd.
There each fair hope, each tenderness of life,
Each nameless charm of soft obliging strife,
Delight, love, fancy, pleasure, genjus fled,
And the best passions of my soul lie dead;
All, all is there in cold oblivion laid,
But pale remembrance bending o'er a shade.
  O come, ye softer sorrows, to my breast!
Ye lenient sighs, that slumber into rest! [wave,
Come, soothing dreams, your friendly pinions
We'll bear the fresh rose to yon honour'd grave;
For once this pain, this frantic pain forego,
And feel at last the luxury of woe!
Ye holy suff'rers, that in silence wait
The last sad refuge of relieving fate!
That rest at eve beneath the cypress' gloom,
And sleep familiar on your future tomb;
With you I'll waste the slow-departing day,
And wear with you th' uncolour'd hours away.
  Oh! lead me to your cells, your lonely ailes,
Where resignation folds her arms and smiles:
Where holy faith unwearied vigils keeps,
And guards the urn where fair Constantia[a] sleeps:
There, let me there in sweet oblivion lie,
And calmly feel the tutor'd passions die.

---

## MONODY.

### SUNG BY A REDBREAST.

The gentle pair that in these lonely shades,
Wand'ring, at eve or morn, I oft have seen,
Now, all in vain, I seek at eve or morn,
With drooping wing, forlorn,
Along the grove, along the daisied green.
For them I've warbled many a summer's day,
Till the light dews impearled all the plain,
And the glad shepherd shut his nightly fold;
Stories of love, and high adventures old
Were the dear subjects of my tuneful strain.
  Ah! where is now the hope of all my lay?
Now they, perchance, that heard them all are
        dead!
With them the meed of melody is fled,
And fled with them the list'ning ear of praise.
Vainly I dreamt, that when the wint'ry sky
Scatter'd the white flood on the wasted plain,
When not one berry, not one leaf was nigh,
To sooth keen hunger's pain,
Vainly I dreamt my songs might not be vain.
That oft within the hospitable hall
Some scatter'd fragment haply I might find,
Some friendly crumb perchance for me design'd,
When seen despairing on the neighbouring wall.
Deluded bird, those hopes are now no more!
Dull Time has blasted the departing year,
And Winter frowns severe,
Wrapping his wan limbs in his mantle hoar;

    [a] See Spectator, No. 164.

Yet not within the hospitable half
The cheerful sound of human voice I hear;
No piteous eye is near,
To see me drooping on the lonely wall.

---

## TO A REDBREAST.

Little bird, with bosom red,
Welcome to my humble shed!
Courtly domes of high degree
Have no room for thee and me;
Pride and pleasure's fickle throng
Nothing mind an idle song.
  Daily near my table steal,
While I pick my scanty meal.
Doubt not, little though there be,
But I'll cast a crumb to thee;
Well rewarded, if I spy
Pleasure in thy glancing eye;
See thee, when thou'st eat thy fill,
Plume thy breast, and wipe thy bill.
  Come, my feather'd friend, again,
Well thou know'st the broken pane.
Ask of me thy daily store;
Go not near Avaro's door;
Once within his iron hall,
Woeful end shall thee befall.
Savage!—He would soon divest
Of its rosy plumes thy breast;
Then, with solitary joy,
Eat thee, bones and all, my boy!

---

## A CONTEMPLATION.

O Nature! grateful for the gifts of mind,
  Duteous I bend before thy holy shrine;
To other hands be Fortune's goods assign'd,
  And thou, more bounteous, grant me only
    thine.

Bring gentlest Love, bring Fancy to my breast;
  And if wild Genius, in his devious way,
Would sometimes deign to be my ev'ning guest,
  Or near my lone shade not unkindly stray:

I ask no more! for happier gifts than these,
  The suff'rer, man, was never born to prove;
But may my soul eternal slumbers seize,
  If lost to Genius, Fancy, and to Love!

---

## MENALCAS.

### A PASTORAL.

Now cease your sweet pipes, shepherds! cease
    your lays,
Ye warbling train, that fill the echoing groves
With your melodious love-notes! Die, ye winds,
That o'er Arcadian valleys blow! ye streams,
Ye garrulous old streams, suspend your course,
And listen to Menalcas.—

### MENALCAS.

Come, fairest of the beauteous train that sport
On Ladon's flow'ry side, my Delia, come!
For thee thy shepherd, silent as he sits
Within the green wood, sighs: for thee prepares

The various wreathes in vain; explores the shade
Where lowly lurks the violet blue, where droops,
In tender beauty, its fair spotted bells,
The cowslip: oft with plaintive voice he calls
The wakeful Echo—What are streams or flowers,
Or songs of blithe birds? What the blushing rose,
Young health, or music, or the voice of praise,
The smile of vernal suns, the fragrant breath
Of ev'ning gales, when Delia dwells afar?

---

## INSCRIPTIONS ON A BEECH TREE,

### IN THE ISLAND OF SICILY.

Sweet land of Muses! o'er whose favour'd plains
Ceres and Flora held alternate sway;
By Jove refresh'd with life-diffusing rains,
By Phœbus blest with ev'ry kinder ray!

O with what pride do I those times survey,
When Freedom, by her rustic minstrels led,
Danc'd on the green lawn many a summer's day,
While pastoral Ease reclin'd her careless head.

In these soft shades: ere yet that shepherd fled,
Whose music pierc'd Earth, air, and Heav'n and Hell,
And call'd the ruthless tyrant of the dead
From the dark slumbers of his iron cell.

His ear unfolding caught the magic spell:
He felt the sounds glide softly through his heart; [tell;
The sounds that deign'd of Love's sweet power to
And, as they told, would point his golden dart.

Fix'd was the god: nor power had he to part,
For the fair daughter of the sheaf-crown'd queen,
Fair without pride, and lovely without art,
Gather'd her wild flowers on the daisied green.

He saw, he sigh'd; and that unmelting breast,
Which arms the hand of death, the power of love confest.

---

## A MONODY,

INSCRIBED TO MY WORTHY FRIEND

### JOHN SCOTT, ESQ.

BEING WRITTEN IN HIS GARDEN AT AMWELL, IN HERTFORDSHIRE, THE BEGINNING OF THE YEAR 1769.

Friend of my genius! on whose natal hour,
Shone the same star, but shone with brighter ray;
Oft as amidst thy Amwell's shades I stray,
And mark thy true taste in each winding bower,
From my full eye why falls the tender shower,
While other thoughts than these fair scenes convey,
Bear on my trembling mind, and melts its powers away?

Ah me! my friend! in happier hours I spread,
Like thee, the wild walk o'er the varied plain;
The fairest tribe of Flora's painted train,
Each bolder shrub that grac'd her genial bed,
When old Sylvanus, by young wishes led,
Stole to her arms, of such fair offspring vain,
That bore their mother's beauties on their head.
Like thee, inspir'd by love—'twas Delia's charms!
'Twas Delia's taste the new creation gave:
For her my groves in plaintive sighs would wave,
And call her absent to their master's arms.

She comes—Ye flowers, your fairest blooms unfold,
Ye waving groves, your plaintive sighs forbear,
Breathe all your fragrance to the am'rous air,
Ye smiling shrubs whose heads are cloth'd with gold!
She comes, by truth, by fair affection led,
The long lov'd mistress of my faithful heart!
The mistress of my soul, no more to part,
And all my hopes and all my vows are sped.
Vain, vain delusions! dreams for ever fled!
Ere twice the spring had wak'd the genial hour,
The lovely parent bore one beauteous flower,
And droop'd her gentle head,
And sunk, for ever sunk, into her silent bed.

Friend of my genius! partner of my fate!
To equal sense of painful suffering born!
From whose fond breast a lovely parent torn,
Bedew'd thy pale cheek with a tear so late—
Oh! let us mindful of the short, short date,
That bears the spoil of human hopes away,
Indulge sweet mem'ry of each happier day!
No, close, for ever close the iron gate
Of cold oblivion on that dreary cell,
Where the pale shades of past enjoyments dwell,
And, pointing to their bleeding bosoms, say,
" On life's disastrous hour what varied woes await!"

Let scenes of softer, gentler kind,
Awake to fancy's soothing call,
And milder on the pensive mind,
The shadow'd thought of grief shall fall.
Oft as the slowly-closing day
Draws her pale mantle from the dew-star's eye,
What time the shepherd's cry
Leads from the pastur'd hills his flocks away,
Attentive to the tender lay
That steals from Philomela's breast,
Let us in musing silence stray,
Where Lee beholds in mazes slow
His uncomplaining waters flow,
And all his whisp'ring shores invite the charms of rest.

---

## IMITATION OF WALLER.

### WALLER TO ST. EVREMOND.

O vales of Penshurst, now so long unseen!
Forgot each shade secure, each winding green;
These lonely paths, what art have I to tread,
Where once young Love, the blind enthusiast, led?
Yet if the genius of your conscious groves
His Sidney in my Sacharissa loves;
Let him with pride her cruel power unfold;
By him my pains let Evremond be told.

## THE DUCHESS OF MAZARINE.

### ON HER RETIRING INTO A CONVENT.

YE holy cares that haunt these lonely cells,
These scenes where salutary sadness dwells;
Ye sighs that minute the slow wasting day,
Ye pale regrets that wear my life away;
O bid these passions for the world depart,
These wild desires, and vanities of heart,
Hide every trace of vice, of follies past,
And yield to Heaven the victory at last.
To that the poor remains of life are due,
'Tis Heaven that calls, and I the call pursue.
  Lord of my life, my future cares are thine,
My love, my duty greet thy holy shrine:
No more my heart to vainer hopes I give,
But live for thee, whose bounty bids me live.
  The power that gave these little charms their
          grace,
His favours bounded, and confin'd their space;
Spite of those charms shall time, with rude essay,
Tear from the cheek the transient rose away.
But the free mind, ten thousand ages past,
Its Maker's form, shall with its Maker last.
  Uncertain objects still our homes employ;
Uncertain all that bears the name of joy!
Of all that feel the injuries of fate
Uncertain is the search, and short the date,
Yet ev'n that boon what thousands wish to gain?
That boon of death, the sad resource of pain!
  Once on my path all Fortune's glory fell,
Her vain magnificence, and courtly swell:
Love touch'd my soul at least with soft desires,
And vanity there fed her meteor fires,
This truth at last the mighty scenes let fall,
An hour of innocence was worth them all.
  Lord of my life! O, let thy sacred ray
Shine o'er my heart, and break its clouds away,
Deluding, flattering, faithless world, adieu!
Long hast thou taught me, God is only true:
That God alone I trust, alone adore,
No more deluded, and misled no more.
  Come, sacred hour, when wav'ring doubts
          shall cease!
Come, holy scenes of long repose and peace!
Yet shall my heart, to other interests true,
A moment balance 'twixt the world and you?
Of pensive nights, of long-reflecting days,
Be yours, at last, the triumph and the praise.
  Great, gracious Master, whose unbounded
          sway,
Felt thro' ten thousand worlds, those worlds obey;
Wilt thou for once thy awful glories shade,
And deign t' espouse the creature thou hast
          made?
All other ties indignant I disclaim,
Dishonour'd those, and infamous to name!
O fatal ties for which such tears I've shed.
For which the pleasures of the world lay dead!
That world's soft pleasures you alone disarm;
That world without you, still might have its
          charm.
But now those scenes of tempting hope I close,
And seek the peaceful studies of repose:
Look on the past as time that stole away,
And beg the blessings of a happier day.
  Ye gay saloons, ye golden-vested halls,
Scenes of high treats, and heart-bewitching balls!

Dress, figure, splendour, charms of play, farewell;
And all the toilet's science to excel;
E'en Love that ambush'd in this beauteous hair,
No more shall lie, like Indian archers, there.
Go, erring Love! for nobler objects given!
Go, beauteous hair, a sacrifice to Heaven!
Soon shall the veil these glowing features hide,
At once the period of their power and pride!
The helpless lover shall no more complain
Of vows unheard, or unrewarded pain;
While calmly sleep in each untutor'd breast
My secret sorrow, and his sighs profest.
  Go, flattering train! and, slaves to me no
          more,
With the same sighs some happier fair adore!
Your alter'd faith I blame not, nor bewail—
And haply yet, (what woman is not frail?)
Yet, haply, might I calmer minutes prove,
If he that lov'd me knew no other love!
  Yet were that ardour, which his breast in-
          spir'd,
By charms of more than mortal beauty fir'd;
What nobler pride! could I to Heaven resign
The zeal, the service that I boasted mine!
O, change your false desires, ye flattering train,
And love me pious, whom you lov'd profane!
  These long adieus with lovers doom'd to go,
Or prove their merit, or my weakness show,
But Heaven, to such soft frailties less severe,
May spare the tribute of a female tear,
May yield one tender moment to deplore
Those gentle hearts that I must hold no more.

---

## THE AMIABLE KING.

THE free-born Muse her tribute rarely brings,
Or burns her incense to the power of kings!
But Virtue ever shall her voice command,
Alike a spade or sceptre in her hand.
Is there a prince untainted with a throne,
That makes the interest of mankind his own;
Whose bounty knows no bounds of time or place,
Who nobly feels for all the human race:
A prince that acts in reason's steady sphere,
No slave to passion, and no dupe to fear;
A breast where mild humanity resides,
Where virtue dictates, and where wisdom guides;
A mind that, stretch'd beyond the years of
          youth,
Explores the secret springs of taste and truth?
These, these are virtues which the Muse shall
          sing;
And plant, for these, her laurels round a king!
Britannia's monarch! this shall be thy praise;
For this be crown'd with never-fading bays!

---

## THE HAPPY VILLAGER.

VIRTUE dwells in Arden's vale;
There her hallow'd temples rise,
There her incense greets the skies,
  Grateful as the morning gale;
There, with humble Peace and her,
Lives the happy villager;
  There, the golden smiles of morn
Brighter every field adorn;

There the Sun's declining ray
Fairer paints the parting day :
There the woodlark louder sings,
Zephyr moves on softer wings,
Groves in greener honours rise,
Purer azure spreads the skies ;
There the fountains clearer flow,
Flowers in brighter beauty blow :
For, with Peace and Virtue, there
Lives the happy villager.
　　Distant still from Arden's vale
Are the woes the bad bewail ;
Distant fell-Remorse, and Pain,
And Frenzy smiling o'er her chain !
Grief's quick pang, Despair's dead groan,
Are in Arden's vale unknown :
For, with Peace and Virtue, there
Lives the happy villager !
　　In his hospitable cell,
Love, and Truth, and Freedom dwell ;
And, with aspect mild and free,
The graceful nymph, Simplicity.
Hail, ye liberal graces, hail !
Natives all of Arden's vale :
For, with Peace and Virtue, there
Lives the happy villager.

---

## HYMENEAL.

ON THE MARRIAGE OF HIS PRESENT MAJESTY.

Awake, thou everlasting lyre !
That once the mighty Pindar strung,
When wrapt with more than mortal fire,
　　The gods of Greece he sung ! Awake !
Arrest the rapid foot of Time again
With liquid notes of joy, and pleasure's melting
　　　　strain.

Crown'd with each beauteous flower that blows
　　On Acidalia's tuneful side ;
　　With all Aonia's rosy pride,
Where numerous Aganippe flows ;
From Thespian groves and fountains wild,
　　Come, thou yellow-vested boy,
　　Redolent of youth and joy,
Fair Urania's favour'd child[1] !
　　George to thee devotes the day :
　　Io ! Hymen, haste away !

Daughter of the genial main !
　　Queen of youth and rosy smiles,
　　Queen of dimple-dwelling wiles ;
Come with all thy Paphian train :
O, give the fair that blooms for Britain's throne,
Thy melting charms of love, thy soul-enchanting
　　　　zone !

Daughter of the genial main !
　　Bring that heart-dissolving power,
　　Which once in Ida's sacred bower
The soul of Jove oppos'd in vain :
The sire of gods thy conquering charms confess'd ;
And, vanquish'd, sunk, sunk down of Juno's fos-
　　t'ring breast.

She comes, the conscious sea subsides ;
　　Old Ocean curbs his thund'ring tides :
　　Smooth the silken surface lies,
Where Venus' flow'ry chariot flies :

[1] See Catullus.

Paphian airs in ambush sleep
On the still bosom of the deep ;
Paphian maids around her move,
Keen-ey'd Hope, and Joy, and Love :
Their rosy breasts a thousand Cupids lave,
And dip their wanton wings, and beat the buxom
　　wave.

But mark, of more than vulgar mein,
　　With regal grace and radiant eye,
　　A form in youthful majesty !
Britain, hail thy favour'd queen !
　　For her the conscious sea subsides ;
　　Old Ocean curbs his thund'ring tides,
　　O'er the glassy-bosom'd main
　　Venus leads her laughing train ;
The Paphian maids move graceful by her side,
And o'er the buxom waves the rosy Cupids ride.

Fly, ye fairy-footed hours !
Fly, with aromatic flowers !
Such as bath'd in orient dews,
Beauty's living glow diffuse ;
Such as in Idalia's grove
Breathe the sweets, the soul of love !

Come, genial god of chaste delight,
　　With wreathes of festive roses crown'd,
And torch that burns with radiance bright,
　　And liberal robe that sweeps the ground !
　　Bring the days of golden joy,
　　Pleasures pure, that never cloy !
Bring to Britain's happy pair,
All that's kind, and good, and fair !
George to thee devotes the day :
Io ! Hymen, haste away.

Daughters of Jove ! ye virgins sage,
　　That wait on Camus' hoary age ;
　　That oft his winding vales along
Have smooth'd your silver-woven song ;
O wake once more those lays sublime,
That live beyond the wrecks of time !
To crown your Albion's boasted pair,
The never-fading wreath prepare ;
While her rocks echo to this strain,
" The friends of freedom and of Britain reign."

---

## SONG.

'Tis o'er, the pleasing prospect's o'er !
My weary heart can hope no more—
　　Then welcome, wan Despair !
Approach with all thy dreadful train !
Wild Anguish, Discontent and Pain,
　　And thorny-pillow'd Care.

Gay Hope, and Ease, and Joy, and Rest,
All, all that charms the peaceful breast,
　　For ever I resign.
Let pale Anxiety instead,
That has not where to lay her head,
　　And lasting woe, be mine.

It comes ! I feel the painful woe—
My eyes for Solyman will flow
　　In silent grief again ;
Who, wand'ring o'er some mountain drear,
Now haply sheds the pensive tear,
　　And calls on me in vain.

Perhaps, along the lonely shores,
He now the sea's blue breast explores,

To watch the distant sail ;
Perhaps, on Sundah's hills forlorn,
He faints, with aching toil o'erborn,
And life's last spirits fail.

Ah, no! the cruel thought forbear!
Avaunt, thou fiend of fell despair,
That only death canst give!
While Heav'n eternal rules above,
Almena yet may find her love,
And Solyman may live!

---

WRITTEN IN

## A COTTAGE-GARDEN,

### AT A VILLAGE IN LORRAIN.

OCCASIONED BY A TRADITION CONCERNING A
TREE OF ROSEMARY,

Arbustum loquitur.

O THOU, whom love and fancy lead
To wander near this woodland hill,
If ever music smooth'd thy quill,
Or pity wak'd thy gentle reed,
Repose beneath my humble tree,
If thou lov'st simplicity.

Stranger, if thy lot has laid
In toilsome scenes of busy life,
Full sorely may'st thou rue the strife
Of weary passions ill repaid.
In a garden live with me,
If thou lov'st simplicity.

Flowers have sprung for many a year
O'er the village maiden's grave,
That, one memorial sprig to save,
Bore it from a sister's bier;
And, homeward walking, wept o'er me
The true tears of simplicity.

And soon, her cottage window near,
With care my slender stem she plac'd;
And fondly thus her grief embrac'd;
And cherish'd sad remembrance dear :
For love sincere and friendship free
Are children of simplicity.

When past was many a painful day,
Slow-pacing o'er the village green,
In white were all its maidens seen,
And bore my guardian friend away.
Ah death! what sacrifice to thee,
The ruins of simplicity.

One gen'rous swain her heart approv'd,
A youth whose fond and faithful breast,
With many an artless sigh confess'd,
In Nature's language, that he lov'd :
But, stranger, 'tis no tale to thee,
Unless thou lov'st simplicity.

He died—and soon her lip was cold,
And soon her rosy cheek was pale ;
The village wept to hear the tale,
When for both the slow bell toll'd—
Beneath yon flow'ry turf they lie,
The lovers of simplicity.

Yet one boon have I to crave ;
Stranger, if thy pity bleed,
Wilt thou do one tender deed,
And strew my pale flowers o'er their grave?

So lightly lie the turf on thee,
Because thou lov'st simplicity.

---

### THE PASTORAL PART OF

## MILTON'S EPITAPHIUM DAMONIS.

O FOR the soft lays of Himeria's maids !
The strains that died in Arethusa's shades ;
Tun'd to wild sorrow on her mournful shore.
When Daphnis, Hylas, Bion breath'd no more !
Thames' vocal wave shall ev'ry note prolong,
And all his villas learn the Doric song,
How Thyrsis mourn'd his long lov'd Damon
      dead,
What sighs he utter'd, and what tears he shed—
Ye dim retreats, ye wandering fountains know,
Ye desert wilds bore witness to his woe :
Where oft in grief he past the tedious day,
Or lonely languish'd the dull night away.
      Twice had the fields their blooming honours
      bore;
And Autumn twice resign'd his golden store,
Unconscious of his loss, while Thyrsis staid
To woo the sweet Muse in the Tuscan shade :
Crown'd with her favour, when he sought again
His flock forsaken, and his native plain ;
When to his old elm's wonted shade return'd—
Then—then, he miss'd his parted friend—and
      mourn'd.
And go, he cry'd, my tender lambs, adieu !
Your wretched master has no time for you.
      Yet are there pow'rs divine in Earth or sky ?
Gods can they be who destin'd thee to die ?
And shalt thou mix with shades of vulgar name ;
Lost thy fair honours, and forgot thy fame ?
Not he, the god whose golden wand restrains
The pale ey'd people of the gloomy plains,
Of Damon's fate shall thus regardless be,
Or suffer vulgar shades to herd with thee.
      Then go, he cry'd, &c.

      Yet while one strain my trembling tongue
      may try,
Not unlamented, shepherd, shalt thou die.
Long in these fields thy fame shall flourish fair,
And Daphnis only greater honours share ;
To Daphnis only purer vows be paid,
While Pan or Pales loves the vulgar shade.
If truth or science may survive the grave,
Or, what is more, a poet's friendship save.
      Then go, &c.

      These, these are thine : for me what hopes
      remain ?
Save of long sorrow, and of anguish vain.
For who, still faithful to my side, shall go,
Like thee, through regions clad with chilling
      snow ?
Like thee, the rage of fiery summers bear,
When fades the wan flower in the burning air ?
The lurking dangers of the chase essay,
Or sooth with song and various tales the day ?
      Then go, &c.

      To whom shall I my hopes and fears impart ?
Or trust the cares and follies of my heart ?
Whose gentle councils put those cares to flight ?
Whose cheerful converse cheat the tedious night ?

The social hearth when autumn's treasures store,
Chill blow the winds without, and through the
    bleak elm roar.
      Then go, &c.

When the fierce suns of summer noons invade,
And Pan reposes in the green-wood shade,
The shepherds hide, the nymphs plunge down
    the deep,       [sleep.
And waves the hedge-row o'er the ploughman's
Ah! who shall charm with such address refin'd,
Such attic wit, and elegance of mind?
      Then go, &c.

Alas! now lonely round my fields I stray,
And lonely seek the pasture's wonted way,
Or in some dim vale's mournful shade repose—
There pensive wait the weary day's slow close,
While showers descend, the gloomy tempest
    raves,
And o'er my head the struggling twilight waves.
      Then go, &c.

Where once fair harvest cloth'd my cultur'd
    plain,
Now weeds obscene and vexing brambles reign;
The groves of myrtle and the clustering vine
Delight no more, for joy no more is mine.
My flocks no longer find a master's care;
Ev'n piteous as they gaze with looks of dumb
    despair.
      Then go, &c,

Thy hazel, Tyt'rus, has no charms for me;
Nor yet thy wild ash, lov'd Alphesibee,
No more shall fancy wave her rural dream,
By Ægan's willow, or Amynta's stream,
The trembling leaves, the fountains cool serene,
The murmuring zephyr, and the mossy green—
These simle unseen, and those unheeded play,
I cut my shrubs, and careless walk'd away.
      Then go, &c.

Mopsus, who knows what fates the stars dis-
    pense,
And solves the grove's wild warblings into sense,
Thus Mopsus mark'd—" what thus thy spleen
    can move?
Some baleful planet, or some hopeless love?
The star of Saturn oft annoys the swain,
And in the dull cold breast long holds his leaden
    reign.''
      Then go, &c.

The nymphs too, piteous of their shepherd's
Came the sad cause solicitous to know.   [woe,
" Is this the port of jocund youth," they cry,
That look disgusted, and that downcast eye?
Gay smiles and love on that soft season wait;
He's twice a wretch whom beauty wounds too
    late [1] .''
      Then go, &c.

[1] Milton seems to have borrowed this sentiment from Guarini:

    Che,se t' assaie a la canuta etate
      Amoroso talento,
    Havrai doppio tormento,
    E di quel, che potendo non volesti,
    E di quel, che volendo non potrai.

One gentle tear the British Chloris gave,
Chloris the grace of Maldon's purple wave—
In vain—my grief no soothing words disarm,
No future hopes, nor present good can charm.
      Then go, &c.

The happier flocks one social spirit moves,
The same their sports, their pastures and their
    loves;
Their hearts to no peculiar object tend,
None knows a fav'rite, or selects a friend.
So herd the various natives of the main,
And Proteus drives in crowds his scaly train;
The feather'd tribes too find an easier fate,
The meanest sparrow still enjoys his mate;
And when by chance or wearing age she dies,
The transient loss a second choice supplies.
Man, hapless man, for ever doom'd to know
The dire vexations that from discord flow,
In all the countless numbers of his kind,
Can scarcely meet with one congenial mind;
If haply found, Death wings the fatal dart,
The tender union breaks, and breaks his heart.
      Then go, &c.

Ah me! what errour tempted me to go
O'er foreign mountains, and thro' Alpine snow?
Too great the price to mark in Tyber's gloom
The mournful image of departed Rome!
Nay, yet immortal, could she boast again
The glories of her universal reign,
And all that Maro left his fields to see,
Too great the purchase to abandon thee!
To leave thee in a land no longer seen!—
Bid mountains rise, and oceans roll between!—
Ah! not embrace thee!—not to see thee die!
Meet thy last looks, or close thy languid eye!
Not one fond farewell with thy shade to send,
Nor bid thee think of thy surviving friend!
      Then go, &c.

Ye Tuscan shepherds, pardon me this tear!
Dear to the Muse, to me for ever dear!
The youth I mourn a Tuscan title bore—
See Lydian Lucca [2] for her son deplore!
O days of ecstacy! when wrapt I lay
Where Arno wanders down his flow'ry way,—
Pluck'd the pale violet, press'd the velvet mead,
Or bade the myrtle's balmy fragrance bleed!—
Delighted, heard amid the rural throng,
Menalcas strive with Lycidas in song.
Oft would my voice the mimic strain essay,
Nor haply all unheeded was my lay.
For, shepherds, yet I boast your gen'rous meed,
The osier basket, and compacted reed:
Francino crown'd me with a poet's fame,
And Dati [3] taught his beechen groves my name.

[2] The Tuscans were a branch of the Pelasgi
that migrated into Europe, not many ages after
the dispersion. Some of them marched by land
as far as Lydia, and from thence detached a
colony under the conduct of Tyrsenus to Italy.

[3] When Milton was in Italy, Carlo Dati was
professor of philosophy at Florence—a liberal
friend to men of genius and learning, as well
foreigners as his own countrymen. He wrote a
panegyric and some poems on Lewis XIV. besides other tracts.

## TO THE REV. MR. LAMB.

Lamb, could the Muse that boasts thy forming
                care,
Unfold the grateful feelings of my heart,
Her hand for thee should many a wreath prepare,
And cull the choicest flowers with studious art.

For mark'd by thee was each imperfect ray
    That haply wander'd o'er my infant mind ;
The dawn of genius brighten'd into day,
    As thy skill open'd, as thy lore refin'd.

Each uncouth lay that faulter'd from my tongue,
    At eve or morn from Eden's murmurs caught ;
Whate'er I painted, and whate'er I sung,
    Tho' rude the strain, tho' artless was the
                draught ;

You wisely prais'd, and fed the sacred fire
    That warms the breast with love and honest
                fame ;
You swell'd to nobler heights the infant lyre,
    Rais'd the low thought, and check'd th' exu-
                berant flame.

O could the Muse in future times obtain
    One humble garland from th' Aonian tree !
With joy I'd bind thy favour'd brows again,
    With joy I'd form a fairer wreath for thee.

## EPISTLE TO MR. ———

From scenes where fancy no excursion tries,
Nor trusts her wing to smoke-envelop'd skies ;
Far from the town's detested haunts remov'd,
And nought but thee deserted that I lov'd ;
From noise and folly and the world got free,
One truant thought yet only stays for thee.
What is that world which makes the heart its
                slave?
A restless sea, revolving wave on wave :
There rage the storms of each uncertain clime ;
There float the wrecks of fortune and of time :
There hope's smooth gales in soft succession
                blow,
While disappointment hides the rock below.
The syren pleasures tune their fatal breath,
And lull you to the long repose of death.
What is that world ? ah !—'tis no more
Than the vext ocean while we walk the shore.
Loud roar the winds and swell the wild waves
                high,
Lash the rude beach, and frighten all the sky ;
No longer shall my little bark be rent,
Since Hope resign'd her anchor to Content.
    Like some poor fisher that, escap'd with life,
Will trust no more to elemental strife ;
But sits in safety on the green-bank side,
And lives upon the leavings of the tide ;
Like him contented you your friend shall see,
As safe, as happy, and as poor as he.

## TO A LADY,

### ON READING AN ELEGY WRITTEN BY HER ON THE SEARCH OF HAPPINESS.

To seek the lovely nymph you sing,
    I've wander'd many a weary mile,
From grove to grove, from spring to spring ;
    If here or there she deign'd to smile.

Nay what I now must blush to say,
    For sure it hap'd in evil hour ;
I once so far mistook my way,
    To seek her in the haunts of power.

How should success my search betide,
    When still so far I wander'd wrong ?
For Happiness on Arrowe's side,
    Was list'ning to Maria's song.

Delighted thus with you to stay,
    What hope have I the nymph to see ;
Unless you cease your magic lay,
    Or bring her in your arms to me ?

## TO ALMENA.

### FROM THE BANKS OF THE IRWAN.

" Where trembling poplars shade their parent
                vale,
And tune to melody the mountain gale ;
Where Irwan murmurs musically slow,
And breathing breezes through his osiers blow ;
Friend of my heart, behold thy poet laid
In the dear silence of his native shade !
Ye sacred vales, whereof the Muse, unseen,
Led my light steps along the moon-light green ;
Ye scenes, where peace and fancy held their
                reign,
For ever lov'd, and once enjoy'd again !
Ah ! where is now that nameless bliss refin'd,
That tranquil hour, that vacancy of mind ?
As sweet the wild rose bears its balmy breast ;
As soon the breeze with murmurs sooths to rest ;
As smooth the stream of silver Irwan flows ;
As fair each flower along his border blows ;
Yet dwells not here that nameless bliss refin'd,
That tranquil hour, that vacancy of mind.
Is it that knowledge is allied to woe ;
And are we happy only e'er we know ?
Is it that Hope withholds her golden ray,
That Fancy's fairy visions fade away ?
Or can I, distant far from all that's dear,
Be happy only when Almena's near ?
That truth, the feelings of my heart disclose :
Too dear the friendship for the friend's repose."
Thus mourn'd the Muse, when thro' his osiers
                wild,
The hill-born Irwan rais'd his head and smil'd :
" Child of my hopes,"–he fondly cried, " for-
Nor let thy Irwan witness thy despair.   [bear ;
Has peace indeed forsook my flow'ry shore ?
Shall Fame, and Hope, and Fancy charm no
                more ?
Tho' Fame and Hope in kindred air depart,
Yet Fancy still should hold thee to her heart ;
For, at thy birth, the village hind has seen
Her light wings waving o'er the shadowy green.
With rosy wreaths she crown'd the new-born
                hours,
And rival fairies fill'd thy bed with flowers ;

In vain—if grief shall waste thy blooming years,
And life dissolve in solitude and tears."

## TO GEORGE COLMAN, ESQ.

PREFIXED TO THE CORRESPONDENCE OF THEODOSIUS
AND CONSTANTIA.

To live beneath the golden star of love,
  With happier fancy, passions more refin'd,
Each soft'ning charm of tenderness to prove,
  And all the finer movements of the mind—
From gifts like these say, what the boasted gain
  Of those who exquisitively feel or know?
The skill from pleasure to extract the pain,
  And open all the avenues of woe.

Yet shall we, Colman, at these gifts repine?
  Implore cold apathy to steel the heart?
Would you that sensibility resign,
  And with those powers of genius would you
    part?

Ah me! my friend! nor deem the verse divine
  That weakness wrote in Petrarch's gentle
    strain!
When once he own'd at love's unfav'ring shrine
  "A thousand pleasures were not worth one
    pain."

The dreams of fancy sooth the pensive heart;
  For fancy's urn can new delights dispense:
The powers of genius purer joys impart;
  For genius brightens all the springs of sense.

O charm of every muse-ennobl'd mind,
  Far, far above the grovelling crowd to rise!—
Leave the low train of trifling cares behind,
  Assert its birthright, and affect the skies!

O right divine, the pride of power to scorn!
  On fortune's little vanity look down!
With nobler gifts, to fairer honours born,
  Than fear, or folly, fancies in a crown!

As far each boon that Nature's hand bestows
  The worthless glare of fortune's train exceeds,
As yon fair orb, whose beam eternal glows,
  Outshines the transient meteor that it feeds.

To Nature, Colman, let thy incense rise,
  For, much indebted, much hast thou to pay;
For taste refin'd, for wit correctly wise,
  And keen discernment's soul-pervading ray.

To catch the manners from the various face,
  To paint the nice diversities of mind,
The living lines of character to trace,
  She gave thee powers, and the task assign'd.

Seize, seize the pen! the sacred hour departs!
  Nor, led by kindness, longer lend thine ear:
The tender tale of two ingenuous hearts
  Would rob thee of a moment and a tear.

## AN ODE

TO THE GENIUS OF WESTMORELAND.

Hail, hidden power of these wild groves,
These uncouth rocks, and mountains grey!
Where oft, as fades the closing day,
  The family of Fancy roves.

In what lone cave, what sacred cell,
Coeval with the birth of Time,
Wrapt in high cares, and thoughts sublime,
  In awful silence dost thou dwell?

Oft in the depth of winter's reign,
As blew the bleak winds o'er the dale;
Moaning along the distant gale,
  Has Fancy heard thy voice complain.
Oft in the dark wood's lonely way,
Swift has she seen thee glancing by;
Or down the summer evening sky,
  Sporting in clouds of gilded day.

If caught from thee the sacred fire,
That glow'd within my youthful breast;
Those thoughts too high to be exprest,
  Genius, if thou didst once inspire,

O pleas'd accept this votive lay,
That, in my native shades retir'd,
And once, once more by thee inspir'd,
  In gratitude I pay.

## HYMN TO HOPE.

Μυνη δ' αυτοθι 'ΕΛΠΙΣ εν αρρηκτοισι δομοισιν
Ενδον εμιμνε ——                        HES.

WRITTEN IN 1761.

Sun of the soul! whose cheerful ray
  Darts o'er this gloom of life a smile;
Sweet Hope, yet further gild my way,
  Yet light my weary steps awhile,
Till thy fair lamp dissolve in endless day.

O come with such an eye and mien,
  As when by amorous shepherd seen;
While in the violet-breathing vale
He meditates his evening tale!
Nor leave behind thy fairy train,
Repose, Belief, and Fancy vain;
That towering on her wing sublime,
Outstrips the lazy flight of Time,
Riots on distant days with thee,
And opens all futurity.

O come! and to my pensive eye
Thy far-foreseeing tube apply,
Whose kind deception steals us o'er
The gloomy waste that lies before;
Still opening to the distant sight
The sunshine of the mountain's height;
Where scenes of fairer aspect rise,
Elysian groves, and azure skies.

Nor, gentle Hope, forget to bring
The family of Youth and Spring;
The hours that glide in sprightly round,
The Mountain-nymphs with wild thyme crown'd;
Delight that dwells with raptur'd eye
On stream, or flower, or field, or sky:
And foremost in thy train advance
The Loves and Joys in jovial dance;
Nor last be Expectation seen,
That wears a wreath of ever-green.

Attended thus by Beleau's streams,
Oft hast thou sooth'd my waking dreams,

When, prone beneath an osier shade,
At large my vacant limbs were laid;
To thee and Fancy all resign'd,
What visions wander'd o'er my mind!
Illusions dear, adieu! no more
Shall I your fairy haunts explore;
For Hope withholds her golden ray,
And Fancy's colours faint away.
To Eden's shores, to Enon's groves,
Resounding once with Delia's loves,
Adieu! that name shall sound no more
O'er Enon's groves or Eden's shore:
For Hope withholds her golden ray,
And Fancy's colours faint away.

Life's ocean slept,—the liquid gale
Gently mov'd the waving sail.
Fallacious Hope! with flattering eye
You smil'd to see the streamers fly.
The thunder bursts, the mad wind raves,
From slumber wake the 'frighted waves:
You saw me, fled me thus distrest,
And tore your anchor from my breast.

Yet come, fair fugitive, again;
I love thee still, though false and vain.
Forgive me, gentle Hope, and tell
Where, far from me, you deign to dwell.
To sooth Ambition's wild desires;
To feed the lover's eager fires;
To swell the miser's mouldy store;
To gild the dreaming chymist's ore;
Are these thy cares?—Or more humane,
To loose the war-worn captive's chain,
And bring before his languid sight
The charms of liberty and light:
The tears of drooping Grief to dry;
And hold thy glass to Sorrow's eye?

Or do'st thou more delight to dwell
With Silence in the hermit's cell?
To teach Devotion's flame to rise,
And wing her vespers to the skies;
To urge, with still returning care,
The holy violence of prayer;
In rapt'rous visions to display
The realms of everlasting day,
And snatch from Time the golden key,
That opens all eternity?

Perchance, on some unpeopled strand,
Whose rocks the raging tide withstand,
Thy soothing smile, in deserts drear,
A lonely mariner may cheer,
Who bravely holds his feeble breath,
Attack'd by Famine, Pain, and Death.
With thee, he bears each tedious day
Along the dreary beach to stray:
Whence their wide way his toil'd eyes strain
O'er the blue bosom of the main;
And meet, where distant surges rave,
A white sail in each foaming wave.

Doom'd from each native joy to part,
Each dear connection of the heart,
You the poor exile's steps attend,
The only undeserting friend.
You wing the slow-declining year;
You dry the solitary tear;
And oft, with pious guile, restore
Those scenes he must behold no more,

O most ador'd of Earth or skies!
To thee ten thousand temples rise;
By age retain'd, by youth carest,
The same dear idol of the breast.
Depriv'd of thee, the wretch were poor
That rolls in heaps of Lydian ore:
With thee the simple hind is gay,
Whose toil supports the passing day.

The rose-lip'd Loves that, round their queen,
Dance o'er Cythera's smiling green,
Thy aid implore, thy power display
In many a sweetly-warbled lay,
For ever in thy sacred shrine,
Their unextinguish'd torches shine;
Idalian flowers their sweets diffuse,
And myrtles shed their balmy dews.
Ah! still propitious, may'st thou deign
To sooth an anxious lover's pain!
By thee deserted, well I know,
His heart would feel no common woe.
His gentle prayer propitious hear,
And stop the frequent-falling tear.

For me, fair Hope, if once again
Perchance, to smile on me you deign,
Be such your sweetly-rural air,
And such a graceful visage wear,
As when, with Truth and young Desire,
You wak'd the lord of Hagley's lyre;
And painted to her poet's mind,
The charms of Lucy, fair and kind.

But ah! too early lost!—then go,
Vain Hope, thou harbinger of woe.
Ah! no;—that thought distracts my heart;
Indulge me, Hope, we must not part.
Direct the future as you please;
But give me, give me present ease.

Sun of the soul! whose cheerful ray
Darts o'er this gloom of life a smile;
Sweet Hope, yet further gild my way,
Yet light my weary steps awhile,
Till thy fair lamp dissolve in endless day.

## HYMN TO PLUTUS.

Great god of wealth, before whose sacred
　　　throne　　　　　　　　　　[prone!
Truth, Honour, Genius, Fame, and Worth lie
To thy throng'd temples take one vot'ry more:
To thee a poet never kneel'd before.
　Adieu the gods that caught my early prayer!
Wisdom that frown'd, and Knowledge fraught
　　　with care,
Friendship that every veering gale could move!
And tantalizing Hope, and faithless Love!
These, these are slaves that in thy liv'ry shine:
For Wisdom, Friendship, Love himself is thine!
　For thee I'll labour down the mine's dark way,
And leave the confines of enliv'ning day;
For thee Asturia's shining sands explore,
And bear the splendours of Potosi's ore;
Scale the high rock, and tempt the raging sea,
And think, and toil, and wish, and wake for thee.
Farewell the scenes that thoughtless youth could
　　　please;
The flow'ry scenes of indolence and ease.

Where you the way with magic power beguile,
Bassora's deep, or Lybia's deserts smile.

Foes of thy worth, that, insolent and vain,
Deride thy maxims, and reject thy reign,
The frantic tribe of virtue shall depart,
And make no more their ravage in my heart.
Away "The tears that pity taught to flow!"
Away that anguish for a brother's woe!
Adieu to these, and ev'ry tiresome guest,
That drain'd my fortunes, or destroy'd my rest!

Ah, good Avaro! could I thee despise?
Thee, good Avaro: provident and wise?
Plutus, forgive the bitter things I've said!
I love Avaro; poor Avaro's dead.

Yet, yet I'm thine; for Fame's unerring tongue
In thy sooth'd ear thus pours her silver song,
"Immortal Plutus! god of golden ease!
Form'd ev'ry heart, and ev'ry eye to please!
For thee Content her downy carpet spreads,
And rosy Pleasure swells her genial beds.
'Tis thine to gild the mansions of Despair,
And beam a glory round the brows of Care;
To cheat the lazy pace of sleepless hours
With marble fountains, and ambrosial bowers."

O grant me, Plutus, scenes like those I sung,
My youthful lyre when vernal fancy strung.
For me their shades let other Studleys rear,
Tho' each tree's water'd with a widow's tear.

Detested god!—forgive me! I adore.
Great Plutus, grant me one petition more,
Should Delia, tender, gen'rous, fair and free,
Leave love and truth, and sacrifice to thee,
I charge thee, Plutus, be to Delia kind,
And make her fortunes richer than her mind.
Be her's the wealth all Heaven's broad eye can
  view;
Grant her, good god, Don Philip and Peru.

---

## HYMN TO HUMANITY.

Parent of Virtue, if thine ear
Attend not now to Sorrow's cry;
If now the pity-streaming tear
Should haply on thy cheek be dry;
Indulge my votive strain, O sweet Humanity.

Come, ever welcome to my breast,
A tender, but a cheerful guest;
Nor always in the gloomy cell
Of life-consuming sorrow dwell;
For sorrow, long-indulg'd and slow,
Is to humanity a foe;
And grief, that makes the heart its prey,
Wears sensibility away.
Then comes, sweet nymph, instead of thee,
The gloomy fiend Stupidity.

O may that fiend be banish'd far,
Though passions hold eternal war!
Nor ever let me cease to know
The pulse that throbs at joy or woe.
Nor let my vacant cheek be dry,
When sorrow fills a brother's eye;
Nor may the tear that frequent flows
From private or from social woes,
E'er make this pleasing sense depart;
Ye cares, O harden not my heart.

If the fair star of fortune smile,
Let not its flatt'ring power beguile :

Nor borne along the fav'ring tide,
My full sails swell with bloating pride.
Let me from wealth but hope content,
Rememb'ring still it was but lent;
To modest Merit spread my store;
Unbar my hospitable door!
Nor feed, for pomp, an idle train,
While Want unpity'd pines in vain.

If Heav'n, in ev'ry purpose wise,
The envy'd lot of wealth denies;
If doom'd to drag life's painful load
Thro' poverty's uneven road,
And, for the due bread of the day,
Destin'd to toil as well as pray;
To thee, Humanity, still true,
I'll wish the good I cannot do;
And give the wretch that passes by,
A soothing word—a tear—a sigh.

Howe'er exalted, or deprest,
Be ever mine the feeling breast.
From me remove the stagnant mind
Of languid indolence, reclin'd;
The soul that one long Sabbath keeps,
And thro' the Sun's whole circle sleeps;
Dull Peace, that dwells in Folly's eye,
And self-attending Vanity.
Alike, the foolish, and the vain,
Are strangers to the sense humane.

O, for that sympathetic glow
Which taught the holy tear to flow,
When the prophetic eye survey'd
Sion in future ashes laid;
Or, rais'd to Heav'n, implor'd the bread
That thousands in the desert fed!
Or when the heart o'er Friendship's grave
Sigh'd,—and forgot its power to save—
O, for that sympathetic glow,
Which taught the holy tear to flow!

It comes: it fills my labouring breast!
I feel my beating heart opprest.
Oh! hear that lonely widow's wail!
See her dim eye! her aspect pale!
To Heav'n she turns in deep despair,
Her infants wonder at her prayer,
And, mingling tears they know not why,
Lift up their little hands and cry.
O God! their moving sorrows see!
Support them, sweet Humanity.

Life, fill'd with grief's distressful train,
For ever asks the tear humane.
Behold in yon unconscious grove
The victims of ill-fated love!
Heard you that agonizing throe?
Sure this is not romantic woe!
The golden day of joy is o'er;
And now they part—to meet no more.
Assist them, hearts from anguish free!
Assist them, sweet Humanity.

Parent of Virtue, if thine ear
Attend not now to Sorrow's cry;
If now the pity-streaming tear
Should haply on thy cheek be dry,
Indulge my votive strain, O sweet Humanity.

## HYMN TO THE RISING SUN.

From the red wave rising bright,
　Lift on high thy golden head;
　O'er the misty mountains spread
Thy smiling rays of orient light!
See the golden god appear;
Flies the fiend of darkness drear;
Flies, and in her gloomy train,
Sable Grief, and Care, and Pain!
See the golden god advance!
On Taurus' heights his coursers prance:
With him haste the vernal Hours,
Breathing sweets, and drooping flowers.
Laughing Summer at his side,
Waves her locks in rosy pride;
And Autumn bland with aspect kind,
Bears his golden sheaf behind.
O haste, and spread the purple day
O'er all the wide ethereal way!
Nature mourns at thy delay:
God of glory haste away!
From the red wave rising bright,
　Lift on high thy golden head;
　O'er the misty mountains, spread
Thy smiling rays of orient light!

## A FAREWELL HYMN

### TO THE VALLEY OF IRWAN.

Farewell the fields of Irwan's vale,
　My infant years where Fancy led;
And sooth'd me with the western gale,
　Her wild dreams waving round my head,
While the blythe blackbird told his tale.
Farewell the fields of Irwan's vale!

The primrose on the valley's side,
　The green thyme on the mountain's head,
The wanton rose, the daisy pied,
　The wilding's blossom blushing red;
No longer I their sweets inhale
Farewell the fields of Irwan's vale!

How oft, within yon vacant shade,
　Has ev'ning clos'd my careless eye!
How oft, along those banks I've stray'd,
　And watch'd the wave that wander'd by;
Full long their loss shall I bewail.
Farewell the fields of Irwan's vale!

Yet still, within yon vacant grove,
　To mark the close of parting day;
Along yon flow'ry banks to rove,
　And watch the wave that winds away;

Fair Fancy sure shall never fail,
Tho' far from these, and Irwan's vale!

## HYMN TO THE ETERNAL PROVIDENCE.

Life of the world, Immortal Mind,
Father of all the human kind!
Whose boundless eye that knows no rest,
Intent on Nature's ample breast;
Explores the space of Earth and skies,
And sees eternal incense rise!
To thee my humble voice I raise;
Forgive, while I presume to praise.

Tho' thou this transient being gave,
That shortly sinks into the grave;
Yet 'twas thy goodness, still to give
A being that can think and live;
In all thy works thy wisdom see,
And stretch its tow'ring mind to thee.
To thee my humble voice I raise;
Forgive, while I presume to praise.

And still this poor contracted span,
This life, that bears the name of man;
From thee derives its vital ray,
Eternal Source of life and day!
Thy bounty still the sunshine pours,
That gilds its morn and ev'ning hours,
To thee my humble voice I raise;
Forgive, while I presume to praise.

Thro' Errour's maze, thro' Folly's night,
The lamp of Reason lends me light.
When stern Affliction waves her rod,
My heart confides in thee, my God!
When Nature shrinks, oppress'd with woes,
E'en then she finds in thee repose.
To thee my humble voice I raise;
Forgive, while I presume to praise.

Affliction flies, and Hope returns;
Her lamp with brighter splendour burns;
Gay Love with all his smiling train,
And Peace and Joy are here again.
These, these, I know, 'twas thine to give;
I trusted; and, behold, I live!
To thee my humble voice I raise;
Forgive, while I presume to praise.

O may I still thy favour prove!
Still grant me gratitude and love.
Let truth and virtue guide my heart;
Nor peace, nor hope, nor joy depart;
But yet, whate'er my life may be,
My heart shall still repose on thee!
To thee my humble voice I raise;
Forgive, while I presume to praise.

# TRANSLATIONS.

## THE DEATH OF ADONIS.

FROM THE GREEK OF BION [1].

1759.

Adonis dead, the Muse of woe shall mourn ;
Adonis dead, the weeping Loves return.
  The queen of beauty o'er his tomb shall shed
Her flowing sorrows for Adonis dead ;
For earth's cold lap her velvet couch forego,
And robes of purple for the weeds of woe.
Adonis dead, the Muse of woe shall mourn ;
Adonis dead, the weeping Loves return.

[1] Bion, the pastoral poet, lived in the time of
Ptolemy Philadelphus. By the epithet Σμυρναι☉
every where applied to him, it is probable that
he was born at Smyrna. Moschus confirms this,
when he says to the river Meles, which had before wept for Homer,

———Νυν παλιν αλλον
Υἷα δακρυεις———

  It is evident, however, that he spent much of
his time in Sicily, Moschus, as he tells us, was
his scholar ; and by him we are informed, that
his master was not a poor poet. " Thou hast left
to others thy riches, " says he, " but to me thy
poetry." It appears from the same author,
that he died by poison. The best edition of his
works, is that of Paris, by M. de Longe-Pierre,
with a French translation.
  *Adonis dead*, &c.] Adonis, the favourite of Venus, was the son of Cynaras, king of Cyprus. His
chief employment was hunting, though he is represented by Virgil as a Shepherd,

Oves ad flumina pavit Adonis.

He was killed by a wild boar, if we may believe Propertius, in Cyprus :

——— Percussit Adonim
Venantem Idalio vertice durus Aper.

The anniversary of his death was celebrated
through the whole Pagan world. Aristophanes,
in his Comedy of Peace, reckons the feast of Adonis among the chief festivals of the Athenians.
The Syrians observed it with all the violence of
grief, and the greatest cruelty of self-castigation.
It was celebrated at Alexandria in St. Cyril's
time ; and when Julian the apostate made his
entry at Antioch, in the year 362, they were celebrating the feast of Adonis.
  The ancients differ greatly in their accounts
of this divinity. Athenæus says, that he was the
favourite of Bacchus. Plutarch maintains, that
he and Bacchus are the same, and that the Jews
abstain'd from swine's flesh because Adonis was
killed by a boar. Ausonius, Epig. 30, affirms
that Bacchus, Osiris, and Adonis, are one and
the same.

Stretch'd on this mountain thy torn lover lies:
Weep, queen of beauty ! for he bleeds—he
    dies.
Ah ! yet behold life's last drops faintly flow,
In streams of purple, o'er those limbs of snow !
From the pale cheek the perish'd roses fly ;
And death dims slow the ghastly gazing eye.
Kiss, kiss those fading lips, ere chill'd in death ;
With soothing fondness stay the fleeting breath.
'Tis vain—ah ! give the soothing fondness o'er !
Adonis feels the warm salute no more.
Adonis dead the Muse of woe shall mourn !
Adonis dead the weeping Loves return.
His faithful dogs bewail their master slain,
And mourning dryads pour the plaintive strain.
Not the fair youth alone the wound opprest,
The queen of beauty bears it in her breast.
Her feet unsandal'd, floating wild her hair,
Her aspect woeful, and her bosom bare,
Distrest she wanders the wild wastes forlorn,
Her sacred limbs by ruthless brambles torn.
Loud as she grieves, surrounding rocks com-
    plain,
And Echo thro' the long vales calls her absent
    swain.
Adonis hears not : life's last drops fall slow,
In streams of purple, down his limbs of snow.
The weeping Cupids round their queen deplore,
And mourn her beauty, and her love no more.
Each rival grace that glow'd with conscious
    pride,
Each charm of Venus, with Adonis dy'd.
Adonis dead, the vocal hills bemoan,
And hollow groves return the sadd'ning groan.
The swelling floods with sea-born Venus weep,
And roll in mournful murmurs to the deep:

  *His faithful dogs*, &c.—*The queen of beauty*,
&c.] The lines in the original run thus :

Αγριον αγριον ἑλκ☉ ἔχει κατα μηρον Ἀδονις.
Μειζον δ' ἁ' Κυθερεια φερει ποτι καρδιον ἑλκ☉.
Κεινον μεν περι παιδα φιλοι κυνες ὡρυσαντο,
Και Νυμφαι κλαιυσιν ὀρειαδες.

The two first of these lines contain a kind of
witticism, which it was better to avoid.—The
author had, however, too much true genius to be
fond of these little affected turns of expression,
which Musæus and others have been industrious
to strike out.
  These four verses are transposed in the translation for the sake of the connection.

  *Distrest, she wanders*, &c.] This image of
the sorrow of Venus is very affecting, and is introduced in this place with great beauty and propriety. Indeed, most modern poets seem to have
observed it, and have profited by it in their
scenes of elegiac woe.

  *The swelling floods*, &c ] When the poet makes
the rivers mourn for Venus, he very properly
calls her Αφροδιτα; but this propriety perhaps

In melting tears the mountain-springs comply;
The flowers, low drooping, blush with grief,
  and die.
Cythera's groves with strains of sorrow ring;
The dirge funereal her sad cities sing.
Hark! pitying Echoes Venus' sighs return;
When Venus sighs, can aught forbear to
  mourn?
But when she saw her fainting lover lie,
The wide wound gaping on the with'ring thigh;
But streaming when she saw life's purple tide,
Stretch'd her fair arms, with trembling voice
  she cry'd:
" Yet stay,lov'd youth! a moment ere we part,
O let me kiss thee!—hold thee to my heart!
A little moment, dear Adonis! stay!
And kiss thy Venus, ere those lips are clay.
Let those dear lips by mine once more be prest,
'Till thy last breath expire into my breast;
Then, when life's ebbing pulse scarce, scarce
  can move,
I'll catch thy soul, and drink thy dying love.
That last-left pledge shall sooth my tortur'd
  breast,
" When thou art gone —————
When, far from me, thy gentle ghost explores
Infernal Pluto's grimly-glooming shores.
" Wretch that I am! immortal and divine,
In life imprison'd whom the Fates confine.
He comes! receive him to thine iron-arms;
Blest queen of death! receive the prince of
  charms.
Far happier thou, to whose wide realms repair
Whatever lovely, and whatever fair.
The smiles of joy, the golden hours are fled:
Grief, only grief, survives Adonis dead."
The Loves around in idle sorrow stand,
And the dim torch falls from the vacant hand.
Hence the vain zone! the myrtle's flow'ry
  pride!
Delight and beauty with Adonis died,
" Why didst thou, vent'rous, the wild chase
  explore,
From his dark lair to rouse the tusky boar?

was merely accidental, as he has given her the
same appellation when she wanders the desert.

*The flowers, low-drooping, blush,* &c.]

Ανθεα δ' εξ οδυνας ερυθραινεται. —————

Paleness being the known effect of grief, we
do not at first sight accept this expression; but
when we consider that the first emotions of it
are attended with blushes, we are pleased with
the observation.

*Cythera's groves,* &c.]

α δε Κυθηρη
Παντας ανα κναμω και ααν πολιν οιχΤρον αειδει.

This passage the scholiasts have entirely mis-
understood. They make Κυθηρη Venus, for
which they have neither any authority, the Doric name she borrows from that island being always Κυθερεια, nor the least probability from
the connection.
This proves that the island Cythera was the
place where Adonis perished, notwithstanding
the opinion of Propertius and others to the contrary.

Far other sport might those fair limbs essay,
Than the rude combat, or the savage fray."
Thus Venus griev'd—the Cupids round
  deplore;
And mourn her beauty, and her love no more.
Now flowing tears in silent grief complain,
Mix with the purple streams, and flood the
  plain,
Yet not in vain those sacred drops shall flow,
The purple streams in blushing roses glow:
And catching life from ev'ry falling tear,
Their azure heads anemonies shall rear.
But cease in vain to cherish dire despair,
Nor mourn unpitied to the mountain-air;
The last sad office let thy hand supply,
Stretch the stiff limbs, and close the glaring
  eye.
That form repos'd beneath the bridal vest
May cheat thy sorrows with the feint of rest.
For lovely smile those lips, tho' void of breath,
And fair those features in the shade of death.
Haste, fill with flowers, with rosy wreaths his
  bed.
Perish the flowers! the prince of beauty's
  dead.
Round the pale corse each breathing essence
  strew,
Let weeping myrtles pour their balmy dew.
Perish the balms, unable to restore
Those vital sweets of love that charm no more.
'Tis done.—Behold, with purple robes ar-
  ray'd,
In mournful state the clay-cold limbs are laid,
The Loves lament with all the rage of woe,
Stamp on the dart, and break the useless bow.
Officious these the wat'ry urn supply.
Unbind the buskin'd leg, and wash the bleed-
  ing thigh.
O'er the pale body those their light wings wave,
As yet, tho' vain, solicitous to save.
All, wild with grief, their hapless queen de-
  plore,
And mourn her beauty and her love no more.
Dejected Hymen droops his head forlorn,
His torch extinct, and flow'ry tresses torn:
For nuptial airs, and songs of joy, remain
The sad slow dirge, the sorrow-breathing strain.
Who wou'd not, when Adonis dies, deplore?
Who wou'd not weep when Hymen smiles no
  more;
The Graces mourn the prince of beauty slain,
Loud as Dione on her native main:
The Fates relenting join the general woe,
And call the lover from the realms below.
Vain, hopeless grief! can living sounds pervade
The dark, dead regions of eternal shade?
Spare, Venus, spare that too luxuriant tear
For the long sorrows of the mournful year.

*For the long,* &c.] Numa seems to have borrowed the custom he instituted of mourning a
year for the deceased, from the Greeks. For
though it is said only ten months were set apart,
yet ten months were the year of Romulus, till regulated by his successor.

EXTRAIT D'UNE ODE SUR LA
MEDIOCRITÉ.

PAR M. GRESSET.

Seduits par d'aveugles idoles
Du bonheur; fantômes frivoles,
Le vulgaire et les grands ne te suivirent pas :
Tu n'eus pour sujets que ses sages
Qui doivent l'estime des âges
A la sagesse, acquise en marchant sur tes pas.

Tu vis naître dans tes retraites
Ces nobles et tendres poëtes,
Dont la voix n'eut jamais formé de sons brillans.
Si le fracas de la fortune,
Ou si indigence importune
Eût troublé leur silence, ou caché leurs talens.

Mais en vain tu fuyois la gloire.
La renommé, et la victoire
Vinrent dans tes déserts se choisir des héros ;
Mieux formés par tes loix stoïques,
Aux vertus, aux faits héroïques,
Que parmi la mollesse, et l'orgueil des faisceaux.

Pour Mars tu formois, loin des villes
Les Fabrices, et les Camilles,
Et ses sages vainqueurs, philosophes guerriers
Qui, du char de la Dictature
Descendant à l'agriculture,
Sur tes secrets autels rapportoient leurs lauriers.

Trop heureux, déïté paisible,
Le mortel sagement sensible,
Qui jamais loin de toi a porte ses desirs,
Par sa douce mélancolie,
Sauvé de l'humaine folie,
Dans la vérité seul il cherche ses plaisirs.

Ignoré de la multitude,
Libre de tout servitude,
Il n'envia jamais, les grands biens, les grand noms,
Il n'ignore point que la foudre
A plus souvent réduit en poudre
Le pin de monts altiers, que l'ormeau des
valons.

Sourd aux censures populaires,
Il ne craint point les yeux vulgaires,
Son œil perce au-delà de leur foible horison :
Quelques bruits que la foule en sème,
Il est satisfait de lui même,
S'il a scû mériter l'aveu de la raison.

Il rit du sort, quand les conquêtes
Promènent de têtes en têtes
Les couronnes du nord, ou celles du midi :
Rien n'altère sa paix profonde,
Et les derniers instans du monde
N'épouvanteroient point son cœur encore hardi.

Amitié, charmante immortelle,
Tu choisis à si cœur fidèle
Peu d'amis mais constans, vertueux comme lui :
Tu ne crains point que le caprice,
Que l'intérêt les désunisse,
Ou verse sur leurs jours les poisons de l'ennui.

Ami des frugales demeures,
Sommeil, pendant les sombres heures,
Tu répans sur ses yeux tes songes favoris ;
Ecartant ces songes funèbres
Qui, parmi l'effroi des ténèbres.
Vont reveiller les grands sous les riches lambris.

THE HAPPINESS OF A MODERATE
FORTUNE, AND MODERATE DÉ-
SIRES.

FROM THE FRENCH OF MR. GRESSET.

O goddess of the golden mean,
Whom still misjudging folly flies,
Seduc'd by each delusive scene ;
Thy only subjects are the wise.
These seek thy paths with nobler aim,
And trace them to the gates of fame.

See foster'd in thy fav'ring shade,
Each tender bar of verse divine !
Who lur'd by fortune's vain parade,
Had never form'd the tuneful line ;
By fortune lur'd or want confin'd,
Whose cold hand chills the genial mind.

In vain you slight the flow'ry crown,
That fame wreathes round the favour'd head !
Whilst laurell'd victory and renown
Their heroes from thy shades have led ;
There form'd, from courtly softness free,
By rigid virtue and by thee.

By thee were form'd, from cities far,
Fabricius just, Camillus wise,
Those philosophic sons of war,
That from imperial dignities
Returning, plough'd their native plain,
And plac'd their laurels in thy fane.

Thrice happy he, on whose calm breast
The smiles of peaceful wisdom play,
With all thy sober charms possest,
Whose wishes never learnt to stray.
Whom truth, of pleasures pure but grave,
And pensive thoughts from folly save.

Far from the crowd's low-thoughted strife,
From all that bounds fair freedom's aim,
He envies not the pomp of life,
A length of rent-roll, or of name :
For safe he views the vale-grown elm,
While thunder-sounding storms the mountain
pine o'erwhelm,

Of censure's frown he feels no dread,
No fear he knows of vulgar eyes,
Whose thought, to nobler objects led,
Far, far o'er their horizon flies :
With reason's suffrage at his side,
Whose firm heart rests self-satisfied.

And while alternate conquest sways
The northern, or the southern shore,
He smiles at fortune's giddy maze,
And calmly hears the wild storm roar.
Ev'n Nature's groans, unmov'd with fear,
And bursting worlds he'd calmly hear.

Such are the faithful hearts you love,
O Friendship fair, immortal maid ;
The few caprice could never move,
The few whom int'rest never sway'd :
Nor shed unseen, with hate refin'd,
The pale cares o'er the gloomy mind.

Soft Sleep, that lov'st the peaceful cell,
On these descends thy balmy power ;
While no terrific dreams dispel
The slumbers of the sober hour ;
Which oft, array'd in darkness drear,
Wake the wild eye of pride to fear.

C'est pour ce bonheur légitime
Que le modeste Abdolonyme
N'acceptoit qu'á regret le sceptre de Sidon:
Plus libre dans un sort champêtre.
Et plus heuréux qu'il ne scût l'être
Sur le trône éclatant des ayeux de Didon.

C'est pas ces vertus pacifiques,
Par ces plaisirs philosophiques,
Que tu scais, cher R***, remplir d'utiles jours,
Dans ce Tivoli solitaire,
Où le Cher de son onde claire
Vient à l'aimable Loire associer le cours.

Fidèle à ce sage sistême,
Là, dans l'étude de toi-même,
Chaque soleil te voit occuper tes loisirs ;
Dans le brillant fracas du monde,
Ton nom, ta probité profonde
T'eut donné plus d'éclat, mais moins de vrais
plaisirs.

Content with all a farm would yield,
Thus Sidon's monarch liv'd unknown,
And sigh'd to leave his little field,
For the long glories of a throne—
There once more happy and more free,
Than rank'd with Dido's ancestry.

With these pacific virtues blest,
These charms of philosophic ease,
Wrapt in your Richmond's tranquil rest,
You pass, dear C——, your useful days,
Where Thames your silent vallies laves,
Proud of his yet untainted waves.

Should life's more public scenes engage
Your time that thus consistent flows,
And following still these maxims sage
For ever brings the same repose ;
Your worth may greater fame procure,
But hope not happiness so pure.

## TRANSLATIONS FROM PETRARCH.

### 1765.

### SONETTO CLXXIX.

In nobil sangue vita umile e queta,
Ed in alto intelletto un puro core ;
Frutto senile in sul giovenil fiori,
E'n aspetto pensoso anima lieta,
Raccolto ha 'n quessa donna 'l suo pianeta,
Anzi 'l re delle stelle ; e 'l vero onore,
Le degne lode, e 'l gran pregio, e 'l valore,
Ch' è da stancar ogni divin poeta.
Amor s' è in lei con onestate aggiunto ;
Con beltà naturale abito adorno ;
Ed un atto, che parla con silenzio ;
E non so, che negli occhi, che 'n un punto
Può far chiara la notte, oscuro il giorno,
E 'l mel amaro, ed addolcir l' assenzio.

### SONNET CLXXIX.

Tho' nobly born, to humble life resign'd ;
The purest heart, the most enlighten'd mind ;
A vernal flower that bears the fruits of age !
A cheerful spirit, with an aspect sage,——
The power that rules the planetary train
To her has given, nor shall his gifts be vain.
But on her worth, her various praise to dwell,
The truth, the merits of her life to tell,
The Muse herself would own the task too hard,
Too great the labour for the happiest bard.
Dress that derives from native beauty grace,
And love that holds with honesty his place ;
Action that speaks—and eyes whose piercing ray
Might kindle darkness, or obscure the day!
\*      \*      \*      \*      \*      \*

### SONETTO CCLXXIX.

Rotta è l' alta colonna, e 'l verde lauro,
Che facean ombra al mio stanco pensiero:
Perdut' ho quel, che ritrovar non spero
Dal Borea all' Austro, O dal Mar Indo al
Mauro;
Tolto m'hai, morte, il mio doppio tesauro,
Che mi fea viver lieto, e gire altero ;
E ristorar nol può terra, nè impero,
Nè gemma oriental, nè forza d'auro,
Ma se consentimento è di destino ;
Che poss' io più, se no aver l' alma trista ;
Umidi gli occhi sempre, e 'l viso chino ?
O nostra vita, ch' é si bella in vista ;
Com' per de agevolmente in un mattino
Quel, che 'n molt' anni a gran pena s'aquista !

### SONNET CCLXXIX.

Fall'n the fair column, blasted is the bay,
That shaded once my solitary shore !
I've lost what hope can never give me more.
Tho' sought from Indus to the closing day.
My twofold treasure death has snatch'd away,
My pride, my pleasure left me to deplore ;
What fields far-cultur'd, nor imperial sway,
Nor orient gold, nor jewels can restore.
O destiny severe of human kind !
What portion have we unbedew'd with tears !
The downcast visage, and the pensive mind
Thro' the thin veil of smiling life appears ;
And in one moment vanish into wind
The hard-earn'd fruits of long, laborious
years.

### SONETTO CCLVII.

Ov' è la fronte' che con picciol cenno
Volgea 'l mio core in questa parte, e' in quella?
Ov' è 'l bel ciglio, e l' una, e l' altra stella
Ch' al corso di mia viver lume denno ?

### SONNET CCLVII.

Where is that face, whose slightest air could
move
My trembling heart, and strike the springs of love?
That Heaven, where two fair stars, with genial
ray,
Shed their kind influence on my life's dim way ?

Ov' è 'l valor, la conoscenza, e 'l senno,
   L' accorta, onesta, umil, dolce favella ?
Ove son le bellezze accolte in ella,
Che gran tempo di me lor voglio fenno ?
Ov' è l'ombra gentil del viso humano;
   Ch' ora e riposo dava all' alma stanca,
   E là, 've i miei pensier scritti eran tutti ?
Ov' e' colei, che mia vita ebbe in mano ?
   Quanto al misero mondo, e quanto manca
   A gli occhi miei ! che mai non sieno asciutti.

---

## SONETTO CCXXXVIII.

Se lamentar augelli, o verdi fronde
   Mover soavemente all' aura estiva,
   O roco mormorar di lucid' onde
   S' ode d' una fiorita e fresca riva;
Là, v' 'io seggia d' amor pensoso, e scriva;
   Lei che 'l ciel ne mostrò, terra n' asconde,
   Veggio, ed odo, ed intendo : ch' ancor viva
   Di sì lontano a' sospir miei risponde.
Deh, perchè innanzi tempo ti consume ?
   Mi dice con pietate : " a che pur versi
   Degli occhi tristi un doloroso fiume?
Di me non pianger tu, che miei dè fersi,
   Morendo, eterni, e nell 'eterno lume,
Quando mostrai pi chiuder gli occhi apersi."

Where are that science, sense and worth confest,
   That speech by virtue, by the graces drest ?
Where are those beauties, where those charms
       combin'd,
That caus'd this long captivity of mind !
Where the dear shade of all that once was fair,
The source, the solace of each amorous care ;
My heart's sole sovereign, Nature's only boast ?
—Lost to the world, to me for ever lost !

---

## SONNET CCXXXVIII.

Wail'd the sweet warbler to the lonely shade ;
   Trembled the green leaf to the summer gale ;
   Fell the fair stream in murmurs down the dale,
Its banks, its flow'ry banks with verdure spread,
Where, by the charm of pensive Fancy led,
   All as I fram'd the love-lamenting tale,
   Came the dear object whom I still bewail,
Came from the regions of the cheerless dead :
   " And why," she cried, " untimely wilt thou
       die ?
Ah why, for pity, shall those mournful tears,
   Start in wild sorrow from that languid eye ?
Cherish no more those visionary fears,
   For me, who range yon light-invested sky !
For me, who triumph in eternal years !"

---

# MILTON'S

## ITALIAN POEMS TRANSLATED,

### AND ADDRESSED TO A GENTLEMAN OF ITALY.

## ADDRESS TO SIGNOR MOZZI,

### OF MACERATA.

To thee, the child of classic plains,
   The happier hand of Nature gave
Each grace of Fancy's finer strains,
   Each Muse that mourn'd o'er Maro's grave.

Nor yet the harp that Horace strung
   With many a charm of easy art ;
Not yet what sweet Tibullus sung,
   When Beauty bound him to her heart ;

Nor all that gentle Provence knew,
   Where each breeze bore a lover's sigh,
When Petrarch's sweet persuasion drew
   The tender woe from Laura's eye ;

Nor aught that nobler Science seeks,
   What truth, what virtue must avoid,
Nor aught the voice of Nature speaks,
   To thee unknown, or unenjoy'd ?

O wise beyond each weaker aim,
   That weds the soul to this low sphere,
Fond to indulge the feeble frame,
   That holds awhile her prisoner here !

Trust me, my friend, that soul survives,
   (If e'er had Muse prophetic skill)    1
And when the fated hour arrives,
   That all her faculties shall fill,

Fit for some nobler frame she flies,
   Afar to find a second birth,
And, flourishing in fairer skies,
   Forsakes her nursery of Earth.

Oh ! there, my Mozzi, to behold
   The man that mourn'd his country's wrong,
When the poor exile left his fold,
   And feebly dragg'd his goat along ! !

On Plato's hallow'd breast to lean,
   And catch that ray of heavenly fire,
Which smooth'd a tyrant's sullen mien,
   And bade the cruel thought retire !

Amid those fairy-fields to dwell
   Where Tasso's favour'd spirit saw
What numbers none but his could tell,
   What pencils none but his could draw !

And oft at eve, if eve can be
   Beneath the source of glory's smile,
To range Elysian groves, and see
   That nightly visitant—'ere while,

Who, when he left immortal choirs,
   To mix with Milton's kindred soul,
The labours of their golden lyres
   Would steal, and " whisper whence he stole."

1 Hanc etiam vix Tityre duco.    Virg.

Ausonian bard, from my fond ear
　By seas and mountains sever'd long,
If, chance, these humble strains to hear,
　You leave your more melodious song,

Whether, adventurous, you explore
　The wilds of Apenninus' brow,
Or musing near Loretto's 2 shore,
　Smile piteous on the pilgrim's vow;

The Muse's gentle offering still
　Your ear shall win, your love shall woo,
And these spring-flowers of Milton fill
　The favour'd vales where first they grew.

For me, depriv'd of all that's dear,
　Each fair, fond partner of my life,
Left with a lonely oar to steer,
　Thro' the rude storms of mortal strife;—

When Care, the felon of my days,
　Expands his cold and gloomy wing,
His load when strong affliction lays
　On hope, the heart's elastic spring:

For me what solace yet remains,
　Save the sweet Muse's tender lyre;
Sooth'd by the magic of her strains,
　If, chance, the felon Care, retire?

Save the sweet Muse's tender lyre,
　For me no solace now remains!
Yet shall the felon, Care, retire;
　Sooth'd by the magic of her strains.

Blagdon-House,
June 26, 1776.

-------

### SON. I.

O LADY fair, whose honour'd name is borne
　By that soft vale where Rhyne so loves to
　　stray,
And sees the tall arch crown his wat'ry way!
Sure, happy he, tho' much the Muse's scorn,
Too dull to die beneath thy beauty's ray,
Who never felt that spirit's charmed sway,
Which gentle smiles, and gentle deeds adorn,
Tho' in those smiles are all love's arrows worn,
Each radiant virtue tho' those deeds display!
Sure, happy he who that sweet voice should hear
Mould the soft speech, or swell the tuneful
　　strain,　　　　　　　　　[vain,
And, conscious that his humble vows were
Shut fond attention from his closed ear;
Who, piteous of himself, should timely part,
Ere love had held long empire in his heart!

-------

### SON. II.

As o'er yon wild hill, when the browner light
　Of evening falls, the village maiden hies
To foster some fair plant with kind supplies,
Some stranger plant, that, yet in tender plight,
But feebly buds, ere Spring has open'd quite
The soft affections of serener skies:
So I, with such like gentle thought devise

2 Within a few miles of Macerata.

This stranger tongue to cultivate with care,
All for the sake of lovely lady fair,
　And tune my lays in language little try'd
By such as wont to Tamis' banks repair,
　Tamis' forsook for Arno's flow'ry side,
So wrought Love's will that ever ruleth wide!

-------

### SON. III.

CHARLES, must I say, what strange it seems to
　　say,
　This rebel heart that Love hath held as naught,
　Or, haply, in his cunning mazes caught,
Would laugh, and let his captive steal away;
This simple heart hath now become his prey.
　Yet hath no golden tress this lesson taught,
Nor vermeil cheek that shames the rising day:
Oh! no—'twas Beauty's most celestial ray,
　With charms divine of sov'reign sweetness
　　fraught!
The noble mien, the soul-dissolving air,
　The bright arch bending o'er the lucid eye,
The voice that, breathing melody so rare,
　Might lead the toil'd Moon from the middle sky!
Charles, when such mischief arm'd this foreign
　　fair,
Small chance had I to hope this simple heart
　should fly.

-------

### SON. IV.

In truth I feel my sun in those fair eyes,
　So strongly strike they, like that powerful ray,
　Which falls with all the violence of day
On Lybia's sands—and oft, as there, arise
Hot wasting vapours from the source where lies
　My secret pain; yet, haply, those may say,
Who talk love's language, these are only sighs,
That the soft ardours of the soul betray [1].

-------

### SON. V.

An artless youth, who, simple in his love,
　Seem'd little hopeful from his heart to fly,
　To thee that heart, O lady, nor deny
The votive gift, he brings; since that shall prove
All change and fear and falsity above,
　Of manners to gentle deeds comply,
　And courteous will, that never asketh why;
Yet mild, as is the never wrathful dove,
Firmness it hath, and fortitude to bear
The wrecks of nature, or the wrongs of fate,
From envy far, and low-designing care,
And hopes and fears that vulgar minds await,
With the sweet Muse, and sounding lyre elate.
　And only weak, when love had entrance there,

[1] The concetti of the Italian in the conclusion
of this Sonnet were so obstinate, that it seemed
scarce possible to reduce them into any reputable form of translation. Such trifling liberties
as the translator shall appear to have taken with
these poems, must be imputed to a desire of
getting over blemishes of the same kind.

## CANZON.

Gay youths and frolic damsels round me throng,
And smiling say, "Why, shepherd, wilt thou
    write
Thy lays of love adventurous to recite
In unknown numbers and a foreign tongue?
Shepherd, if Hope hath ever wrought thee wrong,
    Afar from her and Fancy's fairy light
Retire"—So they to sport with me delight;
And "other shores," they say, "and other streams
    Thy presence wait; and sweetest flowers that
    blow,
Their ripening blooms reserve for thy fair brow,
Where glory soon shall bear her brightest beams:"
Thus they, and yet their soothing little seems;
    If she, for whom I breathe the tender vow,
Sing the soft lays, and ask the mutual song,
This is thy language, Love, and I to thee belong!

## TRANSLATION FROM CATULLUS.

Lesbia, live to love and pleasure,
    Careless what the grave may say:
When each moment is a treasure,
    Why should lovers lose a day?

Setting suns shall rise in glory,
    But when little life is o'er,
There's an end of all the story:
    We shall sleep; and wake no more.

Give me then a thousand kisses,
    Twice ten thousand more bestow,
Till the sum of boundless blisses
    Neither we nor envy know.

THE

# POEMS

OF

## *RICHARD JAGO.*

# LIFE OF JAGO,

## BY MR. CHALMERS.

RICHARD JAGO, descended of a Cornish family, was the third son of the rev. Richard Jago, rector of Beaudesert[1], in Warwickshire, by Margaret, the daughter of William Parker, gent. of Henly in Arden; and was born October 1, 1715. He received his classical education under the rev. Mr. Crumpton, an excellent schoolmaster, at Solihull, in the same county, but one whose severity our poet has thought proper to record in his Edge-Hill,

> Hail, Solihull! respectful I salute
> Thy walls: more awful once, when, from the sweets
> Of festive freedom, and domestic ease,
> With throbbing heart, to the stern discipline
> Of pedagogue morose I sad return'd.

At this school he formed an intimacy, which death only dissolved, with the poet Shenstone, whose letters to him have since been published. In their early days they probably exchanged their juvenile verses, and afterwards communicated to each other their more serious studies and pursuits. Somervile also appears to have encouraged our author's first attempts, which were made at a yet earlier period, when under his father's humble roof.

> O Beaudesert!.........
> Haunt of my youthful steps! where I was wont
> To range, chanting my rude notes to the wind,
> While Somervile disdain'd not to regard
> With candid ear, and regulate the strain.

From school he was entered as a servitor of University College, Oxford, where Shenstone, then a commoner of Pembroke, the late rev. Richard Greaves, Mr. Whistler, and others who appear among Shenstone's correspondents, showed him every respect, notwithstanding the inferiority of his rank. A young man of whatever merit, who was servitor, was usually visited, if visited at all, with secresy; but this prejudice is now so

Or Beldesert, a living conferred upon him by Lloyd, bishop of Worcester, in 1709. C.

much abolished, that the same circumspection is not thought necessary. He took his master's degree July 9, 1738, having entered into the church the year before, and served the curacy of Snitterfield, near Stratford upon Avon. His father died in 1740. In 1744, or, according to Shenstone's Letters, in 1743, he married Dorothea Susanna Fancourt, daughter of the rev. ——— Fancourt of Kilmcote in Leicestershire, a young lady whom he had known from her childhood[2].

For several years after his marriage, he resided at Harbury, to which living he was presented in 1746. Lord Willoughby de Broke gave him also the living of Chesterton, at a small distance from Harbury. These two benefices together did not produce more than one hundred pounds a year. In 1751 he had the misfortune to lose his wife, who appears to have been an amiable and accomplished woman, and was left with the care of seven very young children.

In 1754 lord Clare, the late earl Nugent, procured for him from Dr. Madox, bishop of Worcester, the vicarage of Snitterfield, worth about 140*l.* In 1759, he married a second wife, Margaret, daughter of James Underwood, esq. of Rudgely, in Staffordshire, who survived him, but by whom he had no children.

Some of his smaller pieces of poetry had before this time been inserted in Dodsley's Collection, but he put in for higher claims, by publishing the poem of Edge-Hill, in the year 1767 ; and in 1768 his more popular fable of Labour and Genius. In 1771, he was presented by his kind patron, lord Willoughby de Broke, to the living of Kilmcote, formerly held by his first wife's father, which being worth near 300*l.* a year, enabled him to maintain his family with ease and comfort, especially as he retained Snitterfield, and resigned only the trifling living of Harbury. During the latter part of his life, when the infirmities of age made their approach, he resided almost entirely at Snitterfield, where he amused himself with improving the vicarage house, and ornamenting his grounds, a taste he probably caught from Shenstone, but which he contrived to indulge at a much less expense.

He died after a short illness, May 8, 1781, aged sixty-five years, and was buried, according to his desire, in a vault which he had made for his family in the church at Snitterfield. Three of his daughters, by the first wife, survived him.

His personal character is thus given by his biographer—" Mr. Jago, in his person, was about the middle stature. In his manner, like most people of sensibility, he appeared reserved among strangers : amongst his friends he was free and easy : and his conversation sprightly and entertaining. In domestic life, he was the affectionate husband, the tender parent, the kind master, the hospitable neighbour, and sincere friend ; and both by his doctrine and example, a faithful and worthy minister of the parish over which he presided."

In 1784, his poems, as corrected, improved, and enlarged by the author a short time before his death, with some additional pieces, were published by his friend, the late John Scott Hylton, esq. of Lapall-House near Hales Owen, who was likewise the correspondent of Shenstone. To this publication Mr. Hylton prefixed some account of Jago's life, which, however meagre and unsatisfactory, is all that can now be procured. A very few particulars, indeed, but perhaps of no great importance, have been gleaned from Shenstone's Letters, &c. His life, it may be presumed, was that of a man not dependent on fame, and whose productions formed the amusement of his leisure hours. It would

---

[2] Shenstone's Letters. Letter xlix. *C.*

appear by one of Shenstone's letters that he occasionally used his pencil as well as his pen.

His rank as a poet cannot be thought very high. Yet we have few more beautiful specimens of tenderness and sensibility than in his Elegies on the Blackbirds and Gold-finches. The fable of Labour and Genius has a pleasing mixture of elegance and humour.

The Elegy on the Blackbirds appeared first in The Adventurer, to the editor of which it was sent by Gilbert West, and published as his. The author claimed it, however, when added to Dodsley's collection, a circumstance which Dr. Johnson has noted, but not with sufficient precision, in his life of West. Even when Mr. Jago put his name to it, a manager of the Bath theatre endeavoured to make it pass for his own, and with great effrontery asserted that *Jago* was a fictitious name adopted from the play of Othello.

His longest poem, Edge-Hill, has some passages not destitute of animation, but it is so topographically exact, that to enjoy it the reader must have a map constantly before him ; and perhaps with that aid, if he is not conversant with the various scenery, the effect will be languor and indifference. Even his friend Shenstone seems to speak coldly of it. " You must by no means lay aside the thoughts of perfecting Edge-hill, at your leisure. It is possible, that in order to keep clear of flattery, I have said less in its favour than I really ought—but I never considered it otherwise than as a poem which it was very adviseable for you to complete and finish." Shenstone did not live to see it published in its finished state, and whatever his objections, probably bestowed the warmest praise on the tender and simple episode of Lydia and the Blind Lover, taken from a story in The Tatler.

His other pieces requires no distinct notice.—Shenstone, in a letter dated 1759, mentions an Essay on Electricity written by Jago, but whether published, I have not been able to discover. In 1755, he printed a very sensible and seasonable discourse, entitled The Causes of Impenitence considered, preached at Harbury, May 4, 1755, on occasion of a conversation said to have passed between one of the inhabitants and an apparition, in the churchyard belonging to that place. From this incident, which he does not consider it as his business either to confirm or disprove, he takes an opportunity to enforce the necessity of repentance. Another sermon, 1763, is attributed to him in Cooke's Historical Register, of which I can find no mention any where else.

# HINTS

# PREFACE,

## FOR ANY AUTHOR, AND FOR ANY BOOK.

─────────

THE following sheets were fairly transcribed, the title-page was adjusted, and every thing, as the writer thought, in readiness for the press, when, upon casting his eyes over them for the last time, with more than usual attention, something seemed wanting, which, after a short pause, he perceived to be the Preface. Now it is fit the reader should know, as an apology for this seeming inattention, that he had formerly rejected this article under a notion of its being superfluous, and uninteresting to the reader; but now, when matters were come to a crisis, and it was almost too late, he changed his mind, and thought a preface as essential to the figure of a book, as a portico is to that of a building.

Not that the author would insinuate by this comparison, that his paper edifice was entitled to any thing superb and pompous of this sort; but only that it wanted something plain and decent, between the beggarly style of Quarles, or Ogilby, and the magnificence of the profuse Dryden. Far be it from him, by calling this small appendage to his work by the name of a portico, or an antechamber, or a vestibule, or the like, to raise the reader's expectations, or to encourage any ideas but those of the most simple kind, as introductory to his subsequent entertainment: neither would he, like some undertakers in literary architecture, bestow as much expense on the entrance, as, prudently managed, might furnish the lofty town apartments, or pastoral villa of a modern poet. On the contrary, he reserves all his finery of carving and gilding, as well as his pictures and cabinets, for their proper places within.

But for the further illustration of his meaning, he chooses to have recourse to allusions more nearly related to his subject, such as the prelude to a song, or the prologue to a play, there being evidently a great affinity between rhyming and fiddling, writing verses and playing the fool.

Another consideration, which greatly influenced the author in this point, was the respect which he bears to the public. For conceiving himself now in the very act of making his appearance before every circle of the polite and learned world, he was struck with awe, and felt as if he had been guilty of some indecorum, like a person abruptly breaking into good company with his hat on, or without making a bow. For though by his situation in life he is happily relieved from any personal embarrassment of this kind, yet he considered his book as his proxy, and he would by no means have his proxy guilty of such an impropriety as to keep his hat on before all the learned men of Europe, or to omit making his bow upon being admitted to an audience, or presented in the drawing-room.

Great is the force of this little article of gesticulation, from the lowest class of orators in the street, to those in the highest departments in life; insomuch that it has been thought a prudent, attentive, and skilful manager, either on the stage, or at the bar, as well as the bowing dean in his walk, may acquire as much success amongst polite and well-bred people, and particularly the ladies, who are the best judges, by the magic of his bow, as by any other part of his action or oratory.

Yet, notwithstanding all that the author has said concerning this external mark of reverence, he is sensible that there is a set of cynical philosophers, who are so far from paying it due regard, that they count it no better than a refined species of idolatry, and an abomination utterly unbecoming so noble and erect a creature as man. Upon these gentlemen it is not to be expected that the best bow which the author or his book could make, would have any effect; and therefore he shall decline that ceremony with them, to take them by the hand in a friendly manner, hoping that they will make some allowance for his having been taught against his own consent to dance, and scribble from his infancy.

He is aware likewise that there is another sect of philosophers, whom his ingenious friend Mr. G. author of the Spiritual Quixote, distinguishes by the name of *censorious Christians*, " who," as he expresses it, " will not suffer a man to nod in his elbow-chair, or to talk nonsense without contradicting or ridiculing him."—But as the writer of this admirable work has shown himself so able and successful a casuist in a similar instance of a petulant and over officious zeal, he hopes these gentlemen will, in imitation of Mr. Wildgoose, for the future refrain from a practice so injurious to their neighbours' repose, and so contrary to all the laws of civility and good manners.

It is true, some of these literati may be considered under a more formidable character, from their custom of holding a monthly meeting, or office for arraigning the conduct of all whom they suspect of maintaining heretical opinions contrary to their jurisdiction. In this view these good fathers scruple not to put an author upon the rack for the slightest offence, and not content with their claims of inspiration and infallibility, will torture his own words to prove his guilt. In the execution of this office they judge all men by their own standard, and, like the tyrant Procrustes, regardless of the acute pain they inflict at every stroke, will lop off a foot, or any other portion of an author's matter, or lengthen it out, as best suits their purpose, to bring him to their measure.

But to the inexpressible comfort of himself, and of every free-born English writer, the author reflects that the competence of such a court cannot be admitted in a protestant country: and to speak the truth, from experience, its power, as exercised amongst us, though still very tremendous, is tempered with a gentleness and moderation unknown to those of Spain and Portugal.

But though the author is not without hopes, by his complaisance and condescension, to conciliate the affections of all those various sects of the learned in every part of the world, yet his principal dependence is upon the gentle and humane, whose minds are always open to the feelings of others, as well as to the gratification of their own refined taste and sentiments; and to these he makes his appeal, which he hopes they will accept as a tribute due to their superior merit, and a testimony of the profound respect with which he is their

most obedient,

humble servant,

THE AUTHOR.

# POEMS

OF

# RICHARD JAGO.

---

*EDGE-HILL:*

A POEM.

IN FOUR BOOKS.

Salve, magna parens frugum, Saturnia tellus,
Magna virum! tibi res antiquæ laudis, et artes
Ingredior, sanctos ausus recludere fontes.     Virg.

Our sight is the most perfect and most delightful of all our senses.  It fills the mind with the largest variety of ideas, converses with its objects at the greatest distance, and continues the longest in action without being tired, or satiated with its proper enjoyment.

Spect. No. 411, On the Pleasures of Imagination.

---

## PREFACE.

THE following poem takes its name from a ridge of hills, which is the boundary between the counties of Oxford and Warwick, and remarkable for its beautiful and extensive prospect, of which the latter forms a considerable part.  This circumstance afforded the writer an opportunity, very agreeable to him, of paying a tribute to his native country, by exhibiting its beauties to the public in a poetical delineation; divided, by an imaginary line, into a number of distinct scenes, corresponding with the different times of the day, each forming an entire picture, and containing its due proportion of objects and colouring.

In the execution of this design, he endeavoured to make it as extensively interesting as he could, by the frequent introduction of general reflections, historical, philosophical, and moral; and to enliven the description by digressions and episodes, naturally arising from the subject.

*EDGE-HILL.*

BOOK I.  MORNING.

---

### ARGUMENT.

The subject proposed.  Address.  Ascent to the hill.  General view.  Comparison.  Philosophical account of the origin and formation of mountains, &c.  Morning view, comprehending the southwest part of the scene, interspersed with elements and examples of rural taste; showing, at the same time, its connection with, and dependence upon civil government; and concluding with an historical episode of the Red-horse.

---

BRITANNIA'S rural charms, and tranquil scenes,
 Far from the circling ocean, where her fleets,
Like Eden's nightly guards [1], majestic ride,
I sing; O may the theme and kindred soil
Propitious prove, and to th' appointed hill
Invite the Muses from their cloister'd shades,
With me to rove, and harmonize the strain!
 Nor shall they, for a time, regret the loss
Of their lov'd Isis, and fair Cherwel's stream,
While to the north of their own beauteous fields
The pictur'd scene they view, where Avon shapes
His winding way, enlarging as it flows,
Nor hastes to join Sabrina's prouder wave.
Like a tall rampart! here the mountain rears
Its verdant edge; and, if the tuneful maids
Their presence deign, shall with Parnassus vie.
Level and smooth the track, which thither leads!
Of champaign bold and fair! its adverse side
Abrupt and steep! Thanks, Miller [2]! to thy paths,
That ease our winding steps! Thanks to the fount,

[1] Milton.   Paradise Lost, book iv.
[2] Sanderson Miller, esq. of Radway.

541

The trees, the flow'rs, imparting to the sense
Fragrance or dulcet sound of murm'ring rill,
And stilling ev'ry tumult in the breast !
And oft the stately tow'rs, that overtop
The rising wood, and oft the broken arch,
Or mould'ring wall, well taught to counterfeit
The waste of time, to solemn thought excite,
And crown with graceful pomp the shaggy hill.
    So Virtue paints the steep ascent to Fame³ :
So her aerial residence displays.
    Still let thy friendship, which prepar'd the way,
Attend, and guide me, as my ravish'd sight
O'er the bleak hill or shelter'd valley roves.
Teach me with just observance to remark
Their various charms, their storied fame record,
And to the visual join the mental search.
    The summit 's gain'd ! and, from its airy height,
The late-trod plain looks like an inland sea,
View'd from some promontory's hoary head,
With distant shores environ'd; not with face
Glassy and uniform, but when its waves
Are gently ruffled by the southern gale,
And the tall masts like waving forests rise.
    Such is the scene! that, from the terrac'd hill,
Displays its graces; intermixture sweet
Of lawns and groves, of open and retir'd.
Vales, farms, towns, villas, castles, distant spires,
And hills on hills, with ambient clouds enrob'd,
In long succession court the lab'ring sight,
Lost in the bright confusion.  Thus the youth,
Escap'd from painful drudgery of words,
Views the fair fields of science wide display'd ;
Where Phebus dwells, and all the tuneful Nine;
Perplex'd awhile he stands, and now to this,
Now that blest seat of harmony divine
Explores his way, with giddy rapture tir'd :
Till some sage Mentor, whose experienc'd feet
Have trod the mazy path, directs his search,
And leads him wond'ring to their bright abodes.
Come then, my friend! guide thou th' advent'rous
        Muse,
And with thy counsel regulate her flight.
    Yet, ere the sweet excursion she begins,
O ! listen, while, from sacred records drawn,
My daring song unfolds the cause, whence rose
This various face of things—of high, of low—
Of rough and smooth.  For with its parent Earth
Coeval not prevail'd what now appears
Of hill and dale; nor was its new-form'd shape,
Like a smooth polish'd orb, a surface plain,
Wanting the sweet variety of change,
Concave, convex, the deep, and the sublime:
Nor, from old Ocean's watry bed, were scoop'd
Its neighb'ring shores ; nor were they now depress'd,
Now rais'd by sudden shocks; but fashion'd all
In perfect harmony by laws divine⁴,
On passive matter, at its birth impress'd.

³ See Lord Shaftsbury's Judgment of Hercules.
⁴ Amongst the many fanciful conceits of writers
on the subject, a learned divine, in his Confutation
of Dr. Burnett's Theory, supposes that hills and
mountains might be occasioned by fermentation,
after the manner of leaven in dough; while others
have attributed their production to the several different causes mentioned above.
    The following solution, by the descent of water
from the surface of the Earth to the centre, seemed
most easy and natural to the author, and is therefore adopted. Vide Warren's Geologiæ, 1698.

When now two days, as mortals count their time,
Th' Almighty had employ'd on man's abode;
To motion rous'd the dead, inactive mass,
The dark illumin'd, and the parts terrene
Impelling each to each, the circle form'd,
Compact and firm, of Earth's stupendous orb,
With boundless seas, as with a garment cloth'd,
On the third morn he bade the waters flow
Down to their place, and let dry land appear ;
And it was so.  Straight to their destin'd bed,
From every part, th' obedient waters ran,
Shaping their downward course, and, as they found
Resistance varying with the varying soil,
In their retreat they form'd the gentle slope,
Or headlong precipice, or deep-worn dale,
Or valley, stretching far its winding maze,
As further still their humid train they led,
By Heav'n directed to the realms below⁵.
    Now first was seen the variegated face
Of Earth's fair orb shap'd by the plastic flood :
Now smooth and level like its liquid plains,
Now, like its ruffled waves, sweet interchange
Of hill and dale, and now a rougher scene,
Mountains on mountains lifted to the sky.
Such was her infant form, yet unadorn'd !
And in the naked soil the subtle stream⁶
Fretted its winding track.  So he ordain'd!
Who form'd the fluid mass of atoms small,
The principles of things ! who moist from dry,
From heavy sever'd light, compacting close
The solid glebe, stratum of rock, or ore,
Or crumbling marl, or close tenacious clay,
Or what beside, in wondrous order rang'd,
Orb within orb, Earth's secret depths contains.
    So was the shapely sphere, on ev'ry side,
With equal pressure of surrounding air
Sustain'd, of sea and land harmonious form'd.
Nor beauteous covering was withheld, for straight,
At the divine command, the verd'rous grass
Upsprang unsown, with ev'ry seedful herb,
Fruit, plant, or tree, pregnant with future store;
God saw the whole—And lo! 't was very good.
But man, ungrateful man! to deadly ill
Soon turn'd the good bestow'd, with horrid crimes
Polluting Earth's fair seat, his Maker's gift !
Till mercy could no more with justice strive.
    Then wrath divine unbarr'd Heav'n's watry gates,
And loos'd the fountains of the great abyss.
Again the waters o'er the Earth prevail'd.
Hills rear'd their heads in vain.  Full forty days
The flood increas'd, nor, till sev'n Moons had wan'd,
Appear'd the mountain tops.  Perish'd all flesh,
One family except! and all the works
Of art were swept into th' oblivious pool,
In that dread time what change th' avenging flood
Might cause in Earth's devoted fabric, who
Of mortal birth can tell ? Whether again

⁵ Called in scripture, the deep, the great deep,
the deep that lieth under or beneath the Earth—
the Tartarus or Erebus of the Heathens.

⁶ ........ .. .........So the watry throng
With serpent errour wand'ring found their way,
And on the washy ooze deep channels wore.
Easy ! ere God had bid the ground be dry,
All but within those banks, where rivers now
Stream, and perpetual draw their humid train.
                Milton. Paradise Lost, book vii.

'T was to its first chaotic mass reduc'd [7],
To be reform'd anew ? or, in its orb,
What violence, what disruptions it endur'd [8] ?
What ancient mountains stood the furious shock?
What new arose? For doubtless new there are,
If all are not; strong proof exhibiting
Of later rise, and their once fluid state,
By stranger-fossils, in their inmost bed
Of looser mould, or marble rock entomb'd,
Or shell marine, incorp'rate with themselves:
Nor less the conic hill [9], with ample base,
Or scarry slope [9] by rushing billows torn,
Or fissure deep [9], in the late delug'd soil
Cleft by succeeding draught, side answering side,
And curve to adverse curve exact oppos'd,
Confess the watry pow'r ; while scatter'd trains,
Or rocky fragments, wash'd from broken hills,
Take up the tale, and spread it round the globe.
Then, as the flood retir'd, another face
Of things appear'd, another, and the same !
Taurus, and Libanus, and Atlas, feign'd
To prop the skies ! and that fam'd Alpine ridge,
Or Appenine, or snow-clad Caucasus,
Or Ararat, on whose emergent top
First moor'd that precious bark, whose chosen crew
Again o'erspread Earth's universal orb.
For now, as at the first, from ev'ry side
Hasted the waters to their ancient bounds,
The vast abys ! perhaps from thence ascend,
Urg'd by th' incumbent air, through mazy clefts
Beneath the deep, or rise in vapours warm,
Piercing the vaulted Earth, anon condens'd
Within the lofty mountains' secret cells,
Ere they their summits gain, down their steep sides
To trickle in a never-ceasing round [10].
So up the porous stone, or crystal tube,
The philosophic eye with wonder views
The tinctur'd fluid rise; so tepid dews
From chymic founts in copious streams distil.
Such is the structure, such the wave-worn face
Of Earth's huge fabric! beauteous to the sight,
And stor'd with wonders [11], to the attentive mind

[7] According to Mr. Hutchinson and his followers.

[8] According to Dr. Burnett's Theory.

[9] There are some remarkable traces of the great
event here treated of, in each of these kinds, at
Welcombe, near Stratford upon Avon, formerly a
seat of the Combe family, the whole scene bearing
the strongest marks of some violent conflict of Nature, and particularly of the agency of water.

[10] May not the ebbing and flowing of the sea, to
whatever cause it is owing, tend to assist this operation, as the pulsation of the heart accelerates
the circulation of the blood in animal bodies ?
The reader may see this hypothesis very ably
supported by Mr. Catcot, in his Essay on the Deluge, second edit., together with many respectable
names, ancient and modern, by whom it is patronised. The following passage from Lucretius is
quoted by him, as well expressing their general
meaning :

Partim quod subter per terras diditur omnes.
Percolatur enim virus, retroque remanat
Materies humoris, et ad caput amnibus omnis
Convenit, unde super terras fluit agmine dulci,
Quà via secta semel liquido pede detulit undas.

[11] Trees of a very large size, torn up by the roots,
and other vegetable and animal bodies, the spoils of
VOL. XVII.

Confirming, with persuasive eloquence
Drawn from the rocky mount or watry fen,
Those sacred pages, which record the past,
And awfully predict its future doom.
Now, while the Sun its heav'nly radiance sheds
Across the vale, disclosing all its charms,
Emblem of that fair light, at whose approach
The Gentile darkness fled ! ye nymphs, and swains !
Come haste with me, while now 't is early morn,
Through Upton's airy fields [12], to where yon point
Projecting hides Northampton's ancient seat [13],
Retir'd, and hid amidst surrounding shades:
Counting a length of honourable years,
And solid worth ; while painted Belvideres,
Naked, aloft, and built but to be seen,
Shrink at the Sun, and totter to the wind.
So sober sense oft shuns the public view,
In privacy conceal'd, while the pert sons
Of folly flutter in the glare of day.
Hence, o'er the plain, where, strip'd with alleys
  green,
The golden harvest nods, let me your view
Progressive lead to Verney's sister walls [14],
Alike in honour, as in name allied !
Alike her walls a noble master own,
Studious of elegance. At his command,
New pillars grace the dome with Grecian pomp
Of Corinth's gay design. At his command,
On hill, or plain, new culture clothes the scene
With verdant grass, or variegated grove ;
And bubbling rills in sweeter notes discharge
Their liquid stores. Along the winding vale,
At his command, observant of the shore,
The glitt'ring stream, with correspondent grace,
Its course pursues, and o'er th' exulting wave
The stately bridge a beauteous form displays.
On either side, rich as th' embroider'd floor
From Persia's gaudy looms, and firm as fair,
The chequer'd lawns with count'nance blithe pro-
  claim
The Graces reign. Plains, hills, and woods reply
" The Graces reign," and Nature smiles applause.
Smile on, fair source of beauty, source of bliss !
To crown the master's cost, and deck her path
Who shares his joy, of gentlest manners join'd
With manly sense, train'd to the love refin'd
Of Nature's charms in Wroxton's beauteous groves [15],
Thy neighb'ring villa's ever open gate,
And festive board, O Walton [16] ! next invite
The pleasing toil. Unwilling, who can pay
To thee the votive strain ? For Science here
And Candour dwell, prepar'd alike to cheer
The stranger-guest, or for the nation's weal
To pour the stores mature of wisdom forth,
In senatorial councils often prov'd,

the Deluge, are found in every part of the Earth,
but chiefly in fens, or bogs, or amongst peat-earth,
which is an assemblage of decayed vegetables.
  See Woodward's Nat. Hist. of the Earth, &c.

[12] Upton, the seat of Robert Child, esq.

[13] Compton-Winyate, a seat of the right hon.
the earl of Northampton, at the foot of Edge-Hill.

[14] Compton-Verney, a seat of the right hon.
lord Willoughby de Broke.

[15] Wroxton, the seat of the right hon. the earl
of Guilford, father of lady Willoughby de Broke.

[16] Walton, the seat of sir Charles Mordaunt,
bart. many years a member of parliament for the
county of Warwick.
U

And, by the public voice attested long,
Long may it be! with well-deserv'd applause.
And see beneath the shade of full-grown elm,
Or near the border of the winding brook,
Skirting the grassy lawn, her polish'd train
Walk forth to taste the fragrance of the grove,
Woodbine, or rose, or to the upland scene
Of wildly-planted hill, or trickling stream
From the pure rock, or moss-lin'd grottos cool,
The Naiads' humid cell! protract the way
With learned converse, or ingenuous song.
The search pursue to Charlecote's fair domain [17],
Where Avon's sportive stream delighted strays
Through the gay smiling meads, and to his bed,
Hele's gentle current wooes, by Lucy's hand
In ev'ry graceful ornament attir'd,
And worthier, such, to share his liquid realms !
  Near, nor unmindful of th' increasing flood,
Stratford her spacious magazines unfolds,
And hails th' unwieldly barge from western shores,
With foreign da'nties fraught, or native ore
Of pitchy hue, to pile the fuel'd grate
In woolly stores, or husky grain repay'd.
To speed her wealth, lo ! the proud bridge [18] extends
His num'rous arches, stately monument
Of old munificence, and pious love
Of native soil ! There Stower exulting pays
His tributary stream, well pleas'd with wave
Auxiliary her pond'rous stores to waft;
And boasting, as he flows, of growing fame,
And wondrous beauties on his banks display'd—
Of Alcot's swelling lawns [19], and fretted spires
Of fairest model, Gothic or Chinese—
Of Eatington's [20], and Tolton's [21] verdant meads,
And groves of various leaf, and Honington [22],
Profuse of charms, and attic elegance ;
Nor fails he to relate, in jocund mood,
How liberally the masters of the scene
Enlarge his current, and direct his course
With winding grace—and how his crystal wave
Reflects th' inverted spires and pillar'd domes—
And how the frisking deer play on his sides,
Pict'ring their branched heads, with wanton sport,
In his clear face.  Pleas'd with the vaunting tale,
Nor jealous of his fame, Avon receives
The prattling stream, and, towards thy nobler flood,
Sabrina fair, pursues his length'ning way.
  Hail, beauteous Avon, hail ! on whose fair banks
The smiling daisies, and their sister tribes,
Violets, and cuckoo-buds, and lady-smocks,
A brighter dye disclose, and proudly tell
That Shakspeare, as he stray'd these meads along,
Their simple charms admir'd, and in his verse
Preserv'd, in never-fading bloom to live.
  And thou, whose birth these walls unrival'd boast,
That mock'st the rules of the proud Stagyrite,
And learning's tedious toil, hail, mighty bard !
Thou great magician, hail ! Thy piercing thought
Unaided saw each movement of the mind,
As skilful artists view the small machine,

The secret springs and nice dependencies,
And to thy mimic scenes, by fancy wrought
To such a wondrous shape, th' impassion'd breast
In floods of grief or peals of laughter bow'd,
Obedient to the wonder-working strain,
Like the tun'd string responsive to the touch,
Or to the wizard's charm, the passive storm.
Humour and wit, the tragic pomp, or phrase
Familiar, flow'd spontaneous from thy tongue,
As flowers from Nature's lap.—Thy potent spells
From their bright seats aerial sprites detain'd,
Or from their unseen haunts, and slumb'ring shades,
Awak'd the fairy tribes, with jocund step
The circled green and leafy hall to tread :
While, from his dripping caves, old Avon sent
His willing Naiads to their harmless rout.
  Alas ! how languid is the labour'd song,
The slow result of rules and tortur'd sense,
Compar'd with thine! thy animated thought,
And glowing phrase ! which art in vain essays,
And schools can never teach.  Yet, though deny'd
Thy pow'rs, by situation more allied,
I court the genius of thy sportive Muse
On Avon's bank, her sacred haunts explore,
And hear in ev'ry breeze her charming notes.
  Beyond these flow'ry meads, with classic streams
Enrich'd, two sister rills their currents join,
And Ikenild displays his Roman pride.
There Alcester [23] her ancient honour boasts.
But fairer fame, and far more happy lot
She boasts, O Ragley [24] ! in thy courtly train
Of Hertford's splendid line! Lo ! from these shades,
Ev'n now his sov'reign, studious of her weal,
Calls him to bear his delegated rule
To Britain's sister isle.  Hibernia's sons
Applaud the choice, and hail him to their shore
With cordial gratulation.  Him, well-pleas'd
With more than fil.al rev'rence to obey,
Beauchamp attends.  What son, but would rejoice
The deeds of such a father to record !
What father, but were blest in such a son !
Nor may the Muse omit with Conway's name [25]
To grace her song.  O ! might it worthy flow
Of those her theme involves!  The cider land,
In Georgic strains by her own Philips sung,
Should boast no brighter fame, though proudly
                                        grac'd
With loftiest-titled names—The Cecil line,
Or Beaufort's, or, O Chandos' ! thine, or his
In Anna's councils high, her fav'rite peer,
Harley ! by me still honour'd in his race.
  See, how the pillar'd isles and stately dome
Brighten the woodland shade ! while scatter'd hills,
Airy and light, in many a conic form,
A theatre compose, grotesque and wild,
And, with their shaggy sides, contract the vale
Winding, in straiten'd circuit, round their base.
Beneath their wav:ng umbrage Flora spreads
Her spotted couch, primrose, and hyacinth
Profuse, with ev'ry simpler bud that blows
On hill or dale.  Such too thy flow'ry pride,

[17] Charlecote, the seat of George Lucy, esq.
[18] This bridge was built in the reign of king
Henry VII. at the sole cost and charge of sir Hugh
Clopton, knt. lord mayor of the city of London, and
a native of this place.
[19] The seat of James West, esq.
[20] The seat of the hon. George Shirley, esq.
[21] The seat of sir Henry Parker, bart.
[22] The seat of Joseph Townsend, esq.

[23] So called from its situation on the river Ale-
nus, or Alne, and from its being a Roman station
on the Ikenild-street.
[24] A seat of the right hon. the earl of Hertford.
[25] The right hon. Henry Seymour Conway, esq.
one of his majesty's principal secretaries of state,
and brother to the right hon. the earl of Hertford.

O Hewel [26] ! by thy master's lib'ral hand
Advanc'd to rural fame ! Such Umberslade [27] !
In the sweet labour join'd, with culture fair,
And splendid arts, from Arden's woodland shades [28]
The pois'nous damps and savage gloom to chase.
  What happy lot attends your calm retreats,
By no scant bound'ry, nor obstructing fence,
Immur'd or circumscrib'd ; but spread at large
In open day : save what to cool recess
Is destin'd voluntary, not constrain'd
By sad necessity, and casual state
Of sickly peace ! Such as the moated hall,
With close circumference of watry guard,
And pensile bridge proclaim ! or, rear'd aloft,
And inaccessible the massy tow'rs,
And narrow circuit of embattled walls,
Rais'd on the mountain precipice ! Such thine
O Beaudesert [29] ! old Montfort's lofty seat !
Haunt of my youthful steps ! where I was wont
To range, chanting my rude notes to the wind,
While Somervile disdain'd not to regard
With candid ear, and regulate the strain.
  Such was the genius of the Gothic age,
And Norman policy ! Such the retreats
Of Britain's ancient nobles ! less intent
On rural beauty, and sweet patronage
Of gentle arts, than studious to restrain,
With servile awe, barbarian multitudes ;
Or, with confed'rate force, the regal pow'r
Control. Hence proudly they their vassal troops
Assembling, now the fate of empire plann'd :
Now o'er defenceless tribes, with wanton rage,
Tyrannic rul'd ; and in their castled halls
Secure, with wild excess their revels kept,
While many a sturdy youth, or beauteous maid,
Sole solace of their parents' drooping age !
Bewail'd their wretched fate, by force compell'd
To these abhorr'd abodes ! Hence frequent wars [30],
In ancient annals fam'd ! Hence haply feign'd
Th' enchanted castle, and its cursed train
Of giants, spectres, and magicians dire !
Hence gen'rous minds, with indignation fir'd,
And threat'ning fierce revenge, were character'd
By gallant knights on bold achievements bent,
Subduing monsters, and dissolving spells.
  Thus, from the rural landscape, learn to know
The various characters of time and place.
To hail, from open scenes, and cultur'd fields,
Fair Liberty, and Freedom's gen'rous reign,
With guardian laws, and polish'd arts adorn'd.
While the portcullis huge, or moated fence,
The sad reverse of savage times betray—
Distrust, barbarity, and Gothic rule.
  Would ye, with faultless judgment, learn to plan
The rural seat ? To copy, as ye rove,
The well-form'd picture, and correct design ?
First shun the false extremes of high and low.
With watry vapours this your fretted walls
Will soon deface; and that, with rough assault,
And frequent tempests shake your tott'ring roof.
Me most the gentle eminence delights
Of healthy champaign, to the sunny south

Fair-op'ning, and with woods, and circling hills,
Nor too remote, nor, with too close embrace,
Stopping the buxom air, behind enclos'd.
But if your lot hath fall'n in fields less fair,
Consult their genius, and, with due regard
To Nature's clear directions, shape your plan.
The site too lofty shelter, and the low
With sunny lawns, and open areas cheer.
The marish drain, and with capacious urns,
And well-conducted streams, refresh the dry.
So shall your lawns with healthful verdure smile,
While others, sick'ning at the sultry blaze,
A russet wild display, or the rank blade,
And matted tufts the careless owner shame.
Seek not, with fruitless cost, the level plain
To raise aloft, nor sink the rising hill.
Each has its charms though diff'rent, each in kind
Improve, not alter. Art with art conceal.
Let no straight terrac'd lines your slopes deform ;
No barb'rous walls restrain the bounded sight;
But to the distant fields the closer scene
Connect. The spacious lawn with scatter'd tr es
Irregular, in beauteous negligence,
Clothe bountiful. Your unimprison'd eye,
With pleasing freedom, through the lofty maze
Shall rove, and find no dull satiety.
The sportive stream with stiffen'd line avoid
To torture, nor prefer the long canal,
Or labour'd fount, to Nature's easy flow.
Your winding paths, now to the sunny gleam [31]
Directed, now with high embow'ring trees
Or fragrant shrubs conceal'd, with frequent seat
And rural structure deck. Their pleasing form
To fancy's eye suggests inhabitants
Of more than mortal make, and their cool shade,
And friendly shelter to refreshment sweet,
And wholesome meditation shall invite.
  To ev'ry structure give its proper site.
Nor, on the dreary heath, the gay alcove,
Nor the lone hermit's cell, or mournful urn,
Build on the sprightly lawn. The grassy slope
And shelter'd border for the cool arcade
Or Tuscan porch reserve. To the chaste dome,
And fair rotunda, give the swelling mount
Of freshest green. If to the Gothic scene
Your taste incline, in the well-water'd vale,
With lofty pines embrown'd, the mimic fane,
And mould'ring abbey's fretted windows, place.
The craggy rock, or precipicious hill,
Shall well become the castle's massy walls.
In royal villas the Palladian arch,
And Grecian portico, with dignity,
Their pride display : ill suits their lofty rank
The simpler scene. If chance historic deeds
Your fields distinguish, count them doubly fair,
And studious aid, with monumental stone
And faithful comment, fancy's fond review.
  Now other hills, with other wonders stor'd,
Invite the search. In vain ! unless the Muse
The landscape order. Nor will she decline
The pleasing task. For not to her 't is hard
To soar above the mountain's airy height,
With tow'ring pinions, or, with gentler wing,
T' explore the cool recesses of the vale.
Her piercing eye extends beyond the reach
Of optic tube, levell'd by midnight sage,
At the Moon's disk, or other distant Sun,

[26] The seat of the right hon. the earl of Ply-
mouth.
[27] The seat of the right hon. lord Archer.
[28] The forest, or woodland part of Warwickshire.
[29] So called from its pleasant rural situation.
[30] Called the barons' wars.

[31] Hæc amat obscurum, volet hæc sub luce videri.
                                   Hor.

And planetary worlds beyond the orb
Of Saturn.  Nor can intervening rocks
Impede her search.  Alike the sylvan gloom,
Or Earth's profoundest caverns, she pervades,
And, to her fav'rite sons, makes visible
All that may grace or dignify the song,
Howe'er envelop'd from their mortal ken.
So Uriel, winged regent of the Sun !
Upon its evening beam to Paradise
Came gliding down ; so, on its sloping ray,
To his bright charge return'd.  So th' heav'nly guest
From Adam's eyes the carnal film remov'd,
On Eden's hill, and purg'd his visual nerve
To see things yet unform'd, and future deeds.
Lo ! where the southern hill, with winding course,
Bends tow'rd the west, and from his airy seat
Views four fair provinces in union join'd ;
Beneath his feet, conspicuous rais'd, and rude,
A massy pillar rears its shapeless head.
Others in stature less, an area smooth
Enclose, like that on Sarum's ancient plain [32].
And some of middle rank apart are seen :
Distinguish'd those ! by courtly character
Of knights, while that the regal title bears [33].
What now the circle drear, and stiffen'd mass
Compose, like us, were animated forms,
With vital warmth, and sense, and thought endued ;
A band of warriors brave !  Effect accurs'd
Of necromantic art, and spells impure.
So vulgar fame.  But clerks, in antique lore
Profoundly skill'd, far other story tell :
And, in its mystic form, temple, or court
Espy, to fabled gods, or throned kings
Devote ; or fabric monumental, rais'd
By Saxon hands, or by that Danish chief
Rollo [34] ! the builder in the name imply'd.
Yet to the west the pleasing search pursue,
Where from the vale, Brails lifts his scarry sides,
And Illmington, and Campden's hoary hills
(By Lyttelton's sweet plaint, and thy abode
His matchless Lucia! to the Muse endear'd)
Impress new grandeur on the spreading scene,
With champaign fields, broad plain, and covert vale
Diversify'd : by Ceres, some adorn'd
With rich luxuriance of golden grain,
And some in Flora's liv'ry gaily dight,
And some with sylvan honours graceful crown'd.
Witness the forest glades, with stately pride,
Surrounding Sheldon's venerable dome [35] !
Witness the sloping lawns of Idlicot [36] !
And Honington's irriguous meads !  Some wind
Meand'ring round the hills disjoin'd, remote,
Giving full licence to their sportive range;
While distant, but distinct, his Alpine ridge
Malvern erects o'er Esham's vale sublime,
And boldly terminates the finish'd scene.
Still are the praises of the Red-Horse Vale
Unsung ; as oft it happens to the mind
Intent on distant themes, while what 's more near,
And, nearer, more important, 'scapes its note.
From yonder far-known hill, where the thin turf
But ill conceals the ruddy glebe, a form
On the bare soil portray'd, like that fam'd steed,

Which, in its womb, the fate of Troy conceal'd,
O'erlooks the vale.—Ye swains, that wish to learn,
Whence rose the strange phenomenon, attend !
    Britannia's sons, though now for arts renown'd,
A race of ancestors untaught, and rude,
Acknowledge ; like those naked Indian tribes,
Which first Columbus in the Atlantic isles
With wonder saw.  Alike their early fate,
To yield to conquering arms !  Imperial Rome
Was then to them what Britain is to these,
And through the subject land her trophies rear'd.
    But haughty Rome, her ancient manners flown,
Stoop'd to barbaric rage.  O'er her proud walls
The Goths prevail, which erst the Punic bands
Assail'd in vain, though Cannæ's bloody field
Their valour own'd, and Hannibal their guide !
Such is the fate which mightiest empires prove,
Unless the virtues of the son preserve
What his forefather's ruder courage won !
    No Cato now [37] the list'ning senate warm'd
To love of virtuous deeds, and public weal.
No Scipios led her hardy sons to war,
With sense of glory fir'd.  Through all her realms
Or hostile arms invade, or factions shake
Her tott'ring state.  From her proud capitol
Her tutelary gods retire, and Rome,
Imperial Rome, once mistress of the world,
A victim falls, so righteous Heav'n ordains,
To pride and luxury's all-conq'ring charms.
    Meantime her ancient foes, erewhile restrain'd
By Roman arms, from Caledonia's hills
Rush like a torrent, with resistless force,
O'er Britain's fenceless bounds, and through her
Pour the full tide of desolating war.    [fields
Ætius, thrice consul !  now an empty name,
In vain her sons invoke.  In vain they seek
Relief in servitude.  Ev'n servitude
Its miserable comforts now denies.
From shore to shore they fly.  The briny flood,
A guardian once, their further flight restrains.
Some court the boist'rous deep, a milder foe,
Some gain the distant shores, and fondly hope
In each to find a more indulgent home.
The rest, protracting still a wretched life,
From Belgia's coast in wild despair invite
Its new inhabitants, a Saxon race !
On enterprise and martial conquest bent.
With joy the Saxons to their aid repair,
And soon revenge them on their northern foes,
Revenge too dearly bought !  These courted guests
Give them short space for joy.  A hostile look
On their fair fields they cast, (for feeble hands
Alas ! too fair) and seize them for their own.
    And now again the conquer'd isle assumes
Another form ; on ev'ry plain and hill
New marks exhibiting of servile state,
The massy stone with figures quaint inscrib'd—
Or dyke by Woden [38], or the Mercian king [39],

[32] Stone-henge.

[33] Called the king's stone, or koning stone.

[34] Called Roll-rich stones.

[35] Weston, the seat of William Sheldon, esq.

[36] The seat of the late baron Legge, now belonging to Robert Ladbroke, esq.

[37] Non his juventus orta parentibus
    Infecit æquor sanguine Punico,
    Pyrrhumque, et ingentem cecidit
    Antilochum, Hannibalemque dirum.        Hor.

[38] Wansdyke, or Wodensdyke, a boundary of the kingdom of the West Saxons, in Wiltshire.

[39] Offa, from whom the boundary between the kingdom of the Mercians and the Britons in Wales took its name.

Vast bound'ry made—or thine, O Ashbury [40]!
And Tysoe's [41] wondrous theme, the martial horse,
Carv'd on the yielding turf, armorial sign
Of Hengist, Saxon chief! of Brunswick now,
And with the British lion join'd, the bird
Of Rome surpassing. Studious to preserve
The fav'rite form, the treach'rous conquerors
Their vassal tribes compel, with festive rites,
Its fading figure yearly to renew,
And to the neighb'ring vale impart its name [42].

---

## EDGE-HILL.

### BOOK II. NOON.

---

#### ARGUMENT.

Noon. The mid-scene from the castle on Ratley-hill. More particular accounts of the several parts of this scene, and of whatever is most remarkable in it. Warwick. Its antiquity. Historical account of the earls of Warwick. Story of Guy. Guy's Cliffe. Kenelworth. Its castle. History of it. Balsal. Wroxal. Coventry. Its environs. Manufactures. Story of Godiva. Peroration.

---

THE Sun, whose eastern ray had scarcely gilt
The mountain's brow while up the steep ascent
With early step we climb'd, now wide displays
His radiant orb, and half his daily stage
Hath nearly measur'd. From th' illumin'd vale
The soaring mists are drain'd, and, o'er the hill,
No more breathes grateful the cool, balmy air,
Cheering our search, and urging on our steps
Delightful. See, the languid herds forsake
The burning mead, and creep beneath the shade
Of spreading tree, or shelt'ring hedge-row tall:
Or, in the mant'ling pool, rude reservoir
Of wintry rains, and the slow, thrifty spring!
Cool their parch'd limbs, and lave their panting sides.

Let us too seek the shade. Yon airy dome,
Beneath whose lofty battlements we found
A covert passage to these sultry realms,
Invites our drooping strength, and well befriends
The pleasing comment on fair Nature's book,
In sumptuous volume, open'd to our view.
Ye sportive nymphs! that o'er the rural scene
Preside, you chief! that haunt the flow'ry banks
Of Avon, where, with more majestic wave,
Warwick's illustrious lord, through the gay meads
His dancing current guides, or round the lawn
Directs th' embroider'd verge of various dyes,
O! teach me all its graces to unfold,
And with your praise join his attendant fame.

'T is well! Here shelter'd from the scorching
At large we view the subject ale sublime, [heat,
And unimpeded. Hence its limits trace
Stretching, in wanton bound'ry, from the foot
Of this green mountain, far as human ken

Can reach, a theatre immense! adorn'd
With ornaments of sweet variety,
By Nature's pencil drawn—the level meads,
A verdant floor! with brightest gems inlaid,
And richly painted flow'rs—the tillag'd plain,
Wide waving to the Sun a rival blaze
Of gold, best source of wealth!—the prouder hills,
With outline fair, in naked pomp display'd,
Round, angular, oblong; and others crown'd
With graceful foliage. Over all her horn
Fair Plenty pours, and cultivation spreads,
Her height'ning lustre. See, beneath her touch,
The smiling harvests rise, with bending line
And wavy ridge, along the dappled glebe
Stretching their lengthen'd beds. Her careful hand
Piles up the yellow grain, or rustling hay
Adust for wintry store—the long-ridg'd mow,
Or shapely pyramid, with conic roof,
Dressing the landscape. She the thick-wove fence
Nurses, and adds, with care, the hedge-row elm.
Around her farms and villages she plans
The rural garden, yielding wholesome food
Of simple viands, and the fragrant herb
Medicinal. The well-rang'd orchard now
She orders, or the shelt'ring clump, or tuft
Of hardy trees, the wintry storms to curb,
Or guard the sweet retreat of village swain,
With health and plenty crown'd. Fair Science next,
Her offspring! adds towns, cities, vaulted domes,
And splendid palaces, and chases large,
With lake, and planted grove. Hence Warwick, fair
With rising buildings, Coventry's tall spires,
And Kenelworth! thy stately castle rose,
Which still, in ruin, charms th' astonish'd sight.
To crown the beauteous scene, the curtain'd sky,
Its canopy divine of azure tint,
Spreads heav'nly fair, and softens ev'ry charm.

Now yet again, with accurate survey,
The level plain, hills rising various, woods,
And meadows green, the simple cot, and towns,
Nurs'ries of arts and commerce! Warwick, fair
With rising buildings, Coventry's tall spires,
Magnificent in ruin Kenelworth!
And still more distant scenes, with legends strange,
And smoky arts, taught in the dusky schools
Of Tubal's sons, attentive let us scan,
And all their charms and mysteries explore.

First view, but cautious, the vast precipice;
Lest, startled at the giddy height, thy sense
Swimming forsake thee, and thy trembling limbs,
Unnerv'd, and fault'ring, threaten dang'rous lapse.
Along th' indented bank, the forest tribes,
The thin-leav'd ash, dark oak, and glossy beech,
Of polish'd rind, their branching boughs extend,
With blended tints and amicable strife,
Forming a checker'd shade. Below, the lawns,
With spacious sweep and wild declivity,
To yellow plains their sloping verdure join. [herds
There, white with flocks, and in her num'rous
Exulting, Chadsunt's pastures [1], large and fair,
Salute the sight, and witness to the fame
Of Litchfield's mitred saint [2]. The furzy heaths
Succeed ; close refuge of the tim'rous hare,
Or prowling fox, but refuge insecure!
From their dark covert oft the hunter-train
Rouse them unwilling, and o'er hill and dale,
With wild tumultuous joy, their steps pursue.

---

[40] Ashbury, in Berkshire, near which is the figure of a horse cut on the side of a hill, in whitish earth, which gives name to the neighbouring valley.

[41] The figure of the red horse, here described, is in the parish of Tysoe.

[42] Called, from this figure, the Vale of Red-Horse.

[1] The seat of James Newsam Craggs, esq.

[2] St. Chadd.

Just vengeance on the midnight thief! and life
With life aton'd ! But that poor, trembling wretch!
" Who doubts if now she lives," what hath she done;
Guiltless of blood, and impotent of wrong ?
How num'rous, how insatiate yet her foes !
Ev'n in these thickets, where she vainly sought
A safe retreat from man's unfeeling race,
The busy hound, to blood and slaughter train'd,
Snuffs her sweet vapour, and, to murth'rous rage
By mad'ning sounds impell'd, in her close seat
With fury tears her, and her corse devours:
Or scares her o'er the fields, and, by the scent,
With keen desire of reeking gore inflam'd,
Loud bellowing tortures her with deathful cries.
Nor more secure her *path!* Man even there,
Watching, with foul intent, her secret haunts,
Plants instruments of death, and round her neck
The fatal snare entwines. Thus innocence,
In human things, by wily fraud ensnar'd,
Oft helpless falls, while the bold plund'rer 'scapes.
Next the wide champaign, and the cheerful downs
Claim notice; chiefly thine, O Chesterton [3] !
Pre-eminent. Nor 'scape the roving eye
Thy solemn wood, and Roman vestiges,
Encampment green, or military road !
Amusive to the grave historic mind.
Thee Tachbroke [4] joins with venerable shade.
Nor distant far, in Saxon annals fam'd,
The rural court of Offa [5], Mercian king !
Where, sever'd from its trunk, low lies the head
Of brave Fermundus, slain by coward hands,
As on the turf supine in sleep he lay,
Nor wist it sleep from which to wake no more !
   Now Warwick claims the song; supremely fair
In this fair realm ; conspicuous rais'd to view
On the firm rock, a beauteous eminence
For health and pleasure form'd. Full to the south
A stately range of high embattled walls
And lofty tow'rs, and precipices vast,
Its guardian worth and ancient pomp confess [6].
The northern hills [7], where Superstition long
Her gloomy rites maintain'd, a tranquil scene
Of gentler arts, and pleasures more refin'd,
Displays. Lawns, parks, and meadows fair,
And groves around their mingled graces join,
And Avon pours his tributary stream.
   On thee contending kings their bounty pour'd [8],
And call'd the favour'd city by their names.
Thy worth the Romans publish'd [9], when to thee
Their legions they consign'd. Thee, Ethelflede [10],
Thy guardian fair! with royal grace restor'd,
When Pagan foes had raz'd thy goodly streets.
A monarch's care, those walls to learning rais'd [11],

These an asylum to declining age [12]
A Leicester's love proclaim. Nor pass unsung
The train of gallant chiefs, by thy lov'd name
Distinguish'd, and by deeds of high renown
Gracing the lofty title. Arthgal [13] first,
And brave Morvidus, fam'd in Druid song,
And British annals. Fair Felicia's sire,
Rohand ! and with her join'd in wedded love,
Immortal Guy ! who near Wintonia's walls
With that gigantic braggard Colebrand hight!
For a long summer's day sole fight maintain'd.
But huge gigantic size, and braggart oaths,
And sword, or massy club, dismay'd thee not.
Thy skill the stroke eluded, or thy shield
Harmless receiv'd, while on his batter'd sides
Fell thick thy galling blows, till from his hands
Down dropp'd the pond'rous weapon, and himself
Prostrate, to thy keen blade his grizly head
Reluctant yielded. Lamentations loud,
And shouts victorious, in strange concert join'd,
Proclaim the champion's fall. Thee Athelstan
His great deliverer owns, and meditates
With honours fair, and festive pomp to crown.
But other meed thy thoughtful mind employ'd,
Intent in heav'nly solitude to spend
The precious eve of life. Yet shall the Muse
Thy deed record, and on her patriot list
Enrol thy name, though many a Saxon chief
She leaves unsung. A Norman race succeeds,
To thee, fair town [14]! by charitable deeds
And pious gifts endear'd. The Beauchamps too
Thou claim'st, for arms and courtly manners fam'd !
Him chief [15], whom three imperial Henrys crown'd
With envied honours. Mirror fair was he
Of valour, and of knightly feats, achiev'd
In tilt and tournament. Thee Nevil [16] boasts
For bold exploits renown'd, with civil strife
When Britain's bleeding realm her weakness
And half her nobles in the contest slain [mourn'd,
Of York and Lancaster. He, sworn to both,
As int'rest tempted, or resentment fir'd,
To Henry now, and now to Edward join'd
His pow'rful aid ; now both to empire rais'd,
Now from their summit pluck'd, till in the strife
By Edward's conquering arms at length he fell.
Thou, Clarence [17], next, and next thy hapless son,
The last Plantagenet [18], awhile appears
To dignify the list; both sacrific'd
To barb'rous policy ! Proud Dudley [19] now

[12] The hospital.
[13] The first earl of Warwick, and one of the knights of king Arthur's round table.
[14] Henry de Novo Burgo, the first Norman earl, founded the priory at Warwick, and Roger, his son, built and endowed the church of St. Mary.
[15] Richard earl of Warwick, in the reigns of king Henry IV. V. and VI. was governor of Calais, and lieutenant-general of France. He founded the lady's chapel, and lies interred there, under a very magnificent monument.
[16] Called Make-king. He was killed at the battle of Barnet.
[17] He married the earl of Warwick's daughter, and was put to death by his brother, Edward IV.
[18] Beheaded in the Tower, by Henry VII. under a pretence of favouring the escape of Peter Warbeck.
[19] Made earl of Warwick by Edward VI. and afterwards duke of Northumberland.

[3] A seat of the right hon. lord Willoughby de Broke, so called from its being a Roman station on the Foss-Way.
[4] A seat of sir Walter Bagot, bart.
[5] Offchurch, the seat of Whitwick Knightley, esq.
[6] The castle.
[7] The priory, now the seat of Henry Wise, esq.
[8] Called Caer-Leon, from Guth-Leon, also Caer-Gwayr, or Guaric, from Gwar, two British kings. Its present name is said to be taken from Warremund, a Saxon.
[9] It was the Præsidium of the Romans.
[10] She rebuilt it when it had been destroyed by the Danes.
[11] The free-school.

From Edward's hand the bright distinction bore,
But soon to Mary paid his forfeit head,
And in his fate a wretched race involv'd:
Thee chief, thee wept by ev'ry gentle Muse,
Fair Jane [20]! untimely doom'd to bloody death,
For treason not thy own. To Rich's [21] line
Was then transferr'd th' illustrious name, to thine,
O Greville [22]! last. Late may it there remain!
With promise fair, as now, (more fair what heart
Parental craves?) of long, transmissive worth,
Proud Warwick's name, w'th growing fame to grace,
And crown, with lasting joy, her castled hill.

Hail, stately pile; fit mansion for the great!
Worthy the lofty title! Worthy him [23],
To Beauchamp's gallant race allied! the friend
Of gentle Sidney! to whose long desert,
In royal councils prov'd, his sov'reign's gift
Consign'd the lofty structure: worthy he!
The lofty structure's splendour to restore.

Nor less intent who now, by lineal right,
His place sustains, with reparations bold,
And well-attemper'd dignity to grace
Th' embattled walls. Nor spares his gen'rous mind
The cost of rural work, plantation large,
Forest, or fragrant shrub, or shelter'd walks,
Or ample, verdant lawns, where the sleek deer
Sport on the brink of Avon's flood, or graze
Beneath the rising walls; magnificence
With grace uniting, and enlarg'd delight
Of prospect fair, and Nature's smiling scenes!

Still is the colouring faint. O! could my verse,
Like their Louisa's [24] pencil'd shades, describe
The tow'rs, the woods, the lawns, the winding stream,
Fair like her form, and like her birth sublime!
Not Windsor's royal scenes by Denham sung,
Or that more tuneful bard on Twick'nam's shore,
Should boast a loftier strain, but in my verse
Their fame should live, as lives, proportion'd true,
Their beauteous image in her graven lines.

Transporting theme! on which I still could waste
The ling'ring hours, and still protract the song
With new delight; but thy example, Guy!
Calls me from scenes of pomp, and earthly pride,
To muse with thee in thy sequester'd cell [25].

Here the calm scene lulls the tumultuous breast
To sweet composure. Here the gliding stream,
That winds its wat'ry path in many a maze,
As loth to leave the enchanted spot, invites
To moralize on fleeting time and life,
With all its treacherous sweets and fading joys,
In emblem shown, by many a short-liv'd flow'r,
That on its margin smiles, and smiling falls
To join its parent earth. Here let me delve,
Near thine, my chamber in the peaceful rock,
And think no more of gilded palaces,
And luxury of sense. From the till'd glebe,
Or ever-teeming brook, my frugal meal
I 'll gain, and slake my thirst at yonder spring.
Like thee, I 'll climb the steep, and mark the scene
How fair! how passing fair! in grateful strains
Singing the praises of creative love.
Like thee, I 'll tend the call of mattin bell [26]
To early orisons, and latest tune
My evening song to that more wondrous love,
Which sav'd us from the grand apostate's wiles,
And righteous vengeance of Almighty ire,
Justly incens'd. O, pow'r of grace divine!
When mercy met with truth, with justice, peace.
Thou, holy hermit! in this league secure,
Did'st wait Death's vanquish'd spectre as a friend,
To change thy mortal coil for heav'nly bliss.

Next, Kenelworth! thy fame invites the song.
Assemblage sweet of social and serene!
But chiefly two fair streets, in adverse rows,
Their lengthen'd fronts extend, reflecting each
Beauty on each reciprocal. Between,
A verdant valley, slop'd from either side,
Forms the mid-space, where gently gliding flows
A crystal stream, beneath the mould'ring base
Of an old abbey's venerable walls.
Still further in the vale her castle lifts
Its stately tow'rs, and tott'ring battlements,
Dress'd with the rampant ivy's uncheck'd growth
Luxuriant. Here let us pause awhile,
To read the melancholy tale of pomp
Laid low in dust, and, from historic page,
Compose its epitaph. Hail, Clinton [27]! hail!
Thy Norman founder still yon neighb'ring Green [28],
And massy walls, with style imperial grac'd [29],
Record. The Montforts [30] thee with hardy deeds,
And memorable siege by Henry's arms [31],
And senatorial acts, that bear thy name,
Distinguish. Thee the bold Lancastrian line [32],
A royal train! from valiant Gaunt deriv'd,
Grace with new lustre; till Eliza's hand
Transferr'd thy walls to Leicester's favour'd earl [33].
He long, beneath thy roof, the maiden queen,

[20] Lady Jane Grey, married to a son of the earl of Warwick.

[21] Robert lord Rich, created earl of Warwick by James I.

[22] Greville lord Brook, first created earl Brook of Warwick castle, and afterwards earl of Warwick, by king George II.

[23] Sir Fulke Greville, made baron Brook of Beauchamp's-court, by James I. had the castle of Warwick, then in a ruinous condition, granted to him; upon which he laid out 20,000*l.* He lies buried in a neat octagon building, on the north side of the chancel at Warwick, under a fine marble monument, on which is the following very significant, laconic inscription:

" TROPHOEVM PECCATI!
FULKE GREVILLE, Servant to Queen ELIZABETH, Counsellor to King JAMES, and Friend to Sir PHILIP SIDNEY."

[24] The right hon. lady Louisa Greville, daughter to the right hon. the earl of Warwick.

[25] Called Guy's Cliff, the seat of the right hon. lady Mary Greatheed.

[26] Here was anciently an oratory, where, tradition says, Guy spent the latter part of his life in devotional exercises.

[27] Geoffry de Clinton, who built both the castle and the adjoining monastery, Tem. Hen. I.

[28] Clinton Green.

[29] Cæsar's Tower.

[30] The Montforts, earls of Leicester, of which Simon de Montfort, and his son Henry, were killed at the battle of Evesham.

[31] Henry III. who besieged this castle, and called a convention here, which passed an act for redeeming forfeited estates, called Dictum de Kenelworth.

[32] From whom a part of this structure is called Lancaster's Buildings.

[33] Granted by queen Elizabeth to Dudley earl of Leicester.

And all her courtly guests, with rare device
Of mask, and emblematic scenery,
Tritons, and sea-nymphs, and the floating isle,
Detain'd.   Nor feats of prowess, joust, or tilt
Of harness'd knights, nor rustic revelry
Were wanting; nor the dance, and sprightly mirth
Beneath the festive walls, with regal state,
And choicest lux'ry serv'd.   But regal state,
And sprightly mirth, beneath the festive roof,
Are now no more.   No more assembled crowds
At the stern porter's lodge admittance crave.
No more, with plaint, or suit importunate,
The thronged lobby echoes, nor with staff,
Or gaudy badge, the busy pursuivants
Lead to wish'd audience. · All, alas! is gone,
And Silence keeps her melancholy court
Throughout the walls ; save, where, in rooms of state,
Kings once repos'd! chatter the wrangling daws,
Or screech-owls hoot along the vaulted isles.
No more the trumpet calls the martial band,
With sprightly summons, to the guarded lists;
Nor lofty galleries their pride disclose
Of beauteous nymphs in courtly pomp attir'd,
Watching, with trembling hearts, the doubtful strife,
And, with their looks, inspiring wondrous deeds.
No more the lake displays its pageant shows,
And emblematic forms.   Alike the lake
And all its emblematic forms are flown,
And in their place mute flocks, and heifers graze,
Or buxom damsels ted the new-mown hay.
   What art thou, Grandeur! with thy flatt'ring train
Of pompous lies, and boastful promises?
Where are they now, and what 's their mighty sum?
All, all are vanish'd ! like the fleeting forms
Drawn in an evening cloud.   Nought now remains,
Save these sad relics of departed pomp,
These spoils of time, a monumental pile!
Which to the vain its mournful tale relates,
And warns them not to trust to fleeting dreams.
   Thee too, though boasting not a royal train,
The Muse, O Balshal [34]! in her faithful page
Shall celebrate : for long beneath thy roof
A band of warriors bold, of high renown,
To martial deeds and hazardous emprise
Sworn, for defence of Salem's sacred walls,
From Paynim foes, and holy pilgrimage.
Now other guests thou entertain'st,
A female band, by female charity
Sustain'd.   Thee, Wroxal [35]! too, in fame allied,
Seat of the poet's, and the Muse's friend !
My verse shall sing, with thy long-exil'd knight,
By Leonard's pray'rs, from distant servitude,
To these brown thickets, and his mournful mate,
Invisibly convey'd.   Yet doubted she
His speech and alter'd form, and better proof
Impatient urg'd.   (So Ithaca's chaste queen
Her much-wish'd lord, by twice ten absent years
And wise Minerva's guardian care disguis'd,
Acknowledg'd not: so, with suspended faith,
His bridal claim repress'd.)   Straight he displays
Part of the nuptial ring between them shar'd,
When in the bold crusade his shield he bore.

[34] Formerly a seat of the Knights Templars, now
an almshouse for poor widows, founded by the lady
Katharine Levison, a descendant of Robert Dudley,
earl of Leicester.
[35] The seat of Christopher Wren, esq. ; once a
nunnery, dedicated to St. Leonard.—See Dugdale's
Antiquities.

The twin memorial of their plighted love
Within her faithful bosom she retain'd.
Quick from its shrine the hallow'd pledge she drew,
To match it with its mate, when, strange to tell !
No sooner had the separated curves
Approach'd each other, but, with sudden spring,
They join'd again, and the small circle clos'd.
So they, long sever'd, met in close embrace.
   At length, O Coventry ! thy neighb'ring fields,
And fair surrounding villas, we attend,
Allesley [36], and Whitley's [37] pastures, Stivichale [38],
That views with lasting joy thy green domains,
And Bagington's [39] fair walls, and Stonely [40] ! thine,
And Coombe's [41] majestic pile, both boasting once
Monastic pomp, still equal in renown !
And, as their kindred fortunes they compare,
Applauding more the present than the past.
Ev'n now the pencil'd sheets, unroll'd, display
More sprightly charms of beauteous lawn, and
                                          grove,
And sweetly-wand'ring paths, and ambient stream,
To cheer with lasting flow th' enamell'd scene,
And themes of song for future bards prepare.
   Fair city ! thus environ'd ! and thyself
For royal grants and silken arts renown'd !
To thee the docile youth repair, and learn,
With sidelong glance and nimble stroke, to ply
The flitting shuttle, while their active feet,
In mystic movements, press the subtle stops
Of the loom's complicated frame, contriv'd,
From the loose thread, to form, with wondrous art,
A texture close, inwrought with choice device
Of flow'r, or foliage gay, to the rich stuff,
Or silky web, imparting fairer worth.
Nor shall the Muse, in her descriptive song,
Neglect from dark oblivion to preserve
Thy mould'ring cross [42], with ornament profuse
Of pinnacles, and niches, proudly rais'd,
Height above height, a sculptur'd chronicle !
Less lasting than the monumental verse.
Nor scornful will she flout thy cavalcade,
Made yearly to Godiva's deathless praise,
While gaping crowds around her pageant throng,
With prying look and stupid wonderment.
Not so the Muse ! who, with her virtue fir'd,
And love of thy renown, in notes as chaste
As her fair purpose, from memorials dark,
Shall, to the list'ning ear, her tale explain.
   When Edward [43], last of Egbert's royal race,
O'er sev'n united realms the sceptre sway'd,
Proud Leofric, with trust of sov'reign pow'r,
The subject Mercians rul'd.   His lofty state
The loveliest of her sex ! a noble dame
Of Thorold's ancient line, Godiva shar'd.
But pageant pomp charm'd not her saintly mind
Like virtuous deeds, and care of others' weal.

[36] The seat of M. Neale, esq.
[37] The seat of Ed. Bowater, esq. ; now belonging
to Francis Wheeler, esq.
[38] The seat of Arthur Gregory, esq. ; commanding a pleasant view of Coventry Park, &c.
[39] The seat of William Bromley, esq. ; one of
the representatives in parliament for the county of
Warwick.
[40] The seat of the right hon. lord Leigh.
[41] The seat of the right hon. lord Craven.
[42] Built by sir William Hollies, lord mayor of
London, in the reign of king Henry VIII.
[43] Edward the Confessor.

Such tender passions in his haughty breast
He cherish'd not, but with despotic sway
Control'd his vassal tribes, and, from their toil,
His luxury maintain'd.  Godiva saw
Their plaintive looks; with grief she saw thy sons,
O Coventry ! by tyrant laws oppress'd,
And urg'd her haughty lord, but urg'd in vain!
With patriot-rule, thy drooping arts to cheer.
Yet, though forbidden e'er again to move
In what so much his lofty state concern'd,
Not so from thought of charitable deed
Desisted she, but amiably perverse
Her hopeless suit renew'd.  Bold was th' attempt !
Yet not more bold than fair, if pitying sighs
Be fair, and charity which knows no bounds.
What had'st thou then to fear from wrath inflam'd
At such transcendent guilt, rebellion join'd
With female weakness and officious zeal ?
So thy stern lord might call the gen'rous deed;
Perhaps might punish as befitted deed
So call'd, if love restrain'd not: yet though love
O'er anger triumph'd, and imperious rule,
Not o'er his pride ; which better to maintain,
His answer thus he artfully return'd.
" Why will the lovely partner of my joys,
Forbidden, thus her wild petition urge ?
Think not my breast is steel'd against the claims
Of sweet humanity.  Think not I hear
Regardless thy request.  If piety,
Or other motive, with mistaken zeal,
Call'd to thy aid, pierc'd not my stubborn frame,
Yet to the pleader's worth, and modest charms,
Would my fond love no trivial gift impart.
But pomp and fame forbid.  That vassalage,
Which, thoughtless, thou would'st tempt me to
    dissolve,
Exalts our splendour, and augments my pow'r.
With tender bosoms form'd, and yielding hearts,
Your sex soon melts at sights of vulgar woe ;
Heedless how *glory* fires the *manly* breast
With love of rank sublime.  This principle
In female minds a feebler empire holds,
Opposing less the specious arguments
For milder rule, and freedom's popular theme.
But plant some gentler passion in its room,
Some virtuous instinct suited to your make,
As glory is to ours, alike requir'd
A ransom for the vulgar's vassal state,
Then would'st thou soon the strong contention own,
And justify my conduct.  Thou art fair,
And chaste as fair; with nicest sense of shame,
And sanctity of thought.  Thy bosom thou
Didst ne'er expose to shameless dalliance
Of wanton eyes ; nor, ill-concealing it
Beneath the treach'rous cov'ring, tempt aside
The secret glance, with meditated fraud.
Go now, and lay thy modest garments by:
In naked beauty mount thy milk-white steed,
And through the streets, in face of open day,
And gazing slaves, their fair deliv'rer ride:
Then will I own thy pity was sincere,
Applaud thy v rtue, and confirm thy suit.
But if thou lik'st not such ungentle terms,
And sure thy soul the guilty thought abhors !
Know then that Leofric, like thee, can feel,
Like thee, may pity, while he seems severe,
And urge thy suit no more." His speech he clos'd,
And, with strange oaths, confirm'd the sad decree.
    Again, within Godiva's gentle breast
New tumults rose.  At length her female fears

Gave way, and sweet humanity prevail'd.
Reluctant, but resolv'd, the matchless fair
Gives all her naked beauty to the Sun :
Then mounts her milk-white steed, and, through
    the streets,
Rides fearless ; her dishevell'd hair a veil !
That o'er her beauteous limbs luxuriant flow'd,
Nurs'd long by Fate for this important day !
Prostrate to earth th' astonish'd vassals bow,
Or to their inmost privacies retire.
All, but one prying slave! who fondly hop'd,
With venial curiosity, to gaze
On such a wondrous dame.  But foul disgrace
O'ertook the bold offender, and he stands,
By just decree, a spectacle abhorr'd,
And lasting monument of swift revenge
For thoughts impure, and beauty's injur'd charms.
    Ye guardians of her rights, so nobly won !
Cherish the Muse, who first in modern strains
Essay'd to sing your lovely patriot's [44] fame,
Anxious to rescue from oblivious time
Such matchless virtue, her heroic deed
Illustrate, and your gay procession grace.

---

## EDGE-HILL.

### BOOK III.  AFTERNOON.

---

#### ARGUMENT.

Address to the right hon. the earl of Clarendon.
    Metaphysical subtleties exploded.  Philosophical
    account of vision, and optic glasses.  Objects of
    sight not sufficiently regarded on account of
    their being common.  Story relative thereto.
    Return to the mid-scene.  Solihul.  School scene.
    Bremicham.  Its manufactures.  Coal mines.
    Iron ore.  Process of it.  Panegyric upon iron.

---

AGAIN, the Muse her airy flight essays.
Will Villers, skill'd alike in classic song,
Or, with a critic's eye, to trace the charms
Of Nature's beauteous scenes, attend the lay ?
Will he, accustom'd to soft Latian climes,
As to their softer numbers, deign awhile
To quit the Mantuan bard's harmonious strain,
By sweet attraction of the theme allur'd ?
The Latian poet's song is still the same.
Not so the Latian fields.  The gentle Arts
That made those fields so fair, when Gothic rule,
And Superstition, with her bigot train,

44 See Dugdale's Antiquities of Warwickshire.
    It is pleasant enough to observe, with what gravity
the above-mentioned learned writer dwells on the
praises of this renowned lady.  " And now, before I
proceed," says he, " I have a word more to say of
the noble countess Godeva, which is, that besides her
devout advancement of that pious work of his, i. e.
her husband Leofric, in this magnificent monastery,
viz. of monks at Coventry, she gave her whole treasure thereto, and sent for skilful goldsmiths, who,
with all the gold and silver she had, made crosses,
images of saints, and other curious ornaments."
Which passages may serve as a specimen of the devotion and patriotism of those times.

Fix'd there their gloomy seat, to this fair isle
Retir'd, with Freedom's gen'rous sons to dwell,
To grace her cities, and her smiling plains
With plenty clothe, and crown the rural toil.
    Nor hath he found, throughout those spacious
Where Albis flows, and Ister's stately flood, [realms
More verdant meads, or more superb remains
Of old magnificence, than his own fields
Display, where Clinton's [1] venerable walls
In ruin, still their ancient grandeur tell.
    Requires there aught of learning's pompous aid
To prove that all this outward frame of things
Is what it seems, not unsubstantial air,
Ideal vision, or a waking dream,
Without existence, save what fancy gives?
Shall we, because we strive in vain to tell
How matter acts on incorporeal mind,
Or how, when sleep has lock'd up ev'ry sense,
Or fevers rage, imagination paints
Unreal scenes, reject what sober sense
And calmest thought attest? Shall we confound
States wholly diff'rent? Sleep with wakeful life?
Disease with health? This were to quit the day,
And seek our path at midnight. To renounce
Man's surest evidence, and idolize
Imagination. Hence then banish we
These metaphysic subtleties, and mark
The curious structure of these visual orbs,
The windows of the mind; substance how clear,
Aqueous or crystalline! through which the soul,
As through a glass, all outward things surveys.
    See, while the Sun gilds, with his golden beam,
Yon distant pile, which Hyde, with care refin'd,
From plunder guards, its form how beautiful!
Anon some cloud his radiance intercepts,
And all the splendid object fades away.
Or, if some incrustation o'er the sight
Its baleful texture spread, like a clear lens,
With filth obscur'd! no more the sensory,
Through the thick film, imbibes the cheerful day,
" But cloud instead, and ever-during night
Surround it!" So, when on some weighty truth
A beam of heav'nly light its lustre sheds,
To reason's eye it looks supremely fair.
But if foul passion, or distemper'd pride,
Impede its search, or phrensy seize the brain,
Then ignorance a gloomy darkness spreads,
Or superstition, with misshapen forms,
Erects its savage empire in the mind.
    The vulgar race of men, like herds that graze,
On instinct live, not knowing how they live;
While reason sleeps, or waking stoops to sense.
But sage philosophy explores the cause
Of each phenomenon of sight, or sound,
Taste, touch, or smell; each organ's inmost frame,
And correspondence with external things:
Explains how diff'rent texture of their parts
Excites sensations diff'rent, rough, or smooth,
Bitter, or sweet, fragrance, or noisome scent:
How various streams of undulating air,
Through the ear's winding labyrinth convey'd,
Cause all the vast variety of sounds.
Hence too the subtle properties of light,

[1] The magnificent ruins of Kenelworth castle,
built by Geofry de Clinton, and more particularly
described in the preceding book, belonged to the
right hon. the earl of Clarendon, many years resident in Italy, and envoy to most of the courts in
Germany.

And sev'n-fold colour are distinctly view'd
In the prismatic glass, and outward forms
Shown fairly drawn, in miniature divine,
On the transparent eye's membraneous cell.
By combination hence of diff'rent orbs,
Convex, or concave, through their crystal pores,
Transmitting variously the solar ray,
With line oblique, the telescopic tube
Reveals the wonders of the starry sphere,
Worlds above worlds; or, in a single grain,
Or wat'ry drop, the penetrative eye
Discerns innumerable inhabitants
Of perfect structure, imperceptible
To naked view. Hence each defect of sense
Obtains relief; hence to the palsy'd ear
New impulse, vision new to languid sight,
Surprise to both, and youthful joys restor'd!
    Cheap is the bliss we never knew to want!
So graceless spendthrifts waste unthankfully
Those sums, which merit often seeks in vain,
And poverty would kneel to call its own.
So objects, hourly seen, unheeded pass,
At which the new-created sight would gaze
With exquisite delight. Doubt ye this truth?
A tale shall place it fairer to your view.
    A youth [2] there was, a youth of lib'ral mind,
And fair proportion in each lineament
Of outward form; but dim suffusion veil'd
His sightless orbs, which roll'd, and roll'd in vain,
To find the blaze of day. From infancy,
Till full maturity glow'd on his cheek,
The long, long night its gloomy empire held,
And mock'd each gentle effort, lotions,
Or cataplasms, by parental hands,
With fruitless care employ'd. At length a Leech,
Of skill profound, well-vers'd in optic lore,
An arduous task devis'd aside to draw
The veil, which, like a cloud, hung o'er his sight,
And ope a lucid passage to the Sun.
Instant the youth the promis'd blessing craves.
But first his parents, with uplifted hands,
The healing pow'rs invoke, and pitying friends
With sympathizing heart, the rites prepare:
Mongst these, who well deserv'd th' important trust,
A gentle maid there was, that long had wail'd
His hapless fate. Full many a tedious hour
Had she, with converse, and instructive song,
Beguil'd. Full many a step darkling her arm
Sustain'd him; and, as they their youthful days
In friendly deeds, and mutual intercourse
Of sweet endearment pass'd, love in each breast
His empire fix'd; in her's with pity join'd,
In his with gratitude and deep regard.
    The friendly wound was giv'n; th' obstructing film
Drawn artfully aside; and on his sight
Burst the full tide of day. Surpris'd he stood,
Not knowing where he was, nor what he saw!
The skilful artist first, as first in place
He view'd, then seiz'd his hand, then felt his own,
Then mark'd their near resemblance, much per-
          plex'd,
And still the more perplex'd, the more he saw.
Now silence first th' impatient mother broke,
And, as her eager looks on him she bent,
" My son," she cried, " my son!" On her he gaz'd
With fresh surprise. " And, what?" he cried, " art
          thou,

[2] For the general subject of the following story,
see The Tatler, number 55, and Smith's Optics.

My mother? for thy voice bespeaks thee such,
Though to my sight unknown."—" Thy mother I !"
She quick reply'd, " thy sister, brother these."
" O ! 't is too much," he said ; " too soon to part,
Ere well we meet! But this new flood of day
O'erpow'rs me, and I feel a death-like damp
Chill all my frame, and stop my fault'ring tongue."
    Now Lydia, so they call'd his gentle friend,
Who, with averted eye, but, in her soul,
Had felt the lancing steel, her aid apply'd,
" And stay, dear youth," she said, " or with thee
            take
Thy Lydia, thine alike in life or death."
    At Lydia's name, at Lydia's well-known voice,
He strove again to raise his drooping head,
And ope his closing eye, but strove in vain,
And on her trembling bosom sunk away.
    Now other fears distract his weeping friends.
But short this grief! for soon his life return'd,
And, with return of life, return'd their peace.
Yet, for his safety, they resolve awhile
His infant sense from day's bright beams to guard,
Ere yet again they tempt such dang'rous joy.
As, when from some transporting dream awak'd,
We fondly on the sweet delusion dwell,
And, with intense reflection, to our minds
Picture th' enchanted scene—angelic forms—
Converse sublime—and more than waking bliss !
Till the coy vision, as the more we strive
To paint it livelier on th' enraptur'd sense,
Still fainter grows, and dies at last away :
So dwelt the youth on his late transient joy,
So long'd the dear remembrance to renew.
At length, again the wish'd-for day arriv'd.
The task was Lydia's ! her's the charge, alone
From dangers new to guard the dear delight ;
But first th' impatient youth she thus address'd.
    " Dear youth ! my trembling hands but ill essay
This tender task, and, with unusual fear,
My flutt'ring heart forebodes some danger nigh."
    " Dismiss thy fears," he cried, " nor think so ill
I con thy lessons, as still need be taught
To hail, with caution, the new-coming day.
Then loose these envious folds, and teach my sight,
If more can be, to make thee more belov'd."
    " Ah ! there 's my grief," she cried : " 't is true
        our hearts
With mutual passion burn, but then 't is true
Thou ne'er hast known me by that subtle sense
Through which love most an easy passage finds ;
That sense ! which soon may show thee many a
            maid
Fairer than Lydia, though more faithful none.
And may she not cease then to be belov'd ?
May she not then, when less thou need'st her care,
Give place to some new charmer ? 'T is for this
I sigh ; for this my sad foreboding fears
New terrours form."—" And can'st thou then," he
            cried,
" Want aught that might endear thee to my soul ?
Art thou not excellence ? Art thou not all
That man could wish ? Goodness, and gentlest love ?
Can I forget thy long assiduous care ?
Thy morning-tendance, surest mark to me
Of day's return, of night thy late adieu ?
Do I need aught to make my bliss complete,
When thou art by me ? when I press thy hand ?
When I breathe fragrance at thy near approach ;
And hear the sweetest music in thy voice ?
Can that, which to each other sense is dear,

So wondrous dear, be otherwise to sight ?
Or can sight make, what is to reason good
And lovely, seem less lovely and less good ?
Perish the sense, that would make Lydia such !
Perish its joys, those joys however great !
If to be purchas'd with the loss of thee.
O my dear Lydia ! if there be indeed
The danger thou report'st, O ! by our love,
Our mutual love, I charge thee, ne'er unbind
These hapless orbs, or tear them from their seat,
Ere they betray me thus to worse than death."
    " No, Heav'n forbid !" she cried, " for Heav'n
        hath heard
Thy parents' pray'rs, and many a friend now waits
To mingle looks of cordial love with thine.
And should I rob them of the sacred bliss ?
Should I deprive thee of the rapt'rous sight ?
No ! be thou happy ; happy be thy friends ;
Whatever fate attends thy Lydia's love ;
Thy hapless Lydia !—Hapless did I say ?
Ah ! wherefore ? wherefore wrong I thus thy worth ?
Why doubt thy well-known truth, and constant
            mind ?
No, happiest she of all the happy train,
In mutual vows and plighted faith secure !"
    So saying, she the silken bandage loos'd,
Nor added further speech, prepar'd to watch
The new surprise, and guide the doubtful scene,
By silence more than tenfold night conceal'd.
When thus the youth. " And is this then the world,
In which I am to live ? Am I awake ?
Or do I dream ? Or hath some pow'r unknown,
Far from my friends, far from my native home,
Convey'd me to these radiant seats ? O thou !
Inhabitant of this enlighten'd world !
Whose heav'nly softness far transcends his shape,
By whom this miracle was first achiev'd,
O ! deign thou to instruct me where I am ;
And how to name thee by true character,
Angel or mortal ! Once I had a friend,
Who, but till now, ne'er left me in distress.
Her speech was harmony, at which my heart
With transport flutter'd ; and her gracious hand
Supplied me with whate'er my wish could form ;
Supply and transport ne'er so wish'd before !
Never, when wanted, yet so long denied !
Why is she silent now, when most I long
To hear her heav'nly voice ? why flies she not
With more than usual speed to crown my bliss?
Ah ! did I leave her in that darksome world ?
Or rather dwells she not in these bright realms,
Companion fit for such fair forms as thine ?
O ! teach me, if thou canst, how I may find
This gentle counsellor ; when found, how know
By this new sense, which, better still to rate
Her worth, I chiefly wish'd." The lovely form
Reply'd, " In me behold that gentle friend,
If still thou own'st me such."—" O ! yes, 't is she,"
He cried ; " 't is Lydia ! 't is her charming voice !
O ! speak again ; O ! let me press thy hand :
On these I can rely. This new-born sense
May cheat me. Yet so much I prize thy form,
I willingly would think it tells me true—
    " Ha ! what are these ? Are they not they, of
        whom
Thou warn'dst me ? Yes—true—they are beautiful.
But have they lov'd like thee, like thee convers'd ?
They move not as we move, they bear no part
In my new bliss. And yet methinks, in one,
Her form I can descry, though now so calm !

Who call'd me son."—" Mistaken youth !" she
    cried,
These are not what they seem ; are not as we,
Not living substances, but pictur'd shapes,
Resemblances of life ! by mixture form'd
Of light and shade, in sweet proportion join'd.
But hark ! I hear, without, thy longing friends,
Who wait my summons, and reprove my stay."
    " To thy direction," cried th' enraptur'd youth,
" To thy direction I commit my steps.
Lead on, be thou my guide, as late, so now,
In this new world, and teach me how to use
This wondrous faculty; which thus, so soon
Mocks me with phantoms.   Yet enough for me !
That all my past experience joins with this
To tell me I am happier than I know.
To tell me thou art Lydia ! from whose side
I never more will part ! with whom compar'd,
All others of her sex, however fair,
Shall be like painted, unsubstantial forms."
    So when the soul, inflam'd with strong desire
Of purer bliss, its earthly mansion leaves,
Perhaps some friendly genius, wont to steer
With ministerial charge his dang'rous steps ;
Perhaps some gentle partner of his toil,
More early blest, in radiant lustre clad,
And form celestial, meets his dazzled sight ;
And guides his way, through trackless fields of air,
To join, with rapt'rous joy, th' ethereal train.
    Now to the midland search the Muse returns.
For more, and still more busy scenes remain ;
The promis'd schools of wise artificers
In brass and iron.   But another school
Of gentler arts demands the Muse's song,
Where first she learn'd to scan the measur'd verse,
And awkwardly her infant notes essay'd.
    Hail Solihul ! respectful I salute
Thy walls; more awful once ! when, from the sweets
Of festive freedom and domestic ease,
With throbbing heart, to the stern discipline
Of pedagogue morose I sad return'd.
But though no more his brow severe, nor dread
Of birchen sceptre awes my riper age,
A sterner tyrant rises to my view,
With deadlier weapon arm'd.   Ah ! Critic ! spare,
O ! spare the Muse, who feels her youthful fears
On thee transfer'd, and trembles at thy lash.
Against the venal tribe, that prostitutes
The tuneful art, to soothe the villain's breast,
To blazon fools, or feed the pamper'd lust
Of bloated vanity ; against the tribe
Which casts its wanton jests at holy truths,
Or clothes, with virtue's garb, th' accursed train
Of loathsome vices, lift thy vengeful arm,
And all thy just severity exert.
Enough to venial faults, and hapless want
Of animated numbers, such as breathe
The soul of epic song, hath erst been paid
Within these walls, still stain'd with infant blood.
    Yet may I not forget the pious care
Of love parental, anxious to improve
My youthful mind.   Nor yet the debt disown
Due to severe restraint and rigid laws,
The wholesome curb of passion's headstrong reign.
To them I owe that ere, with painful toil,
Through Priscian's crabbed rules, laborious task !
I held my course, till the dull, tiresome road
Plac'd me on classic ground, that well repaid
The labours of the way.   To them I owe
The pleasing knowledge of my youthful mates

Matur'd in age and honours.   These among,
I gratulate whom Augusta's senate hails
Father ! and, in each charge and high employ,
Found worthy all her love, with amplest trust
And dignity invests.   And well I ween,
Her tribunitial pow'r, and purple pomp
On thee confers, in living manners school'd
To guard her weal, and vindicate her rights,
O Ladbroke ! once in the same fortunes class'd
Of early life ; with count'nance unestrang'd,
For ev'ry friendly deed still vacant found !
    Nor can the Muse, while she these scenes surveys,
Forget her Shenstone, in the youthful toil
Associate; whose bright dawn of genius oft
Smooth'd my incondite verse; whose friendly voice
Call'd me from giddy sports to follow him
Intent on better themes—call'd me to taste
The charms of British song, the pictur'd page
Admire, or mark his imitative skill ;
Or with him range in solitary shades,
And scoop rude grottos in the shelving bank.
Such were the joys that cheer'd life's early morn !
Such the strong sympathy of soul, that knit
Our hearts congenial in sweet amity !
On Cherwel's banks, by kindred science nurs'd ;
And well-matur'd in life's advancing stage,
When, on Ardenna's plain, we fondly stray'd,
With mutual trust, and amicable thought ;
Or in the social circle gaily join'd :
Or round his Leasowe's happy circuit rov'd ;
On hill and dale invoking ev'ry Muse,
Nor Tempe's shade, nor Aganippe's fount
Envied; so willingly the Dryads nurs'd
His groves; so lib'rally their crystal urns
The Naiads pour'd, enchanted with his spells ;
And pleas'd to see their ever-flowing streams
Led by his hand, in many a mazy line ;
Or, in the copious tide, collected large,
Or tumbling from the rock, in sportive falls,
Now, from the lofty bank, precipitate ;
And now, in gentler course, with murmurs soft
Soothing the ear; and now, in concert join'd,
Fall above fall, oblique and intricate,
Among the twisted roots.   Ah ! whilst I write,
In deeper murmur flows the sad'ning stream ;
Wither the groves; and from the beauteous scene
Its soft enchantments fly.   No more for me
A charm it wears, since he, alas ! is gone,
Whose genius plann'd it, and whose spirit grac'd.
Ah ! hourly does the fatal doom, pronounc'd
Against rebellious sin, some social band
Dissolve, and leave a thousand friends to weep,
Soon such themselves, as those they now lament !
This mournful tribute to thy mem'ry paid !
The Muse pursues her solitary way ;
But heavily pursues, since thou art gone,
Whose counsel brighten'd, and whose friendship
    shar'd
The pleasing task.   Now, Bremicham ! to thee
She steers her flight, and, in thy busy scenes,
Seeks to restrain awhile the starting tear.
    Yet ere her song describes the smoky forge,
Or sounding anvil, to the dusky heath
Her gentle train she leads.   What ? though no grain,
Or herbage sweet, or waving woods adorn
Its dreary surface, yet it bears, within,
A richer treasury.   So worthy minds
Oft lurk beneath a rude, unsightly form.
More hapless they ! that few observers search,
Studious to find this intellectual ore,

And stamp, with gen'rous deed, its current worth.
Here many a merchant turns adventurer,
Encourag'd, not disgusted. Interest thus,
On sordid minds, with stronger impulse works,
Than virtue's heav'nly flame. Yet Providence
Converts to gen'ral use man's selfish ends.
Hence are the hungry fed, the naked cloth'd,
The wintry damps dispell'd, and social mirth
Exults, and glows before the blazing hearth.
    When likely signs th' adventrous search invite,
A cunning artist tries the latent soil:
And if his subtle engine, in return,
A brittle mass contains of sable hue,
Straight he prepares th' obstructing earth to clear,
And raise the crumbling rock. A narrow pass
Once made, wide, and more wide the gloomy cave
Stretches its vaulted isles, by num'rous hands
Hourly extended. Some the pick-axe ply,
Loos'ning the quarry from its native bed.
Some waft it into light. Thus the grim ore,
Here useless, like the miser's brighter hoard,
Is from its prison brought, and sent abroad,
The frozen hours to cheer, to minister
To needful sustenance, and polish'd arts.
Meanwhile the subterraneous city spreads
Its covert streets, and echoes with the noise
Of swarthy slaves, and instruments of toil.
They, such the force of custom's pow'rful laws!
Pursue their sooty labours, destitute
Of the Sun's cheering light, and genial warmth.
And oft a chilling damp, or unctuous mist,
Loos'd from the crumbly caverns, issues forth,
Stopping the springs of life. And oft the flood,
Diverted from its course, in torrents pours,
Drowning the nether world. To cure these ills
Philosophy two curious arts supplies,
To drain th' imprison'd air, and, in its place,
More pure convey, or, with impetuous force,
To raise the gath'ring torrents from the deep.
One from the wind [3] its salutary pow'r
Derives, thy charity to sick'ning crowds,
From cheerful haunts, and Nature's balmy draughts
Confin'd; O friend of man, illustrious Hales [4]!
That, stranger still! its influence owes to air [5],
By cold and heat alternate now condens'd,
Now rarefied [6]. Agent! to vulgar thought
How seeming weak, in act how pow'rful seen!
So Providence, by instruments despis'd,
All human force and policy confounds.
    But who that fiercer element can rule?
When, in the nitrous cave, the kindling flame,
By pitchy vapours fed, from cell to cell,
With fury spreads, and the wide fewell'd earth,
Around, with greedy joy, receives the blaze.
By its own entrails nourish'd, like those mounts
Vesuvian, or Ætnean, still it wastes,
And still new fewel for its rapine finds
Exhaustless. Wretched he! who journeying late,
O'er the parch'd heath, bewilder'd, seeks his way.
Oft will his snorting steed, with terrour struck,
His wonted speed refuse, or start aside,
With rising smoke, and ruddy flame annoy'd.
While, at each step, his trembling rider quakes,
Appall'd with thoughts of bog, or cavern'd pit,

Or treach'rous earth, subsiding where they tread,
Tremendous passage to the realms of death!
    Yet want there not ev'n here some lucid spots
The smoky scene to cheer, and, by contrast,
More fair. Such Dartmouth's cultivated lawns [7]!
Himself, distinguish'd more with ornament
Of cultur'd manners, and supernal light!
Such thine, O Bridgman [8]! Such—but envious time
Forbids the Muse to these fair scenes to rove,
Still minding her of her unfinish'd theme,
From russet heaths, and smould'ring furnaces,
To trace the progress of thy steely arts,
*Queen of the sounding anvil* [9]! Aston [10] thee,
And Edgbaston [11] with hospitable shade,
And rural pomp invest. O! warn thy sons;
When for a time their labours they forget,
Not to molest these peaceful solitudes.
So may the masters of the beauteous scene
Protect thy commerce, and their toil reward.
    Nor does the barren soil conceal alone
The sable rock inflammable. Oft-times
More pond'rous ore beneath its surface lies,
Compact, metallic, but with earthy parts
Incrusted. These the smoky kiln consumes,
And to the furnace's impetuous rage
Consigns the solid ore. In the fierce heat
The pure dissolves, the dross remains behind.
This push'd aside, the trickling metal flows
Through secret valves along the channel'd floor,
Where in the mazy moulds of figur'd sand,
Anon it hardens. Now the busy forge
Reiterates its blows, to form the bar
Large, massy, strong. Another art expands,
Another yet divides the yielding mass
To many a taper length, fit to receive
The artist's will, and take its destin'd form.
    Soon o'er thy furrow'd pavement, Bremicham!
Ride the loose bars obstrep'rous; to the sons
Of languid sense, and frame too delicate
Harsh noise perchance, but harmony to thine.
    Instant innumerable hands prepare
To shape, and mould the malleable ore.
Their heavy sides th' inflated bellows heave,
Tugged by the pulley'd line, and, with their blast
Continuous, the sleeping embers rouse,
And kindle into life. Straight the rough mass,
Plung'd in the blazing hearth, its heat contracts,
And glows transparent. Now, Cyclopean chief!
Quick on the anvil lay the burning bar,
And with thy lusty fellows, on its sides
Impress the weighty stroke. See, how they strain
The swelling nerve, and lift the sinewy [12] arm
In measur'd time; while with their clatt'ring blows,
From street to street the propagated sound
Increasing echoes, and, on ev'ry side,
The tortur'd metal spreads a radiant show'r.
    'T is noise, and hurry all! The thronged street,
The close-pil'd warehouse, and the busy shop!
With nimble stroke the tinkling hammers move;

---

[3] The ventilator.
[4] Dr. Stephen Hales.
[5] The fire-engine.
[6] " Densat erant quæ rara modo, et quæ densa relaxat."

[7] Sandwel, the seat of the right hon. the earl of Dartmouth.
[8] Castle Bromwick, the seat of sir Henry Bridgman, bart.
[9] Bremicham, alias Birmingham.
[10] The seat of sir Lister Holt, bart.
[11] The seat of sir Henry Gouch, bart.
[12] Illi inter sese magnâ vi brachia tollunt
    In numerum, versantque tenaci forcipe ferrum.
                        Virg.

While slow and weighty the vast sledge descends,
In solemn base responsive, or apart,
Or socially conjoin'd in tuneful peal.
The rough file [13] grates; yet useful is its touch,
As sharp corrosives to the schirrhous flesh,
Or, to the stubborn temper, keen rebuke.
How the coarse metal brightens into fame
Shap'd by their plastic hands! what ornament!
What various use! See there the glitt'ring knife
Of temper'd edge! The scissars' double shaft,
Useless apart, in social union join'd,
Each aiding each! Emblem how beautiful
Of happy nuptial leagues! The button round,
Plain, or imbost, or bright with steely rays!
Or oblong buckle, on the lacker'd shoe,
With polish'd lustre, bending elegant
In shapely rim. But who can count the forms
That hourly from the glowing embers rise,
Or shine attractive through the glitt'ring pane,
And emulate their parent fires? what art
Can, in the scanty bounds of measur'd verse [14],
Display the treasure of a thousand mines
To wondrous shapes by stubborn labour wrought?
Nor this alone thy praise. Of various grains
Thy sons a compound form, and to the fire
Commit the precious mixture, if perchance
Some glitt'ring mass may bless their midnight toil,
Or glossy varnish, or enamel fair
To shame the pride of China, or Japan.
Nor wanting is the graver's pointed steel,
Nor pencil, wand'ring o'er the polish'd plate,
With glowing tints, and mimic life endu'd.
Thine too, of graceful form, the letter'd type!
The friend of learning, and the poet's pride!
Without thee what avail his splended aims,
And midnight labours? Painful drudgery!
And pow'rless effort! But that thought of thee
Imprints fresh vigour on his panting breast,
As thou ere long shalt on his work impress;
And, with immortal fame, his praise repay.
Hail, native British ore! of thee possess'd,
We envy not Golconda's sparkling mines,
Nor thine Potosi! nor thy kindred hills,
Teeming with gold. What though in outward form
Less fair, not less thy worth. To thee we owe
More riches than Peruvian mines can yield,
Or Motezuma's crowded magazines,
And palaces could boast, though roof'd with gold.
Splendid barbarity! and rich distress!
Without the social arts, and useful toil;
That polish life, and civilize the mind!
These are thy gifts, which gold can never buy.
Thine is the praise to cultivate the soil;
To bare its inmost strata to the Sun;
To break and meliorate the stiffen'd clay,
And, from its close confinement, set at large
Its vegetative virtue. Thine it is
The with'ring hay, and ripen'd grain to sheer,
And waft the joyous harvest round the land.
Go now, and see if, to the silver's edge,
The reedy stalk will yield its bearded store,
In weighty sheafs. Or if the stubborn marle,
In sidelong rows, with easy force will rise

[13] Tum ferri rigor, et argutæ lamina serræ,
      Tum variæ venere artes, &c.     Virg.
[14] Sed neque quàm multæ species, nec nomina
           quæ sint,
    Est numerus: neque enim numero comprên-
        dere refert.            Virg.

Before the silver ploughshare's glitt'ring point.
Or would your gen'rous horses tread more safe
On plated gold? Your wheels, with swifter force
On golden axles move? Then grateful own,
Britannia's sons! Heàv'n's providential love,
That gave you real wealth, not wealth in show,
Whose price in bare imagination lies,
And artificial compact. Thankful ply
Your iron arts, and rule the vanquish'd world.
    Hail, native ore! without thy pow'rful aid,
We still had liv'd in huts, with the green sod
And broken branches roof'd. Thine is the plane,
The chissel thine; which shape the well-arch'd
The graceful portico, and sculptur'd walls. [dome,
    Would ye your coarse, unsightly mines exchange
For Mexiconian hills? to tread on gold,
As vulgar sand? with naked limbs to brave
The cold, bleak air? to urge the tedious chase,
By painful hunger stung, with artless toil,
Through gloomy forests, where the sounding axe,
To the Sun's beam, ne'er op'd the cheerful glade,
Nor culture's healthful face was ever seen?
In squalid huts to lay your weary limbs,
Bleeding and faint, and strangers to the bliss
Of home-felt ease, which British swains can earn,
With a bare spade; but ill alas! could earn,
With spades of gold? Such the poor Indian's lot!
Who starves midst gold, like misers o'er their bags;
Not with like guilt! Hail, native British ore!
For thine is trade, that with its various stores
Sails round the world, and visits ev'ry clime,
And makes the treasures of each clime her own,
By gainful commerce of her woolly vests,
Wrought by the spiky comb; or steely wares,
From the coarse mass, by stubborn toil, refin'd.
Such are thy peaceful gifts! And war to thee
Its best support, and deadliest horrour owes,
The glitt'ring falchion, and the thund'ring tube!
At whose tremendous gleam, and volley'd fire,
Barbarian kings fly from their useless hoards,
And yield them all to thy superior pow'r.

---

## EDGE-HILL.

### BOOK IV. EVENING.

---

#### ARGUMENT.

Evening walk along the hill to the N. E. point.
Scene from thence. Dasset-hills. Farnborough.
Wormleighton. Shuckburg. Leame and Ichene.
Places near those two rivers. Bennones, or High
Cross. Foss Way. Watling Street. Inland
Navigation. Places of note. Return. Pane-
gyric on the country. The scene moralized.
Though beautiful, yet transient. Change by
approach of winter. Of storms and pestilential
seasons. Murrain. Rot amongst the sheep.
General thoughts on the vanity and disorders of
human life. Battle of Edge-Hill. Reflections.
Conclusion.

---

In purple vestments clad, the temper'd sky
Invites us from our hospitable roof,
To taste her influence mild; while to the west
The jocund Sun his radiant chariot drives,

With rapid course, untir'd. Ye nymphs and swains!
Now quit the shade, and, with recruited strength,
Along the yet untrodden terrace urge
Your vig'rous steps.  With moderated heat,
And ray oblique, the Sun shall not o'erpow'r,
But kindly aid your yet unfinish'd search.

Not after sable night, in silence hush'd,
More welcome is th' approach of op'ning morn,
" With song of early birds," than the fresh breeze
Of soften'd air succeeding sultry heat,
And the wild tumult of the buzzing day.

Nor think, though much is past, that nought re-
mains,
Or nought of beauty, or attractive worth,
Save what the morning Sun, or noon-tide ray,
Hath, with his rising beam, distinctly mark'd,
Or more confus'dly, with meridian blaze,
Daz'ling display'd imperfect.  Downward he
Shall other hills illumine opposite,
And other vales as beauteous as the past ;
Suggesting to the Muse new argument,
And fresh instruction for her closing lay.

There Dasset's ridgy mountain courts the song.
Scarce Malvern boasts his adverse boundary
More graceful.  Like the tempest-driven wave,
Irregularly great, his bare tops brave
The winds, and, on his sides, the fat'ning ox
Crops the rich verdure.  When at Hastings' field,
The Norman conqueror a kingdom won
In this fair isle, and to another race
The Saxon pow'r transferr'd ; an alien lord [1],
Companion of his toil !  by sov'reign grant,
These airy fields obtain'd.  Now the tall mount,
By claim more just, a nobler master owns ;
To tyrant force, and slavish laws a foe.
But happier lands, near Ouse's reedy shore,
(What leisure ardent love of public weal
Permits) his care employ ; where Nature's charms
With learned art combin'd ; the richest domes,
And fairest lawns, adorn'd with ev'ry grace
Of beauty, or magnificent design,
By Cobham's eye approv'd, or Grenville plann'd,
The villas of imperial Rome outvie ;
And form a scene of statelier pomp—a Stowe.
Her walls the living boast, these boast the dead,
Beneath their roof, in sacred dust entomb'd.
Lie light, O earth !  on that illustrious dame [2],
Who, from her own prolific womb deriv'd,
To people thy green orb, successive saw
Sev'n times an hundred births.  A goodlier train !
Than that, with which the Patriarch journey'd erst
From Padan-Aram, to the Mamrean plains :
Or that more num'rous, which, with large increase,
At Joseph's call, in wondrous caravans,
Reviving sight !  by Heav'n's decree prepar'd,
He led to Goshen, Egypt's fruitful soil.

Where the tall pillar lifts its taper head,
Her spacious terrace, and surrounding lawns,
Deck'd with no sparing cost of planted tufts,
Or ornamented building, Farnborough [3] boasts.
Hear they her master's call ?  in sturdy troops,
The jocund labourers hie, and, at his nod,
A thousand hands or smooth the slanting hill,

Or scoop new channels for the gath'ring flood,
And, in his pleasures, find substantial bliss.

Nor shall thy verdant pastures be unsung
Wormleighton [4] !  erst th' abode of Spenser's race,
Their title now !  What ?  though in height thou
yield'st
To Dasset, not in sweet luxuriance
Of fat'ning herbage, or of rising groves ;
Beneath whose shade the lusty steers repose
Their cumbrous limbs, mix'd with the woolly tribes,
And leisurely concoct their grassy meal.

Her wood-capt summit Shuckburgh [5] there dis-
plays ;
Nor fears neglect, in her own worth secure,
And glorying in the name her master bears.
Nor will her scenes, with closer eye survey'd,
Frustrate the searcher's toil, if steepy hills,
By frequent chasms disjoin'd, and glens profound,
And broken precipices, vast and rude,
Delight the sense; or Nature's lesser works,
Though lesser, not less fair !  or native stone,
Or fish, the little astroit's [6] doubtful race,
For starry rays, and pencil'd shades admir'd !
Invite him to these fields, their airy bed.

Where Leame and Ichene own a kindred rise,
And haste their neighb'ring currents to unite,
New hills arise, new pastures green, and fields
With other harvests crown'd ; with other charms
Villas, and towns with other arts adorn'd.
There Ichington its downward structures views
In Ichene's passing wave, which, like the mole,
Her subterranean journey long pursues,
Ere to the Sun she gives her lucid stream.
Thy villa, Leamington [7] !  her sister nymph
In her fair bosom shows ; while, on her banks,
As further she her liquid course pursues,
Amidst surrounding woods his ancient walls
Birb'ry [8] conceals, and triumphs in the shade.
Not such thy lot, O Bourton [9] !  nor from sight
Retirest thou, but, with complacent smile,
Thy soc al aspect courts the distant eye,
And views the distant scene reciprocal,
Delighting and delighted.  Dusky heaths
Succeed, as oft to mirth, the gloomy hour!
Leading th' unfinish'd search to thy fam'd seat
Bennones [10] ! where two military ways
Each other cross, transverse from sea to sea,
The Roman's hostile paths ! There Newnham's [11] walls
With graceful pride ascend, th' inverted pile
In her clear stream, with flow'ry margin grac'd,
Admiring.  Newbold [12] there her modest charms
More bashfully unveils, with solemn woods
And verdant glades enamour'd.  Here her lawns,
And rising groves for future shelter form'd,
Fair Coton [13] wide displays.  There Addison,
With mind serene, his moral theme revolv'd,
Instruction dress'd in learning's fairest form !

---

[1] The earl of Mellent.

[2] Dame Hester Temple, of whom this is recorded by Fuller, in his account of Buckinghamshire,
and who lies buried, with many of that ancient
family, in the parish-church of Burton-Dasset.

[3] The seat of William Holbech, esq.

[4] An estate, an ancient seat, belonging to the
right hon. earl Spenser.

[5] The seat of sir Ch. Shuckburgh, bart.

[6] The astroites, or star-stones, found here.

[7] The seat of sir William Wheeler, bart.

[8] The seat of sir Theophilus Biddulph, bart.

[9] The seat of John Shuckburgh, esq.

[10] A Roman station, where the Foss-way and
Watling-street cross each other.

[11] The seat of the right hon. the earl of Denbeigh.

[12] The seat of sir Francis Skipwith, bart.

[13] The seat of Dixwell Grimes, esq.

The gravest wisdom with the liveliest wit
Attemper'd ! or, beneath thy roof retir'd,
O Bilton '4 ! much of peace and liberty
Sublimely mus'd, on Britain's weal intent,
Or in thy shade the coy Pierians woo'd.
Another theme demands the varying song.
Lo ! where but late the flocks and heifers graz'd,
Or yellow harvests wav'd, now, through the vale,
Or o'er the plain, or round the slanting hill,
A glitt'ring path attracts the gazer's eye,
Where sooty barks pursue their liquid track
Through lawns, and woods, and villages remote
From public haunt, which wonder as they pass.
The channel'd road still onward moves, and still
With level course the flood attendant leads.
Hills, dales oppose in vain. A thousand hands
Now through the mountain's side a passage ope,
Now with stupendous arches bridge the vale,
Now over paths and rivers urge their way
Aloft in air. Again the Roman pride
Beneath thy spacious camp embattled hill,
O Brinklow '5 ! seems with gentler arts return'd.
But Britain now no bold invader fears,
No foreign aid invokes. Alike in arts
Of peace, or war renown'd. Alike in both
She rivals ancient Rome's immortal fame.
    Still villas fair, and populous towns remain—
Polesworth and Atherstone, and Eaton's walls
To charity devote ! and, Tamworth, thine
To martial fame ! and thine, O Merival [16] !
Boasting thy beauteous woods, and lofty scite !
And Coleshill [17] ! long for momentary date
Of human life, though for our wishes short,
Repose of Digby's honourable age !
    Nor may the Muse, though on her homeward way
Intent, short space refuse his alleys green,
And decent walls with due respect to greet
On Blythe's [18] fair stream, to whose laborious toil
She many a lesson owes, his painful search
Enjoying without pain, and, at her ease,
With equal love of native soil inspir'd,
Singing in measur'd phrase her country's fame.
    Nor, Arbury [19] ! may we thy scenes forget,
Haunt of the Naiads, and each woodland nymph !
Rejoicing in his care, to whom adorn'd
With all the graces which her schools expound,
The gowny sons of Isis trust their own
And Britain's weal. Nor shall thy splendid walls,
O Packington [20] ! allure the Muse in vain.

[14] The seat of the right hon. Joseph Addison, esq.
[15] The canal designed for a communication between the cities of Oxford and Coventry, passes through Brinklow, where is a magnificent aqueduct, consisting of twelve arches, with a high bank of earth at each end, crossing a valley beneath the vestiges of a Roman camp and tumulus, on the Foss-way.
[16] The seat of the late Edward Stratford, esq. an extensive view to Charley Forest and Bosworth Field.
[17] Seat of the late right hon. lord Digby, commonly called, the good lord Digby.
[18] Blythe Hall, the seat of sir William Dugdale, now belonging to Richard Geast, esq.
[19] The seat of sir Roger Newdigate, bart. member of parliament for the university of Oxford.
[20] The seat of the right hon. the earl of Aylesford.

The Goths no longer here their empire hold.
The shaven terrac'd hill, slope above slope,
And high impris'ning walls to Belgia's coast
Their native clime retire.—In formal bounds
The long canal no more confines the stream
Reluctant.—Trees no more their tortur'd limbs
Lament—no more the long-neglected fields,
Like outlaws banish'd for some vile offence,
Are hid from sight—from its proud reservoir
Of amplest size, and fair indented form,
Along the channel'd lawn the copious stream
With winding grace the stately current leads.
The channel'd lawn its bounteous stream repays,
With ever-verdant banks, and cooling shades,
And wand'ring paths, that emulate its course.
On ev'ry side spreads wide the beauteous scene,
Assemblage fair of plains, and hills, and woods,
And plants of od'rous scent—plains, hills, and woods,
And od'rous plants rejoice, and smiling hail
The reign of Nature, while attendant Art
Submissive waits to cultivate her charms.
    Hail happy land ! which Nature's partial smile
Hath robed profusely gay ! whose champaigns wide
With plenteous harvests wave; whose pastures swarm
With horned tribes, or the sheep's fleecy race;
To the thronged shambles yielding wholesome food,
And various labour to man's active pow'rs,
Not less benign than to the weary rest.
Nor destitute thy woodland scenes of wealth,
Or sylvan beauty ! there the lordly swain
His scantier fields improves; o'er his own realms
Supreme, at will to sow his well-fenc'd glebe,
With grain successive; or with juicy herbs,
To swell his milky kine; or feed, at ease,
His flock in pastures warm. His blazing hearth,
With copious fewel heap'd, defies the cold ;
And housewife-arts or tease the tangled wool,
Or, from the distaff's hoard, the ductile thread
With sportive hand entice ; while to the wheel
The sprightly carol join'd, or plaintive song
Diffuse, and artless sooths th' untutor'd ear
With heartfelt strains, and the slow task beguiles.
    Nor hath the Sun, with less propitious ray,
Shone on the masters of the various scene.
Witness the splendid train ! illustrious names,
That claim precedence on the lists of fame,
Nor fear oblivious time ! enraptur'd bards !
Or learned sages ! gracing, with their fame,
Their native soil, and my aspiring verse.
    Say, now my dear companions ! for enough
Of leisure to descriptive song is giv'n ;
Say, shall we, ere we part, with moral eye,
The scene review, and the gay prospect close
With observation grave, as sober eve
Hastes now to wrap in shades the closing day ?
Perhaps the moral strain delights you not !
Perhaps you blame the Muse's quick retreat ;
Intent to wander still along the plain,
In coverts cool, lull'd by the murm'ring stream,
Or gentle breeze ; while playful fancy skims,
With careless wing, the surfaces of things :
For deep research too indolent, too light
For grave reflection. So the syren queen
Tempted Alcides, on a flow'ry plain,
With am'rous blandishment, and urg'd to waste
His prime inglorious : but fair Virtue's form
Rescued the yielding youth, and fir'd his breast
To manly toil, and glory's well-earn'd prize.
O ! in that dang'rous season, O ! beware
Of vice, envenom'd weed ! and plant betimes

The seeds of virtue in th' untainted heart.
So on its fruit th' enraptur'd mind shall feast
When, to the smiling day, and mirthful scene
Night's solemn gloom, cold Winter's chilling blasts,
And pain, and sickness, and old age succeed.
Nor slight your faithful guide, my gentle train !
But, with a curious eye, expatiate free
O'er Nature's moral plan. Though dark the theme,
Though formidable to the sensual mind ;
Yet shall the Muse, with no fictitious aid,
Inspir'd, still guide you with her friendly voice,
And to each seeming ill some greater good
Oppose, and calm your lab'ring thoughts to rest.
　　Nature herself bids us be serious,
Bids us be wise ; and all her works rebuke
The ever-thoughtless, ever-titt'ring tribe.
What though her lovely hills and valleys smile
To day, in beauty dress'd ? yet, ere three moons
Renew their orb, and to their wane decline,
Ere then the beauteous landscape all will fade ;
The genial airs retire ; and shiv'ring swains
Shall, from the whiten'd plain and driving storm,
Avert the smarting cheek and humid eye.
　　So some fair maid to time's devouring rage
Her bloom resigns, and, with a faded look,
Disgusts her paramour ; unless thy charms,
O Virtue ! with more lasting beauty grace
Her lovelier mind, and, through declining age,
Fair deeds of piety, and modest worth,
Still flourish, and endear her still the more.
　　Nor always lasts the landscape's gay attire
Till surly Winter, with his ruffian blasts,
Benumbs her tribes, and dissipates her charms.
As sickness oft the virgin's early bloom
Spoils immature, preventing hoary age,
So blasts and mildews oft invade the fields
In all their beauty, and their summer's pride.
And oft the sudden show'r or sweeping storm [21]
O'erflows the meads, and to the miry glebe
Lays close the matted grain ; with awful peal,
While the loud thunder shakes a guilty world,
And forked lightnings cleave the sultry skies.
　　Nor does the verdant mead or bearded field
Alone the rage of angry skies sustain.'
Oft-times their influence dire the bleating flock
Or lowing herd assails, and mocks the force
Of costly med'cine, or attendant care.
Such late the wrathful pestilence, that seiz'd
In pastures far retir'd, or guarded stalls,
The dew-lap'd race ! with plaintive lowings they,
And heavy eyes, confess'd the pois nous gale,
And drank infect on in each breath they drew.
Quick through their veins the burning fever ran,
And fro n their nostrils stream'd the putrid rheum
Malignant ; o'er their limbs faint languors crept,
And stupefaction all their senses bound.
In vain their master, with officious hand,
From the pil'd mow the sweetest lock presents ;
Or anxiously prepares the tepid draught
Balsamic ; they the proffer'd dainty loath,
And Death exulting claims his destin'd prey [22].

[21] Sæpe etiam immensum cælo venit agmena quarum,
　Et fædam glomerant tempestatem imbribus atris
　Collectæ ex alto nubes ; ruit arduus æther,
　Et pluviâ ingenti sata læta, boumque labores
　Diluit.　　　　　　　　　　　Virg.
[22] Hinc lætis vituli vulgo moriuntur in herbis,
　Et dulces animas plena ad præsepia reddunt.
　　　　　　　　　　　　　　　Virg.

　　Nor seldom coughs and watry rheums afflict
The woolly tribes [23], and on their vitals seize ;
Thinning their folds ; and, with their mangled limbs,
And tatter'd fleeces, the averted eye
Disgusting, as the squeamish traveller,
With long-suspended breath, hies o'er the plain.
And is their lord, proud man ! more safe than they ?
More privileg'd from the destroying breath,
That, through the secret shade, in darkness walks,
Or smites whole pastures at the noon of day ?
Ah ! no, Death mark'd him from his infant birth ;
Mark'd for his own, and, with envenom'd touch,
His vital blood defil'd. Through all his veins
The subtle poison creeps ; compounded joins
Its kindred mass to his increasing bulk ;
And, to the rage of angry elements,
Betrays his victim, poor, ill-fated man ;
Not surer born to live, than born to die !
In what a sad variety of forms
Clothes he his messengers ? Deliriums wild !
Inflated dropsy ! slow consuming cough !
Jaundice, and gout, and stone ; convulsive spasms ;
The shaking head, and the contracted limb ;
And ling'ring atrophy, and hoary age ;
And second childhood, slack'ning ev'ry nerve,
To joy, to reason, and to duty dead !
I know thee, who thou art, offspring of Sin,
And Satan ! nurs'd in Hell, and then let loose
To range, with thy accursed train, on Earth,
When man, apostate man ! by Satan's wiles,
From life, from bliss, from God, and goodness fell !
Who knows thee not ? who feels thee not within,
Plucking his heart-strings ? whom hast thou not
　　robb'd
Of parent, wife, or friend, as thou hast me ?
Glutting the grave with ever-crowding guests,
And, with their image, sad'ning ev'ry scene,
Less peopled with the living than the dead !
　　Through populous streets the never-ceasing bell
Proclaims, with solemn sound, the parting breath ;
Nor seldom from the village-tow'r is heard
The mournful knell. Alike the grassy ridge,
With osiers bound, and vaulted catacomb,
His spoils enclose. Alike the simple stone,
And mausoleum proud, his pow'r attest,
In wretched doggrel, or elab'rate verse.
　　Perhaps the peasant's humble obsequies ;
The flowing sheet, and pall of rusty hue,
Alarm you not. You slight the simple throng ;
And for the nodding plumes, and scutcheon'd hearse,
Your tears reserve. Then mark, o'er yonder plain,
The grand procession suited to your taste.
I mock you not. The sable pursuivants
Proclaim th' approaching state. Lo ! now the
　　plumes !　　　　　　　　　　　[pear !
The nodding plumes and scutcheon'd hearse ap-
And clad in mournful weeds, a long sad train
Of slowly-moving pomp, that waits on death !
Nay—yet another melancholy train !
Another triumph of the ghastly fiend
Succeeds ! 'T is so. Perhaps ye have not heard
The mournful tale. Perhaps no messenger
Hath warn'd you to attend the solemn deed !
Then from the Muse the piteous story learn ;

[23] Non tam creber agens hyemem ruit æthere turbo,
　Quam multæ pecudum pestes, nec singula morbi
　Corpora corripiunt, sed tota æstiva repentè
　Spernque, gregemque simul, cunctamque ab
　　origine gentem.　　　　　　Virg.

X

And, with her, on the grave procession wait,
That to their early tomb, to mould'ring dust
Of ancestors, that crowd the scanty vault,
Near which our song began, Northampton [24] bears,
The gay Northampton, and his beauteous bride [25] !
Far other pageants in his youthful breast
He cherish'd, while, with delegated trust,
On stately ceremonials, to the shore,
Where Adria's waves the sea-girt city lave,
He went; and, with him, join'd in recent love,
His blooming bride, of Beaufort's royal line,
The charming Somerset ! But royal blood,
Nor youth, nor beauty, nor employment high,
Could grant protection from the rude assault
Of that barbarian, Death ; who, without form,
To courts and cottages unbidden comes ;
And his unwelcome embassy fulfils,
Without distinction, to the lofty peer,
The graceful bride, or peasant's homely race.
Ere, from her native soil, she saw the Sun
Run half his annual course, in Latian climes,
She breath'd her last ; him, ere that course was
    done,
Death met returning on the Gallic plains,
And sent to join her yet unburied dust :
Who, but this youthful pair's untimely fate
Must weep, who, but in theirs, may read their own ?
    Another lesson seek ye, other proof
Of vanity, and lamentable woe
Betiding man ? Another scene to grace
With troops of victims the terrific king,
And humble wanton folly's laughing sons ?
The Muse shall from her faithful memory
A tale select ; a tale big with the fate
Of kings and heroes on this now fair field
Embattled ! but her song shall to your view
Their ranks embody, and, to future peace,
Their fierce designs and hostile rage convert.
    Not on Pharsalia's plain a *bolder strife*
Was *held*, though twice with Roman blood distain'd,
Than when thy subjects, first imperial Charles !
Dared, in these fields, with arms their cause to plead.
Where once the Romans pitch'd their hostile tents [26],
Other Campanias fair, and milder Alps
Exploring, now a nobler warrior stood,
His country's sov'reign liege ! Around his camp
A gallant train of loftiest rank attend,
By loyalty, and love of regal sway,
To mighty deeds impell'd. Meanwhile below
Others no less intrepid courage boast,
From source as fair, the love of liberty !
Dear Liberty ! when rightly understood,
Prime social bliss ! Oh ! may no fraud
Usurp thy name, to veil their dark designs
Of vile ambition, or licentious rage !
    Long time had they, with charge of mutual blame,
And fierce debate of speech, discordant minds
Avow'd, yet not to desp'rate chance of war
Till now their cause referr'd : rude arbiter
Of fit and right ! Unhappy native land !
Nought then avail'd that Nature form'd thy fields
So fair, and with her wat'ry barrier fenc'd !

[24] The right hon. the earl of Northampton, who
died on his return from an embassy to Venice, while
the author was writing this poem.
[25] The right hon. the countess of Northampton,
daughter to the duke of Beaufort.
[26] A Roman camp at Warmington, on the top
of Edge-Hill.

Nought then avail'd thy forms of guardian laws,
The work of ages, in a moment lost,
And ev'ry social tie at once dissolv'd !
For now no more sweet peace, and order fair,
And kindred love remain'd, but hostile rage
Instead, and mutual jealousy, and hate,
And tumult loud ! nor, hadst thou then been there,
O Talbot [27] ! could thy voice, so often heard
On heav'nly themes ! nor his fraternal [28] ! skill'd
In social claims, the limits to define
Of law and right, have calm'd the furious strife,
Or still'd the rattling thunder of the field.
    Across the plain, where the slight eminence
And scatter'd hedge-rows mark a midway space
To yonder town [29], once deem'd a royal court ;
Now harbouring no friends to royalty !
The popular troops the'r martial lines extend.
High on the hill, the royal banners wave
Their faithful signals. Rang'd along the steep,
The glitt'ring files, in burnish'd armour clad,
Reflect the downward Sun ; and, with its gleam,
The distant crowds affright, who trembling wait
For the dire onset, and the dubious fight.
As pent-up waters, swell'd by sudden rains,
Their former bounds disdain, and foam and rage
Impatient of restraint ; till, at some breach,
Outward they burst impetuous, and mock
The peasant's feeble toil, which strives to check
Their headlong torrent ; so the royal troops,
With martial rage inflam'd, impatient wait
The trumpet's summons. At its sprightly call,
The airy seat they leave, and down the steep,
Rank following rank, like wave succeeding wave,
Rush on the hostile wings. Dire was the shock,
Dire was the clash of arms ! The hostile wings
Give way, and soon in flight their safety seek.
They with augmented force and growing rage
The flying foe pursue. But too secure,
And counting of cheap conquest quickly gain'd
O'er dastard minds, in wordy quarrels bold,
But slack by deeds to vindicate their claim,
In chase and plunder long they waste the day,
And late return, of order negligent.
Meanwhile the battle in the centre rag'd
With diff'rent fortune, by bold Essex led,
Experienc'd chief ! and to the monarch's cause,
And youthful race, for martial deeds unripe,
Menac'd destruction. In the royal breast
High passions rose, by native dignity
Made more sublime, and urg'd to pow'rful act
By strong paternal love [30], and proud disdain
Of vulgar minds, arraigning in his race
The rights of sov'reignty, from ancient kings
In order fair deriv'd. Amidst his troops
With haste he flies, their broken ranks reforms,
To bold revenge re-animates their rage,
And from the foe his short-liv'd honour wrests.
    Now Death, with hasty stride, stalks o'er the field,

[27] The rev. Mr. Talbot, of Kineton.
[28] C. Henry Talbot, esq. of Marston, at the bottom of Edge-Hill.
[29] Kineton, alias Kington. So called, as some
conjecture, from a castle on a neighbouring hill,
said to have been a palace belonging to king John.
[30] Prince Charles, afterwards king Charles II.
and his brother the duke of York, afterwards king
James II. were then in the field, the former being
in the 13th, and the latter just entered into the
10th year of his age.

Grimly exulting in the bloody fray.
Now on the crested helm or burnish'd shield,
He stamps new horrours; now the levell'd sword
With weightier force impells, with iron-hoof
Now tramples on th' expiring ranks; or gores
The foaming steed against th' opposing spear.
But chiefly on the cannon's brazen orb
He sits triumphant, and, with fatal aim,
Involves whole squadrons in the sulph'rous storm.
 Then Lindsey 31 fell, nor from the shelt'ring straw
Ceas'd he to plead his sov'reign's slighted cause
Amidst surrounding foes; nor but with life
Expir'd his loyalty. His valiant son 32
Attempts his rescue, but attempts in vain!
Then Verney 33 too, with many a gallant knight
And faithful courtier, anxious for thy weal,
Unhappy prince! but mindless of their own,
Pour'd out his life upon the crimson plain.
Then fell the gallant Stewart 34, Aubigny 35,
And Kingsmill 36! He whose monumental stone
Protects his neighb'ring ashes and his fame.
 The closing day compos'd the furious strife:
But for short time compos'd! anon to wake
With tenfold rage, and spread a wider scene
Of terrour and destruction o'er the land!
 Now mark the glories of the great debate!
Yon grass-green mount, where waves the planted
 pine,
And whispers to the winds the mournful tale,
Contains them in its monumental mould;
A slaughter'd crew, promiscuous lodg'd below!
Still as the ploughman breaks the clotted glebe
He ever and anon some trophy finds,
The relics of the war 37—or rusty spear,
Or canker'd ball; but, from sepulchral soil,
Cautious he turns aside the shining steel,
Lest haply, at its touch, uncover'd bones
Should start to view, and blast his rural toil.
 Such were the fruits of passion, froward will,
And unsubmitting pride! Worse storms than those
That rend the sky, and waste our cultur'd fields!
Strangers alike to man's primeval state,
Ere evil entrance found to this fair world,
Permitted, not ordain'd, whatever pride
May dream of order in a world of sin,
Or pre-existent soul, and penal doom
For crimes unknown. More wise, more happy he!
Who in his breast oft pond'ring, and perplex'd
With endless doubt and learning's fruitless toil,
His weary mind at length reposes sure
On Heav'n's attested oracles. To them
Submiss he bows, convinc'd, however weak
His reason the mysterious plan to solve,

That all He wills is right, who, ere the worlds
Were form'd, in his all-comprehensive mind,
Saw all that was, or is, or e'er shall be.
Who to whate'er exists, or lives, or moves,
Throughout creation's wide extent, gave life,
Gave being, pow'r, and thought to act, to move
Impelling or impell'd, to all ordain'd
Their ranks, relations, and dependencies,
And can direct, suspend, control their pow'rs,
Else were he not supreme! Who bids the winds
Be still, and they obey; who to the sea
Assigns its bounds, and calms its boisterous waves.
Who, with like ease can moral discord rule,
And all apparent evil turn to good.
 Hail then, ye sons of Eve! th' unerring guide,
The sovereign grant receive, sin's antidote!
A cure for all our griefs! So heav'nly Truth
Shall wide display her captivating charms,
And Peace her dwelling fix with human race.
So Love through ev'ry clime his gentle reign
Shall spread, and at his call discordant realms
Shall beat their swords to ploughshares, and their
 spears
To pruning-hooks, nor more learn murth'rous war.
So when revolving years, by Heav'n's decree,
Their circling course have run, new firmaments,
With blessings fraught, shall fill the bright expanse,
Of tempests void, and thunder's angry voice.
New verdure shall arise to clothe the fields:
New Edens! teeming with immortal fruit!
No more the wing'd inhabitants of air,
Or those that range the fields or skim the flood,
Their fierceness shall retain, but brute with brute,
And all with man in amicable league
Shall join, and enmity for ever cease.
 Remains there aught to crown the rapt'rous theme?
'T is this, unfading joy, beyond the reach
Of elemental worlds, and short-liv'd time.
This too is yours—from outward sense conceal'd,
But, by resemblance of external things,
Inward display'd, to elevate the soul
To thoughts sublime, and point her way to Heav'n.
So, from the top of Nebo's lofty mount,
The patriot-leader of Jehovah's sons
The promis'd land survey'd; to Canaan's race
A splendid theatre of frantic joys
And fatal mirth, beyond whose scanty bounds
Darkness and horrour dwell! Emblem to *him*
Of fairer fields, and happier seats above!
Then closed his eyes to mortal scenes, to wake
In the bright régions of eternal day.

---

31 Earl of Lindsey, the king's general.

32 Lord Willoughby, son to the earl of Lindsey.

33 Sir Edmund Verney, standard-bearer to the king.

34 Lord Stewart.

35 Lord Aubigny, son to the duke of Lenox.

36 Captain Kingsmill, buried at Radway.

37 Scilicet et tempus veniet, cum finibus illis,
Agricola incurvo terram molitus aratro,
Exesa inveniet scabrâ rubigine pila,
Aut gravibus rastris galeas pulsabit inanes,
Grandiaque effossis mirabitur ossa sepulchris.
 Virg.

*LABOUR AND GENIUS:*

OR,

THE MILL-STREAM AND THE CASCADE.

A FABLE.

Nature, with lib'ral hand, dispenses
Her apparatus of the senses,
In articles of gen'ral use,
Nerves, sinews, muscles, bones profuse,
Distinguishing her fav'rite race
With form erect, and featur'd face:
The flowing hair, the polish'd skin—
But, for the furniture within,

Whether it be of brains or lead,
What matters it, so there 's a head?
For wisest noddle seldom goes,
But as 't is led by corp'ral nose.
Nor is it thinking much, but doing,
That keeps our tenements from ruin.
And hundreds eat, who spin or knit,
For one that lives by dint of wit.
　　The sturdy thresher plies his flail,
And what to this doth wit avail?
Who learns from wit to press the spade?
Or thinks 't would mend the cobler's trade?
The pedlar, with his cumb'rous pack,
Carries his brains upon his back.
Some wear them in full-bottom'd wig,
Or hang them by with *queue* or *pig.*
Reduc'd, till they return again,
In dishabille, to common men.
Then why, my friend, is wit so rare?
That sudden flash, that makes one stare!
A meteor's blaze, a dazzling show!
Say what it is, for well you know.
Or, if you can with patience hear
A witless fable, lend an ear:
　　Betwixt two sloping verdant hills
A current pour'd its careless rills,
Which unambitious crept along,
With weeds and matted grass o'erhung.
Till *rural Genius,* on a day,
Chancing along its banks to stray,
Remark'd with penetrating look
The latent merits of the brook,
Much griev'd to see such talents hid,
And thus the dull by-standers chid.
　　" How blind is man's incurious race,
The scope of Nature's plans to trace?
How do ye mangle half her charms,
And fright her hourly with alarms?
Disfigure now her swelling mounds,
And now contract her spacious bounds?
Fritter her fairest lawns to alleys,
Bare her green hills, and hide her valleys?
Confine her streams with rule and line,
And counteract her whole design?
Neglecting, where she points the way,
Her easy dictates to obey?
To bring her hidden worth to sight;
And place her charms in fairest light?
　　" Alike to *intellectuals* blind,
'T is thus you treat the youthful mind;
Mistaking gravity for sense,
For dawn of wit, impertinence.
　　" The boy of genuine parts and merit,
For some unlucky prank of spirit,
With frantic rage is scourg'd from school,
And branded with the name of fool,
Because his active blood flow'd faster
Than the dull puddle of his master.
While the slow plodder trots along,
Through thick and thin, through prose and song,
Insensible of all their graces,
But learn'd in words and common phrases:
Till in due time he's mov'd to college,
To ripen these choice seeds of knowledge.
　　" So some taste-pedant, wondrous wise,
Exerts his genius in dirt-pies.
Delights the tonsile yew to raise,
But hates your laurels and your bays,
Because too rambling and luxuriant,
Like forward youths, of brains too prurient.

Makes puns, and anagrams in box,
And turns his trees to bears and cocks.
Excels in quaint jette-d'eau or fountain,
Or leads his stream across a mountain,
To show its shallowness and pride,
In a broad grin, on t' other side.
Perverting all the rules of sense,
Which never offers violence,
But gently leads where Nature tends,
Sure, with applause, to gain its ends.
　　" But one example may teach more,
Than precepts hackney'd o'er and o'er.
Then mark this *rill,* with weeds o'erhung,
Unnotic'd by the vulgar throng!
Ev'n this, conducted by my laws,
Shall rise to fame, attract applause;
Instruct in fable [1], shine in song,
And be the theme of ev'ry tongue."
He said: and, to his fav'rite son,
Consign'd the task, and will'd it done.
　　Damon his counsel wisely weigh'd,
And carefully the scene survey'd.
And, though it seems he said but little,
He took his meaning to a tittle.
And first, his purpose to befriend,
A bank he rais'd at th' upper end:
Compact, and close its outward side,
To stay and swell the gath'ring tide:
But, on its inner, rough and tall,
A ragged cliff, a rocky wall.
The channel next he op'd to view,
And, from its course, the rubbish drew.
Enlarg'd it now, and now with line
Oblique pursued his fair design.
Preparing here the mazy way,
And there the fall for sportive play.
The precipice abrupt and steep,
The pebbled road, and cavern deep.
The rooty seat, where best to view
The fairy scene, at distance due.
He last invok'd the Dryads aid,
And fring'd the borders round with shade.
Tap'stry, by Nature's fingers wove,
No mimic, but a real grove:
Part hiding, part admitting day,
The scene to grace the future play.
　　Damon perceives, with ravish'd eyes,
The beautiful enchantment rise.
Sees sweetly blended shade and light,
Sees ev'ry part with each unite.
Sees each, as he directs, assume
A livelier dye or deeper gloom.
So, fashion'd by the painter's skill,
New forms the glowing canvass fill.
So, to the summer's Sun, the rose
And jessamin their charms disclose.
　　While, all intent on this retreat,
He saw his fav'rite work complete,
Divine enthusiasm seiz'd his breast,
And thus his transport he express'd.
　　" Let others toil, for wealth or pow'r,
I court the sweetly-vacant hour:
Down life's smooth current calmly glide,
Nor vex'd with cares, nor rack'd with pride.
Give me, O Nature! to explore
Thy lovely charms, I ask no more.

[1] See Fable XLI. and LI. in Dodsley's new-invented fables, and many little pieces printed in the public papers.

For thee I fly from vulgar eyes,
For thee I vulgar cares despise.
For thee ambition's charms resign;
Accept a vot'ry, wholly thine.
  " Yet still let Friendship's joys be near,
Still, on these plains, her train appear.
By Learning's sons my haunts are trod,
And Stamford's feet imprint my sod.
For Stamford oft hath deign'd to stray
Around my Leasow's flow'ry way.
And, where his honour'd steps have rov'd,
Oft have his gifts those scenes improv'd.
To him I 'll dedicate my cell,
To him suspend the votive spell.
His name shall heighten ev'ry charm,
His name protect my groves from harm,
Protect my harmless sport from blame,
And turn obscurity to fame."
He spake. His hand the pencil guides,
And Stamford [2] o'er the scene presides.
The proud device, with borrow'd grace,
Conferr'd new lustre on the place:
As books, by dint of dedication,
Enjoy their patron's reputation.
  Now, lanching from its lofty shore,
The loosen'd stream began to roar:
As, headlong, from the rocky mound,
It rush'd into the vast profound.
There check'd awhile, again it flow'd
Glitt'ring along the channel'd road:
From steep to steep, a frequent fall,
Each diff'rent, and each natural.
Obstructing roots and rocks between,
Diversify th' enchanted scene;
While winding now, and intricate,
Now more develop'd, and in state,
Th' united stream, with rapid force,
Pursues amain its downward course,
Till at your feet absorb'd, it hides
Beneath the ground its bustling tides.
  With prancing steeds, and liv'ried trains,
Soon daily shone the bord'ring plains.
And distant sounds foretold th' approach
Of frequent chaise, and crowded coach.
For sons of Taste, and daughters fair,
Hasted the sweet surprise to share:
While Hagley [3] wonder'd at their stay,
And hardly brook'd the long delay.
  Not distant far below, a mill
Was built upon a neighb'ring rill:
Whose pent-up stream, whene'er let loose,
Impell'd a wheel, close at its sluice,
So strongly, that, by friction's pow'r,
'T would grind the firmest grain to flow'r.
Or, by a correspondence new,
With hammers, and their clatt'ring crew,
Would so bestir her active stumps,
On iron-blocks, though arrant lumps,
That, in a trice, she 'd manage matters,
To make them all as smooth as platters.
Or slit a bar to rods quite taper,
With as much ease, as you 'd cut paper.
For, though the lever gave the blow,
Yet it was lifted from below;

And would for ever have lain still,
But for the bustling of the rill;
Who, from her stately pool or ocean,
Put all the wheels and logs in motion;
Things in their nature very quiet,
Though making all this noise and riot.
  This stream, that could in toil excel,
Began with foolish pride to swell:
Piqu'd at her neighbour's reputation,
And thus express'd her indignation.
  " Madam! methinks you 're vastly proud,
You was 'nt us'd to talk so loud.
Nor cut such capers in your pace,
Marry! what antics, what grimace!
For shame! do n't give yourself such airs,
In flaunting down those hideous stairs.
Nor put yourself in such a flutter,
Whate'er you do, you dirty gutter!
I 'd have you know, you upstart minx!
Ere you were form'd, with all your sinks,
A lake I was, compar'd with which,
Your stream is but a paltry ditch:
And still, on honest labour bent,
I ne'er a single *flash* misspent.
And yet no folks of high degree
Would e'er vouchsafe to visit me,
As, in their coaches, by they rattle,
Forsooth! to hear your idle prattle.
Though half the business of my flooding
Is to provide them cakes and pudding;
Or furnish stuff for many a trinket,
Which, though so fine, you scarce would think it,
When Boulton's [4] skill has fix'd their beauty,
To my rough toil first ow'd their duty.
But I 'm plain *Goody* of the Mill;
And you are—*Madam Cascadille!*"
  " Dear coz," reply'd the beauteous torrent,
" Pray do not discompose your current.
That we all from one fountain flow,
Hath been agreed on long ago.
Varying our talents, and our tides,
As chance or education guides.
That I have either note or name,
I owe to him who gives me fame.
Who teaches all our kind to flow,
Or gaily swift, or gravely slow.
Now in the lake, with glassy face,
Now moving light, with dimpled grace.
Now gleaming from the rocky height,
Now, in rough eddies, foaming white.
Nor envy me the gay or great,
That visit my obscure retreat.
None wonders that a clown can dig,
But 't is some art to dance a jig.
Your talents are employ'd for use,
Mine to give pleasure and amuse.
And though, dear coz, no folks of taste
Their idle hours with you will waste,
Yet many a grist comes to your mill,
Which helps your master's bags to fill.
While I, with all my notes and trilling,
For Damon never got a shilling.
Then, gentle coz, forbear your clamours,
Enjoy your hoppers and your hammers:
We gain our ends by diff'rent ways,
And you get bread, and I get—praise."

[2] The scene here referred to, was inscribed to the right hon. the earl of Stamford; but since to William Shenstone, esq.

[3] The seat of the right hon. lord Lyttelton, distant but a few miles from the Leasows.

[4] An eminent merchant, and very ingenious mechanic, at the Soho manufactory, near Birmingham.

## ARDENNA.

### A PASTORAL ECLOGUE.

#### TO A LADY.

#### DAMON AND LYCIDAS.

WHEN o'er the western world fair Science spread
Her genial ray, and Gothic darkness fled,
To Britain's isle the Muses took their way,
And taught her list'ning groves the tuneful lay.
'T was then two swains the Doric reed essay'd
To sing the praises of a peerless maid.
On Arden's blissful plain her seat she chose,
And hence her rural name Ardenna rose.
In sportive verse alternately they vied,
Thus Damon sang, and Lycidas replied.

#### DAMON.

Here, gentle swain, beneath the shade reclin'd,
Remit thy labours, and unbend thy mind.
Well with the shepherd's state our cares agree,
For Nature prompts to pleasing industry.
'T is this to all her gifts fresh beauty yields,
Health to our flocks, and plenty to our fields.
Yet hath she not impos'd unceasing toil,
Not restless ploughshares always vex the soil.
Then, shepherd, take the blessings Heav'n bestows,
Assist the song, and sweeten our repose.

#### LYCIDAS.

While others, sunk in sleep, or live in vain,
Or, slaves of indolence, but wake to pain,
Me let the call of earliest birds invite
To hail th' approaches of returning light;
To taste the freshness of the cheerful morn,
While glist'ring dew-drops hang on ev'ry thorn.
Hence all the bliss that centres in our kind,
Health to the blood, and vigour to the mind.
Hence ev'ry task its meet attendance gains,
And leisure hence to listen to thy strains.

#### DAMON.

Thrice happy swain, so fitly form'd to share
The shepherd's labour, and Ardenna's care!
To tell Ardenna's praise the rural train
Inscribe the verse, or chant it o'er the plain.
Plains, hills, and woods return the well-known sound,
And the smooth beech records the sportive wound.
Then, Lycidas, let us the chorus join,
So bright a theme our music shall refine.
Escap'd from all the busy world admires,
Hither the philosophic dame retires;
For in the busy world, or poets feign,
Intemp'rate vice and giddy pleasures reign;
Then, when from crowds the Loves and Graces flew,
To these lone shades the beauteous maid withdrew,
To study Nature in this calm retreat,
And with confed'rate art her charms complete.
How sweet their union is, ye shepherds, say,
And thou who form'dst the reed inspire my lay.
Her praise I sing by whom our flocks are freed
From the rough bramble and envenom'd weed;
Who to green pastures turns the dreary waste,
With scatter'd woods in careless beauty grac'd.
'T is she, Ardenna! guardian of the scene,
Who bids the mount to swell, who smooths the green,
Who drains the marsh, and frees the struggling flood
From its divided rule and strife with mud.

She winds its course the copious stream to show,
And she in swifter currents bids it flow;
Now smoothly gliding with an even pace,
Now dimpling o'er the stones with roughen'd grace:
With glassy surface now serenely bright,
Now foaming from the rock all silver white.
'T is she the rising bank with beeches crowns,
Now spreads the scene, and now contracts its bounds.
Clothes the bleak hill with verdure ever gay,
And bids our feet through myrtle-valleys stray.
She for her shepherds rears the rooty shed,
The checquer'd pavement, and the straw-wove bed.
For them she scoops the grotto's cool retreat,
From storms a shelter, and a shade in heat.
Directs their hands the verdant arch to bend,
And with the leafy roof its gloom extend.
Shells, flint, and ore their mingled graces join,
And rocky fragments aid the chaste design.

#### LYCIDAS.

Hail, happy lawns! where'er we turn our eyes,
Fresh beauties bloom, and opening wonders rise.
Whilom these charming scenes with grief I view'd
A barren waste, a dreary solitude!
My drooping flocks their russet pastures mourn'd,
And lowing herds the plaintive moan return'd.
With weary feet from field to field they stray'd,
Nor found their hunger's painful sense allay'd.
But now no more a dreary scene appears,
No more its prickly boughs the bramble rears,
No more my flocks lament th' unfruitful soil,
Nor mourn their ragged fleece, or fruitless toil.

#### DAMON.

As this fair lawn excels the rushy mead,
As firs the thorn, and flow'rs the pois'nous weed,
Far as the warbling sky-larks soar on high,
Above the clumsy bat or buzzing fly;
So matchless moves Ardenna o'er the green,
In mind alike excelling as in mien.

#### LYCIDAS.

Sweet is the fragrance of the damask rose,
And bright the dye that on its surface glows,
Fair is the poplar rising on the plain,
Of shapely trunk, and lofty branches vain;
But neither sweet the rose, nor bright its dye,
Nor poplar fair, if with her charms they vie.

#### DAMON.

Grateful is sunshine to the sportive lambs,
The balmy dews delight the nibbling dams;
But kindlier warmth Ardenna's smiles impart,
A balm more rich her lessons to the heart.

#### LYCIDAS.

No more Pomona's guiding hand we need,
Nor Flora's help to paint th' enamell'd mead,
Nor Ceres' care to guard the rising grain,
And spread the yellow plenty o'er the plain;
Ardenna's precepts ev'ry want supply,
The grateful lay what shepherd can deny?

#### DAMON.

A theme so pleasing, with the day begun,
Too soon were ended with the setting Sun.
But see o'er yonder hill the parting ray,
And hark! our bleating flocks reprove our stay.

## THE SCAVENGERS.

### A TOWN ECLOGUE.

Dulcis odor lucri ex re quâlibet.

Awake, my Muse, prepare a loftier theme.
The winding valley and the dimpled stream
Delight not all: quit, quit the verdant field,
And try what dusty streets and alleys yield.
  Where Avon wider flows, and gathers fame,
Stands a fair town, and Warwick is its name.
For useful arts entitled once to share
The gentle Ethelfleda's guardian care.
Nor less for deeds of chivalry renown'd,
When her own Guy was with her laurels crown'd.
Now Syren sloth holds here her tranquil reign,
And binds in silken bonds the feeble train.
Now frowning knights in uncouth armour lac'd,
Seek now for monsters on the dreary waste:
In these soft scenes they chase a gentler prey,
No monsters! but as dangerous as they.
In diff'rent forms as sure destruction l'es,
They have no claws 't is true—but they have eyes.
Last of the toiling race there liv'd a pair,
Bred up in labour, and inur'd to care!
To sweep the streets their task from Sun to Sun,
And seek the nastiness which others shun.
More plodding wight or dame you ne'er shall see,
He Gaffer Pestel hight, and Gammer she.
  As at their door they sat one summer's day,
Old Pestel first essay'd the plaintive lay:
His gentle mate the plaintive lay return'd,
And thus alternately their cares they mourn'd.

#### OLD PESTEL.

Alas! was ever such fine weather seen,
How dusty are the roads, the streets how clean!
How long, ye almanacs! will it be dry?
Empty my cart how long, and idle I!
Ev'n at the best the times are not so good,
But 't is hard work to scrape a livelihood.
The cattle in the stalls resign their life,
And baulk the shambles, and th' unbloody knife.
While farmers sit at home in pensive gloom,
And turnpikes threaten to complete my doom.

#### WIFE.

Well! for the turnpike, that will do no hurt,
Some say the managers are friends to dirt.
But much I fear this murrain where 't will end,
For sure the cattle did our door befriend.
Oft have I hail'd them, as they stalk'd along,
Their fat the butchers pleas'd, but me their dung.

#### OLD PESTEL.

See what a little dab of dirt is here!
But yields all Warwick more, O tell me where?
Yet, on this spot, though now so naked seen,
Heaps upon heaps, and loads on loads have been.
Bigger, and bigger, the proud dunghill grew,
Till my diminish'd house was hid from view.

#### WIFE.

Ah! Gaffer Pestel, what brave days were those,
When higher than our house our muckhill rose!
The growing mount I view'd with joyful eyes,
And mark'd what each load added to its size.

Wrapt in its fragrant steam we often sat,
And to its praises held delightful chat.
Nor did I e'er neglect my mite to pay,
To swell the goodly heap from day to day.
A cabbage once I bought; but small the cost—
Nor do I think the farthing all was lost.
Again you sold its well-digested store,
To dung the garden where it grew before.

#### OLD PESTEL.

What though the beaux and powder'd coxcombs
    jeer'd,
And at the scavenger's employment sneer'd,
Yet then at night content I told my gains,
And thought well paid their malice, and my pains.
Why toils the tradesman, but to swell his store?
Why craves the wealthy landlord still for more?
Why will our gentry flatter, fawn, and lie?
Why pack the cards, and what d' ye call 't—the
    die?
All, all the pleasing paths of gain pursue,
And wade through thick and thin as we folks do.
Sweet is the scent that from advantage springs,
And nothing dirty which good interest brings.

#### WIFE.

When goody Dobbins call'd me nasty bear,
And talk'd of kennels and the ducking-chair,
With patience I could hear the scolding quean,
For sure 't was dirtiness that kept me clean.
Clean was my gown on Sundays, if not fine,
Nor Mrs. ———'s cap so white as mine.
A slut in silk, or kersey is the same,
Nor sweetest always is the finest dame.

Thus wail'd they pleasure past, and present cares,
While the starv'd hog join'd his complaint with
    theirs.
To still his grunting diff'rent ways they tend,
To West Street he, and she to Cotton End [1].

---

## ABSENCE.

With leaden foot Time creeps along
  While Delia is away,
With her, nor plaintive was the song,
  Nor tedious was the day.

Ah! envious pow'r! reverse my doom,
  Now double thy career,
Strain ev'ry nerve, stretch ev'ry plume,
  And rest them when she's here.

---

## TO A LADY.

When Nature joins a beauteous face
With shape, and air, and life, and grace,
To ev'ry imperfection blind,
I spy no blemish in the mind.

[1] Names of the most remote and opposite parts
of the town.

When wit flows pure from Stella's tongue,
Or animates the sprightly song,
Our hearts confess the pow'r divine,
Nor lightly prize its mortal shrine.

Good-nature will a conquest gain,
Though wit and beauty sigh in vain.
When gen'rous thoughts the breast inspire,
I wish its rank and fortunes higher.

When Sidney's charms again unite
To win the soul, and bless the sight,
Fair, and learn'd, and good, and great!
An earthly goddess is complete.

But when I see a sordid mind
With affluence and ill-nature join'd,
And pride without a grain of sense,
And without beauty insolence,
The creature with contempt I view,
And sure 't is like Miss —— you know who.

TO

## A LADY WORKING A PAIR OF RUFFLES.

WHAT means this useless cost, this wanton pride?
To purchase fopp'ry from yon foreign strand!
To spurn our native stores, and arts aside,
And drain the riches of a needy land!

Pleas'd I survey, fair nymph, your happy skill,
Yet view it by no vulgar critic's laws:
With nobler aim I draw my sober quill,
Anxious to list each art in virtue's cause.

Go on, dear maid, your utmost pow'r essay,
And if for fame your little bosom heave,
Know patriot-*hands* your merit shall display,
And amply pay the graces they receive.

Let ev'ry nymph like you the gift prepare,
And banish foreign pomp and costly show;
What lover but would burn the prize to wear,
Or blush by you pronounc'd his country's foe?

Your smiles can win when patriot-speeches fail,
Your frowns control when justice threats in vain,
O'er stubborn minds your softness can prevail,
And placemen drop the bribe if you complain.

Then rise the guardians of your country's fame,
Or wherefore were ye form'd like angels fair?
By beauty's force our venal hearts reclaim,
And save the drooping virtues from despair.

## FEMALE EMPIRE.

### A TRUE HISTORY.

LIKE Bruin's was Avaro's breast,
No softness harbour'd there;
While Sylvio some concern express'd,
When beauty shed a tear.

In Hymen's bands they both were tied,
As Cupid's [1] archives show ye;
Proud Celia was Avaro's bride,
And Sylvio's gentle Chloe.

Like other nymphs, at church they swore
To honour and obey,
Which, with each learned nymph before,
They soon explain'd away.

If Chloe now would have her will,
Her streaming eyes prevail'd,
Or if her swain prov'd cruel still,
Hysterics never fail'd.

But Celia scorn'd the plaintive moan,
And heart-dissolving show'r;
With flashing eye, and angry tone,
She best maintain'd her pow'r.

Yet once the mandates of his Turk
Avaro durst refuse;
For why? important was his work,
" To register old shoes!"

" And does," said she, " the wretch dispute
My claim such clowns to rule?
If Celia cannot charm a brute,
She can chastise a fool."

Then straight she to his closet flew,
His private thoughts she tore,
And from its place the poker drew,
That fell'd him on the floor.

" Henceforth," said she, " my calls regard,
Own mine the stronger plea,
Nor let thy vulgar cares retard
The female rites of tea."

Victorious sex! alike your art,
And puissance we dread;
For if you cannot break our heart,
'T is plain you'll break our head.

Place me, ye gods, beneath the throne
Which gentle smiles environ,
And I'll submission gladly own,
Without a rod of iron.

## ON MR. SAMUEL COOKE'S POEMS.

### WRITTEN IN THE YEAR 1749.

INDEED, master Cooke!
You have made such a book,
As the learned in pastry admire:
But other wits joke
To see such a smoke
Without any visible fire.

What a nice bill of fare,
Of whatever is rare,
And approv'd by the critics of taste!
Not a classical bit,
Ev'ry fancy to hit,
But here in due order is plac'd.

[1] The parish-register.

Yet, for all this parade,
  You are but a dull blade,
And your lines are all scragged and raw;
  And though you 've hack'd, and have hew'd,
  And have squeez'd, and have stew'd,
Your forc'd-meat is n't all worth a straw.

Though your satire you spit,
  'T is n't season'd a bit,
And your puffs are as heavy as lead;
  Call each dish what you will,
  Boil, roast, hash, or grill,
Yet still it is all a calf's-head.

I do n't mind your huffing,
  For you 've put such vile stuff in,
I protest I 'm as sick as a dog;
  Were you leaner or fatter,
  I 'd not mince the matter,
You 're not fit to dress Æsop a frog.

Then, good master Slice!
  Shut up shop, if your wise,
And th' unwary no longer trepan;
  Such advice indeed is hard,
  And may stick in your gizzard,
But digest it as well as you can.

### THE MISTAKE.

#### ON CAPTAIN BLUFF.  1750.

Says a gosling, almost frighten'd out of her wits,
" Help, mother, or else I shall go into fits.
I have had such a fright, I shall never recover,
O ! that *hawke*, that you 've told us of over and
    over.
See, there, where he sits, with his terrible face,
And his coat how it glitters all over with lace.
With his sharp hooked nose, and his sword at his
    heel,
How my heart it goes pit-a-pat, pray, mother, feel."
Says the goose, very gravely, " Pray do n't talk so
    wild,
Those looks are as harmless as mine are, my child.
And as for his sword there, so bright and so nice,
I 'll be sworn 't will hurt nothing besides frogs and
    mice.
Nay, prithee do n't hang so about me, let loose,
I tell thee he dares not say—bo to a goose.
In short there is not a more innocent fowl,
Why, instead of a *hawke*, look ye child, 't is an
    *owl*.'

TO

### A LADY WITH A BASKET OF FRUIT.

Once of forbidden fruit the mortal taste
Chang'd beauteous Eden to a dreary waste.
Here you may freely eat, secure the while
From latent poison, or insidious guile.
Yet O ! could I but happily infuse
Some secret charm into the sav'ry juice,

Of pow'r to tempt your gentle breast to share,
With me the peaceful cot, and rural fare:
A diff'rent fate should crown the blest device,
And change my desert to a paradise.

### PEYTOE'S GHOST[1].

To Craven's health, and social joy,
  The festive night was kept,
While mirth and patriot spirit flow'd,
  And Dullness only slept.

When from the jovial crowd I stole,
  And homeward shap'd my way ;
And pass'd along by Chesterton,
  All at the close of day.

Thy sky with clouds was overcast,
  An hollow tempest blow'd,
And rains and foaming cataracts
  Had delug'd all the road ;

When through the dark and lonesome shade
  Shone forth a sudden light ;
And soon distinct an human form
  Engag'd my wondering sight.

Onward it mov'd with graceful port,
  And soon o'ertook my speed ;
Then thrice I lifted up my hands,
  And thrice I check'd my steed.

" Who art thou, passenger," it cry'd,
  " From yonder mirth retir'd ?
That here pursu'st thy cheerless way,
  Benighted, and be-mir'd."

" I am," said I, " a country clerk,
  A clerk of low degree,
And yonder gay and gallant scene
  Suits not a curacy.

" But I have seen such sights to day,
  As make my heart full glad,
Although it is but dark, 't is true,
  And eke—my road is bad.

" For I have seen lords, knights, and 'squires,
  Of great and high renown,
To choose a knight for this fair shire,
  All met at Warwick town.

" A wight of skill to ken our laws,
  Of courage to defend,
Of worth to serve the public cause
  Before a private end.

[1] Was lord Willoughby de Broke.—This is a
mistake, as that nobleman had neither the name
nor the estate of Mr. Peytoe. The late lord, indeed, his godson and heir, had both. This poem
refers to Mr. Peytoe, who lived at Chesterton, where
the scene lies, and formerly represented the
county. *C.*

' And such they found, if right I guess—
    Of gentle blood he came;
Of morals firm, of manners mild,
    And Craven [2] is his name.

" Did half the British tribunes share
    Experienc'd Mordaunt's [3] truth,
Another half, like Craven boast
    A free unbiass'd youth:

" The Sun I trow, in all his race,
    No happier realms should find;
Nor Britons hope for aught in vain,
    From warmth with prudence join'd.

" Go on, my country, favour'd soil,
    Such patriots to produce!"
" Go on, my countrymen," he cry'd,
    " Such patriots still to choose."

This said, the placid form retir'd
    Behind the veil of night;
Yet bade me, for my country's good,
    The solemn tale recite.

---

## TO A LADY,

### FURNISHING HER LIBRARY, AT ****, IN WARWICKSHIRE.

WHEN just proportion in each part,
And colours mix'd with nicest art,
Conspire to show the grace and mien
Of Chloe, or the Cyprian queen:
With elegance throughout refin'd,
That speaks the passions of the mind,
The glowing canvass will proclaim
A Raphael's or a Titian's name.
So where through ev'ry learned page
Each distant clime, each distant age
Display a rich variety
Of wisdom in epitome;
Such elegance and taste will tell
The hand, that could select so well.
But when we all their beauties view,
United and improv'd by you,
We needs must own an emblem faint,
T' express those charms no art can paint.
Books must, with such correctness writ,
Refine another's taste and wit;
'T is to your merit only due,
That theirs can be refin'd by you.

---

## TO WILLIAM SHENSTONE, ESQ.

### ON RECEIVING A GILT POCKET-BOOK.    1751.

THESE spotless leaves, this neat array,
    Might well invite your charming quill,
In fair assemblage to display
    The power of learning, wit, and skill.

[2] Hon. William Craven, of Wykin; he was afterwards lord Craven.
[3] The late sir Charles Mordaunt, bart.

But since you carelessly refuse,
    And to my pen the task assign;
O! let your genius guide my Muse,
    And every vulgar thought refine.

Teach me your best, your best lov'd art,
    With frugal care to store my mind;
In this to play the miser's part,
    And give mean lucre to the wind:

To shun the coxcomb's empty noise,
    To scorn the villain's artful mask;
Nor trust gay pleasure's fleeting joys,
    Nor urge ambition's endless task.

Teach me to stem youth's boisterous tide,
    To regulate its giddy rage;
By reason's aid my bark to guide,
    Into the friendly port of age:

To share what classic culture yields,
    Through rhetoric's painted meads to roam;
With you to reap historic fields,
    And bring the golden harvest home.

To taste the genuine sweets of wit;
    To quaff in humour's sprightly bowl;
The philosophic mean to hit,
    And prize the dignity of soul.

Teach me to read fair Nature's book,
    Wide opening in each flow'ry plain;
And with judicious eye to look
    On all the glories of her reign.

To hail her, seated on her throne,
    By awful woods encompass'd round,
Or her divine extraction own,
    Though with a wreath of rushes crown'd.

Through arched walks, o'er spreading lawns,
    Near solemn rocks, with her to rove;
Or court her, mid her gentle fawns,
    In mossy cell, or maple grove.

Whether the prospect strain the sight,
    Or in the nearer landscapes charm,
Where hills, vales, fountains, woods unite,
    To grace your sweet Arcadian farm:

There let me sit, and gaze with you,
    On Nature's works by art refin'd;
And own, while we their contest view,
    Both fair, but fairest, thus combin'd!

---

## AN ELEGY ON MAN.

### WRITTEN JANUARY 1752.

BEHOLD Earth's lord, imperial man,
    In ripen'd vigour gay;
His outward form attentive scan,
    And all within survey.

Behold his plans of future life,
His care, his hope, his love,
Relations dear of child and wife,
The dome, the lawn, the grove.

Now see within his active mind,
More gen'rous passions share,
Friend, neighbour, country, all his kind,
By turns engage his care.

Behold him range with curious eye,
O'er Earth from pole to pole,
And through th' illimitable sky
Explore with daring soul.

Yet pass some twenty fleeting years,
And all his glory flies,
His languid eye is bath'd in tears,
He sickens, groans, and dies.

And is this all his destin'd lot,
This all his boasted sway?
For ever now to be forgot,
Amid the mould'ring clay!

Ah, gloomy thought! ah, worse than death!
Life sickens at the sound;
Better it were not draw our breath,
Than run this empty round.

Hence, cheating Fancy, then, away;
O let us better try,
By reason's more enlighten'd ray,
What 't is indeed to die.

Observe yon mass of putrid earth,
It holds an embryo-brood,
Ev'n now the reptiles crawl to birth,
And seek their leafy food.

Yet stay till some few suns are past,
Each forms a silken tomb,
And seems, like man, imprison'd fast,
To meet his final doom.

Yet from this silent mansion too
Anon you see him rise,
No more a crawling worm to view,
But tenant of the skies.

And what forbids that man should share,
Some more auspicious day,
To range at large in open air,
As light and free as they?

There was a time when life first warm'd
Our flesh in shades of night,
Then was th' imperfect substance form'd,
And sent to view this light.

There was a time, when ev'ry sense
In straiter limits dwelt,
Yet each its task could then dispense,
We saw, we heard, we felt.

And times there are, when through the veins
The blood forgets to flow,
Yet then a living pow'r remains,
Though not in active show.

Times too there be, when friendly sleep's
Soft charms the senses bind,
Yet fancy then her vigils keeps,
And ranges unconfin'd.

And reason holds her sep'rate sway,
Though all the senses wake,
And forms in mem'ry's storehouse play,
Of no material make.

What are these then, this eye, this ear,
But nicer organs found,
A glass to read, a trump to hear,
The modes of shape, or sound?

And blows may maim, or time impair
These instruments of clay,
And Death may ravish what they spare,
Completing their decay.

But are these then that living pow'r
That thinks, compares, and rules?
Then say a scaffold is a tow'r,
A workman is his tools.

For aught appears that Death can do,
That still survives his stroke,
Its workings plac'd beyond our view,
Its present commerce broke.

But what connections it may find,
Boots much to hope [1] and fear,
And if instruction courts the mind,
'T is madness not to hear.

## ON RECEIVING A LITTLE IVORY BOX

### FROM A LADY,

#### CURIOUSLY WROUGHT BY HER OWN HANDS.

Little box of matchless grace!
Fairer than the fairest face,
Smooth as was her parent-hand,
That did thy wondrous form command.
Spotless as her infant mind,
As her riper age refin'd,
Beauty with the graces join'd.
Let me clothe the lovely stranger,
Let me lodge thee safe from danger.
Let me guard thy soft repose,
From giddy fortune's random blows,
From thoughtless mirth, barbaric hate,
From the iron hand of Fate,
And oppression's deadly weight.
Thou art not of a sort, or number,
Fashion'd for a poet's lumber;
Though more capacious than his purse,
Too small to hold his store of verse.
Too delicate for homely toil,
Too neat for vulgar hands to soil.
O! would the Fates permit the Muse
Thy future destiny to choose!
In thy circle's fairy round,
With a golden fillet bound:
Like the snow-drop silver white,
Like the glow-worm's humid light,

[1] Vide Butler's Analogy.

Like the dew at early dawn,
Like the moon-light on the lawn,
Lucid rows of pearls should dwell,
Pleas'd as in their native shell;
Or the brilliant's sparkling rays,
Should emit a starry blaze.
   And if the fair, whose magic skill
Wrought thee passive to her will,
Deign to regard thy poet's love,
Nor his aspiring suit reprove,
Her form should crown the fair design,
Goddess fit for such a shrine!

---

## VALENTINE'S DAY.

The tuneful choir in amorous strains
   Accost their feather'd loves;
While each fond mate, with equal pains,
   The tender suit approves.

With cheerful hop from spray to spray
   They sport along the meads;
In social bliss together stray,
   Where love or fancy leads.

Through spring's gay scenes each happy pair
   Their fluttering joys pursue;
Its various charms and produce share,
   For ever kind and true.

Their sprightly notes from ev'ry shade
   Their mutual loves proclaim;
Till winter's chilling blasts invade,
   And damp th' enlivening flame.

Then all the jocund scene declines,
   Nor woods nor meads delight;
The drooping tribe in secret pines,
   And mourns th' unwelcome sight.

Go, blissful warblers! timely wise,
   Th' instructive moral tell!
Nor thou their meaning lays despise,
   My charming Annabelle!

---

## HAMLET'S SOLILOQUY,

### IMITATED.

To *print*, or not to *print*—that is the question.
Whether 't is better in a trunk to bury
The quirks and crotchets of outrageous fancy,
Or send a well-wrote copy to the press,
And by disclosing, end them? To print, to doubt
No more; and by one act to say we end
The head-ach, and a thousand natural shocks
Of scribbling frenzy—'t is a consummation
Devoutly to be wish'd. To print—to beam
From the same shelf with Pope, in calf well bound:
To sleep, perchance, with Quarles—Ay, there's the
For to what class a writer may be doom'd, [rub—
When he hath shuffled off some paltry stuff,
Must give us pause.—There 's the respect that makes
Th' unwilling poet keep his piece nine years.
For who would bear th' impatient thirst of fame,
The pride of conscious merit, and 'bove all,
The tedious importunity of friends,

When as himself might his *quietus* make
With a bare inkhorn? Who would fardles bear?
To groan and sweat under a load of wit?
But that the tread of steep Parnassus' hill,
That undiscover'd country, with whose bays
Few travellers return, puzzles the will,
And makes us rather bear to live unknown,
Than run the hazard to be known and damn'd.
Thus critics do make cowards of us all.
And thus the healthful face of many a poem
Is sickly'd o'er with a pale manuscript;
And enterprises of great fire and spirit,
With this regard from Dodsley turn away,
And lose the name of authors.

---

## ROUNDELAY,

### WRITTEN FOR THE JUBILEE AT STRATFORD UPON AVON,

#### CELEBRATED BY MR. GARRICK IN HONOUR OF SHAKSPEARE, SEPTEMBER, 1769.

#### SET TO MUSIC BY MR. DIBDIN.

Sisters of the tuneful train,
Attend your parent's jocund strain,
'T is Fancy calls you; follow me
To celebrate the jubilee.

On Avon's banks, where Shakspeare's bust
Points out and guards his sleeping dust;
The sons of scenic mirth agree
To celebrate the jubilee.

Come, daughters, come, and bring with you
Th' aerial sprites and fairy crew,
And the sister Graces three,
To celebrate the jubilee.

Hang around the sculptur'd tomb
The 'broider'd vest, the nodding plume,
And the mask of comic glee,
To celebrate the jubilee.

From Birnham wood, and Bosworth field,
Bring the standard, bring the shield,
With drums and martial symphony,
To celebrate the jubilee.

In mournful numbers now relate
Poor Desdemona's hapless fate,
With frantic deeds of jealousy,
To celebrate the jubilee.

Nor be Windsor's wives forgot,
With their harmless merry plot,
The whitening mead, and haunted tree,
To celebrate the jubilee.

Now in jocund strains recite
The humours of the braggard knight,
Fat knight, and ancient Pistol he,
To celebrate the jubilee.

But see in crowds the gay, the fair,
To the splendid scene repair,
A scene as fine as fine can be,
To celebrate the jubilee.

## THE BLACKBIRDS.

### AN ELEGY.

THE Sun had chas'd the mountain snow,
  His beams had pierc'd the stubborn soil,
The melting streams began to flow,
  And ploughmen urg'd their annual toil.

'T was then, amidst the vocal throng,
  Whom Nature wak'd to mirth and love,
A blackbird rais'd his am'rous song,
  And thus it echo'd through the grove.

" O fairest of the feather'd train !
  For whom I sing, for whom I burn,
Attend with pity to my strain,
  And grant my love a kind return.

" For see, the wintry storms are flown,
  And zephyrs gently fan the air;
Let us the genial influence own,
  Let us the vernal pastime share.

" The raven plumes his jetty wing,
  To please his croaking paramour,
The larks responsive carols sing,
  And tell their passion as they soar:

" But does the raven's sable wing
  Excel the glossy jet of mine?
Or can the lark more sweetly sing,
  Than we, who strength with softness join?

" O let me then thy steps attend !
  I 'll point new treasures to thy sight:
Whether the grove thy wish befriend,
  Or edge-rows green, or meadows bright.

" I 'll guide thee to the clearest rill,
  Whose streams among the pebbles stray;
There will we sip, and sip our fill,
  Or on the flow'ry margin play.

" I 'll lead thee to the thickest brake,
  Impervious to the schoolboy's eye;
For thee the plaster'd nest I 'll make,
  And to thy downy bosom fly.

" When, prompted by a mother's care,
  Thy warmth shall form th' imprison'd young;
The pleasing task I 'll gladly share,
  Or cheer thy labours with a song.

" To bring thee food I 'll range the fields,
  And cull the best of ev'ry kind,
Whatever Nature's bounty yields,
  And love's assiduous care can find.

" And when my lovely mate would stray,
  To taste the summer sweets at large,
I 'll wait at home the live-long day,
  And fondly tend our little charge.

" Then prove with me the sweets of love,
  With me divide the cares of life,
No bush shall boast in all the grove,
  A mate so fond, so bless'd a wife.''

He ceas'd his song—the plumy dame
  Heard with delight the love-sick strain,
Nor long conceal'd the mutual flame,
  Nor long repress'd his am'rous pain.

He led her to the nuptial bow'r,
  And perch'd with triumph by her side;
What gilded roof could boast that hour
  A fonder mate, or happier bride?

Next morn he wak'd her with a song,
  " Behold," he said, " the new-born day,
The lark his mattin-peal has rung,
  Arise, my love, and come away."

Together through the fields they stray'd,
  And to the murm'ring riv'let's side,
Renew'd their vows, and hopp'd, and play'd
  With artless joy, and decent pride.

When, O! with grief my Muse relates
  What dire misfortune clos'd the tale,
Sent by an order from the Fates,
  A gunner met them in the vale.

Alarm'd, the lover cried, " My dear,
  Haste, haste away, from danger fly;
Here, gunner, point thy thunder here,
  O spare my love, and let me die."

At him the gunner took his aim,
  Too sure the volley'd thunder flew !
O had he chose some other game,
  Or shot—as he was wont to do!

Divided pair ! forgive the wrong,
  While I with tears your fate rehearse,
I 'll join the widow's plaintive song,
  And save the lover in my verse.

---

## THE GOLDFINCHES.

### AN ELEGY.

#### TO WILLIAM SHENSTONE, ESQ.

.........Ingenuas didicisse fideliter artes
Emollit mores, nec sinit esse feros.

To you, whose groves protect the feather'd choirs,
  Who lend their artless notes a willing ear,
To you, whom pity moves, and taste inspires,
  The Doric strain belongs, O Shenstone hear.

'T was gentle spring, when all the plumy race,
  By Nature taught, in nuptial leagues combine,
A goldfinch joy'd to meet the warm embrace,
  And with her mate in love's delights to join.

All in a garden, on a currant bush,
  With wondrous art they built their airy seat;
In the next orchard liv'd a friendly thrush,
  Nor distant far a woodlark's soft retreat.

Here bless'd with ease, and in each other bless'd,
  With early songs they wak'd the neigbb'ring
    groves,
Till time matur'd their joys, and crown'd their nest
  With infant pledges of their faithful loves.

And now what transport glow'd in either's eye ?
  What equal fondness dealt th' allotted food?
What joy each other's likeness to descry,
  And future sonnets in the chirping brood !

But ah ! what earthly happiness can last ?
  How does the fairest purpose often fail ?
A truant schoolboy's wantonness could blast
  Their flatt'ring hopes, and leave them both to wail.

The most ungentle of his tribe was he,
  No gen'rous precept ever touch'd his heart,
With 'concord false, and hideous prosody,
  He scrawl'd his task, and blunder'd o'er his part.

On mischief bent, he mark'd, with rav'nous eyes,
  Where wrapp'd in down the callow songsters lay,
Then rushing, rudely seiz'd the glitt'ring prize,
  And bore it in his impious hands away !

But how shall I describe, in numbers rude,
  The pangs for poor Chrysomitris decreed,
When from her secret stand aghast she view'd
  The cruel spoiler perpetrate the deed ?

" O grief of griefs !" with shrieking voice she cried,
  " What sight is this that I have liv'd to see !
O ! that I had in youth's fair season died,
  From love's false joys and bitter sorrows free.

" Was it for this, alas ! with weary bill,
  Was it for this I pois'd th' unwieldy straw ?
For this I bore the moss from yonder hill,
  Nor shun'd the pond'rous stick along to draw ?

" Was it for this I pick'd the wool with care,
  Intent with nicer skill our work to crown ?
For this, with pain, I bent the stubborn hair,
  And lin'd our cradle with the thistle's down ?

" Was it for this my freedom I resign'd,
  And ceas'd to rove at large from plain to plain ?
For this I sat at home whole days confin'd,
  To bear the scorching heat, and pealing rain ?

" Was it for this my watchful eyes grow dim ?
  For this the roses on my cheek turn pale ?
Pale is my golden plumage, once so trim !
  And all my wonted mirth and spirits fail !

" O plund'rer vile ! O more than adders fell !
  More murth'rous than the cat, with prudish face !
Fiercer than kites in whom the furies dwell,
  And thievish as the cuckow's pilf'ring race !

" May juicy plumbs for thee forbear to grow,
  For thee no flow'r unveil its charming dies ;
May birch-trees thrive to work thee sharper woe,
  And list'ning starlings mock thy frantic cries."

Thus sang the mournful bird her piteous tale,
  The piteous tale her mournful mate return'd,
Then side by side they sought the distant vale,
  And there in secret sadness inly mourn'd.

---

## THE SWALLOWS.

### AN ELEGY.

### PART I.

Ere yellow autumn from our plains retir'd,
  And gave to wintry storms the varied year,
The swallow race with prescient gift inspir'd,
  To southern climes prepar'd their course to steer.

On Damon's roof a large assembly sate,
  His roof a refuge to the feather'd kind !
With serious look he mark'd the grave debate,
  And to his Delia thus address'd his mind.

" Observe yon twitt'ring flock, my gentle maid !
  Observe, and read the wondrous ways of Heav'n !
With us through summer's genial reign they stay'd,
  And food and sunshine to their wants were giv'n.

" But now, by secret instinct taught, they know
  The near approach of elemental strife,
Of blust'ring tempests, and of chilling snow,
  With ev'ry pang and scourge of tender life.

" Thus warn'd they meditate a speedy flight,
  For this ev'n now they prune their vig'rous wing,
For this each other to the toil excite,
  And prove their strength in many a sportive ring.

" No sorrow loads their breast, or dims their eye,
  To quit their wonted haunts, or native home,
Nor fear they lanching on the boundless sky,
  In search of future settlements to roam.

" They feel a pow'r, an impulse all divine,
  That warns them hence ; they feel it, and obey ;
To this direction all their cares resign,
  Unknown their destin'd stage, unmark'd their
    way.

" Peace to your flight ! ye mild, domestic race !
  O ! for your wings to travel with the Sun !
Health brace your nerves, and zephyrs aid your
    pace,
  Till your long voyage happily be done.

" See, Delia, on my roof your guests to day,
  To morrow on my roof your guests no more,
Ere yet 't is night with haste they wing away,
  To morrow lands them on some happier shore."

How just the moral in this scene convey'd !
  And what without a moral ? would we read !
Then mark what Damon tells his gentle maid,
  And with his lesson register the deed.

So youthful joys fly like the summer's gale,
  So threats the winter of inclement age,
Life's busy plot a short, fantastic tale !
  And Nature's changeful scenes the shifting stage !

And does no friendly pow'r to man dispense
  The joyful tidings of some happier clime ?
Find we no guide in gracious Providence
  Beyond the gloomy grave, and short-liv'd time ?

Yes, yes, the sacred oracles we hear,
  That point the path to realms of endless joy,
That bid our trembling hearts no danger fear,
  Though clouds surround, and angry skies annoy.

Then let us wisely for our flight prepare,
  Nor count this stormy world our fix'd abode,
Obey the call, and trust our leader's care,
  To smooth the rough, and light the darksome road.

Moses, by grant divine, led Israel's host
Through dreary paths to Jordan's fruitful side;
But we a loftier theme than theirs can boast,
A better promise, and a nobler guide.

---

## PART II.

At length the winter's howling blasts are o'er,
Array'd in smiles the lovely spring returns,
Now fuel'd hearths attractive blaze no more,
And ev'ry breast with inward fervour burns.

Again the daisies peep, the violets blow,
Again the vocal tenants of the grove,
Forgot the patt'ring hail or driving snow,
Renew the lay to melody and love.

" And see, my Delia, see o'er yonder stream,
Where, on the bank, the lambs in gambols play,
Alike attracted by the sunny gleam,
Again the swallows take their wonted way.

" Welcome, ye gentle tribe, your sports pursue,
Welcome again to Delia and to me,
Your peaceful councils on my roof renew,
And plan new settlements from danger free.

" Again I 'll listen to your grave debates,
Again I 'll hear your twitt'ring songs unfold
What policy directs your wand'ring states,
What bounds are settled, and what tribes enroll'd.

" Again I 'll hear you tell of distant lands,
What insect nations rise from Egypt's mud,
What painted swarms subsist on Lybia's sands,
What Ganges yields, and what th' Euphratean
flood.

" Thrice happy race! whom Nature's call invites
To travel o'er her realms with active wing,
To taste her various stores, her best delights,
The summer's radiance, and the sweets of spring.

" While we are doom'd to bear the restless change
Of varying seasons, vapours dank and dry,
Forbid like you in milder climes to range,
When wintry storms usurp the low'ring sky.

" Yet know the period to your joys assign'd,
Know ruin hovers o'er this earthly ball,
As lofty tow'rs stoop prostrate to the wind,
Its secret props of adamant shall fall.

" But when yon radiant Sun shall shine no more,
The spirit, freed from sin's tyrannic sway,
On lighter pinions borne than yours, shall soar
To fairer realms, beneath a brighter ray.

" To plains ethereal, and celestial bow'rs,
Where wintry storms no rude access obtain,
Where blasts no lightning, and no tempest low'rs,
But ever-smiling spring and pleasure reign."

## ADAM:

OR,

### THE FATAL DISOBEDIENCE.

#### AN ORATORIO.

COMPILED FROM THE PARADISE LOST OF MILTON,
AND ADAPTED TO MUSIC.

---

#### ADVERTISEMENT.

The Comus, Allegro, Il Penseroso, Lycidas, and
Samson Agonistes of Milton, have each of them had
the good fortune to be made choice of as proper
subjects for musical composition; but no one appears hitherto to have entertained any thoughts of
adapting any part of Paradise Lost to the same use,
though confessedly the most capital of all his works,
and containing the greatest variety both of sentiment, and language susceptible of the graces of that
harmonious art[1]. Indeed the plan for this purpose
was not so obvious. The others were in a great
measure ready prepared to the composer's hands;
here the case was different. The several beautiful
passages contained in this poem lay scattered
through a wide compass, and it appeared difficult to
assemble, and unite them into any regular and
compendious form adapted to public representation.
This the compiler has attempted by confining himself to those passages which have a more immediate
reference to the principal story, and omitting what
was more remote, and digressive. In executing this
design he has varied as little as was possible from the
order of time and language of Milton, and endeavoured not to offend the judgment, at the same
time that he consulted the entertainment of the
public.

He will not say that he has omitted no particular
beauties of this poem, for not to do this would be
to transcribe the whole; but he can truly say that
he has taken some pains to include as many as could
with any propriety be brought within the compass
of his undertaking, and that it will be no small pleasure to him to be the occasion of making them more
universally admired, by means of an alliance with
that sister-art, whose expressive strains are the
only additional ornament of which they were capable.

So far was written after the following piece was
entirely finished, and at a time when the compiler
thought that no one had engaged in the same
design. In this however he finds he was mistaken,
and can truly say, that had he been so much conversant in the musical world as to have known more

---

[1] What Dr. Gregory says of religion in general
as a subject for musical composition, may be applied with the strictest propriety to this work in
particular, viz. that it affords almost all the variety
of subjects which music can express; the sublime,
the joyous, the cheerful, the serene, the devout, the
plaintive, the melancholy.
      Comparative View of the State and
            Faculties of Man, p. 73, 74.

early that a person of Mr. Stillingfleet's merit and abilities had undertaken this work, he would certainly have declined it: but having spent some time in it, and finding that this gentleman's plan does not entirely coincide with his, he hopes he may be excused for presenting it to the world after him.

He will no further detain the reader than to say, that his aim was to furnish the composer with Milton's own beauties, so adapted as that the capital lines and most striking sentiments might naturally offer themselves to musical distinction, rather than form words for that purpose, as he thought had been done in other compositions of a like nature, in a manner very forced and unnatural; and where, though the ear is gratified, the understanding is generally disgusted.

## ADAM:

### AN ORATORIO.

*The persons here represented are*

ADAM, and
EVE; with the
Guardian Angels of Paradise, and others.

*The scene is Paradise.*

## ACT I. SCENE I.

### RECITATIVE.

UNDER a tuft of shade, that, on a green,
Stood whisp'ring soft, on Eden's blissful plain,
Sat the first human pair. (Not that fair field
Of Enna, where Proserpine, gath'ring flow'rs,
Herself, a fairer flow'r, by gloomy Dis
Was gather'd; nor that sweet Elysian grove
Of Daphne by Orontes, and th' inspir'd
Castalian spring, might with this Paradise
Of Eden strive: nor that Nysean isle,
Girt with the river Triton, where old Cham,
Whom Gentiles Ammon call, and Lybian Jove,
Hid Amalthea, and her florid son,
Young Bacchus from his step-dame Rhea's eye—
Nor where Abassine kings their issue guard,
Mount Amara! enclos'd with shining rock,
A whole day's journey high.) Around them grew
All trees of noblest kind for sight, smell, taste,
And all amid them grew the tree of life,
High eminent, blooming ambrosial fruit
Of vegetable gold; and next to Life,
Our death! the tree of knowledge grew fast by.
Here waving boughs wept od'rous gums and balm:
On others fruit, burnish'd with golden rind,
Hung amiable: betwixt them lawns, and downs,
Or palmy hillock, or the flow'ry lap
Of some irriguous valley spread her store,
Flow'rs of all hues, and without thorn the rose.
Another side umbrageous grots, and caves
Of cool recess! o'er which the mantling vine
Lays forth her purple grape, and gently creeps
Luxuriant. Meanwhile murm'ring waters fall
Down the slope hills dispers'd, or, in a lake,

That to the fringed bank, with myrtle crown'd,
Her crystal mirror holds, unite their streams.
The birds their quire apply—airs, vernal airs
Breathing the smell of field, or grove attune
The trembling leaves, and whisper whence they stole
Their balmy spoils. About them frisking play'd
All beasts of th' earth, since wild, and of all chase
In wood, or wilderness, forest, or den.
Sporting the lion ramp'd, and, in his paw,
Dandled the kid. Bears, tigers, ounces, pards
Gambol'd before them. Th' unwieldly elephant,
To make them mirth, us'd all his might, and wreath'd
His lithe proboscis. Close the serpent sly,
Insinuating wove, with Gordian twine,
His braided train, and of his fatal guile
Gave proof unheeded. They superior sat
As lords of all, of godlike shape erect!
For valour he, and contemplation form'd,
For softness she, and sweet attractive grace!

### AIR.

..........................They superior sat,
As lords of all, of godlike shape erect!
For valour he, and contemplation form'd,
For softness she, and sweet attractive grace!

## SCENE II.

### RECITATIVE.

On the soft downy bank, damask'd with flow'rs,
Reclin'd they sat, when Adam first of men
To first of women Eve thus smiling spake.

### ADAM.

Sole partner, and sole part of all these joys,
Dearer thyself than all! needs must the Pow'r,
That made us, and, for us, this ample world,
Be infinitely good, and, of his good
As liberal, and free as infinite;
Who rais'd us from the dust, and plac'd us here,
In all this happiness; who yet requires
From us no other service, than to keep
This one, this easy charge—Of all the trees
In Paradise, that bear delicious fruit
So various, not to taste that only tree
Of knowledge, planted by the tree of life.

### SONG.

Then let us ever praise him, and extol
His bounty, following our delightful task,
To prune these growing plants, and tend these flow'rs,
Which, were it toilsome, yet with thee were sweet.

### RECITATIVE.

### EVE.

..........................O thou! for whom
And from whom I was form'd! Flesh of thy flesh!
And without whom am to no end! My guide,
And head! what thou hast said is just and right:
For we indeed to him all praises owe,
And daily thanks: I chiefly, who enjoy
So much the happier lot, enjoying thee.

### AFFETUOSO.

That day I oft remember, when from sleep
I first awak'd, and found myself repos'd
Under a shade of flow'rs, much wond'ring where,

And what I was, whence thither brought, and how.
Nor distant far from thence, a murm'ring sound
Of waters issued from a cave, and spread
Into a liquid plain, then stood unmov'd
Pure as th' expanse of Heav'n.    I thither went,
With unexperienc'd thought, and laid me down
On the green bank to look into the clear,
Smooth lake, that to me seem'd another sky.
As I bent down to look, just opposite,
A shape within the watry gleam appear'd,
Bending to look on me.    I started back,
It started back.    But, pleas'd, I soon return'd,
Pleas'd it return'd as soon, with answ'ring looks
Of sympathy and love.    There I had fix'd
Mine eyes till now, and pin'd with vain desire,
Had not a voice thus warn'd me.  "What thou see'st,
What there thou see'st, fair creature! is thyself.
With thee it came, and goes.    But follow me,
And I will bring thee where no shadow stays
Thy coming, and thy soft embraces—He!
Whose image thou art—him thou shalt enjoy
Inseparably thine, to him shalt bear
Multitudes like thyself, and thence be call'd
Mother of human race."    What could I do,
But follow straight, invisibly thus led?
Till I espied thee, fair, indeed, and tall,
Under a platan.    Yet methought less fair,
Less winning soft, less amiably mild,
Than that smooth watry image.    Back I turn'd.
Thou following cry'dst aloud ;

### AIR.

................................'  Return, fair Eve!
Whom fly'st thou? whom thou fly'st, of him thou
art,
His flesh, his bone !  To give thee being I lent
Out of my side to thee, nearest my heart,
Substantial life, to have thee by my side,
Henceforth an individual solace dear.
Part of my soul I seek thee, and thee claim
My other half.'   With that thy gentle hand
Seiz'd mine ;  I yielded—and from that time see
How beauty is excell'd by manly grace,
And wisdom, which alone is truly fair.

### RECITATIVE.

So spake our gen'ral mother, and with eyes
Of conjugal affection, unreprov'd,
And meek surrender, half embracing lean'd
On our first father.    Half her swelling breast
Naked met his, under the flowing gold
Of her loose tresses hid.   He, in delight
Both of her beauty and submissive charms,
Smil'd with superior love, and press'd her lip
With kisses pure.    Thus they in am'rous sport,
As well beseems fair couple, link'd as they,
In happy nuptial league, their minutes pass'd,
Crown'd with sublime delight.    The loveliest pair
That ever yet in love's embraces met :
Adam the goodliest man of men since born
His sons, the fairest of her daughters Eve !

### CHORUS.

"  Hail !  Hymen's first, accomplish'd pair !
    Goodliest he of all his sons !
Of her daughters she most fair !
    Goodliest he !
    She most fair !
Goodliest he of all his sons !
    Of her daughters she most fair."
VOL. XVII.

### SCENE III.

#### RECITATIVE.

Now came still ev'ning on, and twilight grey
Had, in her sober liv'ry all things clad,
Silence accompanied : for beast, and bird,
They to their grassy couch, these to their nests
Were slunk : all but the wakeful nightingale !
She all night long her am'rous descant sung.
Silence was pleas'd.   Now glow'd the firmament
With living sapphires.   Hesperus, that led
The starry host, rode brightest, till the Moon,
Rising in clouded majesty, at length,
Apparent queen ! unveil'd her peerless light,
And o'er the dark her silver mantle threw.
When Adam thus to Eve.

#### ADAM.

........................ ...... Fair consort ! th' hour
Of night, and all things now retir'd to rest,
Mind us of like repose : since God hath set
Labour and rest, as day and night, to men
Successive ; and the timely dew of sleep,
Now falling with soft slumb'rous weight, inclines
Our eye-lids.   Ere fresh morning streak the east
With first approach of light, we must be ris'n,
And at our pleasant labour to reform
Yon flow'ry arbours, yonder alleys green,
Our walk at noon, with branches overgrown.
Meanwhile, as Nature wills, night bids us rest.

#### EVE.

My author and disposer, what thou bid'st
Unargu'd I obey, so God ordains.
God is thy law, thou mine.   To know no more
Is woman's happiest knowledge, and her praise.

#### AIR.

" With thee conversing, I forget all time,
All seasons, and their change, all please alike.
Sweet is the breath of morn, her rising sweet,
With charm of earliest birds ! Pleasant the Sun !
When first on this delightful land he spreads
His orient beams on herb, tree, fruit, and flow'r,
Glist'ring with dew : fragrant the fertile Earth,
After soft show'rs ! and sweet the coming on
Of grateful evening mild ; the silent Night,
With this her solemn bird ; and this fair Moon,
And those the gems of Heav'n, her starry train !
But neither breath of Morn, when she ascends,
With charm of earliest birds, nor rising Sun
On this delightful land, nor herb, fruit, flow'r,
Glist'ring with dew, nor fragrance after show'rs,
Nor grateful evening mild, nor silent Night,
With this her solemn bird, nor walk by Moon,
Or glitt'ring star-light without thee is sweet."

#### RECITATIVE.

Thus talking, hand in hand, alone they pass'd
On to their blissful bow'r.   It was a place,
Chos'n by the Sov'reign Planter, when he fram'd
All things to man's delightful use ; the roof,
Of thickest covert, was in woven shade,
Laurel and myrtle, and what higher grew
Of firm and fragrant leaf ; on either side,
Acanthus, and each od'rous bushy shrub,
Fenc'd up the verdant wall, each beauteous flow'r,
Iris, all hues, roses, and jessamine        [wrought
Rear'd high their flourish'd heads between, and

mosaic; under foot the violet,
Crocus, and hyacinth, with rich inlay,
Broider'd the ground, more colour'd than with stone
Of costliest emblem.   Other creature here
Beast, bird, insect, or worm, durst enter none,
Such was their awe of man.   In shady bow'r,
More sacred and sequester'd, though but feign'd,
Pan or Sylvanus never slept, nor Nymph,
Or Faunus haunted.   Here, in close recess,
With flow'rs, and garlands, and sweet smelling herbs,
Espoused Eve deck'd first her nuptial bed,
And heav'nly quires the Hymenæan sung.
    Thus at their shady lodge arriv'd, both stood,
Both turn'd, and, under open sky, ador'd
The God that made both sky, air, Earth, and
        Heav'n,
Which they beheld, the Moon's resplendent globe,
And starry pole.

EVENING HYMN.

..................... " Thou also mad'st the night,
Maker omnipotent! and thou the day,
Which we, in our appointed work employ'd,
Have finish'd, happy in our mutual help,
And mutual love, the crown of all our bliss,
Ordain'd by thee, and this delicious place,
For us too large, where thy abundance wants
Partakers, and uncrop'd falls to the ground.
But thou hast promis'd from us two a race,
To fill the Earth, who shall, with us, extol
Thy goodness infinite, both when we wake,
And when we seek, as now, thy gift of sleep."

ACT II.   SCENE I.

RECITATIVE.

O! FOR that warning voice, which he, who saw
Th' Apocalypse, heard cry in Heav'n aloud,
Then when the Dragon, put to second rout,
Came furious down, to be reveng'd on men,
*Woe to the inhabitants of th' Earth!* that now
While time was, our first parents had been warn'd
The coming of their secret foe, and 'scap'd,
Haply so 'scap'd his mortal snare; for now
Satan, now first inflam'd with rage, came down,
The tempter, ere th' accuser of mankind.

CHORUS.

He, who sits enthron'd on high,
Above the circle of the sky,
Sees his rage, and mocks his toil,
Which on himself shall soon recoil:
In the snare, with malice, wrought
For others, shall his feet be caught.

SCENE II.

RECITATIVE.

Now Morn her rosy steps in th' eastern clime
Advancing, sow'd the earth with orient pearl,
When Adam wak'd, so custom'd, for his sleep
Was airy light, from pure digestion bred,
And temp'rate vapours bland, which th' only sound
Of leaves, and fuming rills, Aurora's fan,
Lightly dispers'd, and the shrill matin song
Of birds on ev'ry bough.   Unwaken'd Eve

Close at his side, in naked beauty lay,
Beauty! which, whether waking, or asleep,
Shot forth peculiar charms.   He, on his side,
Leaning, half rais'd, with looks of cordial love
Hung over her enamour'd : then, with voice,
Mild as when Zephyrus on Flora breathes,
Her hand soft-touching, whisper'd thus.

SONG.

.................................." Awake!
My fairest, my espous'd, my latest found,
Heav'n's last, best gift, my ever new delight,
Awake!  the morning shines, and the fresh field
Calls us; we lose the prime, to mark how spring
Our tended plants, how blows the citron grove,
What drops the myrrh, and what the balmy reed;
How Nature paints her colours; how the bee
Sits on the bloom, extracting liquid sweets."

RECITATIVE.

EVE.

Adam!  well may we labour still to dress
This garden, still to tend herb, plant, and flow'r,
Our pleasant task enjoin'd; but till more hands
Aid us, the work under our labour grows
Luxurious by restraint.   Let us divide
Our labours then, for while together thus
Our task we choose, what wonder if so near
Looks intervene, and smiles, or object new
Casual discourse draw on, which intermits
Our day's work, brought to little, though begun
Early, and th' hour of supper comes unearn'd.

ADAM.

These paths and bow'rs doubt not but our joint
        hands
Will keep from wilderness with ease as wide
As we need walk, till younger hands ere long
Assist us.   But if much converse perhaps
Thee satiate, to short absence I could yield,
For solitude sometimes is best society,
And short retirement urges sweet return.
But other doubt possesses me, lest harm
Befall thee sever'd from me; for thou know'st
What hath been warn'd us, what malicious foe,
Envying our happiness, and of his own
Despairing, seeks to work us woe, and shame,
By sly assault; and somewhere, nigh at hand,
Watches no doubt, with greedy hope, to find
His wish, and best advantage!  us asunder;
Hopeless to circumvent us join'd, where each
To other speedy aid might lend at need.
Then leave not, I advise, the faithful side
Which gave thee being, shades thee, and protects.

AIR.

" The wife, where danger or dishonour lurks,
Safest, and seemliest near her husband stays,
Who guards her, or with her the worst endures."

RECITATIVE.

EVE.

Offspring of Heav'n and Earth, and all Earth's lord!
That such an enemy we have, who seeks
Our ruin, oft inform'd by thee, I learn.
But that thou should'st my firmness therefore doubt,
To God, or thee, because we have a foe
May tempt it, I expected not to hear.

### ADAM.

Daughter of God and man, immortal Eve!
For such thou art, from sin and blame entire:
Nor diffident of thee, do I dissuade
Thy absence from my sight, but to avoid
Th' attempt, which thou thyself with virtuous scorn
And anger would'st resent.   Misdeem not then,
If such affront I labour to avert
From thee alone, which on us both at once
The enemy, though bold, will hardly dare,
Or daring, first on me th' assault shall light.
Nor thou his malice and false guile contemn.
Subtle he needs múst be, who could seduce
Angels; nor think superfluous others' aid.
" I, from the influence of thy looks, receive
Access in ev'ry virtue; in thy sight,
More wise, more watchful, stronger, if need were,
Of outward strength; while shame, thou looking on,
Shame to be overcome, or over-reach'd!
Would utmost vigour raise, and rais'd unite."
Why should'st not thou like sense within thee feel,
When I am present, and thy trial choose
With me, best witness of thy virtue tried?

### EVE.

If this be our condition, thus to dwell
In narrow circuit straiten'd by a foe,
Subtle, or violent, we not endued,
Single, with like defence, wherever met,
How are we happy, still in fear of arm?

#### AIR.

" Frail is our happiness, if this be so,
And Eden were no Eden thus expos'd."

#### RECITATIVE.

### ADAM.

O, woman!  best are all things as the will
Of God ordain'd them.   His creating hand
Nothing imperfect or deficient left
Of all that he created, much less man,
Or aught that might his happy state secure:
Secure from outward force.  Within himself
The danger lies, yet lies within his pow'r.
Against his will he can receive no harm;
But God left free the will, for what obeys
Reason is free, and reason he made right,
And bid her still beware, and still erect,
Lest by some fair, appearing good surpris'd,
She dictate false, and misinform the will
To do what God expressly hath forbid.
Not then mistrust, but tender love enjoins
That I should mind thee oft, and mind thou me,
Firm we subsist, yet possible to swerve.

#### AIR.

" But if thou think'st trial unsought may find
Us both securer than thus warn'd thou seem'st,
Go! for thy stay, not free, absents thee more.
Go in thy native innocence.  Rely
On what thou hast of virtue: summon all,
For God towards thee hath done his part, do thine."

## SCENE III.
#### RECITATIVE.

So haste they to the field, their pleasing task!
But first, from under shady, arb'rous roof,

Soon as they forth were come to open sight
Of day-spring, and the Sun, who scarce upris'n,
With wheels yet hov'ring o'er the ocean brim,
Shot parallel to the Earth his dewy ray,
Discov'ring, in wide circuit, all the bounds
Of Paradise and Eden's happy plains,
Lowly they bow'd adoring, and began
Their orisons, each morning duly paid,
In various style: for neither various style
Nor holy rapture wanted they to praise
Their Maker in fit strains, pronounc'd, or sung,
Unmeditated; such prompt eloquence
Flow'd from their lips, in prose, or num'rous verse,
More tuneable than needed lute, or harp
To add more sweetness: and they thus began.

#### MORNING HYMN.

" These are thy glorious works, parent of good,
Almighty! thine this universal frame!
Thus wondrous fair! thyself how wondrous then!
Unspeakable! who sit'st above these Heav'ns,
To us invisible; or dimly seen
In these thy lowest works : yet these declare
Thy goodness beyond thought, and pow'r divine.
" Speak ye, who best can tell, ye sons of light!
Angels, for ye behold him, and, with songs,
And choral symphonies, day without night,
Circle his throne rejoicing; ye in Heav'n,
On Earth join all ye creatures to extol
Him first, him last, him midst, and without end.
" Fairest of stars, last in the train of night,
If better thou belong not to the dawn,
Sure pledge of day! that crown'st the smiling morn
With thy bright circlet, praise him in thy sphere,
While day arises, that sweet hour of prime.
" Thou Sun, both eye and soul of this great world!
Acknowledge him thy greater, sound his praise
In thy eternal course, both when thou climb'st,
And when high noon hast gain'd, and when hast fall'n.
" Moon! that now meet'st the orient Sun, now fly'st
With the fix'd stars, fix'd in their orb that flies,
And ye five other wand'ring fires, that move
In mystic dance, not without song, resound
His praise, who out of darkness call'd up light.
" Air ! and ye elements, th' eldest birth
Of Nature's womb, that, in quaternion, run
Perpetual circle multiform, and mix,
And nourish all things, let your ceaseless change
Vary to your great Maker still new praise.
" Ye mists and exhalations that now rise
From hill, or steaming lake, dusky, or grey,
Till the Sun paint your fleecy skirts with gold,
In honour to the world's great Maker rise,
Whether to deck with clouds th' uncolour'd sky,
Or wet the thirsty earth with falling show'rs,
Rising, or falling, still advance his praise.   [blow,
" His praise, ye winds, that from four quarters
Breathe soft, or loud; and wave your tops, ye pines,
With ev'ry plant, in sign of honour wave.
" Fountains! and ye that warble, as ye flow,
Melodious murmurs, warbling tune his praise.
" Join voices, all ye living souls! ye birds!
That singing up to Heav'n's bright gates ascend,
Bear on your wings, and in your notes his praise.
" Ye that in waters glide, and ye that walk
The earth; and stately tread, or lowly creep,
Witness if I be silent morn, or ev'n,
To hill, or valley, fountain, or fresh shade
Made vocal by my song, and taught his praise.

" Hail, universal Lord! be bounteous still
To give us only good ; and, if the night
Have gather'd aught of evil, or conceal'd,
Disperse it, as now light dispels the dark."

RECITATIVE.

So pray'd they innocent ; then to their task
They diff'rent ways repair—he, where his choice
Leads him, or where most needs, whether to wind
The woodbine round his arbour, or direct
The clasping ivy where to twine ; while she
In yonder spring of roses, intermix'd
With myrtle, seeks what to redress till noon.
Her long, with ardent look, his eye pursu'd
Delighted, but desiring more her stay.
She, like a wood-nymph light of Delia's train,
Betook her to the groves, but Delia's self
In gait surpass'd, and goddess-like deport.
Grace was in all her steps, Heav'n in her eye ;
In ev'ry gesture dignity and love.

AIR.

" Grace was in all her steps, Heav'n in her eye;
In ev'ry gesture dignity and love."

ACT III.   SCENE I.

THE GUARDIAN ANGELS.

RECITATIVE.

Our charge, though unsuccessful, is fulfill'd.
The tempter hath prevail'd, and man is fall'n.
Earth felt the wound, and Nature, from her seat
Sighing through all her works, gave signs of woe,
That all was lost.   The fatal omens reach'd
Our glitt'ring files, and through th' angelic guard
Spread sadness, mix'd with pity, not with guilt,
Or conscious negligence.   After short pause,
Earth trembled from her entrails, as again
In pangs, and Nature gave a second groan ;
Sky lower'd, and, mutt'ring thunder, some sad drops
Wept at completing of the mortal sin.
Now up to Heav'n we haste, before the throne
Supreme, t' approve our faithful vigilance.

CHORUS.

" Righteous art thou, O Lord ! and just are thy
      judgments.
            Hallelujah !"

RECITATIVE.

But see ! with visage discompos'd, and dim'd
With passions foul, like this late azure clime
With clouds and storms o'ercast, the human pair
Bend hitherward their steps disconsolate.

SCENE II.

ADAM AND EVE.

RECITATIVE.

ADAM.

O Eve ! in evil hour thou didst give ear
To that false worm, of whomsoever taught
To counterfeit man's voice, true in our fall,
False in our promis'd rising, since our eyes
Open'd we find indeed, and find we know

Both good and evil, good lost, and evil got,
Bad fruit of knowledge !

AIR.

..............................." How shall I behold
Henceforth or God, or angel, erst with joy,
And rapture oft beheld ?   O ! might I here
In solitude live savage, in some glade
Obscur'd, where highest woods, impenetrable
To star or sun-light, spread their umbrage broad,
And brown as evening.   Cover me, ye pines,
Ye cedars, with innumerable boughs
Hide me, where I may never see them more."

RECITATIVE.

Would thou had'st hearken'd to my words, and stay'd
With me, as I besought thee, when that strange
Desire of wand'ring, this unhappy morn,
I know not whence possess'd thee ! we had then
Remain'd still happy ; not as now despoil'd
Of all our good, shamed, naked, mis'rable !

AIR.

" Let none henceforth, seek needless cause t' ap-
        prove
The faith they owe ; when earnestly they seek
Such proof, conclude they then begin to fail."

EVE.

Imput'st thou that to my desire, or will
Of wand'ring, as thou call'st it, which who knows
But might as ill have happen'd thou being by,
Or to thyself perhaps, had'st thou been there ?
" Was I t' have never parted from thy side,
As good have grown there still a lifeless rib.
Being as I am, why did'st not thou, the head,
Command me absolutely not to go,
Going into such danger as thou said'st."
Too facil then, thou did'st not much gainsay,
Nay, didst permit, approve, and fair dismiss.
Had'st thou been firm, and fix'd in thy dissent,
Neither had I transgress'd, nor thou with me.

ADAM.

AIR.

...........................…" Thus it shall befall
Him, who to worth in woman overtrusting,
Lets her will rule ; restraint she will not brook,
And left t' herself, if evil thence ensue,
She first his weak indulgence will accuse,"

SCENE III.

RECITATIVE.

ADAM.

O mis'rable of happy ! Is this the end
Of this new glorious world, and me so late
The glory of that glory ? who now become
Accurs'd of blessed ! Hide me from the face
Of God, whom to behold was then my height
Of happiness.   Yet well, if here would end
The mis'ry ; I deserv'd it, and would bear
My own deservings ; but this will not serve.
All that I eat, or drink, or shall beget,
Is propagated curse.   O voice once heard
Delightfully, " Increase, and multiply."
Now death to hear ! For what can I increase,
Or multiply, but curses on my head,

Heavy! though in their place? O fleeting joys
Of Paradise, dear bought with lasting woe!
" Did I request thee, Maker! from my clay,
To mould me man? Did I solicit thee
From darkness to promote me, or to place
In this delicious garden? As my will
Concurr'd not to my being, 't were but right
And equal to reduce me to my dust,
Desirous to resign, and render back
All I receiv'd."

#### EVE.

O Adam! can I thus behold thee wretched,
Thus mis'rable through my default, nor strive
To soothe thy grief, and soften thy distress?

#### ADAM.

Out of my sight, thou serpent! that name best
Befits thee, with him leagu'd, thyself as false,
And hateful................
.............................:....But for thee,
I had continued happy, had not thy pride,
And wand'ring vanity, when least was safe,
Rejected my forewarning, and disdain'd
Not to be trusted; longing to be seen,
Though by the Devil himself.

#### AIR.

.........................." O! why did God,
Creator wise! that peopled highest Heav'n
With spirits masculine, create at last
This novelty on Earth, this fair defect
Of Nature! and not fill the world at once
With men, as angels without feminine?"

#### EVE.

Forsake me not thus, Adam! Witness Heav'n!
What love sincere, and rev'rence in my heart
I bear thee, and unweeting have offended,
Unhappily deceiv'd! Thy supplicant
I beg, and clasp thy knees; "bereave me not,
Whereon I live, thy gentle looks—thy aid—
Thy counsel in this uttermost distress:
My only strength, and stay! Forlorn of thee,
Whither shall I betake me, where subsist?"
While yet we live, scarce one short hour perhaps,
Between us two let there be peace, both joining,
As join'd in injuries, one enmity
Against a foe, by doom express assign'd us,
That cruel serpent. On me exercise not
Thy hatred for this misery befallen,
On me already lost, me than thyself
More miserable: both have sinn'd, but thou
Against God only, I against God and thee:
And to the place of judgment will return,
There with my cries importune Heav'n, that all
The sentence, from thy head remov'd, may light
On me, sole cause to thee of all this woe,
Me! me! just object only of his ire.

#### ADAM.

Alas! ill able art thou to sustain
His full wrath, whose thou feel'st as yet least part,
And my displeasure bear'st so ill. If pray'rs
Could alter high decrees, I to that place
Would speed before thee, and be louder heard,
That on my head all might be visited,
Thy frailty, and infirmer sex forgiv'n,
To me committed, and by me expos'd.
But rise—let us no more contend, and blame

Each other, blam'd enough elsewhere, but strive
In offices of love, how we may lighten
Each other's burthen in our share of woe.
Then to the place repairing, where our judge
Pronounc'd our doom, there let us both confess
Humbly our faults, and pardon beg, with tears
Wat'ring the ground, and with our sighs the air
Frequenting, sent from hearts contrite, in sign
Of sorrow unfeign'd, and humiliation meek.

#### RECITATIVE ACCOMPANIED.

So spake our father penitent, nor Eve
Felt less remorse. They forthwith to the place
Repairing, where he judg'd them, prostrate fell
Before him reverent, and both confess'd
Humbly their faults, and pardon beg'd, with tears
Wat'ring the ground, and with their sighs the air
Frequenting, sent from hearts contrite, in sign
Of sorrow unfeign'd, and humiliation meek.

### SCENE IV.

#### RECITATIVE.

#### EVE.

What tidings bring'st thou, Adam! from this new
Angelical, so late arriv'd? Alas!            [guest
My trembling heart forebodes some further ill;
For far less mild me thought his aspect seem'd
Than Raphael's, social spirit! who wont so oft
To sit indulgent with us, and partake
Rural repast, permitting us the while
Venial discourse unblam'd. What tidings?—say.

#### ADAM.

Our pray'rs are heard in Heav'n, and death our due
By sentence then, when first we did transgress,
Is of his prey defeated many days
Giv'n us of grace, wherein we may repent.
So God appeas'd, from his rapacious claim
Will quite redeem us, and to life restore.
But longer in this Paradise to dwell,
As not befitting creatures stain'd with sin,
He suffers not, but sends us forth to till
The ground from whence he took us, fitter soil!

#### EVE.

#### AIR. AFFETUOSO.

" O! unexpected stroke, worse than of death!
Must I then leave thee, Paradise, thus leave
Thee, native soil! these happy walks, and shades,
Fit haunt of gods! where I had hope to spend
Quiet, though sad, the respite of that day,
That must be mortal to us both. O flow'rs!
That never will in other climate grow,
My early visitation, and my last
At ev'n, which I bred up with tender hand,
From the first op'ning bud, and gave you names,
Who now shall rear you to the Sun, and rank
Your tribes, and water from th' ambrosial fount?
Thee lastly, nuptial bow'r! by me adorn'd
With what to sight or smell was sweet; from thee
How shall I part, and whither wander down
Into a lower world, to this obscure,
And wild; how shall we breathe in other air
Less pure, accustom'd to immortal fruits?"

#### ADAM.

Lament not, Eve! but patiently resign
What justly we have lost, nor set thine heart

Thus overfond on that which is not ours.
Thy going is not lonely—I will guard
Thy steps from harm, and all thy wants supply.  •

### EVE.

Adam! I feel within new life, new hopes
By Heav'n and thee inspir'd.   Then now lead on,
In me is no delay.   " With thee to go,
Is to stay here.   Without thee here to stay,
Is to go hence unwilling.   Thou to me
Art all things under Heav'n, all places thou!
Who for my wilful crime art banish'd hence."
This further consolation yet secure
I carry hence—though all by me is lost,
Such favour I unworthy am vouchsaf'd,
By me the promis'd seed shall all restore.
   So spake our mother Eve.   And Adam heard
Well pleas'd, but answer'd not.   For now too nigh
The cherubim advanc'd ; and in their front
The brandish'd sword of God before them blaz'd,
Fierce as a comet, which, with torrid heat,
Smote on that clime so late their bless'd abode !
Some nat'ral tears they drop'd, but wip'd them soon:
The world was all before them, where to choose
Their place of rest, and Providence their guide.

CHORUS.   ALLEGRO.

" The world was all before them, where to choose
Their place of rest, and Providence their guide."

---

### TO THE COMPOSER.

The form of this piece is an historical drama, for this
reason amongst others, viz. the better to preserve
the very words and manner of Milton, which must
have been frequently altered, and in many instances greatly injured, by any other method. The
recitative consequently is of two kinds, *narrative*
and *interlocutory*.   Again, the *narrative* is either
*descriptive*, as in Act I.   Scene I. and other places,
or else *introductory* to the dialogue, as Scene II.
and elsewhere.   The composer will do well to have
an eye to these distinctions, as mere *description*,

or the *introductory narrative*, will admit of a different
kind of recitative from the *conversation part* ; the
one being like *painting* in *still life*, the other resembling the *portraits* of *living manners*.
   Perhaps he will wish that the dialogue contained
less of the recitative, and more of the air and chorus.   The compiler, however, is of opinion that
there is a due proportion of each.   And if there is
less opportunity for flourishes and repetitions, there
is more room for spirited and sensible expression,
to assist the effect of the dialogue upon the passions of the hearers, by means of an animated and
pathetic recitative, as well as by a full exertion
of the force of musical language in the airs, where
the length of the performance will but seldom admit of dwelling for a long time together in a display of the minute excellencies of this art.
   If the composer should think that in some places
the recitative is continued too long without the intervention of *airs*, in this case he will find fit places
for airs, besides what his own judgment will suggest
to him, marked in this manner, page 323, &c.

" I, from the influence of thy looks, receive."

Again, if he should think the parts assigned for
musical airs too prolix, in some places they may be
shortened, as in the Morning Hymn, from

Fairest of stars, last in the train of night,
to
Made vocal by my song, and taught his praise.

   The compiler is sensible that he ought to make
an apology to a composer, for presuming to interfere so much in his province, and he hopes the
true reason will be accepted as such, viz. that
having bestowed more attention upon this work
than it was likely any other person would, he
thought himself capable of pointing out the divi-
sion of it into its several parts of act, scene, recitative, air, song, chorus, and the like ; and of suggesting some few hints concerning the musical expression in general, though he confesses himself
incapable, at the same time, of executing the most
minute article of it.

THE

# POEMS

OF

## *HENRY BROOKE.*

THE

# LIFE OF HENRY BROOKE, ESQ.

## BY MR. CHALMERS.

This amiable and ingenious writer was a native of Ireland, where he was born in the year 1706. His father, the rev. W. Brooke of Rantavan, rector of the parishes of Killinkare, Mullough, Mybullough, and Licowie, is said to have been a man of great talents and worth : his mother's name was Digby. Our poet's education appears to have been precipitated in a manner not very usual; after being for some time the pupil of Dr. Sheridan, he was sent to Trinity College, Dublin, and from thence removed, when only seventeen years old, to study law in the Temple. Dr. Sheridan was probably the means of his being introduced in London to Swift and Pope, who regarded him as a young man of very promising talents. How long he remained in London we are not told ; but on his return to Ireland he practised for some time as a chamber counsel, when an incident occurred which interrupted his more regular pursuits, and prematurely involved him in the cares of a family.

An aunt, who died at Westmeath about the time of his arrival in Ireland, committed to him the guardianship of her daughter, a lively and beautiful girl between eleven and twelve years old. Brooke, pleased with the trust, conducted her to Dublin, and placed her at a boarding-school, where during his frequent visits he gradually changed the guardian for the lover, and at length prevailed on her to consent to a private marriage. In the life prefixed to his works, this is said to have taken place before she had reached her fourteenth year ; another account, which it is neither easy nor pleasant to believe, informs us that she was a mother before she had completed that year. When the marriage was discovered, the ceremony was again performed in the presence of his family.

For some time this happy pair had no cares but to please each other, and it was not until after the birth of their third child, that Brooke could be induced to think seriously how such a family was to be provided for. The law had long been given up, and he had little inclination to resume a profession which excluded so many of the pleasures of imagination, and appeared inconsistent with the feelings of a mind tender, benevolent, and somewhat romantic. Another journey to London, however, promised the advantages of literary society, and the execution of literary schemes by which he might indulge his genius, and be rewarded by fame and wealth. Accordingly, soon after his arrival, he renewed his acquaintance with his former friends, and published his philosophical poem, entitled Universal Beauty. This had been submitted to Pope, who probably contributed his assistance, and whose manner at least is certainly followed. At what time this occurred is uncertain. The second part was published in 1735, and the remainder about a year after. What fame or advantage he derived from it we know not, as no mention is made of him in the extensive correspondence of Pope or Swift. He was, however, obliged to return to Ireland, where for a short time he resumed his legal profession.

In 1737, he went a third time to London, where he was introduced to Lyttelton and others, the political and literary adherents of the prince of Wales, "who," it is said, "caressed him with uncommon familiarity, and presented him with many elegant and valuable tokens of his friendship." Amidst such society, he had every thing to point his ambition to fame and independence, and readily caught that fervour of patriotic enthusiasm which was the bond of union and the ground of hope in the prince's court.

In 1738, he published a Translation of the First Three Books of Tasso, of which it is sufficient praise that Hoole says, "It is at once so harmonious and so spirited, that I think an entire translation of Tasso by him would not only have rendered my task unnecessary, but have discouraged those from the attempt whose poetical abilities are much superior to mine."

He was, however, diverted from completing his translation by his political friends, who, among other plans of hostility against the minister of the day, endeavoured to turn all the weapons of literature against him. Their prose writers were numerous, but principally essayists and pamphleteers; from their poets they had greater expectations; Paul Whitehead wrote satires; Fielding comedies and farces; Glover, an epic poem; and now Brooke was encouraged to introduce Walpole in a tragedy. This was entitled Gustavus Vasa, the Deliverer of his Country, and was accepted by Drury Lane theatre and almost quite ready for performance, when an order came from the lord chamberlain to prohibit it. That it contains a considerable portion of party-spirit cannot be denied, and the character of Trollio, the Swedish minister, however unjustly, was certainly intended for sir Robert Walpole; but it may be doubted whether this minister gained much by prohibiting the acting of a play which he had not the courage to suppress when published, and when the sentiments, considered deliberately in the closet, might be nearly as injurious as when delivered by a mouthing actor. The press, however, remained open, and the prohibition having excited an uncommon degree of curiosity, the author was more richly rewarded than he could have been by the profits of the stage. Above a thousand copies were subscribed for at five shillings each, and by the sale of the subsequent editions the author is said to have cleared nearly a thousand pounds. The editor of the Biographia Dramatica says that it was acted, in 1742, with some alterations, on the Irish stage, by the title of The Patriot. Dr. Johnson, who at this time ranked among the discontented, wrote a very ingenious satirical pamphlet, in favour of the author, entitled A complete Vindication of the Licensers of the Stage from the malicious and scandalous Aspersion of Mr. Brooke, Author of Gustavus Vasa; 4to. 1739.

The fame Brooke acquired by this play, which has certainly many beauties, seemed the earnest of a prosperous career, and as he thought he could now afford to wait the slow progress of events, he hired a house at Twickenham, near to Pope's, furnished it genteelly, and sent for Mrs. Brooke and his family. But these flattering prospects were soon clouded. He was seized with an ague so violent and obstinate that his physicians, after having almost despaired of his life, advised him, as a last resource, to try his native air; with this he complied, and obtained a complete recovery. It was then expected that he should return to London; and such was certainly his intention; but to the surprise of his friends he determined to remain in Ireland. For a conduct so apparently inconsistent, not only with his interest but his inclination, he was long unwilling to account. It appeared afterwards, that Mrs. Brooke was alarmed at the zeal with which he espoused the cause of the opposition, and dreaded the consequences with which his next intemperate publication might be followed. She persuaded him therefore to remain in Ireland; and for so singular a measure, at this favourable crisis in his history, he could assign no adequate reason, without exposing her to the imputation of caprice, and himself to that of a too yielding temper.

During his residence in Ireland, he kept up a literary correspondence with his London friends; but all their letters were consumed by an accidental fire. Two from Pope, we are told, are particularly to be lamented, as, in one of these, he professed himself in heart a protestant, but apologized for not publicly conforming, by alleging that it would render the eve of his mother's life unhappy. Pope's filial affection is the most amiable feature in his character; but this story of his declining to conform because it would give uneasiness to his mother, falls to the ground when the reader is told that his mother had been dead six or seven years before Brooke went to Ireland. In another letter he is said, with more appearance of truth, to have advised Brooke to take orders, " as being a profession better suited to his principles, his disposition, and his genius, than that of the law, and also less injurious to his health." Why he did not comply with this advice cannot now be known; but before this time he appears to have been of a religious turn, although it is not easy to reconcile his principles, which were those of the strictest kind, with his continual ambition to shine as a dramatic writer.

For some years after his arrival in Ireland little is known of his life, except that lord Chesterfield, when viceroy, conferred upon him the office of barrack-master. His pen, however, was not idle. In 1741, he contributed to Ogle's version of Chaucer, Constantia, or the Man of Law's Tale; and in 1745, according to one account, his tragedy of The Earl of Westmoreland was performed, on the Dublin stage; but the editor of the Biographia Dramatica informs us that it was first acted at Dublin in 1741, under the title of The Betrayer of his Country; and again in 1754, under that of Injured Honour. Its fame, however, was confined to Ireland; nor was it known in England until the publication of his poetical works in 1778. A more important publication was his Farmer's Letters, written in 1745, on the plan of Swift's Drapier's Letters, and with a view to rouse the spirit of freedom among the Irish, threatened as they were, in common with their fellow-subjects, by rebellion and invasion. On this occasion Garrick addressed the following lines to him :

> Oh, thou, whose artless free-born genius charms;
> Whose rustic zeal each patriot bosom warms;
> Pursue the glorious task, the pleasing toil,
> Forsake the fields, and *till* a nobler soil;
> Extend the *farmer's* care to human kind,
> *Manure* the heart and *cultivate* the mind;
> There *plant* religion, reason, freedom, truth,
> And *sow the seeds* of virtue in our youth.

Let not *rank weeds* corrupt, or *brambles* choke,
And shake the *vermin* from the British oak;
From *northern blasts* protect the vernal bloom,
And guard our pastures from the *wolves of Rome;*
On Britain's liberty *engraft* thy name,
And *reap the harvest* of immortal fame!

In 1746, he wrote an Epilogue on the birth-day of the duke of Cumberland, spoken by Mr. Garrick in Dublin, and a Prologue to Othello, which are now added to his works. In 1747, he contributed to Moore's volume of Fables four of great poetical merit, viz. The Temple of Hymen, The Sparrow and Dove, The Female Seducer, and Love and Vanity. In 1748, he wrote a Prologue to The Foundling, which is now added to this edition, and a dramatic opera, entitled Little John and the Giants. This was acted only one night in Dublin, being then prohibited on account of certain political allusions. On this occasion, he wrote The Last Speech of John Good, alias, Jack the Giant Queller, a satirical effusion, not very pointed, and mixed with political allegory, and a profusion of quotations from scripture against tyrants and tyranny. In 1749, his Earl of Essex, a tragedy, was performed at Dublin, and afterwards, in 1760, at Drury Lane theatre, with so much success as to be preferred to the rival plays on the same subject, by Banks and Jones. At what time his other dramatic pieces were written, or acted, if acted at all, is uncertain[1].

His biographer informs us, that " wearied, at length, with fruitless efforts to rouse the slumbering genius of his country—disgusted with her ingratitude—and sick of her venality, he withdrew to his paternal seat, and there, in the society of the Muses, and the peaceful bosom of domestic love, consoled himself for lost advantages and disappointed hopes. An only brother, whom he tenderly loved, accompanied his retirement, with a family almost as numerous as his own; and there, for many years, they lived together with uninterrupted harmony and affection : the nephew was as dear as the son—the uncle as revered as the father—and the sister-in-law almost as beloved as the wife."

In 1762, he published a pamphlet entitled The Trial of the Roman Catholics; the object of which was to remove the political restraints on that class, and to prove that this may be done with safety. In this attempt, however, his zeal led him so far as to question incontrovertible facts, and even to assert that the history of the Irish massacre in 1641 is nothing but an old wife's fable; and upon the whole, he leans more to the principles of the Roman Catholic religion than an argument professedly political, or a mere question of extended toleration, seemed to require.

His next work excited more attention in England. In 1766, appeared the first volume of The Fool of Quality, or the History of the Earl of Moreland, a novel replete with knowledge of human life and manners, and in which there are many admirable traits of moral feeling and propriety, but mixed, as the author advances towards the close, with so much of religious discussion, and mysterious stories and opinions, as to leave it doubt-

---

[1] These were, The Contending Brothers, The Female Officer, and The Marriage Contract, comedies; The Impostor, a tragedy, and Cymbeline, an injudicious alteration from Shakspeare. Montezuma, a tragedy, is printed among his works, but is said to have been the production of another hand. Of these, The Female Officer only is said to have been once acted, when Mrs. Woffington personated the officer; probably at her benefit. *C.*

ful whether he inclined most to Behmenism or Popery. It became, however, when completed in five volumes, 1770, a very popular novel, and has often been reprinted since.

In 1772, he published Redemption, a poem, in which that great mystery of our religion is explained and amplified by bolder figures than are usually hazarded. His taste was, indeed, evidently on the decline; and in this, as well as all his later performances, he seems to have yielded to the enthusiasm of the moment, without any reserve in favour of his better judgment. In this poem too he appears to have left his pronunciation of the English so far as to introduce rhymes which must be read according to the vulgar Irish. His last work was Juliet Grenville, a novel in three volumes, which appeared in 1774. This is very justly entitled The History of the Human Heart, the secret movements of which few novelists have better understood; but there is such a mixture of the most sacred doctrines of religion with the common incidents and chit-chat of the modern romance, that his best friends could with difficulty discover among these ruins some fragments which indicated what his genius had once been.

In this year (1774) we are told that Garrick pressed him earnestly to write for the stage, and offered to enter into articles with him, at the rate of a shilling *per* line for all he should write during life, provided that he wrote for him alone. " This Garrick," says his biographer, " looked upon as an extraordinary compliment to Mr. Brooke's abilities; but he could not, however, bring him over to his opinion, nor prevail with him to accept of his offer ; on the contrary, he rejected it with some degree of haughtiness— for which Garrick never forgave him. He was then in the full and flattering career to fortune and to fame, and would have thought it a disgrace to hire out his talents, and tie himself down to necessity."

In this story there is enough to induce us to reject it. Brooke was so far from being, at this time, in the full and flattering career to fortune and to fame, that he had outlived both. And, supposing that there may be some mistake in the date of Garrick's proposal, and that for 1774 we should read 1764, or even 1754, the proposal itself is too ridiculous to bear examination.

Our author's tenderness of heart, and unsuspecting temper, involved him in pecuniary difficulties. He was ever prone to give relief to the distressed, although the immediate consequence of his liberality was that he wanted relief himself; and at length was compelled to dispose of his property, and remove to Kildare. After living some time here, he took a farm near his former residence. Where this residence was, his biographers have not mentioned; but soon after his return, they inform us that he lost his wife, to whom he had been happily united for nearly fifty years. The shock which this calamity gave to a mind never, I suspect, very firm, and the wreck of a family of seventeen children now reduced to two, was followed by a state of mental imbecility from which he never recovered. The confusion of his ideas, indeed, had been visible in most of his latter writings; and the infirmities of age completed what his family losses and personal disappointments had begun. His last days, however, were cheered by the hopes of religion, which became brighter as he approached the hour in which they were to be fulfilled. He died, October 10, 1783 [2], leaving a son, since dead, and a daughter, the child of his old age.

[2] He was in possession of the place of barrack-master of Mullingar at his death *C.*

His poetical works were collected in 1778, in four volumes octavo, printed very incorrectly, and with the addition of some pieces which were not his. In 1792 another edition was published at Dublin, by his daughter, who procured some memoirs of her father prefixed to the first volume. In this she informs us she found many difficulties. He had lived to so advanced an age that most of his contemporaries departed before him, and this young lady remembered nothing of him previous to his retirement from the world. Such an apology cannot be refused, while we must yet regret that Miss Brooke was not able to collect information more to be depended on, and arranged with more attention to dates. The narrative, as we find it, is confused and contradictory.

From all, however, that can now be learned, Brooke was a man of a most amiable character and ingenuous temper, and perhaps few men have produced writings of the same variety, the tendency of all which is so uniformly in favour of religious and moral principle. Yet even in this there are inconsistencies which we know not how to explain, unless we attribute them to an extraordinary defect in judgment. During a great part of his life, his religious opinions approached to what are now termed methodistical, and one difficulty, in contemplating his character, is to reconcile this with his support of the stage, and his writing those trifling farces we find among his works. Perhaps it may be said that the necessities of his family made him listen to the importunity of those friends who considered the stage as a profitable resource, but by taking such advice he was certainly no great gainer. Except in the case of his Gustavus and Earl of Essex, there is no reason to think that he was successful, and the greater part of his dramas were never performed at all, or printed, until 1778, when he could derive very little advantage from them. Nor can we impute it to any cause, except a total want of judgment and an ignorance of the public taste, that he intermixed the most awful doctrines of religion and the lighter incidents and humorous sketches of vulgar or fashionable life, in his novels.

He lived, however, we are told, more consistently than he wrote. No day passed in which he did not collect his family to prayer, and read and expounded the scriptures to them[3]. Among his tenants and humble friends he was the benevolent and generous character which he had been accustomed to depict in his works, and while he had the means, he literally went about doing good.

As a poet, he delights his readers principally by occasional flights of a vivid imagination, but has in no instance given us a poem to which criticism may not suggest many reasonable objections. The greater part of his life, he lived remote from the friends of whose judgment he might have availed himself, and by whose taste his own might have

---

[3] The following anecdote is given by his biographer, with some regret that he had not been educated for the church. " One Sunday, while the congregation were assembled in the rural church of the parish in which he lived, they waited a long time the arrival of their clergyman. At last, finding he was not likely to come that day, they judged that some accident had detained him; and being loth to depart entirely without their errand, they with one accord requested that Mr. Brooke would perform the service for them, and expound a part of the scriptures.—He consented, and the previous prayers being over, he opened the Bible, and preached extempore on the first text that struck his eye. In the middle of his discourse, the clergyman entered, and found the whole congregation in tears. He entreated Mr. Brooke to proceed; but this he modestly refused; and the other as modestly declared, that after the testimony of superior abilities, which he perceived in the moist eyes of all present, he would think it presumption and folly to hazard any thing of his own. Accordingly, the concluding prayers alone were said, and the congregation dismissed for the day." C.

been regulated.   His first production, Universal Beauty, has a noble display of fancy in many parts.   It is not improbable that Pope, to whom he submitted it, gave him some assistance, and he certainly repaid his instructor by adopting his manner, yet he has avoided Pope's monotony, and would have done this with more effect, if we did not perceive a mechanical lengthening of certain lines, rather than a natural variety of movement.   On the other hand, the sublimity of the subject, by which he was inspired, and which he hoped to communicate, sometimes betrays him into a species of turgid declamation.   Harmony appears to be consulted, and epithets multiplied, to please the ear at the expense of meaning.

The three books of Tasso have already been noticed, and the reader of the present collection may have an opportunity of comparing them with Hoole's translation.   The Man of Law's Tale, from Chaucer, will incline every reader to wish that he had contributed more to Ogle's translation.   Of all his original poems, the most correct are the four fables, first published in Moore's collection.   They are perhaps too long for fables, but as moral *tales* we have few that exceed them in poetical spirit, and sprightly turns of thought.   The Fox Chase and his lesser pieces, if we except some of the songs composed for his dramas, will add but inconsiderably to his fame.

# POEMS

OF

# *HENRY BROOKE.*

---

## *UNIVERSAL BEAUTY:*

### A PHILOSOPHICAL POEM,

### IN SIX BOOKS.

Πάντα δὶ αυτῶ ἐγένετο· καὶ χωρὶς αυτῶ ἐγένετο ἐδὲ ἕν, ὃ γέγονεν.
Εν αυτῷ ζωη ἦν, καὶ ἡ ζωη ἦν 'το φως των ἀνθρώπων.
Καὶ τὸ φῶς ἐν τῆ σκοτία φαίνει, καὶ ἡ σκοτία αὐτὸ ἐ κατέλαβεν.

---

### BOOK I.

The author introduces his work with a general survey of the whole, in nature of the plan or argument; and then commences a-new with a demonstration, a priori, of the being and attributes of God. Thence proceeds to creation, in which he endeavours at an opinion of the manner, as near as possible he may; as also of the nature and difference of the substances of spirit and matter; the economy of the universe; the astronomic system, physics, anatomy, and most branches of natural philosophy; in which the technical terms are as few, and the whole explained and made as easy and obvious as possible. The connection, dependence, use, and beauty, of the whole. Man considered; the nature of his being; the manner of his attaining knowledge; the analysis of the mind, faculties, affections, and passions; how they consist in each individual, and in the species. The nature of freedom; that it is not in the will; what it is, and wherein it consists, demonstrated. Of vice, misery, virtue, and happiness; their nature and final tendency. The whole being wrought into one natural and connected scheme, the author rises whence he began, and ends with a poetical rhapsody in the contemplation of the beauty of the whole.

VOL. XVII.

## UNIVERSAL BEAUTY.

TRITONIA! goddess of the new-born skies,
 Birth-day of Heav'n, wise daughter of th' All-
  wise;
When from Jove's head in perfect sapience born,
Of Heaven you rose the first empyreal morn,
As erst descend——
To mortals thy immortal charms display,
And in our lake thy heavenly form survey!
 Or rather thou, whom ancient prophet styles
Venus Urania! born the babe of smiles,
When from the deep thy bright emergence sprung,
And Nature on thy form divinely hung;        11
Whose steps, by Loves and Graces kiss'd, advance,
And laughing Hours lead on the sprightly dance;
While Time, within eternal durance bound,
Harmonious moves on golden hinges round—
Such, goddess! as when Silence wondering gaz'd,
And even thyself beheld thyself amaz'd;
Such haply by that Côon artist known,
Seated apparent queen on Fancy's throne;

Ver. 1. *Tritonia.*] Minerva, the goddess of wisdom, is fabled to have sprung from the head of Jupiter; and, coming down on Earth, to have viewed her own perfections in the lake Triton in Africa, from whence she was called Tritonia. She is here addressed as the *idea* of the self-existent author of all things, as first containing in itself the beauty of all created things; and, after, surveying that beauty by reflection from the things so created.

Ver. 9. *Venus Urania.*] This Venus, whom the ancients styled Urania, or heavenly, is addressed as representing nature, or the creation, rising out of chaos in the perfection of beauty.

Ver. 18. *Côon artist.*] Apelles, born in the island Cos or Côos.

Z

---

From thence thy shape his happy canvass bless'd,
And colours dipt in Heaven thy heavenly form
　　confess'd——　　　　　　　　　　21
Such, goddess! through this virgin foliage shine;
Let kindling beauties glow through every line,
And every eye confess the work divine.
　O say, while yet, nor time, nor place was found,
And space immense in its own depth was drown'd;
If nothing was, or something yet was not,
Or though *to be*, e'erwhile was *unbegot*;
If caus'd, then how?—if causeless, why effect?
(No hand to form, nor model to direct)　　30
Why ever made?—so soon?—or why so late?
What chance, what will, what freedom, or what
　　fate?——
Matter, and spirit, fire, air, ocean, earth;
All Nature born, nor conscious of its birth!——
Alike unconscious did the womb disclose,
And nothing wonder'd whence this something rose—
Then, by what power?—or what such power could
　　move?
Wisdom, or chance?—necessity, or love?　　38
O, from what root could such high plenty grow?
From what deep fount such boundless oceans flow?
What fund could such unwearied wealth afford?
Subjects unnumber'd! where, O where's your lord?
Whence are your attributes of time and place
Won from eternity and boundless space?
Motion from rest? just order from misrule?
A world from nought?—all empty, now all full!
From silence harmony? from darkness light?
And beamy day from everlasting night?
Light, matter, motion, music, order, laws!
And silent dark nonentity the cause?　　50
But chance, you'll say—I ask you, chance of what,
If nothing was?—'t is answer'd, chance of nought.
Alike from matter mov'd, could Beauty rise,
The florid planets, and gay ambient skies;
Or painted skies, and rolling orbs, dispense
Perception, life, thought, reason, judgment, sense.
Mysterious Thought! swift angel of the mind!
By space unbounded, though to space confin'd,
How dost thou glow with just disdain, how scorn,
That thought could ever think thee earthly born?
Thou who canst distance motion in thy flight,　61
Wing with aspiring plume the wondrous height,
Swifter than light outspeed the flame of day,
Pierce through the dark profound, and shame the
　　darting ray;
Throughout the universal system range,
New form old systems, and new systems change;
Through nature traffic on, from pole to pole,
And stamp new worlds on thy dilated soul;
(By time unlimited, unbound by space)
Sure demonstration of thy heavenly race,　　70
Deriv'd from that, which is deriv'd from none,
Which ever *is*—but of Himself alone!　[in vain,
　O could'st thou search—nor may'st thou search
Haply some glimpse, some dawning to obtain,
Some taste divine of thy eternal spring,
Above those Heliconian bards to sing—
How He who inaccessible remains,
Yet omnipresent through all nature reigns;

Ver. 48. ...... *from everlasting night.*] Such supposed as originally so, and being eternal.
Ver. 53. ...... *from matter mov'd.*] One of the
atheistical unaccountable evasions, is to account
for the order of nature by matter and motion.

Whose age blooms ever in eternal youth,
His substance, beauty, and essential truth,　　80
Essential truth! and beauty's charm! in course,
Of boundless love the ever boundless source!
Of boundless love, which would not, could not miss,
To be the boundless source of boundless bliss!—
Beatitude, rejecting all access!
Repletion, never to be more, nor less!,
Why this ineffable, this inexpress'd,
This fulness in himself, past utterance bless'd,
Spontaneous pour'd these wondrous worlds around,
And fill'd with blessings this immense profound?
　Swift roll'd the spheres to their appointed place,
Jocund through Heaven to run the various race;
Orb within orb in living circlets turn,　　　93
And central suns through every system burn;
Revolving planets on their gods attend,
And tow'rds each sun with awful reverence bend;
Still tow'rds the lov'd enliv'ning beam they wheel,
And pant, and tremble, like the amorous steel.
They spring, they revel in the blaze of day, [ray,
Bathe in the golden stream, and drink the orient
Their blithe satellites with lively glance,　　101
Celestial equipage, around them dance;
All, distance due, and beauteous order keep,
And spinning soft, upon their centres sleep:
The eternal clue the mazy labyrinth guides,
While each in his appointed movement glides;
Transverse, elliptic, oblique, round they run;
Like atoms wanton in the morning Sun;
The seeming vagrants joy to cheat the view,　109
These turn, these change, these fly, and these pur-
Th' implicit discipline to order tends,　[sue;
And still in regular confusion ends—
Each to his native vortex is assign'd,
And magic circles every system bind;
A deeper charm each individual holds,
And firm within its atmosphere enfolds;
The secret spell, through every part, and whole,
Distinct, entire, invades it like a soul;
Its atoms at the amorous touch cohere,
And knit, in universal wedlock share.　　120
　All-teeming wedlock! on the genial hour,
Space furnish'd out one boundless nuptial bow'r;
Ten thousand thousand worlds, profusely gay,
The pomp of bridal ornament display—
How modified, here needless to be told;
Whether terrene, or of ethereous mould;
Gross, porous, firm, opaque, condense, or rare;
Or argent, with celestial tempering clear;
Pellucid, to imbibe the streaming light;
Or dun, but with reflected radiance bright;　130
Or dazzling shrine, or of corporeal leaven,
Terrestrial, that unfold an earthly Heaven
Unspeakable! their landscape hill, and dale,
The lowly sweetness of the flowery vale,
The mount elate that rises in delight,
The flying lawns that wanton from the sight,
The florid theatres, romantic scenes,
The steepy mountains, and luxuriant plains,　138
Delicious regions! plants, woods, waters, glades,
Grots, arbours, flowrets, downs, and rural shades,
The brooks that sportive wind the echoing hills,
The pearly founts, smooth lakes, and murmuring
Myriads of Edens! blissful, blissful seats! [rills—
Arcadian groves, sweet Tempe's blest retreats,

Ver. 115. *A deeper charm.*] Attraction or gravitation.

Delightful Ennas, and Hesperian isles,
And round, and round throughout, Elysium smiles—
Consummate joy, peace, pleasure without end,
Through mansions numberless their guests attend,
Nor long inanimate—As when some cloud
Throws on the beamy noon her sable shroud, 150
Wide o'er the green a dusk and stillness creep,
And glittering swarms beneath the verdure sleep;
Quick, and at once, the drowsy shade gives way;
At once breaks forth the bright enlivening ray;
At once, the gay, the quickening insects rise,
And gilded squadrons strike our wond'ring eyes;
Music flies wanton from ten thousand wings,
And life and joy through every region rings—
Or when glad news some sudden transport start,
The flood swells instant in the labouring heart;
The limbs its lively energy attest, 161
And catch contagion from th' exulting breast;
Tumultuous, through our little world it flies,
Smiles in the dimpling cheek, and lightens from
the eyes—
Or so—or yet beyond compare—as wide
As spaces endless from some point divide,
Sudden the universal world conceives;
As sudden, Nature with her burden heaves;
Quick pulses through each throbbing art'ry beat,
And all the matron glows with genial heat; 170
At once reveals her offspring to the sight;
Up spring the numbers numberless, to light!
The one, the various, blessed, glorious birth,
Of every world, Heaven, ocean, air, and earth—
Diverse, throughout their infinite abodes;
Their essence, nature, virtues, forms, and modes
Ineffable! that mock where fancy soars,
Or what the deep of deepest thought explores,
By visionary semblance, quaint device,
By gloss, trope, type abstruse, or emblem nice—
Ideal, how untoward to convey, 181
Or reach conception by the dark assay.
All perfect, yet alike not perfect found,
With differing virtues, differing glories crown'd;
The prime pre-eminent, and heavenly born,
Whom splendours next to deity adorn,
Lightnings divine, endued with native right
Of regal sceptre and transcending might,
Such, whom eternal Prescience might invest
Far blazing, with monarchal titles grac'd; 190
Of bright, the brightest; pure, the most refin'd;
All intellect, quintessence of the mind;
Cherubic harmonies, seraphic flames,
Empyreal natures with empyreal names,
Natives of Heaven!—Nor want the lucid spheres,
Of bless'd inheritance the blissful heirs;
Angelic shapes that wing th' ethereal space,
And scarce inferior to the heavenly race;
An incompounded radiant form they claim,
Nor spirit all—nor yet corporeal frame; 200
Than one, more dense—than t'other, more refin'd;
If spirit, organiz'd—if matter, mind:
Their essence one, imperishable, bright,
Vital throughout, all heart, ear, sense, and sight.
Through various worlds still varying species
range,
While order knits, and beautifies by change;
While from th' Unchangeable, the One, the Wise
Still changing endless emanations rise,
Of substance duplicate, or triple, mix'd,
Single, ambiguous, or free, or fix'd, 210
From those array'd in Heaven's resplendent robes,
To the brute essence on terrestrial globes;

Nor such inelegant, nor less demand
The curious texture of th' Almighty hand:
Thrice happy all, and lords of wide domains,
Celestial vales and elemental plains!
One is the flood which universal flows;
And hence the reptile, hence the seraph glows:
Still equal, though inequal, that and this; 219
Since fulness bounds, and all are fill'd with bliss.
Now had the Eternal Architect supreme,
In amplitude stretch'd out this wondrous frame,
Equip'd magnificent the house of God, [abode!
Through height, and depth, his boundless, blest
One house, one world, one universe divine,
Where countless orbs through countless systems
shine;
Systems, which, view'd throughout the circuit wide,
Or lost, or scarce the pointed sight abide,
(Through space immense with diminution seen)
Yet boundless to those worlds that roll within; 230
Each world as boundless to its native race,
That range and wanton through its ample space,
Frequent, through fields, through clouds of fra-
grance stray,
Or skim the wat'ry or ethereal way:
For now, with vivid action, nature swarms,
And life's dear stream the purpling conduit warms;
The continent, blithe air, and floating seas,
The smiling lakes, swift floods, and winding bays,
The nooks, the crannies, nurse a numerous brood,
And aptly yield their alimental food, 240
Adjusted to the trunk's unwieldy size,
As nice proboscis of luxurious flies,
Or azure tribes that o'er the damson bloom,
And paint the regions of the ripening plum.
From every root, the lavish plenty grows;
In every stream, perpetual pleasure flows;
Each ravish'd sense with endless bounty feast,
The soul, and ear, and eye, and smell, and touch,
and taste. [queath;
Their sweets, the blossoms plants and flowers be-
Elixirs from the steaming vapours breathe; 250
In balm imbosom'd every region lies,
Of ambient ether and infolding skies;
As the great Mover wrap'd each wheeling sphere
In the soft down of elemental air
Transparent, to imbibe the golden beam,
And wide around spun out th' ethereal stream,
Where worlds in endless revolutions move,
And swim on the abyss of endless Love.
Urania! Nature! from thy heights descend,
And low to Earth thy bright irradiance bend; 260
Dispell the clouds that round our fancy stray,
The mist that damps our intellectual ray;
And show what power all height of power transcends,
And in one act performs ten thousand ends.
Say, why this globe has its appointed place,
And why not vagrant through the boundless space?
Why here preferr'd, sagacious to refuse
What thwarts propriety, convenience, use?
Why not more neighbour to the burning ray,
Or more remote from the declining day? 270
Or here, not sedentary fix'd and still,
Admonish'd by no voice, obsequious to no will?
Or moving, why in circling eddies round,
And not progressive through th' immense profound?

Ver. 265. *Say, why this globe.*] The advantage of
the Earth's situation——
Ver. 271. *Or here.*] of its motions——

Or endless while the dizzy drunkard reels,
And round the Sun its annual motion wheels,
Whence that innate and delegated pow'r,
Central to spin the swift diurnal tour?
Not self-revolv'd, throughout its airy race,
It might expose one constant sultry face,          280
Damn its antipodes with endless night,
And curse with fire the restless sons of light;
These ne'er to slumber on the dewy lawn,
Nor those to rise and bless the golden dawn.
Or though rotation duplicate endears
Sweet change of days and nights and rolling years;
What new vicissitudes of motion bring
The seasons, circling, to the vernal spring?
Whether through Heav'n the winding compass steers,
Or pendulous by mutual balance veers?          290
What Secret Hand the trepidation weighs,
Or through the zodiac guides the spiral pace?
What magic wand the floating orb confines
With polar circles and the tropic lines?
Or does some Voice the potent charm command?
Too potent for unwieldy worlds to stand!—
" Here, nor elsewhere, thou Earth, thy station keep;
Here, roll thy progress through the boundless deep!
My word 's the bias, and my will 's the way,          299
That wheels thy circlet round the lord of day;
That round thy axis spins thy cumbrous frame;
That cheers thee with the still-returning beam;
That whirls thy wondrous motions, one in three,
Where time and place, still varying, still agree."
Omniscience here no lower mean admits;
One slip had maim'd ten thousand thousand hits,
Where to one point unnumber'd causes tend,
Concurring to effect one destin'd end,
Which once attain'd pours forth ten thousand more;
A blessed sea, that never knows a shore!          310
" Ye learn'd! who wisely can deny your God,
And banish Omnipresence with a nod;
In shrewd contempt, at final causes sneer;
In wilful deafness shut the tortuous ear,
Nor think it suited to the sounds ye hear;
Who, in your wisdoms, negatively spy
How vain 's the texture of the useless eye;
While fondly thus prime reasoners you 'd commence,
By literally exploding common sense,
And plead for one concession (only due)          320
That Nature must have err'd—in forming you—
Approach, ye sages, to your parent Earth,
Much wiser than the clods on whom she lavish'd
     birth!"
With deepest art, her skilful plan she lays;
With equal scale, the least advantage weighs;


Ver. 277. Whence that innate.] Diurnal, giving
to its inhabitants the grateful vicissitude of day
and night, adjusted to the times of labour and rest.
     Ver. 287. What new vicissitudes.] The manner
of its annual motion, calculated for the useful and
delightful variety of the seasons; the mutual allay
of immoderate heat and cold; as also for the successive growth and recruit of vegetative nature.
     Ver. 311. Ye learn'd.] The stupidity of those
who will not perceive.
     Ver. 324. With deepest art.] How, even to the
extent of infinite wisdom, as nothing less could be
the author, (vide supra, l. 305) all is formed and
contrived, and in that contrivance adapted, and in
that adaption directed, and in that direction extended distinctly, and in that distinction entirely,

How apt for time, place, circumstance, and use,
She culls all means, that to all ends conduce!
Nice to a point, each benefit selects;
As prudent, every mischief she rejects;
In due proportions, time and motion, metes,          330
Advances to a hair, and to a hair retreats:
Constant to good, for that alone she veers,
And with the varying beam her offspring cheers;
Cools all beneath her equinoctial line,
And gives the day throughout the world to shine;
The nitre from the frozen pole unseals,
And to the tropic speeds the pregnant gales;
Here, leaves th' exhausted fallow to recruit;
Here, plumps and burnishes the ripening fruit;
Superfluous hence withdraws the sultry beam,          340
Here drinks anew the vivifying flame;
Returns, still faithful to the labouring steer—
Wide waves the harvest of the golden year;
Trades universal on from pole to pole,
Inspires, revives, and cultivates the whole;
Frugal, where lack, supplies with what redounds,
And here bestows what noxious there abounds;
This with the gift, and that with giving, bless'd,
Alike throughout, of every wish possess'd.
Wrap'd in her airy car the matron glides,          350
And o'er the firmament ascending rides;
The subtile mass its copious mantle spreads,
Its mantle wove of elemental threads;
Th' elastic flue of fluctuating air,
Transfus'd invisible, enfolds the sphere;
With poinance delicate pervades the whole,
Its ear, eye, breath, and animating soul;
Active, serene, compress'd, rare, cool'd, or warm'd,
For life, health, comfort, pleasure, business,
     form'd;
Useful around, throughout, above, beneath!          360
By this, the quadrupeds, the reptiles breath;
This gives the bloom of vegetative life;
Corrects the seeds of elemental strife;


for the life, light, and comfort of the whole, and
through that whole of every part of this our globe!
of infinitely possible inconveniences, no one avoid-
able inconvenience being admitted; as of infinite
advantages attainable, there is not one, consistent
with the nature of this Earth, left out.
     Ver. 350. Wrap'd in her airy car.] The wonderful
texture of the air or atmosphere.
     Ver. 356. With poinance delicate.] its surprising
subtlety, penetrating even deep below the surface
of the Earth——
     Ver. 357. Its ear.] by which it is as it were one
universal sense to this our globe——
     Ver. 358. Active, serene.] its modification, ad-
mitting various, contrary, and even seemingly inconsistent qualities, suited as well to the single and
separate interests of every individual, as to the entire and uniform weal of the whole——
     Ver. 361. By this, the quadrupeds.] communi-
cating and continuing respiration to the animal
creation——
     Ver. 362. This gives the bloom.] as also an in-
ferior or analagous respiration to all plants and
vegetables——
     Ver. 363. Corrects the seeds.] raising harmony
from disorder, and friendship from enmity, by fermenting and reconciling heat and cold, the fiery
and watery particles, for the better conception
and genial production of the beauties of nature.

Broods o'er the eggs, in airy caverns laid,
Warm'd in the down of their ethereal bed ;
Gives motion to the swimmers of the flood ;
Gives music to the warblers of the wood ;
Rebounds in echo from the doubling vale,
And wafts to Heaven th' undulating gale:
Here hush'd, translucid smiles the gentle calm ;   370
And here impearl'd, sheds meek the show'ry balm ;
Salubrious here, a lively rapture claims,
And winnows pure the pestilential steams ;
Here buoys the bird high on the crystal wave,
Whose level plumes the azure concave shave ;
Here sits voluptuous in the swelling sail,
The vessel dancing to the sprightly gale!
Its varied power to various uses tends,
And qualities occult achieve contrarious ends ; `
With generative warmth fomenting breed,        380
Or alimental with nutrition feed ;
In opposition reconcil'd to good,
Alike the menstruum, as sustaining food:
Or here restorative, destructive here ;
Here Nature's cradle, here her fun'ral bier ;
With keen dispatch on all corruption preys,
And grateful from our aching sense conveys ;
Returns the bane into its native earth,
And there revives it to a second birth,
Renew'd and brighten'd like the minted ore,   390
To shoot again to life, more gorgeous than before!

---

## UNIVERSAL BEAUTY.

### BOOK II.

This, and the two ensuing books, contain and finish
the general survey or epitome of the whole, being a piece in itself distinct and complete.  The
author then commences de novo, and proposes to
answer. every doubt, and illustrate at full every
part of the foregoing abridgment.

---

Thus does the maz'd inexplicable round,
The aspiring bard and all his flights confound ;
Ambitious through his airy tour to sing,
High born above the soar of Pegasean wing ;

Ver. 364. *Broods o'er the eggs.*] affording a commodious receptacle or nursery for the eggs of
numberless animalcules——
   Ver. 366. *Gives motion.*] conveying the watery
inhabitants in their element by the assistance of
the swimming bladder——
   Ver. 367. *Gives music.*] modulating and com-
posing as it were one universal organ for sound
and music, so as the atmosphere becomes an entire harmony——
   Ver. 370. *Here hush'd.*] affording the pleasure
and sweetness of serenity——
   Ver. 371. *And here impearl'd.*] the nourishment
of dews——
   Ver. 372. *Salubrious here.*] and the health of
winds, or ventilations, that purge the noxious vapours and preserve nature fresh and vigorous——
   Ver. 374. *Here buoys the bird.*] wafting the
winged tribes in their airy voyages——
   Ver. 376. *Here sits voluptuous.*] and, by a speedy
navigation, spreading commerce and society
throughout the globe.
   Ver. 378. *Its varied power.*] The various influence

Or rais'd sublime in prospect, while he turns,
Views nature round, and still with rapture burns:
Now in this light the charmer he surveys,
This light he hopes her ev'ry charm displays ;
But here unthought-of charms discover'd lie,
And flash new wonders on th' admiring eye ;   10
While Beauty, changing with alternate grace,
Varies the Heaven of her all-lovely face.
Bewilder'd thus, from scheme to scheme he's toss'd,
And in inextricable windings lost ;
Where to begin, proceed, or how conclude,
This part omit, or hopeless thus elude,
Doubtful.  Again elated in his theme,
A daring unexampl'd task he 'd claim,
And wide unfold the universal frame ;
In mortal draught immortal Beauty snare,      20
And stamp this leaf as Nature's volume fair.
   High argument!  nor hopeless to prevail,
Though for the flight Dedalian plumage fail ;
Though erst of that ambitious youth we read,
Dismounted from the Muse's fabled steed,
And story with alluding caution tell,
How from the Sun's bright car the headlong driver
Nature, unerring tutoress, shall preside,   [fell:
And through her endless revolutions guide ;
Her various maze its windings shall unbraid,   30
Her doublings trace themselves, while self betray'd
Her complications to connection lead.
   For while the circumambient air we sing,
Its springy tension and elastic spring ;
The quick vibration of the yielding mass ;
How objects through its lucid medium pass ;
For Nature how the smiling glass expands ;
Narcissus-like, how beauteous Nature stands,
Self-lov'd within the splendid mirror shines,
But self-enjoy'd, nor like Narcissus pines ;   40
How, as a talisman of magic frame,
This atmosphere conveys th' enlight'ning beam,

of the air on all bodies, animate or inanimate: first,
in the generation of particular beings ; then, in
their nutrition ; thirdly, affording a healing balsam to the hurts or wounds of all creatures, when
recoverable ; but if past remedy, fourthly, hastening their dissolution, to rid the world of the nuisance,
by restoring the matter to its original principle of
nativity ; fifthly, to send again the new-modelled
being blooming afresh in animal life, or vegetation.
   For the use of the atmosphere as a medium and
mirror, vide book ii. line 33, &c.
   Ver. 23. .........*Dedalian plumage fail.*] Icarus.
   Ver. 24. .........*youth we read.*] Bellerophon.
   Ver. 27. .........*driver fell.*] Phaeton.
   Ver. 33. *For while the circumambient air.*] The
advantage of the atmosphere's elastic texture ; by
which it yields to, and closes imperceptibly upon,
all moving bodies——
   Ver. 36. *How objects.*] the surprising transpa-
rency, continuity, and coherence of its parts, forming an uninterrupted medium for the conveyance
of all objects to the eye——
   Ver. 37. *For Nature.*] by which it is, as it were,
an universal looking-glass, wherein all Nature beholds, admires, and enjoys her own complete perfections——
   Ver. 41. *How, as a talisman.*] Its curious disposition for the conveyance of light ; which would be
of no use in vacuo, as it is only perceptible itself,
by rendering other objects visible.

Reflects, inflects, refracts the orient ray;
Anticipating sheds the rising day—
High from his seat the solar glory heaves,
(Whose image fires the horizontal waves)
Abridging, shears the sable robe of night,
And through the globe protracts the cheerful light;
With sweet preambling twilight blends the shade,
And gently lets our evening beam recede.　50
　　Thus, borne on airy wings, the radiance flies,
Quickening the vision of poetic eyes;
Whence we may pierce into the deep profound,
And, searching, view the wondrous system round:
For wide as universal.Nature spreads,
Light's sacred fount its streaming lustre sheds;
Still orient, to the parting beam succeeds;
Through azure climes a sumless journey speeds;
Its restless longitude the glory darts,
Nor less a boundless latitude imparts;　60
Where matter borders on retiring space,
Impulsive urges the perpetual race ;
Stupendous length, illimited by aught
Of numbers summ'd or multiply'd by thought !
But whence the light's invigorating force,
Its active energy, or secret source,
Must be ascrib'd to that Eternal Spring,
Whom first, and last, and ever bless'd, we sing—
Who only could his effluent angel send ;
Athwart the gulf the radiant blaze extend;　70

　Ver. 43. *Reflects, inflects.*] Its still more wonderful quality, in not only reflecting, but refracting,
and inflecting the morning and evening beam ; in
appearance, lifting the Sun about four degrees
above his station, and refracting the light to us
when the Sun is about eighteen degrees below
the horizon; by which means our day is prolonged
about two hours, and the tedious night in the frigid zones shortened annually about thirty-two
days——
　Ver. 49. *With sweet preambling.*] by refraction of
the rays creating the dawn and gradual twilight ;
without which we should be suddenly immersed
in an intolerable flood of day, and without a moment's warning shut up in immediate darkness.
　Ver. 51. *Thus, born on airy wings.*] The use of
light must be apparent to as many as have eyes to
enjoy its benefit; but much more to those who, the
further they pry into Nature, by the assistance of
this element, will still more and more discover an
inexhaustible fund for delight and admiration——
　Ver. 55. *For wide as universal Nature.*] What can
be more amazing than the expansion and extension
of light, which, though a body, propagated from
body, and ponderous in its nature, is so thin and
subtile, as to reach and dilate through an inconceivable compass of space, before the whole content would amount to one drachm of weight——
　Ver. 61. *Where matter borders.*] The swiftness
and length of its progress is no less admirable, extending possibly ad infinitum, and moving in one
second of time near two hundred thousand of our
miles; without which miraculous velocity, its useful and glorious effect and influence could never be
preserved——
　Ver. 65. *But whence the light's.*] and as this
perpetuated motion and vigour has not the least
relation to any property inherent in matter, it can
only be accounted for as flowing from the original
Fountain of light and truth——
　Ver. 69. *Who only could.*] who alone could speed

Kindle the mass to incorporeal speed ;
The flame with never-dying splendours feed;
With heat the universal page unseal;
With light the universal charm reveal ;
In prospect wide th' illustrious work display,
And gem the pavement of the milky way ;
Make grace from use, and use from beauty flow ;
With florid pencil shade the jasper bow ;
The warring elements in wedlock bind,
Water and fire, dull earth and active wind ;　80
Knit by Almighty order they cohere,
And in their ever-varying offsprings share.
　First to the deep he speeds his eldest born,
Whose rosy progress paints the purpling morn ;
The mingling glories o'er the surface play,
And ocean dances to the trembling ray.
　Wide to the beam his ample sea he spreads,
And deep beneath subside the briny beds;
'The spacious beds the liquid realms contain ;
The seasoning tinctures purge the foamy main;　90
But, pois'd by balance of eternal weight,
The salts perpetual hold their wat'ry seat,
Nor in the tepid exhalations mount,
To fire the crystal of the cooling fount.
Th' Almighty Fiat bade the deep conceive,
And finn'd with clustring tribes the vital wave,
From huge leviathan's enormous frame,
To those who tincturing paint the crimson stream;
With wat'ry wings they skim the yielding seas;
Their central poise its gravitation weighs,　100
Adjusted, steady to their varying size,
By geometric rule, and calculation nice :
These have their palaces and coral groves,
Their latent grots, and pearly bright alcoves;
Wide is the copious hand of Bounty spread,
And myriads at the plenteous feast are fed.

and support this his winged messenger, on his universal errand to Nature——
　Ver. 73. *With heat.*] giving power to him only
of unsealing her treasures, and unfolding her beauties; whereby the world's glorious and harmonious
system becomes obvious, and the whole evidently
as elegant as it is useful.
　Ver. 79. *The warring elements.*] Is it not wonderful, that even Almighty power, out of one principle
of matter, should constitute four; and by an endless compounding, modifying, and changing those
four, should produce that infinite variety which is
visible in the universe ?
　Ver. 83. ........ *eldest born.*] Light. Beside the
two elements of air and light, already treated of,
what a spacious field do the waters, and first the
ocean, yield for contemplation and praise !
　Ver. 87. *Wide to the beam.*] In the expansion of
its superficies, without which it would never afford
a sufficient quantity of vapours, to supply the
thirsty land——
　Ver. 88. *And deep beneath.*] the methods by
which its waters are preserved pure from corruption, by the mixture of salts, whose weight is
calculated to prevent their exhaling——
　Ver. 95. *Th' Almighty Fiat.*] the number, size,
and qualities of its inhabitants, all adapted to its
gross and tempestuous medium——
　Ver. 103. *These have their palaces.*] being provided, without their own labour, with all the delights
and conveniences of life——
　Ver. 105. *Wide is the copious hand.*] as well as
nourishment for the support of it——

Nor less the grateful light salutes their eye,
And solar glories gild the nether sky;
Their ocean blushes with the lord of day,
And nightly glitters at the twinkling ray.  110
The Moon, attended by her starry train,
Reflects reflection to the floating plain,
Its murm'ring flux with pale dominion guides,
And swells the pride of its returning tides;
The deep those wholesome agitations purge,
And drive stagnation from the rolling surge;
Their rage the Sovereign Moderator cools,
And riding, as a steed the bounding billow rules;
Whence rising floods their stated empire know,
Nor wasteful o'er the neighbouring regions flow.  120
   Low as the sea's capacious basin sinks,
The thirsty soil th' incumbent ocean drinks;
Whence through the globe diluting liquors pass,
And circulate, as in our smaller mass;
The salts with curious percolation strain,
And kindly through the porous strata drain,
Attracted, in a maze of tubes exhale;
(A stiffening clay cements the spacious vale)
From whence oppos'd, the mountain's height they claim,
And thence perpetual pour the winding stream;  130
Or lower, in perennial fountains rise,
Nor dread the star that fires autumnal skies.
   While ocean thus the latent store bequeaths,
Above its humid exhalation breathes;

Ver. 107. *Nor less.*] their ocean being a medium and atmosphere to them, as our atmosphere is to us; and equally suited to their natures, for respiration, as the conveyance of light from the heavenly luminaries——
   Ver. 113. *Its murm'ring flux.*] How admirably is the Moon's influence on tides (which preserves the great body of waters from stagnation) regulated, to the very point that can alone conduce to order and advantage: were she nearer, or larger; further off, or less; or were there more moons, so as on any hand the influence should be in the least altered; the whole Earth would be rendered uninhabitable, by being poisoned with stagnated vapours, or perpetually overflowed with deluges——
   Ver. 123. *Whence through the globe.*] as there is no point from whence the riches of Nature do not flow in upon us; so there are two (though seemingly most opposite) methods of supplying us with sweet and refreshing waters; one perennial, and from beneath, being thence attracted through our globe, as any liquid when touched by a piece of sugar; which cannot be ascribed to the pressure of our atmosphere, as it is readier performed in vacuo; the salts being separated by filtration through the strata, and the rising waters being opposed by a clayey substance that generally lies near the surface of the lower lands, they proceed to the mountains, from whence, by the advantage of a descent, they spread wealth and pleasure round all the Earth——
   Ver. 133. *While ocean thus.*] The other method being by exhalation, the manner as above described; for heat being the most subtile, light, and agile of all bodies (if it may be called more than a quality of body) by its subtilty penetrates, and by its levity rarifies the humid parts of matter; and then, by its agility, breaking loose, carries off the parts so rarified; which being by that means rendered lighter than the air, mount till they rest or

Its bosom pants beneath the vigorous heat,
And eager beams th' expanding surface beat;
Insinuating, form the lucid cell;
To bladders the circumfluous moisture swell;
Th' inflated vapours spurn the nether tide,
And mounted on the weightier ether ride:  140
As though in scorn of gravitating power,
Sublime the cloudy congregations tower;
O'er torrid climes collect their sable train,
And form umbrellas for the panting swain;
Or figur'd wanton in romantic mould,
Careering knights and airy ramparts hold,
(Emblazoning beams the flitting champions gild,
And various paint the visionary field);
Sudden the loose enchanted squadrons fly,
And sweep delusion from the wond'ring eye;  150
Thence on the floating atmosphere they sail,
And steer precarious with the varying gale;
Or hovering, with suspended wing delay,
And in disdain the kindred flood survey:
When lo! the afflicting ether checks their pride,
Compressing chills the vain dilated tide;
Their shivering essence to its centre shrinks,
And a cold nuptual their coherence links;
With artful touch the curious meteor forms,
Parent prolific of salubrious storms;  160
When from on high the rapid tempest's hurl'd,
Enlivening as a sneeze to man's inferior world:
The frigid chymist culls the mineral store,
The glossy spherules of metallic ore;
Sublimes with nitre the sulphureous foam,
And hoards contagion in Heaven's ample dome,
Where Nature's magazine fermenting lies,
Till the bright ray athwart the welkin flies;
High rage the small incendiary inspires,
Whose kindling touch the dread artillery fires;  170
Quick, with effusion wide, the lightnings glare;
Disploding bolts the cloudy entrails tear;  [room,
The cleansing flames sweep through th' ethereal
And swift the gross infectious steam consume:
Our vital element the blaze refines,
While man, ingrateful, at his health repines.

float in that part of the atmosphere that bears a specific or proportionable gravity; and hence arises——
   Ver. 144. *And form umbrellas.*] the use, beauty, and variety of our meteors; for as the chief operator in raising the vapours is heat, so on the other hand——
   Ver. 155. *When lo!*] the chief artist in forming the several meteors out of those vapours, is cold; as——
   Ver. 157. *Their shivering essence.*] first rain, by expulsion of the rarifying heat; upon which the little bladders or vesicles, knocking against each other, conglobe in the contact, and growing heavier than the atmosphere, fall down in larger or smaller drops, according as the constituent parts of the cloud were more or less contiguous——
   Ver. 161. *When from on high.*] frequently causing storms of wind, by condensing, and thereby destroying the equilibrium of the atmosphere; the parts so condensed, pressing upon the parts more rare, and dilated, by warmth; which pressure produces the wind, which is no other than a current of air——
   Ver. 163. *The frigid chymist.*] thunder and lightning.

With various skill the chilling artist works,
And operator chief in every meteor lurks:
Oft, where the zenith's lofty realms extend,
Ere mists, conglobing, by their weight descend,    180
With sudden nitre captivates the cloud,
And o'er the vapour throws a whitening shroud;
Soft from the concave hovering fleeces fall,
Whose flaky texture clothes our silver ball.
Or when the shower forsakes the sable skies,
Haply the cold in secret ambush lies,
Couching awaits in some inferior space,
And chills the tempest with a quick embrace;
The crystal pellets at the touch congeal,
And from the ground rebounds the rattling hail. 190
Or constant where this artificer dwells,
And alg.d from his heights the mist repels,
The Almighty Alchymist his limbeck rears,
His lordly Taurus, or his Alpine peers;
Suspending fogs around the summit spread,
And gloomy columns crown each haughty head,
Obstructed drench the constipating hill,
And soaking through the porous grit distil:
Collected from a thousand thousand cells,
The subterraneous flood impatient swells;      200
Whence issuing torrents burst the mountain's side,
And hence impetuous pour their headlong tide.
   Still central from the wide circumfluous waves,
(Whose briny dash each bounded region laves)

Ver. 181. *With sudden nitre.*] Snow.

Ver. 188. *And chills the tempest.*] Hail.

Ver. 191. *Or constant.*] Or where the cold is a
constant inhabitant in the upper regions, which,
by reason of their distance from the Earth, are but
little affected by the reflection of the sun-beams,
which reflection chiefly promotes the intenseness
of heat; there the rising vapours are repelled, because, meeting with the cold, they, in a great
measure, lose that active principle of heat, which
was the chief motive of their ascension; and floating as the gale veers, are obstructed in their march
by the mountains, or higher lands; and more vapours still gathering as they are obstructed, their
parts, or little spherules, become more neighbourly,
or contiguous, than when they had a freedom of
ranging wide from each other; and so jostling, run
into, or incorporate one with the other; and descending by the laws of gravity——

Ver. 198. *And soaking.*] soak into the hills, that
are generally of a gravelly, mineral, or lax substance, through which the moisture distills; till
finding, or making a vent to issue at, by the advantage of a descent, they pour their fertile and
delicious streams over all the Earth——

Ver. 203. *Still central from the wide.*] and this
advantage of a descent is the more wonderful and
happy, inasmuch as without it we should have no
rivers, and consequently be poisoned and overflowed
with the standing and stagnating waters: for who,
but the Almighty Director, could lead the currents
from their first source, by a gradual winding, and
nice declivity, frequently through a miraculous
length of about three thousand English miles?
while flowing perpetually through various climates,
and nations of different manners and languages,
they bear and spread around society, trade, commerce, riches, plenty, refreshment, luxuriant
health, blooming verdure, and endless delight——

The soil still rising from the deep retires,
And mediate to the neighb'ring Heaven aspires.
Hence, where the spring its surging effluence boils,
The stream ne'er refluent on the fount recoils,
But trips progressive, with descending pace,
And tunes, through many a league, its warbling
   maze;                                        210
Here blended swells with interfering rills;
And here the lake's capacious cistern fills;
Or, wanton, here a snaky labyrinth roams;
Impervious here with indignation foams;
Or here with rapture shoots the nether glade,
And whit'ning silvers in the steep cascade;
Or slack'ning here, its length of labour sooths;
And slumb'ring soft its sleepy surface smooths;
Wide, deep, and slow the doubtful current glides,
And o'er the flux the tilting vessel rides.    220
The embroider'd banks their gaudy fringes dip,
And pendent flowers the smiling liquors sip;
Or gently where the humid mirrors pass,
The forest rises to the wat'ry glass;
Self-worshipping the stately shade admires,
And to a double Heaven its height aspires.
The social stream a winding motion steers,
And mindful of the neighb'ring region veers;
With traverse or inverted circuit bends,
Nor leaves unvisited remotest friends;         230
With genial bounty spreads the verdant wealth,
And pours large draughts of ever-blooming health:
Delight diffusive down the current flows,
And pleasure on the flow'ry margin grows. [reign,
Through many a realm, where mighty monarchs
The stately flood protracts its floating train;
Revolving suns the wondrous length pursue,
Nor in one day the liquid wanderer view;
Its facil maze the varying seasons wind,
And crystal flakes the struggling fountain bind,
Which distant glows beneath the fervid beam, 241
And into ocean pours the copious stream.
   Thus beauty flows in one perpetual ring,
And uses circling from our oceans spring;
Beneath, attracted, through the strata rise;
Above, exhal'd, usurp the ambient skies;
Meet in the limpid source, or purling rill,
And bathe the vale, or sweep the shelving hill:
From hence their tributary floods repay,
And grateful nourish the recruited sea;        250
The sea replenish'd traffics as before,
And back to earth returns the fruitful store.
To earth! for here, concentring, air, and fire,
And flood, in mutual triple league conspire:
Since he, on whom the mighty fabric leans,
The Eternal, from eternity ordains
Variety, which union must produce;
And order knit consummate, into use;

Ver. 242. *And into ocean pours.*] and disem-
boguing their floods into the sea, there finish——

Ver. 243. *Thus beauty flows.*] only still to repeat and continue the eternal circle and order in
all things——

Ver. 255. *Since he.*] that order, which the Supreme Self-Existence, to manifest his own power
and goodness, has caused to flow through an infinite variety of creatures; and yet has founded
that infinite variety on the union of a few principles; which few principles are further and ulti-
mately resolvable, and united in him, the only
Original, and Self Eternal Principle.

That Deity throughout the world may shine,
And Nature's birth confess her Sire Divine.　260
Nature, bright effluence of the One Supreme!
O how connected is thy wondrous frame!
(Thy grand machine, through many a wanton maze,
Steer'd where it winds, and strait'ning where it
　　　strays,
There most direct where seeming most inflex'd,
Most regular when seemingly most perplex'd,
As though perfection on disorder hung,
And perfect order from incaution sprung)
Still, endless as thy beauteous scenes arise,
Still, endless multiplies our deep surprise.　　270
Say, does each mote know its peculiar place,
All conscious, through the gulf of boundless space?

Ver. 271. *Say, does each mote.*] The reason why
I represent, as above, the various opinions of atheists, in one ridiculous light (when they may be
supposed to differ much in their notions, and the
learned treatises they have written for our instruction to carry a great appearance of ingenious and
metaphysical argumentation) is, that the truth,
and matter of fact, upon inquiry and reflection,
will be found exactly and literally as I have represented it; and that all their ambages and cir-
cumlocutions centre and turn upon one point,
which is this, that whoever attempts to rob the
world of a Superintendant Providence, or Designing Wisdom, does thereby necessarily ascribe all
that is of connection, order, or beauty in the world,
to blind and insensible matter; and is, therefore,
guilty of the ridiculous absurdities and contradictions above set forth. For, as the wit or invention
of men has never yet laid down any atheistical hypothesis, however subtile or various, but what is
evidently resolvable into, first, a fortuitous concourse of atoms; secondly, an eternal operating
necessity; or, thirdly, an endless round or succession of causes and effects; if those gentlemen,
who would thus point out our God, mean, as they
often pretend, that he is any thing more than
bare matter, we shall soon find their intention, by
separating the terms they have annexed as ope-
rators for the assistance of stupid matter: and on
our part it will be but common gratitude to inquire
to which of these three pretended causes we are
obliged for the particular benefits we receive, or
(as members of the great whole) for the formation
and order of the universe, or nature itself.

First then, as chance is the operator assigned in
a fortuitous concourse of atoms, we would know
what this chance, this wise and ingenious artist,
is—is it a substance? No, that is not pretended.
Matter? nor that.—Quality of matter? nor that
neither. What, neither subject nor attribute?—
No.—It is then, what is not; or is not any thing
that is: it is, in truth, what, by way of apology,
we assign as a cause of any effect produced, when
our ignorance, or idleness, will not permit us to
inquire or find any other; a meaning without an
idea; or even less—a word without a meaning.
And thus, when chance is introduced for the solution, chance unluckily happens to leave all the
operating burden upon that poor matter it was
called to assist. As, in the second place, I also
fear there will be immediate occasion for calling
upon chance to help out their necessity, and that
it will prove equally treacherous as before. For as

Can atoms be omniscient, to discern
(What human wisdom strives, but strives in vain
　　　to learn)
What mode mysterious paints the purpling rose,
What melts the current when Mæander flows?

necessity is the supposed operator here, if it be
asked, is this necessity distinct from the things it
necessitates? the answer is, yes, by all means; 
since, to assert otherwise, is allowing it to be the
thing operated, and not the operator; and so the
original superior cause be as far to seek as ever.
If then it be asked, is this necessity conscious, intelligent, free, or designing? that doubtless is denied, else we have there the very God we desire.
But then, if it should be unluckily started, that if
this necessity is neither designing, conscious, nor
intelligent, it is altogether as blind as matter; and
if not free, is as much in need of, and equally
subjected to a higher cause as matter can possibly
be; being consequently a necessity necessitated,
and not acting, but acted upon; if this, I say,
should be objected, there must either be recourse
to the old wise solution, that so it happens, or a
higher necessity or unintelligent cause be alleged,
and so another to support the second, and another
the third, ad infinitum; like the elephant bearing
the Earth, the crab the elephant, and so on; which
procedure, ad infinitum, to assign a cause, shows
that, ad infinitum, they will be as far as ever from
assigning a true cause, and so, ad infinitum, no
cause at all will be assigned.

The third and last shift, is an endless succession
of causes and effects, where all the subtilty consists
in the word endless; for whatever is incapable of
being a cause in any time, ever was, and ever will,
through eternity, continue equally incapable. And
here, if the question be asked, whether any of these
effects be original, independent, or superintendent?
the answer is negative, if it were only to avoid a
direct absurdity and contradiction: if then it be
asked, what these effects are? the answer is, that
the effects are no other than matter variously modified and actuated; for that is the utmost degree
of perfection they will allow them, for fear of bor-
dering too near upon spirit. Again, if it be asked
on the other hand, whether, among the causes,
there is any one original or independent? the answer
doubtless is, no; for to allow there were, would be
contrary to the hypothesis laid down. But then
observe the necessary consequence of all this; for
first, if none of these effects are original, independent, or superintendent; and they all consist of
matter variously modified and actuated, they are
no other than matter still, whatever action or modification be produced. And secondly, if on the
other hand, among the endless causes, there is not
any one cause original or independent, there is
not any one cause but what is effected; and every
one being effected, the whole, which consists of
them, is effected, and therefore is all effect; and
all the effects being matter actuated and modified,
the whole is consequently no other than matter
actuated and modified; and so finally recurs, and
in every light, view, shift, and evasion, resolves in
this, that matter alone operates upon itself; and,
though destitute of design, wisdom, foresight, order,
or direction, yet wisely foresees, designs, directs,
and orders all things.

What modes our adamantine marble bind?
What ruffle active in the blust'ring wind?
From inky jet exclude the piercing day;
Or through the brilliant drink the trembling ray;
Nip in the frost, or in the furnace glow;          281
With gay enamel arch the showery bow;
With various influence our senses greet,
Point in the sour, grow luscious in the sweet,
Scent in the civet, stifle in the draught,
Light from the doe the tainting odour waft,
Excite the nostril of the opening hound;
More subtile still the organic sense compound;
Through elements, plant, reptile, man, and brute,
This thing to that, and all to other suit?          290
Can clay, such virtues, forms, and modes assign?
Debating, methodise, conspire, combine?
Studious deliberate on the public weal,
And ne'er like human politicians fail?
Each particle its separate province choose,
Nor that prefer, nor froward this refuse;
Each for itself, and for the whole advise;
All good, all right, all perfect, and all wise?
Prophetic, through eternity foreknow,
From past, what future revolutions flow?          300
Can each be omnipresent, to perceive
What endless links the blended fabric weave,
On every various consequence reflect,
Prepare each cause to yield the just effect,
Sum up the whole, and thence the whole connect?
O dotage! dreamers! who could once suppose
The passive mass its Maker should enclose,
And the form'd clay its forming Lord compose.
" Ye atheists! if ye will be atheists still,
And will, no cause but this, because ye will;   310
If stubborn, in your little reason's spite,
Ye will judge wrong, because ye wo' nt judge
          right;
Thus argue—Since the clue of boundless space
Winds worlds on worlds, and wonders wonders
          trace;
'T is order above rule that guides the plan,
And wisdom, far beyond what wisdom can;
The bounty boundless, beauty without end:
And would believe a God, he cannot comprehend?"
For deep, indeed, the Eternal Founder lies,
And high above his work the Maker flies:   320
Yet infinite that work, beyond our soar;
Beyond what Clarkes can prove, or Newtons can ex-
          plore!
Its union, as of numbers to the sound
Of minstrelsy, to heavenly rapture wound,
On harmony suspended, tunes the whole,
Thrills in our touch, and lives upon our soul;
Each note inclusive melody reveals,
Soft'ning within th' Eternal Finger dwells,
Now sweetly melts, and now sublimely swells;
Yet relative each social note extends,   330
Throughout is blended, while throughout it blends
Symphonious, echoing the Supreme's design,
Beauty of Love, and Symmetry Divine!

---

## UNIVERSAL BEAUTY.

### BOOK III.

Thus Beauty mimick'd in our humbler strains,
Illustrious through the world's great poem reigns!

The One grows sundry by creative power;
The Eternal 's found in each revolving hour;
The Immense appears in every point of space;
The Unchangeable in Nature's varying face;
The Invisible conspicuous to our mind;
And Deity in every atom shrin'd;
From whence exults the animated clod,
And smiling features speak the Parent God;   10
Who here, and there, and every where abounds:
Air uttering, tells his harmony in sounds;
The light reveals the Fountain of its rays,
And like the seraph kindles in his praise;
The floods ambitious to his glory rise,
And seek their source throughout his ambient skies;
Thence, in united congregations fall,
And tune their anthems o'er the warbled ball;
The ball enliv'ning at his order springs,
And rounding to its central Maker clings:   20
The Maker! ample in his bounty, spread
The various strata of Earth's genial bed;
Temper'd the subject mass with pregnant juice,
And subtile stores of deep and sacred use;
Salts, oils, and bitumen, and unctuous pitch,
With precious, though mysterious, influence rich;
Mercurial, nitrous, and sulphureous spume,
Fermenting virtual the terrestrial womb.
Hence, where the solar heat and searching air,
Transgressive, pierce our actuated sphere,   30
The arch-chymists work as in a secret mine,
And Nature's crude originals refine;
Here blending mix, here separate, here select,
And purging here th' incongruous parts reject;
Perennial bind the flint's impervious rock,
And strict its adamantine texture lock;
The future monumental marble stain,
And wanton through its variegated vein;
Salubrious here the mineral medicine mix,
Here the once potable utensil fix;   40
Here modify with ever varying change;
And here the similar effluvia range;
Compact the lustre of metallic ore,
The steely, argent, or Corinthian store;
Or severing, cast in Nature's purest mould
The dense elixir of refulgent gold.
Through sparkling gems the plastic artists play,
And petrify the light's embody'd ray;
Now kindle the carbuncle's ruddy flame;
Now gild the chrysolite's transparent beam;   50
Infuse the sapphire's subterraneous sky,
And tinge the topaz with a saffron dye;
With virgin blush within the ruby glow,
And o'er the jasper paint the show'ry bow.
Endless the task, and arduous, to unfold
What secrets Earth's prolific entrails hold;
In Nature's womb what embryon treasures sleep,
The wondrous natives of the hoary deep:
Whence happy oft, oft hapless they aspire;
Supply what want can wish, or pride require—   60
Bless'd are the blameless means, the curse is the
          desire.

Ver. 22.   .........strata of Earth's genial bed.] For
the use of the strata or layers of earth in the conveyance of fountains and sweet waters, see book ii.
Ver. 23.   .........subject mass.] The mere matter,
or caput mortuum, supposed in all terrestial
bodies——
Ver. 31. The arch-chymists.] which so impregnated, and modified by air and heat as above recited, supplies——

Hence comfort kindles in the cheerful blaze,
Though fire upon th' expiring martyr preys;
The peasant hence manures th' exhausted soil,
Though lordlings share the product of his toil;
Hence artists in the princely dome survive,
Though drones may occupy its ample hive;
Hence medicines yield the salutiferous pill,
But gently qualified can learn to kill:
Hence medals may reveal the patriot's face, 70
Although a tyrant gild the nether space;
Once more return great Socrates to light,
Or with an Alexander blast the sight—
(Who here approves the infamy of fame,
Shares Alexander's guilt, and Alexander's shame)
Nor less the plough-share needs the Lydian blade,
Though steel and pride the neighbouring realm
    invade;
The tools to life subservient we allege,
Though deadly cruelty can whet their edge:
Such we approve the trade supporting ore, 80
Though avarice purloin the shining store;
In Maro's hand the precious treasure view,
It spreads all bounteous as the heavenly dew.
Shall Nature check the purple colouring globe,
Lest magistrates should trail the splendid robe?
Nor beauteous her adorning brilliants wear,
Lest gems should deck the follies of the fair?
" Ah, Nature ! thou hadst scap'd thy only blot,
Could man but cease to be—or hitherto were not:
Ay, there's the task, the labour of our song— 90
To prove that all is right, though man be wrong."
   Emergent from the deep view Nature's face,
And o'er the surface deepest wisdom trace;
The verdurous beauties charm our cherish'd eyes—
But who 'll unfold the Root from whence they rise?
Infinity within the sprouting bower!
Next to enigma in Almighty Power;
Who only could infinitude confine,
And dwell *immense* within the minim shrine;
The eternal species in an instant mould, 100
And endless worlds in seeming atoms hold.

Plant within plant, and seed enfolding seed,
For ever—to end never—still proceed;
In forms complete, essentially retain
The future semen, alimental grain;
And these again, the tree, the trunk, the root,
The plant, the leaf, the blossom, and the fruit;
Again the fruit and flower the seed enclose,
Again the seed perpetuated grows,
And Beauty to perennial ages flows. 110
   Such the Supreme his wondrous sata made,
Ere yet their foliage cloth'd the novel glade;
Gave each a texture of peculiar frame,
And nature correspondent to its name;
Gave different pow'rs to propagate their kind,
And varying means to various ends assign'd;
Then o'er the globe the missive treasure strow'd,
And first th' Eternal Hand Earth's spacious bosom
    sow'd.
Here elemental principles unite,
To give the new consummate birth to light: 120
The glebe, now pregnant, yields nutritious food;
Lymphatic dews, their mild diluting flood;
The Sun affords his rarifying sphere,
And ether breathes its actuating air;
Quatruple, round the temper'd embryon meet,
And its fine tegument fermenting greet;
Whence subtle juices pierce the filmy skin,
Repeating vigorous their attacks within;
Thence through the lobes with percolation strain,
And thence infusing through their radix drain;
Thence limpid to the plantal root distill, 131
And each impregnated aperture fill,
With swoln repletion through the portals float,
And now unclasp the nice cutaneous coat;
The radicle now obvious they unfold,
And to its infant lips their liquors hold;
The instinctive lips imbibe the gentle tide,
And through the veins the milky liquids glide,
Ascending visit the inclusive plume,
(Where Nature wantons in minutest room, 140
Where folded close, her implicated size
Of trunk, branch, leaf, and future semen lies)
Conspicuous its dilated form display,
And give its texture to apparent day.

Ver. 62. *Hence comfort.*] the comfort of firing, in coals and other combustibles——

Ver. 64. *The peasant hence.*] the manure of lime, marle, and other mooring——

Ver. 66. *Hence artists.*] variety of curious and beautiful stone, for the benefit of habitation, and exercise of art——

Ver. 68. *Hence medicines.*] many medicinal and healing drugs——

Ver. 70. *Hence medals.*] metals for the conveyance of useful history to future ages in sculpture, statuary, embossment, &c.——

Ver. 76. *Nor less the plough-share.*] those metals affording also many engines, utensils, &c. for procuring and accelerating nourishment, and other conveniences and delights in life——

Ver. 80. *Such we approve.*] as also coin, for ascertaining the value, and speeding the transmigration of property in trade and commerce; as may best suit each person's convenience and advantage——

Ver. 84. *Shall Nature check.*] the beauty of colours——

Ver. 86. *Nor beauteous.*] and lustre of jewels.

Ver. 96. ...... *sprouting bower.*] The seed, which, as here described in its vegetative state, may be said to contain or be divided into——

Ver. 126. *And its fine tegument.*] its teguments or coats; the main body included in the coats, and the root and plume or plant included in the main body——

Ver. 129. ...... *lobes with percolation strain.*] the main body (though single in some, and in some more numerous) is generally and distinctly divisible into two equal parts, which are called lobes; and these lobes contain——

Ver. 130. ...... *radix drain.*] the seminal root, whose branches being spread through each lobe in equal moieties, unite at the extremity of the seed in——

Ver. 131. ...... *plantal root distil.*] the plantal root, or——

Ver. 135. ...... *radicle now obvious.*] radicle; which being supplied with juices in the two methods as above described, (i. e. first from the seminal root, and after from the earth to which it becomes obvious) communicates the nourishment to its plume or young plant, which is closely included, and shut up in a narrow cavity within the lobes——

Around the plume the guardian lobes arise,
And fence their minor from inclement skies;
With pious dews his early verdure bathe,
Perform their trust with never failing faith;
Till, self-sufficient, they retire to earth,
And leave the stripling to his right of birth.      150
Now fervid beams the rising sap exhale,
And air ingredient wings the vital gale;
The solids in diluting moisture pass,
And colds condense the vegetating mass.
The labial pores of every various root
Their orifice to varying natures suit,
Admit effluvia of peculiar mode,
And delicate the incongruous parts explode.
Salts, oils, and sulphurs, through the entrance tend,
And similar, with proper members blend;      160
To sight, smell, taste, their several powers dispense,
And aptly ravish each luxuriant sense;
Still graceful, vary in some new delight;
Still obvious, please th' involuntary sight.
Our transient optic o'er the surface plays,
And Nature's superficial mien surveys;
But rare with deeper inquisition pries,
Where Beauty's wrapt, recluse from vulgar eyes,
Essential, sits on Truth's eternal throne,
And universal, reigns o'er worlds unknown;      170
Displays her sway through unimagin'd scenes,
Elysian tracts, and philosophic plains:
These, these are climes of ever-living joy;
Truth ne'er can satiate, reason ne'er can cloy.
O worthy! far more worthy to explore,
Than treasur'd lustre of Peruvian ore;
Or supererogated store, acquir'd
By pilgrimage, to saintship long expir'd.
In Nature's realms no wretched levees wait,
No monarchs hold their arbitrary seat;      180
Far different law her beauteous empire sways,
And Order dictates her unerring ways.
Here may we spy, from the Supreme of things,
How first the originate material springs;
How substituted Nature moulds her forms,
What tender love her infant-embryo warms,
What tempering skill the boon conception frames;
And trace her maze of complicated schemes,
Where differing parts identity compose,
Yet endless how, from One! each varying essence flows;
Each vegetable set in beds of bliss,      191
Their sap exhaling from the Prime Abyss.

Ver. 145. ...... lobes arise.] which lobes, upon a further growth, are effoliated, and rise about the young plant in two dissimilar leaves, (being now nourished in their turn by the radicle which they had formerly fostered) and thus protect and embrace it round, and nourish its infancy with refreshing dews, which they hold to it as in a basin, embalming it round, while yet the scanty moisture of the radicle is insufficient for its support; till having acted their part on the vegetable stage, nature gives them their discharge, and they rot off or fall away.

Ver. 152. And air ingredient wings.] This very principle in our air or atmosphere, which chiefly conduces to, or is the very essence of animal and vegetable life, is also the very principle of corruption, or the dissolution of the parts of matter, as shall hereafter be made evident.

See, bashful why the downward roots retire,
(While up to Heaven their kindred trunks aspire)
Obliquely some, and some with steep descent;
Some level, with direct or tortuous bent;
Some to a root their tether'd trunks condemn,
Attracting prone the yet reluctant stem;
While some peep up, to view the gladsome skies;
And some rotund, with bold projected size,      200
And intersected horizon, arise.
See, wondrous thus how each sagacious root,
As marksmen, to their several signals shoot;
What Cause revers'd the sep'rate bias guides,
And whence the still dissenting movement glides.
Their figures, pliant to some plastic skill,
Alike obsequious to its secret will,
With pointed cone the yielding strata pass;
Or here, accumulate their bulbous mass;
Here bulky, taper, parted or entire;      210
Here writhing, twist their complicated wire;
Here ramified, their forky branches spread;
Or tassell'd here, their fibrous fringes shed;
Adjusted through each multifarious sect,
And efficacious to some point elect—
Elect, within while Wisdom dwells replete,
Incomprehensive through his sacred seat.
Hence, hence alone, the final causes tend,
And reach unerring each appointed end;
The maze of endless implication wind,      220
Directed by the clue of All-perceiving Mind.
Hence from the seraph's intellectual ray,
To reason's spark, that gilds our sensual clay;
To life (scarce conscious) in th' instinctive brute;
To reptile, plant, and vegetating root;
The features in conspicuous semblance shine,
And speak, through all, One Parent all Divine.
Thus answering lively to organic sense,
The plants half animate their powers dispense:
The mouth's analogy their root displays,      230
And for th' intestine viscera purveys;
Their liquors through respondent vessels flow,
And organ-like their fibrous membranes grow:
Nor yet inadequate their congruous use
Of mucilages, lymph, and lacteal juice;
The flood consimilary ducts receive,
And glands refine the separated wave;
Redounding vapours through the pores transpire,
And for the fresh ingredient guests retire.
Revers'd, their trachæ op'rate from beneath,      240
And through the trunk aerial conduits breathe;
Their lignous fibres with continuous length,
Equivalent, compact a bony strength;
But form'd elastic, with inclining shade,
Their yielding stems each stormy gust evade:
So forest pines th' aspiring mountain clothe,
And self-erected towers the stately growth.
But where the strength of mighty fabric fails,
There art with ample recompense avails,
By interposing skill to poise th' eternal scales;      250

Ver. 193. See, bashful.] The various motions of roots.

Ver. 206. Their figures.] The various figures of roots.

Ver. 228. Thus answering lively.] Analogy or similitude of animal and vegetable life.

Ver. 248. But where the strength.] The various provision of Nature for the security and preservation of every species——

While these, more valid through dependence gain,
And strong in indigence on Nature lean.
Thus from the couch of Earth's embroider'd bed,
In elegance of vernal foliage spread;
From pulse leguminous, of verdurous hue;
From herbal tribes, bedropp'd with morning dew;
The gourd, inhabiting the pastur'd glade;
The tufted bush and umbelliferous shade;
The feeble stems that luscious viands bear,
Nor less sublime their pamper'd tension rear: 260
Through botany, through every sylvan scene,
That various deck the vegetating plain,
Even to the proud primeval sons of Earth,
That rise superior in their right of birth,
Whose heights the blasting volley'd thunder stand,
In ruin still magnificently grand;
Distinct, each species of peculiar frame,
Distinct, peculiar love and fondness claim;
Indulg'd by Nature's kind parental care,
As each alone were her appointed heir.      270
    Thus mantling snug beneath a verdant veil,
The creepers draw their horizontal trail;
Wide o'er the bank the plantal reptile bends,
Adown its stem the rooty fringe depends,
The feeble boughs with anchoring safety binds,
Nor leaves precarious to insulting winds.
The tendrils next, of slender helpless size,
Ascendant through luxuriant pampering rise;
Kind Nature sooths their innocence of pride,
While buoy'd aloft the flow'ring wantons ride;
With fond adhesion round the cedar cling,   281
And wreathing circulate their amorous ring;
Sublime with winding maturation grow,
And clench'd retentive gripe the topmost bough;
Here climb direct the ministerial rock,
And clasping firm its steepy fragments lock;
Or various, with agglutinating guile,
Cement tenacious to some neighbouring pile;
Investing green, some fabric here ascend,
And clustering o'er its pinnacles depend.   290
    Defective, where contiguous props evade,
Collateral they spring with mutual aid;
Officious brace their amicable band,
And by reciprocal communion stand:
Bless'd model! (by humanity expell'd)    [held.
The whole upholding each, the whole by each up-
Their social branch the wedded plexures rear,
(Proximity of combination dear)
High arching, cipher love's enamour'd knot,
And wave the fragrance of inviting grot,    300
Or cool recess of odoriferous shade,
And fan the peasant in the panting glade;
Or lace the coverture of painted bower,  [shower.
While from the enamell'd roof the sweet profusions
Here duplicate, the range divides beneath,
Above united in a mantling wreath;

Ver. 271. *Thus mantling snug.*] protecting and supplying the indigent, as the strawberry, cinque-foil, &c.——
Ver. 277. *The tendrils next.*] and supporting the feeble, as the vine, bryony, ivy, &c. and thus equally propagating a perpetuity, as spreading a universality of delights, pleasures, and enjoyments, in——
Ver. 291. *Defective, where.*] the harmony of connection, fragrance of thickets, refreshment of shades, and beauty of colours——
Ver. 305. *Here duplicate.*] charming the eye of

With continuity protracts delight,
Imbrown'd in umbrage of ambiguous night;
Perspicuous the vista charms our eye,
And opens, Janus like, to either sky;       310
Or stills attention to the feather'd song,
While echo doubles from the warbling throng.
    Here, winding to the Sun's magnetic ray,
The solar plants adore the lord of day,
With Persian rites idolatrous incline,
And worship towards his consecrated shrine;
By south from east to west obsequious turn,
And mov'd with sympathetic ardours burn.
To these adverse, the lunar sects dissent,
With convolution of opposed bent;           320
From west to east by equal influence tend,
And towards the Moon's attractive crescence bend;
There, nightly worship with Sidonian zeal,
And queen of Heaven Astarte's idol hail.
    " O Nature, whom the song aspires to scan!
O Beauty, trod by proud insulting man,
This boasted tyrant of thy wondrous ball,
This mighty, haughty, little lord of all;
This king o'er reason, but this slave to sense,
Of wisdom careless, but of whim immense;     330
Towards Thee, incurious, ignorant, profane!
But of his own, dear, strange, productions vain!
Then, with this champion let the field be fought,
And Nature's simplest arts 'gainst human wisdom
    brought:
Let elegance and bounty here unite—
There kings beneficent and courts polite;
Here Nature's wealth—there chymist's golden
    dreams;
Her texture here—and there the statesman's
    schemes;
Conspicuous here let sacred truth appear—    339
The courtier's word and lordling's honour there;
Here native sweets in boon profusion flow—
There smells that scented nothing of a beau;
Let justice here unequal combat wage—
Nor poise the judgment of the law-learn'd sage;
Though all-proportion'd with exactest skill,
Yet gay as woman's wish, and various as her
    will."
    O say, ye pitied, envied, wretched great,
Who veil pernicion with the mask of state!
Whence are those domes that reach the mocking
    skies,
And vainly emulous of Nature rise?           350
Behold the swain projected o'er the vale!
See slumbering peace his rural eyelids seal;
Earth's flowery lap supports his vacant head;
Beneath his limbs her broider'd garment's spread;
Aloft her elegant pavilion bends,
And living shade of vegetation lends,
With ever propagated bounty bless'd,
And hospitably spread for every guest:
No tinsel here adorns a tawdry woof,
Nor lying wash besmears a varnish'd roof;    360
With native mode the vivid colours shine,
And Heaven's own loom has wrought the weft
    divine,
Where art veils art and beauties beauties close,
While central grace diffus'd throughout the system
    flows.

proportion with the regularity of vistas, and other various dispositions; and forming tuneful mansions and choirs for the feathered musicians.

The fibres, matchless by expressive line,
Arachne's cable or ethereal twine,
Continuous, with direct ascension rise,
And lift the trunk, to prop the neighbouring skies.
Collateral tubes with respiration play,
And winding in aerial mazes stray.    370
These as the woof, while warping, and athwart
The exterior cortical insertions dart
Transverse, with cone of equidistant rays,
Whose geometric form the Forming Hand displays.
Recluse, the interior sap and vapour dwells
In nice transparence of minutest cells;
From whence, through pores or transmigrating veins
Sublim'd the liquid correspondence drains,
Their pithy mansions quit, the neighbouring choose,
And subtle through the adjacent pouches ooze;
Refin'd, expansive or regressive pass,    381
Transmitted through the horizontal mass;
Compress'd the lignous fibres now assail,
And entering thence the essential sap exhale:
Or lively with effusive vigour spring,
And form the circle of the annual ring,
The branch implicit of embow'ring trees,
And foliage whispering to the vernal breeze;
While 'Zephyr tun'd, with gentle cadence blows,
And lull'd to rest consenting eyelids close.    390
Ah! how unlike those sad imperial beds,
Which care within the gorgeous prison spreads;
Where tedious nights are sunk in sleepless down,
And pillows vainly soft, to ease the thorny crown!
Nor blush, thou rose, though bashful thy array,
Transplanted chaste within the raptur'd lay;
Through every bush and warbled spray we sing,
And with the linnet gratulate the spring;
Sweep o'er the lawn or revel on the plain,
Or gaze the florid or the fragrant scene;    400
The flowers' forensic beauties now admire,
The impalement, foliation, down, attire,
Couch'd in the pannicle or mantling veil,
That intercepts the keen or drenching gale;
Its infant bud here swath'd with fostering care,
Or fledg'd and opening to the ambient air;
Or bloom dilated in the silken rose,
That flush'd mature, with kindling radiance glows;
Or shrunk in covert of its mantling bower,
(Now ushers evening cool or chilling shower)    410
And skill'd prophetic, with eluding form,
Anticipates approach of ruffling storm.
Or now we pore with microscopic eye,
And Nature's intimate contextures spy;
Her economics, her implicit laws,
The effects how wondrous deep!—how wondrous
    high the Cause!
Now view the floret's miniature of state,
And scorn the scepter'd mansions of the great;
Not architrave embellish'd so adorn,
Whose fretted gold reflects the beamy morn; 420

Ver. 365. *The fibres.*] The interior texture of vegetables.
Ver. 366. *Arachne's cáble.*] The cobweb, or——
Ver. 566. ...... *ethereal twine.*] viscous threads that float in the air.
Ver. 375. *Recluse, the interior sap.*] The motion of the fluids——
Ver. 379. *Their pithy mansions.*] the pith, bark, and insertions being of one texture and coherence.
Ver. 401. *The flower's forensic beauties.*] Of flowers.

Within, the guests of animalcule race
Luxuriant range at large its ample space;
Or now in elegance the banquet spread,
While millions at the sumptuous feast are fed.
Now see whence various propagations breed,
The sucker, scion, sprout, and embryon seed,
In wall concrete of peachy stone secur'd,
Or in the bower of wainscot core immur'd;
Or fœtus in the secondine contain'd,
Its juices through the umbilic fibres drain'd;    430
With birth of prosperous generation spring,
And round and round, hold on the eternal ring.
While pleasure whispers in the balmy gale,
Or wantons venial in the revell'd dale,
Delight reclin'd attends the purling rill;
Health bounds luxuriant o'er the topmost hill;
The mount aspiring contemplation climbs,
And outward forms to inward truth sublimes;
Surveys the worlds that deck the azure skies,
Reflects how beauteous Earth's productions rise;
The system one, One Maker stands confess'd,    441
The Prime, the One, the Wondrous and the Bless'd;
The One in various forms of Unity express'd!

## UNIVERSAL BEAUTY.

### BOOK IV.

The author having, in the third book, taken a short survey of vegetable nature, proceeds to consider the animal system: and first life in general. That life, perception, &c. are terms applicable to some being of whose essence we can form no adequate idea, verse 7th, &c. Yet that such perception and consciousness are an evident demonstration both of the existence and simplicity of such essence; and in this simplicity consists what we call personal identity or sameness, 13: that, nevertheless, we are not to conclude that every organized being is informed with such an essence, so as to have an actual principle of motion and perception; since many such may possibly be no other than pieces of Almighty mechanism, and matter so curiously acted upon, may deceive us with the appearance of internal action, 23. That if ever matter is wrought to such an appearance of life, it is the utmost perfection its nature is capable of; and that it is impossible it should be endued with any real act or perception; demonstrated, 51. That therefore what we call the soul, or such essence so distinct from matter, must exist the same for ever, as it is simple, indissoluble, and unchangeable, 65. The wonderful and inconceivable obligation incumbent on all who have received such a benefit, 75. That as no other return can be made to the Author of beneficence, gratitude and benediction should be universal in their praises from all animate creatures, 97. As all, the most minute and even invisible animalcules, partake his regard and providence, 110. As also the wonders of almighty artifice, in the tex-

Ver. 426. ...... *and embryon seed.*] The seed in its generative state.

ture of their frame; which is here given as an instance of general organization and bodily economy, 120. The circulation of the blood continued contrary to all the known laws of motion, by the operation of two oppositely acting causes, 142. This illustrated by a comparison, 163. Which comparison, though seemingly disproportioned, is not really so, the terms great and little being barely relative, and One alone being absolutely great, in respect of whom all things else are as nothing, 205. All motion and sensation conveyed by the mediation of the nerves to and from the brain, 243, where the soul is seated; and there receiving her intelligencies from the senses (which are here described) informs the whole bodily system, and through the organ of vision, surveys the beauties of nature, 263, to the end.

---

FRESH from his task, the rising bard aspires,
And all his bosom glows with recent fires:
Life, life, new forms and constitutes the theme!
The song too kindles in the vital flame,
Whose vivid principle diffusive spreads,
And through our strain contagious rapture sheds.
Whate'er the spark, the light, the lamp, the ray,
Essence or effluence of Essential Day,
Substance or transubstantiate, and enshrin'd,
Soul, spirit, reason, intellect or mind;    10
Or these but terms, that dignify the use
Of some unknown, some entity abstruse—
Perception specifies the sacred guest,
Appropriate to the individual breast;
Whence, independence through dependence flows,
And each unknowing his existence, knows;
Existence, varied by Almighty plan,
From lowly reptiles, to the pride of man;
While incorporeal in corporeal dwells,
Distinct in union, of associate cells;    20

---

Ver. 13. *Perception specifies.*] Though (upon the reasons and authority of an eminent author) it has long been admitted, that personal identity or sameness, consists in consciousness; yet as consciousness, whether by direct or reflex perception, may, at most, be no other than the inseparable operation or active principle of some simple, unchangeable, or individual substance; it is obvious to dispute, that such identity, or sameness, may more truly exist in the simplicity or unchangeableness of such substance, than in any operation, whether separable or inseparable: and yet, on the other hand, it is most evident, that a consciousness agreeing through differently distant points of duration, or (if I may be allowed the expression) a consentaneous perception, is the highest demonstration of the identity of such substance, as no one substance, or being, can perceive for another; which again is a further demonstration of the simplicity or unchangeableness of such substance, as it now perceives for that very self, which it also perceives was the same or identical self, from the first instant of its perception, notwithstanding all the various changes and revolutions it has observed through all nature beside——
Ver. 16. ... *each unknowing his existence.*] whence we know, that we who now are, were in times past; though what we are, or were, we know not——

Whence powers their prime informing acts dispense'
And sovereign guide the ministry of sense.
Though what! if oft, while Nature works unseen,
And locomotive forms the nice machine,
Sublim'd and quick through elemental strife,
The insensate boasts its vegetative life;
A steaming vapour through the mass exhales,
And warming breathes its imitative gales;
Fomenting in the heart's vibration plays,
And circling winds the tubulary maze;    30
With conscious act the vivid semblance vies,
And subtle now the sprightly nerve supplies;
Unconscious lifts the lucid ball to light,
And glares around with unperceiving sight;
Or studious seems to muse with thought profound,
Or lists as 'wak'd to catch the flying sound—
So temper'd wondrous by mechanic scheme,
The Sovereign Geometrician knits the frame;
In mode of organizing texture wrought,
And quick with spirited quintessence fraught:    40
When objects on the exterior membrane press,
The alarm runs inmost through each dark recess,
Impulsive strikes the corresponding springs,
And moves th' accord of sympathetic strings;
Effects like acts inevitable rise,
(Preordinate in the Design Allwise)
Yet still their earthly origin retain,
Reductive to the principle terrene,
Though curious to deceive with mimic skill,
And feint the dictate of interior will.    50

---

Ver. 19. *While incorporeal.*] neither the manner in which the union between such substance and matter is made, so as to inform the stupid mass with an action utterly alien to its nature.
Ver. 23. *Though what.*] In the account to which this note is annexed, I have doubtless assigned a capacity of higher perfections to matter than it will easily be admitted susceptible of; and therefore I was obliged to call in no less than——
Ver. 38. *Sovereign Geometrician.*] Omnipotence to support the scheme, who actuating and informing all nature by his wisdom, as he created it by his will, the creature so subjected cannot possibly withstand the creating power, and nothing to him is impossible, but impossibility, that is impotence, or what in the very supposition destroys that very power it would assert; nor are such impotential hypotheses unfrequently started and defended by a misguided zeal, which in the behalf of Omnipotence would destroy the very nature of power, indistinctly confounding truth and falsehood, and thereby ascribing and subjecting all things rather to an unaccountable arbitrary will, than to an infinite power ever guided equally by that infinite wisdom which equally and infinitely contemplates and actuates nature, agreeable to that order and those laws originally by that wisdom impressed on all things.—I should be unwilling to lay an errour of this kind to the charge of a worthy prelate of a neighbouring nation, author of a late most learned treatise, wherein he denies that brutes or the inferior animal system is endued with any being distinct from matter, and yet does not seem to me to account for the existence of actions of such animals as mere machines; but if I do not grossly misapprehend him, he ascribes to them, and consequently to mere matter under the term of animal life, an inferior kind of perception and ideas, and thus has

Here, matter's fix'd eternal barriers stand ;
Though wrought beneath th' Almighty's forming
　　hand,
Though subtiliz'd beyond the kindling ray,
Or sacred flame of Heaven's empyreal day,
No plexur'd mode, no aptitude refin'd,
Can yield one glimpse of all-informing mind ;

carried the perfections of matter to a higher pitch
than I can pretend to with any appearance of reason or even possibility. I shall hereafter have a
more ample and proper opportunity to show the
absurdity of this hypothesis, and shall at present
only hint a few reasons that are applicable to the
occasion, which are these——

Ver. 51. *Here, matter's fix'd.*] Whether matter
be divisible ad infinitum or not, if it is capable of
any degree of perception, such perception must
either be naturally inherent, or arise from some
peculiar modification :—now as no two parts of
matter can exist in the same place, (for then neither part would exist in any place, as each would
occupy the place of the other) the parts however
harmoniously modified, or closely united, are absolutely distinct from each other, since their coherence can only consist in neighbourhood or conti-
guity, and not in corporation :—if therefore the
parts so distinct have any inherent perception, they
must have a perception as distinct from each other
as their parts ; and if divisible ad infinitum, there
is such a confusion of indistinct distinct perceptions, as is too absurd for any thing but a jest.—
But if matter is reducible to atoms, and every
atom supposed to perceive, I would ask how atoms
can be organized so as to see, hear, smell, &c. and
if organization is necessary to the perception of
matter, either such perception arises entirely new
from the organization, or the organization only
gives a liberty of action to the perception that was
prior and distinctly latent in every part :—but if
in the former supposition such perception is solely
produced by the organization or modification, organization or modification, however nice or mechanic, being no other than a mode of form or
figure, the most extraneous and incidental of any
property of matter, and perception being the most
absolute and simple of any thing we know, and by
which alone we know all that we do know ; such
hypothesis I say carries in itself such a palpable
contradiction and confutation, as to make what is
simple, absolute, and invariable, to be produced
by what is most compound, precarious, and change-
able, nay, by a mere relative term, figure being no
other than the circumscription of space surrounding a finite body.—But if in the last case and refuge, organization or modification is supposed only
to give a power of action to what was before latent
in the parts of matter, if the perceptions continue
still as distinct as the parts, here must arise such
a multiplicity of perceptions, as must destroy and
confound the very operation of the organs by which
the parts perceive. And lastly, if it be alleged
that by the modification, the parts become so loving and neighbourly, as by sharing the perception
of each other to make one amicable union of the
whole, each part must still retain its proper right
to its portion of perception ; and if upon any accident a member of the system should be lopped off,
why then truly a piece of such united perception

The parts distinct in firm cohesion lie,
Distinct as those that range the distant sky ;
Time's fleeting points the unreal self devour,　　59
Varied and lost through every changeling hour ;
Whence the precarious system, though compact,
Can ne'er arrive to individual act ;
Since impotence absurdly should ensue,
Distinction be the same, and one be ten or two.
Not so, in intellectual splendours bright,
The soul's irradiance burns with native light,
With vision of internal powers profound,
A pure essential unit, incompound ;
Celestial queen, with conscious sceptre grac'd,
And rights in prime of vital action plac'd !　　70
Hence by identity all thought subsists,
And one, in the existing one, exists ;
The one indissoluble must exist,
And deathless through eternity subsist.
Thou Sole Prerogative, Supreme of Right,
Deep Source of Principle, and Light of Light,
Whose *is* will *be*, whose *will be* ever was,
Of Self Essential Coessential Cause !
If not unhallow'd, nor the song profane,
Nor voice of matin elevation vain ;　　　　80
Prime, as the lark with earliest rapture springs,
And warbling soars to Goodness, warbling sings,
To thee permissive sings with venial lays,
And wings his pittance of ascending praise—
O ! whence to us ? or whence to aught ? but
　　thee !
The word, the bliss, the privilege,—to be—
Or if to be, for thee alone to be,
Derivative Great Author Sole ! from thee
Thou Voluntary Goodness ! thus immense
To pour the largess of perceptive sense,　　90
Sense to perceive, to feel, to find, to know,
That we enjoy, and you alone bestow.

being gone, we have only a piece of perception remaining ; and thus also perception the most simple of all units must be daily and hourly divided
by the perpetual flux of matter——

Ver. 65. *Not so, in intellectual.*] whence I must
necessarily and inevitably conclude, that whatever
being is endued with the least degree of perception, must be a being, substance, or essence, as
widely and oppositely distinct from matter, as any
two things can be imagined : and though I do not
see but such essences may be of infinitely different
natures, and consequently differ in their manners
and degrees of powers and perfections ; yet as no
being can perish but by annihilation, which though
no contradiction to Almighty power, can yet never
be admitted consistent with that creating wisdom
which does nothing in vain ; since even matter is
otherwise imperishable, however its variation may
deceive us, which only arises from its accidental
properties of divisibility and cohesion : I must
from the whole as necessarily and inevitably conclude, that whatever being is endued with any
degree of real perception, as it cannot be affected
with those accidental properties of matter, neither
can it be affected with the variation that arises
thereon, and must consequently exist in a higher
enjoyment of powers and perfections, and that for
ever.

Ver. 76. *Deep Source.*] The meaning of the expression is, that the reason or necessity of the
Deity's existence is included in himself.

Could increation crave thy vital skill,
The virtual Fiat of creative will?
Less can thy flow of plentitude receive
Reversion from the goods its bounty gave.
  Come then, O Gratitude, endearing guest,
In all thy feeling soft suggestions dress'd,
And heave the swell of each exulting breast!
Thou sentiment of friendship's cordial tie!      100
Thou thanks expressive from the moist'ning eye!
Thou pledge assur'd of firm dependence dear,
Repos'd on Omnipresence, ever near——
Through all that breathe, waft, waft thy hallow'd
      gale,
And let the universal wish exhale;
In symphony of vocal transport raise,
And mount to Heaven the tributary praise!
Whence, happy creatures! all your blessings flow,
Your voice to praise him, and your skill to know;
Whence, as the drops that deck the morning's robe,
And gem the bosom of the twinkling globe,      111
Profusive gifts the Smiling Goodness sheds,
And boon around his boundless plenty spreads;
Nought, nought exempt; the myriad minim race
Inscrutable amid the ethereal space,
That mock unseen, while human optic pries
Or aids the search with microscopic eyes,
The sweets of Deified Complacence claim;
To him display the wonders of their frame,
His own contexture, where Eternal Art,      120
Emotive, pants within the alternate heart:

Ver. 115. *Inscrutable amid.*] As I claim no advantage from a poetical licence, to assert any thing contrary to what I apprehend as truth; it may reasonably be demanded here, how it comes to be known that there are animalcules so minute, as cannot come under the cognizance of our senses, by which alone we can perceive them. But I think it may more reasonably be answered; that since for many ages past the continual and successive improvements that have been made in natural philosophy, by perpetually displaying new and unimagined scenes of knowledge, do at the same time demonstrate there are many yet unopened; and since the use of glasses shows us how much our eyes were defective, and that farther invention and improvements of such glasses still show the defect of all the former, and yet can never arrive to the perception of any part of matter or inanimate body more minute than many systems and species of beings endued with animal life; I say, upon such consideration, it would be extremely absurd to stop here, and assert there is nothing further left for an Infinite and All Operating Wisdom.

Ver. 121. *Emotive, pants.*] And further—As equivocal generation, upon the soundest reasons, search, and experiments, is most justly exploded—however difficult it may appear to our apprehension, it is most certain, that such animal life in any material being, however minute, cannot exist without organization; since upon its supposition of being a mere machine, it must still have within, and throughout, those secret wheels and springs of motion, to which the machines of human artists may bear an inferior analogy or resemblance. And on the supposition of its being immaterial, but in union with a material vehicle; if the being in such union is perceptive, there then must consequently be a proper medium or organization for the convey-
VOL. XVII.

Here from the lungs the purple currents glide,
And hence impulsive bounds the sanguine tide,
With blithe pulsation beats the arterial maze,
And through the branching complication plays;
Its wanton floods the tubal system lave,
And to the veins resign their vital wave;
Through glands refining, shed specific juice,
Secreted nice to each appropriate use;
Or here expansile, in meanders bend,      130
While through the pores nutritive portions tend,
Their equal aliment dividual share,
And similar to kindred parts adhere.
From thousand rills the flux continuous drains,
Now swells the porta, now the cava veins;
Here rallies last the recollected blood,
And on the right pours in the cordial flood:
While gales ingredient to the thorax pass,
And breathing lungs imbibe th' ethereal mass;
Whence, their licentious ducts dilation claim,      140
And open obvious to the welcome stream,
Which salient, through the heart's contractile force,
Expulsive springs its recontinual course.
The captive air, impatient of retreat,
Refines expansive with internal heat,
Its levity too rare to poise the exterior weight;
Compressive round the incumbent ether lies,
And strict its elemental fold applies,
Whence either.pulmonary lobe expires,
And all the interior subtle breath retires;      150
Subsiding lungs their labouring vessels press,
Affected mutual with severe distress,
While towards the left their confluent torrents gush,
And on the heart's sinister cavern rush;
Collected there complete their circling rout,
And vigorous from their venal engine shoot.
Again the heart's constrictive powers revive,
And the fresh fountain through the aorta drive;
Arterial valves oppose the refluent blood,
And swift injections push the lingering flood;      160
Sped by the last, the foremost currents bound,
And thus perennial run the purpling round.
  So where beneath the culminating beam
From India south the expanded oceans steam,

ance to such perception—And again, this organization in the present flux and incertain state of matter, must be supported, continued, and supplied by as proper and equivalent means, as——
Ver. 128. *Through glands refining.*] secretion——
Ver. 130. *Or here expansile.*] nutrition——
Ver. 138. *While gales ingredient.*] respiration, and——
Ver. 151. *Subsiding lungs.*] sanguification; the manner of which (so long and often debated) is as clearly and intelligibly represented, as the conciseness of this plan will admit; and is in some measure illustrated by the following——
Ver. 163. *So where beneath.*] allusion; where the earth may be considered as representing the solids of the animal system—the exhalations and streams as representing the circulating fluids—the wind or gales conveying those exhalations, the interior breath—and the influence of the Moon on tides, the external influence of the atmosphere, which, by compressing the thorax and lungs, acts as antagonist to the natural contraction of the heart's muscular texture; and by embracing the outward members of the body, thereby, in some measure, actuates and assists the blood to mount in its return and ascent, contrary to all the known laws of motion.

A a

Intense their fervid exhalations rise,
And scale the steep of equinoctial skies;
Collected now progressive proudly sail,
And ride high borne upon the trading gale;
Now 'thwart the trope, or zone antarctic steer,
And now aloof the Cape's emergence veer;        170
Now wheeling dext'rous wind the Æthiop main,
And shading now the' Atlantic ocean stain;
Now westward hang o'er Montezuma's throne,
And view the worlds to ancient worlds unknown:
Around the antipodes th' adventurers roam,
And exil'd never hope their native home ;
Some pious drops the restless vagrants shed,
And now afresh their wing'd effusion spread;
Askance, or cross the broad Pacific deep,
Obliquely north the floating squadrons sweep;   180
Still arctic ply to reach the frozen pole,
Now hurry'd on Sarmatian tempests roll ;
Sinister round extreme Imaus bend,
And glooming o'er the Scythian realms depend ;
Now driven before the keen Septentrion fly,
And intercept the clear Norossian sky ;
Now view where swath'd the mighty Tartar lay ;
Now sidelong hover on the Caspian sea;
Now gather black'ning from the further shore,
And o'er Armenia sluice th' impetuous store;    190
Euphrates here and rapid Tigris swell,
And weep their streams where great Darius fell.
Primeval there, the blissful garden stood,
Here, youthful Ammon stemm'd the torrent flood.
Circumfluous rolls the long disparted tide,
And mighty realms the wand'ring flux divide:
Here, Nineveh, and fair Seleucia rise;
There, Babel vain, attempts the laughing skies,
While proudly round the female structures gleam,
And break and tremble in the blazing stream;    200
Proficient whence, the liquid confluence meet,
And through the gulf their kindred ocean greet;
Urg'd by the Moon, abjure the pearly shore,
And travel whence they sprung—to travel as before.
    How the song smiles, should deeming censure
        chide
As disproportion'd, through allusion wide !
What though we join this globe's encumber'd frame,
The deep unfathom'd, and the copious stream,
With all the appendage of incumbent skies,
To match the frame of animalcule size—          210
Our theme no great (of One exclusive) knows ;
No little, when from One, that One, it flows;
This globe an atom to the native space,
Where vortical it wheels its annual race;

Ver. 205. *How the song smiles.*] That the former
comparison is by no means inadequate; great and
little, being but relative terms, in respect of finite
essences; and magnitude, or minuteness, as they
appear or disappear reciprocally by comparison,
depending barely on the relations, and not the
essences or nature of things; as the term little is
greater than what is less, and is only little by being
compared with something greater; so that, properly
speaking, whatever is finite, in respect of what is
finite, is not really little ; whereas, on the other
hand, in respect of infinity, all things finite are
equally diminutive; being equally remote from——
    Ver. 211 .... *One exclusive.*] What is Infinite, who
alone is absolute, great, and independent.——
    Ver. 213. *This globe an atom.*] thus to any person,
who should compare this stupendous globe of earth

Its vortex (by adjacent whirlpools bound)
A point to worlds that circling blaze around ;
Lost in the whole, these vanish in their turn,
And but with relative effulgence burn :
But where finite to Infinite aspires,
Shrunk from its Lord, the universe retires ;    220
A shade its substance, and a blank its state,
Where One, and only One, is only Great !
All equidistant, or alike all near,
The reptile minim, or the rolling sphere;
Alike minutely great, or greatly less,
In form finite Infinitude express;
Express the seal of Character Divine,
And bright, through his informing radiance shine.
    Just so as when sublime the fancy soars,
And worlds on worlds illimited explores ;       230

and ocean, to its vortex, or the vast extent of space
that includes our planetary system, in which Saturn takes thirty years to finish his circle round the
Sun; upon the supposition that such person were
transported to the Sun in the centre of our vortex,
and the Earth transported beyond the planet Saturn,
to the uttermost verge of the vortex; this Earth,
though shining with reflected light, would not then
appear even as a point, and would only be visible by
the assistance of a telescope.
    Ver. 215. *Its vortex.*] Again, should such person
contemplate the surrounding vortexes within his
ken, where all the planets or inhabited worlds
disappear, and nothing is perceived but a glimmering ray shed from the several suns that shine each in
the centre of their proper vortex; upon comparing
our vortical system to those other worlds or systems
that appear numberless in his view; it is evident,
that in the comparison, our system would barely
hold the proportion of a unit in number, or a point
in magnitude——
    Ver. 217. *Lost in the whole.*] and yet further,
should our thoughts extend to take in those other
vortexes, systems, and suns, that are only visible by
the help of glasses; and extending yet further,
comprehend the whole imaginable and grand material system or universe; in this comparison, all
the visible worlds in their turn would shrink to a
proportionate point——
    Ver. 219. *But where finite.*] But should we at-
tempt yet higher, and compare the universe of matter, to immensity, the attribute of Deity ; here the
whole universal system, with which our thoughts
were so greatly expanded, quite vanishes; since
whatever is finite, as finite, will admit of no compa-
rative relation with infinity; for whatever is less
than infinite, is still infinitely distant from infinity,
and lower than infinite distance the lowest or least
cannot sink——
    Ver. 223. *All equidistant.*] in respect therefore of
the Creator, all creatures are upon a level——
    Ver. 226. *In form finite.*] and yet by being crea-
tures, even the most seemingly despicable, bear
such relation to their Creator, as expresses his
stamp and character sufficient to make it most
highly valuable to all its fellow-creatures; who are
themselves only valuable, by sharing and partaking
the same Divine Influence——
    Ver. 229. *Just so as when sublime.*] which Divine
Influence or character not only declares the immediate operation and art of omnipotence, but even so
far is expressive of the very attribute of Deity, that

No end of thought, or time, or space is found,
And each immense, are each, in either drown'd:
So when the mind to central beauty tends,
And strict to fix some certain period bends,
In vain its ultimate contraction's sought,
And still delusive, shuns the labouring thought;
While that Immense! whence ev'ry essence came,
Still endless reigns in each minutest frame.
   Attentive then inspect the wondrous scene,
Nor deem our animalcule's texture vain;   240
Where tun'd through ev'ry corresponding part,
Its system closes in consummate art,
Quick, from the mind's imperial mansion shed,
With lively tension spins the nervous thread,
With flux of animate effluvia stor'd,
And tubes of nicest perforation bor'd,
Whose branching maze through every organ tends,
And unity of conscious action lends ;
While spirits through the wand'ring channels wind,
And wing the messsage of informing mind;   250
Or objects to the ideal seat convey ;
Or dictate motion with internal sway.
   As when, beneath the sultry Lybian ray,
Coop'd in his camp the Julian hero lay;

Full on the ditch the dusk Numidians bound,
And Rome's last hopes recruited rage around ;
Serenely still, amid the dread alarms,
See, Cæsar sits, the mighty soul of arms !
See, at his nod, the various combat burns,
And the wing'd scout still turns, and still returns!
While he, the war sedately weigh'd informs,   261
Himself unmov'd amid surrounding storms.
   Just so supreme, unmated, and alone,
The soul assumes her intellectual throne;
Around their queen attendant spirits watch,
Each rising thought with prompt observance catch,
The tidings of internal passion spread,
And through each part the swift contagion shed.
With motive throes the quick'ning limbs conceive;
The blood tempestuous pours a flushing wave;   270
With raging swell alternate pantings rise ;
And terrours roll within the kindling eyes.
The mind thus speeds her ministry abroad,
And rules obedient matter with a nod;
Th' obsequious mass beneath her influence yields,
And e'en her will th' unwieldy fabric wields.
Through winding paths her sprightly envoys fly,
Or watchful in the frontier senses lie;
Brisk on the tongue the grateful gusto greet,
And through the nerves return the ideal sweet;
Or incense from the nostrils' gate exhale,   281
And to their goddess waft the odorous gale;
Or musical to charm the list'ning soul,
Attentive round the tortuous ear patrole,
There each sonorous undulation wait,
And thrill in rapture to the mental seat ;
Or wondrous to the organic vision pass,
And to the mind inflect the magic glass ;
Here borne elate upon ethereal tides,
The blithe illuminated glory glides,   290
And on the beam the painted image rides;
Those images that still continuous flow,
Effluviated around, above, below,

whereas outwardly we can assign no certain bounds to the works of an infinite energy——
   Ver. 233. *So when the mind.*] so, on the other hand, within we are as much lost and bewildered, in attempting to find or assign any point or period in the texture of the most minute animalcule——
   Ver. 237. *While that Immense.*] while the harmony and infinity of the Eternal Artist are, in some degree, impressed on his works; and as outwardly we can find no bounds, so inwardly we can find no end of art and beauty——
   Ver. 239. *Attentive then inspect.*] Shall we then slight, or deem that little, in which immensity is so conspicuous? or trivial, which could employ no less than infinite wisdom and power?
   Ver. 243. *Quick, from the mind's.*] It has already been proved in this book, where the circulation of the blood was treated of (vide supra) that the least animalcule must distinctly and perfectly have all the proportion, symmetry, and adjustment of that organized texture, which is indispensably necessary for the several functions of animal life: and as I there chose the smallest of imaginable animal creatures for the general instance of the economy of an animal body ; so here I continue it as an instance of general motion and sensation, both of which are performed by the mediation of the nerves, that all tend to and arise from the brain and spinal marrow. And though formerly I showed that matter when so curiously organized, might possibly be susceptible of motion, and even the appearance of sensation, by the correspondence of its inward texture with the outward impulse or impressions made on it, like the answering harmony of a musical instrument (vide supra); yet I further demonstrated, that bare matter cannot possibly be susceptible of the least real sensation, or perception (vide supra.) I am therefore obliged, upon this occasion, and on the supposition of actual sensation, to introduce——
   Ver. 250 ...... *informing mind.*] a being of a nature distinct from matter, which being situate in the original point of motion and sensation——
   Ver. 254. *Coop'd in his camp.*] (like Julius Cæsar in his camp at Ruspina in Afric, when attacked by

Scipio and the confederate forces of Juba) without moving from that situation, receives all the concurrent intelligences from abroad, by which means it is instructed to send forth its orders and emissaries as occasions require, and thus directs and informs the whole bodily system.
   Ver. 263. *Just so supreme.*] It is an observation of an author learned in the law, that non omne simile quatuor pedibus currit ; yet as our passions (the operation of which is above described) may be called a state of warfare, the simile even in that respect is not unjust.
   Ver. 277. *Through winding paths.*] I did not think it necessary to insert here the sense of feeling, not only because there is no special or peculiar organ to which it bears relation, but because I take it for a sort of universal sense, all sensation being performed by contact; and so——
   Ver. 279. *Brisk on the tongue.*] tasting——
   Ver. 281. *Or incense.*] smelling——
   Ver. 283. *Or musical to charm.*] hearing, and——
   Ver. 287. *Or wondrous.*] seeing, being but a different kind of touch, or feeling, agreeable and accommodated to the difference of objects that are thereby perceived.
   Ver. 289. *Here born elate.*] The manner in which the——
   Ver. 291. ...... *image rides.*] object is conveyed to the eye——

True to the colour, distance, shape, and size,
That from essential things perpetual rise,
And obvious gratulate our wond'ring eyes;
Convey the bloom of Nature's smiling scene,
The vernal landscape, and the wat'ry main;
The flocks that nibble on the flow'ry lawn,
The frisking lambkin, and the wanton fawn; 300
The sight how grateful to the social soul,
That thus imbibes the blessings of the whole,
Joys in their joy, while each inspires his breast
With blessings multiply'd from all that 's bless'd!
Nor less yon heights th' unfolding Heaven display,
Its nightly twinkle, and its streaming day;
The page impress'd conspicuous on the skies,
A preface to the book of glory lies;
We mount the steep, high borne upon delight,
While hope aspires beyond—and distances the sight. 310
Thus Heav'n and Earth, whom varying graces deck,
In full proportions paint the visual speck;
So awful did th' Almighty's forming will,
Amazing texture, and stupendous skill,
The visionary net and tunics weave,
And the bright gem with lucid humours lave;
So gave the ball's collected ray to glow,
And round the pupil arch'd his radiant bow;
Full in a point unmeasur'd spaces lie,
And worlds inclusive dwell within our eye. 320
Yet useless was this textur'd wonder made,
Were Nature, beauteous object! undisplay'd;
Those, both as vain, the object, and the sight,
Wrapt from the radiance of revealing light;
As vain the bright illuminating beam,
Unwafted by the medium's airy stream:

Yet vain the textur'd eye, and object fair,
The sunny lustre, and continuous air;
Annull'd and blank this grand illustrious scene,
All, all its grace, and lifeless glories, vain; 330
Till from th' Eternal sprung this effluent soul,
Bless'd to inspect, and comprehend the whole!
O whence, say whence this endless beauty springs,
This awful, dear, delightful depth of things?
Whence but from thee! thou Great One! thou Divine!
Placid! and Mild! All Gracious! All Benign!
Thou Nature's Parent! and Supreme Desire!
How lov'd the offspring! and how bless'd the Sire!
How ever bless'd! as blessings from thee flow,
And spread all bounteous on thy works below:
The reptile, wreath'd in many a wanton play; 341
And insect, basking in the shine of day;
The grazing quadruped, and plumy choir
That earthly born to heavenly heights aspire;
All species, form'd beneath the solar beam,
That numberless adorn our future theme,—
Fed in thy bounty, fashion'd in thy skill,
Cloth'd in thy love, instructed in thy will,
Safe in thy conduct, their unerring guide,
All-save the child of ignorance and pride— 350
The paths of Beauty and of Truth pursue,
And teach proud man those lectures which ensue!

---

## UNIVERSAL BEAUTY.

### BOOK V.

Thus Nature's frame, and Nature's God we sing,
And trace even life to its Eternal Spring—
The Eternal Spring! whence streaming bounty flows;
The Eternal Light! whence ev'ry radiance glows;
The Eternal Height of indetermin'd space!
The Eternal Depth of condescending grace!
Supreme! and Midst! and Principle! and End!
The Eternal Father! and the Eternal Friend!
The Eternal Love! who bounds in ev'ry breast; 9
The Eternal Bliss! whence ev'ry creature's bless'd—
While man, e'en man, the lavish goodness shares,
The wretch offends, and yet his Goodness spares;
Still to the wayward wight indulgent turns,
And kindly courts him to the peace he spurns;
Emits the beam of intellectual light—
Bright is the beam, and wilful is the night—
While Nature amply spreads th' illustrious scene,
And renders all pretext of errour vain:
Unfolded wide her obvious pages lie,
To win attention from the wand'ring eye; 20
Full to convince us, to instruct us sage,
Strict to reform, and beauteous to engage.

Ver. 296. *And obvious gratulate.*] by whose second mediation the perceiving soul rejoices——
Ver. 297. ......*bloom of Nature's smiling scene.*] beholding the elegance and beauty of nature——
Ver. 299. *The flocks that nibble.*] but chiefly those animated beings who through life are susceptible of happiness——
Ver. 301. *The sight.*] as every generous person increases his happiness by rejoicing in the happiness of others——
Ver. 305. *Nor less yon heights.*] and as by means of this miraculous organ of sight, the beauties of Earth are conspicuous, so in the first page of Heaven expanded before us, to raise our hope to an assurance of further bliss.
Ver. 313. *So awful did.*] The wonderful texture of the eye——
Ver. 315. *The visionary net.*] its retina (continued from the optic nerve) which is the proper organ of vision——
Ver. 315. ...... *tunics weave* ] its coats——
Ver. 316. ...... *humours lave.*] humours——
Ver. 318. ...... *radiant bow.*] and iris, or circle surrounding the pupil, within which——
Ver. 319. *Full in a point.*] the images of things are distinctly painted.
Ver. 321. *Yet useless was.*] The infinitely wise adjustment of nature demonstrated; inasmuch as the eye had been useless without the object, both eye and object useless without light, the eye, the object, and the light, still useless without the medium of air for conveyance, and altogether as useless without——

Ver. 331. *Till from the Eternal.*] the mind, which only can perceive.
Ver. 341. *The reptile.*] This paragraph was added as a hint of the following part, which chiefly treats of the arts and instincts of the inferior animal system: which subject, as it is less abstruse, so, it is probable, it will be more agreeable than any hitherto treated of.

Like Nature's law no eloquence persuades,
The mute harangue our ev'ry sense invades;
Th' apparent precepts of the Eternal Will,
His ev'ry work, and ev'ry object fill;
Round with our eyes his revelation wheels,
Our ev'ry touch his demonstration feels.
And, O Supreme! whene'er we cease to know
Thee, the sole Source, whence sense and science
   flow!        30
Then must all faculty, all knowledge fail,
And more than monster o'er the man prevail.
Not thus he gave our optic's vital glance,
Amid omniscient art, to search for chance,
Blind to the charms of Nature's beauteous frame;
Nor made our organ vocal, to blaspheme:
Not thus he will'd the creatures of his nod,
And made the mortal, to unmake his God;
Breath'd on the globe, and brooded o'er the wave,
And bid the wide obsequious world conceive:  40
Spoke into being myriads, myriads rise,
And with young transport gaze the novel skies;
Glance from the surge, beneath the surface scud,
Or cleave enormous the reluctant flood;
Or roll vermicular their wanton maze,
And the bright path with wild meanders glaze;
Frisk in the vale, or o'er the mountains bound,
Or in huge gambols shake the trembling ground;
Swarm in the beam; or spread the plumy
   sail—
The plume creates, and then directs the gale:  50
While active gaiety, and aspect bright,
In each expressive, sums up all delight.
But whose unmeasur'd prose, memorial long!
Or volubility of num'rous song,
Can Nature's infinite productions range,
Or with her ever-varying species change?
Not the fam'd bard, in whose surviving page
Troy still shall stand, and fierce Pelides rage;
Not this the Mantuan's rival Muse could hope;
Nor thou, sole object of my envy,—Pope!  60
Then let the shoals of latent nations sleep,
Safe in the medium of their native deep;
Haply, when future beauteous scenes invite,
Haply our line may draw those scenes to light.
Meanwhile, Earth's minim populace inspect,
With just propriety of beauties deck'd;
Consummate each, adapted to its state,
And highly in the lowest sphere complete.

Ver. 27. *Round with our eyes.*] The Deity necessarily inferred from the contemplation of every object——
Ver. 41. *Spoke into being,*] But more especially visible in the animate creation, so infinitely diversified in the several species and kinds of——
Ver. 43. *Glance from the surge.*] fish——
Ver. 45. *Or roll vermicular.*] reptiles——
Ver. 47. *Frisk in the vale.*] quadrupeds——
Ver. 49. *Swarm in the beam.*] insects——
Ver. 49. ...... *or spread the plumy sail.*] and birds; as this diversity unites in one universal evidence of One Sole Operator——
Ver. 67. *Consummate each.*] whose characteristic of infinite power and wisdom is equally conspicuous in all, since even the lowest can be derived from no less than the Highest; and, in that respect, the lowest, though apparently despicable, is most highly valuable, since the same Extensive Benignity condescends even to the——

Sublime the theme, and claims th' attentive ear,
Well worth the song, since worth the Almighty's
   care;        70
Since e'en the smallest from the Great One
   springs,
Great and conspicuous in minutest things!
The reptile first, how exquisitely form'd,
With vital streams through ev'ry organ warm'd!
External round the spiral muscle winds,
And folding close th' interior texture binds;
Secure of limbs or needless wing he steers,
And all one locomotive act appears:
His rings with one elastic membrane bound,
The prior circlet moves th'-obsequious round;  80
The next, and next, its due obed'ence owes,
And with successive undulation flows.
The mediate glands, with unctuous juice replete,
Their stores of lubricating guile secrete;
Still opportune, with prompt emission flow,
And slipping frustrate the deluded foe;
When the stiff clod their little augers bore,
And all the worm insinuates through the pore.
Slow moving next, with grave majestic pace,
Tenacious snails their silent progress trace;  90
Through foreign fields secure from exile roam,
And sojourn safe beneath their native home.
Their domes self-wreath'd, each architect attend,
With mansions lodge them, and with mail defend:
But chief, when each his wint'ry portal forms,
And mocks secluded from incumbent storms;
Till gates, unbarring with the vernal ray,
Give all the secret hermitage to day;
Then peeps the sage from his unfolding doors,  99
And cautious Heaven's ambiguous brow explores:

Ver. 73. *The reptile first.*] earth-worm, and has had a peculiar regard towards it——
Ver. 74. *With vital streams.*] in the organization of its frame——
Ver. 75. *External round.*] its wonderful apparatus for motion, by a most especial and accurate provision——
Ver. 83. *The mediate glands.*] With every other mean and method accommodated to its sphere of action; and conducting to the safety and perfection of its state.
Ver. 89. *Slow moving next.*] The same infinite Wisdom operating ever equally, though variously, is no less admirable in the different apparatus for the snail's motion, as differently adapted to its different state and occasions——
Ver. 90. *Tenacious snails.*] by a broad and strong skin on either side the belly, and the emission of a glutinous slime; by the assistance of which they adhere to any surface more firmly than they could do with claws or talons.
Ver. 93. *Their domes self-wreathed.*] The advantage of their shells, which they form by a froth or petrifying juice, which they secreted from their body; and at any time repair a fracture or breach in their building, which serves them both for house and armour.
Ver. 95. *But chief.*] And which they close up during the winter, to shut out the inclemency of the weather, and also to prevent any consumption of the fluids; by which means they want no nourishment at a time that they cannot be readily provided.

Towards the four winds four telescopes he bends,
And on his own astrology depends;
Assur'd he glides beneath the smiling calm,
Bathes in the dew, and sips the morning balm;
The peach this pamp'ring epicure devours,
And climbing on the topmost fruitage towers.
Such have we cull'd from nature's reptile scene,
Least accurate of all the wondrous train,
Who plung'd recluse in silent caverns sleep;
Or multipede, Earth's leafy verdure creep;    110
Or on the pool's new mantling surface play,
And range a drop, as whales may range the sea:
Or ply the rivulet with supple oars,
And oft, amphibious, course the neighb'ring shores;
Or shelt'ring, quit the dank inclement sky,
And condescend to lodge where princes lie;
There tread the ceiling, an inverted floor,
And from its precipice depend secure:
Or who nor creep, nor fly, nor walk, nor swim,
But claim new motion with peculiar limb,    120
Successive spring with quick elastic bound,
And thus transported pass the refluent ground.
Or who all native vehicles despise,
And buoy'd upon their own inventions rise;
Shoot forth the twine, their light aerial guide,
And mounting o'er the distant zenith ride.
Or who a twofold apparatus share,
Natives of Earth, and habitants of air;
Like warriors stride, oppress'd with shining mail,
But furl'd, beneath, their silken pennons veil:    130
Deceiv'd, our fellow reptile we admire,
His bright endorsement, and compact attire,
When lo! the latent springs of motion play,
And rising lids disclose the rich inlay;
The tissu'd wing its folded membrane frees,
And with blithe quavers fans the gath'ring breeze;

Ver. 101. *Towards the four winds.*] I have inserted this opinion of snails having eyes at the ends of
their horns, rather in submission to authority, than
that I am really persuaded it is so. However, they
may, in a great measure, be said to see with their
touch, which in this part is extremely sensible, and
equally serves their purpose——
Ver. 107. *Such have we cull'd.*] and since the
common earth-worm and snail (which seem the
most despicable of all reptiles) are so curiously
adorned, and provided in all respects, how amazing
must the same conduct, care, and artifice be,
through the several scenes of minute animalcules!
who leave no place empty of suitable inhabitants,
and are doubtless of greater consequence in nature,
than our partial and narrow way of thinking may
imagine.
Ver. 119. *Or who nor creep.*] Such as grasshop-
pers, crickets, and frogs.
Ver. 123. *Or who all native.*] Spiders, &c. whose
flights are owing to a thread of inconceivable fineness and levity, which they dart, on occasion, from
their bodies, and which being buoyed up by the
least breeze, bears off the animalcule to which it is
annexed.
Ver. 127. *Or who a twofold.*] Of this kind are
beetles and lady-cows; and nothing can be more
entertaining than to see them, by a surprising machinery of little springs and hinges, erect the smooth
covering of their backs, and unfolding their wings
that were most neatly disposed within their cases,
prepare for flight——

Elate tow'rds Heav'n the beaut'ous wonder flies,
And leaves the mortal wrapp'd in deep surprise.
So when the guide led Tobit's youthful heir,
Elect, to win the seven times widow'd fair,    140
Th' angelic form, conceal'd in human guise,
Deceiv'd the search of his associate's eyes;
Till swift each charm bursts forth like issuing flame,
And circling rays confess his heavenly frame;
The zodiac round his waste divinely turns,
And waving radiance o'er his plumage burns:
In awful transports rapt, the youth admires,
While light from earth the dazzling shape aspires.
O think, if superficial scenes amaze,
And e'en the still familiar wonders please,    150
These but the sketch, the garb, the veil of things,
Whence all our depth of shallow science springs;
Think, should this curtain of Omniscience rise,
Think of the sight! and think of the surprise!
Scenes inconceivable, essential, new,
Whelm'd on our soul, and lightning on our view!——

Ver. 149. *O think* ] But what is there in nature
that is not equally surprising? We are ashamed
not to account for objects that are daily obvious to
our senses; and yet every work of the Deity——
Ver. 151. *These but the sketch.*] in many respects,
is to us as really incomprehensible as the Divine
Operator; for who can give rule or measure to the
works of an Infinite Artist? and if we only super-
ficially behold, and reason from the qualities of
things——
Ver. 153. *Think, should this curtain.*] were this
veil at once laid aside, how insupportably conspicuous would the fullness of Infinite Wisdom and
Essential Beauty appear; pouring on our weak and
unequal senses! We should then be convinced of
the equal folly and impiety of presumption on one
side; or scepticism on the other: of pretending to
know all things; or (because we know not all
things) of inferring that nothing is to be known.
Our reason indeed is not infallible; but neither is
it useless: reason, throughout its sphere of knowledge, perceives a wisdom and art that is obvious
and inimitable; and hence cannot avoid to infer,
that the same wisdom and art is universal; and that
there must be One Sole Omnipresent and
Adorable Artist. But when reason attempts a
higher pitch, and forms to itself independent
schemes of the courses of nature, or fitnesses of
things; nothing can be more vain than such a dic-
tating arrogance.
That there is, and ever will be, a fitness and propriety in things, is evident even to reason; because
reason perceives sufficient wisdom and goodness,
to demonstrate that wisdom and goodness now are,
and ever will be, the sole directing principles. But
to say to what infinitely wise and good purposes
such direction tends; to say how far, and in what
particulars, the nature of such tendency may alter
the appearance of fitness in things; so as to determine what now is, or hereafter may be fit, possible,
or impossible; is generally as absurd as to attempt
to grasp the universe in our hand, or circumscribe
immensity with a carpenter's compass.
Hence this one great truth is evident, that though
our reason apprehends a propriety and fitness in
the relations of many things and actions both natural and moral, yet as we cannot comprehend the
whole of Infinite Wisdom——

How would the vain disputing wretches shrink,
And shiv'ring wish they could no longer think ;
Reject each model, each reforming scheme,
No longer dictate to the Grand Supreme,      160
But, waking, wonder whence they dar'd to dream!
All is phenomenon, and type on Earth,
Replete with sacred and mysterious birth,
Deep from our search, exalted from our soar ;
And reason's task is, only to adore.
Who that beholds the summer's glist'ring
      swarms,
Ten thousand thousand gaily gilded forms,
In volant dance of mix'd rotation play,
Bask in the beam, and beautify the day ;
Would think these airy wantons so adorn,      170
Were late his vile antipathy and scorn,
Prone to the dust, or reptile through the mire,
And ever thence unlikely to aspire ?

Ver. 162. *All is phenomenon.*] there is doubtless a further design, and more latent fitness and beauty in things and their relations, than we can apprehend or are aware of : and as this fitness may be relative in respect of duration, and in respect of the difference between the present and future state of things ; many things may now appear unfit and improper in our way of thinking, which in reality are most perfective of future infinitely wise and directing purposes, to which our notions are by no means adequate.
What has been here offered in the way of hypothesis, is evidently rational ; but when more nearly attended to, will admit of the highest demonstration : for either there is a present absolute fitness in things ; or a fitness in futuro, that is, in prospect or tendency, and only relative here to what must be absolute hereafter. But if there were an absolute fitness in the present state of things, there could then be no change in any thing ; since what is best can never change to better : but things do change, and must therefore have a present relative fitness, tending to, and productive of some future, absolute, and unchangeable fitness or perfection ; to which this present relative fitness is by a moral, wise, and orderly necessity, precedent.
The sum of all (which has so long and copiously employed the pens of the learned) is this,—First, that there is a present fitness or beauty sufficiently obvious in things, to demonstrate an Over-ruling Wisdom.—Secondly, that this Over-ruling Wisdom, or God, now does, and ever will conduct all things for the best.—But, thirdly, since things change, they cannot be now in their state of perfection.—Therefore, fourthly, there must be some other or future state, to which all things tend and are directed, for the final and unchangeable perfection of all things.
Ver. 166. *Who that beholds.*] If any thing in the preceding lines seems too much tinctured with mystery ; I must beg leave to ask the enemies of mystery, were it not for repeated experience, whether every thing in nature would not appear a mystery ? or, whether, when they contemplate a gnat or butterfly, &c. they can perceive, by the bare light of nature or reason, the relation its present state and form bears to the several changes, states, and forms, through which it has passed, all in appearance as distinct as difference could make them ?——

Or who with transient view, beholding, loathes
Those crawling sects, whom vilest semblance
      clothes ;
Who, with corruption, hold their kindred state,
As by contempt, or negligence of fate ;
Could think, that such, revers'd by wondrous
      doom,
Sublimer powers and brighter forms assume ;
From death, their future happier life derive,      180
And though apparently entomb'd, revive ;
Chang'd, through amazing transmigration rise,
And wing the regions of unwonted skies ;
So late depress'd, contemptible on Earth,
Now elevate to Heav'n by second birth ?
No fictions here to willing fraud invite,
Led by the marvellous, absurd delight ;
No golden ass, no tale Arabians feign ;
Nor flitting forms of Naso's magic strain,
Deucalion's progeny of native stone,      190
Or armies from Cadmean harvests grown ;
With many a wanton and fantastic dream,
The laurel, mulberry, and bashful stream ;
Arachne shrunk beneath Tritonia's rage ;
Tithonus chang'd and garrulous with age.
Not such mutations deck the chaster song,
Adorn'd with nature, and with truth made strong ;
No debt to fable, or to fancy due,
And only wondrous facts reveal'd to view.      199
Though numberless these insect tribes of air,
Though numberless each tribe and species fair,
Who wing the noon, and brighten in the blaze,
Innumerous as the sands which bend the seas ;

Ver. 174. *Or who with transient view.*] or, whether, by contemplating an animalcule's egg, they can foresee that this will produce a maggot or caterpillar, &c. that the maggot or caterpillar will build its own sepulchre ; (and having continued therein for a certain term, in an apparent state of mortality, and laid aside its former limbs and organized members) will at length break through the gates of death, and put on a state and form of higher beauty and perfection, than could enter into any heart to conceive, or could have employed the dreams of the deepest philosopher ?——

Ver. 186. *No fictions here.*] How would the refined reasoners of the present age argue against the absurdity and impossibility of such unaccountable contradictions, were not the facts too obvious to sense and perpetual experience to be disputed ? facts altogether as wonderful, though not so fabulous, as the——

Ver. 188. *No golden ass.*] marvellous metamorphoses in romance ; or——

Ver. 189. *Nor flitting forms.*] those of Ovid, in his tales of——

Ver. 190. *Deucalion's progeny.*] Deucalion and Pyrrha re-peopling the world after the flood——

Ver. 191. *Or armies from.*] of Cadmus sowing the serpent's teeth, from whence sprung armed men——

Ver. 193. *The laurel.*] Of Daphne——

Ver. 193. *..... mulberry.*] Pyramus and Thisbe——

Ver. 193. *...... and bashful stream.*] Arethusa——

Ver. 194. *Arachne shrunk.*] Arachne turned into a spider——

Ver. 195. *Tithonus chang'd.*] and Tithonus to a grasshopper.

These have their organs, arts, and arms, and tools,
And funct:ons exercised by various rules;
The saw, axe, auger, trowel, piercer, drill;
The neat alembic, and nectareous still:
Their peaceful hours the loom and distaff know;
But war, the force and fury of the foe,
The spear, the falchion and the martial mail,   210
And artful stratagem where strength may fail.
Each tribe peculiar occupations claim,
Peculiar beauties deck each varying frame;
Attire and food peculiar are assign'd,
And means to propagate their varying kind.
  Each, as reflecting on their primal state,
Or fraught with scientific craft innate,
With conscious skill their oval embryon shed,
Where native first their infancy was fed:
Or on some vegetating foliage glu'd;   220
Or o'er the flood they spread their future brood;
A slender cord the floating jelly binds,
Eludes the wave, and mocks the warring winds;
O'er this their sperm in spiral order lies,
And pearls in living ranges greet our eyes.
In firmest oak they scoop a spacious tomb,
And lay their embryo in the spurious womb:
Some flow'rs, some fruit, some gems, or blossoms
    choose,
And confident their darling hopes infuse;
While some their eggs in ranker carnage lay,   230
And to their young adapt the future prey.

  Ver. 204. *These have their organs.*] However
merry or hyperbolical these assertions may appear,
in respect of creatures, whom our ignorance, or
want of inspection, have rendered despicable to us;
there is nothing more certain, than that they have
more trades and utensils than are here specified.
The inimitable fineness, and mathematical proportion of their works, is a double demonstration
of their skill, and the accuracy of their instruments; to which the most exquisite manufacture of
man may bear just such relation, as a cumbrous
windmill to the neatest tool or machine in a watch-
maker's shop——
  Ver. 216. *Each as reflecting* ] No less admirable
is their reason, precaution, instinct, or what you
please to call their care and skill, in the disposition
of their eggs or embryo; not scattered at random,
but situated agreeable to the nature of every
species, in such places, and among such supplies
of nutriment, as will alone contribute to the perfection, and be acceptable to the several appetites of
their young ones——
  Ver. 220. *Or on some vegetating foliage.*] if on the
leaves of vegetables, then situated and glued in
such a manner, as not to be subject to the influence
of winds or rain——
  Ver. 222. *A slender cord.*] For the mathematical
order in which gnats dispose their eggs or sperm on
the water, vide Derham's Phys. Theology, fig. IX.
and X.——
  Ver. 226. *In firmest oak.*] And so, in like manner, the various receptacles which are suitable to
the sperm of each species, are almost infinite; and
yet the art and prophetic precaution, which, by a
several and distinct method, is peculiar to each,
carries the air of as much wisdom and importance,
as if the harmony and connection of nature had depended on the regular and uniform propagation of
every several sect or species——

  Meantime the Sun his fost'ring warmth be-
    queaths,
Each tepid air its motive influence breathes,
Mysterious springs the wav'ring life supply,
And quick'ning births unconscious motion try;
Mature their slender fences they disown,
And break at once into a world unknown.
  All by their dam's prophetic care receive
Whate'er peculiar indigence can crave: ˉ
Profuse at hand the plenteous table's spread,   240
And various appetites are ap ly fed.
Nor less each organ suits each place of birth,
Finn'd in the flood, or reptile o'er the earth;
Each organ, apt to each precarious state,
As for eternity design'd complete.
Thus nurs'd, these inconsiderate wretches grow,
Take all as due, still thoughtless that they owe.
  When lo! strange tidings prompt each secret
And whisper wonders not to be express'd; [breast,

  Ver. 232. *Meantime the Sun.*] The generality of
these wonderful animals having thus performed all
the requisites, take no further care for their young;
but (like the ostrich, who covers her eggs with the
sands) they are sensible their duty is over, and
leave the rest to the clemency of the seasons, and
the sufficiency of nature, who, in these instances,
renders all further caution needless——
  Ver. 240. *Profuse at hand.*] and alone furnishes
and provides for all, with a more than parental care
and tenderness——
  Ver. 242. *Nor less each organ.*] But among all
the instances of a universal and benign Providence,
nothing can be more signal or expressive of the extensive Goodness than the occasional and temporary
parts and organs of many animals in their change-
able state, still accommodated, suited, and adapted with the most circumstantial and minute exactness to the immediate manner and convenience of
their existence; and yet as immediately shifted
and thrown aside upon the animal's commencing a
new state and scene of action, and a set of limbs
and garniture furnished de novo, as it were a new
suit of clothes fitted and contrived agreeable to
every season. This observation may have escaped
many, who thought it beneath them to inquire into
the economy of these minute animals; but it is
obvious to all persons in the tadpole estate of frogs,
who, in their minority, are provided with a fin-like
tail, which seems to constitute the chief part of
their bulk, but drops off as the growing limbs extend, and gives notice that its continuance is superfluous and unnecessary.
  Though the state and conduct of these animals,
as here described, may be looked on as allegorical,
and representative of the present state of man and
his future hopes; yet the case with them is already
real, and their change and resurrection most evident
to sense. The moment they are hatched——
  Ver. 246. *Thus nu s d.*] they set about pampering their little carcases, without any other apparent
thought or concern——
  Ver. 248. *When lo!*] within a certain period of
time, they conceive a disrelish to all past enjoyment, and by a profound revery seem, as it were,
studious of some great event. During this interval,
new judgments are acquired, and resolutions taken;
they foresee and rejoice at their approaching mortality——

Each owns his errour in his later cares,　250
And for the new unthought of world prepares:
New views, new tastes, new judgments are acquir'd,
And all now loathe delights so late admir'd.
In confidence the solemn shroud they weave,
Or build the tomb, or dig the deadly grave;
Intrepid there resign their parting breath,
And give their former shape the spoils of death;
But reconceiv'd as in a second womb,
Through metamorphoses, new forms assume:
On death their true exalted life depends,　260
Commencing there, where seemingly it ends.
The fullness now of circling time arrives;
Each from the long, the mortal sleep revives;
The tombs pour forth their renovated dead,
And, like a dream, all former scenes are fled.
But O! what terms expressive may relate
The change, the splendour of their new-form'd
　　　　state?
Their texture nor compos'd of filmy skin,
Of cumbrous flesh without, or bone within,
But something than corporeal more refin'd,　270
And agile as their blithe informing mind.
In ev'ry eye ten thousand brilliants blaze,
And living pearls the vast horizon gaze;
Gemm'd o'er their heads the mines of India gleam,
And Heav'n's own wardrobe has array'd their
　　　　frame;
Each spangled back bright sprinkling specks adorn,
Each plume imbibes the rosy tinctur'd morn;
Spread on each wing the florid seasons glow,
Shaded and verg'd with the celestial bow,
Where colours blend an ever varying dye,　280
And wanton in their gay exchanges vie.
Not all the glitter fops and fair ones prize,
The pride of fools, and pity of the wise;
Not all the show and mockery of state,
The little, low, fine follies of the great;

Ver. 254. *In confidence.*] they frame and prepare
the mansions of death with the same cheerful alac-
rity and elegance, as a bridal chamber, or wedding
garment——
Ver. 257. *And give their former shape.*] here the
texture of their former organs suffers an actual dissolution; and whatever the pr nc ple of regenera-
tion be, a new, and, in appearance, a quite different
creature, is conceived from the remains of the old
one——
Ver. 262. *The fullness now.*] their consummation
is at hand——
Ver. 264. *The tombs pour forth.*] their sepulchres
give way; they spring forth, and wing the air in inexpressible beauty and magnificence.
Ver. 268. *Their texture.*] Insecta non videntur
nervos habere, nec ossa, nec spinas, nec cartilagi-
nem, nec pingu a, nec carnes, nec crustam quidem
fragilem, ut quædam marina, nec quæ jure d catur
cut s: sed mediæ cujusdam inter omnia hæc naturæ
corpus. Plin. Nat. Hist. lib. xi. cap. 4.
Ver. 272. *In ev'ry eye.*] These creatures, though,
in appearance, they have but two eyes, are rea ly
multocular. Every lens (of which there are an innumerable number) is a distinct eye, which has a
branch of the optic nerve ministring to it: by
which provision no object escapes them; they at
once view almost all round them; and as their eyes
are immovable, this multiplicity amply supplies the
absence of the motory nerves.

Not all the wealth which eastern pageants wore,
What still our idolizing worlds adore;
Can boast the least inimitable grace,
Which decks profusive this illustrious race.　289
Hence might the song luxuriant range around,
Or plunge the nether ocean's dread profound;
There mete leviathan's enormous length,
Adorn'd with terrours, and unmatch'd in strength,
The sea his pool of pastime when he bathes,
And tempests issue while his nostril breathes,
See where behemoth's pillar'd fabric stands!
His shade extensive cools the distant lands;
Encamp'd, an army on his shoulder lies,
And o'er his back proud citadels arise.
But vain those gifts, those graces to relate,　300
Which all perceive, and envy deems complete.
" O Nature!" cries the wretch of human birth,
" O, why a step-dame to this lord of Earth?
To brutes indulgent bends thy partial care,
While just complainings fill our na al air.
Helpless, uncloth'd, the pride of Nature lies,
And Heaven relentless hears his viceroy's cries.
O, wherefore not with native bounties bless'd,
Nor thus in humble poor dependance dress'd?
Give me the self-born garb, the bark of trees,　310
The downy feather, and the wintry fleece;
The crocodile's invulnerable scale,
Or the firm tortoise's impervious mail;
The strength of elephants, the rein deer's speed,
Fleet and elastic as the bounding steed;
The peacock's state of gorgeous plumage add,
Gay as the dove in golden verdure clad;.
Give me the scent of each sagacious hound;
The lynx's eye, and linnet's warbling sound;
The soaring wing and steerage of the crane,　320
And spare the toil and dangers of the main:
O, why of these thy bounteous goods bereft,
And only to interior reason left?
There, there alone, I bless thy kind decree;
Nor cause of grief, or emulation see."
Thus needless prayers for needless gifts are sent,
And man is, only in his wants, content;
Indocile where he needs instruction most,
His only errour is his only boast.
Ye self-sufficient sons of reasoning pride,　330
Too wise to take Omniscience for your guide,
Those rules from insects, birds, and brutes discern,
Which from the Maker you disdain to learn!—
The social friendship, and the firm ally,
The filial sanctitude, and nuptial tie,
Patience in want, and faith to persevere,
The endearing sentiment, and tender care,

Ver. 300. *But vain those gifts.*] Cujus causa videtur cuncta alia genuisse natura, magna et sæva
mercede contra tanta sua munera; ut non sit
satis æstimare, parens melior homini, an tristior
noverca fuerit——
Ver. 304. *To brutes indulgent.*] Ante omnia
unum animantium cunctorum, alienis velat opibus:
cæter s variè tegumenta tribuit; testas, cortices,
coria, spinas, villos, setas, pilos, plumam, pennas,
squamas, vellera. Truncos etiam arboresque cor-
tice, interdum gemino, a frigoribus et calore tutata
est. Hominem tantum nudum, et in nuda humo,
natali die abjicit ad vagitus statim et ploratum,
nullumque tot animalium aliud ad lacrymas, et
has protinus vitæ principio. Plin. Nat. Hist. L.
VII. Prœm.

Courage o'er private int'rest to prevail,
And die all Decii for the public weal.
  Nor less for geometric schemes renown'd,    340
And skill'd in arts and sciences profound,
Their textur'd webs with matchless craft surprise,
Their buildings in amazing structures rise :
To them each clime and longitude is known,
Each finds a chart and compass of his own ;
They judge the influence of ev'ry star,
And calculate the seasons from afar ;
Through devious air pursue the çertain way,
Nor ever from the conscious dictate stray.

---

## UNIVERSAL BEAUTY.

### BOOK VI.

" Ye human offsprings of distinguish'd birth,
So justly substituted lords of Earth ;
Who boast the seal of highest Heav'n impress'd,
Thence with supremacy of reason bless'd,
Attend the song, and vindicate your claim !
Recall your ancestry of antique fame,
Prime artizans of each sagacious craft,
The curious model, or designing draft,
All talents technical for each device,
The skilful fabric, and the texture nice !    10
  " Or, if ye pride in science more refin'd,
Judicial product of the studious mind,
The scheme politic, or the moral plan,
To form the conduct, or the heart of man ;
Attend the depth of maxims which ensue,
More than e'er Solon, or great Cecil knew ;
The moral, with diviner precepts fraught,
Than stories, or than eastern magi taught."
  First let the botanist his art forego,
And o'er the mountain trace the Cretan doe :    20
Behold the critic stand with curious mien,
And cull the virtues of the various green,
Secrete her foliage from the noxious weed,
And conscious of her skill securely feed !
  Where did this sylvan leech her lore acquire,
From Æsculapius, or his radiant sire ?
When to her panting flank the weapon flies,
And deep within the feather'd mischief lies,
She seeks the well-known med'cine of the plain,
Nor yet despairs where human art were vain ;    30
Mild through her frame the sov'reign balsams glide,
And the keen shaft falls guiltless from her side.
  Ye wanderers of the faithless main ! relate,
Whose science then averts impending fate,
When haply on the distant climate thrown,
Ye view strange objects, and a world unknown ;
Each tree uncouth, with foreign fruitage crown'd,
And unacquainted plenty blooming round :
But who shall dare, with rash advent'rous hand,
To pluck the bane of a suspected land ?    40
Half famish'd, they devour with wistful eyes ;
But fear dissuades to tempt the dangerous prize :
Yet should they spy, amid the fruitful brake,
The skilful trace of some luxurious beak,
With birds their elegant repast they share,
And bless the learn'd inhabitants of air.
  Bear, bear my song, ye raptures of the mind !
Convey your bard through Nature unconfin'd,
Licentious in the search of wisdom range,
Plunge in the depth, and wanton in the change ; 50

Waft me to Tempe, and her flow'ry dale,
Borne on the wings of ev'ry tuneful gale ;
Amid the wild profusions let me stray,
And share with bees the virtues of the day.
  Soon as the matin glory gilds the skies,
Behold the little virtuosi rise !
Blithe for the task, they preen their early wing,
And forth to each appointed labour spring.
Now Nature boon exhales the morning steam,
And glows and opens to the welcome beam ;    60
The vivid tribes amid the fragrance fly,
And ev'ry art and ev'ry business ply.
Each chymist now his subtle trunk unsheaths,
Where, from the flow'r, the treasur'd odour breathes ;
Here sip the liquid, here select the gum,
And o'er the bloom with quiv'ring membrane
     hum.
Still with judicious scrutiny they pry,
Where lodg'd the prime essential juices lie ;
Each luscious vegetation wide explore,
Plunder the spring of ev'ry vital store :    70
The dainty suckle, and the fragrant thyme,
By chymical reduction, they sublime ;
Their sweets with bland attemp'ring suction strain,
And, curious, through their neat alembics drain ;
Imbib'd recluse, the pure secretions glide,
And vital warmth concocts th' ambrosial tide.
  Inimitable art ! do thou atone
The long lost labours of the latent stone ;
Though the five principles so oft transpire,
Fin'd, and refin'd, amid the tort'ring fire.    80
Like issue should the daring chymist see,
Vain imitator of the curious bee,
Nor arts improv'd through ages once produce
A single drachm of this delicious juice.
Your's then, industrious traders ! is the toil,
And man's proud science is alone to spoil.
  " Sweet 's the repast where pains have spread
     the board,
And deep the fund incessant labours hoard ;
A friendly arm makes ev'ry burden light ;
And weakness, knit by union, turns to might." 90
  Hail, happy tribes ! illustrious people hail !
Whose forms minute such sacred maxims veil ;
In whose just conduct, fram'd by wondrous plan,
We read revers'd each polity of man.
Who first in council form'd your embryon state ?
Who rose a patriot in the deep debate ?
Greatly propos'd to reconcile extremes,
And weave in unity opposing schemes ?
From fears inferr'd just reason of defence,
And from self-int'rest rais'd a public sense ;    100
Then pois'd his project with transposing scale,
And from the public, show'd the private weal ?
Whence aptly summ'd, these politicians draw
The trust of power, and sanctitude of law ;
Power in dispensing benefits employ'd,
And healing laws, not suffer'd, but enjoy'd.
The members, hence unanimous, combine
To prop that throne on which the laws recline ;
The law 's protected e'en for private ends,
Whereon each individual's right depends ;    110
Each individual's right by union grows,
And one full tide for ev'ry member flows ;
Each member, as the whole communion great,
Back'd by the pow'rs of a defending state ;
The state by mutual benefits secure,
And in the might of ev'ry member sure !
  The public thus each private end pursues :
Each in the public drowns all private views :

By social commerce and exchange they live,
Assist supported, and receiving give.        120
  High on her throne, the bright imperial queen
Gives the prime movement to the state machine:
She, in the subject, sees the duteous child;
She, the true parent, as the regent mild,
With princely grace invested sits elate,
Informs their conduct, and directs the state.
Around, the drones, who form her courtly train,
Bask in the rays of her auspicious reign;
Beneath, the sage consulting peers repair,
And breathe the virtues of their prince's care;   130
Debating, cultivate the public cause,
And wide dispense the benefit of laws.
  So have I seen, when breathing organs blow,
One board sonorous fill the various row ;
The pipes divide the unity of sound,
And spread the charms of symphony around.
  The clust'ring populace obsequious wait,
Or speed the different orders of the state ;
Here greet the labourer on the toilsome way,
And to the load their friendly shoulder lay ;   140
Or frequent at the busy gate arrive,
And fill with amber sweets their fragrant hive ;
Or seek repairs to close the fractur'd cell ;
Or shut the waxen wombs where embryos dwell ;
The caterers prompt, a frugal portion deal,
And give to diligence a hasty meal ;
In each appointed province all proceed,
And neatest order weds the swiftest speed ;
Dispatch flies various on ten thousand wings,
And joy throughout the gladsome region rings. 150
  Distinctly canton'd is their spacious dome:
Here infants throb within the quicken'ng comb ;
Here vacant seats invite to sweet repose,
And here the tide of balmy nectar flows;
While here their frugal reservoirs remain,
And not one act of this republic 's vain.
  As oft the North, or Gallia's fruitful coast,
Pour'd forth their sons, a wide superfluous host !
To distant climes the banded legions stray'd,
And many a plan of future empire laid ;       160
Like powers these wise prolific people send,
And o'er the globe their colonies extend.
  When swarms tumult'ous claim an ampler space,
And through the straitening citadel increase,
An edict issu'd in this grand extreme,
Proclaims the mandate of the power supreme.
Then exil'd crowds abjure their native home,
And sad, in search of foreign mansions roam;
A youthful empress guides their airy clan,
And wheels and shoots illustrious from the van. 170
Fatigu'd at length, they wish some calm retreat,
The rural settlement, and peaceful state;
When man presents his hospitable snare,
And wins their confidence with traitorous care.
Suspicion never flies a gen'rous breast—
Betray'd, each enters an unwary guest;
Here every form of ancient maxim trace,
And emulate the glories of their race.
  As when from Tyre imperial Dido fled,
And o'er the main her future nation led ;      180
Then staid her host on Afric's meted land,
And in strait bounds a mighty empire plann'd:
So works this rival of the Tyrian queen ;
So founds and models with assiduous mien ;
Instructs with little to be truly great,
And in small limits forms a mighty state.
Intent, she wills her artists to attend,
And from the zenith bids her towers descend:

Nor like to man's, the aerial structures rise ;
But point to earth, their base amid the skies.   190
  Swift for the task the ready builders part,
Each band assign'd to each peculiar art ;
A troop of chymists scour the neighb'ring field,
While servile tribes the cull'd materials wield,
With tempering feet the labour'd cement tread,
And ductile now its waxen foliage spread.
The geometricians judge the deep design,
Direct the compass, and extend the line;
They sum their numbers, provident of space,
And suit each edifice with answering grace.   200
  Now first appears the rough proportion'd frame,
Rough in the draught, but perfect in the scheme ;
When lo ! each little Archimedes nigh,
Meets ev'ry angle with judicious eye;
Adjusts the centring cones with skill profound,
And forms the curious hexagon around.
  The cells indors'd with doubled range adhere,
Knit on the sides, and guarded on the rear ;
Nought of itself, with circling chambers bound,
Each cell is form'd, to form the cells around ; 210
While each still gives what each alike demands,
And but supported by supporting stands ;
Jointly tran ferring and transferr'd exists ;
And, as by magic union, all subsists.
  Amazing elegance ! transcendent art !
Contriv'd at once to borrow and impart ;
In action notable, as council great,
Their fabrics rise, just emblems of their state.
  Nor be the wasp exclusive of our lays ;
Though in a foe, still merit claims its praise,  220
Claims the revealing song, and claims the light,
Though long conceal'd in all-obscuring night.
For deep these subterranean tribes retire,
Nor work like man, that mortals may admire ;
In Earth's dark womb their pompous structures
                                      rise,
Worthy the sight of Heaven's all-seeing eyes ;
While they recluse, o'er nether kingdoms reign,
And wrapt as in a little world remain.
  Around this world a waxen vault extends,
And wide like yon enfolding concave bends ;   230
Magnific cupola ! on either hand,
Unfolded, two mysterious portals stand,
Emblems of human life, precarious state,
At entrance born, and dying in retreat.
Thousands within retiring taste repose;
Or through the streets the busy concourse flows :
Yet not as ours their costly pavements spread,
But high on terrasses and towers they tread,
With which not Roman aqueducts may vie,
Not the fam'd gardens pendent from the sky : 240
Here cities pil'd o'er cities may be seen,
And sumptuous intervals display'd between,
Where columns each proud architrave support,
And form the pomp of many an ample court ;
The weight through ten successive stories bear,
And to the top th' incumbent fabrics rear.
  So have I seen in all the pride of show,
Some splendid theatre divide below,
With charms of gay machinery surprise,
Scenes over scenes, and stage on stage arise,   250
Lost in the glory of descending skies.
  Not so the multipede aurelias dwell,
But form, sole architects, the pensive cell ;
Like seers of old, they seek some lonely seat,
And from the vain the busy world retreat ;
Here fondly form a structure of their own,
And bind the vault of solitary stone;

Or clay, or timber, oft attemp'ring, mould,
And round their form the ductile mansion fold;
Or in peculiar occupations skill'd,     260
A wondrous dome of silken fabric build:
No debt to foreign implements they owe,
But from themselves the mantling tissues flow;
Themselves the gorgeous canopy they spread,
Themselves the loom, the distaff, and the thread—
The thread as fam'd Arachne's texture fine,
When thwart the morn she darts her floating line,
Or spins the scheme of implicated wiles,
And o'er her great Newtonian rival smiles;
Reveals the deep enigma of his trade,     270
And squares the circle in the vernal glade;
The sportive plans of matchless art displays,
While round, and round, the dext'rous wanton plays.

   How might the song with endless rapture pry,
Secluded deep where latent nations lie,
And scar'd from man, a mighty hunter, fly?
He follows panting with a savage joy,
Rapt in his favourite transport to destroy:
To man, even man becomes a mutual prey;
No gain can satiate, and no limits stay;     280
Down the dread depths his boundless lucre dives;
Warr'd on himself, with passion passion strives.
Fly him, ye rangers of the rolling flood!
Fly him, ye songsters of the warbling wood!
Ye dwellers subterrene, the tyrant fly!
And safe in your remote asylums lie;
Where mice, innoxious cottagers, remain,
Meek in the covert of the flow'ry plain;
Recluse their cautious hermitage explore,
And treasure provident the wintry store.     290
With kindred crafts, deep mining burrows work,
And sunk amid Dedalean lab'rinths lurk;
Their various habitation nightly change,
And through a length of maz'd apartments range.

   The beaver too, great architect! immur'd,
With his associate train, retires secur'd;
Their wary mansion elegantly stands,
Where the smooth stream or smiling lake expands,
Whose gentle wave in friendly visit glides,
And swells the tenement with grateful tides.     300
Two posterns gape with deep deceit below,
And o'er the pass fair mantling waters flow;
Evasive whence, they scape the dang'rous train,
Or wide expatiate on the yielding plain;
Through trading currents sail to distant shores,
Or homeward laden with returning stores.
Laborious here, they hew the sounding wood,
And lift the prize triumphant o'er the flood;
Here, lightly some vimineous burdens bear,
Or jointly here the pond'rous rafter share:     310
Spread o'er their tails, they waft the temper'd
    clay,
And deep, and broad, their firm foundations lay;
Assign each chamber its commodious size,
Till rooms o'er rooms and trodden ceilings rise;
Their tail the trowel, as adorning train,
Their teeth the saw, the chissel, and the plane.

   While ardent Sirius shoots a thirsty ray,
And autumn yet withholds retreating day,
They range at large, and gambol through the stream,
Frisk on the beach, or batten in the beam;     320
Or Nature's bounteous vegetation taste,
And opportune indulge the transient feast.
But when pale Phosphor points the morning gale,
Curls on the wave and chills along the vale,
Domestic cares their conscious breast employ;
The frolic hours and luscious banquets cloy;

Intent they furnish the prophetic hoard,
And pile the treasures of their homely board,
With friendship's charm beguile the sullen year,
And barter luxury for social cheer.     330
For them Astrea holds th' impartial scale,
Her frugal hands unenvy'd portions deal;
Health quaffs satiety from Nature's bowl;
Peace gives the constant banquet of the soul;
High in the midst chaste Temperance is crown'd,
And Time leads on the smiling Hours around.

   Thou awful Depth of Wisdom unexplor'd!
Thou Height, where never human fancy soar'd!
Supreme Irradiance! speed the distant ray,
Far speed the dawn of thy internal day;     340
And O! if such, inform the fav'rite line,
And be the praise as inspiration thine!

   Say! when the nest thy little halcyons form,
Brood on the wave, and mock the threat'ning storm;
Who quells the rage of thy reluctant main,
Or o'er thy winter throws a lordly rein?
Lulls the rock'd mansion on the slumb'ring tide,
And bids the care of guardian depths subside?
Till, volatile, the new-fledg'd infants rise;
The surge mounts free, and breaks upon the skies.
   Eternal! thine is ev'ry round of time,     351
The circling season, and the varying clime;
Thine! ev'ry dictate of the conscious breast;
Thine! ev'ry texture of the genial nest,
The oval embryon, and the fost'ring ray;
And thine the life that struggles into day!

   To thee thy callow importuners cry,
Gracious thy ear, and bounteous thy supply;
Till the flown choirs the revel consort raise,
And hymn to Heav'n the rhapsody of praise!     360
   Dispers'd through ev'ry copse, or marshy plain,
Where haunts the woodcock, or the annual crane,
Where else encamp'd the feather'd legions spread,
Or bathe incumbent on their oozy bed,
The brimming lake thy smiling presence fills,
And waves the banners of a thousand hills.
Thou speed'st the summons of thy warning voice;
Wing'd at thy word, the distant troops rejoice,
From ev'ry quarter scour the fields of air,
And to the general rendezvous repair:     370
Each from the mingled rout disparting turns,
And with the love of kindred plumage burns:
Thy potent will instinctive bosoms feel,
And here arranging, semilunar, wheel;
Or marshal'd here the painted rhomb display,
Or point the wedge that cleaves the aerial way:
Uplifted on thy wafting breath they rise;
Thou pavest the regions of the pathless skies, [host,
Through boundless tracts support'st the journey'd
And point'st the voyage to the certain coast;
Thou the sure compass, and the sea they sail,
The chart, the port, the steerage, and the gale!

   Thus through the maze of thy eternal round,
Through yon steep Heav'n, and nether gulfs pro-
The dusky planet, and the lucid sphere,   [found,
Earth's pond'rous ball, and soft enfolding air,
The fish who glance or tempest through the main,
The beasts who trip or thunder o'er the plain,
The reptile wreathing in the wanton ring,
The bird high wafted on the tow'ring wing,     390
All, all from thee, Sole Cause Essential! tend,
Thence flow effusive, thither cent'ring end;
The bliss of providential vision share,
And the least atom claims peculiar care!

   Yet ere material entity begun,
Or from the vast this universe was won;

While finitude erewhile was unconfin'd,
Nor space grew relative, to form assign'd ;
Thou didst thy own eternal now sustain,
And space was swallow'd in thy boundless main ;
Thyself the filler of thy own abyss,    401
Thyself the great eternity of bliss !
All when, and where, in thee imbosom'd lay,
The blaze of majesty, and self-born day ;
No void was found, where Endless Beauty beam'd ;
No darkness, where Essential Glory flam'd ;
No want, no solitude, where thou wer't bless'd,
And in thyself th' unbounded whole possess'd.
Of reason thou the co-eternal cause,
Thyself all reason, and thy will all laws ;  410
All-reasoning will with pow'rful wisdom fraught!
Thy wisdom, one unchanging endless thought,
Where all potential natures were survey'd,
And even in pre-existence lay display'd—
All, all—things past—now present—yet to be,
Great Intellect! were present all to thee ;
While thou sole infinite essential reign'd,
And of finites the infinite contain'd,
Ideal entities in One Supreme,    420
Distinguish'd endless, yet with thee the same,
Thy pow'r their essence, and thy will their claim.
Whence—at thy word, worlds caught the potent
And into being leap'd this wondrous round. [sound,
Pois'd on thy will the universal hung ;
Attraction to its central magnet clung ;
Thy spacious grasp the mighty convex clos'd ;
Soft on thy care incumbent worlds repos'd :
Within, throughout, no second cause presides,
And One Sole Hand the maz'd volution guides !
Hence endless good, hence endless order springs ;
Hence that importance in minutest things ;
And endless hence dependence must endure,
Bless'd in his will, and in his pow'r secure!

---

## JERUSALEM DELIVERED.

### AN EPIC POEM.

TRANSLATED FROM THE ITALIAN OF TORQUATO TASSO.

### BOOK I.

Of arms, devote to Heav'n's Eternal King,
Of sainted hosts the sacred Chief I sing,
Who freed that tomb, to infidels a prey,
Where once the Lord for all the living lay :
Alike his might and conduct claim applause ;
And much he suffer'd in the glorious cause :
In vain infernal fury rais'd alarms,
And half the world oppos'd contending arms ;
Sedition, rul'd, beneath his sceptre lay,
Foes learn'd to fear, and rebels to obey :
So Heaven would crown its hero with success,
And virtue triumph'd in the power to bless.
O Muse! whom mortal trophy would profane,
And thy chaste brow with fading laurel stain ;
While circling glories round thy temples play,
And circling angels hymn th' eternal lay,
O! breathe celestial ardours to my breast,
Inspire the song to Albion's prince address'd ;
And pardon fiction mix'd with truths divine,
Or arts to please which, goddess, are not thine !
Well dost thou know the purport of my song,
Though dress'd to charm, with secret virtue strong ;
While veil'd, beneath the verse the moral lies,
And captivates the soul with kind disguise.

His bitter thus the friendly leech conceals,
And with the fraud of latent med'cine heals ;
To the sick taste he promises delight,
And obvious sweets the infant lip invite ;
Health, ambush'd, in the potion is imbib'd,
For man must e'en to happiness be brib'd.
Six suns had now their annual journey run,
And seen the war that with the first begun ;
Still in his cause Messiah's hosts engage,
And eastward bid the kindling combat rage.
Antioch, and Nice, were now the victor's prize,
Or won by storm, or captive by surprise :
In vain all Asia rises to repel,
Beneath their force unnumber'd Persians fell ;
And last Tortosa vanquish'd, they retire,
Till war shall with returning spring respire.
Scarce winter, warm'd before the golden ray,
Restor'd the battle with the length'ning day,
When God, self rais'd from his eternal throne,
Sublime o'er Heav'n's high empyrean shone.
Aw'd from his seat, though patent to his view,
The rolling universe holds distance due :
He looks ; unnumber'd worlds before him lie,
And Nature lives collected in his eye.
To Syria, on the Christian peers intent,
All-piercing the Divine Perception bent ;
Where Godfrey stood, conspicuous in his sight,
Above the princes eminently bright :
Nor wealth allures him, nor ambition charms,
But faith refines, and heavenly ardour arms ;
While zeal alone his placid bosom fires,
And with the warrior all the saint conspires.
Not such the thoughts that Heav'n in Baldwin
From virtue alien, though by blood ally'd ; [spy'd,
Ambitious phantasms haunt his idle brain,
And pride still prompts him to be greatly vain.
With silent anguish Tancred stood oppress'd,
While love, fond passion, languish'd in his breast.
But Boemond's cares on Antioch's glory wait,
And model in his mind her new-form'd state ;
While the great chief, late terrible in arms,
With arts of peace and social conduct charms,
At once of Earth and Heaven asserts the cause,
Instructs with piety, and forms with laws.
Rinaldo then, to war and nature new,
Gave all his brave, his open soul to view ;
Untam'd that restless bosom wish'd the fight,
And circling perils gave his eyes delight :
Wisdom and fame, but fame the most refin'd,
By turns prevail'd, and fir'd or form'd his mind ;
While he on Guelpho, sage instructor, hung,
And caught the maxims falling from his tongue.
This saw the Deity—through ev'ry breast,
Each latent inclination lay confess'd ;
Then call'd, and from the bright angelic round,
Forth issu'd Gabriel to the sacred sound ;
He, of the prime celestial splendours came,
Obsequious to the will of Heaven's Supreme :
Gracious to man the social spirit stands,
To saints the messenger of bless'd commands ;
Thence, breathes the cordial incense to his King,
And wafts their vows on his returning wing.
(Expressive then th' inutterable Name)
" To Godfrey his Creator's will proclaim—
Ask, wherefore are my Sion's bonds unty'd ?
The hero's sword why dormant at his side ?
To council bid him cite each Christian peer,
Reprove the tardy, and the valiant cheer :
Him I elect, superior in his sway ;
And let his rivals and the world obey."

Nor now Heaven's flaming minister delays;
He heard with transport, and with speed obeys:
Air organiz'd his casual limbs compos'd,
Attemp'ring radiance round his essence clos'd;
A human form the dazzling shape display'd,
But in the majesty of Heav'n array'd;
While youth smil'd o'er him with celestial grace,
And beamy ringlets wanton'd round his face.

He spread for flight his many-tinctur'd wings,
And light from Heaven's high firmament he springs:
All feather'd as the darting shaft he flies,
Cuts the bright steep, and cleaves the yielding skies,
Divides the sphere of many a shining star;
And sends the coming glory from afar;
Then stands on Lebanon reveal'd to view,
And shakes his plumes bedropp'd with morning
   Now half appear'd the horizontal Sun,   [dew.
And west, and east, with equal glory shone;
There shed his evening, here his morning ray,
And gave to diff'rent worlds dividual day—
When wing'd from Lebanon's aspiring head,
The angelic message to Tortosa sped,
What time the duke his orizons address'd,
And breath'd to Heav'n the rapture of his breast:
In usher'd graceful with the morning beam,
A brighter morn the dazzling angel came;
And placid, to the much admiring man,
The bright, the social intellect began.

" Attend, thou favour'd of Supreme Decree!
Thus sends the Deity, and sends to thee—
In Bulloign's breast what kindling zeal should glow,
What fires impel him forceful on the foe?
When Sion calls, when list'ning Heav'n commands,
And consecrates her cause in Godfrey's hands,
'T is thine to vindicate her just complaints,
To strike the shackles from her captive saints;
'T is thine to summon ev'ry christian peer,
Reprove the tardy, and the valiant cheer;
Their gen'ral thou, superior in thy sway—
God so appoints, and mortals must obey."

He ceas'd; and less'ning from the hero's view,
Back to his native Heav'n the brightness flew;
Nor Godfrey yet supports excess of light,
New to the shape, and dizzy'd at the sight;
Not the wide blaze his darkling eye sustains,
And chillness thrill'd unwonted through his veins.

But soon he calls the vision to his mind,
And ponders on the glorious charge assign'd;
Fresh to his soul the high behest returns,
And with redoubled zeal his bosom burns:
Nor yet, that Heav'n preferr'd its warrior saint,
Did pride dilate him, or ambition taint;
But through Almighty will, his will aspires,
As the spark mounts amid the kindling fires.

Straight where they lay, each chieftain he invites;
Now mild requires, and now by mandate cites:
Dispatch'd around his posting envoys fly,
And prayers are mix'd with counsels to comply.
Persuasive here, the gallant soul he charms;
But here provokes, and here impels to arms;
Here blows the slumb'ring virtue to a flame,
And breathes throughout the noble thirst of fame.
·Such Godfrey's conduct, nor his conduct vain;
Each comes, attended by his warlike train:
Tortosa but a scant reception yields,
And tented armies throng the neighb'ring fields.
All awful, to consult the peers repair;
Save Boemond, each majestic fills his chair;
When graceful, to the senate Godfrey rose,
And deep the stream of elocution flows.

" Ye warriors! Heaven elected, to restore
The sacred faith of him those Heavens adore;
Preserv'd for this through many a fearful day,
The foreign climate, and the deadly fray,
Well may ye rush, thus arm'd, upon the foe,
And fight secure where Heaven averts the blow.
Nor vain I deem the purchase of your toil,
The vanquish'd province, and the glorious spoil;
Since trophies through reforming nations rise,
And bear Christ's name triumphant to the skies.
" But not for this we left our native place,
The known endearment, and the chaste embrace;
Each social sweet for distant battle chang'd,
And wand'ring, through the faithless ocean rang'd:
For this, an end unequal to your arms,
Nor bleeds the combat, nor the conquest charms;
Nor such the prize your matchless labours claim,
Barbarian kingdoms, and ignoble fame.
" Was not the scope of our united powers
To scale the steep of Sion's hallow'd towers?
High o'er her walls to force resistless way?
Deep on her dungeons pour the long-lost day?
To lift oppression from her house of pain,
Snap the vile yoke, and burst the pagan chain?
Restore to piety her sacred seat,
And build for virtue a secure retreat;
Where each devoted pilgrim might repair,
And Christ receive the tributary prayer?
" Where triumph stands, defeated of its aim,
How vain the victory! how fruitless fame!
While still the wish'd achievement turns aside,
And conquest flows, but with a diff'rent tide.
For wherefore is the might of Europe arm'd,
Asia invaded, and the world alarm'd,
If ruin be alone the victor's praise,
And states subverted, while we meant to raise?
" Frail is the strength of sublunary things,
The pomp of titles, and the pride of kings;
Nor such the hope a faithful few may boast,
Hemm'd in by nations, and a barb'rous coast;
Our country distant, fickle Greece untry'd,
Nor aught but Heav'n to combat on our side.
" True, we have fought, nor have we fought in vain—
Proud Antioch won, and hostile armies slain!
But these, achiev'd by many a wondrous way,
Show God still guides the fortune of the day;
Then if we seek or conquest, or applause,
Through means averse to his victorious cause,
The pride of triumph, and the thirst of fame,
In death shall vanish, or be quench'd in shame.
" Ah! never may our arms such issue find,
Nor we rebel ingrate, while Heav'n is kind;
But still conform'd to the divine behest,
Be the great period, as commencement, bless'd!
Then, then, while time, while ev'ry pass is ours,
And prompt occasion chides our ling'ring powers,
Quick let us rise, toss high the spacious mound,
And circling gird Jerusalem around.
" For me, ye princes! hear what I presage—
Be witness Heav'n! and ev'ry future age!
Now is the conquering crisis mark'd by fate;
Now is the time to give the world a date,
The time to consecrate your deeds to fame,
To bless your arms, or ever blast your name:
But once elaps'd, though panting to regain,
Vain are our hopes, our labours wake in vain;
Each Sun shall set, a witness to our woe,
And Egypt succour the recruiting foe."

He ceas'd; a solemn whisp'ring fill'd the pause,
And the whole senate murmur'd deep applause:
When Peter, sage and ven'rable man,
Slow rising, to the circling chiefs began.
(Though distant from the war and world retir'd,
Prime author, he the distant war inspir'd;
Which once in act, he issu'd from his cell,
And thus promotes what he commenc'd so well:)
  " With transport I survey the truth express'd
Warm in each eye, and big in ev'ry breast;
When Bulloign speaks it with prevailing charms,
No task remains but to enforce with arms:
Yet pardon one reflection still behind,
A weight long since incumbent o'er my mind.
  " Where friendships are by light suspicions cool'd,
And rulers are themselves by passions rul'd,
Incongruous orders issu'd by the great,
Sedition pregnant in the lower state;
Occasions opportune are ever lost,
And ev'ry good and glorious end is cross'd:
Ill does it seem, when discord thus attaints
The cause of christians, and a host of saints;
A host, whom breach eternal must divide,
While various minds in various powers preside.
  " The mutual weal divided pow'r withstands,
Nor Justice holds her scale with various hands;
Corruption ev'ry partial view attends,
And the torn state each selfish member rends.
Not so has Nature, in the frame of man,
Drawn the true scheme of each politic plan;
Gave various parts to form one beauteous whole,
And gave a head in prudence to control;
Like ruler should ye choose, could I advise,
And form your own, as Nature's conduct, wise."
He said, when, mantling from each hero's breast,
Ambition mounts in ev'ry eye express'd:
But soon a beam, emissive from above,
Shed mental day, and touch'd the heart with love;
Gave jealous rage to know divine control,
And rul'd the tempest rising in the soul.
Calm reason the recoiling tumult sways;
The sage's speech attentive judgment weighs;
To merit ev'ry partial view expands,
And Godfrey! Godfrey! ev'ry voice demands.
  His will, they vote, their future test of right,
His leading arm their ensign to the fight,
Their Atlas fit to bear th' incumbent weight,
The trust of empire, and the task of state;
Submiss, to him they yield unrival'd sway,
And willing princes, late his peers, obey.
The consult ended, and the royal name
Was borne wide wafted on the wings of fame;
The news a thousand busy tongues impart,
Cheer ev'ry brow, and gladden ev'ry heart.
  For not unconscious was the warlike crowd,
Of worth to ev'ry vulgar eye avow'd;
Approving throngs their Godfrey's presence greet,
Charm'd to his sight, or prostrate at his feet,
Proclaim their monarch with united voice,
And loudly consecrate the public choice.
He mild returns, while corresponding grace
Speaks from his mien, and answers in his face;
Then bids his host prepare their bright array,
And light with early arms th' ensuing day.
  The ruddy Sun, now orient, chas'd the dawn,
Shot o'er the sea, and reach'd the dewy lawn;
Up with the morn arose the ready train,
Each seiz'd his arms, and issu'd on the plain.
The driving squadrons fill the spacious coast;
Wide wave the banners of the various host,

Whose burnish'd mail, with flitting lustre gay,
Reflect thick lightnings, and return the day.
Superior the observant Godfrey stands,
Orders the field, and marshals all the bands;
Directs the moving legions from on high,
And rules a host with his experienc'd eye.
Say thou, my soul, with gifts divinely bless'd,
And all thy treasures of a conscious breast!
What chiefs conspicuous then adorn'd the plain,
Their ancient glory, and attending train?
So may'st thou recollect the spoils of age,
And from oblivion snatch the future page:
To thee old Time shall ev'ry trophy yield,
And all the pristine honours of the field,
Transplanted fair on each immortal line,
And ev'ry ear, in ev'ry age, be thine.
  First came the Gauls, Clothario at their head,
Whom Hugo late, unhappy warrior, led:
Where four fair streams an ample nation fold,
And Gallia's isle with soft embraces hold,
He in the front of levy'd numbers shone,
Prime of their host, and brother of the throne;
But early death suppress'd the vital flame,
Secure of Heav'n, and still surviving fame.
Nor now the troops an equal leader scorn,
Great as the first, though not of princes born:
A thousand arm'd, sedate they move along,
In weighty mail indissolubly strong;
Attend their chief with boasted ensigns gay,
And the proud arms of ancient France display.
  To these, each clasp'd within his steely case,
Alike in stature, and in martial grace,
From celtic Gaul a kindred band succeeds,
A thousand warriors on a thousand steeds;
Normania's Robert in the van presides,
And the clos'd files with native sceptre guides.
  Two prelates next their dreaded arms unite,
Renown'd for piety, as fam'd in fight;
Great Ademare with standards richly spread,
And William reverend at his people's head;
Great William, chief amid four hundred known,
From Orange and the deep meander'd Rhone;
Like dangers Ademare from Poget sought,
And in the front of equal numbers fought.
Awful in arms, in ministry divine,
Rever'd alike, in lawn or mail they shine;
Their docile troops with bold example teach,
And fearless combat for the faith they preach.
  Then Baldwin o'er his powers appear'd supreme,
From Bouillon seated on the silver Seme,
Chief of the bands whom late duke Godfrey led,
Now chief of chiefs, and of their host the head.
Carinto o'er four hundred next presides,
With valour fires them, and with wisdom guides;
But thrice that number mightier Baldwin leads,
And arm'd and haughty in the van precedes.
  To these ensue, amid the beaten fields,
Whom Guelpho governs, and whom Suabia yields;
Guelpho, with merit, as with fortune crown'd,
And greatly e'en among the great renown'd:
The princely house of Est, and Roman sire,
Their offspring's emulating acts inspire;
But distant, he his native country sway'd,
And where the chief was born the soil obey'd.
  Two neighb'ring floods his bounded realms contain,
The rising Danaw, and the circling Rhene,
Maternal heritage, with plenty bless'd,
By Rhetians erst, and northern Sweves possess'd!
With nations added by his conq'ring sword,
Carinthian too confess'd the Guelphian lord;

A race addicted much to free delights,
To social joys, and hospitable rites,
While o'er their huts the wintry tempests pass,
Warm'd by the genial fire and sparkling glass:
Five thousand hence the sage commander drew,
A cheerful, faithful, and intrepid crew;
Sad chance of war, the greater number slain,
To mirth no longer wakeful, press the plain.

The Belgi next, in helm and polish'd mail,
Their snowy limbs and flaxen ringlets veil;
Whose narrow realms unbounded wealth contain,
Hemm'd in by France, Almania, and the main.
Where the Moselle and blended Rhine extend,
Wide o'er the banks their weighty harvests bend:
A people valiant, and inur'd to toil,
Domestic industry, and fore gn spoil.
With these appear, dispos'd in armed files,
The subject powers of their associate isles;
Who w th steep mounds repair those dang'rous shores,
Where the breach threatens, and the tempest roars;
Where the proud flood disdains inferior prey,
And o'er a nation pours the headlong sea.

Beneath another Robert all unite,
A thousand arm'd, and eager for the fight,
They pass, and to the British squadrons yield
The next succession of the moving field.
But these superior to the Belgi shone,
Array'd by William, Albion's younger son;
From their broad backs their graceful weapons flow,
The swift wing'd quiver, and the twanging bow:
With them, Hibernia sends her sons to war,
Hibernia, neighbour of the northern star,
Where her bleak hills and hoary woods aspire,
And less'ning from the distant world retire.

Then Tancred caught the eye with heedless grace,
Strength in his arm, and beauty in his face:
Of all that valiant, that unnumber'd host,
Rinaldo might superior prowess boast;
Of worth untainted, fearless in the fight,
And else, unmatch'd, in glory, as in might.
One sole default his nobler ardour chain'd,
While love amid his strength of virtues reign'd,
Caught from a glance of momentary charms,
And nurs'd with anguish in the din of arms.

So fame relates, on that triumphant day,
When Persians fell an undistinguish'd prey,
Far from his host the slaughter Tancred led,
And singly follow'd where the foremost fled.;
Till feverish, and fatigu'd, he sought repose,
And to his wish a rural arbour rose,
Where a cool stream, beneath the whisp'ring shade,
With pendent flow'rs, and quiv'ring willows play'd;
Thither he turn'd, but, with unwary thought,
Soon lost the sweets of that repose he sought.

By the clear stream unlook'd for perils lay,
In all the charms of virgin beauty gay;
Her body arm'd with Amazonian grace,
But obvious all the dangers of her face:
His captive step the warrior stopp'd amaz'd,
Sigh'd as he look'd, and trembled while he gaz'd;
His eyes ran o'er the maid, with hasty art
Thence drew her form, and fix'd it in his heart.

But soon alarm'd the beauteous Pagan rose;
With lovely threats her kindling visage glows;
She brac'd her helm, and fierce the hero view'd,
In act to combat whom her charms subdu'd.
His troops approach'd; the virgin fled like wind,
But hop'd in vain to leave the chief behind:
The place, the person, present to his view,
The nymph still flies, and still his thoughts pursue;

Within his eyes the loved ideas roll,
Heave in his heart, and sicken in his soul.
Hence o'er his cheek distemper'd anguish spread,
Prey'd on his strength, and on his beauty fed;
Despair lay sad, but silent in his breast,
And sighs alone the length'ning woe express'd.
Proud to attend Campania's valiant bands,
Eight hundred horse await the chief's commands;
Campania, bless'd with all the bloom of health,
A seat of pleasures, and a fund of wealth,
Where the rich odours breathe along her vales,
And feed old ocean with the fragrant gales.

Behind, two hundred hardy warriors came,
The only warriors of the Grecian name:   [field,
Light arm'd, and swift, they range th' embattl'd
Nor poise the lance, nor bear the pond'rous shield;
But in close fight, or distant skirmish, know
The dextrous falchion, and the bending bow.
Spare were their steeds, and slender their repast,
But blithe and agile as an eastern blast;
Untir'd, and practis'd to the nimble rein,
They stop, and turn, and dart along the plain :
Thus borne, the riders confidently go,
Deface the battle, and fatigue the foe ;
Expert to charge, to traverse, and to fly,
Pursu'd they combat, and the conquerors die.

Tatino points their progress o'er the fields,
He the sole chief the Grecian empire yields;
Inglorious Greece! in indolence profound
Repos'd, while arm'd contention rang'd around:
" But now the sad equivalent is paid;
Left by the cause you once refus'd to aid,
The haughty Pagan lords it o'er your plains,
And wakes the shameful lethargy with chains."

To close the rear the bold adventurers came,
The last in order, though the first in fame;
A troop of heroes, Europe's proudest boast,
And the dire terrour of the Asian host!
Whate'er through t mes of high memorial rung,
By prose recorded, or by poet's sung,
Achievements valorous, and knights renown'd,
In chivalry, or antique fable found—
Transferr'd to these, may real credence find,
And sum th' excellence of human k nd.

Though each might claim, as of peculiar right,
To lead a host, and rule the ranks of fight,
Dudon that high pre-eminence demands,
By joint assent of the advent'rous bands.
Where Aufidus first rolls an infant wave,
This chief of chiefs Hesperian Conza gave:
Sage were his words, and hoary was his head,
To constant toil, and early battle bred;
Yet ever was his boiling courage young,
And his try'd nerve to vivid action strung;
His bosom nobly trench'd with many a scar,
Old to the field, the father of the war.

Amid the prime of those illustrious peers
Eustatio, Bulloign's youngest son appears;
Great was his challenge of peculiar fame,
But more through his imperial brother's name.
With him, Gernando, heir of Norway, rides,
And in his pomp of vaunted title prides:
Nor less distinguish'd, in the peerless train,
Rode the fam'd Roger, and bold Engerlane ;
Gentonio and Rambaldo, far renown'd;
And the twin Gerrards with like honours crown'd.

Nor here Obizo, or Ubaldo there,
With Rosmond Lancaster's redoubted heir,
Consign'd to latest annals shall accuse,
The mute neglect of our injurious Muse;

Nor brave Achilles, Sforza, Palameed,
Well worthy praise for many a worthy deed;
From Lombardy the valiant brethren came,
To form the great triumvirate of fame.
With these rode Otton, who, in single fight,
Won the dire trophy of the Paynim knight,
High on whose helm a naked infant lay,
Curl'd by a snake voracious o'er the prey.
  The like memorial Guaschar, Raphe, demand,
Who boldly join the voluntary band;
To Eberard and Guernier too belong,
The force and fame of an immortal song;
And the two Guidos equal honours claim,
Alike in glory and alike in name.
  But you, bright pair! shall ever foremost shine;
Shall still survive, to deck the mournful line—
Gildippe, in thy dearer Edward blest;
And Edward, only in thy cares distress'd !
Too fond the knot which wedded faith supplies,
When mutual merit holds what beauty ties !
One life inspir'd them, nor could death divide;
They fought together, and together died.
  Ah Love, all subtle tutor, thou can'st teach
What, uninstructive else, the world might preach;
Give the soft sex to loathe inglorious rest,
String the weak arm, and steel the snowy breast !
You brac'd the fair-one's helm, her corselet tied,
And gave the guardian to her Edward's side !
Thus on they pass'd, inseparably pair'd;
For him she battled, and for her he fear'd :
By each, for each alone, was life desir'd;
And, wounded in the other, each expir'd.
  Last in the rear of that embattled train,
Shone the young comet of the glitt'ring plain,
Rinaldo—in whose fair, majestic face,
Soft beauty sweeten'd ev'ry martial grace :
The youth impatient of his manly prime,
Fled from his years, and stripp'd the speed of time;
Proud on his arm the force of battle lay,
And round his snowy limbs the Graces play.
  This chief, by Adige on the winding shore,
Sophia, spouse to great Bertoldo, bore :
But soon Matilda takes their infant heir,
Caresses fondly, and conducts with care;
To early honour fires his growing youth,
The thirst of glory, and the love of truth;
When to his ears the warlike tidings came,
And sent the stripling to the fields of fame.
  Five summers thrice had bloom'd around his head,
When to the wond'ring camp the warrior fled :
Alone he past, all eager on his way,
And reach'd the shore, and cross'd the Egean sea;
Then sped along by many an unknown coast,
And mix'd exulting with the Christian host.
And now three years were spent amid alarms,
Since first the princely fugitive took arms,
When manhood early dawning from within,
Shed the smooth down to deck his ivory chin.
  The horsemen past, the num'rous foot succeed,
And trace the marches of the bounding steed;
But these, Tolosa's monarch, Raimond heads,
And in the front majestically treads :
From the proud cliffs of Pyrenêan hills,
From lucid Garonne, and the neighbouring rills,
Wide o'er a placid climate stretch'd his reign,
And eastward overlook'd the midland-main.
Four thousand vet'rans hence the hero drew,
Who all the arts of various battle knew :
Compos'd they march, to ev'ry toil address'd;
But he, their bulwark, tow'rs before the rest.
  VOL. XVII.

Five thousand Stephen from Ambasia brings,
And Tours, and shelving Blesæ, seat of kings,
Where Loire the too delicious region laves,
And cities float reflected o'er the waves;
Impatient, hence, of discipline or toil,
They caught the native softness of the soil :
Yet the fair troops, in martial semblance arm'd,
With show of lively preparation charm'd;
Their valour as the lightly flaming fire,
Furious they charge, and fainting soon retire.
  Alcasto then stepp'd forth with haughty pace;
Fierce was his mien, and menacing his face:
Where o'er the clouds the steepy Alps extend,
Six thousand from Helvetia's tow'rs attend;
In shining mail their temper'd ploughshares glance,
Spread in the shield, and pointed in the lance;
While the right arm, that rul'd the flocks so late,
Now threats the mighty, and insults the great.
  Last, in the papal standard, they display
The triple crown, and apostolic key;
Sev'n thousand valiant Romans march behind,
And great Camillo had the charge assign'd
The moving cuishes, and their corselets bright,
Exchange quick lightnings, and fatigue the sight :
Elate in hope, and cheer'd amid alarms,
They bless the cause that calls the world to arms;
So to revive, and vindicate the fame,
That once, unrival'd, mark'd the Roman name.
  Now, summ'd to view, the invincible array
Stands on the plain, and brightens in the day :
The general calls—obsequious to the sound,
His peers approach, and range attentive round;
When Bulloign his imperial will express'd,
And thus reveal'd the counsels of his breast.
  " Soon as the next succeeding morn shall rise,
And dawning purple streak the eastern skies,
Prepar'd, and arm'd with best appointed speed,
Be ev'ry warrior, and be ev'ry steed;
For then we mean to visit Salem's tow'rs,
By secret march, and swift invading pow'rs:
The mighty crisis to the combat calls,
And the foe trembles in her sacred walls."
  Bold was the hope his ardent words inspire;
As the plied fan provokes the slumb'ring fire,
Impatient they regret the ling'ring night,
Fierce for the day, and for the promis'd fight.
But other cares hold Godfrey from repose,
Nor tastes the chief those transports he bestows:
Yet deep he held the secret of his breast,
From ev'ry ear and ev'ry eye suppress'd.
  Small cause of joy his late advices bring—
How Lybia, arm'd beneath the Memphian king,
From Damiata, eastward in the way
To Gaza, on the Syrian frontiers lay.
Innumerous there such warriors he unites,
As force made confident or fame excites;
Nor Godfrey hopes advances can be slow,
From so inveterate, so renown'd a foe :
How best to frustrate or oppose, he seeks;
And to his legate, trusty Henry, speaks.
  " Go, speed thee, Henry—spread the flying sail,
Cut the green wave, and catch the favouring gale;
Nor give indulgence to the labouring oar,
Till the crook'd keel divides the Grecian shore.
There should arrive, as private seals impart,
From one who knows not the deceiving art,
The royal Dane, for matchless force renown'd,
As with the grace of every virtue crown'd;
Zeal sends the northern youth its warmest ray,
And glory wings him to the toilsome way,

From the cold circle, and the polar star,
The friend and brave companion of the war.
  " But, for I know the Greekish monarch's heart,
Stor'd with old wiles, and well dissembled art,
I fear lest he divert the princely youth,
And wrest his purpose from the paths of truth;
Or other specious enterprise persuade,
And rob our armies of the promis'd aid.
But you, my messenger and faithful friend,
Dispose his journey to its destin'd end;
Alike his honour and our arms shall need
His utmost forces, and his swiftest speed.
  " Nor you return, but to the Grecian sue
For aids, by previous obligation due,
Such aids as with his kingly compact stands;
And more than compact—what the cause de-
      mands."
The guardian chief thus wakeful shuns repose,
While in his care ten thousand eye-lids close :
The herald, speeding to the breezy shore,
The seals of trust and royal greeting bore;
And late, the duke, from every task reclin'd,
Gave to his couch the labours of his mind.
  And now the night embalm'd in early dew,
Slow ebbing, from the paler dawn withdrew;
Aurora on the purpling ocean rose;
The reddening east with warmer lustre glows;
His previous beam the solar brightness shed,
And from the wave uprais'd his peerless head—
While through the camp loud echoing clarions ring;
Rous'd to the note, the sprightly soldiers spring;
Their ears delighted drink the warlike sounds,
And every heart with answering motion bounds.
So joys the peasant on the sultry plain,
When thunders roll, the messengers of rain.
  With quick impatience every bosom glows;
Apt to their limbs, the wonted armours close :
Each conscious soldier on his chief attends,
And o'er the plain the ranging host extends :
The banners stream, redundant to the wind;
All move, as rul'd by one informing mind;
While high towards Heaven, the Cross in triumph
      spread,
Waves from the van, and blazes at their head.
  Now up the steep of Heaven the cloudless Sun,
Fresh in his pomp of rising splendour shone—
He strikes the squadrons with a trembling light;
The flash gleams restless, and rejects the sight :
All ether flames, and sparkles round the host,
And the wide glory fires the distant coast;
The coursers neigh, the clanging arms resound,
And deafening hills return the din around.
  Meanwhile the chief, great guardian of his train,
Renders all slights of lurking ambush vain :
He sends the light-arm'd horse detach'd before,
To scour the woodland and the winding shore;
The pioneers with previous labours go,
Pull down the lofty, and supply the low,
Unfold the strait, detect the covert way,
And give large travel to the wide array.
  Not the rude onsets of encountering foes,
Soon scatter'd, could the impervious march oppose;
Not the proud rampart, and the steepy mound,
The guarded battlement, and trench profound—
In vain by thickets, rocks, and hills, withstood,
The rising forest, and the rushing flood !
So when the Po, imperial torrent, swells,
No power resists him, and no force repels :
Deep from the root the sylvan shade he heaves,
The ruin rolls ingulf'd within his waves;

He foams, he roars, he bounds along the plain,
And bears his prey triumphant to the main.
  Meantime, the king of Tripoli, alarm'd,
Mann'd every hold, and every man he arm'd;
But still restrain'd his pow'rs, his wealth suppress'd,
And rul'd the wrath rebellious in his breast;
With specious gifts, and ill dissembled cheer,
Beneath feign'd friendship he disguis'd his fear;
Sign'd ev'ry term that Godfrey would impose,
And gave wide progress to his potent foes.
  Where, south from Salem, Seir's hills arise,
And eastward range, incumbent o'er the skies,
Promiscuous pours a numerous troop of friends,
And, joyful, every sex and age descends :
Large gifts, the tribute of their love, they bring
To the great chief, of Christian armies king;
They view the wondrous man with strange delight,
Press to his touch, and dwell upon his sight;
Through ways well known conduct his journey'd host,
And point his passage o'er the hostile coast.
  Still toward the deep, the windings they explore,
On sea-beat shallows, and the sanded shore;
Off to the right the ships of burden ride,
And plough the surge that murmurs at their side.
Convenient here, the flying barge from far
Imports the various implements of war;
Replete from Scios, and the Greekish isles,
All autumn in the copious navy smiles;
While luscious Crete her generous juice bestows,
And to the host the purple vintage flows.
  From Britain, Belgia, and the Gallic bays,
From Venice, native of the circling seas;
The gulf of Genoa, and Tuscan shores,
And where Sicilia piles her naval stores;
Ships, barks, and gallies, cut the midland-main,
And join in arms, a complicated train.
For here no Pagan to the driving gale,
With daring hand unfurls his timorous sail;
Unrival'd round, the huge armada rides,
And with a forest veils the nether tides;
Beneath the load, indignant, Ocean swells,
The vessel labours, and the surge rebels.
  Wing'd from the circling world the fleet unites;
One wish informs them, and one cause invites :
Their murmuring keels divide the side-long coast,
With large provision to the landed host;   [shore,
Then lanch'd, they shout, and scour the winding
Hoist every sail, and ply with every oar;
All bound, where Christ the dear ablution shed,
And, for a sinful world, a sinless victim bled.
  Fame flies through Sion with preceding sound,
And hastes to spread the fearful news around;
The pow'rs, the names, the numbers, all she sums—
" See, see," she cries, " the dreaded victor comes!
His steps a troop of matchless heroes wait,
Known to the field, the delegates of fate :
Fear ye, whose short enduring power detains
The sacred city, and her saints in chains !
He comes; and on his conquering weapon brings
Death to her foes, and terrour to her kings !"
  Those ills, that present we might learn to bear,
In prospect spread, and magnify by fear;
The phantom realiz'd in fancy's eye,
Is greater ill than all those ills we fly.
With busy face, and ever listening ear,
Restless they run to learn, but dread to hear;
Throughout the city and adjacent plains,
Tumultuous haste, distrust, and rumour reigns;
While in her old malicious tyrant's soul,
Black thoughts and hoary machinations roll.

For Aladine in Sion newly thron'd,
Beneath the proud usurper Judah groan'd:
Dire was the native purpose of his mind,
To ev'ry act of early ill inclin'd;
But as his years increase, his fires assuage,
Allay with time, and mitigate with age.
He learns the progress of the Christian pow'rs,
That like a torrent comes to sap his tow'rs;
And a new doubt his anxious bosom tears—
Treason within, and force without, he fears.
    For Salem's sacred city, then enclos'd,
Two different sects, of different faith, compos'd;
In Christ, divine instructor, those believ'd;
And these, in Macon, carnally deceiv'd:
In number, and in pow'r, the last excel;
The former, only, in believing well.
But late, when he the imperial seat attain'd,
And scepter'd o'er the pow'rs of Judah reign'd,
The Paynims lighten'd from the tax of state,
He whelms the Christians with the unequal weight.
Suspicious hence, he trembles in his turn,
Lest injury with due resentment burn.
Rous'd at the thought, his native wrath respires,
And wakes the fury of his slumb'ring fires;
The glut of future carnage feasts his soul,
And in his eye new scenes of slaughter roll.
Thus numb and peaceful lies some poisonous snake,
Chill'd in the dropping of a wintry brake;
Till, warm'd beneath the Sun's returning ray,
He stirs and curls, and kindles with the day;
Reviv'd to ill, his burnish'd spires arise,
And venom lightens from his sanguine eyes.
    "Behold," he said, "malicious in their joy,
How the smile lurks, when Christians would destroy!
In transport hush'd, they wait the coming foe,
Their hearts exulting in the public woe:
Nor less such secret meditations mean,
Than nightly treasons, and some murd'rous scene;
Or through our gates yon hostile pow'rs to guide,
To us though hostile, yet to them allied.
    "But prudence bids to disappoint the blow,
And turn its force, retorted on the foe;
The traitor's scheme shall on himself recoil,
And take him, with his own invented toil.
Stabb'd on the breast let bleeding infants die;
Each sex and age in mingling slaughter lie;
While hoary on the shrine their priests expire,
And ev'ry temple flames a funeral pyre!"
    So brew'd the murd'rous mischief in his mind,
Dubious to act, what deadly he design'd;
The threatful storm, superior fears control,
And do the work of mercy in his soul;
While the fell purpose through his bosom boils,
With rancour rises, and with dread recoils,
Lest to himself like fortune might betide,
Compell'd to crave that mercy he denied,
And all the war, with desperate vengeance sped,
Should pour its wrath on his devoted head.
    The tyrant hence, irresolute in rage,
Diverts the fury which he can't assuage;
Lays the wide suburbs level with the ground,
And further spreads consuming fires around;
Fell poison with the living fount he blends,
Where death amid the rolling streams descends;
Acts all a cruel prudence can suggest,
And feeds the fiend that ravens in his breast.
    Defensive next, the city claims his cares;
The mound he deepens, and the breach repairs:
Three sides, impregnable, disdain'd the fray;
Sole on the north the doubt of battle lay:

But here, with utmost vigilance he plies;
The bars are doubled, and the ramparts rise;
And last, with native and auxiliar pow'rs,
He arms her wards, and fortifies her tow'rs.

———

## BOOK II.

THE king in each anticipating thought
Thus foil'd his foes, and future combats fought;
When lo! Ismeno, horrid seer, drew nigh,
A vicious counsellor and dread ally;
Ismeno, deep in all the pow'rs of Hell,
The mystic philter, and infernal spell!—
The monumental corse Ismeno warm'd,
And the pale dead with mimic life inform'd;
Compell'd the fiends to issue to his aid,
And Hell's dread king in his own realms obey'd.
A Christian once, he late transferr'd his vows,
And now to Macon, fitter master, bows;
Nor well the form of either system knew,
False to the first, nor to the latter true:
Still were the terms of sacred phrase retain'd,
Mix'd in his songs, and in his rites profan'd;
With lore divine the abhorrent charm he yokes,
And highest Heav'n with deepest Hell invokes.
Dire from his cave, where, impiously retir'd,
His arts he practis'd and his skill acquir'd,
He issu'd, grateful to a tyrant's will;
And thus advis'd the minister of ill.
    "You see, O king, the fury of our foes,
Flush'd with the past, for future conquest glows;
But fury is by answering force controll'd,
And Heav'n is prompt in favour to the bold.
Thrice happy Judah, doubly arm'd in thee!
Expert to act, as cautious to foresee,
Who singly boast the twofold pow'r to save,
Mature for counsel, as for combat brave.
Ah, would your subjects catch the kindred fire,
And bravely emulate as you inspire,
Then Godfrey, soon entomb'd, might here obtain
Unenvied tenure, and a still domain.
For me, whate'er sage science may devise,
Whate'er of trust in deepest magic lies,
I bring, prepar'd, through each advent'rous state,
To ward your danger, or to share your fate;
Bow'd to the lore of necromantic laws,
The host exil'd from Heav'n shall aid your cause:
Then list to what my first instructions move;
And what I counsel, let my king approve.
    "Remote and deep withdrawn from vulgar eyes,
A shrine beneath the Christian temple lies,
With show of pompous consecration plac'd,
And the bright image of their goddess grac'd:
A mortal deity this virgin bore,
And her those sects idolatrous adore;
His vows to her the travell'd pilgrim pays,
The lights perpetual round her idol blaze;
While veil'd, and passive, she attends the throng,
Their various offering, and their saintly song.
But thence, by your imperial hand convey'd,
Transport the form of this maternal maid,
And laid within our prophet's sacred fane,
Let ritual song and circling charms retain:
For such the force of our mysterious art,
And such the pow'rs my wondrous spells impart,
That while this new palladium we possess,
Your arms shall ever meet the wish'd success,

These walls impregnable ensure your reign,
And hostile fury storm around in vain."
　　He spoke; and prompt to ill the tyrant rose :
Impatience through his kindling aspect glows;
Unhallow'd, to the latent shrine he flies,
And grasps, with arms impure, the virgin prize :
In vain the zealous ministry withstands,
Opprobrious, he insults their reverend bands;
Then bears his sacrilege to Macon's fane,
Where Heav'n was ever deaf, and prayer profane :
The sorcerer with dread action stalks around,
And shocks with blasphemy the trembling ground.
　　And now succeeding morn, array'd in white,
Had silver'd Solyma with new-born light;
His charge in vain the anxious keeper sought,
As quickly vanish'd as profanely brought:
All pale, the tidings to his prince he bears,
Who scarce the messenger in madness spares,
But o'er the Christians all his rage renews,
For malice ne'er wants colour to accuse.
Yet, whether mortal arm may boast the deed,
Or Heav'n's high hand the captive image freed,
Remote the goddess from pollution bore,
And left the tyrant blindly to explore—
The times declare not; but in silence choose
To leave the deep decision to the Muse,
Who would all praise in piety assign
As due to pow'r superior and divine.
　　Strict was the search the chafing monarch made,
And wide his ministers of wrath invade;
His threats and vows, or menace, or invite,
Whom rack could terrify, or gold requite:
The wizard too his impious art applies,
And to his aid emerging demons rise:
Nor art, nor yet demoniac aid avails,
Nor deepest Hell imparts what Heav'n conceals.
But when, no more with baffled charms amus'd,
The king in wrath conceiv'd his pow'r abus'd,
His limbs all trembled, and his eyes shot flame,
And vengeful fury shook his labouring frame:
Rous'd in the wrath of unforgiving age,
Against the faithful burn'd his endless rage;
" Perish !" he cried, " destruction seize on all!
So, with the race, the curs'd offender fall.
Yes, ere the guilty 'scape the wrath decreed,
Perish the just, and let the guiltless bleed !
What said I, guiltless ?—O ill-suited name!
Alike all Christians all our vengeance claim;
Foes to our prophet, traitors to our state,
They justly suffer by the laws they hate.
Up, up, my subjects, with the sword and fire;
Quick be their doom, and let their name expire !"
　　So spoke the tyrant; Fame receiv'd the sound,
And, cloth'd in terrour, pours the news around:
The blood from ev'ry Christian cheek she drains,
Strikes to their hearts, and shudders in their veins:
No force of prayer, no bold defence they try,
Fear froze their limbs, nor left the pow'r to fly;
While o'er their souls impending horrours wait,
And half anticipate the stroke of fate:
But succour, least foreseen, deceiv'd the grave;
For Heav'n is prompt, as potent still to save.
　　Then dwelt in Solyma a blooming maid,
With inward truth as outward charms array'd,
Heroic sentiment her bosom warm'd,
And her bright limbs the infant Graces form'd;
Yet with unconscious, or regardless eyes,
She saw no charm, or, seen, refus'd to prize;
Within herself her treasur'd sweetness clos'd,
And private in domestic peace repos'd.

But merit vainly from esteem retires;
The world pursues, discloses, and admires:
In vain from love the bashful charmer flies,
A bashful youth perceives, pursues, and dies;
To him, intruding love the maid reveal'd,
And kill'd with graces from herself conceal'd.
Love through the shade of deepest covert spies,
A blindfold Argus with a thousand eyes;
A various influence his pow'rs impart,
And warm the chaste, and cool the wanton heart.
　　Sophronia she, whose charms his love inspir'd;
Olindo he, whose love those charms admir'd;
In ev'ry grace, to ev'ry virtue train'd,
One faith instructed, and one town contain'd.
Yet he, nor hopes, nor ventures to complain,
Hush'd as th' eternal calm beneath the main;
With awful glance at distance eyes the fair,
Breathes but to sigh, and loves but to despair;
A prey to silent anguish, mourns alone,
Unseen, unmark'd, unpitied, and unknown.
　　The dire decree arrests Sophronia's ear,
Nor taught the Christian for herself to fear;
To nobler views her ample soul makes room,
With her own death to ward the public doom;
The generous maid would greatly bleed for all,
And one a sacrifice for thousands fall.
Strong zeal inspir'd, and native courage taught,
But female decency reproves the thought;
Nor so prevail'd, for resolutely sham'd,
The bolder blush through bashfulness inflam'd.
On through the gazing crowd she pass'd alone,
And like a star new risen the virgin shone;
A veil thrown o'er her charms with thin disguise,
But half eclips'd the danger of her eyes;
Adorn'd, with easy negligence she moves,
And ev'ry eye engages, and reproves;
For mildness, bright'ning through majestic grace,
Spoke in her mien, and lighten'd in her face.
　　Thus gaz'd by all, on pass'd the lovely dame,
And fearless to the royal presence came;
Dire was the form the tyrant's visage wore,
Which she in innocence, regardless, bore.
" O turn," she cried, " the terrours of thy ire,
Nor thou, O king, against thyself conspire;
Taint not the guardian glories of thy reign,
With bleeding innocents and subjects slain:
'Tis mine to give the traitor to thy view,
To point thy wrath, and point the vengeance due."
　　That decent confidence, and awful grace,
Mix'd with the glories of that loveliest face,
Surpris'd the monarch; half abash'd he stands,
And feels, that beauty, more than kings, commands:
Low sunk before the fair all forms of pride,
And bend for mercy to the suppliant side,
For mutual grace unbind the sov'reign brow,
Wishful to find, and willing to allow;
But the fond hope no answering smiles impart,
And wayward beauty damps the kindling heart.
Not love, but sullen pleasure, seiz'd his sense,
A short amazement, and a still suspense:
" At your request," the monarch mild replies,
" Fate is no more, and scarce the guilty dies."
Then she—" Behold the criminal attends !
This hand perform'd, what still my heart commends;
From strange pollution bore our sacred dame,
And I alone your dreaded vengeance claim."
　　Thus, arm'd for pain, unterrified by death,
Thus the sweet innocence resigns her breath;
Her life a ransom for her country yields,
And a whole state with wide protection shields.

Surpris'd he paus'd, yet seeming to require
A form less fair, and apter to his ire :
" Say, who conspir'd, who prompted to the deed ?
Nor give a breast so soft as thine to bleed."
" All rivals," she return'd, " my works disclaim,
Nor brook a partner in the deeds of fame:
My courage prompted what my thoughts conspir'd ;
Alone I counsell'd, and alone acquir'd."
" On thee alone," the tyrant then replied,
" Be the full weight of my resentment tried !"
" 'T is just, 't is just," she cried, " nor I repine;
Mine be the penalty, the glory mine !"
New choler now his gathering visage swells,
And all the tyrant in his heart rebels :
" How, where, hast thou presum'd thy theft to hide ?
Say, quick, nor further urge thy fate !" he cried.
" Not rescu'd," bold she said, " to be betray'd,
Is the bless'd shape of that celestial maid.
Vain you require what, now consum'd with flame,
Nor infidels can touch, nor kings reclaim.
What would you more ? your former captive freed,
You hold the criminal who boasts the deed.
But why the criminal to me transferr'd ?
Must subjects bleed, when kings alone have err'd ?
What you unjustly seiz'd, I justly gain'd ;
And, guiltless, purified what you profan'd."
She spoke ; and, from within, the labouring storm
Rose in his voice, and spread o'er all his form :
The dire distemper of the tyrant's soul,
No mercy mitigates, no bounds control ;
In vain officious love his favourite arms,
And lends an unavailing shield of charms.
By doom severe, he judg'd the fearless dame
With beauty's gifts to feed devouring flame :
Officious villains on his wrath attend ;
Her veil and floating robe they rudely rend ;
Strict round her arms the livid cordage wind,
And to the stake the lamb-like victim bind ;
While meek and silent, she attends her fate,
In pain unalter'd, and in death sedate,
Save that the rose its wonted mansion fled,
And like the lily droop'd her beauteous head.
The busy rumour spread with murmuring sound;
The vulgar ran, and clust'ring pour'd around.
Olindo too in trembling haste drew near,
With love prophetic, and all pale with fear.
But when, by soul distracting woe oppress'd,
The dreaded truth his hapless eyes confess'd,
His love condemn'd, in cruel fetters bound,
And the dire ministers of death around ;
The youth all frantic through the tumult broke,
And thus the king in rage and haste bespoke :
" Not so, not so, my lord, this vaunting dame
Shall arrogate, what only I can claim :
She did not, would not, could not singly dare
A work so weighty, and a deed so rare ;
The guard with unexperienc'd craft deceive,
And from her seat the massy substance heave:
This arm achiev'd what she assumes in vain."
(Ah, thus he lov'd, though hopeless to obtain !)
He added,—" Favour'd by the friendly night,
Where your proud fane admits the eastern light,
I scal'd the steep, and gain'd the dang'rous pass,
And through the postern bore the sacred mass :
Nor shall she thus usurp a foreign spoil,
With hazard enterpris'd, and earn'd with toil ;
Mine are these welcome tortures, chains, and flame,
The trophied monument, and deathless name."
Her eyes from earth the grateful charmer rais'd,
And gently chiding, on her lover gaz'd :

" Say whence the frenzy that infects thy mind,
And why, ah why, to me severely kind ?
Sufficient to my fate, howe'er I seem,
Thy life would but more cruelly redeem :
I want not such society in pain ;
Whate'er he dares inflict, I dare sustain."
The maid, in vain, the enamour'd youth address'd,
Nor shook the steady purpose of his breast :
His fate, in vain, the stedfast you.h demands ;
The maid, as stedfast. and as kind, withstands.
O wond'rous pair !—Unpleasing, pleasing sight !
Where love and virtue amicably fight ;
Where death alone is to the victor dear,
And safety's all the vanquish'd wretch can fear.
But now his wrath the king no longer rein'd,
Who vengeful judg'd his regal pow'r disdain'd :
" Cease, cease !" with cruel irony he cries ;
" You both have won, and shall obtain the prize."
Quick, at his beck, the guards, who waited round,
With chains, the brave, the blooming stripling bound;
Then back to back the lovely pair they tied,
And whom they join in death, in death divide.
And now, applied to the surrounding pyre,
Contagious breath provokes the lingering fire.
A mournful pause the plaintive lover broke,
And to his lov'd, his patient partner, spoke :
" Are then my vows, my tedious sufferings crown'd,
With thee in such eternal spousals bound ?
Far other ties my flatt'ring fancy fram'd,
Far other fire my faithful breast inflam'd !
Nor these the ties that bind connubial hearts ;
Nor these the fires the bridal lamp imparts !
" Sad is the scene our nuptial pomp displays,
And long I earn'd what fate severely pays,
While life still sunder'd whom the grave unites,
And death my fond unfailing faith requites.
But yet, with thee, even agony finds ease ;
Death knows to charm, and pain can learn to please :
Thy fate alone can teach me to repine,
And all the pangs you feel are doubly mine.
Ah ! could I but obtain, that, breast to breast,
Of thee in this my latest hour possess'd,
I might but catch thee with my closing eye,
And my last breath within thy bosom sigh—
That were a bliss, beyond what life could give;
It were indeed too much to feel and live !"
Thus he, with various agitation mov'd ;
And thus the maid with gentle speech reprov'd.
" Not these the griefs, the cares, you should attend ;
Far other griefs, far other cares, impend—
The dreadful summons of offended pow'r,
The doubtful sentence, and the mortal hour !
The lapse of frailty, and the kindling flame,
Alike thy penitence and transport claim ;
The martyr, with peculiar splendours bright,
Selected sits above the sons of light !
View yon fair azure with desiring eye,
Nor fear to tread the glories of the sky :
But O—beyond, beyond—what scenes invite !
O'er Heav'n, another Heav'n, still opening to our
sight !"
Soft sorrows seiz'd the pale deploring crowd :
The pagans wept their pitying griefs aloud ;
But not the Christians the still tempest show,
They drink their tears, and choke the swelling woe.
The king, who felt unwonted pity rise,
Melt in his soul, and moisten in his eyes,
Retir'd, the soft emotion to control,
And fix the flinty temper of his soul.

But you, bright maid, transcendent greatness prov'd,
By weeping floods and circling flames unmov'd;
Inspir'd an anguish you refus'd to own,
In grief superior, and in crowds alone!
Thus hope was far from ev'ry weeping eye,
And death amid involving fires drew nigh;
When, mounted like some favourite son of fame,
A stranger to the mourning concourse came:
In foreign semblance, and unwonted mode,
Proud through the parting throng the hero rode;
Clorinda's corselet grac'd the warrior's breast,
And the fam'd tigress raven'd on her crest;
The admiring crowds her awful signal own,
To routed hosts and trembling nations known.
  With nobler gifts of native worth adorn'd,
The heroic maid her sex's softness scorn'd;
Scorn'd each important toil of female hearts,
The tricking ornament, and needled arts,
The silken indolence, the soft fatigue,
The chamber'd spleen, and closeted intrigue:
Nor envious breath her virgin honour stain'd,
Through wander'd climes and foughten fields retain'd;
While o'er the beauties of her loveliest face,
Delight sat fierce, and smil'd with dreaded grace.
  With early thirst of each adventurous deed,
She steer'd the manage of the bounding steed;
With infant arm would lanch the whistling spear,
Whirl the rough disk, and wield the sword in air;
And foil'd each rival with contending grace,
Strain'd in the grasp, or distanced in the race.
Now from the hills the shaggy spoils she tore,
The brinded lion, and the tusky boar;
And last whole hosts beneath her prowess yield,
She riots like a tigress o'er the field.
From Persia late the fair destroyer came,
And bore deep hatred to the Christian name;
Oft had she bath'd the mountains with their blood,
And with their bodies chok'd the purpling flood:
At Salem just arriv'd, her wand'ring view,
Aspiring flames and murmuring tumults drew.
When curious to inquire she turn'd with speed,
And o'er the pavement urg'd her flying steed.
  The crowd gave way; the Amazonian fair
With strict regard beheld the captive pair—
The virgin silent, while the youth repin'd;
The stronger plaintive, and the weak resign'd;
But plaintive he, as in her sufferings pain'd;
No pangs but for the dearer maid sustain'd;
She silent, as her speech were in her eyes,
To hold superior converse with the skies,
As though her soul had took a previous flight,
The mortal sufferings pass'd, and Heav'n in sight.
  Clorinda's breast divine compassion fill'd,
Her silver lids the pitying drops distill'd;
But chief she mourn'd, and chief admir'd the maid,
Placid in pain, nor even in death dismay'd;
Then fervent thus a neighbouring sage address'd:
" Ah! whence this lovely pair, and why distress'd?
Such death, where such apparent virtues shine,
What crime can merit, or what heart design?"
  She spoke; the man of courtesy explain'd
Whate'er of note the mournful tale contain'd:
Her soul, with kindred dignity inspir'd,
Their guilt acquitted, and their worth admir'd;
And soon her enterprising thoughts presume
By suit or battle, to reverse their doom:
Quick from the stake th' approaching fire she drew,
And thus spoke terrour to the list'ning crew:

" Let none, with cruel or adventurous hand,
Officious dare to act what I withstand,
Till from the court returning orders bring
Freedom or fate, determin'd by your king:
Nor fear in this to rouse the monarch's rage;
My will's your warrant, and my word your gage.''
So saying, to their souls she look'd dismay,
As only born for others to obey;
Then swift to court the lovely suitor ran,
But obvious met the king, and brief began.
  " Ere this, O king, Clorinda's distant fame
Has haply taught your ear a stranger's name,
Who comes, you'll say presumptuous, thus alone,
To guard our faith, and vindicate your throne.
Whate'er of war the various terms comprise,
Within my sphere of copious battle lies;
Nor aught above me, nor beneath I know,
From the proud bulwark to repel the foe,
To form the phalanx, or to lead the field,
Or hand to hand the deadly weapon wield.''
  She ceas'd; and thus the king—" O glorious maid!
Arm of the host you condescend to aid,
From pole to pole thy honour'd name is known,
Thy fame unbounded by the distant Lone:
Not all this warlike confidence of tow'rs,
The force of native and auxiliar pow'rs,
Such trust defensive of our throne provide,
As that right hand, that weapon at thy side.
Come, Godfrey, come, with laurels on thy brow,
Thy march too swift, so late, is tedious now;
Nor less than his Clorinda's glories claim,
Thy word as absolute, as great thy fame!
Thine be the sphere of arbitrary sway,
The secret council, and the bold array;
Beneath thy scepter'd hand my pow'rs I yield,
First in the throne, as foremost in the field!
  He spoke; with easy grace the virgin bow'd,
And suppliant thus her gen'rous plea avow'd:
" Though Aladine may deem the matter new,
Where gifts precede, and services ensue,
So highly your munificence I hold,
Your bounty bids the diffident be bold.
Then for the aid I bring, the life would spend,
For all I shall perform, or may intend,
To my request those wretched captives give,
And grant the lovely criminals may live.
Their sentence merely on suspicion built,
Much might be urg'd abating of their guilt;
But ev'ry plea of innocence I wave,
And sole, in lieu of future service, crave.
Yet, mighty king, permit me to disclaim
The guilt imputed to the Christian name;
Nor should I from receiv'd opinion lead,
Were reason not resistless to persuade;
For ill the wizard's pedant arts retain
That sanctitude which Macan's laws ordain,
Whose tenets, all replete with lore divine,
Prohibit idols from his hallow'd shrine.
To him miraculous ascribe the deed,
His fane from guilt, from profanation freed;
Nor thou repine, when guardian pow'rs reject
What rites might innovate, or arts infect.
Let Ismen exercise, remote from arms,
His maze of tricks, and unavailing charms;
But the keen use of more decisive pow'rs,
The magic of the circling blade be ours!''
  She said; and though the monarch's stubborn breast
Was proof to aught soft pity could suggest,

Yet high observance of the gallant maid,
Her honour'd presence, and her promis'd aid,
'Prevail'd: " All pleading," he return'd, " is vain;
Clorinda ne'er can ask, but to obtain:
Nor I their innocence or guilt debate;
Be you alike sole mistress of their fate!"
Thus were they freed. Olindo, happiest youth!
Great is the recompense that waits thy truth;
Pure was thy constant flame, severe the test,
And Heav'n with equal retribution bless'd.
Now beyond hope exulting, from despair
He pass'd associate with the yielding fair:
To death he lov'd her; and the grateful maid,
With a long life of mutual love repaid.
But, ever to a tyrant's soul ingrate,
He held such virtue dang'rous in the state;
And distant far the bridal exiles sent,
Rich in their love, and each in each content.
With these he banishes the brave and young,
And ev'ry Christian arm with vigour strung;
In hostage then the softer sex retains,
The tender infant binds in needless chains,
Whose helpless cries the wonted names require,
Th' endearing husband, and protecting sire.
Some through the devious wild, or mountain
        shade,
Where chance or sadness tempted, pensive stray'd;
While some, with glory and resentment fir'd,
To heights of more determin'd worth aspir'd,
Bold to Emmaus bend their warlike course,
And with new arms augment the Christian force;
For to Emmaus now approach'd their pow'rs,
Emmaus, west from Salem's regal tow'rs.
Who treads the fresh of April's early dew,
(A thousand scenes of rural scope in view)
At leisure may the mediate space beguile,
By the third hour, the third of Hebrew style.
While distant yet, the town and neighb'ring coast,
With the first ken, salute the Christian host,
" Emmaus !" loud, triumphing legions cry,
And catch the place with long desiring eye.
And now, down Heav'n, the swift careering Sun
His ev'ning course of steep direction run;
At Godfrey's word the travell'd armies stand,
And canvass cities rise to his command,
Whose tented canopy, and flaxen shed,
O'er many a field with ready structure spread.
Nor yet Heav'n's lamp forsook th' ethereal
        plain,
But hover'd verging on the western main,
When lo! two peers, attractive of the eye,
In mode of foreign ornament drew nigh:
Peace in their hands and open brow they bear,
Complacence in their gentle mien and air;
While gorgeous equipage attendant wait
Their embassy from Egypt's scepter'd state.
The first Aletes, vers'd in ev'ry vice;
Base was his birth, conspicuous was his rise :
O'er Nile his proud vicegerence widely spread,
And stor'd with wiles was his sagacious head;
Soft on his lips persuasive fiction hung,
Guile fill'd his heart, and eloquence his tongue;
His manners easy, though his genius shrewd,
Fair to engage, and subtle to delude;
Smooth to persuade with false illusive phrase,
To vindicate with blame, or kill with praise.
With him Argantes, huge Circassian, came,
A stranger late, but quickly known to fame;
Through Egypt, prime in arms, the warrior shone,
And now a satrap grac'd the Memphian throne.

Furious the bent of his unconquer'd soul,
Nor knew his heart or pity or control;
Slave to his will, his will by passion sway'd,
Proud, restless, fierce, untir'd, and undismay'd,
Nor Earth he thought his match in arms could
        yield,
As yet unrival'd through the sanguine field !
His impious arm the only God ador'd,
His reason perch'd upon his conqu'ring sword.
Admittance to the gen'ral's ear they sue,
And introduc'd the royal Godfrey view.
Low on a couch, in unaffected state,
Amid surrounding chiefs the hero sat:
Plain was his vestment, negligence with grace,
And awe with meekness liv'd within his face ;
As Godfrey only could his state adorn,
Too great to value, though too meek to scorn.
Argantes ent'ring, scarce his head inclin'd ;
Haughty his mien, expressive of his mind:
As from due rite he purposely abstain'd,
For conscious merits in himself retain'd.
Not so Aletes; struck with decent awe,
Ent'ring he seem'd half-wishing to withdraw;
As one surpris'd, his forward step repress'd,
And bore his hand respectful to his breast;
Then easy, bow'd with deference profound,
And fix'd his eyes half-closing on the ground.
Spontaneous through his lips, a wonted road,
The stream of voluntary diction flow'd,
Gentle as dews or summer's ev'ning rain
To slake the fevers of the sultry plain ;
While thus the Syriac melted from his tongue,
And list'ning princes on the cadence hung.
" O, mightiest thou ! sole worthy of the sway,
Where circling heroes, chiefs like these obey,
Who bear fresh wreaths on each victorious head,
Fir'd by thy deeds, and by thy conduct led.
Beyond the Herculean pillar flies thy fame,
And Egypt e'en to Nubia tells thy name.
But chief our monarch marks thy wondrous
        ways,
Lists to thy name, and dwells upon thy praise:
No envy his superior bosom fires,
He hears with pleasure, with esteem admires;
To worth like thine perceives his heart ally'd,
And is by love, if not religion ty'd.
Yet well appriz'd of what your arms intend,
Oppos'd where he in honour must defend,
From us his amicable purpose know,
A faithful friend, but a reluctant foe.
" With thee in arms, in council, and in mind,
In equal amity and hate combin'd,
He vows, whate'er encount'ring dangers wait,
To fix the fortunes of thy wav'ring state;
Be Sion only sacred to repose,
He joins with Godfrey, should the world oppose.
" Transcendent chief ! whose memorable page
Shall send a tale to ev'ry future age,
Short is the span that gives thy deeds a date,
But long the time that wond'ring ages shall relate !
Thy rapid progress knows nor rest, nor bound—
What cities forc'd, or levell'd with the ground !
What battles fought ! what victories obtain'd !
What provinces subdu'd ! what empires gain'd !
Amazement flies, or trembles at thy name;
Nor is there left a further work for fame;
New added power can add no new applause;
And glory, spread to either pole, must pause.
" Soar'd to the zenith of a cloudless day,
Thy fortune culminates her warmest ray ;

Her next advance the western steep invites,
Prone she descends, and suddenly benights.
Ah think, great chief!—the dang'rous venture shun,
Where all thy deeds may be at once undone:
Doubtful thy hope, and thy advantage small;
But great the loss, and wondrous deep the fall.

" Yet, Godfrey may reject our fond address;
He views the future in the past success:
His sword with blood of routed armies stain'd,
Beneath his hand reluctant nations rein'd,
With all the bold the boundless wish can crave,
That bribes the fortunate, or fires the brave—
These, these may win him to the waste of war,
And passions prompt what reason would abhor.
Delusive orators! they still persuade,
Unsheath'd to brandish that redoubted blade;
Still to pursue where fortune would betray,
Where glory smooths the faithless arduous way,
Till Macon be no more; and waste, forlorn,
Sad Asia like some widow'd matron mourn:
Fair hopes, high projects, and allurements sweet,
But covert ruin, and assur'd deceit.

" If zeal exhibits no intemp'rate dream,
Nor clouds of wrath eclipse thy reas'ning beam;
How just, how diff'rent would the scene arise,
Nor hope, but apprehension meet thine eyes!
Will Fortune, false as the alternate sea,
For thee perpetual flow, alone for thee?
High the ascent her hourly favourites know,
But steep the precipice that sinks below;
One step alone 'twixt triumph and defeat,
The gulfy ruin and the tow'ry height.
Say, chief! should Nile with all his dread allies,
Potent of wealth and arms, in vengeance rise;
The Turk, the Persian, and Cassano's heir,
Frown in the van, and deepen in the rear;
What mortal pow'r could such a storm assuage,
Or check the thunder lanch'd in all its rage?

" Perhaps, to western aid thy prospects bend;
Aid from the Greek,—that try'd, that trusty friend!
Yes, yes, his faith attesting nations own;
'T is Punic all, and to a proverb known!
His plighted powers we then may learn to fear,
When you grow credulous, or he sincere;
When those who late thy peaceful march withstood,
To buy thy progress will expend their blood;
Who late retail'd the venal air for hire,
Fight in thy cause, and at thy side expire.

" Shrunk to the limits of this warlike round,
All hope is to thy proper squadrons bound;
To these, who, distant from their native soil,
By death diminish, and decline with toil;
And is it hence, thy brave presumption grows,
To foil the fury of united foes?
Not slight the fray thy former conquests boast,
When with full pow'rs you quell'd each sep'rate
        host;
How then should such combining hosts dismay,
When Egypt lengthens out their dread array?

" Yet, should I yield thee more than man for
        might,
In terrours dress'd, invincible in fight,
In heavenly panoply thy warriors cas'd,
With heavenly ardour ev'ry sinew brac'd;
Still Godfrey, still thy mightier foe remains,
More fierce than millions on encount'ring plains—
Go, whirl thy sword, go, lanch th' impetuous spear,
And let remorseless famine learn to fear!
Alas! too soon thy matchless force must feel,
That hunger's sharper than the wounding steel.

" No harvests here wave hopeful to thy eye;
Consum'd around, the blasted pastures lie;
The tiller has himself undone his toil,
Nor left for him to reap, or thee to spoil;
While wasting fires have robb'd thy fainting steed,
And wide devour'd, lest fiercer foes should feed:
Deep guarded battlements the grain immure,
From force defend, and from access secure.
But then your fleet shall waft the large supply,
And seas shall yield, what hostile lands deny;
Yes, you shall live as please the tide and wind,
When gales are constant, and when storms are kind.

" Yet could thy pow'r the struggling tempest
        rein,
Direct the blast, and rule th' indignant main;
How will thy feeble, thy unequal fleet,
Such joint, such formidable forces meet,
When lanch'd around our naval powers unite,
And from the boundless ocean snatch the sight?

" Strange is the turn of thy capricious state,
Where double conquest must prevent defeat;
As strange our fav'ring fate, where one success
Shall with a sure, a double conquest bless:
If we, by land or sea, thy pow'rs sustain,
Vain are thy pow'rs, by land and ocean vain;
And if by sea or land thy forces fail,
By land and sea alike our arms prevail.
In vain by land the fruitless field you boast,
When famine triumphs o'er thy conqu'ring host;
In vain thy fleet shall waft the plenty o'er,
Thy conqu'ring fleet, when armies are no more.

" If yet, nor love, nor interest can invite,
And only wars remorseless wars delight,
How has thy soul her former praise disclaim'd,
Through ev'ry clime, for ev'ry virtue fam'd!
But ah, if war thy milder thoughts deform,
May Heav'n with gentle hand appease the storm;
Through Asia may the horrid conflicts cease,
And Godfrey rule the conquer'd realms in peace!

" And you! whose arms, in dubious battle try'd,
The virtues of your matchless chief divide,
Who share, alike, his council and his care,
Who ev'ry toil and ev'ry peril share;
Let heav'nly peace the swelling passion sway,
Nor smiling fortune, faithless fair, betray.
The mariner, though sails and cordage torn,
Through sands, and rocks, and whirling eddies borne,
At length within the friendly haven cast,
With transport sees that ev'ry danger's pass'd:
Escap'd like him the trusty port retain,
Nor tempt the future tempest on the main."

    He ended smooth; but, through the warlike
        round,
Of deep disgust the murm'ring accents sound;
Impassion'd gestures all their soul avow,
And indignation bends in ev'ry brow.
Thrice and again, his quick discerning view
The chief around his circling heroes threw;
And thus sedate the much-experienc'd man,
With gentle but determin'd voice began.

" Aletes! deep thy art, and smooth thy phrase;
And well you mix the menace with the praise.
If, in sincerity, as it should seem,
Our acts are honour'd with your king's esteem,
You may assure the monarch, on our part,
Of all due deference, and a grateful heart.
But where your words with threat'ning ardour warm,
Collect all Asia in the coming storm,
I answer in my plain accustom'd style,
Not grac'd with eloquence, yet free from guile.

" Know then, that all our suff'ring pow'rs sustain,
Through hostile climes, and the tempestuous main,
Sole cent'ring to one glorious object tends,
And only leads where all our labour ends—
To free yon sacred, venerable wall !
Let ev'ry threat, let ev'ry ruin fall,
Nor death can terrify, nor toil distress,
Since Heav'n with future recompense will bless.
" 'T is not the transient gust of mortal joys,
Gems, crowns, or pageant sceptres, glitt'ring toys !
Nor fame in all her pomp of titles dress'd,
Inspires the fervour of a Christian breast:
Who to the spheres their constant course assign'd,
Alone directs the movements of our mind;
He is the Pole whose fix'd attraction charms,
The Voice that dictates, and the Cause that arms.
His Hand alone the whirling surge restrains,
And o'er his tempest throws the lordly reins.
Alike to us the wintry gusts arise,
Or Syrius fires th' equinoctial skies;
Warm'd by his breath, or shaded by his wing,
His Presence tempers our eternal spring.
Smooth'd, where he leads, the strong ribb'd hills
     subside,
The dangers vanish, and the floods divide;
Low lie proud heads, and ev'ry hostile pow'r,
And from its basis smokes the tumbling tow'r.
" Not from the cumbrous shield, or brittle
     spear,
Or strength of mortal arm, we hope—or fear;
Nor list if Grecia or the world be foes;
We trust a Pow'r, who can alone oppose;
Nor shall the world against our host abide,
Against one man, if Heav'n be on his side.
" But if, before yon consecrated wall,
His Will, inscrutable, ordains our fall,
Our bones shall mingle with that hallow'd clay,
Where once the Prince of Life, Messiah lay :
So will we fall, triumphant, though o'erthrown ;
So will we die!—but, trust me, not alone—
Sad Asia shall the mournful vigil keep,
And (friendless) we will give the foe to weep.
" Yet think not we in savage wars delight,
That terms of honourable peace we slight;
Or, vain of conquest, equally despise
Such formidable foes, such strong allies.
But why your monarch prop these distant walls,
Where neither interest claims, nor justice calls?
If east or west, his conqu'ring ensigns bend,
Pleas'd with his pow'r, we rise not to defend;
Still with his glory may his sway increase,
Still may he rule his native realms in peace,
Nor toil to find unnecessary foes,
But take and grant reciprocal repose !"
He ceas'd; when, passion madd'ning in his eye,
Argantes in a storm of wrath drew nigh,
Th' impetuous gust disdaining to control;
And thus loos'd all the fury of his soul.
" Yes, chief, henceforward let the sword decide;
War is thy wish, nor be thy wish deny'd.
Ill hast thou answer'd to our terms of peace ;
But cause of strife to mortals ne'er can cease."
So saying, quick his flowing garb he seiz'd,
And fold ng with terrific action rais'd :
" Here, thou contemner of events !" he cries,
" Here, peace and war within my vesture lies.
If war be in thy bold election, say;
Choose as you list, but choose without delay."
Such utt'ring arrogance, and scornful air,
Not likely such a princely round should bear :

Incens'd, no voice attends their chief's reply ;
" War, war !" at once, " War, war !" aloud they
     cry.
With rising wrath the fierce Circassian burn'd,
And " War, eternal, mortal war !" return'd.
His robe with hasty furious hand expos'd,
The gates of Janus seem at once disclos'd:
Peace, scar'd, on trembling pinions urg'd her flight;
And Hate and Discord, issuing, claim'd the light.
All dread and terrible, Argantes stands :
Dire as Tiphoius with his hundred hands,
Or Babel, that in spite of Heav'n arose ;
So tow'rs the chief, and menaces his foes.
With awful grace superior, Godfrey smil'd,
And thus rejoin'd more menacingly mild.
" Our answer let your Memphian monarch hear,
Who better knows to threat than we to fear—
If here he means we should attend the fight,
Swift be his march, and well assur'd his might;
Or soon we 'll wait him on Egyptian soil;
For we are, haply, more inur'd to toil."
The hero spoke, and gracefully humane
Dismiss'd the chiefs with their attending train :
Aletes had a helm of richest price,
With plumage proud, the beamy spoil of Nice:
But to Argantes' mightier hand he gave
A massy sword, fit present for the brave;
Though gold the hilt, and gem'd with costliest stone,
Superior to the mass the model shone;
Curious to view, but pond'rous 't was to feel,
And like a meteor gleam'd the length'ning steel.
The bounty quick the proud Circassian took,
Ey'd with delight, and with dread action shook:
" Soon Bulloign! much too soon," he cried, " you 'll
     find,
Such trust was ne'er to better hands assign'd."
They parted thus; and, to his peer address'd,
Argantes spoke the boldness of his breast :
" Go thou to Egypt with the morning light;
I go to Sion, and I go this night.
My pen or presence to no end conduce,
Where deeds are dead, and only words of use:
Talk is thy province, and may have its charms ;
Be mine the war, the nobler clash of arms !"
Brief spoke the Pagan, nor reply attends,
But turn'd with haughty step to Salem bends;
The dictates of his swift impetuous soul
No rites of embassy, no laws control:
Beneath the glimm'ring of the starry ray,
Impatient, he directs his warlike way ;
While warm in ev'ry act, and ev'ry thought,
Contention bled, and future combats fought.
And now still night, diffus'd to either pole,
From Heav'n her balmy visitation stole ;
With soft constraint the drowsied sense oppress'd,
And weigh'd the weary bustling world to rest.
Through nature, peace and short oblivion reign:
The tempest slumbers on the silent main ;
Hush'd through the sylvan shade, and dreary den,
Smooth lake, and peopled flood, and willow'd fen,
Each foot, and fin, and feather, finds repose;
With gentler pace each lazy current flows;
Exil'd from ev'ry heart oppression fled,
And labour sunk upon the grateful bed.
But not the shade with kindly opiate bless'd,
That lull'd the remnant of the world to rest,
Nor toil persuasive of profound repose,
Through Godfrey's camp could give an eye to close:
Impatience hangs upon the lingering night,
Counts the long hour, and claims the promis'd light ;

Still through the gloom exploring looks essay
The dawning whiteness of the eastern ray,
That shall o'er long-sought Solyma arise,
And give her spires to their expecting eyes.

----

## BOOK III.

THE eastern breeze, fresh harbinger of dawn,
Sprung from the surge, and whisper'd o'er the lawn:
Aurora wak'd, suffus'd with early dew,
And round her form the purpling vesture threw;
Her orient locks increasing glory shed,
And Eden's rose adorn'd her radiant head.
The soldiers arm; ten thousand shouts arise,
Ring through the camp, and burst upon the skies;
Triumphant clarions answer to the sound,
And boundless joy and clamour pours around.
  Wild were the transports of the madding host,
Wild as the waves on the Trinacrian coast,
Or winds that o'er the ridgy mountain sweep,
That rend the clouds, and rush upon the deep:
Yet to their chief the ranging troops conform,
He rules the rapture, and directs the storm;
In order'd file arrays th' impetuous train;
Rapid they march, but rapid with the rein.
  Wing'd were their hearts, with previous trans-
                        port fleet,
And wing'd, like feather'd Mercury, their feet;
Nor travel tires, nor obstacles impede,
So warm their ardour and so swift their speed.
But when careering up the ethereal road,
The disk of Heav'n with rising fervour glow'd,
Jerusalem the ravish'd squadrons spy,
" Jerusalem!" triumphing thousands cry;
Jerusalem, their acclamations sweet,
Expanding arms, and reaching raptures, greet.
  So when beneath the keen Septentrion pole,
Or where the tides of Austrial oceans roll,
Advent'rous mariners, a desp'rate band,
Roam in the search of yet untrodden land,
Where skies unknown the dreary prospect bound,
With gulfs that gape, and storms that rage around;
If, haply, now some azure hill they spy,
How is the voice responsive to the eye!
Their cheeks with mutual gratulation glow,
And shouts in scorn dismiss all former woe.
  To the first hurry of that wild delight
When Salem rose transporting to their sight,
Contrition soon with rev'rent check succeeds;
With dulcet anguish ev'ry bosom bleeds:
Their humble eyes all trembling they withhold
From walls too dear, too awful to behold,
Where Christ his seat of mortal passion chose,
Expiring suffer'd, and renew'd arose:
Griefs, joys, unknown, their mingling soul possess'd,
And thrill'd the nerve in ev'ry martial breast.
Soft is their step along the sacred ground,
And hoarse and deep the murm'ring accents sound—
Hoarse as the rustling of autumnal breeze;
Deep as the break of rough assuaging seas,
Where denser woods the shatt'ring blast oppose,
Or craggy shores the surging spume enclose.
  The warriors, by their chief's example led,
With naked feet the sultry causeway tread;
Of boastful trim their arms they all divest,
And all unplum'd is ev'ry bending crest;
Timid their voice, and sweet their whisp'ring woe,
Short breathe their sighs, and fast their eyes o'erflow,

While thus the penitent, the dear distress,
Low fault'ring tongues and speaking hearts express:
  " O Lamb! who here for all the living died,
Love's purple fountain issuing from thy side,
Whose currents through the maze of mercy ran,
To wash the ways, the sinful ways of man;
Receive, receive the contrite tears we shed,
Due tribute where our suff'ring Saviour bled;
Nor common tears should thy memorial keep,
But pour'd to thee our bleeding hearts should
                        weep!"
  Meanwhile the watch, who, from his tow'ry stand,
In spacious prospect held the neigb'ring land,
To right, to left, slow gath'ring on the skies,
Perceiv'd wide wreaths of curling dust arise.
As fraught with coming storm when clouds ascend
And sable wing'd from north to east extend,
The nimble lightnings pour upon the sight,
And the dark vapour labours with the light;
So through th' eclipse, shields, helms, and corslets
                        gleam,
Thick ported spears project a quiv'ring beam,
With man and steed the wide-womb'd cloud is fill'd,
And glitt'ring arms the skirted region gild.
  The hasty centinel the town alarms—
" To arms, ye citizens," he cries, " to arms!
Heavens! what a horrid cloud involves the sky!
What ranks of steely war, what hosts I spy!
Up, up, the foe's at hand; your walls ascend;
Your law, your lives, your native rights defend!"
  The female's feeble sex, and silver'd sage,
Too soft by nature, or unnerv'd by age,
With trembling infants to the mosques repair,
And tire their prophet with a length of prayer.
But those of limb assur'd, and courage bold,
Seiz'd their keen weapons with a hasty hold:
Some run to line the portals, some the wall;
The king informs, directs, and governs all.
Then to a tower that brow'd the northern coast,
And front to front o'erlook'd th' approaching host,
His city here, and here his foe in view,
The monarch, to inspect the whole, withdrew.
Erminia, to his royal house ally'd,
Erminia, gentle charmer! grac'd his side,
Whom late (her kingdom seiz'd, and slain her sire)
The victor's chain permitted to retire.
  Meantime Clorinda, issuing at their head,
The force of many a gallant warrior led;
While, with his squadron couch'd, Argantes lay,
Prepar'd to sally, and sustain the day.
Clorinda's daring voice each ear inspir'd;
Each eye, her warlike presence fill'd and fir'd:
" This day," she cried, " let grateful Asia bless,
That to our arms assign'd the first success."
She said—when straight appear'd a Christian band,
Whose search with early forage scour'd the land,
And now returning with the low'ng prey,
To the main host they held their hasty way.
The virgin, by intemp'rate valour push'd,
Full on the troop, but first on Guardo, rush'd,
Their mighty leader, fam'd for strength in fight,
But much too weak to match her matchless might:
Him from his seat, in either army's view,
O'erturn'd behind his steed Clorinda threw;
Glad omen hence the Pagan hosts portend,
And shouts, by shouts upborne, to Heav'n ascend:
But she, where join'd the thickest squadrons, press'd,
Cleft the bright helm, and tore the plaited breast;
Her men fast follow'd on the road she made,
And fought secure beneath her conqu'ring shade.

Repell'd, with speed the Christians quit the spoil,
And step by step their shatter'd pow'rs recoil;
Till the kind summit of a hill they gain'd,
And rallying thence the stronger foe sustain'd:
When lo! impetuous as loos'd whirlwinds rise,
Or the red bolt that shoots athwart the skies,
His arms and eager eyes ejecting flame,
Far wing'd before his squadron Tancred came.

As in a tempest stands some stable mast,
Brac'd to the board, yet lab'ring in the blast;
So great, so firm, the spear which Tancred takes,
Sits in his grasp, and in his anger shakes.

The king beheld him dreadful in his charms,
Blooming in strength, and eminent in arms.
His presence fill'd the careful monarch's breast,
Who thus Erminia, trembling maid, address'd:
" Well should thy eye, through long acquaintance,
know
The hated shape of each distinguish'd foe;
Say then, what 's he, whose hot and warlike form
Before him sends the terrour of a storm?"

He said; nor answer save the sigh receiv'd,
That in the whiteness of her bosom heav'd,
That half suppress'd in its sweet prison lay,
And through her lips half wing'd its odorous way;
While round her eyes the crimson circlets glow'd,
And bright, within, the liquid anguish flow'd.

At length o'er love she threw aversion's cloke,
And thus, with feign'd yet real passion, spoke:
" Ah me! too well, too well his form I know,
Whose steed so proudly bears my deadliest foe;
Him from my eyes nor mingling hosts can hide,
Him from my thoughts nor time nor place divide.
Great prophet! in what heaps from Antioch's wall,
Beneath that arm I saw my people fall!
The wound he gives no mortal may endure,
No armour ward, and ah!—no med'cine cure.
Tancred his name,—O! cruel,—may he live,
And 'scape the death he knows too well to give,
Till captive once, and to my rage assign'd,
He feels how strait a woman's chains can bind:
A thousand deaths my vengeful thoughts prepare,
And one, which Heav'n avert! would only spare."
She said; involuntary sighs expire,
And just, though great, the monarch deem'd her ire;
But ah! how sweet the vengeance she design'd!
How soft the fetters! and the rage how kind!

Meantime Clorinda ey'd the warrior's speed,
And full to thwart the tempest urg'd her steed.
Couch'd at the head each aim'd a deadly stroke;
Her weapon, shiver'd to the gauntlet, broke:
But the rude welcome of the hero's spear,
Nor silken thongs nor golden buckles bear;
From her fair front the plumed helm he cast,
Her hair dishevelling revell'd in the blast;
Gem'd in the curling radiance shone her face,
The fiercest ardour, and the sweetest grace.
Forth from her glance keen flash'd the living
fire;
Ah! what her smiles—since lovely was her ire?
Why, Tancred! wherefore stops thy late career?
Here 's but one foe, and can the mighty fear?
Or can a face like spelful magic charm,
Freeze the bold nerve, and chain the lifted arm?
Yes, Tancred's eye bears witness to his heart,
And owns a charm beyond the mystic art;
Still on that heart, indelibly impress'd,
Still liv'd that form which now his eyes confess'd:
The shade ill shelt'ring to his soul returns,
And gazing now, as at the fount he burns.

Her shield she rais'd, and on the warrior flew;
Fierce she advanc'd, and gentle he withdrew:
On other foes he would his force have try'd;
But " Here! turn here!" the threatful virgin
cry'd.
Ah, barb'rous maid! one death would not suffice;
Thy sword would trace the progress of thy eyes.

Furious she strikes, while faintly he defends,
And only to her killing face attends:
" Ah!" thought the chief, " sweet combatant forbear!
'T is not thy sword that Tancred knows to fear;
Far deeper than the wounds thy arms impart,
Thou 'st found the way to reach thy soldier's heart.
Strong though thy arm, the strongest arm may fail;
But fate is in thy eyes, and must prevail."

Yet, ere he died, determin'd yet to tell,
Why thus the unresisting victim fell;
Half timorous, half embolden'd by despair,
With troubl'd accent he address'd the fair:
" If the steel'd ranks of this embattled field,
No apter object of thy prowess yield;
If me alone thy vengeance would pursue,
Thy valour combat, and thy arms subdue;
Hence from the mingling hosts with me retire,
And prove whose arm can best express our ire."
The maid assented, though unhelm'd her head,
And rode intrepid where the challenge led.
And now she aim'd, and now discharg'd a stroke,
When, scarce preventing, thus the warrior spoke:
" Hold! lovely heroine, hold! and let thy rage
First hear the terms that won me to engage."
She stay'd; his fault'ring tongue despair made
bold,
And gave the love long latent to unfold:
" Ah my fair foe," th' impassion'd Tancred cried,
" Since peace is in thy endless wrath deny'd,
The terms of war to speedy conquest lead,
Give you to strike and me alone to bleed;
Too bless'd, if so I may thy rage appease,
And learn, so hap'ly, learn in death to please.
Long since, the joys of irksome life are fled,
Nor mine the heart you pierce, or blood you shed:
Mistaken maid! in ev'ry part you reign,
And pour the vital flood through ev'ry vein.
Of me, more nearly than thyself, possess'd,
Thine 's all the int'rest in thy Tancred's breast!
See to thy sword his bosom I impart;
Too well thou know'st thy passage to the heart—
Strike, strike! it leaps to bleed at thy command,
And welcomes death endear'd beneath thy hand."

Yet, Tancred! further had thy lips essay'd,
And haply touch'd the much admiring maid;
But here, by luckless interruption led,
Before their foes some routed Paynims fled.
A Gallic soldier, as he pass'd the fair,
Mark'd the bright flow of her redundant hair;
His coward hand the base advantage seiz'd,
And high in air the cruel steel he rais'd;
But Tancred on his weapon caught the stroke,
And the first force of its encounter broke;
Yet lightly edg'd the glancing sabre hit,
Where the fair head and pillar'd neck were knit.

As when, prepar'd some regal brow to grace,
Or raise the lustre of some fair-one's face,
An artist bids the golden circlets shine,
And calls the ruby from the blushing mine;
So the bright drops of bleeding crimson show'd,
And gem'd amid her mingling tresses glow'd.
Then, then, no limit Tancred's fury knew,
But lanch'd in vengeance on the ruffian flew;

As swiftly loos'd to flight he urg'd his steed,
For instant fear gave feathers to his speed.
Suspens'd awhile, and much at both amaz'd,
On the strange chase the thoughtful virgin gaz'd;
But turn'd, she saw her shatter'd squadrons yield,
And chang'd the fortune of the flying field:
With shame, grief, rage, all kindling at the sight,
She rush'd to turn her routed bands from flight;
Now, singly bold, against a host made head,
And now, o'erpower'd by pressing numbers, fled;
Yet mutual flight to her pursuers taught,
For still she flew, and as she fled she fought.
'As on the wilds of Plessa's bord'ring wood,
Or where broad Volga rolls a deep'ning flood,
The savage Ure, by circling mastiffs press'd,
Shakes the dread dewlap of his bellowing chest;
Outnumber'd, now prepares his flanks for flight,
Now wheeling lifts his horny front in fight;
Clorinda so, half chasing, and half chas'd,
Repelling, and repell'd, now fled, now fac'd;
When flying fear'd, and fatal though pursu'd,
She rather seem'd subduing than subdu'd.
    The Pagans, push'd before the Christian pow'rs,
Now reach'd the bases of their shatt'ring tow'rs;
Whence rallied, for the field again they burn,
And with a shout upon their hunters turn.
    Meantime Argantes with his troop impends,
And plum'd in horrour from the mount descends.
Well might the stoutest tremble at the sight,
For fearful rush'd the giant fam'd in fight:
Pierc'd by his sword, or by his lance o'erthrown,
The prostrate ranks beneath his fury groan;
Deform'd, the battle bleeds at ev'ry vein,
And man and steed lie tumbled on the plain.
With equal death Clorinda heap'd the field,
And made the pride of manly prowess yield.
Ardelio, whose brave spirit, warm though sage,
Felt a fresh spring in his autumnal age,
With rash essay advent'ring to repel,
A victim to the fond presumption fell.
Two sons he had who felt their father's fire,
Two valiant sons to guard a valiant sire;
But wounded lay the brave Alcander's might,
And scarce was Poliphernes sav'd by flight.
    But Tancred, who untimely o'er the plain
Pursu'd the ruffian, but pursu'd in vain,
Now turning saw th' unequal combat wag'd,
And his brave troop by circling hosts engag'd:
With double grief his errour pierc'd his sight,
But double valour would restore the fight;
He ran, he shot, confirm'd his fainting bands,
Recall'd their hearts, and fortified their hands.
    Nor he alone; for now, by Dudon led,
The Advent'rous troop their dreaded ensigns
    spread.
Strength of their strength, and in himself a host,
Their flow'r, their nerve, their beauty, and their
    boast,
Whom by his mien and arms Erminia knew,
Before the foremost young Rinaldo flew.
" Behold," she cry'd, " behold Rinaldo there,
Than man more valiant, more than woman fair!
Whose fame is full ere promise could presage,
And shames in infancy the toils of age.
His arm more forceful than an engine falls,
And threats more ruin to these tott'ring walls.
Had Europe sent six champions to the field,
Six boys like this could ample Europe yield,
The world were conquer'd to the southern pole;
Beneath their yoke should India's Ganges roll,

In chains all Niger's tawny kings should tread,
And Nile in vain would hide his sacred head.
    " But turn where Dudon thy attention claims,
Who there in gold and mingling verdure flames!
He rules yon band whose actions task belief,
Where ev'ry soldier is himself a chief;
Yet justly his experienc'd step precedes,
And hundreds that were born to empire leads.
    " Lo there (unprais'd who in his prowess prides)
The brother of imperial Norway rides,
Gernando, whose huge stature loads the plain!
What boots to say he 's valiant, since he 's vain?
    " But here, O king, in radiant silver dress'd,
Fair as the faith that whitens in their breast,
Behold, ah sweet associates! side by side,
Two friends espous'd, the lover and the bride;
Gildippe, Edward, paradis'd in bliss,
Her Edward that, and his Gildippe this!
No force can foil them, and no fate can part,
Fam'd in the fight, and wedded in the heart."
    While thus she gave due honour to the foe,
Wild was the riot in the vale below:
For now in Tancred and Rinaldo's ire,
The slaughter rages and the ranks expire;
Through the firm depth of hemming foes they
    broke,
And some arm'd Paynim died on ev'ry stroke;
Not e'en Argantes could the shock sustain,
But, fall'n beneath Rinaldo, spread the plain.
And now, O mighty chief, in arms surpass'd,
This thy first foil had haply prov'd thy last,
But chance depriv'd the victor of his prey,
Who press'd beneath his prostrate courser lay.
    Meantime pale fear deform'd the face of fight,
And, mingling, wing'd the Pagan feet for flight;
All, save Argantes and the martial maid,
Who still to stem the conqu'ring army staid;
The bank and bulwark of their host they rose,
And each stood equal to a thousand foes.
Nor so restrain'd, th' impetuous Dudon flew,
Still urg'd the chase, and still the hindmost slew:
Swift, as the victor by Tigranes pass'd,
Lopp'd from the trunk the headed helm he cast:
What, Corban, what, Algazar, could avail,
Your casque well temper'd, and your circling mail?
For his keen sword cleft Corban to the chest,
And through Algazar's back transfix'd the breast:
Beneath his steel Mahammed press'd the plain,
Almanzer's bulk was number'd with the slain;
Before the chief great Amurath expir'd,
And e'en Argantes slow and stern retir'd.
With bridled wrath the indignant warrior burn'd,
He labour'd, rag'd, withdrew, stopp'd, chaf'd, and
    turn'd;
Till now the wish'd advantage he essay'd,
And in brave Dudon's bosom sheath'd the blade;
Prone o'er the field his sully'd armour rung,
And o'er his eyes th' eternal slumber hung.
    Thrice, to the cheer of Heav'n's all-dulcet light,
He lift the pain'd and sickly lids of sight;
And thrice, vain toil, he struggled to arise,
And thrice he fell, and clos'd his umber'd eyes:
From the cold limbs the vital heat retir'd,
And in a parting sigh his soul expir'd.
    Back stepp'd the stern Circassian from the dead,
And shook the reeking steel, and scornful said:
" Go, warriors, let the gen'rous Godfrey know,
What quick effusions from his bounty flow!
When to our arm this weapon he assign'd,
Wise was the trust, as sure the gift was kind;

Nor can he learn, without a secret pride,
To what rare use his favours are apply'd;
Freely he gave, nor I his bounty spare,
Which here return'd his foremost champion's share:
Yet, tell him, yet I languish for that day,
When hand to hand I shall in person pay."
He spoke, when hundreds on the boaster press'd,
And launch'd a mingling tempest at his breast;
But prudence timely prompted to evade,
And the tall towers held forth their friendly shade.
Now shower'd tempest'ous from the embattled wall,
Stones, darts, and flints, and engin'd quarries fall;
Wing'd from the nerve of many a bending bow,
Death points a cloud, and rains the storm below;
The Christian pow'rs receding seek the plain,
And their wide gates the cover'd Pagans gain.
When disencumber'd now Rinaldo rose,
To vengeance loos'd he pour'd upon his foes;
For Dudon's fate had reach'd the warrior's ear,
And gave a fury which e'en friends might fear.
" On, on!" he cried, " why, wherefore stop? O, shame!
Your arms, revenge, revenge and Dudon claim.
In vain their ramparts veil yon trembling rout,
Walls rise in vain to keep the valiant out;
Though fenc'd with adamant, or towers of steel,
Argantes should my ent'ring vengeance feel."
He said, and forward on the ramparts sprung;
A storm of darts around his temples sung:
Yet he gave all his dauntless front to view;
E'en danger aw'd before his eyes withdrew;
The towers appear'd to totter at the sight,
And quailing thousands trembled from their height.
But Sigiere now by royal Godfrey sent,
(Sage herald) bade the rage of war relent:
" Retire, retire, nor vainly hope," he cried,
" That one day's arm shall Salem's fate decide:
Steep are her towers, and boldly mann'd her walls;
And dire must be the shock by which she falls."
They staid reluctant—As the fiery steed
Rein'd in his pride and lorded in his speed,
So far'd Rinaldo's fury, scarce repress'd;
And still the battle struggled in his breast. [gore,
Meantime, with dust deform'd and stain'd with
Brave Dudon from the fated field they bore;
The soldiers press to touch his great remains,
And round his corse the copious sorrow rains.
But Bulloign, from a summit's neighb'ring height,
Survey'd fair Solyma's imperial site;
Her pow'rs, her force, and her defects he scann'd,
And the deep schemes of future conquest plann'd.
High eminent amid the circling lands,
Fair Solyma in ancient glory stands:
Rear'd on two hills her regal spires arise;
Between a vale in rich expansion lies:
From three proud sides she overlooks her foe,
And smiles, impervious, on the war below;
But, weak by nature on the northern part,
She stoops to arm her in the strength of art.
The frugal trough and cistern's vase retain
Her wat'ry stores of Heav'n-descending rain;
Around her walls no lively verdures grow;
Few founts to slake the sultry region flow;
No grove extends its hospitable shade
To the tir'd pilgrim, or the fev'rish glade,
Save where, two leagues divided from the town,
A baleful forest rears its umbrage brown,
Whose silent shades in antique horrours rise,
Brood o'er the soil, and intercept the skies.

Clear to the dawning of th' eastern beam,
The hallow'd Jordan pours a plent'ous stream;
A sanded billow bounds the western side,
And rolls alternate on the midland tide;
Samaria stretch'd upon the north expands,
Where Bethel in opprobrious prospect stands;
But Bethlem, Israel's gem and Judah's boast,
Rears to the south, and consecrates the coast.
While Bulloign thus surveys the hostile ground,
And sends his eye in large experience round,
Metes the proud height of Sion's tower'd wall,
Marks her defects, and meditates her fall;
Erminia intermitted silence breaks,
And thus observant of the hero speaks.
" Behold, O king, in regal purple dress'd,
Strength in his arm, and wisdom in his breast,
Behold where Godfrey takes his awful stand,
All form'd for fame, to act as to command!
In him the hero and the sage unite,
The clue of conduct, and the force of fight:
Raimond alone, of you unnumber'd hosts,
A rival in the nightly council boasts;
Alike young Tancred's and Rinaldo's charms,
Their flame of courage, and their force of arms!"
" I know," the monarch with a sigh replied,
" I know him well, and saw his prowess tried.
When I the seals of Egypt's sultan bore,
And trod a friend upon the Gallic shore,
A stripling in the lists, he struck my eyes,
And matchless bore from ev'ry arm the prize;
Then, ere his spring of bearded down began,
In ev'ry excellence a more than man:
Too sure presages of impending woe
To such, whom fate should mark for Bulloign's foe!
" But say, what 's he, whose scarf with Tyrian pride
Flows o'er his arms, and glows at Godfrey's side?
Though Godfrey treads superior to the sight,
In mien and majesty they both unite."
I see, 't is Baldwin," cried the princely dame,
" His brother, less in features than in fame."
" But mark, intently turn'd how Godfrey hears,
While Raimond speaks the judgment of his years,
Whose hostile hairs bring terrours to my sight,
Grown sage in war, and in experience white;
Beyond ten thousand hands that head alarms,
The ward and leading wisdom of their arms.
" There William, England's younger hope, behold,
His figur'd buckler, and his casque of gold!
Guelfo the next, whose thirst of glory springs
From a long race of heroes and of kings;
I know him well, amid a host express'd,
By his square shoulders and his ample chest.
But ah! in vain I send my eyes about,
To find my foe, the cruel Boemond, out;
The dire usurper, whose relentless hand
Slew my great sire, and seiz'd my native land!"
Thus while they spoke observant of the foe,
The duke descends, and joins his host below:
For now resolv'd, and hopeless to prevail
Where Salem's eminence o'erlook'd the vale,
Incumbent on the opener north he lay,
Spread out his camp, and made his engines play,
Where ev'ry rampart shook beneath his power,
From the far portal to the utmost tower—
In compass near a third; for such the space
That circles Sion in a wide embrace;
Not with thin ensigns length'ning tow'rd the mound,
Could Godfrey's army hem the wondrous round:

Yet ev'ry lane and ev'ry pass he barr'd,
And fix'd the frequent terrours of a guard;
Around his camp the spacious lines he drew,
And broad and deep his guardian trenches threw,
To shield his legions from untimely fight,
And ev'ry dark hostility of night.
     These orders given, the gen'ral held his way
Where Dudon, much lamented hero, lay:
High on a bier, with warlike honours grac'd,
In woeful pomp the great remains were plac'd;
Snapp'd arms and sable ensigns spread the ground,
And mingling princes pour'd their griefs around.
     At Bulloign's sight, the sadly silent crowd,
Renew'd in rising sorrows, wept aloud ;
But he, with majesty that bore the show
Of dirge in triumph, or of cheer in woe,
Approaching, touch'd the bier, repress'd his grief;
And thus pathetic spoke the mourning chief.
     " Hail, Dudon ! hail to thy eternal birth,
Reviv'd in Heav'n from all thy toils on Earth !
Nor yet shall Heav'n the total hero claim,
Still found on Earth, immortal in his fame !
In life, my friend, in death thou didst excel ;
Valiant you fought, and valiantly you fell !
Clos'd is thy warfare, finish'd is thy fight,
And stars of living glory crown thy might !
Not, not for thee, this sable cloud of woe ;
But for ourselves our juster sorrows flow :
Our arm of war 's unnerv'd upon thy bier,
And broke with thine is ev'ry pointless spear ;
Despoil'd of thee, thou chiefest earth'y aid,
Our banners droop, and all our laurels fade !
Yet the great cause that might inform the dead,
The cause survives, for which thy bosom bled;
Survives to warm thee with its wonted charms,
And wing thy soul asisstant to our arms,
When in the powers of heavenly mission bright,
Once more thou shalt descend to rule the fight,
In terrours wrapp'd to thunder on the foe,
To lay the pride of all oppressors low,
To raze the height of yon embattled wall,
And lift thy friends victorious from thy fall !"
He said—and now the slumb'rous dew of night
Mix'd with the shade, and sunk upon the sight;
O'er care-swoln lids effus'd the balm of sleep,
And clos'd those eyes that daily learn'd to weep.
But Bulloign on his pensive pillow lay,
Revolv'd through ev'ry labour of the day,
While forming in his wakeful round of thought
Machines arose, and novel combats fought.
     The bright-ey'd morn from early vapour won,
Saw Godfrey arm'd, and orient with the Sun;
At Dudon's hearse, the friendly melting chief
Pour'd the last tribute of attending grief.
Him a long train of fun'ral pomp convey'd,
And low in earth the warrior's corse they laid,
Where a tall palm its branching honours spread,
Wove in the wind, and worship'd o'er the dead ;
His dust the priestly consecration bless'd,
And sung the great departed soul to rest.
     High o'er his tomb, amid the branches strung,
Ensigns, and arms, and blazon'd trophies hung;
The pride and spoils of many a valiant knight,
Seiz'd by the victor in his days of fight.
Full on the trunk his proper arms were plac'd,
His plumy helm the joining corslet grac'd ;
And thus the marble bore his sacred name—
" Here Dudon lies—yet fills the world with fame."
     The last sad rites of social woes express'd,
And Dudon left to his eternal rest,

The chief of chiefs, on public cares intent,
A convoy to the secret forest sent,
Where silent grew its unfrequented shade,
Now by a Syrian to the duke betray'd,
Who meditates from hence on Sion's fall,
And plans machines the rivals of her wall.
     The woodmen now dispose their ranging bands,
Th' alternate axe high brandish'd in their hands ;
Unwonted noise the affrighted forest fills,
And echo sighs from all the circling hills.
Beneath their strokes the victor palms subside ;
Down falls the pine from its aerial pride ;
Still breathes the cedar o'er a length of ground;
The firs in weeping amber mourn around;
Fell'd with her elm the viny consort lies,
And faithful o'er the folded trunk she dies.
     The poplar, beech, and alder's wat'ry shade,
Sink on the marsh, or wither o'er the glade :
Imperial oaks, that, through ten ages past,
Had brav'd Heaven's bolt and rough encount'ring [blast,
The period now of mortal glory feel,
And fall subdu'd beneath the conq'ring steel :
Th' exil'd pard abjures his wonted den,
And ev'ry feather flies the voice of men :
Wide lie the realms of long usurping night,
And scenes unfold that never saw the light !

---

## CONSTANTIA:

#### OR,

#### THE MAN OF LAW'S TALE,

MODERNIZED FROM CHAUCER. 1741.

TO WHICH IS NOW ADDED,

#### THE TALE,

AS WRITTEN BY CHAUCER, TAKEN FROM THE ACCURATE EDITION OF THE CANTERBURY TALES, PRINTED AT LONDON, 1775.

HENCE Want, ungrateful visitant, adieu !
Pale empress hence, with all thy meager crew—
Sour Discontent and mortified Chagrin ;
Lean hollow Care, and self-corroding Spleen;
Distress and Woe, sad parents of Despair,
With wringing hands, and ever rueful air;
The tread of Dun, and Bum's alarming hand,
Dire as the touch of Circe's circling wand ;
Keen Hunger, with his sharp but famish'd eye,
And dusky Theft, a desp'rate prompter nigh ;
While agues shudder to the whistling gale,
And jointly Law and Infamy assail !
But worse, O worse, than all the hideous train,
Hot-mouth'd Reproach, and saucy writh'd Disdain !
These in the rear of thy assembly wait ;
Still point th' anguish, and augment the weight.
     The worst oppression, who, ah ! who could bear,
If Virtue, hov'ring angel, was not there ?

---

### THE MAN OF LAWES TALE.

O SCATHFUL harm, condition of poverte,
With thirst, with cold, with hunger so confounded,
To asken helpe thee shameth in thin herte,
If thou non ask, so sore art thou ywounded,
That veray nede unwrappeth al thy wound hid.

Where Poverty her blasting progress bends,
The goddess with superior wing attends:
Around the fair her bless'd associates play,
Bask in her eye, and whiten in her ray—
Bright Purity, with firm unalter'd cheek,
The mild, the kind, the gentle, and the meek;
Humility's benignly placid grace,
And Innocence with sweet seraphic face;
Calm Piety that smiles amidst the storm,
And Charity with boundless wishes warm.
Bold in the front, to guard the heavenly band,
Behold the masculine adherents stand!
Patience, with Atlantean shoulders spread;
Hail Temperance, on thrifty viands fed ;
Firm Fortitude, unknowing how to yield ;
And Perseverance with his batter'd shield;
And honest Industry, whose early toil
Wins health and plenty from the labour'd soil.
The genuine arts behind the goddess wait,
Her reign illustrate, and improve her state;
With eye elate here Contemplation soars,
And Learning piles his intellectual stores ;
Here mental sciences arranging shine ;
Here manual crafts the various task design ;
While Diligence the busy finger plies,
And wing'd, from rank to rank, Invention flies.
Such wide extremes on Indigence attend !
There Vice assails, the Virtues here defend :
Below, the gloom of ev'ry passion storms ;
Above, calm Virtue mod'rates and reforms ;
Here, highly elevate; there, deep depress ;
And give, or bliss, or anguish, in excess.
Hail Virtue ! chaste eternal beauty, hail !
Still on the foe, O goddess, still prevail !
The world, ere fram'd, lay open to thy view ;
You form'd the whole, and shall again renew !
Ere I thy arduous pleasing toils decline,
Be want, ah, still be each disaster mine ;
Till e'en oppression be itself subdu'd,
Nor yet a wish for wealth or power intrude!
Nor be the poor alone thy fav'rite care ;
Fly, fly to courts, and let the mighty share!
The silken lethargy at once awake;
Debauch from his intemp'rate opiate shake ;
Thence ev'ry vice and ev'ry folly drive,
That sting or glitter round the gorgeous hive.
Before thy touch let insolence retire,
And vanity, an empty breath, expire;
Hypocrisy cast off the fair disguise,
And starting in his native gloom arise.

---

Maugre thin hed thou must for indigence·
Or stele, or begge, or borwe thy dispence.

Thou blamest Crist, and sayst ful bitterly,
He misdeparteth richesse temporal ;
Thy neighebour thou witest sinfully,
And sayst, thou hast to litel, and he hath all :
Parfay (sayst thou) somtime he reken shall,
Whan that his tayl shall brennen in the glede,
For he nought helpeth needful in hir nede.

Herken what is the sentence of the wise,
Bet is to dien than have indigence.
Thy selve neighebour wol thee despise,
If thou be poure, farewel thy reverence.
Yet of the wise man take this sentence,
Alle the dayes of poure men ben wicke,
Beware therfore or thou come to that pricke.

Now, goddess, ent'ring, view the dome of state !
Do thou inform, and give me to relate ;
Let demons obvious to my eye appear,
(Which known, could sure find no admittance here.)
Amid the buzzing, busy, idle crowd,
The mix'd assembly of the mean and proud,
See, Treason smiles, a suitor to his king,
See, Promise flutters on a cypress wing;
Her pinion like autumnal foliage falls,
And on the pavement Disappointment crawls.
A friendly aspect Enmity assumes ;
Beneath applause, deep lurking Envy glooms;·
The tempting mammon Subornation shows ;
And in the patriot's zeal Dissention glows.
Oppression there with gently winning grace,
And Ignorance with solemn thinking face,
And Pride with mortify'd and Christian guise,
And Infidelity with saintly eyes,
Four rival candidates, their monarch sue;
Two for the bench, and for the mitre two.
Lo, there Ambition, from his height elate !
And Pleasure lolling on a couch of state!
On these the pageantry of pomp attends ;
To these th' idolizing tumult bends;
The poor, the rich, the peasant. and the peer,
And all religions, join in worship here.
Ambition, reaching from his airy stand,
Grasps at a globe that shuns his desp'rate hand:
Around the glitt'ring sphere, confusedly gay,
Crowns, truncheons, gems, and trophy'd radiance
    lay,
But changing with alternate light and shade,
The lures appear, and vanish, shine, and fade ;
Vain as the cloudy meteor of the morn,
Which fancy forms, and transient rays adorn.
The prime rewards four suppliant sons of fame,
Lust, Rapine, Violence, and Slaughter, claim;
And though essential happiness is due,
For toys the wise, for toys the virtuous sue.
Deluded men the ready ambush fly !
Dire lurking deaths behind ambition lie—
The murdering block, keen axe, and racking wheel,
The poison'd goblet, and the bosom'd steel !
Here Pleasure on her velvet couch reclines,
Smiles to undo, and in destruction shines;
With seeming negligence displays her charms ;
The strong she withers, and the steel'd disarms.
Imagination, specious handmaid, waits,
And serves a pomp of visionary cates :
The sorceress still essays the fresh repasts;
But mock'd eternally, she feeds, and fasts.
Around her couch unnumber'd votaries meet,
And wish to share th' imaginary treat ;

---

If thou be poure, thy brother hateth thee,
And all thy frendes fleen fro thee, alas !
O riche marchants, ful of wele ben ye,
O noble, O prudent folk, as in this cas,
Your bagges ben not filled with ambes as,
But with sis cink, that renneth for your chance;
At Christenmasse mery may ye dance.

Ye seken lond and see for your winninges,
As wise folk ye knowen all th' estat
Of regnes, ye ben fathers of tidinges,
And tales, both of pees and of debat :
I were right now of tales desolat,
N'ere that a marchant, gon is many a yere,
Me taught a tale, which that ye shull here.

Devour each morsel with desiring eye,
And for large draughts of fancy'd nectar sigh:
A thousand nymphs of wanton sprightly mien,
Trip round the sofa, and amuse their queen;
With transport she surveys the darling train,
All daughters of her light fermenting brain :
Here laughter, mirth, and dalliance unite,
Illusive joy, and volatile delight,
Conceits, sports, gambols, titillations gay,
Hopes that allure, and projects that betray.
Prime sister of th' inessential bands,
Erect, persuasive Expectation stands;
On each pursuit she flourishes with grace,
And gives a butterfly to lead the chase;
Or wafts a bubble on the parting gale,
And bids surrounding multitudes assail;
With sweets the fond pursuit alone is fraught,
The game still vanishes, when once it 's caught;
Vain is the joy—but not the anguish vain ;
And empty pleasure gives essential pain :
Couch'd as a tiger, watchful to surprise,
Grim death beneath the false enchantress lies ;
The fiends around invisibly engage,
Guilt stings, pains rack, and disappointments rage;
Aches, asthmas, cholics, gouts, convulsions, rheums,
Remorse that gnaws, and languor that consumes.
    Far other train, apparent queen ! you lead;
True bliss attends, though arduous toils precede:
Serene thy bosom, though thy brow severe;
Pain points thy path, but Heav'n is in thy rear.
Wondrous th' influence thy power supplies,
Where triumphs only from oppression rise ;
Peace springs from passion, and from weakness
        might;
Calm ease from travel, and from pain delight ;
No sweets that vanish, and no gusts that cloy—
Clear is the rapture, and serene the joy ;
Reflection culls from ev'ry labour past,
And gives the same eternal bliss to last.
Thus, by long trial, and severe distress,
You, Virtue ! truly, though severely, bless;
Through each tradition, each recorded page,
Through ev'ry nation, and through ev'ry age,
From purpled monarchs to the rural hind,
By pain you purify'd, by toil refin'd :
The mightier weight thy fav'rite heroes bore;
Chief you depress'd, whom chief you meant should
Still with the foe gave forces to prevail,    [soar;
And with this moral form'd the following tale.
    While yet the Turk his early claim avow'd,
And rul'd beneath the sceptre, Judah bow'd ;
A set of worthy wealthy merchants chose
The world for trade, and Sion for repose.
Here they select the gems of brightest rays,
Rich stuffs, wrought silks, and golden tissues blaze;
Through ev'ry climate, and to ev'ry gale,
They lanch the cargo, and expand the sail:
Wide, with their name, their reputation grew,
And to their mart concurring chapmen drew.
    The lure of novelty, and thirst of gain,
Now points their passage o'er the midland main ;

In Surrie whilom dwelt a campagnie
Of chapmen rich, and therto sad and trewe,
That wide where senten hir spicerie,
Clothes of gold, and satins riche of hewe.
Hir chaffare was so thrifty and so newe,
That every wight hath deintee to chaffare
With hem, and eke to sellen hem hir ware.

The Tiber now their spumy keels divide,
And stem the flow of his descending tide.
To Rome, imperial Rome, the traders came ;
Rome heard the voice of their preceding fame :
Free mart and splendid mansion she affords;
Joy crown'd their nights, and elegance their boards.
With mutual chat they gratify desire,
What 's curious now relate, and now inquire;
Alike for knowledge and for wealth they trade,
And are with usury in both repaid.
But Fame surpris'd them with a wonder new,
Beyond what times of brightest record drew,
The poet's fancy, or the lover's tongue ;
And thus the darling excellence she sung.
    " To crown our monarch's age with fond delight,
His cares alleviate, and his toils requite,
Beyond whate'er paternal wish could crave,
Indulgent Heav'n a peerless infant gave:
The softer sex her beauteous body forms,
But her bright soul each manly virtue warms;
Youth without folly, greatness without pride,
And all that 's firm to all that 's sweet ally'd.
Rich as the land by sacred promise bless'd,
Lies the fair vale of her expanded breast;
Mild on a parian pillar turns her head,
Her front, like Lebanon, divinely spread ;
There sit the chaste, the placid, and the meek,
And morn smiles fresh upon her open cheek.
Babes learn distinction at Constantia's sight,
And wither'd age revives to strange delight;
Tumult'ous wishes breathe along her way,
Hands rise, tongues bless, and cent'ring eyes survey;
All run to bend the voluntary knee,
The blind to hear her, and the deaf to see.
Ah ! were she born to universal sway,
How gladly would the willing world obey ?

_____

Now fell it, that the maisters of that sort
Han shapen hem to Rome for to wende,
Were it for chapmanhood or for disport,
Non other message wold they thider sende,
But comen hemself to Rome, this is the ende:
And in swiche place as thought hem avantage
For hir entente, they taken hir herbergage.

Sojourn'd han these marchants in that toun
A certain time, as fell to hir plesance :
And so befell, that the excellent renoun
Of the emperoure's doughter dame Custance
Reported was, with evrey circumstance,
Unto these Surrien marchants, in swiche wise
Fro day to day, as I shal you devise.

This was the commun vois of every man:
" Our emperour of Rome, God him se,
A doughter hath, that sin the world began,
To reken as wel hire goodnesse as beaute,
N'as never swiche another as is she :
I pray to God in honour hire sustene,
And wold she were of all Europe the quene.

" In hire is high beaute withouten pride,
Youthe, withouten grenehed or folie :
To all hire werkes vertue is hire guide;
Humblesse hath slaien in hire tyrannie:
She is mirrour of all curtesie,
Hire herte is veray chambre of holinesse,
Hire hond ministre of fredom for almesse."

And now with wealthy manufacture stow'd,
Lanch'd on the tide their freighted vessels rode;
The pendants vainly point the fav'ring gale,
Court the weigh'd anchor, and th' opening sail,
Till first the fair perfection they beheld,
Who all report, in fatal hour, excell'd:
For Syria then they ply the lab'ring oar,
And the crook'd keels divide their native shore.

Exulting now they touch the fav'rite land,
Unlade, and moor along the yielding strand.
Now duteous, on their youthful sultan wait,
Unfold new treasures, and new tales relate.
With usual grace, and curious ear he hears;
With usual courtesy and bounty cheers;
The strange, the wondrous narrative admires,
And all that 's foreign, all that 's new requires.

Ah, hapless prince, thy further search restrain;
Couch'd in the tale, death lurks to entertain!
Constantia's charms their raptur'd tongues disclose;
In ev'ry word some kindling beauty glows;
Her form, her features, mien, and soul they breathe,
Unpraise all praise, and leave all terms beneath.

Strong eloquence can picture to the blind,
Create new forms, and people all the mind;
Can pain or mitigate, can heal or wound,
Enchant with sentences, and kill with sound.
The fancy'd sweets his ear impatient drinks;
Deep on his soul the imag'd beauty sinks; [reigns,
Through all his thoughts, his powers, she lives,
Pants in each pulse, and thrills along his veins.

Sure, through the tracts of yon celestial maze,
Where mystic planets dance, and glories blaze;

More wonders typical impress the sky,
Than e'er was trac'd with astrologic eye!
There haply, ere his natal hour express'd,
First burn'd the flame that glow'd within his breast:
There might the nymph with previous beauty bloom,
With previous languishment the youth consume;
Expire the victim of successless care;
Die ere he liv'd, and ere he lov'd despair.
There the dear friendly stream, ere Julius bled,
Great Brutus to his dearer country shed;
With destin'd tyranny there pride enslaves,
With destin'd virtue there the patriot saves;
There Pompey glow'd for freedom and for fame,
There Socrates, of Greece the pride and shame:
Alcides there each horrid monster slew;
There triumph'd Sampson, the heroic Jew;
There all, or doom'd to save, or to destroy,
The chiefs who fought at Thebes, or fought at Troy!

Long mourn'd the youth, with secret woe oppress'd;
The latent vulture prey'd within his breast:
Constrain'd at length, nor able to sustain
The wasting malady, and mental pain;
The sage the bearded pillars of his state
He calls, and privily unfolds his fate:
" No mean," he cries, " my cruel stars assign;
Swift death, or else Constantia must be mine!"

Alternate, each their hopes or fears disclose,
Invent, reject, and now again propose;
While some, with mystic rites of wondrous art,
Engage to gain the sympathetic heart;
By philter'd science, and infernal charms,
To win the bright perfection to his arms:
Th' abhorrent scheme his gen'rous thoughts disdain,
Resolv'd to die, or justly to obtain;
And all their arguments, howe'er renew'd,
In rites of nuptial sanctitude conclude.
But here again new obstacles appear'd,
And much for this their latest hope they fear'd;
Fear'd that diversity of faith might prove
Alike diversity, and breach in love;
Nor the fair Christian e'er consent to wed
A prince in Macon's sacred precepts bred.

---

And al this vois was soth, as God is trewe,
But now to purpos let us turn agein.
These marchants han don fraught hir shippes newe,
And whan they han this blisful maiden sein,
Home to Surrie ben they went ful fayn,
And don hir nedes, as they han don yore,
And liven in wele, I can say you no more.

Now fell it, that these marchants stood in grace
Of him that was the soudan of Surrie:
For whan they came from any strange place
He wold of his benigne curtesie
Make hem good chere, and besily espie
Tidings of sundry regnes, for to lere
The wonders that they mighte seen or here.

Amonges other thinges especially
These marchants han him told of dame Custance
So gret noblesse, in ernest seriously,
That this Soudan hath caught so gret plesance
To han hire figure in his remembrance,
That all his lust, and all his besy cure
Was for to love hire, while his lif may dure.

Paraventure in thilke large book,
Which that men clepe the Heven, ywriten was
With sterres, whan that he his birthe took,
That he for love shuld han his deth, alas!
For in the sterres, clerer than is glas,
Is writen, God wot, who so coud it rede,
The deth of every man withouten drede.

In sterres many a winter therbeforn
Was writ the deth of Hector, Achilles,
Of Pompey, Julius, or they were born;
The strif of Thebes; and of Hercules,
Of Sampson, Turnus, and of Socrates

The deth; but mennes wittes ben so dull,
That no wight can wel rede it at the full.

This Soudan for his prive council sent,
And shortly of this matere for to pace,
He hath to hem declared his entent,
And sayd hem certain, but he might have grace
To han Custance, within a litel space,
He n'as but ded, and charged him in hie
To shapen for his lif some remedie.

Diverse men, diverse thinges saiden;
They argumentes casten up and doun;
Many a subtil reson forth they laiden;
They speken of magike, and abusion;
But finally, as in conclusion,
They cannot seen in that non avantage,
Ne in non other way, save mariage.

Than saw they therin swiche difficultee
By way of reson, for to speke all plain,
Because ther was swiche diversitee
Betwene hir bothe lawes, that they sayn,
They trowen that no Cristen prince wold fayn

The monarch then, " Ah ! wherefore doubt my
     friends ;
Why yet dispute where love and life depends ?
That faith must sure have most prevailing charms,
That gives Constantia to my circling arms :
No obstacles shall bar, no doubts deter ;
Nor will I think that she was form'd to err."
     The voice determin'd, and imperial eye,
Leave no pretence for courtiers to reply :
With the fond speed of love's impatience warm'd,
Now embassies are sent, and treaties form'd.
All zealous to promote the cause divine,
The pope, the church, and Christian powers com-
The royal long-reluctant parents yield,    [bine ;
And contracts are by mutual proxy seal'd.
     High was the trust the regal writings bore,
And solemn th' attesting parties swore,
That the young Syrian, and his barons bold,
Each sex and state, the infant and the old,
Should all Messiah's hallow'd faith embrace,
And bright Constantia be the bond of grace.
     We list not here of pompous phrase to say,
What order'd equipage prepares the day ;   [train,
Grooms, prelates, peers, and nymphs, a shining
To wait the beauteous victim o'er the main :
All Rome attend in wish the lovely maid ;
And Heav'n their universal vows invade.

---

Wedden his child under our lawe swete,
That us was yeven by Mahound our prophete.

And he answered : " Rather than I lese
Custance, I wol be cristened douteles :
I mote ben hires, I may non other chese,
I pray you hold your arguments in pers,
Saveth my lif, and beth not reccheles
To geten hire that hath my lif in cure,
For in this wo I may not long endure."

What nedeth greter dilatation ?
I say, by tretise and ambassatrie,
And by the popes mediation,
And all the chirche, and all the chevalrie,
That in destruction of Maumetrie,
And in encrese of Cristes lawe dere,
They ben accorded so as ye may here ;

How that the Soudan and his baronage,
And all his liege shuld ycristened be,
And he shal han Custance in mariage,
And certain gold, I n'ot what quantitee,
And hereto finden suffisant suretee.
The same accord is sworne on eyther side ;
Now, fair Custance, Almighty God thee gide.

Now wolden som men waiten, as I gesse,
That I shuld tellen all the purveiance,
The which that the emperour of his noblesse
Hath shapen for his doughter dame Custance.
Wel may men know that so gret ordinance
May no man tellen in a litel clause,
As was arraied for so high a cause.

Bishopes ben shapen with hire for to wende,
Lordes, ladies, and knightes of renoun,
And other folk ynow, this is the end.
And notified is thurghout al the toun,
That every wight with great devotioun
Should prayen Crist, that he this mariage
Receive in gree, and spede this viage.

At length the day, the woful day arrives,
And ev'ry face of wonted cheer deprives ;
The fatal hour admits no fond delay,
That shall the joy from ev'ry heart convey.
Ye men of Rome ! your parting glory mourn ;
Far from your sight your darling shall be torn ;
No more the morn with usual smiles arise,
Or with Constantia bless your longing eyes,
Of ev'ry tongue, of ev'ry pen the theme,
The daily subject, and the nightly dream !
     But, O Constantia ! say, thou fair distress'd,
What woes that hour thy lovely soul possess'd ?
Its native cheek the bright carnation fled,
And charg'd with grief, reclin'd thy beauteous head ;
To lands unknown those limbs must now repair,
Nurs'd in the down of fond paternal care.
Peace spread thy nightly couch to sweet repose,
Delight around thy smiling form arose ;
Each scene familiar to thy eye appear'd,
And custom long thy native soil endear'd ;
Eas'd by thy bounty, at thy sight exil'd,
Grief was no more, or in thy presence smil'd ;
Each rising wish thy glad attendants seiz'd ;
To give thee pleasure, ev'ry heart was pleas'd :
But now to strange, to foreign climes convey'd,
Strange objects must thy loathing sense invade,
Strange features to thy weeping eyes appear,
Strange accents pierce thy undelighted ear ;
In distant unacquainted bondage tied,
The gilded slave of insolence and pride,
Perhaps of form uncouth, and temper base,
Thy lord shall clasp thee with abhorr'd embrace.
     Thus sad the fair revolv'd ; soft sorrows flow,
And all her sighing soul was loos'd to woe :
" Father !" she cried, " your fond, your wretched
     child !—
And you, my mother ! you, my mother mild !—
My parents dear, beneath whose kindly view,
Bless'd by whose looks, your cherish'd infant grew ;

---

The day is comen of hire departing,
I say the woful day fatal is come,
That ther may be no longer tarying,
But forward they hem dressen all and some.
Custance, that was with sorwe all overcome,
Ful pale arist, and dresseth hire to wende,
For wel she seth ther n'is non other ende.

Alas ! what wonder is it though she wept ?
That she be sent to straunge nation
Fro frendes, that so tenderly hire kept,
And to be bounde under subjection
Of on, she knoweth not his condition.
Housbondes ben all good, and han ben yore,
That knowen wives, I dare say no more.

" Fader," she said, " thy wretched child Custance,
Thy yonge doughter, fostered up so soft,
And ye, my moder, my soveraine plesance
Over all thing, (out taken Crist on loft)
Custance your child hire recommendeth oft
Unto your grace ; for I shal to Surrie,
Ne shal I never seen you more with eye.

" Alas ! unto the Barbare nation
I muste gon, sin that it is your will :
But Crist, that starfe for our redemption,
So yeve me grace his hestes to fulfill,
I wretched woman no force though I spill ;

When far, O far from your embraces torn,
Will you then think a wretch like me was born?
Shall then your child some sad remembrance claim?
And some dear drops embalm Constantia's name?
Your face—ah, cruel fortune, can it be?—
These eyes shall never, never, never see!
For ever parted by the rolling main,
I now must feel a lordly husband's chain;
From every friend, from every joy remove,
And the rough yoke of rude barbarians prove:
But so may Heav'n the precious issue bless,
And all find happiness through my distress!
Woman was doom'd, ere yet the world began,
The prey of sorrow, and the slave of man."
  She could no more; her voice by sobs suppress'd,
And tears, pour'd forth in anguish, told the rest.
Wide through the crowd the sad contagion flew;
Each hoary beard is drench'd with mournful dew;
In shortening throbs ten thousand bosoms rise,
Grief showers its tempest from ten thousand eyes;
Along the shore the deepening groans extend,
And louder shrieks the cloudy concave rend:
Not through old Rome when desolation reign'd,
And bleeding senators her forum stain'd;
Not in the wreck of that all dismal night,
When Ilion tumbled from her tow'ry height;
Such utt'ring plaints the deep despair betray'd,
As now attend the dear departing maid.
  To the tall ship, with slow desponding tread,
All drown'd in grief the beauteous victim 's led:

---

Women arn borne to thraldom and penance,
And to ben under mannes governance."

I trow at Troye whan Pirrus brake the wall,
Or Ilion brent, or Thebes the citee,
Ne at Rome for the harm thurgh Hanniball,
That Romans hath venqueshed times three,
N'as herd swiche tendre weping for pitee,
As in the chambre was for hire parting,
But forth she mote, wheder she wepe or sing.

O firste moving cruel firmament,
With thy diurnal swegh that croudest ay,
And hurtlest all from est til occident,
That naturally wold hold another way;
Thy crouding set the heven in swiche array
At the beginning of this fierce viage,
That cruel Mars hath slain this marriage.

Infortunat ascendent tortuous,
Of which the lord is helpeles fall, alas!
Out of his angle into the derkest hous.
O Mars, O Atyzar, as in this cas;
O feble Mone, unhappy ben thy pas,
Thou knittest thee ther thou art not received,
Ther thou were wel fro thennes art thou weived.

Imprudent emperour of Rome, alas!
Was ther no philosophre in al thy toun?
Is no time bet than other in swiche cas?
Of viage is ther non electioun,
Namely to folk of high conditioun,
Nat whan a rote is of a birth yknowe?
Alas! we ben to lewed, or to slow.

To ship is brought this woful faire maid
Solempnely, with every circumstance:
" Now Jesu Crist be with you all," she said.
Ther n'is no more, but " farewel fair Custance."
She peineth hire to make good countenance,

---

She turn'd, and with an aching wistful look,
A long farewel of ev'ry field she took;
" Adieu!" to all the melting crowd she cried—
" Adieu! Adieu !" the melting crowd reply'd;
Her lanching bark the mournful notes pursue,
And echoing hills return, " Adieu! Adieu !"
  Here let us leave the virgin on the main,
With all her peerage, and her pompous train;
To Syria let the swifter Muse repair,
And say what cheer prepares her welcome there.
The dame, from whom his birth the prince de-
Imperial dowager, had yet surviv'd:      [riv'd,
Ambitious, greedy of supreme control,
And born with all the tyrant in her soul,
At filial government she long repin'd,
Nor yet the reins of secret rule resign'd.
Her savage sentiments her sex belied,
And vers'd in wiles with deepest statesmen vied;
Yet o'er her soft'ning tongue, and soothing face,
The subtle varnish spread with easy grace:
The sage discern'd, but still confess'd her sway;
And whom their hearts detest, their fears obey.
Tenacious zeal her prophet's lore rever'd,
The practice scorn'd, but to the text adher'd;
And far as faith with fury could inflame,
She was indeed a most religious dame.
When she her son's determin'd bent perceiv'd,
Her breast with cruel agitation heav'd;
Her call, each hoary, each experienc'd friend,
In haste, and midnight privacy, attend;
When dire, amid the dusky throng she rose,
And from her tongue contagious poison flows.
  " Ye peers, ye pillars of our falling state!
Too faithful subjects of a prince ingrate;
A son, whom these detesting breasts have fed,
A serpent grown, to your destruction bred!
Say, shall a single hand such patriots awe?
Insult your prophet, and supplant your law?
First, Heav'n! be all the bonds of Nature broke,
Ere I assume the curs'd, the Christian yoke:
For, what import these innovating rites,
But here a living death of all delights?
Such threats as penitence can ne'er appease,
The body's penance, and the mind's disease?—

---

And forth I let hire sayle in this manere,
And turne I wol againe to my matere.

The mother of the Soudan, well of vices,
Espied hath hire sones pleine entente,
How he wol lete his olde sacrifices:
And right anon she for her conseil sente,
And they ben comen, to know what she mente,
And whan assembled was this folk in fere,
She set hire doun, and sayd as ye shul here.

" Lordes," she sayd, " ye knowen everich on,
How that my sone in point is for to lete
The holy lawes of our Alkaron,
Yeven by Goddes messager Mahomete:
But on avow to grete God I hete,
The lif shal rather out of my body sterte,
Than Mahometes lawe out of myn herte.

" What shuld us tiden of this newe lawe
But thraldom to our bodies and penance,
And afterward in Helle to ben drawe,
For we reneied Mahound our creance?
But, lordes, wol ye maken assurance,

Yet, were I of some faithful hearts secure,
Not such the malady, but we can cure."
She spoke, and all with swift compliance swear,
The glorious deed with all their pow'rs to dare;
Her charge, though ne'er so bloody, to fulfill,
Though ne'er so dang'rous, to effect her will.
"Doubt not a birth," she cried, "so well conceiv'd,
Great acts are more by fraud than force achiev'd;
To gain the conquest, we must seem to yield,
And feign to fly, that we may win the field.
Let each in public wear a Christian face,
And counterfeit the saintly signs of grace:
What though our skin the sprinkling priest baptize?
Our skin 's unsully'd, while our hearts despise.
Not such the tricks our bolder hands shall play,
When revels end th' unsuspecting day;
Nor such the stream our purpling points shall shed,
When we shall, in our turn, baptize with red."
Ah, sex! still sweet, or bitter, to extreme;
Gloomy as night, or bright as morning beam!
No fiend's may with a female's wrath compare;
No angel's purity like woman's fair!
To save or damn, for bliss or ruin given,
Who has thee feels a Hell, or finds a Heav'n.
Smooth as the surface of the dimpled main,
While brooding storms the gath'ring ruin rein,
Her son, with dire dissembling leer she seeks,
And in the depth of smiling malice speaks.

---

As I shal say, assenting to my lore?
And I shal make us sauf for evermore."

They sworen, and assented every man
To live with hire and die, and by hire stond:
And everich on, in the best wise he can,
To strengthen hire shal all his freudes fond.
And she hath this emprise ytaken in hond,
Which ye shull heren that I shall devise,
And to hem all she spake right in this wise.

"We shul first feine us Cristendom to take;
Cold water shal not greve us but a lite:
And I shal swiche a feste and revel make,
That, as I trow, I shal the Soudan quite.
For tho his wife be cristened never so white,
She shal have nede to wash away the rede,
Though she a font of water with hire lede."

O Soudannesse, rote of iniquitee,
Virago thou Semyramee the second,
O serpent under femininitee,
Like to the serpent depe in Helle ybound:
O feined woman, all that may confound
Vertue and innocence, thurgh thy malice
Is bred in thee, as nest of every vice.

O Sathan envious, sin thilke day
That thou were chased from our heritage,
Wel knowest thou to woman the olde way.
Thou madest Eva bring us in servage,
Thou wolt fordon this cristen mariage:
Thin instrument so (wala wa the while!)
Makest thou of women whan thou wolt begile.

This Soudannesse, whom I thus blame and warrie,
Let prively hire conseil gon hir way:
What shuld I in this tale longer tarie?
She rideth to the Soudan on a day,
And sayd him, that she would reneie hire lay,

"My child! though froward age is over wise,
Let no offence against a parent rise;
Long habits gain a privilege from time,
And frequent custom mellows ev'ry crime:
Repugnant hence I dar'd to thwart your will;
I fear'd the novelty, I fear'd the ill:
But now, convinc'd by Christ's superior grace,
His law I rev'rence, and his faith embrace.
Bless'd be thy bed! thy bridal transports bless'd!
Nor you refuse a mother's fond request—
Mine be the joy to entertain the fair;
To form the festival, be mine the care;
To show the peers who on thy bride attend,
As she in beauty, we in love transcend.'"
The royal youth in silent wonder stood;
Joy held his voice, and rapture thrill'd his blood:
Around her knees his prostrate arms he threw,
And duteous tears distill'd the grateful dew:
Her son she rais'd, all innocent of ill,
And smiling kiss'd whom soon she meant to kill.
At length the bride, and all her solemn train,
Past o'er the danger of the midland main:
The main is past, but not the danger o'er;
The sea less cruel than the Syrian shore!
Applauding crowds the landed beauty greet,
And Juda's peers in rich procession meet;
Great was the throng, and splendid the array,
And guards arranging lin'd the glitt'ring way.
Such were the triumphs of imperial Rome,
When conquest led some darling victor home;
While meeting millions his approach withstand,
And walls, and trees, and clamber'd roofs are mann'd.
All gem'd in ornaments of curious mode,
Gay in the van, the false sultana rode;

---

And Cristendom of prestes hondes fong,
Repenting hire she hethen was so long;

Beseching him to don hire that honour,
That she might han the Cristen folk to fest:
To plesen hem I wol do my labour.
The Soudan saith, "I wol don at your hest,"
And kneling, thanked hire of that request;
So glad he was, ne n'iste not what to say,
She kist hire sone, and home she goth hire way.

Arrived ben these Cristen folk to lond
In Surrie, with a gret solempne route,
And hastily this Soudan sent his sond,
First to his mother, and all the regne aboute,
And sayd, his wif was comen out of doute,
And praide hem for to riden again the quene,
The honour of his regne to sustene.

Gret was the presse, and riche was th'array
Of Surriens and Romanes met in fere.
The mother of the Soudan riche and gay
Received hire with all so glad a chere,
As any mother might hire doughter dere:
And to the nexte citee ther beside
A softe pas solempnely they ride.

Nought trow I, the triumph of Julius,
Of which that Lucan maketh swiche a bost,
Was realler, or more curious,
Than was th' assemblee of this blissful host:
But yet this scorpion, this wicked gost,
The Soudannesse, for all hire flattering
Cast under this ful mortally to sting.

Oft to her breast she clasp'd the heav'nly maid,
And wond'ring oft with cruel gaze survey'd.
Last came the sultan, royal, hapless youth,
Grace in his form, and in his bosom truth!
The last he came, for timorous love controll'd,
He fear'd, and long'd, and trembled to behold:
A faint salute his faultering voice supplied;
Scarce, "Welcome! O divinely fair!" he cried.
He blush'd, and sigh'd, and gaz'd with wav'ring
Nor dar'd to hope the blissful vision true.   [view,
Thus onward to a neighbouring town they far'd,
In purpos'd pomp, and regal state prepar'd;
And here the old maternal fiend invites,
To order'd feasts, and dearly bought delights.
Down sit the guests, triumphing clarions blow,
Drums beat, mirth sings, and brimming goblets flow;
In boundless revel ev'ry care is drown'd,
And clamour shouts, and freedom laughs around.
Ah, hapless state of ev'ry human mind,
Wrap'd in the present, to the future blind!
In the gay vapour of a lucky hour,
Light folly mounts, and looks with scorn on pow'r:
Nor sees how swift the tides of fortune flow,
The swelling happiness and ebbing woe;
That man should ne'er indulge, or bliss, or care,
The prosperous triumph, or the wretch despair;
So close, so sudden, each reverse succeeds,
And mischief treads where'er success precedes.
And now the night, with brooding horrours still,
Gloom'd from the brow of each adjacent hill;
Slow heav'd her bosom with distemper'd breath,
And o'er her forehead hung the weights of death.
Oppress'd with sleep, and drown'd in fumy wine,
The prostrate guards their regal charge resign;
But far within, still wakeful to delight,
The prince and peers protract the festal night—
When from the portal, lo! a sudden gloom
Projects its horrours through the spacious room:
Fearful and dark the ruffian bands appear,
The dire sultana storming in the rear.
The bloody task invading treason plies:
Quick, and at once alarm'd, the nobles rise;
But these, as faith or faction led, divide,
And traitors most with entering traitors side:

---

The Soudan cometh himself sone after this
So really, that wonder is to tell:
And welcometh hire with all joye and blis.
And thus in mirth and joye I let hem dwell.
The fruit of this matere is that I tell.
Whan time came, men thought it for the best
That revel stint, and men go to hir rest.

The time come is, this olde Soudannesse
Ordeined hath the feste of which I tolde,
And to the feste Cristen folk hem dresse
In general, ya bothe yonge and olde.
Ther may men fest and realtee beholde,
And deintees mo than I can you devise,
But all to dere they bought it or they rise.

O soden wo, that ever art successour
To worldly blis, spreint is with bitternesse
Th' ende of the joye of our worldly labour:
Wo occupieth the fyn of our gladnesse.
Herken this conseil for thy sikernesse:
Upon thy glade day have in thy minde
The unware wo of harm, that cometh behinde.

Boards, bowls, and seats o'erturn'd, the pavement
strow;   [strow;
Of blood with wine the mingling currents flow;
Vain is the fear that wings their feet for flight,
They fall who basely fly or bravely fight;
With screams and groans the echoing courts re-
sound,
And gasping Romans bite the trait'rous ground.
Say, royal Syrian! in that hour of death,
Say, didst thou tamely then resign thy breath?
Surprise, and shame, and love, and boundless rage,
Flash from his eyes, and in his breast engage.
Threat'ning aloft, his flaming steel he drew,
And swift to save his lov'd Constantia flew;
Before his bride a beauteous bulwark stands,
Now presses on, and backwards bears the bands:
Bold to his aid surviving Romans spring,
Some Syrians too could dare to join their king;
Invaded late, they in their turn invade,
And traitors are with mutual death repaid.
But what may courage, what may strength avail,
Where still o'erpow'ring multitudes assail;
Where number with increasing number grows,
And ev'ry sword must match a thousand foes?
As melting snows with gradual waste subside,
So sink the warriors from their hero's side:
Thin'd are the remnants of his bleeding train,
And scarce, but scarce, th' unequal strife sustain;
Their veins exhausted and o'ertoil'd their might,
And struggling, but to fall the last, they fight.
The monarch thus on ev'ry side distress'd,
And hope extinguish'd in his valiant breast,
Turn'd to his queen, he sent the parting look,
And brief th' eternal last adieu he took:   [end!
"Since here," he cried, "our hapless loves must
Where this arm fails, may mightier Heav'n defend!
This is my last, my only, fond desire:
Too bless'd am I, who in thy cause expire."
So saying, with recruited pow'rs he glows,
Exalted treads, and overlooks his foes:
Of more than mortal size the warrior seems,
And terrour from his eye imperial streams.
The circling host his single voice defies;
Amid the throng, with fury wing'd, he flies:
Deep bites his sword, in heaps on heaps they fall;
Hands, arms, and heads, bespread the sanguin'd hall;
Untir'd with toil, resistless in his course,
Disdain gave fury, and despair gave force.
As here and there, his conquering steps he bends,
Down his fair form the purpling stream descends;
Exhausted nature would persuade to yield,
But courage, still tenacious, holds the field.
As when the lamp its wavering light essays,
The source consum'd that fed the vital blaze,
Extinguish'd now its kindly flame appears,
And now aloft a livelier radiance rears;
Subsides by fits, by fits again aspires,
And bright, but doubtful, burn its fainting fires;
Till recollected to one force of light,
Sudden she flashes into endless night—
So the brave youth the blaze of life renews,
Reels, stands, defends, attacks, and still subdues;
Till ev'ry vein, and ev'ry channel drain'd,
One last effort his valiant arm sustain'd:
As lightning swift, he sped the latest blow,
And greatly fell, expiring on his foe.
As should an oak within some village stand,
Young, tall, and straight, the favourite of the land,
Beneath the dews of Heav'n sublime he grows,
Beneath his shade the wearied find repose;

To deck his boughs each morn the maidens rise,
And youths around his form contest the prize:
Yet haply if a sudden storm descend,
Sway'd by the blast, his beauteous branches bend;
But vig'rous, to their tow'ring height recoil,
Mainta'n the combat, and outbrave the toil;
Till the red bolt with levell'd ruin shoots,
And cuts the pillar'd fabric from the roots:
Swift falls the beauty o'er a length of ground;
The nymphs and swains incessant mourn around.
So did the youth with living form excel,
So fair, so tall, and so lamented, fell!
Relenting traitors would revive the dead,
And weep the blood their ruthless weapons shed:
One tender pang the dire sultana felt,
And nature, spite of Hell, compels to melt.
Whi e sudden thus each bloody arm suspends,
And round their prince the satiate tumult bends;
Regardless of her fate, Constantia goes
Through pointed javelins, and a host of foes.
Amaze before the daring virgin yields,
And innocence from ev'ry weapon shields;
Till mourning by the great remains she stood,
And o'er her lover pour'd the copious flood:
" Ah, valiant arm! a waste of worth in vain!
Ah, royal youth," she cried, " untimely slain!
O! had I perish'd, ere I reach'd thy shore,
The surge devour'd, or wat'ry monsters tore;
To bless the world your worth had yet surviv'd,
Nor I, too fatally belov'd, arriv'd.
'T is I, who have this dear effusion shed;
For me, for me, a luckless bride, you bled!"
So saying—furious, the sultana cries,
" Strike, strike; the source of all our mischief dies!"
"Yes, strike!" the bright, th' intrepid maid replies.
But vainly this consents, or that commands;
Heav'n check'd their hearts, and pity bound their
        hands:
At once a thousand javelins rise in air;
A thousand wishes whisper—" Ah, forbear!"
Recoiling arms the bloody task refuse,
And beauty with resistless charm subdues.
Alone relentless, the sultana cries,
" 'T is well, the death she wish'd, may still suffice:
Hence with that form, that knows so well to reign;
Hence with the witch, and plunge her in the main!
Her passage thence to Rome she may explore,
And tell her welcome on the Syrian shore."
So saying, quick to a selected band
She gave to execute the dire command;
Reluctant to the charge, they yet obey,
And to the shore the mourning fair convey.
Slow as she mov'd, soft sorrows bathe the ground;
Her guards too melt, and pitying weep around;
Though vers'd in blood, detest the stern commands,
And feel their hearts rebellious to their hands.
When now upon th' appointed beach they stood,
That look'd with horror o'er the deep'ning flood,
Each ey'd his fellow with relenting look,
And each to each the cruel task forsook;

---

For shortly for to tellen at a word,
The Soudan and the Cristen everich on
Ben all to-hewe, and stiked at the bord,
But it were only dame Custance alone.
This old Soudannesse, this cursed crone,
Hath with hire frendes don this cursed dede,
For she hireself wold all the contree lede.

With distant awe the heav'nly maid survey,
Nor once her harm in act or thought essay.
The still suspense at length their leader broke,
And bow'd before the trembling beauty, spoke:
" O thou, endow'd with more than mortal charms,
Who ev'ry foe of all his force disarms!
Say, how shall we our pow'r or will employ;
Where both are weak, to spare thee, or destroy—
Both impotent alike our pow'r and will,
The means to save thee, or the thoughts to kill?
Yet one extreme may cruelly remain,
To yield thee haply to the pitying main;
And Heav'n, who form'd thee so divinely fair,
If Heav'n has pow'r, will sure have will to spare."
He said; the rest assent, and to the bay
With secret step the virgin-bride convey.
Convenient here a Roman bark they find;
They hoist the hasty canvass to the wind:
The bark with Roman wealth and plenty stow'd,
Now lanching with the lonely sailor rode;
The gale from shore with ready rapture blew,
And to her vessel bore the last adieu.
Now, stain'd with blood, the self-convicted night
Fled from the face of all inquiring light;
And morn, unconscious of the murd'rous scene,
O'er Syria, guilty Syria, rose serene.
The mountains sink before Constantia's eyes;
Wing'd o'er the surge, her bounding galley flies;
From sight of land, and human face conveys,
The skies alone above, and all around the seas.
Go, lovely mariner! imperial fair!
The warring winds and angry ocean dare;
Strange climes and spheres, a lone advent'rer view,
New to the main, and to misfortune new;
Without the chart, or polar compass steer,
Nor storms, in which the stoutest tremble, fear.
But ill those limbs, for gentle office form'd,
And in the down of nightly softness warm'd,
Shall now, obsequious to the ruder gale,
Command the frozen cord, and pond'rous sail;
Shall now, beneath the wat'ry sky obscure,
The nightly damp and piercing blast endure.
Thus all disconsolate, and sore distress'd,
And sorrow heaving in her beauteous breast,
Down sinks the fair; her hands in anguish rise,
And up to Heav'n she lifts her streaming eyes:
" O thou!" she said, " whence ev'ry being rose,
In whom they safe exist, and soft repose;
Fix'd in whose pow'r, and patient to whose eye,
Immense, those copious worlds of wonders lie;
To me, the meanest of thy works, descend;
To me, the last of ev'ry being, bend!

---

Ne ther was Surrien non that was converted,
That of the conseil of the Soudan wot,
That he n'as all to-hewe, er he asterted:
And Custance han they taken anon fote-hot,
And in a ship all stereles (God wot)
They han hire set, and bidden hire lerne sayle
Out of Surrie againward to Itaille.

A certain tresor that she thither ladde,
And soth to sayn, vitaille gret plentee,
They han hire yeven, and clothes eke she hadde,
And forth she sayleth in the salte see:
O my Custance, ful of benignitee,
O emperoures yonge doughter dere,
He that is lord of fortune be thy stere.

Since not exempt, in thy paternal care,
The lowest triumph, and minutest share;
Thy subjects all, and all their sov'reign know,
The seas that eddy, and the winds that blow;
The winds thy ruling inspiration tell;
The seas, exulting in thy presence, swell:
O'er these, o'er those, supreme, do thou preside;
For I desire no other star to guide:
In want and weakness, be thy pow'r display'd,
And thou assist, where else no arm can aid.
But if, as surely ev'ry mortal must,
If now I hasten to my native dust,
From the dread hour, and this devouring deep,
The spark of deathless animation keep;
Then may my soul, as bright instinctive flame,
Aspiring then, thy kindred radiance claim;
Or to some humbler Heav'n the trembler raise,
Though there the last, the first to sing thy praise:
Some lowly, vacant seat, Eternal, deign,
Nor be creation, and redemption vain!"
So pray'd the maid, and peace, a wonted guest,
Sought the known mansion of her spotless breast;
To ev'ry peril arm'd, and pain resign'd,
Cheer in her looks, and patience in her mind.
The wind fresh blowing from the Syrian shore,
Swift through the floods her spooming vessel bore.
Long breath'd the current of the eastern gale,
And swell'd th' expanse of each distended sail:
And now the hills of Candia rise to view,
As ev'ning clouds and settled vapours blue;
And now, still driven before the orient blast,
Morea, and her lengthening capes, are past:
Now land again her wistful prospect flies,
And gives the unvarying ocean to her eyes;
Till Malta's rocks, emerging from the main,
The circling war of earth and sea maintain.
Alike unknown, each varying clime appear'd;
The land and main alike the virgin fear'd;
While ev'ry coast her wand'ring eyes explore,
Reminds her soul of Syria's hostile shore;
And more than ever'ry monster seas can yield,
From man, from man, she begs that Heav'n would
   shield.
Full many a day, and many a night, forlorn,
Through shelves, and rocks, and eddying tempest
   borne,

Through drizzling sky, and nightly damp severe,
No fire to warm, no social face to cheer;
On many a meal of tainted viands fed,
The chill blast whistling round her beauteous head;
The pensive innocence attends her fate,
Amidst surrounding deaths and storms, sedate.
Ye silken sons of affluence and pride!
Whose fortunes roll a soft superfluous tide,
Who yet on visionary wants refine,
And rack'd with false fantastic woes repine;
And ye, whom penury and sharp distress,
With better, but salubrious med'cine, bless—
Behold that sex, whose softness men despise;
Behold a maid, who might instruct the wise,
Give patience precedent, fierce frenzy 'suage,
And with philosophy new-form the sage!
For her the tides of regal fullness flow'd;
For her oppression heap'd the cumbrous load;
In affluence humble, in misfortune great,
She stands the worst alternatives of fate!
At length, her galley wing'd before the blast,
Swift lanching, through the straits of Ceuta past;
And winding now before the varying gale,
Tempestuous Auster rends her labouring sail:
Hispania's realm the obsequious vessel coasts;
Now Gallia's surge the beauteous burthen boasts;
Till last, Britannia's wave the charge receives,
And from the Atlantic main, exalting, heaves;
The destin'd freight with pleas'd emotion bore,
And gently wafted to Northumbria's shore.
But haply now't were obvious to demand,
How borne from Solyma's far-distant land,
Through many a clime and strait that might restrain,
The gust of winter, and the whelming main,
Britannia's coast should fix the wand'ring maid,
Through such a length of devious tracts convey'd?
Say first, when ships in dizzy whirlwinds wheel,
Who points the fervour of the amorous steel?
Wing'd by whose breath the bidden tempests blow?
Heav'd in whose fulness mighty oceans flow?
Yet what are winds that blow, or seas that roll?
The globe stupendous, or the poising pole?
What the seven planets on their axis spun?
What the wide system of our centering Sun?
A point, an atom, to the ambient space,
Where worlds on worlds in circling myriads race!

---

She blesseth hire, and with ful pitous vois
Unto the crois of Crist thus sayde she.
" O clere, o weleful auter, holy crois,
Red of the Lambes blood ful of pitee,
That wesh the world fro the old iniquitee,
Me fro the fende, and fro his clawes kepe,
That day that I shal drenchen in the depe.

" Victorious tree, protection of trewe,
That only were ordeined for to bere
The King of Heven, with his woundes newe,
The white Lamb, that hurt was with a spere;
Flemer of fendes, out of him and here
On which thy limmes faithfully extenden,
Me kepe, and yeve me might my lif to amenden."

Yeres and dayes fleet this creature
Thurghout the see of Grece, unto the straite
Of Maroc, as it was hire aventure:
On many a sory mele now may she baite,
After hire deth ful often may she waite,
Or that the wilde waves wol hire drive
Unto the place ther as she shal arive.

Men mighten asken, why she was not slain?
Eke at the feste who might hire body save?
And I answer to that demand again,
Who saved Daniel in the horrible cave,
Ther every wight, save he, master or knave,
Was with the leon frette, or he asterte?
No wight but God, that he bare in his herte.

God list to show his wonderful miracle
In hire, for we shuld seen his mighty werkes:
Crist, which that is to every harm triacle,
By certain menes oft, as knowen clerkes,
Doth thing for certain ende, that ful derke is
To mannes wit, that for our ignorance
Ne can nat know his prudent purveiance.

Now sith she was not at the feste yslawe,
Who kepte hire fro the drenching in the see?
Who kepte Jonas in the fishes mawe,
Til he was spouted up at Ninivee?
Wel may men know, it was no wight but he
That kept the peple Ebraike fro drenching,
With drye feet thurghout the see passing.

Yet these the inanimate volution keep,
And roll eliptic through the boundless deep;
While One Hand weighs the infinite suspense,
The insensate loads and measures the immense;
Within, without, through height and depth presides;
With equal arm, the bark, or planet, guides.
By thee uplifted, through the pathless skies,
With conscious plume, the birds of passage rise;
Through thee their patent longitude is known,
The stated climate, and the varying zone.
Thy Will informs the universal plan,
The ways of angels, and the ways of man;
The moral and material world connects,
Through each, Supreme, both governs and inspects;
Conducts the blood through each arterial round,
Conducts each system through the vast profound:
One Rule, the joint, the boundless model forms,
And the small ant to love of order warms;
Alike, through high, and low, and great, and small,
Nor aught 's mysterious, or mysterious all.

What time the wafting tide, and favouring blast,
The fair on Britain's fated region cast;
Young Alla then Northumbria's sons obey'd,
Whose substituted sceptre Offa sway'd:
Illustrious Offa, who in worth excell'd
Whate'er the rolls of Saxon heroes held!
Alone Rodolphus, to the chief allied,
Excell'd in arms, but much excell'd in pride.

High on the brow of a commanding steep,
And full in prospect of the eastern deep,
His seat, address'd for war, as for repose,
And fix'd with elegance, brave Offa chose.
And now the hero, at his wonted hour,
Where trees o'er-arching form'd the sylvan bow'r,
With Hermigilda sought the evening air,
His bride, the fairest of the Saxon fair—

When from the main, and obvious to the view,
Th' apparent wreck their fix'd attention drew;
And quickly by innate compassion led,
Attended, to the neighbouring shore they sped.
Constantia here sole mariner they found,
Admiring gaze, and silently surround:
Her eyes to Heav'n the grateful charmer rais'd,
And with mute thanks of swift acceptance prais'd;
Then turn'd, with suppliant mien her arms extends,
And lowly at their feet for mercy bends.
Though Pagans, yet with native virtues bless'd,
The sentiment humane inform'd their breast:
They her sad narrative of woes inquire,
Prompt to redress, as courteous to desire.
With moving eloquence the maid began,
And through a length of strange disasters ran:
What truth requir'd, with artless grace reveal'd;
What prudence check'd, with graceful art conceal'd;
Pathetic gave her sufferings to the view,
But o'er her state a specious covering threw.
Sweet flow'd the accents of her gentle tongue;
Attention on the mournful music hung:
Each heart a sympathetic anguish felt—
Who saw that face, and could refuse to melt?
Great Offa's bride with answering woes distress'd,
With streaming eyes and clasping arms caress'd:
Officious now to please, and prompt to aid,
They to the palace lead the peerless maid;
With feast and song, and social aspect cheer,
And, as of more than mortal mould, revere.
Here, pleas'd with privacy, and long content,
Her days the universal charmer spent;
To office apt, and each obliging art,
She kindly stole the voluntary heart;
Ador'd around, a mental empire gain'd,
And still a queen through ev'ry bosom reign'd.

---

Who bade the foure spirits of tempest,
That power han to anoyen lond and see,
Both north and south, and also west and est,
Anoyen neyther see, ne lond, ne tree?
Sothly the commander of that was he
That fro the tempest ay this woman kepte,
As wel whan she awoke as whan she slepte.

Wher might this woman mete and drinke have?
Three yere and more, how lasteth hire vitaille?
Who fed the Egyptian Mary in the cave
Or in desert? no wight but Crist *sans faille.*
Five thousand folk it was as gret marvaille
With loves five and fishes two to fede:
God sent his foyson at hire grete nede.

She driveth forth into our ocean
Thurghout our wide see, til at the last
Under an hold, that nempnen I ne can,
Fer in Northumberlond, the wave hire cast,
And in the sand hire ship stiked so fast,
That thennes wolde it not in all a tide:
The wille of Crist was that she shulde abide.

The constable of the castle doun is fare
To seen this wrecke, and al the ship he sought,
And fond this wery woman ful of care;
He fond also the tresour that she brought:
In hire langage mercy she besought,
The lif out of hire body for to twinne,
Hire to deliver of wo that she was inne.

A maner Latin corrupt was hire speche,
But algate thereby was she understond.
The constable, whan him list no lenger seche,
This woful woman brought he to the lond.
She kneleth doun, and thanketh Goddes sond;
But what she was, she wolde no man seye
For foule ne faire, though that she shulde deye.

She said, she was so mased in the see,
That she forgate hire minde, by hire trouth.
The constable hath of hire so gret pitee
And eke his wif, that they wepen for routh:
She was so diligent withouten slouth
To serve and plesen everich in that place,
That all hire love, that loken in hire face.

The constable and dame Hermegild his wif
Were Payenes, and that contree every wher;
But Hermegild loved Custance as hire lif;
And Custance hath so long sojourned ther
In orisons, with many a bitter tere,
Til Jesu hath converted thurgh his grace,
Dame Hermegild, constablesse of that place.

In all that lond no Cristen dorste route;
All Cristen folk ben fled fro that contree
Thurgh Payenes, that conquereden all aboute
The plages of the North by lond and see.
To Wales fled the Cristianitee
Of olde Bretons, dwelling in this ile;
Thir was hir refuge for the mene while.

What winning pow'r on beauty's charm attends !
The rude it softens, and the bigot bends.
What precept from Constantia's lips can fail ?
What truth so musical, and not prevail ?
Persuasive while she pleads, the priest might learn,
The deaf find ears, and even the blind discern.
Soon through the house of gen'rous Offa spread,
Her pleasing tongue its sacred influence shed ;
And all the cordial proselytes of grace,
The Christian law, the law of love, embrace.
But ah, sweet maid, how short is thy repose !
Nor hope that here thy scenes of suffering close ;
Heav'n speeds the planet that o'er-rul'd thy birth,
And hastes to make one angel, ev'n on Earth.

 Rodolphus to the Saxon chief allied,
Whose strength of limb with mightiest giants vied,
Of feature crude, and insolent of soul,
Whose heart nor knew, or mercy, or control—
He saw ; and though to deeds of discord bred,
He saw, and on the lovely vision fed :

---

But yet n'ere Cristen Bretons so exiled,
That ther n'ere som which in hir privitee
Honoured Crist, and hethen folk begiled ;
And neigh the castle swiche ther dwelten three :
That on of hem was blind, and might not see,
But it were with thilke eyen of his minde,
With which men mowen see whan they ben blinde.

Bright was the Sonne, as in that sommer's day,
For which the constable and his wif also
And Custance, han ytake the righte way
Toward the see, a furlong way or two,
To plaien, and to romen to and fro ;
And in her walk this blinde man they mette,
Croked and olde, with eyen fast yshette.

" In the name of Crist," cried this blinde Breton,
" Dame Hermegild, yeve me my sight again."
This lady wexe afraid of that soun,
Lest that hire husband, shortly for to sain,
Wold hire for Jesu Cristes love have slain,
Til Custance made hire bold, and bade hire werche
The will of Crist, a doughter of holy cherche.

The constable wexe abashed of that sight,
And sayde ; " What amounteth all this fare ?"
Custance answer'd : " Sire, it is Cristes might,
That helpeth folk out of the fendes snare :"
And so ferforth she gan our lay declare,
That she the constable, er that it were eve,
Converted, and on Crist made him beleve.

This constable was not lord of the place
Of which I speke, ther as he Custance fond,
But kept it strongly many a winter space,
Under Alla, king of Northumberlond,
That was ful wise, and worthy of his hond
Againe the Scottes, as men may wel here ;
But tourne I wol againe to my metere.

Sathan, that ever was waiteth to begile,
Saw of Custance all hire perfectioun,
And cast anon how he might quite hire wile,
And made a yonge knight, that dwelt in that town,
Love hire so hote of foule affectioun,
That veraily him thought that he shuld spille,
But he of hire might ones han his wille.

Swift through his veins the sulphurous poison run,
But women seem'd all obvious to be won.
Malicious fervour prompts him to enjoy ;
Dire is the love that 's eager to destroy !
Vows, prayers, and oaths, and menaces he tried,
And priz'd alike the prostitute and bride.
But when repuls'd with merited disdain,
He found all threats, as all entreaties vain,
The flame, that gloomy in his bosom burn'd,
To deadly hate by swift transition turn'd ;
And nightly, in his dark designing soul,
Dire future scenes and schemes infernal roll.

 Meantime, the sons of hostile Scotia arm,
And fame through Albion gives the loud alarm.
Young Alla at the warlike call arose,
And speeds with answering boldness to oppose ;
While Offa, with glad heart, and honours due,
To welcome his approaching sov'reign flew.

 And now Rodolphus, of whose baleful breast
The fiends and ev'ry fury stood possess'd,
On ills of cruellest conception bent,
To perpetrate his deadly purpose meant.
 All wrap'd in clouds, from Heaven's nocturnal
  steep
Mid darkness hung, and weigh'd the world to sleep ;
When Offa's consort, and the Roman maid,
By unsuspecting innocence betray'd,
Divinely pious, and divinely fair,
Tir'd with long vigil and the nightly pray'r,
Together lock'd in calm oblivion lay ;
Not both to rise and greet returning day.
Rodolphus, unperceiv'd, invades the room,
His bosom darker than the midnight gloom :
Dire o'er the gentle pair the felon stands,
A poniard thirsting in his impious hands.
As should some cottager, with hourly care,
Two lambs, his sole delight and substance, rear,
With fondness at his rural table fed,
Beneath his eye, and in his bosom bred ;
Till fierce for blood, and watchful to devour,
Some prowling wolf perceives the absent hour,
His nightly tread through some sly postern bends,
And the meek pair with savage fury rends—
So sweet, so innocent, the fair-ones lay ;
So stern, the human savage views his prey !
His steel swift plung'd through Hermegilda's breast,
From the pure form, dismiss'd the purer guest ;
Without one sigh her gentle soul expires,
And wak'd in bliss, the wondrous change admires,
Beyond, beyond what utt'rance e'er can name,
Or vision of ecstatic fancy frame.
Not so, bright maid ! thy harder fate intends ;
A simple death was only meant for friends :

---

He woeth hire, but it availeth nought,
She wolde do no sinne by no wey :
And for despit, he compassed his thought
To maken hire on shameful deth to dey.
He waiteth whan the constable is away,
And prively upon a night he crepte
In Hermegildes chambre while she slepte.

Wery, forwaked in hire orisons,
Slepeth Custance, and Hermegilde also.
This knight, thurgh Sathanas temptations,
All softely is to the bed ygo,
And cut the throte of Hermegilde atwo,
And layd the blody knif by dame Custance,
And went his way, ther God yeve him mischance.

For thee, he hoards the fund of future ill,
And spares with tenfold cruelty to kill.
Close by Constantia, lovely sleeping maid,
His reeking steel the murd'rous ruffian laid:
Revolv'd within his breast new mischiefs brew,
And smiling horridly the fiend withdrew.
Thick darkness yet withstood approaching day,
And camp'd upon the western summits lay;
And scarce the straggling rays of orient light,
Excursive, pierc'd the paler realms of night;
Their passage through Constantia's casement won,
And view'd the brightest form beneath the Sun—
When the first glories of her opening eyes
With prompt, with early elevation rise,
Its wing tow'rds Heav'n her waking soul extends,
And in a rhapsody of praise ascends.
But ah, not long those lively transports burn!
Confus'd, alarm'd, her thoughts to Earth return:
All chill, and in the vital current drown'd,
Pale at her side, her lovely friend she found;
A cloud of horrour quick involv'd the fair,
And uttering shrieks express'd the loud despair.
Wak'd to her griefs, the scar'd domestics rose:
In rush'd the train, shrill echoing to her woes;
O'er the pale dame a mourning torrent shed,
And with repeated cries invoke the dead.
Rodolphus too, with well-dissembled fears,
And face of busy feign'd concern, appears:
From Heav'n's high wrath, with swift perdition sped,
He calls down vengeance on the guilty head;
Apparent zeal his earnest visage fires,
And loud the murd'rer for himself inquires.
With bloody marks of dire conjecture stain'd,
Constantia, hapless virgin, stands arraign'd:
The fair with fears her guiltless cause essays;
But ah! each specious circumstance betrays:
Rude cords around her polish'd arms they strain;
Strong pleads the innocent, but pleads in vain.
Far were thy friends, Constantia, lovely maid!
Far distant all, that had the pow'r to aid;
From guilt, from death, from infamy to save,
Or shed a tear upon a stranger's grave.
And now the tale, with deadly tidings fraught,
To Offa's ear a speedy courier brought.
Heart-pierc'd with anguish stood the mourning
     chief;
No plaints express'd th' inutterable grief;
No sighs exhale, no streaming sorrows flow,
Fix'd and immoveable in speechless woe.
Compassion touch'd the gen'rous Alla's breast,
For his brave subject, for his friend distress'd;
Each circumstance the royal youth inquires,
And the dire act his just resentment fires.

By specious proofs of false suggestion led,
He vows full vengeance on Constantia's head;
To doom the luckless innocent he speeds,
And in his wrath the previous victim bleeds.
Fame flies before with voluntary wing;
A thousand distant shouts proclaim their king:
Pour'd from all parts, the populace unite,
And on his form insatiate feed their sight;
For Alla, bright in each perfection, shone,
That grac'd the cottage, or enrich'd the throne:
The nerve Herculean brac'd his youthful arm,
His cheek imbib'd the virgin's softest charm:
Mild was his soul, all spotless as his form;
His virtues not severe, but chaste and warm;
His manners sweet and sprightly, yet sincere;
His judgment calm and deep, yet quick and
     clear:
Graceful his speech, above the flow'rs of art;
Open his hand, more bounteous yet his heart;
As mercy soft, kind, social, and humane,
Vice felt alone, that Alla held the rein:
To all the pride of courts, and pomp of show,
The brightest ornament, yet greatest foe!
Within, without, thus rich in ev'ry grace,
And all the angel in his soul and face,
Not form'd to feel love's passion, but impart,
No charms were yet found equal to his heart:
For him each virgin sigh'd, but sigh'd in vain,
By him unpitied, since unknown the pain.
Detesting flattery, yet fond of fame,
Through deadly fields he sought a deathless name;
Still foremost there, he sprung with youthful heat,
And war, not love, gave Alla's breast to beat;
Each foe he conquer'd, and each friend retain'd,
And scepter'd in his subjects' bosoms reign'd.
And now arriv'd—severe in solemn state,
Whence no appeal, the grand tribunal sat.
Great Alla, thron'd conspicuous to the view,
Attention, love, and centering rev'rence drew.
In form, the deadly process straight began;
Wide through the crowd a doubtful murmur ran;
Rodolphus chief the friendless prisoner charg'd,
Enforc'd the pain, and on the guilt enlarg'd.
The fair unknown to her defence they cite:
Guarded she comes, as pure as angels bright;
As though delight and grief at once combin'd,
And fled to her, displeas'd with all mankind;
Or as delight would grief, in grief, excell,
Or grief could find delight with her to dwell.
Pensive she moves, majestically slow,
And with a pomp of beauty decks her woe:
All murmurs, silenc'd by her presence, cease,
And from her eye the yielding crowd gives place;

---

Sone after cometh this constable home again,
And eke Alla, that king was of that lond,
And saw his wife despitously yslain,
For which ful oft he wept and wrong his hond;
And in the bed the blody knif he fond
By dame Custance, alas! what might she say?
For veray wo hire wit was all away.

To king Alla was told all this mischance,
And eke the time, and wher, and in what wise,
That in a ship was fonden this Custance,
As here before ye han herd me devise:
The kinges herte of pitee gan agrise,
Whan he saw so benigne a creature
Falle in disese and in misadventure.

For as the lamb toward his deth is brought,
So stant this innocent beforn the king:
This false knight, that hath this treson wrought,
Bereth hire in hond that she hath don this thing:
But natheles ther was gret murmuring
Among the peple, and sayn they cannot gesse
That she had don so gret a wickednesse.

For they han seen hire ever so vertuous,
And loving Hermegild right as hire lif:
Of this bare witnesse everich in that hous,
Save he that Hermegild slow with his knif:
This gentil king hath caught a gret motif
Of this witness, and thought he wold enquere
Deper in this cas, trouthe for to lere.

E'en Alla's looks his soft'ning soul confess'd,
And all resentment died within his breast.
But ah! while shame with injur'd honour vies,
While yet her tongue its fault'ring task denies,
More than all phrase, or study'd quaint address,
Her down-cast eyes and speaking looks express.
At length pathetic, with a starting tear,
She thus to bow'd attention charm'd the ear.
"Where may the wretched for protection bend?
Or when, ah when, shall my misfortunes end?
Sure, persecution in the grave will cease;
And death bestow, what life denies me, peace.
Driv'n from before the face of humankind,
Earth, air, and sea, with cruel man combin'd;
Each hour, each element, prepar'd a foe,
And nature seem'd exhausted in my woe.
At length, with ev'ry grace and virtue crown'd,
One friend, one pitying faithful friend I found;
With her, retir'd, to pass my days I chose,
And here presum'd to taste a late repose:
But peace to me, alike all climes refuse,
And mischief to the furthest pole pursues;
'T is e'en a crime to be Constantia's friend,
Nor less than death to those who would defend.
Ah, Hermigilda! could my forfeit life,
To the fond husband give the faithful wife;
From her recall thy chastely feather'd charms,
And yield thee to the gen'rous Offa's arms;
Ah! gladly would I then resign my breath,
If life so dear could be reviv'd by death.
But thus to die with foul suspicion stain'd,
For murder, murder of my friend, arraign'd!—
Alas! unskill'd in ev'ry cruel art,
Had I the pow'r to hurt, I want the heart:
No creature e'er Constantia's malice felt;
Ev'n suff'ring foes have taught my heart to melt,
My heart, for birds, for insects oft distress'd;
And pity is its known, its only guest.
O youth! thy happy people's boasted theme,
O Alla! sacred to the breath of fame,
To whom subjected realms their rights submit,
Who thron'd in judgment like an angel sit;
Still more extensive be thy guardian care,
And let the innocent, the stranger share!"
Here rudely on her plea Rodolphus broke,
And all-inflam'd, and interrupting, spoke:
"List not, O king, to that bewitching tongue!
So sweetly false the tempting Syrens sung;
Her words would give the knotted oak an ear,
And charm the Moon from her enchanted sphere.
That by her hand our dear relation bled,
This sword shall witness on her guilty head,

Whatever champion, or bold odds oppose,
And, arm'd by justice, dare a thousand foes:
Then be her purity by combat try'd;
And by the conqu'ring arm let Heav'n decide."
"Alas, O Alla!" cry'd the trembling maid,
"My sex, not arms but innocence must aid.
Helpless I stand, and distant ev'ry friend,
That has the pow'r, or courage to defend.
If justice is ordain'd to crown the strong,
Then the weak arm is ever in the wrong;
The hawk may triumph in his lawless deeds,
While doom'd beneath his gripe the turtle bleeds,
Yet that I 'm guiltless, ev'n my charge admits,
And malice, meaning to arraign, acquits:
What though the sword lay treach'rous at my side?
Sure, guilt could never want the craft to hide!
The spots of bloody circumstance explain,
That inward truth fears no exterior stain;
And last my capture with the slain implies,
That guilt, not innocence, from vengeance flies.
I fear not death, but that surviving shame,
Which must to ages blast my spotless name—
Be that from taint of guilty censure freed,
And all that malice can inflict, decreed!"
Thus while she spake, with secret passion tost,
And in a world of new-found wonders lost,
Scarce Alla could his struggling heart control:
Fix'd were his eyes, but restless was his soul;
His breast with various agitation burn'd;
Now pale, now red, his varying aspect turn'd:
Her accents dwell upon his list'ning ears;
When now she ceas'd, delighted still he hears;
Her form with chang'd, with fev'rish look surveys,
And could for ever hear, for ever gaze.
At length collected, as from bonds he broke,
And with cold speech, and feign'd indiff'rence spoke:
"Thy charge, bright maid! my secret soul acquits;
But public law no private voice admits:
Kings sit not here, with arbitrary sense
To form new laws, or cavil, but dispense;
Though law is fallible, yet law should sway,
And kings, more fallible than law, obey.
Say, gallant warriors! who, unmatch'd in arms,
May yield uncensur'd to resistless charms;

---

Alas! Custance, thou hast no champion,
Ne fighten canst thou not, so wala wa!
But he that starf for our redemption,
And bond Sathan, and yet lith ther he lay,
So be thy stronge champion this day:
For but if Crist on thee miracle kithe,
Withouten gilt thou shalt be slaine as swithe.

She set hire doun on knees, and thus she sayde;
"Immortal God, that savedest Susanne
Fro false blame, and thou merciful mayde,
Mary I mene, doughter to seint Anne,
Beforn whos child angels singen Osanne,
If I be gilteles of this felonie,
My socour be, or elles shal I die."

Have ye not seen somtime a pale face
(Among a prees) of him that hath ben lad
Toward his deth, wher as he geteth no grace,
And swiche a colour in his face hath had,
Men mighten know him that was so bestad,
Amonges all the faces in that route,
So stant Custance, and loketh hire aboute.

O quenes living in prosperitee,
Duchesses, and ye ladies everich on,
Haveth som routhe on hire adversitee;
An emperoures doughter stant alone;
She hath no wight to whom to make hire mone;
O blood real, that stondest in this drede,
Fer ben thy frendes in thy grete nede.

This Alla king hath swiche compassioun,
As gentil herte is fulfilled of pitee,
That fro his eyen ran the water doun.
"Now hastily do fecche a book," quod he;
"And if this knight wol sweren, how that she
This woman slow, yet wol we us avise,
Whom that we wol that shal ben our justice."

Say, is there one, who, singularly brave,
At his own peril-greatly dares to save;
From pain, from death, from slander, to defend,
And give the stranger,·and the fair, a friend ?"
　The hero said; but mute was ev'ry tongue,
Blank ev'ry face, and ev'ry nerve unstrung ;
So much Rodolphus, never match'd in arms,
Each weaker hand and conscious heart alarms ;
So was the giant fam'd for brutal pow'r,
Strode like an arch, and menac'd l.ke a tow'r !
　Then Alla—" Soon as Phosphor's dewy ray
Shall gild the shade, bright promiser of day,
Prepar'd and meted with the morning light,
Be the rail'd barrier, and the lists of fight;
Then, ere the Sun, swift mounting up the sky,
Views the wide world with his meridian eye,
While issuing from the trumpet's brazen throat
Defiance loudly breathes its martial note,
If haply Heav'n, not impotent to aid,
With interposing arm protect the maid,
Some angel, or unlook'd-for champion send,
And with prevailing ministry defend;
Freed be the fair, and spotless be her fame—
Ere ev'ning else, she feeds the hungry flame !"
So spake the prince, descending from his throne:
Sad through the concourse went the length'ning
The maid, to death inevitably doom'd,　[groan;
A guiltless victim ev'ry heart presum'd ;
To her they consecrate the pitying tear,
Nor e'er, till then, could think their prince severe.
　Constantia (when with firm though hopeless eye
She now perceiv'd the fatal hour drew nigh)
In conscious innocence erects her head :
With doubt exil'd, all care and terrour fled;
Death stole from triumph to adorn her state,
And gave a smile beyond the reach of fate.
All night, in pray'r and mental song, the maid,
With angels choir'd, her soul for Heav'n array'd :
Light from her heart, as summer's careless robe,
Drop'd each affection of this sin-worn globe ;
O'er honour, late so lov'd, o'er brutal foes,
And ev'ry sense of mortal coil she rose ;
Till tow'rd the dawn she gently sunk to rest,
With all Elysium open'd in her breast.

---

A Breton book, written with Evangiles,
Was fet, and on this book he swore anon
She giltif was, and in the mene whiles
An hond him smote upon the nekke bone,
That doun he fell at ones as a stone :
And both his eyen brost out of his face
In sight of every body in that place.

A vois was herd, in general audience,
That sayd ; " Thou hast desclandred gilteles
The doughter of holy chirche in high presence ;
Thus hast thou don, and yet hold I my pees."
Of this mervaille agast was all the prees,
As mased folk they stonden everich on
For drede of wreche, save Custance alone.

Gret was the drede and eke the repentance
Of hem that hadden wrong suspection
Upon this sely innocent Custance ;
And for this miracle, in conclusion ;
And by Cus'ances mediation,
The king, and many another in that place,
Converted was, thanked be Cristes grace.

　Gray morning now involv'd in rising dew,
O'er the capt hills her streaming mantle threw ;
While, far beyond, the horizontal Sun
With beam of intersected brightness shone;
Gold pav'd o'er ocean stretch'd his glitt'ring road,
And to the shore the length'ning radiance glow'd.
Full in his sight, and open to the main,
Concurring squadrons throng'd Northumbria's plain :
To learn what fate attends the foreign fair,
Each sex and age in mingling routs repair,
Whom, pour'd by millions to the listed field,
Dispeopled towns, and empty'd hamlets yield.
Within the lists, conspicuous to the sight,
Rode the proud stature of the Saxon knight:
His mien, with thirst of opposition fir'd,
Appear'd to menace what it most desir'd ;
Gave all to wish some champion for the fair,
Gave all to wish the fight, but none to dare.
His bold defiance o'er the measur'd ground,
The brazen blasts of winding clarions sound ;
While strong-lung'd heralds challenge to the fight,
And seem, at once, to threaten and invite.
　And now, expectant of the murd'rous flame,
In sable pomp the lovely victim came :
On her, all looks and cent'ring hearts were fix'd,
Love, grief, and awe, with soft compassion mix'd ;
To Heav'n, the voice of wide affliction cries;
Earth drinks the tribute of ten thousand eyes—
Such sighs, as from the dying breast expire,
And tears, as meant to quench a world on fire.
To the tall pyre, in sad procession led,
The tranquil maid ascends her sylvan bed ;
And fearless on the fun'ral summit plac'd,
Her seat of fearful preparation grac'd.
Hence, with wide gaze, she threw her eyes around,
Nor Alla, cruel, lovely Alla, found.
　" Ah," soft she said, " where 's this heroic youth,
So fam'd for clemency, so fam'd for truth ;
So sage, so cautious in the casuist's chair,
Too firm to deviate, and too just to spare ;
To strangers cruel, though to subjects kind;
In law discerning, yet to mercy blind ?
Why comes not he to feast his savage eyes,
And view the pains he can so well devise ?
Heav'n fram'd thee, Alla, with exterior art,
Soften'd thy form, but left a flinty heart;
Too perfect else had been the beauteous plan,
And Alla had been something more than man !"
　Thus while she spoke, a distant murmur rose,
As when the wind through rustling forest blows ;
And gath'ring now still louder and more near,
To mute attention turn'd each list'ning ear.
Distinctly heard along the lifted ground,
To trumpets, now, shrill answ'ring trumpets sound;
A clamorous cheer from rank to rank extends,
And sudden shout the deafen'd welkin rends.
Straight, usher'd to the field with loud acclaim,
A knight unknown, and unattended came :
No trophy'd boast, no outward shine of arms,
Nor love device, with quaint attraction charms ;
Unplum'd the motion of his sable crest,
And black the guardian corselet on his breast ;
Black was the steed that bore him to the field,
And black the terrour of his ample shield.
　As when, to slake Ierne's fev'rish plain,
And check the dog-star's short but sultry reign,
A cloud, full freighted with the coming storm,
Black brow'd o'er ocean lifts its cumb'rous form,
Dread, to the shore its gloomy progress bends,
And charg'd with Heav'n's avenging bolt suspends—

So to the field the gloomy champion show'd;
So charg'd with mercy, as with vengeance rode.
  Where the bright victim bless'd the circling view,
Close to the pyre the sable warrior drew;
" Guilty," aloud, " or innocent?" he cry'd—
" Ah, guiltless—so help Heav'n !" the maid reply'd;
" So by this arm," he said, " may Heav'n for thee
    decide !"
  Surpris'd Rodolphus stood; abash'd the bold,
And like a torrent in mid course control'd ;
Abash'd to find that any mortal wight
Could singly dare to match his matchless might.
But soon, of conscious force, and scorn, and pride,
With two-fold fury swell'd th' impetuous tide:
Resistless, dreadful, in his wrath he rose ;
For courage still with opposition grows.
  Attending heralds straight divide the field,
And the dire interval for combat yield.
To either goal retir'd each threatful knight,
Fierce through restraint, and trembling for the fight,
On each by turns was ev'ry look intent,
Now here, now there, with swift emotion bent:
Perch'd on the summit of the stranger's crest,
Here conquest seem'd to ev'ry eye confess'd;
Not long confess'd, for from his rival, there,
Again the varying judgment learns despair ;
For ev'ry wish assum'd the stranger's part,
And quick expectance throbb'd in ev'ry heart.
  Fix'd in his seat, each waits the dread career,
And in each rest firm sits the pond'rous spear ;
Each conscious steed impatient beats the ground ;
Eager and wan was ev'ry face around.
The signal giv'n, they vanish from the goals;
Earth backward spurn'd from either courser rolls;
Space gathers quick beneath their nimble feet,
And horse to horse, tremendous shock ! they meet.
Nor yet blind wrath, or head-long valour rul'd;
More forceful was their force, by judgment cool'd;
The deadly aim each hostile eye selects,
Each eye too marks where either arm directs;
With art they ward, and with dread action wield,
Point with the lance, and parry with the shield.
Full at the bosom of his active foe,
Rodolphus levell'd the resistless blow ;
But from his oblique buckler glanc'd the spear,
Which else, nor targe, nor mortal arm could bear.
Not so his lance the sable champion sped,
Feign'd at the breast, then brandish'd at the head;
Through his foe's shield the verging weapon press'd,
And raz'd the plume that wanton'd on his crest.
Together, with impetuous onset push'd,
Thus horse to horse, and man to man, they rush'd;
Then backward, driv'n by mutual shock, they
    bound :
Beneath the conflict shakes the suff'ring ground.
  So wing'd, in war, or darkness, on the deep,
Two ships adverse the mediate ocean sweep:
With horrid brunt joins each encount'ring prow;
Loud roars the rifled surge, and foams below;
Sails, shrouds, and masts, all shiver in the toil,
And backward to their sterns the found'ring keels
    recoil.
  But each well skill'd in ev'ry warlike meed,
New to the charge revives his sinking steed ;
Swift from his side his steely terrour drew,
And on his foe with answ'ring fury flew.
The sway long time intemp'rate valour bore,
While artless rage unlearn'd the warrior's lore :
On their hack'd arms the restless peal descends,
Targe, plate, and mail, and riven corselet, rends;

Struck from their helms, the steely sparks aspire,
And from their swords forth streams the mingling
  As in the glow of some Vulcanian shed,   [fire.
Two brawny smiths heave high the pond'rous sled,
Full front to front, a grizzly pair they stand ;
Between their arms extends the fiery brand :
Huge strokes from the tormented anvil bound ;
Thick flames the air, and groans the lab'ring
    ground—
So toil'd these heroes with commutual rage,
And such reciprocated combat wage.
Around them, trembling expectation waits ;
With speechless horrour ev'ry bosom beats ;
For either seem'd resistless in the fight,
But each too seem'd to match resistless might.
Surpris'd at length the wary warriors own
A rival to their arms till then unknown;
With mutual wile defensive now they fought,
And mutual wounds a mutual caution taught :
All dint of force, and stratagem, they try,
Reach with their arms, and measure with their eye;
They feint, they ward, strike out, and now evade,
Foin with the point, and parry with the blade;
Probe each defect, some purpos'd limb expose,
Now grappling seize, and with dread union close;
Their waists with unenamour'd grasp they wind ;
Their arms, like cramps, and forceful engines, bind ;
Each strives to lift the other from his seat,
Heav'd thick, and short, their lab'ring bosoms beat ;
Struggling they gripe, they pull, they bend, they
    strain,
But firm and still unsway'd their seats retain ;
Till loos'd as by consent again they turn,
And with reviving force and fury burn.
Thus future ages had this fight beheld,
Where both all might excelling, none excell'd,
Had not Rodolphus with impassion'd pride,
High heav'd a blow that should at once decide,
His utmost pow'rs collected in the stroke—
Like thunder o'er the yielding foe he broke:
The foe elusive of the dire intent,
His force in air th' embarrass'd Pagan spent,
And by his bulk of cumb'rous poise o'ersway'd,
Full on his helm receiv'd th' adverse blade :
Prone fell the giant o'er a length of ground ;
With ceaseless shouts th' echoing Heav'ns resound.
  As from the brow of some impending steep,
The sportive diver views the briny deep,
From his high stand with headlong action flies,
And turns his heels retorted to the skies ;
Inverted so the bulky chief o'erturns,
And Heav'n, with heel of quick elation, spurns.
  Light from his steed the conqu'ring hero sprung,
And threatful o'er the prostrate monster hung :
He, with feign'd penitence, and humbled breath,
Fond to evade the fear'd, th' impending death,
(The instant weapon glitt'ring at his breast)
The murd'rous scene and nightly guilt confess'd.
  Meanwhile, attended by the shouting crew,
The fair, now freed, to greet her champion flew ;
For not of mortal arm the chief she thought,
But Heav'n's own delegate with vengeance fraught.
When now, enchanting to the warrior's sight,
The maid drew near, the maid as angels bright,
His beaver from his lovely face he rais'd,
And all on Alla, conqu'ring Alla, gaz'd :
Earth, sea, and air, with endless triumph ring,
And shouting thousands hail their victor king.
Not so Constantia,—struck with strange surprise,
Her great deliverer in her judge she eyes ;

Conquest and love upon his regal brow,
A cruel judge, but kind deliverer now:
Soft shame, and trembling awe, her step repress'd,
And wondrous gratitude disturb'd her breast;
Joys, fainting fears, quick thrill'd through ev'ry vein,
And scarce her limbs their beauteous charge sustain.
  How widely devious from the ways of man,
Is the great maze of providential plan!
Vain man, short-sighted politician! dreams,
That things shall move subservient to his schemes;
But Heav'n the fond projector undermines,
And makes the agent thwart his own designs;
Against itself the instrument employs,
And with the means the end propos'd destroys.
What shall prevent Omniscience to direct?
And what, what can 't Omnipotence effect?
He to th' event subdues th' opposing cause,
And light from darkness, wondrous influence, draws;
Defeat from conquest, infamy from fame;
And oft to honour paves the path of shame.
Why then this toil, and coil, and anxious care?
Why does man triumph, why does man despair?
Why does he choose by vicious steps to scale,
Where virtue may, at least as well, prevail?
Since not in him his proper fortune lies,
And Heav'n alone ordains his fall or rise:
Man may propose, but only Heav'n must speed;
And though the will is free, th' event 's decreed.
Be then the scope of ev'ry act, and thought,
To will, and do, still simply as we ought;
The less shall disappointment's sting annoy,
And each success will bring a double joy:
To boundless Power and Prescience leave the rest;
But thou enjoy the province in thy breast!
  Lo! in one hour, by fortune unforeseen,
The lowly criminal becomes the queen;
From shame to glory, anguish to repose,
From death to life, and bonds to freedom rose.
In love, as war, resistless, Alla woo'd,
And whom he won by arms, by suit subdu'd:
Constantia with her secret wish comply'd,
For Alla would not, could not be deny'd.
  Nor list we here, with pomp of long array,
To blazon forth that chaste connubial day;

To tell what numbers numberless, what knights
And glitt'ring dames adorn'd the festal rites;
What joys the banquet or the bowl could yield,
Or what the trophies of the tilting field.
Loud were the revels, boundless was the mirth,
That hail'd the sweetest brightest pair on Earth—
Of men, the wisest, bravest, fairest, he;
Of all that 's beautiful most beauteous, she!
Love, nature, harmony, the union claim'd,
And each for each, and both for one were fram'd.
But we of subsequent adventure treat,
And hasten to unfold their future fate.
  Some months young Alla and his peerless bride,
In cordial bond of dear accordance ty'd,
Had look'd and smil'd the precious hours away,
And fed on bliss that ne'er could know decay:
He, whose charm'd ear on that enchanting tongue
With thirst of fondest inclination hung,
Won by a preacher with so fair a face,
Becomes the zealous proselyte of grace;
And subjects too their heathenish rites forego,
For still from courts, or vice, or virtues flow.
But ah! too soon, from beauty's softer charms,
War, rig'rous war, and Scotia call to arms;
Constantia must her blooming hero yield,
For honour sends him to th' embattled field.
  Meanwhile, the pregnant fruit of chaste delight
With a male infant crown'd the nuptial rite;
All sweet and lovely as the smiling morn,
Mauritius was to bless a nation born:
Their pledge of future bliss, their princely boy,
The Britons hail with universal joy;
Their fancy frames him what their pray'rs require,
Sweet as their queen, and valiant as his sire.
Offa, to whom the king's departing care,
Inestimable charge! consign'd the fair,
Advice of loyal gratulation sent,
To glad his sov'reign with the bless'd event.
  But Donnegilda [1], cruel, crafty dame,
Great Alla's mother, over-fond of fame,
She, (as all antique parents, wondrous sage,
For youth project th' inappetence of age,

---

This false knight was slain for his untrouthe
By jugement of Alla hastily;
And yet Custance had of his deth gret routhe;
And after this Jesus of his mercy
Made Alla wedden ful solempnely
This holy woman, that is so bright and shene,
And thus hath Crist ymade Custance a quene.

But who was woful (if I shal not lie)
Of this wedding but Donegild and no mo,
The kinges mother, ful of tyrannie?
Hire thoughte hire cursed herte brast atwo;
She wolde not that hire sone had do so;
Hire thoughte a despit, that he shulde take
So strange a creature unto his make.

Me list not of the chaf ne of the stre
Maken so long a tale, as of the corn.
What shulde I tellen of the realtee
Of this mariage, or which cours goth beforn,
Who bloweth in a trompe or in an horn?
The fruit of every tale is for to say;
They ete and drinke, and dance, and sing, and play.

They gon to bed, as it was skill and right,
For though that wives ben ful holy thinges,
They mosten take in patience a night
Swiche maner necessaries, as ben plesinges
To folk that han ywedded hem with ringes,
And lay a lite hir holinesse aside
As for the time, it may no bet betide.

On hire he gat a knave childe anon,
And to a bishop, and his constable eke
He toke his wif to kepe, whan he is gon
To Scotland ward, his fomen for to seke.
Now faire Custance, that is so humble and meke,
So long is gon with childe til that still
She halt hire chambre, abiding Cristes will.

The time is come, a knave child she bere;
Mauricius at the fontstone they him calle.
This constable doth forth come a messager,
And wrote unto his king that cleped was Alle,
How that this blissful tiding is befalle,
And other tidings spedeful for to say.
He hath the lettre, and forth he goth his way.

Each sense endearing and humane despise,
And on the mammon feast their downcast eyes)
Malevolent beheld a stranger led,
Unknown, unfriended, to the regal bed:
For in the secret closet of her breast,
Constantia her imperial birth suppress'd,
Till Heav'n should perfect the connubial band,
And with her royal offspring bless the land.
Ah! ill-tim'd caution! were this truth declar'd,
What a vast cost of future woe was spar'd!
But where Heav'n's will th' unequal cause supplies,
To set the world on fire a spark may well suffice.

  The subtile dame, who now th' occasion spy'd
To tear Constantia from her Alla's side,
Debauch'd the messenger, his mandate stole,
And forg'd in Offa's name the crafty scroll ;
Wherein she fram'd a tale with wondrous art,
" How the feign'd fair by witchcraft won his heart,
Seduc'd his senses with infernal lore,
And a dread monster, hideous offspring! bore."
But Alla, of whose fond, whose faithful breast,
His consort was the dear eternal guest,
Unmov'd, return'd—" His bliss was too refin'd,
Without the just allay that Heav'n assign'd;
And what Constantia bore, or Heav'n decreed,
To be unwelcome must be strange indeed !"

---

This messenger, to don his avantage,
Unto the kinges mother rideth swithe,
And salueth hire ful faire in his langage.
" Madame," quod he, " ye may be glad and blithe,
And thanken God an hundred thousand sithe;
My lady quene hath child, withouten doute,
The joye and blisse of all this regne aboute.

" Lo here the lettre seled of this thing,
That I most bere in all the hast I may:
If ye wol ought unto your sone the king,
I am your servant bothe night and day."
Donegilde answerd, " As now at this time nay;
But here I wol all night thou take thy rest,
To morwe wol I say thee what me lest."

This messenger drank sadly ale and wine,
And stolen were his lettres prively
Out of his box, while he slept as a swine;
And contrefeted was ful subtilly
Another lettre, wrought ful sinfully,
Unto the king directe of this matere
Fro his constable, as ye shal after here.

This lettre spake, the quene delivered was
Of so horrible a fendliche creature,
That in the castle non so hardy was
That any while dorste therein endure:
The mother was an elfe by aventure
Ycome, by charmes or by sorcerie,
And everich man hateth hire compagnie.

Wo was this king whan he this lettre had sein,
But to no wight he told his sorwes sore,
But of his owen hand he wrote again ;
" Welcome the sonde of Crist for evermore
To me, that am now lerned in his lore:
Lord, welcome be thy lust and thy plesance,
My lust I put all in thyn ordinance.

This letter too the courier as before,
To Britain's dowager unweeting bore ;
And in the surfeit of oblivious wine
Left her to perpetrate the black design.
This too she cancell'd, forg'd the regal hand,
And pityless inscrib'd " the dire command,
With threats, that Offa, to the wonted sea,
Should the false queen and hated imp convey ;
And there permit the now detested dame
To seek the shore from whence the sorceress came."
  When Offa had the barb'rous mandate read,
To Heav'n his eyes and lifted hands he spread.

---

" Kepeth this child, al be it foule or faire,
And eke my wif, unto min home coming :
Crist whan him-list may senden me an heire,
More agreable than this to my liking."
This lettre he seled, prively weping,
Which to the messager was taken sone,
And forth he goth, ther is no more to done.

O messager fulfilled of drunkenesse,
Strong is thy breth, thy limmes faltren ay,
And thou bewreiest alle secrenesse ;
Thy mind is lorne, thou janglest as a jay;
Thy face is tourned in a new array;
Ther dronkenesse regneth in any route,
Ther is no conseil hid withouten doute.

O Donegild, I ne have non English digne
Unto thy malice, and thy tirannie ;
And therfore to the fende I thee resigne,
Let him enditen of thy traitorie.
Fy mannish, fy; o nay by God I lie;
Fy fendliche spirit, for I dare wel telle,
Though thou here walke, thy spirit is in Helle.

This messager cometh fro the king again,
And at the kinges modres court he light,
And she was of this messager ful fayn,
And plesed him in all that ever she might.
He dranke, and wel his girdel underpight ;
He slepeth, and he snoreth in his gise
All night, until the sonne gan arise.

Eft were his lettres stolen everich on,
And contrefeted lettres in this wise,
" The king commanded his constable anon
Up peine of hanging and of high jewise,
That he ne shulde soffren in no wise
Custance within his regne for to abide
Three daies and a quarter of a tide ;

" But in the same ship as he hire fond,
Hire and hire yonge sone, and all hire gere
He shulde put, and croude hire fro the lond,
And charge hire, that she never eft come there."
O my Custance, wel may thy ghost have fere,
And sleping in thy dreme ben in penance,
When Donegild cast all this ordinance.

This messager on morwe whan he awoke,
Unto the castel halt the nexte way ;
And to the constable he the lettre toke;
And whan that he this pitous lettre sey,
Ful oft he sayd " Alas, and wala wa ;        [dure ?
Lord Crist," quod he, " how may this world en-
So ful of sinne is many a creature.

Like Niobe to marble turn'd, he stood;
Grief, fear, and horrour, froze the gen'rous blood!
Again he stirr'd, as from some wistful dream;
Again he read—alas! he read the same.

But, though in terms of soothing phrase express'd,
When now Constantia learn'd her lord's behest,
Keen anguish, piercing to the springs of life,
At once arrests the mother and the wife:
For not, to her alone confin'd, as late
When bold she stood the weightiest stroke of fate,
A thousand cares of soft endearing kind,
Now share with Heav'n the motions of her mind;
And with fond thoughts of sweet concern divide,
The melting mother, and the clasping bride:
And these alone her bursting bosom rend,
And o'er the couch her lifeless limbs extend.

Fame pour'd the mourning populace around:
In gushing anguish ev'ry eye is drown'd;
Compassion set her virtues full to view,
And with their queen bade ev'ry joy adieu;
Swift from his throne they wish their Alla hurl'd,
And her crown'd empress of the peopled world:
But ah! in vain their pray'rs and tears delay;
Strict was the charge, and Offa must obey.

With heavy heart and faint reluctant hand,
He led the mourner to the neighb'ring strand:
She to the heaving whiteness of her breast,
With melting looks, her helpless infant press'd;

And thus, while sobs her piteous accent broke,
Her little inattentive child bespoke. [father's will,
" Weep not, sweet wretch! though such thy
Yet hast thou one, one tender parent still.
Peace, peace! to thee thy mother means no harm;
Nor let our lot thy little heart alarm:
O'er thee, till death, o'er thee my cares shall wake,
And love thee for thy cruel father's sake."

Had ev'ry sire as on the banks of Nile,
Lost his first-born throughout Britannia's isle;
Or death with undistinguish'd carnage swept
Wives, sons, and sires, by all the living wept;
Such haply were the woes that now deplore
Their queen attended to the echoing shore:
They tear their locks, their rueful bosoms smite,
And trace her bark with long pursuing sight.

Tedious it were, though wondrous strange to tell,
What new adventures o'er the main befel;
How fondly prattling, while her infant smil'd,
She the long hours and wint'ry nights beguil'd;
Till seiz'd by pirates on th' Atlantic wave,
A prince of Gallia bought th' imperial slave:
How, in calm peace and friendship long retain'd,
High trust and grace her winning sweetness gain'd;
Till she to Rome, predestinate event!
Associate with her lord and mistress went.

But now to Britain let the Muse repair;
For there the valiant Alla claims her care.

---

" O mighty God, if that it be thy will,
Sin thou art rightful juge, how may it be
That thou wolt soffren innocence to spill,
And wicked folk regne in prosperitee?
A good Custance, alas! so wo is me,
That I mote be thy turmentour, or dey
On shames deth, ther is non other wey."

Wepen both yong and old in all that place,
Whan that the king this cursed lettre sent:
And Custance with a dedly pale face
The fourthe day toward the ship she went:
But natheles she taketh in good entent
The will of Crist, and kneling on the strond
She sayde, " Lord, ay welcome be thy sond.

" He that me kepte fro the false blame,
While I was in the lond amonges you,
He can me kepe fro harme and eke fro shame
In the salt see, although I se not how:
As strong as ever he was, he is yet now,
In him trust I, and in his mother dere,
That is to me my sail and eke my stere."

Hire litel child lay weping in hire arm,
And kneling pitously to him she said,
" Pees, litel sone, I wol do thee no harm:"
With that hire couverchief of hire hed she braid,
And over his litel eyen she it laid,
And in hire arme she lulleth it ful fast,
And into the Heven hire eyen up she cast.

" Mother," quod she, " and mayden bright Marie,
Soth is, that thurgh womannes eggement
Mankind was lorne, and damned ay to die,
For which thy child was on a crois yrent:
This blisful eyen saw all his turment,
Than is ther no comparison betwene
Thy wo, and any wo man may sustene.

" Thou saw thy child yslain before thin eyen,
And yet now liveth my litel child parfay:
Now, lady bright, to whom all woful crien,
Thou glory of womanhed, thou faire may,
Thou haven of refute, bright sterre of day,
Rew on my child, that of thy gentillesse
Rewest on every rewful in distresse.

" O litel child, alas! what is thy gilt,
That never wroughtest sinne as yet parde?
Why wol thin harde fader have the spilt?
O mercy, dere constable," quod she,
" As let my litel child dwell here with thee:
And if thou darst not saven him fro blame,
So kisse him ones in his fadres name."

Therwith she loketh backward to the lond,
And saide; " Farewel, housbond routheles!"
And up she rist, and walketh doun the strond
Toward the ship, hire foloweth all the prees:
And ever she praieth hire child to hold his pees,
And taketh hire leve, and with an holy entent
She blesseth hire, and into the ship she went.

Vitailled was the ship, it is no drede,
Habundantly for hire a ful long space:
And other necessaries that shuld nede
She had ynow, heried be Goddes grace:
For wind and wether, almighty God purchace,
And bring hire home, I can no better say,
But in the see she driveth forth hire way.

Alla the king cometh home sone after this
Unto his castel, of the which I told,
And asketh wher his wif and his child is;
The constable gan about his herte cold,
And plainly all the matere he him told
As ye han herd, I can tell it no better,
And shewed the king his sele and his letter;

Triumphant soon from Scotia he return'd,
And to behold his lov'd Constantia burn'd:
This wings his feet along the toilsome way—
But thoughts are swifter, swifter far than they;
Hope, elevate, the distant journey metes,
And to his march his heart the measure beats.

But when o'er Tweed he led his conqu'ring host,
And trode the verdure of Northumbria's coast,
While laurels round their trophy'd temples twin'd,
And banners wanton'd in the curling wind,
No wonted crowds their once-lov'd Alla meet,
No prostrate knees, or hailing voices greet:
Blank was his passage o'er the pensive ground,
And silence cast a mournful gloom around;
Or if his prince some straggling peasant spy'd,
As from a basilisk he slunk aside.
What this might mean, revolv'd within his breast,
Conjecture dire, and whisp'ring doubts suggest;
More dread than death, some hideous ill impart—
This the first fear e'er seiz'd on Alla's heart.
But worse, O worse than fancy yet could fear,
When now the killing truth arrests his ear!
Athwart his eyes, and mantling round his soul,
Thick clouds of grief and dreary darkness roll;
His sense, nor tears, nor utt'ring groans could tell,
But froze and lock'd in speechless woe he fell.
At length by care, by cruel kindness, brought
To all the anguish of returning thought,
Swift from the sheath he drew the deadly guest,
And would have pierc'd this vulture in his breast;
Such was the sting of agonizing pain,
His frenzy would th' immortal soul have slain!
But this prevented, round th' attending crew,
With baleful glance, his eager eyes he threw:
" Constantia!" he requires with frantic tongue,
" Constantia!" still the restless accents sung:
To her, as present, now his fondness speaks;
As absent, into desp'rate action breaks.
" O never, never more, my queen!" he cries,
" Shall that known form attract these dying eyes!
Never?—O, 't is the worst, the last despair—
Never is long, is wondrous long to bear! [stoop;
Down, down, ye cloud-topt hills, your summits
With me, in sign of endless mourning, droop!
Snapt be the spear, bright armour ground to dust;
Repose, thou corslet, in eternal rust;

---

And saide; " Lord, as ye commanded me,
Up peine of deth, so have I don certain."
This messager turmented was, til he
Moste beknowe, and tellen plat and plain,
Fro night to night in what place he had lain:
And thus by wit and subtil enquering
Imagined was by whom this harm gan spring.

The hand was knowen that the lettre wrote,
And all the venime of this cursed dede;
But in what wise, certainly I n'ot.
The effect is this, that Alla out of drede
His moder slew, that moun men plainly rede,
For that she traitour was to hire ligeance;
Thus endeth this old Donegild with meschance.

The sorwe that this Alla night and day
Maketh for his wif and for his child also,
Ther is no tonge that it tellen may.
But now wol I agen to Custance go,
That fleteth in the see in peine and wo
Five yere and more, as liked Cristes sonde,
Or that hire ship approched to the londe.

VOL. XVII.

---

Still'd be each tube, the trumpet's warlike swell—
Empire, and fame, all, all, with thee, farewell!
For thee alone, thy conqu'ring soldier arm'd,
The banner wav'd, and sprightly clangour charm'd:
But arms and loath'd desire with thee are dead;
And joy—no, never to return—is fled!"
Thus rav'd the youth, to wilful woes resign'd;
And offer'd aid was sickness to his mind,
To frenzy by uxorious transports rais'd,
His vengeance on his aged parent seiz'd;
Who, doom'd to lose that too designing head,
A victim to his lov'd Constantia bled.
But violence in nature cannot last:
What region's known to bear eternal blast?
Time changes all, dissolves the melting rock,
And on fix'd water turns the crystal lock.
Time o'er his anguish shed a silent balm,
A peace unsmiling, and a gloomy calm;
By ill untaught to mourn, by joy to glow,
And still insensible to bliss or woe.

---

Under an hethen castel at the last,
(Of which the name in my text I not find)
Custance and eke hire child the see up cast.
Almighty God, that saved all mankind,
Have on Custance and on hire child som mind,
That fallen is in hethen hond eftsone
In point to spill, as I shal tell you sone.

Doun fro the castel cometh ther many a wight
To gauren on this ship, and on Custance:
But shortly fro the castel on a night,
The lordes steward (God yeve him meschance)
A theef, that had reneyed our creance,
Came into the ship alone, and said he wolde
Hire lemman be, whether she wolde or n'olde.

Wo was this wretched woman tho begon,
Hire childe cried, and she cried pitously:
But blisful Mary halpe hire right anon,
For with hire strogling wel and mightily
The theef fell over bord al sodenly,
And in the see he drenched for vengeance,
And thus hath Crist unwemmed kept Custance.

O foule lust of luxurie, lo thin ende,
Nat only that thou faintest mannes mind,
But veraily thou wolt his body shende,
Th' ende of thy werk, or if thy lustes blind,
Is complaining: how many may men find,
That not for werk somtime, but for th' entent
To don this sinne, ben other slain or shent.

How may this weke woman han the strength
Hire to defend again this renegate?
O Golias, unmesurable of length,
How mighte David maken thee so mate?
So yonge, and of armure so desolate,
How dorst he loke upon thy dredful face?
Wel may men seen it was but Goddes grace.

Who yaf Judith corage or hardinesse
To sleen him Holofernes in his tent,
And to deliver out of wretchednesse
The peple of God? I say for this entent,
That right as God spirit of vigour sent
To hem, and saved hem out of meschance,
So sent he might and vigour to Custance.
D d

To him, thus careless of the circling year,
Five annual suns had roll'd their bright career:
To Heav'n alone, his earthly ardours turn'd;
There, late to 'neet the dear Constantia, burn'd:
Still that fond hope remain'd—his sole desire!
And gave new wings to the celestial fire.
" But yet—hereafter!—what might there betide
The blood-stain'd hand, by whom a parent dy'd ?"
This, this gave doubtful thought, unhing'd his rest,
And shook the region of his contrite breast;
At length taught satiate vengeance to relent,
And shipp'd for Rome, the royal pilgrim sent.

Forth goth hire ship thurghout the narwe mouth
Of Jubaltare and Septe, driving alway,
Somtime west, and somtime north and south,
And somtime est, ful many a wery day:
Til Cristes moder (blessed be she ay)
Hath shapen thurgh hire endeles goodnesse
To make an end of all hire hevinesse.

Now let us stint of Custance but a throw,
And speke we of the Romane emperour,
That out of Surrie hath by lettres knowe
The slaughter of Cristen folk, and dishonour
Don to his doughter by a false traitour,
I mene the cursed wicked Soudannesse,
That at the fest let sleen both more and lesse.

For which this emperour hath sent anon
His senatour, with real ordinance,
And other lordes, God wote, many on,
On Surriens to taken high vengeance:
They brennen, sleen, and bring hem to meschance
Ful many a day: but shortly this is th' ende,
Homward to Rome they shapen hem to wende.

This senatour repaireth with victorie
To Rome ward, sayling ful really.
And met the ship driving, as saith the storie,
In which Custance sitteth ful pitously:
Nothing ne knew he what she was, ne why
She was in swiche array, ne she wil sey
Of hire estat, though that she shulde dey.

He bringeth hire to Rome, and to his wif
He yaf hire, and hire yonge sone also:
And with the senatour she lad hire lif,
Thus can our Lady bringen out of wo
Woful Custance, and many another mo:
And longe time dwelled she in that place,
In holy werkes ever, as was hire grace.

The senatoures wif hire aunte was,
But for all that she knew hire never the more:
I wol no longer tarien in this cas,
But to king Alla, which I spake of yore,
That for his wif wepeth and siketh sore,
I wol returne, and let I wol Custance
Under the senatoures governance.

King Alla, which that had his moder slain,
Upon a day fell in swiche repentance,
That if I shortly tellen shal and plain,
To Rome he cometh to receive his penance;
And putte him in the popes ordinance,
In high and low, and Jesu Crist besought,
Foryeve his wicked werks that he had wrought.

O'er Tiber soon the far-fraught tidings sped,
(For far beyond the warrior's fame had spread)
And Gallia's Hugo, to whose gen'rous care
Protecting Heav'n consign'd the wand'ring fair,
With those whom virtuous approbation fir'd,
(As still the brave are by the brave admir'd)
To see, to touch the gallant Alla glow'd,
And rank'd to meet the regal pilgrim rode.
With all due rite and answ'ring grace humane,
The courteous prince receiv'd the shining train:
But Hugo chief, with port of winning view,
The hero's eye and prime affection drew;
And him, with note selected from the rest,
The prince solicits for a frequent guest.
But ah! when now it reach'd Constantia's ear,
That Alla, lovely, barb'rous man, was near,
Her soul a thousand diff'rent thoughts assail;
Expell'd by turns, by turns they all prevail:
With melting joy and burning love she glows,
With cooling grief and icy hate she froze;
Dear to her heart, though horrid to her will,
He was the lov'd, the charming Alla still.
Nor Hugo now, in pompous dress array'd,
To wait Britannia's potent lord delay'd.
With him Mauritius frequent chat supply'd,
A little gay companion at his side—
He beams a Ganymede, in whose sweet face
The sire and mother liv'd with mingling grace:
Here still they met, in beauty reconcil'd;
Here still, in soft delicious union, smil'd;
So join'd, so blended, with divinest art,
As left it not in any power to part!
Upon the prattler's aspect, with surprise,
And charm'd attention, Alla fix'd his eyes:
Somewhat of wonted semblance there he spy'd,
Dear to his sense, and to his heart ally'd;

The fame anon thurghout the toun is born,
How Alla king shal come on pilgrimage,
By herbergeours that wenten him beforn,
For which the senatour, as was usage,
Rode him againe, and many of his linage,
As wel to shewen his high magnificence,
As to don any king a reverence.

Gret chere doth this noble senatour
To king Alla, and he to him also;
Everich of hem doth other gret honour;
And so befell, that in a day or two
This senatour is to king Alla go
To fest, and shortly, if I shal not lie,
Custances sone went in his compagnie.

Som men wold sain at requeste of Custance
This senatour hath lad this child to feste:
I may not tellen every circumstance,
Be as be may, ther was he at the leste:
But soth is this, that at his mothers heste
Beforn Alla, during the metes space,
The child stood, loking in the kinges face.

This Alla king hath of this child gret wonder,
And to the senatour he said anon,
" Whos is that faire child that stondeth yonder ?"
" I n'ot," quod he, " by God, and by Seint John;
A moder he hath, but fader hath he non,
That I of wote: but shortly in a stound
He told Alla how that this child was found.

Somewhat that touch'd beyond all mortal view,
And inly with the link of nature drew.
Disturb'd he rose; upon his secret soul,
Unweeting thaw, and cordial earnings stole:
Big with the soft distress, aside he stepp'd,
And much the warrior wonder'd why he wept.
Compos'd, he clasp'd the infant to his breast,
And ask'd, what sire with such a son was bless'd?
" That," Hugo cried, " his dame alone must show;
Sire hath he none, or none of whom we know:
But mother, sure, he hath, that 's such a mate
No man can boast, nor boastful tongue relate:
Though fancy, to give semblance of her face,
From all her sex should cull each sep'rate grace,
To speak her soul should rob from ev'ry saint;
Low yet were phrase, and all description faint!"

   Thus, while his tongue with free encomium flow'd,
With strange emotion Alla's aspect glow'd:
Full on his heart the dear idea rush'd;
His cheek with hope and lively ardour flush'd;
When straight despondence sick'ning in his soul,
From its known seat the rosy tincture stole:
" Once, once," he cry'd, (the lab'ring sigh sup-
     press'd)
" Such treasure once these widow'd arms possess'd!
Nature is rich—yet gladly should I know,
If the world's round can such another show."
" Be that," reply'd the Gallic chief, " confess'd,
Whene'er my house boasts Alla for a guest."
   They went. But when the long-dissever'd pair,
Her Alla here, and his Constantia there—
By doubts, loves, fears, and rushing joys dismay'd,
Unmov'd, each face with mutual gaze survey'd—
Such was the scene, th' impassion'd gesture such,
As phrase can 't reach, nor liveliest pencil touch!
Three times the fair-one sought the shades of death,
Three times reviv'd by Alla's balmy breath;

---

" But God wot," quod this senatour also,
" So vertuous a liver in all my lif
Ne saw I never, as she, ne herd of mo
Of worldly woman, maiden, widewe, or wif:
I dare wel sayn hire hadde lever a knif
Thurghout hire brest, than ben a woman wikke,
Ther is no man coude bring hire to that prikke."

Now was this child as like unto Custance
As possible is a creature to be;
This Alla hath the face in remembrance
Of dame Custance, and theron mused he,
If that the childes moder were aught she
That is his wif, and prively he sighte,
And sped him fro the table that he mighte.

" Parfay," thought he, " fantome is in min hed.
I ought to deme of skilful jugement,
That in the salte see my wif is ded."
And afterward he made his argument;
" What wot I, if that Crist have hider sent
My wif by see, as wel as he hire lent
To my contree, fro thennes that she went ?"

And after noon home with the senatour
Goth Alla, for to see this wonder chance.
This senatour doth Alla gret honour,
And hastily he sent after Custance:
But trusteth wel, hire luste not to dance.
Whan that she wiste wherfore was that sonde,
Unnethe upon hire feet she mighte stonde.

And thrice his guiltless plea he would essay,
And thrice she turn'd, Constantia turn'd away.
" Now, by this hand," Britannia's hero cry'd,
" This hand, by whom a cruel parent dy'd,
Long since for thee, for thee thou dear one, bled,
A victim sacred to that injur'd head—
Of all thy wrongs thy Alla is as clear,
As here my son, thy other Alla here!
Ah! could you know the anguish, the distress—
But who can know what words can ne'er express ?—
What racks, what deaths, thy tort'ring absence cost;
What restless toil this suff'ring bosom tost—
'T was such a ruin, such a breach of care,
As this and only this could e'er repair !"
   So saying, swift resistless to his breast,
The yielding fair repeated transport press'd.
But when all doubt and cold suspicion clear'd,
Her lord still faithful as belov'd appear'd;
By her so oft, so cruelly accus'd,
Still kind and true, and as herself abus'd;
She in his bosom, all with joy o'erpower'd,
Of sobs and tears the copious tempest shower'd—
All eyes around the melting measure kept,
And pleasure through contagious transport wept:
For Heav'n, alone, can emulate the sweet
Of one hour's bliss, when two such lovers meet.
   Still had Constantia, lock'd within her breast,
The royal secret of her birth suppress'd,

---

Whan Alla saw his wif, faire he hire grette,
And wept, that it was routhe for to see,
For at the firste look he on hire sette
He knew wel veraily that it was she:
And she for sorwe, as domb stant as a tree:
So was hire herte shette in hire distresse,
Whan she remembered his unkindnesse.

Twies she swouneth in his owen sight,
He wepeth and him excuseth pitously:
" Now God," quod he, " and all his halwes bright
So wisly on my soule as have mercy,
That of your harme as gilteles am I,
As is Maurice my sone, so like your face,
Elles the fend me fetche out of this place."

Long was the sobbing and the bitter peine,
Or that hir woful hertes mighten cese,
Gret was the pitee for to here hem pleine,
Thurgh whiche pleintes gan hir wo encrese.
I pray you all my labour to relese,
I may not tell hir wo until to morwe,
I am so wery for to speke of sorwe.

But finally, whan that the soth is wist,
That Alla gilteles was of hire wo,
I trow an hundred times han they kist,
And swiche a blisse is ther betwix hem two,
That save the joye that lasteth evermo,
Ther is non like, that any creature
Hath seen or shal, while that the world may dure.

Tho praied she hire husbond mekely
In releef of hire longe pitous pine,
That he wold pray hire fader specially,
That of his magestee he wold encline
To vouchesauf som day with him to dine:
She praied him eke, he shulde by no way
Unto hire fader no word of hire say.

When Rome's imperial monarch wide invites
To social cheer and festival delights:
For now triumphant from the Syrian coast,
Though long detain'd, return'd his vengeful host;
And to reward their toils and drown their cares,
The monarch on a solemn day prepares.
With festal robes adorn'd each warrior came;
In glitt'ring vesture many a Roman dame:
And there, amid the peers, a peerless guest,
There Alla came in regal splendours dress'd,
All India beaming at the hero's side;
O'er beaming India shone his brighter bride;
While the young joy of each applauding tongue,
Mauritius on his smiling parents hung,
As though a stripling cherub should attend,
Where two of prime angelic rank descend.
Struck at the pleasing prospect all admire,
But mute with wonder stood th' imperial sire;
For haply, since our primal parents fell,
Ne'er met a pair that could this pair excel.

He at his left Britannia's monarch plac'd,
And his right hand th' unknown Constantia grac'd;
When with a starting tear the rev'rend man,
To Alla turn'd, in placid speech began:
" Young though thou art, with earliest vigour strung,
And the fond theme of fame's applauding tongue,
'T is said thou hast the stings of fortune felt;
And such can learn from others' woes to melt.
I had a daughter—once my only care!
As virtuous as thy consort, and as fair:
But her (sad cause of folly to repent)
To Syria with a num'rous train I sent;
And there the tale, the treach'rous toil was spread,
And there Constantia, there, my child, you bled!
Around the maid her brave attendants fell,
Nor one was left the fatal tale to tell:
Hence age through grief has doubly known decay,
And care untimely turn'd my locks to grey.
This day selected from the circling year,
To her I consecrate the annual tear;
And these the chiefs, who, in her quarrel crown'd,
Have late in vengeance bath'd the hostile ground.
But vain is vengeance where all hope is fled;
Nor hosts of victims can revive the dead!

---

Som men wold sayn, how that the child Maurice
Doth this message until this emperour;
But as I gesse, Alla was no so nice,
To him that is so soveraine of honour,
As he that is of Cristen folk the flour,
Send any child, but it is bet to deme
He went himself, and so it may well seme.

This emperour hath granted gentilly
To come to dinner, as he him besoughte;
And wel rede I, he loked besily
Upon this child, and on his doughter thought.
Alla goth to his inne, and as him ought
Arraied for this feste in every wise,
As ferforth as his conning may suffice.

The morwe came, and Alla gan him dresse,
And eke his wif, this emperour to mete:
And forth they ride in joye and in gladnesse,
And whan she saw hire fader in the strete,
She light adoun and falleth him to fete.
" Father," quod she, " your yonge child Custance
Is now ful clene out of your remembrance.

My child! thou 'st robb'd my life of all delight—
But death shall soon our happier souls unite !"
Nor yet he ended,—when, with troubled mien,
Quick at his knees low bow'd Britannia's queen:
" Not so, not so, my father !" loud she cry'd—
" See here thy child, thy daughter at thy side !
Why look you thus with wild and piercing eye ?
Your daughter here, your daughter you descry !
Constantia, who through many a death survives,
And yet to see her king and sire, arrives."
"Yes, yes, you are my child,—these accents tell !"—
He could no more, but on her neck he fell.
Down her soft cheek his mingling tears o'erflow;
Joy, joy too great, assum'd the form of woe !
The roof, surprise and echoing transport tore;
And eyes then wept, that never wept before.

Wing'd as an arrow from some vig'rous arm,
Through Rome's wide city flew the glad alarm—
" Constantia's here,—she lives !—she lives !"—they
    cry'd;
" Constantia, now the British hero's bride !"
Around the palace pour'd in wild delight,
On thousands gath'ring thousands straight unite:
With ceaseless clamours and extended hands,
Constantia's presence ev'ry voice demands;
Constantia, Alla, and their lovely boy
They claim, the blooming pledge of future joy !
Forth straight they come conspicuous to the view,
And greet with graceful mien th' applauding crew:
In shouts to Heav'n their exultations fly,
And universal joy torments the sky.

---

" I am your doughter, your Custance." quod she,
" That whilom ye han sent into Surrie :
It am I, fader, that in the salte see
Was put alone, and dampned for to die.
Now, goode fader, I you mercy crie,
Send me no more into non hethenesse,
But thanketh my lord here of his kindenesse."

Who can the pitous joye tellen all
Betwix hem thre, sin they ben thus ymette?
But of my tale make an ende I shal,
The day goth fast, I wol no longer lette.
Thise glade folk to dinner ben ysette,
In joye and blisse at mete I let hem dwell,
A thousand fold wel more than I can tell.

This child Maurice was sithen emperour,
Made by the pope, and lived cristenly,
To Cristes chirche did he gret honour:
But I let all his storie passen by,
Of Custance is my tale specially,
In the olde Romane gestes men may find
Maurices lif, I bere it not in mind.

This king Alla, whan he his time sey,
With his Custance, his holy wif so swete,
To Englond ben they come the righte wey,
Ther as they live in joye and in quiete.
But litel while it lasteth I you hete,
Joye of this world for time wold not abide,
Fro day to night it changeth as the tide.

Who lived ever in swiche delite o day,
That him ne meved other conscience,
Or ire, or talent, or som kin affray,
Envie, or pride, or passion, or offence ?
I ne say but for this end this sentence,
That litel while in joye or in plesance
Lasteth the bliss of Alla with Custance.

# *FABLES.*

## THE TEMPLE OF HYMEN.

As on my conch supine I lay,
Like others, dreaming life away;
Methought, expanded to my sight,
A temple rear'd its stately height.
All ready built, without omitting
One ornament, for temples fitting.
    Large look'd the pile, sublime and fair;
But " Who the godhead worship'd there?"
This to inquire, appearing meet,
Imagination lent me feet,
And thither, without further cavil,
I fairly undertook to travel.
    At once, in bright procession spied,
The female world was at my side,
Mingled, like many-colour'd patterns,
Nymphs, mesdames, trollops, belles, and slatterns,
From point, and saucy ermine, down
To the plain coif, and russet gown;
All, by inquiry as I found,
On one important errand bound.
    Their van, to either tropic spread,
Forerunning Expectation led;
Pleasure the female-standard bore,
And Youth danc'd lightly on before;
While Prudence, Judgment, Sense, and Taste,
The few directing virtues, plac'd
To form and guide a woman's mind,
Discarded, sigh'd and slunk behind.
    At length, in jubilee, arriving,
Where dwelt the jolly god of wiveing,
All press'd promiscuously to enter,
Nor once reflected on the venture.
But here, the Muse, affecting state,
Beckon'd her clamorous sex to wait,
Lest such a rendezvous should hinder
To say what pass'd, the while, within door.
    Against the portal, full in sight,
His sable vesture starr'd like night,

---

For deth, that taketh of hie and low his rente,
Whan passed was a year, even as I gesse,
Out of this world this king Alla he hente,
For whom Custance hath ful gret hevinesse.
Now let us praien God his soule blesse:
And dame Custance finally to say,
Toward the toun of Rome goth hire way.

To Rome is come this holy creature,
And findeth ther hire frendes hole and sound:
Now is she scaped all hire aventure:
And whan that she hire fader hath yfound,
Doun on hire knees falleth she to ground,
Weping for tendernesse in herte blithe
She herieth God an hundred thousand sithe.

In vertue and in holy almesse dede
They liven alle, and never asonder wende;
Till deth departeth hem, this lif they lede:
And fareth now wel, my tale is at an ende.
Now Jesu Crist, that of his might may sende
Joye after wo, governe us in his grace,
And kepe us all that ben in this place.

High thron'd upon an ebon seat,
Beneath a canopy of state,
That o'er his dusky temples nodded,
Was fix'd the matrimonial godhead.
    Low at his feet, in pomp display'd,
The world's collected wealth was laid;
Where bags of mammon, pil'd around,
And chests on chests, o'erwhelm'd the ground,
With bills, bonds, parchments, the appointers
Of doweries, settlements, and jointures;
From whence, in just proportion weigh'd,
And down, by special tail, convey'd,
The future progenies inherit
Taste, beauty, virtue, sense, and merit.
    Whatever titles here may suit us
For this same god, Hymen, or Plutus,
Who, from his trade of a gold-finder,
Might now become a marriage-binder,
And, haply, use that precious metal
To solder sexes, like a kettle;
No earthly god, in my opinion,
Claim'd such an absolute dominion.
    To prove his right to adoration
Through ev'ry age, and ev'ry nation,
Around the spacious dome, display'd
By many a fabled light and shade,
Was emblematically told
The great omnipotence of gold.
    And first, in yonder panel seen,
A lad, call'd Paris, stroll'd the green,
Poor, hungry, witless, and dejected,
By country, and by kin, neglected;
Till Fortune, as she cross'd the plain,
Conceiv'd a crotchet in her brain,
And, laughing at the bashful blockhead,
Took a huge pippin from her pocket,
Of the true glittering tempting kind,
And gold throughout from core to rind;
This, in a whim, the dame bestow'd,
Then, smiling, turn'd, and went her road.
    The neighbours, now, when Fame had shown them
The youth had got the summum bonum,
From many a hut and hamlet crowd,
And, duly, at his levee bow'd.
His reputation spreads apace—
O, such a shape, and such a face!
His mouth he opens, and they swear
The Delphic oracle is there.
    Now, see the king of Troy aspire
To be the wealthy shepherd's sire.
For him, the brightest nymphs contended;
To him, three goddesses descended,
And show'd, in fair and open day,
Where honour, wit, and beauty lay,
O'er which, our poem, to conceal
From vulgar optics, drops a veil.
    In the next panel, you discover
Olympic Jove, that thundering lover,
Who, charm'd with old Acrisius' daughter,
In many a shape had vainly sought her,
And run the round of all his tricks,
Yet still was doubtful where to fix;
Till, by some wiser head inclin'd,
To cast his blustring bolt behind,
His duller light'ning to withhold,
And wear the brighter form of gold,
He took the hint, he storm'd the tow'r,
And drop'd in yon omnific show'r.
    In the next board, the tale so common is,
'Twixt Atalanta and Hippomenes,

I shall but slightly stop a minute,
To drop one observation in it;
Remarking, that howe'er prefer'd to
Their sex, for many a course in virtue,
The bright allurement, well applied,
May tempt good nymphs to turn aside.
  Next, Lybia's golden orchard grew
Blooming temptation to the view,
In which a dragon, call'd the Law,
Kept conscientious fools in awe:
Yet Power, superior to the crime,
And tall Ambition, skill'd to climb,
With traitors of a new invention,
Who sell their country for a pension,
Through many a thicket won their way,
And spoil'd the grove, and shar'd the prey.
  On the same golden system laid,
The world was in the fifth display'd:
The Earth a golden axis turn'd;
The Heavens, with golden planets, burn'd;
And thence, as astrologians know,
Deriv'd their influence below:
A girdle, call'd the zodiac, grac'd
The glittering round of Nature's waste,
Whose mystic charm from gold arises,
For this the Cæstus of the skies is:
And as in Homer's works, we read
(And Homer is the poet's creed)
Of a well twisted golden tether,
That tied the Heavens and Earth together,
Such was the cord, or such the cable,
That tied the spheres within this table;
By which, the artist, underhand,
Would give the wise to understand,
That interest, in ev'ry creature,
Throughout religion, law, and nature,
From east to west, and pole to pole,
Moves, binds, suspends, and turns the whole.
  While thus, in passing slightly o'er, I
Survey'd the scenes of ancient story;
Or ey'd, with more minute attention,
What prudence, here, forbids to mention;
The Muse my shoulder tapp'd, to mind me
Of things that pass'd, the while, behind me.
  I turn'd and view'd, with deep surprise,
The phantom that assail'd my eyes:
His hinder-head disrob'd of hair,
His sapless back and shoulders bare,
Confess'd the wrinkles of a sage
Who past ten Nestors in his age;
But cloth'd before with decent grace,
And infant sweetness in his face,
Not Smintheus with such vigour strung,
Nor blooming Hebe look'd so young.
  On his left hand a palette lay,
With many a teint of colours gay;
While, guided with an easy slight,
The flying pencil grac'd his right.
  Unnumber'd canvasses appear'd,
Before the moving artist rear'd,
On whose inspirited expanse he
Express'd the creatures of his fancy;
So touch'd, with such a swift command,
With such a magic pow'r of hand,
That Nature did, herself, appear
Less real than her semblance here,
And, not a mortal, so betray'd,
Could know the substance from the shade!
  Whate'er the world conceives, in life,
Worth toil, anxiety, and strife;

Whate'er by ignorance is bought,
By madness wish'd or folly sought,
The mitres, coronets, and garters,
To which Ambition leads his martyrs;
With ev'ry joy and toy, that can
Amuse the various child of man,
Was painted here in many a scene,
A trifling, transient, charming train!
  Awhile I stood, in thought suspended,
To guess what these affairs intended;
When, lo, the Muse, in whispers, told,
" 'T is father Time whom you behold;
In part discover'd to the wise,
In part conceal'd from human eyes.
A slave to yon gold-giving pow'r,
For him he spends each restless hour;
The product of his toil intends
As gifts to those his god befriends,
And paints what other mortals view
As substances, though shades to you."
  She ceas'd, and, turning to the sentry,
Desir'd he 'd give the ladies entry;
And straight the portal open'd wide,
And in they delug'd like a tide.
So, to some grove, by stress of weather,
Fast flock the fowl of ev'ry feather;
A mighty, pretty, prating rabble,
Like Iris rigg'd, and tongued like Babel;
Then crowding toward the nuptial throne,
By bags of strong attraction known,
Low bending to their god they bow'd,
And vented thus their pray'r aloud:
  " Great power! in whom our sex confides,
Who rul'st the turns of female tides,
Who kenst, while varying fancy ranges
Through all its doubles, twirls, and changes,
To what a woman's heart is prone,
A secret to ourselves unknown—
O, give us, give us, mighty pow'r!
The wedded joy of ev'ry hour:
Assign thy favourites, in marriage,
To coaches of distinguish'd carriage;
To all the frippery of dressing;
A nameless, boundless, endless blessing;
To drums, ridottos, sights, and sounds;
To visits in eternal rounds;
To card and counter, rake and rattle;
To the whole lust of tongue and tattle;
And all the dear delightful trances
Of countless frolics, fits, and fancies.
You have heard, that men, unpolish'd boors!
Lay naughty passions at our doors;
'T is your's to contradict the liar,
Who are, yourself, our chief desire.
O then, as widow, or as wife,
To you we yield each choice in life;
Or would you ev'ry pray'r fulfil,
Wed us! O! wed us, to our will!"
  They ceas'd, and, without more addition,
The god confirm'd their full petition:
To Time he beckon'd, and desir'd
He 'd give the good each nymph requir'd;
And, from his visionary treasure,
Wed ev'ry woman to her pleasure.
  The first, who came, resolv'd to fix
Upon a gilded coach and six;
The suit was granted her on sight,
The nymph with ardour seiz'd her right.
A wonder! by possession banish'd,
The coach and dappled coursers vanish'd;

And a foul waggon held the fair
Full laden with a weight of care .
She sigh'd ; her sisters caught the sound,
And one insulting laugh went round.

The second was a dame of Britain,
Who by a coronet was smitten ;
With boldness she advanc'd her claim,
Exulting in so just a flame.
But ah, where bliss alone was patent,
What unsuspected mischief latent !
The worst in all Pandora's box,
Her coronet contain'd a —.

With this example in her eye,
The third, a widow'd dame, drew nigh,
And fix'd her sight and soul together
Upon a raking hat and feather ;
Nor sigh'd in vain, but seiz'd her due,
And clasp'd old age in twenty-two.

Thus, through the difference and degrees
Of sword-knots, mitres, and toupees,
Prim bands, pert bobs, and well-hung blades,
Long robes, smart jackets, fierce cockades,
And all the fooleries in fashion,
Whate'er became the darling passion,
The good for which they did importune,
Was straight revers'd into misfortune ;
And ev'ry woman, like the first,
Was, at her own entreaty, curst.

At length, was introduc'd a fair,
With such a face, and such an air,
As never was, on Earth, I ween,
Save by poetic organs, seen.

With decent grace and gentle cheer,
The bright adventurer drew near ;
Her mild approach the godhead spied,
And, " Fairest," with a smile, he cried,
" If aught you seek in Hymen's pow'r,
You find him in a happy hour."

At this, the virgin, half amaz'd,
As round the spacious dome she gaz'd,
With caution ev'ry symbol ey'd,
And, blushing, gracefully replied.

" If you are he, whose pow'r controls
And knits the sympathy of souls,
Then, whence this pomp of worthless geer,
And why this heap of counters here ?
Is this vain show of glittering ore,
The bliss that Hymen has in store ?
Love sees the folly with the gloss,
And laughs to scorn thy useless dross.

" Where are the symbols of thy reign ?
And where thy robe of Tyrian grain,
Whose teint, in virgin-colours dy'd,
Derives its blushing from the bride ?
Where is thy torch, serenely bright,
To lovers yielding warmth and light,
That from the heart derives its fire,
And only can, with life, expire ?

" Will this unactive mass impart
The social feelings of the heart ?
Or can material fetters bind
The free affections of the mind ?
Through ev'ry age, the great and wise,
Behold thee with superior eyes ;
Love spurns thy treasures with disdain,
And Virtue flies thy hostile reign.

" By love, congenial souls embrace,
Celestial source of human race !
From whence, the cordial sense within,
The bosom'd amities of kin,

The call of Nature to her kind,
And all the tunings of the mind,
That, winding Heaven's harmonious plan,
Compose the brotherhood of man."

She said, and gracefully withdrew ;
Her steps the Muse and I pursue.
Along an unfrequented way
The virgin led, nor led astray ;
Till, like the first, in form and size,
A second fabric struck our eyes :
We enter'd, guided by the fair,
And saw a second Hymen there.

A silken robe of saffron hue
About his decent shoulders flew ;
While a fair taper's virgin light
Gave Ovid to his soul and sight.

An hundred Cupids wanton'd round,
Whose useless quivers strow'd the ground ;
While, careless of their wonted trade,
They with the smiling Graces play'd.

Along the wall's extended side,
With teints of varying nature dy'd,
In needled tapestry, was told
The tale of many a love of old.

In groves, that breath'd a citron air,
Together walk'd the wedded pair ;
Or toy'd upon the vernal ground,
Their beauteous offspring sporting round ;
Or, lock'd in sweet embracement, lay,
And slept and lov'd the night away.

There sat Penelope in tears,
Besieg'd, like Troy, for ten long years :
Her suitors, in a neighbouring room,
Wait the long promise of the loom,
Which she defers from day to day,
Till death determin'd to delay.
With thoughts of fond remembrance wrung,
Deep sorrowing, o'er her work she hung ;
Where, in the fields, at Ilium fought,
The labours of her lord she wrought,
The toil, the dust, the flying foe,
The rallied host, the instant blow ;
Then, sighing, trembled at the view,
Scar'd at the dangers which she drew.

There too, suspended o'er the wave,
Alcione was seen to rave,
When, as the foundering wreck she spied,
She on her sinking Ceÿx cried :
Her Ceÿx, though by seas oppress'd,
Still bears her image in his breast ;
And, with his fondest latest breath,
Murmurs, " Alcione !" in death.

Panthea there, upon a bier,
Lay'd the sole lord of her desire :
His limbs were scatter'd through the plains ;
She join'd, and kiss'd, the dear remains.
Too pond'rous was her weight of woe,
For sighs to rise, or tears to flow ;
On the lov'd corse she fix'd her view,
Nor other use of seeing knew ;
While high and stedfast as she gaz'd,
Her snowy arm a poniard rais'd,
Nor yet the desperate weapon stay'd,
But, for a longer look, delay'd,
Till, plunged within her beauteous breast,
She on his bosom sunk to rest.

But, O, beyond whate'er was told
In modern tales, or truths of old,
One pair, in form and spirit twin'd,
Out-lov'd the loves of human kind ;

She Hero, he Leander, nam'd,
For mutual faith, as beauty, fam'd !
Their story, from its source, begun,
And, to the fatal period, ruh.
    While, bow'd at Cytherea's shrine,
The youth adores her pow'r divine,
He sees her blooming priestess there,
Beyond the sea-born goddess, fair :
She, as some god, the stripling eyes,
Just lighted from his native skies—
The god, whose chariot guides the hour ;
Or, haply, love's immortal pow'r.
    At once, their conscious glances spoke,
Like fate, the strong and mutual stroke ;
Attracted by a secret force,
Like currents meeting in their course,
That, thence, one stream for ever rolls,
Together rush'd their mingling souls,
Too close for fortune to divide,
For each was lost in either tide.
    In vain, by ruthless parents torn,
Their bodies are asunder borne,
And tow'ring bulwarks intervene,
And envious ocean rolls between ;
Love wings their letters o'er the sea,
And kisses melt the seals away.
    And now the sable night impends,
Leander to the shore descends,
Exults at the appointed hour,
And marks the signal on the tow'r—
A torch, to guide the lover's way,
Endear'd beyond the brightest day !
    At once, he plunges in the tide ;
His arms the Hellespont divide ;
The danger and the toil he braves,
And dashes the contending waves.
    While near, and nearer to his sight,
The taper darts a ruddier light,
Recruited at the view, he glows ;
Aside the whelming billow throws :
The winds and seas oppose in vain ;
He spurns, he mounts, he skims the main.
    Now, from the tow'r, where Hero stood,
And threw a radiance o'er the flood,
Leander, in the deep, she spied,
And would have sprung to join his side ;
Howe'er, her wishes make essay,
And clasp and warm him on his way.
    The main is cross'd, the shore is gain'd,
The long wish'd hour, at last, attain'd.
But lovers, if there e'er arose
A pair, so form'd and fond as those,
So lov'd, so beauteous, and so bless'd,
Alone can speak or think the rest ;
Nor will the weeping Muse unfold
The close, too tragic to be told !
    Long were the loving list to name,
With Portia's faith, that swallow'd flame :
But much the longer list were those
Whose joys were unallay'd by woes ;
Whose bliss no cruel parents cross'd,
Whose love not ages could exhaust,
Where not a cloud did intervene,
Or once o'ercast their bright serene,
But, through the summer's day of life,
The husband tender as the wife,
Like Henry and his nut-brown maid,
Their faith nor shaken nor decay'd,
Together ran the blissful race,
Together liv'd, and slept in peace.

Long time the much inquiring maid,
From story on to story stray'd ;
Joy'd in the joys that lovers know,
Or wept her tribute to their woe ;
Till Hymen, with a placid air,
Approaching, thus address'd the fair.
    " Hail to the Nymph, whose sacred train
Of virtues shall restore my reign !
Whate'er the wishes of thy soul,
But speak them, and possess the whole."
    " Thanks, gentle pow'r," the maid replied ;
" Your bounty shall be amply tried.
I seek not titles, rank, or state,
Superfluous to the truly great ;
Nor yet, to sordid wealth inclin'd,
The poorest passion of the mind ;
But, simply fix'd to Nature's plan,
I seek the associate in the man.
    " Yet, O beware ! for much depends
On what that syllable intends.
    " Give him a form that may delight
My inward sense, my mental sight ;
In ev'ry outward act, design'd
To speak an elegance of mind.
    " In him, by science, travel, taste,
Be nature polish'd, not defac'd ;
And set, as is the brilliant stone,
To be, with double lustre, shown.
    " Sweet be the music of his tongue,
And, as the lyre of David, strung,
To steal, from each delighted day,
Affliction, care, and time, away.
    " Within his comprehensive soul
Let Heaven's harmonious system roll ;
There let the great, the good, the wise,
Of fam'd antiquity arise,
From ev'ry age and ev'ry clime,
Eluding death, and circling time !
There let the sacred virtues meet,
And range their known and native seat !
There let the charities unite,
And human feelings weep delight !"
    " Kind power ! if such a youth you know,
He 's all the Heav'n I ask, below."
    So wish'd the much-aspiring maid ;
Pale turn'd the power, and, sighing, said :
    " Alas ! like him you fondly claim,
Through ev'ry boasted form and name,
That graces Nature's varying round,
A second is not to be found !
Your suit, fair creature, must miscarry,
Till CHARLEMONT resolves to marry."

THE SPARROW AND THE DOVE.

IT was, as learn'd traditions say,
Upon an April's blithsome day,
When Pleasure, ever on the wing,
Return'd companion of the Spring,
And cheer'd the birds with amorous heat,
Instructing little hearts to beat ;
A Sparrow, frolic, gay, and young,
Of bold address and flippant tongue,
Just left his lady of a night,
Like him, to follow new delight.
    The youth, of many a conquest vain,
Flew off to seek the chirping train ;
The chirping train he quickly found,
And with a saucy ease bow'd round,

For ev'ry she his bosom burns,
And this, and that, he wooes by turns;
And here a sigh, and there a bill,
And here—" those eyes, so form'd to kill!"
And now, with ready tongue, he strings
Unmeaning, soft, resistless things;
With vows and demmes skill'd to woo,
As other pretty fellows do.
Not that he thought this short essay
A prologue needful to his play;
No, trust me, says our learned letter,
He knew the virtuous sex much better:
But these he held as specious arts,
To show his own superior parts;
The form of decency to shield,
And give a just pretence to yield.

Thus finishing his courtly play,
He mark'd the favourite of a day;
With careless impudence drew near,
And whisper'd Hebrew in her ear;
A hint, which, like the mason's sign,
The conscious can alone define.

The fluttering nymph, expert at feigning,
Cried, " Sir—pray, sir, explain your meaning—
Go, prate to those that may endure ye—
To me this rudeness!—I 'll assure ye!"——
Then off she glided, like a swallow,
As saying—you guess where to follow.

To such as know the party set,
'T is needless to declare they met;
The parson's barn, as authors mention,
Confess'd the fair had apprehension.
Her honour there secure from stain,
She held all further trifling vain,
No more affected to be coy,
But rush'd licentious on the joy.

" Hist, love!"—the male companion cried;
" Retire a while, I fear we 're spy'd."
Nor was the caution vain; he saw
A turtle rustling in the straw,
While o'er her callow brood she hung,
And fondly thus address'd her young.

" Ye tender objects of my care!
Peace, peace, ye little helpless pair!
Anon he comes, your gentle sire,
And brings you all your hearts require.
For us, his infants, and his bride,
For us, with only love to guide,
Our lord assumes an eagle's speed,
And like a lion dares to bleed.
Nor yet by wintry skies confin'd,
He mounts upon the rudest wind;
From danger tears the vital spoil,
And with affection sweetens toil.
Ah cease, too venturous! cease to dare;
In thine, our dearer safety spare!
From him, ye cruel falcons, stray;
And turn, ye fowlers, far away!

" Should I survive to see the day,
That tears me from myself away,
That cancels all that Heav'n could give,
The life by which alone I live;
Alas, how more than lost were I,
Who, in the thought, already die!"

Ye powers, whom men and birds obey,
Great rulers of your creatures, say,
Why mourning comes, by bliss convey'd,
And e'en the sweets of love allay'd?
Where grows enjoyment, tall and fair,
Around it twines entangling care;

While fear for what our souls possess,
Enervates ev'ry pow'r to bless:
Yet friendship forms the bliss above;
And, life! what art thou, without love?

Our hero, who had heard apart,
Felt something moving in his heart;
But quickly, with disdain, suppress'd
The virtue rising in his breast:
And first he feign'd to laugh aloud;
And next, approaching, smil'd and bow'd.

" Madam, you must not think me rude;
Good manners never can intrude.
I vow I come through pure good nature—
Upon my soul, a charming creature!—
Are these the comforts of a wife?
This careful, cloister'd, moaping life?
No doubt, that odious thing, call'd duty,
Is a sweet province for a beauty.
Thou pretty ignorance! thy will
Is measur'd to thy want of skill;
That good old-fashion'd dame, thy mother,
Has taught thy infant years no other—
The greatest ill in the creation,
Is sure the want of education!

" But think ye?—tell me without feigning,
Have all these charms no further meaning?
Dame Nature, if you do n't forget her,
Might teach your ladyship much better.
For shame, reject this mean employment;
Enter the world, and taste enjoyment,
Where time, by circling bliss, we measure;
Beauty was form'd alone for pleasure!
Come, prove the blessing, follow me;
Be wise, be happy, and be free."

" Kind sir," reply'd our matron chaste,
" Your zeal seems pretty much in haste.
I own, the fondness to be bless'd,
Is a deep thirst in ev'ry breast:
Of blessings too I have my store;
Yet quarrel not, should Heav'n give more.
Then prove the change to be expedient,
And think me, sir, your most obedient."

Here turning, as to one inferior,
Our gallant spoke, and smil'd superior.
" Methinks, to quit your boasted station,
Requires a world of hesitation!
Where brats and bonds are held a blessing,
The case, I doubt, is past redressing.
Why, child, suppose the joys I mention
Were the mere fruits of my invention,
You 've cause sufficient for your carriage,
In flying from the curse of marriage;
That sly decoy, with vary'd snares,
That takes your widgeons in by pairs;
Alike to husband, and to wife,
The cure of love, and bane of life;
The only method of forecasting,
To make misfortune firm and lasting;
The sin, by Heaven's peculiar sentence,
Unpardon'd, through a life's repentance:
It is the double snake, that weds
A common tail to diff'rent heads,
That lead the carcass still astray,
By dragging each a diff'rent way.
Of all the ills that may attend me,
From marriage, mighty gods, defend me!

" Give me frank Nature's wild demesne,
And boundless tract of air serene,
Where Fancy, ever wing'd for change,
Delights to sport, delights to range.

There, Liberty! to thee is owing
Whate'er of bliss is worth bestowing:
Delights, still vary'd, and divine,
Sweet goddess of the hills! are thine.
    " What say you now, you pretty pink you?
Have I for once spoke reason, think you?
You take me now for no romancer—
Come, never study for an answer;
Away, cast ev'ry care behind ye,
And fly where joy alone shall find ye."
    " Soft yet," return'd our female fencer,
" A question more, or so—and then, sir.
You have rally'd me with sense exceeding,
With much fine wit, and better breeding:
But pray, sir, how do you contrive it?
Do those of your world never wive it?"
" No, no."—" How then?"—" Why dare I tell?—
What does the business full as well."
" Do you ne'er love?"—" An hour at leisure."
" Have you no friendships?"—" Yes, for pleasure."
" No care for little ones?"—" We get them;
The rest the mothers mind, and let them."
    " Thou wretch," rejoin'd the kindling Dove,
" Quite lost to life, as lost to love!
Whene'er misfortune come, how just!
And come misfortune surely must;
In the dread season of dismay,
In that your hour of trial, say,
Who then shall prop your sinking heart;
Who bear affliction's weightier part?
    " Say, when the black-brow'd welkin bends,
And winter's gloomy form impends,
To mourning turns all transient cheer,
And blasts the melancholy year;
For times, at no persuasion, stay,
Nor vice can find perpetual May;
Then where 's that tongue, by folly fed?
That soul of pertness, whither fled?
All shrunk within thy lonely nest,
Forlorn, abandon'd, and unbless'd!
No friends, by cordial bonds ally'd,
Shall seek thy cold unsocial side;
No chirping prattlers, to delight
Shall turn the long-enduring night;
No bride her words of balm impart,
And warm thee at her constant heart.
    " Freedom, restrain'd by reason's force,
Is as the Sun's unvarying course,
Benignly active, sweetly bright,
Affording warmth, affording light;
But torn from virtue's sacred rules,
Becomes a comet, gaz'd by fools,
Foreboding cares, and storms, and strife,
And fraught with all the plagues of life.
    " Thou fool! by union, every creature
Subsists through universal nature;
And this, to beings void of mind,
Is wedlock of a meaner kind.
    " While womb'd in space, primeval clay
A yet unfashion'd embryo lay,
The Source of Endless Good above
Shot down his spark of kindling love:
Touch'd by th' all-enlivening flame,
Then motion first exulting came;
Each atom sought its sep'rate class,
Through many a fair enamour'd mass;
Love cast the central charm around,
And with eternal nuptials bound.
Then form and order, o'er the sky,
First train'd their bridal pomp on high;

The Sun display'd his orb to sight,
And burnt with hymeneal light.
    " Hence Nature's virgin-womb conceiv'd,
And with the genial burden heav'd:
Forth came the oak, her first-born heir,
And scal'd the breathing steep of air;
Then infant stems, of various use,
Imbib'd her soft maternal juice;
The flowers, in early bloom disclos'd,
Upon her fragrant breast repos'd;
Within her warm embraces grew,
A race of endless form and hue;
Then pour'd her lesser offspring round,
And fondly cloth'd their parent ground.
    " Nor here alone the virtue reign'd,
By matter's cumb'ring form detain'd;
But thence, subliming, and refin'd,
Aspir'd, and reach'd its kindred mind:
Caught in the fond, celestial fire,
The mind perceiv'd unknown desire;
And now with kind effusion flow'd,
And now with cordial ardours glow'd;
Beheld the sympathetic fair,
And lov'd its own resemblance there;
On all with circling radiance shone,
But, cent'ring, fix'd on one alone;
There clasp'd the heaven-appointed wife,
And doubled ev'ry joy of life.
    " Here ever blessing, ever bless'd,
Resides this beauty of the breast;
As from his palace, here the god
Still beams effulgent bliss abroad.
Here gems his own eternal round,
The ring by which the world is bound;
Here bids his seat of empire grow,
And builds his little Heav'n below.
    " The bridal partners thus ally'd,
And thus in sweet accordance tied,
One body, heart, and spirit live,
Enrich'd by ev'ry joy they give;
Like Echo, from her vocal hold,
Return'd in music twenty fold.
Their union firm, and undecay'd,
Nor time can shake, nor power invade;
But as the stem and scion stand,
Ingrafted by a skilful hand,
They check the tempest's wintry rage,
And bloom and strengthen into age.
A thousand amities unknown,
And powers perceiv'd by love alone,
Endearing looks, and chaste desire,
Fan and support the mutual fire,
Whose flame, perpetual as refin'd,
Is fed by an immortal mind.
    " Nor yet the nuptial sanction ends;
Like Nile it opens, and descends,
Which, by apparent windings led,
We trace to its celestial head:
The sire, first springing from above,
Becomes the source of life and love,
And gives his filial heir to flow,
In fondness down on sons below.
Thus roll'd in one continu'd tide,
To time's extremest verge they glide;
While kindred streams, on either hand,
Branch forth in blessings o'er the land.
    " Thee, wretch! no lisping babe shall name,
No late-returning brother claim,
No kinsman on thy road rejoice,
No sister greet thy ent'ring voice,

With partial eyes no parents see,
And bless their years restor'd in thee.
"  In age rejected, or declin'd,
An alien e'en among thy kind,
The partner of thy scorn'd embrace
Shall play the wanton in thy face;
Each spark unplume thy little pride,
All friendship fly thy faithless side;
Thy name shall like thy carcass rot,
In sickness spurn'd, in death forgot.
"  All giving Pow'r! great Source of Life!
O hear the parent! hear the wife!
That life thou lendest from above,
Though little, make it large in love;
O bid my feeling heart expand
To ev'ry claim, on ev'ry hand;
To those from whom my days I drew,
To these in whom those days renew;
To all my kin, however wide,
In cordial warmth, as blood ally'd;
To friends, with steelly fetters twin'd,
And to the cruel not unkind!
"  But chief, the lord of my desire,
My life, myself, my soul, my sire,
Friends, children, all that wish can claim,
Chaste passion clasp, and rapture name;
O spare him, spare him, gracious Power!
O give him to my latest hour!
Let me my length of life employ,
To give my sole enjoyment joy;
His love, let mutual love excite;
Turn all my cares to his delight;
And ev'ry needless blessing spare,
Wherein my darling wants a share.
When he with graceful action wooes,
And sweetly bills, and fondly cooes,
Ah! deck me, to his eyes alone,
With charms attractive as his own;
And in my circling wings caress'd,
Give all the lover to my breast.
Then in our chaste, connubial bed,
My bosom pillow'd for his head,
His eyes with blissful slumbers close,
And watch, with me, my lord's repose;
Your peace around his temples twine,
And love him, with a love like mine.
"  And, for I know his gen'rous flame,
Beyond whate'er my sex can claim,
Me too to your protection take,
And spare me for my husband's sake.
Let one unruffled calm delight
The loving, and belov'd unite;
One pure desire our bosoms warm,
One will direct, one wish inform;
Through life, one mutual aid sustain,
In death, one peaceful grave contain!"
While, swelling with the darling theme,
Her accents pour'd an endless stream,
The well-known wings a sound impart,
That reach'd her ear, and touch'd her heart;
Quick dropp'd the music of her tongue,
And forth, with eager joy, she sprung;
As swift her en'tring consort flew,
And plum'd and kindled at the view;
Their wings their souls embracing meet,
Their hearts with answering measure beat,
Half lost in sacred sweets, and bless'd
With raptures felt, but ne'er express'd.
Straight to her humble roof she led
The partner of her spotless bed:

Her young, a flutt'ring pair, arise,
Their welcome sparkling in their eyes;
Transported, to their sire they bound,
And hang with speechless action round.
In pleasure wrapt, the parents stand,
And see their little wings expand;
The sire, his life-sustaining prize
To each expecting bill applies,
There fondly pours the wheaten spoil,
With transport given, though won with toil;
While, all collected at the sight,
And silent through supreme delight,
The fair high Heaven of bliss beguiles,
And on her lord and infants smiles.
The Sparrow, whose attention hung
Upon the Dove's enchanting tongue,
Of all his little slights disarm'd,
And from himself, by virtue charm'd,
When now he saw, what only seem'd
A fact, so late a fable deem'd,
His soul to envy he resign'd,
His hours of folly to the wind;
In secret wish'd a turtle too,
And sighing to himself withdrew.

---

## THE FEMALE SEDUCERS.

'T is said of widow, maid, and wife,
That honour is a woman's life;
Unhappy sex! who only claim
A being in the breath of fame,
Which tainted, not the quick'ning gales
That sweep Sabæa's spicy vales,
Nor all the healing sweets restore,
That breathe along Arabia's shore.
The traveller, if he chance to stray,
May turn uncensur'd to his way;
Polluted streams again are pure,
And deepest wounds admit a cure:
But woman no redemption knows;
The wounds of honour never close!
Though distant ev'ry hand to guide,
Nor skill'd on life's tempestuous tide,
If once her feeble bark recede,
Or deviate from the course decreed,
In vain she seeks the friendless shore—
Her swifter folly flies before;
The circling ports against her close,
And shut the wanderer from repose;
Till, by conflicting waves oppress'd,
Her found'ring pinnace sinks to rest.
"  Are there no offerings to atone,
For but a single errour?"—None.
Though woman is avow'd, of old,
No daughter of celestial mould,
Her temp'ring not without allay,
And form'd but of the finer clay,
We challenge from the mortal dame
The strength angelic natures claim;
Nay more; for sacred stories tell,
That e'en immortal angels fell.
"  Whate'er fills the teeming sphere
Of humid earth, and ambient air,
With varying elements endu'd,
Was form'd to fall, and rise renew'd.
"  The stars no fix'd duration know;
Wide oceans ebb, again to flow;
The Moon repletes her waining face,
All-beauteous, from her late disgrace;

And suns, that mourn approaching night,
Refulgent rise with new-born light.
" In vain may death and time subdue,
While Nature mints her race anew,
And holds some vital spark apart,
Like virtue, hid in ev'ry heart:
'T is hence, reviving warmth is seen
To clothe a naked world in green;
No longer barr'd by winter's cold,
Again the gates of life unfold ;
Again each insect tries his wing,
And lifts fresh pinions on the spring ;
Again, from ev'ry latent root,
The bladed stem and tendril shoot,
Exhaling incense to the skies,
Again to perish, and to rise.
" And must weak woman then disown
The change, to which a world is prone ?
In one meridian brightness shine,
And ne'er like evening suns decline ?
Resolv'd and firm alone ?—Is this
What we demand of woman ?"—Yes.
" But should the spark of vestal fire,
In some unguarded hour expire ;
Or should the nightly thief invade
Hesperia's chaste and sacred shade,
Of all the blooming spoil possess'd,
The dragon, Honour, charm'd to rest ;
Shall virtue's flame no more return ?
No more with virgin splendour burn ?
No more the ravag'd garden blow
With spring's succeeding blossom ?"—No :
Pity may mourn, but not restore ;
And woman falls, to rise no more!
Within this sublunary sphere,
A country lies—no matter where ;
The clime may readily be found,
By all who tread poetic ground.
A stream, call'd Life, across it glides,
And equally the land divides:
And here, of Vice the province lies ;
And there, the hills of Virtue rise !
Upon a mountain's airy stand,
Whose summit look'd to either land,
An ancient pair their dwelling chose,
As well for prospect as repose ;
For mutual faith they long were fam'd,
And Temperance, and Religion, nam'd.
A numerous progeny divine,
Confess'd the honours of their line :
But in a little daughter fair,
Was center'd more than half their care ;
For Heaven, to gratulate her birth,
Gave signs of future joy to Earth:
White was the robe this infant wore,
And Chastity the name she bore.
As now the maid in stature grew,
A flower just opening to the view !
Oft through her native lawns she stray'd,
And wrestling with the lambkins play'd :
Her looks diffusive sweets bequeath'd,
The breeze grew purer as she breath'd ;
The morn her radiant blush assum'd,
The spring with earlier fragrance bloom'd ;
And Nature yearly took delight,
Like her, to dress the world in white.
But when her rising form was seen
To reach the crisis of fifteen,
Her parents up the mountain's head,
With anxious step, their darling led ;

By turns they snatch'd her to their breast,
And thus the fears of age express'd.
" O joyful cause of many a care !
O daughter, too divinely fair !
Yon world, on this important day,
Demands thee to a daug'rous way ;
A painful journey all must go,
Whose doubtful period none can know ;
Whose due direction who can find,
Where reason 's mute, and sense is blind ?
Ah, what unequal leaders these,
Through such a wide perplexing maze !
Then mark the warnings of the wise,
And learn what love and years advise.
" Far to the right thy prospect bend,
Where yonder tow'ring hills ascend :
Lo, there th' arduous path 's in view,
Which Virtue and her sons pursue ;
With toil o'er less'ning Earth they rise,
And gain, and gain, upon the skies !
Narrow 's the way her children tread ;
No walk for pleasure smoothly spread,
But rough, and difficult, and steep,
Painful to climb, and hard to keep.
" Fruits immature those lands dispense,
A food indelicate to sense,
Of taste unpleasant ; yet from those
Pure health with cheerful vigour flows,
And strength unfeeling of decay,
Throughout the long laborious way.
" Hence, as they scale that heavenly road,
Each limb is lighten'd of its load ;
From Earth refining still they go,
And leave the mortal weight below :
Then spreads the strait, the doubtful clears,
And smooth the rugged path appears ;
For custom turns fatigue to ease,
And, taught by Virtue, pain can please.
" At length, the toilsome journey o'er,
And near the bright celestial shore,
A gulf, black, fearful, and profound,
Appears, of either world the bound,
Through darkness leading up to light :
Sense backwards shrinks, and shuns the sight ;
For there the transitory train,
Of time, and form, and care, and pain,
And matter's gross encumb'ring mass,
Man's late associates, cannot pass,
But sinking, quit th' immortal charge,
And leave the wond'ring soul at large ;
Lightly she wings her obvious way,
And mingles with eternal day.
" Thither, O thither, wing thy speed,
Though pleasure charm, or pain impede !
To such th' all-bounteous Power has given,
For present Earth, a future Heaven ;
For trivial loss, unmeasur'd gain ;
And endless bliss, for transient pain.
" Then fear, ah ! fear to turn thy sight,
Where yonder flow'ry fields invite ;
Wide on the left the path-way bends,
And with pernicious ease descends :
There sweet to sense, and fair to show,
New planted Edens seem to blow,
Trees that delicious poison bear,
For death is vegetable there.
" Hence is the frame of health unbrac'd,
Each sinew slack'ning at the taste ;
The soul to passion yields her throne,
And sees with organs not her own ;

While, like the slumberer in the night,
Pleas'd with the shadowy dream of light,
Before her alienated eyes,
The scenes of fairy land arise;
The puppet world's amusing show,
Dip'd in the gayly colour'd bow,
Sceptres, and wreaths, and glitt'ring things,
The toys of infants, and of kings,
That tempt, along the baneful plain,
The idly wise, and lightly vain;
Till verging on the gulfy shore,
Sudden they sink, 'and rise no more.
   " But list to what thy fates declare;
Though thou art woman, frail as fair,
If once thy sliding foot should stray,
Once quit yon heaven-appointed way,
For thee, lost maid, for thee alone,
Nor prayers shall plead, nor tears atone :
Reproach, scorn, infamy, and hate,
On thy returning steps shall wait;
Thy form be loath'd by ev'ry eye,
And ev'ry foot thy presence fly."
   Thus arm'd with words of potent sound,
Like guardian-angels plac'd around,
A charm by Truth divinely cast,
Forward our young adventurer pass'd:
Forth from her sacred eye-lids sent,
Like morn, forerunning radiance went;
While Honour, hand-maid late assign'd,
Upheld her lucid train behind.
   Awe-struck, the much admiring crowd
Before the virgin vision bow'd,
Gaz'd with an ever new delight,
And caught fresh virtue at the sight :
For not of Earth's unequal frame
They deem the heaven-compounded dame;
If matter, sure the most refin'd,
High wrought, and temper'd into mind !
Some darling daughter of the day,
And body'd by her native ray !
Where'er she passes, thousands bend;
And thousands, where she moves, attend;
Her ways observant eyes confess,
Her steps pursuing praises bless;
While to th' elevated maid
Oblations, as to Heaven, are paid.
   'T was on an ever blithsome day,
The jovial birth of rosy May,
When genial warmth, no more suppress'd,
New melts the frost in ev'ry breast,
The cheek with secret flushing dyes,
And looks kind things from chastest eyes;
The Sun with healthier visage glows,
Aside his clouded 'kerchief throws,
And dances up th' ethereal plain,
Where late he us'd to climb with pain;
While Nature, as from bonds set free,
Springs out, and gives a loose to glee.
   And now, for momentary rest,
The nymph her travell'd step repress'd;
Just turn'd to view the stage attain'd,
And glory'd in the height she 'd gain'd.
   Outstretch'd before her wide survey,
The realms of sweet perdition lay,
And pity touch'd her soul with woe,
To see a world so lost below;
When straight the breeze began to breathe
Airs gently wafted from beneath,
That bore commission'd witchcraft thence,
And reach'd her sympathy of sense;

No sounds of discord, that disclose
A people sunk and lost in woes,
But as of present good possess'd,
The very triumph of the bless'd.
The maid in wrapt attention hung,
While thus approaching Sirens sung.
   " Hither, fairest, hither haste!
Brightest beauty, come and taste
What the powers of bliss unfold,
Joys too mighty to be told !
Taste what ecstasies they give—
Dying raptures taste, and live.
   " In thy lap, disdaining measure,
Nature empties all her treasure;
Soft desires that sweetly languish,
Fierce delights that rise to anguish !
Fairest, dost thou yet delay ?
Brightest beauty, come away !
   " List not, when the froward chide,
Sons of pedantry and pride;
Snarlers, to whose feeble sense
April's sunshine is offence;
Age and envy will advise,
Even against the joy they prize.
   " Come, in pleasure's balmy bowl,
Slake the thirstings of thy soul,
Till thy raptur'd powers are fainting,
With enjoyment past the painting :
Fairest, dost thou yet delay ?
Brightest beauty, come away !"
   So sung the Sirens, as of yore,
Upon the false Ausonian shore;
And O ! for that preventing chain,
That bound Ulysses on the main,
That so our fair-one might withstand
The covert ruin now at hand.
   The song her charm'd attention drew,
When now the tempters stood in view—
Curiosity, with prying eyes,
And hands of busy bold emprise;
Like Hermes feather'd were her feet,
And, like forerunning Fancy, fleet :
By search untaught, by toil untir'd,
To novelty she still aspir'd;
Tasteless of ev'ry good possess'd,
And but in expectation bless'd.
   With her, associate, Pleasure came,
Gay Pleasure, frolic-loving dame;
Her mien all swimming in delight,
Her beauties half reveal'd to sight;
Loos'd flow'd her garments from the ground,
And caught the kissing winds around.
As erst Medusa's looks were known
To turn beholders into stone,
A dire reversion here they felt,
And in the eye of Pleasure melt.
Her glance with sweet persuasion charm'd,
Unnerv'd the strong, the steel'd disarm'd;
No safety e'en the flying find,
Who, venturous, look but once behind.
   Thus was the much-admiring maid,
While distant, more than half betray'd.
With smiles, and adulation bland,
They join'd her side, and seiz'd her hand :
Their touch envenom'd sweets instill'd,
Her frame with new pulsations thrill'd;
While half consenting, half denying,
Reluctant now, and now complying,
Amidst a war of hopes and fears,
Of trembling wishes, smiling tears,

Still down, and down, the winning pair
Compell'd the struggling yielding fair.
　As when some stately vessel, bound
To bless'd Arabia's distant ground,
Borne from her courses, haply lights
Where Barca's flow'ry clime invites,
Conceal'd around whose treach'rous land,
Lurk the dire rock, and dang'rous sand;
The pilot warns, with sail and oar
To shun the much suspected shore—
In vain; the tide, too subtly strong,
Still bears the wrestling bark along;
Till found'ring she resigns to fate,
And sinks o'erwhelm'd with all her freight.
　So, baffling ev'ry bar to sin,
And Heav'n's own pilot plac'd within,
Along the devious smooth descent,
With pow'rs increasing as they went,
The dames, accustom'd to subdue,
As with a rapid current drew;
And o'er the fatal bounds convey'd
The lost, the long reluctant maid.
　Here stop, ye fair-ones, and beware,
Nor send your fond affections there:
Yet, yet your darling, now deplor'd,
May turn, to you and Heav'n restor'd;
Till then, with weeping Honour wait,
The servant of her better fate,
With Honour left upon the shore,
Her friend and handmaid now no more;
Nor, with the guilty world, upbraid
The fortunes of a wretch betray'd,
But o'er her failing cast a veil,
Rememb'ring you yourselves are frail.
　And now, from all-inquiring light,
Fast fled the conscious shades of night;
The damsel, from a short repose,
Confounded at her plight, arose.
　As when, with slumb'rous weight oppress'd,
Some wealthy miser sinks to rest,
Where felons eye the glitt'ring prey,
And steal his hoard of joys away;
He, borne where golden Indus streams,
Of pearl and quarry'd diamond dreams;
Like Midas, turns the glebe to oar,
And stands all wrapt amidst his store;
But wakens, naked, and despoil'd
Of that, for which his years had toil'd.
So far'd the nymph—her treasure flown,
And turn'd, like Niobe, to stone;
Within, without, obscure and void,
She felt all ravag'd, all destroy'd:
And, " O thou curs'd, insidious coast!
Are these the blessings thou can'st boast?
These, Virtue! these the joys they find,
Who leave thy Heav'n-topt hills behind?
Shade me, ye pines, ye caverns hide,
Ye mountains cover me!" she cry'd.
　Her trumpet Slander rais'd on high,
And told the tidings to the sky;
Contempt discharg'd a living dart,
A side-long viper to her heart;
Reproach breath'd poisons o'er her face,
And soil'd and blasted ev'ry grace:
Officious Shame, her handmaid new,
Still turn'd the mirror to her view,
While those, in crimes the deepest dy'd,
Approach'd to whiten at her side,
And ev'ry lewd insulting dame
Upon her folly rose to fame.

What should she do?—attempt once more
To gain the late-deserted shore?
So trusting, back the mourner flew;
As fast the train of fiends pursue.
　Again the further shore 's attain'd,
Again the land of Virtue gain'd;
But echo gathers in the wind,
And shows her instant foes behind.
Amaz'd, with headlong speed she tends,
Where late she left an host of friends;
Alas! those shrinking friends decline,
Nor longer own that form divine:
With fear they mark the following cry,
And from the lonely trembler fly;
Or backward drive her on the coast,
Where peace was wreck'd, and honour lost.
　From Earth thus hoping aid in vain,
To Heav'n not daring to complain,
No truce by hostile clamour given,
And from the face of friendship driven;
The nymph sunk prostrate on the ground,
With all her weight of woes around.
　Enthron'd within a circling sky,
Upon a mount, o'er mountains high,
All radiant sat, as in a shrine,
Virtue, first effluence divine,
Far, far above the scenes of woe,
That shut this cloud-wrapt world below;
Superior goddess, essence bright,
Beauty of uncreated light,
Whom should mortality survey,
As doom'd upon a certain day,
The breath of frailty must expire;
The world dissolve in living fire;
The gems of Heav'n, and solar flame,
Be quench'd by her eternal beam;
And Nature, quick'ning in her eye,
To rise a new-born phenix, die.
　Hence, unreveal'd to mortal view,
A veil around her form she threw,
Which three sad sisters of the shade,
Pain, Care, and Melancholy, made.
　Through this her all-inquiring eye,
Attentive from her station high,
Beheld, abandon'd to despair,
The ruins of her favourite fair;
And with a voice, whose awful sound
Appall'd the guilty world around,
Bid the tumultuous winds be still,
To numbers bow'd each list'ning hill,
Uncurl'd the surging of the main,
And smooth'd the thorny bed of pain;
The golden harp of Heav'n she strung,
And thus the tuneful goddess sung.
　" Lovely penitent, arise!
Come, and claim thy kindred skies;
Come, thy sister angels say,
Thou hast wept thy stains away.
　" Let experience now decide,
'Twixt the good, and evil try'd:
In the smooth, enchanted ground,
Say, unfold the treasures found?—
Structures rais'd by morning dreams,
Sands that trip the flitting streams,
Down that anchors on the air,
Clouds that paint their changes there!
Seas that smoothly dimpling lie,
While the storm impends on high,
Showing, in an obvious glass,
Joys that in possession pass;

Transient, fickle, light, and gay,
Flattering only to betray!
What, alas! can life contain?
Life, like all its circles, vain!
 " Will the stork, intending rest,
On the billow build her nest?
Will the bee demand his store
From the bleak and bladeless shore?
Man alone intent to stray,
Ever turns from wisdom's way;
Lays up wealth in foreign land,
Sows the sea, and ploughs the sand.
 " Soon this elemental mass,
Soon th' encumbering world shall pass,
Form be wrap'd in wasting fire,
Time be spent, and life expire.
Then, ye boasted works of men,
Where is your asylum then?
Sons of pleasure, sons of care,
Tell me mortals, tell me where?
Gone, like traces on the deep,
Like a sceptre grasp'd in sleep,
Dews exhal'd from morning glades,
Melting snows, and gliding shades!
 " Pass the world, and what 's behind?—
Virtue's gold, by fire refin'd;
From an universe deprav'd,
From the wreck of nature sav'd:
Like the life-supporting grain,
Fruit of patience, and of pain,
On the swain's autumnal day,
Winnow'd from the chaff away.
 " Little trembler, fear no more!
Thou hast plenteous crops in store,
Seed by genial sorrows sown,
More than all thy scorners own.
 " What though hostile Earth despise,
Heaven beholds with gentler eyes;
Heaven thy friendless steps shall guide,
Cheer thy hours, and guard thy side.
When the fatal trump shall sound,
When th' immortals pour around,
Heaven shall thy return attest,
Hail'd by myriads of the bless'd.
 " Little native of the skies,
Lovely penitent, arise!
Calm thy bosom, clear thy brow,
Virtue is thy sister now.
 " More delightful are my woes,
Than the rapture pleasure knows;
Richer far the weeds I bring,
Than the robes that grace a king.
 " On my wars of shortest date,
Crowns of endless triumph wait;
On my cares, a period bless'd;
On my toils, eternal rest.
 " Come, with Virtue at thy side,
Come, be ev'ry bar defy'd,
Till we gain our native shore:
Sister, come, and turn no more!"

<hr>

## LOVE AND VANITY.

THE breezy morning breath'd perfume,
The wak'ning flow'rs unveil'd their bloom;
Up with the Sun, from short repose,
Gay Health and lusty Labour rose;
The milk-maid carol'd at her pail,
And shepherds whistl'd o'er the dale;
When Love, who led a rural life,
Remote from bustle, state, and strife,
Forth from his thatch'd-roof'd cottage stray'd,
And stroll'd along the dewy glade.
 A nymph, who lightly trip'd it by,
To quick attention turn'd his eye:
He mark'd the gesture of the fair,
Her self-sufficient grace and air,
Her steps that mincing meant to please,
Her study'd negligence and ease;
And curious to inquire what meant
This thing of prettiness and paint,
Approaching spoke, and bow'd observant;
The lady, slightly,—" Sir, your servant."
 " Such beauty in so rude a place!
Fair-one, you do the country grace:
At court, no doubt, the public care—
But Love has small acquaintance there!"
 " Yes, sir," reply'd the flutt'ring dame,
" This form confesses whence it came:
But dear variety, you know,
Can make us pride and pomp forego.
My name is Vanity. I sway
The utmost islands of the sea:
Within my court all honour centres,
I raise the meanest soul that enters;
Endow with latent gifts and graces,
And model fools for posts and places.
 " As Vanity appoints at pleasure,
The world receives its weight and measure;
Hence all the grand concerns of life,
Joys, cares, plagues, passions, peace, and strife.
 " Reflect how far my pow'r prevails,
When I step in, where Nature fails,
And ev'ry breach of sense repairing,
Am bounteous still, where Heav'n is sparing.
 " But chief, in all their arts and airs,
Their playing, painting, pouts, and pray'rs,
Their various habits and complexions,
Fits, frolics, foibles, and perfections,
Their robing, curling, and adorning,
From noon till night, from night till morning,
From six to sixty, sick or sound,
I rule the female world around."
 " Hold there a moment," Cupid cry'd,
" Nor boast dominion quite so wide.
Was there no province to invade,
But that by love and meekness sway'd?
All other empire I resign;
But be the sphere of beauty mine.
For in the downy lawn of rest,
That opens on a woman's breast,
Attended by my peaceful train,
I choose to live, and choose to reign.
 " Far-sighted Faith I bring along;
And Truth, above an army strong;
And Chastity, of icy mould,
Within the burning tropics cold;
And Lowliness, to whose mild brow,
The pow'r and pride of nations bow;
And Modesty, with downcast eye,
That lends the morn her virgin dye;
And Innocence, array'd in light;
And Honour, as a tow'r upright;
With sweetly winning Graces, more
Than poets ever dream'd of yore,
In unaffected conduct free,
All smiling sisters, three times three;

And rosy Peace, the cherub bless'd,
That nightly sings us all to rest.
 " Hence, from the bud of Nature's prime,
From the first step of infant time,
Woman, the world's appointed light,
Has skirted ev'ry shade with white ;
Has stood for imitation high,
To ev'ry heart and ev'ry eye ;
From ancient deeds of fair renown,
Has brought her bright memorials down ;
To time affix'd perpetual youth,
And form'd each tale of love and truth
 " Upon a new Promethean plan,
She moulds the essence of a man,
Tempers his mass, his genius fires,
And, as a better soul, inspires.
 " The rude she softens, warms the cold,
Exalts the meek, and checks the bold ;
Calls Sloth from his supine repose ;
Within the coward's bosom glows ;
Of Pride unplumes the lofty crest ;
Bids bashful Merit stand confess'd ;
And, like coarse metal from the mines,
Collects, irradiates, and refines.
 " The gentle science she imparts,
All manners smooths, informs all hearts :
From her sweet influence are felt
Passions that please, and thoughts that melt ;
To stormy rage she bids control,
And sinks serenely on the soul ;
Softens Deucalion's flinty race,
And tunes the warring world to peace.
 " Thus, arm'd to all that's light and vain,
And freed from thy fantastic chain,
She fills the sphere, by Heav'n assign'd,
And, rul'd by me, o'errules mankind."
 He spoke. The nymph impatient stood ;
And laughing, thus her speech renew'd.
 " And pray, sir, may I be so bold
To hope your pretty tale is told ;
And next demand, without a cavil,
What new Utopia do you travel ?—
Upon my word, these high flown fancies
Show depth of learning—in romances.
 " Why, what unfashion'd stuff you tell us,
Of buckram dames, and tiptoe fellows !
Go, child ; and when you 're grown maturer,
You 'll shoot your next opinion surer.
 " O such a pretty knack at painting !
And all for softening, and for sainting !
Guess now, who can, a single feature,
Through the whole piece of female nature !
Then mark ! my looser hand may fit
The lines, too coarse for Love to hit.
 " 'T is said that woman, prone to changing,
Through all the rounds of folly ranging,
On life's uncertain ocean riding,
No reason, rule, nor rudder guiding,
Is like the comet's wand'ring light,
Eccentric, ominous, and bright ;
Trackless, and shifting, as the wind ;
A sea, whose fathom none can find ;
A moon, still changing, and revolving ;
A riddle, past all human solving ;
A bliss, a plague, a Heav'n, a Hell,
A—something, that no man can tell.
 " Now learn a secret from a friend ;
But keep your counsel, and attend.
 " Though in their tempers thought so distant,
Nor with their sex, nor selves consistent,

'T is but the diff'rence of a name,
And ev'ry woman is the same.
For as the world, however vary'd,
And through unnumber'd changes carry'd,
Of elemental modes, and forms,
Clouds, meteors, colours, calms, and storms,
Though in a thousand suits array'd,
Is of one subject matter made ;
So, sir, a woman's constitution,
The world's enigma, finds solution ;
And let her form be what you will,
I am the subject essence still.
 " With the first spark of female sense,
The speck of being, I commence ;
Within the womb make fresh advances,
And dictate future qualms and fancies ;
Thence in the growing form expand,
With childhood travel hand in hand,
And give a taste to all their joys,
In gewgaws, rattles, pomp, and noise.
 " And now, familiar, and unaw'd,
I send the flutt'ring soul abroad.
Prais'd for her shape, her face, her mien,
The little goddess, and the queen,
Takes at her infant shrine oblation,
And drinks sweet draughts of adulation.
 " Now blooming, tall, erect, and fair,
To dress becomes her darling care :
The realms of beauty then I bound ;
I swell the hoop's enchanted round,
Shrink in the waist's descending size,
Heav'd in the snowy bosom rise,
High on the floating lappet sail,
Or curl'd in tresses kiss the gale.
Then to her glass I lead the fair,
And show the lovely idol there ;
Where, struck as by divine emotion,
She bows with most sincere devotion ;
And, numb'ring ev'ry beauty o'er,
In secret bids the world adore.
 " Then all for parking, and parading,
Coquetting, dancing, masquerading ;
For balls, plays, courts, and crowds, what passion !
And churches, sometimes—if the fashion :
For woman's sense of right, and wrong,
Is rul'd by the almighty throng ;
Still turns to each meander tame,
And swims the straw of ev'ry stream.
Her soul intrinsic worth rejects,
Accomplish'd only in defects ;
Such excellence is her ambition ;
Folly, her wisest acquisition ;
And ev'n from pity and disdain,
She 'll cull some reason to be vain.
 " Thus, sir, from ev'ry form and feature,
The wealth and wants of female nature,
And ev'n from vice, which you 'd admire,
I gather fewel to my fire ;
And, on the very base of shame,
Erect my monument of fame.
 " Let me another truth attempt,
Of which your godship has not dreamt.
 " Those shining virtues, which you muster,
Whence, think you, they derive their lustre ?
From native honour, and devotion ?—
O yes, a mighty likely notion !
Trust me, from titl'd dames to spinners,
'T is I make saints, whoe'er makes sinners ;
'T is I instruct them to withdraw,
And hold presumptuous man in awe ;

For female worth, as I inspire,
In just degrees still mounts the higher,
And virtue so extremely nice,
Demands long toil, and mighty price:
Like Sampson's pillars, fix'd elate,
I bear the sex's tott'ring state;
Sap these, and in a moment's space
Down sinks the fabric to its base.
  " Alike from titles, and from toys,
I spring, the fount of female joys;
In ev'ry widow, wife, and miss,
The sole artificer of bliss.
For them each tropic I explore;
I cleave the sand of ev'ry shore;
To them uniting Indias sail,
Sabæa breathes her furthest gale:
For them the bullion I refine,
Dig sense and virtue from the mine;
And from the bowels of invention
Spin out the various arts you mention.
  " Nor bliss alone my pow'rs bestow,
They hold the sov'reign balm of woe:
Beyond the stoic's boasted art,
I soothe the heavings of the heart;
To pain give splendour and relief,
And gild the pallid face of grief.
  " Alike the palace, and the plain,
Admit the glories of my reign:
Through ev'ry age, in ev'ry nation,
Taste, talents, tempers, state, and station,
Whate'er a woman says, I say;
Whate'er a woman spends, I pay:
Alike, I fill and empty bags,
Flutter in finery and rags,
With light coquets through folly range,
And with the prude disdain to change.
  " And now you 'd think, 'twixt you and I,
That things were ripe for a reply——
But soft; and, while I 'm in the mood,
Kindly permit me to conclude,
Their utmost mazes to unravel,
And touch the furthest step they travel.
  " When ev'ry pleasure 's run aground,
And folly tir'd through many a round,
The nymph, conceiving discontent hence,
May ripen to an hour's repentance,
And vapours, shed in pious moisture,
Dismiss her to a church or cloister:
Then on I lead her, with devotion
Conspicuous in her dress and motion;
Inspire the heav'nly-breathing air,
Roll up the lucid eye in pray'r,
Soften the voice, and in the face
Look melting harmony and grace.
  " Thus far extends my friendly pow'r,
Nor quits her in her latest hour:
The couch of decent pain I spread,
In form incline her languid head,
Her thoughts I methodise in death,
And part not, with her parting breath:
Then do I set, in order bright,
A length of funeral pomp to sight,
The glitt'ring tapers and attire,
The plumes that whiten o'er her bier;
And last, presenting to her eye
Angelic fineries on high,
To scenes of painted bliss I waft her,
And form the Heav'n in she hopes hereafter."
  " In truth," rejoin'd love's gentle god,
" You have gone a tedious length of road;

And strange, in all the toilsome way,
No house of kind refreshment lay;
No nymph, whose virtues might have tempted,
To hold her from her sex exempted."
  " For one, we 'll never quarrel, man;
Take her; and keep her—if you can:
And, pleas'd, I yield to your petition,
Since ev'ry fair, by such permission,
Will hold herself the one selected;
And so my system stands protected."
  " O, deaf to virtue, deaf to glory,
To truths divinely vouch'd in story!"—
The godhead in his zeal return'd,
And, kindling, at her malice burn'd:
Then sweetly rais'd his voice, and told
Of heav'nly nymphs, rever'd of old—
Hypsipyle, who sav'd her sire;
And Portia's love, approv'd by fire;
Alike Penelope was quoted,
Nor laurel'd Daphne pass'd unnoted;
Nor Laodamia's fatal garter,
Nor fam'd Lucretia, honour's martyr;
Alceste's voluntary steel,
And Catherine smiling on the wheel!
But who can hope to plant conviction,
Where cavil grows on contradiction?
Some she evades, or disavows;
Demurs to all, and none allows—
" A kind of ancient things, call'd Fables!"
And thus the goddess turn'd the tables.
  Now both in argument grew high,
And choler flash'd from either eye;
Nor wonder each refus'd to yield
The conquest of so fair a field.
When happily arriv'd in view
A goddess, whom our grandames knew;
Of aspect grave, and sober gait,
Majestic, awful, and sedate;
As Heav'n's autumnal eve serene,
When not a cloud o'ercasts the scene;
Once Prudence call'd, a matron fam'd,
And in old Rome Cornelia nam'd.
Quick at a venture, both agree
To leave their strife to her decree.
  And now by each the facts were stated,
In form and manner as related.
The case was short. They crav'd opinion,
" Which held o'er females chief dominion?"
When thus the goddess, answering mild,
First shook her gracious head, and smil'd:
  " Alas, how willing to comply,
Yet how unfit a judge am I!
In times of golden date, 't is true,
I shar'd the fickle sex with you;
But from their presence long precluded,
Or held as one whose form intruded,
Full fifty annual suns can tell,
Prudence has bid the sex farewell."
  In this dilemma what to do,
Or who to think of, neither knew;
For both, still biass'd in opinion,
And arrogant of sole dominion,
Were forc'd to hold the case compounded,
Or leave the quarrel where they found it.
  When in the nick, a rural fair,
Of inexperienc'd gait and air,
Who ne'er had cross'd the neighb'ring lake,
Nor seen the world beyond a wake,
With cambric coif, and kerchief clean,
Tript lightly by them o'er the green.
  E e

" Now, now !" cried love's triumphant child,
And at approaching conquest smil'd ;
" If Vanity will once be guided,
Our diff'rence may be soon decided :
Behold yon wench ! a fit occasion
To try your force of gay persuasion.
Go you, while I retire aloof,
Go, put those boasted powers to proof ;
And if your prevalence of art
Transcends my yet unerring dart,
I give the fav'rite contest o'er,
And ne'er will boast my empire more."
　　At once, so said, and so consented,
And well our goddess seem'd contented ;
Nor, pausing, made a moment's stand,
But tript, and took the girl in hand.
Meanwhile the godhead, unalarm'd,
As one to each occasion arm'd,
Forth from his quiver cull'd a dart,
That erst had wounded many a heart ;
Then bending, drew it to the head—
The bow-string twang'd, the arrow fled ;
And, to her secret soul-address'd,
Transfix'd the whiteness of her breast.
　　But here the dame, whose guardian care
Had to a moment watch'd the fair,
At once her pocket mirror drew,
And held the wonder full in view ;
As quickly, rang'd in order bright,
A thousand beauties rush to sight,
A world of charms till now unknown,
A world reveal'd to her alone !
Enraptur'd stands the love-sick maid,
Suspended o'er the darling shade ;
Here only fixes to admire,
And centres ev'ry fond desire.

　　　　　　═══════

　　　　　　*CONRADE :*

　　　　　　A FRAGMENT.

THE SONG OF THE FILEA OF ANCIENT DAYS, PHELIN THE
GRAY-HAIRED SON OF THE SON OF KINFADDA.

WHAT do I love—what is it that mine eyes
Turn round in search of—that my soul longs after,
But cannot quench her thirst ?—'T is beauty, Phe-
　　lin !
I see it wide beneath the arch of Heaven,
When the stars peep upon their evening hour,
And the Moon rises on the eastern wave,
Hous'd in a cloud of gold !—I see it wide
In Earth's autumnal teints of various landscape,
When the first ray of morning tips the trees,
And fires the distant rock !—I hear its voice,
When thy hand sends the sound along the gale,
Swept from the silver strings ; or, on mine ear
Drops the sweet sadness !—At my heart I feel
Its potent grasp, I melt beneath the touch,
When the tale pours upon my sense humane
The woes of other times !—What art thou, Beauty ?
Thou art not colour, fancy, sound, nor form—
These but the conduits are, whence the soul quaffs
The liquor of its Heaven.—Whate'er thou art,
Nature, or Nature's spirit, thou art all
I long for !—O, descend upon my thoughts !
To thine own music tune, thou power of grace,
The cordage of my heart ! fill every shape
That rises to my dream, or wakes to vision ;

And touch the threads of every mental nerve
With all thy sacred feelings !
　　The Sun now hasten'd down his western Heaven,
And saw his beams reflected from the spires
Of fair Emania. High, within the hall,
With all his heroes, names of wide renown,
With all his sages, heads grown white in council,
With all his bards, the sires of song, around him—
Conrade the mighty, sat !
　　Wide o'er the festal board, in many a bowl,
The various liquor flow'd. In various cups,
Metal, or wrought from veiny adamant,
Or of the treasures of the pearly deep,
The social pledge of health went round.　Before
The king of chiefs, the hoar and reverend brow
Of wisdom was unbent, and ev'ry heart
Caught gladness from his aspect.　Near the seat
Of lifted majesty, stood the young bloom
Of Erin's hope, Slemfannon, as a sapling
Sprouting aloft beneath the parent oak,
That overlooks the forest.　Now, and oft,
He turn'd his face of filial sweetness upward,
To catch the glance of the paternal eye,
That dropp'd indulgence and delight upon him :
Now, with both hands, fast by the sinewy wrist
He grasp'd the first of heroes—" O," he cried,
" Will ever, ever, your Slemfannon wield
The crashing mace, or bend the bow of steel,
With such an arm as this ?"—He spoke, and rear'd
The pond'rous hand on high ! The shout of joy
Pour'd round the table !—for in that right hand
Lay Erin's glory, and the sure resource
Of nations from the wasters of the world !
　　Soft smiling, gently bending from his seat,
The monarch answer'd—" Yes, thou pride of Con-
In whom he fondly joys to live renew'd,　[rade,
Fresh born, a dearer growth of young existence—
Thou art the vessel that shall pour his fame
On future times ! The day is yet to come,
When nations, to exalt the name of Conrade,
Shall say, he was the father of Slemfannon ! [ous ;
　　" Thine arm is young, my son, but not inglori-
The Romans, from the Rhodane to the Po,
Have felt it through their steel ! The ear of heroes
Lists not to its own praise—yet know, thy name
Is in the song of bards ; and Phelin oft
To me gives up the music of thy deeds,
And tunes my soul to joy. But, mark, Slemfannon !
Th' arm of power is ever worthiest seen
In preservation—he who saves, is next
To him who gives existence. O, Slemfannon,
That we might save !—that we might save all, then,
Without offence to any ! In this hall,
O, might yon length of sword, yon shining mail,
Hang indolent for ever !—and, in days
Of ages yet to come, the sons of peace,
Gazing and wond'ring, question with each other,
What once had been their use !—Attend, my heroes !
　　" Man comes into this passing world of weakness,
And cries for help to man : for feeble is he,
And many are his foes—thirst, hunger, nakedness ;
Diseases infinite within his frame ;
Without, th' inclemency and wrath of seasons,
Famines, plagues, pests, devouring elements,
Earthquakes beneath, and thunders rolling o'er him ;
Age and infirmity on either hand ;
And Death, who lifts the certain dart behind him !
　　" These we might deem (had any pitying power
Ordain'd the ways of man) were ills sufficient !
Man thinks not so—on his own race he turns

The force of all his talents, exquisite
To shorten the short interval, by art,
Which Nature left us! Fire and sword are in
His hand; and, in his thought, are machinations
For speeding of perdition! Half the world,
Down the steep gulf of dark futurity,
Push off their fellows—pause upon the brink—
And then drop after!——
" Tell me, ye sages, tell me, if ye can,
Whence is the stream of life! It rises fresh
In smiling infancy; and pours along,
Short, turbulent, and murmuring in its course,
To its capacious sea. The sea fills not;
The sea, from whence it never has return'd;
Nor ceases yet the stream. Where lies the fund
From whence it flows?—will it be ever thus?—
And to no end, no purpose?"
While thus the hero question'd on the height
And depth of vast infinitude, intent
To plumb it with his fathom; through the hall
A sudden radiance broke! All turn'd their eyes
Upon the coming glory; for of Earth
They did not deem the vision! On she came,
Shulama, daughter of the gold-thron'd king
Of Scandinavia—on she came, in all
Her pleasantness of beauty, as the morn,
Blushing amidst the brightness of its east,
Rises on human sight! A train of virgins
Follow'd her steps; to them, twice twenty heroes,
Lords of wide lands, and fam'd in northern fields,
Succeeded; and yet, distant, far behind,
Was seen the long retinue! Through the hall,
Silent and still, as in the noon of night,
Attention held its breath—the white-hair'd sages
Rear'd their spread hands, in wonder—and Slem-
fannon
Gaz'd, as a blind-born man endow'd with sight,
When first he looks upon a new-found world!
Toward the gem'd throne of awful majesty
The maiden bent the lustre of her eye,
And grace of motion. Lowly on her knee
She sunk, imploring—" Hail, thou first of heroes,
The conqueror of the conquerors of the world,
King over kings uplifted!—Have I then
Beheld the face of Conrade, and surviv'd it?
" Ruthamor, monarch of the golden throne,
Whose deeds light up the north, hath sent Shulama
To seek alliance with the might of Conrade!—
I come from far, ambassadress of love;
And claim a partner for my father's throne,
Even your beloved daughter, Segaleme,
The witch who rolls th' eyes of young enchantment!"
Rising, and slow descending from his throne,
Conrade advanc'd. He rais'd the awe-struck maid,
And, to his war-imprinted bosom, clasp'd
The dangers of her beauty—" Welcome, welcome,
Welcome," he cried, " to Conrade, to his Erin,
Thou daughter of delight!—for fav'ring Heaven
Hath made thee in its pride of workmanship,
And planted loveliness, as light, around thee!
" Hadst thou, O daughter of the bless'd Ruthamor,
Requir'd a province at the hands of Conrade,
It had been given—or gold, and costly jewels;
He would have stor'd your shipping with the burden,
Till you cried, hold! But, here, alas, you ask
Th' only thing I covet!—Segaleme,
And young Slamfannon, are the eyes of Conrade—
The precious eyes by which he guides his steps,
And looks, alone, for joy! And shall I, then,
Shall I send off the treasure from my soul,

To enrich the land of strangers?—No, Shulama!
Haply, when grown infirm, and dim with age,
When I can only feel around for comfort,
How shall my hands stretch forth to foreign climes,
And to my knees draw up the little ones
Of Segaleme?"—While the monarch spoke,
A distant portal open'd: Segaleme
Appear'd to sight, and fill'd the pass with brightness!
As, should two moons, at east and west, arise
In aspect opposite; and each, in other,
Behold the image of its own perfection;
So shone, so mov'd, so gaz'd, the rival lights
Of Conrade and Ruthamor! They approach'd—
Their steps seem'd measur'd by the sound of music;
And each had lost the memory of herself,
In admiration of the other's beauty!
Silent, their arms of ivory they expand;
They fold each other to a polish'd bosom,
And mix their rays of brightness!—Segaleme
First broke the stillness in the hall of heroes.
" Welcome," she cried, " thrice welcome to the
vale
Of Erin, that shall gladden in thy presence,
O beam of northern hills!"—" And have I, then,
Have I, at length, beheld thee," cried Shulama,
" Thou praise of every tongue?—mine eyes are
satisfied, [joy,
And take their rest with thee!"—" Thou art the
The sister of my soul!" said Segaleme—
She spoke, and kiss'd her forehead. Whispering soft,
Shulama then inquir'd—" Say, which is he,
The force of your Slemfannon, so renoun'd,
For feats of warfare in the field of Romans?
Which is your mighty brother, Segaleme?—
For mine eye dare not venture in his search,
Amid the groups of heroes that surround us."
" There, there he grows, the flower of Erin's gar-
Fast by the royal pillar of the land! [den,
There stands the young Slemfannon, in his sweet-
ness!"
Full on the youth the maid of Scandinavia
Roll'd the young lightning of the glance of beauty—
His eyes met hers; and down they sunk abash'd,
As caught in some transgression.
" Ah, thou deceiver, beauteous witch of Erin,"
Rejoin'd Shulama, " this is not thy brother!
I ween'd to meet some giant, as in tales
Of old renown, and terrible to sight!
But here I view the infant of the spring,
Like one of us, who pale to look on blood,
And o'er the dying songster of the cage
Shed tears of mourning!"—Segaleme smil'd;
And from the dimpling of her radiant cheek
A glory went abroad! Forth, by the hand,
She led the lovely stranger to her bower.
Mean-season, to the peers of Scandinavia
The monarch bow'd benevolent, and said—
" Welcome, ye heroes of the sky-topp'd hills!
Thrice welcome all, though each had been an hun-
dred—
For plenty dwells upon the vales of Erin,
And Conrade's palace is the home of strangers!
The night descends, light up my many halls;
Spread wide the boards; pour plenteous, to the brim,
The juice of every region!" It was done.
By hundreds, and by fifties, sat the chiefs
Commix'd with bards and sages; while the voice
Of festal joy was heard throughout Emania.
But far within, in regal majesty,
Sat Erin's strength! Slemfannon bless'd his side;

And, full in view, he plac'd the high-born maids,
And fed his soul upon the work of Beauty.
  Phelin, the seer and song of ancient days,
The sage instructor of his lov'd Slemfannon,
Was seated here—and here, again, Siffrenna,
The white-hair'd guardian of Shulama's beauties.
  Soon as the board lay lighten'd of the banquet,
Fair boys and maidens, into crystal cups,
Pour'd the rich vintage of the Greekish isles
Of Archipelago. The joy went round;
The wish of pleasing, and the sweets of converse!
  " Slemfannon," said the monarch, " take the
      harp—
Thou arm, of Conrade, take the strings of story,
And, to the ear of Erin's lovely guest,
Tune some of thine adventures, when thou stood'st,
In southern climates, by the side of Conrade,
Then, like a glimpse of lightning, shot abroad,
And overturn'd the foe!" Yet still obedient
To the high call, the blushing youth replied:
" I turn'd, and shelter'd me behind your buckler,
As though behind the walls of Arisphellan !"
  Old Phelin from its chain releas'd the lyre,
And gave it, smiling. O'er the silver strings
Light flew the fingers of the shamefac'd boy,
Scarce audible. At length the tale began:
  " Our tent was pitch'd amid the field of Narbon—
The dead lay wide around—the night came down,
To veil their ghastliness—no star appear'd—
And the Moon, sick'ning at the sight of blood,
Had shrouded up her visage !—Through the gloom
Mine ear was stricken with the voice of wailing,
Sad as a thousand sighs, when the dark winds
Sob through the yews that stand amid the graves
Of Arnel !—Forth I went to seek the mourner.
  " Through the night's glimpse, that struck upon
I saw a warrior, tall and fair of stature. [his mail,
Upon his strenuous arm he lightly bore
The corse of his companion. On a bank
He laid the body down, and sunk beside it.
  " ' Art thou then gone ?' he cried; ' for ever gone,
Companion of my soul! in whom I liv'd,
The dearer self of desolated Hugon!
Wilt thou no more arise, like light, upon me ?
Nor give the smile of friendship to mine eyes ;
Nor cheer my spirit with thy voice of music ?
  " ' Why didst thou step before me in the battle?
Wast thou not safe, behind my wheeling sword,
As in the fort of Delma?—That my breast,
O, that my naked breast had met the dart
That slew my brother !—Thou hast left me, Berith,
With grief alone companion'd. O, stern grief,
Sad is thy fellowship ! I will not bide it.
I will o'ertake thee, Berith !—We will live,
Perchance, in happier climes ; or in one grave
Silent lie down, and sleep in peace together !
  " ' Look not, my mother, from the wonted pride
Of thine high battlements, to see thy son
Returning, in the front of all his trophies !
Mistake not Arden's forest for his flags;
Nor the wind's western clangour for his trumpets !
Thou shalt look upward, with a tearful eye,
And sigh to see how empty is his armour !
Thy hall, it shall be hung around with black,
And one lone lamp shall light thee !'
  " Straight, by th' accent of the hero's tongue,
I knew him for an enemy to Conrade:
But well I knew that Conrade was the friend
Of humankind !—With gentle voice, the voice
As of a brother, I the chief accosted :

" ' My heart, O warrior ! takes a kindred share
In all thy sufferings. In the field, indeed,
My falchion rises in my country's quarrel ;
But my soul knows no warfare with the brave,
The good, or the unhappy !—Know, great Hugon,
That the dristress'd are held as sons and brothers
To Conrade and Slemfannon ! Near at hand
Extends our camp—whate'er of friendly aid
Can there be given, is thine !' He answer'd not ;
But, with a grateful and assenting clasp,
Confin'd me to his bosom—while our souls,
Mingling their friendships, coalesced together.
  " Attendants straight I call'd ; then to my tent
Convey'd the corse, and gently on a bed
Reclin'd, and soon the steelly mail unbrac'd—
When, strange to tell ! upon th' astonish'd sight
Rose two twin orbs of beauty !—Back, abash'd,
Starting I turn'd, and sent the female train ;
Then sought where Hugon, all involv'd in grief,
Sat with my sire. In panting haste I told
The wondrous tale. The hero cried, ' 'T is she,
'T is she herself !—it must be Eliphene !
My heart confess'd her, though my eyes refus'd
Its attestation, turning love's fierce ardours
To friendship's gentler flame !'—At once they rose,
And follow'd where the beauteous body lay,
Decent, in virgin sheets. We sent in haste,
And call'd Elphenor, sovereign of all herbs
And arts for healing. He the deadly wound
Ere long discover'd ; for it still ooz'd crimson,
Like a rose springing midst a bed of lilies !
The vital heat, unwilling to forego
Its lovely mansion, feebly held the centre ;
And still a thread of life gave faint pulsation !
From his elixir'd crystal, drop by drop,
Through the pale lips, the cautious sage infused
The potent cordial. Thus, while doubtful life
Hung, fearfully suspended, generous Hugon
Address'd my sire—
  " ' O Conrade,' cried the chief,
' Thou dread of tyrants ; hateful to oppressors,
But, to the feeble and oppress'd, a name
Of sure asylum—lov'd of all the valiant !—
Yes, Hugon swears the valiant love thee, Conrade,
Even while as foes they draw the sword against thee !
O, monarch, lend the ear of thy compassion !
Thine ear, still open to the tale of mourning,
Lend it a while to Hugon ! He 's a Tuscan,
By clime and birth thine enemy—although
His kindred spirit long has held thee dear,
Even with the dearest. Hear then, hear my tale
Of sad distress !—That lovely, hapless maid,
Of noblest lineage, to my guardian care
Was by her parents left. She was address'd
By all the potentates, whose station warranted
To lift an eye so lofty. I was then
In foreign climes, on travel—I return'd.
  " ' Upon a stated festival, the chiefs
And princes of the land, with princely dames,
Conven'd a galaxy !—I too was there ;
And there was Eliphene, as the star
Of beauty, regent, midst the smaller sparklers !
With fond attraction she compell'd me to her,
As the touch'd needle to the frozen north ;
For so I did misdeem it. From that day,
Amidst the noblest of her princely suitors,
I too preferr'd my claim. She first receiv'd me
With smiling, kind, encouraging complacence :
But soon her looks grew more constrain'd—whene'er
Her eyes met mine, she blush'd and turn'd aside,

As wishing to avoid me. To all others
She look'd an elegance of ease, and spoke
In terms as free as air—to me, her speech,
Unfrequent, was abrupt and cautious. Stung
With scorpion jealousy, I, to my soul,
Thus spoke indignant—' What have these to boast,
These favour'd rivals, o'er rejected Hugon?
Does their pre-eminence consist in shape,
Or feature?—eyes, that are not Eliphene's,
Will answer, no. And, as to feats of prowess,
Compar'd with me, they 're nameless!—O shame,
⠀⠀⠀⠀⠀⠀⠀⠀shame,
Shame on this weakness, this degrading passion!
Henceforth, I will wage war on my own heart—
And conquer it, or perish!'
⠀⠀" ' At the time,
The tidings of your dread invasion reach'd us.
Quick, at the name of Conrade, my whole soul
Kindled to generous rivalship—' Yes, yes,
Thou shalt be met, thou mighty one!' I cried,
' Thou shalt be met—thy best esteemer shall
Oppose thee, front to front!—I ask of Heaven
No boon, no other bounty, than to have
My death ennobled by the arm of Conrade!'
⠀⠀" ' Straight I address'd for war; but love, un-
Obtruded, whispering to my secret soul, ⠀[call'd,
' First take thy last adieu of Eliphene!'
Pride, haughty champion, rose, with stern rebuke
Against the gentler power. He frown'd, and cried,
' What, are we not, as yet, enough debased?
Shall we add further forces to the foe;
And furnish arms, against our nobleness,
To the tried scorn and insolence of beauty?'
⠀⠀" ' Dire was the contest—Love long kept his
But Pride, at last, was prevalent—I rent, [ground;
I tore myself away from my belov'd,
From my true lover—
As a self-murderer, desperate of his state,
Makes a divorce betwixt his soul and body!
⠀⠀" ' I lay encamp'd, my legions tented round me,
When word was brought me of a youthful warrior,
Of graceful mien, and more than matchless beauty,
Who ask'd admission. To my presence led
He bow'd submiss; and, blushing, pray'd the grace
Of being privileg'd to do me service. ⠀[aspect—
⠀⠀" ' My heart straight took acquaintance with his
Some strange similitude fond memory found
'Twixt him and Eliphene!—but, my soul
Conceiv'd no thought, that she her tender frame
Should vest in steel—should seek the man she
⠀⠀⠀⠀⠀hated—
Should trace her Hugon into death and dangers!
⠀⠀" ' Instant, our hearts commenced a friendship,
Fondly inviolate, as caught together ⠀[tender,
By hooks of golden grappling. I, no more,
Sought Conrade on the perilous edge of conflict;
I now had one to care for! and my eye,
My guardian eye pursued and watch'd his motions,
On this side, and on that. In this day's battle,
I charg'd him, on his duty, on his love,
To hold him rearward. Still I turn'd, and turn'd,
Even as a timid deer accompanied
By her lov'd fawn, to see if he was near—
But yet, alas, in fear of losing fame,
I led my friend too deeply into dangers!
⠀⠀" ' At length, toward eve—for who can cope with
⠀⠀⠀⠀⠀Conrade?—
Your host prevail'd! Indignant I oppos'd,
And would have reinforc'd the fight—when, lo,
A random shaft rush'd, rudely, through the mail,

The light fram'd mail of my belov'd companion,
And ting'd his arms with blood! Upon the instant,
Our legions sounded a retreat. Then, then—
Must I confess that Hugon trembled? Straight
Into my arms I caught my best belov'd,
And fled the hindmost: night came on apace,
And parted all affray. Upon a bank
I laid her down, and, to the pitying Moon, [broke,
Whose doubtful glimpses through the darkness
Utter'd my wailings. Then, our lov'd Slemfannon
Came, provident of comforts, to console;
And did console, by showing that, on Earth,
Such virtue still was extant!'—Here the hero
Clos'd his sad narrative!
⠀⠀" Meantime, Elphenor, pendent o'er the corse,
Still plied his tender offices. At length,
The beauteous form began to move—each heart
Bounded with expectation—when her eyes
Open'd their faint refulgence to the light,
Look'd wild around her with a sickly gleam,
And clos'd their orbs for ever! Then Elphenor:
' By Death's cold hand this rose of beauty cropp'd,
Fades, and shall bloom no more—except in Hea-
⠀⠀⠀⠀⠀ven!'
⠀⠀" Meantime, astonish'd, o'er the lifeless corse
The hero speechless stood—then, all at once,
As some high cliff, far jutting o'er its base,
Disparts and dashes on the sea-beat shore,
Bereft of sense he fell—bless'd pause of being!
But O, how fearfully to be succeeded
By anguishes unutterable! Long,
Long lay he tranc'd. I thought, I wish'd him dead.
For what had life, midst all its stores of bliss,
For him, save misery extreme? At length,
He wak'd to all the pangs of mental feeling!
⠀⠀" Five days, and five soul-tort'ring nights, he lay
By th' embalm'd remains—in all which time,
Nor food, nor word of utterance, pass'd his lips;
Nor word of consolation to his ear
Obtain'd admission. By his side fast laid,
I press'd his hand in mine, and on it dropp'd
The tear of sad condolence! Through the camp
Sudden I heard the shout of joint lament.
I rose, and issu'd forth."

⸻

⸻

### RUTH:

## AN ORATORIO.

⸻

### PERSONS.

| | |
|---|---|
| BOAZ. | RUTH. |
| HIGH PRIEST. | ISRAELITES, |
| NAOMI. | MOABITES. |

⸻

### PART I.

SCENE I.—*A Field in Moab.*

ISRAELITE TRAVELLERS, AND NAOMI.

RECITATIVE.—FIRST ISRAELITE.

STAY, brother—see, in yonder shade,
Some sable daughter of affliction laid!

She rises—mark her mournful air !
She looks, she moves, she breathes despair !
   Too great appears her woe,     [flow.
To suffer words to break away, or swelling tears to

### RECITATIVE ACCOMPANIED.—SECOND ISRAELITE.

'T is nought to us—come, let's be gone—
This land for us no friendship knows :
   All are strangers here, and foes !   [—pass on.
Shall we regard a foe's distress ?—no, brother, no !

### AIR.—FIRST ISRAELITE.

Through ev'ry clime, the heart humane
Is pleas'd to share in ev'ry pain—
There dwells a secret sense within,
To frail mortality a-kin ;
And to the child of humbling grief,
Or friend, or foe, it brings relief !

### CHORUS.

Or friend, or foe, the child of grief,
From hearts humane will find relief !

### RECITATIVE.—FIRST ISRAELITE.

Unhappy sister ! whence the care,
That seems above thy strength to bear ?

### RECITATIVE.—NAOMI.

'T is an incurable despair !—

### RECITATIVE.—FIRST ISRAELITE.

Yet if our power cannot relieve, our pity sure may
   share.

### RECITATIVE.—NAOMI.

Lopp'd from the trunk of Israel's tree,   [you see !
And stripp'd of foliage and of fruit, a blasted branch

### RECITATIVE.—SECOND ISRAELITE.

Of Israel ?—O, declare thy grief !—
I hasten, now, to bring relief.

### AIR.—NAOMI.

Ah, cease—your comforts come in vain !
   As a barren rock they fall ;
Whence soft descending stores of rain,
   No blade of kindly growth can call.

### AIR.—FIRST ISRAELITE.

From desolated lands,
From rugged rocks, and parching sands,
The powerful word of Israel's King
Can call the beauties of the spring !

### RECITATIVE.

His hand the wounded heart can heal—
But O, whence springs thy grief, reveal !

### RECITATIVE.—NAOMI.

Once I was bless'd, supremely bless'd !
These arms a lov'd and loving consort press'd—
Two sons, beside, were mine—all now, alas, no more !
Husband and children lost I'm destin'd to deplore !

### RECITATIVE.—FIRST ISRAELITE.

Alas, sad matron !—May we claim
Thy tribe, thy native place, and name ?

### RECITATIVE.—NAOMI.

Of Judah's tribe, in Bethlehem's town,
Naomi once was known.
But late, when famine ravag'd all our plains,
I, with my household, succour sought from Moab's
   foreign swains.

### RECITATIVE.—SECOND ISRAELITE.

Our sister !——

### FIRST ISRAELITE.

—————— O, our sister dear !

### SECOND ISRAELITE.

Return !——

### FIRST ISRAELITE.

—————— Thy kin, thy country, cheer !

### RECITATIVE.—SECOND ISRAELITE.

The Lord hath visited our land,      [hand !
And on his chosen people pour'd the bounty of his

### AIR. DUET.

Rich verdure and blossoms again deck the spring,
Again in the groves the wing'd choristers sing ;
Again the blithe milkmaid is heard at her pail,
And the ploughman's glad whistle descends on the
   vale.

### RECITATIVE.—NAOMI.

Though fall my ills so heavy from his hand,
I bless the Lord who saves my native land.
Yes, happy soil ! ye hills and vales of grace !
   Thou sacred, pleasing, promis'd place !   [sight,
With thee, once more, these eyes shall glad their
Then, closing, bid adieu to mortal life and light !

### AIR.

Dear natal Earth, prepare my grave,
Receive the fading form you gave !
Dear natal Earth, upon your breast,
The fading form you gave shall rest !

### RECITATIVE.—SECOND ISRAELITE.

Cease, cease, O hapless sister ! cease to mourn—
Thy joyful friends shall hail thy wish'd return ;
Bethlehem exulting thy approach shall greet,
And her throng'd ways spread flow'rs beneath thy
   feet.

### AIR.

Let no wretched offspring of Adam despair—
As passes our pleasure, so passes our care !
Man's life is an April, now gloomy, now gay ;
His shade and his shine fleet successive away !
To the pain thy Creator appoints thee resign,
And seize the glad moment allow'd to be thine.

### RECITATIVE.—NAOMI.

My friends, my country, now Naomi scarce will
   own—
To haughty wealth, in prosperous state, the poor remain unknown !

### RECITATIVE.—FIRST ISRAELITE.

As o'er a treasure lost and found,
O'er thee thy kindred will rejoice around.

AIR.

O Israel, receive to thy breast,
  This thy daughter, so virtuous and dear !
In thy songs be her welcome express'd,
  And her diffidence lost in thy cheer !
As her morning in clouds has begun,
  Let her noon in its progress be bright ;
And her evening, like summer's fair sun,
  Leave behind it a glory of light !

## PART II.

### SCENE I.

### NAOMI, RUTH, AND MOABITES.

RECITATIVE.—NAOMI.

DAUGHTERS of Moab, hear ! By famine's hand
Oppress'd, erewhile I left my native land—
To you I came ; ye took the stranger in,
And fill'd the place of country and of kin.
Now home recall'd, for leave to part I sue,
And my full heart must take the last adieu !

RECITATIVE.—MOABITES.

Would'st thou their blessing from thy servants take ?
Your Lord loves Moab for Naomi's sake.

AIR.

Where'er thy visit is address'd,
The household and the house are bless'd !

RECITATIVE.—NAOMI.

Though you, my friends, I quit, my broken heart
Leaves in your hospitable earth its better, dearer
    part !

AIR.

A long, long adieu, my kind neighbours, I take,
Ye wealth of the wealthless, ye strength of the weak !
While worth shall endear, or beneficence bind,
Your mem'ry shall hold the first place in my mind :
And if ever your lot should oblige you to stray,
May others the friendship you show'd me repay !

RECITATIVE.—RUTH.

Come, mother, come ! no more indulge delay !
Towards your Israel's pleasant land I long to bend
    my way.

RECITATIVE.—NAOMI.

What means my daughter ? would she leave
Her friends of Moab for her loss to grieve ?

AIR.—RUTH.

Yes, mother, yes ; with thee,
Though faint from travel and from toil,
Each land will prove a native soil,
  Each house a home to me !
Companion'd with thee, as we journey along,
No time can be tedious, no road can be wrong !

RECITATIVE.

By wedlock, Ruth, ally'd to thee,
Became a gift of Israel's tree—
So firmly fix'd, so strongly tied,
No storm can shake, no stroke divide !

AIR.—NOAMI.

O, flower of Moab, passing fair !
  Say, shall my unpropitious hand
Thee, from thy native garden, bear,
  To wither in a foreign land ?

RECITATIVE.—RUTH.

Some power, unconquerably strong,
Impells thy daughter's steps along.

AIR.

As the Lord of thy Israel now reigneth above,
In his kingdom of peace, and his regions of love,
      'T is in vain
      To restrain ;
With thee I will wander, with thee will remain.
    To the lot that is thine,
Or pleasant, or painful, with joy I resign ;
Thy people, thy God, and thy grave, shall be mine !

RECITATIVE.—NAOMI.

O child, above all kindred dear,
Thou bless'd of our Jehovah, hear !

AIR.

I see, I see with other eyes,
From darkness distant radiance rise !
Soon shall the promis'd Son be born,
And come on Solyma like morn,
    Enlight'ning all her skies !

CHORUS OF MOABITES.

Amid the great, the glorious thought,
Our souls to future times are caught.
    We see, with other eyes,
From darkness distant radiance rise !
Soon shall the promis'd Son be born,
And come on Moab like the morn,
    Enlight'ning all her skies !

## PART III.

### SCENE I.

### NAOMI AND RUTH.

RECITATIVE.—NAOMI.

TURN, O daughter, turn thy eyes,
Where Bethlehem's glittering spires arise—
How fair her flowery vales extend !
How bold her swelling hills ascend !

AIR.

Dear native soil ! do I again
  Thy kindly breeze inhale ?
No air of any foreign plain
  Could thus my sense regale.

RECITATIVE.—RUTH.

Fair is thy land, O mother ! wondrous fair !
My bosom from the view strange transport seems
    to share.

AIR.

New scenes, and new prospects, my spirit employ,
  And with hopes of new happiness cheer me ;
My heart all enliven'd indulges its joy,
  And some sudden blessing seems near me.

RECITATIVE.—NAOMI.

Behold, my lovely child, behold,
How Bethlehem's streets at our approach pour
    forth their young and old!

SCENE II.

NAOMI, RUTH, BOAZ, ISRAELITES.

CHORUS.

Naomi?—lost and found again,
O welcome to thy native plain!
Raise all your voices, brethren, raise,
And hail your sister's glad return with gratulating
    lays.

RECITATIVE.—NAOMI.

Say, brethren, who is he that leads the throng,
And like a hero moves majestical along?

RECITATIVE.—FIRST ISRAELITE.

'T is Boaz, Bethlehem's prince, your near allied—
Your first of kindred by your husband's side!

AIR, DUET.—ISRAELITE.

His step is at a distance from thousands discern'd!
When he speaks in the gate, elders hear and grow
    learn'd!
His couches are spread for the stranger's repose;
For the naked he shears, for the hungry he sows!
He stands like a tree in the midst of his ground,
With the widow and orphan rejoicing around!

RECITATIVE.—BOAZ.

Hail, mother of thy people!—this embrace
Bids thee thrice welcome to thy native place.
Oft have those arms my infant years caress'd,
And clasp'd thy little kinsman to thy breast!

RECITATIVE.—NAOMI.

Hail, son!—May Heaven in bounty heap on thee
Tenfold the blessings it has rent from me!

RECITATIVE.—BOAZ.

In this our present happy lot,
Be past calamities forgot!
But where is she, our new allied—
Of Moab's land so late the pride?

AIR.—NAOMI.

Lo, there! like a mist on the morning, her veil
    Strives in vain to obscure her from sight;
It betrays what it means to conceal,
    A beauty for vision too bright!

RECITATIVE.—BOAZ.

Thee, fairest Ruth, by Israel's law I claim,
A glad succeeder to thy husband's name!
Thrice have the visions of the night
Brought to my view thy semblance fair, that fill'd
    my tent with light!

RECITATIVE.—RUTH.

If so your laws ordain,
Your handmaid will not of her lot complain.

RECITATIVE.—HIGH PRIEST.

Hear, men of Bethlehem, and rejoice!
The LORD informs his servant's voice—

Yon portion fair of Moab's earth,
To Israel's Chosen Plant gives birth!
Hence the mighty tree shall spring,
The glory of the grove, of every tree the king!

CHORUS OF PRIESTS.

To the centre, shall reach the vast depth of his root!
To the stars, the vast height of his summit shall
    shoot!
Through the world, the vast length of his boughs
    shall extend!
For their food, on his fruit, shall all nations de-
    pend!

GRAND CHORUS.

Hail, mother of approaching grace!
Hail, parent of the promis'd race!
Far distant I see him!—The young and the old
Rush to meet the Messiah, by prophets foretold!
    The lame, with a bound,
    Lightly leap from the ground;
The deaf run to hear, and the blind to behold—
And the dead rise triumphant around!

---

## PROLOGUES AND EPILOGUES.

### PROLOGUE

#### TO GUSTAVUS VASA.

BRITONS! this night presents a state distress'd:
Though brave, yet vanquish'd; and though great,
    oppress'd.
Vice, rav'ning vulture, on her vitals prey'd;
Her peers, her prelates, fell corruption sway'd:
Their rights, for pow'r, the ambitious weakly sold;
The wealthy, poorly, for superfluous gold.
Hence wasting ills, hence severing factions rose,
And gave large entrance to invading foes:
Truth, justice, honour, fled th' infected shore;
For freedom, sacred freedom, was no more.
    Then, greatly rising in his country's right,
Her hero, her deliverer, sprung to light:
A race of hardy northern sons he led,
Guiltless of courts, untainted, and unread;
Whose inborn spirit spurn'd th' ignoble fee,
Whose hands scorn'd bondage, for their hearts were
    free.
    Ask ye, what law their conquering cause con-
    fess'd?—
Great Nature's law, the law within the breast;
Form'd by no art, and to no sect confin'd,
But stamp'd by Heav'n upon th' unletter'd mind.
    Such, such, of old, the first-born natives were,
Who breath'd the virtues of Britannia's air,
Their realm when mighty Cæsar vainly sought;
For mightier freedom against Cæsar fought,
And rudely drove the fam'd invader home,
To tyrannise o'er polish'd—venal Rome.
    Our bard, exalted in a freeborn flame,
To ev'ry nation would transfer this claim:
He, to no state, no climate, bounds his page,
But bids the moral beam through ev'ry age.
Then be your judgment gen'rous as his plan;
Ye sons of freedom!—save the friend of man.

## PROLOGUE

### TO THE EARL OF ESSEX,

#### A TRAGEDY.

THIS night, to your free censure, are expos'd
Scenes, now almost two hundred winters clos'd:
Scenes, yet, that ought to be for ever near,
To freedom sacred, and to virtue dear!
  Deep is the spring, whose stream this night we
    draw;
Its source is truth—'tis liberty made law:
A draught divine to ev'ry generous breast;
The cordial of the wretched—of the bless'd!
The juice, by which the strength of souls is fed;
Without whose aliment, who lives—is dead.
  If aught is honest, noble, kind, or great,
Which yet may give some British hearts to beat;
If aught has been by mighty fathers won,
Which yet descends to animate a son;
However weak the warmth, or dim the beam,
We show from whence the distant glory came;
And lead you backward, by the kindred ray,
To the full blaze of Britain's brightest day—
Elizabeth!—a light till then unknown,
The virgin sun, of truth's meridian, shone,
And in the subject's freedom fix'd a living throne.
  Is there, to whom one privilege is sure,
Who holds fair property, as yet, secure?—
Is there, to whom religion stands endear'd,
So hardly rescued, so divinely clear'd?—
Is there, who claims, who feels, who prizes aught,
For which the hero bled, the patriot wrought?—
Elizabeth, as one inspiring soul,
Reform'd, connected, and affirm'd the whole;
And sent the blessings down, through ev'ry reign,
For you to clasp, to cherish, and retain!
  Like Cynthia, peerless queen, supremely crown'd,
Her guardian constellations blaz'd around—
Selected chiefs, for council, as for fight;
Her men of wisdom, and her men of might;
Whose acts, illustrating our annals, stand
The grace, the good, the glory of the land!
For then no courtly faction stood confess'd—
Who serv'd his country, serv'd his queen the best!
  If yet, among those godlike men of old,
Some taint of earth lay mingled with the mould;
On human frailty if misfortune grew,
And sufferings, such as all who read must rue—
Through time descending let the sorrow flow,
And you who share the virtue, share the woe!

---

## ANOTHER PROLOGUE

### TO THE EARL OF ESSEX.

#### SPOKEN BY MR. SHERIDAN.

WHENE'ER the brave, the gen'rous, and the just,
Whene'er the patriot sinks to silent dust,
The tragic Muse attends the mournful hearse,
And pays her tribute of immortal verse.
Inspir'd by noble deeds, she seeks the plain,
In honour's cause where mighty chiefs are slain;
And bathes with tears the sod that wraps the dead,
And bids the turf lie lightly on his head.
  Nor thus content she opens death's cold womb,
And bursts the cearments of the awful tomb

To cast him up again—to bid him live,
And to the scene his form and pressure give.
  Thus once-fam'd Essex at her voice appears,
Emerging from the sacred dust of years.
  Nor deem it much, that we retrace to night
A tale to which you have listen'd with delight.
How oft of yore, to learned Athens' eyes,
Did new Electras and new Phædras rise?
In France, how many Theban monarchs groan
For Laius' blood, and incest not their own?
When there new Iphigenias heave the sigh,
Fresh drops of pity gush from ev'ry eye:
On the same theme though rival wits appear,
The heart still finds the sympathetic tear.
  If there soft pity pours her plenteous store,
For fabled kings and empires now no more;
Much more should you—from freedom's glorious
    plan,
Who still inherit all the rights of man—
Much more should you with kindred sorrows glow
For your own chiefs, your own domestic woe;
Much more a British story should impart
The warmest feelings to each British heart.

---

## PROLOGUE

### TO THE EARL OF WESTMORLAND,

#### A TRAGEDY.

CHARM'D to this spot, concurring to this night,
Wide nations close, and centuries unite.
Scenes long eras'd, past ages rise to view, [you!
Realms change their place, and time returns—for
  The merchant, vent'rous in his search of gain,
Who ploughs the winter of the boist'rous main,
From various climes collects a various store,
And lands the treasure on his native shore.
Our merchant yet imports no golden prize,
What wretches covet, and what you despise!
A different store his richer freight imparts—
The gem of virtue, and the gold of hearts;
The social sense, the feelings of mankind,
And the large treasure of a godlike mind!
  When Westmorland, unhappy, brave, and great,
Appears conflicting with the pow'rs of fate,
Guilty yet good, deserving yet forlorn,
And by the strife of warring passions torn—
Although our author brings the distant woe,
From eyes that wept a thousand years ago,
He claims your kindred tears for the distress'd,
Nor thinks one virtue foreign to your breast!
  But when the bright Rowena shall appear,
First of her sex—except her rivals here—
No more let man assert his lordly claim,
No more presume to step the first for fame;
But to the fair their native rights allow,
Look round, and with becoming homage bow!

---

## ANOTHER PROLOGUE

### TO THE EARL OF WESTMORLAND.

THERE was a time, these polish'd times preceding,
Ere our good sires of Britain—knew fine breeding;
Ere honesty was elbow'd from the nation,
Or life's learn'd lie entitled " Education."

Bold Nature then disdain'd the mask of art;
Man, on his open aspect, wore his heart.
Passion then knew nor cover, nor control;
Each action spoke the dictate of the soul:
Worth claim'd its triumphs, guilt confess'd its
  stings,
And truth was known at courts—and told to kings!
  Such were your sires, humanely, nobly rude;
And such the good old times, for you renew'd!
  From the still regions of enduring night,
Our author calls the dead to life and light.
He bids your hearts to heave, your eyes to flow,
O'er griefs that pass'd nine hundred years ago:
Bids truth in person tread Hibernia's stage,
And action preach her sermon to the age;
The sermon to which Nature sets her seal—
For none can doubt the doctrine that they feel.
  Sweet as a field that vernal breezes fan,
Sweet are emotions in the heart of man;
Sweet are the tears of worth, the ties of kin,
And all the home-bred charities within!
When human feelings warm breast inspire,
When pity softens, and when passions fire;
Then glows the mint of Nature, apt, refin'd,
And virtue strikes her image on the mind.
  If the distinguish'd hero of this night
Is urg'd to leap the sacred mound of right;
If, wildly toss'd on passion's stormy wave,
He wrecks the country he was born to save;
Know it is man's to err—and let that move,
To pity frailties that you can't approve.
  But when you see Rowena greatly soar,
A height that virtue never dar'd before;
A summit, to aspiring man unknown,
And, first and last, achiev'd by her alone;
Then turn, and in her sex the saint revere—
Then bend with reverence, to the chaste and fair!

---

## PROLOGUE,

### FOR THE OPENING OF A THEATRE.

WHEN lazy moralists from cloisters taught
The frosty precepts of unpractis'd thought,
Howe'er the judgment coldly was inform'd,
No worth was kindled, for no heart was warm'd.
But when some good men to the public read
The generous lecture of a life well led:
When patriots stood for liberty and laws,
Or fell the victims of their country's cause:
Then hearts were taught to glow, and eyes to melt,
And hands to act the lesson that was felt.
  In languid maxims, which we barely hear,
The voice of truth sounds distant to our ear;
But action bids the substance to arise,
And gives the living beauty to your eyes.
Hence was the stage, from earliest times, design'd
A vital school of virtue to mankind.
In real life, if scant the good and fair,
If truth be foreign, and if worth be rare,
For these through ev'ry clime and age we steer;
And thence unlade the precious purchase here!
  Though Time and Death have clos'd their ancient
They bar their everlasting gates in vain—  [reign,
The fatal valves shall to your eyes unfold,
Recall the past and renovate the old:
And, from the realms of silence and of night,
Pour down a flood of eloquence and light.

Whate'er of worth informs the social breast,
Upon humanity by Heaven impress'd,
The sympathy that proves great souls of kin,
The touch that tries the hidden gold within:
Whate'er of generous, courteous, fond and kind,
Strikes the lin'd unison of mind to mind:
Whate'er may teach a virtuous eye to flow,
For griefs that pass'd nine hundred years ago:
All those we bring—Confess to modern eyes,
The deed of fam'd antiquity shall rise:
Friends, lovers, heroes, patriots, to this stage
Shall come, from every land, from every age:
Old Time shall render, to your eyes and ears,
The truths and trophies of four thousand years:
Cato again shall abdicate his tomb,
And Brutus strike for liberty and Rome!

---

## PROLOGUE

### TO OTHELLO.

#### SPOKEN IN DUBLIN, BY MR. GARRICK.

My term expir'd with this concluding play.
I 've cast the buskin and the sock away.
No more to kindle the poetic rage,
Nor in mock-majesty to awe the stage,
The hero shrinks into his native span—
This little sketch and miniature of man.
" Where 's Garrick?" says the beau: and as I pass,
To mark the noted insect—takes his glass.
Plac'd in yon box, to publish my disaster,
" Mamma," cries miss, " who is that little master?"
"Zounds!" says the captain, "what! is that Othello?
Ha, ha, ha!——
" A good joke, damme—a rare hulking fellow!"
Thus on defects I dare to build a name:
And imperfection gives me up to fame.
O, could my stature with your bounty rise,
And swelling gratitude extend my size!
What ample measure would that change impart,
When every limb should answer to my heart.
  Great are the favours which my soul avows;
Great are the thanks with which your servant bows!
My faults are debtors to your generous sense—
Quick to observe, yet gracious to dispense!
And should I but presume that something, too,
Is to your judgment, to your justice due;
Blame not the vanity you kindly raise,
Sprung from your smiles, and heighten'd by your
  praise!                                   [pole,
  Hail, generous isle! though neighbouring to the
Thy warmth is in the virtues of the soul!
Though clouds, above, may intercept the light:
Below, thy sun of beauty cheers our sight!
Where'er my distant fortunes may command,
I sigh for thee as for my natal land.
Or east, or west, howe'er the region lies,
A country takes its name from social ties;
The heart alone appoints its favourite place,
And I 'm a native by your special grace.
  Then take the warmest wishes of my mind—
As your own favours, great and unconfin'd,
May peace and smiling pleasure, hand in hand,
Walk the wide limits of your plenteous land!
May Gallia curse the day of William's [1] might,
And Chesterfield return to bless your sight!

  [1] William, duke of Cumberland.

## EPILOGUE

### ON THE BIRTH-DAY OF HIS ROYAL HIGHNESS THE DUKE OF CUMBERLAND.

#### SPOKEN BY MR. GARRICK, IN DUBLIN.

'T is not a birth to titles, pomp, or state,
That forms the brave, or constitutes the great:
To be the son of George's just renown,
And brother to the heir of Britain's crown,
Though proud these claims, at best they but adorn,
For heroes cannot be, like princes, born:
Valour and worth must consecrate their name,
And virtue give them to the rolls of fame.

Hail to the youth, whose actions mark this year,
And in whose honour you assemble here!
'T is not to grace his natal day we meet,
His birth of glory is the birth we greet.
How quick does his progressive virtue run,
How swift ascend to its meridian sun,
Before its beam the northern storms retire,
And Britons catch the animating fire.

Yet rush not too precipitate, for know
The fate you urge would prove our greatest foe,
Religion, law, and liberty 's at stake,
Repress your ardour for your country's sake,
The life you prize not, Britain may deplore,
And chance may take, what ages can 't restore.

O! did the gallant Cumberland but head
Such troops as here our glorious William [1] led!
Bold names, in Britain's history renown'd,
Who fix'd her freedom on Hibernian ground,
Till death, embattled for their country, stood,
And made the Boyne immortal by their blood.
Such were your sires, who still survive in fame;
Such are the sons who would achieve the same.
Young William then should rival trophies raise,
And emulate our great deliverer's days,
By equal actions win the like applause,
Alike their name, their glory, and their cause.

May Heav'n's peculiar angel shield the youth!
Who draws the sword of liberty and truth,
By mask in Britannia's injuries redress,
And crown his toil, his virtue, with success,
Make him the scourge of France, the dread of Rome,
The patriot's blessing, and the rebel's doom.

Then seize, Hibernia, seize the present joy,
This day is sacred to the martial boy!—
The morrow shall a different strain require,
When, with thy Stanhope [2], all delights retire,
And (a long polar night of grief begun)
Thy soul shall sigh for its returning sun.

## PROLOGUE

### TO THE FOUNDLING.

Unpractis'd in the drama's artful page,
And new to all the dangers of the stage,
Where judgment sits to save or damn his play,
Our poet trembles for his first essay.
He, like all authors, a conforming race!
Writes to the taste and genius of the place:
Intent to fix, and emulous to please
The happy sense of these politer days,

[1] King William III.
[2] Lord Chesterfield left Ireland about this time.

He forms a model of a virtuous sort,
And gives you more of moral than of sport:
He rather aims to draw the melting sigh,
Or steal the pitying tear from beauty's eye:
To touch the strings that humanise our kind,
Man's sweetest strain, the music of the mind.

Ladies, he bids me tell you, that from you,
His first, his fav'rite character he drew:
A young, a lovely, unexperienc'd maid,
In honest truth and innocence array'd;
Of fortune destitute, with wrongs oppress'd,
By fraud attempted, and by love distress'd:
Yet guarded still: and every suff'ring pass'd,
Her virtue meets the sure reward at last.

From such examples shall the sex be taught,
How virtue fixes whom their eyes have caught:
How honour beautifies the fairest face,
Improves the mien, and dignifies the grace.

And hence the libertine, who builds a name
On the base ruins of a woman's fame,
Shall own, the best of human blessings lie
In the chaste honours of the nuptial tie:
There lives the home-felt sweet, the near delight,
There peace reposes, and there joys unite:
And female virtue was by Heav'n design'd
To charm, to polish, and to bless mankind.

---

## EPILOGUE

### TO THE

### PLAY OF WHAT WE MUST ALL COME TO.

What all must come to!—what?—debate and strife!
Must all wed plague and broils—who wed a wife?
If that 's the sage conclusion of our poet,
The man 's a fool—you happy husbands know it!

Your dames are form'd upon a gentler plan—
To sooth and smooth the rough-hewn mass of man;
To bid the tumult of your souls to cease,
And smile your warring passions into peace.

Like Rome's fam'd matrons, scorning all excess
In mask or mummery, in dance or dress,
Your wives are busied in the nobler cares
Of planting their own virtues in your heirs,
And scarce depart their house—except to prayers!
They neither take nor give the world a handle
For tittle-tattle, gossiping, or scandal;
And, as for that strange vice of gaming—lard!
I dare be sworn, they scarce can tell a card.

In times of yore, indeed, when 't was the fashion,
And drums, routs, rackets, cards, the favourite
    passion;
With ev'ry husband, gambling was the flame,
And even their precious spouses—play'd the game.

Plumb, in the reigning vice, your statesmen jump;
And factions in rotation turn'd up trump:
Honours, on all hands, they agree to wave;
Some play'd the fool, who meant to play the knave.
The vizier, vers'd in all the gambling trade,
The court against his simpler country play'd;
But, dubious of the pow'rs that might withstand,
He wisely kept the impending king in hand—
The people thought the advantage somewhat hard;
But deem'd their Magna Charta a sure card!
Now heats and bets all terms of truce confound;
Craft, perjury, prostitution, wait around;
While high o'er head Astrea's beam behold,
Weighing light conscience against pond'rous gold.

But how the game did end, or may end—why—
Time, if it choose, may tell—in sooth, not I.
 Ye fair, intended, by the powers above,
With silken chains to bind the world in love;
On whose soft sway, to Earth's extremest end,
The race, the brotherhood of man depend!
O, never, never answer rage with rage,
But shun the tempest which you can't assuage;
Your tyrants, then, shall spend their wrath in
  vain,
Return quite tame, and reassume their chain;
So shall submission win despotic sway,
And the world's lord shall willingly obey!

---

## EPILOGUE

### ON HUMBUGGING.

Of all trades and arts in repute or possession,
Humbugging is held the most ancient profession.
'Twixt nations, and parties, and state politicians,
Prim shopkeepers, jobbers, smooth lawyers, phy-
  sicians,
Of worth and of wisdom the trial and test
Is—mark ye, my friends!—who shall humbug the
  best.
 Our neighbour of France, with his prologue so
  kind,
And his epilogue spoke by his cannon behind;
Who, in banter and bully, in cringing and hugging,
Is counted of old, the great prince of humbugging;
For once stands amaz'd, howsoe'er it was hit on,
To find he 's humbugg'd by his cullies of Britain.
 But why, honest friends, should we ramble and
  roam,
To look for humbuggers so distant from home?
Poor Ireland, as well as her neighbours, of late
Has begun to remove the fool's cap from her pate.
Our hummers in state, physic, learning, and law,
Do not all sit, as chiefs, in the court of Nassau:
And, once, a whole house of humbuggers was seen
In a place—let me think—ay—'t is call'd Col-
  lege-green!
 Since Galen, in slopping, and doseing, and drug-
  ging,
Gave rules for the physical branch of humbugging;
The patient, when once duly drain'd of his treasure,
Is welcome to die—or recover—at leisure.
 'T other day, in the four courts—sweet pow'rs!
  how I wonder'd
To see, of my friend Harry Lone, a whole hundred!
With gowns, bands, and faces, so smooth and so
  smug'd,
And the world crowding in to be surely humbug'd!
So much for the lawyer and doctor—what lacks?—
The parson, you think, should come in for his snacks.
We doubt not his will—but, in these learned days,
We are all grown too knowing, to mind what he
  says.
 But, what are all hummers, their tricks and their
  arts,
To yon roguish round, the humbuggers of hearts—
By whose sweet enchantment, grey wisdom is fool'd,
And prowess is conquer'd, and courage is cool'd?
For beauty, by ancient tradition, we find,
Has delightfully humm'd the whole race of man-
  kind.

---

TO

## THE MEMORY

OF

### LIEUTENANT COLONEL HENRY CLEMENTS

Shall boastful pomp, the high imperial name,
Or title, only, swell the trump of Fame?
To equal worth be equal glory due,
And wreaths that bloom'd for Clayton bloom for
  you!
 O, once endow'd with ev'ry pleasing pow'r,
To cheer the sad or charm the social hour;
To sweeten life with many a gentle art,
And win the whole dominion of the heart;
I deem'd, far other than the Fates allow,
The laurels bound upon your living brow,
To greet my friend returning from his toil,
Grac'd with his deeds, and laden with his spoil.
Too fond of what the martial harvests yield,
Alas, too forward to the dangerous field,
As one of old renown in battle tried,
The glory of the dusty plain you died!
The tongues of Dettingen your triumph tell,
And weeping Tournay points where Clements fell.
 O, in some future day of loud alarms,
When virtue and my country call to arms
For freedom—struggling nations to unbind,
And snap the sceptres that would bruise man-
  kind—
At such an hour, in such a cause as thine,
The honour'd close of such a death be mine!
Then may some kindred bard appoint my grave,
Snatch forth my name, and roll it with the brave;
Assign my pen and sword the wish'd applause,
And say that both were drawn in virtue's cause!
Then drop the salutation given to you—
" Companion, countryman, and friend—adieu!"

---

## A CHARACTER.

When o'er the canvass flows the master's line,
He adds no name to mark the just design;
The portrait, midst a mingling world, is known,
And stands admir'd, distinguish'd, and alone!
 Behold him, full of virtues as of days,
Laden with worth, infirmities, and praise!
Down the hoar flowings of his silver'd head,
Wisdom and time their equal honours shed;
Truth and benevolence, with equal grace,
Rise from his breast, and lighten in his face.
 His languid limbs expect the peaceful bier;
His head and heart still active, free, and clear!
On his own frame, though dire distemper preys,
He 's borne around, to give all others ease;
Before his healing presence life respires,
And sickness, with his rueful train, retires!
 Great Leach[1] both of our persons and our state!
When thou, at some sad hour, shalt yield to fate—
O then, adieu Hibernia's chiefest wealth;
Adieu to liberty! adieu to health!

---

[1] Dr. Lucas, member of parliament for Dublin.

## TO MR. B———

ON ADVERTISING HIS TREATISE ON THE INTERESTS OF
IRELAND.

Say, B ———, what demon has possess'd
  A brain, that better should discern,
Than thus to choose a theme, confess'd
  No creature's study or concern?

Hadst thou but writ of Mat the miller,
  Or frolics of the fairy-tribe,
Or even of John the Giant Killer;
  There's not a soul but would subscribe.

But, here, though from a seraph's wing
  Thy manna-dropping quill were shed;
Morpheus his leaden mace shall bring,
  Or ere the second page be read.

———

## THE

## PATRIOTISM OF IRELAND,

### AN

### HISTORICAL BALLAD.

TO THE TUNE OF—*Ye commons and peers.*

In the year, do you see,
Of fifty and three,
  A year of facetious renown;
A conjurer came,
Old R———r by name,
  For the pastime of country and town!

At once to surprise
And cozen our eyes,
  He show'd us of courtiers ten brace;
All courtiers as true
To the minister's cue,
  As ever took pension or place!

But R———r, anon,
Cries, " Pass and be gone !"
  The coast it is instantly clear;
And straight, in the place
Of prostitutes base,
  Ten brace of good patriots appear!

The rabble and rout
Clap, caper, and shout;
  The multitude see and believe:
They hail, with acclaim,
Each patriot name!
  But the knowing-ones laugh in their sleeve.

For R———r, once more
Our wits to restore,
  Repeats his charm backwards—and then,
On this patriot-host,
He throws powder of post,
  And he shows them all rascals again!

## THE QUESTION.

INSCRIBED TO LADY CAROLINE RUSSEL.

From our frail sire, who first knew sin,
  Through every stage of age and youth,
The world's grand question still hath been,
  " Whence is beauty, what is truth ?"

This to resolve, or to inquire,
  Employ'd the learn'd of every age;
Alike perplex'd the son and sire,
  The dull, the subtle, and the sage.

At length, impatient of delay,
  The world agreed no more to wait;
But cast disputed truth away,
  As well from practice, as debate.

Then beauty, on unrivall'd ground,
  Sole cause of contest, stood alone;
And every knight hath form'd, or found,
  A favourite princess of his own.

To magic numbers, one confines
  The castle, where the charmer dwells;
And one, to corresponding lines
  Of angles, cubes, and parallels.

By sounds of soft attraction led,
  Her power the man of music feels:
The scholar dreams she's in his head;
  The dancer swears she's in his heels.

In pleasure some, and some in state,
  Their cloud-compos'd enchantress spy [1];
And, from ambition's tow'ry height,
  She catches many a wishful eye.

In symmetry, discerners view
  A glance of beauty's real queen;
And nearer, by a chosen few,
  The sentimental fair is seen.

But each, like knights of old emprise,
  (Whate'er his present flame) requires,
That all should find conforming eyes,
  And join to bow—where he admires.

To fix this fire of wand'ring love,
  Supernal Power resolv'd to show,
That what was truth in Heav'n above,
  Alone made beauty here below.

For this, he purpos'd to condense
  What angels felt of good or bright,
With sentiment to strike the sense,
  And give the charm of soul to sight.

At length the plastic power descends
  With Heav'n's select ingredients fraught:
To Earth his beamy flight he bends,
  And into substance features thought.

[1] Ixion was enamoured of a cloud that represented Juno.

From Zembla's frozen clime, he chose
  A quantity of virgin air,
For lucid organs, to compose
  The moving fabric of his fair.

With this he blends the portion due,
  Nine solar rays of morning light,
To give a blush of chastest hue,
  As deep and warm, as pure and bright.

From Hybla's sweets, that breathe in fame,
  He press'd the prime of bloom and bud;
And, through the soft transparent frame,
  He pour'd the aromatic flood.

Spher'd in the centre, as a sun,
  Within he hung the cordial freight,
Which from Eternal Truth he won,
  And bid th' embosom'd Heav'n to beat.

From number, music, sisters twin,
  He caught the magic of the face;
And, from the sentiment within,
  He pictur'd motion, mien, and grace,

Thus folding, in one radiant frame,
  Each beauty humanely-divine,
He gave his system up to fame,
  And mortals call her—Caroline!

---

## SONGS FROM HIS DRAMATIC PIECES.

### FROM

### JACK THE GIANT-QUELLER.

#### AIR I.

THE laws they were made for the little,
The laws they were made for the little,
  In the hands of the strong,
  All the ties, that belong
To justice and honour, are brittle.

The laws they were made for the little,
The laws they were made for the little,
  Though churchmen may preach,
  And philosophers teach,
The great will not list to a tittle.

The laws they were made for the little,
The laws they were made for the little;
  It is not by right,
  But by wrong-doing might,
That giants still 'scape a committal.

#### AIR II.

This scepter'd hand all nations own;
  All religions hold divine—
I the king of ev'ry throne;
  I the god of ev'ry shrine!

Gold is every woman's lust;
  Gold is every man's desire;
Gold the covert patriot's gust;
  Kneel my sons, and own your sire!

#### AIR III.

#### TUNE—*Moll Roe.*

WOULD you silence a patriot committee,
  Touch their lips with this magical wand;
Through country, and senate, and city,
  'T is the lock and the key of the land.

Take a piece of this same from your coffer,
  Display to the voter your pelf;
And the wretch, having nothing to offer,
  Will frugally sell you—himself.

'T is a shot for the fowl of all feather,
  A bait for the gust of all fish;
To this ev'ry gudgeon will gather,
  And plump, ready dress'd, in your dish.

If the booby, your pupil, so dull is,
  He scarce can remember his name;
Yet his mouth it shall open, like Tully's,
  When fed with a spoon of this same.

To a rascal, a bear, and a blockhead,
  Unconscious of mood or of tense,
This plastic receipt, in his pocket,
  Gives grace, figure, virtue, and sense.

Old saints will for this sell their manuals;
  O'er this, at your sov'reign nod,
Old judges will skip like young spaniels,
  And cardinals kiss you this rod.

To study aught else is but nonsense;
  From hence all philosophy springs—
'T is the crown, beauty, cause, and good conscience,
  Of priests, ladies, lawyers, and kings.

#### AIR IV.

#### TUNE—*Peggy Benson.*

In the church, where your dignified doctors you
  Such holy men refrain, son;   [find,
For, uplifted by us, and our offices kind,
  Their sanctify'd pride they sustain, son.

Let governors thrive, and each prince, on his throne,
  In peace and plenty reign, son;
Till you find that by talents, and virtue, alone,
  One man shall to honour attain, son.

Let party in turbulent senates debate,
  Nor matters it who shall gain, son;
Till you find that one act for the good of the state,
  Shall have enter'd in either's brain, son.

Let the law be your care, nor one tittle retrench,
  But support each furr'd robe in its station;
For they, as our substitutes, sit on the bench,
  To decide the affairs of the nation.

In cities, though czars of a pitiful sphere,
  Would you know who would be our relation?
'T is the alderman's worship, and sudden lord
     mayor,
  Who struts through his yearly creation.

Each fox-hunting justice and landlorded youth,
  Are prone to your point, when they may, son;
For these, too, are little grand signiors, forsooth,
  And giants, each man in his way, son.


### AIR V.

*Tune—If all the fair maids.*

Ambition like jack-o'-the-lantern bewitches;
Ambition like jack-o'-the-lantern bewitches;
And leads you benighted through dirt and through
        ditches.          Dol de dol, &c.

Your griping for gold, a beggarly itch is;
Your griping for gold, a beggarly itch is;
And virtue, though humble, looks down upon riches.
                  Dol de dol, &c.

Your great men and statesmen, the higher their
        pitch is,          [pitch is,
Your great men and statesmen, the higher their
By climbing the broader, but show us their breeches.
                  Dol de dol, &c.


### AIR VI.

*Tune—Dole and woe fa our cat.*

How often our mother has told,
  And sure she is wondrous wise!
In cities, that all you behold,
  Is a fair, but a faithless disguise:
That the modes of a court education
  Are train-pits, and traitors to youth;
And the only fine language in fashion,
  A tongue that is foreign to truth.

Where honour is barely an oath;
  Where knaves are with noblemen class'd;
Where nature's a stranger to both;
  And love an old tale of times pass'd;
Where laughter no pleasure dispenses,
  Where smiles are the envoys of art;
Where joy lightly swims on the senses,
  But never can enter the heart.

Where hopes and kind hugs are trepanners;
  Where virtue's divorc'd from success;
Where cringing goes current for manners,
  And worth is no deeper than dress.
Where favour creeps lamely on crutches;
  Where friendship is nothing but face;
And the title of duke, or of dutchess,
  Is all that entitles to grace.


### AIR VII.

*Tune—Lochaber.*

Farewell to my Gracey, my Gracey so sweet,
How painful to part!—but again we shall meet.
Thy Jack, he will languish, and long for the day
That shall kiss the dear tears of his sister away.
Though honour, in groves of tall laurel, should
        grow;
And fortune, in tides, should eternally flow;
Nor honour, nor fortune, thy Jack shall detain,
But he'll come to his Gracey, his sister again.

Again, at our door, in the morning of spring,
To see the Sun rise, and hear goldfinches sing!
To rouse our companions, and maids of the May,
In copses to gambol, in meadows to play.
Or, at questions and forfeits, all rang'd on the grass;
Or to gather fresh chaplets, each lad for his lass;
To sing, and to dance, and to sport on the plain,
Thy Jack shall return to his Gracey again.

Or alone, in his Gracey's sweet company bless'd,
To feed thy young robins that chirp on the nest;
To help at her med'cines, and herbs for the poor,
And welcome the stranger that stops at the door.
At night, o'er our fire, and a cup of clear ale,
To hear the town-news, and the traveller's tale;
To smile away life, till our heads they grow hoar,
And part from my sheep, and my Gracey no more.


### AIR VIII.

*Tune—Dremondoo.*

O now he has left me, what care shall employ,
What object afford me the shadow of joy?
To a heart so o'erladen, all sorrows are meet;
Misfortune is welcome, and mourning is sweet!

Away, ye companions of daily delight,
And pastimes that gently could steal on the night;
Away, ye fond sports of the wake and the fair!
Your pleasures are vanish'd—no brother is there!

Of the ball, and the hurling, the dance, and the
        race,
His skill was the victor, his person the grace:
The maidens throng'd round him, delighted to see,
And wish'd they had all been his sisters, like me.

Thus, ev'ry dear scene of my former delight,
To my mind will recall him, but not to my sight;
The trees will all droop, and the meadows look lone;
And all say—poor maid! thy companion is gone!


### AIR IX.

*Tune—Grana Weil.*

Though passions contend, and afflictions storm,
And shake the frail state of the human form;
If virtue the base of our pile sustain,
Afflictions shall rage and assault in vain.

The paths for the steps of all mortals made,
Is simply to follow where truth shall lead:
Nor thou from its rectitude turn aside;
The rest, let hereafter and Heaven provide.


### AIR X.

*Tune—I have sixpence under my thumb.*

How sweet the gossiping birds that sing!
How sweet the treasure the zephyrs bring,
Light wafted on each odorif'rous wing
That winnows the breast of flowery spring!

How sweet the showers with balm replete!
The fawns that frolic, and lambs that bleat!
But O! above all, though all should meet,
Our Justice, our queen of sweets is sweet!

## AIR XI.

*Tune—To you fair ladies now on land.*

The world, a faithless ocean, toss'd
   By passion's stormy wind,
Is spread with spoils of thousands lost,
   The wreck of human kind !
Where all the freight their vessels bear
Is but a wilful weight of care.
            Dol lol, &c.

For what can Reason's feeble hand
   Before the helm perform,
Where he can spy nor port, nor land,
   To 'scape from stress or storm—
Where Hope, amid the raging main,
Her anchor casts,—but casts in vain ?
            Dol lol, &c.

O turn, misguided wights !—return
   To us, who smile on shore !
To us, who yet your errours mourn,
   Your safety who implore !
Your forfeit peace with us renew,
Who shed no tears—except for you.
            Dol lol, &c.

## AIR XII.

*Tune—Twang dillo dee.*

But we to Nature who adhere, nor further bliss re-
      quire,             [desire.
To lop the root of all our care, we lop each vain

We ask no cynic law, nor saw, nor scrolls of beard-
      ed men ;           [can ken.
For Nature's the most learned book that innocence

To baffle want, and sweeten toil, from debt and
      danger free;      [trious bee.
We learn instruction from the ant, and the indus-

From dogs we learn unfailing faith, affection from
      the dove;        [circling love.
And from the hen, who guards her chick, a parent's

And, last, we to all bounteous Heav'n our daily
      tribute yield;      [grateful field.
Taught by the fragrant incense breath'd from ev'ry

## AIR XIII.

*Tune—Ye commons and peers.*

The time to beguile,
   Now listen a while,
And I 'll show you an excellent plot;
   How husband and wife,
   Through the crosses of life,
May be held by the true-lover's knot.

As mortals are frail,
   Let indulgence prevail,
And all mutual infirmities blot ;
   Let the husband but own
   His wife errs not alone,
And I 'll vouch for the true-lover's knot.

My Dolly so bright,
   Should your Hob, over night,
Be surpris'd by his pipe or his pot;
   Let him sleep his dose out,
   Nor, by scolding or pout,
Strive to lessen the true-lover's knot.

When your wives they grow grey,
   And their graces decay,
Of all mortal beauty the lot;
   Remember their youth,
   And, by friendship and truth,
Make eternal the true-lover's knot.

## AIR XIV.

*Tune—A begging we will go.*

However some in coaches, on barrows some may
      beg ;         [wooden leg.
'T is want that makes the mendicant, and not the
      When a begging they do go, &c.

'T is thus, by greater poverty, that nobles grow re-
      nown'd ;      [want a pound.
For where we want a penny, friend, state beggars
      And a begging they do go, &c.

Your courtier begs for honour—and that 's a want
      indeed !      [need,
As many should for honesty, but will not own their
      When a begging they should go, &c.

Your vizier begs for subsidies, your party-man for
      place ;      [for grace,
Your church-man, for a benefice ;—but not a man
      When a begging they do go, &c.

Thus all from Rome to London are of the begging
      train ;      [vain,
But we, who beg for charity—must look to beg in
      When a begging we do go, &c.

## AIR XV.

*Tune—Fie, let us awa to the wedding.*

Yet many, when beggars are pressing,
   Of bounty are nothing loth;
The bishop will give you—his blessing ;
   The officer give you—his oath,
Of his promise, to be a free donor,
   The courtier is little nice;
And great-ones will give you—their honour !
   For these are of little price.

## AIR XVI.

*Tune—A cobbler there was.*

You yet may behold the surprise of the town,
To see truth elated, dishonour pull'd down ;
All tricks, low and little, despis'd by the great,
And honesty fix'd for a maxim of state !
            Derry down, &c.

To see our lac'd lordlings deserving of trust;
Our clergymen pious, our justices just ;
Our court ladies blush ; and our thing of a beau,
A something, beside a mere nothing but show.
            Derry down, &c.

To see worth and talents to office preferr'd;
The virtuous rewarded; the vicious deterr'd;
And the streams of polution, where people resort,
New fed from the clarify'd springs of our court.
Derry'down, &c.

To see freedom loyal; elections unbrib'd;
All faction exil'd, and corruption proscrib'd:
Pure Nature exalted o'er masking and art;
And Dominion possess'd of its seat in the heart.
Derry down, &c.

To see Mirth, with Innocence, walking tne land;
And Probity taking Free-trade by the hand;
And the courts of our law from iniquity clear,
O then, what a rare revolution were here!
Derry down, &c.

CHORUS.

And the courts, &c.

### AIR XVII.

TUNE—*Chevy chase.*

BUT since by mortals 't is confess'd,
  The shafts of Fate mu*t fall;
I 'll take firm patience to my breast,
  And smile, secure of all.

### AIR XVIII.

TUNE—*Delia, by Arne.*

O FORM'D of harmony and light!
  Too bright for sense to bear!
Art thou to feeling as to sight?
  Essential as thou 'rt fair?

If some illusion from the skies,
  In pity yet delay;
Nor melt, sweet object, from my eyes,
  In fleeting air away!

### AIR XIX.

TUNE—*Two gossips they luckily met.*

THE Indies thy toilet shall grace;
  For thee shall earth, ocean, and air,
From the gin, and the net, and the chase,
  Each costly collation prepare.

All seasons their sweets shall dispense,
  And a round of long happiness roll;
And bliss, through the gates of each sense,
  Shall enter and mix with thy soul.

Fair Phœbe shall light up her horn,
  To watch the repose of thy charms;
And each blushing and rapturous morn
  Shall find thee reclin'd in my arms.

### AIR XX.

TUNE—*Who 'll see my gallantee show.*

I 'LL first present you a prime minister,
Free from thought or action sinister!
Public good his square and measure;
Himself his country's trust and treasure.
And is not this a show?

VOL. XVII.

Here 's humility in high station!
Dignity strip'd of ostentation!
Friendship, here, outgoes profession;
Here is pow'r, without oppression!
Oh, the finest show!

Who 'll see honesty in a miser?
Fops, from France, return the wiser?
Wealthy poets, and poor receivers?
Lawyers in future rewards believers?
Oh, the curious show!

Here 's dependance, without servility;
Peers, to virtue who owe nobility;
Next, where piety weds with prelacy:
But you scarce will credit, till you see,
Such a wondrous show!

### AIR XXI.

TUNE—*Foddreen mare.*

COME all you gay gallants, for pleasure who prowl!
Come all you young racers, who strain for the goal!
Come all you stout wrestlers, who strive on the
  plain! [main!
Come all you fond merchants, who trade on the
Come all, who expend your short candle, in quest
Of phantoms, still follow'd, but still unpossess'd!
In vain you search, wander, strain, struggle, and
  steer!
The prize you all wrestl'd, and run for, lay here.

[*Two trifling airs omitted here.*]

### AIR XXIV.

TUNE—*My father and mother sent me far.*

FOR lo! her wealth all spent on want,
  Where Charity's reclin'd!
The moving tale of wretchedness
  Still rolling in her mind.
Her sighs and tears are still a fund
  Of bounty to distress;
And she delights to share the woe
  She can no more redress.

### AIR XXV.

TUNE—*My dog and my gun.*

ON what a firm rock here does fortitude fix!
Around him, in war, all the elements mix!
The hurricane rages! the tempest it boils!
Loud thunders are lanch'd at his head—and he
  smiles!

### AIR XXVI.

TUNE—*Æneas wandering prince of Troy.*

HUMILITY, her crown aside,
Here stoops to wash the feet of Pride.
Averse from all the world calls great,
She fain would fall, and sink from state!
But sink or fall, howe'er she will,
She finds the world beneath her still.

F f

## AIR XXVII.

### TUNE—*Past one o'clock.*

How mild, in this ruby, pale Chastity flushes;
 And tinctures with crimson her form of light!
Unconscious of guilt ;—at her beauty she blushes,
 And wraps each proportion and charm from sight.
All hush'd as rock'd infants, all sweet as the fold-
  ing rose,                              [disclose!
Her lips, with reluctance, the balm of her breath
Her eyes look abash'd at their brightness, yet still
  she shows
Brighter by veiling whate'er is bright!

## AIR XXVIII.

### TUNE—*The bonny Christ-church bells.*

WOULD you wear this pearl so rare ?
Then, fair one, list to me,
First learn the skill your tongue to still;
And leave the name and honest frame of others free.
Your tittle-tattle, prate and prattle—rake and rattle,
  all
Due victims to this pearl must fall.
Your joys in toys, of folly, fops, and noise,
That, noon and night, the toy-shop of your heart
  employs;
The side-long glance, and kindling dance,
Minc'd mien, and conscious eye ;       [show;
With foibles which, you know, in shame I spare to
A price, I fear, too high.

## AIR XXIX.

### TUNE—*Bumpers, 'squire Jones.*

'SINCE, sir, you require
Me with freedom to tell you the price I desire ;
  If duly obey'd,
I must claim all your shifts,
Mean resources, sly drifts,
  And whole system of trade.
Each method of weaving
Court nets for enslaving ;
Your chaffer for conscience, by barter and lure :
State quacks, and state nurses ;
Your purging of purses ;
And skinning of wounds, which you wish not to cure.

Each subtle essay
Of spreading corruption, in order for sway ;
  All projects for rule,
By the bate and the bribe,
And political tribe,
  Of trick, traffic, and tool.
Your court-broom, that gathers
Motes, chaff, straw, and feathers,
And sweeps up all trash from the surface of life.
With your largess of graces,
Posts, pensions, and places,
Where talents and office are ever at strife.

With these, I must claim
Your entry of red-coated gentry, who dream
  That heroes are made,
And enabl'd to kill,
  By the courage and skill
  Of a dreadful cockade!

A race, who are prouder
To spend their *sweet powder*
At *balls*, than on *bullets*,—a terrible train
  Of crimp petit-maitres,
  Nice seamsters and plaiters,
Beau'd out, for the dance of a dainty campaign !

## AIR XXX.

### TUNE—*Ye fairy elves that be.*

COME follow, follow me,
You jolly boys all, who be
Divested of constraint,
From mortify'd saw, or saint !
To pleasure and boundless licence free,
Come follow, follow, follow me !
Come all to measureless licence free,
And follow, follow, follow me !

Let lean-ey'd honesty bear
His merited weight of care ;
And phlegm and conscience dwell
In cynical tub, or cell ;
But all ye lovers of game and glee,
And feast and frolic, come follow me !
To Nature's measureless licence free,
Come follow, follow, follow me !

The pedanted priest, who fain
Would ride, but wants a rein ;
To moral us into control,
Would sour the jovial soul !!
The priest is cunning, and so are we ;
Then priest and people, come follow me !
From scruple and qualm, and conscience free,
Come follow, follow me !

## AIR XXXI.

### TUNE—*Tiptelera.*

THESE gauntlets, we understand,
  From annals, time out of mind,
Have giv'n due weight to each hand
  Of the bruisers of mankind.
Still apt to his occupation
  Whom no restriction awes;
Whose courage would cuff a nation,
  And quell both land and laws.

## AIR XXXII.

### TUNE—*Ye commons and peers.*

BEHOLD, from old times,
Through all customs, and climes,
  The meed of ambition and pride !
'T is a gift, my good sirs,
For him who, with spurs,
  On the back of his country would ride.
                         Dol de rol, &c.

*[A trifling air omitted here.]*

## AIR XXXIV.

### TUNE—*Ye fairy elves that be.*

DUET BETWEEN JUSTICE AND JACK.

ARISE, arise, arise !
Each shape, and sort, and size

Of honesty, where ye lie,
Unheeded, on dank or dry;
From cottages, shades, and sheds, to court,
My brothers of worth, and want, resort!
Arise to labour, arise to play,
For virtue dawns a new-born day!
     CHORUS.   Arise to labour, &c.

To court, to court repair;
Though destitute, poor, and bare;
And yet unskill'd in aught
That Euclid or Machiavel taught.
By naked probity, you acquire
A garb beyond the silk of Tyre;
And more than talents, and more than art,
Is furnish'd in an upright heart!
     CHORUS.  And more than, &c.

Let jollity e'en devour
His interval of an hour;
Yet pity his transient roar,
For list—and he laughs no more!
The purest pleasures that guilt can bring,
Are like the tickling of a sting;
The tickling leaves no sweet behind;
The sting remains, and stabs the mind!
     CHORUS.  The tickling leaves, &c.

But virtue, in the breast,
Composes her halcyon nest;
And sooths and smooths each storm,
That would the fair seat deform;
Herself most frolic, and sweetly free
To cordial jollity, cordial glee!
The fountain of all that 's bless'd and bright;
Of orient pleasure, of orient light!
     CHORUS.  The fountain, &c.

And from this mental dawn,
O'er village, and lake, and lawn;
New radiance shall expand,
To brighten each dusky land;
While truth, from this approving stage,
Shall beam through ev'ry act and age!

CHORUS.

While truth, from this approving stage,
Shall beam through ev'ry act and age.

FROM

## THE EARL OF WESTMORLAND.

### THE INSIDE OF THE ABBEY.

*Rowena and Nuns ranged on each side, with tapers.*

ANTHEM.

HERE, in ev'ry sacred aisle,
Solemn walk, and silent cell,
Truth and Peace serenely smile,
Hope and warm Devotion dwell.

Safely landed, here we mourn,
Found'ring mortals, left behind;
Wretches, on the deep forlorn,
Toss'd and wreck'd with ev'ry wind.

What has grandeur to supply,
What has pleasure to impart?
Mere illusion to the eye,
Real anguish to the heart!

Here, from time and transience won,
Beauty has her charms resign'd;
Heav'n already is begun,
Opening in an humble mind.

Fount of truth, seraphic bowl,
Pour the nectar from above!
O, descend into the soul,
Thirsting after life and love!

Death is conquer'd, time is pass'd,
Heav'n is present to our view—
Welcome, welcome, joys that last!
Short seducing world, adieu!

FUNERAL PROCESSION, AND DIRGE.

WRETCHED mortals, doom'd to go
Through the vale of death and woe!
Let us travel sad and slow.

Care and sickness, toil and pain,
Here their restless vigils keep:
Sighs are all the winds that blow,
Tears are all the streams that flow!
Virtue hopes reward in vain—
The gentlest lot she can obtain,
Is but to sit and weep!

Ye dreary mansions of enduring sleep,
Where pale mortality lies dark and deep!
Thou silent, though insatiate grave,
Gorg'd with the beauteous and the brave,
Close, close thy maw—thy feast is o'er,
Time and death can give no more!

In Rowena thou hast
Thy consummate repast!
All that Earth could boast divine,
All we held of Heav'n is thine!
Time and death no more can gain—
They have all perfection slain!
O grave, thy festival is o'er;
The beggar'd world can give no more!

SONG OF CONSOLATION.

YE desolate mortals who stray,
Dark, devious, and wilfully blind;
O turn, and distinguish the way
That leads to the bliss of mankind!

The titles ye falsely assign,
With their symbols are ever at strife;
And death, by appointment divine,
Is our birth and our portal to life.

The Framer of Nature from chaos and night,
Who drew yon fair system of order and light,
On extremes hath the plan of his universe built,
On frailty perfection, and pardon on guilt; [pain,
And through the short transience of death and of
Appoints human weakness to rise and to reign.

'T is virtue, 't is virtue, o'er grief and the grave,
   That rises secure and sublime ;
The prize that eternity watches to save
   From the wrecks and the ruins of time !

---

## FROM MONTEZUMA.

### HYMN TO BEAUTY.

TELL us, ye gods, what power is this,
   That rules with such resistless sway ;
To whom the mightiest bow submiss,
   Whom crowds adore, whom kings obey ?

It is the power of Beauty's charm,
   That can all other powers subdue,
The savage tame, the fierce disarm,
   And teach subjected pride to sue.

Great monarch ! if you haply find
   The force of her enchantment here,
Her temples with your garland bind,
   And crown her empress of the year.

### INCANTATION.

MOON, pale regent of the night,
Goddess of each magic rite—
In this dread and dreary hour
Aid us with thy light and power !

O, ye stars, ye seeds of light,
Radiant gems of gloomy night,
  n whose ever-varying round
Present, past, and future 's found ;
Who, in characters, comprise
Falls of kingdoms, ere they rise,
To our favour'd sight reveal      [ceal !
Whate'er, from vulgar eyes, with caution ye con-

Ye spirits infernal, dark partners of woe !
Ye demons, who wield ebon sceptres below !
Ye goblins and fairies, or dusky or fair,
Who mine in the earth, or who dance in the air !

My wand demands ye, from Hell, earth, and skies—
     Arise, arise, arise !

     [A terrestial Spirit ascends.]

Spirit.—Prince, mourn your search—your gods are
   all control'd ;
Silent, and bow'd before superior power !
     I dare no more.     [Descends.

High Priest.—Hence, dark and dastard sprite !—
Calib, my ever-smiling friend !
Circled with radiant light, descend ;
Our bosoms with thy wonted tidings cheer,
Speak comfort to our heart, and music to our ear !

     [Calib descends in white, and sings.]

Mighty emperor, attend ;
Heavy, heavy things impend !

Many a conflict, many a fight,
Desolation, fear, and flight,
Loss of empire, life, and light,
   All rush upon my sight !

Yet, through the horrours of this threat'ning sky,
One radiant beam I spy.
It comes, the singly smiling hour,
That puts our Indian world again into thy power !

   They stand, they stand,
     Within thine hand,
This horrid, hostile, ruthless band—
Strike, strike, and save the land !     [Ascends.

### SONG OF TRIUMPH AND THANKSGIVING,

#### BY PRIESTS AND PRIESTESSES.

THUNDER sleeps—the storm is o'er ;
War and terrour are no more.
See their horrid hosts retire—
Fainting worlds again respire !
By our conq'ring hero fell'd,
Spain is shackled, force is quell'd !
Peace revisits India's shore—
Thunder sleeps —the storm is o'er !

Peace revisits, &c.

Now, through ev'ry glen and glade,
In the sunshine, in the shade,
Vacant innocence shall stray,
Fearing neither wile nor way !
Sons shall laugh within the shed,
By their sires and grandsires spread ;
Peace shall slumber, toil shall snore—
Wars and terrours are no more.

Peace shall, &c.

In wedlock, again, loving pairs shall be tied,
And children shall run by their glad father's side ;
Long poles shall be fix'd, where the minstrel shall
   sound,     [around ;
And where holy-day crowds shall dance cheerly
Birds shall chirp in the groves, and beasts frisk in
   the plain,     [Spain.
Nor be scar'd by the thunders and lightnings of
Through our clime, mirth shall carol, and laughter
   shall roar ;
For war, tumult, terrour, and Spain are no more !
Through our clime, &c.

---

## THE FOX-CHASE.

YOUNG Marcus with the lark salutes the morn—
" Saddle your horses, huntsman ; wind your horn."
We start, we rise at the enliv'ning sound—
The woods all ring—and wind the horn around :
We snatch a short repast within the hall ;
" To horse ! to horse !"—We issue at the call.
As when, to rid his country from alarms
Of Russian inroads, and of Gallic arms,

Great Prussia bids the patriot trump to blow,
The free-born gather, and around him glow:
So, at the call of Marcus—grateful sound—
Men, steeds, and dogs, tumult'ous pour around.

The youth upon their coursers vault with grace;
The coursers neigh, impatient for the chase :,
Their short and eager steps the bit restrains :
They paw and pant, reluctant to the reins.
Unfolding gates a spacious passage yield—
Forward we move, and issue to the field.

Far within cover thoughtless Reynard lay,
And slept the riots of the night away.
Late, from the ravage of a neighb'ring farm,
He had withdrawn, impenitent of harm ;
The tainted gales his felon steps pursue,
And tell his travels to the conscious dew.
But he, whom many a 'scape had render'd sure,
For slights and wiles unrivall'd, slept secure,
In unsuspecting spirits blithe and bland,
Nor dreams the dreadful reck'ning is at hand.

Trueman, whom for sagacious nose we hail
The chief, first touch'd the scarce-distinguish'd gale;
His tongue was doubtful, and no hound replies :
" Haux ! — wind him !—haux !" — the tuneful
          huntsman cries.
At once the list'ning pack asunder spread,
With tail erect, and with inquiring head :
With busy nostrils they foretaste their prey,
And snuff the lawn-impearling dews away.

Now here, now here, they chop upon the scent,
Their tongues in undulating ether spent :
More joyous now, and louder by degrees,
Warm, and more warm, they catch the coming
          breeze.
Now with full symphony they jointly hail
The welcome tidings of a surer gale ;
Along the vale they pour the swelling note ;
Their ears and dewlaps on the morning float.

How vainly art aspires, by rival sounds,
To match the native melody of hounds !
Not eunuchs, warbling in the vocal choir,
Though join'd by pipe and string, such bliss inspire,
When with joint sense they quaff the tainted gale,
And in full concert ring their morning peal :
The list'ning planets from their orbits bend,
And the still elements with joy attend.

Again the doubtful scent our hope defeats :
" To cover—hark !"—the huntsman's voice repeats.
Wide on the left a neighb'ring copse was spread,
And thither th' obsequious pack he led.
But more aloof the parting sportsmen scout,
Watch ev'ry path, and skirt the wood about.
The huntsman now, with expectation flush, [bush:
" Haux, fox !" he cries, and strikes the hopeful
To cover straight the spreading hounds now take,
Snuff ev'ry tuft, and spy in ev'ry brake.
Again the breeze betrays the tainted ground,
And Lovely tells the gladsome tidings round ;
" Hark !—Lovely !—hark !"—deep echoing glens
          resound.

Ah, hapless foxes ! ever blind to fate !
Without a cause dejected and elate.
Darkling ye walk, unconscious of your end,
Nor mark the gath'ring mischiefs that impend!
The shrewd and simple share an equal lot—
In death the wizard finds himself a sot.,
That luckless morn, when first along the glade
The tell-tale dews his nightly steps betray'd,
Wrapp'd in soft slumbers Reynard press'd his bed,
And there on visionary poultry fed.

He dream'd, as by a neighb'ring grange he crept,
Crouch'd while he mov'd, and linger'd as he stept,
Two virgin pullets fix'd his side regard,
Plump from the sounding barn and pamp'ring yard:
Near, and more near, he steals with winking eyes,
Then springs at once, and seizes on his prize.
Loud piercing screams th' affrighted welkin fill,
And down his jaws the luscious streams distil.
Ev'n in this rapturous moment, while his taste
Gorg'd the full riot of a fancy'd feast,
Lovely's near note, far echoing, pierc'd his ears—
He wakes, and inward shrinks to shun his fears.
Upward he starts—erects his ears—and then
Hears the loud " Hark !".—and down he sinks again.
Trembling he strives to re-assure his heart
With a fresh promise of long prosp'ring art ;
Then with sly caution, crouching as he rose,
From his warm kennel's ancient seat he goes ;
The seat to which he shall return no more,
Now with chill moss and dropping branches hoar.

Through frizzled thickets, and through yielding
          sprays,
He thwarts each path, and treads a puzzling maze.
So steer'd, some devious vessel shifts her sail,
And, veering, gains upon th' adverse gale.

Now, from the mansion of his late repose
Rank steams and reeking exhalations rose ;
The tepid vapours are diffus'd around,
And reach the nerves of each inquiring hound :
With answering notes, their heads tow'rds Heav'n
          they cast,
And in full concert hail the rich repast.

The sculking caitiff, who beneath the spread
Of fav'ring umbrage veil'd his luckless head,
Close at his ear believes the distant peals,
And a whole host of demons at his heels.
His instant terrours cast all wiles away,
He breaks from cover, and demands the day :
O'er the fair field he flies his num'rous foes,
And down the wind, as swift as wind he goes.
A watchful scout his bold elopement spies—
" Ho !—tally-ho !"—triumphantly he cries.
His rash alarm the gen'rous Marcus blames—
" Law !—give him law !"—as loudly he exclaims.
The distant sportsmen gather at the shout,
As bees they buzz and close their chief about ;
The fervid youth attending crowd the plain,
And bind the crested coursers to the rein. [throats,

The choiring hounds, with deep harmonious
Fill the charm'd wood, and swell the doubling notes ;
Sweeter than those of that enchanting strain
That still'd the surge on the Trinacrian main,
When to the mast, the Grecian, wisely bound,
Scarce dar'd the tempting magic of the sound.

The dogs, a travers'd labyrinth unwind,
Subtler than that which Dædalus design'd.
By slow degrees the doubling wile is won,
Trac'd through the shade, and push'd into the sun ;
There the broad airs a livelier scent assume,
And greet their senses with a full perfume.
Then, as a shaft from the withholding thong,
They shoot away, and pour the plains along.

No more the youth their eager steeds restrain ;
Ardent they start, and loose the granted rein :
The steeds spring forth, and from the rein unbound,
Devour the less'ning distance of the ground ;
They stretch and strain each nerve and active limb,
Sweep down the slopes, and o'er the levels skim.
Their force a gen'rous emulation fires ;
Beneath our speed the fleeting earth retires.

In a glad frenzy we attempt the sky;
Nor seem to run, or ride, but mount and fly!
Now lightly o'er opposing walls we bound,
Clear the broad trench, and top the rising mound:
No stop, no time for respite or recess;
On, and still on, fox, dogs, and horses press.
    The hounds outbreath'd, from their late tuneful
                                                throat
Now break—half short—the disappointed note.
Now o'er the smoking vale each gen'rous steed
Relaxes from the fervour of his speed:
Push'd up the bray, indignantly they feel
The clanking lash, and the retorted steel;
Then down the steep with quick'ning rapture go,
And stretch and sweat upon the plain below.
    Athwart one way a tumbling stream was laid
That to the lake its daily tribute paid:
Here the first stop our rapid course delays,
And with a grateful interruption stays.
Upon the bank, in watchful silence still,
We breathe the rising freshness of the rill;
We pant—we drop our languid limbs—and all,
Like fainting Cephalus, on Aura call.
Dark as a mist that to the distant view
Caps the brown mountains with a murky blue;
So from our steeds the thick'ning vapours rise,
Infold their riders, and obscure the skies.
The glowing dogs, forgetful of their foe,
Full on the stream their headlong bodies throw,
Like iron on the whizzing smithy flung,
And lap, and pant, and loll the length'ning tongue.
    Now, from the west, a livelier gale upsprings,
And with new nerves each listless member strings.
In terms still varying their harmonious sounds,
The huntsman calls, and cheers his circling hounds.
Now up, now down, now cross the stream he beats—
" Haux!—wind him!—haux!—Fox, find him!"
                                            he repeats.
Now round and round a fruitless search he plies,
And now a tour of wider circuit tries.
But no intelligence rewards his care;
No note confess'd the fox was ever there—
As though some opening gulf had gorg'd our prey,
Or sudden power had snatch'd him quite away.
    But Reynard, hotly push'd, and close pursu'd,
Yet fruitful in expedients to elude,
When to the bourn's refreshing bank he came,
Had plung'd, all reeking, in the friendly stream.
The folding waves his failing pow'rs restore,
And close the gates of every fuming pore.
Then down the channel, over flats and steeps,
He steals, and trots—or wades, or swims, or creeps;
Till, where the pebbled shores the surges break,
He quits his feet, and lanches on the lake.
    As when some coasting skiff, with shatter'd geers,
A cautious course 'twixt land and ocean steers,
Fearful alike on either dang'rous hand
To trust the boist'rous sea or faithless land:
Possess'd of equal fears and equal lore,
So Reynard coasts aloof, and shuns the shore,
Lest the uncover'd odour should exhale,
And tell sure tidings to the trait'rous gale.
    Not distant far, upon the beach there stood
The hoary growth of a majestic wood,
Whose age of oak and intervening yew
Not the great-grandsires of the living knew:
The flooring, deep beneath the distant shade,
With thorn and frizzling brush was thick inlaid,
While clamouring rooks, scarce heard above our
Amid the cloud-commingling branches bred. [head,

Here Reynard lands, all dripping from the lake,
And seeks the shelter of his wonted brake.
Arriv'd, he shakes, and rolls, and turns him round;
Then entering, sinks o'ertoil'd upon the ground:
Stretch'd at full length, secure of care he lies,
And instant slumbers seal his willing eyes.
    The chop-fall'n hounds meantime are heard no
                                                more,
But silent range along the winding shore.
Hopeless alike the hunters lag behind,
And give all thoughts of Reynard to the wind—
All, save one wily rival of his art,
Who vows unpitying vengeance ere they part.
Along the coast his watchful course he bent,
Careful to catch and wind the thwarting scent;
And last, to make his boastful promise good,
Enter'd the precincts of the fatal wood.
    There, through the gloom, he leads one hopeless
                                                train,
And cheers the long-desponding pack in vain;
Till Ringwood first the faint effluvia caught,
And with loud tongue reform'd their old default.
Rous'd at the swell of that reviving sound,
Our hopes rekindle, and our hearts rebound!
Eager we spread through furze and mingling brush,
And lash the woof of each afflicted bush;
While here and there the busy dogs reveal
The languid tidings of the dubious gale.
    Meanwhile the fox, unconscious of the chase,
Repair'd his late fatigues, and slept in peace;
Nor mark'd the cry of many a hostile tongue
That through the copious forest loudly rung,
Till a bold youth approach'd his thoughtless bed,
And struck the bower that trembl'd o'er his head.
    As when amaz'd upstarted Manoah's heir,
Shorn of his strength and his enchanted hair,
While his peal'd ears receiv'd the hostile sound
Of shouting foes that girt his couch around;
So Reynard wakes with sudden horrours chill,
Scant of his force, and shorten'd of his skill.
Bold through despair, he breaks at once away,
Bounds through the brush, and rushes into day!
The fields, the shores, the hills, each wood resounds
With echoing hunters, and with op'ning hounds:
Rocks, waters, undulating air, and sky,
Become one peal, and propagate the cry.
From the firm land, and from the trembling lake,
Full on our ears the tuneful thunders break,
Roll o'er the waves, and strike the distant coast,
And far beyond, mid heav'n-top'd hills, are lost.
    Again we start, we bound, we stretch amain,
O'er the brown heath, and o'er the bright champaign:
Again o'er gates we fly, through hedges rush,
Through moorlands labour, and through thickets
                                                push.
Intense again our gath'ring fervour grows—
Again the coursers smoke—the rider glows:
Distinguish'd steeds their fellow steeds outwind,
And leave their late associates far behind;
While laggard hounds, that form a lengthen'd train,
Run, hoarse and mute, and panting o'er the plain.
    O'erbreath'd we come where, 'twixt impending
Ran the joint current of two gurgling rills; [hills,
On either hand, adown each fearful steep,
Hung forth the shaggy horrours, dark and deep:
Here, through brown umbrage, glow'd the vivid
                                                green,
And headlong slopes, and winding paths between;
Growth above many a growth, tall trees arose,
The tops of these scarce veil'd the roots of those;

A winding court, where wand'ring Fancy walk'd,
And to herself responsive Echo talk'd.
Here stay'd again, we hail the kind delay,
And down the shadowy paths delighted stray;
'The gath'ring pack unite, and enter in,
Then spread, and pierce the darkness of the glen.
Now here, now there, now sole, and now combin'd,
They catch the wand'ring odour from the wind;
Through many a traverse, many-twirling maze,
And all the wondrous wisdom of his ways,
The fox they trace, unrav'ling as they go,
Discreetly sure, and musically slow;
Now in joint harmony they pour their notes,
And echo answers from ten thousand throats.
From hill to hill, with replicated sounds,
The peal rolls down the glen, and still rebounds,
Packs beyond packs seem sweetly to reply,
And waft to distant climes the less'ning cry.
    At length, from path to path, and glade to glade,
Midst woven thickets and impending shade,
Through the steep wilderness their way they won,
And reach'd the shelve that open'd to the Sun:
Then up the slope they speed them, swift as wind,
As swift the hunters press, and shout behind.
    But now no more our coursers pull the rein
O'er the firm greensward, or expanded plain,
Through rude and craggy grounds, through miry
          clay,
We urge with peril our o'erlabour'd way.
Cast, here and there, along the dang'rous course,
Lies spread the rider, and the flound'ring horse;
But onward still the foremost press, nor mind
To ask for luckless friends that limp behind.
At last the bottom of a mount we reach'd,
Whose top from sea to sea its prospect stretch'd,
And seem'd a look of stately scorn to throw
On the proud works of little men below.
    With half a pack, and scarcely half a train,
We dare all dangers, and all toil disdain;
The dogs near faint, yet still on slaughter bent,
With tongues abrupt avow the burning scent;
The pendent cliffs audaciously essay,
And trot, or crawl, or climb their desp'rate way.
While, slanting, we avoid the headlong deep,
Yet bend, press on, and labour up the steep.
    Where the brow beetling from the mountain
          sprung,
With stunted thorn and shaggy rocks o'erhung,
Beneath whose base a sanded bench, with shade
Of furze and tangling thicket was o'erlaid,
Reynard his palace kept, his regal seat,
His fort of sure resource, and last retreat;
The rest were but the mansions of a night,
For casual respite, or for fresh delight.
Here a vulcanian Cacus erst was said
To hale the carcasses whose blood he shed;
Or as in rolls of old romance we read
Of rav'ning giants, an enormous breed,
With grizly bones who hung their spacious bower,
Dire trophies of their cruelty and pow'r:
So bones and blood did Reynard's hall distain,
And whit'ning skeletons confess'd the slain;
Hens, leverets, lambs—sad trophies of his art,
His raging appetite, and ruthless heart.
To this dread fort, with many a hard essay,
We win with peril our o'er-labour'd way;
At length our journey, not our work, is done,
The way indeed, but not the fort is won.
    Here had the felon carth'd;—with many a hound
And many a horse we gird his hold around:

The hounds 'fore Heav'n their accusation spread,
And cry for justice on his caitiff head.
    Meanwhile, with cutlasses we clear each bush
Of platted blackthorn, and of stubborn brush,
Remove the covert of befriending night,
And on the cavern's entrance pour the light.—
Aghast, and trembling in the burst of day,
With haggard eyes the shrinking savage lay;
In vain he glares his desp'rate glance around,
No scape—no stratagem—no hope is found!
" He dies!—he dies!" the echoing hills reply,
And the loud triumph rends the vaulted sky.

------

## REDEMPTION.

### A POEM.

It comes; the wish'd, the long-expected morn—
" Thou Son of Man, thou Son of God, be born!"
Lo, he descends, and bows the yielding skies:
To meet him, the exulting valleys rise:
Death shrinks and trembles, fearing to be slain;
And all Hell quakes throughout its deep domain.
    Yet comes he not, array'd in worldly show,
Nor in the weakness of man's power below:
In human flesh, his Godhead he conceals;
In human form, immensity he veils:
Eternal, he assumes a mortal frame:
And, in subjection, lo, the world's supreme!
    'T is come; the day of health, the saving morn—
The Son of God, the Babe of Love is born!
Behold, all Heaven descends upon the wing,
And choiring angels " Glory, glory!" sing;
" Glory to God, from whom such bounties flow!
And peace on Earth, good-will to man below!"
    " Tidings we bring, glad tidings of free grace,
Tidings of joy to all of human race!
The promis'd day is come, the great event—
To you a child is born, a son is sent;
A Saviour, Christ, the lowly, the supreme,
Gracious to pardon, mighty to redeem!
Within his hand the nations shall be weigh'd,
The world upon his infant-shoulder laid.
His name is Wonderful; he shall be styl'd
The God of Power, the all-embracing child;
Th' embosom'd Sun, whose inward beam imparts
Wisdom to souls, the Counsellor of hearts,
Whose days nor know commencement nor increase;
The everlasting Father, Prince of Peace!
Your saving God, in Bethlehem ye shall find,
Swath'd in a crib, on humbling straw reclin'd;
He, who all things unites and comprehends,
To stable with his lowliest brutes descends.
Your songs, your songs, ye morning stars, employ;
And, all ye sons of glory, shout for joy!"
    Approaching seraphim the babe surround,
And, with adoring reverence, bow profound;
Amaz'd to see their Infinite confin'd,
The Ancient of all days in infancy enshrin'd.
With wond'ring eye, they pierce his filmy skin
And lucid flesh, when, lo, a Heaven within,
Wide as the round where yonder planets roll,
Though stretch'd to infinite from either pole;
Love, to whose depth no measure can descend;
And bliss, encircling blessings, without end.
    See the dear, little, helpless, mighty hands,
So meekly yielded to maternal bands!
'T is theirs the powers of darkness to repel,
To crush the pride of Earth, and wrath of Hell;

To lift the fall'n, to prop the feeble knee,
To set the pris'ners of his Israel free;
To burst the iron gates of sin and pain,
To number time and death among the slain;
Captive to lead captivity on high,
Follow'd by blood-bought myriads through the sky;
His kingdom in eternal peace to found,
And beam forth blessings without end or bound.

Ye sophists, who, with scientific lore,
Nature's recluse arcana would explore;
Who, in your dreams of fancy, mould and wield
The mazy worlds of yon empyreal field,
And boast to have retrac'd, by reason's force,
Th' unmeasur'd chain of sequels to their source;
Come forward with your length and depth of thought,
And see all human learning set at nought:
Here, try to mete, to compass, to define,
And plumb your God with your five-fathom'd line!
Ye mighty too, beneath whose tyrant brow
Pale vassals shake, and servile nations bow,
Perish your pride! and let your glories fade!
Lo, Nature's monarch in a manger laid!
Behold, the Word, at whose creative might
The Heavens and Earth sprnng forth to form and
In love descends, unutterably mild,    [light,
And smiles the world's salvation—in a child!

No clarions yet proclaim him King of Kings;
No ensigns speak him the Supreme of things:
Humbly he lays his purple robe aside,
Until, for man, it shall in blood be dy'd;
Nor shall the crown his regal brow adorn,
Till his love twist it of the pointed thorn!
Ah, Father, Author, God of boundless grace!
What, what is man, with all his recreant race,
That they with thine own Jesus should be weigh'd;
And, for their ransom, such a price be paid?
'T is true, that man from his Creator came
All-bright, as from the Sun his effluent beam;
Lord of these Heavens and Earth, the seas that flow,
The lands that germinate, and stars that glow.
Lovely without, and glorious all within,
He knew no sorrow, for he knew no sin:
His will was with the Father's will inform'd;
His love was with the love of Jesus warm'd;
The Eternal Light, that lights the solar ray,
Shed forth the peace of his diviner day;
He felt the bliss of the supremely bless'd,
And God's own Heaven was open'd in his breast.

But ah! he yet was frail, nor understood
There's but one Will, all-just, all-wise, all-good;
The Will, throughout the universe, who knows,
Alone, to make, to fit, and to dispose.
The wretch who dares a diff'rent will to frame,
Brings war into the works of Heaven's supreme;
Of pow'r would e'en Omnipotence defraud,
And blasts his being in the will of God.

Hence, man, so great, so glorious, and so good,
Was tempted from the tow'r in which he stood,
Lur'd by external baits of sensual taste,
He wish'd to gratify, he long'd to feast;
The good of his subjected world to know;
Distinct from God, to win a Heav'n below;
To found a new dominion of his own,
And reign sufficient to himself alone.
" Ingrate—O stop thee on the headlong brink!
Ere thou dost take the fearful venture,—think!
Think, from the God thou wishest to forego,
All that thou art, thy bliss and being flow;
And, can the creatures yield thee, should they list,
More than the source where thou and they exist?

Of thy Creator if thou art bereft,
Think, to redeem, no other God is left!"
He listens not,—th' infernal powers impel:
He long'd, he pluck'd, he tasted—and he fell.
O, what a fall! a steep from high to low!
Extremes of bliss, to what extremes of woe!
Plump, from his Heav'n, this second angel fell
Down his own depth, his God-abandon'd Hell:
Horrour of horrours! darkness and despair!
He look'd for comfort—but no gleam was there!
O Love, Love, Love! stupendous, wide and
steep!
High o'er all heights, below damnation deep!
In vain the desp'rate rebel would essay,
From thee to tear his being, far away
Thy saving hand arrests his prone career;
For, to thy presence, ev'ry place is—here!

For him thou hadst prepar'd a mediate seat,
Meet for his taste, and fitting to his state;
A seat of fleshy organs, gross and frail,
To dissolution doom'd, and form'd to fail.
He wakes to a new world, and, with new eyes,
Sees unknown elements, and unknown skies;
The husk and surface of that bless'd abode,
Where late he dwelt, internal, with his God.

He turns his eyes upon his carnal frame,
And sees it, all, a seat of filth and shame;
Fellow'd with brutes, with brutes to take his bed,
Like brutes to propagate, be born, and fed:
But diff'rent far the table and the treat;
Earth is their Heav'n, their home, and native seat:
For brutes, unearn'd, the ready banquet lies,
Apt to their taste, and obvious to their eyes;
But man must wring it from a grudging soil,
And win scant sustenance with sweat and toil.

He looks abroad, and sees the new-dropp'd fawn
Cloth'd without care, and frisking on the lawn;
But finds his own new carcass bleak and bare,
And shiv'ring in a strange and hostile air.
Yet know, O man, that all which can betide
From hard-fang'd avarice, or o'erbearing pride,
That art can compass from the flood or field,
All that these four-fold elements can yield,
Is barely to afford thee warmth and bread,
Like fellow brutes to be array'd and fed;
But ah, all, all, incapable, as wind,
To yield one morsel to the famish'd mind!

This the wretch finds (beguil'd by devilish fraud)
The sum of all, for which he left his God;
The sum of all the good—he yet was blind
To half the evils that came close behind.

Late lord of land and water, air and flame,
He wielded, at his will, their cumbrous frame;
Could pierce Earth's dark and various entrails
through;
Could call forth all their wonders to his view;
Through minim forms th' internal maze could trace,
And lift the broad-back'd mountains from their base.
To him of ev'ry foliage, flow'r, and blade,
The fabric, use, and beauty, lay display'd;
Of living specks he pierc'd the fine machine,
And open'd to himself the world within;
Saw all with glory, as with skill, replete,
And trac'd the artist to his inmost seat.

But now, fall'n, fall'n from his imperial tow'r,
'Reft of his glory, empty'd of his pow'r;
Degraded, hurl'd from his celestial steep,
And sunk in flesh, a dungeon dark and deep;
(Distance immense in nature, not in space,
But wider, wider far, than place from place!)

Th' insulting elements their lord control,
And cast their four-fold fetters round his soul.

Dethron'd, debas'd, without as from within,
Enslav'd by matter, since enslav'd by sin,
Corruption to its kindred mass lays claim,
And, ent'ring, seizes his devoted frame.

Distemper follows, with his gloomy throng,
Bearing pests, stings, and fires, and racks along;
Languor that saps, and rueful throes that grind;
With Death, who shakes the certain dart behind.

Already, o'er the sad subjected wight,
The lordly elements exert their right;
And on his limbs their baneful influence cast,
Parch'd in the beam, or shiv'ring in the blast:
While high o'er head, the gath'ring vapours frown,
And on his anguish look unpitying down;
Then flash in thunders, or in tempest pour,
And on his members dash the pelting show'r.

But worse, far worse within, black storms infest
And shake the sphere of his benighted breast.
Still, round and round, the whirling passions tend,
And his sad heart with horrid conflict rend;
Impatience, rage, despair, untam'd desire,
And hate, impregnate with infernal fire:
He calls for death, and would have ruin hurl'd
At Heav'n, himself, the tempter, and the world.

But God, THE ONE ETERNAL THIRST TO BLESS,
Ey'd his estate, and pity'd his distress.

" Adam," he said, and look'd unmeasur'd grace,
" Adam, thou 'rt fall'n, and fall'n is all thy race!
Such as the tree is, such will be the fruit;
The branch must bear the flavour of the root.

" Late I was in thee love, and pow'r, and will;
My glory did thy soul and body fill;
But, laps'd from me, thy spirit and thy frame
Sink to the principles from whence they came—
Thy soul to its own helpless fierce desire,
A rueful whirl of dark tormenting fire!
Thy body to the grossness of its birth,
Corruption to corruption, earth to earth!

" If, in thy strength, thou didst not hold thy state,
How shall thy weakness reassume its seat?
How, from thy pit of flesh, so dull and deep,
Cast off the cumbrance. and ascend the steep?
For, by the road thou hast fall'n, as is most just,
Through the same road, O man, return thou must;
To strength through weakness, and to peace through strife,
To bliss through anguish, and through death to life.

" But this no creature, not the seraph can;
Though once in God so mighty, less can man:
This, therefore, Adam, thou canst never do;
Thou in thy God then must be born anew;
Born a new creature of a seed divine,
Reborn, O Adam, of thy son and mine;
Thou the old father of man's fall'n estate,
He the New Sire who shall regain their seat.

" Foil'd by a devilish foe, thy weakness fell,
Captive to sense, and sin, and death, and Hell;
In weakness, therefore, must his strength prevail,
Though sense, and sin, and death, and Hell assail;
As man, in human flesh and frailty, he
Must conquer all, O man, that conquer'd thee.

" Yes, from my bosom my belov'd I give,
That my lost creatures may return, and live.
He, for your sakes, shall lay his glory by;
For you be born, and suffer, gasp, and die;
The price of guilt my Holy-One shall pay,
And tread, of death and Hell, the bitterest way.

" You, by his fetters, can alone be freed;
To wash your stains, the Lamb of Love must bleed;
So shall his woe turn all your woe to weal,
His bruises medicine, and his woundings heal.

" Hence man, apostate man, so deeply lost,
Shall weigh the curs'd commission, by the cost;
Shall learn, as meet, to hold himself at nought;
Shall feel he 's all a folly, all a fault;
In deep abasement lift his suppliant eyes,
In lowliness alone be taught to rise;
In tears, in anguish, shall his guilt deplore,
Shall call on Christ who can alone restore;
By him supported, shall affirm his ground,
Shall struggle with the chains by which he 's bound;
Disclaim, detest the world, in which he fell;
Oppose his champion'd soul to flesh and Hell;
Wish his old worm, his sin, and self undone,
And catch, and cling to my all-saving Son!

" This in due time.

Jesus, meanwhile, shall steal, like doubtful morn,
Into the breasts of all of woman born;
There shed his dawn of coeternal light,
There struggle with their length and depth of night;
A solid gloom! which he alone can melt;
Which, like Egyptian darkness, may be felt.

" His seed, in flesh, my Holy-One shall sow,
And give it strength to root, and grace to grow;
Man within man, begotten from above,
Bearing the likeness of the Son of Love;
Sons of my son, ordain'd to see my face;
All embryon heirs of glory and of grace;
But not mature to-wing their native skies,
Till their new Adam shall from death arise.

" Thus the new offspring shall the old put on,
Making a double manhood, two in one;
Of diff'rent principles, of diff'rent sires,
Conceptions, tastes, enjoyments, and desires:
The one, as Earth, crude, grudging, grappling all
To the dark centre of its craving ball;
The other, as the Sun, benign and bright,
A going forth on all in life and light.

" Hence through the course of their sublunar life,
Though brother'd, they shall be at truceless strife:
What one approves, the other shall reject;
What one detests, the other shall affect.
So man, at once, shall court what he 'll contemn,
Neglect yet rev'rence, do what he 'll condemn;
At once transgress, and wish he could fulfil;
Be righteous and unrighteous, good and ill;
Bearing the witness and the seal, within,
Of new and old, the man of grace and sin,
The heart-writ story of his rise and fall,
The gospel of his freedom and his thrall.

" Thy elder offspring, Adam, grown and strong,
Frequent, shall drag his younger mate along;
Like huge Leviathan, shall trust to play,
And rule at large in his congenial sea:
But mine within his jaws a bard shall place,
And check the headlong monster in his race.
The younger heir, invisibly, within,
Shall oft convict his outward mate of sin;
Reprove with judgment, and reform betimes;
Or, with a whip, call'd conscience, lash his crimes:
So may the bless'd the accursed one subdue,
And the old man, at length, refine into the new!

" Nor grudge I, Adam, those fall'n sons of thine,
Flesh of thy flesh, to share a seat with mine,
By him sublim'd into a nobler sphere;
So they slay not their younger brothers, here.

"But, through much grief, this glory must be won;
Flesh, soil'd by sin, by death must be undone;
Must drop the world, wherein it felt its force,
And, giant-like, rejoic'd to run its course;
Must drop each organ of its late delight;
Must bid a long adieu to sense and sight,
A long adieu to ev'ry darling lust;
Must yield its passive members, dust to dust,
Within the potter's furnace to be fin'd,
And leave its grossness, with its guilt, behind.
"Meanspace, those forms of flesh, those sons of sin,
Shall serve to hold my priceless pearls within;
As golden grain within prolific clay,
To shoot and ripen toward a future day.
"Yon maggot, vilest offspring of vile earth,
Answers the genial baseness of his birth:
Lo, where he rolls and battens, with delight,
In filth, to smell offensive, foul to sight!
Well pleas'd, he drinks the stench, the dirt devours,
And prides him in the puddle of his powers;
Careless, unconscious of the beauteous guest,
The internal speck committed to his breast.
Yet in his breast the internal speck grows warm,
And quickens into motion, life, and form;
Far other form than that its fosterer bore,
High o'er its parent-worm ordain'd to soar:
The son, still growing as the sire decays,
In radiant plumes his infant shape arrays;
Matures, as in a soft and silent womb;
Then, opening, peeps from his paternal tomb;
Now, struggling, breaks at once into the day,
Tries his young limbs, and bids his wings display,
Expands his lineaments, erects his face,
Rises sublime o'er all the reptile race;
From dew-drop'd blossoms sips the nectar'd stream,
And basks within the glory of the beam.
"Thus, to a sensual, to a sinful shrine,
The Saviour shall entrust his speck divine;
In secret animate his chosen seed,
Fill with his love, and with his substance feed;
Inform it with sensations of his own,
And give it appetites to flesh unknown:
So shall the lusts of man's old worm give place,
His fervour languish, and his force decrease;
Till spoil'd of ev'ry object, gross or vain,
His pride and passions humbl'd, crush'd, and slain;
From a false world to his first kingdom won,
His will, and sin, and sense, and self, undone;
His inward man from death shall break away,
And soar, and mingle with eternal day!"
This (in a word) the Father spoke—and straight
The Son descended from above all height.
Upon the chaos of man's world he came,
And pierc'd the darkness with his living beam;
Then cast a rein on the reluctant will,
And bid the tempest of the soul be still.
The good from evil he did then divide,
And set man's darkness from God's light aside:
Wide, from the heart, he bids his will be done,
And there plac'd conscience as a central Sun;
Whence reason, like the Moon, derives, by night,
A weak, a borrow'd, and a dubious light.
But, down the soul's abyss, a region dire!
He caus'd the Stygian horrours to retire;
From whence ascends the gloom of many a pest,
Dark'ning the beam of Heav'n within the breast;

Atrocious intimations, causeless care,
Distrust, and hate, and rancour, and despair.
As in creation, when the Word gave birth
To ev'ry offspring of the teeming Earth,
He now conceiv'd high fruits of happier use,
And bid the heart and head of man produce:
Then branch'd the pregnant will, and went abroad
In all the sweets of its internal God;
In ev'ry mode of love, a fragrant throng,
Bearing the heart-sent charities along;
Divine effusions of the human breast,
Within the very act of blessing, bless'd;
Desires that press another's weight to bear,
To soothe their anguish, to partake their care;
Pains that can please, and griefs that joys excite;
Bruises that balm, and tears that drop delight.
God saw the seed was precious; and began
To bless his own redeeming work, in man.
Nor less, the pregnant region of the mind
Brought forth conceptions suited to its kind;
Faint emblems, yet of virtue to proclaim
That parent-spirit, whence our spirits came;
Spirits that, like their God, with mimic skill,
Produce new forms and images at will;
Thoughts that from Earth, with wing'd emotion soar,
New tracts expatiate, and new worlds explore;
Backward, through space and through duration, run,
Passing the bounds of all that e'er begun;
Then, as a glance of lightning, forward flee,
Straining to reach at all that e'er shall be.
Thus, in the womb of man's abyss are sown
Natures, worlds, wonders, to himself unknown.
A comprehension, a mysterious plan
Of all the almighty works of God, is man;
From Hell's dire depth to Heav'n's supremest height,
Including good and evil, dark and light.
What shall we call this son of grace and sin,
This demon, this divinity within,
This flame eternal, this foul mould'ring clod—
A fiend, or seraph—A poor worm, or God?
O, the fell conflict, the intestine strife,
This clash of good and evil, death and life!
What, what are all the wars of sea and wind,
Or wreck of matter, to this war of mind?
Two minds in one, and each a truceless guest,
Rending the sphere of our distracted breast!
Who shall deliver, in a fight so fell;
Who save from this intestine dog of Hell?
God! thou hast said, that Nature shall decay,
And all yon starr'd expansion pass away:
That, in thy wrath, pollution shall expire,
The Sun himself consume with hotter fire;
The melting Earth forsake its form and face,
These elements depart, but find no place;
Succeeded by a peaceful bless'd serene,
New Heav'ns and Earth, wherein the just shall reign.
O then, upon the same benignant plan,
Sap, crush, consume this mass of ill, in man!
Within this transient frame of mould'ring clay,
Let death's cerberean demon have his day;
Let him tear off this world, the nurse of lust,
Grind flesh, and sense, and sin, and self to dust—
But O, preserve the principle divine;
In mind and matter, save whate'er is thine!
O'er time, and pain, and death, to be renew'd;
Fill'd with our God, and with our God endu'd!

THE

# POEMS

OF

# *JOHN SCOTT.*

# LIFE OF JOHN SCOTT,

## BY MR. CHALMERS.

T HIS very amiable man, the youngest son of Samuel and Martha Scott, was born on the ninth day of January 1730, in the Grange Walk, in the parish of St. Mary Magdalen, Bermondsey. His father was a draper and citizen of London, a man of plain and irreproachable manners, and one of the society of the people called Quakers, in which persuasion our poet was educated, and continued during the whole of his life, although not with the strictest attention to all the peculiarities of that sect[1].

His father does not appear to have intended him for a classical education. In his seventh year he was put under the tuition of one John Clarke, a native of Scotland, who kept a school in Bermondsey Street, but attended young Scott at his father's house, where he instructed him in the rudiments of the Latin tongue. Little is known of his proficiency under this tutor, whom, however, in his latter days, he remembered with pleasure, although he was a man of severe manners. In his tenth year, his father retired with his family, consisting of Mrs. Scott and two sons, to the village of Amwell in Hertfordshire, where, for some time, he carried on the malting trade.

Here our poet was sent to a private day-school, in which he is said to have had few opportunities of polite literature, and those few were declined by his father from a dread of the small-pox, which neither he nor his son had yet caught. This terrour, perpetually recurring as the disorder made its appearance in one quarter or another, occasioned such frequent removals as prevented his son from the advantages of regular education. The youth, however, did not neglect to cultivate his mind by such means as were in his power. About the age of seventeen, he discovered an inclination to the study of poetry, with which he combined a delight in viewing the appearances of rural nature. At this time he derived much assistance from the conversation and opinions of one Charles Frogley, a person in the humble station of a bricklayer, but who had improved a natural taste for poetry, and arrived at a considerable degree of critical dis-

---

[1]. He used *thee* and *thou* in conversation and correspondence, and conformed to the Quaker-garb, but on the title-page of the edition of his poems published by himself the year before his death, he is called John Scott, *esq. C.*

cernment. This Mr. Scott thankfully acknowledged when he had himself attained a rank among the writers of his age, and could return with interest the praise by which Frogley had cheered his youthful attempts. The only other adviser of his studies, in this sequestered spot, was a Mr. John Turner, afterwards a dissenting preacher. To him he was introduced in 1753 or 1754, and on the removal of Mr. Turner to London and afterwards to Colliton in Devonshire, they carried on a friendly correspondence on matters of general taste.

Mr. Scott's first poetical essays were published in the Gentleman's Magazine, " the great receptacle for the ebullitions of youthful genius." Mr. Hoole, his biographer, has not been able to discover all the pieces inserted by him in that work, but has reprinted three of them, which are now added to the collection originally formed by himself. Other pieces which he occasionally communicated to his friend Turner, were either mis-laid, or on more mature deliberation kept back from the press. He appears to have looked up to Turner's opinions with much deference, and it was probably at his solici-tation that he first ventured to come before the public as a candidate for poetical fame.

With the taste of the public during his retirement at Amwell, he could have little ac-quaintance. He had lived here about twenty years, at a distance from any literary society or information. His reading was chiefly confined to books of taste and criticism, but the latter at that time were not many, nor very valuable. In the ancient or modern languages it does not appear that he made any progress. Mr. Hoole thinks he knew very little of Latin, and had no knowledge of either French or Italian. Those who know of what importance it is to improve genius by study, will regret that such a man was left, in the pliable days of youth, without any acquaintance with the noble models on which English poets have been formed. They will yet more regret that the cause of this distance from literary society, the source of all generous and useful emulation, was a superstitious dread of the small-pox, already mentioned as obstructing his early studies, and which continued to prevail with his parents to such a degree, that although at the distance of only twenty miles, their son had been permitted to visit London but once in twenty years. His chief occupation, when not in a humour to study, was in cultivating a garden, for which he had a particular fondness, and at length rendered one of the most attractive objects to the visitors of Amwell.

About the year 1760, he began to make occasional, though cautious and short visits to London, and in the spring of this year published his Four Elegies, descriptive and moral, epithets which may be applied to almost all his poetry. These were very fa-vourably received, and not only praised by the public critics, but received the valuable commendations of Dr. Young, Mrs. Talbot, and Mrs. Carter, who loved poetry, and loved it most when in conjunction with piety.

Although Mr. Scott had not given his name to this publication, he was not long un-discovered, and began to be honoured with the notice of several of the literati of the day, which, however, did not flatter him into vanity or carelessness. For many years he abstained from further publication, determined to put in no claims that were not strengthened by the utmost industry, and frequent and careful revisal. This, I am apt to think, in some cases checked his enthusiasm, and gave to his longer poems an appear-ance of labour.

In 1761, during the prevalence of the small-pox at Ware, he removed to St. Marga-ret's, a small hamlet about two miles distant from Amwell, where Mr. Hoole informs us he became first acquainted with him, and saw the first sketch of his poem of Amwell, to which he then gave the title of A Prospect of Ware and the Country adjacent. In 1766, he became sensible of the many disadvantages he laboured under by living in continual dread of the small-pox, and had the courage to submit to the operation of inoculation, which was successfully performed by the late baron Dimsdale. He now visited London more frequently, and Mr. Hoole had the satisfaction to introduce him, among others, to Dr. Johnson. "Notwithstanding the great difference of their political principles, Scott had too much love for goodness and genius, not to be highly gratified in the opportunity of cultivating a friendship with that great exemplar of human virtues, and that great veteran of human learning; while the doctor, with a mind superior to the distinction of party, delighted with equal complacency in the amiable qualities of Scott, of whom he always spoke with feeling regard [2]."

In 1767, he married Sarah Frogley, the daughter of his early friend and adviser Charles Frogley. The bride was, previous to her nuptials, admitted a member of the society of Quakers. For her father he ever preserved the highest respect, and seems to have written his eleventh Ode, with a view to relieve the mind of that worthy man from the apprehension of being neglected by him. The connection he had formed in his family, however, was not of long duration. His wife died in child-bed in 1768, and the same year he lost his father, and his infant child. For some time he was inconsolable, and removed from Amwell, where so many objects excited the bitter remembrance of all he held dear, to the house of a friend at Upton. Here, when time and reflection had mellowed his grief, he honoured the memory of his wife by an elegy, in which tenderness and love are expressed in the genuine language of nature. As he did not wish to make a parade of his private feelings, a few copies only of this elegy were given to his friends, nor would he ever suffer it to be published for sale. It procured him the praise of Dr. Hawkesworth, and the friendship of Dr. Langhorne, who about this time had been visited by a similar calamity.—His mother, it ought to have been mentioned, died in 1766; and in 1769, he lost his friend and correspondent Mr. Turner.

In November 1770, he married his second wife, Mary de Horne, daughter of the late Abraham de Horne, " a lady whose amiable qualities promised him many years of uninterrupted happiness." During his visits in London, he increased his literary circle of friends by an introduction to Mrs. Montague's parties. Among those who principally noticed him with respect, were lord Lyttelton, sir William Jones, Mr. Potter, Mr. Mickle, and Dr. Beattie, who paid him a cordial visit at Amwell in 1773, and again in 1781, and became one of his correspondents.

Although we have hitherto contemplated our author as a student and occasional poet, he rendered himself more conspicuous as one of those reflectors on public affairs who employ much of their time in endeavouring to be useful. He appears to have acquired the spirit and patriotism of the *country gentleman* whose abilities enable him to do good, and whose fortune adds the influence which is often necessary to render that good effectual and permanent. Among other subjects, his attention had often been called to that glaring defect in human polity, the state of the poor, and having revolved it in his mind, with the assistance of many personal inquiries, he published, in 1773, Observations on the present State of the parochial and vagrant Poor. It is needless to add that his advice in this matter was rather approved than followed. Some of his propositions,

---

[2] Hoole's Life of Scott, p. 35—36. *C.*

indeed, were incorporated in Mr. Gilbert's Bill, in the year 1782, but the whole was lost for want of parliamentary support.

In 1776 he published his Amwell, a descriptive poem, which he had long been preparing, and in which he fondly hoped to immortalize his favourite village. His biographer, however, has amply demonstrated the impossibility of communicating local enthusiasm by any attempt of this kind. The reflections occasionally introduced, and the historical or encomiastic digressions, are generally selected as the most pleasing passages in descriptive poetry, but all that is really descriptive, all that would remove us from the closet to the scene is a hopeless attempt to do that by the pen which can only be done by the pencil. Of all writers, whether in prose or verse, who have attempted picturesque description, Gilpin alone has succeeded, not indeed completely, for language will not admit of it, but in bringing objects the nearest to the eye.

At such intervals as our author could spare, he wrote various anonymous pamphlets and essays, on miscellaneous subjects, and is said to have appeared among those enemies of the measures of government who answered Dr. Johnson's Patriot, False Alarm, and Taxation no Tyranny. On the commencement of the Rowleian controversy, he took the part of Chatterton, and was among the first who questioned the authenticity of the poems ascribed to Rowley. This he discussed in some letters inserted in the Gentleman's Magazine. Of course he was led to admire the wonderful powers of the young impostor, and in his twenty-first Ode pays a poetical tribute to his memory, in which, with others of his brethren at that time, he censures the unfeeling rich for depriving their country of a new Shakspeare or Milton.

These, however, were his amusements; the more valuable part of his time was devoted to such public business as is ever best conducted by men of his pure and independent character. He gave regular attendance at turnpike meetings, navigation trusts, and commissions of land tax [3], and proposed and carried various schemes of local improvement, particularly the fine road between Ware and Hertford, and some useful alterations in the streets of Ware. Among his neighbours he frequently, by a judicious interference or arbitration, checked that spirit of litigation which destroys the felicity of a country life. During the meritorious employments of his public and political life, it can only be imputed to him that in his zeal for the principles he espoused, he sometimes betrayed too great warmth; and in answering Dr. Johnson's pamphlets, it has been allowed that he made use of expressions which would better become those who did not know the worth of that excellent character.

In 1778, he published a work of great labour and utility, entitled, A Digest of the Highway and General Turnpike laws. In this compilation, Mr. Hoole informs us, all the acts of parliament in force are collected together, and placed in one point of view; their contents are arranged under distinct heads, with the addition of many notes, and an appendix on the construction and preservation of public roads, probably the only scientific treatise on the subject. A part of this work appeared in 1773, under the title of a Digest of the Highway Laws.

---

[3] When once asked whether he was in the commission of the peace, he answered without hesitation, that his principal objection to taking the oath, was the offence which it would give to *the society*. His own opinion was, that an oath and an affirmative are substantially the same, and that the mode of appeal to the searcher of hearts is of little consequence, though he certainly preferred the latter. Monthly Review, vol. vii. number v. p. 237. *C.*

In the spring of 1782, he published what he had long projected, a volume of poetry, including his Elegies, Amwell, and a great variety of hitherto unpublished pieces. On this volume it is evident he had bestowed great pains, and added the decorations of some beautiful engravings. A very favourable account was given of the whole of its contents in the Monthly Review; but the Critical having taken some personal liberties with the author, hinting that the ornaments were not quite suitable to the plainness and simplicity of a quaker, Mr. Scott thought proper to publish a letter addressed to the authors of that journal, in which he expostulated with them on their conduct, and defended his poetry. Every friend, however, must wish he had passed over their strictures in silence. His defence of his poetry betrays him into the error of which he complained, and we see far more of the conceited egotist than could have been supposed to belong to his simple and humble character.

After this contest, he began to prepare a work of the critical kind. He had been dissatisfied with some of Dr. Johnson's Lives of the Poets, and had amassed in the course of his own reading and reflection a number of observations on Denham, Milton, Pope, Dyer, Goldsmith, and Thomson, which he sent to the press under the title of Critical Essays, but did not live to publish. On the 25th of October 1783, he accompanied Mrs. Scott to London for the benefit of medical advice for a complaint under which she laboured at that time; but on the first of December, while at his house at Ratcliff, he was attacked by a putrid fever, which proved fatal on the 12th of that month, and he was interred on the 18th in the quaker's burying ground at Ratcliff. He had arrived at his fifty fourth year, and left behind him a widow and a daughter, their only child, then about six years old. His death was the more lamented as he was in the vigour of life, and had the prospect of many years of usefulness. " In his person he was tall and slender, but his limbs were remarkably strong and muscular: he was very active, and delighted much in the exercise of walking: his countenance was cheerful and animated." The portrait prefixed to his works is not a very correct likeness, nor was he himself satisfied with it.

His public and private character appears to have been in every respect worthy of imitation, but what his religious opinions were, except that he cherished a general reverence for piety, is somewhat doubtful. Professedly, he was one of the society called Quakers, but the paper which that society, or some of his relations, thought it necessary to publish after his death, seems to intimate, that in their opinion, and finally in his own, his practice had not in all respects been consistent. Mr. Hoole has suppressed this document, while he has thrown out a hint which is altogether unintelligible without a reference to it. He says, that " he had been told that the *state of his mind did not a little contribute to strengthen his malady.*" Whether this was the case, the reader may judge from a perusal of the following statement, originally drawn up for the use of *The Friends*, and which is now reprinted, without any suspicion that it will injure the memory of Mr. Scott, and certainly without any intention to produce such an effect. Those who have admired him as the active and benevolent citizen, and the favoured poet, will not, it is hoped, whatever their religious opinion may be, view him with less complacency on his death-bed as the humble Christian.

" John Scott was favoured with strength of body, and an active and vigorous mind: he was esteemed regular and moral in his conduct, and extensive in his knowledge, being remarkably diligent and attentive in promoting works of public utility: in assisting individuals in cases of difficulty, and in the conciliation of differences. His removal hence is generally lamented by his neighbours, both in superior and inferior stations. Notwithstanding these qualifications, there is reason to believe he frequently experienced the conviction of the spirit of truth, for not faithfully following the Lord, and adhering to the cross of Christ, by which true believers are crucified to the world and the world to them.

" During the yearly meeting in London, in the year 1783, he attended many of the meetings for worship, and appeared to be more religiously concerned than for some years preceding.

" On the 1st of the 12th month he was seized with a fever; and, expecting it would prove fatal, he was greatly humbled in spirit, saying to his wife, that his father was a good man, and he believed was gone to Heaven, expressing a sense of the happiness of the righteous in futurity; but being convinced of his own low and unprepared state, he said, he himself was unworthy of the lowest place in the heavenly mansions, but hoped he should not be a companion of accursed and wrathful spirits.

" In the early part of his illness, he discoursed with his wife concerning some outward affairs, particularly desiring that his only and beloved daughter might be brought up among friends.

" Notwithstanding the severity of the distemper, he was favoured with a clear and unimpaired understanding, and the exercise of his spirit seemed to be almost continual for peace and reconciliation with his Maker; having a hope, that if it should please the Lord to spare him, he should become a new man; but, in much diffidence, he expressed a fear lest the old things should again prevail; he also said to the person who attended him, that ' he had been too proud.' But it is well known, that his behaviour to his inferiors was the reverse, for to them he was remarkably easy of access.

" Speaking frequently of his brother, and expressing a desire to see him, on the 9th of the 12th month a special messenger was sent to Hertford, from Ratcliff, requesting his attendance there. His brother, on being informed next morning, by letter, of his continual solicitude to see him, and him only, reached his house at Ratcliff about four that afternoon. Being introduced to his bed-side, on asking him how he did, he answered, ' Very bad: I wanted to see thee, and if thee had come sooner, I had a great deal to say to thee, but I fear now I cannot.' What afterwards passed between them was as follows. After a short space of silence, John Scott began to speak, with a voice full of power:—' I wanted to see thee, to tell thee that I have nothing to trust to but the blessed Jesus; and that, if I die, I do not die an unbeliever. If I die, I die a believer, and have nothing to trust to but mere unmerited mercy.' Finding him brought down, as from the clefts of the rocks, and the heights of the hills, into the valley of deep humiliation, his brother rejoiced in spirit, and spake comfortably to him, expressing the deeply humiliating views he had of his own state. J. Scott replied—' O! if it is so with thee, how must it have been with me who have been the chief of sinners?' The insufficiency of self-righteousness being mentioned, ' Oh,' said he, with great earnestness, ' righteousness! I have no righteousness, nor any thing to trust to, but the blessed Jesus and his merits.' Pausing awhile, he proceeded—' There is something within me which keeps me from despairing. I dare not despair, although I have as much reason to despair as any one, were it not for him who showed mercy to the thief upon the cross. The thief upon the cross, and Peter, who denied his master, are much before me.' Being advised to trust in the Lord, he replied, ' I have none else to trust in. Oh!' said he, ' the Saviour! he is the way, and there is no other; I now see there is no other. Oh, the Saviour! I have done too much against him; and if I live, I hope I shall be able to let the world know it, and that, in many respects, my mind is altered.  But I dare not make resolutions.'  His brother mentioning former times, and the days of his youth, in which they frequently conversed about, and were both clearly convinced of, the necessity of inward and experimental piety, he answered—' I was then very deficient, but I have 'since been much more shaken.'  Visiting the sick in a formal customary manner, being represented as unprofitable, he replied, ' Oh ! it is not a time to be solicitous about forms ! Here is a scene, indeed, enough to bring down the grandeur of many, if they could see it.  I buoyed myself up with the hope of many days.'  Recommending him to the great object, Christ within, the hope of glory, to which his mind was measurably turned, his brother seemed to withdraw, on which he clasped his hand, and took a solemn farewell.

" He continued in mutability about two days longer, altogether in a calm and rational state.  About twelve hours before his decease, his speech much faltered : but, by some broken expressions, it appeared that the religious concern of his mind was continued.

" On the 12th day of the 12th month, 1783, he departed this life in remarkable quietness, without sigh or groan, and was buried in friends' burying ground on the 18th, being nearly 54 years of age.

" The publication of these Memoirs proceeds not from partiality to our deceased friend : they are preserved as a word of reproof to the careless, and of comfort to the mourners in Zion.

" May none, in a day of health and prosperity, reject the visitation of his divine grace and favour, who hath declared, that ' his spirit shall not always strive with man, for that he also is flesh.'  Nor, on the other, may the penitent, and truly awakened, at no time despair of that mercy and forgiveness which the Lord hath promised to them who sincerely repent."

His Critical Essays were published in 1785, by Mr. Hoole, who prefixed a life, written with much affection, yet with impartiality.  He loved the man, and he freely criticises the poet.  Of his peculiar habits we have only one anecdote :—" He preferred the time for poetical composition, when the rest of the family were in bed ; and it was frequently his custom to sit in a dark room, and when he had composed a number of lines, he would go into another room where a candle was burning, in order to commit them to paper.  Though in general very regular in his hour of retiring to rest, he would sometimes be up great part of the night, when he was engaged in any literary work."

As a poet, he may be allowed to rank among those who possess genius in a moderate degree ; who please by short efforts and limited inspirations ; but whose talents are better displayed in moral reflection and pathetic sentiment than in flights of fancy.  His Elegies, as they were the first, are among the best of his performances.  Simplicity appears to have been his general aim, and he was of opinion that it was too little studied by modern writers.  In the Mexican Prophecy, however, and in Serim, there is a fire and spirit worthy of the highest school.  His Amwell will ever deserve a distinguished place among descriptive poems ; although it is liable to all the objections attached to descriptive poetry.  But he cannot be denied the merit of being original in many individual passages ; a d he appears to have viewed Nature with the eye of a genuine poet.  He has himself pointed out some coincidences with former poets, which were accidental ; and perhaps others may be discovered, without detracting from the independence of his Muse.  His feeblest effort is the Essay on Painting, a hasty sketch, in which he professed himself, and that not in very humble terms, to be the rival of Hayley[4], on the same subject. The public, I am afraid, has decided against him. Upon the whole, however, the vein of pious and moral reflection, and the benevolence and philanthropy, which pervade all his poems, will continue to make them acceptable to those who read to be improved, and are of opinion that pleasure is not the sole end of poetry.

[4] See his two letters in Forbes's Life of Dr. Beattie, vol. ii. but especially his letter to the Critical Reviewers. *C.*

# ADVERTISEMENT.

---

Such of the following pieces as were formerly published having been honoured with general approbation, any apology for reprinting them must be unnecessary. The others, which constitute the principal part of this volume, it is apprehended, are not of inferior merit; and the whole may perhaps afford an innocent and agreeable amusement to the lovers of nature and poetry.

AMWELL, 1782.

# POEMS

OF

# *JOHN SCOTT.*

## ÉPIDEMIC MORTALITY,

### FROM ECCL. XII.

PUBLISHED IN THE GENTLEMAN'S MAGAZINE 1753.

TO move unthinking youth to just regard,
  On Judah's plains thus sung the royal bard.
" Thy Maker, God, in early time revere !
Ere evil days, those dreadful days, draw near,
When health shall fly, and pleasure leave the plain,
And woe, and languor, and distress remain;
When stars, nor Moon, nor Sun, shall cheer the skies;
On Earth, when pestilence enrag'd shall rise;
The rain scarce past, when threat'ning clouds return,
And sickly mists ascend, and south winds burn;
When the bold guarders of the house shall shake,
And, pain'd, their station at the door forsake;
When the fierce heroes, dreadless in the field,
Bow with disease, and slowly drooping yield;
When, freed from labour, captives idle lie,
Nor, though their numbers lessen'd, find employ;
When the proud daughters, of their beauty vain,
Griev'd for their friends, or for themselves in pain,
At the high windows spread their charms no more,
But all sequester'd in the dark deplore;
When barr'd the gates, and clos'd the doors appear,
And scarce of grinding the faint sounds they hear;
Long ere the dawn, when early mourners rise,
The solemn rites of grief to exercise.
Nor songs are heard, nor mirthful minstrels meet;
Death 's in the house, and silence in the street !
When e'en high places shall be seats of fear;
Still in the way when danger shall be near;
When the thick, sultry, foul, and stagnant air
Unseen infection scatters ev'ry where;
When the ripe almond shall be pluck'd no more,
Despis'd untasted all its luscious store!
Wide o'er the land when locusts shall be spread,
Dead all the crowds that on their numbers fed:
When fairest objects fail to move desire,
Of youth extinguish'd all the sprightly fire:

Because the time of desolation 's come,
And man swift passes to his final home;
And pensive mourners range about the street,
And rend their garments, and their bosoms beat."

## *VERSES*

OCCASIONED BY THE DESCRIPTION OF THE ÆOLIAN HARP,
IN FEBRUARY MAGAZINE, 1754.

UNTAUGHT o'er strings to draw the rosin'd bow,
Or melting strains on the soft flute to blow,
With others long I mourn'd the want of skill
Resounding roofs with harmony to fill.
Till happy now th' Æolian lyre is known,
And all the powers of music are my own.
Swell all thy notes, delightful harp, O! swell !
Inflame thy poet to describe thee well,
When the full chorus rises with the breeze,
Or, slowly sinking, lessens by degrees,
To sounds more soft than amorous gales disclose,
At evening panting on the blushing rose;
More sweet than all the notes that organs breathe,
Or tuneful echoes, when they die, bequeathe;
Oft where some Sylvan temple decks the grove,
The slave of easy indolence I rove;
There the wing'd breeze the lifted sash pervades,
Each breath is music, vocal all the shades.
Charm'd with the soothing sound, at ease reelin'd,
To Fancy's pleasing pow'r I yield my mind:
And now enchanted scenes around me rise,
And some kind Ariel the soft air supplies:
Now lofty Pindus through the shades I view,
Where all the Nine their tuneful art pursue :
To me the sound the panting gale conveys,
And all my heart is ecstasy and praise.
Now to Arcadian plains at once convey'd,
Some shepherd's pipe delights his favourite maid;
Mix'd with the murmurs of a neighbouring stream,
I hear soft notes that suit an amorous theme !

Ah! then a victim to the fond deceit,
My heart beg'ns with fierce desires to beat;
To fancy'd sighs I real sighs return,
By turns I languish, and by turns I burn.
Ah! Delia, haste! and here attentive prove,
Like me, that "music is the voice of love:"
So shall I mourn my rustic strains no more,
While pleas'd you listen, who could frown before.

Hertfordshire, Nov. 15, 1754.          R. S.

## TO FEAR.

### FROM THE GENTLEMAN'S MAGAZINE, JULY, 1758.

O THOU! dread foe of honour, wealth, and fame,
Whose touch can quell the strong, the fierce can tame,
Relentless Fear! ah! why did fate ordain
My trembling heart to own thy iron reign?
There are, thrice happy, who disdain thy sway:
The merchant wand'ring o'er the wat'ry way;
The chief serene before th' assaulted wall;
The climbing statesman thoughtful of his fall;
All whom the love of wealth or pow'r inspires,
And all who burn with proud ambition's fires:
But peaceful bards thy constant presence know,
O thou! of ev'ry glorious deed the foe!
Of thee the silent studious race complains,
And learning groans a captive in thy chains.
The secret wish when some fair object moves,
And cautious reason what we wish approves,
Thy Gorgon front forbids to grasp the prize,
And seas are spread between, and mountains rise!
Thy magic arts a thousand phantoms raise,
And fancy'd deaths and dangers fill our ways:
With smiling hope you wage eternal strife,
And envious snatch the cup of joy from life.
O leave, tremendous pow'r! the blameless breast,
Of guilt alone the tyrant and the guest.
Go, and thy train of sable horrours spread,
Where Murder meditates the future dead;
Where Rapine watches for the gloom of night,
And lawless Passion pants for other's right;
Go, to the bad—but from the good recede,
No more the foe of ev'ry glorious deed!

## MORAL ECLOGUES.

At secura quies, et nescia fallere vita,
Dives opum variarum; at latis otia fundis,
Speluncæ, vivique lacus; at frigida Tempe,
Mugitusque boum, mollesque sub arbore somni
Non absunt. Illic saltus, ac lustra ferarum,
Et patiens operum parvoque assueta juventus,
Sacra deûm, sanctique patres: extrema per illos
Justitia excedens terris vestigia fecit.
                    Virg. Georg. II. l. 467.

### ADVERTISEMENT.

THE most rational definition of pastoral poetry seem to be that of the learned and ingenious Dr. Johnson, in the 37th Number of his Rambler. "Pastoral," says he, "being the representation of an action or passion, by its effects on a country life, has nothing peculiar, but its confinement to rural imagery, without which it ceases to be pastoral." This theory the author of the following Eclogues has endeavoured to exemplify.

## ECLOGUE I.

### THERON; OR, THE PRAISE OF RURAL LIFE.

#### SCENE, A HEATH:

#### SEASON—SPRING; TIME—MORNING.

FAIR Spring o'er Nature held her gentlest sway;
Fair Morn diffus'd around her brightest ray;
Thin mists hung hovering on the distant trees,
Or roll'd from off the fields before the breeze.
The shepherd Theron watch'd his fleecy train,
Beneath a broad oak, on the grassy plain.
A heath's green wild lay pleasant to his view,
With shrubs and field-flow'rs deck'd of varied hue:
There hawthorns tall their silver bloom disclos'd,
Here flexile broom's bright yellow interpos'd;
There purple orchis, here pale daisies spread,
And sweet May-lilies richest odour shed.
From many a copse and blossom'd orchard near,
The voice of birds melodious charm'd the ear;
There shrill the lark, and soft the linnet sung,
And loud through air the throstle's music rung.
The gentle swain the cheerful scene admir'd;
The cheerful scene the song of joy inspir'd.
"Chant on," he cry'd, "ye warblers on the spray!
Bleat on, ye flocks, that in the pastures play!
Low on, ye herds, that range the dewy vales!
Murmur, ye rills! and whisper soft, ye gales!
How bless'd my lot, in these sweet fields assign'd,
Where Peace and Leisure soothe the tuneful mind;
Where yet some pleasing vestiges remain
Of unperverted Nature's golden reign,
When Love and Virtue rang'd Arcadian shades,
With undesigning youths and artless maids!
For us, though destin'd to a later time,
A less luxuriant soil, less genial clime,
For us the country boasts enough to charm,
In the wild woodland or the cultur'd farm.
Come, Cynthio, come! in town no longer stay;
From crowds, and noise, and folly, haste away!
The fields, the meads, the trees, are all in bloom,
The vernal show'rs awake a rich perfume,
Where Damon's mansion, by the glassy stream,
Rears its white walls that through green willows gleam,
Annual the neighbours hold their shearing-day;
And blithe youths come, and nymphs in neat array:
Those shear their sheep, upon the smooth turf laid,
In the broad plane's or trembling poplar's shade;
These for their friends th' expected feast provide,
Beneath cool bow'rs along th' inclosure's side.
To view the toil, the glad repast to share,
Thy Delia, my Melania, shall be there;
Each, kind and faithful to her faithful swain,
Loves the calm pleasures of the pastoral plain.
Come, Cynthio, come! If towns and crowds invite,
And noise and folly promise high delight;
Soon the tir'd soul disgusted turns from these—
The rural prospect, only, long can please!"

## ECLOGUE II.

### PALEMON ; OR, BENEVOLENCE.

SCENE, A WOOD-SIDE ON THE BROW OF A HILL:

SEASON—SUMMER ; TIME—FORENOON.

BRIGHT fleecy clouds flew scattering o'er the sky,
And shorten'd shadows show'd that noon was nigh;
When two young shepherds, in the upland shade,
Their listless limbs upon the greensward laid.
Surrounding groves the wand'ring sight confin'd—
All, save where, westward, one wide landscape shin'd.
Down in the dale were neat enclosures seen,
The winding hedge-row, and the thicket green;
Rich marshland next a glossy level show'd,
And through grey willows silver rivers flow'd:
Beyond, high hills with tow'rs and villas crown'd,
And waving forests, form'd the prospect's bound.
Sweet was the covert where the swains reclin'd!
There spread the wild rose, there the woodbine
                       twin'd;                [ground,
There stood green fern ; there, o'er the grassy
Sweet camomile and alehoof crept around ;
And centaury red and yellow cinquefoil grew,
And scarlet campion, and cyanus blue ;
And tufted thyme, and marjoram's purple bloom,
And ruddy strawberries yielding rich perfume.
Gay flies their wings on each fair flow'r display'd,
And labouring bees a lulling murmur made.
Along the brow a path delightful lay ;
Slow by the youths Palemon chanc'd to stray,
A bard, who often to the rural throng,
At vacant hours, rehears'd the moral song !
The song the shepherds crav'd; the sage reply'd:
" As late my steps forsook the fountain side,
Adown the green lane by the beechen grove,
Their flocks young Pironel and Larvon drove;
With us perchance they'll rest awhile"—The swains
Approach'd the shade ; their sheep spread o'er the
Silent they view'd the venerable man,        [plains:
Whose voice melodious thus the lay began :
" What Alcon sung where Evesham's vales extend,
I sing ; ye swains, your pleas'd attention lend !
There long with him the rural life I led,
His fields I cultur'd, and his flocks I fed.
Where, by the hamlet road upon the green,
Stood pleasant cots with trees dispers'd between,
Beside his door, as waving o'er his head
A lofty elm its rustling foliage spread,
Frequent he sat ; while all the village train
Press'd round his seat, and listen'd to his strain.
And once of fair Benevolence he sung,
And thus the tuneful numbers left his tongue :
' Ye youths of Avon's banks, of Bredon's groves,
Sweet scenes, where Plenty reigns, and Pleasure
Woo to your bow'rs Benevolence the fair,  [roves!
Kind as your soil, and gentle as your air.
She comes ! her tranquil step and placid eye,
Fierce Rage, fell Hate, and ruthless Avarice fly.
She comes ! her heav'nly smiles, with powerful
           charm,                          [arm.
Smoothe Care's rough brow, and rest Toil's weary
She comes ! ye shepherds, importune her stay !
While your fair farms exuberant wealth display,
While herds and flocks their annual increase yield,
And yellow harvests load the fruitful field ;
Beneath grim Want's inexorable reign,
Pale Sickness, oft, and feeble Age complain !

Why this unlike allotment, save to show,
That who possess, possess but to bestow' ?"
Palemon ceas'd.—" Sweet is the sound of gales
Amid green osiers in the winding vales ;
Sweet is the lark's loud note on sunny hills,
What time fair Morn the sky with fragrance fills;
Sweet is the nightingale's love-soothing strain,
Heard by still waters on the moonlight plain !
But not the gales that through green osiers play,
Nor lark's nor nightingale's melodious lay,
Please like smooth numbers by the Muse inspir'd!"—
Larvon reply'd, and homeward all retir'd.

---

## ECLOGUE III.

### ARMYN ; OR, THE DISCONTENTED.

SCENE, A VALLEY:

SEASON—SUMMER ; TIME—AFTERNOON.

SUMMER o'er Heav'n diffus'd serenest blue,
And painted Earth with many a pleasing hue ;
When Armyn mus'd the vacant hour away,
Where willows o'er him wav'd their pendent spray.
Cool was the shade, and cool the passing gale,
And sweet the prospect of th' adjacent vale :
The fertile soil, profuse of plants, bestow'd
The crowfoot's gold, the trefoil's purple show'd,
And spiky mint rich fragrance breathing round,
And meadsweet tall with tufts of flowrets crown'd,
And comfrey white, and hoary silver-weed,
The bending osier, and the rustling reed.
There, where clear streams about green islands
                   spread,
Fair flocks and herds, the wealth of Armyn, fed ;
There, on the hill's soft slope, delightful view !
Fair fields of corn, the wealth of Armyn, grew ;
His sturdy hinds, a slow laborious band,
Swept their bright scythes along the level land :
Blithe youths and maidens nimbly near them pass'd,
And the thick swarth in careless wind-rows cast.
Full on the landscape shone the westering Sun,
When thus the swain's soliloquy begun :
    " Haste down, O Sun ! and close the tedious day :
Time, to the unhappy, slowly moves away.
Not so to me, in Roden's sylvan bowers,
Pass'd youth's short blissful reign of careless hours;
When to my view the fancy'd future lay,
A region ever tranquil, ever gay.
O then, what ardours did my breast inflame !
What thoughts were mine, of friendship, love, and
           fame !
How tasteless life, now all its joys are try'd,
And warm pursuits in dull repose subside !"
He paus'd : his closing words Albino heard,
As down the stream his little boat he steer'd ;
His hand releas'd the sail, and dropt the oar,
And moor'd the light skiff on the sedgy shore.
" Cease, gentle swain," he said ; " no more, in vain,
Thus make past pleasure cause of present pain !
Cease, gentle swain," he said ; " from thee, alone,
Are youth's bless'd hours and fancy'd prospects flown?
Ah, no !—remembrance to my view restores
Dear native fields, which now my soul deplores ;
Rich hills and vales, and pleasant village scenes
Of oaks whose wide arms stretch'd o'er daisied greens,
And windmill's sails slow-circling in the breeze,
And cottage walls envelop'd half with trees—

Sweet scenes, where beauty met the ravish'd sight,
And music often gave the ear delight;
Where Delia's smile, and Mira's tuneful song,
And Damon's converse, charm'd the youthful throng!
How chang'd, alas, how chang'd!—O'er all our
          plains,
Proud Norval, now, in lonely grandeur reigns;
His wide-spread park a waste of verdure lies,
And his vast villa's glittering roofs arise.
For me, hard fate!—But say, shall I complain?
These limbs yet active life's support obtain.
Let us, or good or evil as we share,
That thankful prize, and this with patience bear.''
The soft reproach touch'd Armyn's gentle breast;
His alter'd brow a placid smile express'd.
" Calm as clear ev'nings after vernal rains,
When all the air a rich perfume retains,
My mind,'' said he, " its murmurs driv'n away,
Feels truth's full force, and bows to reason's sway!"
He ceas'd : the Sun, with horizontal beams,
Gilt the green mountains, and the glittering streams.
Slow down the tide before the sinking breeze
Albino's white sail gleam'd among the trees;
Slow down the tide his winding course he bore
To watry Talgar's aspin-shaded shore.
Slow cross the valley, to the southern hill,
The steps of Armyn sought the distant vill,
Where through tall elms the moss-grown turret rose;
And his fair mansion offer'd sweet repose.

---

ECLOGUE IV.

LYCORON; OR, THE UNHAPPY.

SCENE, A VALLEY :

SEASON—AUTUMN; TIME—EVENING.

THE matron, Autumn, held her sober reign
O'er fading foliage on the russet plain :
Mild Evening came; the Moon began to rise,
And spread pale lustre o'er unclouded skies.
'T was silence all—save, where along the road
The slow wane grating bore its cumb'rous load ;
Save, where broad rivers roll'd their waves away,
And screaming herons sought their watry prey—
When hapless Damon, in Algorno's vale,
Pour'd his soft sorrows on the passing gale.
" That grace of shape, that elegance of air,
That blooming face so exquisitely fair;
That eye of brightness, bright as morning's ray,
That smile of softness, soft as closing day,
Which bound my soul to thee ; all, all are fled—
All lost in dreary mansions of the dead !
Ev'n him, whom distance from his love divides,
Toil'd on scorch'd sands, or tost on rolling tides,
Kind hope still cheers, still paints, to sooth his pain,
The happy moment when they meet again.
Far worse my lot ! of hope bereft, I mourn !—
The parted spirit never can return !"
Thus Damon spoke, as in the cypress gloom
He hung lamenting o'er his Delia's tomb.
In the still valley where they wander'd near,
Two gentle shepherds chanc'd his voice to hear:
Lycoron's head Time's hand had silver'd o'er,
And Milo's cheek youth's rosy blushes bore.
" How mournful," said Lycoron, " flows that
          strain !
It brings past miseries to my mind again.

When the blithe village, on the vernal green,
Sees its fair daughters in the dance convene;
And youth's light step in search of pleasure strays,
And his fond eyes on beauty fix their gaze ;
Shouldst thou then, lingering midst the lovely train,
Wish some young charmer's easy heart to gain,
Mark well, that reason love's pursuit approve,
Ere thy soft arts her tender passions move :
Else, though thy thoughts in summer regions range,
Calm sunny climes that seem to fear no change ;
Rude winter's rage will soon the scene deform,
Dark with thick cloud, and rough with battering
          storm !
When parents interdict, and friends dissuade,
The prudent censure, and the proud upbraid ;
Think ! all their efforts then shalt thou disdain,
Thy faith, thy constancy, unmov'd, maintain ?
To Isca's fields, me once ill-fortune led ;
In Isca's fields, her flocks Zelinda fed :
There oft, when Ev'ning, on the silent plain,
Commenc'd with sweet serenity her reign,
Along green groves, or down the winding dales,
The fair-one listen'd to my tender tales;
Then when her mind, or doubt, or fear, distress'd,
And doubt, or fear, her anxious eyes express'd,
' O no !' said I, ' let oxen quit the mead,
With climbing goats on craggy cliffs to feed ;
Before the hare the hound affrighted fly,
And larks pursue the falcon through the sky ;
Streams cease to flow, and winds to stir the lake,
If I, unfaithful, ever thee forsake !—'
What my tongue utter'd then, my heart believ'd :
O wretched heart, self-flatter'd and deceiv'd !
Fell Slander's arts the virgin's fame accus'd ;
And whom my love had chose, my pride refus'd.
For me, that cheek did tears of grief distain ?
To me, that voice in anguish plead in vain ?
What fiend relentless then my soul possess'd ?
Oblivion hide ! for ever hide the rest !
Too well her innocence and truth were prov'd ;
Too late her pity and my justice mov'd !"
He ceas'd, with groans that more than words
And smote in agony his aged breast.   [express'd ;
His friend reply'd not; but, with soothing strains
Of solemn music, sought to ease his pains:
Soft flow'd the notes, as gales that waft perfume
From cowslip meads, or linden boughs in bloom.
Peace o'er their minds a calm composure cast;
And slowly down the shadowy vale in pensive mood
          they pass'd.

---

*ELEGIES,*

DESCRIPTIVE AND MORAL.

---

ELEGY I.

WRITTEN AT THE APPROACH OF SPRING.

STERN Winter hence with all his train removes,
     And cheerful skies and limpid streams are seen;
Thick-sprouting foliage decorates the groves ;
     Reviving herbage clothes the fields with green.

Yet lovelier scenes th' approaching months prepare;
     Kind Spring's full bounty soon will be display'd;
The smile of beauty ev'ry vale shall wear ;
     The voice of song enliven ev'ry shade.

O Fancy, paint not coming days too fair!
  Oft for the prospects sprightly May should yield,
Rain-pouring clouds have darken'd all the air,
  Or snows untimely whiten'd o'er the field:

But should kind Spring her wonted bounty show'r,
  The smile of beauty, and the voice of song;
If gloomy thought the human mind o'erpower,
  Ev'n vernal hours glide unenjoy'd along.

I shun the scenes where madd'ning passion raves,
  Where Pride and Folly high dominion hold,
And unrelenting Avarice drives her slaves
  O'er prostrate Virtue in pursuit of gold.

The grassy lane, the wood-surrounded field, [gay,
  The rude stone fence with fragrant wall-flow'rs
The clay-built cot, to me more pleasure yield
  Than all the pomp imperial domes display;

And yet even here, amid these secret shades,
  These simple scenes of unreprov'd delight,
Affliction's iron hand my breast invades,
  And Death's dread dart is ever in my sight.

While genial suns to genial show'rs succeed
  (The air all mildness, and the earth all bloom;)
While herds and flocks range sportive o'er the mead,
  Crop the sweet herb, and snuff the rich perfume;

O why alone to hapless man deny'd
  To taste the bliss inferior beings boast?
O why this fate, that fear and pain divide
  His few short hours on Earth's delightful coast?

Ah, cease—no more of Providence complain!
  'T is sense of guilt that wakes the mind to woe,
Gives force to fear, adds energy to pain,
  And palls each joy by Heav'n indulg'd below:

Why else the smiling infant-train so bless'd,
  Ere ill propension ripens into sin,
Ere wild desire inflames the youthful breast,
  And dear-bought knowledge ends the peace within?

As to the bleating tenants of the field,
  As to the sportive warblers on the trees,
To them their joys sincere the seasons yield,
  And all their days and all their prospects please;

Such mine, when first, from London's crowded streets,
  Rov'd my young steps to Surry's wood-crown'd hills,
O'er new-blown meads that breath'd a thousand
  By shady coverts and by crystal rills. [sweets,

O happy hours, beyond recov'ry fled!
  What share I now that can your loss repay,
While o'er my mind these glooms of thought are
    spread,
  And veil the light of life's meridian ray?

Is there no power this darkness to remove?
  The long-lost joys of Eden to restore?
Or raise our views to happier seats above,
  Where fear, and pain, and death shall be no more?

Yes, those there are who know a Saviour's love
  The long-lost joys of Eden to restore,
And raise their views to happier seats above,
  Where fear and pain, and death, shall be no more:

These grateful share the gifts of Nature's hand;
  And in the varied scenes that round them shine
(Minute and beautiful, or rude and grand)
  Admire th' amazing workmanship divine.

Blows not a flow'ret in th' enamel'd vale,
  Shines not a pebble where the riv'let strays,
Sports not an insect on the spicy gale,
  But claims their wonder, and excites their praise.

For them ev'n vernal Nature looks more gay,
  For them more lively hues the fields adorn;
To them more fair the fairest smile of day,
  To them more sweet the sweetest breath of morn.

They feel the bliss that hope and faith supply;
  They pass serene th' appointed hours that bring
The day that wafts them to the realms on high,
  The day that centres in Eternal Spring.

---

## ELEGY II.

WRITTEN IN THE HOT WEATHER, JULY, 1757.

THREE hours from noon the passing shadow shows,
  The sultry breeze glides faintly o'er the plains,
The dazzling ether fierce and fiercer glows,
  And human nature scarce its rage sustains.

Now still and vacant is the dusty street,
  And still and vacant all yon fields extend,
Save where those swains, oppress'd with toil and heat,
  The grassy harvest of the mead attend.

Lost is the lively aspect of the ground,
  Low are the springs, the reedy ditches dry;
No verdant spot in all the vale is found,
  Save what yon stream's unfailing stores supply.

Where are the flow'rs, the garden's rich array?
  Where is their beauty, where their fragrance fled?
Their stems relax, fast fall their leaves away,
  They fade and mingle with their dusty bed:

All but the natives of the torrid zone,
  What Afric's wilds, or Peru's fields display,
Pleas'd with a clime that imitates their own,
  They lovelier bloom beneath the parching ray.

Where is wild Nature's heart-reviving song,
  That fill'd in genial spring the verdant bow'rs?
Silent in gloomy woods the feather'd throng
  Pine through this long, long course of sultry hours.

Where is the dream of bliss by summer brought?
  The walk along the riv'let-water'd vale?
The field with verdure clad, with fragrance fraught?
  The Sun mild-beaming, and the fanning gale?

The weary soul Imagination cheers,
  Her pleasing colours paint the future gay:
Time passes on, the truth itself appears,
  The pleasing colours instant fade away.

In diff'rent seasons diff'rent joys we place,
  And these will spring supply, and summer these;
Yet frequent storms the bloom of spring deface,
  And summer scarcely brings a day to please.

O for some secret shady cool recess,
  Some Gothic dome o'erhung with darksome trees,
Where thick damp walls this raging heat repress,
  Where the long aisle invites the lazy breeze !

But why these plaints?—reflect, nor murmur more—
  Far worse their fate in many a foreign land,
The Indian tribes on Darien's swampy shore,
  The Arabs wand'ring over Mecca's sand.

Far worse, alas ! the feeling mind sustains,
  Rack'd with the poignant pangs of fear or shame;
The hopeless lover bound in Beauty's chains,
  The bard whom Envy robs of hard-earn'd fame;

He, who a father or a mother mourns,
  Or lovely consort lost in early bloom ;
He, whom fell Febris, rapid fury ! burns,
  Or Phthisis slow leads ling'ring to the tomb—

Lest man should sink beneath the present pain ;
  Lest man should triumph in the present joy ;
For him th' unvarying laws of Heav'n ordain,
  Hope in his ills, and to his bliss alloy.

Fierce and oppressive is the heat we bear,
  Yet not unuseful to our humid soil ;
Thence shall our fruits a richer flavour share,
  Thence shall our plains with riper harvests smile.

Reflect, nor murmur more—for, good in all,
  Heav'n gives the due degrees of drought or rain;
Perhaps ere morn refreshing show'rs may fall,
  Nor soon you Sun rise blazing fierce again :

Ev'n now behold the grateful change at hand !
  Hark, in the east loud blust'ring gales arise ;
Wide and more wide the dark'ning clouds expand,
  And distant lightnings flash along the skies !

O, in the awful concert of the storm,
  While hail, and rain, and wind, and thunder join ;
May deep-felt gratitude my soul inform,
  May joyful songs of rev'rent praise be mine !

---

### ELEGY III.

#### WRITTEN IN HARVEST.

Farewell the pleasant violet-scented shade,
  The primros'd hill, and daisy-mantled mead ;
The furrow'd land, with springing corn array'd ;
  The sunny wall, with bloomy branches spread :

Farewell the bow'r with blushing roses gay ;
  Farewell the fragrant trefoil-purpled field ;
Farewell the walk through rows of new-mown hay,
  When ev'ning breezes mingled odours yield :

Of these no more—now round the lonely farms,
  Where jocund Plenty deigns to fix her seat ;
Th' autumnal landscape op'ning all its charms,
  Declares kind Nature's annual work complete.

In diff'rent parts what diff'rent views delight,
  Where on neat ridges waves the golden grain ;
Or where the bearded barley dazzling white,
  Spreads o'er the steepy slope or wide champaign.

The smile of Morning gleams along the hills,
  And wakeful Labour calls her sons abroad ;
They leave with cheerful look their lowly vills,
  And bid the fields resign their ripen'd load.

In various tasks engage the rustic bands,
  And here the scythe, and there the sickle wield ;
Or rear the new-bound sheaves along the lands,
  Or range in heaps the swarths upon the field.

Some build the shocks, some load the spacious wains,
  Some lead to shelt'ring barns the fragrant corn ;
Some form tall ricks, that tow'ring o'er the plains
  For many a mile, the homestead yards adorn.—

The rattling car with verdant branches crown'd,
  The joyful swains that raise the clam'rous song,
Th' enclosure gates thrown open all around,
  The stubble peopled by the gleaning throng,

Soon mark glad harvest o'er—Ye rural lords,
  Whose wide domains o'er Albion's isle extend ;
Think whose kind hand your annual wealth affords,
  And bid to Heav'n your grateful praise ascend !

For though no gift spontaneous of the ground
  Rose these fair crops that made your vallies smile,
Though the blithe youth of ev'ry hamlet round
  Pursu'd for these through many a day their toil ;

Yet what avail your labours or your cares?
  Can all your labours, all your cares, supply
Bright suns, or soft'ning show'rs, or tepid airs,
  Or one indulgent influence of the sky ?

For Providence decrees, that we obtain
  With toil each blessing destin'd to our use ;
But means to teach us, that our toil is vain
  If he the bounty of his hand refuse.

Yet, Albion, blame not what thy crime demands,
  While this sad truth the blushing Muse betrays—
More frequent echoes o'er thy harvest lands,
  The voice of riot than the voice of praise.

Prolific though thy fields, and mild thy clime,
  Realms fam'd for fields as rich, for climes as fair,
Have fall'n the prey of famine, war, and time,
  And now no semblance of their glory bear.

Ask Palestine, proud Asia's early boast,     [oil ;
  Where now the groves that pour'd her wine and
Where the fair towns that crown'd her wealthy coast;
  Where the glad swains that till'd her fertile soil :

Ask, and behold, and mourn her hapless fall !
  Where rose fair towns, where toil'd the jocund
    swain,
Thron'd on the naked rock and mould'ring wall,
  Pale Want and Ruin hold their dreary reign.

Where Jordan's vallies smil'd in living green,
  Where Sharon's flow'rs disclos'd their varied hues,
The wand'ring pilgrim views the alter'd scene,
  And drops the tear of pity as he views.

Ask Grecia, mourning o'er her ruin'd tow'rs ;
  Where now the prospects charm'd her bards of old,
Her corn-clad mountains and Elysian bow'rs,
  And silver streams through fragrant meadows
    roll'd ?

Where Freedom's praise along the vale was heard,
   And town to town return'd the fav'rite sound;
Where patriot War her awful standard rear'd,
   And brav'd the millions Persia pour'd around?

There Freedom's praise no more the valley cheers,
   There patriot War no more her banner waves;
Nor bard, nor sage, nor martial chief appears,
   But stern barbarians rule a land of slaves.

Of mighty realms are such the poor remains?
   Of mighty realms that fell, when mad with pow'r,
They call'd for Vice to revel on their plains;
   The monster doom'd their offspring to devour!

O Albion! wouldst thou shun their mournful fate,
   To shun their follies and their crimes be thine;
And woo to linger in thy fair retreat,
   The radiant virtues, progeny divine!

Fair Truth, with dauntless eye and aspect bland;
   Sweet Peace, whose brow no angry frown deforms;
Soft Charity, with over-open hand;
   And Courage, calm amid surrounding storms.

O lovely train! O haste to grace our isle!
   So may the pow'r who ev'ry blessing yields,
Bid on her clime serenest seasons smile,
   And crown with annual wealth her far-fam'd fields.

---

## ELEGY IV.

### WRITTEN AT THE APPROACH OF WINTER.

THE Sun far southward bends his annual way,
   The bleak north-east wind lays the forests bare,
The fruit ungather'd quits the naked spray,
   And dreary Winter reigns o'er earth and air.

No mark of vegetable life is seen,
   No bird to bird repeats his tuneful call;
Save the dark leaves of some rude evergreen,
   Save the lone red-breast on the moss-grown wall.

Where are the sprightly prospects Spring supply'd,
   The may-flower'd hedges scenting ev'ry breeze;
The white flocks scatt'ring o'er the mountain's side,
   The woodlarks warbling on the blooming trees?

Where is gay Summer's sportive insect train,
   That in green fields on painted pinions play'd?
The herd at morn wide-pasturing o'er the plain,
   Or throng'd at noon-tide in the willow shade?

Where is brown Autumn's ev'ning mild and still,
   What time the ripen'd corn fresh fragrance yields,
What time the village peoples all the hill,
   And loud shouts echo o'er the harvest fields?

To former scenes our fancy thus returns,
   To former scenes, that little pleas'd when here!
Our winter chills us, and our summer burns,
   Yet we dislike the changes of the year.

To happier lands then restless fancy flies,      [flow;
   Where Indian streams through green savannahs
Where brighter suns and ever tranquil skies
   Bid new fruits ripen, and new flow'rets blow.

Let Truth these fairer happier lands survey—
   There frowning months descend in wat'ry storms;
Or Nature faints amid the blaze of day,
   And one brown hue the sun-burnt plain deforms.

There oft, as toiling in the sultry fields,
   Or homeward passing on the shadeless way,
His joyless life the weary lab'rer yields,
   And instant drops beneath the deathful ray.

Who dreams of Nature, free from Nature's strife?
   Who dreams of constant happiness below?
The hope-flush'd ent'rer on the stage of life;
   The youth to knowledge unchastis'd by woe.

For me, long toil'd on many a weary road,
   Led by false hope in search of many a joy;
I find in Earth's bleak clime no bless'd abode,
   No place, no season, sacred from annoy:

For me, while Winter rages round the plains,
   With his dark days I human life compare; [rains,
Not those more fraught with clouds, and winds, and
   Than this with pining pain and anxious care.

O! whence this wondrous turn of mind our fate—
   Whate'er the season or the place possess'd,
We ever murmur at our present state;
   And yet the thought of parting breaks our rest?

Why else, when heard in Ev'ning's solemn gloom,
   Does the sad knell, that sounding o'er the plain
Tolls some poor lifeless body to the tomb,
   Thus thrill my breast with melancholy pain?

The voice of Reason thunders in my ear:
   "Thus thou, ere long, must join thy kindred clay;
No more those nostrils breathe the vital air,
   No more those eyelids open on the day!"—

O Winter, o'er me hold thy dreary reign!
   Spread wide thy skies in darkest horrours drcss'd!
Of their dread rage no longer I 'll complain,
   Nor ask an Eden for a transient guest.

Enough has Heav'n indulg'd of joy below,
   To tempt our tarriance in this lov'd retreat;
Enough has Heav'n ordain'd of useful woe,
   To make us languish for a happier seat.

There is, who deems all climes, all seasons fair;
   There is, who knows no restless passion's strife;
Contentment, smiling at each idle care;
   Contentment, thankful for the gift of life!

She finds in Winter many a view to please; [gay,
   The morning landscape fring'd with frost-work
The Sun at noon seen through the leafless trees,
   The clear calm ether at the close of day:

She marks th' advantage storms and clouds bestow,
   When blust'ring Caurus purifies the air;
When moist Aquarius pours the fleecy snow, [bear:
   That makes th' impregnate glebe a richer harvest

She bids, for all, our grateful praise arise,
   To him whose mandate spake the world to form;
Gay Spring's gay bloom, and Summer's cheerful
   skies,                           [sounding storm.
And Autumn's corn-clad field, and Winter's

## ELEGY.

WRITTEN AT AMWELL, IN HERTFORDSHIRE, 1768.

O FRIEND ! though silent thus thy tongue remains,
   I read inquiry in thy anxious eye,
Why my pale cheek the frequent tear distains,
   Why from my bosom bursts the frequent sigh.

Long from these scenes detain'd in distant fields,
   My mournful tale perchance escap'd thy ear :
Fresh grief to me the repetition yields ;
   Thy kind attention gives thee right to hear !

Foe to the world's pursuit of wealth and fame,
   Thy Theron early from the world retir'd,
Left to the busy throng each boasted aim,
   Nor aught, save peace in solitude, desir'd.

A few choice volumes there could oft engage,
   A few choice friends there oft amus'd the day ;
There his lov'd parents' slow-declining age,
   Life's calm unvary'd ev'ning, wore away.

Foe to the futile manners of the proud,
   He chose an humble virgin for his own ;
A form with Nature's fairest gifts endow'd,
   And pure as vernal blossoms newly blown :

Her hand she gave, and with it gave a heart
   By love engag'd, with gratitude impress'd,
Free without folly, prudent without art,
   With wit accomplish'd, and with virtue bless'd.

Swift pass'd the hours ; alas, to pass no more !
   Flown like the light clouds of a summer's day !
One beauteous pledge the beauteous consort bore ;
   The fatal gift forbad the giver's stay.

Ere twice the Sun perform'd his annual round,
   In one sad spot where kindred ashes lie,
O'er wife, and child, and parents, clos'd the ground ;
   The final home of man, ordain'd to die !

O cease at length, obstrusive Mem'ry ! cease,
   Nor in my view the wretched hours retain,
That saw disease on her dear life increase,
   And med'cine's lenient arts essay'd in vain.

O the dread scene ! (in misery how sublime !)
   Of love's vain pray'rs to stay her fleeting breath !
Suspense that restless watch'd the flight of time,
   And helpless dumb despair awaiting death !

O the dread scene ! 'T is agony to tell,
   How o'er the couch of pain declin'd my head,
And took from dying lips the long farewell,
   The last, last parting, ere her spirit fled.

" Restore her, Heav'n, as from the grave retrieve—
   In each calm moment all things else resign'd,
Her looks, her language, show how hard to leave
   The lov'd companion she must leave behind.

" Restore her, Heaven ! for once in mercy spare."
   Thus love's vain prayer in anguish interpos'd ;
And soon suspense gave place to dumb despair,
   And o'er the past, Death's sable curtain clos'd—

In silence clos'd—My thoughts rov'd frantic round,
   No hope, no wish, beneath the Sun remain'd ;
Earth, air, and skies, one dismal waste I found,
   One pale, dread, dreary blank, with horrour
      stain'd.

O lovely flow'r, too fair for this rude clime !
   O lovely morn, too prodigal of light !
O transient beauties, blasted in their prime !
   O transient glories, sunk in sudden night !

Sweet excellence, by all who knew thee mourn'd !
   Where is that form, that mind, my soul admir'd ;
That form, with ev'ry pleasing charm adorn'd ;
   That mind, with ev'ry gentle thought inspir'd ?

The face with rapture view'd, I view no more ;
   The voice with rapture heard, no more I hear :
Yet the lov'd features Mem'ry's eyes explore ;
   Yet the lov'd accents fall on Mem'ry's ear.

Ah, sad, sad change ! (sad source of daily pain !)
   That sense of loss ineffable renews ;
While my rack'd bosom heaves the sigh in vain,
   While my pale cheek the tear in vain bedews.

Still o'er the grave that holds the dear remains,
   The mould'ring veil her spirit left below,
Fond Fancy dwells, and pours funereal strains,
   The soul-dissolving melody of woe.

Nor mine alone to bear this painful doom,
   Nor she alone the tear of song obtains ;
The Muse of Blagdon [1], o'er Constantia's tomb,
   In all the eloquence of grief complains.

My friend's fair hope, like mine, so lately gain'd ;
   His heart, like mine, in its true partner bless'd ;
Both from one cause the same distress sustain'd,
   The same sad hours beheld us both distress'd.

O human life ! how mutable, how vain !
   How thy wide sorrows circumscribe thy joy—
A sunny island in a stormy main,
   A spot of azure in a cloudy sky !

All-gracious Heav'n ! since man, infatuate man,
   Rests in thy works, too negligent of thee,
Lays for himself on Earth his little plan,
   Dreads not, or distant views mortality ;

'T is but to wake to nobler thought the soul,
   To rouse us ling'ring on Earth's flow'ry plain,
To virtue's path our wand'rings to control,
   Affliction frowning comes, thy minister of pain !

———————

## AMWELL :

### A DESCRIPTIVE POEM.

THERE dwells a fond desire in human minds,
When pleas'd, their pleasure to extend to those
Of kindred taste ; and thence th' enchanting arts
Of picture and of song, the semblance fair

[1] See Verses written at Sandgate Castle, in memory of a lady, by the late ingenious Dr. Langhorne.

Of Nature's forms produce. This fond desire
Prompts me to sing the lonely sylvan scenes
Of Amwell; which, so oft in early youth,
While novelty enhanc'd their native charms,
Gave rapture to my soul; and often, still,
On life's calm moments shed serener joy.

Descriptive Muse! whose hand along the stream
Of ancient Thames, through Richmond's shady
    groves,
And Sheen's fair vallies, once thy Thomson led [1];
And once o'er green Carmarthen's woody dales,
And sunny landscapes of Campania's plain,
Thy other favour'd bard [2]; thou, who so late,
In bowers by Clent's wild peaks [3], to Shenstone's ear
Didst bring sweet strains of rural melody,
(Alas, no longer heard !)—vouchsafe thine aid:
From all our rich varieties of view,
What best may please, assist me to select,
With art dispose, with energy describe,
And its full image on the mind impress.

And ye, who e'er in these delightful fields
Consum'd with me the social hour, while I
Your walk conducted o'er their loveliest spots,
And on their fairest objects fix'd your sight;
Accept this verse, which may to memory call
That social hour, and sweetly vary'd walk !
And thou, by strong connubial union mine;
Mine, by the stronger union of the heart;
In whom the loss of parents and of friends,
And her, the first fair partner of my joys,
All recompens'd I find; whose presence cheers
The soft domestic scene; Maria, come!
The country calls us forth; blithe Summer's hand
Sheds sweetest flowers, and Morning's brightest smile
Illumines earth and air; Maria, come!
By winding pathways through the waving corn,
We reach the airy point that prospect yields,
Not vast and awful, but confin'd and fair;
Not the black mountain and the foamy main;
Not the throng'd city and the busy port;
But pleasant interchange of soft ascent,
And level plain, and growth of shady woods,
And twining course of rivers clear, and sight
Of rural towns and rural cots, whose roofs
Rise scattering round, and animate the whole.

Far tow'rds the west, close under sheltering hills,
In verdant meads, by Lee's cerulean stream,
Hertford's grey towers [4] ascend; the rude remains
Of high antiquity, from waste escap'd
Of envious time, and violence of war.
For war there once, so tells th' historic page,
Led Desolation's steps : the hardy Dane,
By avarice lur'd, o'er ocean's stormy wave,
To ravage Albion's plains, his fav'rite seat,
There fix'd awhile; and there his castles rear'd

[1] Thomson, author of the Seasons, resided part
of his life near Richmond.

[2] Dyer, author of Grongar Hill; The Ruins of
Rome; and that excellent neglected poem, The
Fleece.

[3] The Clent-hills adjoin to Hagley-park, and are
not far distant from the Leasowes.

[4] In the beginning of the heptarchy, the town
of Hertford was accounted one of the principal
cities of the East Saxons, where the kings of that
province often kept their courts, and a parliamentary council, or national synod, was held, Sept. 24,
673. Chauncy's Hertfordshire, p. 237.

Among the trees; and there, beneath yon ridge
Of piny rocks, his conq'ring navy moor'd,
With idle sails furl'd on the yard, and oars
Recumbent on the flood, and streamers gay
Triumphant flutt'ring on the passing winds.
In fear, the shepherd on the lonely heath
Tended his scanty flock; the ploughman turn'd
In fear his hasty furrow : oft the din
Of hostile arms alarm'd the ear, and flames   [far
Of plunder'd towns through night's thick gloom from
Gleam'd dismal on the sight : till Alfred came,
Till Alfred, father of his people, came,
Lee's rapid tide into new channels turn'd,
And left aground the Danian fleet, and forc'd
The foe to speedy flight [5]. Then Freedom's voice
Reviv'd the drooping swain; then Plenty's hand
Recloth'd the desert fields, and Peace and Love
Sat smiling by ; as now they smiling sit,
Obvious to Fancy's eye, upon the side
Of yon bright sunny theatre of hills,
Where Bengeo's villas rise, and Ware-park's lawns
Spread their green surface, interspers'd with groves
Of broad umbrageous oak, and spiry pine,
Tall elm, and linden pale, and blossom'd thorn,
Breathing mild fragrance, like the spicy gales
Of Indian islands. On the ample brow,
Where that white temple rears its pillar'd front
Half hid with glossy foliage, many a chief
Renown'd for martial deeds, and many a bard
Renown'd for song, have pass'd the rural hour.
The gentle Fanshaw [6] there, from "noise of camps,
From court's disease retir'd [7]," delighted view'd
The gaudy garden fam'd in Wotton's page [8];
Or in the verdant maze, or cool arcade,
Sat musing, and from smooth Italian strains
The soft Guarini's amorous lore transfus'd
Into rude British verse. The warrior's arm
Now rests from toil; the poet's tuneful tongue

[5] Towards the latter end of the year 879, the
Danes advanced to the borders of Mercia, and
erected two forts at Hertford on the Lee, for the
security of their ships, which they had brought up
that river. Here they were attacked by the Lon-
doners, who were repulsed. But Alfred advanced
with his army, and viewing the nature of their situation, turned the course of the stream, so that their
vessels were left on dry ground; a circumstance
which terrified them to such a degree, that they
abandoned their forts, and, flying towards the Severn,
were pursued by Alfred as far as Quatbridge.—
Smollet's Hist. of England, 8vo. edit. vol. i. p. 182.

[6] Sir Richard Fanshaw, translator of Guarini's
Pastor Fido, the Lusiad of Camoens, &c. He was
son of sir Henry Fanshaw of Ware-park, and is said
to have resided much there. He was ambassador
to Portugal, and afterwards to Spain, and died at
Madrid in 1666. His body was brought to England, and interred in Ware church, where his monument is still existing. In Cibber's Lives of the
Poets, it is erroneously asserted that he was buried
in All-Saints church, Hertford.

[7] The words marked with inverted commas are
part of a stanza of Fanshaw's.

[8] See Reliquiæ Wottonianæ, where the author
makes a particular mention of the garden of sir
Henry Fanshaw at Ware-park, "as a delicate and
diligent curiosity," remarkable for the nice arrangement of its flowers.

In silence lies; frail man his lov'd domains
Soon quits for ever! they themselves, by course
Of nature often, or caprice of art,
Experience change: even here, 't is said of old
Steep rocky cliffs rose where yon gentle slopes
Mix with the vale; and fluctuating waves
Spread wide, where that rich vale with golden flowers
Shines; and where yonder winding crystal rill
Slides through its smooth shorn margin, to the brink
Of Chadwell's azure pool. From Chadwell's pool
To London's plains, the Cambrian artist brought
His ample aqueduct [9]; suppos'd a work
Of match!ess skill, by those who ne'er had heard
How, from Preneste's heights and Anio's banks,
By Tivoli, to Rome's imperial walls,
On marble arches came the limpid store,
And out of jasper rocks in bright cascades
With never-ceasing murmur gush'd; or how,
To Lusitanian Ulysippo's towers [10],
The silver current o'er Alcant'ra's vale
Roll'd high in air, as ancient poet's feign'd
Eridanus to roll through Heaven: to these
Not sordid lucre, but the honest wish
Of future fame, or care for public weal,
Existence gave; and unconfin'd, as dew
Falls from the hand of Evening on the fields,
They flow'd for all. Our mercenary stream,
No grandeur boasting, here obscurely glides
O'er grassy lawns or under willow shades.
As, through the human form, arterial tubes
Branch'd every way, minute and more minute,
The circulating sanguine fluid extend;
So, pipes innumerable to peopled streets
Transmit the purchas'd wave. Old Lee, meanwhile,
Beneath his mossy grot o'erhung with boughs
Of poplar quivering in the breeze, surveys
With eye indignant his diminish'd tide [11]
That laves yon ancient priory's wall [12], and shows
In its clear mirror Ware's inverted roofs.

Ware once was known to Fame; to her fair fields
Whilom the Gothic tournament's proud pomp
Brought Albion's valiant youth and blooming maids:
Pleas'd with ideas of the past, the Muse
Bids Fancy's pencil paint the scene, where they
In gilded barges on the glassy stream
Circled the reedy isles, the sportive dance
Along the smooth lawn led, or in the groves
Wander'd conversing, or reclin'd at ease
To harmony of lutes, and voices sweet
Resign'd th' enchanted ear; till sudden heard
The silver trumpet's animating sound
Summon'd the champions forth; on stately steeds,
In splendid armour clad, the pond'rous lance
With strenuous hand sustaining, forth they came.
Where gay pavilions rose upon the plain,
Or azure awnings stretch'd from tree to tree,

Mix'd with thick foliage, form'd a mimic sky
Of grateful shade (as oft in Agra's streets
The silken canopy from side to side
Extends to break the Sun's impetuous ray,
While monarchs pass beneath); there sat the fair,
A glittering train on costly carpets rang'd,
A group of beauties all in youthful prime,
Of various feature and of various grace!
The pensive languish, and the sprightly air,
The engaging smile, and all the nameless charms
Which transient hope, or fear, or grief, or joy,
Wak'd in th' expressive eye, th' enamour'd heart
Of each young hero rous'd to daring deeds.
Nor this aught strange, that those whom love in-
Prov'd ev'ry means the lovely sex to please: [spir'd
'T is strange, indeed, how custom thus could teach
The tender breast complacence in the sight
Of barb'rous sport, where friend from hand of friend
The fatal wound full oft receiv'd, and fell
A victim to false glory; as that day
Fell gallant Pembroke, while his pompous show
Ended in silent gloom [13]. One pitying tear
To human frailty paid; my roving sight
Pursues its pleasing course o'er neighb'ring hills,
Where frequent hedge-rows intersect rich fields
Of many a different form and different hue,
Bright with ripe corn, or green with grass, or dark
With clover's purple bloom; o'er Widbury's mount
With that fair crescent crown'd of lofty elms,
Its own peculiar boast; and o'er the woods
That round immure the deep sequester'd dale
Of Langley [14], down whose flow'ry-embroider'd
      meads
Swift Ash through pebbly shores meandering rolls,
Elysian scene! as from the living world
Secluded quite; for of that world, to him
Whose wand'rings trace thy winding length, appears
No mark, save one white solitary spire
At distance rising through the tufted trees—
Elysian scene! recluse as that, so fam'd
For solitude, by Warwick's ancient walls,
Where under umbrage of the mossy cliff
Victorious Guy, so legends say, reclin'd
His hoary head beside the silver stream,
In meditation rapt——Elysian scene!
At ev'ning often, while the setting Sun
On the green summit of thy eastern groves
Pour'd full his yellow radiance; while the voice

[13] " In the 25th of Henry III. on the 27th of
June, Gilbert Marshall, earl of Pembroke, a potent
peer of the realm, proclaimed here (at Ware) a
disport of running on horseback with lances, which
was then called a tournament." Chauncy's Hist.
of Hertfordshire.
   " At this tournament, the said Gilbert was slain
by a fall from his horse; Robert de Say, one of his
knights, was killed, and several others wounded."
Smollet's Hist. of England.
[14] This delightful retreat, commonly called
Langley-bottom, is situated about half a mile from
Ware, and the same distance from Amwell. The
scene is adapted to contemplation, and possesses
such capabilities of improvement, that the genius
of a Shenstone might easily convert it to a second
Leasowes. The transition from this solitude to
Widbury-Hill, is made in a walk of a few minutes,
and the prospect from that hill, in a fine evening,
is beautiful beyond description.

[9] The New River brought from Chadwell, a
spring in the meadows between Hertford and Ware,
by sir Hugh Middleton, a native of Wales.
[10] The ancient name of Lisbon.
[11] A considerable part of the New River water
is derived from the Lee, to the disadvantage of the
navigation on that stream.
[12] " About the 18th of Henry III. Margaret,
countess of Leicester, and lady of the manor,
founded a priory for friars in the north part of this
town of Ware, and dedicated the same to St. Francis " Chauncy's Hertfordshire.

Of Zephyr whisp'ring midst the rustling leaves,
The sound of water murm'ring through the sedge,
The turtle's plaintive call, and music soft
Of distant bells, whose ever varying notes
In slow sad measure mov'd, combin'd to sooth
The soul to sweet solemnity of thought;
Beneath thy branchy bowers of thickest gloom,
Much on th' imperfect state of man I 've mus'd:
How Pain o'er half his hours her iron reign
Ruthless extends; how Pleasure from the path
Of innocence allures his steps; how Hope
Directs his eye to distant joy, that flies
His fond pursuit; how Fear his shuddering heart
Alarms with fancy'd ill; how Doubt and Care
Perplex his thought; how soon the tender rose
Of beauty fades, the sturdy oak of strength
Declines to earth, and over all our pride
Stern Time triumphant stands.   From gen'ral fate
To private woes then oft has memory pass'd,
And mourn'd the loss of many a friend belov'd;
Of thee, De Horne, kind, gen'rous, wise, and good!
And thee, my Turner, who, in vacant youth,
Here oft in converse free, or studious search
Of classic lore, accompanied my walk!
From Ware's green bowers, to Devon's myrtle vales,
Remov'd a while, with prospect op'ning fair
Of useful life and honour in his view;
As falls the vernal bloom before the breath
Of blasting Eurus, immature he fell!
The tidings reach'd my ear, and in my breast,
Aching with recent wounds [15], new anguish wak'd.
When melancholy thus has chang'd to grief,
That grief in soft forgetfulness to lose,
I 've left the gloom for gayer scenes, and sought
Through winding paths of venerable shade,
The airy brow where that tall spreading beech
O'ertops surrounding groves, up rocky steeps,
Tree over tree dispos'd; or stretching far
Their shadowy coverts down th' indented side
Of fair corn-fields; or pierc'd with sunny glades,
That yield the casual glimpse of flowery meads
And shining silver rills; on these the eye
Then wont to expatiate pleas'd; or more remote
Survey'd yon vale of Lee, in verdant length
Of level lawn spread out to Kent's blue hills,
And the proud range of glitt'ring spires that rise
In misty air on Thames's crowded shores.
  How beautiful, how various, is the view
Of these sweet pastoral landscapes! fair, perhaps,
As those renown'd of old, from Tabor's height,
Or Carmel seen; or those, the pride of Greece,
Tempè or Arcady; or those that grac'd
The banks of clear Elorus, or the skirts
Of thymy Hybla, where Sicilia's isle
Smiles on the azure main; there once was heard
The Muse's lofty lay.——How beautiful,
How various is yon view! delicious hills [streams
Bounding smooth vales, smooth vales by winding
Divided, that here glide through grassy banks
In open sun, there wander under shade
Of aspen tall, or ancient elm, whose boughs
O'erhang grey castles, and romantic farms,
And humble cots of happy shepherd swains.
Delightful habitations! with the song
Of birds melodious charm'd, and bleat of flocks
From upland pastures heard, and low of kine
Grazing the rushy mead, and mingled sounds
Of falling waters and of whisp'ring winds—

Delightful habitations! o'er the land
Dispers'd around, from Waltham's osier'd isles
To where bleak Nasing's lonely tower o'erlooks
Her verdant fields; from Raydon's pleasant groves
And Hunsdon's bowers on Stort's irriguous marge,
By Rhye's old walls, to Hodsdon's airy street;
From Haly's woodland to the flow'ry meads
Of willow-shaded Stansted, and the slope
Of Amwell's mount, that crown'd with yellow corn
There from the green flat, softly swelling, shows
Like some bright vernal cloud by Zephyr's breath
Just rais'd above th' horizon's azure bound.
  As one long travell'd on Italia's plains,
The land of pomp and beauty, still his feet
On his own Albion joys to fix again;
So my pleas'd eye, which o'er the prospect wide
Has wander'd round, and various objects mark'd,
On Amwell rests at last, its fav'rite scene!
How picturesque the view! where up the side
Of that steep bank, her roofs of russet thatch
Rise mix'd with trees, above whose swelling tops
Ascends the tall church tow'r, and loftier still
The hill's extended ridge.   How picturesque!
Where slow beneath that bank the silver stream
Glides by the flowery isle, and willow groves
Wave on its northern verge, with trembling tufts
Of osier intermix'd.   How picturesque
The slender group of airy elm, the clump
Of pollard oak, or ash, with ivy brown
Entwin'd; the walnut's gloomy breadth of boughs,
The orchard's ancient fence of rugged pales,
The haystack's dusky cone, the moss-grown shed,
The clay-built barn; the elder-shaded cot,
Whose white-wash'd gable prominent through green
Of waving branches shows, perchance inscrib'd
With some past owner's name, or rudely grac'd
With rustic dial, that scarcely serves to mark
Time's ceaseless flight; the wall with mantling vines
O'erspread, the porch with climbing woodbine
                                wreath'd,
And under sheltering eves the sunny bench,
Where brown hives range, whose busy tenants fill,
With drowsy hum, the little garden gay, [flowers,
Whence blooming beans, and spicy herbs, and
Exhale around a rich perfume! Here rests
The empty wain; there idle lies the plough:
By Summer's hand unharness'd, here the steed,
Short ease enjoying, crops the daisy'd lawn;
Here bleats the nursling lamb, the heifer there
Waits at the yard-gate lowing.   By the road,
Where the neat ale-house stands, (so once stood
Deserted Auburn! in immortal song          [thine,
Consign'd to fame [16]) the cottage sire recounts
The praise he earn'd, when cross the field he drew
The straightest furrow, or neatest built the rick,
Or led the reaper band in sultry noons
With unabating strength, or won the prize
At many a crowded wake.   Beside her door,
The cottage matron whirls her circling wheel,
And jocund chants her lay.   The cottage maid
Feeds from her loaded lap her mingled train
Of clamorous hungry fowls; or o'er the style
Leaning, with downcast look, the artless tale
Of ev'ning courtship hears.   The sportive troop
Of cottage children on the grassy waste
Mix in rude gambols, or the bounding ball
Circle from hand to hand, or rustic notes

[15] See Elegy written at Amwell, 1768, p. 462.
  VOL. XVII.

[16] See The Deserted Village, a beautiful poem,
by the late Dr. Goldsmith.
                    H h

Wake on their pipes of jointed reed : while near
The careful shepherd's frequent-falling strokes
Fix on the fallow lea his hurdled fold.
   Such rural life! so calm, it little yields
Of interesting act, to swell the page
Of history or song; yet much the soul
Its sweet simplicity delights, and oft
From noise of busy towns, to fields and groves,
The Muse's sons have fled to find repose.
Fam'd Walton [17], erst, the ingenious fisher swain,
Oft our fair haunts explor'd; upon Lee's shore,
Beneath some green tree oft his angle laid,
His sport suspending to admire their charms.
He, who in verse his country's story told [18], [scene,
Here dwelt awhile; perchance here sketch'd the
Where his fair Argentile, from crowded courts
For pride self-banish'd, in sequester'd shades
Sojourn'd disguis'd, and met the slighted youth

[17] Isaac Walton, author of The Complete Angler, an ingenious biographer, and no despicable poet. The scene of his Anglers' Dialogues is the vale of Lee, between Tottenham and Ware; it seems to have been a place he much frequented: he particularly mentions Amwell Hill.

[18] William Warner, author of Albion's England, an historical poem; an episode of which, entitled Argentile and Curan, has been frequently reprinted, and is much admired by the lovers of old English poetry. The ingenious Dr. Percy, who has inserted this piece in his collection, observes, that " though Warner's name is so seldom mentioned, his contemporaries ranked him on a level with Spenser, and called them the Homer and Virgil of their age;" that " Warner was said to have been a Warwickshire man, and to have been educated at Magdalen Hall; that, in the latter part of his life, he was retained in the service of Henry Cary, lord Hunsdon, to whom he dedicates his poem; but that more of his history is not known." Mrs. Cooper, in her Muses' Library, after highly applauding his poetry, adds, " What were the circumstances and accidents of his life, we have hardly light enough to conjecture; any more than, by his dedication, it appears he was in the service of the lord Hunsdon, and acknowledges very gratefully, both father and son, for his patrons and benefactors."—By the following extract from the parish register of Amwell, it may be reasonably concluded, that Warner resided for some time at that village; and, as his profession of an attorney is particularly mentioned, it is pretty evident that, whatever dependence he might have on lord Hunsdon, it could not be in the capacity of a menial servant. Though Warner's merit, as a poet, may have been too highly rated, it was really not inconsiderable; his Argentile and Curan has many beauties; but it has also the faults common to the compositions of his age, especially a most disgusting indelicacy of sentiment and expression.

" Ma. William Warner, a man of good yeares and honest reputation, by his profession an attorney at the Common Please, author of Albion's England; dying suddenly in the night in his bedde, without any former complaynt or sicknesse, on Thursday night, beeing the 9th of March, was buried the Saturday following, and lieth in the church at the upper end, under the stone of Gwalter Fader." Parish register of Amwell, 1608—9.

Who long had sought her love—the gentle bard
Sleeps here, by Fame forgotten; (fickle Fame
Too oft forgets her fav'rites!) By his side
Sleeps gentle Hassal [19], who with tenderest care
Here watch'd his village charge; in nuptial bonds
Their hands oft join'd; oft heard, and oft reliev'd
Their little wants; oft heard, and oft compos'd,
Sole arbiter, their little broils; oft urg'd
Their flight from folly and from vice; and oft
Dropp'd on their graves the tear, to early worth
Or ancient friendship due. In dangerous days,
When Death's fell fury, pale-ey'd Pestilence,
Glar'd horrour round, his duty he discharg'd
Unterrified, unhurt; and here, at length,
Clos'd his calm inoffensive useful life
In venerable age: her life with him
His faithful consort clos'd; on Earth's cold breast
Both sunk to rest together.——On the turf,
Whence Time's rude grasp has torn their rustic
    tombs,
I strew fresh flowers, and make a moment's pause
Of solemn thought; then seek th' adjacent spot,
From which, through these broad lindens' verdant
The steeple's Gothic wall and window dim [arch,
In perspective appear; then homeward turn
By where the Muse, enamour'd of our shades,
Deigns still her fav'ring presence; where my friend,
The British Tasso [20], oft from busy scenes
To rural calm and letter'd ease retires.
As some fond lover leaves his fav'rite nymph,
Oft looking back, and ling'ring in her view,
So now reluctant this retreat I leave,
Look after look indulging; on the right,
Up to yon airy battlement's broad top
Half veil'd with trees, that, from th' acclivious steep
Jut like the pendent gardens, fam'd of old,
Beside Euphrates' bank; then, on the left,

[19] Thomas Hassal, vicar of Amwell; he kept the above-mentioned parish register with uncommon care and precision, enriching it with many entertaining anecdotes of the parties registered. He performed his duty in the most hazardous circumstances, it appearing that the plague twice raged in the village during his residence there; in 1603, when twenty-six persons, and in 1625, when twenty-two persons died of it, and were buried in his church-yard. The character here given of him must be allowed, strictly speaking, to be imaginary; but his composition, in the said register, appeared to me to breathe such a spirit of piety, simplicity, and benevolence, that I almost think myself authorised to assert that it was his real one. He himself is registered by his son Edmund Hassal, as follows:
" Thomas Hassal, vicar of this parish, where he had continued resident fifty-seven years, nine months, and sixteen days, in the reigns of queen Elizabeth, king James, and king Charles, departed this life September 24th, Thursday, and was buried September 26th, Saturday. His body was laid in the chancel of this church, under the priests or marble stone. Ætatis 84. Non erat ante, nec erit post te similis. Edmund Hassal." Register of Amwell, 1657.

Elizabeth Hassal, wife of the said Thomas Hassal, died about the same time, aged 78 years 8 months, married 46 years and 4 months.

[20] Mr. Hoole, translator of Tasso's Jerusalem Delivered.

Down to those shàded cots, and bright expanse
Of water softly sliding by : once, where
That bright expanse of water softly slides,
O'erhung with shrubs that fringe the chalky rock,
A little fount pour'd forth its gurgling rill,
In flinty channel trickling o'er the green,
From Emma nam'd ; perhaps some sainted maid
For holy life rever'd ; to such, erewhile,
Fond Superstition many a pleasant grove,
And limpid spring, was wont to consecrate.
Of Emma's story nought Tradition speaks ;
Conjecture, who, behind Oblivion's veil,
Along the doubtful past delights to stray,
Boasts now, indeed, that from her well the place
Receiv'd its appellation [21].——Thou, sweet Vill,
Farewell ! and ye, sweet fields, where Plenty's horn
Pours liberal boons, and Health propitious deigns
Her cheering smile ! you not the parching air
Of arid sands, you not the vapours chill
Of humid fens, annoy ; Favonius' wing,
From off your thyme-banks and your trefoil meads,
Wafts balmy redolence ; robust and gay
Your swains industrious issue to their toil,
Till your rich glebe, or in your granaries store
Its gen'rous produce : annual ye resound
The ploughman's song, as he through reeking soil
Guides slow his shining share ; ye annual hear
The shouts of harvest, and the prattling train
Of cheerful gleaners :—and th' alternate strokes
Of loud flails echoing from your loaded barns,
The pallid Morn in dark November wake.
But, happy as ye are, in marks of wealth
And population ; not for these, or aught
Beside, wish I, in hyperbolic strains
Of vain applause, to elevate your fame
Above all other scenes ; for scenes as fair
Have charm'd my sight, but transient was the view :
You, through all seasons, in each varied hour
For observation happiest, oft my steps
Have travers'd o'er ; oft Fancy's eye has seen
Gay Spring trip lightly on your lovely lawns,
To wake fresh flowers at morn ; and Summer spread
His listless limbs, at noon-tide, on the marge
Of smooth translucent pools, where willows green
Gave shade, and breezes from the wild mint's bloom
Brought odour exquisite ; oft Fancy's ear,
Deep in the gloom of evening woods, has heard
The last sad sigh of Autumn, when his throne
To Winter he resign'd ; oft Fancy's thought,
In ecstasy, where from the golden east,
Or dazzling south, or crimson west, the Sun
A different lustre o'er the landscape threw,
Some Paradise has form'd, the blissful seat
Of Innocence and Beauty ! while I wish'd
The skill of Claude, or Rubens, or of him
Whom now on Lavant's banks, in groves that breathe
Enthusiasm sublime, the sister nymphs [22]
Inspire [23]; that, to the idea fair, my hand

[21] In Doomsday book, this village of Amwell is written Emmevelle, perhaps originally Emma's-Well. When the New River was opened, there was a spring here which was taken into that aqueduct. Chadwell, the other source of that river, evidently received its denomination from the tutelar saint, St. Chad, who seems to have given name to springs and wells in different parts of England.

[22] Painting and Poety.

[23] Mr. George Smith of Chichester, a justly celebrated landscape painter, and also a poet. La-

Might permanence have lent !—Attachment strong
Springs from delight bestow'd ; to me delight
Long ye have given, and I have given you praise !

## AMOEBAEAN ECLOGUES.

### ADVERTISEMENT.

MUCH of the rural imagery which our country
affords, has already been introduced in poetry ;
but many obvious and pleasing appearances seem
to have totally escaped notice. To describe these
is the business of the following Eclogues. The
plan of the Carmen Amoebaeum, or responsive
verse of the ancients, inconsistent as it may be
deemed with modern manners, was preferred on
this occasion, as admitting an arbitrary and desultory disposition of ideas, where it was found difficult to preserve a regular connection.

### ECLOGUE I.

#### RURAL SCENERY; OR, THE DESCRIBERS.

DECEMBER's frost had bound the fields and streams,
And noon's bright Sun effus'd its cheerful beams :
Where woodland, northward, screen'd a pleasant
    plain,
And on dry fern-banks brows'd the fleecy train,
Two gentle youths, whom rural scenes could please,
Both skill'd to frame the tuneful rhyme with ease,
Charm'd with the prospect, slowly stray'd along,
Themselves amusing with alternate song.

#### FIRST.

These pollard oaks their tawny leaves retain,
These hardy hornbeams yet unstripp'd remain;
The wintry groves all else admit the view
Through naked stems of many a vary'd hue.

#### SECOND.

Yon shrubby slopes a pleasing mixture show ;
There the rough elm and smooth white privet grow,
Straight shoots of ash with bark of glossy grey,
Red cornel twigs, and maple's russet spray.

#### FIRST.

These stony steeps with spreading moss abound,
Grey on the trees and green upon the ground ;
With tangling brambles ivy interweaves,
And bright mezerion [1] spreads its lust'ring leaves.

vant is the name of the river at Chichester, which city gave birth to the sublime Collins.

[1] Mezerion : laureola sempervirens: *vulg.* spurge-laurel. This beautiful little evergreen is frequent among our woods and coppices. Its smooth shining leaves are placed on the top of the stems in circular tufts or clusters. Its flowers are small, of a light green, and perfume the air at a distance in an agreeable manner. It blows very early in mild seasons and warm situations. The common deciduous mezerion, frequently planted in gardens, though very different in appearance, is another species of this genus.

SECOND.

Old oaken stubs tough saplings there adorn,
There hedge-row plashes yield the knotty thorn;
The swain for different uses these avail,
And form the traveller's staff, the thresher's flail.

FIRST.

Where yon brown hazels pendent catkins bear,
And prickly furze unfolds its blossoms fair,
The vagrant artist oft at ease reclines,
And broom's green shoots in besoms neat combines.

SECOND.

See, down the hill, along the ample glade,
The new-fallen wood in even ranges laid!
There his keen bill the busy workman plies,
And bids in heaps his well-bound faggots rise.

FIRST.

Soon shall kind Spring her flowery gifts bestow,
On sunny banks when silver snowdrops blow,
And tufts of primrose all around are spread,
And purple violets all their fragrance shed.

SECOND.

The woods then white anemonies array,
And lofty sallows their sweet bloom display,
And spicy hyacinths azure bells unfold,
And crowfoot clothes the mead with shining gold.

FIRST.

Then soon gay Summer brings his gaudy train,
His crimson poppies deck the corn-clad plain;
There scabious blue [2], and purple knapweed [3] rise,
And weld [4] and yarrow show their various dyes.

SECOND.

In shady lanes red foxglove bells appear,
And golden spikes the downy mulleins rear [5];
Th' enclosure ditch luxuriant mallows hide,
And branchy succory crowds the pathway side.

FIRST.

The autumnal fields few pleasing plants supply,
Save where pale eyebright grows in pastures dry,
Or vervain blue for magic rites renown'd,
And in the village precincts only found [6].

[2] Scabious: scabiosa vulgaris.
[3] Knapweed: jacea vulgaris.
[4] Weld: luteola vulgaris, or dyers' weed. —
These plants, with many others not inferior in
beauty, are frequent on the balks, or ridges, which
separate different kinds of corn in our common
fields.
[5] The digitalis, or foxglove, is a very beautiful
plant; there are several varieties of it which are
honoured with a place in our gardens. The mul-
lein is not inferior in beauty, consequently merits
equal notice.
[6] It is a vulgar opinion, .at vervain never
grows in any place more than a quarter of a mile
distant from a house.—Vide Miller's Gardener's
Dictionary, article Verbena.

SECOND.

Th' autumnal hedges withering leaves embrown,
Save where wild climbers spread their silvery down [7],
And rugged blackthorns bend with purple sloes,
And the green skewerwood seeds of scarlet shows [8].

FIRST.

When healthful salads crown the board in spring,
And nymphs green parsley from the gardens bring,
Mark well lest hemlock mix its poisonous leaves—
Their semblance oft th' incautious eye deceives.

SECOND.

Warn, O ye shepherds! warn the youth who play
On hamlet wastes, beside the public way;
There oft rank soils pernicious plants produce,
There nightshade's berry swells with deadly juice.

FIRST.

What vary'd scenes this pleasant country yields,
Form'd by th' arrangement fair of woods and fields!
On a green hillock, by the shady road,
My dwelling stands—a sweet recluse abode!
And o'er my darken'd casement intertwine
The fragrant briar, the woodbine, and the vine.

SECOND.

How different scenes our different tastes delight!
Some seek the hills, and some the vales invite.
Where o'er the brook's moist margin hazels meet,
Stands my lone home—a pleasant, cool retreat!
Gay loosestrife there, and pale valerian spring [9],
And tuneful reed-birds midst the sedges sing.

FIRST.

Before my door the box-edg'd border lies,
Where flowers of mint, and thyme, and tansy rise;
Along my wall the yellow stonecrop grows,
And the red houseleek on my brown thatch blows.

SECOND.

Among green osiers winds my stream away,
Where the blue halcyon skims from spray to spray,
Where waves the bulrush as the waters glide,
And yellow flag-flowers deck the sunny side.

FIRST.

Spread o'er the slope of yon steep western hill,
My fruitful orchard shelters all the vill;
There pear-trees tall their tops aspiring show,
And apple-boughs their branches mix below.

[7] Wild climbers: clematis, viorna, or traveller's
joy. The white downy seeds of this plant make a
very conspicuous figure on our hedges in autumn.
[8] Skewerwood: evonymus; or, spindle-tree.—
The twigs of this shrub are of a fine green; the
capsules, or seed-vessels, of a fine purple; and the
seeds of a rich scarlet. In autumn, when the capsules open and show the seeds, the plant has a most
beautiful appearance.
[9] Loosestrife: lysimachia lutea vulgaris. Dr.
Hill observes, that it is so beautiful a plant, in its
erect stature, regular growth, and elegant flowers,
that it is every way worthy to be taken into our
gardens. It is frequent in moist places. The
flowers are of a bright gold colour.

### SECOND.

East from my cottage stretch delightful meads,
Where rows of willows rise, and banks of reeds;
There roll clear rivers; there, old elms between,
The mill's white roof and circling wheels are seen.

### FIRST.

Palemon's garden hawthorn hedges bound,
With flow'rs of white, or fruit of crimson, crown'd;
There vernal lilacs show their purple bloom,
And sweet syringas all the air perfume;
The fruitful mulberry spreads its umbrage cool,
And the rough quince o'erhangs the little pool.

### SECOND.

Albino's fence green currants hide from view,
With bunches hung of red or amber hue;
Beside his arbour blows the jasmine fair,
And scarlet beans their gaudy blossoms bear;
The lofty hollyhock there its spike displays,
And the broad sunflow'r shows its golden rays.

### FIRST.

Where moss-grown pales a sunny spot enclos'd,
And pinks and lilies all their hues expos'd,
Beneath a porch, with mantling vines enwreath'd,
The morning breeze the charming Sylvia breath'd:
Not pink nor lily with her face could vie,
And, O how soft the languish of her eye!
I saw and lov'd; but lov'd, alas, in vain!
She check'd my passion with severe disdain.

### SECOND.

When o'er the meads with vernal verdure gay
The village children wont at eve to stray,
I pluck'd fresh flow'rets from the grassy ground,
And their green stalks with bending rushes bound;
My wreaths, my nosegays, then my Delia dress'd,
Crown'd her fair brow, or bloom'd upon her breast.
Young as I was, the pleasing thought was mine,
" One day, fond boy, that beauty will be thine!"

### FIRST.

Beside his gate, beneath the lofty tree,
Old Thyrsis' well-known seat I vacant see;
There, while his prattling offspring round him play'd,
He oft to please them toys of osiers made:
That seat his weight shall never more sustain,
That offspring round him ne'er shall sport again.

### SECOND.

Yon lone church tow'r that overlooks the hills!—
The sight my soul full oft with sorrow fills:
There Damon lies;—in prime of youth he died!—
A ford unknown by night he vent'rous tried:
In vain he struggled with the foaming wave;
No friendly arm, alas, was near to save!

### FIRST.

Cease, friend! and homeward as we bend our way,
Remark the beauties of the closing day;
See, tow'rds the west, the redd'ning Sun declines,
And o'er the fields his level lustre shines.

### SECOND.

How that bright landscape lures the eye to gaze,
Where with his beams the distant windows blaze!
And the gilt vane, high on the steeple spire,
Glows in the air—a dazzling spot of fire!

### FIRST.

Behind yon hill he now forsakes our sight,
And yon tall beeches catch his latest light;
The hamlet smokes in amber wreaths arise;
White mist, like water, on the valley lies.

### SECOND.

Where yon chalk cliffs th' horizon eastward bound,
And spreading elms the ancient hall surround,
The Moon's bright orb arises from the main,
And night in silence holds her solemn reign.

---

## ECLOGUE II.

### RURAL BUSINESS; OR, THE AGRICULTURISTS.

May's lib'ral hand her fragrant bloom disclos'd,
And herds and flocks on grassy banks repos'd;
Soft evening gave to ease the tranquil hour,
And Philomel's wild warblings fill'd the bow'r,
Where near the village rose the elm-crown'd hill,
And white-leav'd aspins trembled o'er the rill,
Three rural bards, the village youth among,
The pleasing lore of rural business sung.

### FIRST.

The care of farms we sing—attend the strain—
What skill, what toil, shall best procure you gain;
How diff'rent culture, diff'rent ground requires;
While wealth rewards whom industry inspires.

### SECOND.

When thy light land on scorching gravel lies,
And to the springing blade support denies;
Fix on the wintry tilth the frequent fold,
And mend with cooling marl or untry'd mould.

### THIRD.

If thy strong loam superfluous wet retain,
Lead through thy fields the subterraneous drain,
And o'er the surface mellowing stores expand
Of fiery lime, or incoherent sand.

### FIRST.

In vacant corners, on the hamlet waste,
The ample dunghill's steaming heap be plac'd;
There many a month fermenting to remain,
Ere thy slow team disperse it o'er the plain.

### SECOND.

The prudent farmer all manure provides,
The mire of roads, the mould of hedge-row sides;
For him their mud the stagnant ponds supply;
For him their soil, the stable and the sty.

### THIRD.

For this the swain, on Kennet's winding shore,
Digs sulphurous peat along the sable moor;
For this, where ocean bounds the stormy strand,
They fetch dank sea-weed to the neighb'ring land.

### FIRST.

Who barren heaths to tillage means to turn,
Must, ere he plough, the greensward pare and burn;
Where rise the smoking hillocks o'er the field,
The saline ashes useful compost yield.

### SECOND.

Where sedge or rushes rise on spongy soils,
Or rampant moss th' impoverish'd herbage spoils,
Corrosive soot with lib'ral hand bestow;
Th' improving pasture soon its use will show.

### THIRD.

Hertfordian swains on airy hills explore
The chalk's white vein, a fertilizing store;
This from deep pits in copious baskets drawn,
Amends alike the arable and lawn.

### FIRST.

Who spends too oft in indolence the day,
Soon sees his farm his base neglect betray;
His useless hedge-greens docks and nettles bear,
And the tough cammoc clogs his shining share [1].

### SECOND.

Thy weedy fallows let the plough pervade,
Till on the top th' inverted roots are laid;
There left to wither in the noon-tide ray,
Or by the spiky harrow clear'd away.

### THIRD.

When wheat's green stem the ridge begins to hide,
Let the sharp weedhook's frequent aid be try'd,
Lest thy spoil'd crop at harvest thou bemoan,
With twitch and twining bindweed overgrown.

### FIRST.

Much will rank melilot thy grain disgrace,
And darnel, fellest of the weedy race:
T' extirpate these might care or cost avail,
T' extirpate these nor care nor cost should fail.

### SECOND.

When the foul furrow fetid mayweed fills,
The weary reaper oft complains of ills;
As his keen sickle grides along the lands,
The acrid herbage oft corrodes his hands.

### THIRD.

Wield oft thy scythe along the grassy layes,
Ere the rude thistle its light down displays;
Else that light down upon the breeze will fly,
And a new store of noxious plants supply.

### FIRST.

Would ye from tillage ample gains receive,
With change of crops th' exhausted soil relieve;
Next purple clover let brown wheat be seen,
And bearded barley after turnips green.

### SECOND.

Bid here dark peas or tangled vetches spread,
There buckwheat's white flow'r faintly ting'd with red;
Bid here potatoes deep green stems be born, [
And yellow cole th' enclosure there adorn.

### THIRD.

Here let tall rye or fragrant beans ascend,
Or oats their ample panicles extend ;
There rest thy glebe, left fallow not in vain,
To feel the summer's Sun and winter's rain.

[1] Cammoc: ononis, or restharrow. The roots of this troublesome plant are so strong, that it is credibly asserted they will stop a plough drawn by several horses.

### FIRST.

The skill'd in culture oft repay their toil
By choice of plants adapted to their soil ;
The spiky saintfoin best on chalk succeeds,
The lucern hates cold clays and moory meads.

### SECOND.

Best on loose sands, where brakes and briars once
            rose,
Its deep fring'd leaves the yellow carrot shows:
Best on stiff loam rough teasels [2] rear their heads,
And brown coriander's od'rous umbel spreads.

### THIRD.

On barren mountains, bleak with chilly air,
Forbidding pasturage or the ploughman's care,
Laburnum's boughs a beauteous bloom disclose,
Or spiry pines a gloomy grove compose.

### FIRST.

On rushy marshes, rank with watry weeds,
Clothe the clear'd soil with groves of waving reeds;
Of them the gard'ner annual fences forms,
To shield his tender plants from vernal storms.

### SECOND.

Cantabrian hills the purple saffron show;
Blue fields of flax in Lincoln's fenland blow;
On Kent's rich plains, green hop-grounds scent the
            gales;
And apple-groves deck Hereford's golden vales [3].

### THIRD.

Shelter'd by woods the weald of Sussex lies;
Her smooth green downs sublime from ocean rise :
That, fittest soil supplies for growth of grain ;
These, yield best pasture for the fleecy train.

### FIRST.

Say, friends! whoe'er his residence might choose,
Would these sweet scenes of sylvan shade refuse,
And seek the black waste of the barren wold,
That yields no shelter from the heat or cold?

### SECOND.

Dull are slow Ousa's mist-exhaling plains,
Where long rank grass the morning dew retains :
Who pastures there in autumn's humid reign,
His flock from sickness hopes to save in vain.

### THIRD.

The bleak, flat, sedgy shores of Essex shun,
Where fog perpetual veils the winter Sun;
Though flatt'ring Fortune there invite thy stay,
Thy health the purchase of her smiles must pay.

### FIRST.

When, harvest past, thy ricks of yellow corn
Rise round the yard, and scent the breeze of morn;
Rude Winter's rage with timely care t' avert,
Let the skill'd thatcher ply his useful art.

[2] Teasel: dipsacus sativus. This plant is cultivated, in many places, for the use of the woollen manufacture.   There are large fields of it in Essex; where the coriander is also grown.

[3] There is a part of Herefordshire, from its extraordinary fertility and pleasantness, usually denominated The Golden Vale.

### SECOND.

When thy ripe walnuts deck the glossy spray,
Ere pilf'ring rooks purloin them fast away,
Wield thy tough pole, and lash the trees amain,
Till leaves and husks the lawn beneath distain.

### THIRD.

When thy green orchards fraught with fruit appear,
Thy lofty ladder midst the boughs uprear;
Thy basket's hook upon the branch suspend,
And with the fragrant burden oft descend.

### FIRST.

Spread on the grass, or pil'd in heaps, behold
The pearmain's red, the pippin's speckled gold;
There shall the russet's auburn rind be seen,
The redstreak's stripes, and nonpareil's bright
    green.

### SECOND.

These on dry straw, in airy chambers, lay,
Where windows clear admit the noon-tide ray;
They, safe from frosts, thy table shall supply,
Fresh to the taste, and pleasing to the eye.

### THIRD.

When fav'ring seasons yield thee store to spare,
The circling mill and cumbrous press prepare;
From copious vats, the well-fermented juice
Will sparkling beverage for thy board produce.

### FIRST.

From red to black when bramble-berries change,
And boys for nuts the hazel copses range,
On new-reap'd fields the thick strong stubble mow,
And safe in stacks about thy homestead stow.

### SECOND.

With purple fruit when elder-branches bend,
And their bright hues the hips and cornels blend,
Ere yet chill hoar-frost comes, or sleety rain,
Sow with choice wheat the neatly furrow'd plain.

### THIRD.

When clam'rous fieldfares seek the frozen mead,
And lurking snipes by gurgling runnels feed;
Then midst dry fodder let thy herds be found,
Where shelt'ring sheds the well-stor'd crib surround.

### FIRST.

Though Winter reigns, our labours never fail:
Then all day long we hear the sounding flail;
And oft the beetle's strenuous stroke descends,
That knotty block-wood into billets rends.

### SECOND.

Then in the barns in motion oft are seen
The rustling corn-fan, and the wiry screen:
In sacks the tasker measures up his grain,
And loads for market on the spacious wain.

### THIRD.

Th' enclosure fence then claims our timely care,
The ditch to deepen, and the bank repair;
The well-plash'd hedge with frequent stakes confine,
And o'er its top tough wyths of hazel twine.

### FIRST.

Where in the croft the russet hayrick stands,
The dextrous binder twists his sedgy bands,
Across the stack his sharp-edg'd engine guides,
And the hard mass in many a truss divides [4].

### SECOND.

When frost thy turnips fixes in the ground,
And hungry flocks for food stand bleating round,
Let sturdy youths their pointed peckers ply,
Till the rais'd roots loose on the surface lie.

### THIRD.

When stormy days constrain to quit the field,
The house or barn may useful business yield;
There crooked snaths [5] of flexile sallow make,
Or of tough ash the fork-stale and the rake.

### FIRST.

Full many a chance defeats the farmer's pains,
Full many a loss diminishes his gains;
Wet spoils the seed, or frosts its growth o'erpow'r,
Beasts break the stalk, and birds the grain devour.

### SECOND.

While plenteous crops reward thy toil and care,
Thy lib'ral aid may age and sickness share!
Nor let the widow'd cottager deplore
Her fireless hearth, her cupboard's scanty store.

### THIRD.

The haughty lord, whom lust of gain inspires,
From man and beast excessive toil requires:
The gen'rous master views with pitying eyes
Their lot severe, and food and rest supplies.

### FIRST.

Amid Achaia's streamy vales of old,
Of works and days th' Ascrean pastor told;
Around him, curious, came the rustic throng,
And wond'ring listen'd to th' informing song.

### SECOND.

Where fam'd Anapus' limpid waters stray,
Sicilia's poet tun'd his Doric lay;
While o'er his head the pine's dark foliage hung,
And at his feet the bubbling fountain sprung.

### THIRD.

The Latian Maro sung, where Mincio's stream
Through groves of ilex cast a silv'ry gleam;
While down green vallies stray'd his fleecy flocks,
Or slept in shadow of the mossy rocks.

### FIRST.

Fair fame to him, the bard whose song displays
Of rural arts the knowledge and the praise!
Rich as the field with ripen'd harvest white—
A scene of profit mingled with delight!

### SECOND.

As dewy cherries to the taste in June,
As shady lanes to travellers at noon,

[4] Hay is usually cut with an oblong, triangular instrument, called a cutting-knife.
[5] Snath is the technical term for the handle of a scythe.

To me so welcome is the shepherd's strain;
To kindred spirits never sung in vain!

### THIRD.

While lindens sweet and spiky chesnuts blow,
While beech bears mast, on oaks while acorns grow;
So long shall last the shepherd's tuneful rhyme,
And please in ev'ry age and ev'ry clime!

## ORIENTAL ECLOGUES.

### ADVERTISEMENT.

THE Oriental Eclogues of Collins have such excellence, that it may be supposed they must preclude the appearance of any subsequent work with the same title. This consideration did not escape the author of the following poems; but as the scenery and sentiment of his predecessor were totally different from his own, he thought it matter of little consequence.

This kind of composition is, in general, subject to one disadvantage, for which allowance should be made. He, who describes what he has seen, may describe correctly: he, who describes what he has not seen, must depend for much on the accounts of others, and supply the rest from his own imagination.

## ZERAD;

### OR, THE ABSENT LOVER.

#### AN ARABIAN ECLOGUE.

THE learned and ingenious Mr. Jones, in his elegant and judicious Essay on the Poetry of the Eastern Nations, speaking of the Arabians, has the following passage: " It sometimes happens," says he, " that the young men of one tribe are in love with the damsels of another; and, as the tents are frequently removed on a sudden, the lovers are often separated in the progress of the courtship. Hence, almost all the Arabic poems open in this manner: The author bewails the sudden departure of his mistress, Hinda, Maia, Zeineb, or Azza, and describes her beauty; comparing her to a wanton fawn that plays among the aromatic shrubs. His friends endeavour to comfort him; but he refuses consolation; he declares his resolution of visiting his beloved, though the way to her tribe lie through a dreadful wilderness, or even through a den of lions."—The author of the following Eclogue was struck with this outline, and has attempted to fill it up. An apology for expatiating on the pleasing subjects of love and beauty, when nothing is said to offend the ear of chastity, he supposes needless. If any, however, there be, who question the utility of at all describing those subjects; such may remember, that

there is an eastern poem, generally esteemed *sacred*, which abounds with the most ardent expressions of the one, and luxuriant pictures of the other.

KORASA's tribe, a frequent-wand'ring train,
From Zenan's pastures sought Negiran's plain.
With them Semira left her fav'rite shades,
The loveliest nymph of Yemen's sportive maids!
Her parting hand her fair companions press'd;
A transient sorrow touch'd each tender breast;
As some thin cloud across the morning ray
Casts one short moment's gloom, and glides away:
Their cares, their sports, they hasted soon to tend,
And lost in them the memory of their friend.
  But gallant Zerad ill her absence bore,—
A wealthy emir from Katara's shore;
A warrior he, the bravest of his race;
A bard high-honour'd in his native place;
Age oft learn'd knowledge from his tuneful tongue,
And list'ning beauty languish'd while he sung.
What time the tribes in camp contiguous lay,
Oft with the fair-one he was wont to stray;
There oft for her fresh fruits and flow'rs he sought,
And oft her flocks to crystal fountains brought.
  Where the tall palm-grove grac'd Alzobah's green,
And sable tents in many a rank were/seen [1];
While ev'ning's steps the setting Sun pursu'd,
And the still fields her balmy tears bedew'd;
The pensive lover, there reclin'd apart,
Indulg'd the sorrows of his anxious heart.
His graceful head the costly turban dress'd;
The crimson sash confin'd his azure vest;
His hand the sounding arabeb [2] sustain'd;
And thus his voice in melody complain'd—
Soft as the night-bird's amorous music flows,
In Zibit's gardens, when she woos the rose [3]:
  " Bright star of Sora's sky, whose matchless blaze
Gilds thy proud tribe with mild, benignant rays!
Sweet flow'r of Azem's vale, whose matchless bloom
O'er thy fam'd house spreads exquisite perfume!
Blithe fawn of Kosa, at the break of dawn,
Midst groves of cassia, sporting on the lawn!
Too charming beauty! why must I bemoan
Thee from my presence thus abruptly flown?
Ere the shrill trump to march the signal gave,
And banners high in air began to wave;
Ere the tall camel felt his wonted load,
And herds and flocks slow mov'd along the road;
Ere slow behind them march'd the warrior train,
And the struck tents left vacant all the plain;
Could no fond plea obtain a longer stay.;
Would no kind hand th' intelligence convey?
Ah, hapless me! to Aden's port I stray'd,
Sought gold and gems, but lost my lovely maid!
  " My friends, they come my sorrows to allay—
Azor the wise, and Soliman the gay—
One cries, ' Let Reason hold her sober reign,
Nor Love's light trifles give thy bosom pain!

[1] The Arabian tents are black. Vide Canticles, i. 5.

[2] Arabebbah, an Arabian and Moorish instrument of music. Vide Shaw's Travels, and Russell's History of Aleppo.

[3] Alluding to an eastern fable of the Nightingale courting the Rose.

For thee kind Science all her lore displays,
And Fame awaits thee with the wreath of praise.'
' O why,' cries one, ' is she alone thy care?
She 's fair, indeed, but other maids are fair :
Negima's eyes with dazzling lustre shine,
And her black tresses curl like Zebid's vine ;
On Hinda's brow Kushemon's lily blows,
And on her cheek unfolds Nishapor's rose !
With them, the tale, the song, the dance shall please,
When Mirth's free banquet fills the bow'r of ease.'
' Ah cease,' said I; ' of love he little knows,
Who with sage counsel hopes to cure its woes !
Go, bid in air Yamama's lightnings stay,
Or Perath's lion quit his trembling prey :
Kind Science' lore with Beauty best we share,
And Beauty's hands Fame's fairest wreaths prepare.
I praise Negima's lovely hair and eyes;
Nor Hinda's lily, nor her rose despise ;
But Omman's pearls diffuse a brighter beam
Than the gay pebbles of Kalafa's stream.'—
  " O lov'd Semira ! whither dost thou rove ?
Tread thy soft steps by Sada's jasmine grove ?
Dost thou thy flocks on Ocah's mountain keep ?
Do Ared's olives whisper o'er thy sleep ?—
Ah, no !——the maid, perhaps, remote from these,
Some hostile troop, in ambush laid, may seize :
Too lovely captive ! she, in triumph borne,
The proud pacha's throng'd haram shall adorn.
Vain fear! around her march her valiant friends ;
Brave Omar's hand the bow of Ishmael bends ;
Strong Hassan's arm Kaaba's spear can wield,
And rear on high El-makin's pond'rous shield !
Ah, shame to me ! shall Sloth's dishonouring chain
From love, from glory, Zerad here detain,
Till grief my cheek with sickly saffron spread,
And my eyes, weeping, match th' argavan's red 4 ?
Haste, bring my steed, supreme in strength and grace,
First in the fight, and fleetest in the chase ;
His sire renown'd on Gebel's hills was bred,
His beauteous dam in Derar's pastures fed :
Bring my strong lance that ne'er impell'd in vain,
Pierc'd the fierce tiger on Hegesa's plain.
Across the desert I her steps pursue ;
Toil at my side, and danger in my view !
There Thirst, fell demon! haunts the sultry air,
And his wild eye-balls roll with horrid glare;
There deadly Sumiel 5, striding o'er the land,
Sweeps his red wing, and whirls the burning sand ;
As winds the weary caravan along,
The fiery storm involves the hapless throng,
I go, I go, nor toil nor danger heed;
The faithful lover Safety's hand shall lead.
The heart that fosters virtue's gen'rous flames,
Our holy prophet's sure protection claims.
  " Delightful Irem 6 (midst the lonely waste
By Shedad's hand the paradise was plac'd)

4 D' Herbelot informs us, that saffron faces, and argavan eyes, are expressions commonly used in the east, to describe passionate lovers, whose melancholy appears in their countenances, and whose eyes become red with weeping. The argavan is supposed to be the arbor judæ ; whose blossoms are of a bright purple. Vide Harmer's Commentary on Solomon's Song, page 162.
5 Sumiel; the fiery blasting wind of the desert.
6 " Mahommed, in his Alcoran, in the chapter of the Morning, mentions a garden, called Irem,

Each shady tree of varied foliage shows,
And ev'ry flow'r and ev'ry fruit bestows ;
There drop rich gums of ev'ry high perfume;
There sing sweet birds of ev'ry gaudy plume ;
There soft-ey'd Houries tread th' enamell'd green—
Once, and no more, the happy seat was seen ;
As his stray'd camel midst the wild he sought,
Chance to the spot the wand'ring Esar brought ;
A blissful Irem, midst the desert drear,
Semira's tent my love-sick sight shall cheer.
  " What palm of beauty tow'rs on Keran's hills?
What myrrh with fragrance Sala's valley fills?
'T is she, who left so late her fav'rite shades,
The loveliest nymph of Yemen's sportive maids !
Look from thy tent, the curtains fair unfold,
Give to my view thy veil of silk and gold;
O lift that veil ! thy radiant eyes display—
Those radiant eyes shall light me on my way !
On Hejar's wild rocks from the Persian main,
Thus the Moon rising lights the wilder'd swain.
O raise thy voice ! the sound shall give delight,
Like songs of pilgrims distant heard by night!
I come, I come !"—He spoke, and seiz'd the rein,
And his fleet courser spurn'd the sandy plain.

————

SERIM ;

OR, THE ARTIFICIAL FAMINE.

AN EAST-INDIAN ECLOGUE.

————

THE following account of British conduct and its consequences, in Bengal and the adjacent provinces, some years ago, will afford a sufficient idea of the subject of the following Eclogue. After describing the monopoly of salt, betel-nut, and tobacco, the historian thus proceeds : " Money, in this current, came but by drops; it could not quench the thirst of those who waited in India to receive it. An expedient, such as it was, remained to quicken its pace.—The natives could live with little salt, but not without food. Some of the agents saw themselves well situated for collecting the rice into stores; they did so. They knew the Gentoos would rather die, than violate the precepts of their religion by eating flesh. The alternative would therefore be, between giving what they had, and dying. The inhabitants sunk ; they that cultivated the land, and saw the harvest at the disposal of others, planted in doubt; scarcity ensued; then the monopoly was easier managed. The people took to roots, and food they had been unaccustomed to eat. Sickness ensued. In some districts, the languid living left the bodies of their numerous dead unburied."——Short History of English Transactions in the East-Indies, p. 145. The above quotation sufficiently proves, that the general plan of the following poem is founded on

which is no less celebrated by the Asiatic poets, than that of the Hesperides by the Greeks. It was planted, as the commentators say, by a king named Shedad ; and was once seen by an Arabian, who wandered far into the desert, in search of a lost camel." Jones's Essay on the Poetry of the Eastern Nations.

fact. And, even with regard to its particular incidents, there can be little doubt, but that, among the varied miseries of millions, every picture of distress, which the author has drawn, had its original.

---

" O GUARDIAN genius of this sacred wave [1]!
O save thy sons, if thine the pow'r to save!"
So Serim spoke, as sad on Ganges' shore
He sat, his country's miseries to deplore—
" O guardian genius of this sacred wave!
O save thy sons, if thine the pow'r to save!
From Agra's tow'rs to Muxadabat's [2] walls,
On thee for aid the suff'ring Hindoo calls:
Europe's fell race control the wide domain,
Engross the harvest, and enslave the swain.
Why rise these cumbrous piles along thy tide ?
They hold the plenty to our prayers deny'd !
Guards at their gates perpetual watch maintain,
Where Want in anguish craves relief in vain.
' Bring gold, bring gems,' th' insatiate plunderers cry;
' Who hoards his wealth by Hunger's rage shall die.'
Ye fiends ! ye have ravish'd all our little store;
Ye see we perish, yet ye ask for more!
Go ye yourselves, and search for gold the mine ;
Go, dive where pearls beneath the ocean shine !
What right have ye to plague our peaceful land ?
No ships of ours e'er sought your western strand :
Ne'er from your fields we snatch'd their crops away,
Nor made your daughters or your sons our prey.
Not ev'n in thought we quit our native place—
A calm, contented, inoffensive race!
By Avarice led, ye range remotest climes,
And ev'ry nation execrates your crimes.
" When Timur's house [3] renown'd, in Delhi reign'd,
Distress, assistance unimplor'd obtain'd :
When Famine o'er th' afflicted region frown'd,
And Sickness languish'd on the barren ground,
The imperial granaries wide display'd their doors,
And ships provision brought from distant shores ;
The laden camels crowded Kurah's vales,
From Colgon's cliffs they hail'd the coming sails.
But ye !—e'en now, while fav'ring seasons smile,
And the rich glebe would recompense our toil,

[1] The Hindoos worship a god or genius of the Ganges.

[2] Muxadabat, or Morshedabat, a large city of India, about two hundred miles above Calcutta. The name is commonly pronounced with the accent on the last syllable; Muxadabát. I have taken the liberty to accommodate this, and some few other words, to my verse, by altering the accentuation ; a matter, I apprehend, of little consequence to the English reader.

[3] The famous Mahometan tyrant, Auranzebe, during a famine which prevailed in different parts of India, exerted himself to alleviate the distress of his subjects. " He remitted the taxes that were due; he employed those already collected in the purchase of corn, which was distributed among the poorer sort. He even expended immense sums out of the treasury, in conveying grain, by land and water, into the interior provinces, from Bengal, and the countries which lie on the five branches of the Indus." Dow's Indostan, vol. iii. p. 340.

Dearth and disease to you alone we owe;
Ye cause the mischief, and enjoy the woe!
" This beauteous clime, but late, what plenty bless'd !
What days of pleasure, and what nights of rest !
From Gola's streets, fam'd mart of fragrant grain !
Trade's cheerful voice resounded o'er the plain ;
There now sad Silence listens to the waves
That break in murmurs round the rocky caves.
Sweet were the songs o'er Jumal's level borne,
While busy thousands throng'd to plant the corn ;
Now tenfold tax the farmer forc'd to yield,
Despairs, and leaves unoccupy'd the field.
Sweet were the songs of Burdwan's mulberry grove,
While the rich silk the rapid shuttle wove;
Now from the loom our costly vestments torn,
Th' insulting robbers meanest slaves adorn.
In Malda's shades, on Purna's palmy plain,
The hapless artists, urg'd to toil in vain,
Quit their sad homes, and mourn along the land,
A pensive, pallid, self-disabled band [4] !—
" The year revolves—' Bring choicest fruits and flow'rs !
Spread wide the board in consecrated bow'rs ;
Bring joy, bring sport, the song, the dance prepare !
'T is Drugah's [5] feast, and all our friends must share !'
The year revolves—nor fruits nor flow'rs are seen ;
Nor festive board in bow'rs of holy green ;
Nor joy, nor sport, nor dance, nor tuneful strain:
'T is Drugah's feast—but grief and terrour reign.
Yet there, ingrate ! oft welcome guests ye came,
And talk'd of honour's laws and friendship's flame.
" The year revolves—and Bishen's [6] fast invites
On Ganges' marge to pay the solemn rites ;
All, boons of Bishen, great preserver, crave ;
All, in the sacred flood, their bodies lave :
No more, alas!—the multitude no more
Bathe in the tide, or kneel upon the shore ;
No more from towns and villages they throng,
Wide o'er the fields, the public paths along :

[4] " Those who now made the things the English most wanted, were pressed on all sides—by their own necessities, their neighbours, and the agents employed to procure the company's investments, as the goods sent to Europe are called. These importunities were united, and urged so much, so often, and in such ways, as to produce, among the people in the silk business, instances of their cutting off their thumbs, that the want of them might excuse them from following their trade, and the inconveniences to which they were exposed beyond the common lot of their neighbours." History of English Transactions in the East Indies.

[5] Drugah ; a Hindoo goddess. " Drugah Poojah is the grand general feast of the Gentoos, usually visited by all Europeans, (by invitation) who are treated by the proprietors of the feast with the fruits and flowers in season, and are entertained every evening with bands of singers and dancers." Vide Holwell's Indostan, vol. ii.

[6] Bishen, Bistnoo, or Jaggernaut, is one of the principal Hindoo deities. " This fast, dedicated to him, is called the Sinan Jattra, or general washing in the Ganges; and it is almost incredible to think the immense multitude, of every age and sex, that appears on both sides the river, throughout its whole course, at one and the same time." Vide Mr. Holwell, vol. ii. p. 124—128.

Sad on our ways, by human foot unworn,
Stalks the dim form of Solitude forlorn!—
From Ava's mountains Morn's bright eyes survey
Fair Ganges' streams in many a winding stray;
There fleecy flocks on many an island feed;
There herds unnumber'd pasture many a mead;
(While noxious herbs our last resource supply,
And, dearth escaping, by disease we die)
' Take these,' ye cry, ' nor more for food complain!
Take these, and slay like us, and riot on the slain!'
Ah no! our law the crime abhorr'd withstands;
We die—but blood shall ne'er pollute our hands.
O guardian genius of this sacred wave!
Save, save thy sons, if thine the pow'r to save!"
    So Serim spoke—while by the Moon's pale beam,
The frequent corse came floating down the stream [7].
He sigh'd, and rising turn'd his steps to rove
Where wav'd o'er Nizim's vale the coco-grove;
There, midst scorch'd ruins, one lone roof remain'd,
And one forlorn inhabitant contain'd.
The sound of feet he near his threshold heard;
Slow from the ground his languid limbs he rear'd:
" Come, tyrant, come! perform a gen'rous part,
Lift thy keen steel, and pierce this fainting heart!
Com'st thou for gold? my gold, alas, I gave,
My darling daughter in distress to save!
Thy faithless brethren took the shining store,
Then from my arms the trembling virgin tore!
Three days, three nights, I 've languish'd here
        alone—
Three foodless days, three nights to sleep unknown!
Come, tyrant, come! perform a gen'rous part,
Lift thy keen steel, and pierce this fainting heart!"
    " No hostile steps the haunt of Woe invade,"
Serim reply'd—and, passing where the glade
A length of prospect down the vale display'd,
Another sight of misery met his view;
Another mournful voice his notice drew!
There, near a temple's recent ruin, stood
A white-rob'd Bramin, by the sacred flood:
His wives, his children, dead beside him lay—
Of hunger these, and those of grief the prey!
Thrice he with dust defil'd his aged head;
Thrice o'er the stream his hands uplifted spread:
" Hear, all ye pow'rs to whom we bend in pray'r!
Hear, all who rule o'er water, earth, and air!
'T is not for them, though lifeless there they lie;
'T is not for me, though innocent I die:—
My country's breast the tiger, Avarice, rends,
And loud to you her parting groan ascends.
Hear, all ye pow'rs to whom we bend in pray'r!
Hear, all who rule o'er water, earth, and air!
Hear, and avenge!——         [sphere,
    " But, hark! what voice, from yonder starry
Slides, like the breeze of ev'ning, o'er my ear?
Lo, Birmah's [8] form! on amber clouds enthron'd;
His azure robe with lucid emerald zon'd;

He looks celestial dignity and grace,
And views with pity wretched human race!
    " ' Forbear, rash man! nor curse thy country's
        foes;
Frail man to man forgiveness ever owes.
When Moisasoor [9] the fell on Earth's fair plain
Brought his detested offspring, Strife and Pain;
Revenge with them, relentless Fury, came,
Her bosom burning with infernal flame!
Her hair sheds horrour, like the comet's blaze;
Her eyes, all ghastly, blast where'er they gaze;
Her lifted arm a poison'd crice [10] sustains;
Her garments drop with blood of kindred veins!
Who asks her aid, must own her endless reign,
Feel her keen scourge, and drag her galling chain!'
    " The strains sublime in sweetest music close,
And all the tumult of my soul compose.
Yet you, ye oppressors! uninvok'd on you [11],
Your steps, the steps of justice will pursue!
Go, spread your white sails on the azure main;
Fraught with our spoils, your native land regain;
Go, plant the grove, and bid the lake expand,
And on green ills the pompous palace stand:
Let Luxury's hand adorn the gaudy room,
Smooth the soft couch, and shed the rich per-
        fume—
There night's kind calm in vain shall sleep invite,
While fancied omens warn, and spectres fright:
Sad sounds shall issue from your guilty walls,
The widow'd wife's, the sonless mother's calls;
And infant rajahs' bleeding forms shall rise,
And lift to you their supplicating eyes:
Remorse intolerable your hearts will feel,
And your own hand plunge deep th' avenging
        steel [12].
(For Europe's cowards Heav'n's command disdain,
To Death's cold arms they fly for ease in vain.)
For us, each painful transmigration o'er,
Sweet fields receive us to resign no more;
Where Safety's fence for ever round us grows,
And Peace, fair flow'r, with bloom unfading blows;
Light's Sun unsetting shines with cheering beam;
And Pleasure's river rolls its golden stream!" .
    Enrapt he spoke—then ceas'd the lofty strain,
And Orel's rocks return'd the sound again.—
A British ruffian, near in ambush laid,
Rush'd sudden from the cane-isle's secret shade;
" Go to thy God!" with rage infernal cry'd,
And headlong plung'd the hapless sage into the
        foaming tide.

[7] The Hindoos frequently cast the bodies of their deceased into the Ganges; with the idea, I suppose, of committing them to the disposal of the god or genius of the river.

[8] Birmah is a principal deity of the Hindoos, in whose person they worship the divine attribute of wisdom. From the best accounts we have of India, the intelligent part of the natives do not worship " stocks and stones," merely as such; but rather the Supreme Existence, in a variety of attributes or manifestations.

[9] Moisasoor: the Hindoo author of evil, similar to our Satan.

[10] Crice, an Indian dagger.

[11] The reader must readily perceive the propriety of this turn of thought in a poem designed to have a moral tendency. There is much difference between a person wishing evil to his enemy, and presaging that evil will be the consequence of that enemy's crimes  The first is an immoral act of the will; the second, a neutral act of the judgment.

[12] The Hindoo religion strongly prohibits suicide. Mr. Holwell gives us the following passage from the Shastah : " Whosoever, of the delinquent Debtah, shall dare to free himself from the mortal form wherewith I shall enclose him; thou, Sieb, shalt plunge him into the Onderah for ever: he shall not again have the benefit of the fifteen Boboons of pur- gation, probation, and purification.

## LI-PO;

### OR, THE GOOD GOVERNOR.

#### A CHINESE ECLOGUE.

Those who are conversant in the best accounts of China, particularly Du Halde's History, must have remarked, that the Chinese government, though arbitrary, is well regulated and mild; and that a prince, in that country, can acquire no glory, but by attention to the welfare of his subjects. On this general idea is founded the plan of the following poem.

Where Honan's hills Kiansi's vale enclose,
And Xifa's lake its glassy level shows;
Li-po's fair island lay—delightful scene!
With swelling slopes, and groves of every green:
On azure rocks his rich pavilion plac'd,
Rear'd its light front with golden columns grac'd;
High o'er the roof a weeping willow hung,
And jasmine boughs the lattice twin'd among;
In porcelain vases crested amaranth grew,
And starry aster, crimson, white, and blue;
Lien-hoa flow'rs upon the water spread;
Bright shells and corals varied lustre shed;
From sparry grottos crystal drops distill'd
On sounding brass, and air with music fill'd;
Soft through the bending canes the breezes play'd,
The rustling leaves continual murmur made;
Gay shoals of gold-fish glitter'd in the tide,
And gaudy birds flew sportive by its side.
The distant prospects well the sight might please,
With pointed mountains, and romantic trees:
From craggy cliffs, between the verdant shades,
The silver rills rush'd down in bright cascades;
O'er terrac'd steeps rich cotton harvests ¹ wav'd,
And smooth canals the rice-clad valley lav'd;
Long rows of cypress ² parted all the land,
And tall pagodas crown'd the river's strand!
'T was here, from business and its pomp and pain,
The pensive master sought relief in vain.
Li-po, mild prince, a viceroy's sceptre sway'd,
And ten fair towns his gentle rule obey'd:
The morn's transactions to his memory came,
And some he found to praise, and some to blame;
Mark'd here how justice, pity there prevail'd,
And how from haste or indolence he fail'd.
Beneath a bow'r of sweet ka-fa, whose bloom
Fill'd all th' adjacent lawn with rich perfume,
His slaves at distance sat—a beauteous train!—
One wak'd the lute, and one the vocal strain:
They saw his brow with care all clouded o'er,
And wish'd to ease the anxiety he bore.
Amusive tales their soothing lay disclos'd,
Of heroes brave to perils strange expos'd,

¹ The Chinese reduce the steep slopes of their hills into little terraces, on which they grow cotton, potatoes, &c. They plant the edges of their terraces with trees, which keep up the ground, and make a very fine appearance.

² Their rice-grounds are separated by broad ditches, the sides of which are planted with cypresses. Vide Osbeck's Voyage to China.

Of tyrants proud, from pow'r's high summit cast;
And lovers, long desponding, bless'd at last.
They ceas'd; the warblings softly died away,
Like zephyrs ceasing at the close of day.      [sight,
" This scene," said he, " how fair! to please the
How Nature's charms, Art's ornaments unite!
Those maids, what magic in the strains they sung!
Song sweetliest flows from Beauty's tuneful tongue.
Yet say, did Tien bid pow'r and wealth be mine,
For me my soul to pleasure to resign?
" What boots that annual, on our fathers' tombs,
We strew fair flow'rs, and offer choice perfumes;
Our veneration of their memories show,
And not their steps in virtue's path pursue?
When, from his province as the prince returns,
Rich feasts for him are spread, and incense burns,
And gilded barks unfold their streamers gay,
And following crowds their loud applauses pay;
Avails all this, if he from right has swerv'd,
And conscience tells him all is undeserv'd?
" Arise, Li-po! 't is duty calls, arise!
The Sun sinks redd'ning in Tartarian skies.
Yon walls that tow'r o'er Xensi's neighb'ring plain,
Yon walls unnumber'd miseries contain.
Think, why did Tien superior rank impart,
Force of the mind, or feelings of the heart.
Last night in sleep, to Fancy's sight display'd,
Lay lovelier scenes than e'er my eyes survey'd;
With purple shone the hills, with gold the vales,
And greenest foliage wav'd in gentlest gales:
Midst palmy fields, with sunshine ever bright,
A palace rear'd its walls of silvery white;
The gates of pearl a shady hall disclos'd,
Where old Confucius' rev'rend form repos'd:
Loose o'er his limbs the silk's light texture flow'd,
His eye serene ethereal lustre show'd:
' My son,' said he, as near his seat I drew,
' Cast round this wondrous spot thy dazzled view;
See how, by lucid founts in myrtle bow'rs,
The bless'd inhabitants consume their hours;
They ne'er to War, fell fiend! commission gave
To murder, ravish, banish, and enslave;
They ne'er bade Grandeur raise her gorgeous pile,
With tribute ravish'd from the hand of Toil;
But parents, guardians of the people reign'd,
The weak defended, and the poor sustain'd.'
Smiling he ceas'd—the vision seem'd to fly,
Like fleecy clouds dispersing in the sky.
" Arise, Li-po! and cast thy robes aside,
Disguise thy form, thy well-known features hide;
Go forth, yon streets, yon crowded streets pervade,
Mix with the throng, and mark who seeks thy aid:
There Avarice stern o'er poverty bears sway,
And age and sickness fall his easy prey;
There hands that Justice' sacred ensigns bear,
Protect the plunderer, and the plunder share;
Perhaps there Discord's desp'rate rage prevails,
And Wisdom's voice to calm the tumult fails;
Perhaps Revenge gives victims to the grave,
Perhaps they perish, ere I haste to save!"
He spoke, and rose; but now along the way
That from the city-gate fair-winding lay,
Stretch'd through green meads where lowing cattle
Amid the lake's wide silver level rais'd,      [graz'd,
Led up steep rocks by painted bridges join'd,
Or near thin trees that o'er the tide inclin'd,
Slow tow'rds his palace came a suppliant train;—
Whoe'er his presence sought ne'er sought in vain—
The ready vessel, waiting at his call,
Receiv'd, and bore him to the audience-hall.

# *O D E S.*

The Horatian, or lesser ode, is characterized principally by ease and correctness. The following little pieces, attempted on that plan, were the production of very different periods, and, on revisal, were thought not undeserving a place in this collection.

## ODE I.

### TO LEISURE.

Gentle Leisure, whom of yore
To Wealth the fair Contentment bore,
When Peace with them her dwelling made,
And Health her kind attendance paid;
As wand'ring o'er the sunny plains
They fed their herds and fleecy trains:—
O thou! who country scenes and air
Preferr'st to courts, and crowds, and care;
With thee I 've often pass'd the day,
To thee I wake the grateful lay.
  With thee on Chadwell's [1] thymy brow,
Beneath the hazels bending bough,
I 've sat to breathe the fragrance cool
Exhaling from the glassy pool;
Where, through th' unsully'd crystal seen,
The bottom show'd its shining green:
As, all-attentive, these I view'd,
And many a pleasing thought pursu'd,
Whate'er of pleasure they bestow'd,
Still I to thee that pleasure ow'd!
  With thee, on Mussla's [2] corn-clad height,
The landscape oft has charm'd my sight;
Delightful hills, and vales, and woods,
And dusty roads, and winding floods;
And towns, that through thin groups of shade
Their roofs of vary'd form display'd:
As, all-attentive, these I view'd,
And many a pleasing thought pursu'd,
Whate'er of pleasure they bestow'd,
Still I to thee that pleasure ow'd!
  With thee, where Easna's [3] hornbeam grove
Its foliage o'er me interwove,
Along the lonely path I 've stray'd,
By banks in hoary moss array'd,
Where tufts of azure orpine grew,
And branchy fern of brighter hue:
As, all-attentive, these I view'd,
And many a pleasing thought pursu'd,
Whate'er of pleasure they bestow'd,
Still I to thee that pleasure ow'd!
  With thee by Stansted's [4] farms enclos'd,
With aged elms in rows dispos'd;
Or where her chapel's walls appear,
The silver winding river near,
Beneath the broad-leav'd sycamore,
I 've linger'd on the shady shore:

[1] The New River Head, near Ware.
[2] A hill on the north side of Ware.
[3] A pleasant wood, east of Ware.
[4] A village in the same neighbourhood.

As, all-attentive, these I view'd,
And many a pleasing thought pursu'd,
Whate'er of pleasure they bestow'd,
Still I to thee that pleasure ow'd!
  With thee, where Thames his waters leads
Round Poplar's isle [5] of verdant meads,
Along the undulating tide,
I 've seen the white-sail'd vessels glide;
Or gaz'd on London's lofty towers,
Or Dulwich hills, or Greenwich bowers:
As, all-attentive, these I view'd,
And many a pleasing thought pursu'd,
Whate'er of pleasure they bestow'd,
Still I to thee that pleasure ow'd!
  O gentle Leisure!—absent long—
I woo thee with this tuneful song:
If e'er, allur'd by grateful change,
O'er scenes yet unbeheld I range,
And Albion's east or western shore
For rural solitudes explore:
As, all-attentive, these I view,
And many a pleasing thought pursue,
Whate'er of pleasure they bestow,
To thee that pleasure I must owe!

## ODE II.

### THE EVENING WALK.

What time fair Spring, with dewy hand,
  Awakes her cowslip bloom;
And hawthorn boughs, by breezes fann'd,
  Diffuse a rich perfume;

Young Theron down the valley stray'd
  At ev'ning's silent hour;
When bright the setting sunbeams play'd
  On Hertford's distant tower.

He sigh'd, and cast around his eye
  O'er all the pleasing scene;
Now tow'rds the golden-clouded sky,
  Now on the fields of green.

" Thrice has fair Spring her cowslip bloom
  Awak'd with dewy hand;
And hawthorn boughs diffus'd perfume,
  By western breezes fann'd,

" Since here, at ev'ning's silent hour,
  Delighted oft I stray'd;
While bright on Hertford's distant tower
  The setting sunbeams play'd:

" 'T was then the flatterer Hope was near;
  And sung this soothing strain:
' Where through the trees yon tow'rs appear
  Far o'er the level plain;

" ' There oft thy pleasant evening walk
  Thy fav'rite maid shall join,
And all the charms of tender talk
  And tuneful song be thine:

[5] Commonly called the Isle of Dogs, opposite Greenwich.

" ' With thee she 'll hear the bleat of flocks,
　The throstle's mellow lay ;
The rills that murmur o'er the rocks,
　The whispers of the spray.'—'

" So sung false Hope—deceiv'd I heard,
　And set my heart at ease ;
The future then so fair appear'd,
　It made the present please.

" So sung false Hope—the approaching years,
　That distant look'd so gay,
With clouds of cares and storms of fears
　All fraught, have pass'd away.

" As glides yon Sun adown the sky,
　As rolls yon rapid stream ;
So fast our joys and sorrows fly,
　And, flown, appear a dream.

" Be then the events that Time has brought,
　To me not brought in vain ;
By painful disappointment taught,
　Let wisdom be my gain !"

Thus Theron spoke, and earnest ey'd
　The Sun's departing ray ;
Again he look'd, again he sigh'd,
　And homeward bent his way.

---

## ODE III.

### TO CHILDHOOD.

CHILDHOOD ! happiest stage of life,
Free from care and free from strife,
Free from Memory's ruthless reign,
Fraught with scenes of former pain ;
Free from Fancy's cruel skill,
Fabricating future ill ;
Time, when all that meets the view,
All can charm, for all is new ;
How thy long-lost hours I mourn,
Never, never, to return !
　Then to toss the circling ball,
Caught rebounding from the wall ;
Then the mimic ship to guide
Down the kennel's dirty tide ;
Then the hoop's revolving pace
Through the dusty street to chase ;
O what joy !—it once was mine,
Childhood, matchless boon of thine !—
How thy long-lost hours I mourn,
Never, never to return !

---

## ODE IV.

### HEARING MUSIC.

YON organ ! hark !—how soft, how sweet,
The warbling notes in concert meet !
　The sound my fancy leads
To climes where Phœbus' brightest beams
Gild jasmine groves and crystal streams,
　And lily-mantled meads ;

Where myrtle bowers their bloom unfold,
Where citrons bend with fruit of gold,

Where grapes depress the vines ;
Where, on the bank with roses gay,
Love, Innocence, and Pleasure play,
　And Beauty's form reclines.

Now diff'rent tones and measures flow,
And, gravely deep, and sadly slow,
　Involve the mind in gloom ;
I seem to join the mournful train,
Attendant round the couch of Pain,
　Or leaning o'er the tomb:

To where the orphan'd infant sleeps,
To where the love-lorn damsel weeps,
　I pitying seem to stray ;
Methinks I watch his cradle near ;
Methinks her drooping thoughts I cheer,
　And wipe her tears away.

Now loud the tuneful thunders roll,
And rouse and elevate the soul
　O'er Earth and all its care ;
I seem to hear from heavenly plains
Angelic choirs responsive strains,
　And in their raptures share.

---

## ODE V.

### A LANDSCAPE.

ON the eastern hill's steep side
Spreads the rural hamlet wide ;
Cross the vale, where willows rise,
Further still another lies ;
And, beneath a steeper hill,
Lies another further still :
Near them many a field and grove—
Scenes where Health and Labour rove !
　Northward swelling slopes are seen,
Clad with corn-fields neat and green ;
There, through grassy plains below,
Broad and smooth the waters flow ;
While the town, their banks along,
Bids its clust'ring houses throng,
In the sunshine glitt'ring fair,
Haunts of business, haunts of care !
　Westward o'er the yellow meads
Wind the rills through waving reeds ;
From dark elms a shadow falls
On the abbey's whiten'd walls :
Wide the park's green lawns expand ;
Thick its tufted lindens stand:
Fair retreat ! that well might please
Wealth, and Elegance, and Ease.
　Hark ! amidst the distant shades
Murm'ring drop the deep cascades ;
Hark ! amidst the rustling trees
Softly sighs the gentle breeze ;
And the Eolian harp, reclin'd
Obvious to the stream of wind,
Pours its wildly-warbled strain,
Rising now, now sunk again.
　How the view detains the sight !
How the sounds the ear delight !—
Sweet the scene ! but think not there
Happiness sincere to share :
Reason still regrets the day
Passing rapidly away ;
Less'ning life's too little store ;
Passing, to return no more !

## ODES.

ODES.

### ODE VI.

#### TO A FRIEND,

ON HIS MARRIAGE AND REMOVAL INTO THE COUNTRY.

WRITTEN AT STANWAY-HALL, IN ESSEX.

WHATE'ER of lighter strain the Muse
Essay'd, in vacant hours of ease,
At thy expense to raise a smile,
I deem thy candour will excuse;
For sure I meant not to displease,
For sure I wish'd thee well the while [1].

And now the nuptial knot is tied,
That Muse no idle flatt'ry brings,
Nor talks of joy unmix'd with care—
I trust that none whoe'er has try'd
The sober state of human things,
Will give thee hope such joy to share.

Domestic life must soon be thine—
'T is various as an April day;
'T is pleasure now, and now 't is pain:
Through storms of foul and gleams of fine
Contented hold thy steady way,
And these enjoy, and those sustain.

From London's streets to solitude,
From brilliant shops to dirty fields,
From beaux and belles to rugged hinds—
The change I own is strange and rude:
Yet scarce a place so little yields,
But he who seeks amusement finds.

Perchance thou 'lt not disdain to hear
The ploughman's history of the plain;
Thy sight the prospect's scenes may charm:
And sure fastidious is the ear,
That slights the milkmaid's simple strain,
At ev'ning echoing from the farm.

The market lore of artful swains
The price of cattle and of corn,
The sportsman's feats of dogs and guns;—
To practise that will cost thee pains;
And these with patience must be borne,
For he will be dislik'd who shuns.

Courage, my friend! whate'er our fate!
So versatile the human mind,
That oft, when novelty is o'er,
To objects of our former hate
Assimilated and resign'd,
We wonder they displeas'd before.

'T was on the festive, social day,
Where Beauty cast her smiles around,
And Mirth the mind from care reliev'd;
What time our hands in harmless play
Thy brow with wreaths of myrtle bound,
My thoughts this grateful lay conceiv'd.

[1] The author alludes to some trifling pieces of humour, written on his friend, for the amusement of a few intimate acquaintance.

From Stanway's groves, from fields of Layer [2],
To other scenes and other friends
To morrow calls my steps away;
Yet memory them in view shall bear;
Yet them the wish of health attends,
And many a moment calm and gay.

### ODE VII.

#### WRITTEN IN WINTER.

WHILE in the sky black clouds impend,
And fogs arise and rains descend,
And one brown prospect opens round
Of leafless trees and furrow'd ground;
Save where unmelted spots of snow
Upon the shaded hill-side show;
While chill winds blow, and torrents roll,
The scene disgusts the sight, depresses all the soul.

Yet worse what polar climates share—
Vast regions, dreary, bleak, and bare!—
There, on an icy mountain's height,
Seen only by the Moon's pale light,
Stern Winter rears his giant form,
His robe a mist, his voice a storm:
His frown the shiv'ring nations fly,
And hid for half a year in smoky caverns lie.

Yet there the lamp's perpetual blaze
Can pierce the gloom with cheering rays;
Yet there the heroic tale or song
Can urge the ling'ring hours along;
Yet there their hands with timely care
The kajak [3] and the dart prepare,
On summer seas to work their way, [prey.
And wage the wat'ry war, and make the seals their

Too delicate! reproach no more
The seasons of thy native shore—
There soon shall Spring descend the sky,
With smiling brow and placid eye;
A primrose wreath surrounds her hair,
Her green robe floats upon the air;
And scatter'd from her lib'ral hand, [land.
Fair blossoms deck the trees, fair flowers adorn the

### ODE VIII.

#### TO A FRIEND.

WHERE Grove-hill [4] shows thy villa fair,
But late, my Lettsom, there with thee
'T was mine the tranquil hour to share—
The social hour of converse free;
To mark th' arrangement of thy ground,
And all the pleasing prospect round,
Where, while we gaz'd, new beauties still were found.

There, as th' impending cloud of smoke
Fled various from the varying gale,
Full on the view fresh objects broke
Along th' extensive peopled vale,

[2] Layer Breton, a village in Essex.
[3] A Greenland fishing boat.
[4] At Camberwell, in Surry.

Beside Thamesis' bending stream,
From ancient Lambeth's west extreme,
To Limehouse glitt'ring in the ev'ning beam.

And now and then the glancing eye
Caught glimpse of spots remoter still,
On Hampstead's street-clad slope so high,
Or Harrow's fair conspicuous hill ;
Or eastward wander'd to explore
All Peckham's pleasant level o'er,
To busy Deptford's vessel-crowded shore:

Or sought that southern landscape's bound,
Those swelling mounts—one smooth and green,
And one with oaken coverts crown'd,
And one where scatt'ring trees are seen [5].
'T was these, with Summer's radiance bright,
That gave my earliest youth delight,
Of rural scenes the first that met my sight [6].

That business, with fatiguing cares,
For this delightful seat of thine
Such scanty store of moments spares,
Say, friend, shall I for thee repine ?
Were it the commerce of the main,
Or culture of the teeming plain,
From blame or pity I should scarce refrain.

But O! to alleviate human woes,
To banish sickness, banish pain,
To give the sleepless eye repose,
The nerveless arm its strength again ;
From parent eyes to dry the tear,
The wife's distressful thought to cheer,
And end the husband's and the lover's fear.

Where Want sits pining, faint, and ill,
To lend thy kind, unpurchas'd aid,
And hear the exertions of thy skill
With many a grateful blessing paid—
'T is luxury to the feeling heart,
Beyond what social hours impart,          [Art !
Or Nature's beauteous scenes, or curious works of

-----

## ODE IX.

### LEAVING BATH.   1776.

BATH ! ere I quit thy pleasing scene,
Thy beachen cliff I 'll climb again,
To view thy mountains' vivid green,
To view thy hill-surrounded plain :
    To see distinct beneath the eye,
    As in a pictur'd prospect nigh,
Those attic structures shining white,
That form thy sunny crescent's bend,
Or by thy dusty streets extend,
Or near thy winding rivers site.

Did Commerce these proud piles upraise ?
For thee she ne'er unfurl'd her sails—
Hygeia gave thy fountains praise,
And Pain and Languor sought thy vales :

-----

[5] The Dulwich hills.
[6] The author was born in the environs of London,
on the Surry side.

-----

But these suffic'd an humble cell,
If they with Strength and Ease might dwell.
Then Fashion call'd ; his potent voice
Proud Wealth with ready step obey'd,
And Pleasure all her arts essay'd,
To fix with thee the fickle choice.

Precarious gift !—Thy mansions gay,
Where peers and beauties lead the ball,
Neglected, soon may feel decay ;
Forsaken, moulder to their fall.—
    Palmyra, once like thee renown'd,
    Now lies a ruin on the ground.—
But still thy environs so fair,
Thy waters' salutary aid,
Will surely always some persuade
To render thee their care.

-----

## ODE X.

### TO J. PAYNE, ESQ.

#### ACCOUNTANT-GENERAL OF THE BANK OF ENGLAND.

O FRIEND ! to thee, whose lib'ral mind
Was form'd with taste for joys refin'd,
For all the extended country yields,
Of azure skies and verdant fields ;
For all that Genius' hand displays,—
The painter's forms, the poet's lays :—
To thee, restraint to that dull room,
Where sunshine never breaks the gloom ;
To thee, restraint to that dull lore
Of books, with numbers cypher'd o'er—
How hard the lot ! I see with pain,
And wish it oft exchang'd in vain.

Yet not for thee I ask the stores
Which Rapine rends from foreign shores,
Nor those Oppression's pow'r procures
From ills that Poverty endures.
Far happier thou ! thy honest gain
Can life with decency sustain ;
For thee, Content, with thought serene,
Surveys the present changeful scene ;
And Piety her view sublime
Extends beyond the realm of time.

-----

## ODE XI.

### TO A FRIEND

#### APPREHENSIVE OF DECLINING FRIENDSHIP.

Too much in man's imperfect state
    Mistake produces useless pain.—
Methinks, of friendship's frequent fate
    I hear my Frogley's voice complain.

This heart, I hope, forgives its foes ;
    I know it ne'er forgets its friends ;
Where'er may chance my steps dispose,
    The absent oft my thought attends.

Deem not that Time's oblivious hand
    From Memory's page has ras'd the days,
By Lee's green verge we wont to stand,
    And on his crystal current gaze.

From Chadwell's cliffs, o'erhung with shade,
From Widbury's prospect-yielding hill,
Sweet look'd the scenes we then survey'd,
While fancy sought for sweeter still:

Then how did Learning's stores delight!
From books what pleasures then we drew!
For then their charms first met our sight,
And then their faults we little knew.

Alas! life's summer swiftly flies,
And few its hours of bright and fair!
Why bid Distrust's chill east-wind rise,
To blast the scanty blooms they bear?

## ODE XII.

### TO A FRIEND.

No, Cockfield, no! I'll not disdain
Thy Upton's elm-divided plain;
Nor scorn the varied views it yields,
O'er Bromley's creeks and isles of reeds,
Or Ham's or Plaistow's level meads,
To Woolwich streets, or Charlton fields:
Thy hedge-row paths I'll pleasant call,
And praise the lonely lane that leads
To that old tow'r upon the wall.

'T was when Misfortune's stroke severe,
And Melancholy's presence drear,
Had made my Amwell's groves displease,
That thine my weary steps receiv'd,
And much the change my mind reliev'd,
And much thy kindness gave me ease;
For o'er the past as thought would stray,
That thought thy voice as oft retriev'd,
To scenes which fair before us lay.

And there, in happier hours, the walk
Has frequent pleas'd with friendly talk;
From theme to theme that wander'd still—
The long detail of where we'd been,
And what we'd heard, and what we'd seen;
And what the poet's tuneful skill,
And what the painter's graphic art,
Or antiquarian's searches keen,
Of calm amusement could impart.

Then oft did Nature's works engage,
And oft we search'd Linnæus' page;
The Scanian sage, whose wondrous toil
Had class'd the vegetable race:
And, curious, oft from place to place
We rang'd, and sought each different soil,
Each different plant intent to view,
And all the marks minute to trace,
Whence he his nice distinctions drew.

O moments these, not ill employ'd!
O moments, better far enjoy'd
Than those in crowded cities pass'd;
Where oft to Luxury's gaudy reign
Trade lends her feeble aid in vain,
Till pride, a bankrupt wretch at last,
Bids Fraud his specious wiles essay,
Youth's easy confidence to gain,
Or Industry's poor pittance rend away!
VOL. XVII.

## ODE XIII.

I HATE that drum's discordant sound,
Parading round, and round, and round:
To thoughtless youth it pleasure yields,
And lures from cities and from fields,
To sell their liberty for charms
Of tawdry lace and glitt'ring arms;
And when Ambition's voice commands,
To march, and fight, and fall, in foreign lands.

I hate that drum's discordant sound,
Parading round, and round, and round:
To me it talks of ravag'd plains,
And burning towns, and ruin'd swains,
And mangled limbs, and dying groans,
And widows tears, and orphans' moans;
And all that Misery's hand bestows,
To fill the catalogue of human woes.

## ODE XIV.

### WRITTEN

### AFTER READING SOME MODERN LOVE-VERSES.

TAKE hence this tuneful trifler's lays!
I'll hear no more the unmeaning strain
Of Venus' doves, and Cupid's darts,
And killing eyes, and wounded hearts;
All Flattery's round of fulsome praise,
All Falsehood's cant of fabled pain.

Bring me the Muse whose tongue has told
Love's genuine plaintive tender tale;
Bring me the Muse whose sounds of woe
Midst Death's dread scenes so sweetly flow,
When Friendship's faithful breast lies cold,
When Beauty's blooming cheek is pale:
Bring these—I like their grief sincere;
It sooths my sympathetic gloom:
For, oh! Love's genuine pains I've borne,
And Death's dread rage has made me mourn;
I've wept o'er Friendship's early bier,
And dropt the tear on Beauty's tomb.

## ODE XV.

### THE MUSE; OR, POETICAL ENTHUSIASM.

THE Muse! whate'er the Muse inspires,
My soul the tuneful strain admires:
The poet's birth, I ask not where,
His place, his name, they're not my care;
Nor Greece nor Rome delights me more
Than Tagus' bank[1], or Thames's shore[2]:
From silver Avon's flowery side
Though Shakspeare's numbers sweetly glide,
As sweet from Morven's desert hills,
My ear the voice of Ossian fills.

[1] Alluding to Camoens, the epic poet of Portugal; of whose Lusiad we have a well-known masterly translation by Mr. Mickle.
[2] Alluding to Milton, Pope, &c.
I i

The Muse ! whate'er the Muse inspires,
My soul the tuneful strain admires:
Nor bigot zeal, nor party rage
Prevail, to make me blame the page;
I scorn not all that Dryden sings
Because he flatters courts and kings;
And from the master lyre of Gray
When pomp of music breaks away,
Not less the sound my notice draws,
For that 't is heard in Freedom's cause.

The Muse ! whate'er the Muse inspires,
My soul the tuneful strain admires:
Where Wealth's bright sun propitious shines.
No added lustre marks the lines;
Where Want extends her chilling shades,
No pleasing flower of Fancy fades;
A scribbling peer's applauded lays
Might claim, but claim in vain, my praise
From that poor youth, whose tales relate
Sad Juga's fears and Bawdin's fate [3].

The Muse ! whate'er the Muse inspires,
My soul the tuneful strain admires:
When Fame her wreaths well-earn'd bestows,
My breast no latent envy knows;
My Langhorne's verse I lov'd to hear,
And Beattie's song delights my ear;
And his, whom Athens' tragic maid
Now leads through Scarning's lonely glade;
While he for British nymphs bid flow
Her notes of terrour and of woe [4].

The Muse ! whate'er the Muse inspires,
My soul the tuneful strain admires:
Or be the verse or blank or rhyme,
The theme or humble or sublime;
If Pastoral's hand my journey leads
Through harvest fields or new-mown meads;
If Epic's voice sonorous calls
To Œta's cliffs [5] or Salemn's walls [6];
Enough—the Muse, the Muse inspires !
My soul the tuneful strain admires.

---

## ODE XVI.

### VIEWING THE RUINS OF AN ABBEY.

#### TO A FRIEND.

How steep yon mountains rise around,
How bold yon gloomy woods ascend !
How loud the rushing torrents sound
That midst these heaps of ruin bend,
Where one arch'd gateway yet remains,
And one lone aisle its roof retains,
And one tall turret's walls impend !

, [3] See Rowley's poems, supposed to have been
written by Chatterton, an unhappy youth born at
Bristol.

[4] See Mr. Potter's excellent translation of Æschylus and Euripides.

[5] See Mr. Glover's Leonidas, alluded to as an
example of classical dignity and simplicity.,

[6] See Tasso's Jerusalem Delivered, alluded to as
an example of Gothic fancy and magnificence.

Here once a self-sequester'd train
Renounc'd life's tempting pomp and glare;
Rejected pow'r, relinquish'd gain,
And shun'd the great, and shun'd the fair:
The voluntary slaves of toil,
By day they till'd their little soil,
By night they woke, and rose to prayer.

Though Superstition much we blame,
That bade them thus consume their years;
Their motive still our praise must claim,
Their constancy our thought reveres:
And sure their solitary scheme
Must check each passion's wild extreme,
And save them cares, and save them fears.

Their convent's round contain'd their all;
Their minds no sad presage oppress'd,
What fate might absent wealth befall,
How absent friends might be distress'd:
Domestic ills ne'er hurt their ease;
They nought of pain could feel from these,
Who no domestic joys possess'd.

But imperfection haunts each place:
Would this kind calm atone to thee
For Fame's or Fortune's sprightly chase,
Whose prize in prospect still we see;
Or Hymen's happy moments bless'd,
With Beauty leaning on thy breast,
Or childhood prattling at thy knee?

---

## ODE XVII.

### PRIVATEERING.

How custom steels the human breast
To deeds that Nature's thoughts detest !
How custom consecrates to fame
What reason else would give to shame !
Fair Spring supplies the favouring gale,
The naval plunderer spreads his sail,
And ploughing wide the wat'ry way,
Explores with anxious eyes his prey.

The man he never saw before,
The man who him no quarrel bore,
He meets, and Avarice prompts the fight;
And Rage enjoys the dreadful sight
Of decks with streaming crimson dy'd,
And wretches struggling in the tide,
Or, midst th' explosion's horrid glare,
Dispers'd with quivering limbs in air.

The merchant now on foreign shores
His captur'd wealth in vain deplores;
Quits his fair home, O mournful change !
For the dark prison's scanty range;
By Plenty's hand so lately fed,
Depends on casual alms for bread;
And, with a father's anguish torn,
Sees his poor offspring left forlorn.

And yet, such man's misjudging mind,
For all this injury to his kind,
The prosperous robber's native plain
Shall bid him welcome home again;

His name the song of ev'ry street,
His acts the theme of all we meet,
And oft the artist's skill shall place
To public view his pictur'd face!

If glory thus be earn'd, for me
My object glory ne'er shall be;
No, first in Cambria's loneliest dale
Be mine to hear the shepherd's tale!
No, first on Scotia's bleakest hill
Be mine the stubborn soil to till!
Remote from wealth, to dwell alone,
And die, to guilty praise unknown!

## ODE XVIII.

### TO HOSPITALITY.

DOMESTIC pow'r! erewhile rever'd
  Where Syria spread her palmy plain,
Where Greece her tuneful Muses heard,
Where Rome beheld her patriot train;
  Thou to Albion too wert known,
  Midst the moat and moss-grown wall
That girt her Gothic-structur'd hall
  With rural trophies strown.

The traveller, doubtful of his way,
  Upon the pathless forest wild;
The huntsman, in the heat of day,
And with the tedious chase o'ertoil'd;
  Wide their view around them cast,
  Mark'd the distant rustic tow'r,
And sought and found the festive bower,
  And shar'd the free repast.

E'en now, on Caledonia's shore,
  When Eve's dun robe the sky arrays,
Thy punctual hand unfolds the door,
Thy eye the mountain road surveys;
  Pleas'd to spy the casual guest,
  Pleas'd with food his heart to cheer,
With pipe or song to sooth his ear,
  And spread his couch for rest.

Nor yet e'en here disdain'd thy sway,
  Where Grandeur's splendid modern seat
Far o'er the landscape glitters gay;
  Or where fair Quiet's lone retreat
Hides beneath the hoary hill,
  Near the dusky upland shade,
Between the willow's glossy glade,
  And by the tinkling rill.

There thine the pleasing interviews
  That friends and relatives endear,
When scenes not often seen amuse,
When tales not often told we hear;
  There the scholar's liberal mind
  Oft instruction gives and gains,
And oft the lover's lore obtains
  His fair-one's audience kind.

O gentle power! where'er thy reign,
  May Health and Peace attend thee still;
Nor Folly's presence cause thee pain,
  Nor Vice reward thy good with ill;

Gratitude thy altar raise,
  Wealth to thee her offerings pay,
And Genius wake his tuneful lay
  To celebrate thy praise.

## ODE XIX.

### THE APOLOGY.

" PASTORAL, and elegy, and ode!
Who hopes by these applause to gain,
Believe me, friend, may hope in vain—
These classic things are not the mode;
Our taste polite, so much refin'd,
Demands a strain of different kind.

" Go, court the Muse of Chevy Chase,
To tell in Sternhold's simple rhymes
Some tale of ancient English times;
Or try to win rude Satire's grace,
That scold, who dirt around her throws,
And many a random stain bestows.

" Or dull trite thoughts in songs combine,
And bid the tuneful accents fall,
To wake the echoes of Vauxhall;
Or tow'rds the stage thy thoughts incline,
And furnish some half-pilfer'd play,
To shine the meteor of the day."

O! no—though such the crowd amuse,
And peals of noisy praise procure;
Will they the critic eye endure,
And pass the ordeal of reviews?
And who is he for whom they'll gain
A niche in Fame's immortal fane?

The plan that Virgil's choice could claim,
The plan that Horace deign'd to choose,
Trust me, I wish not to refuse:—
To Akenside's or Shenstone's name
The praise that future days shall pay,
Methinks may well content my lay.

## ODE XX.

THIS scene how rich from Thames's side,
While evening suns their amber beam
Spread o'er the glassy-surfac'd tide,
And midst the masts and cordage gleam;
Blaze on the roofs with turrets crown'd,
And gild green pastures stretch'd around,
And gild the slope of that high ground,
Whose corn-fields bright the prospect bound [1]!

The white sails glide along the shore,
Red streamers on the breezes play,
The boatmen ply the dashing oar,
And wide their various freight convey;
Some Neptune's hardy thoughtless train,
And some the careful sons of gain,
And some th' enamour'd nymph and swain
Listening to music's soothing strain.

[1] Shooter's Hill. This view was taken on the
north side of the Thames, at Ratcliff.

But there, while these the sight allure,
Still Fancy wings her flight away
To woods recluse, and vales obscure,
And streams that solitary stray ;
To view the pine-grove on the hill,
The rocks that trickling springs distill,
The meads that quivering aspins fill,
Or alders crowding o'er the rill.


And where the trees unfold their bloom,
And where the banks their floriage bear,
And all effuse a rich perfume
That hovers in the soft calm air ;
The hedge-row path to wind along,
To hear the bleating fleecy throng,
To hear the skylark's airy song,
And throstle's note so clear and strong.


But say, if there our steps were brought,
Would these their pow'r to please retain ?
Say, would not restless, roving thought
Turn back to busy scenes again ?
O strange formation of the mind !
Still, though the present fair we find,
Still tow'rds the absent thus inclin'd,
Thus fix'd on objeots left behind !

---

### ODE XXI.

#### WRITTEN AFTER A JOURNEY TO BRISTOL.


THEE, Bristol, oft my thoughts recall,
  Thy Kingsdown brow and Brandon hill;
The space, once circled by thy wall,
  Which tow'rs and spires of churches fill ;
And masts and sails of vessels tall,
With trees and houses intermingled still !


From Clifton's rocks how grand the sight,
  When Avon's dark tide rush'd between!
How grand, from Henbury's woody height,
  The Severn's wide-spread wat'ry scene,
Her waves with trembling sunshine bright,
And Cambrian hills beyond them rising green !


To Mendip's ridge how stretch'd away
  My view, while Fancy sought the plain
Where Blagdon's groves secluded lay,
  And heard my much-lov'd poet's strain [1] !
Ah ! why so near, nor thither stray
To meet the friend I ne'er shall meet again ?


Occasion's call averse to prize,
  Irresolute we oft remain—
She soon irrevocably flies,
  And then we mourn her flown in vain ;
While Pleasure's imag'd forms arise,
Whose fancied loss Regret beholds with pain.

---

[1] The late ingenious Dr. John Langhorne, then
resident at Blagdon, near Bristol.

And Bristol ! why thy scenes explore,
  And why those scenes so soon resign,
And fail to seek the spot that bore
  That wondrous tuneful youth of thine,
The bard [2], whose boasted ancient store
Rose recent from his own exhaustless mine [3] !


Though Fortune all her gifts deny'd,
  Though Learning made him not her choice,
The Muse still plac'd him at her side,
  And bade him in her smile rejoice—
Description still his pen supply'd,
Pathos his thought, and Melody his voice !


Conscious and proud of merit high,
  Fame's wreath he boldly claim'd to wear:
But Fame, regardless, pass'd him by,
  Unknown, or deem'd unworth her care :
The Sun of Hope forsook his sky ;
And all his land look'd dreary, bleak, and bare!


Then Poverty, grim spectre, rose,
  And horrour o'er the prospect threw—
His deep distress too nice to expose;
  Too nice for common aid to sue,
A drear alternative he chose,
And rashly from the painful scene withdrew.


Ah ! why for Genius' headstrong rage
  Did Virtue's hand no curb prepare ?
What boots, poor youth ! that now thy page
  Can boast the public praise to share,
The learn'd in deep research engage,
And lightly entertain the gentle fair ?


Ye, who superfluous wealth command,
  O why your kind relief delay'd ?
O why not snatch'd his desp'rate hand ?
  His foot on Fate's dread brink not stay'd ?
What thanks had you your native land
For a new Shakspeare or new Milton paid ?


For me—Imagination's power
  Leads oft insensibly my way,
To where at midnight's silent hour,
  The crescent Moon's slow-westering ray
Pours full on Redcliff's lofty tow'r,
And gilds with yellow light its walls of grey.


Midst Toil and Commerce slumb'ring round,
  Lull'd by the rising tide's hoarse roar,
There Frome and Avon willow-crown'd,
  I view sad-wandering by the shore,  [sound,
With streaming tears, and notes of mournful
Too late their hapless bard, untimely lost, deplore.

---

### ODE XXII.

#### TO CRITICISM.

FAIR nymph ! of Taste and Learning born,
Whom Truth's and Candour's gifts adorn,

---

Chatterton.
[3] This is at least the author's opinion, notwithstanding all that has hitherto appeared on the
other side of the question. The last line alludes to
one of the ingenious Mr. Mason in his Elegy to a
young nobleman :
  See from the depths of his exhaustless mine
  His glitt'ring stores the tuneful spendthrift throws.

The Muse's friend to thee she sings:
Accept the grateful verse she brings.
When Genius, ranging Nature o'er,
Collects his tributary store,
What matter's tract immense supplies,
Or wide in mind's vast region lies,
And ev'ry thought with skill combines,
And all transmits in tuneful lines;
Then rap'ure sparkling in thine eye,
Then rais'd thy solemn voice on high;
Thy comment still his work pursues,
The plan explains, the style reviews,
And marks its strength, and marks its ease;
And tells us why and how they please.
And when, perhaps, disdaining care,
He blends with faults his products fair;
Whate'er of such thy sight surveys,
Thy tongue in tr'umph ne'er displays,
But hints, as spots that dim thé Sun,
Or rocks that future sails should shun.
  'T was thee whom once Stagyra's grove
Oft with her sage [1] allur'd to rove;
'T was thee to whom in Tadmor's bow'rs,
Her statesman [2] vow'd his vacant hours;
'T was thee whom, Tibur's vines among,
Her bard [3] in careless measures sung;
'T was thou who thence to Albion's plain
Remov'd, to teach her tuneful train,
When Dryden's age, by thee inspir'd,
Condemn'd the flights his youth admir'd;
And Pope, intent on higher praise,
So polish'd all his pleasing lays:
And now by thee our favour'd coast
A Warton, Hurd, and Burke can boast;
And her, whose pen from Gallic rage
Defended Shakspeare's injur'd page [4].
  Give me, bright power! with ready ear
Another's plea for fame to hear,
And bid my willing voice allow
The bays to Merit's modest brow:
And when the Muse her presence deigns,
And prompts my own unstudy'd strains,
Instruct me then, with view severe,
To inspect, and keep from errour clear;
Nor spare, though fancy'd e'er so fine,
One ill-plac'd thought, or useless line.

---

## ODE XXIII.

### TO DISEASE.

DISEASE! man's dread, relentless foe,
Fell source of fear, and pain, and woe!
O say, on what ill-fated coast
They mourn thy tyrant reign the most?
On Java's bogs, or Gambia's sand,
Or Persia's sultry southern strand;
Or Egypt's annual-flooded plain,
Or Rome's neglected, waste domain;

[1] Aristotle.
[2] Longinus.
[3] Horace.
[4] The ingenious Mrs. Montague, who has so ably vindicated Shakspeare from the çavils of Voltaire.

Or where her walls Byzantium rears,
And mosques and turrets crescent-crown'd,
  And from his high serail the sultan hears
The wide Propontis' beating waves resound [1].

  I'll ask no more—Our clime, though fair,
  Enough thy tyrant reign must share;
And lovers there, and friends, complain,
By thee there friends and lovers slain:
And yet our avarice and our pride
Combine to spread thy mischiefs wide;
While that the captive wretch confines,
To hunger, cold, and filth resigns,—
And this the funeral pomp attends
To vaults, where mould'ring corses lie,—
  Amid foul air thy form unseen ascends,
And like a vulture hovers in the sky [2].

---

## ODE XXIV.

### THE TEMPESTUOUS EVENING.

THERE's grandeur in this sounding storm,
That drives the hurrying clouds along
That on each other seem to throng,
And mix in many a varied form;
While, bursting now and then between,
The Moon's dim misty orb is seen,
And casts faint glimpses on the green.

Beneath the blast the forests bend,
And thick the branchy ruin lies,
And wide the shower of foliage flies;
The lake's black waves in tumult blend,
Revolving o'er and o'er and o'er,
And foaming on the rocky shore,
Whose caverns echo to their roar.

The sight sublime enrapts my thought,
And swift along the past it strays,
And much of strange event surveys,
What History's faithful tongue has taught,
Or fancy form'd, whose plastic skill
The page with fabled change can fill
Of ill to good, or good to ill.

But can my soul the scene enjoy,
That rends another's breast with pain?
O hapless he, who, near the main,
Now sees its billowy rage destroy!
Beholds the found'ring bark descend,
Nor knows, but what its fate may end
The moments of his dearest friend!

---

## ODE XXV.

### THE MELANCHOLY EVENING.

O HASTE, ye hov'ring clouds, away,
  Ye clouds so fleecy, dim, and pale,
Through which the Moon's obstructed ray
  Sheds this sad whiteness o'er the vale!

[1] *Byzantium:* Constantinople; subject to frequent visitations of that dreadful fever, the plague.
[2] Alluding to the too frequent miserable situation of prisoners of war, debtors, &c.; and the absurd custom of burying in churches; circumstances contributing greatly to the propagation of disease.

Forbear, ye bells, that languid strain!
The sight, the sound, are fraught with pain;
The words of dying friends I hear,
The open grave I linger near,
Take the last look, and drop the parting tear!

Before my view dire phantoms rise,
The plagues of hapless humankind!
Pale Fear, who unpursu'd still flies,
    And starts, and turns, and looks behind;
Remorse, whose own indignant aim
Deforms with useless wounds her frame;
Despair, whose tongue no speech will deign,
Whose ghastly brow looks dark disdain,
And bends from steep rocks o'er the foaming main.

And Rage, whose bosom inly burns,
    While Reason's call he scorns to hear;
And Jealousy, who ruthless turns
    From suppliant Beauty's pray'r and tear;
Revenge, whose thoughts tumultuous roll
To seek the poniard or the bowl;
And Phrensy, wildly passing by,
With her chain'd arm and starting eye,
And voice that with loud curses rends the sky!

Ambition, here, to heights of pow'r
    His course with daring step pursues,
Though Danger's frown against him lour,
    Though Guilt his path with blood bestrews;
There Avarice grasps his useless store,
Though Misery's plaints his aid implore,
Though he her ruin'd cottage nigh,
Beholds her famish'd infants lie,
And hears their faint, their last expiring cry!

Ye dreadful band! O spare, O spare!
    Alas, your ear no prayers persuade!
But, ah! if man your reign must bear,
    Sure man had better ne'er been made!
Say, will Religion clear this gloom,
And point to bliss beyond the tomb?
Yes, haply for her chosen train;
The rest, they say, severe decrees ordain
To realms of endless night, and everlasting pain [1]!

---

### ODE XXVI.

#### THE PLEASANT EVENING.

DELIGHTFUL looks this clear, calm sky,
With Cynthia's orb on high!
Delightful looks this smooth green ground,
With shadows cast from cots around:
Quick-twinkling lustre decks the tide;
And cheerful radiance gently falls
On that white town, and castle walls,
That crown the spacious river's further side.

And now along the echoing hills
The night-bird's strain melodious trills;

[1] The author does not give these as his own sentiments, but merely such as the gloomy moment
described might naturally suggest. That the above
dreadful idea is adopted by a large body of Christians, is sufficient to authorize its admission into
a poem professing to paint the dark side of things.

And now the echoing dale along
Soft flows the shepherds tuneful song:
And now, wide o'er the water borne,
The city's mingled murmur swells,
And lively change of distant bells,
And varied warbling of the deep-ton'd horn.

Their influence calms the soften'd soul,
The passions feel their strong control:
While Fancy's eye, where'er it strays,
A scene of happiness surveys;
Through all the various walks of life
No natural ill nor moral sees,
No famine fell, nor dire disease,
Nor war's infernal unrelenting strife.

For these, behold a heav'nly band,
Their white wings waving o'er the land!
Sweet Innocence, a cherub fair,
And Peace and Joy, a sister pair:
And Kindness mild, their kindred grace,
Whose brow serene complacence wears,
Whose hand her lib'ral bounty bears
O'er the vast range of animated space!

Bless'd vision! O for ever stay!
O far be guilt and pain away!
And yet, perhaps, with him, whose view
Looks at one glance creation through,
To gen'ral good our partial ill
Seems but a sand upon the plain,
Seems but a drop amid the main,
And some wise unknown purpose may fulfil.

---

### ODE XXVII.

#### AFTER READING AKENSIDE'S POEMS.

To Fancy's view what visions rise,
Remote amid yon azure skies!
    What goddess-form descends in air?
The Grecian Muse, severely fair!
What sage is he, to whom she deigns
Her lyre of elevated strains?
The bard of Tyne—his master hand
Awakes new music o'er the land;
And much his voice of right and wrong
Attempts to teach th' unheeding throng.
    What mean those crystal rocks serene,
Those laureate groves for ever green,
Those Parian domes?—Sublime retreats,
Of Freedom's sons the happy seats!—
There dwell the few who dar'd disdain
The lust of power and lust of gain;
The patriot names of old renown'd,
And those in later ages found;
The Athenian, Spartan, Roman boast,
The pride of Britain's sea-girt coast!
    But, oh! what darkness intervenes!
But, oh! beneath, what diff'rent scenes!
What matron she, to grief resign'd,
Beside that ruin'd arch reclin'd?
Her sons, who once so well could wield
The warrior-spear, the warrior-shield,
A turban'd ruffian's scourge constrains
To toil on desolated plains!—
    And she who leans that column nigh,
Where trampled arms and eagles lie;

Whose veil essays her blush to hide,
Who checks the tear that hastes to glide?
A mitred priest's oppressive sway
She sees her drooping race obey:
Their vines unprun'd, their fields untill'd,
Their streets with want and misery fill'd.
  And who is she, the martial maid
Along that cliff so careless la:d,
Whose brow such laugh unmeaning wears,
Whose eye such insolence declares,
Whose tongue descants, with scorn so vain,
On slaves of Ebro or of Seine?
What grisly churl [1], what harlot bold [2],
Behind her, chains enormous hold?
Though Virtue's warning voice be near,
Alas, she will not, will not hear!
And now she sinks in sleep profound,
And now they bind her to the ground.
  O what is he, his ghastly form
So half obscur'd in cloud and storm,
Swift striding on [3]?—beneath his strides
Proud Empire's firmest base subsides;
Behind him dreary wastes remain,
Oblivion's dark chaotic reign!

---

## THE MEXICAN PROPHECY.

### AN ODE.

---

De Solis, in his History of the Conquest of Mexico,
informs us, that, on the approach of Cortez to the
neighbourhood of that city, the emperor Motezuma sent a number of magicians to attempt the
destruction of the Spanish army. As the sorcer-
ers were practising their incantations, a demon
appeared to them in the form of their idol Tlcatlepuca, and foretold the fall of the Mexican empire. On this legend is founded the following
poem. The conquest of Mexico was undertaken
from motives of avarice, and accompanied with
circumstances of cruelty; but it produced the
subversion of a tyrannical government, and the
abolition of a detestable religion of horrid rites
and human sacrifices.

---

From Cholula's hostile plain [4],
Left her treach'rous legions slain,
Left her temples all in flame,
Cortes' conquering army came.
High on Chalco's stormy steep
Shone their phalanx broad and deep;
High the Hispanian banner rais'd,
Bore the cross in gold emblaz'd [5].

---

[1] Avarice.    [2] Luxury.    [3] Ruin.

[4] Cholula was a large city, not far distant from
Mexico. The inhabitants were in league with the
Mexicans; and after professing friendship for the
Spaniards, endeavoured to surprise and destroy
them.

[5] The device on Cortes's standard was the sign of
the cross. Vide de Solis.

Thick the gleaming spears appear'd,
Loud the neighing steeds were heard;
Flash'd the musquets lightnings round,
Roll'd their thunders o'er the ground,
Echo'd from a thousand caves,
Down to Tenustitan's waves [6];—
Spacious lake, that far below
Bade its lucid level flow:
There the ever-sunny shore
Groves of palm and coco bore;
Maize-fields rich, savannas green,
Stretch'd around, with towns between.
Tacubà, Tezeùco fair,
Rear'd their shining roofs in air;
Mexico's imperial pride
Glitter'd midst the glassy tide,
Bright with gold, with silver bright,
Dazzling, charming all the sight [7].
From their post the war-worn band
Raptur'd view'd the happy land:
" Haste to victory, haste to ease,
Mark the spot that gives us these!"
  On the exulting hero strode,
Shunn'd the smooth insidious road,
Shunn'd the rock's impending shade,
Shunn'd the expecting ambuscade [8].
  Deep within a gloomy wood
Motezume's magicians stood:
Tlcatlepuca's horrid form,
God of famine, plague, and storm,
High on magic stones they rais'd;
Magic fires before him blaz'd;
Round the lurid flames they drew,
Flames whence steams of sulphur flew;
There, while bleeding victims smok'd,
Thus his aid they loud invok'd:
" Minister supreme of ill,
Prompt to punish, prompt to kill,
Motezuma asks thy aid!
Foreign foes his realms invade;
Vengeance on the strangers shed,
Mix them instant with the dead!
By thy temple's sable floor,
By thy altar stain'd with gore,
Stain'd with gore, and strew'd with bones,
Echoing shrieks, and echoing groans!
Vengeance on the strangers shed,
Mix them instant with the dead!"
  Ordaz heard, Velasquez heard—
Swift their falchions' blaze appear'd;
Alvarado rushing near,
Furious rais'd his glitt'ring spear;

[6] Tenustitan, otherwise Tenuchtitlan, the ancient
name of the lake of Mexico.

[7] The Spanish historians assert, that the walls
and houses of the Indian cities were composed of a
peculiar kind of glittering stone or plaster, which at
a distance resembled silver.

[8] The Indians had blocked up the usual road to
Mexico, and opened another broader, and smooth
at the entrance, but which led among rocks and
precipices, where they had placed parties in ambush. Cortes discovered the stratagem, and ordered his troops to remove the obstructions. Being
asked by the Mexican ambassadors the reason of
this procedure, he replied, that the Spaniards always
chose to encounter difficulties.

Calm, Olmedo mark'd the scene[9],
Calm he mark'd, and stepp'd between:
" Vain their rites and vain their pray'r,
Weak attempts beneath your care ;
Warriors ! let the wretches live !
Christians ! pity, and forgive !"
Sudden darkness o'er them spread,
Glow'd the woods with dusky red ;
Vast the idol's stature grew,
Look'd his face of ghastly hue,
Frowning rage, and frowning hate,
Angry at his nation's fate ;
Fierce his fiery eyes he roll'd,
Thus his tongue the future told ;
Cortes' veterans paus'd to hear,
Wondring all, though void of fear :
" Mourn, devoted city, mourn !
Mourn, devoted city, mourn !
Doom'd for all thy crimes to know
Scenes of battle, scenes of woe !
Who is he—O spare the sight !—
Rob'd in gold, with jewels bright ?
Hark ! he deigns the crowd to call ;
Chiefs and warriors prostrate fall [10].
Rev'rence now to fury yields ;
Strangers o'er him spread your shields !
Thick the darts, the arrows, fly ;
Hapless monarch ! he must die !
Mark the solemn funeral state
Passing through the western gate !
Chàpultèqua's cave contains
Mighty Motezume's remains.
" Cease the strife ! alas, 't is vain !
Myriads throng Otumba's plain ;
Wide their feathery crests they wave,
All the strong and all the brave [11].
Gleaming glory through the skies,
See the imperial standard flies !
Down by force resistless torn,
Off in haughty triumph borne.
Slaughter heaps the vale with dead,
Fugitives the mountains spread.
" Mexico, 't is thine to know
More of battle, more of woe !—
Bright in arms the stranger train
O'er thy causeways move again.
Bend the bow, the shaft prepare,
Join the breastplate's folds with care,
Raise the sacrificial fire,
Bid the captive youths expire [12] ;

Wake the sacred trumpet's breath,
Pouring anguish, pouring death [13] ;
Troops from every street repair,
Close them in the fatal snare ;
Valiant as they are, they fly,
Here they yield, and there they die.
" Cease the strife ! 't is fruitless all,
Mexico at last must fall !
Lo ! the dauntless band return,
Furious for the fight they burn !
Lo ! auxiliar nations round,
Crowding o'er the darken'd ground !
Corses fill thy trenches deep ;
Down thy temple's lofty steep
See thy priests, thy princes thrown—
Hark ! I hear their parting groan !
Blood thy lake with crimson dyes,
Flames from all thy domes arise !
" What are those that round thy shore
Lanch thy troubled waters o'er ?
Swift canoes that from the fight
Aid their vanquish'd monarch's flight ;
Ambush'd in the reedy shade,
Them the stranger barks invade ;
Soon thy lord a captive bends,
Soon thy far-fam'd empire ends [14] ;
Otomèca shares thy spoils,
Tlascalà in triumph smiles [15].
Mourn, devoted city, mourn !
Mourn, devoted city, mourn !
" Cease your boast, O stranger band,
Conquerors of my fallen land !
Avarice strides your van before,
Phantom meagre, pale, and hoar !
Discord follows, breathing flame,
Still opposing claim to claim [16] ;
Kindred demons, haste along !,
Haste, avenge my country's wrong !"
Ceas'd the voice with dreadful sounds,
Loud as tides that burst their bounds ;
Roll'd the form in smoke away,
Amaz'd on earth th' exorcists lay ;
Pondering on the dreadful lore,
Their course the Iberians downward bore ;
Their helmets glittering o'er the vale,
And wide their ensigns fluttering in the gale.

[9] Bartholeme de Olmedo, chaplain to Cortes : he seems to have been a man of enlarged ideas, much prudence, moderation, and humanity.

[10] Motezuma, who was resident in the Spanish quarters when they were attacked by the Mexicans, proposed showing himself to the people, in order to appease the tumult. At his first appearance he was regarded with veneration, which was soon exchanged for rage, to the effects whereof he fell a victim.

[11] Cortes, in his retreat from Mexico, after the death of Motezuma, was followed and surrounded by the whole collective force of the empire, in the plains of Otumba. After repelling the attacks of his enemies on every side, with indefatigable valour, he found himself overpowered by numbers ; when, making one desperate effort, with a few select friends, he seized the imperial standard, killed the general, and routed the army.

[12] De Solis relates, that the Mexicans sacrificed to their idols a number of Spaniards, whom they had taken prisoners, and whose cries and groans were distinctly heard in the Spanish camp, exciting sentiments of horrour and revenge in their surviving companions.

[13] The above author observes, that the sacred trumpet of the Mexicans was so called, because it was not permitted to any but the priests to sound it ; and that only when they denounced war, and animated the people on the part of their gods.

[14] When the Spaniards had forced their way to the centre of Mexico, Guatimozin, the reigning emperor, endeavoured to escape in his canoes across the lake ; but was pursued and taken prisoner by Garcia de Holguin, captain of one of the Spanish brigantines.

[15] The Otomies were a fierce, savage nation, never thoroughly subdued by the Mexicans. Tlascala was a powerful neighbouring republic, the rival of Mexico.

[16] Alluding to the dissentions which ensued among the Spaniards after the conquest of America.

# EPISTLES.

## EPISTLES.

### EPISTLE I.

#### THE GARDEN.

##### TO A FRIEND.

From Whitby's rocks steep rising o'er the main,
From Eska's vales, or Ewecot's lonely plain,
Say, rove thy thoughts to Amwell's distant bow'rs,
To mark how pass thy friend's sequester'd hours?
" Perhaps," think'st thou, " he seeks his pleas-
ing scenes
Of winding walks, smooth lawns, and shady greens:
Where China's willow hangs its foliage fair,
And Po's tall poplar waves its top in air,
And the dark maple spreads its umbrage wide,
And the white bench adorns the bason side;
At morn reclin'd, perhaps, he sits to view
The bank's neat slope, the water's silver hue.
" Where, midst thick oaks, the subterraneous
To the arch'd grot admits a feeble ray;      [way
Where glossy pebbles pave the varied floors,
And rough flint-walls are deck'd with shells and
ores,
And silvery pearls, spread o'er the roofs on high,
Glimmer like faint stars in a twilight sky;
From noon's fierce glare, perhaps, he pleas'd retires,
Indulging musings which the place inspires.
" Now where the airy octagon ascends,
And wide the prospect o'er the vale extends,
Midst evening's calm, intent perhaps he stands,
And looks o'er all that length of sun-gilt lands,
Of bright green pastures, stretch'd by rivers clear,
And willow groves, or osier islands near."
Alas, my friend, how strangely men mistake,
Who guess what others most their pleasure make!
These garden scenes, which Fashion o'er our plains
Spreads round the villas of our wealthy swains,
Though Envy grudge, or Friendship wish to share,
They claim but little of their owners' care.
For me, my groves not oft my steps invite,
And far less oft they fail to offend my sight:
In vain the senna waves its glossy gold,
In vain the cistus' spotted flow'rs unfold,
In vain the acacia's snowy bloom depends,
In vain the sumach's scarlet spike ascends,
In vain the woodbine's spicy tufts disclose,
And green slopes redden with the shedding rose:
These neat-shorn hawthorns useless verdant bound,
This long straight walk, that pool's unmeaning
round,      [trees,
These short-curv'd paths that twist beneath the
Disgust the eye, and make the whole displease.
" No scene like this," I say, " did Nature raise,
Brown's fancy form, or Walpole's [1] judgment praise;
No prototype for this did I survey
In Woollett's landscapes [2], or in Mason's lay."

[1] See Mr. Walpole's ingenious History of modern Taste in Gardening, at the end of the fourth
volume of his Anecdotes of Painting.
[2] The above-named excellent artist, several years
ago, drew and engraved a number of beautiful
views in some of our most celebrated modern gardens.

But might thy genius, friend, an Eden frame,
Profuse of beauty, and secure from blame;
Where round the lawn might wind the varied way,
Now lost in gloom, and now with prospect gay;
Now screen'd with clumps of green, for wintry
bow'rs;
Now edg'd with sunny banks for summer flow'rs;
Now led by crystal lakes with lilies dress'd,
Or where light temples court the step to rest—
Time's gradual change, or tempest's sudden rage,
There with thy peace perpetual war would wage.
That tyrant oak, whose arms so far o'ergrow,
Shades some poor shrub that pines with drought
below;
These rampant elms, those hazels branching wide,
Crowd the broad pine, the spiry larix hide.
That lilac brow, where May's unsparing hand
Bade one vast swell of purple bloom expand,
Soon past its prime, shows signs of quick decay,
The naked stem, and scanty-cover'd spray.
Fierce Boreas calls, and Ruin waits his call;
Thy fair catalpa's broken branches fall;
Thy soft magnolia mourns her blasted green,
And blighted laurel's yellowing leaves are seen.
But Discontent alone, thou 'lt say, complains
For ill success, where none perfection gains:
True is the charge; but from that tyrant's sway
What art, what power, can e'er redeem our day?
To me, indeed, short ease he sometimes yields,
When my lone walk surrounds the rural fields;
There no past errours of my own upbraid,
No time, no wealth expended unrepaid:
There Nature dwells, and throws profuse around
Each pastoral sight and ev'ry pastoral sound;
From Spring's green copse, that pours the cuckoo's
And evening bleatings of the fleecy train,   [strain,
To Autumn's yellow field and clam'rous horn [3]
That wakes the slumb'ring harvesters at morn.
There Fancy too, with fond delighted eyes,
Sees o'er the scene ideal people rise;
There calm Contentment, in his cot reclin'd,
Hears the grey poplars whisper in the wind;
There Love's sweet song adown the echoing dale
To Beauty's ear conveys the tender tale;
And there Devotion lifts his brow to Heav'n,
With grateful thanks for many a ble sing given.
Thus oft through Maylan's shady lane I stray,
Trace Rushgreen's paths, or Postwood's winding
Thus oft to Eastfield's airy height I have;   [way,
(All well known spots thy feet have frequent trac'd!)
While Memory, as my sight around I cast,
Suggests the pleasing thought of moments past;
Or Hope, amid the future, forms again
The dream of bliss Experience broke in vain.

### EPISTLE II.

#### WINTER AMUSEMENTS IN THE COUNTRY.

##### TO A FRIEND IN LONDON.

While thee, my friend, the city's scenes detain,—
The cheerful scenes where Trade and Pleasure reign;
Where glittering shops their varied stores display,
And passing thousands crowd the public way;

[3] There is a custom, frequent in many parts of
England, of calling the harvest-men to and from

Where Painting's forms and Music's sounds delight,
And Fashion's frequent novelties invite,
And conversation's sober social hours
Engage the mind, and elevate its pow'rs—
Far different scenes for us the country yields,
Deserted roads and unfrequented fields:
Yet deem not, lonely as they are, that these
Boast nought to charm the eye, the ear to please.
Though here the tyrant Winter holds command,
And bids rude tempests desolate the land;
Sometimes the Sun extends his cheering beam,
And all the landscape casts a golden gleam:
Clear is the sky, and calm and soft the air,
And through thin mist each object looks more fair.
    Then, where the villa rears its sheltering grove,
Along the southern lawn 't is sweet to rove:
There dark green pines, behind, their boughs extend,
And bright spruce firs like pyramids ascend,
And round their tops in many a pendent row,
Their scaly cones of shining auburn show;
There the broad cedar's level branches spread,
And the tall cypress lifts its spiry head;
With alaternus ilex interweaves,
And laurels mix their glossy oval leaves;
And gilded holly crimson fruit displays,
And white viburnum [4] o'er the border strays.
    Where these from storms the spacious greenhouse screen,
Ev'n now the eye beholds a flow'ry scene;
There crystal sashes ward the injurious cold,
And rows of benches fair exotics hold;
Rich plants, that Afric's sunny cape supplies,
Or o'er the isles of either India rise.
    While strip'd geranium shows its tufts of red,
And verdant myrtles grateful fragrance shed;
A moment stay to mark the vivid bloom,
A moment stay to catch the high perfume,
And then to rural scenes—Yon path, that leads
Down the steep bourn and 'cross the level meads,
Soon mounts th' opponent hill, and soon conveys
To where the farm its pleasing group displays:
The rustic mansion's form, antiquely fair;
The yew-hedg'd garden, with its grass-plat square;
The barn's long ridge, and doors expanded wide;
The stable's straw-clad eves and clay-built side;
The cartshed's roof, of rough-hewn roundwood made,
And loose on heads of old sere pollards laid;
The granary's floor that smooth-wrought posts sustain,
Where hungry vermin strive to climb in vain;
And many an ash that wild around them grows,
And many an elm that shelter o'er them throws.
    Then round the moat we turn, with pales enclos'd,
And midst the orchard's trees in rows dispos'd,
Whose boughs thick tufts of misletoe adorn
With fruit of lucid white on joints of yellow borne.

work by the sound of a horn. This practice, as well as that of the harvest-shouting, seems much on the decline. The latter could boast its origin from high antiquity, as appears from that beautiful stroke of eastern poetry, Isaiah, chap. xvi.:
" I will water thee with my tears, O Heshbon and Elealeh; for the shouting for thy summer fruits, and for thy harvest, is fallen!"
    [4] That well-known beautiful flowering evergreen, commonly called laurustinus.

    Thence up the lane, romantic woods among,
Beneath old oaks with ivy overhung,
(O'er their rough trunks the hairy stalks entwine,
And on their arms the sable berries shine:)
Here oft the sight, on banks bestrewn with leaves,
The early primrose' opening bud perceives;
And oft steep dells or ragged cliffs unfold
The prickly furze with bloom of brightest gold;
Here oft the red-breast hops along the way,
And midst grey moss explores his insect prey;
Or the green woodspite [5] flies with outcry shrill,
And delves the sere bough with his sounding bill;
Or the rous'd hare starts rustling from the brake,
And gaudy jays incessant clamour make;
Or echoing hills return from stubbles nigh
The sportsman's gun, and spaniel's yelping cry.
    And now the covert ends in open ground,
That spreads wide views beneath us all around;
There turbid waters, edg'd with yellow reeds,
Roll through the russet herd-forsaken meads;
There from the meads th' enclosures sloping rise,
And, midst th' enclosures, dusky woodland lies;
While pointed spires and curling smokes, between,
Mark towns, and vills, and cottages unseen.
And now,—for now the breeze and noontide ray
Clear the last remnants of the mist away,—
Far, far o'er all extends the aching eye,
Where azure mountains mingle with the sky:
To these the curious optic tube applied
Reveals each object distance else would hide;
Their seats or homesteads, plac'd in pleasant shades,
Show their white walls and windows through the glades;
There rears the hamlet church its hoary tow'r;
(The clock's bright index points the passing hour)
There green-rob'd huntsmen o'er the sunny lawn
Lead home their beagles from the chase withdrawn,
And ploughs slow-moving turn the broad champaign,
And on steep summits feed the fleecy train.
    But wint'ry months few days like these supply,
And their few moments far too swiftly fly:
Dank thaws, chill fogs, rough winds, and beating rain,
To sheltering rooms th' unwilling step detain;
Yet there, my friend, shall liberal Science find
Amusement various for th' inquiring mind.
    While History's hand her sanguine record brings,
With woes of nations fraught, and crimes of kings;
Plague thins the street, and Famine blasts the plain,
War wields his sword, Oppression binds his chain;
Curiosity pursues the unfolding tale,
Which Reason blames, and Pity's tears bewail.
    While Fancy's pow'rs th' eventful novel frame,
And Virtue's care directs its constant aim;
As Fiction's pen domestic life pourtrays,
Its hopes, and fears, and joys, and griefs displays;
By Grandison's or Clinton's [6] story mov'd,
We read delighted, and we rise improv'd.
    Then with bold voyagers our thought explores
Vast tracts of ocean and untrodden shores;
Now views rude climes, where ice-rocks drear aspire,
Or red volcanos shoot their streams of fire:

    [5] The green woodpecker. Vide Pennant's British Zoology, folio, p. 78.
    [6] Vide The Fool of Quality, a well-known novel, by Mr. Henry Brooke, author of Gustavus Vasa, &c.

Now seeks sweet isles, where lofty palm-groves wave,
And cany banks translucent rivers lave;
Where Plenty's gifts luxuriant load the soil,
And Ease reposes, charm'd with Beauty's smile.
Such, hapless Cook[7]! amid the southern main,
Rose thy Taheitè's peaks and flow'ry plain;—
Why, daring wanderer! quit that blissful land,
To seek new dangers on a barbarous strand?
Why doom'd, so long escap'd from storms and foes,
Upon that strand thy dying eyes to close;
Remote each place by habit render'd dear,
Nor British friends nor Otaheitean near?

Nor less than books the engraver's works invite,
Where past and distant come before the sight;
Where, all the painter's lively tints convey'd,
The skilful copyist gives in light and shade:
While faithful views the prospect's charms display,
From coast to coast, and town to town, we stray;
While faithful portraits human features trace,
We gaze delighted on the speaking face;
Survey the port that bards and heroes bore,
Or mark the smiles that high-born beauties wore.

Cease these to please? Philosophy attends
With arts where knowledge with diversion blends;
The Sun's vast system in a model shows;
Bids the clear lens new forms to sight expose;
Constructs machines, whose wondrous powers de-
Th' effects of light, and properties of air; [clare
With whirling globes excites electric fires,
And all their force and all their use inquires.
O Nature! how immense thy secret store,
Beyond what ev'n a Priestley can explore!

Such, friend, the employments may his time
       divide,
Whom rural shades from scenes of business hide;
While o'er his ear unnotic'd glide away
The noise and nonsense of the passing day[8]!

---

## AN ESSAY ON PAINTING.

### TO A YOUNG ARTIST.

---

The author had conceived a design of writing a
  pretty extensive poem on the subject of painting, long before Mr. Hayley's ingenious Poetical
  Epistle to an eminent Painter appeared. That
  performance anticipated and precluded part of
  his intended work, but seemed not to render the
  suppression of the following lines necessary.

---

FROM sunny Adria's sea-surrounded tow'rs,
From Tiber's vales and Arno's viny bow'rs,
The Muse of painting seeks Britannia's plain,
And leads to Thames's bank her favourite train:

[7] This celebrated circumnavigator, after sur-
mounting numerous difficulties, and escaping many
dangers, was at length slain by the inhabitants of
Owhyhee, a little island in the Pacific Ocean.

[8] A short Epistle, partly on the same plan as
the foregoing, was, some years ago, inadvertently
suffered to appear in a Collection of Poems, by
several hands, published by G. Pearch.—Such lines
of that piece as were thought worth preservation,
are here retained.

There, where a nation's wealth her dome has plac'd,
With her kind sister's[1] Attic beauties grac'd,
She, like the Spring, as liberal and as gay,
Bids her rich hand its annual stores display;
And mimic Being glowing round the walls,
From scene to scene the rapt attention calls.
There, where the public gives the palm of praise,
And only Merit to renown can raise,
Doubtless, my friend, the just ambition's thine
To see thy future works distinguish'd shine.
Hear then thy poet's monitory lay,
That hints not useless may perchance convey:
No artist I, like him of Gallia's shore[2],
Whose pencil practis'd, ere he taught his lore;
Yet Taste incites me others' works to view,
And risk a judgment haply not untrue.

Were Painting's path my pleasing road to fame,
The choice of subject much my care should claim;
His graphic pow'r he sure but ill bestows,
Who best a trifle's nice resemblance shows.
Though the rich tints so finely blended fall,
When carps and pheasants deck the rural hall,
That oft, like Zeuxis' grapes, they scarcely fail
To tempt to touch the feather or the scale;—
Yet not ev'n Elmer's[3] skill can make us prize
What ev'ry field or ev'ry pond supplies;
Regret gives pain to view such wondrous art
Tried on no theme that interests the heart.
The pride of genius should thy hand restrain
From all that life's inferior ranks contain[4];
Thy conscious pallet ne'er its hues should spare
To draw a sportsman's hound or racer's mare;
Nor thy reluctant crayon stoop to trace
A fool's dull eye or villain's ill-mark'd face.

But deem not portrait's gifts I mean to slight,—
Portrait, the source of many a pure delight!
When bards' or sages' works our wishes fire
To see their forms whose minds we there admire,
The featur'd canvass full to view displays
Reason's deep calm or Fancy's glowing rays.
When Beauty's charms their varied graces wear,
Love's gentle smile, or Mirth's vivacious air,
The pleasing image strikes remotest climes,
And goes unalter'd down to distant times.
When Death's relentless hand in dust has laid
The school-companion, or the first-lov'd maid;
The father kind, with filial awe rever'd;
The tender mother, by her cares endear'd;
When from our arms the darling child is torn,
Or when the husband or the wife we mourn—
As on their picture many a glance we cast,
Remembrance wanders to the vanish'd past;

[1] Architecture.
[2] C. A. Du Fresnoy, a well-known French painter;
author of a Latin poem, De Arte Graphica.
[3] The author must here once for all remark,
that whatever he may say respecting the works of
any painter, is solely the result of impartial, though
possibly mistaken opinion. He cannot be misled
by friendship; for, excepting a slight acquaintance
with those amiable characters, Mr. West and Mrs.
Kauffman, he has not the pleasure of knowing any
artist whose name he has taken the liberty to mention.
[4] This is meant only of such objects, when considered as the principal subject of a picture. Almost every class of animals may be occasionally
introduced as ornaments in landscape, and often
in history.

Our thoughts o'er numberless minutiæ roll,
And pain-mix'd pleasure solaces the soul.
To portrait's study should thy choice incline,
Ev'n there to aim at excellence be thine ;
And strive to reach the point that few can gain,
Preserve the likeness, yet the spirit retain.

Of landscape's province wide extends the range,
From the deep vale and humble rural grange,
To Cambrian heaths sublimely brown and bare [5],
Or Alpine ice-points glitt'ring white in air :
And not from Nature only she designs,
But different parts of different scenes combines;
Or new creations of her own she forms,
Illumes with sunshine, or involves in storms [6].

Familiar prospects would thy hand bestow ?
Mark what our hay-fields and our hop-grounds
        show ;
Where in neat rows the russet cocks are seen,
Or from tall poles depend festoons of green;
And long straight paths in perspective extend,
And yellow sandhills close behind ascend [7].
Nor sweeter contrast sure can meet the eye
Than village lanes in vernal months supply,
When amber clouds, in sky of soft bright blue,
Hang o'er the copse just crown'd with verdure
        new ;
Or where the orchard's sun-gilt branches spread
Their bloom of white or faintly-blushing red.
The fairest scenes, when peopled, look more fair,
But these to people asks peculiar care :
We wish not here for Virgil's classic swains,
Nor Dryad nymphs light tripp'ng o'er the plains ;
Nor yet the grinning Hobbinols of Gay,
Nor cottage Marians in their torn array :
The rustic life, in ev'ry varied place,
Can boast its few of beauty and of grace ;
From them select the forms that most may please,
And clothe with simple elegance and ease :
Such forms in Smith's [8] delightful spots we prize,
And such in Sandby's pleasant fields arise.

The observant artist much from travel gains ;
Increase of knowledge well rewards his pains.
Now his pleas'd eye o'er Tuscan prospects roves,
Their sunny corn-fields and their cypress groves ;
Their roads, where sports from tree to tree the
        vine,
And through broad leaves its crystal clusters shine [9];
Their white cassines, with olive groves around ;
And glitt'ring cliffs with towns and castles crown'd.
Now his pleas'd step a wider circuit tries,
Where Nile's vast flood on Egypt's level lies ;
While midst the tide tall palms their tops uprear,
And causeways broad and cities fair appear [10].

[5] That celebrated artist, Mr. Wilson, has painted
a set of beautiful Views from Nature, in different
parts of Wales.
[6] These circumstances, termed by the painters
*accidents of nature*, often agreeably diversify landscape.
[7] For this imagery the author is indebted to Mr.
Walpole, who in his Anecdotes of Painting, vol. iv.
p. 65, proposes our hay-fields and hop-grounds as
new subjects of landscape.
[8] The late Mr. George Smith of Chichester.
[9] The hedge-row trees in Tuscany are covered
with vines. Vide Smollet's Travels, vol. ii. p. 46.
[10] Vide Rollin's Ancient History, 18mo. vol. i.
p. 22.

Now Indian climes he east or west explores,
Quits the dull factory and the sandy shores [11],
Climbs craggy hills, pervades romantic woods,
Or winds along the cataracts of the floods ;
Through beasts, and birds, and insects, fruits and
        flow'rs,
In shape and colour all distinct from ours ;
Or strays o'er isles that spicy vales unfold,
Midst skies of glory and midst seas of gold ;
Such skies, such seas, as Hodges' pencil drew,
And round the rocks of Ulitea threw [12].

Whate'er we copy, or whate'er we feign,
Through all the piece one character should reign :
When Claude's bright morn on Mola's precincts
        dawns,
What sweet quiescence marks the groves and lawns!
How calm his herds among the ruins graze !
How calm his curious peasant stands to gaze [13]!
When bold Salvator under turbid skies
Bids his scath'd hills and blasted trees arise,
Behind wild rocks bids his wild streams be lost,
And from vast cliffs shows broken fragments tost ;
Midst them no shepherds lead their flocks along,
Nor village maidens seem to tune their song ;
But solemn augurs flights of birds survey,
Or stern-ey'd robbers wait the passing prey [14].
In Rubens' forest, when the wounded boar,
Plung'd in the stream, attempts the further shore,
How the fierce dogs retard his awkward speed !
How the fierce hunters urge the straining steed !
And, eager, one the winged arrow sends,
And one firm-fix'd th' expectant spear protends [15].

        To History's group, where passion'd thought ex-
        press'd
Strikes kindred feelings on the gazer's breast,—
To History's group, the epic of thy art,
Proceed we now, and what we can, impart.
The mighty masters of Italian name
All Rome, all Florence, and Bo'ogna claim ;
Whose fresco forms still animate their walls,
Whose living canvass decks their domes and halls :
What various pow'rs for these their glory won,
And what of theirs to choose, and what to shun,
Illustrious Reynolds much in prose has told,
And more my verse pretends not to unfold.
These still thy study but with caution make,
Nor prize the picture for the painter's sake ;

[11] Several of our artists have attended to this
circumstance of foreign scenery. The ingenious
Mr. George Robertson has painted several fine romantic views in Jamaica, which have been engraved.
[12] Several beautiful landscapes, taken in different
parts of the new discovered islands, by Mr. Hodges,
who attended captain Cook in one of his voyages,
must be well remembered by those who attend the
annual exhibitions of the Royal Academy.
[13] Vide a beautiful engraving, by Vivarez, from
a capital picture of Claude Lorrain, called the
Morning, in which he introduces himself drawing
an antique temple on the banks of the Tiber, between Ponte Mola and Rome.
[14] Vide Salvator Rosa's landscapes, engraved
by Goupy. See also sir Joshua Reynold's Discourses, p. 175.
[15] Vide Rubens's landscape of boar-hunting,
engraved by Bolswert.

Raffaelle himself, beneath himself oft fell,
And meaner hands' best works his worst excel [16].
'T is general nature, in thy art and mine,
Must give our fame in future times to shine:
Sublime and pathos, like the Sun's fix'd flame,
Remain, and please through ev'ry age the same;
Humour's light shapes, like vapours in the sky,
Rise, pass, and vary, and for ever fly:
Hogarth and Swift, if living, might deplore
Half their keen jokes, that now are jokes no more.

What Truth's rich page of real event supplies,
What Fancy's pow'rs of fabled act devise,
Before thee lie—but where the field so wide,
There Judgment's hand Selection's step must guide.
To Horrour's forms the mind aversion feels,
To Spaniolet's [17] flay'd saints and torturing wheels;
Nor praise for nauseous images we win,
For Spenser's Errour, or for Milton's Sin.

Mythology, that Greek enchantress, long
Has reign'd the idol of the painting throng:
But Reason's thought disdains Ovidian dreams
Absurd, of nymphs transform'd to trees and streams;
And Virtue Homer's wanton gods abhors,
With all their lewd amours and all their idle wars.
The battle's conflicts ample scope bestow,
Th' effects of fury, fear, and pain to show;
As different features these unlike express,
The contrast's force affects us more or less.
But here Confusion holds his crowded reign,
And the tir'd eye attempts to rest in vain;
And o'er the scene Humanity complains, [tains.
Where mangled corses lie, and blood the land dis-
When in the fore-ground kings or generals stand,
Direct the attack, or head the charging band,
Their graceful forms we unconcern'd survey,
Who fight for conquest, or who fight for pay:
Nor in their postures can there much be prais'd,
Their pistols levell'd, or their falchions rais'd;
And to dull sameness here so oft we fall,
That who beholds one piece, beholds them all.

But War's dire field, not all confin'd to these,
Affords us often incidents that please:
For oft the historian's, oft the poet's art,
Can win our wishes on some hero's part;
His country nam'd, his place and parents known,
Our busy thought his perils makes its own.
To fierce Pelides, midst Scamander's waves,
When young Lycaon's voice for pity craves [18];
The chief's stern brow and lance suspended high,
The youth's bent knee and deprecating eye,

Not West's rich pencil need disdain to trace,
Or Romney's stroke with glowing colours grace.
When Dithyrambus, on Oëta's plain,
Mourns the brave Persian whom his hand has slain,
Nor marks his danger from th' approaching foe,
Nor his bold friend prepar'd to ward the blow;
In one what grief, in one what vengeful rage,
In one what ardour, might the sight engage [19]!
The gentle Kauffman's traits can best declare
The sentimental feelings of the fair,
When soft Erminia in the sylvan shade
Leaves Tancred's name on ev'ry tree display'd [20];
Or kind Louisa pens the friendly scroll,
To sooth the mournful sister of her soul [21].
The same skill'd hand more strong expression tries,
At Edward's feet when Woodville's daughter lies [22];
Or, midst th' admiring weeping train around,
Fond Eleanora sucks the poison'd wound [23].
Delightful artist!—Grace her pencil guides,
And Delicacy o'er its stroke presides!
Th' immortal swans, appointed to redeem
Genius and Worth from Lethe's silent stream,
Pleas'd with their charge, shall bear her medall'd name
To the fair priestess of the fane of Fame [24].
Such tender subjects, if thy choice they gain,
Enough for thee as yet untouch'd remain.
Now from the page of Richardson bestow
On Clementina's face the lines of woe;
Or let sweet Harriet's livelier beauty wear
The soul-fraught eye and apprehensive air;
Or draw the proud Olivia's rage-flush'd charms,
When the calm hero seiz'd her deadly arms;

Achilles, at the moment when the death of Patroclus, occurring to his thought, determined him to kill Lycaon, would afford a fine expression:

> Talk not of life or ransom, he replies;
> Patroclus dead, whoever meets me dies.

[19] Vide Leonidas, book viii. l. 355.

> He ended, rushing furious on the Greek,
> Who, while his gallant enemy expir'd,
> While Hyperanthes tenderly receiv'd
> The last embraces of his gasping friend,
> Stood nigh reclin'd in sadness on his shield,
> And in the pride of victory repin'd.
> Unmark'd his foe approach'd. But forward sprung
> Diomedon. Before the Thespian youth
> Aloft he rais'd his targe——

[20] Vide Tasso's Jerusalem Delivered.

[21] See Emma Corbett, an interesting novel, by Mr. S. I. Pratt, vol. i. letter 34.

[22] See the story of Elizabeth Grey, daughter of sir Richard Woodville, suing to Edward IV. for restitution of her lands. Rapin, vol. i. p. 601.

[23] The well-known story of Eleanor of Castile, queen of Edward I. sucking the poison from her husband's arm, when he was wounded by an assassin in Palestine.

[24] See a painting of Mrs. Kauffman's, from a passage in Ariosto, where swans are introduced bringing the names of ingenious persons, inscribed on medals, to a nymph who deposits them in the temple of Fame.

[16] For this assertion the author has the highest authority, viz. that of sir Joshua Reynolds. "I have no desire," says he, "to degrade Raffaelle from the high rank he deservedly holds; but, in comparing him with himself, he does not appear to me to be the same man in oil as in fresco." Discourses, p. 165.

[17] Gioseppe Ribera, a native of Valencia in Spain. He was noted for painting horrid subjects; such as Prometheus with the vulture feeding on his liver; Ixion tortured on the wheel; and St. Bartholomew with the skin flayed from his body. Vide Dryden's translation of Fresnoy, p. 352.

[18] Vide the Iliad, book xxi. This story of Lycaon is perhaps one of the most affecting passages in the whole poem. Vide Pope's note, vol. v. p. 208. of his translation. The countenance of

And paint that hero, firm in trial prov'd,
Unaw'd by danger, and by vice unmov'd [25].
To Sterne's soft maniac let thy hand impart
The languid cheek, the look that pierc'd his heart,
When to her virgin saint the vesper song she rais'd,
Or earnest view'd him as he sat and gaz'd [26].
Mark, if thou can'st, philanthropy divine,
That swells the breast, and bids the features shine,
When the tear glist'ning starts from Toby's eyes
Fix'd on the couch where poor Le Fevre dies.

The Grecian classics' venerable lore
I see thee often diligent explore;
What Homer's Muse to Chian cities taught,
Or Pity's priest [27] to Athens' audience brought.
Methinks, now rising from thy plastic hand,
Troy's hoary monarch shall a suppliant stand;
To stern Achilles all his griefs explain,
And ask his Hector's corse, nor ask in vain [28].
Now Jove's kind son to Thebes's sorrowing king
Shall his restor'd unknown Alcestis bring;
Admetus' eyes his anguish'd thoughts declare,
And turn disgusted from the proffer'd fair [29].

The dark sublime of extra-natural scenes
The vulgar magic's puerile rite demeans;
Where hags their caldrons fraught with toads pre-
pare,
Or glide on broomsticks through the midnight air.
Chain'd on the rock let bold Prometheus lie,
And cast wild looks, upbraiding, to the sky [30];
Bid Milton's Satan from the burning steep
Call his wide legions, slumb'ring on the deep;
Or Camoens' spirit of the Cape upraise,
And show him only by the lightning's blaze;
Or place sad Hosier's ghost amid the tide,
Where by the pale Moon anchor'd navies ride [31].
O where is he, whose thought such grandeur gave
To bold Fitzwalter and the barons brave,

[25] The History of sir Charles Grandison, vol. iv. p. 176. The interview between Grandison and Olivia, at the instant of his seizing her poinard, would make a noble picture. This work of Richardson's abounds with fine situations. Brookes's Fool of Quality, and the Adventurer of Hawkesworth, are also books worthy the perusal of an artist who wishes for choice of interesting incidents.

[26] This subject has been attempted by several ingenious artists, who have given very pleasing figures; but perhaps none that convey the precise idea of Sterne. This author being mentioned, a trite observation must be indulged, viz. That there probably never was a more striking instance of mis-application of talents than in him. With superior powers for the pathos, he chose to descend to ribaldry, that affronted the taste and corrupted the morals of the public. What pity that the gold had not been separated from the dross, and the latter consigned to that oblivion it so richly merits!

[27] Euripides.

[28] Vide the Iliad, book xxiv.

[29] Vide the Alcestis of Euripides. Hercules restores to life Alcestis, the deceased wife of Admetus, and brings her to her husband, disguised with a veil, and represented as a stranger; whom Admetus, in the height of distress for the loss of his beloved consort, refuses to admit into his palace.

[30] See the Prometheus of Æschylus.

[31] See that admirable song, entitled Hosier's Ghost; by the author of Leonidas.

When, rang'd in arms along their Thames's strand,
They snatch'd their charter from a tyrant's hand [32]?
Through all the scenes his rapid stroke bestow'd,
Rosa's wild grace and daring spirit glow'd;
In him—ah, lost ere half his powers were shown!—
Britain perhaps an Angelo had known!
Would'st thou his honours emulous pursue,
And give the patriot energy to view,—
Deep in the gloom of Dalecarlia's mine,
Bid Freedom's flame in Vasa's visage shine [33];
The pass of fam'd Thermopylæ display,
And Sparta's monarch's port august portray [34].
For pontiffs and for kings, the painter's skill
From sacred story toils their walls to fill;
Where'er we turn, its subjects strike the eye,
And few untried are left for us to try.
Yet who has Jepthah's matchless woe express'd,
By his lov'd daughter's sudden sight distress'd;
Or shown the patriarchs, struck with wild amaze,
As on the viceroy's hidden cup they gaze [35]?
Or who, when Israel's hosts on Edom's plain
Despairing lie,—a thirst-afflicted train!—
Has bade the prophet and his minstrel stand,
And call new waters o'er the burning sand [36]?
When David's chiefs, with gen'rous thought inspir'd,
Bring the clear wave his sick'ning soul desir'd;
What dignity might to his act be given,
The pure libation pouring out to Heaven [37]!
No more of theme; design must now succeed—
The mind's strong picture when we hear or read [38],
Where every person finds his proper place,
And turn of attitude and turn of face:

[32] Vide the late Mr. Mortimer's picture of king John delivering magna charta to the barons. That ingenious artist's obvious powers of imagination promised the attainment of a high degree of excellence in his profession.

[33] Brooke's Gustavus Vasa, act i. scene 2. where Gustavus discovers himself to Anderson and Arnoldus in the copper-mines of Dalecarlia, See another fine subject in the same Tragedy, act iv. scene xi.

[34] Vide Leonidas, book x. where the hero of the poem repeats to the assembled council the message of Argestes; while Alpheus, at the same instant, brings news of the Persians having passed the Upper Strait. This would make a noble picture; the dauntless appearance of the Greeks might be well contrasted with the fear and shame of the ambassador of Xerxes. The banquet of Melissa, priestess of the Muses, where Leonidas and Æschylus are supposed present, book vii. is another fine subject. Such pictures would hardly be popular; but to some minds they would afford singular pleasure.

[35] The author does not recollect seeing or hearing of any celebrated picture on those interesting subjects, of Jepthah's return, and the discovery of Joseph's cup in the sack of Benjamin.

[36] Vide 2 Kings, chap. iii. This subject would afford a variety of noble expression in the different characters of the kings, the pious confidence of Jehosaphat, and the desponding anxiety of Jehoram, the distress of the soldiers, and the enthusiasm of Elisha. The streams of water might appear in the distance, seemingly visible only to the prophet, from his situation.

[37] 2 Samuel, chap. xxiii.

[38] See sir Joshua Reynolds's Discourses, p. 104.

ESSAY ON PAINTING.

The artist's powers in this must greatly fail,
Whose figures point not out at once his tale [39].
When Lystra's crowd around the apostles throng,
And joyful lead the victim ox along ;
Ask we the cause, while he that cause explains
Whose limb, late useless, strength and use ob-
tains [40]?
When West's young warrior, bleeding on the ground,
His mournful group of martial friends surround ;
Their gallant gen'ral instantly we know,
Their griefs, their cares, his life's importance show ;
Quebec's proud tower, the encount'ring troops be-
tween,
In distant view discriminates the scene [41].
As in the drama all events should tend
In course unbroken to the purpos'd end ;
So must the picture's business still maintain
The same connective unity of train.
When Copley's youth, swift struggling through the
wave,
The anxious boatmen strain each nerve to save ;
As strives the rav'nous shark to reach his prey,
One lifts the javelin to arrest his way ;
And now, as near his dreadful jaws expand,
One casts the cord, and one extends the hand :
What care, what pity, mark their eager eyes !
What hopes, what terrours, in our bosoms rise [42] !
The skilful painter, at whose option lie
Positions various, fails not all to try ;
And those prefers, where every part the best
Accordance keeps, illustrating the rest.
By different modes effect he oft obtains ;
To one chief figure now the attention gains ;
Now force on second characters bestows,
And all his meaning by reflection shows ;
Now through the whole, each rank, and sex, and
age,
One common ruling passion bids engage.
When Raffaelle's Saviour from the tomb ascends,
Such majesty and grace his presence blends,
That the fix'd eye contemplates him alone,
Nor heeds th' astonish'd guards around him
thrown [43].
When Vandyke's gen'ral, whose victorious spear
Sunk Persia's pride, and check'd the Goth's career,
Of service paid with indigence complains,
And sightless age on daily alms sustains ;
As the young chief th' affecting scene surveys,
How all his form the emotion'd soul betrays !

" O, thus has Fortune for the brave decreed ?
Of toils and dangers this at last the meed [44] ?"
When Rome's fair princess, who from Syrian shore
Her late lost consort's sacred ashes bore,
With steps slow-moving o'er Brundusium's strand,
Meets her lov'd friends—a numerous mourning
band—
Her gentle frame no gestures rude disgrace, [
No vulgar grief deforms her beauteous face ;
Her downcast eyes immoveable remain,
Fix'd on the urn her careful hands sustain.
The widow'd mother, by her garment's folds,
Close on each side each tender offspring holds ;
While melancholy all the train o'ershades,
Of hoary warriors and of blooming maids ;
And all their breasts with pity seem to heave,
And for the dead and for the living grieve [45].
The great sublime with energy to express
Exert thy utmost power, nor fear excess.
When passion's tumults in the bosom rise,
Inflate the features, and enrage the eyes ;
To Nature's outline can we draw too true,
Or Nature's colours give too full to view ?
Did Reynolds' hand with force too strong disclose
Those looks that mark th' unutterable woes,
When Ugoline the wretch in prison lies,
And hears his dying children's piercing cries,
And while fell Hunger haunts the impervious walls,
And one by one the suffering victims calls,
Invokes the lightning's bolt those walls to rend,
Or earth to open, and his miseries end [46] ?
Our bards indeed, I own, here often fail,
And spoil with bombast and conceit their tale ;
Their heroes rant in many a curious strain
Of thought, that none could think in anger or in pain.
Celestial scenes with caution must be tried,
Where knowledge fails, and fancy sole can guide :
The great First Cause no form reveals to sight,
We mark his presence by excess of light [47] ;
While angel shapes at ease on wing remain,
Or on thin clouds their airy steps sustain.
But though, fair Painting ! thus by just design,
And strong expression, much to please is thine ;
Yet not from these thy utmost praises rise,
For useful moral oft thy work supplies.
When, midst Poussin's Arcadian vale serene,
The virgin's sculptur'd monument is seen,
And the sad shepherd pointing seems to say,
" O Death, no place is sacred from thy sway !"
Our mournful thoughts the well-known truth recall,
That youth and beauty oft untimely fall [48].

[39] " That composition must be defective, which
cannot, to a careful observer, point out its own
tendency ; and those expressions must be either
weak or false, which do not in some degree mark
the interest of each actor in the drama." Webb's
Inquiry into the Beauties of Painting, Preface, p. 8.
[40] Vide Raffaelle's St. Paul and Barnabas at
Lystra. For the above observation and description the author is indebted to the ingenious Inquiry into the Beauties of Painting, p. 180.
[41] Vide West's celebrated picture of the death
of general Wolfe, engraved by Woollett.
[42] See Mr. Copley's picture of a youth rescued
by sailors from a shark, in the harbour of the Ha-
vannah. There is a fine mezzotinto of this piece
by Green.
[43] Raffaelle's picture of the resurrection of
Christ, engraved by Vivarez and Grignion from a
drawing of Dalton.

[44] Vide the Belisarius of Vandyke ; engraved
by Goupy and Scotin.
[45] This capital picture of Agrippina landing at
Brundusium, with the ashes of Germanicus, is, in
the author's opinion, one of Mr. West's most pleasing compositions. There is a beautiful print of it
by Earlom.
[46] Vide sir Joshua Reynolds's excellent picture
of count Ugolino and his children in the dungeon ;
where they were confined and starved to death by
the archbishop Puggieri. This circumstance is
described by the Italian poet Dante.
[47] The author could not here omit censuring the
practice of some celebrated painters, who have
presumptuously and absurdly represented the Supreme Being in the form of an aged man.
[48] Vide Poussin's picture, called The Shepherds
in Arcadia ; engraved by Ravenet, in Mr. Boydell's

On Carthage' plains when Marius meets the eye,
And the stern prætor's mandate bids him fly;
Fresh from the view the strong reflection springs,
How strange the vast vicissitude of things!
Rome's rival city to the dust depress'd;
Her haughty consul there denied to rest [49]!
When Persia's conqueror, midst her female train,
Appears the chaste, the gen'rous, and humane;
His looks, his act on, on the mind impress
The needful knowledge how to bear success [50].

Thus may thy art, O friend, for ever prove
Of force, to virtue, and from vice to move!
To statesmen, thoughtless on the heights of pow'r,
Mark Wolsey's fall, or show his final hour;
To patriot eyes give Marvell's calm disdain,
When Danby urg'd the tempting bribe in vain [51];
Or bid the inconstant her own doom deplore
In the sad exit of the hapless Shore [52].

Without the entheus Nature's self bestows,
The world no painter nor no poet knows:
But think not mind in its own depth contains
A source of wealth that no disbursement drains:
Quick observation, ever on the wing,
Home, like the bee, its useful stores must bring;
From hills, and vales, and rocks, and streams, and trees,
And towns, and all that people those and these;
From meanest objects that may hints inspire,
Discolour'd walls, or heaps of g owing fire [53].
Care too beside thee still must take her place,
Ret uch each stroke, and polish every grace;
For when we join not dignity with ease,
Nor thou canst paint, nor I can write, to please.

Perfection's point the artist nearest gains,
Who with his work unsatisfy'd remains:
Da Vinci's thought an excellence conceiv'd,
That his eye miss'd in all his hand achiev'd [54].
The clear-obscure how happiest to produce,
And what of various tints the various use,
My lay to that presumes not to aspire,
Nor with trite precept this thy ear shall tire:
Coreggio's practice that describes the best:
In Fresnoy's theory this we find express'd.
No rude incongruence should thy piece disgrace,
No motley modes of diff'rent time and place;
By Grecian chiefs no Gallic airs be worn [55],
Nor in their hands be modern weapons borne;
Nor mix the crested helm and coat of mail
With the vast curl'd peruke, or pointed tail.

---

collection of prints: also the abbé Du Bos's Reflections on Poetry, Painting, and Music; and Dr. Warton's ingenious Essay on Didactic Poetry, in his translation of Virgil.

[49] There is a fine picture of Mortimer's on this subject. The reply of Marius to the messenger who came with orders for him to depart, was nobly concise and affecting: " Go, tell the prætor thou hast seen Marius sitting on the ruins of Carthage."

[50] Vide Le Brun's Alexander in the tent of Darius, engraved by Edelinck.

[51] See the Life of Andrew Marvell, in Cibber's Lives of the Poets.

[52] The interview between Shore and her husband, in the last scene of Rowe's tragedy, would afford a fine picture.

[53] Vide Reynold's Discourses, p. 61.

[54] Vide Graham's Account of Painters, in Dryden's Fresnoy, p. 278.

[55] Vide Reynolds's Discourses, p. 87.

---

And sacred ever be the solemn scene
From base intrusion of burlesque and mean;
Nor in a patriarch's or apostle's sight
Set snarling dogs and growling cats to fight.

One caution further must the Muse impart;
Shun naked form, that scandal of thy art:
Even Dryden blames them who refuse to spare
The painful blushes of the modest fair.
Let Decency her veil of drapery throw,
And Grace diffuse its folds in easy flow [56].

And now, my friend, for thee may Fortune find
Employ congenial to thy liberal mind;
Not tasks impos'd by power, or chosen for gain,
Begun reluctant, and pursu'd with pain.
What warms the heart, the hand with force reveals,
And all that force the charm'd spectator feels:
For genius, piercing as the electric flame,
When wak'd in one, in others wakes the same.

# SONNETS.

The following Sonnets, and the Stanzas addressed to Mrs. Macaulay, appeared in Pearch's Collection of Poems published in 1770. The remaining pieces are now first printed.

## SONNET I.

### APOLOGY FOR RETIREMENT. 1766.

Why asks my friend what cheers my passing day,
Where these lone fields my rural home enclose,
That all the pomp the crowded city shows
Ne'er from that home allures my steps away?

Now through the upland shade I musing stray,
And catch the gale that o'er the woodbine blows;
Now in the meads on river banks repose,
And breathe rich odour from the new-mown hay:

Now pleas'd I read the poet's lofty lay,
Where music fraught with useful knowledge flows;
Now Delia's converse makes the moments gay,
The maid for love and innocence I chose:
O friend! the man who joys like these can taste,
On vice and folly needs no hour to waste.

## SONNET II.

### TO DELIA. 1766.

Thrice has the year its vary'd circuit run,
And swiftly, Delia, have the moments flown,
Since with my love for thee my care begun,
To improve thy tender mind to science prone.

The flatteries of my sex I bade thee shun,
I bade thee shun the manners of thy own;
Fictitious manners, by example won,
That ill for loss of innocence atone!

[56] Vide Dryden's preface to his translation of Fresnoy's Art of Painting, p. 22, &c. where the licence of painters, in the above respect, is severely censured.

Say, gen'rous maiden, in whose gentle breast
Dwells simple Nature, undisguis'd by art,
Now amply tried by time's unerring test,
How just the dictates of this faithful heart;
Which, with the joys thy fav'ring smiles impart,
Deems all its care repaid, itself supremely bless'd.

## SONNET III.

### AFTER READING SHENSTONE'S ELEGIES. 1766.

The gentle Shenstone much of Fortune 'plain'd,
Where Nature's hand the liberal spirit gave ;
Partial, her bounty she too oft restrain'd,
But pour'd it full on Folly's tasteless slave.

By her alike my humble prayer disdain'd,
She stern denies the only boon I crave ;
O'er my fields, fair as those Elysian feign'd,
To bid the green walk wind, the green wood wave.

On the high hill to raise the higher tower,
To ope wide prospects over distant plains,
Where by broad rivers towns and villas rise ;
Taste prompts the wish, but Fortune bounds the
        power :
Yet while Health cheers, and Competence sustains,
These more than all, Contentment bids me prize.

## SONNET IV.

### PREFIXED TO LANGHORNE'S POETICAL WORKS.
1766.

Langhorne! unknown to me (sequester'd swain!)
Save by the Muse's soul-enchanting lay,
To kindred spirits never sung in vain ;
Accept the tribute of this light essay.

Sweet are thy songs, they oft amuse my day
Of Fancy's visions, while I hear thee 'plain,
While Scotland's honours claim thy pastoral strain,
Or Music comes o'er Handel tears to pay.

For all thy Irwan's flow'ry banks display,
Thy Persian lover, and his Indian fair ;
For all Theodosius' mournful lines convey,
When Pride and Avarice part a matchless pair ;
Receive just praise, and wreaths that ne'er decay,
By Fame and Virtue twin'd for thee to wear.

## SONNET V.

### TO BRITAIN. 1766.

Renown'd Britannia! lov'd parental land !
Regard thy welfare with a watchful eye !
Whene'er the weight of Want's afflicting hand
Wakes in thy vales the poor's persuasive cry—

When wealth enormous sets the oppressor high,
When bribes thy ductile senators command,
And slaves in office freemens' rights withstand ;
Then mourn, for then thy fate approacheth nigh !

Not from perfidious Gaul or haughty Spain,
Nor all the neighb'ring nations of the main,
VOL. XVII.

Though leagued in war tremendous round thy shore—
But from thyself, thy ruin must proceed !
Nor boast thy power ; for know it is decreed,
Thy freedom lost, thy power shall be no more !

## STANZAS

### ON READING

### MRS. MACAULEY'S HISTORY OF ENGLAND. 1766.

To Albion's bards the Muse of history spoke :
  " Record the glories of your native land,
How Power's rude chain her sons' brave efforts broke,
  And the keen scourge tore from Oppression's
        hand.

" Give to renown the patriot's noble deeds ;
  Brand with disgrace the tyrant's hated name ;
Though Falsehood oft awhile the mind misleads,
  Impartial Time bestows impartial fame."

She said ; and soon the lofty lyre they strung,
  But artful chang'd the subject and the lore ;
Of kings, and courts, and courtly slaves they sung,
  And gloss'd with vain applause their actions o'er.

The servile strain the Muse indignant heard ;
  Anxious for truth, for public virtue warm,
She Freedom's faithful advocate appear'd,
  And bore on Earth the fair Macaulay's form.

## ELEGY

### IN THE MANNER OF HAMMOND ;

### SUPPOSED TO HAVE BEEN WRITTEN IN THE AUTHOR'S
GARDEN, DURING A STORM. 1756.

Blow on, ye winds! exert your utmost rage,
  Sweep o'er the doom, or through the forest howl!
Could north with south, or east with west engage,
  What were their war to that within my soul?

There adverse passions fierce contention hold,
  There Love and Pride maintain alternate sway,
There fell Despair's dark clouds on clouds are roll'd !
  And veil Hope's transient, faint, delusive ray !

Too charming Sylvia ! dear capricious fair !
  What strange perplexing change of mind is thine !
No more thy smiles I 'll trust, thy frowns I 'll bear ;
  I 'll shun the beauty that must ne'er be mine !

Was it for thee I form'd this fair retreat,    [away,
  Bade through the grove the smooth walk wind
Adorn'd that walk with many a rustic seat,
  And by those seats bade tinkling runnels stray ?

Along my sunny wall the fruit-tree spread,
  Upon my eves expos'd the curling vine,
Around my door the spicy woodbine led,
  Beneath my window saw the jasmine twine ?

Blow on, ye winds ! exert your utmost power,
  Rage through my groves, and bear down ev'ry
        tree ;
Blast the fair fruit, and crush the blooming flower—
  For Sylvia's lost, and these are nought to me !
  K k

## AUTHOR TO HIS WIFE.

### 1776.

Friend of my heart, by fav'ring Heav'n bestow'd,
My lov'd companion on life's various road!
Now six swift years have wing'd their flight away
Since yon bright Sun adorn'd our nuptial day—
For thy sweet smiles, that all my cares remove,
Sooth all my griefs, and all my joys improve;
For thy sweet converse, ever fram'd to please,
With prudence lively, sensible with ease;
To thee the Muse awakes her tuneful lay,
The thanks of gratitude sincere to pay!
Thus long may Hymen hold for us his reign,
And twine with wreaths of flowers his easy chain;
Still may fond love and firmest faith be mine,
Still health, and peace, and happiness be thine!

## STANZAS

### WRITTEN AT MEDHURST, IN SUSSEX,

ON THE AUTHOR'S RETURN FROM CHICHESTER, WHERE HE
HAD ATTEMPTED IN VAIN TO FIND THE BURIAL-PLACE
OF COLLINS.

To view the beauties of my native land,
    O'er many a pleasing distant scene I rove;
Now climb the rock, or wander on the strand,
    Or trace the rill, or penetrate the grove.

From Baia's hills, from Portsea's spreading wave,
    To fair Cicestria's lonely walls I stray;
To her fam'd poet's venerated grave,
    Anxious my tribute of respect to pay [1].

O'er the dim pavement of the solemn fane,
    Midst the rude stones that crowd th' adjoining
The sacred spot I seek, but seek in vain;    [space,
    In vain I ask—for none can point the place.

What boots the eye whose quick observant glance
    Marks ev'ry nobler, ev'ry fairer form?
What the skill'd ear that sound's sweet charms en-
        trance,
    And the fond breast with gen'rous passion warm?

What, boots the power each image to portray,
    The power with force each feeling to express?
How vain the hope that through life's little day,
    The soul with thought of future fame can bless?

While Folly frequent boasts th' insculptur'd tomb,
    By Flattery's pen inscrib'd with purchas'd praise;
While rustic Labour's undistinguish'd doom
    Fond Friendship's hand records in humble phrase;

[1] Collins was born at Chichester, died, and probably was interred there.

Of Genius oft, and Learning, worse the lot;
    For them no care, to them no honour shown [2]:
Alive neglected, and when dead forgot,
    Even Collins slumbers in a grave unknown.

Flow, Lavant, flow! along thy sedgy shore
    Bear the fraught vessel from the neighb'ring main!
Enrich thy sons!—but on thy banks no more
    May lofty poet breathe his tuneful strain!

## VERSES

### TO A FRIEND, PLANTING.

Proceed, my friend, pursue thy healthful toil,
Dispose thy ground, and meliorate thy soil;    [ers,
Range thy young plants in walks, or clumps, or bow-
Diffuse o'er sunny banks thy fragrant flowers;
And, while the new creation round thee springs,
Enjoy uncheck'd the guiltless bliss it brings:
But hope no more. Though Fancy forward stray,
There scenes of distant pleasure to survey,
To expatiate fondly o'er the future grove,
The happy haunt of Friendship and of Love;
Know, each fair image form'd within thy mind,
Far wide of truth thy sick'ning sight shall find!

## TO AN ABSENT FRIEND.

While thou far hence on Albion's southern shore
View'st her white rocks, and hear'st her ocean roar;
Through scenes, where we together stray'd, I stray,
And think o'er talk of many a long-past day.
    That fav'rite park now tempts my steps again,
On whose green turf so oft at ease we 've lain;
While Hertford's turrets rose in prospect fair,
And my fond thought beheld my Sylvia there;
And much the Muse rehears'd in careless lays
The lover's sufferings and the beauty's praise.
    Those elm-crown'd fields, now oft my walk invite,
Whence Lee's wide vale lies pleasant to the sight;
Where, as our view o'er towns and villas roll'd,
Our fancy imag'd how they look'd of old;
When Gothic mansions there uprear'd their towers,
Their halls for banquet, and for rest their bowers.
    But, O my friend! whene'er I seek these scenes
Of lovely prospects and delightful greens;
Regardless idly of the joys possess'd,
I dream of days to come, of days more bless'd,
When thou with me shalt wander here once more,
And we shall talk again our fav'rite topics o'er.
On Time's smooth current as we glide along,
Thus Expectation ever tunes her song:
" Fair these green banks with gaudy flow'rets bloom,
Sweet breathe these gales, diffusing rich perfume;
Heed, heed them not, but carelessly pass by,
To morrow fairer, sweeter will supply."

[2] This censure may seem too general—perhaps
it is so. But must it not be allowed that the
public is capricious in bestowing its honours? Does
not Westminster Abbey show monuments erected to men, as poets, who had little or no title
to the name, while it contains no memorials of
writers of far superior merit?

To morrow comes—the same the Syren's lay—
" To morrow sweeter gales, and flow'rets still more
gay."

## THE SHEPHERD'S ELEGY.

### OCCASIONED BY

### THE DEATH OF AN INGENIOUS FRIEND.

Upon a bank with spreading boughs o'erhung,
Of pollard oak, brown elm, and hornbeam grey,
The faded fern and russet grass among,
While rude winds swept the yellow leaves away,
And scatter'd o'er the ground the wild fruits lay ;
As from the churchyard came the village throng,
Down sat a rural bard, and rais'd his mournful song.

" Nature's best gifts, alas, in vain we prize !
The powers that please, the powers that pleasure
For, O, with them, in full proportion, rise    [gain !
The powers of giving and of feeling pain !
Why from my breast now bursts this plaintive strain ?
Genius, my friend ! with all its charms was thine,
And sensibility too exquisite is mine !

" There low he lies !—that head in dust repos'd
Whose active thought scann'd every various theme !
Clos'd is that eye, for ever, ever clos'd,
Whence wont the blaze of sentiment to beam !
Mute is that tongue, whence flow'd the copious
Of eloquence, whose moral lore so rare    [stream
Delighted and improv'd the list'ning young and fair.

" Witness for me, ye rain-polluted rills ;
Ye desert meads, that one brown hue display ;
Ye rude east-winds, whose breath the dank air chills ;
Ye hov'ring clouds, that veil the Sun's faint ray !
Witness, as annual here my steps shall stray,
How his dear image thought shall still recall,
And oft the sigh shall heave, and oft the tear shall
fall !"

As cease the murmurs of the mantling pool,
As cease the whispers of the poplar spray,
While o'er the vale the white mist rises cool
At the calm sunset of a summer's day—
So softly, sweetly ceas'd the shepherd's lay :
While down the pathway to the hamlet plain
Return'd, with ling'ring steps, the pensive rural train.

### ON THE

## INGENIOUS MR. JONES'S

### ELEGANT TRANSLATIONS AND IMITATIONS OF
### EASTERN POETRY,

#### AND HIS RESOLUTION TO DECLINE TRANSLATING THE PERSIAN POETS.

The Asian Muse, a stranger fair !
Becomes at length Britannia's care ;
And Hafiz' lays, and Sadi's strains,
Resound along our Thames's plains.

They sing not all of streams and bowers,
Or banquet scenes, or social hours ;
Nor all of Beauty's blooming charms,
Or War's rude fields, or feats of arms ;
But Freedom's lofty notes sincere,
And Virtue's moral lore severe,
But ah ! they sing for us no more !
The scarcely-tasted pleasure 's o'er !
For he, the bard whose tuneful art
Can best their vary'd themes impart—
For he, alas ! the task declines ;
And Taste, at loss irreparable, repines.

## HYMN

### FROM PSALM VIII.

Almighty Power ! amazing are thy ways,
Above our knowledge, and above our praise !
How all thy works thy excellence display !
How fair, how great, how wonderful are they !
Thy hand yon wide-extended Heav'n upra, s'd,
Yon wide-extended Heav'n with stars emblaz'd,
Where each bright orb, since Time his course begun,
Has roll'd a mighty world, or shin'd a sun :
Stupendous thought ! how sinks all human race !
A point an atom in the field of space !
Yet ev'n to us, O Lord, thy care extends,
Thy bounty feeds us, and thy pow'r defends ;
Yet e'en to us, as delegates of thee,
Thou giv'st dominion over land and sea ;
Whate'er, or walks on earth, or flits in air ;
Whate'er of life the wat'ry regions bear ;
All these are ours, and for th' extensive claim,
We owe due homage to thy sacred name !
Almighty Pow'r ! how wondrous are thy ways !
How far above our knowledge and our praise !

## CONCLUSION.

### TO A FRIEND.

When erst the enthusiast Fancy's reign,
Indulg'd the wild, romantic thought,
That wander'd midst Arcadian vales,
Sicilian streams, Arabian gales ;
Bless'd climes, with wondrous pleasures fraught,
Sweet pleasures, unalloy'd with pain !

When Observation's calmer view
Remark'd the real state of things ;
Whate'er amusive one obtain'd,
Whate'er of use the other gain'd,
To thee my verse a tribute brings,
A tribute to thy friendship due.

Accept then this, nor more require :
The Muse no further task essays ;
But midst the sylvan scenes she loves,
The falling rills, and whisp'ring groves,
With smiles her labours past surveys,
And quits the syrinx and the lyre.

# POSTSCRIPT.

The author, in the course of his literary inquiries, has had reason to believe that the productions of some writers have not unfrequently received very considerable alterations and improvements from the hands of their friends. What he has been told of others, may possibly be suspected of himself; he therefore takes the liberty to observe, that, although he has often derived advantage from the judicious remarks of a few kind acquaintance, to whom his MSS. have been shown, he is not indebted to them, nor indeed to any person, for the insertion of a single line.

From the works of preceding poets, memory has sometimes supplied him with turns of expression, which, at the instant of composing, he imagined were his own; and at other times he has happened on lines used by writers, whose performances he had not then seen. Some instances of such unconscious plagiarism, and accidental coincidence, are here pointed out, as matter of curiosity; others may possibly exist, though he is not apprised of them.

------

Blows not a flow'ret in the enamell'd vale,
Shines not a pebble, &c.
  Elegies, Descriptive and Moral, p. 459.

Lurks not a stone enrich'd with lively stain,
Blooms not a flower amid the vernal store,
Falls not a plume on India's distant plain,
Glows not a shell on Adria's rocky shore—
  Shenstone's Works, vol. i. 8vo. p. 140.

Perhaps Shenstone was indebted to Akenside:

...................... ............ Not a breeze
Flies o'er the meadow, not a cloud imbibes
The setting Sun's effulgence, not a strain
From all the tenants of the warbling shade
Ascends...............................
  Pleasures of Imagination, b. iii. l. 593.

But claims their wonder and excites their praise.
  Elegies, Descriptive and Moral, p. 459.

Provoke our wonder and transcend our praise.
  Addison to Dryden, Works, vol. i. p. 3.

Or rear the new-bound sheaves along the lands.
  Elegies, Descriptive and Moral, p. 460.

Or range my sheaves along the sunny land.
  Hammond, Elegy xiii. l. 12.

No more those nostrils breathe the vital air.
  Elegies, Descriptive and Moral, p. 461.

That while my nostrils draw the vital air.
  Pope, Rape of the Lock, canto iv.

In one sad spot where kindred ashes lie.
  Elegy written at Amwell, 1768, p. 462.

In one lone spot their mouldering ashes lie.
  Mr. Keate's Ruins of Netley Abbey, 1764.

Of classic lore accompanied my walk.
  Amwell, p. 465.

In sumptuous cars accompanied his march.
  Leonidas, book viii.

And his wild eye-balls roll with horrid glare.
  Arabian Eclogue, p. 473.

And his red eye-balls roll with living fire.
  Dryden's Meleager and Atalanta.

And one forlorn inhabitant contain'd.
  Indian Eclogue, p. 475.

The cities no inhabitant contain'd.
  Fawke's Song of Deborah; Poems, p. 100.

Again he look'd, again he sigh'd.
  Ode ii. p. 478.

And sigh'd and look'd.
  Dryden's Alexander's Feast.

Then Poverty, grim spectre! rose.
  Ode xxi. p. 484.

Scar'd at the spectre of pale Poverty.
  Pope, Imitation of Horace, b. ii. epist. 1.

Each pastoral sight, and every pastoral sound.
  Epistle i. p. 489.

Designedly imitated from Milton:

Each rural sight, each rural sound.——

And pure as vernal blossoms newly blown.
  Elegy written at Amwell, 1768, p. 462.

All pure as blossoms which are newly blown.
  W. Browne's Britannia's Pastorals, v. i. p. 101.

Davies's edition of Browne's Works was published in 1772. The author had never seen any of the old editions, nor any extract from them.

Haste, brings my steed supreme in strength and grace,
First in the fight, and fleetest in the chase.
  Arabian Eclogue, p. 473.

This eclogue was written in 1777. In a volume of poems by the ingenious Mr. Maurice, printed in 1779, the author met with the following near resemblance:

Full fifty steeds I boast of swiftest pace,
Fierce in the fight, and foremost in the race.

In the Amoebaean Eclogue, entitled, The Describers, p. 467, a part of the imagery bears a considerable resemblance to some descriptions in a little collection of pleasing sonnets, by Mr. Bamfylde, 1778; which collection the author never saw till after his own volume was printed. This is a proof that two writers, both painting from Nature, will often unknowingly coincide very nearly in selection, arrangement, and expression.